For Reference

Not to be taken from this room

HILL'S MANUAL.

HILL'S MANUAL

OF

SOCIAL AND BUSINESS FORMS:

A

GUIDE TO CORRECT WRITING

Showing How to Express Written Thought Plainly, Rapidly, Elegantly and Correctly.

EMBRACING INSTRUCTION AND EXAMPLES IN

PENMANSHIP, SPELLING, USE OF CAPITAL LETTERS, PUNCTUATION, COMPOSITION, WRITING FOR THE PRESS, PROOF-READING, EPISTOLARY CORRESPONDENCE, NOTES OF INVITATION, CARDS, COMMERCIAL FORMS, LEGAL BUSINESS FORMS, FAMILY RECORDS, SYNONYMS, SHORT-HAND WRITING, DUTIES OF SECRETARIES, PARLIA-MENTARY RULES, SIGN-WRITING, EPITAPHS, THE LAWS OF ETIQUETTE, BOOK-KEEPING, VALUABLE TABLES OF REFERENCE, WRITING POETRY, ETC., ETC.

BY THOS. E. HILL,

AUTHOR OF "HILL'S ALBUM OF BIOGRAPHY AND ART," "MORALS AND MANNERS, ILLUSTRATED."

CHICAGO:

HILL STANDARD BOOK CO., PUBLISHERS.

1885.

THE ORIGINAL 1885 TITLE PAGE

THE 1885 EDITION OF

HILL'S MANUAL

Of Social and Business Forms

THE HOW-TO-DO-EVERYTHING BOOK OF VICTORIAN AMERICA

WITH AN INTRODUCTION BY

THEODORE M. BERNSTEIN

of The New York Times

A New York Times Book

QUADRANGLE BOOKS

CHICAGO

To

THE MILLIONS

WHO WOULD, AND MAY,

Easily and Gracefully Express the Right Thought,

THIS WORK IS

RESPECTFULLY DEDICATED.

PREFACE.

Written Ten Years after the First Issue of This Work, Giving an Outline Sketch of the Causes Which Produced Hill's Manual.

THE purpose of this book is to teach how to write the document correctly, and do the right thing at the right time in various important positions in life.

Born in a retired part of New England, where school advantages in childhood were few, and possessed of extreme sensitiveness as to his lack of needed education, the author of this volume early realized the want of a work that would serve as a teacher and guide to those who desire an education, but have little opportunity for obtaining it. When quite young, he resolved to acquire not only a knowledge of practical life himself, but to embody in a volume, for the use of others, such information as he, in his own experience, had realized that the people required.

Twenty years went by, during which time, with an ample experience as student, teacher, traveler, editor, publisher and business-man, he was selecting, arranging, and writing that which he designed some day to publish in permanent form. At last, with time and means at command, he sat down to finish that labor which he had resolved in early years to execute, and at the end of two years and two months, from the time his close attention was given to the work, with the aid of skilled workmen in every department of book-making, at an expense of many thousands of dollars, HILL'S MANUAL was issued to the world. Its success was immediate and permanent; and its influence as an educator has been immense, over a quarter of a million of copies having been sold; while imitations of the work, under various names, have had, in the aggregate, also, a large circulation.

Notwithstanding the great sale of this book, its author and publishers are not content to allow it to rest on its past success. With a full realization of the advancing spirit and demand of the age, coupled with superior opportunity and knowledge gathered from large experience, additions and improvements are continually being made, and no expense or effort is spared to maintain the reputation that this work has sustained from the first, as a reliable and Standard Form-Book.

CHICAGO, 1884.

Contents

HILL'S MANUAL, first issued in 1873, though very complete at first, has been from time to time changed. The following are now the principal divisions of the work, each being quite fully treated, and several of them appropriately illustrated with instructive engravings.

Introduction

BY THEODORE M. BERNSTEIN
of The New York Times

HEN you are a guest in someone's home do you know how to stand near a wall so as not to stain the wallpaper? Have you at hand a speech to accompany the presentation of a watch to a clergyman? Are you aware of the way to write a lower-case "a" so that it does not look like a "u"? Are you familiar with the proper wording of a letter requesting the loan of a pistol? Or, if you are a young lady, are you familiar with the proper wording of a letter spurning a young gentleman who professes love at first sight?

If your answer to questions such as these is no, then Hill's Manual is the book for you. If your answer is yes, it is still the book for you.

To use a phrase that Mr. Hill, were he alive, would undoubtedly disapprove on linguistic grounds, this manual is a fun book. Not that it was by any means intended to be such. It was compiled in the utmost seriousness—in deadly seriousness, as witness the section setting forth suitable tombstone inscriptions. And without question it was received with equal seriousness by our forebears of the late nineteenth century. But today it is—well, let's say camp, if that word is still current. As used by Susan Sontag, the camp leader,

and her followers, camp pertains to outgivings in the various artistic fields, but there is no reason why it could not apply elsewhere as well. As she says, "The whole point of camp is to dethrone the serious. Camp is playful, anti-serious." At another point she says—and this may be even more pertinent to the nineteenth century stress on form: "Camp is...the relation to style in a time in which the adoption of style—as such—has become altogether questionable."

Form—i.e., style—is assuredly passé in our age. When did you last see a man surrender his seat in a public conveyance to a woman? When did you last see a woman graciously nod upon being introduced to a man? How many invitations have you received this year that bore the notation "black tie"? How many college students wear jackets and ties to the classroom? How many grammar school pupils show respect to the teacher? When did you last hear of the hazing of a freshman class at your college? Yes, we have gotten away from forms and perhaps in doing so we have in some respects found ourselves in an era of greater sincerity.

The forms of the nineteenth and earlier centuries quite unintentionally cast a cold shield of conventionality over candor, over honesty, over human feeling. All this is evident in the content of Hill's Manual. If the condolence note of a genuinely grieved friend is almost identical with that of the acquaintance who merely feels obligated to send a note, how does human warmth assert itself? There is a note of irony in the Manual that is relevant to this point: The introduction to the section on Letter Writing contains the sentence, "Be original," whereupon the reader is launched upon 40-odd pages of letter forms for every possible occasion.

Few present-day readers would be likely to use the forms presented. Or, for that matter, to follow the rules of etiquette or to utter the toasts set forth for various occasions or to adhere to the guides for facial expression and gesture in oratory. But they all make delicious present-day reading and invite us in an unusual way to live, for the moment, in a bygone day. And, after all, isn't nostalgia one of the in things today?

For scholars interested in researching the period, it is difficult to conceive of a more detailed, more explicit, more comprehensive picture of the American community in the late 1800's than this book.

Hill's Manual first appeared in 1873, then reappeared in ever-larger editions for a decade, reaching a total of 290,000 people who either were ignorant of how to punctuate a sign over a store or needed a synonym for "seduce" or did not know how to go about collecting a debt. The subscribers were able to pick up some quaint things about English usage. They learned that you should never say, "If I am not mistaken," but rather, "If I mistake not"; that it is improper to speak of "a new pair of boots" rather than "a pair of new boots," and that instead of "I know better; that ain't so," you should say, "Pardon me, I understand differently." Naturally the Manual also offers some valuable general rules for writing, such as: "Care should be taken to prune out the unnecessary words with an unsparing hand. Thus, in the sentence, 'I have got back, having returned yesterday,' it is better to say, 'I returned yesterday.'"

Mr. Hill himself—Thomas Edie Hill, to give him his full name—was born at Sandgate, Vt., in 1832 and began his career as a teacher. He then switched to journalism, founding the Aurora, Ill., Herald in 1866. He boasted that he had made the Aurora Silver Plate Factory a success in its early history, and in 1876 he became Mayor of Aurora, in which office his chief claim to fame was that he "shut off 600 cows from running at large in streets." In 1885 he settled at Glen Ellyn, Ill., which he named and which he proceeded to improve. It was there that he died in 1915.

Obviously Mr. Hill thrived on activity. And the extent and thoroughness of his industry are evident in this Manual. Granted that much of what it contains is perishable in the sense of modern utility, yet as amusing documentation of another time it may never perish.

WRITING.

RITING is the art of placing thought, by means of written characters, upon any object capable of receiving the same. The origin of this art is completely veiled in obscurity, no history giving authentic account of its first introduction and use. Its first recorded mention is in the Bible, wherein it is said, referring to the preparation of the Ten Commandments by Moses on Mount Sinai, that "The Tables were *written* on both their sides."

Fifteen hundred years before Christ, Cadmus, the Phœnician, had introduced letters into Greece, being sixteen in number, to which several were afterwards added. It is certain that the Greeks were among the very earliest of the nations of the earth to invent and make use of written characters for the record of ideas, which could be clearly interpreted by succeeding generations; though the invention of the art came from the advancing civilization of mankind, and had its origin with various nations: at first in the form of hieroglyphics, or picture writing, which characters have, as mankind progressed, been simplified, systematized, and arranged in alphabets, giving us the various alphabetical characters now in use.

Writing and penmanship, though nearly synonymous terms, are quite different in meaning. Writing is the expression of thought by certain characters, and embraces penmanship, spelling, grammar and composition.

ENMANSHIP is the combination of peculiar characters used to represent the record of thought; and having, since its first invention, continued to change its form down to the present time, so it is probable the style of penmanship will continue to change in the future. The great defect existing in the present system of penmanship is the superabundance of surplus marks, that really mean nothing. This fault, along with our defective alphabet, consumes in writing, at present, a great amount of unnecessary time and labor. Thus, in writing the word *Though*, we make twenty-seven motions, whereas, being but two sounds in the word, we actually require but two simple marks.

That style of writing whereby we use a character to represent each sound, is known as phonography, which system of penmanship enables the penman to write with the rapidity of speech. The phonetic or phonographic system of spelling, wherein each sound is represented by a character, gives us the nearest approach to a perfect alphabet in existence, and is the method of spelling and the style of writing to which we will, beyond question, ultimately attain.

It has been found extremely difficult, however, to suddenly change a style of alphabet in general use in a living language; and the mass of the American and English people will, without doubt, use the present style of penmanship, with various modifications, many decades in the future. To the perfection of that system in general use, in the English and American method of writing, which the present generation will be most likely to have occasion to use throughout their lifetime, this work is directed, as having thus the most practical value; though Short-hand is illustrated elsewhere.

System of Penmanship.

Two styles of penmanship have been in use, and each in turn has been popular with Americans in the past fifty years; one known as the round hand, the other as the angular writing. The objection attaching to each is, that the round hand, while having the merit of legibility, requires too much time in its execution; and the angular, though rapidly written, is wanting in legibility. The best teachers of penmanship, of late, have obviated the objections attaching to these different styles, by combining the virtues of both in one, producing a semi-angular penmanship, possessing the legibility of the round hand along with the rapid execution of the angular.

To the Duntons, of Boston, and the late P. R. Spencer, as the founders of the semi-angular penmanship, are the people indebted for the beautiful system of writing now in general use in the schools throughout the country.

Copies.

The copies, accompanied by directions in this book, will be found ample in number and sufficiently explicit in detail to give the student a knowledge of writing and flourishing. In acquiring a correct penmanship it is not the practice of many different copies that makes the proficient penman, but rather a proper understanding of a few select ones, for a few copies embrace the whole art.

As will be seen by an examination of the copy plates, each letter of the alphabet is made in a variety of styles, both large and small, succeeded by words alphabetically arranged in fine

and coarse penmanship, which are excellently adapted to the wants of both ladies and gentlemen, according to the dictates of fancy in the selection of coarse and fine hand.

As a rule, however, the bold penmanship, indicating force of character, will be naturally adopted by gentlemen, while the finer hand, exhibiting delicacy and refinement, will be chosen by the ladies.

Principles.

The principles of penmanship, also represented, give the complete analysis of each letter, while the proper and improperly made letters, representing good and bad placed side by side, will have a tendency to involuntarily improve the penmanship, even of the person who makes a casual examination of the letters of the alphabet thus made in contrast.

The illustrations of curves, proportions and shades that accompany these directions should also be carefully studied, as a knowledge of these scientific principles in penmanship will be found of great service to the student in giving a correct understanding of the formation of letters.

Importance of Practice.

It is not sufficient, however, that the student merely study the *theory* of writing. To be proficient there must be actual *practice*. To conduct this exercise to advantage it is necessary to have the facilities for writing well. Essential to a successful practice are good tools with which to write. These comprise the following writing materials:

Pens.

Metallic pens have generally superseded the quill. They are of all styles and quality of metal, gold and steel, however, being the best. In consequence of its flexibility and great durability, many prefer the gold pen; though in point of fine execution, the best penmen prefer the steel pen, a much sharper and finer hair line being cut with it than with the gold pen.

Paper.

For practice in penmanship, obtain of the stationer five sheets of good foolscap paper. Midway from top to bottom of the sheet, cut the paper in two, placing one half inside the other. Use a strong paper for the cover, and sew the whole together, making a writing-book. Use a piece of blotting paper to rest the hand on. The oily perspiration constantly passing from the hand unfits the surface of the paper for receiving good penmanship. The hand should never touch the paper upon which it is designed, afterwards, to write.

Ink.

Black ink is best. That which flows freely, and is nearest black when first used, gives the most satisfaction. The inkstand should be heavy and flat, with a large opening, from which to take ink, and not liable to tip over. The best inkstand is made of thick cut glass, enabling the writer to see the amount of ink in the same, and shows always how deep to set the pen when taking ink from the stand. Care should be observed not to take too much ink on the pen ; and the surplus ink should be thrown back into the bottle, and never upon the carpet or floor. Close the bottle when done using it, thus preventing rapid evaporation of the ink, causing it soon to become too thick.

Other Writing Materials.

An important requisite that should accompany the other writing materials is the pen wiper, used always to clean the pen when the writing exercise is finished, when the ink does not flow readily to the point of the pen, or when lint has caught upon the point. A small piece of buckskin or chamois skin, obtained at the drug store, makes much the best wiper. The student should be provided with various sizes of paper, for different exercises to be written, such as commercial forms, letters, notes of invitation, etc., with envelopes to correspond in size ; together with lead-pencil, rubber, ruler, and mucilage. Thus provided with all the materials necessary, the writing exercise, which otherwise would be an unpleasant task, becomes a pleasure.

How to Practice.

Having the necessary materials in readiness for writing, the student should set apart a certain hour or two each day for practice in penmanship, for at least one month, carefully observing the following directions :

See Plate 1. Carefully examine each copy on this plate. Devote one page in the writing book to the practice of each copy. Commence with copy No. 1. The practice of this copy is an important exercise for two reasons, being : first, to give sufficient angularity for rapidity in writing; and second, to give freedom of movement.

The student who carries a heavy, cramped hand, will find great benefit result from practicing this copy always at the commencement of the writing exercise. Rest the hand on the two lower fingers — never on the wrist, and rest the body and arm lightly upon the forearm. Assume thus a position whereby the pen can take in the entire sweep of the page, writing this exercise, in copy No. 1, from the left to the right side of the page, without removing the pen from the paper while making the same. The student may write both with pen and lead-pencil, and should continue the practice of this exercise until perfect command is obtained of the fingers, hand and arm ; and all evidence of a stiff, cramped penmanship disappears.

Copy No. 2 is a contraction of copy No. 1, making the letter *m.* Great care should be used in writing this letter to make the several  parts of the same, uniform in height, size, and slope ; the downward slope of all the letters being at an angle of 52 degrees. See diagram illustrating slope of letters.

Position while Writing.

AN object early to be attained, is to acquire an easy, graceful and healthful position of body while sitting or standing, when writing. To obtain this, the writer should sit with the right side to the desk, using a table so high as to compel the body to sit erect.

Rest the arm lightly upon the elbow and forearm, and the hand upon the two lower fingers, the wrist being free from the desk. Allow the body and head to incline sufficiently to see the writing, but no more.

Maintain a position such as will give a free expansion of the lungs, as such posture is absolutely indispensable to the preservation of health.

A desk or table, with a perfectly level surface, is best for writing. Where a decided preference is manifested for sitting with the left side, or square, to the desk, such position may be taken. If the desk slopes considerably, the left side is preferable.

Avoid dropping the body down into an awkward, tiresome position. If wearied with continued sitting, cease writing. Lay down the pen, step forth into the fresh air, throw back the arms, expand the chest, inflate the lungs, and take exercise. When work is again resumed, maintain the same erect position, until the habit becomes thoroughly fixed of sitting gracefully and easily, while engaged in this exercise.

Position for Sitting and Holding the Pen.

TO secure the correct slope of a plain, rapid penmanship, when writing, keep the paper at right angles with the arm, holding the same in position with the left hand, the edge of the paper being parallel with edge of the desk.

Hold the pen between the thumb and second finger, resting against the corner of the nail, with the fore-finger on the back of the pen, for the purpose of steadying it; having the thumb sufficiently bent to come opposite the forefinger joint, the two last fingers being bent under, resting lightly on the nails.

Avoid dropping or rolling the hand and pen too much to one side, thereby causing one point of the pen to drag more heavily than the other, thus producing a rough mark in writing. A smooth stroke indicates that the pen is held correctly; a rough one tells us when the position is wrong.

Sit sufficiently close to the desk to avoid the necessity of leaning forward or sidewise in order to reach the same, and occupy a chair that gives support to the back, using a table large enough to comfortably hold all the writing materials that are necessary when writing.

Copy No. 3 shows (see Plate I) the *m,* in words, and illustrates the distinction that should be made between the several letters, to make writing plain. See "Description of the Plates."

Legibility.

Legibility is of the greatest importance in penmanship; and care should be observed to make each letter very distinctly what it is designed to be. While practicing with a view to improvement, the student should beware of writing too fast. The copies are very simple, and are easily imitated by the student who may give the subject earnest attention and care.

Proportion of Small Letters.

The following diagrams represent the relative proportion of the capital and small letters. As will be seen in the diagram for the finer hand, there are eight lines, containing seven spaces. In the middle space are made the contracted letters which occupy one space, excepting *i* and *s,* which are a little higher. The *t, d* and *p* are each of the same height; *p* and *q* extend the same distance below the line. The loop letters are all of the same length above and below the line, the loop being two thirds the length of the letter. Capitals are of the same height as the loop letters above the line.

RELATIVE PROPORTION OF LETTERS IN LARGE, ROUND HAND.

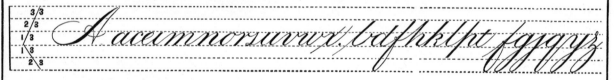

Elements of Small Letters.

By examination of the small letters of the alphabet, it is seen that they can be resolved into a few fundamental elements (or principles, as they are called by many teachers), being five in number, as follows:

¹*i* ²*ı* ³*ı* ⁴*o* ⁵*l*

The 1st principle, *i,* is found in the following letters, viz: last of *a, d,* completely in the *i,* in the *p,* with the lower part omitted; last of the *q,* first of the *i* and *s,* completely in the *t,* completely in the *u* and last of *w.*

The 2nd principle, *ı,* forms the first of *m, n* and upper part of *z.*

The 3rd principle, *ı,* forms the lower part of *h,* the lower part of *k,* last of *m, n* and *p* and first of *u, w, x* and *y.*

The 4th principle, *o,* forms the first part of *a,* left of *c,* lower part of *d,* left of *e,* lower part of *f,* upper part of *g,* the whole of *o,* upper part of *q* and right of *s.*

The 5th principle, *l,* forms the upper part of

f, b, h, k and *l.* Inverted, it forms

the lower part of *g, j, y* and *z.*

General Hints for Small Letters.

Be careful to close the *a* at the top, else it will resemble a *u.* Observe the distinction between the *n* and the *u.* The *t* and *d* are shaded at the top, and made square. The *t* is crossed one third the distance from the top. The loop is of uniform length in all loop letters. Avoid a loop in the upper part of *t* and *d.* The dot of the *i* should be at a point twice the height of the letter. Beware of making the extended letters crooked. The left hand mark of the loop letters should be straight, from the center of the loop to the line, sloping at an angle of 52 degrees. See diagram of slope. Figures are twice the height of the *m.*

Principles of Capital Letters.

No. 1.

No. 2.

No. 3.

The capital stem (see No. 1) can be terminated at the bottom, as shown in the first character. Observe in Nos. 2 and 3 the disposition of shades, curves and parallel lines. Their application in capitals will be seen in the next column.

CAPITAL LETTERS.

THREE standard principles are used in the formation of Capital Letters, viz:

The 1st principle, called the capital stem, is found in *A, B, D, F, G, H, I, J, K, L, M, N, P, R, S, T, X, Y* and *Z.*

The 2nd principle, occurs in *C, D, E, K, M, O, R, U* and *X.*

The 3rd principle, is found in the upper part of *B, F, H, M, N, P* and *T* and forms the first of *Q, U, V, W, X* and *Y.*

Capital letters, in a bold penmanship, are three times the height of the small letter *m.*

VIEWS OF THE CORRECT POSITION FOR HOLDING HAND AND PEN WHILE WRITING.

No. 1.

No. 1 Represents the first position to be taken, when placing the hand in correct position for writing. As will be seen, the hand is squarely on the palm, and not rolled to one side. The wrist is free from the desk, and the two lower fingers are bent under, resting upon the nails.

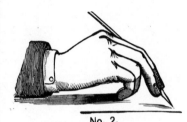

No. 2.

No. 2 Exhibits the hand elevated upon the two lower fingers, with the pen placed in correct position. The end of the large finger drops slightly beneath the penholder, giving a much greater command of the fingers than when it rests at the side or slightly on top of the holder.

No. 3.

No. 3 Shows another view of correct position. It will be seen that no space is shown between the pen and finger, the holder crossing the forefinger in front of the knuckle-joint. The thumb is sufficiently bent to come opposite the forefinger-joint, supporting the holder on the end of the thumb. The end of the large finger should be about three-quarters of an inch from the point of the pen.

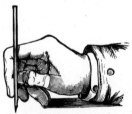

No. 4.

No. 4 Represents the correct position when the pen is at the bottom of an extended letter below the line, the pen being, as shown, nearly perpendicular. With the holder held snugly beneath the forefinger and supported on the end of the thumb, the greatest command is thus given to the fingers.

No. 5.

No. 5 Exhibits the front view of the hand showing the position of the forefinger, which should rest squarely on the top of the holder. The large finger drops beneath the holder, which crosses the corner of the nail. The hand is held, as shown, squarely on the palm and not dropped to one side.

VIEWS REPRESENTING INCORRECT POSITIONS FOR HAND AND PEN WHILE WRITING.

No. 6 Represents the evil effect of rolling the hand too much to one side, and holding all of the fingers so straight as to completely lose command of them. The result is a stiff, heavy, cramped penmanship, and rough marks, resulting from one point of the pen dragging more heavily than the other.

No. 6.

No. 7 Exhibits the pen " held so tightly that the hand is wearied and the letters look frightfully.'' The large finger should be straightened, and the end caused to drop lightly beneath the holder. The forefinger should be brought down snugly upon the holder, and the end of the thumb brought back opposite the forefinger joint. Loosen the fingers, grasping the holder therein just firm enough to guide the pen and no more.

No. 7.

No. 8 Shows the result of dropping the hand too heavily upon the wrist and allowing it to roll to one side. The writer has thus lost command of the hand and arm, and the pen scratches, resulting from one point dragging more heavily than the other. The large finger should drop beneath the holder, and the hand should be brought up squarely upon the palm.

No. 8.

No. 9 Represents another bad position, with pen held too tightly. The writer loses a command of the fingers, in this case, by allowing the holder to fall below the knuckle-joint between the forefinger and thumb. All the fingers are likewise out of position.

No. 9.

The student should institute a rigid comparison between the correct and incorrect positions herewith shown, with an earnest resolve to reject the wrong and to hold fast that which is good.

As is ·exhibited in the above, those letters composed of curved lines present a grace and beauty not shown in those having straight lines and angles. As a rule, never make a straight line in a capital letter when it can be avoided.

NATURE'S RULES.

THERE are a few general principles in Nature that are applicable to penmanship. These principles are eternal, and will never change.

Curved Lines.

The first is that of curved lines. Those objects in Nature that we most admire possess a grace and fullness of curve which elicit our admiration. The edge of the flower curves. The trunk of the tree, the leaf, the bud, the dewdrop, the rainbow, —all that is beautiful in Nature, in fact, is made up of curved lines. The human countenance, rounded and flushed with the rosy hue of health, is beautiful. Wasted by disease and full of angles, it is less attractive. The winding pathway in the park, the graceful bending of the willow, the rounded form of every object that we admire, are among the many illustrations of this principle. This is finely shown in the engraving of birds and flowers at the head of this chapter.

The same applied to the making of capital letters is shown in the following, representing in contrast letters made of curves and straight lines :

Proportion.

Another important principle is that of proportion. Any object, to present a pleasing appearance to the eye, should have a base of sufficient size and breadth to support the same. Nature is full of examples. The mountain is broadest at the base ; and the trunk of every tree and shrub that grows upon its sides, is largest near the earth, the roots spreading broader than the branches.

The good mechanic builds accordingly. The monument is broadest at the base. The house has a foundation large enough for its support, and the smallest article of household use or ornament, constructed to stand upright, is made with reference to this principle of proportion, with base broader than the top. This principle, applied in capital letters, is shown by contrast of various letters made in good and bad proportion, as follows :

Letters should be constructed self supporting in appearance, with a foundation sufficiently broad to support that which is above.

Contrast.

A very important principle, also, is that of contrast. Nature is again the teacher, and affords an endless variety of lessons. Scenery is beautiful that is most greatly diversified by contrast. That is more beautiful which is broken by mountain, hill, valley, stream, and woodland, than the level prairie, where nothing meets the eye but brown grass. The bouquet of flowers is beautiful in proportion to the many colors that adorn it, and the strong contrast of those colors. Oratory is pleasing when accompanied by changes in the tone of voice. Music is beautiful from the variety of tone. The city is attractive from contrast in the style of buildings; and the architecture of the edifice that is broken by striking projections, tall columns, bold cornice, etc., is beautiful from that contrast. Thus in penmanship. Made with graceful curves, and in good proportion, the letter is still more beautiful by the contrast of light and shaded lines, the heavy line giving life to the appearance of the penmanship. If desirous of observing this principle, care should be taken not to bring two shades together, as the principle of contrast is thus destroyed. The effect of shade is shown by the following letters in contrast.

In capitals, where one line comes inside another, it is important for beauty that the lines should run parallel to each other. The equi-distant lines of the rainbow, and the circles around the planets, are among Nature's illustrations. A uniformity of slope and height, in all letters should also carefully be observed.

Again, as the well-trimmed lawn and the cleanly kept park, with no unsightly weeds or piles of rubbish to meet the gaze, are objects of admiration, so the neatly-kept page of writing, marred by no blots or stains, is beautiful to the eye.

Position of the Hand in Flourishing.

In executing broad sweeps with the pen, and assuming a position that will give greatest command of the hand in flourishing, the position of the pen in the hand should be reversed; the end of the penholder pointing *from* the left shoulder, the pen pointing towards the body, the holder being held between the thumb and two first fingers, as shown above.

Plain Penmanship and Flourishing.

The chief merit of business penmanship is legibility and rapidity of execution. Without sacrificing these qualities, the student may add as much beauty as possible. The business penman should beware, however, of giving much attention to flourishing, its practice, aside from giving freedom with the pen, being rather to distract the mind from the completion of a good style of business writing. Especially in plain penmanship should all flourishing be avoided. Nothing is in worse taste, in a business letter, than various attempts at extra ornamentation.

To the professional penman, however, in the preparation of different kinds of pen work, a knowledge of scientific flourishing is essential to the highest development of the art.

The principles of curves, shades and proportion that govern the making of capital letters apply as well also in flourishing.

CORRECT POSITION

FOR STANDING

WHILE WRITING;

Showing Hands, Paper, and
Position of the Feet.

THE desk at which the individual stands when writing, should slightly incline from the front upward. It should so project as to give ample room for the feet beneath, which should be so placed as to be at nearly right angles with each other, the right foot forward, the principal weight of the body resting upon the left. Incline the left side to the desk, resting the body upon the left elbow, as shown in the above engraving, thus leaving the right arm free to use the muscular or whole arm movement, as may be desired.

The desk should be so high as to cause the writer to stand erect, upon which the paper should be placed with the edge parallel with the desk.

Rest the body lightly on the forearm, and the hand upon the two lower fingers, the end of the penholder pointing towards the right shoulder. Practice in the position herewith shown, either with lead pencil or pen, upon waste paper, entirely regardless of the form of letters, until the pen can be held easily and correctly, and writing can be executed rapidly. Strike off-hand exercises, and the whole arm capitals, making each letter as perfectly as may be, the practice, however, being with special reference to acquiring the correct position, and freedom of movement.

Steady the paper firmly with the left hand, holding it near the top of the sheet, as shown in the illustration. Beware of soiling the paper with perspiration from the left hand.

CORRECT & INCORRECT

POSITION

FOR

SITTING and HOLDING

THE PEN.

 EREWITH are shown, in contrast, the correct and incorrect positions for sitting while writing; the upright figure representing the youth who sits erect, graceful and easy, holding the paper at right angles with the arm, steadying the same with the left hand.

As will be perceived, the correct position, here represented is at once conducive to health and comfort, being free from labored effort and weariness.

On the opposite side of the table sits a youth whose legs are tired, whose hands are wearied, and whose head and back ache from his struggles at writing. This boy will be liable to become, ere long, near-sighted, from keeping his eyes so close to his work. He will be round-shouldered, will have weak lungs, and will probably early die of consumption, caused from sitting in a cramped, contracted and unhealthy posture.

The bad positions liable to be assumed in writing, are, first, the one here shown; second, lying down and sprawling both elbows on the table; third, rolling the body upon one side, turning the eyes, and swinging the head, at the same time protruding and twisting the tongue every time a letter is made.

An earnest, determined effort should be made, when writing, to bring the body into an easy, graceful attitude, until the habit becomes thoroughly established.

This illustration should be carefully studied by youth when learning to write; and *all* writers should give the matter attention.

SMALL LETTERS CONTRASTED, SHOWING PROBABLE FAULTS.   RIGHT AND WRONG.

Wrong.   **Right.**

1st *a* is not closed at the top. It resembles a *u*. 2nd *a* contains a loop and resembles an *e*.

Wrong.   **Right.**

1st *b* is crooked. 2nd *b* has a loop too long.

Wrong.   **Right.**

1st *c* has the connecting line too high. 2nd *c* has a loop too large, causing it to resemble the *e*.

Wrong.   **Right.**

1st *d* contains a loop at the bottom. 2nd *d* slopes too much.

Wrong.   **Right.**

1st *e*, loop too small. 2nd *e*, loop too large.

Wrong.   **Right.**

1st *f* is crooked. 2nd *f* has a loop too long, top and bottom.

Wrong.   **Right.**

1st *g* is left open at the top. It resembles a *y*. 2nd *g* contains a loop at the top.

Wrong.   **Right.**

1st *h* is crooked. 2nd *h* has a loop too long.

Wrong.   **Right.**

1st *i* has no dot, and the lines unite too low. 2nd *i* has the dot too near the letter; the lines are not sufficiently united.

Wrong.   **Right.**

1st *j* is crooked and contains too much loop at the bottom. 2nd *j*, loop too short.

Wrong.   **Right.**

1st *k* resembles an *h* and is crooked. 2nd *k*, loop too long; lower part spreads too much.

Wrong.   **Right.**

1st *l* is crooked. 2nd *l*, loop too broad and too long.

Wrong.   **Right.**

1st *m* lacks uniformity of slope and appearance. 2nd *m* lacks uniformity of height, and too angular.

Wrong.   **Right.**

1st *n* lacks uniformity of slope. 2nd *n* resembles a *u* with first part too high.

Wrong.   **Right.**

1st *o* is left open at the top and resembles a *v*. 2nd *o* contains a loop.

Wrong.   **Right.**

1st *p* is crooked. 2nd *p* has been patched and is badly shaded.

Wrong.   **Right.**

1st *q* is left open at the top. 2nd *q* contains a loop in the top.

Wrong.   **Right.**

1st *r* contains a loop. 2nd *r* is too flat

Wrong.   **Right.**

1st *s* is too short. 2nd *s* contains a loop, top and bottom.

Wrong.   **Right.**

1st *t*, not crossed, is too round at the bottom, with bad connecting line. 2nd *t* slopes too much.

Wrong.   **Right.**

1st *u* resembles an *n*. 2nd *u* is irregular in height.

Wrong.   **Right.**

1st *v* is too angular at the top and bottom. 2nd *v* spreads too much.

Wrong.   **Right.**

1st *w* is too angular. 2nd *w* is irregular in height.

Wrong.   **Right.**

1st *x* is spread too much. 2nd *x* is too angular.

Wrong.   **Right.**

1st *y* is too high in the first part. 2nd *y* slopes too much.

Wrong.   **Right.**

1st *z* has a loop at the top. 2nd *z* slopes too much.

Wrong.   **Right.**

The dollar mark should have parallel lines being crossed by a character similar to the letter *S*.

CAPITALS CONTRASTED, SHOWING PROBABLE FAULTS. RIGHT AND WRONG.

Wrong.   **Right.**

1st *A* is too broad at the top.   2nd too much resembles the small *a*.

Wrong.   **Right.**

1st *B* has a bad capital stem. 2nd *B*, like the first, is too large at the top.

Wrong.   **Right.**

1st *C* has the loop too large, with base too small. 2nd *C* contains an angle.

Wrong.   **Right.**

1st *D* contains several angles.   2nd *D* is out of proportion.

Wrong.   **Right.**

1st *E* contains angles.   2nd *E*, out of proportion by being too large at the top.

Wrong.   **Right.**

1st *F* has the top too far to the left.   2nd *F* contains both a bad top and capital stem.

Wrong.   **Right.**

1st *G* is too small at the top.   2nd *G* is too large at the top

Wrong.   **Right.**

1st *H* has a bad capital stem.   2nd *H* resembles an *X*.

Wrong.   **Right.**

1st *I* is too broad, and has the loop too large. 2nd *I* has a bad capital stem.

Wrong.   **Right.**

1st *J* is crooked. 2nd *J* is too broad at the top, and contains a bad loop at the bottom.

Wrong.   **Right.**

1st *K* has a bad capital stem.   2nd *K* has an angular capital stem, and spreads too much.

Wrong.   **Right.**

1st *L* loop too large in upper part.   2nd *L* has the loop in the top too small.

Wrong.   **Right.**

1st *M* spreads too much at the top and has a bad capital stem.   2nd *M* is too close at the top, has a bad capital stem, the last *O* part spreading too much.

Wrong.   **Right.**

1st *N* has a bad capital stem, being too long and angular.   2nd *N* is out of proportion by spreading too much at the top.

Wrong.   **Right.**

1st *O* is too slim.   2nd *O* contains an angle at both top and bottom.

Wrong.   **Right.**

1st *P* is too small at the top.   2nd *P* has the top too large.

Wrong.   **Right.**

1st *Q* contains angles.   2nd *Q* is too large at the top.

Wrong.   **Right.**

1st *R* is too large at the top.   2nd *R* contains angles.

Wrong.   **Right.**

1st *S* has the loop too small at the top.   2nd *S* has the loop too large at the top.

Wrong.   **Right.**

1st *T* has a bad capital stem.   2nd *T* has a bad top.

Wrong.   **Right.**

1st *U* contains angles in the upper part.   2nd *U* spreads too much at the top.

Wrong.   **Right.**

1st *V* contains angles.   2nd *V* spreads too much at the top.

Wrong.   **Right.**

1st *W* contains angles in the upper portion of the first of the letter.   2nd *W* is out of proportion by having too much slope.

Wrong.   **Right.**

1st *X* contains several angles where there should be none.   2nd *X* is spread too much.

Wrong.   **Right.**

1st *Y* has the top too long.   2nd *Y* is too small at the top.

Wrong.   **Right.**

1st *Z* resembles a small letter *y*.   2nd *Z* is also illegible.

Wrong.   **Right.**

1st character & is too slim.   2nd character spreads too much. Both slope badly.

DESCRIPTION OF THE PLATES.

VERY Copy on Plates Nos. 1, 2, 3 and 4 should be written with care by all students desirous of improving their penmanship. Ladies can, if they wish, terminate with the finer hand, while gentlemen will end with the bolder penmanship.

Plate I.

Copy I is a free, off-hand exercise, calculated to give freedom and ease in writing. Observe to make an angle, top and bottom. A sufficient amount of practice on this copy, with pen or pencil, will break up all stiffness in the writing.

Copy 2 is the contraction of copy No. 1 into the letter *m*, giving a free, open, bold, business hand.

Copy 3 is composed of words of greater length, which should be written, if possible, by the student, from the beginning to the end of the word, without removing the pen from the paper until the word is finished. The words are composed principally of the letter *m*, which should be written with much care.

Copies 4 and 5 are the small letters of the alphabet. Carefully observe the shades, and the uniformity in slope of letters.

Copy 6 exhibits the figures, which are twice the height of small letters. The **7** and **9**, in script, extend one-half their length below the line.

Copies 7 and 8 are the capital letters of the alphabet, which are of the same height as the small letter *l*. There is usually but one shade in a letter. Observe the directions, given elsewhere, for the making of capitals, and guard against the probable faults, as there expressed. Study also, carefully, the principles of curves, proportion and shades, as applied in the making of capital letters.

The remainder of copies on Plates 1 and 2 should be written with the greatest care, "Perseverance" being the motto. Do not leave these copies until they are thoroughly mastered.

Plate III.

This plate is composed of copies similar to the others, the same principles being applicable in the making of the letters. As will be seen, this is a much more delicate hand, and is especially adapted to fine epistolary writing.

Plate IV.

Plate IV illustrates the form of writing a letter of introduction, and may be copied by the student as a specimen business letter.

Plate V.

This plate exhibits the off-hand capitals, which should be made purely with the arm movement, the hand resting lightly on the two lower fingers. Practice, at first, in making them with a lead-pencil on waste paper, will be found quite beneficial.

Plate VI.

The copies of Round Hand on this plate should be written with especial care, being the style suitable for headings, etc. Observe in the small letters that each is round, and every down mark shaded. The alphabet of German Text on this page will be found useful for ornamental work.

Plate VII.

Plate VII exhibits a variety of pen work, containing both fine and bold penmanship, and will be found a superior copy in which the student can display a knowledge of penmanship and flourishing.

Plate VIII.

Plate VIII is an original off-hand specimen of flourishing, the curves, proportion and shades in which should be carefully observed. (*See view of holding pen in flourishing*, page 27.)

PLATE I   17

1 ———————————————

2 m. mum. men. ment.

3 mammon. mammoth. m. n.

4 a b c d e f g h i j k l m n o p

5 q r s t u v w x y z. & &c. &c.

6 1 2 3 4 5 6 7 8 9 0. 1st 2nd 3rd 4th 1881.

7 A B C D E F G H I K L M N

8 O P Q R S T U V W X Y Z.

9 Albany. Boston. Chicago. Detroit.

10 Edinburgh. Florence. Gettysburg.

11 Hartford. Indianapolis. Jackson.

12 K London. Montreal. New York. O.

13 Pittsburg. Quincy. Rutland. S.

14 T U V W X Y Z. & &c. &c.

15 A mans manners shape his fortune.

16 Samples of my business writing.

17 My success to day due to good writing.

18   A beautiful hand writing is of itself an ornament and does honor to the executer. It is of that value which cannot be bought or sold, but is obtained only by talents and application.

The Mendel Lithographing Co. Chicago.

PLATE III.   19

1   a b c d e f g h i j k l m n o p q r s t

2   u v w x y z. 1 2 3 4 5 6 7 8 9 0. & &c. &Co.

3   A B C D E F G H I J K L M N

4   O P Q R S T U V W X Y Z

5   Sunday Monday Tuesday Wednesday Thursday

6   Friday Saturday Jan. Feb. March Apr. May.

7   June July Aug. Sept. Oct. Nov. Dec.   1st 2nd 3rd

8   A fine penmanship suitable for epistolary writing.

9   Copies of runninghand penmanship for ladies.

10   Samples of penmanship adapted to rapid writing.

Letter of Introduction.

New York, June 1st 1882

Hill Standard Book Co.
Chicago, Ill.

Dear Sirs:

This will introduce to your honorable house, Mr. Winfield Success of this city, who visits Chicago for the purpose of procuring a situation, as canvassing agent, for Hill's Manual.

From a knowledge of his honesty, industry, and steadiness of purpose, I think him such a person as you will be pleased to employ if you need more canvassers. I therefore take great pleasure in recommending him to your favorable acquaintance.

Yours Very Respectfully,
Daniel Cunningham.

The Mendel Lithographing Co. Chicago.

PLATE V. 21

OFF HAND CAPITALS.

The Mendel Lithographing Co. Chicago.

Specimens of Round Hand,

For

Day Book *and Ledger* *Headings*

and all

Forms where Legibility is Required.

German Text.

𝔄𝔅𝔒𝔇𝔈𝔉𝔊ℌℑ𝔍𝔎𝔏𝔐𝔑𝔒𝔓𝔔
ℜ𝔖𝔗𝔘𝔙𝔚𝔛𝔜ℨ

a b c d e f g h i j k l m n o p q r s t u v w x y z.

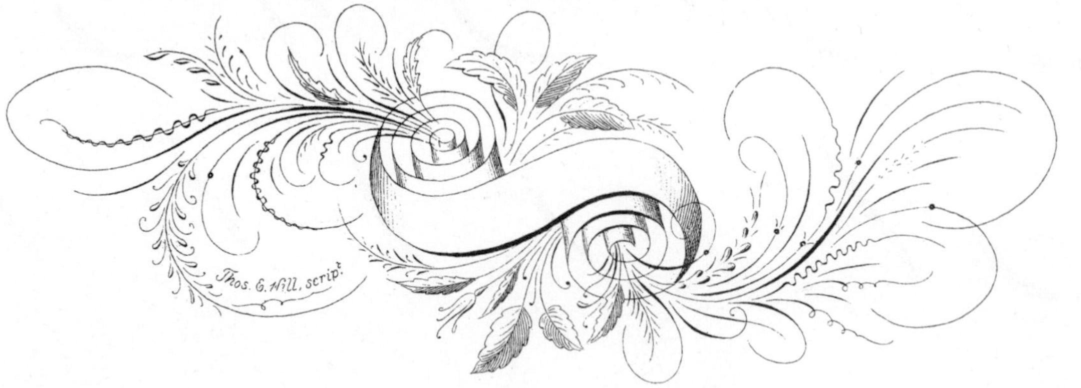

Thos. G. Hill, script.

PLATE VII   23

Poetic Gems.

"Full many a Gem, of purest ray serene,
The dark unfathomed caves of Ocean bear,
Full many a flower is born to blush unseen
And waste its sweetness on the desert air."

"God pity them both! and pity us all,
Who vainly the Dreams of Youth recall,
For of all sad words of tongue or pen,
The saddest are these It might have been."

Written and Flourished by Thos E Hill.

The Mendel Lithographing Co. Chicago.

Flourished by Thos E Hill

The Mendel Lithographing Co. Chicago.

Chalk and pencil Drawing.

Blackboard Flourishing.

The plates, representing flourishing in white lines on dark groundwork, though designed to represent off-hand work upon the blackboard, will be found equally useful for practice with the pen. The figure of the Swan from Packard and Williams' "Gems of Penmanship" is a beautiful piece of flourishing, which finely illustrates how true to nature an object may be made with but very few strokes of the pen. As will be seen, the figures on these plates are composed wholly of curved lines.

TEACHING PENMANSHIP.

DURING the past twenty years great improvement has been wrought in the penmanship of our youth, by the general introduction of writing books into our common schools, containing engraved copy lines; and yet statistics show that vast numbers of people in every State in the Union are unable to write; and some of these are to be found in nearly every locality. A majority of these persons have passed their school days, but the necessity is none the less urgent with them for improvement in penmanship; and they would gladly avail themselves of the opportunity for receiving instruction, if a competent teacher were to open a Writing School in their vicinity.

There exists a general demand for good instructors in Writing throughout the country, and teachers who will properly prepare themselves for the profession, can have excellent remuneration for their services. It is true that many persons attempt to teach writing as a profession, who, through bad management and want of moral principle, deservedly fail; but the earnest, faithful, competent teacher is wanted, and will be well rewarded for his labor.

The "12 Lesson" System.

There are but twenty-six letters in the alphabet to write; fifty-two in all, capital and small letters. The principles from which these letters are formed are, in reality, very few; and to obtain a mastery of these principles is the object of giving instruction. Therefore, to acquire a knowledge of *how* to write, a large number of lessons is not absolutely necessary. The course of instruction may be so arranged as to very completely include all the principles pertaining to penmanship in twelve lessons; and the class may have such practice, each lesson being two hours in length, as will, with many pupils, completely change their penmanship in that time. It is not pretended that any one can *perfect* their writing in twelve lessons. Real ease and grace in penmanship is the result of months and years of practice; but a knowledge of *how* to practice, to impart which is the mission of the teacher, may be learned in a short time. In fact, most people are surprised to see how much may be accomplished in few lessons when the class is properly instructed.

Should, however, the teacher wish to give a more extended term of instruction, it is only necessary to drill longer upon each principle, with elaborate blackboard illustration to correspond. If the time and means of the student prevent the taking of the longer course, the shorter term may be made proportionately beneficial. Should the Twelve-lesson term be adopted by the traveling teacher, the following suggestions may be of service in the organization and management of a Writing class.

Having acquired proficiency in penmanship, and having good specimens of writing to exhibit, let the young teacher, desirous of establishing a Writing school, visit any locality where live a civilized people. While it is true that the more ignorant most greatly need the advantage of such instruction, it is nevertheless a fact that the more intelligent and educated the people of a community, the better will be the teacher's patronage.

How to Organize the Class.

Secure, if possible, a school-room provided with desks and a blackboard. It is no more than justice to present the directors and the teacher of the school, upon whom the responsibility of management of the school building rests, each with a scholarship in the writing class. Having obtained a school-room, the next thing to be done to secure success, is to thoroughly advertise the nature and character of the school, and the time of commencement. The teacher may do this in the following ways:

First, By having editorial mention made in all newspapers published in the vicinity.

Second, By posters, announcing the school, liberally distributed about the town.

Third, By circulars, giving full description of the school, sent to each house.

Fourth, By visiting each school-room, supposing the day schools to be in session, in the vicinity, and, having obtained permission to do so, addressing the pupils of the school, accompanied by blackboard illustrations, showing method of teaching, announcing terms, time of commencing school, etc., and

Fifth, By personally calling at every public business place, and as many private houses as possible, in the neighborhood, exhibiting specimens and executing samples of writing when practicable.

A lady or gentleman well qualified as a teacher, pursuing this plan will seldom fail of obtaining a large class. Having secured an established reputation as a good teacher, personal canvass afterwards is not so necessary. Personal acquaintance with the patrons of the school, however, is always one of the surest elements of success with any teacher.

If the school is held in a rural district, newspaper and printed advertising can be dispensed with. In the village or city it is indispensable.

It is unwise to circulate a subscription paper, the establishment of the school being made contingent upon the number of subscribers to the class. A better way is to announce the school *positively* to commence at a certain time and *certainly* to continue through the course, which announcement inspires confidence and secures a much larger class.

Ask no one to sign a subscription paper, or to pay tuition in advance. The fact of doing so argues that the teacher lacks confidence in the people, who, in turn, suspect the stranger that seeks advanced pay, and thus withhold their patronage. The better way is to announce that no subscription is required to any paper, and no tuition is expected in advance; that all are invited to attend the school, and payment of tuition may be made when students are satisfied of the worth of the school. The fairness of these terms will secure a larger attendance than could otherwise be obtained, and will induce the teacher to put forth the very best efforts to please the patrons of the school.

Commencing about the middle of the term to make collection, by good management on the part of the teacher, if the school has been really meritorious, all the tuition will be paid by the time the last lesson is reached.

How to Maintain Interest.

To secure the best attendance, and the most interest on the part of pupils, the school should be in session every evening or every day, Sundays excepted, until the close of the term. It is a mistaken idea that students do best receiving but one or two lessons per week. During the intervening time between lessons pupils lose their interest, and the probability is that the class will grow smaller from the beginning to the close, if the mind of the student is allowed to become pre-occupied, as it will be, with other matters that occur between lessons so far apart. On the contrary, a writing class that meets every day or evening, under the management of an enthusiastic, skillful master, will grow from the beginning in size and interest, and the student, like the daily attendant at the public school, will exhibit a good improvement, resulting from undivided attention to the study, from the time of commencement to the close.

Each pupil in the class should be provided with pen, ink, and a writing book. Practicing in the evening, each should be provided with a lamp, covered with a shade, throwing as strong light as possible on the writing.

For the writing book, use five sheets of best foolscap paper. Cut in two, midway from top to bottom of the sheet; put one half inside the other; cover with strong paper, and sew the whole together, the cover extending one inch above the writing paper.

How to Arrange Copies.

Slips are best for copies, as they slide down the paper and can be kept directly above the writing of the pupil while practicing. Twenty-four copies will be generally sufficient to occupy the time of most pupils during the term, and should be arranged to embrace all the principles and exercises it is necessary for the student to understand in writing plain penmanship.

The copies may be written or printed. Written, if well executed; printed, if the teacher can obtain them, suitably arranged for the twelve-lesson term, as they are thus more perfect than written copies are likely to be, and save the teacher the drudgery of writing copies. If printed, the copy should be a fine, elegant lithographic *fac simile* of perfect penmanship; —perfect, because it takes the pupil no longer to learn to make a correct than an incorrect letter. Numbered in the order of their succession, from one to twenty-four, these slips should be wrapped together in a package, which should be pasted on the inside, at the top of the cover, whence they can be drawn as required by the student. When the copy is finished, the slip should be placed at the bottom of the package.

The wrapper, holding the copies, should be sufficiently firm and tight to prevent the copies falling from their places when the book is handled. If the copies are kept by the pupil free from wrinkles and blots, an advantage of this arrangement is, that when the book is written through the copies are yet carefully preserved in their place, when new writing paper may be added to the book and the copies used again by the same pupil or by others.

Another plan is, for the teacher to keep the copies and distribute the same at the commencement of the lesson among the members of the class, and collect them at the close. When the teacher is short of copies, this plan may be pursued, though the other is the most systematic, and is attended with the least labor.

The most advanced and rapid penmen of the class, who write out their copies before the close of the term, may be furnished with copies of various commercial forms, for practice, in the last of the term.

Should a *second term* of lessons be given, those students who attend it should review the copies of the first term for about six lessons, after which they may be drilled in the writing of commercial forms, business letters, compositions, etc., according to the capacity and advancement of the pupil.

The copy should always be ready before the class assembles. The teacher should never be compelled to write a copy while the school is in session, especially if the class be large.

Commencement of the School.

The teacher having arranged to give a course of lessons in writing, should open the school at the hour appointed, even if there be no more than one pupil in attendance at the time of commencement, and should *conduct the term through*, unless insurmountable obstacles prevent. If the school possesses real merit the class will steadily increase in size, until a hundred pupils may be in attendance, even though but a half dozen were in the class at the opening lesson.

PROGRAMME OF EXERCISES FOR EACH LESSON.

First Lesson.

ALLING audience to order. Brief statement of what it is proposed to accomplish during the course of instruction. Assembling of the members of the class in front of the teacher, when each pupil, able to do so, should write a sample of penmanship, worded as follows: "*This is a sample of my penmanship before taking lessons in writing*," each signing name to the same.

Pupils should be urged to present the best specimen it is possible for them to write, in order that the improvement made may be clearly shown when the student writes a similar exercise at the close of the term.

Specimens written, assume position for sitting and holding pen, full explanation being given by the teacher concerning correct and incorrect positions. Commence writing on the second page, the first page being left blank on which to write the name of the owner of the book. Let the first be a copy composed of quite a number of extended letters, containing such words as, "*My first effort at writing in this book.*" Writing these words in the first of the term enables the pupils to turn back from the after pages and contrast their writing with their first efforts in the book, on an ordinarily difficult copy, thus plainly showing their improvement as they could not perceive it by commencing with the simplest exercise. Students are encouraged to much greater exertion when they can plainly see their improvement. Having covered the first page with their ordinary penmanship, let the class commence with Copy No. **2**, shown on page 41, in the set of writing-school copies, while the teacher fully explains, from the blackboard, the object of the copy. Give half an hour's practice on position and freedom of movement, making frequent use of the blackboard in illustrating the principles for making letters. The blackboard is, in fact, indispensable to the teacher of penmanship.

Intermission of fifteen minutes. Criticism of position, explanation on blackboard of letter *m*, and practice on the letter by the class. Remarks by the teacher on the importance of a good handwriting, with brief outline of what the next lesson is to be.

Second Lesson.

Drill on position; criticism. Use a separate slip of paper for ten minutes' practice on freedom of movement for hand and arm. See that every pupil has the requisite materials. Explanation again of letter *m* as made in words mum, man, mim, etc. Thorough drill, and examination by teacher of each pupil's writing. *Intermission.* Writing of short words, with special reference to perfecting the letter *m*. Blackboard explanation of slope of letters, with illustrations showing importance of uniformity of slope, etc. Hints in reference to neatness, order, and punctuality, and encouragement, if the improvement of the class warrants the same. Love of appro-

bation is one of the ruling organs of the mind. Nothing is more gratifying, when the student has done well, than to be appreciated; and the pupil is stimulated to much greater exertion, when receiving judicious praise from the teacher for work well performed. Prompt and early attendance of the class at the next lesson should be urged, and close by giving outline of next lesson. The teacher should gather and keep the books. Students may each care for their pens, ink, and light.

Third Lesson.

Drill in movement. Explanation of letter *o* on the blackboard, and letters in which it is made, such as *a, d, g, q, e,* etc., showing, also, faults liable to be made. Careful examination and criticism of the writing of every student in the class individually. Explanation of *t, d,* and *p,* on the board, showing probable faults, with other exercises at the discretion of the teacher. *Intermission.* Explanation of length, size, and form of loop letters, the class being supposed to be practicing similar exercises to those illustrated on the board. Explanation and illustration concerning the writing of all the small letters, representing on the board the principles upon which they are made. During the lesson, two hours in length, the students should always be engaged in writing, except at intermission, and while the attention of the class is engaged with the blackboard illustrations.

Fourth Lesson.

A few minutes' drill on freedom of movement. Explanation of position for sitting and holding the pen, showing faults. Illustrations on the blackboard of the fundamental principles for making capital letters, representing curves, proportion, shades, parallel lines, etc.; students practicing the principles on a loose piece of paper. Careful drill on the capital stem. Caution by the teacher that students do not write too fast. General practice on copies including the capital letters. Individual examination by the teacher of all the writing books. *Intermission.* Blackboard illustration, showing faults in the making of the principles; careful drill on position for sitting, holding pen, and freedom of movement. Representation by teacher of evil effects of cramped penmanship, and weariness resulting from sitting improperly. Earnest effort to induce every pupil to practice as much as possible between lessons, a premium being given to the member of the class who shows greatest improvement at the close of the lessons, and a premium to the best penman.

Fifth Lesson.

Five minutes' drill on off-hand movement, special attention being paid by the class to the position for sitting and holding the pen. Illustration by the teacher, on the blackboard, of capital letters from *A* to *M*, making each capital correctly, beside which should be made the same letter as the pupil is liable to make it, showing probable faults. Examination by the teacher of the writing in each book. *Intermission.* Urgent appeal by the teacher to students to secure the greatest possible excellence in writing, by practice both in and out of the school; showing not only the reputation acquired by receiving the premium in the class, but the lasting advantage resulting from always being able to put thoughts beautifully and readily on paper. Blackboard illustrations, giving the capitals from *M* to *Z*, together with probable faults. Careful drill by pupils on capitals, accompanied by examination and criticism of each pupil by the teacher pleasantly suggesting a change where faults are visible, and praising all where improvement is plain.

Sixth Lesson.

General drill by the class on small letters and capitals. Review by the teacher of the capital stem on the blackboard and the making of all capitals in which it occurs. Examination by teacher of writing books. General remarks on punctuation, showing the importance of being able to punctuate correctly ; followed by making each punctuation mark on the board, its use being explained by sentences written. Each student should give careful attention to all blackboard illustrations. Different sentences should be written, and the various members of the class required to punctuate the same, if possible, correctly. *Intermission.* Continued drill in penmanship. Special explanation of the capital letter *O* on the blackboard, showing faults liable to be made ; that the height of the *O*, correctly formed, is twice its width, is made of a perfect curve, with parallel lines, only one down mark shaded. The teacher will then, on the board, make the capitals in which the same is found. Twenty minutes' practice by the class, applying the principle. Rest occasionally by the class, in which the teacher further illustrates exercises in punctuation.

Seventh Lesson.

Drill in penmanship, the teacher yet watching and exposing every fault to be seen in sitting and holding the pen ; also any marked fault in penmanship ; calling, however, no names of pupils that may be at fault. Blackboard illustration, showing the principle found in the upper part of *Q, W,* etc. Capitals made in which it occurs. Careful drill by pupils on this exercise. Criticism of writing in each book by the teacher. General remarks by the teacher on the use of capital letters, followed by illustrations on the board showing where capitals should be used. Steady practice in penmanship by the class, the pupils being cautioned to write with the utmost care, making it a point to write every letter perfectly, no matter how long it may take to execute the same, remembering that practice will bring rapid writing, but care alone, and attention to principles, will bring perfect penmanship. Brief drill by the class in off-hand penmanship, from copies on the board ; wrist free from the desk, and forearm resting lightly on the desk. The teacher should remind the pupil of the importance of always holding the paper with the left hand, and having now nearly completed the seventh lesson, what is yet the fault with any member of the class? Students should ask themselves, " What lack I yet in my penmanship?" *Intermission.* Continued practice by the class. The pupils may rest while the teacher writes several sentences upon the board without capitals, the members of the class suggesting where capitals belong, and also being required to punctuate. Several words may be given for the students to practice next day, the student presenting the best specimen of the same, at the next lesson, to receive honorable mention.

Eighth Lesson.

Penmanship drill in the writing book. Blackboard illustration, showing any fault yet discovered by the teacher. General remarks on the importance of good penmanship, pecuniarily and intellectually, calculated to inspire the class with a due appreciation of their work. Students can generally write during the time the teacher is talking, except during blackboard illustration. The teacher will now give general remarks on the writing of business forms, concerning the value and use of promissory notes, bills, receipts, orders, checks, drafts, etc., following by writing a promissory note upon the board, accompanying the same by an explanation of the form in which a note should be written to draw six per cent., ten per cent., no per cent., etc. If sold to another person, how it should be endorsed, etc. After writing one hour, at each lesson, should follow *Intermission.* Continued practice in penmanship in the writing. Write one copy to the page, a plain hand, and never anything but what is found in the copy. It is a great mistake to practice many styles of penmanship. In so doing the ordinary pupil becomes proficient in none. Blackboard illustrations, during this lesson, on writing orders, receipts, bills, etc., requiring students to capitalize and punctuate the same. The teacher should urge, at the close of the lesson, the great importance of practice between lessons during the remainder of the term. To whom shall the premiums be given? That will greatly depend upon the practice out of the school-room.

Ninth Lesson.

Require every student to write one page in the writing book with the greatest care. The teacher should examine every book. What faults yet remain? Illustrate them on the board. More practice in the writing books. General remarks by the teacher on superscriptions, followed by illustrations on the blackboard. Illustrate why and where to place name on the envelope, together with name of town, county, state ; where to place postage stamp, how to write straight. Illustrate and explain all the various titles used in addressing Kings, Queens, Presidents, Members of Congress, Governors, Judges, Lawyers, Physicians, Clergymen, Professors, etc., etc. *Intermission.* On a separate slip of paper the students may then each write the superscription they would use were they to address any official, military, or professional man. Continued practice in the writing book, the lesson closing by the teacher requesting each pupil to bring five sheets of note paper and five envelopes for practice in letter writing at the next lesson.

Tenth Lesson.

Twenty minutes' practice in writing books until all the members of the class have assembled. General remarks by the teacher on the subject of letter writing and commercial correspondence, explaining the various kinds of letters for different purposes, size of paper and envelopes required for each, and all the essentials necessary to writing any kind of a letter well. The teacher will then write a brief friendship letter upon the board, explaining where and how to write the dating, the complimentary address, body of the letter, complimentary closing, signature, division of subjects into paragraphs, etc. The students should criticise the letter with reference to punctuation and capital letters, and when the subject is thoroughly understood by the class, let each pupil copy the letter from the board; the teacher in the meantime passing to the desk of each pupil, criticising and making suggestions to pupils that may require assistance. See that all copy the letter. This exercise is invaluable, and every student should be required, if possible, to master it. This lesson, well conducted by the teacher, will give each member of the class information that is worth vastly more than the cost of his tuition for the entire term. *Intermission.* Each member of the class should copy the letter once more. With all the corrections and suggestions that have now been made, many of the class will write the exercise very well. The letter finished, write superscription on envelope, the pupils writing such address as they may choose. At the close of the lesson, the students may take with them their envelopes and letter paper, for practice on the morrow, and the pupil that will present the most correctly and beautifully written letter, at the eleventh lesson, shall be awarded a premium of such character as the teacher may select. This will induce a great deal of practice in the next twenty-four hours in letter writing, and will be very beneficial to the class.

Eleventh Lesson.

General review in penmanship, with practice in writing book for half an hour, followed by writing of last specimens, as follows :

"*This is a specimen of my penmanship after taking lessons in writing,*" each scholar signing name to specimen. Each pupil should write two samples at the commencement of the course of lessons, and two at the close, one of the first to be put with one of the last for the student to keep, showing the advancement made in a course of lessons. The other first and last will be preserved by the teacher, as a memento of the pupil, and also to show, in other localities, the amount of improvement made by students in this and preceding classes. During this lesson the teacher will give general remarks on letters of introduction, and notes of invitation and acceptance, with illustrations on the blackboard, explaining the circumstances under which they are used. Before the recess, the teacher should appoint three ladies and three gentlemen of the class to assemble at intermission, and select three disinterested persons to examine specimens of the class, to determine who shall receive premiums at the last lesson. *Intermission.* Every pupil should write a last specimen. Most students will be surprised to see their advancement in penmanship in the past ten lessons, though no one can actually *see all* the improvement that has been made, as much of the time of the class has been occupied in explanation, thus placing a knowledge of correct writing in the *head.* In after months of practice it will come out at the *fingers.* The remaining blackboard illustrations of the lesson may relate to card writing; the teacher explaining the nature of business cards, wedding cards, visiting cards, and address cards; showing how they should be written, when used, etc.

At the close of the lesson, an invitation should be extended to all the people of the neighborhood to be present at the closing exercises of the last lesson to witness the award of premiums, see the improvement of the class, etc.

Twelfth Lesson.

Students in their seats, and continued practice in the writing books. The teacher has had all the specimens of the class, first and last of each pupil, examined by a committee chosen for that purpose, along with writing books when thought necessary, each pupil's name on the specimen being covered by a small piece of paper pasted across the same. The knowledge of who takes the premiums, however, should be entirely kept from the class until the last minute, when the same is announced, amid a breathless silence, by the teacher. All the members of the class having assembled, the teacher will review the position for sitting, holding pen, kinds of materials to use, how to preserve materials, etc. He should dwell on the importance of frequent composition and letter writing, showing that the writing term, composed as it is of but twelve lessons, cannot be expected to make the student a finished penman in that course of time. That the object of the lessons has been to teach the members of the class *how* to learn ; that it now simply remains for the pupils to build on their knowledge of the principles. Upon the blackboard, the teacher will then review the fundamental principles over which the class has passed, showing how the principles of curves, proportion, shades, and parallel lines will give elegance and grace to the letter. A few perfect and imperfect letters should again be contrasted together for the benefit of the class, and the entertainment of the audience present, the blackboard illustrations comprising the making of birds, eagles, swans, pens, etc., showing the application of the principles in all forms, as well as letters ; thus impressing upon the class the necessity of careful attention to nature's rules, in the execution of beautiful penmanship. The teacher should be provided with a small writing desk, containing every article necessary for writing. This he should open before the class, and follow by showing the use for every article contained therein, the concluding remarks on penmanship being that students should provide themselves with every material necessary for composition and letter writing, thus making their practice in the future agreeable, and hence their continued improvement certain. Adverting now to the promise made in the early part of the term, that those students should be rewarded with honorable mention and premiums who had exhibited greatest improvement and excellence the teacher will explain the course pursued in the examination of writing by the committee, and after showing that perfect impartiality has been observed, he will announce the name of the person presenting the best letter, and present premium ; following with the name of the pupil having made greatest improvement, concluding with the announcement of the student that is regarded the best penman in the class, accompanying the remarks by presentation of prizes. The exercises of the lesson should close with appropriate farewell remarks.

SUGGESTIONS TO TEACHERS.

A WRITING School conducted thus, according to the foregoing arrangement of lessons, the principles of penmanship being explicitly illustrated on the blackboard and taught by a thoroughly competent teacher, will be of great and lasting service to the community in which it is held, and will afford every member of the class a season of highly profitable enjoyment. Of course the success of the school mainly depends upon the teacher. The instructor is, in fact, the life and soul of the class. If he possess love of order, tact, versatility, knowledge of human nature, self-possession, with ability to illustrate, explain and entertain his class with story and anecdote pertaining to writing, he will find his classes large and the profession of teaching writing as profitable to himself and as beneficial to the public as any upon which he can enter.

Should teaching writing be chosen as a profession for a series of years, it is well for the teacher to select a dozen or twenty villages in which to teach, and give instruction in each of these localities, once or twice a twelvemonth for years in succession rather than teach over a very wide range of country. The teacher's reputation thus becomes established, the profession is dignified and ennobled; people knowing the worth of the school are free to patronize, and thus the avocation is made much more pleasant and profitable to the teacher.

The outline of instruction given for the foregoing series of lessons is but a brief epitome of what each lesson ought to be. The enumeration of subjects may guide the young teacher somewhat, but the whole should be greatly elaborated, and will be, by the ingenious teacher, as circumstances demand.

The usual charge for a course of instruction of 12 lessons is from $2 to $5 per pupil.

Teachers should furnish paper for students, and care for the books when not in use by the pupils. Students may take charge of the other materials required.

The strictest order should be maintained. No whispering ought to be allowed. Such stillness should reign in the school that every scratching pen may be distinctly heard.

To secure order the teacher will notice when the first evidence of restlessness begins to manifest itself in the class; certain students becoming tired of writing. If this uneasiness is allowed to continue twenty minutes, the school will be oftentimes a scene of confusion, but upon the first appearance of weariness, the attention of the class should be directed for a short time to the blackboard, or the time may be occupied for a little while by some story, humorous or otherwise, having a bearing upon writing; listening to which the students become rested, and proceed with their practice afterwards with pleasure.

Having invited the leading citizens of the town to visit the school, call upon them frequently for remarks to the class on the subject of writing. From the business and professional men who may thus address the class, the teacher and pupils may oftentimes gain many valuable ideas, the class will be encouraged, and better discipline will be secured. The great secret of preserving good order in school is to keep the mind of the students constantly employed with the work in hand.

The subjects pertaining to writing are abundant, and it becomes the teacher to study and present them to the class in familiar lectures as occasion demands. Many of the succeeding chapters of this book afford subject matter, from which the teacher of penmanship can obtain topics to discuss, that will entertain and instruct the class, while the instructor should, at the same time, be on the alert for practical subjects to illustrate his work, from whatever source they may be obtained. For example, how character can be told from penmanship; what faculties of mind are employed in the execution of writing ; why some pupils are naturally handsome penmen and others not ; why Edward Everett should write elegantly and Horace Greeley with a scrawl ; why gentlemen naturally write a large hand, and ladies fine, etc.

The effect of temperament on penmanship, and the result of using stimulants, should be thoroughly considered, and presented to the class. Students should be urged to avoid the use of tobacco as a noxious habit that lays the foundation for intemperance, and the use of strong drink as the destroyer of the soul ; both tobacco and stimulants being also destructive to that steadiness of nerve essential to the execution of beautiful penmanship.

Many a boy may be deterred from an evil habit by the good example and advice of the teacher, admonishing him that superiority in penmanship and great excellence in life will come from being strictly temperate.

CONCLUDING SUGGESTIONS ON PENMANSHIP TO LEARNERS.

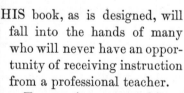 HIS book, as is designed, will fall into the hands of many who will never have an opportunity of receiving instruction from a professional teacher.

To practice penmanship to advantage, unaided by the teacher, students should provide themselves with necessary materials, as detailed elsewhere.

For the purpose of making steady progress in the acquisition of an elegant, plain penmanship, the student will be assisted by copying choice gems of poetry or prose, first writing each exercise on a separate slip of paper and afterwards transcribing the same in a book kept for the purpose. In the writing of original compositions and letters, each exercise should be copied as long as the student is desirous of

improving in penmanship; the copy being always a great improvement upon the original, not only in penmanship, but in spelling, grammar, use of capital letters, and composition.

Writers should not rest satisfied until they have absolutely mastered a plain, rapid, and elegant penmanship. The art, being almost purely mechanical, is more easily acquired by some than others; but every person from eight years of age upwards, until the body becomes tremulous with age, having ordinary command of the hand, who will persevere in the attempt, can write a legible, easy penmanship.

Among the benefits arising from a good handwriting, some are shown in the following

Reasons why we should write well.

Because, 1st. Good penmanship of itself adds greatly to our *happiness*. The consciousness to the lady or gentleman of being able to write a letter that shall win the admiration and praise of the friend to whom it is written is a source of unspeakable pleasure to the writer, and to possess this ability throughout our lifetime is to be proficient in an accomplishment which adds to our happiness, as does excellence in oratory, painting or music. Good writing is a fine art, and is to the eye what good language is to the ear.

2nd. Good writing is of great benefit to us *pecuniarily*. The person who may apply for a situation as teacher, clerk, or any position where intellectual ability is required, finds a beautifully written letter the best recommendation that can be sent when applying for that position. Hundreds of instances are on record, many doubtless within the knowledge of the reader, where lucrative situations have been obtained through good penmanship, that could never have been secured had the applicant not had a good handwriting.

And, 3rd. A mastery of the art of writing is of great service to us *intellectually*. Persons who can write well, taking pleasure in the practice, will write more than they otherwise would. Every time they write a word they spell it, and thus improve in spelling. Every time a sentence is written, an application is made of grammar; and thus knowledge is obtained of how to speak correctly. The subject they write about, they become familiar with; and thus, in the act of writing, they are intellectually improved. The most intelligent and influential in any community are those who can express thought most easily and correctly on paper.

COPIES FOR WRITING-SCHOOL.

STANDARD copies for the twelve lessons may consist of the following script lines, though it is important that they be as perfectly prepared as the copies shown on Plates I, II, III and IV.

The extra practice, beyond the two copies assigned at each lesson, may be on a separate slip of paper, and should comprise the writing of the elements of letters, commercial forms, off-hand capitals, letter writing, etc.

Students may join the class at any time, up to the last half of the term. Whatever may be the time of commencement, however, each pupil should begin with the first copies, and write as many of them as time will permit. The occasional review of the principles, by the teacher, will enable the students that join last to understand them; though it is desirable, for the sake of practice, that each pupil commence, if possible, with the first lesson.

As will be seen by examination, the style of penmanship, for ladies and gentlemen, is equally large up to the 17th copy. Beyond that, the size for ladies is decidedly finer. Though important that ladies should be able to write a bold penmanship for business and other writing, the lady involuntarily chooses a more delicate handwriting, by which she thus expresses her natural delicacy and refinement of character.

First Lesson.

1. *My first effort at writing in this book.*

2.

Second Lesson.

3. *n n m m u u m n n m m u u n*

4. *mum min mam mem mind ment*

Third Lesson.

5. *o a d g g e d t p b f l o a d g g e*

6. *a b c d e f g h i j k l m n*

—————Fourth Lesson.—————

7.   o p q r s t u v w x y z. &. &c. Ho

8.   A B C D E F G H I J K L M

—————Fifth Lesson.—————

9.   N O P Q R S T U V W X Y Z.

10.   America. Bavaria. Canada. Denmark.

—————Sixth Lesson.—————

11.   England. France. Germany. Holland.

12.   India. Japan. Kentucky. Lapland.

—————Seventh Lesson.—————

13.   Mexico. Norway. Oregon. Pennsylvania.

14.   Quito. Russia. Switzerland. Turkey.

—————Eighth Lesson.—————

15.   Uruguay. Vermont Wyoming X. Y. Z.

16.   A sample of my business penmanship.

—————Ninth Lesson.—————

17.   By commendable deportment we gain esteem.

18.   Commendations generally animate men.

—————Tenth Lesson.—————

19.   Improvement should be the object of all.

20. *Honor and shame from no condition rise.*

— Eleventh Lesson. —

21. *Learning is the ornament of youth.*

22. *Prosperity gains friends; adversity tries them.*

— Twelfth Lesson. —

23. *Running hand penmanship for business.*

24. *Samples of my off-hand, business writing*

LADIES EPISTOLARY.

— Ninth Lesson. —

17. *Emulation in acquiring knowledge is commendable. For value received.*

18. *In time of prosperity prepare for adversity. Sunshine and Storm.*

— Tenth Lesson. —

19. *Humiliation and repentance are ornaments of the Christian. Humiliation*

20. *Learn all that is possible to-day; you may require it to-morrow. Learn.*

— Eleventh Lesson. —

21. *Merit shall not go unrewarded. Trust to time and persevere. Persevere.*

22. *Nature unfolds a volume ever profitable for our study. Look and learn.*

— Twelfth Lesson. —

23. *This is a specimen of my hand-writing. Specimens of Penmanship.*

24. *Running-hand penmanship for Ladies Epistolary Writing. Writing*

Short-Hand Writing.

Short-Hand for Business Purposes.

 VERY year adds proof, by the constantly increasing demand for it, how indispensable in a modern education is a knowledge of rapid writing. The young, by all means, should acquire it.

It may be used by the author in his study, the editor in his "sanctum," the clergyman in his library, the lawyer in his office — in fact, everywhere that writing is needed, the simplicity and dispatch of Short-hand make its value apparent.

The beginner should determine, at the outset, whether or not he will, for a time at least, do verbatim writing. If he wishes to do this, he must expect to give much time and close attention to it. The man or system that promises to give verbatim speed in a few weeks' time, is unworthy of confidence. It is useless to expect to be a good reporter and follow some other business at the same time. Reporting is a profession of itself, and requires the undivided attention of the person following it. If, however, the beginner, simply wishing relief from long-hand in his daily writing, is content with a rate of speed that gives a fully written and absolutely legible manuscript, a style that is easy to learn, write, read, and remember, let him take up the simplest style, master it thoroughly, and depend for speed upon perfect familiarity with the word-forms used, and the greatest facility in their execution, as in long-hand, and he will gain his object more easily and quickly than if he seeks it through shorter word-forms, which must necessarily be more difficult to learn and read. Very few people need to become verbatim reporters; every one, however, having much writing to do, can use a simple style of short-hand to advantage.

The grand principle upon which a system of short-hand should be built is that of phonetics. Every sound in the language should be represented by its individual sign, used for that sound and no other. As a simple sound is uttered by one impulse of the voice, so should the sign representing it be made by one movement of the hand; resulting in a single, simple sound being represented by a single, simple line. These lines should be of such a form that they may be easily joined, one to another, so that a word may be completely written without raising the pen. The most frequently occurring sounds should be represented by the most easily written signs; and all the sounds should be represented by such signs as will give a free, flowing, forward direction to the writing, without running either too far above or below the line upon which it is written. There should be a distinct line drawn between the simplest style for general use — which should contain no contracted, irregular, or exceptional word-forms — and the more brief and complicated styles for the reporter's use.

Of the various systems of Short-hand, that called Tachygraphy (*Ta-kig-ra-fe*), a system invented and elaborated by D. P. Lindsley, of Andover, Mass., probably more nearly meets the requirements of the public than any now in use ; the advantage of this system of Short-hand being, that it combines rapidity with completeness of detail in a very large degree. By permission of Mr. Lindsley we are enabled to present the following synopsis and illustrations from his work, " Elements of Tachygraphy," published by Otis Clapp, No. 3 Beacon St., Boston.

THE ALPHABET OF TACHYGRAPHY.

CONSONANTAL SIGNS.

SIGN.	NAME.	SOUND.	SIGN.	NAME.	SOUND.
	Be,	b in bay.		The,	th in they.
	Pe,	p in pay.		Ith,	th in oath.
	Ga,	g in go.		Em,	m in may.
	Ka,	k in key.		En,	n in nay.
	De,	d in do.		Ing,	ng in sing.
	Te,	t in to.		El,	l in lay.
	Ve,	v in eve.		Ra,	r in ray.
	Ef,	f in if.		Wa,	w in we.
	Zhe,	z in azure.		Ya,	y in ye.
	Ish,	sh in show.		Ha,	h in high.
	Ze,	z in ooze.		Ja,	j in jail.
	Es,	s in so.		Cha,	ch in each.

VOCAL SIGNS.

SIGN	NAME	SOUND	SIGN	NAME	SOUND
	E,	e in eve.		ĭ,	i in it ; y in duty.
	A,	a in ace.			
	Ai,	ai in air.		ĕ,	e in ebb.
	Ah,	a in are.		ă,	a in ask, at.
	Oo,	o in do.		ŏŏ,	oo in foot ; u in full.
	O,	o in ode.		ŭ,	ŭ in us, fun, hut.
	Au,	au in aught.		ŏ,	o in on, or.
	Oi,	oy in boy.		I,	i in ice.
	Ow,	ow in now.		Ew,	ew in dew.

In writing Tachygraphy the pen should be held between the first and second fingers, and steadied by the thumb — as shown in the cut at the beginning of this chapter — so that such signs as | \ ___ may be easily made, without changing the position of the pen.

The alphabet should be thoroughly mastered by taking up the signs in pairs, and writing them many times, repeating the sound represented as the sign is made, so as to get the sound allied with the sign, and both well fixed in the mind. It will be noticed that all heavy signs represent vocal sounds, while nearly all the light signs represent whispered sounds.

The signs, | | \ \ )) ((⌐ ⌐, are always written downward; ▬ ▬ ⌒ ⌒ ⌣ ⌣ ⌐ ⌐, from left to right ; / ⌐ /, either upward or downward, and ⌐ ⌐ ⌐, always upward.

In joining consonant signs with each other, acute angles should be made where possible, as they are more easily and rapidly made than obtuse angles. The joining of a vowel sign with a consonant, at its beginning, should always form an angle, thus :

Abe, eke, it, of, owes, on, oil, are.

At the end of a consonant, the semi-circular vowels are written, either in their alphabetic form or as hooks on the consonant, whichever is most convenient and adds most to facility in writing. The vowels ⌒ ⌒ (distinguished mainly by size), are determined by their being written in the direction the hands of a clock move — turning far enough to the right to form a proper angle with the following sign ; and ⌣ ⌣ (also distinguished mainly by size), are determined by their being written in the opposite direction. Examples :

Be, kid, keen, deep, tick, fish, leap, hid, bad, car, tan, narrow, last.

The dash vowels should always form angles with consonant signs ; ⌇ ⟍ are varied in their direction to facilitate this.   Examples :

⟍ ⌣ goat, knowing, | ⟍ up, cut.

Either the first or second, or both strokes of the vowel diphthongs may be made straight or curved to facilitate joining, thus :

Nine,   size,   noise,   now,   hew.

The other vowel signs do not vary from the alphabetic position, and must be disjoined when they will not form a proper angle.

Disjoined vowels should be written to the left of upright and inclined, and above horizontal consonants, when the vowel sound precedes the consonant sound, and to the right of upright and inclined, and below horizontal consonants, when the vowel sound follows the consonantal.

CONSONANTAL DIPHTHONGS.

Br, as in brow.	Dl, as in meddle.
Pr, as in prow.	Tl, as in settle.
Gr, as in grow.	Vl, as in evil.
Cr, as in crow.	Fl, as in fly.
Dr, as in draw.	Zhl, as in ambrosial.
Tr, as in try.	Shl, as in special.
Vr, as in over.	Nl, as in kennel.
Fr, as in free.	
Zhr, as in measure.	Sp, as in spy.
Shr, as in shred.	Sk, as in sky.
Thr, as in other.	St, as in stay.
Thr, as in three.	Sf, as in sphere.
Nr, as in owner.	Sm, as in smith.
Bl, as in blow.	Sn, as in snow.
Pl, as in plow.	Sl, as in slat.
Gl, as in glow.	Sw, as in sweet.
Cl, as in clay.	

Bz, as in hubs.	Mz, as in hems.
Ps, as in hopes. also Gz, Ks, Dz, Ts, etc.	Nz, Ns, as in hens, hence.
Vz, as in loaves.	Ngz, as in brings.
Fs, as in roofs.	Lz, Ls, as in owls, else.
Zz, as in mazes.	Rz, Rs, as in wars, horse.
Sz, as in masses. also Thz, Ths, etc.	Wh, as in when.

These signs, it will be observed, are not new ones, but modifications of those already learned. They should be used only where no vowel sound occurs between the consonant sounds. A few examples will explain their use quite fully.

Blow, glow, meddle, evil, brow, upper, gray, meeker, draw, utter, over, free, measure, shred, other, owner, spy, stay, sphere, smith, snow, sleep, sweet, when, special, kennel.

Where the final consonant of a word is either s or z, preceded by a consonant, a circle is used for the s or z, thus :

Hope, hopes, lad, lads, owl, owls, war, wars. When preceded by a vowel, use the alphabetic form for s and z.

The circle is also used between two consonants, and is then written on the outside of the angle formed by the consonants — when both are straight lines, as | ⟋ ; on the inside of the curve, where one is a curve and the other a straight line, as ⟩ ⟨ ; and on the inside of both curves, when possible, as in

It is sometimes necessary to write the circle on the inside of one curve and outside of the other, as in ⟩

Two or more words, closely allied in sense, may be joined into a phrase, where the signs composing the words unite readily, thus adding to both the speed and legibility of the writing. Example;

Of the, with it, it is, in such a way, I will be, I have.

The first inclined or perpendicular consonant sign should rest upon the line — the other signs following in their proper direction.　Example:

Seek always to form a free, flowing, graceful outline.　The most easily written forms are the most beautiful, and *vice versa*.

We have given, of this system, only a synopsis of the fully written Common Style, but sufficient, however, to explain the merits and principles of Tachygraphy.　Those who wish to fit themselves for verbatim writing are referred to the work entitled, " The Note Taker.　A Treatise on the Second Style of Lindsley's Brief Writing, for the use of Lawyers, Editors, Reporters, Students, and all persons desirous of taking full notes in Courts of Record, Professional Schools, Seminaries, and Public Assemblies."　Published by the firm to which we have before alluded.

The following Extracts are from Pope's Essay on Man.

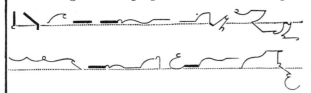

Vice is a monster of so frightful mien,

As, to be hated, needs but to be seen;

Yet seen too oft, familiar with her face,

We first endure, then pity, then embrace.

Pope's Essay on Man.—Second Epistle.

SPELLING.

BEAUTIFUL penmanship should be accompanied by correct spelling. If the person can possess but one accomplishment, it is, in fact, better to spell correctly than to write well. Nothing so mars the effect of beautiful chirography as bad spelling, which is the more conspicuous when set off by good penmanship. True, there are over a hundred thousand words in the English language, and we cannot reasonably be expected to remember the correct orthography of them all; and not until the phonetic system is received, by which every word is represented by a recognized sign, can we spell all words correctly without reference to the dictionary; but the few hundred words in general use are not so difficult to master. At any rate, the writer should have at hand a reliable dictionary, and no word should go from his hand without being correctly spelled.

The following will aid students somewhat in their knowledge of spelling:

Names of Elementary Sounds.

An elementary sound is the simplest sound of the English language, as a, e, b, k.

The English language contains about forty elementary sounds.

These sounds are divided into three *classes*—*vocals*, *sub-vocals*, and *aspirates*.

The *vocals* consist of a pure tone only, as a, e, i, o, u.

The *sub-vocals* consist of tone united with breath; as b, d, l, m, n, r.

The *aspirates* consist of pure breath only; as p, t, k, f.

The following words contain the different elementary sounds of the language:

VOCALS.— N-*a*-me, b-*a*-ll, *a*-t, m-*e*, m-*e*-t, f-*i*-ne, p-*i*-n, s-*o*-ld, m-*o*-ve, n-*o*-t, m-*u*-te, p-*u*-ll, c-*u*-p, f-*ou*-nd.

SUB-VOCALS.— *B*-at, *d*-og, *g*-o, *j*-oy, *l*-ife, *m*-an, *n*-o, so-*ng*, ba-*r*, *th*-ose, *v*-oice, *w*-ise, *y*-es, *z*-one, a-*z*-ure.

ASPIRATES.— *F*-aith, *h*-at, ar-*k*, *p*-ine, *s*-un, *t*-ake, *th*-ink, *sh*-one, *ch*-ur-*ch*, *wh*-en.

Letters.

A letter is a *character* used to represent an elementary sound.

The English Alphabet contains twenty-six letters: A, a; B, b; C, c; D, d; E, e; F, f; G, g; H, h; I, i; J, j; K, k; L, l; M, m; N, n; O, o; P, p; Q, q; R, r S, s; T, t; U, u; V, v; W, w; X, x; Y, y; Z, z.

As will be seen, there are more elementary sounds than letters. It therefore follows that some letters must represent more than one sound each.

Those letters which represent vocals are called *vowels*. They are a, e, i, o, u, and sometimes w and y.

Those letters which represent sub-vocals and aspirates are called *consonants*.

The sub-vocals and consonants are b, d, g, l, m, n, r, v, z.

The aspirates and consonants are f, h, k, c, q, p, t, s.

Rules for Spelling.

1. Words of one syllable ending in F, L, or S, preceded by a single vowel, double the final consonant; as STAFF, MILL, PASS; except IF, OF, AS, GAS, HAS, WAS, YES, IS, HIS, THIS, US, THUS.

2. Words ending in any other consonant except F, L, and S, do not double the final letter; except ADD, ODD, EGG, EBB, INN, ERR, PURR, BUTT, BUZZ, and some proper names.

3. Words of one syllable, and words accented on the last syllable, when they end with a single consonant, preceded by a single vowel, double the final consonant before an additional syllable beginning with a vowel; as ROB, ROBBER; PERMIT, PERMITTING; but X final, being equivalent to KS, is an exception, and is never doubled.

4. A final consonant, when not preceded by a single vowel, or when the accent is not on the last syllable, should remain single before an additional syllable; as TOIL, TOILING; VISIT, VISITED. L and S are often doubled, in violation of this rule, when the accent is not on the last syllable: as TRAVEL, TRAVELLER; BIAS, BIASSED. It is better to write TRAVELER and BIASED.

5. Primitive words ending in LL reject one L before LESS and LY; as SKILL, SKILLESS; FULL, FULLY: but words ending in any other double letter, preserve it double before these terminations; as FREE, FREELY; ODD, ODDLY.

6. The final E of a primitive word is generally omitted before an additional termination beginning with a vowel; as RATE, RATABLE; FORCE, FORCIBLE; but words ending in CE and GE retain the E before ABLE and OUS; as PEACE, PEACEABLE; OUTRAGE, OUTRAGEOUS.

7. The final E of a primitive word is generally retained before an additional termination beginning with a consonant; as PALE, PALENESS; but when the E is preceded by a vowel it is sometimes omitted; as TRUE, TRULY: and sometimes retained; as SHOE, SHOELESS.

8. The final Y of a primitive word, when preceded by a consonant, is changed into I before an additional termination; as MERRY, MER-RILY: but with a vowel before, the Y is not changed; as VALLEY, VALLEYS, and not VALLIES, as frequently written; and before ING the Y is retained to prevent the doubling of the I; as PITY, PITYING.

9. Compounds generally retain the orthography of the simple words of which they are composed; as ALL-WISE, BLUE-EYED.

10. Words ending in F or FE have V substituted for the F in forming the plurals: as WIFE, WIVES; KNIFE, KNIVES, etc., except when ending in FF.

11. Some words are spelt the same in both the singular and plural; as DEER, SHEEP, etc., in which instance, by placing A before the word, one is meant, and by using THE, more than one.

12. Some words are spelt altogether differently in the singular and plural; as MOUSE, MICE; GOOSE, GEESE.

13. In spelling words it is necessary to consider well the different sounds of each part of the word. Every separate sound in a word must have in it one of the following letters, A, E, I, O, or U. Take for instance, CONTEMPLATE, which consists of three different sounds, CON-TEM-PLATE; there are the letters O, E, and A, respectively, in each sound or syllable, as it is called, and each one gives the sound to its syllable. In dividing such words at the end of a line, you must not let the last letter be any one of the above-mentioned five vowels, but must divide according to the syllable.

Another rule to be observed in the spelling of words which have ING added to them, when such words end in E, the E must always be left out; as COME, COMING; DIVIDE, DIVIDING.

It is also found difficult when the letters I and E come together in a word, to know which is to be placed first. The following simple rule will obviate such difficulty: When I and E follow C in a word, the E is usually placed first; as RECEIVE, DECEIVE, CONCEIVE, etc.; in other instances the I comes before the E; as BELIEVE, RELIEVE, etc.

Words of Similar Pronunciation that are Spelled Differently.

Ail, Ale. Ail, unwell; Ale, a liquor.

All, Awl. All, everyone; Awl, shoemaker's tool.

Bear, Bare. Bear, wild animal; Bare, naked.

Bier, Beer. Bier, frame for carrying corpse; Beer, a malt liquor.

Bore, Boar. Bore, carried, or to make a hole; Boar, the male swine.

Birth, Berth. Birth, to be born; Berth, sleeping place.

Bee, Be. Bee, an insect; Be, is used in every other instance.

Call, Caul. Call, to visit, or shout after; Caul, the covering on the heads of some children when born.

Currant, Current. Currant, a fruit; Current, a stream.

Draft, Draught. Draft, commercial form, or current of air; Draught, to draw a load, or a drink.

Dear, Deer. Dear, not cheap, term of affection; Deer, an animal.

Fourth, Forth. Fourth, next after third; Forth, forward.

Four, Fore. Four, the number after three; Fore, the front.

Great, Grate. Great, large; Grate, fire support in the stove.

Hail, Hale. Hail, to shout after, frozen rain; Hale, vigorous.

Hear, Here. Hear, to understand; Here, in this place.

Hole, Whole. Hole, an opening; Whole, entire, complete.

I, Eye. I, myself, used thus it should always be a capital; Eye, organ of sight.

Know, No. Know, to understand; No, a denial.

Lief, Leaf. Lief, willingly; Leaf, part of a tree.

More, Moor, Moore. More, in addition; Moor, a piece of waste land; Moore, a man's name.

None, Nun. None, not any; Nun, a female who secludes herself from all worldly affairs.

Piece, Peace. Piece, a bit; Peace, quietness.

Pare, Pear, Pair. Pare, to peel; Pear, a fruit; Pair, two.

Rain, Rein, Reign. Rain, water falling from clouds; Rein, a strap for guiding a horse; Reign, to rule.

Reed, Read. Reed, a kind of tall grass; Read, the act of reading.

Red, Read. Red, a color; Read, past tense of read.

Sign, Sine. Sign, a token; Sine, a mathematical term.

There, Their. There, in that place; Their, a personal pronoun.

Tow, Toe. Tow, rope material; Toe, a part of the foot.

Vain, Vane. Vain, conceited; Vane, a weathercock.

Vice, Vise. Vice, wickedness; Vise, a blacksmith's tool.

Ware, Wear. Ware, goods, or earthen-ware; Wear, to make use of clothing.

Write, Wright, Rite, Right. Write, to use a pen; Wright, a man's name; Rite, a ceremony; Right, not wrong.

Wrote, Rote. Wrote, having written; Rote, to repeat from memory.

You, Yew, Ewe. You, yourself; Yew, a tree; Ewe, female sheep.

Blew, Blue. Blew, having blown; Blue, a color.

Made, Maid. Made, formed; Maid, female servant.

Pail, Pale. Pail, a vessel; Pale, white.

Words having prefixes and suffixes of different spelling, while having each the same or nearly the same pronunciation.

ible and able.

The following words end in *ible*. Most other words of similar pronunciation end in *able*.

Accessible,	Decoctible,	Fallible,
Admissible,	Deducible,	Feasible,
Appetible,	Defeasible,	Fencible,
Apprehensible,	Defectible,	Flexible,
Audible,	Defensible,	Forcible,
Coercible,	Depectible,	Frangible,
Collectible,	Deprehensible,	Fusible,
Comminuible,	Descendible,	Horrible,
Compatible,	Destructible,	Ignoscible,
Competible,	Digestible,	Illegible,
Comprehensible,	Discernible,	Immarcessible,
Compressible,	Discerptible,	Immiscible,
Conceptible,	Distractible,	Intelligible,
Conclusible,	Distensible,	Irascible,
Congestible,	Divisible,	Legible,
Contemptible,	Docible,	Miscible,
Contractible,	Edible,	Partible,
Controvertible,	Effectible,	Perceptible,
Convertible,	Eligible,	Permissible,
Convincible,	Eludible,	Persuasible,
Corrigible,	Expansible,	Pervertible,
Corrosible,	Enforcible,	Plausible,
Corruptible,	Evincible,	Possible,
Credible,	Expressible,	Producible,
Deceptible,	Extendible,	Quadrible,
Decerptible,	Extensible,	Reducible,

Referrible,
Reflexible,
Refrangible,
Regible,
Remissible,
Reprehensible,

Resistible,
Responsible,
Reversible,
Revertible,
Risible,
Seducible,

Sensible,
Tangible,
Terrible,
Transmissible,
Visible.

The following words end in **able** :

Approvable,
Blamable,
Conversable,
Dilatable,
Dissolvable,
Incondensable,
Inferable,

Manifestable,
Movable.
Probable,
Retable,
Referable,
Reprovable,
Salable,

Solvable,
Tamable,
Tenable,
Transferable,
Unsalable,
Untamable,
Untenable.

The following words in spelling begin with **Im**. Other words of similar pronunciation begin with **Em**.

Imbibe,
Imboil,
Imbound,
Imbrue,
Imbrute,
Imbue,
Imburse,
Immanuel,
Immaculate,
Immense,
Imminent,
Immigrant,
Immerge,
Immerse,
Immigrate,

Immingle,
Immit,
Immix,
Immure,
Impact,
Impale,
Impassioned,
Impawn,
Impeach.
Impearl,
Impel,
Impen,
Imperil,
Impinge,

Implant,
Implead,
Impart,
Impose,
Impound,
Impregnate,
Impress,
Imprint,
Impromptu,
Impugn,
Impulse.
Impunity,
Imputable,
Impute.

ise and ize.

The following words terminate with *ise*. Other words of like pronunciation terminate with *ize*.

Advertise,
Advise,
Affranchise,
Apprise,
Catechise,
Chastise,
Circumcise,
Comprise,
Compromise,

Criticise,
Demise,
Despise,
Devise,
Disfranchise,
Disguise,
Divertise,
Emprise,
Enfranchise,

Exercise,
Exorcise.
Merchandise,
Misprise,
Recognise,
Reprise,
Supervise,
Surmise,
Surprise.

Words ending in **d, de, ge, mit, rt, se**, or **ss**, take **sion** in derivatives. Other words of similar pronunciation in their ending are usually spelled with **tion**.

Abscission,
Abscersion,
Adhesion,
Admission,
Cohesion,
Compulsion,
Condescension,

Confession,
Confusion,
Conversion,
Declension,
Decursion,
Depulsion,
Dissension,

Divulsion,
Emersion,
Evasion,
Evulsion,
Exesion,
Expulsion,
Impression,

Impulsion,
Incursion,
Intrusion,
Propulsion,

Recension,
Recursion,
Remission,
Revision,

Revulsion,
Tension,
Transcursion,
Version.

Exceptional words. Coercion, Suspicion, Crucifixion.

Words in En.

Encage,
Enchant,
Enchase,
Encircle,
Enclose,
Encroach,
Encumber,
Endamage,
Endear,
Endow,
Enfeeble,

Enfranchise,
Engender,
Engorge,
Entrance,
Enhance,
Enjoin,
Enlard,
Enlarge,
Enlighten,
Enlist,
Enroll,

Ensure,
Entail,
Entangle,
Enthrone,
Entice,
Entire,
Entitle,
Entomb,
Entrap,
Entreat,
Enure,

Words in In.

Inclasp,
Incrust,
Indict,
Indite,
Indorse,
Indue,
Infold,
Ingraft,

Ingrain,
Ingulf,
Inquire,
Insnare,
Insure,
Interlace,
Interplead,
Inthrall,

Intrust,
Intwine,
Inure,
Inveigle,
Inwheel,
Inwrap,
Inwreathe.

Words ending in eive.

Conceive,
Receive,

Deceive,

Perceive,

Words ending in ieve.

Achieve,
Aggrieve,
Believe,

Relieve,
Reprieve,
Retrieve,

Sieve,
Thieve.

Nouns which change f or fe into *ves* in the plural.

Beeves,
Calves,
Elves,
Halves,
Knives,

Leaves,
Lives,
Loaves,
Selves,
Sheaves,

Shelves,
Thieves,
Wharves,
Wives,
Wolves.

Nouns ending in f or fe in which s is only used in the plural.

Briefs,
Chiefs,
Fiefs,
Griefs,
Mischiefs,
Kerchiefs,

Turfs,
Kerfs,
Surfs,
Fifes,
Strifes,
Safes,
Scarfs,

Woofs,
Hoofs,
Roofs,
Proofs,
Beliefs,
Reliefs,
Gulfs.

Dwarfs.

Nouns ending in eau, ieu, and ou, terminate the plural in *x*.

Beaux,
Bureaux,
Chapeaux,
Chateaux,

Flambeaux,
Rondeaux,
Plateaux,
Bijoux,

Morceaux,
Rouleaux,
Tableaux,

SPELLING BY SOUND.

SYSTEM OF ORTHOGRAPHY, whereby superfluous letters could be dispensed with, educational reformers have long sought to introduce. Of these, the following method of Spelling by Sound was published some time since by the Hon. Joseph Medill, editor of the Chicago Tribune, its advantage over the strictly phonetic system being that the same alphabet is employed as that in general use, which makes it much easier to introduce. It is at the same time more agreeable to the eye. By this system the student can spell any word after learning the sounds, and the reader can readily pronounce any word when reading. The great advantages gained are less space used in writing, less time, correct pronunciation, and correct spelling.

The application of this system of spelling is shown as follows:

A Specimen of His System.

The extreme iregûlarities ov our orthografy hav long ben a sours ov inconvéniens and anoians. Men eminent az skolars and státsmen hav often pointed out theze absurdities ov speling. Yet the évil remanes. It encumbers our primary edûcásion and robs our yuth ov yeres ov time that shùd be dévóted tu the acquizision ov nolej. It impozes a burden upon the literary man thru life in the ûse ov súperflúus leters, and compels meny persons tu study speling from the cradle tu the grave or fale tu spel corectly. It iz a fereful barier tu foriners hu wish tu lern our langwaje; and wors than aul, it hinders thousands ov persons from lerning tu rede and rite, and thus largly augments the ranks ov ignórans and depravity.

Theze évils ar so énormus in the agrégate that we fele compeled tu endors the words ov the distinguished President ov the American Filólojical Asósiásion, Prof. F. A. March, ûzed in hiz opening adres at the last anûal méting ov the Sósíety:

"It iz no ûse tu try tu caracterize with fiting epithets the monstrous speling ov the English langwaje. The time lost by it is a larj part ov the hole skule time ov the most ov men. Count the ours which éch person wásts at skule in lerning tu rede and spel, the ours spent thru life in képing up and perfecting hiz nolej ov speling, in consulting dicshunáries —a work that never ends—the ours that we spend in ríting sílent leters; and multiplying this time by the number ov persons hu speak English, and we hav a tótal ov milyuns ov yeres wásted by éch jenerásion. The cost ov printing the sílent leters ov the English langwaje iz tu be counted by milyuns ov dolors for éch jenerásion."

"Súner or láter English orthografy must be simplified and réformed."—BENJAMIN FRANKLIN.

"I fele very hopeful that a begining wil be made before long in réforming, not indede everything but at lést sumthing in the unhistorical, unsistematic, unintelijible, untéchable, but by no menes unamendable speling now curent in England."—PROF. MAX MÜLLER.

In spéking ov the disgrásful state ov English orthografy and the best mode ov réforming it. the grate American lexicografer, Dr. Nóah Webster, in the intróducsion tu hiz Quarto Dicshunary, says:

"Nothing can be more disrepútable tu the literáry caracter ov a násion than the históry ov English orthografy, unles it is that ov our orthóepy." * * *

"Dr. Franklin compíled a dicshunary on hiz skeme ov réform, and prócúred típes tu be cast, which he ofered tu me with a vû tu engaje me tu prosecute hiz dezine. This ofer I declíned tu acsept; for I wos then, and am stil, convinsed that the skeme ov intródûcing nu caracters intu the langwaje is néther practicable nor expedient. Eny atempt ov this kind must sertenly fale ov sucses."

"The mode ov asertáning the prónunsiasion ov words by marks, points or trifling olterásions ov the present caracters, semes tu be the ónly won which can be redûsed tu practis."

" Delitful task! to rere the tender thaut,
Tu téch the yung ídéa hou tu shute,
Tu pore fresh instrucsion ó'er the mind,
Tu brethe the enlivening spirit, and tu fix
The jenerus purpos in the glóing brest."

"O, thautles mortals! ever blind tu fate,
Tu sune dejected and tu sune élate."

" Worth makes the man and want ov it the felo·
The rest is aul but lether or prúnela."

Where there iz a wil there iz a wa; and while the evil continûes the nesesity for orthografic réform wil never cese. If there ar eny among us hu hav tu litle regard for there óne children tu smuthe for them the path on which there infant fete must stumble, we conjure them in the name ov God and hûmanity tu beware ov the gráter sin ov crushing by opózing infûens the rising hopes ov milyuns les fortunate, hu hav néther mony nor time tu squonder, but hu nede aul the ades posible tu enáble them tu take a pozision among the intelijent, vertûus and hapy sitizens ov our grate and glórius cuntry.

The foregoing will suffice to represent Mr. Medill's idea of simplified orthography. It is almost phonetic and yet preserves most of the analogies and peculiarities of the English language. He retains the general rule that *e* ending a word and preceding a consonant indicates that the vowel is "long." Thus he spells such words as

bel*ie*ve,	beleve,	guide,	gide,	prove,	pruve,
rece*i*ve,	reseve,	course,	corse,	proof,	prufe,
release,	relese,	pique,	peke,	through,	thru,
fierce,	férse,	chaise,	shaze,	school,	skule,
repeal,	repele,	paid,	pade,	door,	dore,
feel,	fele,	repair,	repare,	four,	fore,
sleeve,	sleve,	gauge,	gage,	boar,	bore,
league,	lege,	pear,	pare,	blow,	blo.

Where the *e* sound does not indicate the long vowel sound, he proposes to use accented vowels, viz.: á, é, í, ó, ú, and for the sound of *u* in full, should, etc., he uses ù: thus, fùl, shùd. For the broad sound of *a* heard in ought, caught, awful, all, broad, he employs *au* and spells them out; caut, auful, aul, braud, etc. For the terminals tion, sion, cian, scion, etc., he uses *sion*. He retains *ed* as the sign of the past tense, and *s* as that of the plural of nouns and singular of verbs. *Ble* as a terminal is also retained. *K* is written for *ch* in all words in which *ch* has the sound of *k*. Ex.: arkitect, monark, skule, etc. All double consonants are reduced to single ones, as only one of them is heard in pronunciation. In all words now spelled with *ck*, as back, beck, lick, rock, luck, he drops the *c* as being wholly superfluous. In words ending in ous, he omits the *o*, as in curius, spurius, and when *ou* has the sound *u* he also drops the *o*, as in duble, jurny. He retains *y* at the end of nouns in the singular, as copy, foly. He writes *f* for *ph* in alfabet, fonetics, flosofy, etc. He omits all silent vowels in digraphs, and writes

head,	hed	said,	sed	tongue,	tung,
earth,	erth	heifer,	hefer,	sieve,	siv,
though,	tho,	leopard,	lepard,	built,	bilt,
phthisic,	tizic,	cleanse,	clens,	myrrh,	mer.

The proposed system is very easily written. After an hour's practice the pen runs naturally into it. The plan is one which would cost adults scarcely an effort to learn to write, and no effort at all to learn to read it. He thinks it is the simplest and most rational compromise with existing usage, prejudice, and etymologies, which can probably be devised with any hope of acceptance, and if accepted and adopted it would secure to the Anglo-American race throughout the world one of the simplest and best orthographies in existence.

CAPITAL LETTERS.

MANY people greatly disfigure their writing, and stamp themselves as illiterate, by the omission or improper use of capital letters.

What do we think of the man who, wishing to place his son in the care of a teacher, wrote a letter, introducing his boy, thus?

"deer sur yeW Bein a man of noleg i Wish tu Put Mi son in yure skull."

Or, of the mother who sends a line by her child to the boot and shoe merchant as follows?

"mister Grean Wunt you let mi Boay hev a Pare ov Esy toad shuz."

Fortunately the rules for using capitals are few, and once acquired, are easily remembered.

Rules for the Use of Capitals.

Begin every paragraph with a capital letter.

Begin every sentence following a period with a capital letter.

Begin each proper name with a capital letter.

Begin the names of places, as Boston, Newport, Niagara, with capital letters.

Begin the words, North, South, East, West, and their compounds and abbreviations, as North-east, S. W., with capital letters, when geographically applied.

Begin the names of the Deity and Heaven, or the pronoun used for the former, as, in His mercy — Thou, Father, etc., with capital letters.

Begin all adjectives formed from the names of places or points of the compass as English, Northern, each with a capital letter.

Begin each line of poetry with a capital letter.

Begin all quotations with a capital letter.

Begin all titles of books, and usually each important word of the title, as Hume's History of England, with capital letters.

Begin the name of any historical event, as the French Revolution, with capital letters.

The pronoun I and the interjection O must invariably be capital letters.

Begin names of the month, as June, April, with capital letters. Also the days of the week, as Monday, Tuesday, etc.

Begin all addresses, as Dear Sir — Dear Madam, with capital letters.

Capital letters must never be placed in the middle of a word.

PUNCTUATION.

WHILE the omission of punctuation may not mar the appearance of writing, as do bad spelling and improper use of capitals, its correct use is, nevertheless, essential to the proper construction of a sentence.

Very ludicrous, and sometimes serious mistakes result from improper punctuation. In the following sentence, the meaning is entirely changed by the location of the semicolon.

" He is an old and experienced hand ; in vice and wickedness he is never found ; opposing the works of iniquity he takes delight."

" He is an old and experienced hand in vice and wickedness ; he is never found opposing the works of iniquity ; he takes delight."

Punctuation Marks.

The following are the principal characters or points used in punctuation :

Comma	,	Exclamation !		Hyphen	-
Semicolon,	;	Interrogation ?		Apostrophe	'
Colon	:	Dash	—	Quotation Marks	" "
Period	.	Ellipsis		Brackets	[ ]
Parenthesis ( )		The Caret	∧		

Rules for Punctuation.

The Comma (,). Wherever occurs a distinct natural division of a sentence ; or where two or more words are connected, without the connecting word being expressed, the comma is used ; as

"Dealer in hats, caps, boots, shoes, etc." " Hedges, trees, groves, houses, and people, all went rushing by." " Towering far above us stood the pines, silent, majestic, and grand." "Verily, verily, I say unto you."

The Semicolon (;) is used where a sentence consists of several members each constituting a distinct proposition, and yet having dependence upon each other ; as

"Some men are born great ; some acquire greatness ; some have greatness thrust upon them." "Contributors: Will. M. Carleton ; Wm. C. Bryant ; B. F. Taylor ; John G. Saxe." "Contents: Riches ; Poverty ; Religion."

The Colon (:) is used to divide a sentence into two or more parts, which, although the sense is complete in each, are not wholly independent ; as

"Temperance begets virtue : virtue begets happiness." "Two questions grow out of the subject: 1st: What is the necessity of a classical education ? 2d: How far can a classical education be made applicable to the ordinary business affairs of life ?"

The Period (.) is placed at the end of every complete and independent sentence ; before decimals ; between pounds and shillings ; after initial letters, and for abbreviations ; as

"Man, know thyself." "Chas. Williams, M.D." "J. Q. Adams." "Genl. Supt. of C., B., and Q. R. R." "£25. 8s. 4d." "4.24 miles."

The Exclamation Point (!) denotes sudden or violent emotion ; as

"O blissful days ! Ah me ! How soon ye passed !" "Charge, Chester, charge ! On, Stanley, on !" "Great bargains ! Clothing sold at forty per cent. below cost !" "Rejoice ! Rejoice ! the summer months are coming."

The Note of Interrogation (?) is used after every sentence in which a question is asked ; as

"What season of the year do you enjoy most ?"

It is also used to denote sneeringly the unbelief of the speaker ; as

"His wise counsels (?) failed to accomplish their end."

Brackets [ ] *and Parentheses* ( ) are employed to enclose words thrown into a sentence by way of explanation, which could be omitted without injury to its construction ; as

"I have met (and who has not) with many disappointments." "Eight (8) miles and one hundred (100) yards." "In conclusion, gentlemen, I am for the constitution, the whole constitution, and nothing but the constitution." [Great applause.]

The Dash (—) is used when the subject breaks off suddenly, and to show the omission of words, letters and figures ; thus :

"I would — but ah ! I fear it is impossible — I would — I *will* reform." "The pulse fluttered — stopped — went on — stopped again — moved — stopped."

"This agreement entered into this —— day of ——, 18—, between ———— of the first part, and ———— of the second part, witnesseth, etc."

The Hyphen (-) is employed as a character between two words to show that they are connected together as a compound word ; thus :

Thirty-fold, super-heated, four-leaved, etc.

It is also used at the end of a syllable when the remainder of the word follows on the next line. Also in dividing a word to show its pronunciation ; as

Pro-cras-ti-nate ; val-e-tud-i-na-ri-an ; co-op-e-rate.

The Ellipsis (. . . .) is used to represent the omission of words, syllables, and letters, and is sometimes represented by a dash ; thus, k — g for king: occasionally by stars ; thus, * * * * : and sometimes by periods ; like these . . . . . The following examples illustrate its use.

"Mrs. W—— ——, of C——, is said to be the fortunate individual." "This was in 1850. * * * * Twenty years later, in 1870, we gather up, again, the thread of our discourse." "If he had married . . . . Ah, well ! it was not so to be."

The Apostrophe (') is employed to distinguish the possessive case ; thus :

"John's Book." "Superintendent's Office." "Wells' Grammar:"

And the omission of letters in the beginning or middle of a word , thus ,

"I'll," for "I will." "Thou'lt," for "Thou wilt." "Prop'r," for "Proprietor." "In'st," for "Interest," etc.

See rules for punctuation, in the chapter relating to "Sign Painting."

The Caret (∧) is employed, in writing, to show where a word, or several words have been omitted in the sentence, and have been placed above the line ; as

handmaid of   e
"Temperance is the virtue." "Improvment."
     ∧   ∧

Quotation Marks (" ") are used by the writer to designate a word or sentence quoted or copied from another author ; as

"Three things bear mighty sway with men,
The Sword, the Sceptre, and the *Pen*."

The Marks of Reference (* † ‡ § ‖ ¶) are used to call attention to notes of explanation at the bottom of the page. If many notes are used and these are all exhausted, they can be doubled. Some writers use letters, and some figures, for reference.

Marks of Pronunciation.

For the purpose of giving inflection to certain words, or to designate the prolongation of occasional syllables in a word, the author frequently finds it convenient to use certain characters to denote such accents. To illustrate:

The Acute (á) gives the rising inflection ; as

"Will you ríde ?"

The Grave (à) the falling ; as

"Will you wàlk or ríde."

The Circumflex (â) indicates the rising and falling inflection in the same syllable ; as,

"Machîne," Montreâl," etc.

The Macron (¯) placed above a letter designates a full, long vowel sound ; as

"Fāte." "Hōme." "Nōte." "Ēve," etc.

A Breve (˘) denotes a short sound, when placed above a vowel ; as

"Ă-dŏre." "Glŏ-rĭ-oŭs."

The Diæresis (ä) is used for the purpose of dividing a diphthong, or syllable into two distinct syllables ; as

"Avengëd." "Belovëd."

Also when two vowels come together, this character is sometimes used to show that they are not contracted into a diphthong ; as

"Coöperate." "Reïterate." "Reäppear."

The Cedilla (ç) is a mark placed under the c to denote that its sound is the same as the letter *s ;* as

"Çhaise." "Façade."

The Tilde (ñ) placed over an n gives it the sound of *ny ;* as

"Miñon." "Señor."

Marks Directing Attention.

The Index (☞) is used to call special attention to an important line or clause in the writing or printing , as :

"☞ Five per cent discount for **cash**."

The Asterism or Stars (⁂) is used to designate a general reference ; as

"⁂ The teacher should make frequent use of the blackboard."

The Brace } is employed to unite two or more parts of speech or names that are brought into juxtaposition   as

Gender { Masculine. Feminine, Neuter.   Committee { Wm. Smith. John Brown.

A Paragraph (¶) is used by the author frequently to designate, in the middle of a sentence, when he re-reads his manuscript, those words that he wishes to have commence a paragraph. It shows where something new begins.

A Section (§) usually designates the smaller distinct parts of a book.

As references they are frequently used with numbers ; thus :

"¶ 87.   Wedding Ceremonies in Different Countries."
"§ 172.   The Law of Usury in Different States."

Leaders (----) are employed to lead the eye from one portion of the page to another across blank space ; as

London _____ 123
Paris _____ 84
New York _____ 304

Underscoring.

Words and sentences that the writer desires should be emphatic, are designated by lines drawn beneath the words that are to be emphasized. Thus one line indicates *italics ;* two lines, SMALL CAPITALS ; three lines, LARGE CAPITALS ; four lines, *ITALIC CAPITALS.* The words

"To arms ! to arms !! to arms !!! they cry,"

Underscored will appear in print thus —

" *To arms !* TO ARMS !! TO ARMS !!! they cry."

" Upward and upward we went! gradually the scene grew more and more entrancing! until at length, *faster,* RICHER, WILDER, *GRANDER* the weird objects came and went, fading away at last in the long dim distance."

The Parts of Speech.

IMPROPER USE OF WORDS.

RAMMAR is the art of writing or speaking a language correctly. There are eight distinct parts of speech, named as follows: *Noun, Pronoun, Adjective, Verb, Adverb, Preposition, Conjunction,* and *Interjection.*

The NOUN is the name of an object or some quality of the same; as, *knife, horse, house, sharpness, speed, beauty.* Nouns are of two classes, proper and common. A proper noun is the name of an individual object; as, *England, William, Washington;* and should always be capitalized. Names given to whole classes are common nouns; as, *sea, land, army, tree, etc.*

A PRONOUN is a word that takes the place of a noun; as, "*He* reads," "*She* studies," "*It* falls."

An ADJECTIVE is a word used to describe a noun; as, "*sweet* cider," "*educated* people," "*fast* horse."

The VERB is a word that expresses action; as, "He *runs,*" "She *sleeps,*" "It *falls.*"

The ADVERB tells how the action is performed, and modifies the meaning of verbs, adjectives, and other adverbs; as, "He walks *rapidly,*" "*Very* soon," "*More* pleasing," "*Directly* under," etc.

A PREPOSITION is a word that connects other words, and shows the relation between them; as, "The snow lies *on* the ground," "He went *to* Europe."

A CONJUNCTION is a part of speech used to connect words and sentences together; as, "Houses *and* lands;" "I walked in the meadows *and* in the groves, *but* I saw no birds *nor* animals of any kind, *because* of the darkness."

An INTERJECTION is a word used to express sudden or strong emotion; as, *O! Alas! Ah!*

As a full consideration of the subject of grammar requires a volume of itself, it is not, therefore, the purpose of this book to enter into a detailed explanation of the use of the various parts of speech, along with the rules for applying the same. Fuller instruction relating to the proper construction of language may be obtained in any of the various text-books on grammar, which may be procured at the bookstores.

Mistakes Corrected.

The object in introducing the subject of grammar here is to call attention to the faults liable to be made by the writer and speaker unacquainted with a knowledge of the correct use of language. To illustrate: special care should be taken to use the plural verb when the plural nominative is used; as, "Trees *grows*" should be "Trees *grow;*" "Birds *flies*" should be "Birds *fly;*" "Some flowers *is* more fragrant than others" should be "Some flowers *are* more fragrant than others."

Care should be exercised in the use of the adjective pronoun; as, "*Them* men" should be "*Those* men."

The past tense of the word *do* is frequently improperly used; as, "I *done* the example" should be "I *did* the example."

Care should be taken with words terminating with *ly;* as, "Birds fly swift" should be "Birds fly *swiftly;*" "She sang beautiful" should be "She sang *beautifully;*" "He walks rapid" should be "*rapidly;*" "He talks eloquent" should be "*eloquently.*"

The word *got* is frequently unnecessarily used; as, "I have *got* the book" should be "I have the book."

The word *learn* is often wrongly used in place of teach; as, "Will you *learn* me to write?" should be "Will you *teach* me to write?"

The verbs *lay* and *lie* are frequently misused. The following examples illustrate the distinctions to be observed in their use: Thus, "I *lie* down; you *lie* down; he *lies* down." But, "I *lay* down the book; you *lay* down the carpet; he *lays* down the rules."

The verbs *sit* and *set* are often used improperly. The following sentences illustrate the difference between them: Thus, "I *sit* down; you *sit* down; he *sits* down." "I *set* the table; you *set* the trap; and he *sets* the saw."

Care should be used not to have two negatives in a sentence when affirmation is meant; thus, "Don't never tell a lie" should be "Never tell a lie;" "I can't see nothing" should be "I can see nothing," or, "I cannot see anything."

Slang Phrases, and Profanity.

A man is known by the company he keeps. He is also known by his language. No amount of good clothes or outside polish can prevent a man from being regarded as vulgar and low-bred who is addicted to the use of profane words. The use of profanity plainly indicates that the person employing it has such a limited knowledge of words suitable to express ideas, that he is compelled to use vulgar language in order to convey his thought. And the same measurably is true of slang phrases. Such terms as "*Level Best,*" "*Right Smart,*" "*Played out,*" "*You Bet,*" "*Bottom dollar,*" etc., while sometimes allowed among familiar acquaintances, are vulgarisms, and in all graver speaking and writing should be avoided.

The uniform use of a chaste, refined and beautiful language is not only an index to a pure, clear and cultivated intellect, but is always, to the lady or gentleman, one of the surest elements of success in any business where language is required.

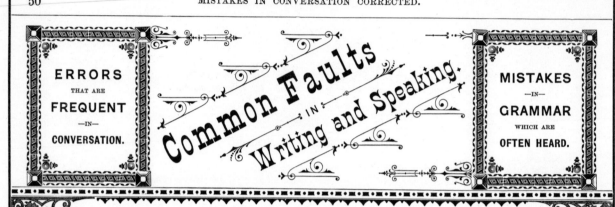

ERRORS THAT ARE FREQUENT —IN— CONVERSATION.

Common Faults IN Writing and Speaking.

MISTAKES —IN— GRAMMAR WHICH ARE OFTEN HEARD.

Superfluous Words, Improper Phrases, and Errors of Grammar.

MANY of the following expressions may be heard in the ordinary conversation of every day life. They indicate a lack of knowledge or want of care in the use of words which those who have been trained to the use of correct language immediately observe.

In this connection it may be said that one of the most important studies is that of Grammar, which should be vigorously pursued until the student can properly construct sentences. On that qualification, in many positions of life, hangs success. Without this training the individual is liable at any time to use those expressions which indicate deficiency in this branch of a primary education.

These phrases are especially common in the language of those who are unskilled in knowledge of grammar. The corrections will aid the student somewhat in the acquisition of a better method of expression, but while they do this it is not pretended that they teach this art. They simply direct attention to the importance of this subject as a branch of education, and point out by example those phrases which are often used incorrectly.

"It is *me*," should be "It is *I*."

"I *done* that," should be "I *did* that."

"I *seen* him," should be "I *saw* him."

"We enter *in*," should be "We enter."

"This *'ere* one," should be "This one."

"Is that *him*?" should be "Is that *he*?"

"Call *upon* him," should be "Call *on* him."

"Do *like* I do," should be "Do *as* I do."

"*Onc't* or twice," should be "*Once* or twice."

"If I *was* him," should be "If I *were* he."

"*In case* I win," should be "*If* I win."

"Let you and *I*," should be "Let you and *me*."

"That *there* one," should be "That one."

"*Be* you cold?" should be "*Are* you cold?"

"Better than *me*," should be "Better than *I*."

"How *fur* is it," should be "How *far* is it."

"I *love* beefsteak," should be "I *like* beefsteak."

"*Was* you there?" should be "*Were* you there?"

"Who *done* that?" should be "Who *did* that?"

"I *don't* think so," should be "I think not."

"How *do* you *do*?" should be "How *are* you?"

"Give me *me* hat," should be "Give me *my* hat."

"A *summer's* day," should be "A *summer* day."

"I have *got* back," should be "I have *returned*."

"Not as I know *of*," should be "Not that I know."

"I am very *dry*," should be "I am very *thirsty*."

"I have *saw* him," should be "I have *seen* him."

"Both *of* these men," should be "Both these men."

"*Who* do you wish?" should be "*Whom* do you wish?"

"I *had* rather do it," should be "I *would* rather do it."

"He had *laid* down," should be "He had *lain* down."

"What *are* the news?" should be "What *is* the news?"

"*Set* down and rest," should be "*Sit* down and rest."

"See that *'ere* bird," should be "See that bird."

"I *had* ought to go," should be "I *ought* to go."

"They *was* talking," should be "They *were* talking."

"*Me* and John saw it," should be "John and *I* saw it."

"*Who* did you say?" should be "*Whom* did you say?"

"*Are* you *uns* going?" should be "*Are* you going?"

"*Such another* error," should be "*Another such* error."

"I can't *stand* it," should be "I cannot *endure* it."

"He was *to* Henry's," should be "He was *at* Henry's."

"He travels *rapid*," should be "He travels *rapidly*."

"As soon *as ever* I can," should be "As soon *as* I can."

"The crops look *finely*," should be "The crops look *fine*."

"*Don't* never do that," should be "*Never* do that."

"Can you *learn* me?" should be "Can you *teach* me?"

"I *have got* the book," should be "I *have* the book."

"I *enjoy* good health," should be "I *have* good health."

"I'll *bet* you'll go," should be "I *think* you will go."

"Let me dress *me*," should be "Let me dress *myself*."

"The man was *beat*," should be "The man was *beaten*."

"He is as good as *him*," should be "He is as good as *he*."

"They returned *back*," should be "They returned."

"The cloth was *wove*," should be "The cloth was *woven*."

"Between you and *I*," should be "Between you and *me*."

"It is three *foot* long," should be "It is three *feet* long."

"She sings *beautiful*," should be "She sings *beautifully*."

"He *won't* never do it," should be "He *will* never do it."

"He made a *dicker*," should be "He made a *bargain*."

"He fell *on* the floor," should be "He fell *to* the floor."

"Cover *over* the well," should be "Cover the well."

"If I am *not mistaken*," should be "If I *mistake not*."

"He is *up* on the house," should be "He is *on* the house."

"I cannot by *no* means," should be "I cannot by *any* means."

"The stone sinks *down*," should be "The stone sinks."

"It was *her* who called," should be "It was *she* who called."

"There *was* some men," should be "There *were* some men."

"He must stay *to* home," should be "He must stay *at* home."

"First *of all* let me say,"
should be
"First, let me say."

"*New* furnished rooms,"
should be
"*Newly* furnished rooms."

"Do you see *them* men?"
should be
"Do you see *those* men?"

"*Is* your hands cold?"
should be
"*Are* your hands cold?"

"*Above* a year since,"
should be
"*More than* a year since."

"These kind of apples,"
should be
"These *kinds* of apples,"
or
"*This* kind of apples."

"He is *in* under the wall,"
should be
"He is *under* the wall."

"I *toted* him across,"
should be
"I *carried* him across."

"I came from *over yer*,"
should be
"I came from *yonder*."

"*Lay* down or *set* down,"
should be
"*Lie* down or *sit* down."

"Two *spoonsful* of tea,"
should be
"Two *spoonfuls* of tea."

"I'll give you *fits*,"
should be
"I will *attend* to you."

"A *new pair* of boots,"
should be
"A *pair of* new boots."

"The *best* of the two,"
should be
"The *better* of the two."

"I have *lit* the fire,"
should be
"I have *lighted* the fire."

"I *belong* to the church,"
should be
"I am a *churchmember*."

"He *climbed up* the hill,"
should be
"He *climbed* the hill."

"What *beautiful* sauce,"
should be
"What *excellent* sauce."

"I *had* rather ride,"
should be
"I *would* rather ride."

"Very *warmish* weather,"
should be
"Very *warm* weather."

"*There is* a great many,"
should be
"*There are* a great many."

"I *only want* five dollars,"
should be
"I *want only* five dollars."

"You *hadn't ought* to go."
should be
"You *ought not* to go."

"*There's lots* of them,"
should be
"*There are many* of them."

"I have *rode* with him,"
should be
"I have *ridden* with him."

"I saw the *Miss Browns*,"
should be
"I saw the *Misses Brown*."

"Peaches were *plenty*,"
should be
"Peaches were *plentiful*."

"*Continue on* in this way,"
should be
"*Continue* in this way."

"*Don't* give him no more,"
should be
"*Give* him no more."

"Walter and *me* went down,"
should be
"Walter and *I* went down."

"*Who* does this belong to,"
should be
"*Whom* does this belong to."

"*As far as* I am concerned,"
should be
"*So far as* I am concerned."

"He had *near* ten dollars,"
should be
"He had *nearly* ten dollars."

"We had an *awful nice* time,"
should be
"We had a *delightful* time."

"He rose *up* from his seat,"
should be
"He rose from his seat."

"He came *ladened* with honor,"
should be
"He came *laden* with honor."

"I expected *to have seen* him,"
should be
"I expected *to see* him."

"Give me a *little bit of* piece,"
should be
"Give me a *small* piece."

"They despised *one another*,"
should be
"They despised *each other*."

"I was *tickled* to see him "
should be
"I was *pleased* to see him."

"He is heavier than I *be*,"
should be
"He is heavier than I *am*."

"When we *was* living here,"
should be
"When we *were* living here."

"He is better than you *be*,"
should be
"He is better than you *are*."

"Similarity *with* each other,"
should be
"Similarity *to* each other."

"When I get *off from* a car,"
should be
"When I get *off* a car."

"Do you *mean* to do that?"
should be
"Do you *intend* to do that?"

"*Either of them are* rich,"
should be
"*Each of them is* rich."

"I have *a couple of dollars*,"
should be
"I have *two* dollars."

"It spread *all over* the town,"
should be
"It spread *over all* the town."

"If I *was him* I would do it,"
should be
"If I *were he* I would do it."

"I'll be blamed if I can tell,"
should be
"I cannot tell."

"Who is there?" "It is *me*,"
should be
"Who is there?" "It is *I*."

"I *took* you for another,"
should be
"I *mistook* you for another."

"His faith has been *shook*,"
should be
"His faith has been *shaken*."

"He died *with* consumption,"
should be
"He died *of* consumption."

"You are stronger than *me*,"
should be
"You are stronger than *I*."

"I *reckon* I'll go to-morrow,"
should be
"I *intend* to go to-morrow."

"I *guess* I'll go to-morrow,"
should be
"I *think of going* to-morrow."

"He has a *tarnal lot* of potatoes,"
should be
"He has a *large quantity of* potatoes."

"*Make haste* and dress *you*,"
should be
"*Make haste* and dress *yourself*."

"The two *first* men are the strongest,"
should be
"The *first two* men are the strongest."

"She sang *to* the Baptist church,"
should be
"She sang *at* the Baptist church."

"*Them is* large enough for you,"
should be
"*Those are* large enough for you."

"We *won't* say one *single* word,"
should be
"We *will not* say one word."

"He is *down in* the basement,"
should be
"He is *in* the basement."

"His manner admits *of* no excuse,"
should be
"His manner admits no excuse."

"Received *of* John Brown five dollars,"
should be
"Received *from* John Brown five dollars."

"No other means *but* this was left,"
should be
"No other means *than* this was left."

"They will go *from* thence next week,"
should be
"They will go thence next week."

"*From now* till Christmas,"
should be
"*From this time* till Christmas."

"He has *got over* his trouble,"
should be
"He has *recovered from* his trouble."

"I *know* better; that ain't so,"
should be
"Pardon me, I *understand* differently."

"I know little *or nothing* of it,"
should be
"I know little, *if anything*, of it."

"He has four *brother-in-laws*,"
should be
"He has four *brothers-in-law*."

"I know *Mr. and Mrs. Dr.* Brown,"
should be
"I know *Dr. and Mrs.* Brown."

"It's *funny* how long she *stays* sick,"
should be
"It is *singular* that she should *remain* sick so long."

"You *lie*; he got *tight*,"
should be
"You are *mistaken*; he was *drunk*."

"*I'll be goll darned if* I know where it is,"
should be
"I do not know where it is."

"*Somehow or another* I'm a failure,"
should be
"*For some reason* I am always a failure."

"Henry and John *is* coming,"
should be
"Henry and John *are* coming."

"He dropped *down* into the water,"
should be
"He dropped into the water."

"They differ *among one another*,"
should be
"They differ *among themselves*."

"Take three-fourths; give me the *balance*,"
should be
"Take three-fourths; give me the *remainder*."

"I see him *every now and then*,"
should be
"I see him *occasionally*."

"I never play if I can *help it*,"
should be
"I never play if I can *avoid it*."

"*Look out* or you'll get hurt,"
should be
"*Be careful* or you'll get hurt."

"Should have gloves like *Henry has*,"
should be
"Should have gloves like *Henry's*."

"I'd like *for you* to go,"
should be
"I would be pleased to have you go."

"May be I *mought* or I *moughtn't*,"
should be
"I *may or I may not*."

"I never *see such a slew* of people before,"
should be
"I never *saw such a large number* of people before."

"His works are approved *of by* many,"
should be
"His works are approved *by* many."

"I *don't* know nothing about it,"
should be
"I know nothing about it."

"He has a *heap* of cattle,"
should be
"He has a *large number* of cattle."

"He had a *right smart crop* of corn last year,"
should be
"He had a *large crop* of corn last year."

"He has a good *bit* of money,"
should be
"He has a good *deal* of money."

"I went to New York, *you know*, and when I *came back, you see*, I commenced attending school,"
should be
"I went to New York, and when I *returned* I commenced attending school."

AIDS TO COMPOSITION.

A SUMMARY OF IMPORTANT SUGGESTIONS.

HAT is said elsewhere in this book in relation to the formation and expression of language is of general interest to all who desire to speak and write correctly, and without these instructions it is simply impossible to acquire proper methods of communicating ideas, either by tongue or pen.

While with some persons it is very easy to convey elaborate intelligence distinctly, concisely and in a pleasing manner with the voice, others again find it extremely difficult to frame a sentence of ten words and utter it in company, with any degree of comfort to themselves or benefit to others.

On the other hand, the most fluent speaker who can face a large audience and instruct and amuse his hearers in an hour's discourse, without notes, may not be able to sit down and write an essay on some other topic than that embraced in his sermon or lecture, that would interest a reader or be accepted for a magazine article.

The art of writing compositions, like that of public speaking, may be acquired by diligent study and practice, but with some persons it is a gift so natural that their ideas and sentences easily flow to-gether and combine with such rapidity that the pen cannot give expression to them as fast as the mind conceives them. Where the ideas are brilliant with deep thought or beauty of expression, the possession of this faculty is called "genius," and fame and fortune are usually at its command.

But without genius a writer for the press or the forum may attain to such excellence of expression and methods of thought, by proper training of the natural faculties, as to rival the works of genius in positive value and interest.

Unless, however, the habit of thinking is duly cultivated by read-ing the works of the best authors, living and dead, and meditating upon them carefully and patiently, superior effort can scarcely be expected in a composition, either for the pulpit, the platform or the press. For thought begets thought, even in slow thinkers, and the suggestion of one author here, and of another there, will often lead to a train of thought in which few, if any, have ever before indulged. One of two things, therefore, is requisite in the construction of a successful composition—the possession of a genius, (which is no common gift), or habits of study, combined with observation in certain directions, which serve to evolve ideas from the writer's own brain and pen.

Practice is a great perfecter of the art of writing compositions. At first, the work may be irksome, but in due time, as it becomes easier, it unlocks the chambers of thought, the ideas begin to form and flow, and the task becomes a lasting pleasure.

In the schools it is a most important feature in the list of studies, and its daily exercise tends to indelibly fix upon the memory the proper spelling of words, the principles of penmanship, punctuation, grammar, sentence-building and the use of capital letters. Even if a literary or journalistic profession is not to be subsequently followed by the pupil, the art of writing a composition, learned under the guidance of an experienced teacher, may be of infinite service to the future man or woman, by inducing systematic methods of thinking.

The Reading of the Essay.

It is a public occasion. Coming to the front, upon the stage, confident, easy and natural, with manuscript held in the left hand, that the right may be free for gesture if required, the lady reads her essay; the exercise being effective by originality of composition, fitting words, new and important thoughts, appropriateness, ease, and clearness of enunciation. Self-possession is manifest in every tone and gesture.

Out of school, in leisure moments, as a recreation, the pupil will find it profitable to plan the outline of a story, or frame a description of something seen or heard, the appearance or character of some peculiar individual in the neighborhood, the natural scenery of that locality, or some remembered incident of other days or climes. This practice fits one for a sudden call to prepare an address or petition, or to draft a letter of public interest, or it might lead to the production of an elaborate literary work that would prove both valuable and famous. Many books have achieved accidental popularity.

The use of compositions in village lyceums, or debating clubs, is productive not only of much genuine recreation, but is really a beneficial practice, especially if each paper is submitted to honest criticism as to its construction, after it has been read. Errors are thus corrected, and suggestions are made that tend greatly to improvement in all future productions.

Those who desire to excel in the composition of an essay, which is one of the noblest forms of literary production, will find the works of Joseph Addison, Dr. Samuel Johnson, Oliver Goldsmith and Lord Macaulay excellent models to study. Their clear-cut sentences, breathing wit, humor, sentiment and elevated thought, are delightful reading, and in beauty of construction cannot be surpassed.

Probably, for discipline in forming a series of connected thoughts, all tending to the establishment of some important truth, the best is the sermon. This species of composition may be as systematically constructed as a house, which has a basement, first floor, chambers, attic and cupola. The foundation of the sermon is a well-chosen *text*, indicating the principal topic to be discussed. Following this is the *exordium*, or introduction, the object of which is to interest the hearer or reader in the subject by a few choice sentences and happy allusions to matters more or less intimately connected with the topical discussion. A good beginning is a great point gained. The next step is the *division of the subject* into two or more heads, suggested by the text, each affording a fine field for the exercise of the intellect in creating and gathering pleasing and appropriate sentiments, and advancing arguments leading to the one great truth to be impressed upon the mind of the reader. This portion of the composition requires skill in placing the arguments properly, and clinching them with logical force and appropriate drafts upon the writings of eminent authors. The arguments finished, their strong points are briefly recounted and accompanied by a direct *appeal to the feelings of the reader*, so that not only his intellect is convinced, but his better nature is affected. Finally comes the *peroration*, or closing summing-up of the whole; and here is afforded one of the finest opportunities possible for a skillful and touching display of literary ability.

Next to the sermon, the platform lecture demands great care and skill, and thus affords a profitable discipline for a youthful writer. The selection of the subject is all-important, for it should be one of general interest—not a trivial one, even if the object is simply to amuse. "Artemus Ward's" best effort was named "The Babes in the Wood," but this title was only a fictitious one, on which to string choice bits of humor for two hours. In that connection any other title would have been as relevant, but, perhaps not so "taking." The subject having been chosen, the next object is to obtain, from sources at hand, all the information possible concerning it. From the mass of matter thus gathered, literary talent is taxed to make such selections as seem best suited in every way to form attractive features, and exhibit them in the most fascinating manner possible. There should be an exordium and a peroration to each lecture, and if the subject is argumentative, or explanatory, it should be systematically and logically presented.

The newspaper article differs from most examples of composition. It is usually written under the pressure of business and in haste, relates to some current topic or event, and should be brief, concise and pointed. A long, dry, argumentative essay, however learned and valuable as a literary effort, would not be suitable for an editor's column in a daily journal. The paragraph style is most commonly esteemed. For instance:

"Garfield is dead; but as he once said, upon another important occasion, 'God reigns, and the republic still lives.'"
—"Chicago may have all the national conventions, but she can't fill all the offices."
—"The price of this paper is two dollars a year, but this sum does not include the editor."
—"We are in favor of the constitution as it is, until it shall be constitutionally amended."

A few suggestions as to the composition of fiction—by which is meant novels, tales, sketches and incidents originating in the writer's own brain, and having no foundation except in his imagination,—may be appropriate here. Such reading-matter is more sought for, and more abundant, than any other. The tendency to write it is a common one, and when the laws of language, the purity of morals, and the probabilities of real existence are not outraged in such works, as too frequently they are, fiction can be made the pleasing vehicle of valuable instruction. It is, perhaps, the easiest to write of all literature, and, too often, is made to bring the largest profits to author and publisher.

Poetry is a peculiar gift, and unless it flows naturally and brilliantly from the mind and heart, should seldom be attempted.

The engraving on this page is significant, and carries with it a powerful lesson. The gentleman on the right may be in every respect the equal of the one on the left—may be quite as learned, quite as witty, quite as strong in real argument—but he is a slave to his manuscript. He dare not lift up his head to speak two consecutive sentences without its aid, and if he takes his eyes from it, he is almost sure to skip words and stumble in his discourse. The speaker on the left hand, standing firmly on his feet, erect in form, graceful in gesture, and with his well-balanced mind filled with the importance of his subject, overflows with spontaneous expressions that instruct and delight his audience. Perhaps he has never written a single paragraph of the splendid discourse that falls from his lips, but every word is weighed, every sentence abounds with earnest argument and sentiment, and the impressions that he makes as his eloquence reaches throughout the hall will be felt for years.

Apparently Extemporaneous.   **Confined to Manuscript.**

Two speakers are seen above. One makes no show of written notes, and speaks so independently as to create the favorable impression which comes from a powerful, extemporaneous address. The other handles his papers and makes such a display of his manuscript, and is so closely confined to its reading, as to greatly weaken the power of the discourse, and thus much of his influence is lost.

Topics Suitable for Composition.

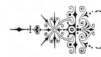

A Visit to Chicago.
Opportunity for Work.
The Bachelor's Home.
Discoveries of Galileo.
Visit to a Poor-House.
Thanksgiving Thoughts.
People whom we Meet.
Memory and Reflection.
The Fate of Joan of Arc.
Visit to a Printing Office.
My First School-Teacher.
How we Spent Christmas.
Pleasures of Suburban Life.
As we Sow, we shall Reap.
The Changes in Twenty Years.
Night Scenes on the Battle-Field.
The School-Ma'am's Noonday Dream.
The First Jewish High Priest.
Honesty, the Poor Man's Riches.
Real Life and Ideal Aspirations.

Charity Toward All.
A Trip on a Railroad.
Some Business Signs.
Benefits of Fine-Art.
Talk in a Sewing-Circle.
To be Hanged To-morrow.
Love Conquers Selfishness.
Things in a Country Store.
Preparing for the Wedding.
The Books we Ought to Read.
A Bar-Tender's Fearful Dream.
The Skeleton in the Household.
My Last Visit to the Old Home.
Home Amusements Considered.
The Man in a Drunkard's Skin.
My Garden, and What was In It.
Old School-House by the Wayside.
Going to Visit Mother Next Week.
Life, Rightly Passed, Worth Living.
New Inventions Discovered by Accident.

What is Worship?
A Drunkard's Fate.
Happiness in a Palace.
The Last Day of School.
Beauty at Seventy-Five.
Bad Habits, Hard Masters.
What Might have been, Was.
Adventures in a Snow-storm.
Description of a Spelling-Bee.
A Man's Lament at Growing Old.
Description of a Writing-School.
Description of a Singing-School.
Mathematics a Finished Science.
Description of a Church Choir.
A Boy's Lament at being Young.
Education Gained by Observation.
An Instance of Presence of Mind.
Lost in the Darkness—City Sketch.
Why Some People are Always Poor.
Description of a Jail and its Inmates.

IDEAS EXPRESSED IN FEW WORDS.

BREVITY IN COMPOSITION.

TO be able to talk correctly, the student should first be able to write properly. Not only should penmanship be plain and easy, words rightly spelled, capitals correctly used, and sentences grammatically constructed and punctuated, but much depends, also, beyond that, upon the style of composition, mode of expression, and language used, whether it be acceptable to readers and hearers or not.

As a rule, with the great sea of literature about us, the writer of to-day who is original and condenses ideas into the smallest space, whether in the sermon, book, business-letter, or newspaper article, is much the most likely to have readers or hearers. The aim of the writer should therefore be, first, to say something new, presenting a subject fraught with original ideas; and, second, to give those ideas in the fewest possible words consistent with agreeable expression.

"Why did you not make that article more brief?" said an editor to his correspondent.

"Because," said the writer, "I did not have time."

The idea sought to be conveyed, concerning brevity, is clearly shown in that answer of the correspondent. It is an easy matter to dress ideas in many words. It requires much more care, however, to clearly state the same idea in fewer words.

The chief merit of Shakespeare is the thought conveyed in few words; the meaning that we catch beyond the words expressed.

Those poets that will live in immortality have

written thus. The reader cannot fail to recognize the truth and thought conveyed in this stanza of Cowper's, beyond the words themselves:

> "Judge not the Lord by feeble sense,
> But trust Him for His grace;
> Behind a frowning providence
> He hides a smiling face."

The idea expressed in these few lines brings up in long review the trials of a past life, and the recollection of sorrows and afflictions which we afterwards, not infrequently, discovered to be blessings in disguise, and in reality seemingly designed for our best good.

There is much food for reflection in the following stanza from Gray's "Elegy":

> Full many a gem, of purest ray serene,
> The dark, unfathomed caves of ocean bear;
> Full many a flower is born to blush unseen,
> And waste its sweetness on the desert air."

With this reading comes up the thought of those of our fellow-men whom *we* know to be good, noble, and worthy, but whose names will go down to the grave unhonored and unknown.

Very plainly we see the meaning beyond the words in the following, also from Gray:

> Perhaps, in this neglected spot, is laid
> Some heart, once pregnant with celestial fire—
> Hand, that the rod of empire might have swayed,
> Or waked to ecstacy the living lyre."

A similar idea is expressed by Whittier, though in fewer words:

> Of all sad words of tongue or pen,
> The saddest are these, 'It might have been.'"

Both stanzas are deeply freighted with thought beyond what is expressed.

Those extracts, whether in prose or poetry, that are destined to go down to coming generations, are so laden with ideas and suggestions that in listening, or reading, the scenes they suggest seem to move before us, and we forget words in contemplating that which the words describe.

Prose writings often contain gems of thought told very briefly, especially in the works of our best authors. In the following, from Irving's description of the grave, the reader becomes so absorbed in the picture portrayed that the words themselves are lost in the emotions they enkindle:

"O the grave! the grave! It buries every error, covers every defect, extinguishes every resentment. From its peaceful bosom spring none but fond regrets and tender recollections. Who can look down upon the grave even of an enemy, and not feel a compunctious throb, that he should ever have warred with the poor handful of earth that lies mouldering before him.

"But the grave of those we loved—what a place for meditation! There it is that we call up in long review the whole history of virtue and gentleness, and the thousand endearments lavished upon us, almost unheeded, in the daily intercourse of intimacy; there it is that we dwell upon the tenderness, the solemn, awful tenderness of the parting scene—the bed of death, with all its stifled griefs, its noiseless attendants, its mute, watchful assiduities—the last testimonies of expiring love—the feeble, fluttering, thrilling—O how thrilling!—pressure of the hand—the last fond look of the glazing eye, turned upon us even from the threshold of existence—the faint, faltering accents struggling in death to give one more assurance of affection.

"Ay, go to the grave of buried love, and meditate! There settle the account with thy conscience for every past benefit unrequited, every past endearment unregarded, of that departed being who can never—never—never return to be soothed by thy contrition."

The Bible abounds in beautiful and expressive sayings, that reveal much in few words, as shown in the following:

"The wicked flee when no man pursueth." "Boast not thyself of to-morrow. Thou knowest not what a day may bring forth."

"A soft answer turneth away wrath." "Better is a dinner of herbs where love is, than a stalled ox and hatred therewith."

"Hope deferred maketh the heart sick." "Cast thy bread upon the waters, for thou shalt find it after many days."

Care should be taken to prune out the unnecessary words with an unsparing hand. Thus, in the sentence, "I have got back, having returned yesterday," it is better to say, "I returned yesterday."

Two young men, upon going into the army during the late civil war, were requested by their friends to telegraph at the close of any battle they might take part in, concerning their condition. At the close of the battle of Perryville, one telegraphed the following:

PERRYVILLE, KY., Oct. 9, 1862.

DEAR FRIENDS:

As requested, I take the first opportunity after the late severe battle, fought at this place, to inform you that I came from the engagement uninjured.

HENRY MOSELY.

The other telegraphed as follows:

PERRYVILLE, KY., Oct. 9, 1862.

Uninjured.

HIRAM MAYNARD.

Hiram well knew that his friends would hear immediately of the battle from the newspapers, and would learn from the same source that his regiment participated in the engagement. Their next question would then be "How is Hiram?" To answer that, he had simply to telegraph one word. In a letter, afterwards, he gave the particulars.

The following rules should be observed in writing:

First. Never use a word that does not add some new thought, or modify some idea already expressed.

Second. Beware of introducing so many subjects into one sentence as to confuse the sense.

Third. Long and short sentences should be properly intermixed, in order to give a pleasing sound in reading. There is generally a rounded harmony in the long sentence, not found in the short, though as a rule, in order to express meaning plainly, it is better to use short sentences.

Fourth. Make choice of such words and phrases as people will readily understand.

Rhetorical Figures.

THE beauty, force, clearness, and brevity of language are frequently greatly enhanced by the judicious use of rhetorical figures, which are named and explained as follows:

A **Simile** is an expressed comparison.

EXAMPLE—"Charity, *like the sun*, brightens every object on which it shines."

The **Metaphor** is an implied comparison, indicating the resemblance of two objects by applying the name, quality or conduct of one directly to the other.

EXAMPLES—"Thy word is a *lamp* to my feet." "Life is an *isthmus* between two eternities." "The morning of life." "The storms of life."

An **Allegory** is the recital of a story under which is a meaning different from what is expressed in words, the analogy and comparison being so plainly made that the designed conclusions are correctly drawn.

EXAMPLE—Thou hast brought a vine (the Jewish nation) out of Egypt; thou hast cast out the heathen and planted it. Thou preparedst room before it and didst cause it to take deep root, and it filled the land. The hills were covered with the shadow of it, and the boughs thereof were like the goodly cedars. —BIBLE.

In **Hyperbole,** through the effect of imagination or passion, we greatly exaggerate what is founded in truth, by magnifying the good qualities of objects we love, and diminish and degrade the objects that we dislike or envy.

EXAMPLES—"That fellow is so tall that he does not know when his feet are cold." "Brougham is a *thunderbolt.*"

Personification consists in attributing life to things inanimate.

EXAMPLE—"*Hatred* stirreth up strife; but *love* covereth all sins."

A **Metonymy** (*me-ton-y-my*) substitutes the name of one object for that of another that sustains some relation to it, either by some degree of mutual dependence. or otherwise so connected as to be capable of suggesting it; thus cause is used for effect, or the effect for the cause, the attribute for the subject, or the subject for the attribute.

EXAMPLES—1. Cause and effect; as "Extravagance is the *ruin* of many,"—that is, the *cause of ruin.*

2. Attribute and that to which it belongs; as "*Pride* shall be brought low,"—that is, *the proud.*

A **Synecdoche** (*sin-ek-do-ke*) is a form of speech wherein something more or something less is substituted for the precise object meant, as when the whole is put for a part, or a part for the whole; the singular for the plural or the plural for the singular.

EXAMPLES—"His *head* is grey,"—that is, his *hair.* "The *world* considers him a man of talent,"—that is, the *people.*

Antithesis is the contrasting of opposites.

EXAMPLES—"Sink or *swim,* live or *die,* survive or *perish,* I give my hand and heart to this vote." "Though *deep* yet *clear.*"

Irony is a form of speech in which the writer or speaker sneeringly means the reverse of what is literally said, the words being usually mockery uttered for the sake of ridicule or sarcasm. Irony is a very effective weapon of attack. the form of language being such as scarcely to admit of a reply.

EXAMPLE—"Have not the Indians been kindly and justly treated? Have not the temporal things, the vain baubles and filthy lucre of this world, which are too apt to engage their worldly and selfish thoughts, been benevolently taken from them; and have they not, instead thereof, been taught to set their affections on things above?"

Paralipsis pretends to conceal what is really expressed.

EXAMPLE—"*I will not call him villain,* because it would be unparliamentary. *I will not call him fool,* because he happens to be chancellor of the exchequer."

Climax is the gradual ascending in the expression of thought, from things lower to a higher and better. Reversed, it is called *anticlimax*.

EXAMPLES—" A Scotch mist becomes a shower; and a shower, a storm; and a storm, a tempest; and a tempest, thunder and lightning; and thunder and lightning, heavenquake and earthquake." "Then virtue became silent, heartsick, pined away, and died."

Allusion is that use of language whereby in a word or words we recall some interesting incident or condition by resemblance or contrast.

EXAMPLES—" Give them the Amazon in South America, and we'll give them the Mississippi in the United States."

After the signing of the Declaration of Independence, Hancock remarked to his fellow-signers that they must all *hang* together. "Yes," said Franklin, "or we shall all *hang separately.*"

The allusion in this case turns to a *pun*, which is a play upon words.

EXAMPLE—'' And the Doctor told the Sexton,
And the Sexton *tolled* the bell."

A continued allusion and resemblance in style becomes a *parody*.

EXAMPLE—" 'Tis the last rose of summer, left blooming alone;
All her lovely companions are faded and gone;
No flower of her kindred, no rosebud is nigh,
To reflect back her blushes, and give sigh for sigh.
I'll not leave thee, thou lone one, to pine on thy stem;
Since the lovely are sleeping, go, sleep thou with them.
Thus kindly I scatter thy leaves o'er the bed
Where thy mates of the garden lie scentless and dead."

PARODY—" 'Tis the last golden dollar, left shining alone;
All its brilliant companions are squandered and gone;
No coin of its mintage reflects back its hue,
They went in mint juleps, and this will go too!
I'll not keep thee, thou lone one, too long in suspense;
Thy brothers were melted, and melt thou, to pence!
I'll ask for no quarter, I'll spend and not spare,
Till my old tattered pocket hangs centless and bare."

PUN—" Ancient maiden lady anxiously remarks,
That there must be peril 'mong so many *sparks:*
Roguish-looking fellow, turning to the stranger,
Says it's his opinion she is out of danger."—*Saxe.*

Exclamation is a figure of speech used to express more strongly the emotions of the speaker.

EXAMPLES—"Oh! the depth of the riches both of the wisdom and the knowledge of God!"
"How poor, how rich, how abject, how august,
How complicate, how wonderful is man!
Distinguished link in being's endless chain!
Midway from nothing to the Deity!
A beam ethereal, sullied and absorbed!
Though sullied and dishonored, still divine!
An heir of glory! a frail child of dust:
A worm! a god! I tremble at myself,
And in myself am lost."

Interrogation is a rhetorical figure by which the speaker puts opinions in the form of questions, for the purpose of expressing thought more positively and vehemently, without expectation of the questions being answered.

EXAMPLES—" He that planned the ear, shall He not hear? He that formed the eye, shall He not see?" "O Death, where is thy sting? O Grave, where is thy victory?"
"But when shall we be stronger? Will it be the next week or the next year? Will it be when we are totally disarmed, and when a British guard shall be stationed in every house? * * * Is life so dear, or place so sweet, as to be purchased at the price of chains and slavery?"
"Can storied urn or animated bust
Back to its mansion call the fleeting breath?
Can Honor's voice provoke the silent dust,
Or Flattery soothe the dull, cold ear of death?"

Euphemism (*u-fe-miz-em*) is a word or sentence so chosen and expressed as to make a disagreeable fact sound more pleasantly than if told in plain language.

EXAMPLES—" Deceased " for " dead;" "stopping payment," instead of "becoming bankrupt;" " falling asleep," instead of "dying;" " you labor under a mistake," for " you lie;" " he does not keep very correct accounts," instead of " he cheats when he can;" " she certainly displays as little vanity in her personal appearance as any young lady I ever saw;" for " she is an intolerable slattern."
"I see Anacreon laugh and sing;
His silver tresses breathe perfume;
*His cheeks display a second spring
Of roses taught by wine to bloom.*"

Apostrophe, like the exclamation, is the sudden turning away, in the fullness of emotion, to address some other person or object. In this we address the absent or dead as if present or alive, and the inanimate as if living.

This figure of speech usually indicates a high degree of excitement.

EXAMPLES—"O gentle sleep,
Nature's soft nurse, how have I frighted thee,
That thou no more wilt weigh my eyelids down,
And steep my senses in forgetfulness?"

Thus King David, on hearing of the death of Absalom, exclaims, "O my son Absalom, my son, my son!"

Ossian's Address to the Moon is one of the most beautiful illustrations of the apostrophe:

"Daughter of heaven, fair art thou! The silence of thy face is pleasant. Thou comest forth in loveliness. The stars attend thy blue steps in the East. The clouds rejoice in thy presence, O Moon! brighten their dark-brown sides. Who is like thee in heaven, daughter of the night? The stars are ashamed in thy presence, and turn aside their sparkling eyes. Whither dost thou retire from thy course, when the darkness of thy countenance grows? Hast thou thy hall like Ossian? Dwellest thou in the shadow of grief? Have thy sisters fallen from heaven? and are they who rejoiced with thee at night no more? Yes, they have fallen, fair light! and often dost thou retire to mourn. But thou thyself shall one night fail, and leave thy blue path in heaven. The stars will then lift their heads; they who in thy presence were astonished will rejoice."
"Thou lingering star with less'ning ray,
That lov'st to greet the early morn,
Again thou usher'st in the day
My Mary from my soul was torn.
O Mary! dear departed shade!"

Vision is a figure of rhetoric by which the speaker represents the objects of his imagination as actually before his eyes and present to his senses.

EXAMPLES—"Soldiers! from tops of yonder pyramids forty centuries look down upon you!"

"We behold houses and public edifices wrapt in flames; we hear the crash of roofs falling in, and one general uproar proceeding from a thousand different voices; we see some flying they know not whither, others hanging over the last embraces of their wives and friends; we see the mother tearing from the ruffian's grasp her helpless babe, and the victors cutting each others' throats wherever the plunder is most inviting."

Onomatopœia is the use of such word or words as by their sound will suggest the sense, as *crash, buzz, roar, etc.* Motion is thus easily imitated, as is also sound, and even the reflections and emotions.

EXAMPLES—"Away they went pell mell, hurry skurry, wild buffalo, wild horse, wild huntsmen, with clang and clatter, and whoop and halloo that made the forest ring." "The ball went *whizzing* past."

"While I nodded nearly napping, suddenly there came a tapping
As of some one gently rapping, rapping at my chamber door."

General Summary.

Dr. Blair's system of rhetoric sums up the most important qualities of style in the six following terms, being thus condensed by Kerl:

"*Purity, propriety,* and *precision* chiefly in regard to words and phrases; and *perspicuity, unity,* and *strength,* in regard to sentences. He who writes with *purity,* avoids all phraseology that is foreign, uncouth, or ill-derived; he who writes with *propriety,* selects the most appropriate, the very best expressions, and generally displays sound judgment and good taste; he who writes with *precision,* is careful to state exactly what he means—all that he means, or that is necessary, and nothing more; he who writes with *perspicuity,* aims to present his meaning so clearly and obviously, that no one can fail to understand him at once; he who observes *unity,* follows carefully the most agreeable order of nature, and does not jumble together incongruous things, nor throw out his thoughts in a confused or chaotic mass; and he who writes with *strength,* so disposes or marshals all the parts of each sentence, and all the parts of the discourse, as to make the strongest impression. A person's style, according as it is influenced by taste and imagination, may be *dry, plain, neat, elegant, ornamental, florid,* or *turgid.* The most common faulty style is that which may be described as being stiff, cramped, labored, heavy and tiresome; its opposite is the easy, flowing, graceful, sprightly, and interesting style. One of the greatest beauties of style, one too little regarded, is simplicity or naturalness; that easy, unaffected, earnest, and highly impressive language which indicates a total ignorance, or rather innocence, of all the trickery of art. It seems to consist of the pure promptings of nature; though, in most instances, it is not so much a natural gift as it is *the perfection of art.*"

Laws of Language.

The following rules by Dr. Campbell, in reference to the construction of sentences and choice of words, will be found of service:

1. When the usage is divided as to any particular words or phrases, and when one of the expressions is susceptible of different meanings, while the other admits of only one signification, the expression which is strictly of one meaning should be preferred.

2. In doubtful cases, analogy should be regarded.

3. When expressions are in other respects equal, that should be preferred which is most agreeable to the ear.

4. When none of the preceding rules takes place, regard should be had to simplicity.

5. All words and phrases, particularly harsh and not absolutely necessary, should be dismissed.

6. When the etymology plainly points to a different signification from what the word bears, propriety and simplicity require its dismission.

7. When words become obsolete, or are never used but in particular phrases, they should be repudiated, as they give the style an air of vulgarity and cant, when this general disuse renders them obscure.

8. All words and phrases which analyzed grammatically, include an imperfection of speech, should be dismissed.

9. All expressions which, according to the established rules of language, either have no meaning, or involve a contradiction, or according to the fair construction of the words, convey a meaning different from the intention of the speaker, should be dismissed.

Specific Directions.

PARAGRAPHS.—One or more sentences form a paragraph. When a deviation or change is made in the subject, a new paragraph is commenced. The first line of each paragraph in writing should commence about one inch from the left side of the sheet. Preserve a space half an inch in width between the left of the writing and the edge of the sheet. Write as close to the right edge of the sheet as possible. When lack of space prevents the completion of a word on the line, place the hyphen (-) at the end of the line and follow with the remaining syllables on the next line. Words may be divided, but never divide syllables.

Rules of Construction.

1. The principal words in a sentence should be placed where they will make the most striking impression.

2. A weaker assertion or argument should not follow a stronger one.

3. The separation of the preposition from the noun which it governs, should be avoided.

4. Concluding the sentence with an adverb, preposition, or other insignificant words, lessens the strength of the sentence.

ORDER OF ARRANGEMENT.—Young writers will find it well to prepare a memorandum of the subjects they wish to treat on a separate slip of paper, and the points they wish to make relating to each subject. Having the subjects clearly fixed in the mind, they should commence with the least important and follow through to the end, considering the most important at the close.

Dictionary of Synonyms.

SEVERAL THOUSAND SYNONYMOUS WORDS.
For the use of Writers and Speakers.

 UITE a common fault is that of using, when writing, the same word several times in a sentence. To avoid this inelegant repetition, the writer should give careful attention to the selection of different words having a similar meaning. Observe the following:

Example.

He is *accurate* in figures, *accurate* in grammar, *accurate* in spelling, *accurate* in writing.

IMPROVED.

He is *accurate* in figures, *correct* in grammar, *exact* in spelling, *precise* in writing.

See the word *accurate* in the dictionary, accompanied by synonymous words.

Example.

He made an excellent *address* in the morning, and his colleague made an excellent *address* in the evening.

IMPROVED.

He made an excellent *address* in the morning, and his colleague entertained the assemblage with an eloquent *speech* in the evening.

Example.

The patient *suffered* untold *agony* for years; during which time he *suffered* not only *agony* of body, but *agony* of mind.

IMPROVED.

The patient *suffered* untold *agony* for years; during which time he *endured* not only *torture* of body, but *anguish* of mind.

A

Abase—humble, lower, degrade, depress, disgrace.

Abate—lessen, reduce, subside, decrease, diminish.

Abbreviate — abridge, curtail, condense, compress, empitomize, lessen, reduce, shorten.

Abhor—abominate, detest, hate, loathe.

Ability—capacity, power, skill, means, talent.

Able—capable, competent.

Abode—dwelling, habitation, residence.

Abominate—abhor, detest, hate, loathe.

Abridge—contract, diminish, lessen, shorten.

Absent—abstracted, inattentive, heedless.

Absorb—engross, engulf, imbibe, swallow.

Abstain—forbear, refrain, withhold.

Abstruse—hidden, obscure, difficult.

Absurd — foolish, unreasonable, preposterous, ridiculous, silly.

Abundant—ample, copious, plentiful.

Abusive—insolent, offensive, scurrilous, disgraceful.

Accede — acquiesce, agree, consent, assent, comply, yield.

Accept—admit, receive, take.

Acceptable—agreeable, grateful, welcome.

Accession — addition, augmentation, increase.

Accommodate — adjust, adapt, serve, suit, fit.

Accomplice—abettor, ally, assistant, accessory, associate.

Accomplish — complete, effect, achieve, fulfill, execute, realize, finish.

Account—explanation, narration, description, recital.

Accumulate—heap, collect, gather, amass.

Accurate—precise, exact, correct.

Accuse—asperse, arraign, censure, impeach, defame, calumniate, detract, vilify.

Achieve—execute, complete, fulfill, realize, accomplish, effect.

Acknowledgment — confession, concession.

Acknowledge — confess, own, avow, grant.

Acquaint—inform, communicate, disclose, make known.

Acquiesce — comply, yield, consent, agree, assent.

Acquire — gain, attain, procure, win, obtain.

Acquirement—attainment, gain.

Acquit — free, pardon, forgive, discharge, clear.

Active — quick, nimble, agile, alert, prompt, industrious, busy, brisk, vigorous.

Actual—real, certain, positive.

Actuate—impel, induce, move.

Acute—sharp, keen, subtle, piercing, shrewd, pointed, penetrating.

Adapt—suit, fit, adjust, accommodate.

Add—join to, put to, increase.

Address—speech, utterance, ability, courtship, skill, direction.

Addition — augmentation, accession, increase.

Adhere — stick, cleave, hold, attach.

Adept—apt, quick, skillful, expert.

Adherent—disciple, follower, partisan.

Adhesion—sticking, attachment, adherence.

Adjacent—close, near, adjoining, contiguous.

Adjourn—postpone, defer, delay.

Adjust—settle, fix, suit, adapt, accommodate.

Administer—give, execute, dispense, manage, supply, serve.

Admiration — regard, esteem, wonder, snrprise, amazement.

Admission—entrance, access, admittance.

Admit — allow, permit, tolerate, concede, grant.

Admonition — warning, advice, counsel, reproof.

Adorn—deck, embellish, beautify.

Adroit—agile, dexterous, clever, skilful.

Adulterate—corrupt, pollute, debase, defile.

Advancement—progression, improvement.

Advantage—profit, benefit, use, good.

Adventure — chance, casualty, contingency, incident, occurrence.

Adversary — opponent, antagonist, enemy.

Adverse — unfortunate, hostile, contrary, repugnant, opposed.

Advert—notice, turn, regard, allude.

Advise — consult, consider, deliberate, admonish.

Advocate—plead, argue, defend, support.

Affability — civility, courteousness, urbanity.

Affable—civil, courteous, urbane, pleasing.

Affair—business, concern, matter, transaction.

Affect—aim, assume, move, pretend, arrogate.

Affecting—feeling, touching, pathetic.

Affection—love, fondness, attachment, kindness, tenderness.

Affiliate—adopt, receive, initiate, associate.

Affinity—relationship, kindred, alliance, conformity, attraction.

Affirm—assure, assert, aver, declare, protest.

Affliction—pain, trouble, distress, grief, sadness, sorrow, tribulation, bereavement, calamity.

Affluence—plenty, abundance, riches, opulence, wealth, concourse, influx.

Afford—yield, grant, give, impart, spare.

Affright—alarm, dismay, shock, terrify, appall, frighten, dishearten, intimidate.

Affront—provoke, outrage, insult, offend.

Afraid—fearful, terrified, timid, timorous.

Aged—elderly, old, senile, advanced in years.

Agent—representative, deputy.

Aggregate—mass, collect, accumulate.

Agile—alert, active, lively, quick, sprightly, nimble, brisk.

Agitate—shake, disturb, move, discuss.

Agitation—disturbance, trepidation, tremor.

Agony—pain, distress, torture, anguish, suffering.

Agree—accede, acquiesce, assent, consent, concur, comply.

Agreeable—suitable, acceptable, pleasing, grateful.

Agreement—harmony, accordance, covenant, concurrence, contract, bargain.

Aid—assist, help, succor, relieve.

Aim—aspire, eudeavor, level, point.

Air—aspect, manner, appearance, look, mien.

Alarm—fear, consternation, dread, apprehension, fright, terror, summons, surprise.

Alienate—transfer, withdraw, estrange.

Allege—adduce, affirm, advance, assert.

Alleviate—ease, abate, lessen, mitigate, relieve, diminish, soothe, lighten.

Alliance—coalition, union, combination, league, confederacy.

Allot—distribute, apportion, assign, appoint.

Allowance—wages, pay, stipend, salary, permission, concession, grant.

Allude—refer, suggest, hint, intimate.

Allure—tempt, entice, seduce, decoy, attract.

Alter—change, vary, modify, rearrange.

Always—ever, perpetually, constantly, continually, incessantly.

Amass—gather, heap, collect, accumulate.

Amazement—astonishment, surprise, wonder, admiration.

Ambiguous—obscure, doubtful, equivocal, uncertain.

Amenable—answerable, responsible, accountable.

Amend—correct, improve, better, rectify, reform, mend.

Amends—recompense, restoration, reparation, restitution.

Amiable—lovely, kind, charming, delightful, obliging.

Ample—large, extended, spacious, copious, abundant, plenteous.

Amusement—entertainment, diversion, sport, pastime, recreation.

Angry—passionate, hot, irascible, hasty.

Anguish—pain, distress, suffering, agony.

Animate—cheer, enliven, exhilarate, impel, incite, inspire, urge, encourage.

Animation—life, spirits, liveliness, buoyancy, gayety, vivacity.

Animosity—hatred, enmity, malignity, hostility.

Annex—attach, affix, add, subjoin.

Announce—proclaim, declare, advertise, publish.

Annul—destroy, revoke, abolish, cancel, repeal, annihilate.

Answer—reply, response, rejoinder.

Answerable—amenable, accountable, responsible.

Antagonist—enemy, foe, opponent, adversary.

Antecedent—previous, former, anterior, preceding, prior, foregoing.

Antipathy—aversion, abhorrence, dislike, detestation, hatred.

Anxiety—caution, care, perplexity, solicitude, uneasiness, disquietude.

Apathy—unfeelingness, indifference, insensibility, unconcern.

Aperture—cavity, opening.

Apology—defense, plea, excuse.

Apparent—evident, clear, plain, visible, distinct.

Appeal—invoke, refer, call upon.

Appearance—aspect, look, air, manner, mien, semblance.

Appease—calm, soothe, pacify, allay, assuage, tranquilize.

Applaud—praise, approve, extol, commend.

Applause—acclamation, shouting, approval.

Appoint—allot, fix, provide, order, prescribe, ordain, depute, constitute.

Appraise—value, estimate.

Appreciate—value, esteem, estimate, prize.

Apprehension—terror, alarm, fear, seizure, dread, suspicion, fright.

Apprise—inform, acquaint, disclose.

Approach—admittance, access, avenue, passage.

Approbation—approval, concurrence, consent, sanction, confirmation.

Appropriate—assume, usurp, set apart.

Appropriate—peculiar, exclusive, adapted.

Approve—allow, like, applaud, esteem, commend.

Arbitrator—judge, umpire, arbiter.

Archives—annals, records.

Ardent—hot, eager, passionate, fervent, fiery, vehement.

Arduous—hard, difficult, laborious.

Argument—proof, reason, dispute.

Arise—mount, ascend, rise, stand up.

Arraign—charge, accuse, impeach.

Arrange—place, dispose, class, range.

Arrogance—assumption, pride, self-conceit, haughtiness, presumption.

Artful—crafty, artificial, deceitful, cunning, dexterous.

Articulate—speak, pronounce, utter.

Artifice—deception, imposition, stratagem, cheat, deceit, finesse.

Attitude—posture, gesture.

Attract—charm, captivate, win, allure, draw, entice.

Attractions—charms, allurements, enticements.

Audacity—impudence, boldness, hardihood, effrontery.

Auspicious—favorable, propitious, prosperous, lucky, fortunate.

Authentic—genuine, authorized, true.

Authority—power, dominion, force, sway, influence, ascendency.

Avarice—greed, covetousness, cupidity.

Averse—loth, unwilling, reluctant, repugnant, unfortunate, unfavorable.

Aversion—dislike, repugnance, antipathy, abhorrence, detestation.

Avidity—eagerness, greediness.

Avocation—calling, trade, profession, office, business, employment, occupation.

Avoid—shun, elude, eschew.

Avow—own, confess, recognize, acknowledge.

Awake—rouse, provoke, excite.

Awe—fear, dread, reverence.

B

Babbling—idle talk, loquacity, chattering, prattling.

Backward—loth, unwilling, reluctant, averse.

Baffle—confound, defeat, disconcert, elude, confuse.

Balance—settle, adjust, regulate, equalize.

Banter—taunt, ridicule, deride, rally, joke, jest.

Bare—stripped, naked, destitute, uncovered, unadorned.

Bargain—purchase, cheapen, contract, buy.

Base—mean, low, vile.

Bashful—shy, modest, diffident, timid.

Basis—foundation, pedestal, base, ground.

Bastard—spurious, illegitimate.

Battle—combat, fight, engagement.

Bear—carry, bring forth, support, suffer, endure, sustain, undergo.

Beat—hit, strike, defeat, overthrow.

Beau—sweetheart, gallant, dandy, fop.

Beautiful—handsome, fine.

Beautify—embellish, decorate, adorn, deck, ornament.

Becoming—suitable, graceful, comely, decent, befitting, meet, fit.

Beg—crave, beseech, entreat, ask, request, implore, solicit, supplicate.

Begin—originate, enter upon, commence.

Beguile—delude, mislead, amuse, deceive, impose upon.

Behavior—conduct, carriage, deportment, manner, demeanor, address.

Behold—see, look, observe, view.

Beholder—spectator, looker on, observer.

Belief—credit, faith, trust, certainty, confidence, reliance, conviction, opinion, assent.

Below—under, beneath.

Bend—lean, incline, distort, bow, subdue.

Beneath—under, below.

Bequeath—devise, give by will.

Beseech—solicit, crave, implore, beg, entreat, request, urge, supplicate.

Bestow—grant, confer, give, present.

Better—improve, mend, reform, ameliorate.

Blame—reprove, reproach, condemn, censure, reprehend, inculpate, upbraid.

Blameless—unblemished, faultless, innocent, guiltless, spotless, irreproachable.

Blast—desolate, destroy, wither up, split.

Blemish—flaw, spot, defect, fault, speck.

Blunt—dull, uncouth, insentient, abrupt.

Blunder—error, mistake.

Boaster—braggard, braggart, braggadocio, vaunter, blusterer.

Boasting—parade, ostentation, vaunting.

Boisterous—violent, furious, impetuous.

Bold—courageous, daring, fearless, impudent, insolent, audacious.

Bondage—servitude, slavery, confinement, imprisonment.

Border—edge, verge, rim, brim, margin, brink, side.

Bore—pierce, penetrate, perforate.

Bound—define, confine, restrict, terminate, limit, circumscribe.

Bounty—liberality, benevolence, generosity, beneficence.

Brave—bold, daring, heroic, undaunted, courageous, intrepid, fearless.

Breach—gap, chasm, break, opening.

Break—destroy, batter, dissolve, rend, tame, demolish, shatter.

Breaker—surge, billow, wave, sand-bank, covered rock.

Brief—short, concise, succinct, compendious, summary, epitomized.

Bright—clear, shining, sparkling, brilliant, glistening, glittering, lucid, resplendent.

Brilliancy—brightness, radiance, splendor, luster.

Broad—far-reaching, ample, extensive, large, wide.

Broil—fight, quarrel, altercation, affray.

Bruise—break, crush, squeeze, pound, compress.

Build—erect, establish, construct, found.

Bulk—greatness, largeness, size, extent, magnitude, dimensions.

Burden—load, freight, weight, cargo.

Burning—ardent, fiery, scorching, hot.

Burst—break, rend, crack, split.

Business—trade, occupation, calling, work, avocation, profession, employment.

Bustle—disorder, hurry, tumult, confusion.

But—except, still, however, save, nevertheless, yet, notwithstanding.

Butchery—havoc, slaughter, carnage, massacre.

Buy—procure, bargain, obtain, purchase.

C

Cabal—coalition, league, combination, conspiracy, intrigue, plot.

Calamity—mishap, disaster, misfortune.

Calculate—count, number, compute, reckon, estimate.

Call—exclaim, cry, invite, name, summon, subpœna.

Calling — trade, occupation, profession, business, employment, avocation.

Calm — soothe, compose, tranquilize, pacify, appease, assuage, allay.

Cancel — erase, destroy, abolish, repeal, annul, revoke.

Candid — frank, open, artless, honest, ingenuous.

Capable — able, fitted, competent, qualified, skillful.

Capacity — capability, faculty, ability, genius, talent.

Caprice — fancy, humor, freak, whim, notion.

Capricious — notional, variable, fickle, changeable, fantastical, whimsical.

Captivate — charm, enslave, attract, enchant, enrapture, take prisoner, fascinate.

Captivity — servitude, bondage, confinement, imprisonment.

Capture — prize, seizure.

Care — anxiety, solicitude, regard, attention, management, concern, disquietude, worry.

Careful — cautious, solicitous, attentive, provident, guarded, prudent, circumspect.

Careless — heedless, thoughtless, remiss, inattentive, negligent, unconcerned.

Caress — fondle, endear, embrace, stroke, soothe.

Carnage — massacre, butchery, slaughter.

Carriage — manner, behavior, deportment, mien, demeanor, walk, bearing.

Carry — transport, convey, bear.

Cast — throw, hurl, turn, direct, fling.

Catch — snatch, seize, lay hold of, grasp, capture, grip.

Cause — origin, source, reason, inducement.

Caution — advice, warning, notice, admonition, care, solicitude, circumspection.

Cautious — careful, wary, watchful, prudent, circumspect.

Cease — leave off, desist, stop, discontinue.

Celebrated — honored, illustrious, famous, renowned.

Celebrate — praise, extol, commend, perpetuate.

Censure — rebuke, reprimand, condemnation, reproach, stricture, blame.

Ceremony — form, rite, observance.

Certain — manifest, actual, real, sure, constant.

Chagrin — vexation, mortification, fretfulness.

Challenge — demand, defy, claim, call, accuse, object, except.

Chance — hazard, casual, fortuitous.

Change — alteration, variety, mutation, conversion, vicissitude.

Changeable — uncertain, variable, fickle, mutable, inconstant, unsteady.

Character — manner, reputation, description, letter, mark, quality.

Charity — kindness, benevolence, good-will, liberality, beneficence, generosity.

Charm — attract, bewitch, delight, enrapture, captivate, fascinate.

Chasten — correct, punish, afflict, chastise.

Chasteness — purity, continence, simplicity, chastity.

Chastise — correct, afflict, punish.

Chattels — effects, movable goods.

Cheat — fraud, deception, deceit, stratagem, imposition.

Cheer — incite, comfort, gladden, encourage, exhilarate.

Cheerfulness — mirth, gladness, liveliness, sprightliness, gayety, jollity, comfort.

Cherish — help, shelter, nurture, warm, foster.

Chide — scold, rebuke, reprove, reprimand.

Chiefly — mainly, principally, particularly, especially.

Childish — simple, puerile, trifling.

Childhood — infancy, minority.

Children — offspring, issue, progeny.

Choke — stifle, smother, suffocate.

Choice — selection, election, option.

Choose — prefer, select, pick, elect.

Circulate — spread, pass, diffuse, propagate.

Circumscribe — limit, confine, enclose, bound.

Circumstance — event, incident, state, situation, condition.

Circumspect — watchful, wary, cautious, particular, vigilant, prudent.

Circumstantial — minute, particular, incidental, accidental.

Civil — obliging, polite, affable, courteous, complaisant, polished, well-bred.

Civilization — refinement, culture.

Claim — demand, pretension, right.

Clandestine — secret, hidden, private.

Class — division, order, degree, rank.

Cleansing — purifying, purging, cleaning.

Clear — free, pure, acquit, absolve, discharge, satisfy, vindicate, apparent, evident, obvious.

Clearly — distinctly, lucidly, plainly, manifestly, obviously, visibly.

Clemency — mercy, mildness, lenity, kindness.

Clever — adroit, skillful, ready, expert.

Climb — mount, scale, ascend.

Cling — stick, hold, cleave, clasp, hang.

Close — shut, firm, compact, concise, confined, near.

Clothes — raiment, garments, covering, attire, habiliments, apparel.

Clouded — obscured, variegated, dark, gloomy, overcast, sullen.

Clumsy — awkward, unhandy, uncouth, bungling.

Coadjutor — assistant, colleague, ally.

Coalition — conspiracy, league, union, combination.

Coarse — gross, inelegant, rough, rude, vulgar, unrefined.

Coax — flatter, wheedle, fawn, cajole.

Coerce — force, compel, restrain.

Cognomen — name, appellation, denomination.

Coherent — consistent, adhesive, tenacious.

Coincide — harmonize, agree, concur.

Cold — reserved, chill, frigid, shy, unaffecting.

Colleague — ally, associate, partner, coadjutor.

Collected — calm, placid, unruffled, composed, gathered.

Collection — gathering, contribution, assemblage, group.

Colloquy — dialogue, conference, talk.

Color — dye, hue, tint, paint, tinge.

Combination — union, league, coalition, conspiracy, alliance, confederacy.

Comely — graceful, handsome, agreeable.

Comfort — solace, console, encourage, enliven.

Comfortless — wretched, desolate, forlorn.

Comic — funny, ludicrous, ridiculous, laughable.

Command — direction, behest, precept, order, injunction.

Commanding — dictatorial, imperative, authoritative, imperious.

Commence — undertake, originate, begin.

Commend — praise, recommend, extol, applaud, approve, laud.

Commensurate — sufficient, adequate, equal, proportionate.

Comment — utterance, explanation, exposition, annotation, note, observation, elucidation, remark.

Commiseration — feeling for, pity, compassion, sympathy, condolence.

Commission — authorize, enable, empower.

Commodious — fit, suitable, convenient.

Commodity — goods, merchandise, wares.

Common — mean, vulgar, frequent, low, general, ordinary, usual.

Commotion — perturbation, disturbance, tumult.

Communicate — tell, report, disclose, make known, impart, reveal.

Communication — commerce, intercourse, conference.

Communion — fellowship, union, converse, intercourse.

Commute — exchange, barter.

Compact — contract, agreement, covenant, firm, solid, close.

Companion — ally, accomplice, associate, comrade, friend, confederate, partner.

Company — assembly, band, crew, corporation, congregation, association.

Compass — attain, enclose, invest, besiege, environ, encircle, consummate.

Compassion — tenderness, pity, sympathy, commiseration.

Compensation — pay, amends, reward, remuneration, requital.

Competent — suitable, fitted, able, qualified, capable, efficient, skillful, effective.

Competition — rivalry, contest, emulation.

Complaining — lamenting, murmuring, bemoaning, bewailing, regretting, repining.

Complaisant — agreeable, affable, courteous, civil.

Complete — conclude, fulfill, terminate, effect, accomplish, finish, consummate, execute.

Complex — intricate, complicate, compound.

Compliment — extol, flatter, congratulate, praise.

Comply — agree, accord, accede, assent, yield, acquiesce, consent.

Compose — put together, form, settle, soothe, calm, quiet, compound.

Comprehend — appreciate, embrace, include, understand, comprise, conceive.

Compress — condense, squeeze, bind.

Compulsion — constraint, force, restraint, coercion.

Compunction — regret, penitence, remorse, repentance, contrition.

Compute — count, number, rate, estimate, calculate.

Concede — yield, grant, allow, deliver, admit, surrender.

Conceal — hide, disguise, cover, secrete.

Conceit — imagination, fancy, notion, freak.

Conceited — vain, proud, egotistical, opinionated.

Conception — perception, knowledge, fancy, idea, imagination, notion.

Concern — care, interest, business, affair, regard, matter.

Concert — contrive, manage, adjust, consult.

Conciliate — win, reconcile, propitiate.

Conclude — finish, terminate, close.

Conclusion — termination, inference, end.

Conclusive — convincing, decisive.

Concord — harmony, agreement, unity, amity, peace.

Concur — agree, coincide, approve, acquiesce.

Condemn — sentence, doom, blame, reproach, reprove.

Condense — abbreviate, shorten, contract.

Condescension — humility, submission, deference.

Condition — rank, state, compact, bond, case, situation, stipulation.

Condolence — compassion, commiseration, sympathy.

Conduce — conduct, tend, lead, contribute.

Conduct — management, behavior, guidance, deportment.

Confederate — ally, accomplice, associate.

Confer — give, bestow, discourse, grant.

Confess — acknowledge, grant, own, admit, avow, recognize, disclose.

Confide — rely, trust, repose, depend.

Confident — impudent, bold, positive, dogmatical, absolute, assured.

Confined — limited, shut up, circumscribed, restrained, contracted, imprisoned.

Confirm — corroborate, establish, strengthen.

Conflict — contest, contention, fight, agony, combat, struggle, warfare, pang.

Conform — submit, yield, comply.

Confuse — stupefy, embarrass, confound, abash, disorder, perplex.

Congruity — agreement, consistency.

Conjecture — guess, think, belief, surmise.

Connected — joined, united, related.

Connection — intercourse, union, commerce, association, communion.

Conquer — subdue, vanquish, overcome, surmount.

Conscious — aware, sensible, apprised.

Consent — yield, agree, assent, comply, acquiesce, accede.

Consequence — result, inference, effect.

Consequently — hence, accordingly, therefore, wherefore.

Consider — ponder, deliberate, regard, reflect.

Consign — entrust, commit, transfer, make over.

Consistent — agreeing, consonant, accordant, firm.

Console — comfort, soothe, cheer.

Conspicuous — prominent, noted, distinguished, illustrious.

Constancy — perseverance, firmness, steadiness, stability.

Constantly — ever, continually, perpetually, unchangeably, incessantly.

Construct — make, build, erect, form.

Consult — consider, deliberate, advise.

Consume — waste, destroy, absorb, complete.

Consummation—perfection, completion.

Contagious—epidemic, infectious.

Contain—hold, include, embrace, comprehend.

Contaminate—pollute, taint, defile, corrupt, poison.

Contemn—scorn, despise, disdain.

Contemplate—consider, meditate, muse.

Contemptible — paltry, vile, disdainful, mean, despicable, disreputable, low.

Contend—quarrel, debate, contest, argue, vie, strive.

Contention—strife, conflict, contest, combat, dispute, dissension.

Contentment—acquiescence, happiness, satisfaction, gratification.

Contiguous — near, approximating, adjacent.

Continual — perpetual, constant, incessant, unceasing, continuous.

Continuation—continuance, duration.

Contract—arrangement, bargain, agreement, compact, covenant.

Contract — curtail, abridge, condense, abbreviate, reduce, shorten.

Contradict — gainsay, deny, oppose.

Contrary — opposite, adverse, inimical.

Contribute — assist, administer, aid, share.

Contrition — remorse, penitence, repentance, compunction, regret.

Contrivance—device, means, invention, plan, scheme.

Control—subdue, restrain, check, govern, curb.

Controversy—argument, debate, disputation, contest.

Convene—call together, assemble, convoke.

Convenient — handy, adapted, suitable.

Conversation — dialogue, discussion, conference, colloquy.

Converse—commune, speak, talk, discourse.

Convey—take, carry, bear, transport.

Conviction — persuasion, detection, satisfaction.

Convivial — agreeable, festal, social, sociable.

Convoke—gather, assemble, convene, call together.

Copious — ample, full, abundant, exuberant, plenteous, bountiful.

Cordial—hearty, warm, sincere.

Correct — mend, amend, reform, better, improve, rectify.

Corroborate—establish, confirm, strengthen.

Corruption—depravity, pollution, defilement, adulteration, contamination, infection, putridity.

Costly—expensive, precious, valuable.

Counsel — advice, instruction, exhortation.

Counteract — change, defeat, oppose, hinder, frustrate, prevent.

Countenance—uphold, favor, encourage, support, sanction.

Counterfeit — forged, feigned, false, spurious, imposture, imitation.

Couple — brace, pair, two, join, connect.

Courage — heroism, valor, bravery, firmness, intrepidity, fearlessness.

Course — mode, way, track, line, career, progress, method, passage, road, route, series, succession.

Courteous — kind, civil, affable, polished, respectful, polite, wellbred.

Covenant — arrangement, agreement, contract, pledge, stipulation.

Covering—concealing, screening, sheltering, hiding, overspreading.

Covetousness — greed, avarice, cupidity, inordinate desire.

Coward — sneak, dastard, poltroon.

Cowardice—fear, timidity, cowardliness.

Crafty — underhanded, cunning, artful, wily, deceitful, sly, subtle.

Crave—beg, pray, beseech, entreat, implore, request, solicit, supplicate.

Create—build, form, make, cause, invent, originate, shape, produce.

Crime—evil, guilt, wickedness, sin, vice.

Crisis—juncture, critical point.

Criticism — stricture, censure, review, remark, judgment.

Crooked—bowed, turned, curved, awry, bent, disfigured, deformed.

Cross—ill-tempered, fretful, peevish, spleeny, petulant, splenetic.

Cruel—barbarous, brutal, pitiless, inhuman, inexorable, unmerciful, harsh.

Cultivation—advancement, civilization, improvement, refinement, tillage.

Cure—heal, restore, remedy.

Curious—prying, inquisitive.

Curse — imprecation, malediction, anathema, execration.

Cursory — hasty, careless, slight, desultory, superficial.

Curtail—shorten, contract, abbreviate, abridge.

Custom — habit, manner, usage, prescription, practice.

D

Damage—injury, hurt, loss, detriment.

Dampness — wet, moisture, humidity.

Danger—hazard, peril, risk, venture.

Daring—bold, fearless, valorous, courageous, intrepid, brave.

Dark — dismal, obscure, gloomy, dim.

Date — time, period, epoch, era, age.

Dead — still, lifeless, inanimate, deceased.

Deadly — fatal, mortal, destructive.

Dealing—trade, practice, traffic, commerce.

Dearth — famine, need, scarcity, want.

Debar — deter, hinder, prevent, exclude, preclude.

Debase — lower, degrade, humble, disgrace.

Debate—argue, wrangle, dispute, controvert, contest.

Debilitate — impair, weaken, enervate, enfeeble.

Debility — infirmity, weakness, incapacity, imbecility, feebleness.

Decay—decline, consumption.

Decease—demise, death, departure of life.

Deceit — fraud, duplicity, deception, cunning, artifice, trickery, guilt.

Decent—comely, fit, seemly, becoming.

Decide—settle, resolve, fix, determine.

Decision — sentence, determination, judgment, resolution, conclusion.

Decisive—conclusive, convincing, ending.

Declare — announce, pronounce, testify, proclaim, assure, assert, affirm.

Decline—droop, decay, shun, reject, repel, sink, refuse.

Decorate — embellish, ornament, beautify, adorn.

Decoy—allure, tempt, seduce, entice, inveigle.

Decrease — lessen, diminish, subside, lower, abate.

Dedicate—devote, consecrate, set apart.

Deduction—abatement, inference, conclusion.

Deed — action, exploit, achievement, feat.

Deface — mar, disfigure, destroy, mutilate.

Defame—slander, vilify, scandalize, calumniate.

Defeat — beat, baffle, conquer, overcome, overthrow, vanquish, frustrate.

Defect—want, flaw, blemish, imperfection.

Defective — wanting, imperfect, deficient.

Defender — protector, advocate, pleader, vindicator.

Defense—apology, excuse, justification, protection, vindication.

Defer—delay, hinder, prolong, retard, postpone, protract, procrastinate.

Deference—respect, regard, condescension, submission, veneration.

Deficient—lacking, wanting, imperfect.

Defile—taint, poison, vitiate, corrupt, contaminate, pollute.

Definite—exact, precise, positive, certain, bounded, limited.

Defraud—swindle, cheat, rob, deceive, trick.

Degrade—lower, disgrace, lessen, reduce, decry, depreciate, disparage.

Degree—rank, position, station, class, order.

Dejection — depression, lowliness, melancholy.

Delay—hinder, defer, detain, prolong, protract, postpone.

Deliberate — slow, hesitating, considerate, thoughtful, cautious.

Delicate—frail, fine, nice, weak, tender, beautiful, elegant, dainty.

Delighted — pleased, glad, grateful, joyful.

Delineate—describe, draw, paint, sketch, depict, represent.

Delinquent — criminal, offender.

Deliver — give up, save, yield, utter, surrender, concede, rescue, transmit.

Delude—mislead, deceive, cheat, beguile.

Delusion—cheat, illusion, deception, fallacy.

Demand—claim, require, ask.

Demolish—overthrow, destroy.

Demonstrate — illustrate, show, prove, manifest.

Denominate—name, title, style, designate.

Denote—imply, signify, mark, betoken.

Deny—refuse, disown, contradict, oppose.

Departure — leaving, forsaking, going away, abandoning, exit.

Dependence—trust, reliance, confidence, connection.

Deplore—bemoan, bewail, mourn, lament.

Deportment—behavior, conduct, character, carriage, demeanor.

Depraved — degraded, corrupt, abandoned, profligate, wicked, vicious.

Deprecate—underrate, disparage, detract, undervalue, degrade, traduce, lower.

Deprive—prevent, hinder, depose, divest, strip, abridge.

Depute—authorize, appoint, constitute.

Deputy—agent, substitute, representative, delegate.

Derange—disarrange, discompose, disorder, confuse, disconcert.

Deride—mock, ridicule, make fun of, banter, laugh at.

Describe—illustrate, narrate, delineate, recount, relate, represent.

Description -- account, illustration, narration, explanation, recital, relation, detail.

Design—intend, plan, scheme, purpose, project, sketch.

Designate — name, show, point out, indicate, choose, distinguish, style.

Desist—stop, leave off, cease, discontinue.

Desperate—desponding, hopeless, mad, careless, furious, regardless.

Despicable — mean, vile, pitiful, worthless, outrageous, contemptible.

Despise—hate, scorn, loathe.

Despotic — arbitrary, self-willed, absolute.

Destination—point, location, lot, design, fate, purpose, appointment.

Destitute — bare, forlorn, poor, scanty, forsaken, needy.

Destroy — ruin, waste, demolish, consume, annihilate, dismantle.

Desultory — hasty, slight, loose, roving.

Detach—sever, separate, disjoin, divide.

Detail—account, tale, description, narration, recital.

Detain — keep, restrain, confine, hold.

Detect—find, discover, convict.

Determine — fix, decide, bound, limit, settle, resolve, adjust.

Determined — firm, resolute, decided, fixed, concluded, ended, immovable.

Detest—hate, loathe, abominate, abhor.

Detestable — hateful, loathsome, abominable, execrable.

Detract—defame, degrade, vilify, slander, calumniate, scandalize, derogate.

Detriment—inconvenience, loss, injury, disadvantage, damage, hurt, prejudice.

Develop — grow, unravel, clear, unfold, disclose, exhibit.

Deviate—stray, wander, err, digress, swerve.

Device — design, scheme, show, plan, contrivance, stratagem, invention.

Devote—give, apply, consecrate, set apart, dedicate.

Devout — pious, holy, religious, prayerful.

Dexterity — adroitness, ability, expertness, aptness, skillfulness, skill, tact.

Dialect—language, speech, tongue.

Dictate — propose, direct, order, prescribe, instruct, suggest.

Die — expire, depart, perish, languish, wither.

Differ—dispute, dissent, contend, vary, disagree.

Different — unlike, various, diverse.

Difficult—trying, arduous, hard, troublesome.

Difficulty — obstacle, obstruction, embarrassment, trouble, perplexity, trial, impediment.

Diffident—retiring, fearful, bashful, distrustful, modest, hesitating.

Dignified — exalted, elevated, honored, stately.

Diligent — industrious, assiduous, laborious, active, persevering, attentive.

Diminish—shorten, curtail, abate, decrease, lessen, subside.

Direct — show, guide, conduct, manage, regulate, sway.

Direction — command, order, address, superscription. .

Directly — at once, quickly, immediately, instantly, promptly, instantaneously.

Disagree—dispute, dissent, differ, quarrel, vary.

Disappoint—foil, defeat.

Disaster — misfortune, calamity, mischance, mishap.

Disavow—disown, deny, disclaim, repudiate.

Discard — cast off, dismiss, discharge.

Discern — distinguish, discriminate, penetrate, behold, discover.

Discernible—plain, evident, perceptible, manifest, apparent.

Disclose — reveal, discover, divulge.

Disconcert — disorder, confuse, defeat, ruffle, fret, vex, unsettle, interrupt, derange.

Discord — contention, dissension, inharmony.

Discover — make known, detect, communicate, reveal, impart, tell, disclose.

Discredit—dishonor, scandal, disgrace, disrepute, ignominy, reproach.

Discretion—prudence, judgment.

Disdain—scorn, contempt, pride, arrogance, haughtiness.

Disease—sickness, distemper, malady, disorder.

Disgrace — degrade, debase, dishonor, abase.

Disguise — cover, disfigure, conceal, dissemble.

Disgust—loathing, nausea, dislike, aversion.

Dishonor—shame, disgrace.

Dislike—antipathy, aversion, repugnance, hatred, contempt, abhorrence.

Dismiss — discharge, divest, discard.

Disorder — confusion, bustle, disease, tumult, malady, distemper, irregularity.

Disparage — lower, undervalue, degrade, detract, decry, depreciate.

Disperse—scatter, dissipate, deal out, spread, distribute.

Display — parade, exhibit, show, ostentation.

Displease—offend, anger, vex.

Dispose—regulate, place, arrange, order, adapt.

Dispute—contest, debate, quarrel, altercation, difference, controversy.

Disseminate—spread, circulate, scatter, propagate.

Dissertation — discourse, essay, treatise, disquisition.

Dissipate — disperse, squander, waste, expend, consume, dispel.

Distaste—aversion, disgust, contempt, dislike, dissatisfaction, loathing.

Distinct—clear, obvious, different, separate, unlike, dissimilar.

Distinguish—discriminate, know, see, perceive, discern.

Distinguished—noted, eminent, conspicuous, celebrated, illustrious.

Distress—grief, sorrow, sadness, suffering, affliction, agony, pain, anguish, misery.

Distribute—deal out, scatter, assign, allot, apportion, divide.

District—locality, section, tract, region, territory, province, circuit, county.

Diversion—enjoyment, pastime, recreation, amusement, deviation, sport.

Divide—separate, part, share, distribute.

Divine—suppose, conjecture, foretell, guess.

Divulge—disclose, impart, reveal, communicate, publish.

Docile—gentle, tractable, pliant, teachable, yielding, quiet.

Doctrine—belief, wisdom, dogma, principle, precept.

Dogmatical—positive, authoritative, arrogant, magisterial, confident.

Doleful—awful, dismal, sorrowful, woeful, piteous, rueful.

Doubt—suspense, hesitation, perplexity, scruple, uncertainty.

Doubtful — unstable uncertain, dubious, precarious, equivocal.

Drag—pull, bring, haul, draw.

Dread—fear, apprehension.

Dreadful—fearful, frightful, terrible, awful, horrible.

Dress—array, apparel, vestments, garments, attire.

Droop—pine, sink, fade, decline, languish.

Dumb—mute, still, silent, inarticulate.

Durable — lasting, constant, permanent, continuing.

Dutiful — submissive, obedient, respectful.

Dwelling — home, house, abode, habitation, residence, domicile.

E

Eager — earnest, excited, ardent, impetuous, quick, vehement.

Earn—acquire, win, make, gain, obtain.

Earth—globe, world, planet.

Ease—rest, quiet, repose, facility, lightness.

Economical—careful, close, saving, frugal, thrifty, sparing.

Ecstasy—happiness, joy, rapture, transport, delight, enthusiasm, elevation.

Edifice — building, fabric, structure.

Education — culture, cultivation, breeding, refinement, instruction, nurture, tuition.

Efface—destroy, obliterate, erase, expunge, eradicate.

Effect — consequence, result, purpose, event, issue, reality, meaning.

Effects — things, goods, chattels, furniture, movables, property.

Efficient — competent, capable, able, effectual, effective.

Effort—endeavor, essay, attempt, exertion, trial.

Elegant—graceful, lovely, beautiful, handsome.

Eligible — suitable, fit, worthy, capable.

Embarrass — trouble, entangle, puzzle, perplex, distress.

Embellish — ornament, decorate, adorn, illustrate, deck, beautify.

Emblem—symbol, figure, type.

Embrace—hold, clasp, hug, comprehend, comprise.

Emergency—necessity, exigency, casualty.

Emolument—reward, profit, gain, advantage, lucre.

Emotion—feeling, tremor, excitement, agitation.

Employment—occupation, trade, profession, business, avocation.

Empower—enable, delegate, commission, authorize.

Empty—untenanted, vacant, void, evacuated, unfurnished, unfilled.

Enchant—beguile, charm, captivate, bewitch, fascinate, enrapture.

Encomium—eulogy, praise.

Encounter—quarrel, assault, attack, combat, engagement, meeting.

Encourage — cheer, stimulate, animate, incite, sanction, support, countenance, instigate.

Encroach—intrude, trespass, infringe.

End—finish, close, stop, extremity, termination, sequel, consequence, cessation, death, purpose.

Endeavor—aim, exertion, effort, attempt.

Endless — unending, everlasting, perpetual, interminable, infinite, incessant, eternal.

Endurance — submission, fortitude, patience, resignation.

Enemy—adversary, opponent, foe, antagonist.

Energy — determination, efficacy, force, vigor, strength, potency, power.

Enervate—weaken, enfeeble, unnerve, debilitate, deteriorate.

Engage — employ, enlist, fight, induce, pledge, promise, attract, win.

Enjoyment—happiness, pleasure, joy, gratification.

Enlarge — extend, widen, lengthen, increase.

Enmity—spite, hatred, hostility, malignity, animosity.

Enough—ample, sufficient, plenty, abundance.

Enrage—excite, irritate, inflame, incense, aggravate, exasperate.

Enrapture—charm, attract, captivate, fascinate, enchant.

Enterprise—business, adventure, attempt, undertaking.

Entertainment—pastime, sport, amusement, recreation, diversion, performance, banquet, feast.

Entice—tempt, decoy, seduce, attract, allure.

Entire—full, whole, perfect, complete, total, integral.

Entirely—perfectly, completely, wholly.

Entitle — style, designate, name, characterize, denominate.

Entreat—ask, solicit, crave, beg, beseech, implore, petition, supplicate.

Envy—suspicion, jealousy, grudging.

Epitomize—lessen, abridge, curtail, reduce, condense.

Equal—commensurate, adequate, uniform.

Equitable — just, right, honest, satisfactory, impartial, reasonable, fair.

Eradicate—exterminate, root out, extirpate.

Erase — expunge, efface, cancel, obliterate.

Erect—build, raise, found, set up, construct, elevate, establish, institute.

Error—blunder, mistake, fault.

Escape—elope, evade, elude, fly, avoid, pass.

Essential—important, necessary, requisite, indispensable.

Esteem — respect, regard, value, appreciate, prize, love.

Estimate—rate, compute, value, calculate, appraise, appreciate, esteem.

Eternal—perpetual, forever, endless, infinite, immortal, continual, everlasting.

Evade—escape, elude, avoid, prevaricate, shun.

Even—smooth, level, plain, equal, uniform.

Event—incident, adventure, issue, occurrence, result, consequence.

Ever—always, constantly, forever, unceasingly, continually, incessantly.

Evidence—proof, deposition, witness, testimony.

Evil—sinful, wicked, bad.

Exact — enjoin, demand, extract, extort.

Exact—sure, strict, punctual, precise, accurate.

Exalted—high, elevated, refined, dignified, raised, sublime, magnificent.

Examination—search, scrutiny, investigation, inquiry, research.

Example — copy, precedent, pattern.

Exasperate—excite, irritate, enrage, vex, provoke, aggravate.

Exceed — improve, outdo, excel, surpass, transcend.

Excellence — goodness, purity, superiority, perfection, eminence.

Except—but, besides, unless, object.

Exchange—barter, trade, traffic.

Excite—provoke, arouse, incite, stimulate, awaken, irritate.

Exculpate — forgive, exonerate, acquit, absolve, justify.

Excuse—pretense, pretext, plea, subterfuge, apology, evasion.

Execrable—hateful, detestable, contemptible, abominable.

Exemption — freedom, privilege, immunity.

Exercise—practice, exert, carry on.

Exhaust—empty, drain, spend.

Exigency—necessity, emergency.

Exonerate—clear, relieve, exculpate, justify, acquit, absolve, forgive.

Expectation—belief, trust, hope, confidence, anticipation.

Expedient — fit, suitable, necessary, requisite.

Expedite — hurry, hasten, accelerate, quicken.

Expeditious — speedy, diligent, quick, prompt.

Expel—exile, banish, cast out.

Expensive — dear, costly, valuable.

Experience — knowledge, trial, experiment, proof, test.

Expert — handy, ready, skillful, adroit, dexterous.

Explain—show, elucidate, unfold.

Explanation — detail, account, description, relation, explication, recital.

Explicit—clear, definite, express, plain.

Exploit — feat, accomplishment, achievement, deed, performance.

Explore—search, examine.

Extend—spread out, stretch out, enlarge, increase, distend, diffuse.

Extensive—wide, comprehensive, large.

Extenuate — palliate, diminish, lessen, excuse.

Exterior — outward, outside, external.

Exterminate — eradicate, extirpate, destroy.

External—outward, exterior.

Extol—commend, praise, admire, laud, eulogize, applaud.

F

Facetious — amusing, jocular, comic, jocose.

Fact—incident, circumstance.

Faculty — ability, gift, talent, power.

Failing—weakness, imperfection, frailty, misfortune, miscarriage, foible, fault.

Fair—clear, consistent, right, impartial, straight, honest, just, equitable.

Faith—trust, belief, credit, fidelity.

Fallacious — illusive, visionary, deceitful, delusive, fraudulent.

Falsehood — falsity, falsification, fabrication, fiction, lie, untruth.

Familiar—free, intimate, unceremonious.

Famous — celebrated, eminent, renowned, distinguished, illustrious.

Fanciful — ideal, imaginative, capricious, fantastical, whimsical, hypochondriac.

Fancy—imagination, taste, whim, caprice, inclination, liking, conceit, notion, conception, humor, ideality.

Fascinate—charm, attract, captivate, bewitch, enchant, enrapture.

Fashion — style, mode, custom, manner, way, practice, form, sort.

Fasten—fix, hold, stick, annex, attach, affix.

Fastidious — particular, disdainful, squeamish.

Fate — destiny, chance, fortune, luck, doom, lot.

Favor—civility, support, benefit, grace.

Favorable—auspicious, suitable, propitious.

Fault—failing, error, shortcoming, blemish, imperfection, offense.

Faultless — guiltless, blameless, spotless, innocent.

Fear—alarm, dread, timidity, terror, fright, trepidation, apprehension.

Fearful—dreadful, horrible, terrible, awful, afraid, timorous, timid.

Fearless—daring, brave, intrepid, undaunted, courageous.

Feasible — reasonable, plausible, practicable.

Feat—exploit, trick, achievement, act, deed.

Feeble—frail, infirm, weak.

Feeling — sensation, sympathy, generosity, sensibility.

Felicity—joy, delight, happiness, prosperity, bliss, blessedness.

Fertile—fruitful, prolific, abundant, productive.

Fervor — warmth, heat, ardor, vehemence, zeal.

Festivity—joyfulness, happiness, gayety, festival.

Fickle—unstable, changeable, inconstant, variable, capricious, impulsive.

Fiction—invention, lie, untruth, falsehood, fabrication.

Fidelity—faith, honesty, loyalty.

Fiery — hot, fervent, impulsive, ardent, passionate, vehement.

Figure — shape, semblance, form, representation, statue.

Fine—delicate, nice, pretty, lovely, showy, beautiful, elegant.

Finish—conclude, end, terminate, close, complete, perfect.

Firm—ready, strong, immovable, solid, steady, sturdy, partnership, resolute.

First—highest, chief, earliest, primary, primitive, pristine, commencement, original.

Fitted—suited, competent, qualified, adapted.

Flag — droop, languish, decline, pine, faint.

Flagitious — wicked, atrocious, flagrant, heinous.

Flavor—taste, odor, fragrance.

Flaw—spot, stain, speck, crack, blemish, defect.

Fleeting — transient, transitory, swift, temporary.

Fleetness — swiftness, rapidity, quickness, velocity, celerity.

Fluctuate—vary, waver, change, hesitate, vacillate.

Follower — adherent, successor, believer, disciple, partisan, pursuer.

Fondness—affection, love, attachment, tenderness.

Foolish—simple, stupid, silly, absurd, preposterous, irrational.

Forbear—refrain, spare, abstain, pause.

Forbid—deny, prohibit, interdict, oppose.

Force—oblige, compel, restrain.

Forcible—powerful, strong, irresistible, mighty, potent, cogent.

Forebode—foretell, presage, betoken, prognosticate, augur.

Forego—quit, give up, resign.

Foregoing—before, former, previous, prior, preceding, anterior, antecedent.

Forethought—expectation, foresight, anticipation, premeditation.

Forfeiture—penalty, fine.

Forge—counterfeit, frame, invent, fabricate.

Forgive—absolve, pardon, remit, acquit, excuse.

Forlorn — forsaken, lost, lonely, destitute, deserted.

Form—ceremony, observance, rite.

Formal — cermonious. particular, methodical, exact, stiff, precise.

Forsake—desert, abandon, leave, abdicate, relinquish, quit.

Fortunate — successful, lucky, prosperous.

Fortune—estate, portion, success, fate.

Forward—confident. eager, bold, ardent, immodest, presumptuous, ready, progressive.

Foster — keep, harbor, nourish, cherish, nurse.

Fragile — brittle, weak, tender, frail.

Frailty—weakness, unsteadiness. instability, failing, foible.

Frame—fabricate, compose, plan, contrive, invent, form, adjust.

Fraternity — society, brotherhood.

Fraud—cheat, imposition, deceit, deception, guile.

Freak — whim, caprice, humor, fancy.

Free — generous, liberal, candid, open, frank, familiar, unconfined, unconstrained, unreserved, munificent, bounteous.

Free — deliver, liberate, rescue, clear, affranchise, enfranchise.

Freedom — liberty, independence, exemption, privilege, familiarity, unrestraint.

Freely — spontaneously, frankly, unreservedly, cheerfully, unhesitatingly, liberally.

Frequently — often, repeatedly, commonly, generally, usually.

Fresh—new, recent, cool, modern, novel.

Fret—chafe, anger, gall, corrode, agitate, vex.

Fretful—captious, peevish, angry, petulant.

Friendly—pleasant, kind, agreeable, sociable, amicable.

Fright—panic, consternation, terror, alarm.

Frighten—terrify, scare, alarm, intimidate, affright, daunt.

Frightful—horrid, horrible, terrible, terrific, dreadful, fearful.

Frugal—careful, saving, prudent, economical.

Fruitful — abundant, plentiful, fertile, productive, prolific.

Frustrate—defeat, hinder, foil, nullify, disappoint.

Fully—largely, amply, completely, copiously, abundantly.

Futile—useless, frivolous, trifling.

G

Gain—obtain, get, win, acquire, attain, profit.

Gait — bearing, mien, walk, carriage.

Gale — breeze, storm, hurricane, tempest.

Gather — collect, muster, infer, assemble, compress, fold.

Gay—dashing, showy, merry, fine, cheerful.

Generally — usually, commonly, frequently.

Generous — liberal, bounteous, beneficent, munificent, noble.

Genius—talent, intellect, wisdom, ingenuity, capacity, ability, taste.

Genteel — polished, refined, mannerly, cultured, polite.

Gentle—tame, meek, mild, quiet, peaceable.

Genuine—real, actual, authentic, unalloyed, unadulterated, true, natural.

Germinate—sprout, shoot, grow, bud, vegetate.

Gesture—action, motion, posture, attitude.

Get—gain, attain, obtain, procure, realize, acquire, possess.

Gift—donation, present, gratuity, benefaction, endowment, ability, talent.

Give — impart, confer, grant, bestow, consign, yield.

Glad—happy, gay, cheerful, joyful, joyous, delighted, gratified.

Glance—sight, look, glimpse.

Glitter — glisten, sparkle, shine, glare, radiate.

Glittering—glistening, sparkling, shining, bright, brilliant.

Gloom — dark, sad, dim, cloudy, dull, sullen, morose, melancholy.

Glory — fame, renown, splendor, praise, honor, reputation, brightness.

Graceful — comely, genteel, becoming, elegant, neat.

Grand — dignified, lofty, exalted, great, elevated, magnificent, sublime, majestic, glorious, superb, splendid.

Grant—give, bestow, cede, confer, concede, sell, yield.

Grasp—grip, seize, catch.

Grateful — thankful, agreeable, delicious, pleasing.

Gratification — indulgence, happiness, enjoyment, fruition, pleasure.

Grave—slow, solemn, thoughtful, serious, important, sedate.

Greatness—size, bulk, grandeur, magnitude, immensity, dignity, power.

Greediness—ravenous, rapacity, voracity, covetousness, eagerness.

Grief—sadness, sorrow, distress, regret, melancholy, affliction, anguish.

Grieve—bemoan, bewail, afflict, lament, hurt, mourn, sorrow.

Group—cluster, collection, assemblage.

Grow—sprout, vegetate, proceed, increase.

Guarantee—warrant, vouch for, secure.

Guard — protect, defend, shield, watch.

Guess—suppose, conjecture, think, surmise, divine.

Guest—stranger, visitor, visitant.

Guide—lead, direct, conduct, control, instruct, regulate.

Guilty—depraved, wicked, sinful, criminal, debauched.

H

Hale—strong, sound, hearty, robust.

Handsome—fine, fair, beautiful, pretty, graceful, lovely, elegant, noble.

Happiness — contentment, luck, felicity, bliss.

Harass—tire, molest, weary, disturb, perplex, vex, torment.

Harbinger — messenger, forerunner, precursor.

Hard—near, close, unfeeling, inexorable, arduous, difficult, firm, hardy, solid.

Hardened—unfeeling, obdurate, insensible, callous.

Hardihood — boldness, presumption, audacity, effrontery, daring, bravery.

Hardly — barely, scarcely, with difficulty.

Hardship—affliction, oppression, grievance, injury.

Harm—evil, injury, damage, misfortune, hurt, ill, mishap.

Harmless — gentle, unoffending, inoffensive, innocent.

Harmony—unison, concord, accordance, melody, agreement.

Harsh—rough, stern, severe, rigorous, austere, morose.

Hasten—hurry, expedite, accelerate, quicken.

Hastiness—dispatch, speed, precipitancy, hurry, rashness.

Hasty—rash, angry, quick, passionate, cursory.

Hate—dislike, abjure, detest, abhor, loathe, abominate.

Hateful — odious, contemptible, execrable, detestable, abominable, loathsome.

Haughtiness — vanity, self-conceit, arrogance, pride, disdain.

Hazard—trial, venture, chance, risk, danger, peril.

Headstrong — self-willed, stubborn, forward, violent, obstinate, venturesome.

Heal—restore, cure, remedy.

Healthy—well, sound, wholesome, salutary, salubrious.

Hear—harken, listen, watch, attend, overhear.

Hearty—sincere, zealous, warm, strong, cordial, ardent, healthy.

Heaviness — sorrow, gloom, dejection, weight, gravity.

Heedless — dilatory, thoughtless, negligent, remiss, careless, inattentive.

Heighten — raise, advance, improve, aggravate.

Heinous—wicked, sinful, flagrant, atrocious.

Help—provide, serve, assist, aid, relieve, support, succor.

Hence—from, thence, so, accordingly, therefore, wherefore, consequently.

Heroic—bold, noble, brave, fearless, valiant, courageous, intrepid.

Heroism—valor, boldness, courage, bravery, gallantry, fortitude.

Hesitate—pause, falter, wait, delay, doubt, demur, stammer.

Hidden — obscure, mysterious, secret, covert, concealed.

Hideous—awful, frightful, horrible, ghastly, grim, grisly.

Hilarity—jollity, joviality, mirth, merriment, cheerfulness, gayety.

Hinder — interfere, impede, embarrass, retard, prevent, oppose, stop, thwart, obstruct.

Hold — keep, occupy, maintain, retain, detain, grasp, possess.

Honesty—honor, fidelity, frankness, integrity, probity, purity, justice, sincerity, rectitude, uprightness, truthfulness.

Honor — exalt, dignify, respect, adorn, revere, esteem, venerate, reverence.

Hope—desire, belief, trust, confidence, expectation, anticipation.

Hopeless—desponding, dejected, despairing.

Horrible—dreadful, terrible, terrific, fearful, frightful, awful.

Hostile—unfriendly, contrary, opposite, repugnant.

Hostility — enmity, opposition, animosity, illwill, unfriendliness.

House—domicile, dwelling, home, habitation, family, race, quorum.

However—notwithstanding, but, nevertheless, yet, still.

Humble—meek, lowly, subdued, submissive, modest, unpretending, unassuming.

Hurry—hasten, expedite, precipitate.

Hurtful — annoying, injurious, detrimental, mischievous, pernicious, prejudicial.

Hypocrisy — dissimulation, pretence, deceit.

I

Idea—notion, thought, conception, imagination, perception.

Idle—unoccupied, unemployed, inactive, indolent, still, lazy, slothful.

Ignorant — untaught, unskilled, uninformed, unlettered, illiterate, unlearned.

Illness — sickness, disorder, disease, malady.

Illusion—falsity, mockery, deception.

Imagine—think, suppose, fancy, conceive, deem, contrive, apprehend.

Imbecility — weakness, languor, feebleness, infirmity, debility, impotence.

Imitate—follow, copy, mimic.

Immaterial—unimportant, insignificant, inconsiderable, inconsequential, uncorporeal, spiritual, unsubstantial, unconditioned.

Immediately—instantly, directly.

Immense—vast, huge, enormous, prodigious, unlimited.

Immodest—impudent, bold, indelicate, shameless, indecent, unchaste.

Impair — lessen, weaken, injure, decrease.

Impart—grant, bestow, disclose, communicate, reveal, divulge.

Impatient — uneasy, eager, restless, hasty.

Impeach—censure, reproach, arraign, accuse.

Impede—hinder, delay, obstruct, retard.

Impediment — obstruction, obstacle, hinderance.

Impel—urge, force, incite, induce, instigate, animate, encourage.

Impending—imminent, threatening.

Imperative — commanding, imperious, authoritative, despotic.

Imperfection—wanting, blemish, fault, defect, failing, frailty, foible, weakness.

Imperious — commanding, domineering, haughty, imperative, proud, lordly, overbearing, tyrannical.

Impertinent—rude, quarrelsome, intrusive, insolent, meddling, irrelevant, troublesome.

Impetuous—hasty, rough, vehement, violent, forcible, boisterous.

Implicate — involve, embarrass, entangle.

Implore — beg, beseech, ask, entreat, supplicate, solicit, request.

Imply—mean, signify, denote, infer, involve.

Importance — weight, moment, signification, consequence.

Imposture—deceit, cheat, fraud, deception, imposition, counterfeit, artifice.

Imprecation—execration, curse, malediction, anathema.

Improve — cultivate, correct, reform, rectify, amend, advance.

Impudent—insolent, bold, rude, saucy, impertinent, uncouth, immodest, shameless.

Impute—charge, ascribe, attribute.

Inability — disability, weakness, impotence.

Inactive — sluggish, lazy, idle, slothful, inert, drowsy.

Inadequate—insufficient, incompetent, unable, incapable.

Inattentive—negligent, heedless, careless, inadvertent, thoughtless, dilatory, remiss.

Incessantly—constantly, continually, unremitingly, unceasingly.

Incident — contingency, circumstance, event.

Incite—provoke, excite, stimulate, arouse, encourage, animate, aggravate.

Include—contain, enclose, comprise, embrace, comprehend.

Incommode—molest, disturb, inconvenience, trouble, annoy.

Incompetent—inapt, insufficient, incapable, inadequate, unsuitable.

Inconsistent—incongruous, contrary, ridiculous, absurd.

Inconstant—unstable, uncertain, fickle, variable, changeable, versatile.

Indecent—unbecoming, impudent, immodest, indelicate.

Indicate—show, mark, point out, reveal.

Indifferent—passive, neutral, regardless, unconcerned, impartial.

Indigence—poverty, need, want, penury.

Indigenous—native.

Indignation—temper, anger, displeasure, contempt, resentment, wrath.

Indiscretion—imprudence, folly, injudiciousness.

Indispensable — important, necessary, essential.

Indisputable — undeniable, indubitable, unquestionable, incontrovertible, conclusive, settled.

Indistinct—confused, ambiguous, doubtful, dark.

Induce—persuade, lead, influence, urge, instigate, actuate.

Industrious — diligent, persevering, laborious, assiduous, active.

Inevitable—unavoidable, certain.

Inexorable — immovable, relentless, unyielding, implacable.

Inexpedient — unsuitable, unfit, inconvenient.

Infect—taint, corrupt, defile, contaminate, pollute.

Inference—deduction, conclusion.

Inferior—less, lower, secondary, subservient, subordinate.

Infested—disturbed, troubled, annoyed, plagued.

Infinite — boundless, unbounded, illimitable, unlimited, immense, eternal.

Infirm — weak, sickly, decrepit, feeble, debilitated, imbecile.

Influence—authority, power, persuasion, credit, favor, sway.

Information — notice, counsel, intelligence, advice, instruction.

Ingenious — inventive, talented, skillful.

Ingenuity — capacity, invention, genius, skill, talent.

Inhabit — dwell, occupy, reside, stay, abide, sojourn.

Inherent—innate, inborn, inbred.

Inhuman—cruel, savage, barbarous, brutal.

Iniquitous—unjust, evil, wicked, nefarious.

Injunction—order, mandate, precept, command.

Injure—harm, hurt, impair, damage, deteriorate.

Innate—natural, inherent, inbred, inborn.

Innocent—pure, blameless, guiltless, faultless, inoffensive, harmless, spotless.

Inordinate—immoderate, intemperate, irregular, excessive.

Inquisitive—curious, inquiring, anxious, prying.

Insanity—derangement, madness, craziness, lunacy, mania.

Insensibility — dullness, apathy, indifference, stupidity, torpor, imperceptibility.

Insidious—deceitful, sly, crafty, cunning, subtle, treacherous.

Insignificant — worthless, meaningless, inconsiderable, trivial, unimportant.

Insinuate — hint, suggest, intimate.

Insolent—insulting, abusive, rude, haughty, saucy, offensive, impertinent.

Inspire—animate, invigorate, enliven, cheer, exhilarate, suggest.

Instigate — tempt, incite, urge, encourage, impel, move, stimulate.

Instill—infuse, implant, sow.

Instruction—education, precept, teaching, suggestion, counsel, advice.

Insufficient — inadequate, incapable, incompetent, unfit, unable, unsuitable.

Insult — abuse, affront, outrage, contempt, insolence, indignity.

Integrity—purity, probity, truthfulness, uprightness, honesty.

Intellect—understanding, genius, ability, capacity, talent.

Intelligence—intimation, understanding, information, notice, knowledge, intellect.

Intemperate—excessive, immoderate, inordinate.

Intend—purpose, mean, design.

Intercede — mediate, interpose, interfere.

Interline—insert, alter, correct, add.

Intermission — cessation, stop, rest, vacation, interruption.

Intermit — abate, suspend, subside, forbear.

Interpose — mediate, interfere, intermeddle.

Interpret—explain, demonstrate, elucidate, expound, decipher.

Interrogate—examine, question, inquire.

Interval—space, interstice, time.

Intervening — coming between, interposing, intermediate.

Intimidate — frighten, alarm, daunt, scare.

Intoxication — infatuation, inebriety, drunkenness.

Intractable—perverse, obstinate, stubborn, ungovernable, uncontrollable, unmanageable.

Intrepid — fearless, undaunted, bold, daring, valiant, courageous, brave.

Intrinsic—real, true, inherent, inward, essential, genuine.

Introductory—preliminary, previous, prefatory.

Intrude — invade, infringe, encroach, obtrude, entrench.

Intrust—confide, commit.

Invade — enter, attack, intrude, encroach, infringe.

Invalid—weak, sick, infirm, null, feeble, void.

Invalidate—weaken, injure, destroy, overthrow.

Invective—censure, abuse, railing, reproach, satire.

Invent—feign, fabricate, frame, conceive, discover, devise.

Invest—enclose, surround, confer, adorn, array, endow, endue.

Investigation—search, inquiry, examination, scrutiny, research.

Inveterate—obstinate, confirmed, constant, fixed.

Invigorate—restore, strengthen, fortify.

Invincible — unyielding, unconquerable.

Involve — envelop, enwrap, entangle, implicate.

Irascible—irritable, hasty, fiery, hot, angry.

Ire — anger, temper, wrath, passion, resentment.

Irony—ridicule, sarcasm, satire, burlesque.

Irrational — unreasonable, foolish, absurd, silly.

Irrefragable—undeniable, indisputable, incontrovertible, unquestionable.

Irritate — plague, anger, tease, excite, provoke, aggravate, exasperate.

Irruption—opening, invasion, inroad, bursting forth.

Issue—offspring, progeny, result, end, sequel, egress, evacuation, effect, consequence.

J

Jade — harass, weary, tire, dispirit.

Jealousy—suspicion, envy.

Jest—fun, joke, sport.

Jocose—funny, witty, merry, jocular, pleasant, facetious, waggish.

Jocund — joyful, lively, merry, gay, sprightly, sportive, lighthearted, vivacious, mirthful.

Join—unite, add, combine, close, adhere, confederate league.

Joke—rally, sport.

Jollity—hilarity, mirth, gayety, merriment, festivity, joviality.

Journey — travel, trip, voyage, tour.

Joy—happiness, delight, gladness, charm, rapture, ecstasy, felicity, exultation, pleasure, transport.

Judgment — sentence, decision, doom, opinion, discernment, discrimination, penetration, intelligence, sagacity.

Just — exact, accurate, correct, honest, barely, upright, righteous, equitable, incorrupt.

Justify — defend, excuse, clear, absolve, maintain.

Justness—exactness, correctness, accuracy, equity, propriety.

K

Keen—sharp, penetrating, acute, cutting, piercing, shrewd.

Keep—hold, detain, support, retain, maintain, guard, reserve, sustain.

Kind—indulgent, compassionate, tender, lenient, gentle, affable, courteous, benignant, bland.

Kind—sort, manner, class, race, species, way, genus.

Knowledge—understanding, perception, learning, erudition, skill, acquaintance.

L

Labor—toil, work, strive, exert, drudge.

Lament—sorrow, mourn, deplore, complain, bewail, grieve, regret.

Language—tongue, speech, dialect, idiom.

Languid — weary, weak, faint, exhausted, dull, drooping.

Large — comprehensive, capacious, extensive, big, great, huge.

Lassitude — prostration, languor, weariness, enervation, fatigue.

Last — latest, hindmost, ultimate, final, end.

Lasting — durable, continuous, forever, continual, permanent, perpetual, eternal.

Latent — unseen, hidden, secret.

Laudable — praiseworthy, commendable.

Laughable — droll, ridiculous, comical, mirthful.

Lavish — profuse, wasteful, extravagant.

Lazy — indolent, idle, slothful, inactive.

Lean — bend, incline, totter, waver.

Learning — intelligence, knowledge, erudition, science, literature, information.

Leave — abandon, desert, resign, relinquish, bequeath.

Legitimate — real, legal, lawful, genuine.

Lengthen — protract, extend, continue, draw out.

Lessen — diminish, decrease, abate, reduce, subside, shrink, degrade.

Let — allow, [permit, suffer, leave, hire.

Lethargic — dull, tired, weary, heavy, drowsy, sleepy.

Level — even, smooth, plain, flat.

Levity — giddiness, gayety, fickleness, vanity, lightness.

Liable — exposed, responsible, subject.

Liberal — benevolent, generous, munificent, charitable.

Liberate — free, set free, deliver, release.

Liberty — freedom, permission, license, leave, exemption, privilege.

Lie — deception, untruth, fiction, fabrication, falsehood.

Life — being, energy, vitality, vivacity, briskness.

Lifeless — deceased, dead, inanimate, inactive, stale, flat, dull.

Lift — raise, elevate, exalt, hoist.

Light — illuminate, enlighten, nimble, kindle.

Like — probable, similar, uniform, resembling.

Likeness — resemblance, picture, portrait.

Liking — inclination, attachment, fondness, affection.

Linger — wait, delay, loiter, hesitate, saunter, tarry, lag.

Liquid — fluid, liquor.

Listen — hearken, attend, hear, overhear.

Little — small, diminutive.

Live — exist, subsist, dwell, abide, reside.

Lively — active, energetic, brisk, nimble, jocund, merry, sprightly, vigorous.

Lodge — accommodate, entertain, shelter, harbor.

Loftiness — height, haughtiness, stateliness, elevation, dignity, pride.

Loiter — lag, saunter, linger.

Lonely — dreary, lonesome, retired, solitary.

Look — see, behold, view, inspect, appearance.

Loose — unconnected, open, unrestrained, dissolute, licentious, unjointed.

Loss — injury, damage, detriment, waste.

Lot — share, portion, fate, fortune, destiny.

Loud — noisy, vociferous, clamorous, turbulent, vehement.

Love — liking, affection, fondness, kindness, attachment, adoration, esteem.

Lovely — attractive, amiable, elegant, charming, handsome, fine, delightful, beautiful.

Lover — beau, wooer, suitor.

Loving — kind, affectionate, attentive, tender, amorous.

Low — humble, mean, base, abject, debased, dejected, despicable.

Lower — humble, humiliate, debase, degrade.

Lucky — successful, fortunate, prosperous.

Ludicrous — amusing, comical, droll, laughable.

Lunacy — mania, derangement, insanity, madness.

Luxuriant — excessive, voluptuous, abundant, exuberant.

Luxury — profusion, abundance, excess.

M

Magnificent — noble, grand, sublime, glorious, splendid, superb.

Magnitude — size, greatness, bulk.

Maintain — sustain, keep, support, help, continue, assert, defend, vindicate.

Malady — evil, disease, affliction, disorder, distemper.

Manage — control, direct, conduct.

Mandate — command, charge, injunction, order.

Mangle — cut, lacerate, mutilate, tear, maim.

Manifest — evident, clear, open, apparent, obvious, plain.

Margin — edge, verge, rim, brim, brink, border.

Mark — stamp, impress, imprint, brand, show, observe.

Marriage — matrimony, wedlock, nuptials.

Marvel — wonder, prodigy, miracle.

Massive — large, heavy, bulky, ponderous.

Master — achieve, overcome, surmount, conquer.

Mature — perfect, complete, ripe.

Maxim — saying, adage, proverb.

Mean — abject, low, despicable, miserly, sordid, penurious, niggardly.

Meaning — sense, import, signification, intention, purpose, design.

Meanwhile — meantime, interim, intervening.

Mechanic — artisan, artificer.

Meddle — interpose, interfere, interrupt.

Mediate — intercede, interpose.

Meek — mild, soft, gentle, humble.

Meet — assemble, join, fit, becoming.

Meeting — assembly, company, auditory, congregation.

Melancholy — sadness, distress, depression, gloom, grief, dejection.

Melody — harmony, unison, happiness, concord.

Melt — dissolve, soften, liquefy.

Memory — remembrance, reminiscence, recollection.

Mend — improve, repair, rectify, correct.

Merciful — mild, tender, gracious, benignant, compassionate, forgiving.

Merciless — hard-hearted, pitiless, cruel, unmerciful.

Mercy — pity, clemency, compassion, lenity.

Merry — happy, joyous, cheerful, gay, lively, mirthful, sportive, sprightly, vivacious.

Messenger — bearer, carrier, harbinger, forerunner, precursor.

Metaphor — similitude, trope, emblem, allegory, symbol.

Method — order, manner, system, mode, rule, plan, regularity.

Mighty — strong, powerful, great, potent.

Mild — meek, gentle, kind, easy, sweet, tender, mellow.

Mindful — heedful, observant, attentive.

Minister — contribute, supply, administer.

Mirth — merriment, joy, hilarity, cheerfulness, vivacity, jollity.

Mischief — damage, harm, hurt, misfortune, injury.

Miserly — stingy, covetous, niggardly, penurious, avaricious.

Misfortune — calamity, harm, disaster, mishap, ill-luck.

Mistake — error, blunder, misconception.

Misuse — ill-treat, pervert, abuse, misapply.

Mitigate — lessen, alleviate, appease, ameliorate, abate, assuage, soothe, mollify.

Model — pattern, copy, sample, mould, specimen.

Moderation — temperance, sobriety, frugality, forbearance, modesty.

Modern — recent, late, new, novel.

Modest — quiet, retiring, reserved, diffident, bashful, unassuming.

Modify — re-arrange, change, extenuate, alter, moderate.

Molest — annoy, vex, tease, incommode, trouble, disturb.

Mollify — ease, appease, moderate, mitigate, assuage, soften.

Morose — sour, sullen, gloomy, peevish, forbidding.

Motive — incentive, reason, cause, principle.

Mourn — grieve, lament, sorrow, bewail, bemoan.

Move — change, pass, stir, incite, influence, persuade, actuate, instigate, impel.

Munificent — bounteous, bountiful, generous, beneficent, liberal, plentiful.

Muse — study, ponder, wonder, reflect, think, meditate, contemplate.

Mutable — changeable, unsteady, inconstant, fickle, wavering, unstable, variable, alterable, irresolute.

Mutilate — deface, injure, destroy, deprive, mangle, maim.

Mutinous — turbulent, seditious, insubordinate.

Mysterious — hidden, dim, dark obscure, mystic, latent.

N

Naked — exposed, nude, unclothed, uncovered, simple, plain.

Name — cognomen, appellation, title, reputation, credit, denomination.

Narrow — contracted, confined, limited, curtailed, close.

Native — indigenous, genuine, intrinsic.

Near — adjoining, adjacent, close, contiguous.

Necessary — needful, expedient, indispensable, essential, important, requisite.

Need — poverty, want, penury, indigence.

Nefarious — evil, wicked, unjust, wrong, iniquitous.

Negligent — careless, heedless, remiss, neglectful, inattentive.

New — fresh, late, modern, novel.

Nigh — close, adjoining, contiguous, near, adjacent.

Noble — distinguished, elevated, exalted, illustrious, great, grand.

Noisy — boisterous, turbulent, high, clamorous, loud sounding.

Noted — renowned, distinguished, conspicuous, celebrated, eminent, notorious, illustrious.

Notice — warning, information, intelligence, advice.

Notion — thought, opinion, sentiment, whim, idea, conception, perception.

Notorious — celebrated, renowned, distinguished, noted, public, conspicuous.

Notwithstanding — nevertheless, however, in spite of, yet.

Nourish — feed, uphold, maintain, cherish, nurture, support.

O

Obdurate — inflexible, unfeeling, callous, impenitent, hardened, insensible, obstinate.

Obedient — submissive, compliant, yielding, dutiful, obsequious, respectful.

Object — end, subject, aim.

Object — oppose, against, except to.

Oblige — compel, coerce, bind, engage, force, favor, please, gratify.

Obnoxious — offensive, liable, disagreeable, unpleasant, exposed.

Obscure — hidden, concealed, indistinct, difficult, dark, abstruse.

Observance — ceremony, rite, attention, form, respect.

Observant — watchful, attentive, mindful, regardful.

Observe — see, notice, watch, follow, remark, keep.

Obsolete — disused, old, worn-out, antiquated, ancient, old-fashioned.

Obstacle — impediment, obstruction, difficulty, hinderance.

Obstinate — stubborn, resolute, headstrong.

Obstruct — impede, hinder, stop, prevent.

Obtain — gain, secure, get, win, acquire, procure, earn.

Obvious — plain, apparent, open, clear, evident, visible, manifest.

Occupation — work, profession, calling, trade, business, avocation, employment.

Occupy — keep, hold, use, possess.

Occurrence — event, contingency, adventure, incident.

Odor — smell, fragrance, perfume, scent.

Offense — trespass, crime, injury, sin, outrage, insult, misdeed, wrong, transgression.

Offensive — mean, abusive, insulting, impertinent, insolent, rude, scurrilous, obnoxious, opprobrious.

Officious — busy, active, forward, obtrusive, intrusive.

Only — solely, singly, alone, simply, merely.

Open — unravel, reveal, disclose, unlock.

Opening — fissure, aperture, hole, cavity.

Operation — performance, action, agency.

Opinion — belief, idea, sentiment, notion.

Opinionated — obstinate, stubborn, stiff, egotistical, conceited, self-willed.

Opponent — opposer, adversary, foe, enemy, antagonist.

Opposite — contrary, repugnant, adverse.

Opprobrious — reproachful, insolent, abusive, offensive, insulting, scandalous, scurrilous.

Opprobrium — shame, disgrace, reproach, infamy, ignominy.

Oration — speech, sermon, lecture, discourse, address, harangue.

Ordain — appoint, invest, order, prescribe.

Order — brotherhood, fraternity, rank, method, succession, series, degree, genus.

Order—mandate, injunction, precept, command.

Orderly—precise, regular, systematic, methodical.

Ordinary—usual, common.

Origin—rise, cause, source, foundation, beginning, descent, fountain.

Original — primitive, first, pristine, primary.

Ornament — decorate, beautify, adorn, deck, embellish.

Ornate—decorated, adorned, embellished, bedecked, garnished.

Ostentation—parade, show, display, boast.

Outrage—insult, injure, affront, violence.

Outward—extraneous, apparent, intrinsic.

Overbearing—repressive, impertinent, haughty, lordly.

Overcome — vanquish, conquer, surmount, subdue.

Overflow—fill, inundate, deluge, abound.

Oversight — mistake, error, misapprehension, inattention.

Overwhelm — overpower, crush, upturn, overthrow, subdue.

Owner—holder, proprietor, master, possessor.

P

Pacify—calm, still, quiet, soothe, conciliate.

Pain—distress, afflict, torture, torment, suffer, hurt.

Paint—portray, represent, depict, sketch, color, describe, delineate.

Pair—join, two, couple, brace.

Pale — fade, wan, white, pallid, fair.

Palpable—gross, plain, apparent, discernible, perceptible.

Palpitate—tremble, throb, beat, flutter, gasp, pant.

Pang—torture, torment, distress, agony, anguish, sorrow.

Pardon — acquit, forgive, clear, free, discharge, release, remit.

Parsimonious — mean, frugal, miserly, avaricious, penurious, niggardly.

Part — share, portion, division, piece, action.

Particular—individual, specific, exact, appropriate, circumstantial, peculiar, exclusive, punctual, distinct.

Particularly — chiefly, mainly, principally, especially, distinctly, specifically.

Partisan—disciple, adherent, follower.

Partner — associate, accomplice, colleague, coadjutor.

Passion — desire, feeling, love, anger, excitement.

Passionate — hot, angry, irascible, hasty, excitable.

Passive—submissive, unresisting, patient, resigned.

Pathetic — affecting, touching, moving.

Patience — endurance, fortitude, resignation.

Patient—resigned, composed, enduring, calm, passive, an invalid.

Peaceable—quiet, calm, serene, tranquil, mild, gentle.

Peevish — fretful, disagreeable, petulant, cross, captious, irritable.

Penalty—punishment, pain, fine, forfeiture, chastisement.

Penitence — contrition, remorse, compunction, repentance.

Penurious — parsimonious, sparing, miserly, niggardly, beggarly.

Penury—want, poverty, distress, indigence, need.

Perceive — observe, discern, distinguish.

Perception—belief, conception, sentiment, idea, sensation, notion.

Peremptory—positive, despotic, arbitrary, dogmatical, absolute.

Perfect—done, complete, finished.

Perfidious — false, treacherous, faithless.

Perforate — pierce, bore, penetrate.

Perform — execute, accomplish, effect, produce, achieve, fulfill.

Perfume—odor, smell, scent, exhalation, fragrance.

Period—circuit, date, age, epoch, era.

Permit — allow, suffer, consent, admit, tolerate, yield.

Pernicious — noisome, ruinous, destructive, mischievous, hurtful, noxious.

Perpetual—uninterrupted, incessant, unceasing, constant, continual.

Perplex — bewilder, annoy, confuse, involve, molest, puzzle, embarrass, harass, entangle.

Persevere — endure, continue, persist, insist, pursue, prosecute.

Perspicuity—clearness, transparency, brilliancy.

Persuade—urge, induce, exhort, influence, entice, prevail upon.

Perverse — stubborn, untractable, unmanageable, crooked, cross.

Pestilential — destructive, mischievous, epidemical, infectious, contagious.

Petition — prayer, supplication, request, suit, entreaty.

Picture—likeness, image, effigy, representation.

Pious — spiritual, devout, godly, religious.

Pique — offense, grudge, dislike, malice, spite, rancor.

Pity — sympathy, commiseration, compassion, condolence, mercy.

Place — site, ground, post, position.

Placid—still, calm, gentle, quiet, tranquil, serene.

Plague—perplex, embarrass, tantalize, annoy, importune, vex, torment.

Plain — perceptible, discernible, manifest, obvious, clear, apparent, evident, distinct.

Plan—design, contrivance, device, scheme, arrangement, project, stratagem.

Pleasant—cheerful, jocular, gay, vivacious, agreeable, facetious, witty.

Please — gratify, satisfy, humor, delight.

Pleasure — satisfaction, delight, happiness, enjoyment, joy.

Pledge—pawn, deposit, security, hostage, earnest.

Plentiful — bounteous, abundant, copious, exuberant, ample, plenteous.

Pliant — lithe, limber, yielding, bending, supple, flexible, pliable.

Plight—predicament, state, case, situation, condition, conjuncture.

Plot—plan, arrangement, project, conspiracy, combination, scheme, intrigue.

Polite—courteous, well-bred, civil, polished, refined, genteel, affable.

Politeness—good manners, civility, courtesy, suavity, good breeding.

Politic—wise, careful, artful, cunning, civil, prudent.

Pollute—corrupt, taint, defile, infect, contaminate.

Pompous—lofty, stately, ostentatious. showy, dignified, magnificent.

Ponder — study, reflect, think, muse, consider.

Portion — piece, part, quantity, share, division, dower, fortune.

Positive—confident, certain, real, dogmatic, sure, absolute.

Possess—keep, hold, have, enjoy, occupy.

Postpone—retard, delay, prolong, protract, defer, procrastinate.

Posture—figure, gesture, action, position, attitude.

Potent—powerful, strong, vigorous, mighty, forcible.

Poverty—want, need, indigence, penury, suffering.

Practicable—possible, feasible, available.

Practice—custom, style, manner, form, use, habit.

Praise—eulogize, applaud, laud, admire, commend.

Prayer—application, petition, request, suit, entreaty, supplication.

Precarious—uncertain, dubious, doubtful, equivocal, unreliable.

Precedence — priority, superiority, preference.

Preceding — anterior, previous, prior, antecedent, former, foregoing.

Precept—maxim, rule, principle, injunction, law, doctrine, mandate, command.

Precious — choice, costly, valuable, expensive, uncommon, rare.

Precise — careful, particular, exact, accurate, correct, nice.

Preclude—intercept, prevent, obviate, hinder.

Predicament—condition, plight, position, situation.

Predict—prophesy, foretell.

Predominant — prevalent, overruling, controlling, supreme, prevailing.

Predominate—prevail, rule over.

Preference — advancement, priority, choice.

Prejudice — bias, injury, hurt, disadvantage.

Preliminary—previous, preparatory, introductory, antecedent.

Prepare — arrange, qualify, fit, equip, make ready.

Preposterous—impossible, ridiculous, absurd, foolish.

Prerogative — immunity, privilege.

Prescribe — dictate, ordain, appoint.

Preserve — uphold, maintain, protect, spare, save.

Pressing—urgent, emergent, importunate, crowding, squeezing, forcing.

Presume—guess, suppose, think, surmise, conjecture, believe.

Presuming — forward, arrogant, presumptuous.

Pretext — excuse, pretense, pretension.

Pretty — lovely, beautiful, fine, agreeable.

Prevailing — dominant, ruling, overcoming, prevalent, predominating.

Prevent — impede, obstruct, hinder, obviate, preclude.

Previous—before, prior, anterior, preliminary, introductory.

Price — value, worth, expense, cost.

Pride — self-esteem, arrogance, haughtiness, conceit, ostentation, loftiness, vanity.

Primary — elemental, first, original, pristine.

Principal—main, chief, capital, head, leading, important.

Principle—motive, tenet, constituent part, doctrine, element.

Print—impress, stamp, mark.

Prior—before, previous, former, antecedent, preceding, anterior.

Priority—preference, precedence, pre-eminence.

Pristine — original, first, primitive.

Privacy — seclusion, solitude, retirement, loneliness.

Privilege — prerogative, right, advantage, immunity, exemption.

Probability—supposition, likelihood, chance.

Probity—reliability, uprightness, honesty, integrity, veracity.

Proceed — progress, arise, issue, advance, emanate.

Proceeding—transaction, course, progression, work.

Proclaim — declare, publish, announce, tell, advertise, promulgate.

Proclivity—liking, tendency, inclination, proneness.

Procure—obtain, acquire, gain.

Prodigal — lavish, extravagant, wasteful.

Prodigious — great, astonishing, vast, large, amazing, monstrous.

Profane—secular, irreverent, impious, irreligious.

Profession—calling, employment, business, vocation, work, labor.

Proficiency — advancement, improvement, progress.

Profit—gain, advantage, benefit, emolument.

Profligate — depraved, wicked, corrupt, sinful, vicious, abandoned.

Profuse—lavish, wasteful, prodigal, extravagant.

Progeny—descendants, offspring, race, issue.

Project—invent, design, scheme, plan.

Prolific--productive, fruitful, fertile.

Prolix—tiresome. long, diffuse.

Prolong—extend, delay, protract, postpone, retard, procrastinate.

Prominent — eminent, conspicuous, distinguished.

Promise — agreement, assurance, engagement, declaration, pledge, word, obligation.

Promote — raise, encourage, forward, advance.

Prompt — quick, active, ready, assiduous.

Pronounce — say, speak, utter, declare, affirm, articulate, enunciate.

Proof—evidence, testimony, argument.

Propagate — multiply, increase, disseminate, diffuse, circulate, spread, extend.

Propensity — liking, inclination, proneness, tendency, bias.

Proper—fit, right, suitable, just, appropriate.

Propitious — favorable, auspicious.

Propitiate—conciliate, appease, reconcile.

Proportionate—equal, adequate, commensurate.

Propose—offer, apply, tender, intend, purpose, bid.

Prospect — view, landscape, survey.

Prospective—future, foreseeing, hereafter, forward.

Prosperous — fortunate, lucky, flourishing, successful.

Protect—uphold, guard, shield, maintain, defend, cherish, foster, patronize.

Protract—withhold, retard, prolong, delay, defer, postpone.

Proud—haughty, assuming, arrogant, lofty, vain, conceited.

Proverb—maxim, saying, adage.

Provide—procure, furnish, supply, prepare.

Provident—cautious, prudent, economical, careful.

Proviso—requirement, condition, stipulation.

Provoke—excite, irritate, enrage, aggravate, exasperate, tantalize.

Prudence—forethought, carefulness, wisdom, discretion, judgment.

Publish—announce, promulgate, proclaim, advertise, declare.

Puerile—infantile, boyish, childish, juvenile.

Pull—bring, haul, draw, drag.

Punctual—prompt, particular, exact.

Punish—whip, chastise, correct, discipline.

Pursue—follow, prosecute, chase, persist, continue, persevere.

Puzzle—confound, perplex, embarrass, bewilder, entangle.

Q

Quack—imposter, pretender, empiric, charlatan.

Qualified—capable, fit, adapted, competent.

Quarrel—fight, affray, riot, contest, battle, contention, altercation, dispute, tumult.

Query—question, interrogatory, inquiry.

Question—ask, examine, doubt, dispute, consider, inquire, interrogate.

Questionable—suspicious, doubtful.

Quick—rapid, active, lively, swift, prompt, expeditious, brisk.

Quiet—calm, repose, tranquillity, rest, ease, peaceable, placid, still.

Quit—depart, leave, resign, abandon, forsake, relinquish.

Quota—rate, share, proportion.

Quote—copy, relate, cite, adduce.

R

Race—lineage, family, breed, generation, course.

Radiance—light, glory, brightness, brilliancy.

Rage—indignation, anger, fury.

Raise—heighten, elevate, exalt, erect, collect, propagate.

Rank—class, degree, place, position.

Ransom—purchase, free, redeem.

Rapacious—voracious, greedy, ravenous.

Rapidity—swiftness, fleetness, celerity, speed, agility, velocity.

Rapture—joy, delight, transport, ecstasy.

Rare—scarce, uncommon, excellent, singular, unusual, incomparable, raw.

Rash—impulsive, hasty, violent, thoughtless, headstrong.

Rate—price, quota, proportion, ratio, value, degree, assessment.

Ravenous—voracious, rapacious, greedy.

Ray—dawn, beam, gleam, streak, glimmer.

Real—certain, true, genuine, positive, actual.

Realize—reach, procure, achieve, consummate, accomplish, effect.

Reason—purpose, proof, motive, argument, origin, understanding.

Reasonable—fair, probable, just, moderate, equitable, honest, rational.

Rebuke—reprimand, reproach, reproof, censure.

Recant—revoke, recall, renounce, withdraw, retract, abjure.

Recede—retire, retrograde, fall back, retreat.

Recite—repeat, rehearse.

Reckon—count, number, estimate, calculate, compute.

Reclaim—reform, recover, correct.

Recollection—memory, remembrance, reminiscence.

Recompense—satisfaction, pay, price, reward, equivalent, remuneration.

Reconcile—propitiate, conciliate.

Recruit—repair, retrieve, replace, recover.

Rectify—mend, improve, correct, amend, reform.

Redeem—restore, rescue, recover, ransom.

Redress—relief, remedy.

Refer—propose, suggest, allude, intimate, hint.

Refined—graceful, genteel, polished, polite, elegant.

Reform—correct, amend, rectify, improve, better.

Refractory—unmanageable, unruly, contumacious, perverse.

Refrain—forego, forbear, spare, abstain.

Regale—refresh, entertain, feast, gratify.

Regard—respect, esteem, value, reverence, mind, heed.

Regardless—careless, negligent, indifferent, unconcerned, unobservant, heedless.

Region—section, quarter, district, country.

Regret—sorrow, complaint, grief, lament.

Regulate—control, rule, direct, govern, dispose, adjust.

Rehearse—detail, repeat, recite, recapitulate.

Reject—refuse, deny, decline, repel.

Rejoinder—response, answer, reply.

Reliance—trust, belief, repose, confidence, dependence.

Relieve—assist, help, succor, aid, alleviate, mitigate, support.

Religious—pious, devout, holy.

Remain—continue, stay, abide, tarry, sojourn.

Remainder—rest, residue, remnant.

Remark—comment, observation, note.

Reminiscence—recollection, remembrance.

Remiss—heedless, negligent, inattentive, careless, thoughtless.

Remit—send, transmit, liberate, abate, forgive, pardon, relax.

Remorse—penitence, contrition, distress.

Renew—revive, refresh, renovate.

Renounce—leave, resign, abdicate, abandon, forego, relinquish, quit.

Renown—reputation, celebrity, fame.

Repair—improve, retrieve, recover, restore.

Reparation—restitution, restoration, amends.

Repeal—cancel, annul, revoke, abolish, abrogate, destroy.

Repeat—detail, rehearse, recite.

Repetition—tautology, prolixity, iteration, reiteration.

Replenish—supply, fill, refill.

Repose—ease, sleep, rest, quiet.

Reproach—blame, reprove, censure, condemn, upbraid, reprimand.

Repugnance—aversion, abhorrence, antipathy, dislike, hatred.

Repugnant—hostile, adverse, opposite, contrary.

Reputation—repute, fame, character, honor, renown, credit.

Request—solicit, ask, demand, entreat, beg, beseech, implore.

Requisite—important, necessary, essential, expedient.

Research—investigation, study, examination, inquiry.

Resemblance—similarity, semblance, similitude, likeness.

Residence—home, abode, house, dwelling, domicile.

Residue—leavings, remainder, rest.

Resign—yield, abdicate, renounce, relinquish, forego.

Resignation—patience, endurance, submission, acquiescence.

Resist—endure, oppose, withstand.

Resolution—firmness, determination, fortitude, courage, decision.

Resort—visit, frequent, haunt.

Respect—esteem, regard, deference, attention, consideration, good-will, estimation.

Respectful—deferential, dutiful, obedient, civil.

Respite—delay, suspension, interval, reprieve.

Response—reply, answer, rejoinder.

Responsible—amenable, answerable, accountable.

Rest—quiet, ease, repose, intermission, stop, cessation, others, remainder.

Restore—cure, renew, return, repay, rebuild.

Restrain—confine, repress, restrict, coerce, limit, constrain.

Restrict—limit, circumscribe, hold, bind.

Result—effect, issue, ultimate, consequence, event.

Retain—hold, detain, keep, reserve.

Retard—hinder, defer, protract, postpone, delay, procrastinate, prolong, prevent, impede.

Retire—recede, withdraw, retreat, secede.

Retract—annul, take back, revoke, recant, recall.

Retrieve—renew, recover, regain.

Reveal—impart, divulge, communicate, disclose, expose.

Revenge—vindicate, avenge.

Revere—adore, worship, reverence, venerate.

Review—examine, survey, notice, revision.

Revive—enliven, renew, reanimate, refresh, renovate.

Revoke—cancel, annul, abolish, repeal, abrogate, efface, retract.

Reward—recompense, remuneration, compensation, satisfaction.

Riches—wealth, opulence, affluence.

Ridicule—deride, banter, laugh at.

Ridiculous—droll, absurd, ludicrous, preposterous, unreasonable, improbable.

Right—correct, just, honest, proper, privilege, claim, direct, straight, immunity.

Righteous—just, godly, upright, honest, incorrupt, virtuous.

Rite—form, custom, ceremony, observance.

Road—path, way, course, route.

Roam—wander, ramble, stroll, range, rove.

Room—chamber, space, place, apartment.

Rough—harsh, uncivil, rude, uncouth, unmannerly, unpolished, rugged, severe, stormy.

Round—globular, spherical, orb, circuit, tour.

Route—path, course, way, road.

Rude—rough, impertinent, coarse, impudent, unpolished, saucy, disgreeable, bold.

Rule—authority, law, regulation, government, custom, maxim, habit, precept, guide.

S

Sacred—holy, divine, devoted.

Sad—sorrowful, mournful, dejected, gloomy, melancholy.

Sagacity—perception, penetration, acuteness, discernment.

Salary—wages, pay, stipend, hire, reward, remuneration.

Sanction—maintain, sustain, uphold, countenance, ratify, support.

Sapient—discreet, wise, sage, sagacious.

Sarcasm—satire, irony, ridicule.

Satisfaction—compensation, remuneration, contentment, atonement, reward.

Saving—prudent, thrifty, frugal, economical, close, sparing, stingy, penurious.

Saying—adage, maxim, proverb, by-word, relating, speaking, uttering, communicating.

Scandal—disgrace, reproach, discredit, baseness, infamy.

Scarce—uncommon, unusual, singular, rare.

Scatter—disseminate, dissipate, spread, disperse.

Scent—odor, smell, perfume, fragrance.

Scoff—ridicule, sneer, jeer, jibe, belittle.

Scope—object, tendency, aim, drift.

Scruple—hesitate, doubt, fluctuate.

Scrupulous—truthful, upright, correct, careful, conscientious, cautious.

Scrutinize—search, examine, investigate.

Scurrilous—disgusting, abusive, offensive, insulting, insolent.

Search—inquiry, examination, scrutiny, pursuit, investigation.

Secede—withdraw, retire, recede.

Seclusion—quietude, privacy, solitude, retirement, loneliness.

Secondary—subordinate, inferior.

Secret—hidden, quiet, still, concealed, latent, mysterious, clandestine.

Secular—temporal, wordly.

Secure—safe, certain, confident, sure, procure, warrant.

Security—pledge, warranty, defense, guard, protection.

Sedate—serene, calm, unruffled, unconcerned, still, quiet, composed.

Seduce—decoy, betray, attract, allure.

See—examine, look, behold, observe, perceive, view.

Sense—idea, feeling, meaning, judgment, import, reason.

Sensitive—keen, susceptible, appreciative.

Sentence—mandate, judgment, decision, period, phrase, proposition.

Sentiment—expression, opinion, notion, feeling.

Separate — dissociate, detach, disengage.

Settle—determine, fix, establish, arrange, adjust, regulate.

Settled—conclusive, decided, confirmed, established.

Sever — separate, disjoin, divide, detach.

Several — sundry, different, various, diverse.

Severe—cold, stern, harsh, sharp, rigid, cruel, heartless, rough, strict, unyielding, austere, rigorous.

Shake — shiver, quiver, shudder, quake, agitate, totter.

Shame—dishonor, disgrace, ignominy.

Shameless — insolent, impudent, immodest, indelicate, indecent.

Shape—form, fashion, mould.

Share—divide, distribute, apportion, participate, partake.

Sharpness—shrewdness, penetration, keenness, acuteness, sagacity, cunning.

Shelter — shield, defend, screen, harbor, protect, cover.

Shine — illumine, glisten, gleam, glitter, glare.

Shining — bright, glittering, radiant, glistening, brilliant.

Shocking — disgusting, terrible, dreadful, horrible.

Short—brief, concise, scanty, defective, brittle.

Shorten—lessen, contract, reduce, abridge, curtail.

Show—display, exhibition, pomp, parade, representation, spectacle, sight.

Showy—grand, ostentatious, gay, gaudy, fine, sumptuous.

Shrewd—sharp, acute, keen, precise.

Shun—evade, avoid, elude.

Sickly—unwell, sick, ill, diseased, indisposed.

Sign—indication, omen, symptom, signal, note, mark, token.

Signify—imply, express, betoken, denote, declare, utter, intimate, testify.

Silence—quietude, stillness, muteness.

Silent — dumb, mute, speechless, still.

Silly—ridiculous, foolish, absurd, stupid, dull, weak, simple.

Similarity — resemblance, likeness, similitude.

Simple—weak, silly, artless, foolish, unwise, stupid, plain, single.

Simply—solely, merely, only.

Since—for, as, inasmuch, after.

Sincere—true, honest, frank, upright, incorrupt, plain.

Singular — particular, eccentric, odd, strange, remarkable, rare, scarce.

Situation — place, position, employment, site, locality, case, condition, plight.

Skillful — expert, adroit, adept, dexterous, accomplished.

Slander—defame, vilify, calumniate, detract.

Slavery — servitude, bondage, captivity.

Slender — slight, slim, fragile, thin.

Slow — tardy, dilatory, tedious, dull.

Small—little, minute, diminutive, narrow, infinitesimal.

Smooth—easy, mild, bland, even, level.

Smother — suffocate, stifle, suppress, conceal.

Snarling — snappish, waspish, surly.

Sober — grave, moderate, temperate, abstemious.

Social—sociable, companionable, convivial, familiar.

Society — fellowship, company, congregation, association, community.

Soft — flexible, ductile, yielding, pliant, mild, compliant.

Solicit—request, ask, entreat, implore, beg, beseech, supplicate, importune.

Solicitation — entreaty, invitation, importunity.

Solicitude — care, earnestness, anxiety.

Solid—enduring, firm, hard, substantial.

Solitary — sole, alone, desolate, only, lonely, remote, retired.

Soothe—quiet, compose, appease, calm, pacify, assuage, tranquilize.

Sorrow—trouble, grief, affliction.

Sort—order, kind, species.

Sound—tone, firm, whole, hearty, healthy, sane.

Sour — tart, acid, acrimonious, sharp.

Source—head, origin, fountain, cause, spring, reason.

Spacious — capacious, ample, large.

Sparkle—glitter, glisten, shine, glare, radiate, corruscate.

Speak — utter, talk, articulate, pronounce, converse, say, tell, recite, relate.

Species—order, kind, class, sort.

Specific—definite, particular, special.

Specimen — sample, model, pattern.

Spectator — beholder, observer, auditor.

Speech—oration, address, lecture, harangue, sermon.

Speechless—dumb, silent, mute.

Spend — expend, exhaust, dissipate, squander, waste.

Sphere—orb, circle, globe.

Spirited — quick, animated, ardent, vivacious, active.

Spiritual—ethereal, immaterial, unearthly, incorporeal.

Spite—pique, malice, grudge, malignity, hate.

Splendid — superb, magnificent, grand, sublime, heavenly.

Splendor — magnificence, luster, brightness, brilliancy.

Splenetic—peevish, melancholy, morose, sullen, gloomy, fretful.

Sport—play, game, amusement, pastime, diversion, recreation.

Spotless—faultless, unblemished, blameless, unsullied, clear, untarnished, pure, innocent, stainless.

Spread—distribute, diffuse, circulate, expand, disperse, disseminate, propagate, scatter, dispense, sow.

Spring—leap, arise, start, flow, proceed, emanate, jump, issue.

Sprinkle—bedew, water, scatter, besprinkle.

Sprout — vegetate, germinate, bud.

Stability — fixedness, continuity, steadiness, firmness.

Stain—mar, soil, tarnish, blemish, blot, flaw, spot, speck, tinge, color, discolor.

Stammer — hesitate, stutter, falter.

Stamp—mark, print, impress.

Standard—test, rule, criterion.

State — situation, condition, position, plight, predicament.

Station — place, situation, post, position.

Stay—dependence, reliance, staff, prop, abide, remain, continue, delay, hinder, support.

Sterility—barrenness, unfruitfulness.

Stern—unfeeling, severe, austere, strict, cold, rigid, rigorous.

Still—quiet, calm, silent, appease, assuage, lull, pacify.

Stimulate—arouse, excite, incite, urge, impel, encourage, instigate.

Stock — supply, collection, fund, accumulation, store, provision, cattle.

Stop—rest, intermission, vacation, cessation, delay, hinder, impede, check.

Story — tale, anecdote, incident, memoir.

Straight—direct, immediate.

Strange — unusual, curious, odd, singular, surprising, eccentric.

Stratagem—deception, cheat, artifice, fraud, trick, imposture, delusion.

Strength — potency, authority, power, force, might.

Strict—precise, exact, particular, accurate, nice, severe, harsh, rigorous, stern.

Strife—disagreement, dissension, discord, contest.

Strong — able, powerful, robust, stout, vigorous, firm, muscular, hardy.

Style — custom, mode, manner, phraseology, diction.

Subdue—vanquish, conquer, overcome, subjugate, subject, surmount.

Subject—control, liable, exposed, object, matter, material.

Subjoin—attach, connect, annex, affix.

Sublime—lofty, elevated, great, exalted, grand, magnificent.

Submissive — obedient, yielding, humble, compliant.

Subordinate — subject, subservient, inferior.

Subsistence — livelihood, living, sustenance, maintenance, support.

Substantial — reliable, strong, solid, stout, real, responsible.

Substitute — agent, representative, exchange, change.

Subtle—sly, artful, cunning, deceitful, crafty, wily, perfidious, insidious, arch, acute, fine.

Subtract—withdraw, deduct, take from.

Subvert — ruin, overthrow, reverse, controvert, invert, reverse.

Successful — prosperous, lucky, winning, fortunate.

Succession — series, order, continuance.

Succor—defend, help, aid, assist, relieve.

Sudden — unexpected, unlooked for, unanticipated, hasty.

Suffer—endure, tolerate, permit, bear, allow.

Suffocate—smother, choke, stifle.

Sufficient — plenty, abundance, enough, competent, adequate.

Suffrage—vote, ballot, aid, voice.

Suggest—propose, insinuate, hint, allude, intimate.

Suitable — appropriate, fit, becoming, agreeable, expedient.

Suitor—beau, wooer, lover, petitioner.

Summon—cite, call, invite, bid, convoke.

Sundry—several, various, diverse, different.

Superficial—flimsy, slight, shallow.

Supersede — supplant, overrule, displace.

Supplicate—solicit, entreat, beg, beseech, ask, implore.

Support—maintain, uphold, sustain, defend, encourage, second,

prop, protect, favor, forward, cherish, assist, endure.

Sure—reliable, confident, certain, infallible.

Surmise—presume, think, guess, suppose, believe, conjecture.

Surmount — subdue, overcome, vanquish, conquer.

Surpass — beat, outdo, outstrip, excel, exceed.

Surprise—astonishment, admiration, wonder, amazement.

Surrender — yield, resign, give up, deliver.

Surround — encompass, enclose, encircle, environ.

Survey—review, prospect, retrospect.

Suspense—hesitation, doubt, uncertainty.

Suspicion — distrust, jealousy, apprehension.

Sustain — carry, bear, support, uphold, maintain.

Sustenance — livelihood, living, maintenance, support.

Swiftness—speed, rapidity, velocity, fleetness, quickness, celerity.

Symbol—illustration, type, figure, emblem, metaphor.

Symmetry — harmony, proportion.

Sympathy — compassion, condolence, agreement, commiseration.

Symptom — evidence, indication, token, sign, mark, note.

System—order, method.

T

Talent — faculty, ability, gift, endowment, capability, intellectuality.

Talk—conference, discourse, chat, conversation, sermon, communication, lecture, dialogue, colloquy.

Tantalize—plague, tease, taunt, provoke, irritate, torment, aggravate.

Taste — perception, discernment, judgment, flavor, savor, relish.

Tax—duty, assessment, rate, toll, tribute, contribution, custom.

Tedious — wearisome, slow, tiresome, tardy.

Tell — inform, communicate, reveal, disclose, acquaint, impart, mention, state, talk, report.

Temper—mood, humor, temperament, disposition.

Temperate — moderate, sober, abstemious, abstinent.

Temporal — worldly, mundane, sublunary, secular.

Temporary—uncertain, fleeting, transitory, transient.

Tempt—allure, induce, entice, attract, decoy, seduce.

Tender—propose, offer, bid.

Tenderness—fondness, love, humanity, affection, benignity.

Tenet — belief, dogma, doctrine, principle, position, opinion.

Terms—conditions, words, expressions, language.

Terminate — close, finish, end, complete.

Terrible—awful, frightful, fearful, shocking, terrific, horrible.

Terror—alarm, fear, dread, consternation, apprehension, fright.

Test — experiment, proof, experience, trial, standard, criterion.

Testify — prove, declare, swear, signify, witness, affirm.

Testimony—proof, evidence.

Therefore — wherefore, accordingly, then, hence, so, consequently.

Think—consider, deliberate, mediate, ponder, conceive, contemplate, imagine, surmise.

Though—allow, while, although.

Thought—contemplation, meditation, fancy, idea, supposition, reflection, conception, conceit.

Thoughtful — anxious, considerate, careful, attentive, discreet, contemplative.

Thoughtless — inconsiderate, indiscreet, careless, foolish, hasty, unthinking.

Throw—heave, cast, hurl, fling.

Time—period, season, age, date, duration, era, epoch.

Timely — opportune, seasonable, early.

Tired — wearied, fatigued, harassed.

Title—name, appellation, claim.

Token—emblem, sign, indication, symptom, mark, note.

Tolerate—permit, allow, suffer.

Tortuous—tormenting, crooked, twisted, winding.

Total — complete, whole, entire, gross, sum.

Touching—moving, pathetic, affecting.

Tour—round, circuit, jaunt, trip, journey, ramble, excursion.

Trace—clue, track, mark, vestige.

Trade—vocation, business, calling, labor, occupation, dealing, traffic.

Traduce—injure, condemn, censure, depreciate, degrade, decry, calumniate, detract.

Tranquillity— stillness, peace, quiet, calm.

Transact—manage, conduct, negotiate.

Transcend — surpass, excel, exceed, outdo.

Transparent — clear, pellucid, pervious, translucent.

Transient—brief, fleeting, short.

Transport — delight, rapture, ecstasy.

Treacherous — insidious, faithless, dishonest, perfidious, heartless.

Trepidation—palpitation, emotion, trembling, tremor, agitation.

Trespass — violation, transgression, offense, misdemeanor.

Trial—endeavor, attempt, effort, experiment, test, proof, temptation.

Trick — cheat, fraud, deception, artifice, imposture, stratagem, jugglery.

Trifling—insignificant, inconsiderable, unimportant, light, futile, petty, frivolous.

Trip—journey, jaunt, excursion, tour, ramble, voyage.

Trouble—anxiety, vexation, adversity, affliction, sorrow, distress.

Troublesome — annoying, disturbing, vexing, perplexing, irksome, teasing, harassing, importunate.

True—honest, candid, sincere, reliable, plain, upright.

Truth—fidelity, veracity, candor, faithfulness, honesty.

Try—endeavor, attempt.

Turbulent—raging, tumultuous, seditious, mutinous, riotous.

Turn—revolve, whirl, twist, circulate, wind, gyrate, contort, bend, distort, wheel.

Type—illustration, symbol, figure, emblem, mark.

U

Ultimate—latest, last, final, end.

Umpire—judge, arbitrator, arbiter.

Unbelief — incredulity, disbelief, skepticism, infidelity.

Unblemished — faultless, blameless, spotless, irreproachable, untarnished, stainless.

Unceasingly—eternally, perpetually, always, constantly, continually.

Unchangeable—unalterable, immutable.

Uncommon — singular, unusual, rare, unique, infrequent, choice, scarce.

Unconcerned—careless, regardless, uninterested, indifferent.

Uncover—reveal, expose, strip, discover.

Undaunted — courageous, bold, fearless, intrepid.

Undeniable — indisputable, incontrovertible, unquestionable.

Under — subordinate, lower, beneath, below, inferior, subject, subjacent.

Understanding—conception, intelligence, comprehension, sense, perception, faculty, reason, intellect.

Undetermined—uncertain, irresolute, hesitating, wavering, unsteady, doubtful, vacillating, fluctuating.

Unfaithful — untruthful, faithless, dishonest, disloyal, treacherous, perfidious.

Unfold—explain, divulge, reveal, unravel, develop, expand, open, display.

Unhandy — ungainly, awkward, uncouth, clumsy.

Unhappy—distressed, miserable, unfortunate, afflicted, wretched.

Uniform — even, alike, equal, same.

Unimportant — trivial, trifling, immaterial, insignificant, petty, inconsiderable.

Unlearned — uninformed, unlettered, ignorant, illiterate.

Unlike — distinct, dissimilar, different.

Unlimited — infinite, boundless, unbounded, illimitable.

Unquestionable — indubitable, undeniable, indisputable, incontrovertible.

Unravel — unfold, disentangle, extricate, reveal.

Unrelenting—unforgiving, hardhearted, inexorable, relentless.

Unruly — unmanageable, uncontrollable, refractory, ungovernable.

Unseasonable — ill-timed, unfit, untimely, unsuitable, late.

Unsettled — doubtful, wavering, undetermined, unsteady, vacillating.

Unspeakable — unutterable, inexpressible.

Unstable — inconstant, mutable, vacillating, changeable, wavering.

Untimely — inopportune, premature, unseasonable, unsuitable.

Unwilling—loth, backward, disinclined, disliking, averse, reluctant.

Upbraid — reprove, censure, reproach, blame.

Uproar—noise, confusion, bustle, tumult, disturbance.

Urbanity — courtesy, affability, suavity, civility.

Urge—press, incite, impel, instigate, stimulate, encourage, animate.

Urgent — importunate, pressing, earnest.

Usage — habit, fashion, custom, treatment, prescription.

Use—practice, custom, habit, service, usage, advantage, utility.

Usually—generally, commonly.

Utility—use, service, benefit, advantage, convenience, usefulness.

Utterly — perfectly, completely, fully.

V

Vacant—void, empty, devoid, unused.

Vague—unsettled, indefinite.

Vain—conceited, useless, fruitless, idle, ineffectual.

Valedictory — farewell, taking leave.

Valuable—expensive, costly, precious, useful, worthy, estimable.

Value—price, worth, rate, appreciation, estimation, account, appraise, assess, compute, regard, respect.

Vanity—pride, haughtiness, conceit, arrogance.

Vanquish — subdue, overcome, slay, conquer, confute, subjugate.

Variable—transitory, capricious, fickle, unsteady, changeable, versatile, wavering.

Variation — deviation, change, variety, vicissitude.

Variety—diversion, change, difference.

Various — sundry, different, diverse.

Vehement— hot, eager, ardent, fiery, passionate, violent, impetuous.

Velocity—speed, celerity, swiftness, fleetness, rapidity, quickness.

Venerate — worship, reverence, respect, adore.

Veracity—honesty, truth, integrity.

Verbal—oral, vocal.

Vestige — evidence, mark, trace, track.

Vexation — chagrin, uneasiness, trouble, sorrow, mortification.

Vicinity—locality, neighborhood, nearness, section.

View—picture, prospect, survey, landscape, see, look, behold.

Vigorous — robust, active, energetic, powerful, agile, forcible, potent.

Violent — turbulent, boisterous, impetuous, furious.

Virtue—chastity, purity, efficacy, goodness.

Visible — apparent, discernible, evident, plain, distinct, manifest, doubtless, obvious.

Visionary — fanatic, enthusiast, dreamer, imaginary, fanatical.

Volatility—lightness, flightiness, levity, giddiness, sprightliness, liveliness.

Vouch—assure, warrant, affirm, aver, protest, attest.

Vulgar—ordinary, common, low, mean.

W

Wages—stipulation, hire, salary, pay, allowance.

Wakeful—vigilant, attentive, observant, watchful.

Wander — roam, stroll, ramble, rove, range, journey.

Want—indigence, need, poverty, lack.

Ware—goods, merchandise, commodity.

Warlike—military, martial.

Warmth — fervor, ardor, cordiality, animation, heat, fervency, vigor, glow, zeal, vehemence.

Warning—notice, advice, monition, caution.

Wary—discreet, guarded, watchful, cautious, circumspect.

Waste — loose, dissipate, spend, expend, consume, lavish, squander.

Wasteful—profuse, extravagant, lavish, prodigal.

Watchful — cautious, observant, vigilant, careful, circumspect, attentive, wakeful.

Waver—hesitate, vacillate, fluctuate, scruple, to be undetermined.

Way—plan, method, course, manner, system, means, fashion, road, route.

Weak—infirm, feeble, enfeebled, debilitated, enervated.

Wealth—opulence, riches, affluence.

Weakness — debility, feebleness, frailty, infirmity, languor, failing, imbecility, silliness, folly.

Weariness — languor, lassitude, tediousness, fatigue.

Weary—annoy, distress, harass, jade, tire, vex, perplex, subdue.

Wedding—marriage, nuptial.

Weight—load, burden, heaviness, gravity, importance, signification.

Welcome — desirable, agreeable, grateful, acceptable.

Wherefore — consequently, accordingly, so, then, therefore, thence, hence.

Whiten—blanch, fade, bleach.

Whole—undivided, complete, entire, perfect, total, uninjured, sum.

Wicked—sinful, guilty, unjust, flagrant, impious, atrocious, villainous, criminal, depraved, outrageous.

Wily — cunning, artful, subtle, crafty.

Wisdom — foresight, prudence, knowledge, understanding.

Withdraw—retreat, recede, go back, retire, take back, retrograde.

Withhold — forbear, refrain, refuse, hinder, keep back.

Wonder—astonishment, marvel, surprise, admiration, amazement.

Wonderful — strange, curious, astonishing, surprising, marvelous, admirable.

Worthy — estimable, deserving, meritorious.

Wretched—unhappy, miserable.

Writer—author, scribe.

Y

Yearly—annually.

Yet—but, however, notwithstanding, still, nevertheless.

Yield—comply, conform, concede, allow, produce, permit, resign, surrender.

Z

Zeal—warmth, ardor, fervor, enthusiasm.

Zealous—concerned, earnest, ardent, fervent, anxious, warm, enthusiastic.

OU have thoughts that you wish to communicate to another through the medium of a letter. Possibly you have a favor to bestow. Quite as likely you have a favor to ask. In either case you wish to write that letter in a manner such as to secure the respect and consideration of the person with whom you correspond.

The rules for the mechanical execution of a letter are few; understanding and observing the rules already considered for composition, the writer has only to study perfect naturalness of expression, to write a letter well.

Style and Manner.

The *expression* of language should, as nearly as possible, be the same as the writer would speak. A letter is but a talk on paper. The *style* of writing will depend upon the terms of intimacy existing between the parties. If to a superior, it should be respectful; to inferiors, courteous; to friends, familiar; to relatives, affectionate.

Originality.

Do not be guilty of using that stereotyped phrase,

Dear Friend:

I now take my pen in hand to let you know that I am well, and hope you are enjoying the same great blessing.

Be original. You are not exactly like any one else. Your letter should be a representative of yourself, not of anybody else. The world is full of imitators in literature, who pass on, leaving no reputation behind them. Occasionally originals come up, and fame and fortune are ready to do them service. The distinguished writers of the past and present have gone aside from the beaten paths. Letter writing affords a fine opportunity for the display of originality. In your letter be yourself; write as you would talk.

* In the preparation of this chapter the author gathered many valuable suggestions from " Frost's Original Letter-Writer," and other works on epistolary correspondence, published by Dick & Fitzgerald, New York.

PARTS OF A LETTER.

_____ *Date.*

Complimentary address.
....

_____ *Body of the Letter.*

Complimentary closing.
....

Signature.
....

Name.
....

Address.
....

faithful daguerreotype of your intellectuality and your moral worth.

You little dream how much that letter may influence your future. How much it may give of hope and happiness to the one receiving it. How much it may be examined, thought of, laughed over and commented on; and when you suppose it has long since been destroyed, it may be brought forth, placed in type, and published broadcast to millions of readers.

When, in after years, the letter you now write is given to the world, will there be a word, an expression, in the same that you would blush to see in print?

Write in the spirit of cheerfulness. It is unkind to the correspondent to fill the sheet with petty complainings, though there are occasions when the heart filled with grief may confide all its troubles and sorrows to the near friend, and receive in return a letter of sympathy and condolence, containing all the consolation it is possible for the written missive to convey.

The length of letters will depend upon circumstances. As a rule, however, business letters should be short, containing just what is necessary to be said, and no more.

Form.

To be written correctly according to general usage, a letter will embrace the following parts: 1st, the date; 2nd, complimentary address; 3rd, body of the letter; 4th, complimentary closing; 5th signature; 6th, superscription.

The above shows the position of the several parts of an ordinary letter.

Purity of Expression.

Bear in mind the importance, in your correspondence, of using always the most chaste and beautiful language it is possible to command, consistent with ease and naturalness of expression. Especially in the long letters of friendship and love — those missives that reveal the heart—the language should show that the heart is pure. Let your letter be the record of the fancies and mood of the hour; the reflex of your aspirations, your joys, your disappointments; the

Position of the Various Parts.

The following position of the several parts of a letter should be observed:

1. Write the date near the upper right hand corner of the sheet.

2. Commence the complimentary address on the line next beneath one inch from the left side of the sheet.

3. The body of the letter should be commenced nearly under the last letter of the complimentary address.

4. Begin the complimentary closing on the line next beneath the body of the letter, one half of the distance from the left to the right side of the page.

5. The center of the signature may be under the last letter of the complimentary closing.

6. The name and address of the person written to should come on the line beneath the signature, at the left of the sheet.

The Complimentary Address.

Of late years it has become common, in business letters, instead of giving name and address at the close, to write the same at the commencement; thus,

To the Business Man.

Mr. William B. Ashton,
    Washington, D. C.
  Dear Sir:
        Your note of the 1st inst. received, etc.

To the Married Woman.

Mrs. Helen E. King,
    Baltimore, Md.
  Dear Madam:
        Enclosed find check for, etc.

To the Unmarried Woman.

Miss Harriet A. Kendall,
    Lowell, Mass.
    In reply to your favor of the 4th ult., etc.

Note.—It is customary to address the married woman by the name which she uses on her cards. It is optional with the lady whether she uses her own name, "Mrs. Helen E. King," or that of her husband, "Mrs. Chas. H. King."

FORM OF A LETTER.

(Date.)
Olney, England, June 16, 1769.

(Complimentary Address.)
My Dear Friend:

(Body of the Letter.)
I am obliged to you for your invitation, but being long accustomed to retirement, which I was always fond of, I am now more than ever unwilling to visit those noisy scenes which I never loved, and which I now more than ever abhor. I remember you with all the friendship I ever professed, which is as much as I ever entertained for any man.

I love you and yours. I thank you for your continued remembrance of me, and shall not cease to be their and your

(Complimentary Closing.)
Affectionate Friend,

(Signature.)
William Cowper.

(Name.)
To Joseph Hill,

(Address.)
London.

Kinds of Paper to Use.

Be particular to use a sheet appropriate in shape to the purpose for which it is employed. Paper is now manufactured of every size adapted to the wants of any article written. The names of the various kinds of paper in general use are *Legal-cap, Bill-paper, Foolscap, Letter-paper, Commercial-note, Note-paper* and *Billet.*

In the writing of all *Legal Documents*, such as wills, taking of testimony, articles of agreement, etc., legal cap is generally used, characterized by a red line running from top to bottom of the sheet.

For *Bills*, paper is commonly ruled expressly for the purpose, and generally bears the name and business advertisement of the person using the same, at the top.

When writing *Notes, Orders, Receipts, Compositions, Petitions, Subscription Headings*, etc., foolscap paper is used.

For the ordinary friendship letter or other

long letter, it is best to use letter paper, which in size is four-fifths the length of foolscap.

The common *Business Letter* should be so brief as generally to require but one page of commercial note, which is somewhat narrower and shorter than letter paper.

Note and billet paper are the smallest sheets made, being suitable for *Notes of Invitation, Parents' Excuses* for children to teachers, and other written exercises that are very brief.

Etiquette of Letter Writing.

As a rule, every letter, unless insulting in its character, requires an answer. To neglect to answer a letter, when written to, is as uncivil as to neglect to reply when spoken to.

In the reply, acknowledge first the receipt of the letter, mentioning its date, and afterwards consider all the points requiring attention.

If the letter is to be very brief, commence sufficiently far from the top of the page to give a nearly equal amount of blank paper at the bottom of the sheet when the letter is ended.

Should the matter in the letter continue beyond the first page, it is well to commence a little above the middle of the sheet, extending as far as necessary on the other pages.

It is thought impolite to use a half sheet of paper in formal letters. As a matter of economy and convenience for business purposes, however, it is customary to have the card of the business man printed at the top of the sheet, and a single leaf is used.

In writing a letter, the answer to which is of more benefit to yourself than the person to whom you write, enclose a postage stamp for the reply.

Letters should be as free from erasures, interlineations, blots and postscripts as possible. It is decidedly better to copy the letter than to have these appear.

A letter of introduction or recommendation, should never be sealed, as the bearer to whom it is given ought to know the contents.

Titles.

IT IS customary, in the heading of petitions to persons in official positions, in the complimentary address of a letter, and in superscriptions, to give each their proper title. These are divided into titles of respect, military, and professional titles.

Titles of respect are:—*Mr.*, from *Master*; *Mrs.*, from *Mistress*; *Miss*, from the French, *De-moi-selle*; *Esq.*, from *Esquire*, an English Justice of the Peace, or member of the legal profession, but applied very indiscriminately to males throughout this country generally.

Two titles of the same class should not be applied to the same name. Thus, in addressing John Smith, do not say *Mr.* John Smith, *Esq.*; though we may say *Mr.* John Smith, or John Smith, *Esq.*

If the profession of the person addressed be known, the professional title alone should be used. If the person be entitled to two titles the highest is given.

Titles of respect are usually placed before the name; as, *Mr.*, *Hon.*, *Rev.*, *Dr.*, and military titles.

Professional titles sometimes precede and sometimes follow the name; as, *Dr.* John Smith, or John Smith, *M.D.*; *Prof.* John Smith, or John Smith, *A.M.*

The following list illustrates the various titles used for the different ranks, among individuals, either in the complimentary address or superscription on the envelope.

To Royalty.

"*To the King's Most Excellent Majesty.*"
"*To the Queen's Most Excellent Majesty.*"
"*To his Royal Highness,* Albert Edward, Prince of Wales."

In like manner all the other members, male and female, of the Royal family are addressed.

To Nobility.

"*To his Grace* the Duke of Argyle."
"*To the Most Noble* the Marquis of Westminster."
"*To the Right Honorable* the Earl of Derby."
"*To the Right Honorable* Lord Viscount Sidney."
"*To the Honorable* Baron Cranworth."

The wives of noblemen have the same titles as their husbands; thus,

"*To her Grace* the Duchess of Argyle."
"*To the Most Noble* the Marchioness of Westminster."
"*To the Right Honorable* the Countess of Derby."
"*To the Right Honorable* the Viscountess Sidney."
"*To the Honorable* the Baroness Cranworth."

The title of *Honorable*, in great Britain, is applied to the younger sons of noblemen (the elder son taking, by courtesy, the title next in rank below that of his father). It is also given to members of parliament and to certain persons holding positions of honor and trust.

To Baronets.

"*Sir* Walter Scott, Bart."

To Knights.

"*Sir* William Armstrong, Kt."

Ellsworth's "Text-Book on Penmanship" gives the following classification of the various titles used in the United States.

Titles of Honor, Profession and Respect.

"*His Excellency* Richard Roe,"	President of the United States, Governor of any State, or Minister to Foreign Countries.
"*Honorable* Richard Roe,"	Vice-President, Senators and Representatives of the U. S., Lieut.-Gov. of State, State Senators and Representatives, Judges, Mayors, Consuls, Ministers Abroad, and Heads of Executive Departments of the General Government.
"*Rev.* Richard Roe, D.D."	Doctor of Divinity.
"Richard Roe, LL.D."	Doctor of Laws.
"Richard Roe."	Minister of the Gospel.
"*Dr.* Richard Roe."	Physician and Surgeon.
"*Prof.* Richard Roe."	Professor or teacher of any art or science.
"Richard Roe, *Esq.*"	Member of the legal Fraternity.
"*Mr.* Richard Roe."	Non-professional gentleman.
"Richard Roe."	Plain signature.
"Richard X Roe."	Unable to write his own name.

Titles of the Dignitaries, Prelates, Clergy, and Other Officers of the Roman Catholic Church.

Of the Pope—*His Holiness* Pope Leo XIII.
Of a Cardinal—*His Eminence* John, Cardinal McCloskey.
Of an Archbishop—*Most Rev.* T. J. Burroughs, D.D.
Of a Bishop—*Rt. Rev.* Thomas Foley, D.D.
Of a Vicar-General—*Very Rev.* J. D. Halbert, D.D.
Of a Priest—*Rev.* Patrick Kelly, P.P.
Of Directors of Parish Schools— { *Rev. Provincial* James Rice. { *Rev. Bro. Director* Henry Baker.
Of a Directress of a Seminary—*Madame* De Vincent.
Of a Teacher of a Seminary—*Sister* Le Clerc.
Of a Lady Superintendent of a Convent—*Sister Superior* Laflange.
Of a Lady Superintendent of a Catholic Orphan Asylum — *Mother Superior* St. Agnes.

Military Titles in the United States.

The following are addressed as *General, Colonel, Major, Captain, Lieutenant, Corporal,* or *Sergeant,* according to their rank:

COMMISSIONED OFFICERS.	
General of the Army.	Captain.
Lieutenant-General of the Army.	Chaplain.
Major-General.	Adjutant.
Adjutant-General.	First Lieutenant.
Inspector-General.	Second Lieutenant.
Quartermaster-General.	NON-COMMISSIONED OFFICERS.
Commissary-General.	Sergeant-Major.
Paymaster-General.	Quartermaster-Sergeant.
Surgeon-General.	Sergeant.
Brigadier-General.	Corporal.
	Company Clerks.

Brigade-Inspector.
Colonel.
Lieutenant-Colonel.
Major.

Drum-Major.
Fife-Major.
Hospital-Stewards.

Titles and Names of Naval Officers.

The only titles generally used among naval officers are those of *Admiral, Commodore, Captain* and *Lieutenant.*

Rear-Admiral.	Second Assistant-Engineer.
Vice-Admiral.	Third Assistant-Engineer.
Commodore.	Naval Constructor.
Captain.	Navy Agent.
Commander.	Purser, or Storekeeper.
Lieutenant-Commander.	Secretary to Commander.
First Lieutenant.	Navy-yard Clerks.
Second Lieutenant.	Bandmaster.
Master.	Musicians.
Ensign.	Mate—First, Second, and Third.
Midshipman.	Quartermaster.
Fleet Surgeon.	Master-at-Arms.
Ship's Surgeon.	Ship's Corporal.
Passed Surgeon.	Section Captain.
Asssistant Surgeon.	Boatswain.
Retired Surgeon.	Coxswain.
Paymaster.	Carpenter.
Assistant Paymaster.	Sailmaker.
Chaplain.	Gunner.
Professor of Mathematics.	Armorer.
Engineer-in-Chief—on shore.	Quarter-Gunner.
Chief Engineer—on ship.	Seamen.
First Assistant-Engineer.	Marines.

Superscriptions.

ENVELOPES that are perfectly plain, for ordinary letter writing, are regarded as in much the best taste. Ladies do well to use white. Buff, light straw color, or manila answer for business purposes, though it is always in good taste to use white.

The upper side of the envelope is that containing the flap. Care should be observed, in writing the superscription on the letter, to have the same right side up.

Extensive practice enables business men to write comparatively straight upon the envelope, without the aid of a line. The inexperienced penman may be aided in writing on the buff colored envelope by lead pencil lines, which should never be used, however, unless completely erased by rubber after the ink is dry.

Care should be taken to write upon the envelope very plainly, giving the full name and title of the person addressed, with place of residence written out fully, including town, county, State, and country if it goes abroad. The designation of the street, number, drawer, etc., when written upon the letter, is explained elsewhere.

For light colored envelopes, a piece of paper a little smaller than the envelope may be ruled with black ink over the blue lines, thus, and placed inside.

A scrap of paper, ruled like this, when placed
inside a light-colored envelope, will enable the
person writing on the same to trace distinctly
these lines, and thus write the superscription
straight.

In writing the superscription, commence the name a little to the left of the center of the envelope. The town, on a line beneath, should extend a little to the right of the name. The State, next below, should stand by itself still further to the right. The county may be on the same line with the State, towards the left side of the envelope; thus,

FORM OF SUPERSCRIPTION ON ENVELOPES.

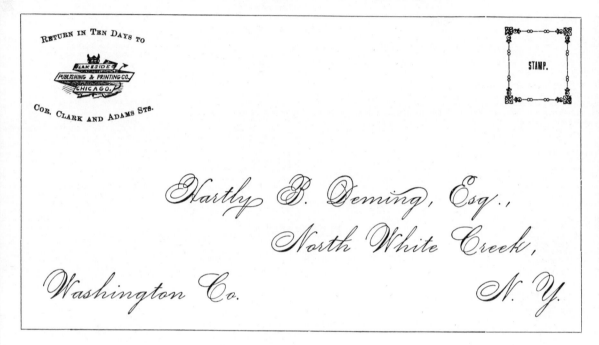

For the convenience of the mailing clerk in handling the letter, the postage stamp should be placed at the upper right hand corner of the envelope.

If the town is a large metropolis, the county may be omitted. In that event the street and number are usually given, or the post office box. Each should be written very conspicuously upon the envelope, for the convenience of the post office clerk and the mail carrier; thus,

If written in the care of any one, the following may be the form :

STAMP.

Rev. Chas. H. Smith,
Care of Col. E. W. King,
Boston,
84 Sumner Street.   *Mass.*

If, after remaining in the office at its destination a certain length of time uncalled for, the writer is desirous of having the letter forwarded or returned, the same may be indicated upon the outside of the envelope ; thus,

STAMP.

Rev. Mrs. D. B. Worth,
London,
If not called for in 10 days,
P. M. please forward to
Hotel de Ville, Paris, France.   *England.*

Letter Sent by a Private Party,
Acknowledging on the envelope obligation to the person carrying the same.

Mr. A. C. Rowe,
No. 3 Euclid Ave.,
By Politeness of   *Cleveland, O.*
Mr. J. E. Brown.

It is usually safest, in nearly all cases, to give the county, even if the town is well known ; thus,

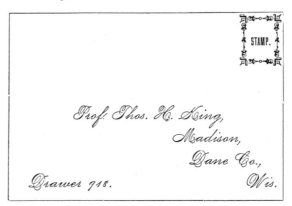

Prof. Thos. H. King,
Madison,
Dane Co.,
Drawer 918.   *Wis.*

Tourists, when receiving letters abroad, frequently have their letters directed in the care of the bankers with whom they deal when on the continent, the form of superscription being thus :

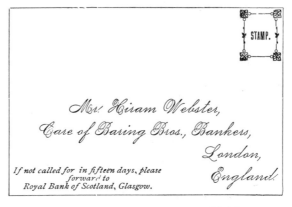

Mr. Hiram Webster,
Care of Baring Bros., Bankers,
London,
If not called for in fifteen days, please
forward to
Royal Bank of Scotland, Glasgow.   *England.*

Letter to a Person in the Immediate Vicinity
Sent by carrier, but not through the mail.

Miss Lizzie Walker.

Presented.

SUPERSCRIPTIONS.

A letter to Germany will be superscribed somewhat as follows:

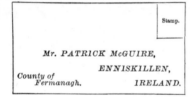

Letter from Germany:

The county, town, etc., on a letter to Ireland, is shown on the envelope as follows:

When it is desired to have the letter returned, if not called for, sooner than it otherwise would be, the direction may be so specified upon the upper left hand corner, similar to the following:

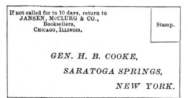

Where it is desired to express the title of the husband, on a letter or note of invitation to the husband and wife, the following form may be used:

> *His Excellency and Mrs. U. S. Grant.*
> *Governor and Mrs. Wm. H. Brown.*
> *Hon. and Mrs. L. B. Henderson.*
> *Rev. and Mrs. Chas. H. Smith.*
> *Professor and Mrs. K. A. Benson.*

Where a letter is addressed to a husband and wife, each of whom have a title, the address may read as follows:

> *Drs. John E. and Jane H. Brown.*

To a man and woman, engaged as partners in business, but unmarried, the address may read:

> *Mr. Wm. H. Smith and Miss Mary H. Boone.*
> Or, *Wm. H. Smith and Mary H. Boone.*

To a husband and wife, where the wife, alone, has the title, the superscription will read:

> *Mr. J. B. and Mrs. Dr. E. L. King.*

To a husband and wife, each of whom have a title, the address may be as follows:

> *Rev. W H. and Mrs. Dr. A. B. Smith.*

Where the wife has a title, and is, alone, addressed, the form may be

> *Rev. Mrs. Chas. D. King.*
> Or, *Rev. Mrs. Jane E. King.*
> Or, *Rev. Jane E. King.*

If the lady's husband, alone, has the title, the address will properly read:

> *Mrs. Rev. Chas. D. King.*

If the lady is unmarried, and is a minister of the gospel or physician, her address may read:

> *Rev. Miss Mary Williams.*
> Or, *Rev. Mary Williams.*
> *Miss Dr. Helen E. Snow.*
> Or, *Dr. Helen E. Snow.*

Suggestions.

If people wish to have their letters perfectly secure from observation it is better to seal them with wax, which cannot be broken without exposure. The ordinary envelope is easily opened, and sealed again, leaving no trace of the fact; though a very heavy fine is imposed as a penalty on any one convicted of opening a letter, that is not authorized to do so.

In the United States, a letter not called for within a certain length of time is then advertised, after which it is held thirty days, when, no owner being found, the letter is forwarded to the Dead-Letter Office at Washington, where it is opened. If the address of the person who wrote the letter can there be learned, the letter is then returned to the writer.

If the name or address be written or printed upon the envelope, instead of going to the Dead-Letter Office, the letter will be returned to the writer at the expiration of thirty days. If desirous of having it sooner returned, the writer should add, "Return in 5 days," or "10 days," etc., as seen in the letter of Jansen, McClurg & Co., shown above.

It is safest for persons sending letters to place stamps upon the envelopes themselves, and not depend upon postmasters or their clerks to do so, as, in their haste, they sometimes forget directions.

It has been suggested that the State be written first upon the envelope; thus,

> MISSOURI,
> CORNING,
> JOHN SMITH.

As the State to which the letter is directed, is, however, no more conspicious at the top of the superscription than at the bottom, there is no advantage gained in this mode of address, on the score of legibility.

Business Letters.

N letters of business, use as few words as possible.

2. Business letters should be promptly answered.

3. Use a clear, distinct writing, avoiding all flourish of penmanship or language.

4. Come at once to your subject, and state it so clearly that it will not be necessary to guess your meaning.

5. Give town, county, State and date explicitly. It is frequently of great importance to know *when* a letter was written.

6. Read your letter carefully when finished, to see that you have made no omissions and no mistakes. Also carefully examine your envelope, to see that it is rightly directed, with postage-stamp affixed.

7. Copy all business letters, of your own, by hand, or with the copying-press made for the purpose.

8. Send money by Draft, P. O. Money-Order, or Express, taking a receipt therefor; thus you have something to show for money, guarantying you against loss. Always state in your letter the amount of money you send, and by what means sent.

9. Write date, and by whom sent, across the end of each letter received, and file for future reference, fastening the letters together with rubber bands, or binding in a letter-file adapted to the purpose. The possession of a letter sometimes prevents litigation and serious misunderstanding.

Ordering Goods.

In ordering goods, state very explicitly the amount, kind, quality, color, shape, size, etc., and on what terms wanted. Whether you wish the same sent by freight or express, and *what* express. Much inconvenience is experienced among business men because of a neglect to designate explicitly what is wanted.

Should the writer wish to make suggestions, ask questions, or add other matter to the letter, which is foreign to the subject, such words should be placed entirely separate from the order. Of fifty or a hundred letters received to-day by the merchant, that one which is mixed up with complaints, enquiries, etc., will probably be laid over till to-morrow, or until time can be spared to read it through. Had the order been explicitly stated, and the suggestions placed elsewhere, the goods would have been forwarded immediately. It is, in fact, better to write the order on a separate sheet from the other matter.

Send your order, also, early enough to give yourself plenty of time in which to receive the goods before they are needed.

Books, being a common article ordered, may be taken as an example showing the importance of giving a careful description of the goods wanted. To illustrate: be explicit in giving name of book, name of author, by whom published, style of binding, price at which it is advertised, etc. Thus, a careless person, ordering of Harper & Brothers a United States History, will say, "Send me a United States History." Of course the first query of the shipping-clerk is, "*Whose* history?" There are many histories of the United States, published by as many different authors, and the clerk is liable to send the one not wanted; in which case the person ordering is very likely to unjustly blame Harper & Brothers.

If the writer should say, "Send me a copy of Willard's History of the United States, by Emma Willard, published by A. S. Barnes & Co., bound in cloth," there would be no liability to mistake. The following will serve as sample forms:

Form of Letter Ordering Books.

ROCKFORD, ILL., March 1, 18—.

MESSRS. JANSEN, McCLURG & Co.,
　　　　Chicago, Ill.
　　Dear Sirs:
　　　　Enclosed find draft for $48.75, for which please send, by American Express,

10 Tennyson's Poems.	Published by Harper & Bros.	$1.25	$12.50
10 Thirty Years in the Harem.	" " "	1.50	15.00
10 Literature and Art, by M. Fuller.	" Fowler & Wells.	1.00	10.00
5 Getting on in the World, Mathews.	S. C. Griggs & Co.	2.25	11.25
			$48.75

Thanking you for the promptitude with which you have filled my orders heretofore, I am,

　　　　　　Very Respectfully,
　　　　　　　　CASH DOWN.

Form of an Order to a Dry-Goods Merchant.

April 5, 18—.

MESSRS. A. T. STEWART & Co.,
　　　　New York.
　　Dear Sirs:
　　　　Enclosed find Post Office Order for $25, for which please send, by American Express, the following goods:

2 Lancaster Table Spreads ($3.50),	$ 7.00
4 prs. Alexandre Kid Gloves ($2.50), No. 6½, Brown, Green, Yellow, Black,	10.00
8 yds. Calico, Brown, with small figure (25c.),	2.00
12 " " White, " " pink dot "	3.00
2 Linen Handkerchiefs (50c.),	1.00
4 prs. Ladies' Cotton Hose (50c.), No. 9,	2.00
	$25.00

Direct to
　　　　MRS. MARY WILSON,
　　　　　　ELKHART, IND.

From a Young Man Commencing Business, to a Wholesale House, with Order.

RACINE, WIS., Aug. 10, 18—.

MESSRS. FIELD, LEITER & Co.,
　　　　Chicago, Ill.
　　Dear Sirs:
　　　　Having recently commenced business for myself, with fair prospects of success, I shall be pleased to open an account with your house, and trust it will be to our mutual advantage. Should you think favorably of the matter, you will please fill the accompanying order with the least possible delay, and on your best terms.

For testimonials, I refer you to Carson, Pirie, Scott & Co., of your city, by whom I have been, until recently, employed; but, as this is my first transaction with your house, upon forwarding me an invoice of goods, and deducting your usual discount for cash, I will remit a sight draft on the First National Bank of your city, for the amount, by return mail. Expecting your usual prompt attention, I am,

　　　　　　Yours Respectfully,
　　　　　　　　HENRY MAYNARD.

Reply from Wholesale House, with Invoice.

CHICAGO, Aug. 12, 18—.

MR. HENRY MAYNARD,
　　　　Racine, Wis.
　　Dear Sir:
　　　　We take pleasure in sending this day, by your order, the enclosed invoice of goods, amounting to $1,400, subject to 5 per cent discount for prompt cash.

Your references being entirely satisfactory, we have no hesitation in opening an account and allowing you our best terms. Trusting that the goods, which are shipped by express, will arrive safely and meet your favor, we are,

　　　　　　Yours Truly,
　　　　　　　　FIELD, LEITER & CO.

Requesting Information Concerning the Opening of a Store.

BOSTON, MASS., Sept. 18, 18—.

CHAS. H. WILLIAMS, ESQ.,
　　　　Bennington, Vt.
　　Dear Sir:
　　　　My partner and myself being desirous of establishing a branch store in the clothing trade, I take the privilege of a friend in asking you to send me the number of clothing stores already in your village, and such other information as may be necessary, concerning the feasibility of establishing our business in your place. An early reply will greatly oblige,

　　　　　　Yours, Very Truly,
　　　　　　　　WM. B. HOPKINS.

Answer to the Foregoing.

BENNINGTON, VT., Sept. 20, 18—.

MR. WM. B. HOPKINS,
　　　　Boston, Mass.
　　Dear Sir:
　　　　I have taken occasion to enquire in relation to the extent and number of clothing stores in this place, and am happy to inform you that, while that department of trade is very fairly represented, there seems to be a good opening for a first-class store, such as your house would undoubtedly establish.

There is also a large store just vacated, in the center of the village, one of the best locations in the town, which can be had at reasonable rent. Hoping that you may carry out your design of locating here, and trusting that you may realize your expectations, I am,

　　　　　　Yours Truly,
　　　　　　　　CHAS. H. WILLIAMS.

Enquiry Concerning Real Estate.

SPRINGLAKE, MICH., Sept. 4, 18—.

MESSRS. S. TOWN & SON,
Aurora, Ill.,

Dear Sirs :
Having heard much said in praise of your beautiful city, particularly concerning railroad privileges, church and educational advantages, I have concluded to make your town my permanent place of abode, if I can locate myself aright, inasmuch as I have a large family of children to educate, and the numerous lines of railway radiating from your city will afford me the desired accommodations in my traveling agency.

My object in writing you at present is to learn your best terms for a residence containing not less than ten rooms, having from six to ten acres of land attached, situated not over a mile from the postoffice.

An immediate answer will oblige,

Your Obedient Servant,

HARVEY B. WILCOX.

Superintendent's Resignation.

GALESBURG, ILL., Sept. 1, 1878.

TO THE GENERAL SUPERINTENDENT OF THE C., B. & Q. R. R.,
Chicago, Ill.,

Dear Sir :
I herewith tender my resignation as local superintendent of the railroad repair works in this city, my labors in behalf of your company to cease October 1, 1878.

Respectfully Yours,

D. B. LAWSON.

Short Form of Resignation.

PITTSBURGH, PA., Dec. 2, 1879.

TO THE DIRECTORS OF THE PITTSBURGH GLASS WORKS,
Pittsburgh, Pa.,

Dear Sirs :
Please accept my immediate resignation as business manager of your manufactory.

Yours Respectfully,

WM. D. WEBSTER.

Clergyman's Resignation.

TO THE TRUSTEES OF FIRST BAPTIST CHURCH,
Pittsfield, Mass.,

Gentlemen :
It has now been seven years since the commencement of my pastoral connection with the First Baptist Church of this city. During this time the church society has grown in numbers, the sabbath school has been continually blessed by a large attendance, and the relations between pastor and congregation have always been of a most pleasant character. For these and other reasons it would be agreeable to continue my connection with the society longer; but other fields of labor affording wider and better opportunities, I feel it but just that I accept the privileges offered.

Thanking the congregation to whom I have ministered for their kind and unwavering support, and praying for your continued prosperity, I desire you to accept my resignation as pastor of your society, to take effect January 15, 1878.   Yours Very Respectfully,

CHAS. B. HANFORD.

Letter Complaining of Error in a Bill.

TROY, N. Y., June 10, 18—.

MESSRS. H. B. CLAFLIN & CO.,
New York,

Dear Sirs :
Upon examining bill accompanying your last lot of goods, I find that I am charged with four dozen pairs of cotton hose which I never ordered nor received. I enclose the bill and copy of the invoice of goods, that the error may be corrected. I am, gentlemen,

Yours Very Respectfully,

H. B. MOORE.

Answer to the Foregoing.

NEW YORK, June 11, 18—.

MR. H. B. MOORE,
Troy, N. Y.,

Dear Sir :
We regret that you were put to any trouble by the carelessness of a clerk, who, having proved himself incompetent, has left our service. We enclose the correct bill to you, and offer apologies for the error.   Truly Yours,

H. B. CLAFLIN & CO.

An Application for a Situation on a Railway.

DAVENPORT, IA., Jan. 15, 18—.

HON. B. C. SMITH,
Dear Sir :
Understanding that you are a shareholder in some of the principal railways, and on intimate terms with several of the directors, I venture to solicit your kind interest in behalf of my eldest son, William, now in his twentieth year. His education has been varied and useful, and his character, so far as I know, is above reproach.

For several years he has expressed a desire to enter the employ of a railroad company, and under the circumstances I venture to write to you, in the hope that, should you have it in your power to oblige me, you will kindly intercede in his favor. By doing so you will confer a lasting obligation both on him and me. I remain, sir,

Your Ob'd't Servant,

Recommending a Successor in Business.

MILWAUKEE, WIS., Dec. 24, 18—.

MESSRS. BELL & HARDY,
Dear Sirs :
We flatter ourselves that there are many friends among our connection who will regret that we are on the point of relinquishing business. In doing so our premises and stock of goods will be transferred to the hands of Messrs. Williams & Co., who will in future carry on the business on the same approved system and extensive scale as ourselves, provided they can rely upon receiving the patronage of our connection; in the hope of which, it is our pleasure and duty to present these gentlemen to your notice. We cannot speak too highly of the confidence we feel in their liberal mode of conducting mercantile transactions; and, in the hope that they may be honored with the same countenance received by ourselves from your respected firm, we beg to sign ourselves

Your Most Obedient Servants,

HOPE, GOOD & CO.

Notice of Having Forwarded Goods.

SOUTH HAVEN, MICH., Sept. 1, 18—.

MESSRS. HAGER, SPIES & CO.,
Chicago, Ill.,

Dear Sirs :
According to your order, I have shipped you this day, per Steamer Morning Star,

200 baskets Peaches,	(Marked H., S. & Co.)	
10 bbls. Sweet Potatoes,	" " "	
12 " Apples,	" " "	

Trusting that these will prove as satisfactory as those heretofore sent, and bring as good a price, I am

Respectfully Yours,

A. M. GOODFELLOW.

Requesting a Friend to Make Purchases.

KANKAKEE, ILL., Jan. 1, 18—.

DEAR MARY :
I am going to trespass on your kindness by asking you to make a few purchases for me. Enclosed find twenty dollars and a memorandum of what I want.

My household duties, combined with the objection I have to leaving my children at this season of the year in the care of servants, very closely confine me to my home, and are my excuse for troubling you.

We are in usual health, and I hope this note will find your family all well. With kind regards to Mr. Webster and love to children, I remain,

Your Sincere Friend,
HELEN D. WELLS.

To Mrs. May Benson,
— Michigan Ave., Chicago.

Requesting Settlement of Account.

MEMPHIS, TENN., Oct. 9, 18—

Hiram Baxter, Esq.,
Nashville, Tenn.
Sir:
I enclose your account. I shall feel obliged by your settlement at an early date, as I have several heavy payments to make.
Trusting that you will excuse my troubling you, I am,
Yours Respectfully,
DELOS HARTWELL.

Reply to the Preceding.

NASHVILLE, TENN., Oct. 12, 18—.

Delos Hartwell, Esq.,
Memphis, Tenn.
Sir:
As I am unable to send you the money for settlement of our account, without inconvenience, I enclose my acceptance for thirty days, which I trust you will be able to use.
Yours Truly,
HIRAM BAXTER.

Urging Payment of Rent.

COLUMBUS, O., March 11, 18—.

Mr. D. P. Hoyt.
Dear Sir:
I have waited patiently for your convenience in the payment of rent for the house you are at present occupying. As, however, you have now been my tenant for four months without meeting any of the payments, which were to be made monthly, I feel obliged to remind you of the fact that there are now $80 due to me.
Trusting that you will give the subject your immediate attention, I am,

Yours Truly,
WEBSTER GREEN.

Letter to a Pioneer Settler in the West.

TOLEDO, OHIO, July 9, 18—.

Mr. Martin Fuller.
Dear Sir:
I take the liberty, though a stranger, of addressing you a few lines relative to the inducements for new settlers in your section of the country, having been recommended to do so through our mutual friend, Artemas Carter.
As I have sold out my business in this city for ten thousand dollars, I am anxious to invest the proceeds in a large farm in a young State, feeling satisfied that a new country, like that you are now in, offers attractions for young and energetic men not found in the old cities.
You will much oblige me by giving information concerning climate, soil, water, timber, and other inducements for settling in your vicinity. Trusting that doing so will not seriously trouble you, and that I may hear from you soon, I remain,
Yours, Very Respectfully,
CHAS. W. CANFIELD.

Answer to the Foregoing.

BIG STRANGER, KANSAS, Aug. 15, 18—.

Mr. Chas. W. Canfield,
Toledo, Ohio.
Dear Sir:
Your welcome letter was received yesterday. I can assure you that I will be only too happy to furnish you all the information you desire relative to the prospects in this portion of Uncle Sam's domains.
I have now been two years in this place, and I can truly say that these years have been the happiest of my life. True, we have endured some hardships incident to pioneer life; but the glorious freedom from the frivolities of fashion and the formalities of aristocratic life, common to the old towns in the East, together with the pleasure one takes in making new improvements, all have combined to render our family perfectly delighted with the country.
For a quarter of the money in your possession, you can purchase all the land you will desire to cultivate; the remainder you can loan hereabouts, on bond and mortgage, at good interest.
The climate here is healthy and invigorating; the soil good, with running streams in sufficient abundance to water most of the farms. Plenty of building material and fuel can be had in the timber skirting the streams; and the prospect for the ultimate opening of the land in this section to a ready market, through several lines of railway now in contemplation, is very flattering. At present, however, the nearest station to my farm, on the stage route, is Chesterfield, thirty-four miles distant, at which place I will take great pleasure in meeting you, with my team, at any time you may appoint.
A very excellent farm, adjoining mine, can be bought for five dollars ($5) per acre. One corner of the land is crossed by a never-failing stream, with considerable timber along the same.
You will have to rough it for a little while after you arrive; but the neighbors will all turn out to aid in getting up your log house, after which you will be at home "under your own vine and fig-tree."
We have two rooms in our house, and, till your house is completed, we will give one of them to your family. It will seem a little odd, at first, for a fashionable family of six or eight persons to occupy one room, with wolf and deer skins for quilts and coverlets; but, by-and-by, when the young ladies find they are in just as good style as anybody else, they will dismiss their fastidiousness, and think it jolly fun. These privations that we at first endure are necessary, perhaps, to enable us to appreciate the fine homes which we all expect to have in the good time coming. Hoping to have the pleasure of welcoming yourself and family as neighbors, I am,
Yours, Very Truly,
MARTIN FULLER.

 # Applications for Situations.

Letters Answering Advertisements.

HE following advertisements, taken from metropolitan papers, are but samples of hundreds of such to be seen every day in the advertising columns of the leading daily newspapers in the great cities; showing that abundant opportunities constantly offer for obtaining employment, the positions to be secured, however, by letters making application for them.

As a hundred different persons will sometimes make application for one position, which will be given to the individual writing the best letter, everything else being equal, this illustrates in a striking manner the importance of being able to write a letter elegantly and correctly.

Answer to an Advertisement for an Assistant Editor.

Maplewood, Mass., April 1, 18—.

Dear Sir:

Observing the enclosed advertisement in this morning's "Herald," I improve the opportunity by writing you an application for the place, as I am at present disengaged.

I graduated four years ago at Mrs. Willard's Seminary, Troy, N. Y., since which time I conducted the literary department of Frank Leslie's "Magazine of Fashion" up to October last, when failing health, resulting from too much close confinement, compelled me to travel abroad, from which journey, principally through England and France, I have just returned, with health completely restored.

I beg to refer you to Mr. Leslie for testimonials. Being exceedingly fond of literary pursuits, I shall be happy to occupy the position you offer, if mutually agreeable.

Yours, Most Respectfully,

Harriet Sibley. (May Myrtle.)

WANTED.

Miscellaneous.

WANTED—AN EDITORIAL ASSISTANT ON A literary paper. A thoroughly competent lady preferred. Address D 71, Herald office, New York.

WANTED—IN A GRAIN COMMISSION HOUSE, a smart lad for office work; must be a good penman. Address, in own handwriting, stating age and salary expected, W 32, Ledger office.

WANTED—A YOUNG LADY CLERK IN A DRY goods store. Must be accustomed to the business. Address, with reference, B 80, Picayune office.

WANTED—AN ASSISTANT BOOKKEEPER, one who writes neatly and rapidly; willing to work for a moderate salary, and who can bring A No. 1 recommendations. Address, stating experience and particulars, X. Y. Z., Bulletin office.

WANTED—AN EXPERIENCED BOOKKEEPER in a bank. Address, with reference, Z 61, Journal office.

WANTED—LADY COPYIST, ABLE TO WRITE A bold, distinct hand. Salary good. Address, in applicant's own handwriting, COPY, Republican office.

WANTED—A COMPETENT SALESMAN TO sell pianos—one who has experience and good references. Address, stating salary expected, PIANOS, Tribune office.

WANTED—AN ACCOMPLISHED, EDUCATED young lady as a companion, to travel for six months in Europe, with a gentleman, wife, and daughter. Must be a ready writer, a good conversationalist, and possess vivacity and pleasing manners. Wardrobe furnished, and money to pay all expenses. Address Z. B M., Commercial office, stating where an interview can be had.

General Directions.

Letters in reply to advertisements should be written immediately, else you may be too late.

Paste the advertisement at the head of your letter; thus it will be known exactly what your communication has reference to.

It is not necessary to speak much in praise of yourself, but you may state your reference, your experience, and qualifications fitting you for the position, the whole being told as briefly as possible.

Write your application yourself, your handwriting and the manner of expressing yourself being the test by which the advertiser judges you. If you have written testimonials, copy the same, marking them as such, and enclose the copy.

From a Boy Applying for a Clerkship.

879 Market Street, PHILADELPHIA, PA., Nov. 4, 18—.
DEAR SIR:
    I notice in this morning's "Ledger" your advertisement of "a boy wanted in a grain commission house," which position I take the first opportunity to apply for.

I am fourteen years old, have been at school most of the time, winters, for the past seven years, and understand bookkeeping and conducting correspondence pretty well, having assisted my father much of the time while he was in the coal trade, which was about three years.

I am perfectly willing and ready to take my coat off and go right to work at handling grain or anything else in your line.

I refer you to Mr. Ira Belden, coal dealer, at 56 Benton street, who has always known me.

I will board at home, and will try to earn for you five dollars a week.
Very Respectfully Yours,
JOHN CLANCY.

From a Young Lady Applying for a Clerkship in a Store.

182 Murray St., BUFFALO, N. Y., May 19, 18—.
DEAR SIR:
    I take the earliest opportunity of replying to the enclosed advertisement.

I have been for the past two years in the employ of Bennett & Hawley, dry-goods dealers, 492 Camden street, until the dissolution of their firm, about four weeks ago. I beg to refer you, for testimonials, to Mr. Chas. H. Bennett, of the firm of Snow, Williams & Bennett, 178 Harvard street, should you entertain my application.
Your Very Obedient Servant,
MARY H. BENSON.

Answering an Advertisement for a Bookkeeper.

1184 Longworth St., CINCINNATI, O., May 1, 18—.
DEAR SIR:
    In reply to your advertisement in to-day's "Commercial" for a clerk or assistant bookkeeper, I beg to offer my services to your firm.

I have been in the employ of Mr. Wm. H. Wilson for the past four years, until he sold out his business a few days ago, having kept the books of his house during the time.

He permits me to refer to him for any testimonial of character or ability which you may require.

Should my application meet your views, it will be my earnest endeavor to faithfully and punctually fulfill the duties required. I have the honor to remain,
Yours, Very Respectfully,
HOMER BUXTON.

Answering an Advertisement for a Cook.

48 Wentworth Ave., PITTSBURGH, PA.,
March 17, 1873.
MRS. D. N. HASKINS.
    Respected Madam:
    Seeing an advertisement in this morning's "Press" for a good plain and fancy cook, I take the opportunity to apply for the situation.

I have been with my present mistress, Mrs. Burton, for three years, and only leave because she has rented her house for the summer, to make an extended visit among her relatives in New England.

I shall remain here until Tuesday next, unless I find a place sooner, and Mrs Burton will give you any information you may desire regarding my capacity.
I Remain, Very Respectfully,
SARAH E. WESTON.

Answer to an Advertisement for a Chambermaid.

(Advertisement pasted in.)

No. —— St., NASHVILLE, TENN.,
Feb. 14, 18—.
DEAR MADAM:
    In answer to the above advertisement, I beg to state that I am about to leave my present situation, as Mrs. Harrington, with whom I have been for the past six years, is about breaking up housekeeping; and I take the opportunity to apply for the position you offer.

Mrs. Harrington assures me that she will take pleasure in recommending me to any person who may apply to her concerning my industry and trustworthiness.
MARGARET BALLENTINE.

Application for a Situation as Gardener.

No. —— 7th St., NEW YORK,
June 10, 18—.
DEAR SIR:
    Understanding that you want a gardener, I beg to offer myself as a candidate to fill the place. I have had constant experience for ten years, both in nursery grounds and private gardens, and am thoroughly acquainted with the management of the greenhouse and hothouse.

The enclosed testimonials, from gentlemen for whom I have worked, will, I trust, prove satisfactory. My last employer, Mr. Snow, I would like to have you see personally concerning my fitness for the position.

I am a married man, thirty-three years of age. If favorable to my application, please address as above, and oblige,
Your Obedient Servant,
JAMES H. HARPER.

Application for a Situation as Coachman.

178 —— St., Boston,
April 10, 18—.

Mr. John H. Williams.

Dear Sir:

Having been informed that you are in want of a coachman, I take the liberty of enclosing you the accompanying testimonials, to which I ask your attention. Though reared in Deerfield, I have been in Boston for the past fourteen years, having constantly had charge of horses during that time, as I did on the farm before leaving home.

As further evidence of my ability, I may mention that I had chief charge of the Tremont Street Livery Stable until the death of the owner, Mr. Paxton, after which the stock was sold and the stable closed.

Should my application meet your favor, I shall be glad to engage as your coachman, and will do all in my power to merit your approval.

Yours Respectfully,
HIRAM WILDER.

Application from a Governess Answering an Advertisement.

(Advertisement pasted in.)

No. 784 —— St., Troy, N. Y.,
July 18, 18—.

Mrs. C. B. Williams.

Dear Madam:

In answer to the above, I would say that I am seeking such a situation as you offer. My present term of teaching will close August 15th, at which time I would be ready to enter upon the work of superintending the education of your daughters.

I have, for several years, taught the higher English studies, besides German, Latin and drawing. For testimonials, I beg to refer you to the principal of my school, Rev. H. B. Watson.

Hoping that I may hear from you soon, and that we may make an arrangement mutually satisfactory, I remain,

Very Respectfully Yours,
HELEN B. CHANDLER.

Requesting the Character of a Governess.

No. 84 —— St., Troy, N. Y.,
July 19, 18—.

Rev. H. B. Watson,
Principal, Glenhaven Seminary.

My Dear Sir:

Having inserted an advertisement in the papers requiring the services of a governess competent to instruct my two daughters, I will esteem it a great favor if you will inform me concerning the ability of Miss Chandler to give instructions in the higher English studies, German and drawing, she having referred me to you.

I am especially desirous of securing the services of a young lady whose moral influence will guard my children from danger—one whose amiability of character will make her a pleasant companion as well as teacher. I am much pleased with the appearance of Miss Chandler, and, if your report is favorable, I shall not hesitate to perfect an engagement with her at once.

Yours, Very Respectfully,
CLARA B. WILLIAMS.

Favorable Reply to the Foregoing.

Glenhaven Seminary, N. Y.
July 21, 18—.

Mrs. Clara B. Williams.

Dear Madam:

Your letter of enquiry in regard to Miss Chandler is before me, in reply to which it affords me much pleasure to bear testimony to the high moral character, and superior intellectual culture, of which she is possessed. During five years' residence in our family she has ever been as one of our own household, and I can thus speak understandingly of her merits. She is thoroughly conversant with the higher English branches, and is quite fluent in Latin and German. Should you complete an engagement with her, I feel confident you will have every reason for being pleased with having done so.

Very Truly Yours,
HARVEY B. WATSON.

Unfavorable Reply to the Foregoing.

Glenhaven Seminary, N. Y.,
July 21, 18—.

Mrs. Clara B. Williams.

Dear Madam:

In reply to your polite inquiries, I am sorry to say that the educational acquirements of Miss Chandler, I fear, will not be up to the standard you require. While she has taught the higher English for some years, knowing, as I do, the proficiency of your daughters, I doubt if she is capable of advancing them in their studies. Another very unfortunate fault of which she is possessed, which causes me to dispense with her services at the close of the present term, is her failure to sufficiently command her temper. In other respects I have nothing to say to her prejudice.

Regretting that I cannot give a more favorable reply to your letter, I remain, Your Most Obedient Servant,
HARVEY B. WATSON.

Answering an Advertisement for an Apprentice to a Dressmaker.

(Advertisement pasted in.)

Mrs. Harriet Munson.   Chicago, Ill., Aug. 1, 18—.

Dear Madam:

In answer to the above, I respectfully apply for the situation. Though I never took up the business as a trade, I have long been in the habit of doing all the dressmaking for our family, and feel myself competent to do all plainer kinds of sewing neatly and rapidly.

Having recently, by the death of an only brother, been thrown upon my own resources, I am thus induced to seek a position which I think I will enjoy.

Hoping that you will accept my services, I remain,

Very Respectfully Yours,
PAMELIA HARRISON.

Answer to an Advertisement for a Music-Teacher.

Walnut Grove Academy, Mass.,
June 9, 18—.

Col. H. B. Darling.

Dear Sir:

Seeing your advertisement in to-day's "Journal," I write to offer my services as music-teacher in your family.

I am a graduate of Music Vale Seminary, and have taught a music-class in this institution for the past three terms. My training has been with special reference to teaching the piano, the guitar, and vocal music.

I am permitted by Professor Weston, the teacher of music in the Academy, to refer to him for any testimonial of ability. I am,

Yours, Very Respectfully,
AMELIA D. PORTER.

Answering an Advertisement for an Apprentice to a Printer.

Troy Grove, Ill.,
Feb. 4, 18—.

Mr. A. B. Cook.

Dear Sir:

Having seen your advertisement in the last *Eagle*, I would respectfully apply for the position for my son Henry, who is anxious to learn printing. He is well versed in the common English branches, having been regular in attendance at the public school for the past seven years. He is now fifteen.

I would like to have you take him on trial for a few weeks, and, if he pleases you, will arrange to have him remain until he masters the trade.

Respectfully Yours,
Z. K. HENDERSON.

Letters of Recommendation.

KNOWLEDGE of persons recommended, of their fitness and capacity for the work they engage in, is always essential, before they can be conscientiously commended to others.

A letter of recommendation should be written in a plain hand, in as few words as can be used to express the idea distinctly.

A recommendation, after considering the moral character of the individual, should relate directly to the work of which the person makes a specialty.

An individual giving a recommendation is, in a certain sense, responsible for the character and ability of the person recommended; hence, certificates of character should be given with caution and care.

Recommending a Salesman.

SYRACUSE, N. Y., April 10, 18—.

MESSRS. DUTTON & BROWN.
    Dear Sirs:
        Your favor of the 4th inst., relative to the ability of Mr. Benjamin Walker, is received. We take great pleasure in testifying to his high moral worth and his business capacity. He was in our employ for four years, as a salesman, during which time his affability and uniform courtesy to customers, coupled with his truthful representations in regard to goods, made him a universal favorite.

Accurate in accounts, ready and graceful as a penman, attentive and kind to all, he is a most useful man in the counting-room; and the firm securing his services may be congratulated on their good fortune.

Very Truly Yours,
        SMITH & PAXTON.

Recommending a Schoolmistress.

GLEN DALE SEMINARY,
        March 1, 18—.

GEN. A. B. COTTRELL.
    Dear Sir:
        It gives me pleasure, in reply to your note of the 24th ult., to most cordially recommend Miss Fannie Chapman to the position of teacher of your village school.

As a graduate of this Seminary, and subsequently as a teacher, much of the time conducting the various classes alone, she has proven herself thoroughly competent to conduct a school under almost any circumstances.

Though very amiable, she is a strict disciplinarian, and thoroughly conversant with the ordinary branches of an English education.

Yours Respectfully,
        DELOS SIMPSON,
            Principal Glen Dale Seminary.

Recommending a Bookkeeper.

WHITEHALL, N. Y., Sept. 10, 18—.

Mr. Ransom Fellows having been in my employ for the past two years as a bookkeeper, it gives me great pleasure to testify to his ability. He is an upright, conscientious, exemplary young man, a good penman and accountant, and a most faithful clerk. He leaves my employ voluntarily, with my best wishes.

MARTIN BIGELOW.

Recommending a Waiter.

TREMONT HOUSE, CHICAGO,
        Aug. 11, 18—.

Arthur Brooks, who has been in my employ for two years, has given entire satisfaction, both to myself and guests, as a table-waiter. Honest, obliging and neat, it affords me pleasure, as he now leaves my employ, to commend him as a first-class hotel waiter.

BROWN PORTER,
        Steward, Tremont House.

Recommending a Cook.

HARRISBURG, PA., Dec. 20, 18—.

This is to certify that Catherine Miller did the cooking for my family some ten months, to my entire satisfaction, serving me both as a plain and fancy cook. She is very attentive to her work, and strictly honest and reliable.

MYRA D. ROWE.

Recommending a Washerwoman.

NEW ORLEANS, LA., May 7, 18—.

This certifies that Hannah Webber, who has been employed in my laundry for the past year, is an excellent washer and ironer, understanding fine starching, crimping, polishing, etc.

HELEN MAYDWELL.

Recommending a Porter.

CHARLESTON, S. C., Sept. 18, 18—.

Donald Kennedy, the bearer of this, has been in my employ, as a porter, for the last eighteen months. He is a strong, honest, reliable man, and always very punctual, careful, and faithful in the discharge of his duty.

JOHN H. BLISS.

Declining to Recommend a Cook.

SAVANNAH, GA., Oct. 10, 18—.

MRS. BALLARD:
        In reply to your note of enquiry, I decline to recommend Bridget Mallory. She is both dishonest and addicted to intemperance.

HENRIETTA SANFORD.

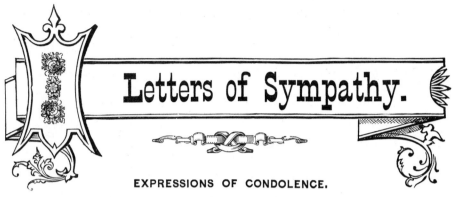

EXPRESSIONS OF CONDOLENCE.

 A LETTER of sympathy and condolence, though unpleasant to write, may afford inexpressible comfort to a friend in the hour of affliction.

Make your letter as brief, but earnest and sincere, as possible.

Do not commit the mistake of insinuating that the misfortune is the fault of your friend. Better leave the letter unwritten.

Admit the loss. Do not attempt to make light of it. If you are satisfied that it will eventuate in a blessing, you may gently point the way, but with a full admission of the present deep affliction.

To a Friend, on the Death of a Husband.

NEWARK, O., Oct. 18, 18—.

DEAR FRIEND:

I know that no words can make amends for the great loss you have sustained. I deeply realize, from having passed through a similar bereavement, that expressions of condolence wholly fail to restore the loved and lost one, yet I cannot but hope that the heartfelt sympathy of a sincere friend will not be deemed intrusion on your grief.

It has been well said, that "we weep for the loved and lost because we know that our tears are in vain." I would ease your sorrow, and yet ı know not how. We can only acknowledge that the affliction is God's will. Over in the beautiful land to which I trust your life-companion has gone, we may not doubt, he is free from the pains that he so long endured here; and when *we* gather at the river, is it not a sweet consolation to think that among the loved and lost he may meet you on the other side?

Commending you to Him who doeth all things well, I remain, in the tenderest friendship,

Your Sincere Friend,
WINFIELD BROWN.

To MRS. CLARA WAYLAND,
Columbus, O.

Reply to the Foregoing.

COLUMBUS, O., Oct. 20, 18—.

MY DEAR FRIEND:

I can scarcely express to you how grateful I am for your sympathizing letter, yet the loss of my husband has so prostrated me that I am hardly able to write this reply.

My friends assure me that time will reconcile me to my great bereavement. Yes, time, and the great consolation that you speak of, which comes from the hope that we will meet our friends in a world where partings are no more, will, I trust, enable me to bear my sorrow. God bless you for your thought of me in the dark hours, and your sweet words of consolation.

Your Friend,
CLARA WAYLAND.

To a Friend, on the Death of a Mother.

EVANSVILLE, TENN., Oct. 16, 18—.

FRIEND ALBERT:

I have just learned, on my return from a visit in the far West, of the death of your mother. Having suffered the loss of my mother when a child, I know how to sympathize with you in your affliction; though, fortunately for you, your mother lived to guide the footsteps of her boy till manhood's years had crowned his intellect with judgment and fixed moral principles. It can truly be said that, in the training of her family, in the church, in the social circle, she always did her duty nobly, and was an ornament to society. Ripened in years, and fully prepared for another state of existence, she passes on now to enjoy the reward of a life well spent on earth.

Restored to maidenhood prime, we cannot doubt that in the flowery walks of spirit life she is the same good woman that we knew so well here.

Truly Yours,
HARTLEY JONES.

To A. H. STEWART,
Belle Plain, Miss.

To a Friend, on the Death of a Brother.

LEXINGTON, Mo., Dec. 10, 18—.

DEAR HENRY:

I have learned with profound regret of the death of your brother. I condole with you most sincerely on the sad event, and, if sympathy of friends can be any consolation under the trying circumstances, be assured that all who knew him share in your sorrow for his loss. There is, however, a higher source of consolation than earthly friendship, and, commending you to that, I remain,

Yours Faithfully,
SANFORD F. BARTON.

To a Friend, on the Death of a Wife.

BURLINGTON, IOWA, Nov. 10, 18—.

MY DEAR DELWIN:

I know that this letter will find you filled with grief at the loss of your dear wife. You have, indeed, suffered a great affliction. A more faithful partner never lived, and few men, I venture to say, ever enjoyed more domestic tranquility than yourself.

A true wife, and a devoted mother! No higher eulogy can be pronounced upon any woman. How the little motherless children will miss her tender care! How those fragile little girls will miss her sweet presence at the evening hour, when she sat by the bedside and listened to their innocent prayers, soothing their little spirits as they dropped off to sleep! Truly the great central sun of your household has gone down, and I most truly, deeply sympathize with you in your affliction.

Let us hope, however, in the language of Scripture, "I go to prepare a place for you," that, in the golden summer of another life, children, mother and father will gather again in a sweet reunion, where partings are unknown.

Though the days are dark now, spring will come once more. Thus, I trust, pleasant days will come again for you and yours.

Send both of the little girls to our home for a month's visit, and come yourself as soon as you can find time to do so. My previously arranged departure, to-morrow, prevents my visiting you.

Your Friend,
S. B. OSGOOD.

To D. B. MAXWELL,
Henderson, Kentucky.

To a Friend, on the Death of a Sister.

AUBURN, N. Y., July 16, 18—.

DEAR FRIEND:

I have learned, with sorrow, of the death of your sister Helen. Though I never knew her personally, I knew her so well through you, that it seems as if I, myself, had lost a very near and intimate friend. I recollect her from that sweet face and gentleness of manner, as I saw her once in your company, that impressed me with the belief that she was one of the angelic ones of earth.

I know how deeply you must have grieved at her death. No one could mourn her loss so truly as yourself. Younger than you, frail and delicate, her guardianship entrusted to yourself, confiding everything to you, it was natural that to a sister's affection should be added, also, almost a mother's love for your gentle sister Helen. She died, too, at a time when life was apparently all blossoming before her. How hard to reconcile ourselves to the loss of dear kindred, when their continued presence is so necessary to our happiness. But may we not hope that the same sweet voice, and gentle, confiding heart, that was so dear to sister and kindred here, is waiting for you in the summer land? "Not dead, but gone before."

The loss of near friends thus calls for our contemplation of another life toward which we are all tending. You and I, dear M., have talked these matters over often. I know you expect to meet her on the other side; so do I. Believing that your faith in that golden, sunny Future, which you and I have so often considered, will sustain you, I am,

Your Ever Faithful Friend,
JAS. D. HENRY.

To a Friend, on the Death of a Daughter.

HARTFORD, CONN., Nov. 14, 18—.

MY DEAR FRIEND:

It is with profound sorrow that I have heard of the death of dear Mary. While you have lost a dutiful and affectionate daughter, I have lost one of the dearest friends on earth. Outside of yourself, I am confident no one could more fully appreciate her loss than myself. We were so much together that I can hardly reconcile myself to the thought that I can no more meet her here. True, her death teaches us that, sooner or later, we must all make the journey across that mystic river. The angels called, and, in the ways of an

all-wise Providence, it was best that she should go. We all have the ordeal to pass. Fortunate it would be if all could be as certain of being among the exalted angels as was our darling Mary. I will come and see you soon. *A propos*, I send you this little poem, "The Covered Bridge."

Your Friend,   MYRA.

THE COVERED BRIDGE.

BY DAVID BARKER.

Tell the fainting soul in the weary form,
    There 's a world of the purest bliss,
That is linked, as the soul and form are linked,
    By a Covered Bridge, with this.

Yet to reach that realm on the other shore
    We must pass through a transient gloom,
And must walk, unseen, unhelped, and alone,
    Through that Covered Bridge—the tomb.

But we all pass over on equal terms,
    For the universal toll
Is the outer garb, which the hand of God
    Has flung around the soul.

Though the eye is dim, and the bridge is dark,
    And the river it spans is wide,
Yet Faith points through to a shining mount,
    That looms on the other side.

To enable our feet in the next day's march
    To climb up that golden ridge,
We must all lie down for one night's rest
    Inside of the Covered Bridge.

To a Friend, on the Death of an Infant.

PEMBERTON, MISS., Nov. 18, 18—.

MY DEAR FRIEND:

I realize that this letter will find you buried in the deepest sorrow at the loss of your darling little Emma, and that words of mine will be entirely inadequate to assuage your overwhelming grief; yet I feel that I must write a few words to assure you that I am thinking of you and praying for you.

If there can be a compensating thought, it is that your darling returned to the God who gave it, pure and unspotted by the world's temptations.

The white rose and bud, I send, I trust you will permit to rest upon your darling's pillow.

With feelings of the deepest sympathy, I remain, dear friend,

Yours, Very Sincerely,
MARION BRADSHAW.

To a Friend, on a Sudden Reverse of Fortune.

HANNIBAL, MO., Aug. 18, 18—.

FRIEND STEWART:

I regret to hear of your sudden and unexpected heavy loss, and hasten to offer you, not only my earnest sympathy, but aid in whatever way I can assist you.

I know your energy and hopeful spirit too well to believe that you will allow this to depress or discourage you from further effort. Perhaps there is, somewhere, a blessing in this reverse. I have had my dark days, but I learned to trust the truth of that little stanza of Cowper:

"Judge not the Lord by feeble sense,
    But trust him for his grace;
Behind a frowning Providence
    He hides a smiling face."

The child learns to walk after many falls, and many of our richest and most prosperous men have attained their eminence and wealth only by the experience resulting from failure.

I predict that you will build on your ruins a brilliant future. How can I serve you? Let me know; by so doing, I shall understand that you have not ceased to value my friendship.

Sincerely Your Friend,
HERBERT D. WRIGHT.

To ROB'T H. STEWART,
Singleton, Me.

Letters of Congratulation.

ETTERS of Congratulation are very properly written upon receiving intelligence of the sudden prosperity of a near and intimate friend.

They should be written as soon as possible after the occasion that calls them forth.

These letters will admit of an abundance of good-natured merriment.

Do not indulge in over-praise, or too much flowery exaggeration, lest your friend may doubt your sincerity.

No envy or discontent should show itself in such a letter. Nor should the same be marred by advice, bad news, the expression of any doubt, or any unfavorable prediction calculated to throw a cloud over the happiness of your friend.

Form of Letter Congratulating a Friend upon Election to Office.

Troy, N. Y., Feb. 1, 18—.

My Dear Friend Callie:

My newspaper informs me that the people of your County have shown their good judgment by selecting you to represent them as Superintendent of Public Schools. It affords me unfeigned pleasure to hear of the choice falling upon yourself. I am confident that no person in your district could fill the place more worthily.

Accept my congratulations.

Yours Truly,

S. D. Willing.

To Miss Callie M. Spencer,
Cedar Grove, Ill.

Congratulating a Friend upon Receiving a Legacy.

APPLETON, WIS., Jan. 1, 18—.

FRIEND GEORGE:

I have learned to-day, through our friend Charlie Goodwin, of your good fortune in receiving a very material addition to your worldly possessions. Good! I congratulate you. I know of no one who more justly deserves good fortune, and of no person who will use it more worthily. You would be ever the same to me, whether good or ill success should attend your pathway. As it is, I take a friend's delight in congratulating you upon your fortune.

Your Friend,

DANIEL TEMPLETON.

Congratulating a Gentleman upon his Marriage.

KINGSTON, CANADA, April 4, 18—.

DEAR WILL:

I have just received a little missive, which informs me of two happy hearts made one. I wish you much joy. You have my earnest congratulations on the event, and good wishes for a long and serenely happy married life. May each succeeding year find you happier than the one before.

God bless you and yours, and surround you ever with his choicest blessings.

Your Friend,

JOHN K. BUEL.

Congratulating a Friend upon the Birth of a Son.

GRACELAND, FLA., Jan. 3, 18—.

DEAR CLARK:

Accept my warmest congratulations upon the birth of your son. May his years be long in the land which the Lord giveth him. May he honor his father and his mother, and be the blessing and support of their declining years. I anticipate holding the young gentleman on my knee, and will be over to see you in a few days.

My kindest regards to Mrs. Henry. I remain,

Faithfully Your Friend,

DEB. HARTWELL.

Congratulating a Friend upon the Twenty-fifth Anniversary of his Wedding Day.

DARTMOUTH, N. H., March 5, 18—.

MY DEAR MR. BANCROFT:

I acknowledge the receipt of a kind invitation to be present at the celebration of the twenty-fifth anniversary of your marriage. I have since learned that large numbers of your friends were present on the occasion, presenting you with an abundant and varied collection of silver, and other elegant and appropriate gifts.

I congratulate you and your good wife upon passing the signal-station indicating a quarter of a century of blissful wedded life. That you may both live to allow your friends to celebrate your golden and diamond weddings, is the hope of,

Your Sincere Friend,

PERRY OLMSTED.

Congratulating a Lady upon her Approaching Marriage.

BANGOR, ME., Dec. 2, 18—.

DEAR CATHERINE:

Two beautiful cards on my table advise me of your approaching nuptials. Allow me to congratulate you upon the choice of such a noble man, to whom you are to entrust your life's happiness. That the mid-day and evening of your married life may be as cloudless and beautiful as the morning, is the earnest wish of,

Your Loving Friend,

NELLIE GRANT.

Congratulating a Friend on Passing a Successful School Examination.

UTICA, N. Y., April 6, 18—.

DEAR HELEN:

I was greatly pleased to hear, through our friend Mary, that you had, through diligent application, passed through the prescribed course of study in the Aurora public schools, and had graduated with honors. Knowing how deeply interested your parents and relatives have been in your success, it is particularly gratifying to have you reward them by the achievement of such rapid progress. Accept my best wishes for your future success.

Your Friend,

DELLA MAYNARD.

Congratulating an Author upon the Success of his Book.

MARENGO, VA., May 7, 18—.

FRIEND KEMPLE:

I have just finished an attentive examination of your most valuable book, and cannot wonder, after a careful reading, that it is meeting so large a sale. The world is greatly indebted to you for presenting in such an attractive form the amount of useful information you have collected within its pages.

Thanking you for the benefit I have obtained from its perusal, I remain,   Yours Truly,

SILAS ACKLEY.

Congratulating a Friend upon Obtaining a Business Situation.

ASHBURY, PA., June 8, 18—.

FRIEND JOHN:

I am greatly pleased to learn that, notwithstanding the general dullness of business, you have succeeded in obtaining a clerkship. I doubt not your firm will regard themselves fortunate in securing your services. In the meantime, accept my congratulations upon your success.

Hoping that your stay may be permanent and prosperous, I am,

Yours Truly,

CHARLES BELSHAW.

JOHN BELDEN.

Letters of Introduction.

LETTERS of Introduction should be written very plainly, and should be brief, as the person introduced is compelled to wait while the letter is being read.

In introducing a person in a business capacity, state distinctly what is his business; if a professional man, his profession, and your knowledge or information of his ability.

The letter of introduction should be left unsealed. It would be a great discourtesy to prevent the bearer from seeing what you have written.

As in letters of recommendation, the person giving a letter of introduction is, in a measure, responsible for the character and ability of the person introduced. Hence, such letters should be guardedly written, or given with full knowledge of the person they introduce.

That the person receiving such a letter may know at a glance its character, the letter should, on the envelope, be addressed thus:

Chas. D. Kingsbury, Esq.,
Introducing   478 Broadway,
Wm. H. Brown,   New York.
of Cleveland, O.

Presenting the letter of introduction at the private house, send it by the servant to the person addressed, accompanied with your card.

At the business house, send the letter to the counting-room, accompanied by your card.

Introducing one Gentleman to Another.

NORWAY, MAINE, July 9, 18—.

FRIEND WILLIAM.

The bearer of this, Mr. Sterling Hepworth, is a dry-goods merchant in our town, who visits your city for the purpose of making purchases for his fall trade. Mr. H. is a heavy dealer in his line, pays cash for all he buys, and expects the discount accompanying cash payment. Any favor you can render him by introduction to your leading wholesale houses, or otherwise, will be appreciated by Mr. Hepworth, and acknowledged by,

Your Friend,
WALTER KIMBALL.

WILLIAM DARLING.

Introducing one Lady to Another.

ROME, GA., Aug. 10, 18—.

DEAR ANNABEL:

I take this occasion to introduce to you the bearer of this letter, Mrs. Pemberton, who is on a visit to her relatives in your city. Mrs. P. is my very dear friend, of whom you have often heard me speak. Believing that your acquaintance with each other would be mutually agreeable, I have urged her to call upon you during her stay. Any attention you may bestow upon her, during her visit, will be highly appreciated by,

Your Friend,
DELIA MAYBORNE.

Introducing a Young Musician to a Lady Friend.

SALEM, MASS., Sept. 12, 18—.

MRS. STEPHEN HAWKINS.
Dear Friend:

The bearer, Miss Serena Snow, visits your city for the purpose of pursuing a musical education, being as yet undetermined whom she will choose as an instructor. Any advice and assistance you may render will be highly appreciated by her, and duly acknowledged by her parents, who have great confidence in your judgment in matters pertaining to music.

Trusting that you will find it agreeable to aid my young friend, I remain,

Yours Sincerely,
MARY A. BARNET.

Introducing an Officer to a Brother-Officer.

HOLYOKE, MASS., Sept. 17, 18—.

DEAR CAPTAIN:

My old-time comrade, Capt. H. M. Benson, visits your town for the purpose of attending the Army Reunion on the 27th. As he will remain some little time, I commend him to your brotherly care. Believing that your acquaintance will be mutually agreeable, I remain,

Fraternally Yours,
T. M. SEYMOUR.

CAPT. A. M. BELLOWS.

Introducing a Gentleman Seeking a Clerkship.

DENVER, COL., Oct. 13, 18—.

FRIEND PATTERSON:

This letter will introduce to you my young friend, Morgan Hatfield, who has been in my employ as a clerk for the past eighteen months, and whom I would still retain, had not the disposing of a portion of my business rendered his services, with those of others of my clerks, unnecessary.

Believing that your wide influence would very materially aid him in securing a good position in the dry-goods trade in your city, I presume upon the acquaintance of an old friend in thus writing you. For reference you can use my name.

Believing that you will not afterwards regret any assistance you render the young man, I am,

Your Friend,
HERBERT HOPKINS.

A. B. PATTERSON, ESQ.

Introducing a Sister to a Schoolmate.

SALEM, OREGON, Nov. 14, 18—.

DEAR FRIEND:

This will be brought you by my sister Callie, of whom you have heard me talk so much. No words of mine are necessary in introducing you. I have told you both so much of each other that you are already acquainted. I bid you love each other as well as I love you both.

Affectionately Yours,
JENNIE.

MISS LIZZIE BRAYTON.

Introducing a Clerk to an Old Fellow-Clerk.

SILVER CITY, NEW MEXICO, Dec. 18, 18—.

DEAR HAL.:

My friend and fellow-clerk, Wm. Bell, will spend a week in your city, and wants to look at the desk where you and I stood, side by side, so long. You will find him a genial, friendly fellow, and will most assuredly not regret my sending him to you.

Ever Your Friend,
CON. BALDWIN.

HALBERT STEBBINS.

Introducing a Student to the Writer's Mother.

SAN FRANCISCO, CAL., Feb. 2, 18—.

DEAR MOTHER:

The bearer of this is my college chum, Harry Worthington. Being about to visit his parents at San Jose, I have persuaded him to stop over one train to see you and sister Kate. Harry is in the same class with myself, and is, I can assure you, a splendid fellow. Of course, you and Kate will treat him so finely as to make him, perhaps, stay longer than one day. He will tell you all the news.

Your Ever Affectionate Son,
SAMMY DOBBIN.

Introducing a Friend to a Member of Congress.

DOVER, DEL., Mar. 3, 18—.

HON. D. B. GRAHAM.

Respected Sir:

The bearer, Mr. D. H. Harmon, is the son of Mrs. Lieut. W. H. Harmon, of this town, whose husband was killed at the battle of Iuka, bravely defending the flag. This young man has just graduated from one of our best schools, and at my suggestion visits Washington, thinking to acquaint himself with the condition of things at the Capitol, and, if the same could be obtained, would gladly occupy a clerkship for a time. Should it be in your power to grant him such a favor, it will be warmly appreciated by his mother and myself. I remain,

Yours Respectfully,
V. H. MARTIN.

Introducing a Literary Lady to a Publisher.

BATON ROUGE, LA., March 4, 18—.

MR. WARREN H. WEBSTER.

Dear Sir:

The bearer, Mrs. Lydia Huntington, visits New York for the purpose of conferring with some publisher relative to introducing her first book to the public. She is a lady of well-known reputation and acknowledged talent throughout the South, and will, I feel sure, assume prominent rank ere long in the literary world. I take the liberty of an old friend to ask of you a consideration of her claims.

Yours, Very Respectfully,
B. H. CAMPBELL.

Introducing a Daughter About to Make a Visit.

CHARLESTON, S. C., May 6, 18—.

MY DEAR MRS. HAMILTON:

In compliance with your oft-repeated request, I send my daughter to spend a few weeks of her vacation in your delightful country home, trusting that her visit may be as delightful for her and yourself as mine was a year ago. Anticipating a visit from you all, ere the close of the present summer, I remain,

As Ever, Your Devoted Friend,
MARY DAVENPORT.

Letters of Advice.

 OUR life has been a success," said an individual to an old and prosperous business man. "To what do you attribute your success?" "To an admonition given me by my father, when a boy, which was this:

"First, to attend strictly to my own business. Second, to let other people's business alone. Observing this, I incurred no ill will by inter-meddling with others, and I saved my time for the development and improvement of my own business."

Be very sparing of letters of advice. As a rule, you will have enough to do to attend to your own affairs; and, as a general thing, advice even when solicited is liable to give offence.

If, however, you are asked to give an opinion, you may plainly state it. Do not give it, however, as a law, nor feel offended if your advice is disregarded.

Beware of giving advice from selfishness. Sooner or later your motive will be discovered. Let your admonition be alone for the interest and welfare of your friend. If you expect, however, to be benefited by the course which you advise the person to pursue, you may frankly state the fact.

Advising a Young Lady to Refuse Gifts from Gentlemen.

Monroeville, O., Feb. 2, 18——.

My Dear Caroline:

Your letter of the 28th ult. is before me. I regret to learn that you accepted of a bracelet at the hands of Wm. Spencer. By all means return it. In its acceptance you place yourself under obligation to him, as you would to any one from whom you accept presents, unless you render an equivalent.

Nothing will more surely injure a young lady's reputation than the acceptance of many presents from different young men. When married, the gifts of your husband will come hallowed with his affection. Until then, refuse gifts from all gentlemen.

I am,

Your Sincere Friend,

Harriet McInhill.

Letter Advising a Young Man to Beware of Bad Company.

WASHINGTON, D. C., Jan. 1, 18—.

MY DEAR YOUNG FRIEND:

I observe, by the tone of your last letter, that you are becoming very intimate with Henry Hubbard and Barney McIntosh. I need not tell you that your letter has given me much uneasiness. These young men are bad characters, and you cannot continue your association with them, without contaminating your morals.

I am an old man, and I write this, my boy, with a most earnest desire for your happiness. You have acquired a fine education, and have entered upon your profession with every prospect of success. You have a widowed mother to support, and an orphaned sister looking to you for guidance. It becomes you, therefore, to maintain a reputation unsullied, and obtain a good credit, which, to a young man in the commencement of a business career, is equal to a large capital of itself.

Association with these young men will certainly carry you downward. They are both without employment, they drive fast horses, they wear flash jewelry, they frequent gambling-houses, they both use intoxicating drink, chew tobacco, and talk profane language. What would you think of another that might be seen in their company? People will judge you as you would judge any one else. There is much truth in the old proverb, " A man is known by the company he keeps," and I would have your company such as will reflect the highest honor upon yourself.

I have written this letter earnestly and strongly, for I believe your good judgment will take it kindly; and I trust, when you sincerely reflect upon the matter, you will at once dismiss that class of associates from your company.

Your Earnest Well-Wisher
and Sincere Friend,
DAVID CLINE.

Advising a Young Man Against a Hurried Marriage.

RUTLAND, VT., April 5, 18—.

FRIEND CHARLES:

You ask me if you will not act the wiser part by marrying Miss Manchester at once, and settling yourself permanently; and yet you inform me that it has been but three weeks since you first made her acquaintance. You may possibly be in jest, and perhaps in earnest; in either case, as you ask my advice, I can but give it.

The choosing of a life-companion, dear Charles, is a too serious matter to be so hastily decided. The selection of a partner for a dance or a ride may be of little moment; the choice of an associate for business may be determined in a short time; but the acceptance of a partner for life requires the most serious deliberation. You should take ample time for the study of the character, temperament, disposition and accomplishments of the lady whom you choose to be the sharer of your labors, joys, sorrows, reverses and prosperity.

Upon this step hangs a large share of your happiness in life. Do not act too hastily. Trusting, however, that I will some day see you happily married and settled, I am, as ever,

Your Most Sincere Friend,
GEORGE BATCHELDER.

Advice to a Gentleman on the Subject of Health.

BOSTON, MASS., May 6, 18—.

MY DEAR FRIEND:

Yours of the 2d inst. is before me. I am pleased with the prospect that you report in your business, but regret that you should be discouraged about your health. You ask me what you had better do; I will answer.

The first great secret of good health is good habits; and the next is *regularity* of habits. They are briefly summed up in the following rules:

1.—*Sleep.* Give yourself the necessary amount of sleep. Some men require five hours of the twenty-four; others need eight. Avoid feather beds. Sleep in a garment not worn during the day. To maintain robust health, sleep with a person as healthy as yourself, or no one.

2.—*Dress.* In cold weather, dress warmly with underclothing. Remove muffler, overcoat, overshoes, etc., when remaining any considerable length of time in a warm room. Keep your feet warm and dry. Wash them, in warm water, two or three times a week. Wear warm stockings, large boots, and overshoes when in the snow or wet. Wear a light covering on the head, always keeping it cool.

3.—*Cleanliness.* Have always a pint or quart of water in the sleeping room. In the morning, after washing and wiping hands and face, then wet, with the hands, every part of the body. Cold water will not be disagreeable when applying it with the bare hands. Wipe immediately; follow by brisk rubbing over the body. The whole operation need not take over five minutes. The result of this wash is, the blood is brought to the surface of the skin, and made to circulate evenly throughout the body. You have opened the pores of the skin, allowing impurities in the body to pass off, and have given yourself in the operation a good, vigorous morning exercise. Pursue this habit regularly, and you will seldom take cold.

4.—*Inflation of the Lungs.* Five minutes spent in the open air, after dressing, inflating the lungs by inhaling as full a breath as possible, and pounding the breast during the inflation, will greatly enlarge the chest, strengthen the lung power, and very effectually ward off consumption.

5.—*Diet.* If inclined to be dyspeptic, avoid mince pie, sausage and other highly seasoned food. Beware of eating too freely of soups; better to eat food dry enough to employ the natural saliva of the mouth in moistening it. If inclined to over-eat, partake freely of rice, cracked wheat, and other articles that are easily digested.

Eat freely of ripe fruit, and avoid excessive use of meats. Eat at regular hours, and lightly near the hour of going to bed. Eat slowly. Thoroughly masticate the food. Do not wash it down with continual drink while eating. Tell your funniest stories while at the table and for an hour afterwards. Do not engage in severe mental labor directly after hearty eating.

6.—*Exercise.* Exercise, not too violent, but sufficient to produce a gentle perspiration, should be had each day in the open air.

7.—*Condition of Mind.* The condition of the mind has much to do with health. Be hopeful and joyous. To be so, avoid business entanglements that may cause perplexity and anxiety. Keep out of debt. Live within your income. Attend church. Walk, ride, mix in jovial company. Do as nearly right as you know how. Thus, conscience will always be at ease. If occasionally disappointed, remember that there is no rose without a thorn, and that the darkest clouds have a silver lining; that sunshine follows storm, and beautiful spring follows the dreary winter. Do your duty, and leave the rest to God, who doeth all things well.

Hoping to hear of your continued prosperity and recovery of health, I am,

Your Very Sincere Friend,
SIBLEY JOHNSON, M. D.

ALLEN MATLOCK.

Advice to an Orphan Boy.

ARLINGTON, N. C., June 7, 18—.

MY DEAR CHARLIE:

I received your letter last evening. I was greatly pleased to hear that you have secured a position with Colby, Henderson & Co., and that your sisters are comfortably situated in their new homes. You ask me for advice as to what you shall do to maintain the good opinion of your employers, and thus ultimately prosperously establish yourself.

This desire that you evince to please is one of the very best evidences that you *will* please. Your question is very commendable. How can you succeed? That should be the great question with all young men. It is best answered, perhaps, by the reply of the wealthy and honored old man, who gave this advice to his grandson:

" My boy, take the admonition of an old man who has seen every phase of human life.

" If I could give you but one precept to follow, it would be, *Keep good company.* But, adding more, I will say:

" Be truthful; you thus always have the confidence of others.

" Be temperate; thus doing, you preserve health and money.

" Be industrious; you will then be constantly adding to your acquisitions.

" Be economical; thus, you will be saving for the rainy day.

" Be cautious; you are not then so liable to lose the work of years.

" Be polite and kind; scattering words of kindness, they are reflected back upon yourself, continually adding to your happiness."

Observe these directions, and you will prosper. With many wishes for your success, remember I am always,

Your Friend,
ABEL MATTOCK.

ETTERS of Excuse should be written as promptly as may be.

Any damage that may have been caused by yourself, you should, if possible, repair immediately, with interest.

In apologizing for misconduct, failing to meet an engagement, or for lack of punctuality, always state the reason why.

By fulfilling every engagement promptly, discharging every obligation when due, and always being punctual, you thereby entirely avoid the necessity for an excuse.

Any article borrowed by measure, be certain to return in larger quantity and better quality, to make up the interest. To fail to make good that which has been borrowed is the certain loss of credit and business reputation in the neighborhood where you live. No letter of apology can make amends for neglecting to pay your debts.

Apologizing for a Broken Engagement.

FREDERICK, MD., July 13, 18—.

MY DEAR MISS MERTON:

I fear that you will feel injured at my failure to keep my appointment this evening. You will, however, I know, forgive me when I explain. When about to proceed to your residence, my horse, being very restive, became so frightened at an object by the roadside as to cause his runaway, throwing me violently to the ground, breaking an arm, and completely demolishing my carriage. Regretting my failure to keep my engagement, I am yet rejoiced that the accident occurred before you had entered the carriage.

Trusting that my excuse is a sufficient apology, I remain,

Your Faithful Friend,

ALBERT BIGBEE.

Apologizing for Failure to Pay Money Promptly.

DANBY, N. Y., July 11, 18—.

MR. D. B. FRISBIE.

Dear Sir:

I very much regret that the failure of H. Cole & Son will prevent my payment of your note on the 20th instant, without serious inconvenience to myself. I shall be able to pay it, however, promptly on the 25th. Should the five days' delay seriously incommode you, please write me at once, and I will aim to procure the money from another source.

Your Obedient Servant,

DANIEL FRAZIER.

Excuse to a Teacher for Non-Attendance of Child at School.

WEDNESDAY MORNING, Sept. 4, 18—.

MISS BLAKE:

You will please excuse Gertrude for non-attendance at school yesterday afternoon, she being detained in consequence of a severe headache.

Very Respectfully,

MARCIA BARROWS

Apology for Breaking a Business Engagement.

MONTICELLO, ILL., Oct. 15, 18—.

MR. PAUL D. WARREN,
Kensington.

Dear Sir:

I very much regret being compelled to apologize for not meeting you at the railroad meeting in Salem last Saturday, as I agreed to do. The cause of my detention was the sudden and severe illness of my youngest child, whose life for a time we despaired of. Please write me the result of the meeting. Hoping that the arrangements we anticipated were perfected, I am,

Yours Truly,

SOLOMON KING.

Apology for Delay in Returning a Book.

KENTLAND, IND., Nov. 19, 18—.

MY DEAR AMY:

You must excuse my long delay in returning your book. The truth is, it has been the rounds for several to read, though it has not been out of our house. When I had nearly finished its reading, Aunt Mary became interested in its contents and read it through. Her glowing description of the character of the work caused mother to peruse it; so that we have kept it from you several weeks. We feel very grateful to you, however, for furnishing us such an intellectual feast, and hope to have the pleasure of doing you a like favor.

Truly Your Friend,

LIZZIE BRAINARD.

Letters Asking Favors.

T is to be hoped that you will not often be compelled to write a letter asking a favor.

Do not urge your claims too strongly. Should you be refused, you will feel the more deeply humiliated.

In conferring a favor, avoid conveying the impression that the recipient is greatly under obligation to you. Rather imply that the granting and accepting of the favor is mutually a pleasure.

Letters refusing a favor should be very kindly worded, and, while expressing regret at your inability to comply with the request, state the reason why.

Requesting the Loan of a Book.

WEDNESDAY MORNING, JAN. 1, 18—.

DEAR BERTHA:

Will you be so kind as to loan me, for a few days, "How I Found Livingstone?" By so doing, you will greatly oblige,

Your Friend,

NANNIE WHITE.

Reply Granting the Favor.

WEDNESDAY MORNING, Jan. 1, 18—.

DEAR NANNIE:

I send you the book with pleasure, and hope you will enjoy its perusal as much as I did. I shall be over to see you next Thursday afternoon.

Affectionately Yours,

BERTHA.

Requesting a Loan of Money.

LISBON, ILL., Feb. 2, 18—.

FRIEND BAKER:

Will you do me the kindness to loan me one hundred dollars until Wednesday of next week. Having several large collections to make during the next three days, I may return the loan before then. Yours Truly,

GEORGE HASKINS.

Answer Refusing the Request.

LISBON, ILL., Feb. 2, 18—.

FRIEND HASKINS:

I regret that all the money I have at liberty I am compelled to use this afternoon; else I would comply with your request with pleasure. Respectfully,

JOHN BAKER.

Requesting a Letter of Introduction.

SPRINGFIELD, MASS., March 4, 18—.

FRIEND RICH:

I start for Boston to-morrow, to make arrangements for our excursion. I shall arrange to have the journey extend as far as the Holy Land. Be so kind, if you please, as to give me a letter of introduction to Prof. Wm. Kidder, whom I hope, also, to enlist in the scheme.

With warmest regards to your family, I remain,

Very Truly Yours,

HENRY FRENCH.

Reply Granting the Request.

SPARTA, R. I., March 6, 18—.

DEAR FRENCH:

I enclose, with pleasure, the letter to Prof. Kidder, who, I think, will be pleased to join us. Wishing you much success, I am,

Yours Truly,

BARTON RICH.

Requesting the Loan of an Opera Glass.

THURSDAY AFTERNOON, April 7, 18—.

DEAR MABEL:

Accompanied by cousin Fred and Jennie Masters, I am going to the theater to-night, and in behalf of Fred I wish you would loan me your opera-glass for the evening.

BECKIE HOWELL.

Answer Refusing the Request.

THURSDAY, April 7, 18—.

DEAR BECKIE:

Charlie Hackney called and borrowed my glass about an hour since; otherwise, I would take the greatest pleasure in granting your request. Wishing you a delightful evening, I am,

Your Devoted Friend,

MABEL GALE.

Requesting the Loan of a Pistol.

FRIDAY MORN., MAY 8, 18—.

FRIEND GODARD:

Please loan me your pistol this forenoon, and oblige

JOHN OGDON.

Reply Granting the Request.

FRIDAY, May 8, 18—.

FRIEND JOHN:

Accept the pistol. Beware that you do not get hurt. I shall want it to-morrow. Truly Yours,

BEN GODARD.

Letters Accompanying Gifts.

Form of Letter Accompanying Photographs.

 SUALLY, in sending gifts, it is customary to accompany the same with a prettily written note. Such letters, with their answers, are very brief, and are usually written in the third person, unless among relatives or very intimate friends.

Though a reply should be given immediately, no haste need be made in repaying the gift, else it would seem that you feel the obligation, and will experience relief by paying the debt.

———◦◦———

Accompanying a Betrothal Gift of a Ring.

No. 84 ELDRIDGE COURT, Jan. 1, 18—.

DEAR ANNIE:

Will you accept the accompanying ring, and wear it as a pledge of the undying affection of,

Yours Constantly,
WILLIAM.

———◦◦———

Reply to the Foregoing.

No. 8 ——— ST., Jan. 2, 18—.

DEAR WILLIAM:

Your beautiful gift is on my finger, where it will be ever worn as a token of your love.

Yours Truly,
ANNIE.

Rockland, Va., Oct. 20, 18—.

Dear Helen.

Will you accept the accompanying photographs of husband, May, Jennie, and your humble servant, in lieu of the visit that we anticipated making you this month?

We want the photos of all your family to make our album complete, and I shall watch the mail, expecting to get them. Hoping to hear from you soon, I remain,

Your Friend,

Emily Gerry.

Answer to the Foregoing.

JACKSON, MISS., Oct. 25, 18—.

DEAR EMILY:

I regret that we are not to have the anticipated visit from you this spring. We are very thankful for the photographs, however, if we can do no better. We regard them very life-like in expression, and truthful in representation. When baby is a few weeks older, we will group ourselves together, and you shall see us as we are. Our love to all your family, and remember me as,

Your Constant Friend,
HELEN STANFORD.

Accompanying a Book Sent by the Author.

SPRINGDALE, N. J., June 1, 18—.

Miss Harmon will please accept the accompanying volume as a token of the high esteem and regard of the Author,

ARTHUR WELLS.

MISS MARTHA HARMON.

Answer to the Foregoing.

No. 9 —— St., Aug. 2, 18—.

Miss Harmon presents her regards to Mr. Wells, and accepts with much gratification his highly esteemed and valuable gift.

ARTHUR WELLS, ESQ.

Accompanying a Boquet of Flowers to a Lady.

Will Miss Beveridge honor Mr. Haines by carrying the accompanying flowers to the concert this evening?

Answer to the Foregoing.

Miss Beveridge's compliments and thanks to Mr. Haines. His beautiful and fragrant gift will be a welcome addition to her toilet for this evening.

Accompanying a Birthday Gift.

BELVIDERE, ILL., Dec. 10, 18—.

FRIEND DAVID:

Sixty years ago, to-day, you and I exchanged birthday greetings, then in our twentieth year. How the years have flown by since then, sprinkling our heads with snow, and finally covering them with white! You will please accept this staff as an evidence that time cannot dim the unchanging friendship of,

Your Friend,
JOSEPH BARLOW.

Answer to the Foregoing.

FREEPORT, ILL., Dec. 10, 18—.

MY FRIEND JOSEPH:

Your very valuable and welcome gift came to-day. I lean on it, and look back. The noonday of our life has passed. Gradually we are descending the slope towards the going-down of our life's sun. It is appointed for all to reach life's meridian, stand there for a little while, and go down on the other side. Youth may not be recovered here, but I doubt not that we may be young again, in that bourne towards which we are fast passing. During my remaining years I will cherish your gift. Accept my warmest thanks, and remember me as,

Your Constant Friend,
DAVID BINNINGER.

Accompanying a Donation to a Clergyman.

To THE REV. WASHINGTON SMITH,
Pastor of the —th St. M. E. Church.

Dear Sir:

Will you confer upon us the great pleasure of appropriating to your own use the accompanying check? It is presented by your many friends in your congregation, as a slight token of the very high esteem in which you are held by the people, as a Christian gentleman and a most eloquent and instructive preacher.

Trusting that its acceptance will afford you as much pleasure as is given us in the presentation, we are,

Very Respectfully,
MARTIN FULLER,
WM. B. KING, } Com. of Presentation.
CHAS. H. SNOW.

Answer to the Foregoing.

ST. LOUIS, MO., Jan. 1, 18—.

MESSRS. MARTIN FULLER, WM. B. KING, AND CHAS. H. SNOW.

Gentlemen:

Your very kind and courteous letter, accompanied by your valuable testimonial, is received, for which please accept my grateful acknowledgments. The gift itself, however, is not more valued than the golden words of sympathy and encouragement that accompany its presentation. Trusting that, through God's blessing, I may be able to serve the generous donors as acceptably in the future as your testimonial leads me to suppose I have in the past, I am,

Your Very Obedient Servant,
WASHINGTON SMITH.

Accompanying a Gift to a Superintendent upon Retirement.

CHICAGO, ILL., Feb. 2, 18—.

MR. ARTHUR P. STEPHENS.

Dear Sir:

The undersigned, employes of the Northwestern Sheet Lead and Zinc Works, deeply regretting your departure from among us, desire your acceptance of the accompanying memorial, in testimony of our affection and respect for you as a gentleman and a mechanic, and as a faint expression of our appeciation of your kindly efforts to render our connection with this manufactory not only pleasant and agreeable to ourselves, but profitable to the company.

Deeply regretting that our connection must be severed, we shall gratefully remember our association in the past, and hope always to be held in pleasurable remembrance by you.

(SIGNED BY THE EMPLOYES.)

Answer to the Foregoing.

CHICAGO, ILL., Feb. 3, 18—.

To THE EMPLOYES OF THE NORTHWESTERN SHEET LEAD AND ZINC WORKS.

Gentlemen:

I am in receipt of your kind letter and testimonial. Wherever fortune may cast my lot, I shall never cease to remember the pleasant associations of the past few years, and the many kind attentions I have received at your hands. If our relations and labors have been pleasant, I do not forget that they were largely made so by your always generous efforts and willing coöperation.

I will ever cherish your beautiful gift as a memorial of our pleasant years together, and can only wish that each of you, when occupying positions of trust, may be as warmly supported and as ably assisted by those in your charge as I have been since my connection with yourselves. Thanking you for this testimonial and your generous words of approval, I remain,

Your Friend,
ARTHUR P. STEPHENS.

Letters of Friendship and Relationship.

WRITE letters to friends and relatives very often. As a rule, the more frequent such letters, the more minute they are in giving particulars; and the longer you make them, the better.

The absent husband should write a letter at least once a week. Some husbands make it a rule to write a brief letter home at the close of every day.

The absent child need not ask, "Do they miss me at home?" Be sure that they do. Write those relatives a long letter, often, descriptive of your journeys and the scenes with which you are becoming familiar. And, if the missive from the absent one is dearly cherished, let the relatives at home remember that doubly dear is the letter from the hallowed hearthstone of the home fireside, where the dearest recollections of the heart lie garnered. Do not fail to write very promptly to the one that is away. Give all the news. Go into all the little particulars, just as you would talk. After you have written up matters of general moment, come down to little personal gossip that is of particular interest. Give the details fully about Sallie Williams marrying John Hunt, and her parents being opposed to the match. Be explicit about the new minister, how many sociables you have a month, and the general condition of affairs among your intimate acquaintances.

Don't forget to be very minute about things at home. Be particular to tell of "bub," and "sis," and the baby. Even "Major," the dog, should have a mention. The little tid-bits that are tucked in around, on the edge of the letter, are all devoured, and are often the sweetest morsels of the feast.

Let the young, more especially, keep up a continual correspondence with their friends. The ties of friendship are thus riveted the stronger, and the fires of love and kind feeling, on the altar of the heart, are thus kept continually burning bright.

From a Husband, Absent on Business, to his Wife.

DETROIT, MICH., Feb. 1, 18—.

MY DEAR HENRIETTA:

I have been to the end of my journey, and am now homeward bound. Another week, and I hope to kiss my wife and babies, and tell them that this is my last journey of the winter. One or two journeys next spring, and then I am done traveling away from home. What better news can I write you than this? Yes, perhaps I have better news yet, which is, that I have completed such arrangements, during my absence from you this time, as will greatly increase my income without it being necessary for me to travel.

Isn't that pleasant? How I long to get home and tell you all about it. At present, when not closely engaged in business, I am busy thinking of many improvements that we will make around our home next summer, being the very changes that you have so long desired, but which our means hitherto have not permitted us to make.

Kiss Sammie and Tillie for me, and accept many kisses for yourself. I will write you from Cleveland, if not before. Good night.

Your Loving Husband,
WM. TILDEN.

From a Young Lady to a Schoolmate just Married.

GALVA, ILL., DEC. 26, 18—.

DEAR MINNIE:

I have just heard, through our mutual friend and former schoolmate, Nellie Crandall, that you are the first of our school-girl circle who has taken upon herself the cares and duties of married life.

Thus, one by one, I expect, our little band of joyous, happy girls, so short a time ago together,

will drop away into happy homes, which, if they do not make them, they will at least adorn.

And so you are married. Well, I had some intimation, months ago, that such an event might sometime take place, but really I did not think you would change your name so soon. Mrs. Charles Blackwell!—well, that *does* sound a little odd, I confess, but then it is a pretty name, nevertheless. I assure you I am impatient to meet you, and witness how you dignify the name.

Accept my most sincere good wishes for your future happiness, and tell your husband that he must be prepared to feel an interest in the welfare of all your old friends, especially,

Your Friend,
CALLIE BROWN.

From a Young Girl, at Boarding-School, to her Mother.

Hopeville Female Seminary,
Oct. 1, 18——.

Dear Mother:

I want you to write me a letter at once, asking me to come home and see you. O dear! I am so homesick! You know, mother, this is the first time I was ever away from you so long. You must let me come right home, or I will certainly die of homesickness.

Your Miserable Child,
Ella Bennett.

To Mrs. D. C. Bennett.

Answer of the Mother.

NEW YORK, Oct. 3, 18—.

MY DEAR CHILD:

I am sorry that you should urge me to grant you such an unreasonable request. Of course, nothing could please me better than to have my darling little Ella sitting on my lap at this very moment; but think how seriously the absence from your school, now, would derange all your recitations for this term. You must not think of it; recollect that all your brothers and sisters have been away at school, and always remained until the vacations. It is true that you, being the youngest, have been petted more than the rest, but it would be very unfortunate to have my indulgence interfere with your studies. You know that you are the idol of our hearts; for that very reason you should endeavor to become proficient in those branches of study that will render you an accomplished lady.

Believe me, my dear child, you will find school more pleasant every day, as you get better acquainted with your schoolmates; and, through improvement in your studies, you will steadily grow in favor with your teachers.

I will write Mrs. Mayhew to render your tasks as light as possible at first, and I have no doubt she will do all in her power to aid you.

Only a few weeks, remember, and you will be home for a long vacation, which will be all the more delightful for the privation you are at present undergoing. Your father, brothers and sisters all unite with me in sending you their love.

I remain, my dear child,
Your Affectionate Mother,
NANCY BENNETT.

To ELLA BENNETT,
Hopeville Female Seminary.

From an Absent Wife to her Husband.

ARGYLE, N. Y., March 2, 18—.

DEAREST LOVE:

I am at last safely under uncle's roof, having arrived here last evening, baby and myself both well, but really very tired. We had no delay, except about two hours at Buffalo. Uncle met me at the depot with his carriage, and, in fifteen minutes from the time of my arrival, I was cosily seated in my room, which was all in readiness for me.

Uncle and aunt seem greatly pleased with my coming, and both are loud in their praise of the baby. They very much regret that you could not have come with me, and say they intend to prevail on you to make them a visit when I am ready to go home.

Baby looks into my eyes once in a while and says, solemnly, "Papa, papa!" I do actually believe he is thinking about home, and wants to keep up a talk about you. Everybody thinks he looks like his papa.

By day after to-morrow I will write a long letter. I want you to get this by the first mail, so I make it short. With dearest love, I am,
Your Wife,
CAROLINE.

Answer to the Foregoing.

MICHIGAN CITY, IND., March 7.

DEAR WIFE:

I was indeed rejoiced to hear of your safe arrival, having felt no little anxiety for you, which is relieved by the receipt of your letter.

I miss you very much, the house looks so dreary without your loved presence; but I am, nevertheless, glad that you are making your visit, as the journey, I trust, will be beneficial to your health.

Kiss baby for me. Only by his absence do I know how much I have enjoyed my play with our little Charlie.

Don't take any concern about me. Enjoy your visit to the utmost extent. In one of my next letters I will write whether I can go East and return with you.

Remember me to uncle and aunt.
Your Ever-Faithful Husband,
ARCHIBALD.

From a Servant in the City, to her Parents in the Country.

NEW YORK, June 1, 18—.

MY DEAR PARENTS:

I take the first opportunity, since I arrived in the city, to write to you. It was a sore trial, I assure you, to leave home, but since coming here I have been quite contented, and I am getting so well accustomed to my work that I begin to like my place very much.

Mr. and Mrs. Benedict are both very kind to me. The family consists of father, mother and three children, the youngest being a little boy three years old—a beautiful little fellow, that always reminds me of brother James. Eliza, the oldest girl, is thirteen, and Martha is eleven. They are both very kind to me, and do so much about the house that it helps me very considerably.

Mr. Benedict is a clothing merchant in the city, and, I judge, is in very good circumstances. The girls are attending school at present. All the family are very regular in their attendance at church.

For the first few days here, everything seemed very strange. I hardly knew what to make of so much noise and so many people on the streets. I have now, however, become accustomed to the multitudes, and would, I presume, consider my native village very dull indeed, compared with the bustle and activity of the city.

I realize every day, dear parents, the worth of your good advice to me, which I never knew the value of so much before; thanking you for the same, I will always endeavor to follow it.

Give my love to Johnny, Mary, Jimmy and all inquiring friends. I shall anxiously look for a letter from you. Write me in the care of Solon Benedict, No.——Thirteenth Street.
Your Dutiful and Affectionate Daughter.
BETSEY ANN FAIRBANKS.

To MR. AND MRS. H. K. FAIRBANKS,
Swallow Hill, Pa.

The Mother's Reply.

SWALLOW HILL, PA., June 7, 18—.

DEAR BETSEY:

Your letter, which has been received, affords great pleasure and satisfaction to your father and myself. Nothing could give our hearts greater happiness than to know of your enjoyment and firm purpose to do right. Now that you are removed from all parental restraint, it is of the most vital importance that you implicitly rely upon the religious precepts which have been instilled into your mind, and that you daily pray to God for guidance and mercy.

We are greatly pleased that you are well situated with Mr. and Mrs. Benedict; in return for their kindness you must be honest, industrious, kind and obliging, always doing your duty faithfully, which will be a real satisfaction to yourself as well as to your employers.

Several of the neighbors, who have called, have wished to be remembered to you; Mary and Jimmy unite with you father and myself in sending you love.

We shall constantly pray for your continued protection and prosperity. I remain, dear Betsey,
Your Affectionate Mother,
HARRIET FAIRBANKS.

Letter from a Father, Remonstrating with his Son.

DANBURY, CONN., July 7, 18—.

MY DEAR SON:

I am sorry to learn that you are not inclined to be as strict in your line of duty as you should be. Remember, my son, that a down-hill road is before you, unless you rouse yourself and shake off immediately the habits of dissipation that are fastening themselves upon you. Be sure, dear boy, that nothing but sorrow and shame can come of bad company, late hours, neglect of duty, and inattention to the obligations of morality. I am willing to think that you have not given this matter sufficient thought heretofore; that your actions are the result of thoughtlessness, rather than a disposition to do wrong.

But be forewarned in time. You must change your course of action immediately, or incur my severe displeasure.

I urge this, my boy, for your sake. Remember that my happiness is bound in your own, and that nothing could give me greater pleasure than your prosperity. I trust that it will not be necessary for me to use more severe language than this.

Your Anxious Father,
RUDOLF MATHEWS.

The Son's Reply.

BOSTON, MASS., June 9, 18—.
DEAR FATHER:

I realize that I need the good advice contained in your letter. I am aware, as I stop to think of my conduct, that I have given you reason for anxiety, but I intend, by attention to my business hereafter, and a complete reformation of my habits, to give you no occasion for concern about me in the future. Believe me, I love and respect you too much to intentionally wound your feelings, or to bring down your gray hairs with sorrow.

Excuse me, dear father, for having given you this uneasiness, and trust me as,

Your Affectionate and Repentant Son,
CHARLES MATHEWS.

From a Married Man to a Friend About to Marry.

ATLANTA, GA., Aug. 20, 18—.
FRIEND BATCHELDER:

Can it be possible? Am I right, or am I dreaming? Has it come to this at last? You, Batchelder Button — you cynic, railer against women, the unalterable, unchangeable bachelor, — is it possible that you have at last been captured, and have surrendered all your ordnance, heavy guns and small arms to the enemy?

What a defeat! That large, strong heart of yours all crumbling to pieces, and surrendering to Cupid's battery!

Well, now, seriously, my friend, from my point of view, I think you have done a very sensible thing. The man who goes the journey alone through life, lives but half a life. If you have found the woman fitted by temperament and accomplishments to render your pathway through life the joyous one that the married state should be, you are certainly to be congratulated for awakening to a true sense of your condition, though rather late in the day.

Though but slightly acquainted with Miss Howell, I have formed a very favorable idea of her intelligence and worth, which opinion, I believe, is generally shared by those who know her best. I doubt not, with her your married life will be a continually happy one.

Your Friend,
HERBERT TRACEY.

From a Young Man Who Has Recently Entered College.

HARVARD COLLEGE, MASS., May 18, 18—.
DEAR FATHER:

I am happy to inform you that I passed my examination with credit, if I am to believe the commendation bestowed upon me by Dr. H——.

I was very agreeably surprised, soon after my arrival, to meet my former schoolmate, Hartley Montague, who is one of the most respected and influential in his class, with whom I am, as formerly, on quite intimate terms. Many things are quite new to me here. The society is very much mixed, and I cannot tell just where my level is; but I trust I shall be able to follow the good advice of my parents, and always do credit to myself and my relatives, who have labored so assiduously to advance me to this position.

I thank you for the check you so kindly sent me, which was fully adequate to cover all expenses of entrance, and leave me a surplus sufficient for the rest of the term.

Love to dear mother and sisters. Hoping to meet you all at our forthcoming commencement, I am,

Your Affectionate Son,
BARFORD D. CLAY.

Descriptive Letter
From a Young Man at the "Old Home," to his Parents in the West.

CAMBRIDGE, N. Y., June 18, 1873.
DEAR PARENTS:

Agreeable to your request, I take the first opportunity, after my visit to the "old home" and a hurried call upon our relatives, to write you how I found the people and scenes that you knew so well in the days lang syne, and that I remember as a boy.

I arrived at Cambridge after a ninety minutes' ride from Troy. What a great change in traveling! When last I was here, it was a day's journey from Troy, by stage-coach. To-day, New York, in time, is nearer to our old home than Troy was then; and Troy, after traveling among the thriving, driving cities of the great West, seems like a wayside village, instead of the great metropolis that it once seemed to be; though it is a beautiful, growing, wealthy manufacturing city to-day, nevertheless. It is not that the villages and cities that we once knew grow less, but by observation and comparison we class them where they belong.

At Cambridge I secured a livery team for a three days' sojourn among the scenes of my boyhood. Up the Battenkill. Could it be that this was the great river in which my parents were in such constant fear of their boy being drowned? Was this the Mississippi of my childhood? Alas! that I had floated down the Ohio River to the real Mississippi, that I had been up the Missouri, two thousand miles from its mouth, and that I had navigated the Father of Waters from its fountain-head to its outlet in the Gulf of Mexico.

Had the Battenkill been drying up? Not at all. Though a brook, comparatively, there are the same milldams, the same trout-holes, and the same bending willows by its side; and the first to meet me among our old neighbors was uncle Nat., the same old jolly fisherman, returning from his daily piscatorial excursion, with a small string of trout. Uncle Nat. complains bitterly of the scarcity of fish at present in the river, caused, he says, by "them city chaps" from Troy, New York and Albany, who are in the habit of sojourning during the summer months in the hotels among the mountains hereabouts.

Stopping first at uncle Henry's, I visited the old homestead towards evening on the day of my arrival. Whatever may be said about the village and rivers growing smaller, it must certainly be admitted that the mountains, hills and rocks hold their own. Up there, on the hillside, was "the old house at home," which I had not seen for fifteen years. I went up the walk. There were the maples that I assisted father in planting, twenty years ago — great, spreading trees now. There was the same rosebush that mother and I cared for sixteen years ago. No other evidence of the flowers and shrubbery that mother so much delighted in remained about the premises.

I had learned that the place had passed into the hands of an Irishman named Sweeny, so I rapped at the front door, and was met by Mrs. S., from whom I obtained permission to stroll around the place. "Oh, yes," said the kind-hearted woman, "go all about, and when Mr. Swainy comes, he'll go wid ye."

So I strolled in the quiet evening hour, alone, among the scenes of my childhood, where we boys picked stones and played ball in the summer, and slid down hill and chopped firewood in the winter. The barn was the same old barn. I clambered to its old girtbeam, and sat looking down on the haymow where I had jumped, hundreds of times, into the hay below. I climbed to the box, close under the rafters, where we boys used to keep doves. The same box is there yet. I went down into the stables, where we hunted hens' eggs. Apparently, the same speckled hens are there now. And down around the barn are the same old maples, and willows beside the brook.

I went out to the fields. What immense tracts of land I thought these ten-acre fields, when I was a boy! The same orchards are there. The old Jones sweet-apple tree is dead, however, and none of the trees are looking thrifty. I took a drink from the upper spring, in the Barnes lot, which tasted just as cool as ever, and getting down on my hands and knees to drink seemed like old times. I saw a woodchuck and several squirrels, in my walk, and heard the same old caw, caw, of the crows, which brought back the past the most vividly of anything I had heard.

Returning, and looking through the house, I found almost everything changed. Two American and three Irish families had occupied it since we left, and they, evidently thinking that they would soon leave, did not pretend to make any improvements for their successors to enjoy. To sum up the description of the house—it has never been painted since we left; the dooryard fence is gone; the woodhouse has been removed; the outdoor cellar has caved in; the wagonhouse leans so badly it is liable to fall over at any time; the house itself, in a few years, will go the way of the fences; and most of the outbuildings are already gone. Nearly every American family that once lived here has gone West; the population of the vicinity, at the present time, being largely made up of Irish. Another generation, and, it is probable, scarcely an American will be left to tell the tale. Though sorrowing to see the wreck of our old home, I am greatly enjoying the visit. The scenery is truly beautiful; though, unfortunately, the people here know nothing of its beauties, and it takes us some years on the level plains of the West to learn to appreciate it.

One thing must be said of the people here, however, especially the Americans that are left—they take their full measure of enjoyment. With continuous snow four months in the year, the winter is made up of sleighriding to parties and festal occasions; the sunshine of spring is the signal for maple-sugar-making, and sugaring-off parties; the hard work of summer is broken up by fishing, berrying, and frequent excursions to various parts of the country; the fall is characterized by apple-parings and corn-huskings; so that, with their maple sugar, berries, cream, trout, honey and pumpkin pies, they are about the best livers and happiest people I ever met. I never knew, till I returned, that they enjoyed themselves so well.

I will continue the record of my visit in my next.

Yours Affectionately,
ALFRED T. WEEKS.

Descriptive Letter.
From a Young Lady Visiting Chicago, to her Parents in the East.

CHICAGO, ILL., June 1, 1873.

DEAR PARENTS:

Having been the rounds among our relatives here, I seat myself to give you something of an idea of this wonderful city—in many respects one of the most remarkable on the face of the earth, having a population to-day of over 300,000.

You have heard so much of the city that I must give you a brief sketch of its history.

The first white man ever known to have set foot on the spot where Chicago now stands, was a French Missionary, from Canada, named Pierre Jacques Marquette, who, with two others, having been on a missionary tour in the southern part of Illinois, when homeward bound was detained at this place in the fall of 1673, in consequence of the severe cold, until the following spring. That was two hundred years ago.

The first settler that came here was Point-au-Sable, a St. Domingo negro, who, in 1796, commenced a few improvements—seventy-seven years since. Au-Sable soon afterwards removed to Peoria, Ill., his improvements passing into the hands of one Le Mai, a Frenchman, who traded considerably with the Indians. The first permanent settler here was John Kinzie, who came over from St. Joseph, Michigan, and commenced his improvements in 1804—sixty-nine years ago. Mr. Kinzie was, indeed, what Romulus was to Rome, the founder of the city. There was a fort built that year, a blockhouse made of logs, a few rods southwest of what is now known as Rush street bridge. Mr. Kinzie had a house near the south end of the bridge, which bridge, of course, had no existence in those days. An employe of Mr. Kinzie, named Ouilmette, a Frenchman, had a cabin a little west of Mr. Kinzie; and a little further west was the log cottage of one Burns, a discharged soldier. South of the fort, on the South Side, a Mr. Lee had a farm, in the low swamp lands, where now stands the heart of the business center of the city, and his cabin was a half mile or so down the river.

For a quarter of a century the growth of the village was remarkably slow, as shown by the fact that in 1830 there were but twelve houses in the village, with three suburban residences on Madison street, the entire population, whites, half-breeds and negroes, making about one hundred. That was forty years ago.

I should have told you that Chicago has a river, which is doubtless the cause of the wonderful commercial growth of the place of late years, which, at the time of its discovery, was two hundred feet wide, and twenty feet deep, with banks so steep that vessels could come up to the water's edge and receive their lading. A half mile or more from the mouth of the river, the stream divides: that portion north of the stream being known as the North Side; that between the forks, the West Side; and that south of the river, the South Side.

At that time, the North Side was covered with a dense forest of black walnut and other trees, in which were bears, wolves, foxes, wild cats, deer and other game in great abundance; while the South Side, now the business center, was a low, swampy piece of ground, being the resort of wild geese and ducks. Where the court house stands, was a pond, which was navigable for small boats. On the banks of the river, among the sedgy grass, grew a wild onion, which the Indians called Chikago, and hence the name of the city.

On a summer day, in 1831, the first vessel unloaded goods at the mouth of the river. In 1832, the first frame house was built, by Geo. W. Dole, and stood on the southeast corner of Dearborn and South Water streets. At an election for township trustees in 1833,—just forty-one years since—there were twenty-eight voters. In 1840, there were less than 5,000 people in the place. Thus you see this city, now the fifth in the order of the population in the United States, has grown from 5,000 to 300,000 in thirty-three years.

It is needless for me to describe the wonderfully rapid up-building of the city since the fire. You have heard all about it. What I want to tell you more especially is concerning our relatives. Uncles John, William and James, you recollect perhaps, all came here in 1836. They worked that summer for different parties, and until the next spring, when, in the summer of 1837, each of the men they had labored for failed. Uncle John had due him $150. Fortunately, as he thought, he was able to settle the claim at fifty cents on the dollar, and with $75 he left the place in disgust, and went to work for a farmer in Dupage County, a little distance west of Chicago. Uncle William could not get a cent. He even proposed to take $50 for the $175 that were due him, but cash could not possibly be obtained. He finally settled his claim by taking six acres of swampy land on the South Side, which he vainly tried to sell for several years that he might leave the city; but, unable to do so, he continued to work in Chicago. Uncle James took fifteen acres in the settlement of his claim, which he also found it impossible to sell, his experience being about the same as that of uncle William. Well, now the luck begins to come in. Uncle William got independent of his land by and by, but at last sold an acre for money enough to put up one of the most elegant residences you ever beheld. He sold afterwards another acre for money with which he bought a farm three miles from the court house, that is now worth $500,000. With two acres more, he got money enough to put up five business blocks, from which he gets a revenue, each year, sufficient to buy several farms.

Uncle James' experience is almost exactly similar to uncle William's. He has sold small portions of his land at various times, re-investing his money in real estate, until he is worth to-day about $2,000,000. Uncle William is said to be worth about the same amount. Uncle John came in from the country a few years ago, and, in various capacities, is working for his brothers around the city, being to-day a poor man; but will, I presume, be just as rich in eternity as uncles James and William.

All have interesting families of intelligent children, among whom I have almost terminated one of the most delightful visits I ever made. Such in brief is the history of Chicago, and a sketch of two of its sample rich men, who were made wealthy in spite of themselves.

In my next I will describe the parks and boulevards about the city. Till then, adieu.

Your Affectionate Daughter,
AMELIA SPARLAND.

Letters of Love.

O F all letters, the love-letter should be the most carefully prepared. Among the written missives, they are the most thoroughly read and re-read, the longest preserved, and the most likely to be regretted in after life.

IMPORTANCE OF CARE.

They should be written with the utmost regard for perfection. An ungrammatical expression, or word improperly spelled, may seriously interfere with the writer's prospects, by being turned to ridicule. For any person, however, to make sport of a respectful, confidential letter, because of some error in the writing, is in the highest degree unladylike and ungentlemanly.

NECESSITY OF CAUTION.

As a rule, the love-letter should be very guardedly written. Ladies, especially, should be very careful to maintain their dignity when writing them. When, possibly, in after time the feelings entirely change, you will regret that you wrote the letter at all. If the love remains unchanged, no harm will certainly be done, if you wrote with judgment and care.

AT WHAT AGE TO WRITE LOVE-LETTERS.

The love-letter is the prelude to marriage — a state that, if the husband and wife be fitted for each other, is the most natural and serenely happy; a state, however, that none should enter upon, until, in judgment and physical development, both parties have completely matured. Many a life has been wrecked by a blind, impulsive marriage, simply resulting from a youthful passion. As a physiological law, man should be twenty-five, and woman twenty-three, before marrying.

APPROVAL OF PARENTS.

While there may be exceptional cases, as a rule, correspondence should be conducted only with the assent and approval of the parents. If it is not so, parents are themselves generally to blame. If children are properly trained, they will implicitly confide in the father and mother, who will retain their love until they are sufficiently matured to choose a companion for life. If parents neglect to retain this love and confidence, the child, in the yearning for affection, will place the love elsewhere, frequently much too early in life.

TIMES FOR COURTSHIP.

Ladies should not allow courtship to be conducted at unseasonable hours. The evening entertainment, the walk, the ride, are all favorable for the study of each other's tastes and feelings. For the gentleman to protract his visit at the lady's residence until a late hour, is almost sure to give offence to the lady's parents, and is extremely ungentlemanly.

HONESTY.

The love-letter should be honest. It should say what the writer means, and no more. For the lady or gentleman to play the part of a coquette, studying to see how many lovers he or she may secure, is very disreputable, and bears in its train a long list of sorrows, frequently wrecking the domestic happiness for a life-time. The parties should be honest, also, in the statement of their actual prospects and means of support. Neither should hold out to the other wealth or other inducements that will not be realized, as disappointment and disgust will be the only result.

MARRYING FOR A HOME.

Let no lady commence and continue a correspondence with a view to marriage, for fear that she may never have another opportunity. It is the mark of judgment and rare good sense to go through life without wedlock, if she cannot marry from love. Somewhere in eternity, the poet tells us, our true mate will be found. Do not be afraid of being an "old maid." The disgrace attached to that term has long since passed away. Unmarried ladies of mature years are proverbially among the most intelligent, accomplished and independent to be found in society. The sphere of woman's action and work is so widening that she can to-day, if she desires, handsomely and independently support herself. She need not, therefore, marry for a home.

INTEMPERATE MEN.

Above all, no lady should allow herself to correspond with an intemperate man, with a view to matrimony. She may reform him, but the chances are that her life's happiness will be completely destroyed by such a union. Better, a thousand times, the single, free and independent maidenhood, than for a woman to trail her life in the dust, and bring poverty, shame and disgrace on her children, by marrying a man addicted to dissipated habits.

MARRYING WEALTH.

Let no man make it an ultimate object in life to marry a rich wife. It is not the possession, but the *acquisition*, of wealth, that gives happiness. It is a generally conceded fact that the inheritance of great wealth is a positive mental and moral injury to young men, completely destroying the stimulus to advancement. So, as a rule, no man is permanently made happier by a marriage of wealth; while he is quite likely to

be given to understand, by his wife and others, from time to time, that, whatever consequence he may attain, it is all the result of his wife's money. Most independent men prefer to start, as all our wealthiest and greatest men have done, at the foot of the ladder, and earn their independence. Where, however, a man can bring extraordinary talent or distinguished reputation, as a balance for his wife's wealth, the conditions are more nearly equalized. Observation shows that those marriages prove most serenely happy where husband and wife, at the time of marriage, stand, socially, intellectually and pecuniarily, very nearly equal. For the chances of successful advancement and happiness in after life, let a man wed a woman poorer than himself rather than one that is richer.

POVERTY.

Let no couple hesitate to marry because they are poor. It will cost them less to live after marriage than before — one light, one fire, etc., answering the purpose for both. Having an object to live for, also, they will commence their accumulations after marriage as never before. The young woman that demands a certain amount of costly style, beyond the income of her betrothed, no young man should ever wed. As a general thing, however, women have common sense, and, if husbands will perfectly confide in their wives, telling them exactly their pecuniary condition, the wife will live within the husband's income. In the majority of cases where men fail in business, the failure being attributed to the wife's extravagance, the wife has been kept in entire ignorance of her husband's pecuniary resources. The man who would be successful in business, should not only marry a woman who is worthy of his confidence, but he should at all times advise with her. She is more interested in his prosperity than anybody else, and will be found his best counselor and friend.

CONFIDENCE AND HONOR.

The love correspondence of another should be held sacred, the rule of conduct being, to do to others as you wish them to do to you. No woman, who is a lady, will be guilty of making light of the sentiments that are expressed to her in a letter. No man, who is a gentleman, will boast of his love conquests, among boon companions, or reveal to others the correspondence between himself and a lady. If an engagement is mutually broken off, all the love-letters should be returned. To retain them is dishonorable. They were written under circumstances that no longer exist. It is better for both parties to wash out every recollection of the past, by returning to the giver every memento of the dead love.

HOW TO BEGIN A LOVE CORRESPONDENCE.

Some gentlemen, being very favorably impressed with a lady at first sight, and having no immediate opportunity for introduction, make bold, after learning her name, to write her at once, seeking an interview, the form of which letter will be found hereafter. A gentleman in doing so, however, runs considerable risk of receiving a rebuff from the lady, though not always. It is better to take a little more time, learn thoroughly who the lady is, and obtain an introduction through a mutual acquaintance. Much less embarrassment attends such a meeting; and, having learned the lady's antecedents, subjects are easily introduced in which she is interested, and thus the first interview can be made quite agreeable.

The way is now paved for the opening of a correspondence, which may be done by a note inviting her company to any entertainment supposed to be agreeable to her, or the further pleasure of her acquaintance by correspondence, as follows:

148 ——St., July 2, 18—.

MISS MYRA BRONSON:

Having greatly enjoyed our brief meeting at the residence of Mrs. Powell last Thursday evening, I venture to write to request permission to call on you at your own residence. Though myself almost entirely a stranger in the city, your father remembers, he told me the other evening, Mr. Williams of Syracuse, who is my uncle. Trusting that you will pardon this liberty, and place me on your list of gentleman acquaintances, I am,

Yours, Very Respectfully,
HARMON WILLIAMS.

Favorable Reply.

944 —— St., July 8, 18—.

MR. HARMON WILLIAMS.
Dear Sir:

It will give me much pleasure to see you at our residence next Wednesday evening. My father desires me to state that he retains a very favorable recollection of your uncle, in consequence of which he will be pleased to continue your acquaintance.

Yours Truly,
MYRA BRONSON.

Unfavorable Reply.

944 —— St., July 2, 18—.

Miss Myra Bronson, making it a rule to receive no gentleman visitors upon such brief acquaintance, begs to decline the honor of Mr. Williams' visits.

HARMON WILLIAMS, ESQ.

An Invitation to a Place of Public Amusement.

462 —— St., April 4, 18—.

MISS FARRINGTON:

May I request the very great pleasure of escorting you to Barnum's Museum, at any time which may suit your convenience? To grant this favor will give me very much pleasure. No pains will be spared by myself to have you enjoy the occasion, and I will consult your wishes in every particular as to time of calling for you and returning. Waiting an early reply to this, I remain,

Most Sincerely,
CHAS. STEVENSON.

Reply Accepting.

876 —— St., April 7, 18—.

MR. STEVENSON.
Dear Sir: I thank you for your very kind invitation, which I am happy to accept. I will appoint next Monday evening, at which time, if you will call for me at our house, I will accompany you.

Yours Sincerely,
CLARA FARRINGTON.

Reply Refusing.

876 —— St., April 4, 18—.

MR. STEVENSON.
Dear Sir: I am grateful to you for your very polite invitation, but, as I should go only with my own family were I to attend any place of amusement, I am unable to avail myself of your kindness. Thanking you, I remain,

Yours Truly,
CLARA FARRINGTON.

Reply with Conditions.

876 —— St., April 4, 18—.

MR. STEVENSON.
Dear Sir: I shall be most happy to visit Barnum's Museum with you, but will prefer being one of a company in which yourself is included, such also being the wish of my mother, who sends her kind regards. A visit from you at our house, next Tuesday evening, will enable us to decide upon the time of going.

Very Sincerely,
CLARA FARRINGTON.

Love at First Sight.

96 —— St., June 1, 18—.

Dear Miss Hawley:

You will, I trust, forgive this abrupt and plainly spoken letter. Although I have been in your company but once, I cannot forbear writing to you in defiance of all rules of etiquette. Affection is sometimes of slow growth, but sometimes it springs up in a moment. I left you last night with my heart no longer my own. I cannot, of course, hope that I have created any interest in you, but will you do me the great favor to allow me to cultivate your acquaintance? Hoping that you may regard me favorably, I shall await with much anxiety your reply. I remain,

Yours Devotedly,

BENSON GOODRICH.

Unfavorable Reply.

694 —— St., June 1, 18—.

Mr. Goodrich.

Sir: Your note was a surprise to me, considering that we had never met until last evening, and that then our conversation had been only on commonplace subjects. Your conduct is indeed quite strange. You will please be so kind as to oblige me by not repeating the request, allowing this note to close our correspondence.

MARION HAWLEY.

Favorable Reply.

694 —— St., June 1, 18—.

Mr. Goodrich.

Dear Sir: Undoubtedly I ought to call you severely to account for your declaration of love at first sight, but I really cannot find it in my heart to do so, as I must confess that, after our brief interview last evening, I have thought much more of you than I should have been willing to have acknowledged had you not come to the confession first. Seriously speaking, we know but very little of each other yet, and we must be very careful not to exchange our hearts in the dark. I shall be happy to receive you here, as a friend, with a view to our further acquaintance. I remain, dear sir,

MARION HAWLEY.

A Lover's Good-bye Before Starting on a Journey.

104 —— St., May 10, 18—.

My Darling Minnie:

I go west, to-morrow, on business, leaving my heart in your gentle keeping. You need be at no expense in placing a guard around it, for I assure you that, as surely as the needle points towards the pole, so surely my love is all yours. I shall go, dearest, by the first train, hoping thereby to return just one train sooner, which means that not an hour, not a minute longer will I be absent from you, than is imperatively necessary. Like the angler, I shall "drop a line" frequently, and shall expect a very prompt response, letter for letter. No credit given in this case; business is business — I must have prompt returns.

Ever Faithfully Yours,

WINFIELD BAKER.

Reply to the Foregoing.

814 —— St., May 10, 18—.

Dear Winfield:

I have had my cry over your letter — a long, hard cry. Of course, I know that does not help the matter any. I suppose you must go, but I shall be *so* lonely while you are gone. However, you promise that you will return at the earliest moment, and that is one little ray of sunshine that lines the cloud. Shall we be enough happier after your return to pay for this separation? Thinking that

we may be, I will let that thought sustain me. In the meantime, from this moment until your return I will think of you, *just once* — a long-drawn-out thought.

Yours Affectionately,

MINNIE LA SURE.

Letter Asking an Introduction through a Mutual Friend.

912 —— St., April 2, 18—.

Friend Henry:

I am very desirous of making the acquaintance of Miss Benjamin, with whom you are on terms of intimate friendship. Will you be so kind as to give me a letter of introduction to her? I am aware that it may be a delicate letter for you to write, but you will be free, of course, to make all needed explanations in your letter to her. I will send her your letter, instead of personally calling upon her myself, thus saving her from any embarrassment that may result from my so doing. By granting this favor, you will much oblige,

Yours, Very Respectfully,

WM. H. TYLER.

Reply.

117 —— St., April 2, 18—.

Friend Tyler:

Enclosed, find the note you wish. As you will observe, I have acted upon your suggestion of giving her sufficient explanation to justify my letter. Your desire to please the lady, coupled with your good judgment, will, I doubt not, make the matter agreeable.

Truly Yours,

HENRY PARSONS.

LETTER OF INTRODUCTION.

Dear Miss Benjamin: This will introduce to you my friend Wm. Tyler, who is very desirous of making your acquaintance, and, having no other means of doing so, asks of me the favor of writing this note of introduction, which he will send you, instead of calling himself, thus leaving you free to grant him an interview or not. Mr. Tyler is a gentleman I very highly respect, and whose acquaintance, I think, you would not have occasion to regret. Nevertheless, you may not regard this a proper method of introduction, in which case, allow me to assure you, I will entertain the same respect for yourself, if you will frankly state so, though it would be gratifying to Mr. Tyler and myself to have it otherwise. With sincere respect, I am,

Very Respectfully,

HENRY PARSONS.

To the Father of the Lady.

Burlington, Iowa, Jan. 1, 18—.

Respected Sir:

I take this means of consulting you on a subject that deeply interests myself, while it indirectly concerns you; and I trust that my presentation of the matter will meet with your approval.

For several months your daughter Mary and myself have been on intimate terms of friendship, which has ripened into affection on my part, and I have reason to think that my attentions are not indifferent to her. My business and prospects are such that I flatter myself I can provide for her future, with the same comfort that has surrounded her under the parental roof. Of my character and qualifications, I have nothing to say; I trust they are sufficiently known to you to give confidence in the prospect of your child's happiness.

Believing that the parents have such an interest in the welfare of the daughter as makes it obligatory upon the lover to consult their desires, before taking her from their home, I am thus induced to request you to express your wishes upon this subject.

I shall anxiously await your answer.

Your Very Obedient Servant,

DANIEL HARRISON.

To Wm. Franklin, Esq.,
184 —— St.

Favorable Reply.

184 —— St., Jan. 1, 18—.

My Dear Mr. Harrison:

I very highly appreciate the manly and honorable way in which you have addressed me in reference to my daughter Mary.

Believing you to be honest, industrious, ambitious to do well, and possessed of an excellent moral character, I unite with Mrs. Franklin in the belief that our darling child may very safely trust her happiness to your protecting care.

If agreeable and convenient to you, we shall be happy to have you dine with us to-morrow.

Very Sincerely Yours,

WM. FRANKLIN.

To Mr. Daniel Harrison.

Unfavorable Reply.

184 —— St.

Dear Sir:

Highly appreciating the straightforward and gentlemanly manner in which you have written me concerning a subject that every parent has an interest in, I am compelled to inform you that, though my daughter has treated you with much friendliness, as she is accustomed to with all her friends, she will be unable to continue with you a love acquaintance with a view to marriage, owing to a prior engagement with a gentleman of worth and respectability, which contract she has no occasion to regret.

Fully sensible of your most excellent qualities, and the compliment paid in your selection of her, my daughter unites with me in the wish that you may meet with a companion in every way calculated to ensure your happiness.

Yours, Very Respectfully,

WM. FRANKLIN.

To Mr. Daniel Harrison.

Reply to a Young Man that Uses Tobacco.

662 —— St., July 18, 18—.

Mr. Bannister.

Dear Sir:

I am in receipt of your courteous letter, containing a declaration of love. I will be frank enough with you to admit that, while I have been sensible of your affectionate regard for me for some months, I have also cherished a growing interest in you. In truth, to make a candid confession, I most sincerely love you. I should, perhaps, say no more, but I feel it due to you, as well as to myself, to be strictly honest in my expression, lest we foster this growing love, which, under present conditions, must be broken off.

I have always admired your natural ability; I appreciate you for your industry; I respect you for your filial conduct towards your parents. In fact, I consider you quite a model young man, were it not for one habit, which has always been, heretofore, a very delicate subject for me to speak of, fearing that it might give you offense. But believing it best that I be true to my convictions and state my objections plainly, I thus freely write them.

I have reference to the use of tobacco. Apparently, this is a little thing. I am aware that ladies generally consider it beneath their notice; but so thoroughly convinced am I that it is one of the most destructive habits, sapping the morality and vigor of our young men, that I could never consent to wed a man addicted to its use, my reasons being as follows:

It would impoverish my home. Only ten cents a day expended for a cigar, in a lifetime of forty years, with its accumulations of interest, amounts to over four thousand dollars! The little sum of eleven cents per day, saved from being squandered on tobacco, and properly put at interest, amounts in that time to $5,160! No wonder so many homes, the heads of which use tobacco, are without the comforts of life.

It might wreck my happiness. It is a well-known physiological fact that the use of tobacco deadens the sense of taste; that water and all common drinks become insipid and tasteless when tobacco is used, so

that the person using the same involuntarily craves strong drink, in order to *taste* it. Therein lies the foundation of a large share of the drunkenness of the country. Observation proves that, while many men use tobacco that are not drunkards, almost every drunkard is a user of tobacco, having nearly always formed the habit from the use of this narcotic weed.

It would surround me with filth. To say nothing of the great drain on the physical health by the constant expectoration of saliva, thus ruining the health of many robust constitutions, I could not endure the fetid breath of the tobacco-user. I sicken at the sight of the brown saliva exuding from between the lips; physiology proving that, with tobacco-chewers, nearly all the waste fluids from the body pass through the mouth. I am immediately faint at the thought of dragging my skirts through spittle in a railway car, or any place where it is thrown upon the floor; I turn with disgust at the atmosphere—God's pure, fresh air—that is tainted with the stench of tobacco smoke.

It would corrupt my husband's morals. All the associations of tobacco are bad. It is true that many good men use tobacco. It is also a truth that nearly every man that is bad is addicted to its use. To smoke in peace, the man must resort to the place where others smoke. In that room are profanity, obscene language and every species of vulgarity. There may be occasionally an exception. The fact is patent, however, that, in the room in which vulgarity and obscenity prevail, there is always tobacco smoke in the air, and the vile spittle on the floor.

You will forgive me for speaking thus plainly. I love you too well to disguise my feelings on the subject. I could not possibly constantly love a tobacco-user, for the reasons that I have given.

While I devotedly love you, I cannot consent that you should bestow your affections upon a person that would instinctively repel you. Believing, therefore, under the circumstances, that our further correspondence should cease, I remain,

Your Friend and Well-Wisher,

MARIETTA WILCOX.

Letter to an Entire Stranger.

478 —— St., Jan. 1, 18—.

Miss Henderson:

I beg to apologize for addressing you thus, being an entire stranger; but having the misfortune to be unknown to you is my excuse for this strange proceeding, which, I am well aware, is entirely at variance with the rules of etiquette. I have for two sabbaths seen you at church, and I am frank to confess that your appearance has made so deep an impression upon me as to make me extremely desirous of forming your acquaintance. I am, at present, a clerk in the ribbon department at Smith & Brown's store. Will you do me the great favor of allowing this to commence a friendship, which, I trust, will never be regretted by yourself. Please deign to give me at least a single line in reply to this, and oblige,

Your Sincere Admirer,

WESLEY BARNUM.

Unfavorable Reply.

Mr. Barnum.

Dear Sir:

I considerably question whether it is due to propriety to answer your note at all. But as you might fear that your letter had miscarried, and thus be induced to write again, it is best, probably, for me to make an immediate reply, and thus settle the affair entirely, and relieve you, possibly, of further suspense. It will be impossible for me to recognize you, or to think under any circumstances of permitting an acquaintance to be commenced by such an introduction as you seem to deem sufficient. More especially should I regret allowing a friendship to be formed by recognitions in the hours of divine service in church, while the mind should be employed in religious observances. You will, therefore, please understand that I am not favorable to further recognition, nor to a continuance of correspondence.

AMELIA HENDERSON.

Reply More Favorable.

355 —— St., June 10, 18—.

Mr. Barnum.

Dear Sir:

I am in receipt of your note, and must confess that I am surprised at your request. I am entirely opposed to commencing, on general principles, an acquaintance with such an introduction, and consider it very improper, especially to allow it to originate in church during the hours of divine service. Were it not that I think your meaning kind and your intentions good, I would return your letter unanswered. As it is, I will take your request under consideration, and, if I think best to grant it, you may know of the fact by my recognition at the close of the service in the Sabbath School.

Respectfully,

AMELIA HENDERSON.

An Advertisement in a Morning Paper.

PERSONAL.—Will the lady who rode up Broadway last Thursday afternoon, about two o'clock, in an omnibus, getting out at Stewart's, accompanied by a little girl dressed in blue suit, please send her address to D. B. M., Herald office?

REMARKS.

It is useless to advise people never to reply to a personal advertisement like the above. To do so is like totally refusing young people the privilege of dancing. People will dance, and they will answer personal advertisements. The best course, therefore, is to properly direct the dancers, and caution the writers in their answers to newspaper personals. If the eye of the young lady referred to meets the above advertisement, she will possibly be indignant at first, and will, perhaps, resolve to pay no attention to it. It will continue to occupy her attention so much, however, and curiosity will become so great, that, in order to ease her mind, she will at last give her address; in which case she makes a very serious mistake, as any lady replying to a communication of such a character, giving her name and residence to a stranger, places herself at a great disadvantage. Should her communication never be answered, she will feel mortified ever afterwards that she committed the indiscretion of replying to the advertisement at all; and, should the person she addresses prove to be some worthless fellow who may presume to press an acquaintance upon the strength of her reply, it may cause her very serious perplexity and embarrassment.

It is clearly evident, therefore, that she should not give her name and address as requested; and yet, as the advertisement may refer to a business matter of importance, or bring about an acquaintance that she will not regret, she may relieve her curiosity on the subject by writing the following note in reply:

THE REPLY.

(Advertisement pasted in.)

D. B. M.:

I find the above advertisement in the "Herald" of this morning. I suppose myself to be the person referred to. You will please state your object in addressing me, with references.

Address, A. L. K., Herald Office.

It is probable that the advertiser, if a gentleman, will reply, giving his reasons for requesting the lady's address, with references, upon receiving which, the lady will do as she may choose relative to continuing the correspondence; in either case, it will be seen that she has in no wise compromised her dignity, and she retains the advantage of knowing the motive and object that prompted the advertisement, while she is yet unknown to the advertiser.

Great caution should be exercised in answering personals. The supposition is, if the advertiser be a gentleman, that he will honorably seek an interview with a lady, and pay court as gentlemen ordinarily do. Still, an occasion may happen to a man, who is in the highest sense a gentleman, wherein he sees the lady that he very greatly admires, and can learn her address in no other way without rendering himself offensive and impertinent; hence, the apparent necessity of the above personal advertisement.

Instances have also occurred where gentlemen, driven with business, and having but little time to mingle in female society, or no opportunity, being strangers comparatively, desirous of forming the acquaintance of ladies, have honestly advertised for correspondence, been honestly answered, and marriage was the result.

Those advertisements, however, wherein Sammy Brown and Coney Smith advertise for correspondence with any number of young ladies, for fun, mutual improvement, "and what may grow out of it, photographs exchanged," etc., young ladies should be very wary of answering. Instances have been known where scores of young ladies, having answered such an advertisement, could they have looked in upon those young men, a week afterwards, would have seen them with a pile of photographs and letters, exhibiting them to their companions, and making fun of the girls who had been so foolish as to answer their advertisement.

It is true that no one but the meanest kind of a rascal would be guilty of such a disgraceful act as to advertise for and expose correspondence thus, and it is equally true that the young lady who gives the advertiser the opportunity to ridicule her shows herself to be very foolish.

Personal Advertisement.

PERSONAL.—A gentleman, a new comer in the city, having a sufficiency of this world's goods to comfortably support himself and wife, is desirous of making the acquaintance of a lady of middle years, with a view to matrimony. Address, in the strictest confidence, giving name, residence and photograph, H. A. B., Station H, Postoffice.

THE REPLY.

To H. A. B.

Sir:

I am led to suppose, from the reading of the above, that it is dictated in sincerity, by a desire to meet with a lady who would be treated with candor and respect. I have at present no acquaintance to whom I am inclined to give a very decided preference, nor have I ever had any very distinct ideas on the subject of marriage. I am free, however, to confess that, should circumstances favor my acquaintance with a gentleman whom I could honor and respect, I might seriously think of a proposal. Believing that you wish, as you intimate, this letter in confidence, I will say that I am — years old, am in receipt of —— annually, from property that is leased. I have been told that I was handsome, though others, probably, have a different opinion. Of that fact, you must be the judge. I am entirely free to select whomsoever I may choose. My social standing, I trust, would be satisfactory, and my accomplishments have not been neglected. It is not necessary that I should write more. I shall be happy to correspond with you with a view to better acquaintance, when, if mutually agreeable, an introduction may take place. You desire me to send name, address and photograph, which, I trust you will perceive, would be improper for me to do. It is due to myself, and, under certain circumstances, to you, that I should be very guarded as to the manner of my introduction. A letter addressed to M. A. L., Station A, Postoffice, will reach me.

I sign a fictitious name, for obvious reasons.

Respectfully,

NANCY HILLIS.

A Gentleman Makes a Frank Acknowledgment. — Gushing with Sentiment, and Running Over with Poetry.

WHITE MOUNTAINS, N. H., Oct. 1, 18—.

MY DEAR MARY:

One by one the brown leaves are falling, reminding us that the golden summer that we have so delightfully loitered through approaches its close. How thickly our pathway has been strewn with roses; how fragrant have been the million blossoms; how sweetly the birds have sung; how beautiful have been the sunny days; how joyous have been the starry nights! Dear M., I do not need to tell you that this delightful summer has been to me one grand Elysian scene. I have gazed on and dreamed of thy beauty. I have been fed by thy sparkling repartee and merriment; I have drank at the fountain of thy intellectuality; but the feast is ended, and gradually the curtain is falling. Dear, beautiful summer; so beautiful to me because of thy loved presence. And standing now on the threshold of a scene all changed, I take a last, fond, long, lingering look on the beautiful picture that will return to me no more; and yet, who knows, but on in that great eternity we may live again these Eden hours.

"Like a foundling in slumber, the summer day lay
      On the crimsoning threshold of even,
And I thought that the glow through the azure-arched way
      Was a glimpse of the coming of Heaven.
There together we sat by the beautiful stream;
      We had nothing to do but to love and to dream
In the days that have gone on before.
      These are not the same days, though they bear the same name,
With the ones I shall welcome no more.

"But it may be the angels are culling them o'er,
      For a Sabbath and Summer forever,
When the years shall forget the Decembers they wore,
      And the shroud shall be woven, no, never!
In a twilight like that, darling M. for a bride—
      Oh! what more of the world could one wish beside,
As we gazed on the river unroll'd
      Till we heard, or we fancied, its musical tide,
Where it flowed through the Gateway of Gold?"

Dearest, you must forgive my ardent expressions in this letter. With a temperament gushing to the brim and overflowing with sentiment and rhapsody, I have passed the fleeting summer in thy charming presence in one continual dream of poesy. I cannot now turn back to the solemn duties before me, without telling you what trembled on my tongue a thousand times, as we gathered flowers together and wove our chaplets in the sunny days gone by. Dear, darling Mary, I love you, I adore you. How often in the beautiful moonlight nights, as we strolled among the lilacs and the primroses, have I been on the verge of clasping your jeweled hand and telling you all my heart. But, oh! I did not quite dare; the hours were so delightful, even as they were. Fearing that I might be repulsed, I chose to accept the joy even that there was, rather than run the risk of losing it all. How many a morning have I arisen and firmly resolved that, ere another day, I would know my fate! But, ah! the twilight would fall, and the evening hour would pass by, and I never completely dared to risk the result of a declaration. The morrow I knew would be joyous if I bridled my impulse; it might not be if I made a mistake. But the dream has passed by. To-morrow, I bid adieu to these silvan groves, the quiet meadows and the gurgling brooks, to go back to the prose duties of business. And now, at the close of this festal season, as I am upon the verge of going, having nothing to lose and everything to gain, I have told you my heart. I have not the slightest idea what your reply will be. You have been to me one continual puzzle. If your answer is adverse, I can only entertain the highest respect for you ever in the future; and memory shall keep alive the recollection of the most blissful summer I have ever known. If your reply is favorable—dearest, may I fondly hope that it will be?—then opens before me a great volume of happiness, of which this joyous summer has been but the opening chapter.

Dear M., may I come again and see you, and address you henceforth as a lover? The messenger who brings you this will return again in an hour for your answer. I need not tell you what an hour of suspense this will be to me. Upon your reply hangs my future. If your reply is favorable, I shall tarry another day; and will you grant me a long interview, as I have much to talk over with you? If unfavorable, please return this letter with your note. Accept my warmest thanks for the entertainment which I, in common with others, have received at your hand in the past; and, if I may not sign myself your devoted lover, I shall at least, I trust, have ever the pleasure of subscribing myself,

Your Sincere Friend,
CLARENCE HARRINGTON.

Favorable Reply.

DEAR CLARENCE:

I shall not attempt in this to answer your missive with the same poetic fervor that colors your letter from beginning to end. While it is given you to tread the emerald pavements of an imaginary Eden, in my plainer nature I can only walk the common earth.

I fully agree with you in your opinion of the beautiful summer just passed. Though in seasons heretofore many people have been here from the cities, I have never known a summer so delightful. Yes, Clarence, these three months have been joyous, because—shall I confess it?—because *you* have been here. I need not write more. You have agreed to stay another day; I shall be at home this afternoon, at two o'clock, and will be happy to see you.

Yours Very Truly,
MARY SINGLETON.

To a Lady, from a Gentleman Confessing Change of Sentiment.

844—ST., April 2, 18—.

MISS MARION THORNTON:

Your note accusing me of coldness is before me. After spending several hours in a consideration of this subject, to determine what is my duty, I have concluded that it is decidedly best for me to be perfectly frank with you, and give my reasons for a change of sentiment.

I do not think we could live happily together if we were married, because, from disparaging remarks I have heard you make concerning people that are not wealthy, I think you would be entirely dissatisfied with my circumstances; and the further fact that you allow your mother to do all the drudgery of the household, you sitting in the parlor entertaining gentlemen, and affecting to have no knowledge of housekeeping, is proof that our tastes would not accord in home matters. I consider it just as honorable, and just as important, that young ladies should do something to support themselves, as that young men should. If the opportunities are not as great for them to go abroad, they can, at least while at home, learn to be good in sewing, cooking and housekeeping, and thus be prepared when opportunities offer, to make prudent, economical, tidy housewives. I do not under-value the importance of being proficient in the lighter accomplishments which go to make a lady at ease in society; but I vastly more prize

the lady who knows how to get an excellent breakfast early in the morning, who is not only a model of neatness herself, but relieves her mother in household duties, keeping her younger brothers and sisters clean and orderly.

I have admired and loved you for your musical talent and your fine conversational powers, but, as I could not keep the necessary servants to enable you constantly to gratify those talents to the exclusion of the more substantial duties, I feel that our marriage would be a mistake for us both.

You asked my reason for my changing love; I have reluctantly, yet plainly, stated it. Hoping, however, that you may always be happy in life, I am,

Your Friend,
CLINTON HOLMES.

Reply to a Young Man Addicted to Intemperance.

669——— St., Nov. 7, 18—

Mr. Spellman.

Dear Sir:

Your kind invitation to accompany you to the opera, to-morrow evening, is received. Under ordinary circumstances, I would be delighted to go with you, believing you at heart to be really a most excellent gentleman. I regret to add, however, that I have undoubted evidence of the fact that you are becoming addicted to the use of the wine-cup. I regard it entirely unsafe for any young lady to continue an intimacy with a young man upon whom is growing the habit of intemperance. With an earnest prayer for your reformation, ere it be too late, I beg you to consider our intimacy at an end.

Respectfully,
Helen Sanford.

One Way of Breaking the Ice.

584 —— St., July 1, 18—.

My Dear Friend Caroline:

I returned yesterday from a brief trip into Canada, my journey being most agreeable; only one little episode breaking the monotony, as I neared home, which was this: in the next seat behind me in the car sat a young couple, who were evidently regretting that their ride was so near an end. Though buried in my reading, I could not avoid hearing much that they said. One question asked by the young man made a striking impression on my mind. "Maggie," said he, "we have now been acquainted a good while; you know me, and I know you. I do not need to tell you that I love you with all my heart; now, do you love me?"

I knew the young fellow had taken that occasion, when the cars were thundering along, so that he might not be knocked down by the beating of his own heart. I confess to have been guilty of eavesdropping, then. I listened intently for the lady's answer, but just at that moment, as my ill luck would have it, another train came thundering by us, and her voice was drowned in the noise. I got to thinking like this: suppose you and I were riding thus, and I should ask precisely the same question; what would be your reply? I am very curious to know what your answer would be, and shall await a letter from you, with much anxiety.

Most Truly Yours,

ROLAND MILLS.

An Offer of Marriage.

248 —— St., Dec. 10, 18—.

Dearest Bertha:

I have intended, oh, how many times! when we have been together, to put the simple question which I intend this note shall ask; but, although apparently a very easy matter to ask the hand in marriage of one I so deeply love as yourself, it is no easy task. I therefore write what I have never found courage in my heart to speak. Dearest, will you bestow upon me the great happiness of permitting me to call you mine? If I have spoken this too boldly, you will forgive; but I fondly hope that you will not be indifferent to my appeal. I trust, if you answer this in the affirmative, that you will never regret doing so. Anxiously awaiting your answer, I remain,

Yours Affectionately,

HARLAN DEMPSTER.

Favorable Reply.

367 —— St., Dec. 10, 18—.

Dear Sir:

Your proposal is quite unexpected to me, but it is made with such candor and frankness that I can take no offence. I cannot, in this note, give you a definite reply. Marriage is a very serious matter; and, while I regard you with the greatest favor, I desire to consult my near relatives, and consider the subject myself carefully for a few days, ere I give you a final answer. I think I can assure you, however, that you may *hope*.

Very Sincerely,

FANNIE KIMBALL.

Letter from a Young Man Who Proposes Marriage and Emigration.

482 —— St., April 16, 18—.

Dear Clara:

You have doubtless heard of my intention to go West in the coming month. Though surrounded here with my relatives and all the many friends of my boyhood, I have an intense desire to try my fortune amid new scenes, feeling that the fetters that now bind me and seem to hinder my upward progress will then be broken.

I shall sunder my ties with some regrets, but, to commence my business career as I am desirous of doing, I must make the sacrifice; in doing so, I do no more than thousands have done before me. In the great, broad fields of the growing West, a young man of resolution, ambition, honesty, temperance and perseverance cannot fail, I believe, to better his condition much more rapidly than he can here; you will, I think, coincide with me in this opinion.

Dear Clara, of all my farewells, none will be so sad to me as that I shall bid to you. Dear, dear Clara, you cannot be indifferent to the fact that I have long devotedly loved you; and, at the hour of parting, I feel that I cannot go without telling you my heart, and asking you if I may not have your love in return. And now, while I am asking, will you not take me and my heart, and in turn allow me to be your protector through life?

Dearest, I am going to press my suit still further. Will you not be mine before I go, and accompany me on my journey? I know this is asking a great deal of you. To accept of this proposition, is to take you from a home of affluence, where you are surrounded with every desired comfort. I have no right to ask the sacrifice; and yet I have resolved to make bold before I go, and tell you all. If you accept my offer, and will consent to cast your fortunes with me out in the great Sea of the Hereafter, I can assure you that no trouble or sorrow will come to you through me; and that, as you will be my dear, dear companion and sacred trust, so will I be to you all that a lover and husband can be.

Now, dearest, if you will accept my future as your own, and place yourself by my side, accepting the sorrow and partaking of the joy that is in store for me, you will make me the happiest of men. If you assent, God grant that you may never regret your faith. Do not decide the question hastily. The sacrifice is such, in leaving home and kindred, that you may not accept of my proposal even though you love. When you have fully determined, however, please send the answer, which I shall most anxiously await. Ever, Dear Clara,

Your Affectionate,

HENRY ADAMS.

Reply.

172 —— St., April 16, 18—.

Dear Henry:

I can make a reply to your candid question at once. I do not need to deliberate upon it long. I love you; I confide in you. I will trust you; I will go with you; I will accept the love and the future you offer. You may have many joys; you may experience some sorrows: I will share and bear them all with you, trusting that patient, earnest, willing effort may crown our labors with success. Believing that God will guide and prosper us, I can only add, hoping to see you soon, that I am,

Ever yours,

CLARA DUNHAM.

WEDDING CARDS.

IF the lady who marries resides with her parents, with relatives, guardians, or friends, and the marriage receives the approval of those parties, the ceremony usually takes place at the residence of the bride, or at the church where she generally attends; a reception being held at her residence soon afterwards or upon the return from the bridal tour.

Some parties prefer to marry very quietly, having but few guests at the wedding. Others make more elaborate display, and observe the time as an occasion of general rejoicing. Where many guests are invited, it is customary to issue notes of invitation to those persons whose attendance is desired, accompanied by wedding cards bearing the name of the bride and groom. The form of wording such notes and cards has changed but little for several years, though the *style* in which such wording appears, changes frequently.

Two methods are pursued in preparing the invitations and cards: one being to have them neatly printed from type; the other, and more expensive manner, is to have them engraved and printed in the metropolis, by a card-engraver, who makes an exclusive business of preparing such cards.

The later style for cards and notes of invitation is to have the most of the wording in a light script, upon very fine, white, billet paper, and the cards upon thin bristol-board, sometimes long, and frequently nearly square, according to fancy.

The following cards and notes of invitation, while expressing the suitable wording, do not,

in all cases, represent the size of the card or note of invitation. They are of various sizes, according to fancy, and generally a little larger than here illustrated.

In sending the note of invitation, it is customary to inclose the cards in the same envelope. In cases where no guests are invited, yet it is desired to inform the acquaintances throughout the country of the marriage, it is usual to inclose the cards alone. Formerly, it was common to use but one card, having Mr. & Mrs. Chas. H. Smith in the center of the card, while the lady's maiden name was placed upon the lower left-hand corner. Of late, it is regarded more in style to use two cards, one considerably larger than the other; the larger bearing the names, Mr. & Mrs. Chas. H. Smith, the smaller, the lady's name alone, thus:

Mr. & Mrs. Chas. H. Smith.

Hattie M. Maynard.

If it is definitely decided where the future permanent residence of the newly wedded couple is to be, it is proper to place the name of the town and state, at the lower left-hand corner of the larger card, as shown herewith.

Invitations to the Wedding.

THE following, are among the many of the various styles of notes of invitation to the wedding ceremony. The form shown here, is printed on paper about the width, but a little shorter than, commercial note paper, the wording being on the lower half of the sheet. In the center of the upper half of the sheet is the monogram, composed of the initial letters of the surnames of the bride and groom, blended together. This monogram is also printed upon the flap of the envelope containing the invitation and cards. The accompanying is the note of invitation issued by Mr. & Mrs. D Collins, on the occasion of the marriage of their daughter, M. Louise, to Jay H. Sabray; the ceremony taking place at their residence. Two cards accompany this note, one reading *Mr. & Mrs. Jay H. Sabray*, the other, *M. Louise Collins*.

Mr. & Mrs. Chas. H. Smith,

NEWARK, N. J.

Actual size of one form of Note of Invitation. This dotted line shows the fold.

Request the pleasure of your Company at the Marriage of their Daughter,

M. Louise to Jay H. Sabray,

Thursday, September 19th, '72, at 8 o'clock, P. M.

AT THEIR HOME, ATLANTA, GA.

If desirous of giving information of the time of return from the bridal tour, and an invitation to receptions afterwards, the address is omitted on the larger card, and a third card may accompany the other two, worded as follows:

This style of invitation, printed on a fine card about the size of a large envelope, is frequently employed. If desirous of using colored cardboard, a light olive or pink tint is sometimes admissible, though white is always in best taste.

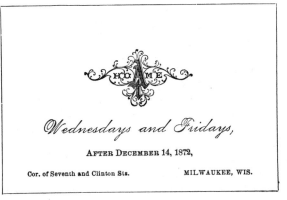

Wednesdays and Fridays,

AFTER DECEMBER 14, 1872,

Cor. of Seventh and Clinton Sts.   MILWAUKEE, WIS.

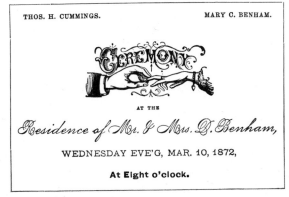

THOS. H. CUMMINGS.   MARY C. BENHAM.

AT THE

Residence of Mr. & Mrs. D. Benham,

WEDNESDAY EVE'G, MAR. 10, 1872,

At Eight o'clock.

This style of invitation, requiring no cards, is frequently used:

The following note, announcing, "At Home," after October 15, requires no cards:

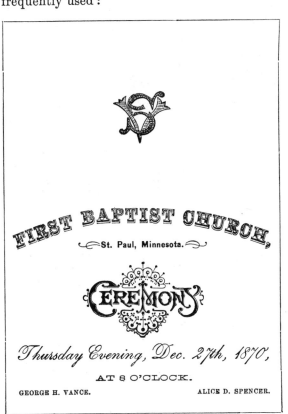

FIRST BAPTIST CHURCH,

St. Paul, Minnesota.

CEREMONY

Thursday Evening, Dec. 27th, 1870,

AT 8 O'CLOCK.

GEORGE H. VANCE.   ALICE D. SPENCER.

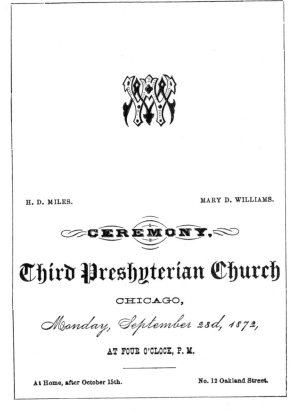

H. D. MILES.   MARY D. WILLIAMS.

CEREMONY,

Third Presbyterian Church

CHICAGO,

Monday, September 23d, 1872,

AT FOUR O'CLOCK, P. M.

At Home, after October 15th.   No. 12 Oakland Street.

The cards are often made in this proportion, and fastened with a ribbon, thus:

The following invitation is accompanied by the cards shown above, fastened by a ribbon in the center. The larger card bears the names of Mr. and Mrs. James Wilson; the other, the name of the bride, Angeline Sherman.

Not unfrequently the cards are fastened at the top, as shown in this illustration:

Jennie L. Henderson.

Henry D. Rand.

The succeeding invitation is issued by the parents of the bride, the reception taking place at their residence, after the ceremony at church. As with the other invitations, this is also accompanied by the monogram.

Mr. & Mrs. Chas. H. Sherman,

Request the pleasure of your Company at the Marriage

Of their Daughter, Angeline, Tuesday Eve'g, Apr. 23d, '72,

CEREMONY, AT 9 O'CLOCK.

112 Clinton St., Boston.

Mr. & Mrs. Samuel Henderson,

Wednesday Evening, June 10th, '71. at 8.30 o'clock.

HENRY D. RAND.   JENNIE L. HENDERSON.

CLEVELAND, O.

WEDDING CEREMONIES.
FOR
Notes of
INVITATION
TO
WEDDINGS
AND
PARTIES

See Preceding Pages.

HAVING resolved upon marriage, the lady will determine when the ceremony shall take place.

No peculiar form of ceremony is requisite, nor is it imperative that it be performed by a particular person. In the United States, marriage is regarded as a civil contract, which may be entered into by a simple declaration of the contracting parties, made in the presence of one or more witnesses, that they, the said parties, do respectively contract to be husband and wife.

In consequence of the recognized vast importance of marriage to the parties contracting the same, long usage has established the custom, almost universally, of having the ceremony performed by, or in presence of, a clergyman or magistrate.

To be entitled to contract marriage, the following requisites are necessary: 1st, That they be willing to marry ; 2d, That they be of sound mind ; 3d, That they have arrived at the age allowed by law ; 4th, That neither of the parties is married already to another who is living, and from whom such party has not obtained a divorce from the bonds of matrimony ; and 5th, That the parties are not so nearly related by consanguinity, as to prohibit their marriage, by the laws of the State in which the marriage is contracted.

In most of the States, the common law requires that the male be fourteen and the female twelve years of age, before the marriage can take place. In certain States, seventeen for males and fourteen for females; in others, the age for males is eighteen, for females, fourteen.

Formerly in certain Eastern States, parties intending to marry were required by statute to record a notice of such intent with the town clerk for three weeks, at the expiration of which time, if no objection was interposed, the clerk was authorized to give a certificate to that effect, and the clergyman or magistrate was empowered to perform the ceremony. In various States, the law requires that parties intending marriage shall previously obtain from the city or town clerk, a certificate of their respective names, occupations, ages, birth-places, and residences upon receipt of which, any clergyman or magistrate is authorized to perform the ceremony.

In several States of the Union, the consent of the parents or guardians is required, before the proper officer can issue a license, if the male be under twenty-one years, or the female under eighteen

In some of the States, a license to marry must first be procured of the city, town, or county clerk, empowering the clergyman or magistrate to marry the contracting parties, which is worded as follows:

Marriage License.

—State of— —County of—

The people of the State of ...., to any person legally authorized to solemnize Marriage, GREETING: You are hereby authorized to join in the holy bonds of Matrimony, and to celebrate the rites and ceremonies of Marriage, between Mr. ...., and M ...., according to the usual custom and laws of the State of ...., and you are required to return this license to me within thirty days, from the celebration of such Marriage, with a Certificate of the same, appended thereto, and signed by you, under the penalty of One Hundred Dollars.

Witness ...., Clerk of our said Court and the Seal thereof, at his office, in ...., in said County, this day of ...., A. D., ...187....

Seal.

County Clerk.

State of ...., } S.S. I, ...
.... County. a ...., hereby certify that on the .... day of ...., 187...., I joined in Marriage, Mr. ...., and M ...., agreeable to the authority given in the above License, and the customs and laws of this State. Given under my hand and seal, this .... day of ...., A. D., 187....

SEAL.

The Ceremony.

The license procured, the ceremony of marriage may take place wherever it best suits the convenience of the parties marrying, and may be performed by a clergyman, justice of the supreme court, judge of an inferior court, justice of the peace, or police justice; one or more witnesses being present to testify to the marriage. The clergyman or magistrate may visit the candidates for matrimony at a private residence, hotel, hall, church or other place; or the parties may call upon the clergyman at his residence, or visit the magistrate in his office, where the rite may be performed. When the ceremony is conducted by the magistrate, the following is the usual form.

Form of Marriage.

(The man and woman rising, the justice will say to the man:)

"Will you have this woman to be your wedded wife, to live together after God's ordinance, in the holy estate of Matrimony, to love her, comfort her, honor and keep her, in sickness and in health, and, forsaking all others, keep thee only unto her, so long as you both shall live?"

(Then, addressing the woman, the justice will say:)

"Will you have this man to be your wedded husband, to live together after God's ordinance, in the holy estate of Matrimony, to love, honor and keep him, in sickness and in health, and, forsaking all others, keep thee only unto him, so long as you both shall live?"

(The parties answering in the affirmative, the justice will then instruct to join hands, and say:

"By the act of joining hands you take upon yourselves the relation of husband and wife, and solemnly promise and engage, in the presence of these witnesses, to love, honor, comfort and cherish each other as such, so long as you both shall live; therefore, in accordance with the laws of the State of————, I do hereby pronounce you husband and wife."

Short Form of Marriage.

(The justice will instruct the parties to rise and join hands, and then say:)

"By this act of joining hands you do take upon yourselves the relation of husband and wife, and solemnly promise and engage, in the presence of these witnesses, to love and honor, comfort and cherish each other as such, as long as you both shall live; therefore in accordance with the laws of the State of————, I do hereby pronounce you husband and wife."

The form used by clergymen is essentially the same, though the wording may vary slightly to suit the occasion and conform to the rites of the church under which the parties marry.

The marriage license is returned by the magistrate or clergyman to the clerk that granted it, for record. At the time of procuring the license, however, the bridegroom or other person should obtain a blank marriage certificate, usually furnished by the clerk, which should be filled by the clergyman or magistrate at the close of the ceremony, certifying to the marriage of the parties; which certificate should be always preserved by the husband and wife, as proof of marriage, if necessary, when they have removed to other parts of the country.

The following is the form of the marriage certificate:

Marriage Certificate.

State of————————————, ———————————— County.

THIS CERTIFIES

That ———— of ———— in the State of ———— and ———— of ———— in the State of ———— were at ———— in the said County, by me joined together in

HOLY MATRIMONY,

On the ————————, day of————————, in the year of our Lord, One Thousand Eight Hundred and Seventy————

IN PRESENCE OF

ASIDE from the entertainments of guests at the residence of the bride, the expenses of the marriage are entirely borne by the groom, who is understood to be the winner of the prize. If the parties marrying are wealthy and of undoubted standing and respectability in society, they can appropriately celebrate the nuptial ceremony in an expensive manner, the occasion being taken by the relatives and friends as an opportunity for the making of every description of present to the bride and groom. If, however, the parties move in the humbler walks of life, an expensive bridal tour, and very great display at the wedding, are not advisable. It is much better for the newly wedded couple to commence life in a manner so plain and modest that succeeding years cannot fail to steadily increase their wealth and give them better opportunities. People always more highly respect those persons who steadily go upward, no matter how slowly, than those that attempt a display beyond their ability honestly to maintain.

To legally marry in the United States, only a few incidental expenses are really necessary. Of these, the license costs, in different States, from one to two dollars, and the magistrate, for performing the ceremony, is allowed by law to charge two dollars. While no law regulates the price, it is customary to quietly present the clergyman five dollars or more, according to the ability and liberality of the groom. In giving notice of the marriage to the newspaper, it is courtesy always to enclose, with the same, a dollar bill.

The wording of the marriage notice will depend upon circumstances. If the parties have a large circle of acquaintances, to whom they desire to offer an apology for not having invited them to the wedding, they will announce, with the notice, that no general invitation was extended, thus:

MARRIED.

LEONARD — REYNOLDS.— In this city, at the residence of the bride's father, January 1, 1873, by the Rev. Chas. G. Robinson, rector of Christ Church, Mr. Theron D. Leonard and Mrs. A. B. Reynolds, daughter of Wm. Fairbanks, Esq., all of Philadelphia. No cards.

Other marriage notices, according to circumstances, will read as follows:

In this city, by the Rev. H. A. Henderson, CHARLES H. WILLIAMS and MYRA B. COOLEY, both of Chicago.

On Tuesday, the 7th inst., by the Rev. Dr. Belmont, at the residence of the bride's uncle, Harvey Baker, Esq., Cyrus E. Maynard, of New York, and Miss Lizzie H. Wentworth, of Cleveland, Ohio.

On Thursday, January 20th, at the residence of Mr. Asa Sprague, 144 Mayberry St., Anton D. Miller, of St. Joseph, Mich., and Harriet A. Sprague, of this city.
St. Joseph papers please copy.

At the Leland house, Springfield, Ill., January 30, by the Rev. J. L. Stoddard, Stephen M. Byron, of Detroit, Mich., and Carrie D. Paine, of Springfield, Ill.

On the evening of the 30th, at the Revere House, by Winfield Gardner, Miss Emma Brown to William Wedgewood, all of this city.

In this city, on Monday, at the residence of the bride's father, Mr. H. A. Waldron and Miss Agnes E. Willett.

The ceremonies took place at the residence of Henry Willett, Esq., on Beverly Place, yesterday morning at nine o'clock, only a select company of friends being present. The happy couple departed at once on their wedding tour, with New York as their main point of destination. Their visit will be protracted until the middle of next month, when, upon their return, Mr. Waldron will assume the secretaryship of the Great Western Mutual Insurance Company, of this city, to which position he has been recently called by the directors of the company.

Invitations to Receptions and Parties.

PRINTED ON CARDS AND CIRCULARS.

Mr. & Mrs. Charles Simmonds,

RECEIVE FRIENDS,

Wednesday Evening, May 10th,

At 8 o'clock.

Mr. & Mrs. W. H. Bartlett,

BURLINGTON,

Friday Evening, Sept. 20th,

At 8 1-2 o'clock.

Dr. & Mrs. William Stewart,

Wednesday Eve'g, Nov. 10th, '71,

AT EIGHT O'CLOCK.

G. C. H.

GRAND CENTRAL HOTEL

Hop,

THURSDAY EVENING, JAN. 4TH, 1871.

— COMPLIMENTARY. —

Mr. _____,

Yourself and Ladies are Cordially Invited.

Committee of Arrangements

D. O. LEWIS,   WM. W. BROWN,   D. B. SNOW,
HIRAM D. KING,   CHAS. WILSON,   H. E. POTWIN.

Family Records.

How to Prepare the Register; giving Names of the Family, Births, Marriages and Deaths.

DURING LIFE, a carefully prepared record of the family, which should be arranged by the head of the household, is of great convenience for reference. This register should contain the name, birth, marriage, and death of each member of the family. It may be kept in the Bible, on a paper prepared especially for the purpose, suitable for framing, or in any manner whereby the same may be preserved. It may also contain brief biographical sketches of members of the family.

IN preparing the register, care should be taken to give the names of the family in full, the town and state where each was born, and date of birth; the state and town where each died, and date of death; town and state where each married, and date, together with the name of the officiating clergyman, or magistrate, and of one or more witnesses to the marriage. In proving claims to pensions, or heirship to estates, this is frequently of great importance. Observe carefully the form of record shown on the opposite page.

BIOGRAPHY OF CHILDREN.

GUARDIANS and parents are also recommended to prepare in a book of blank pages, made for the purpose, a biographical sketch of each child under their charge, noting peculiarities of birth, attending physician, color of hair, eyes, &c., when born; strength of constitution, subsequent disposition, age at which the child first walks, talks, reads, writes, first attends school, and so on upwards until the child is able to take up the record itself.

THE child's record should be made very full and explicit for many reasons, the principal being that it may be of great service to the future biographer of the child, while the physiologist may draw an important lesson by a comparison between the habits of infancy and those of mature years. This record will certainly be a matter of value to the family, and like the infant-picture, it will be of especial interest to the man and woman as a daguerreotype of their early years.

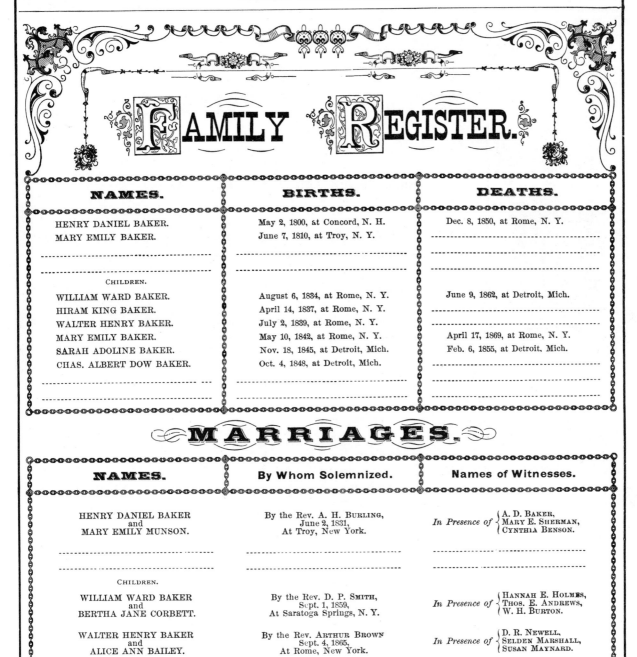

FAMILY REGISTER.

NAMES.	BIRTHS.	DEATHS.
HENRY DANIEL BAKER.	May 2, 1800, at Concord, N. H.	Dec. 8, 1850, at Rome, N. Y.
MARY EMILY BAKER.	June 7, 1810, at Troy, N. Y.	
CHILDREN.		
WILLIAM WARD BAKER.	August 6, 1834, at Rome, N. Y.	June 9, 1862, at Detroit, Mich.
HIRAM KING BAKER.	April 14, 1837, at Rome, N. Y.	
WALTER HENRY BAKER.	July 2, 1839, at Rome, N. Y.	
MARY EMILY BAKER.	May 10, 1842, at Rome, N. Y.	April 17, 1869, at Rome, N. Y.
SARAH ADOLINE BAKER.	Nov. 18, 1845, at Detroit, Mich.	Feb. 6, 1855, at Detroit, Mich.
CHAS. ALBERT DOW BAKER.	Oct. 4, 1848, at Detroit, Mich.	

MARRIAGES.

NAMES.	By Whom Solemnized.	Names of Witnesses.
HENRY DANIEL BAKER and MARY EMILY MUNSON.	By the Rev. A. H. BURLING, June 2, 1831, At Troy, New York.	In Presence of { A. D. BAKER, MARY E. SHERMAN, CYNTHIA BENSON.
CHILDREN.		
WILLIAM WARD BAKER and BERTHA JANE CORBETT.	By the Rev. D. P. SMITH, Sept. 1, 1859, At Saratoga Springs, N. Y.	In Presence of { HANNAH E. HOLMES, THOS. E. ANDREWS, W. H. BURTON.
WALTER HENRY BAKER and ALICE ANN BAILEY.	By the Rev. ARTHUR BROWN Sept. 4, 1865, At Rome, New York.	In Presence of { D. R. NEWELL, SELDEN MARSHALL, SUSAN MAYNARD.
MARY EMILY BAKER and MYRON BURTON ELDRIDGE.	By the Rev. D. O. SMITH, Aug. 16, 1865, At Detroit, Michigan.	In Presence of { CAPT. O. D. KEMPLE, MALVINA SIMPSON, HARRIET PUTNAM.
CHAS. A. D. BAKER and FLORENCE PERCY BRIGGS.	By WM. M. KELLOGG, J. P., March 4, 1872, At St. Louis, Missouri.	In Presence of { ANNA E. MOORE, CHAS. D. WELLS, ABIGAIL MINARD.

Marriage Anniversaries.

GOLD, SILVER AND OTHER WEDDINGS.

ASHION has established the custom, of late years, of celebrating certain anniversaries of the marriage, these being named as follows:

The celebration at the expiration of the first year is called the COTTON wedding; at two years comes the PAPER; at three, the LEATHER; at the close of five years comes the WOODEN; at the seventh anniversary the friends assemble with the WOOLEN, and at ten years comes the TIN. At twelve years the SILK AND FINE LINEN; at fifteen the CRYSTAL wedding. At twenty, the friends gather with their CHINA, and at twenty-five the married couple, that have been true to their vows for a quarter of a century, are rewarded with SILVER gifts. From this time forward, the tokens of esteem become rapidly more valuable. At the thirtieth anniversary, they are presented with PEARLS; at the fortieth, come the RUBIES; and at the fiftieth, occurs the celebration of a glorious GOLDEN wedding. Beyond that time the aged couple are allowed to enjoy their many gifts in peace. If, however, by any possibility they reach the seventy-fifth anniversary, they are presented with the rarest gifts to be obtained, at the celebration of their DIAMOND wedding.

In issuing the invitations for celebrating these anniversaries, it is customary to print them on a material emblematical of the occasion. Thus, thin wood, leather, cloth, tin-foil, silk, silver and gold paper, and other materials are brought into use.

Of course, those who accept of such an invitation, and partake of the hospitalities of the host and hostess, are expected to contribute to the collection of gifts that will grace the occasion.

The form of invitation for such an anniversary is represented in the following:

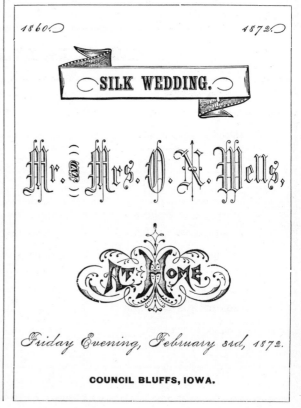

Invitation to the Crystal Wedding.

CRYSTAL   WEDDING.

1858.   1873.

Mr. & Mrs. W. Stevens,

RECEPTION

Thursday Evening, March 25, 1873,
at Four O'clock.

ROME,   N. Y.

Invitation to the China Wedding.

China Wedding.

1850 1870.

Mr. & Mrs. B. Ring

WILL RECEIVE THEIR FRIENDS AT THE

TWENTIETH ANNIVERSARY

OF THEIR

MARRIAGE,

Tuesday Eve., June 14, 1870.

LONG BRANCH.

Invitation to the Silver Wedding.

MR. & MRS. H. R. MEAD,

Cordially invite you to be present at their Twenty=
Fifth Wedding

ANNIVERSARY,

On Monday Evening, June 16, 1873.

No. 700 Broadway, New York.   **Ceremony at 8 o'Clock.**

Invitation to the Golden Wedding.

1823.   1873.

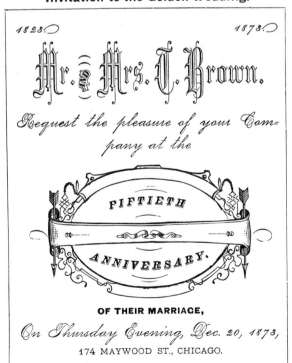

Mr. & Mrs. T. Brown.

Request the pleasure of your Com=
pany at the

FIFTIETH

ANNIVERSARY.

OF THEIR MARRIAGE,

On Thursday Evening, Dec. 20, 1873,

174 MAYWOOD ST., CHICAGO.

Notes of Invitation to Parties

AND ELSEWHERE.

NOTES of invitation to a large party are usually printed and displayed in a style similar to the annexed, being always worded in the third person. If written, and among intimate friends, a more familiar style may be adopted.

Invitations should be written or printed upon a whole sheet of small note-paper, and should be issued at least a week before the time appointed for the party, so that, if necessary, a suitable dress may be obtained. For a costume ball or masquerade, two weeks is the usual time allowed for preparation.

The letters R. S. V. P. are sometimes put at the end of a note. They stand for the French phrase, "*Répondez s'il vous plaît*"--answer, if you please. It is better, however, when an answer is particularly desired, to say, "An answer will oblige."

It is courtesy to reply promptly to a note of invitation requesting an answer.

If no reply is requested, and you send no regrets, it is understood that you accept the invitation.

Send invitations, to persons in your own city or neighborhood, by your own messenger. It is regarded a violation of etiquette to send them by mail.

Invitation to an Intimate Friend.

Mrs. Langford may write to her intimate friend, Miss Burling, as follows:

June 9th, 18____.

Dear Lizzie:

We are to have a little social party on Wednesday evening next, which will be very incomplete without you. Please come, and bring your cousin with you. He will not, I trust, require a more formal invitation, as he knows he will be very welcome.

Your Friend,

Harriet Langford.

Wednesday Evening.

Invitation to a Lawn Soiree.

MR. & MRS. HARRINGTON.
MR. D. C. HARRINGTON.

Request the pleasure of your company, at a Lawn Soiree, Friday evening, from half-past seven to half-past ten o'clock, June 20th, 18—, weather permitting.
R. S. V. P.

Invitation to an Evening Party.

Mrs. Langford requests the pleasure of Mr. and Mrs. Bell's company on Thursday evening, 7th inst., at seven o'clock.
No. 7 —— St., Dec. 1st.

Answer Accepting the Invitation.

Mr. and Mrs. Bell accept, with pleasure, Mrs. Langford's kind invitation for Thursday evening, the 7th inst.
No. 8 —— St., Dec. 2d.

Answer Declining the Invitation.

Mr. and Mrs. Bell regret their inability to accept Mrs. Langford's kind invitation for Thursday evening, the 7th inst.
No. 8 —— St., Dec. 2d.

Invitation to a Dinner Party.

Mr. Conklin presents his warm regards to Mr. Belden, and requests the pleasure of his company to dinner, on Thursday next (18th) at 5 o'clock. Mr. Conklin expects the pleasure, also, of receiving Mr. Wilbur, of Buffalo.
An answer will oblige.
No. 44 —— St., June 16, 18—.

Answer Accepting the Invitation.

Mr. Belden presents his kind regards to Mr. Conklin, and accepts, with pleasure, his polite invitation for Thursday next.
No. 17 —— St., June 17, 18—.

Answer Declining the Invitation.

Mr. Belden regrets that a previously arranged business engagement will prevent his accepting Mr. Conklin's kind invitation for to-morrow. Mr. Belden has delayed answering until to-day, hoping to effect a change of appointment, but has learned this forenoon that no change can be made without serious disappointment to others.
No. 17 —— St., June 17, 18—.

HALLOWEEN

Gertrude, Willie and Carrie Hall's

COMPLIMENTS FOR

Monday Evening, October 31, 1873.

No. 481 MARBLE STREET.

Mr. & Mrs. Harvey Blossom's

COMPLIMENTS FOR

Monday Evening, Sept. 21st, 1873.

DANCING.

Refreshments will be Served at Ten o'Clock.

Familiar Invitation to a Wedding.

No.———St., Dec. 12, 18—.

DEAR HATTIE:

I have issued but few invitations for our Aggie's wedding, as we desire to be almost entirely private; but the presence of a few dear friends will give us all pleasure. Can we count you among those few? The ceremony will be at seven, on Tuesday evening next, December 18th, and at eight we will receive the other invited guests.

Hoping to see you early, I am,

Yours Affectionately,

BERTHA HANSON.

Answer Accepting the Invitation.

No.———St., Dec. 13, 18—.

MY DEAR BERTHA:

I accept with great pleasure your kind invitation to Aggie's wedding, and will be punctual. I most earnestly pray that she may be very happy in her new life and home. Please give her my kindest love and best wishes.

Your Friend,

HATTIE HARMON.

Answer Declining the Invitation.

No.———St., Dec. 13, 18—.

MY DEAR BERTHA:

My recent great bereavement must plead my excuse for not attending the wedding of your dear daughter Aggie. I would not cloud the festal scene by my heavy weeds of mourning, and I could not lay them aside, even for an hour, while the wound in my heart is so fresh with grief.

Deeply regretting that I cannot attend, I can only wish Aggie, in her new relations, the joyous life of happiness she so richly deserves.

Your Sincere Friend,

HATTIE HARMON.

The following exhibits the size of paper, and the wording of a Funeral Notice, in common use in the metropolitan cities, where it is impossible, frequently, for all the friends to know of the death.

Funeral Notice.

—

Yourself and family are respectfully invited to attend the funeral of

William Comstock,

from his late residence, on Oak Street, near Monroe, to-morrow afternoon, at three o'clock.

A discourse, by the Rev. A. W. Kendall, will be delivered, at the First Baptist Church, immediately before the funeral.

Pittsburgh, Nov. 7, 1874.

Invitation to a Picnic.

The Young Ladies of Mt. Hope Seminary

Solicit the presence of Yourself and Friends

AT THEIR

Annual Reunion and Picnic

ON THE GROUNDS OF

HON. WM. STEVENSON, NEAR KENWOOD,

Friday Afternoon, Oct. 5th,

AT TWO O'CLOCK.

Invitation to a Ball.

First Annual Ball

Philadelphian Society,

Wednesday Evening, Nov. 8, '74,

AT

CONTINENTAL HOTEL.

Invitation to a Festival.

Fête Champêtre,

ON THE GROUNDS OF

Henry Mitchell, Esq.

SPRINGDALE,

WEDNESDAY AFTERNOON, JUNE 10, 1874.

Entrance Ticket, 50 Cents.

The above cards may be displayed in this manner, but for actual use should be about four times larger.

Visiting and Address Cards.

OUR kinds of cards are in general use, viz.: Wedding, Autograph or Visiting, Address, and Business cards. The wedding has already been described. The visiting card is used principally by the lady in her calls among acquaintances in the city. The address card is also frequently used for the same purpose, and is useful to present when it may be desired to open future correspondence. The business card is valuable for advertising and as being introductory to business acquaintance. In the autograph card, Chas. H. Briggs will write his name as follows:

> *Chas. H. Briggs.*

His wife will write her name:

> *Mrs. Chas. H. Briggs.*

His daughters will add Miss to their names, thus:

> *Miss Edith W Briggs.*

Or the name may be without the Miss, thus:

> *Emily A. Briggs.*

The address card may read thus:

> *Mrs. Chas. H. Briggs.*
> 18 Beverly Place.

Or it may read thus:

> *Mrs. Chas. H. Briggs.*
> Appleton, Wis.

Autograph cards should be used only among those acquaintances to whom the residence is well known. Business cards should contain upon their face the name, business, address and references, if references are used.

NOTE.—A former rule of etiquette, not now so much observed, was for the eldest daughter, only, to prefix "Miss" to her name.

Selections for the Album.

THE individual is frequently called upon for his or her autograph. In complying, it is customary to couple with the same a sentiment, signing the name beneath. If the matter written is original, be it long or short, it is usually more highly valued. If a brief selection be made, some of the following quotations may be appropriate:

O NATURE! though blessed and bright are thy rays,
O'er the brow of creation enchantingly thrown,
Yet faint are they all to the luster that plays
In a smile from the heart that is dearly own!

TAKE heart, nor of the laws of fate complain,
Though now 'tis cloudy, 't will clear up again.

SO far is it from being true that men are naturally equal, that no two people can be half an hour together but one shall acquire evident superiority over the other.

IF others be as fair,
What are their charms to me?
I neither know nor care,
For thou art all to me.

PURCHASE not friends by gifts; when thou ceasest to give, such will cease to love.

SMALL service is true service while it lasts;
Of friends, however humble, scorn not one:
The daisy, by the shadow that it casts,
Protects the lingering dew-drop from the sun.

OLD Time will end our story,
But no time, if we end well, will end our glory.

THE most delicate, the most sensible of all pleasures, consists in promoting the pleasures of others.

AND what is fame? the meanest have their day;
The greatest can but blaze and pass away.

AH! could you look into my heart
And watch your image there!
You would own the sunny loveliness
Affection makes it wear.

HE who labors with the mind governs others; he who labors with the body is governed by others.

THERE is pleasure in the pathless woods,
There is rapture on the lonely shore,
There is society, where none intrudes,
By the deep Sea, and music in its roar:
I love not Man the less, but Nature more.

HE who surpasses or subdues mankind,
Must look down on the hate of those below.

LET us deal very gently with the erring. We should always remember that had we been born with a like unfortunate organization, and been trained amid as unfavorable circumstances, we would have done as badly ourselves.

I DEEMED that time, I deemed that Pride
Had quenched at length my boyish flame;
Nor knew, till seated by thy side,
My heart in all, save hope, the same.

EARTH holds no other like to thee,
Or if it doth, in vain for me.

OH! many a shaft, at random sent,
Finds mark the archer little meant;
And many a word, at random spoken,
May soothe or wound a heart that 's broken.

THOSE who have finished by making others think with them, have usually been those who began by daring to think with themselves.

DESIRE not to live long, but to live well;
How long we live, not years, but actions tell.

WHO does the best his circumstance allows,
Does well, acts nobly; angels could do no more.

AH, well! for us all some sweet hope lies
Deeply buried from human eyes;
And, in the hereafter, angels may
Roll the stone from its grave away.

HE who sedulously attends, pointedly asks, calmly speaks, coolly answers, and ceases when he has no more to say, is in the possession of some of the best requisites of man.

SOMETIME, when all life's lessons have been learned,
And sun and stars forever more have set,
The things which our weak judgments here have spurned,
The things o'er which we grieved with lashes wet,
Will flash before us out of life's dark night,
As stars shine most in deeper tints of blue;
And we shall see how all God's plans were right,
And how what seemed reproof was love most true.

Peruse these simple rhymes,
 If ever you read any,
And think of me, sometimes,
 Among the many!

May you through life remain the same,
 Unchanged in all except your name.

Fond Memory, come and hover o'er
 This album page of my fair friend;
Enrich her from thy precious store,
 And happy recollections send.
If on this page she chance to gaze
 In years to come—where'er she be—
Tell her of earlier happy days,
 And bring her back one thought of me.

When I, poor elf, shall have vanished in vapor,
 May still my memory live—on paper.

As half in shade, and half in sun,
 This world along its path advances,
Oh! may that side the sun shines on
 Be all that ever meets thy glances;
May Time, who casts his blight on all,
 And daily dooms some joy to death,
On thee let years so gently fall
 They shall not crush one flower beneath.

As flowers bloom'd in Petrarch's favorite grove,
 So glows the heart beneath the smile of love.

Longest joys won't last forever—
 Make the most of every day;
Youth and beauty Time will sever,
 But Content hath no decay.

I care not for beauty, but give me that heart
 Where truth has its dwelling, and goodness a part.

As o'er the cold, sepulchral stone
 Some name arrests the passer-by,
So, when thou view'st this page alone,
 Let mine attract thy pensive eye;
And when by thee that name is read,
 Perchance in some succeeding year,
Reflect on me as on the dead,
 And think my heart is buried here,

If Cupid be blind, as the ancients declare,
 'Tis strange he should always recognize the fair.

Had I the power to carve or print
 Thy future, my dear friend,
It would be fair and ever bright
 Unclouded to the end.

Bright be the years before thee,
 Friend of my childhood days;
Peace weave her olive o'er thee,
 And joy attend thy ways.

When on this page you chance to look,
 Think of me and close the book.

Thy memory, as a spell
 Of love, comes o'er the mind;
As dew upon the purple bell,
 As perfume on the wind,
As music on the sea,
 As sunshine on the river,
So hath it always been to me,
 So shall it be forever.

Good sense and virtue must prevail
 O'er hearts where wit and beauty fail.

The changeful sand doth only know
 The shallow tide and latest;
The rocks have marked its highest flow,
 The deepest and the greatest:
And deeper still the flood-marks grow;—
 So, since the hour I met thee,
The more the tide of time doth flow,
 The less can I forget thee!

When you are gone, oh where has fled my rest?
 When you are near, I feel supremely bless'd.

Fair and flowery be thy way,
 The skies all bright above thee,
And happier every coming day
 To thee and those that love thee.

Sweet is the girl who reads this line;
 I wish her sweetness were all mine!

It may occur in after-life
 That you, I trust, a happy wife,
Will former happy hours retrace,
 Recall each well-remembered face.
At such a moment I but ask,
 I hope 'twill be a pleasant task,
That you'll remember as a friend
 One who'll prove true e'en to the end.

Most noble and generous, benevolent and free,
 My heart beats with affection and friendship for thee.

My Album's open! Come and see!
 What! won't you waste a line on me?
Write but a thought—a word or two,
 That Memory may revert to you.

A DICTIONARY OF THE LANGUAGE OF FLOWERS.

VERY charming and interesting method of communicating thought is by the aid of flowers, their language and sentiment being understood by the parties who present them. Although the following list is very complete, this vocabulary may be still enlarged by the addition of other definitions, the parties having an understanding as to what language the flower shall represent. Thus an extended and sometimes important correspondence may be carried on by the presentation of bouquets, single flowers and even leaves; the charm of this interchange of thought largely consisting in the romance attendant upon an expression of sentiment in a partially disguised and hidden language.

Of course much of the facility with which a conversation may be conducted, thus, will depend upon the intimate knowledge possessed of the language of flowers and the variety from which to select.

ILLUSTRATIONS.

A declaration of feeling between a lady and gentleman may be expressed by single flowers, as follows:

The gentleman presents a Red Rose—"I love you." The lady admits a partial reciprocation of the sentiment by returning a Purple Pansy—"You occupy my thoughts." The gentleman presses his suit still further by an Everlasting Pea—"Wilt thou go with me?" The lady replies by a Daisy, in which she says—"I will think of it." The gentleman, in his enthusiasm, plucks and presents a Shepherd's Purse—"I offer you my all." The lady, doubtingly, returns a sprig of Laurel—"Words, though sweet, may deceive." The gentleman still affirms his declaration by a sprig of Heliotrope—"I adore you." The lady admits a tenderness of sentiment by the Zinnia—"I mourn your absence."

LANGUAGE OF THE BOUQUET.

A collection of flowers in a bouquet may mean very much. Thus a Rose, Ivy and Myrtle will signify "Beauty, Friendship and Love." A Bachelor's Button "Hope," and a Red Rose "Love," will indicate that "I hope to obtain your love."

I DESIRE TO MARRY YOU.
Jonquil—Linden.

I HAVE SWEET MEMORIES IN MY SOLITUDE.
Periwinkle—Heath.

PRAY FOR ME IN MY ABSENCE.
White Verbena—Wormwood.

Thus longer and shorter sentences may be readily expressed by flower-language; and by agreement, if the variety of flowers is not sufficient, a change of definition may be given the more common blossoms and plants, whereby the language and correspondence may be conducted without inconvenience.

Flowers and their Sentiment.

Flower	Sentiment
Acacia, Rose	Friendship.
Acanthus	Art.
Adonis, Flos	Painful recollections.
Agnus Castus	Coldness; life without love.
Agrimony	Gratitude.
Almonds	Giddiness; heedlessness.
Aloe	Bitterness.
Amaranth	Immortality; Unfading.
Amaryllis	Beautiful but timid.
Anemone, Garden	Forsaken; Withered hopes; Illness.
Amethyst	Admiration.
Anemone, Windflower	Desertion.
Angelica	Inspiration.
Apple Blossom	Preference.
Arbor Vitæ	Unchanging Friendship.
Arbutus	Thee only do I love.
Ash	Grandeur.
Aspen	Sighing.
Asphodel	Remembered beyond the tomb.
Aster, Double German	Variety.
Aster, Large flowered	Afterthought; Love of variety.
Bachelors' Button	Hope; Single Blessedness.
Balm, Mint	Pleasantry.
Balm of Gilead	Healing; I am cured.
Balsamine	Impatience.
Barberry	Petulance; Ill temper.
Basil	Give me your good wishes.
Bay Leaf	I change but in death.
Beech	Lovers' tryst; Prosperity.
Begonia	Deformed.
Bindweed	Humility; Night.
Birch	Grace; Elegance.
Bittersweet Nightshade	Truth.
Blackthorn, or Sloe	Difficulties.
Bladder Tree	Frivolous amusement
Blue Bell	Constancy.
Blue Bottle	Delicacy.
Borage	Abruptness.
Box	Stoicism.
Briers	Envy.
Broom	Neatness; Humility.
Bryony, Black	Be my support.
Buckbean	Calmness; Repose.
Bugloss	Falsehood.
Bulrush	Docility.
Burdock	Touch me not; Importunity.
Buttercup	Riches; Memories of childhood.
Cabbage	Profit.
Calla	Delicacy; Modesty.
Camillia	Gratitude; Perfect Loveliness.
Camomile	Energy in Adversity.
Candytuft	Indifference; Architecture.
Canterbury Bell	Constancy.
Cardinal Flower	Distinction; Preferment.
Carnation	Pure and deep love.
China Aster	Love of variety.
Cedar Leaf	I live for thee.
Cherry	A good education.
Chestnut	Do me justice.
Cereus, Night Blooming	Transient Beauty.
Chiccory	Frugality; Economy.
Chrysanthemum	A heart left to desolation.
Cinnamon Tree	Forgiveness of injuries.
Cinquefoil	A beloved daughter.
Cistus	Surety.
Clover, Red	Industry.
Clematis	Mental Beauty; Artifice.
Clover, White	I promise.
Clover, Four Leaved	Be mine.
Cockle	Vain is beauty without merit.
Coltsfoot	Justice shall be done you.
Columbine, Red	Anxious and trembling.
Coreopsis	Always cheerful.
Coriander	Hidden merit.
Corn	Riches; Abundance.
Cornelian, Cherry	Continuance; Duration.
Cowslip	Native grace; Pensiveness.
Coxcomb	Foppery.
Crocus	Cheerfulness.
Cresses	Stability.
Crowfoot	Ingratitude.
Currant	Thy frown will kill me
Crown, Imperial	Power; Pride of birth
Cucumber	Criticism.
Cypress	Despair; Mourning.
Dahlia	Dignity and elegance.
Daffodil	Unrequited love.
Daisy, Garden	I share your feelings.
Daisy, Single Field	I will think of it.
Dandelion	Oracle; Coquetry.
Datura	Deceitful charms.
Dew Plant	Serenade.
Dittany of Crete	Birth.
Dodder	Meanness; Baseness.
Ebony Tree	Blackness.
Eglantine	Poetry; I wound to heal.
Elder	Compassion.
Elecampane	Tears.
Everlasting	Always remembered.
Everlasting Pea	Wilt thou go with me?
Fennel	Force; Strength.
Fern	Sincerity.
Fir	Elevation.
Flax	I feel your benefits.
Flos, Adonis	Painful recollections.
Forget-me-not	Do not forget.
Foxglove	Insincerity; Occupation.
Fraxinella	Fire.
Fuchsia	Taste; Frugality.

Gentian	Intrinsic worth.
Geranium, Ivy	I engage you for the next dance.
Geranium, Oak	A melancholy mind.
Geranium, Rose	I prefer you.
Geranium, Scarlet	Silliness.
Gillyflower, Common	Lasting Beauty.
Gillyflower, Stock	Promptness.
Gladiolus	Ready armed.
Goats' Rue	Reason.
Gold Basket	Tranquility.
Gooseberry	Anticipation.
Grape Vine	Intemperance.
Grass	Utility; Submission.
Greek Valerian	Rupture.
Golden Rod	Encouragement.
Gorse, or Turze	Anger.
Harebell	Retirement; Grief.
Hawthorn	Hope.
Hazel	Reconciliation.
Heath	Solitude.
Heliotrope	I adore you; Devotion
Henbane	Blemish; Fault.
Hibiscus	Delicate beauty.
Hoarhound	Fire.
Holly	Am I forgotten? Foresight.
Hollyhock	Fecundity; Ambition.
Honey Flower	Sweet and secret love.
Honeysuckle	Devoted love; Fidelity
Hop	Injustice.
Hornbean	Ornament.
Horse Chestnut	Luxury.
Houstania	Innocence; Content.
Houseleek	Domestic economy.
Hyacinth	Constancy; Benevolence.
Hydrangea	Vain-glory; Heartlessness.
Ice Plant	Your looks freeze me.
Indian Plum	Privation.
Iris, Common Garden	A message for thee.
Iris, German	Flame.
Ivy	Friendship; Marriage
Jasmine, White	Amiability.
Jasmine, Yellow	Grace and elegance.
Jonquil	Desire; Affection returned.
Jumper	Asylum; Aid; Protection.
Laburnum	Pensive beauty.
Ladyslipper	Capricious beauty.
Larch	Boldness; Audacity.
Larkspur, Pink	Lightness; Fickleness
Laurel, American	Words, though sweet, may deceive.
Lantana	Rigor.
Laurel, Mountain	Glory; Victory; Ambition.
Laurestine	I die if neglected.
Lavatera	Sweet disposition.
Lavender	Mistrust.
Lemon Blossom	Prudence; Discretion.
Lettuce	Cold hearted; Coolness.
Lichen	Dejection.
Lilac, Purple	First emotions of love
Lilac, White	Youth.
Lily, Water	Eloquence.
Lily, White	Majesty; Purity.
Lily of the Valley	Return of happiness.
Linden, or Lime	Conjugal; Marriage.
Liverwort	Confidence.
Locust Tree, Green	Love beyond the grave
Lotus Leaf	Recantation.
Lucern	Life.
Lupine	Dejection.
Madder	Calumny.
Magnolia	Love of Nature.
Maiden Hair	Discretion.
Marjoram	Blushes.
Manchineel Tree	Falseness.
Mandrake	Rarity.
Maple	Reserve.
Marigold	Sacred affection.
Marigold, Garden	Grief; Chagrin.
Marigold, Rainy	A storm.
Marigold and Cypress	Despair.
Marshmallow	Beneficence.
Marvel of Peru	Timidity.
Mayflower	Welcome.

Meadow Saffron	My best days are past
Mezercon	Desire to please.
Mignonette	Your qualities surpass your charms.
Milfoil	War.
Mint	Virtue.
Milkweed	Hope in misery.
Mistletoe	I surmount everything
Mock Orange	Counterfeit; Uncertainty.
Monkshood	Treachery; A foe is near.
Morning Glory	Coquetry; Affection.
Mountain Ash	I watch over you.
Moss	Maternal love.
Mourning Bride	I have lost all.
Mugwort	Good luck; Happiness
Mulberry, Black	I shall not survive you
Mulberry, White	Wisdom.
Mullen	Good nature.
Mushroom	Suspicion.
Musk Plant	Weakness.
Myrtle	Love in Absence.
Myrrh	Gladness.
Narcissus	Egotism; Self-Love.
Nasturtium	Patriotism; Splendor
Nettle	Cruelty.
Nightshade	Dark thoughts; Sorcery.
Oak	Hospitality; Bravery.
Oleander	Beware.
Olive	Peace.
Orange Flower	Chastity.
Orchis, Bee	Error.
Orchis, Spider	Skill.
Osier	Frankness.
Osmunda	Reverie.
Oxalis	Wood sorrel.
Pansy, Purple	You occupy my thoughts.
Parsley	Festivity; Banquet.
Passion Flower	Devotion; Religious fervor.
Peach Blossom	I am your captive.
Peony	Ostentation; Anger.
Persimmons	Bury me amid Nature's beauties.
Peppermint	Warmth of feeling.
Pennyroyal	Flee away.
Periwinkle	Sweet memories.
Phlox	Our hearts are united.
Pimpernel	Rendezvous; Change.
Pine	Endurance; Daring.
Pine Apple	You are perfect.
Pink, Red	Pure love.
Plane, or Platane	Genius.
Plum Tree	Keep your promises.
Plum, Wild	Independence.
Polyanthus	Heart's mystery
Pomegranate	Conceit.
Pompion, or Pumpkin	Grossness; Coarseness
Poplar, Black	Courage.
Poplar, White	Time.
Poppy, Corn	Consolation.
Poppy, White	Sleep; Oblivion.
Potatoe	Benevolence.
Primrose	Modest worth; Silent love.
Privit, or Prim	Prohibition.
Purple Scabious	Mourning.
Queen of the Meadow	Uselessness.
Quince	Temptation.
Ranunculus, Garden	You are radiant with charms.
Reeds	Music.
Rest Harrow	Obstacle.
Rhododendron	Agitation.
Rhubarb	Advice.
Rosebud	Confession of love.
Rosebud, White	Too young to love.
Rose, Cinnamon	Without pretension.
Rose, Hundred leaved	The graces.
Rose, Austrian	Thou art all that is lovely.
Rose Leaf	I never trouble.
Rose, Monthly	Beauty ever new.
Rose, Moss	Superior merit; Voluptuousness.
Rose, Musk	Capricious beauty.
Rose, Red	I love you.
Rose, White	Silence.

Rose, Wild, Single	Simplicity.
Rose, Yellow	Infidelity; Unfaithfulness.
Rosemary	Remembrance; Your presence revives me
Rue	Disdain.
Rush	Docility.
Saffron, Meadow	My best days are past.
Saffron, Crocus	Do not abuse me.
Sage	Domestic Virtue; Esteem.
St. John's Wort	Animosity.
Sardonia	Irony.
Satin Flower	Forgetfulness.
Scratch Weed	Roughness.
Scotch Thistle	Retaliation.
Sensitive Plant	Sensitiveness; Modesty.
Serpent Cactus	Horror.
Service Tree, or Sorb	Prudence.
Shepherd's Purse	I offer you my all.
Silver Weed	Naiveté.
Snapdragon	Presumption.
Snowball	Goodness; Thoughts of Heaven.
Snowdrop	Consolation; A friend in adversity.
Sorrel	Parental Affection.
Speedwell	Fidelity.
Spindle Tree	Your charms are graven on my heart.
Star of Bethlehem	Reconciliation; Purity.
Straw, Broken	Quarrel.
Straw	Agreement; United.
Strawberry	Perfect excellence.
Sumach	Splendid misery.
Sunflower, Tall	Lofty and wise thoughts.
Sunflower	False riches.
Sunflower, Dwarf	Adoration.
Sweet Flag	Fitness.
Sweet Pea	A meeting.
Sweet Sultan	Happiness.
Sweet William	Gallantry; Finesse; Dexterity.
Syringa	Memory; Fraternal love.
Sycamore	Curiosity.
Tare	Vice.
Teasel	Misanthropy.
Thistle	Austerity.
Thorn Apple	Disguise.
Thrift	Sympathy.
Thyme	Activity.
Tremella	Resistance.
Tube Rose	Dangerous Pleasure; Voluptuousness; Sweet voice.
Tulip, Variegated	Beautiful eyes.
Tulip, Red	Declaration of love.
Valerian, Common	Accommodating disposition.
Valerian	Facility.
Venus's Looking Glass	Flattery.
Verbena	Sensibility; Sensitiveness.
Verbena, Purple	I weep for you; Regret.
Verbena, White	Pray for me.
Vervain	Enchantment.
Vernal Grass	Poor, but happy.
Vetch	I cling to thee.
Violet, Blue	Faithfulness.
Violet, White	Purity; Candor; Modesty.
Volkamenia	May you be happy.
Wall Flower	Fidelity in misfortune.
Weeping Willow	Melancholy.
Wheat	Wealth.
Whortleberry	Treachery.
Willow, Common	Forsaken.
Willow Herb	Pretension.
Wood Sorrel	Joy.
Woodbine	Fraternal love.
Wormwood	Absence.
Yarrow	Cure for the heartache.
Yew	Sadness.
Zinnia	I mourn your absence.

PLEASANT WORDS AND AGREEABLE MANNERS.

To be loved is the instinctive desire of every human heart. To be respected, to be honored, to be successful, is the universal ambition. The ever constant desire of all is to be happy. This never varying instinct lies at the foundation of every action; it is the constantly propelling force in our every effort.

To be happy, we strive for the acquisition of wealth, for position and place, for social and political distinction. And when all is obtained, the real enjoyment in its possession comes from the thousand little courtesies that are exchanged between individuals — pleasant words and kindly acts, which the poor may enjoy as well as the rich.

In reality it need not take much to make one happy. Our real wants are very few. To be fed and clothed, and provided with comfortable shelter, are the prime necessities. Added to these are kindness and love from those with whom we associate. Given all these, with a contented spirit, and, however lowly our position, we may be very happy.

There is one perpetual law, however, running through all our intercourse with others, which is that we may rightly possess nothing without rendering therefor just compensation. This law is recognized in the commercial world, and it should be strictly observed in the etiquette of social life.

In short, in the many varied amenities of life, the fundamental rule of action should be the golden rule: "To do unto others as we would that others should do unto us."

We are at ease, we are made peaceful, satisfied and happy, by words and acts of kindly feeling extended to us; and in like manner we may strew the pathway of others with roses and sunshine, by courteous action, and kind, gentle and loving conduct; to do which may cost us no effort, but on the contrary may afford us real pleasure.

In a business, social and artistic view, it is of very great advantage to most people to be possessed of ease and grace of manner. By the possession of confidence and self-command, a single individual will oftentimes cause a large company, that otherwise would be socially very inharmonious, to be satisfied, composed and perfectly at ease; and in a thousand ways such a person will scatter happiness and blessings among those with whom he or she may come in contact.

Natural and Acquired Politeness.

To some, a pleasing manner comes very naturally. If born to the possession of an easy flow of language, agreeableness of address, poetical and imaginative power, and large knowledge of human nature, the whole accompanied by judicious training, good education and wide opportunities, such persons will most surely, without studied effort, be self-possessed and at ease in any company, upon any occasion.

On the contrary, if the natural advantages have been few, and the opportunities for acquiring polished deportment limited, then we may very appropriately make a study of the subject of how to please; and hence the necessity for special instruction on the subject of Etiquette.

It is of the utmost importance, however, that there be no labored effort to behave by rule, and that the forms of etiquette be not carried too far. The law of common sense should rest at the basis of our intercourse with society, and a kindly desire to make happy everybody with whom we come in contact, should actuate our conduct. Still, with all this, there are thousands of people of the kindest intentions, with much breadth of intellect, who continually violate the common usages of society, and who are liable to do the wrong thing at important times, and thus embarrass their warmest friends. Hence, the need of a treatise on general conduct is evidently as much a necessity as is the text-book on grammar, penmanship or mathematics.

If the soldier is more efficient by drill, the teacher more competent by practice, the parliamentarian more influential by understanding the code of parliamentary law, then equally is the general member of society more successful by an understanding of the laws of etiquette, which teach how to appear, and what to do and say in the varied positions in which we may be placed.

In the study of etiquette, much may be learned by observation, but much more is learned by practice. We may listen to the finest oratory for a dozen years, and yet never be able to speak in public ourselves; whereas, by practice in the art of declamation, with passable talent, we may become quite proficient in half that time. We may thoroughly study the theory and art of language for twenty years, and yet be very poor talkers. We may practice the art of conversation by familiar and continuous intercourse with the cultured and refined, and become fluent and easy in communicating thought in a few years.

Such is the difference between theory and practice. Both are necessary—the former in pointing the way; the latter by making use of theory in practical application. Thus we may acquire ease and grace of manner: First, by understanding the regulations which govern social etiquette; and secondly, by a free intermingling in society, putting into continual practice the theories which we understand. To avail ourselves, however, to the fullest extent of society advantages, we must have acquaintance; and hence, we introduce the rules of etiquette by a chapter on the forms of presentation—the art of getting acquainted.

Etiquette of Introductions.

THERE are various forms of introduction to be used, each depending on particular circumstances. Thus, when introducing a gentleman to a lady, the party introducing them will say, bowing to each as the name of each is pronounced, "Miss Williamson, allow me to introduce to you my friend Mr. Grant; Mr. Grant, Miss Williamson."

Some prefer the word "present" instead of the word "introduce." The words are not very material. The form is all that is essential.

Of two gentlemen being introduced, one of whom is more eminent in position, look first at the elder or superior, with a slight bow, saying, "Mr. Durham, I make you acquainted with Mr. Stevens; Mr. Stevens, Mr. Durham."

The last clause repeating the names, "Mr. Stevens, Mr. Durham," may be justly regarded a useless formality, and is not necessary unless for the purpose of making the names more distinct by their repetition.

Parties being introduced have an opportunity for conversation, and are immediately set at ease by the person introducing giving the place of residence and the business of each, with the introduction, thus: "Mr. Snow, allow me to make you acquainted with Mr. Burton. Mr. Burton is extensively engaged in mining in Colorado. Mr. Snow is one of our lawyers in this city." He may still continue, if he wishes to aid the parties he is introducing, by saying, "Mr. Burton comes East for the purpose of disposing of mining stock to some of our capitalists, and it is possible, Mr. Snow, that with your large acquaintance you can give him some information that will aid him." Such an introduction will immediately lead to a general conversation between the parties, and the person having introduced them can then retire if he desires.

It is always gratifying to anyone to be highly esteemed, hence you will confer pleasure by always conveying as favorable an impression as possible when giving the introduction.

Always apply the titles when making introductions, where the parties are entitled to the same, as Honorable, Reverend, Professor, etc. Thus, in introducing a clergyman to a member of the legislature, it is etiquette to say: "Mr. Shelden, permit me to present to you the Reverend Mr. Wing." Addressing Mr. Shelden, he says: "Mr. Wing is the pastor of the First Presbyterian church at Troy, New York." Addressing Mr. Wing, he continues: "Mr. Shelden is at present our representative in the State Legislature, and author of the "Shelden Letters" which you have so much admired."

If there are many introductions to be made, the simple words, "Mr. Smith, Mr. Jones," will serve the purpose. Mr. Smith and Mr. Jones will then take up the weather or some other topic, and proceed with their conversation. A very proper reply for either party to make when introduced is, "I am glad to meet you," or, "I am happy to make your acquaintance."

If several persons are introduced to one, mention the name of the single individual but once, as follows: "Mr. Belden, allow me to introduce Mr. Maynard, Mr. Thompson, Miss Hayward, Mrs. Rice, Mr. Harmon, Mr. Brown," bowing to each as the name is mentioned.

When introducing a couple that may be somewhat diffident, the parties will be materially aided in becoming sociable and feeling at ease, by a very full introduction, thus: "Miss Kennicott, allow me to present to you my friend Miss Swift. Miss Kennicott is from the far-famed city of New Haven, Connecticut; and, upon the close of her visit here, is going to California for a visit of a year. Miss Swift is from Buffalo, New York, and is attending Hopedale Seminary in this city."

General Suggestions About Introductions.

Ladies being introduced should never bow hastily, but with slow and measured dignity.

The inferior is to be introduced to the superior; the younger to the older; the gentleman to the lady.

It is the lady's privilege to recognize the gentleman after an introduction, and his duty to return the bow.

Introductions on the streets or in public places should be made so quietly as not to attract public attention.

Perfect ease and self-possession are the essentials to the making and receiving of graceful and happy introductions.

Etiquette requires that a gentleman always raise his hat (Fig. 2) when introduced to either a lady or gentleman on the street.

Introduce to each other only those who may find acquaintance agreeable. If any doubt exists on the subject, inquire beforehand.

When introducing parties, pronounce the names distinctly. If you fail to understand the name when introduced, feel at liberty to inquire.

One of the duties of the host and hostess of a private party is to make the guests acquainted with each other. Guests may, however, make introductions.

Introductions are often dispensed with at a private ball, it being taken for granted that only those are invited who ought to be acquainted. Thus acquaintance may begin without formal introduction.

If upon any occasion you are introduced at a friend's house to even your bitterest enemy, courtesy requires that you salute him, or her, and give no sign of ill-feeling while you are the guest of your friend.

Fig. 2.   Introduction on the Street.

If casually introduced to a stranger, when making a call at the house of a friend, etiquette does not require a subsequent recognition. It is optional with the parties whether the acquaintance be continued or not after such accidental meeting and introduction.

Always pronounce the surname when giving the introduction. To be introduced to "my cousin Carrie" leaves the stranger at a loss how to address the lady. In introducing a relative, it is well to say, "My brother, Mr. Wells;" "My mother, Mrs. Briggs," etc.

To shake hands when introduced, is optional; between gentlemen it is common, and oftentimes between an elderly and a young person. It is not common between an unmarried lady and a gentleman, a slight bow between them when introduced being all that etiquette requires. The married lady will use her discretion when introduced to gentlemen.

Two parties meeting on the street, accompanied by friends, may stop and speak to each other without the necessity of introducing their friends, though, when parting, it is courtesy for each to give a parting salutation as though acquaintance had been formed.

Parties who may meet by chance at your house, when making calls, need not necessarily be introduced to each other. If, however, they continue their calls together, it may be agreeable to make them acquainted in order to more pleasantly carry forward conversation.

If you are a gentleman, do not let the lack of an introduction prevent you from rendering services to any unattended lady who may need them. Politely offer your protection, escort or assistance, and, when the service has been accomplished, politely bow and retire.

A visitor at your house should be introduced to the various callers, and the acquaintance should continue while the friend remains your guest. All callers should aim to make the visit of the friend as pleasant as possible, treating the guest as they would wish their friends to be treated under similar circumstances.

If thrown into the company of strangers, without the formality of an introduction, as is often the case when traveling and at other times,

acquaintance may be formed between gentlemen and ladies, with proper reserve, but duty requires that the slightest approach toward undue familiarity should be checked by dignified silence.

Persons who have been properly introduced have claims upon the acquaintance of each other which should call for at least a slight recognition thereafter, unless there be very decided reasons for cutting the acquaintance entirely. To completely ignore another to whom you have been rightly introduced, by meeting the person with a vacant stare, is a mark of ill-breeding.

Introductions at Court and Presidential Receptions.

In paying your respects to the President of the United States, you will be introduced by the master of ceremonies on public occasions. At other times, to send in your card will secure you audience, although the better way is to be introduced by a mutual acquaintance, or a member of Congress. Introductions at Court in foreign countries are accompanied by a good deal of formality. At the English Court, the stranger, having the credential of the American Ambassador, will be introduced, if a lady, by a lady; if a gentleman, by a gentleman. Elsewhere abroad the proper method in each case can be best learned from our national representative at each capital. Court etiquette requires that the lady appear in full dress, and the gentleman in black suit, with white vest, gloves and necktie.

 # FORMS OF SALUTATION.

SUGGESTIONS CONCERNING THE BOW.

COMMON forms of salutation, in America, are the bow, the kiss, words of address, and shaking hands.

Acquaintances are usually entitled to the courtesy of a bow. It is poor policy to refuse recognition because of a trifling difference between parties.

The young lady should show a similar deference to an elderly lady, or to one in superior position, that a gentleman does to a lady.

A gentleman who may be smoking when he meets a lady, should in bowing remove the cigar from his mouth and from her presence.

When bowing to ladies, it is etiquette for the gentleman to raise his hat from his head. If passing on the street, the hat should be raised and salute given with the hand farthest from the person addressed.

A bow or graceful inclination should be made by ladies when recognizing their acquaintances of the opposite sex. It is the privilege of the lady to bow first.

A gentleman on horseback should grasp whip and reins in his left hand, and raise his hat with his right, when saluting a lady. The lady salutes by bowing slightly.

To a casual acquaintance you may bow without speaking; but to those with whom you are well acquainted, greater cordiality is due. A bow should always be returned; even to an enemy it is courtesy to return the recognition.

When a gentleman, accompanied by a friend, meets a lady upon the street, it is courtesy, in the salutation, for the gentleman's friend to bow slightly to the lady also, as a compliment to his companion, even though unacquainted with the lady.

On meeting a party, some of whom you are intimately acquainted with, and the others but little, the salutation should be made as nearly equal as possible. A slight recognition of some, and great demonstration of pleasure toward others, is a violation of etiquette.

A gentleman should return a bow made him upon the street, even if the one making the same is not recognized. The person may possibly be a forgotten acquaintance; but, even if a mistake has been made, there will be less embarrassment if the bow is returned.

A gentleman should not bow from a window to a lady on the street, though he may bow slightly from the street upon being recognized by a lady in a window. Such recognition should, however, generally be avoided, as gossip is likely to attach undue importance to it when seen by others.

A warm cordiality of manner, and a general recognition of acquaintances, without undue familiarity, is the means of diffusing much happiness, as well as genial and friendly feeling. In thinly settled localities, the habit of bowing to every one you meet is an excellent one, evincing, as it does, kindliness of feeling toward all.

When meeting a lady who is a stranger, in a hallway, upon a staircase, or in close proximity elsewhere, courtesy demands a bow from the gentleman. In passing up a stairway, the lady will pause at the foot and allow the gentleman to go first; and at the head of the stairway he should bow, pause, and allow her to precede him in the descent.

How to Address Others.—Nicknames.

Use the title, when speaking to others, whenever possible. Thus, addressing John Brown, a Justice of the Peace, say, "Squire;" Dr. Bell, you will address as "Doctor;" Mayor Williams, as "Mayor;" Senator Snow, as "Senator;" Governor Smith, as "Governor;" Professor Stevens, as "Professor," etc.

Before all public bodies, take pains to address those in authority very respectfully, saying to the presiding officer, "Mr. President," or if he be a Mayor, Judge, or Justice, address him as "Your Honor," etc.

When stopping at the house of a friend, ascertain the Christian names of all the children, and of those servants that you frequently have to address; and then always speak respectfully to each, using the full Christian name, or any pet name to which they are accustomed.

To approach another in a boisterous manner, saying, "Hello, Old Fellow!" "Hello Bob!" or using kindred expressions, indicates ill-breeding. If approached, however, in this vulgar manner, it is better to give a civil reply, and address the person respectfully, in which case he is quite likely to be ashamed of his own conduct.

Husbands and wives indicate pleasant conjugal association existing where they address each other in the family circle by their Christian names, though the terms of respect, "Mr." and "Mrs.," may be applied to each among strangers. When speaking of each other among near and intimate relatives, they will also use the Christian name; but among general acquaintances and strangers, the surname.

Never call anyone by a nickname, or a disrespectful name. Treat all persons, no matter how lowly, in addressing them, as you would wish to be addressed yourself. You involuntarily have more respect for people, outside of your family or relatives, who call you "Mr. Smith," or "Mr. Jones," than for those who call you "Jack," or "Jim." Hence, when you speak to others, remember that you gain their favor by polite words of address.

When speaking to a boy, under fifteen years of age, outside of the circle of relatives, among comparative strangers, call him by his Christian name, as "Charles," "William," etc. Above that age, if the boy has attained good physical and intellectual development, apply the "Mr." as "Mr. Brown," "Mr. King," etc. To do so will please him, will raise his self-respect, and will be tendering a courtesy which you highly valued when you were of the same age.

It is an insult to address a boy or girl, who is a stranger to you, as "Bub" or "Sis." Children are sometimes very sensitive on these points, resenting such method of being addressed, while they very highly appreciate being spoken to respectfully. Thus, if the child's name is unknown, to say "My Boy," or "My Little Lad," "My Girl," or "My Little Lady," will be to gain favor and set the child a good example in politeness. Children forever gratefully remember those who treat them respectfully. Among relatives, nicknames should not be allowed. Pet names among the children are admissible, until they outgrow them, when the full Christian name should be used.

THE PRACTICE OF KISSING.

Upon the meeting of intimate friends among ladies, at the private house, the kiss as a mode of salutation is yet common; but even there it is not as customary as formerly. The custom ought to be abolished for physiological and other reasons.

Upon the meeting or departure of a young person, as between parents and children, or guardians and wards, the kiss is not inappropriate in public. Between all other parties it is a questionable propriety in public places, it being etiquette to avoid conduct that will attract the attention of strangers.

ETIQUETTE OF SHAKING HANDS.—SUGGESTIONS ABOUT SHOPPING.

WAYS OF CLASPING HANDS.

ACCOMPANYING the salutation of hand-shaking, it is common, according to the customs of English-speaking people, to inquire concerning the health, the news, etc.

Offer the whole hand. It is an insult, and indicates snobbery, to present two fingers (Fig. 3) when shaking hands. It is also insulting to return a warm, cordial greeting with a lifeless hand (Fig. 4), and evident indifference of manner, when hand-shaking. Present a cordial grasp (Fig. 5) and clasp the hand firmly, shaking it warmly for a period of two or three

Fig. 3. The snob that sticks out two fingers when shaking hands.

seconds, and then relinquish the grasp entirely. It is rude to grasp the hand very tightly or to shake it over-vigorously. To hold it a long time is often very embarrassing, and is a breach of etiquette. It is always the lady's privilege to extend the hand first. In her own house a lady should give her hand to every guest.

If both parties wear gloves, it is not necessary that each remove them in shaking hands; if one, however, has ungloved hands, it is courtesy for the other to remove the glove, unless in so doing it would cause an awkward pause; in which case apologize for not removing it, by saying, "Excuse my glove." The words and forms will always very much

Fig. 4. The cold-blooded, languid person, that exhibits only indifference as you shake the hand.

depend upon circumstances, of which individuals can themselves best judge. Kid and other thin gloves are not expected to be removed in hand-shaking; hence, apology is only necessary for the non-removal of the thick, heavy glove.

As a rule in all salutations, it is well not to exhibit too much haste. The cool, deliberate person is much the most likely to avoid mistakes. The nervous, quick-motioned, impulsive individual will need to make deliberation a matter of study; else, when acting on the spur of the moment, with possibly slight embarrassment, ludicrous errors are liable to be made. In shaking hands, offer the right

Fig. 5. The generous, frank, whole-souled individual, that meets you with a warm, hearty grasp.

hand, unless the same be engaged; in which case, apologize, by saying "Excuse my left hand." It is the right hand that carries the sword in time of war, and its extension is emblematic of friendliness in time of peace.

CONDUCT IN THE STORE.

PURCHASERS should, as far as possible, patronize the merchants of their own town. It is poor policy to send money abroad for articles which can be bought as cheaply at home.

Do not take hold of a piece of goods which another is examining. Wait until it is replaced upon the counter before you take it up.

Injuring goods when handling, pushing aside other persons, lounging upon the counter, whispering, loud talk and laughter, when in a store, are all evidences of ill-breeding.

Never attempt to "beat down" prices when shopping. If the price does not suit, go elsewhere. The just and upright merchant will have but one price for his goods, and he will strictly adhere to it.

It is an insult to a clerk or merchant to suggest to a customer, about to purchase, that he may buy cheaper or better goods elsewhere. It is also rude to give your opinion, unasked, about the goods that another is purchasing.

Never expect a clerk to leave another customer to wait on you; and when attending upon you, do not cause him to wait while you visit with another. When the purchases are made, let them be sent to your home, and thus avoid loading yourself with bundles.

Treat clerks, when shopping, respectfully, and give them no more trouble than is necessary. Ask for what is wanted, explicitly, and if you wish to make examination with a view to future purchase, say so. Be perfectly frank. There is no necessity for practicing deceit.

The rule should be to pay for goods when you buy them. If, however, you are trusted by the merchant, you should be very particular to pay your indebtedness when you agree to. By doing as you promise, you acquire habits of promptitude, and at the same time establish credit and make reputation among those with whom you deal.

It is rude in the extreme to find fault and to make sneering remarks about goods. To draw unfavorable comparisons between the goods and those found at other stores does no good, and shows want of deference and respect to those who are waiting upon you. Politely state that the goods are not what you want, and, while you may buy, you prefer to look further.

If a mistake has been made whereby you have been given more goods than you paid for, or have received more change than was your due, go immediately and have the error rectified. You cannot afford to sink your moral character by taking advantage of such mistakes. If you had made an error to your disadvantage, as a merchant, you would wish the customer to return and make it right. You should do as you would be done by. Permanent success depends upon your being strictly honest.

Etiquette of Calling.

THE morning call should be very brief. This formal call is mainly one of ceremony, and from ten to twenty minutes is a sufficient length of time to prolong it. It should never exceed half an hour.

In making a formal call, a lady does not remove her bonnet or wraps.

Unless there be a certain evening set apart for receiving, the formal call should be made in the morning.

It is customary, according to the code of etiquette, to call all the hours of daylight morning, and after nightfall evening.

Calls may be made in the morning or in the evening. The call in the morning should not be made before 12 M., nor later than 5 P. M.

A gentleman, making a formal call in the morning, must retain his hat in his hand. He may leave umbrella and cane in the hall, but not his hat and gloves. The fact of retaining hat indicates a formal call

When a gentleman accompanies a lady at a morning call (which is seldom), he assists her up the steps, rings the bell, and follows her into the reception-room. It is for the lady to determine when they should leave.

All uncouth and ungraceful positions are especially unbecoming among ladies and gentlemen in the parlor. Thus (Fig. 6), standing with the arms akimbo, sitting astride a chair, wearing the hat, and smoking in the presence of ladies, leaning back in the chair, standing with legs crossed and feet on the chairs — all those acts evince lack of polished manners.

If possible, avoid calling at the lunch or dinner hour. Among society people the most fashionable hours for calling are from 12 M. to 3 P. M. At homes where dinner or lunch is taken at noon, calls may be made from 2 to 5 P. M.

Should other callers be announced, it is well, as soon as the bustle attending the new arrival is over, to arise quietly, take leave of the hostess, bow to the visitors, and retire, without apparently doing so because of the new arrivals. This saves the hostess the trouble of entertaining two sets of callers.

To say bright and witty things during the call of ceremony, and go so soon that the hostess will desire the caller to come again, is much the more pleasant. No topic of a political or religious character should be admitted to the conversation, nor any subject of absorbing interest likely to lead to discussion.

A lady engaged upon fancy sewing of any kind, or needlework, need not necessarily lay aside the same during the call of intimate acquaintances. Conversation can flow just as freely while the visit continues.

FIG. 6. UNGRACEFUL POSITIONS.

No. 1. Stands with arms akimbo.
" 2. Sits with elbows on the knees.
" 3. Sits astride the chair, and wears his hat in the parlor.
" 4. Stains the wall paper by pressing against it with his hand; eats an apple alone, and stands with his legs crossed.
No. 5. Rests his foot upon the chair-cushion.
" 6. Tips back his chair, soils the wall by resting his head against it, and smokes in the presence of ladies.

During the visits of ceremony, however, strict attention should be given to entertaining the callers.

Gentlemen may make morning calls on the following occasions: To convey congratulations or sympathy and condolence, to meet a friend who has just returned from abroad, to inquire after the health of a lady who may have accepted his escort on the previous day. (He should not delay the latter more than a day.) He may call upon those to whom letters of introduction are given, to express thanks for any favor which may have been rendered him, or to return a call. A great variety of circumstances will also determine when at other times he should make calls.

Evening Calls.

Evening calls should never be made later than 9 P. M., and never prolonged later than 10 P. M.

In making a formal call in the evening, the gentleman must hold hat and gloves, unless invited to lay them aside and spend the evening.

In making an informal call in the evening, a gentleman may leave hat, cane, overshoes, etc., in the hall, provided he is invited to do so, and the lady may remove her wraps.

The evening call should not generally be prolonged over an hour. With very intimate friends, however, it may be made a little longer; but the caller should be very careful that the visit be not made tiresome.

General Suggestions.

Calls from people living in the country are expected to be longer and less ceremonious than from those in the city.

When it has been impossible to attend a dinner or a social gathering, a call should be made soon afterwards, to express regret at the inability to be present.

A gentleman, though a stranger, may with propriety escort an unattended lady to the carriage, and afterwards return and make his farewell bow to the hostess.

Should a guest arrive to remain for some time with the friend, those who are intimate with the family should call as soon as possible, and these calls should be returned at the earliest opportunity.

Unless invited to do so, it is a violation of etiquette to draw near the fire for the purpose of warming one's self. Should you, while waiting the appearance of the hostess, have done so, you will arise upon her arrival, and then take the seat she may assign you.

When a lady has set apart a certain evening for receiving calls, it is not usual to call at other times, except the excuse be business reasons.

THE USE OF CARDS WHEN CALLING.

The gentleman's card should bear nothing but the name and address of the caller, in small script or card text. In addition, the lady's card may bear the "Mrs." or the "Miss," thus:

CHARLES BELDEN   MRS. H. B. KING,
Cambridge, Mass.   *17 Belmont Place.*
                 At Home Thursday Evenings.

The eldest daughter and unmarried sisters often adopt the following:

MISS CLARA D. WELLS,   THE MISSES HAMMOND,
No. 44 Birch Street.   *No. 1 Day Street.*

The physician may have his professional title, as

DR. ROBERT HOLLAND, or ROBERT HOLLAND, M. D.
No. 70 Henderson St.   *No. 70 Henderson St.*

The officers of the army and navy may have their titles thus:

LIEUT. HENRY H. WEBSTER, U. S. A.

LIEUT. HARVEY B. SNOW, U. S. N.

A card left, during your illness, should be answered by a call as soon as your health will permit.

The honorary titles of Prof., Hon., Esq., etc., are not allowable upon the calling card in the United States.

When about leaving town, the card which is left will bear on the lower left-hand corner the letters " P. P. C. "—" Presents parting compliments," from the French *" Pour Prendre Conge "*—to take leave. The card may also be sent by mail or private carrier, the latter mode of conveyance showing most respect. *

A card sent to a person who is ill or in affliction, from the loss of a relative, should be accompanied by verbal inquiries regarding the person's health.

Cards may be left immediately where a death is known, but a call of sympathy and condolence is not usually made within a week after the bereavement.

The lady in mourning who may not desire to make calls, will send mourning cards instead of making calls for such period of time as she may not desire to mingle in general society.

Should the servant reply to a gentleman that the lady of the house, to whom the call is made, is not at home, but the daughter is, he should send in his card, as it is not usual for young ladies to receive calls from gentlemen unless they are quite intimate friends.

It is well to have cards in readiness at every call. If a servant meets you at the door, to send up a card will save mispronouncing your name, and if the lady is not at home it will show that you have called. Should there be two or more ladies in the household, to turn down one corner of the card will signify that the call was designed for all the family.

The handsomest style of card is that which is engraved; next is that which is prettily written. Succeeding, comes the printed card, which, with some of the modern script or text types, makes a most beautiful card if neatly printed. Extra ornament is out of place.

When desirous of seeing anyone at a hotel or parlor, send up your card by the waiter, while you wait in the reception-room or office.

The hostess should, if not desiring to see anyone, send word that she is "engaged" when the servant first goes to the door, and not after the card has been sent up. Should she desire certain persons only to be admitted, let the servant understand the names definitely.

* P. P. C. cards are no longer left when leaving home to be absent a few months.

WHAT SHOULD BE AVOIDED WHEN CALLING.

Do not stare around the room.

Do not take a dog or small child.

Do not linger at the dinner-hour.

Do not lay aside the bonnet at a formal call.

Do not fidget with your cane, hat or parasol.

Do not make a call of ceremony on a wet day.

Do not turn your back to one seated near you.

Do not touch the piano, unless invited to do so.

Do not handle ornaments or furniture in the room.

Do not make a display of consulting your watch.

Do not go to the room of an invalid, unless invited.

Do not remove the gloves when making a formal call.

Do not continue the call longer when conversation begins to lag.

Do not remain when you find the lady upon the point of going out.

Do not make the first call if you are a new-comer in the neighborhood.

Do not open or shut doors or windows or alter the arrangement of the room.

Do not enter a room without first knocking and receiving an invitation to come in.

Do not resume your seat after having risen to go, unless for important reasons.

Do not walk around the room, examining pictures, while waiting for the hostess.

Do not introduce politics, religion or weighty topics for conversation when making calls.

FIG. 7. GENTILITY IN THE PARLOR.

The figures in the above illustration represent graceful postures to be assumed by both ladies and gentlemen in the parlor. As will be seen, whether holding hat or fan, either sitting or standing, the positions are all easy and graceful.

To assume an easy genteel attitude, the individual must be self-possessed. To be so, attention must be given to easy flow of language, happy expression of thought, study of cultured society and the general laws of etiquette.

Do not prolong the call if the room is crowded. It is better to call a day or two afterwards.

Do not call upon a person in reduced circumstances with a display of wealth, dress and equipage.

Do not tattle. Do not speak ill of your neighbors. Do not carry gossip from one family to another.

Do not, if a gentleman, seat yourself upon the sofa beside the hostess, or in near proximity, unless invited to do so.

Do not, if a lady, call upon a gentleman, except officially or professionally, unless he may be a confirmed invalid.

Do not take a strange gentleman with you, unless positively certain that his introduction will be received with favor.

Do not, if a gentleman, leave the hat in the hall when making merely a formal call. If the call is extended into a visit, it may then be set aside. Whether sitting or standing (Fig. 7), the hat may be gracefully held in the hand.

Duty of the Hostess.

She should greet each guest with quiet, easy grace.

She should avoid leaving the room while guests are present.

She should furnish refreshments to those callers who come a long distance to see her.

She should be aided, upon important occasions, by a gentleman, in the reception of guests.

She should avoid speaking disrespectfully of those who have previously called upon her; she should equally divide her attentions among the several callers, that none may feel slighted.

Etiquette of Conversation.

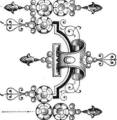

HOW, WHEN AND WHERE TO SPEAK.

TO ACQUIRE the art of conversation in a superior degree, there must be intimacy with those who possess refinement and general information. There must also be observed certain general rules in order to accomplish the best results, prominent among which are the following:

In the first place, in order to converse well, there must be knowledge; there must be a command of language, assisted by imagination; there must be understanding of the rules of construction, to frame sentences aright; there must be confidence and self-possession, and there must be courage to overcome failure.

To be an excellent conversationalist is a very desirable accomplishment. We talk more than we do anything else. By conversation we may make friends, we may retain them, or we may lose them. We may impart information; we may acquire it. We may make the company with whom we associate contented with itself, or we can sow inharmony and discord. Our success in life largely rests upon our ability to converse well; therefore the necessity of our carefully studying what should and what should not be said when talking.

How to Please in Conversation.

Use clear, distinct words to express your ideas, although your voice should be low.

Be cool, collected and self-possessed, using respectful, chaste and appropriate language.

Always defend the absent person who is being spoken of, as far as truth and justice will permit.

Allow people that you are with to do their full share of the talking if they evince a willingness to converse.

Beware of talking much about yourself. Your merits will be discovered in due time, without the necessity of sounding your own praises.

Show the courtesy, when another person joins the group where you are relating an incident, of recapitulating what has been said, for the advantage of the newcomer.

Recollect that the object of conversation is to entertain and amuse; the social gathering, therefore, should not be made the arena of dispute. Even slight mistakes and inaccuracies it is well to overlook, rather than to allow inharmony to present itself.

Aim to adapt your conversation to the comprehension of those with whom you are conversing. Be careful that you do not undervalue them. It is possible that they are as intelligent as yourself, and their conversation can, perhaps, take as wide a range as your own.

Remember that the person to whom you are speaking is not to blame for the opinion he entertains. Opinions are not made *by* us, but they are made *for* us by circumstances. With the same organization, training and circumstances around us, we would have the same opinions ourselves.

Remember that people are fond of talking of their own affairs. The mother likes to talk of her children, the mechanic of his workmanship, the laborer of what he can accomplish. Give everyone an opportunity, and you will gain much valuable information besides being thought courteous and well-bred.

Be patient. The foreigner cannot, perhaps, recall the word he desires; the speaker may be slow of speech; you may have heard the story a dozen times; but even then you must evince interest, and listen patiently through. By so doing, you gain the esteem of the person with whom you are conversing.

What to Avoid in Social Conversation.

Do not manifest impatience.

Do not engage in argument.

Do not interrupt another when speaking.

Do not find fault, though you may gently criticise.

Do not talk of your private, personal and family matters.

Do not appear to notice inaccuracies of speech in others.

Do not allow yourself to lose temper or to speak excitedly.

Do not allude to unfortunate peculiarities of anyone present.

Do not always commence a conversation by allusion to the weather.

Do not, when narrating an incident, continually say, "you see," "you know," etc.

Do not introduce professional or other topics that the company generally cannot take an interest in.

Do not talk very loud. A firm, clear, distinct, yet mild, gentle and musical voice has great power.

Do not be absent-minded, requiring the speaker to repeat what has been said that you may understand.

Do not speak disrespectfully of personal appearance when anyone present may have the same defects.

Do not try to force yourself into the confidence of others. If they give their confidence, never betray it.

Do not use profanity, vulgar terms, slang phrases, words of double meaning, or language that will bring the blush to anyone.

Do not intersperse your language with foreign words and high sounding terms. It shows affectation, and will draw ridicule upon you.

Do not carry on a conversation with another in company about matters which the general company knows nothing of. It is almost as impolite as to whisper.

Do not allow yourself to speak ill of the absent one if it can be avoided; the day may come when some friend will be needed to defend you in your absence.

Do not speak with contempt and ridicule of a locality where you may be visiting. Find something to truthfully praise and commend; thus make yourself agreeable.

Do not make a pretense of gentility, nor parade the fact that you are a descendant of any notable family. You must pass for just what you are, and must stand on your own merit.

Do not contradict. In making a correction say, "I beg your pardon, but I had an impression that it was so and so." Be careful in contradicting, as you may be wrong yourself.

Do not be unduly familiar; you will merit contempt if you are. Neither should you be dogmatic in your assertions, arrogating to yourself much consequence in your opinions.

Do not be too lavish in your praise of various members of your own family when speaking to strangers; the person to whom you are speaking may know some faults that you do not.

Do not feel it incumbent upon yourself to carry your point in conversation. Should the person with whom you are conversing feel the same, your talk will lead into violent argument.

Do not allow yourself to use personal abuse when speaking to another, as in so doing you may make that person a life-long enemy. A few kind, courteous words might have made him a lifelong friend.

Do not discuss politics or religion in general company. You probably would not convert your opponent, and he will not convert you. To discuss those topics is to arouse feeling without any good result.

Do not make a parade of being acquainted with distinguished or wealthy people, of having been to college, or of having visited foreign lands. All this is no evidence of any real genuine worth on your part.

Do not use the surname alone when speaking of your husband or wife to others. To say to another, that "I told Jones,' referring to your husband, sounds badly. Whereas, to say, "I told Mr. Jones," shows respect and good breeding.

Do not yield to bashfulness. Do not isolate yourself, sitting back in a corner, waiting for some one to come and talk with you. Step out; have something to say. Though you may not say it very well, keep on. You will gain courage and will improve. It is as much your duty to entertain others as theirs to amuse you.

Do not attempt to pry into the private affairs of others by asking what their profits are, what things cost, whether Melissa ever had a beau, and why Amarette never got married. All such questions are extremely impertinent, and are likely to meet with rebuke.

Do not whisper in company; do not engage in private conversation; do not speak a foreign language which the general company present may not understand, unless it is understood that the foreigner is unable to speak your own language.

Do not take it upon yourself to admonish comparative strangers on religious topics; the persons to whom you speak may have decided convictions of their own in opposition to yours, and your over-zeal may seem to them an impertinence.

Do not aspire to be a great story-teller; an inveterate teller of long stories becomes very tiresome. To tell one or two witty, short, new stories, appropriate to the occasion, is about all that one person should inflict on the company.

Do not indulge in satire; no doubt you are witty, and you could say a most cutting thing that would bring the laugh of the company upon your opponent, but you must not allow it, unless to rebuke an impertinent fellow who can be suppressed in no other way.

Do not spend your time in talking scandal; you sink your own moral nature by so doing, and you are, perhaps, doing great injustice to those about whom you talk. You probably do not understand all the circumstances. Were they understood, you would doubtless be much more lenient.

Do not flatter; in doing so you embarrass those upon whom you bestow praise, as they may not wish to offend you by repelling it, and yet they realize that if they accept it they merit your contempt. You may, however, commend their work whenever it can truthfully be done; but do not bestow praise where it is not deserved.

NEW YEAR'S CALLING.

OF LATE years it has become fashionable, for ladies in many cities and villages, to announce in the newspapers the fact of their intention to receive calls upon New Year's day, which practice is very excellent, as it enables gentlemen to know positively who will be prepared to receive them on that occasion; besides, changes of residence are so frequent in the large cities as to make the publication of names and places of calling a great convenience.

The practice of issuing personal notes of invitation, which is sometimes done, to a list of gentleman acquaintances, stating that certain ladies will receive on New Year's day, is not to be commended. It looks very much like begging the gentlemen to come and see them; besides, should this practice generally prevail, it would, in a brief time, abolish New Year's calls altogether, as gentlemen would not feel at liberty to make calls unless personally invited; and thus the custom would soon go into disuse.

Upon calling, the gentlemen are invited to remove overcoat and hat, which invitation is accepted unless it is the design to make the call very brief. If refreshments are provided, the ladies will desire to have the gentlemen partake of them, which cannot conveniently be done in overcoat, with hat in hand. Gloves are sometimes retained upon the hand during the call, but this is optional. Cards are sent up, and the gentlemen are ushered into the reception-room. The call should not exceed ten

Fig. 8.   Gentlemen Making New Year's Calls.

or fifteen minutes, unless the callers are few and it should be mutually agreeable to prolong the stay.

Best taste will suggest that a lady having the conveniences shall receive her guests at her own home, but it is admissible and common for several ladies to meet at the residence of one, and receive calls together. Whether ladies make announcement or not, however, it will be usually safe for gentlemen to call on their lady friends on New Year's, as the visit will be generally received with pleasure.

It is customary for the ladies who announce that they will receive, to make their parlors attractive on that day, and present themselves in full dress. They should have a bright, cheerful fire if the weather be cold, and a table, conveniently located in the room, with refreshments, consisting of fruits, cakes, bread and other food, such as may be deemed desirable, with tea and coffee. No intoxicating drinks should be allowed. Refreshments are in no case absolutely essential. They can be dispensed with if not convenient.

Ladies expecting calls on New Year's should be in readiness to receive from 10 A. M. to 9 P. M. It is pleasant for two or more ladies to receive calls together on that occasion, as several ladies can the more easily entertain a party of several gentlemen who may be present at one time. While gentlemen may go alone, they also frequently go in pairs, threes, fours (Fig 8) or more. They call upon all the ladies of the party, and where any are not acquainted, introductions take place, care being taken that persons do not intrude themselves where they would not be welcome. Each gentleman should be provided with a large number of cards, with his own name upon each, one of which he will present to every lady of the company where he calls.

The ladies keep these cards for future reference, it being often pleasant to revive the incidents of the day by subsequent examination of the cards received upon that occasion.

An usher should be present wherever many calls are expected, to receive guests, and care for hats and coats. The calls are necessarily very brief, and are made delightfully pleasant by continual change of face and conversation. But, however genial and free may be the interchange of compliments upon this occasion, no young man who is a stranger to the family should feel at liberty to call again without a subsequent invitation.

The two or three days succeeding New Year's are the ladies' days for calling, upon which occasion they pass the compliments of the season, comment upon the incidents connected with the festivities of the holiday, the number of calls made, and the new faces that made their appearance among the visitors. It is customary upon this occasion of ladies' meeting, to offer refreshments and to enjoy the intimacy of a friendly visit. This fashion of observing New Year's day is often the means of commencing pleasant friendships which may continue through life.

Etiquette of the Party and Ball.

THE DANCE---RULES THAT SHOULD GOVERN IT.

YOU purpose giving a larger entertainment than the dinner party—one to which you will invite a greater number of your friends and associates—so great a number, indeed, of young and middle-aged people, that the serious question is, how they shall be entertained; you conclude that you will allow them to dance, and you will name your entertainment a ball.

In this connection we will express no opinion concerning the propriety or the impropriety of dancing. In the simple act of passing through the figures of the dance, there need be no wrong committed; but, as the ball is often conducted, very serious and unfortunate results follow.

Evils of the Ball.

For the company to assemble at a late hour and engage in unusual, exciting and severe exercise throughout the entire night, is often too great a tax upon the physical system. To dress too thinly, and in a state of perspiration to be exposed, as ladies at the ball frequently are, to draughts of cold, is oftentimes to plant the seeds of a disease from which they never recover. Again, to come in contact, as ladies are liable to, more especially at the public ball, with disreputable men, is sometimes to form alliances that will make a lifetime of sorrow.

Well may the watchful parent look with anxiety and suspicion upon the ball, because its associations are so frequently dangerous. If in this chapter we may give admonitions and suggestions that shall tend to correct some of the evils of the dance, our labors will not be in vain.

The dancing-master should be in the highest sense of the term a gentleman; he should be thoroughly schooled in the laws of etiquette; he should be a man of good moral character; he should be a physiologist; he should be a reformer. Such a man at the head of a dancing-school would be of infinite assistance to the young men and women coming upon the stage of action. In his class he would teach his pupils the laws of good behavior; he would warn them concerning the evils of bad association; he would instruct them in the importance of regularity of habit and of keeping proper hours: with which instruction he would reform many abuses that now exist at public entertainments.

Fortunately we have some instructors who appreciate the importance of their work, and are thus instrumental in doing a great amount of good to those who are so favored as to attend their classes.

How to Conduct the Ball.

The management of the ball will largely depend upon whether it is a public or private entertainment. If public, it will be under the control of managers who will send out tickets to those likely to attend, often several weeks before the ball is given. These tickets are sent only to gentlemen who invite such ladies to attend the ball with them as they may choose.

In tendering the invitation, the gentleman frequently visits the lady personally. If he sends a written note of invitation, the form may be as follows:

Wednesday, Oct. 10.

Miss Hammond:
May I have the pleasure of your company to the ball at the Grand Central Hotel, in New York, on the evening of October 25th, at eight o'clock? *Very Respectfully,*

W. H. SIMPSON.

The following may be the reply:

Thursday, Oct. 11.

Mr. W. H. Simpson:
I shall be happy to accompany you to the ball at the Grand Central, on the evening of October 25th.

CARRIE D. HAMMOND.

Or, if the invitation is declined, the note may have this form:

Thursday, Oct. 11.

Mr. W. H. Simpson:
I regret that absence from the city, (or assign such other cause as may occasion the refusal) *will deprive me of the pleasure of accompanying you to the ball at the Grand Central, on the evening of October 25th.*

CARRIE D. HAMMOND.

If the ball is to be given at a private residence, the notes of invitation should be sent by messenger or post, to each guest, two or three weeks before the dance, and will read as follows:

Mrs. Conklin's compliments to Miss Henry, requesting the pleasure of her company at a ball on Thursday evening, April 12th, at eight o'clock.

This should invariably be answered within a day or two, and, if accepted, the reply may read in the following form:

Miss Henry's compliments to Mrs. Conklin, accepting with pleasure her kind invitation for Thursday evening, April 12th.

If declined, the answer may be—

Miss Henry's compliments to Mrs. Conklin, regretting that the recent death of a relative (or assign such other cause as may occasion the refusal) *will prevent her acceptance of the kind invitation for the evening of April 12th.*

Invitations to all the Family.

In sending invitations to a family where there are parents, sons and daughters, all of whom you desire to invite, enclose an invitation full and complete to the heads of the family, one to the daughters, and one to the sons. Should there be a visitor staying with the family, a distinct card must be sent, but all can be enclosed in one envelope, and addressed to the lady of the house. The invitations to each may read as follows:

(To the Parents.)

Mrs. Hobart's compliments to Mr. and Mrs. Hanson, requesting the pleasure of their company at a ball on the evening of Sept. 8th, at 8 o'clock.
R. S. V. P.*

(To the Daughters.)

Mrs. Hobart's compliments to Misses Ruth and Mary Hanson, requesting the pleasure of their attendance at a ball, Sept. 8th, at 8 o'clock.
R. S. V. P. †

(To the Sons.)

Mrs. Hobart's regards to Messrs. Robert D., Henry H. and Chas. C. Hanson, soliciting their company at a ball on the evening of Sept. 8th, at 8 o'clock.
R. S. V. P.

---

* R. S. V. P. From the French, "Repondez s'il vous plait." Answer if you please.
† R. S. V. P. may be considered unnecessary, as a reply should always be made.

(To the Visitor.)

Mrs. Hobart's respects to Miss Williamson, desiring the pleasure of her company at a ball on the evening of Sept. 8th, at 8 o'clock.
R. S. V. P.

The acceptance or regrets from each party invited should be enclosed in one envelope, and directed to the hostess, being sent by a messenger within from one to three days from the time the invitations are received.

The hostess having considered how many sets may be accommodated in the dancing-room, it may be well to invite twice that number to the entertainment, thus allowing for those who will decline and for those who will desire to rest while the others are engaged in the dance.

The requisites of a room suitable for dancing purposes are a smooth floor and good ventilation; added to these, an elaborate trimming of the room with various decorations will be appropriate. Floral embellishment gives much attraction, and if an abundance of flowers, shrubbery and evergreens are about the music-stand, concealing the musicians from view, the effect will be all the more charming.

The dressing-room should be provided with servants to receive the wraps, to each of which a card should be attached bearing the name of the owner, or checks may be provided and the same system pursued as is ordinarily observed in checking baggage.

A dressing-table in the ladies' room should be supplied with soap, water, towels, brushes, combs, pomade, face-powder, cologne, needles, thread, pins, etc.; while water, soap, towels, brush-broom, comb, hair-brush, bootjack, and blacking-brush with a box of blacking, should be in the gentlemen's dressing apartment.

Unlike the dinner-party, it is not absolutely necessary that each guest come promptly at a certain time; still, for the sake of regularity of sleep, it is well for each to go early and retire early, though it will be allowable to go somewhat later than the hour appointed.

The host and hostess should be near the door to welcome arrivals, occupying any unused time in making the guests acquainted with each other by introductions. Other members of the family will also intermingle with the company, making introductions and seeing that all are provided with partners for dancing.

It is expected that those who accept an invitation to a ball are able to dance; otherwise it is better to decline, as the wall-flower serves but to embarrass the hostess and other members of the company.

A gentleman, having arranged to accompany a lady to a ball, may very appropriately send her a bouquet of flowers in the afternoon, and in the evening he should call promptly with his carriage at the appointed hour. Upon reaching the house where the entertainment is given, he will conduct the lady immediately to the ladies' dressing-room; when, retiring to the gentlemen's apartment and putting his own toilet in order, he will return to the door of the ladies' room, meet his charge, and conduct her to the ball-room and the hostess.

Etiquette requires that the lady dance first with her escort, and afterwards he should see that she is provided with partners, and that she enjoys herself, though she may dance with whom she pleases. He should conduct her to supper, and will hold himself in readiness to escort her home whenever she desires to go.

In inviting a lady to dance, various forms of invitation may be used to avoid repetition, as, "Will you honor me with your hand for the quadrille?" "May I have the honor of dancing this set with you?" "May I have the pleasure?" "Will you give me the pleasure?" etc.

A gentleman who may be at the party unattended, will invite one of the ladies of the house for the first dance, but she, possibly being otherwise occupied or engaged, will quite likely introduce him to another lady, whom he must accept.

The music will first play a march, then a quadrille, a waltz, a polka, a galop, etc., interspersed with several round dances to each quadrille, usually ending with a march, prior to supper, when the gentleman, presenting his arm to the lady he is dancing with at the time, unless she has come with another gentleman, will proceed to the table, where possibly a little more freedom will prevail than at the dinner-party, though essentially the same etiquette will govern it.

If any lady is without an attendant, it should be the duty of the lady of the house to see that she is provided with an escort. After supper,

several dances will follow, the company dispersing, let us hope, at an early, temperate hour.

Each dancer should be provided with a ball-card bearing a printed programme of the dances, having a space for making engagements upon the same, with a small pencil attached. Much care should be taken to keep each engagement. It is a great breach of etiquette to invite a lady to dance, and then fail to remind her of her promise when the time comes for its fulfillment.

It is customary for the lady and gentleman, who accompany each other to the ball, to dance together once or twice only; to dance as partners oftener is likely to excite remark, though, if the parties be indifferent to comment, no harm will be done. To dance together continually is impolite, and will deservedly provoke severe criticism.

While upon the floor, awaiting the music, a lady and gentleman should avoid long conversations, as they are likely to interfere with the dance; but a pleasant word or two in light conversation will be appropriate if the parties are acquainted; if not, they may quietly wait. The bow should be given at the commencement and close of each dance.

General Suggestions to those who Attend Balls.

When all the ladies are provided for at the table, then the gentlemen may think of their own supper.

Ladies will consult their own pleasure about recognizing a ball-room acquaintance at a future meeting.

Gently glide in the dance, wearing a pleasant expression. "Bow the head lightly as you touch hands lightly."

Should you make a mistake in taking a position, apologize to the party incommoded, and take another place in the set.

Any difficulty or misunderstanding at a public ball should be referred to the master of ceremonies, whose decision should be deemed final.

In tendering an invitation to the lady to dance, allow her to designate what set it shall be, and you are expected to strictly fulfill the engagement.

A gentleman who goes to a ball should dance frequently; if he does not, he will not receive many invitations afterwards; he is not invited to ornament the wall and "wait for supper."

After dancing, a gentleman should conduct the lady to a seat, unless she otherwise desires; he should thank her for the pleasure she has conferred, but he should not tarry too long in intimate conversation with her.

A gentleman having taken a lady's seat during a dance, must rise as soon as it is over, and invite her to come and take it again. It is not necessary to bow more than once, though you frequently meet acquaintances upon the promenade; to bow every time would be tiresome.

What Conduct to Avoid at the Ball.

A ball-room engagement should not be broken.

A lady should not enter or cross the hall unattended.

No gentleman should enter the ladies' dressing-room at a ball.

No evidence of ill-nature should ever show itself at the ball.

Never lead a lady in the hall by the hand; always offer the arm.

Guests should remain at the supper-table no longer than is necessary.

A couple should not engage in a long, private, confidential talk in a ball-room.

While one dance is in progress, it is not in good taste to be arranging for another.

Do not engage yourself for the last two or three dances; it may keep you too late.

Neither married nor unmarried ladies should leave a ball-room assemblage unattended.

A gentleman should not wait until the music has commenced, before selecting his partner.

Do not aim to put in all the steps in the quadrille. The figures are now executed in a graceful walk.

A gentleman should not insist upon a lady continuing to dance, when she has expressed a desire to sit down.

Excepting the first set, it is not etiquette for married people to dance together at either a public or private ball.

Do not contend for a position in the quadrille at either head or sides. It indicates frivolity. You should be above it.

A gentleman should not take a vacant seat beside a lady, without asking permission, whether he is acquainted or not.

The lady should never accept of an invitation to dance with one gentleman immediately after having refused another.

No lady at a ball should be without an escort at the supper-table. The hostess should see that she is provided with one.

A gentleman should never presume upon the acquaintance of a lady after a ball; ball-room introductions close with the dancing.

Ladies should not boast to others, who dance but little, of the great number of dances for which they are engaged in advance.

No gentleman should use his bare hand to press the waist of a lady in the waltz. If without gloves, carry a handkerchief in the hand.

A lady should not select a gentleman to hold her bouquet, fan and gloves during the dance, unless he be her husband, escort or a relative.

Gentlemen should never forget that ladies are first to be cared for, to have the best seats, and to always receive the most courteous attention.

A gentleman in waltzing should not encircle the waist of a lady until the dancing commences, and he should drop his arm when the music ceases.

No gentleman whose clothing or breath is tainted with the fumes of strong drink or tobacco, should ever enter the presence of ladies in the dancing-room.

When the company has been divided into two different sets, you should not attempt to change from one to the other, except by permission of the master of ceremonies.

A lady should not refuse to be introduced to a gentleman at a private ball. At a public ball she will use her discretion, and she can with propriety refuse any introduction.

Never eat your supper in gloves. White kids should be worn at other times throughout the dancing. It is well to have two pairs, one before supper, the other afterwards.

Ladies should not be allowed to sit the evening through without the privilege of dancing. Gentlemen should be sufficiently watchful to see that all ladies present are provided with partners.

Do not, unless for very urgent reasons, withdraw from a quadrille or a set where your assistance is required. Even then you should inform the master of ceremonies, that he may find a substitute.

A gentleman should not invite a lady to be his partner in a dance with which he is not perfectly familiar. It is tiresome and embarrassing to a lady to have a partner who appears awkward.

No gentleman should play the clown in the ball-room. Dancing a break-down, making unusual noise, dressing in a peculiar style, swaggering, swinging the arms about, etc., are simply the characteristics of the buffoon.

The lady is not obliged to invite her escort to enter the house when he accompanies her home, and if invited he should decline the invitation. But he should request permission to call the next day or evening, which will be true politeness.

No display should be made when leaving the ball. Go quietly. It is not necessary to bid the host and hostess good-bye. To do so may cause others to think it later than it is, and thus the ball may be broken up sooner than the hostess might desire.

A lady may not engage herself to two gentlemen for the same dance, excepting the waltz, the first of which may be danced with one and the last with another, she explaining the matter to her first partner, that he may not be offended when she leaves him for the other.

The members of the family where the ball is given should not dance too frequently. It is possible that others may desire to fill their places, and they should have the opportunity. It is the duty of the family to entertain the guests, and not usurp their opportunities.

A gentleman should not be offended if a lady that has declined an invitation from him is seen dancing with another. Possibly she did not despise the one, but she preferred the other, or she may have simply redeemed a forgotten promise. Special evidences of partiality should, however, as much as possible be avoided at places where all should be courteous to each other.

 # ETIQUETTE OF A SOCIAL GAME.

The topics of conversation have become exhausted at the party; you have no musicians in the company, possibly, or if you have music, it no longer entertains. Under the circumstances, you bethink yourself of some light, pleasant indoor game that nearly all can play, and very likely you may select cards, about which the following suggestions may be appropriate:

Should you engage in the game, do so simply for recreation and sociability. Never bet on cards. Like all bets, it leads to demoralization. If you cannot play without gambling and spending too much time, then dismiss the game from your mind. In the simple matter of playing cards there is no harm, but in the abuse of the game there is very much injury.

It is the province of the hostess, not of the guests, to introduce the game. New, bright, clean cards should be kept in readiness for occasions like the evening party.

In taking a seat at the table, where there may be a choice, the elder and married ladies take precedence over the younger members of the company, only those persons being urged to join in the game who have no conscientious scruples against playing.

Rules of the Game.

Do not remove the cards from the table until all are dealt.

Partners should give no appearance of an understanding between themselves by signals of any kind.

Never play with an air of indifference. If tired, you will ask to be excused, and retire; but evince interest while you play.

It is a violation of etiquette to converse upon other topics while playing the game, especially if at the table there are those who are interested, and desire to confine their attention to the play.

It is not courtesy to hurry others when playing. It is very annoying to have an opponent, or even a partner, continually saying, "Come, hurry up!" "We are waiting!" "Any time to-day!" etc.

The object of the game is to give rest. Therefore all topics liable to lead to long argument should be avoided when conversing in the pauses of the play. Small talk, that requires no mental effort, is all that should be indulged in while at the game.

If possible, never violate the rules of the game, and never be guilty of cheating. Should you observe any one doing so, quietly and very politely call their attention to the fact, and be careful that you do not get excited. People who lose patience, and experience ill-feeling at the game, should avoid playing.

It is unkind in those who may have continued success to irritate the opponent; and, whatever may be the ill-luck, it is a serious breach of etiquette to lose temper. Neither should there be reflections made upon the playing of the partner nor criticisms upon the opponents.

It is the duty of those who play to make themselves proficient in the game, and thus not embarrass a partner when playing; and courtesy requires that those who play much together should not play with each other in general company, as they would thus be taking unfair advantage of their opponents.

Etiquette of the Table.

THE TABLE--HOW TO SET AND ARRANGE IT.

THE dinner-hour will completely test the refinement, the culture and good breeding which the individual may possess. To appear advantageously at the table, the person must not only understand the laws of etiquette, but he must have had the advantage of polite society. It is the province of this chapter to show what the laws of the table are. It will be the duty of the reader, in the varied relations of life, to make such use of them as circumstances shall permit.

Rules to be Observed.

Sit upright, neither too close nor too far away from the table.

Open and spread upon your lap or breast a napkin, if one is provided—otherwise a handkerchief.

Do not be in haste; compose yourself; put your mind into a pleasant condition, and resolve to eat slowly.

Keep the hands from the table until your time comes to be served. It is rude to take knife and fork in hand and commence drumming on the table while you are waiting.

Possibly grace will be said by some one present, and the most respectful attention and quietude should be observed until the exercise is passed.

It is the most appropriate time, while you wait to be served, for you to put into practice your knowledge of small talk and pleasant words with those whom you are sitting near. By interchange of thought, much valuable information may be acquired at the table.

Do not be impatient to be served. With social chit-chat and eating, the meal-time should always be prolonged from thirty minutes to an hour.

Taking ample time in eating will give you better health, greater wealth, longer life and more happiness. These are what we may obtain by eating slowly in a pleasant frame of mind, thoroughly masticating the food.

If soup comes first, and you do not desire it, you will simply say, "No, I thank you," but make no comment; or you may take it and eat as little as you choose. The other course will be along soon. In receiving it you do not break the order of serving; it looks odd to see you waiting while all the rest are partaking of the first course. Eccentricity should be avoided as much as possible at the table.

The soup should be eaten with a medium-sized spoon, so slowly and carefully that you will drop none upon your person or the table-cloth. Making an effort to get the last drop, and all unusual noise when eating, should be avoided.

Fig. 9   The general arrangement of the table set for a party of twelve persons. The plates are often left off, and furnished by the waiter afterwards.

Fig. 10. Relative position of plate, napkin, goblet, salt-cup, knife and fork, when the table is set.

If asked at the next course what you desire, you will quietly state, and upon its reception you will, without display, proceed to put your food in order for eating. If furnished with potatoes in small dishes, you will put the skins back into the dish again; and thus where there are side-dishes all refuse should be placed in them—otherwise potato-skins will be placed upon the table-cloth, and bones upon the side of the plate. If possible, avoid putting waste matter upon the cloth. Especial pains should always be taken to keep the table-cover as clean as may be.

Eating with the Fork.

Fashions continually change. It does not follow, because he does not keep up with them, that a man lacks brains; still to keep somewhere near the prevailing style, in habit, costume and general deportment, is to avoid attracting unpleasant attention.

Fashions change in modes of eating. Unquestionably primitive man conveyed food to his mouth with his fingers. In process of time he cut it with a sharpened instrument, and held it, while he did so, with something pointed. In due time, with the advancement of civilization, there came the two-tined fork for holding and the broad-bladed knife for cutting the food and conveying it to the mouth. As years have passed on, bringing their changes, the three and four-tined forks have come into use, and the habit of conveying food with them to the mouth; the advantage being that there is less danger to the mouth from using the fork, and food is less liable to drop from it when being conveyed from the plate. Thus the knife, which is now only used for cutting meat, mashing potatoes, and for a few other purposes at the table, is no longer placed to the mouth by those who give attention to the etiquette of the table.

Set the table as beautifully as possible. Use only the snowiest of linen, the brightest of cutlery, and the cleanest of china. The setting of the table (Fig. 9) will have fruit-plates, castors and other dishes for general use, conveniently placed near the center. The specific arrangement (Fig. 10) of plate, knife, fork, napkin, goblet and salt-cup, is shown in the accompanying illustration.

It is customary for the gentleman who is the head of the household, in the ordinary family circle, to sit at the side of the table, in the center, having plates at his right hand, with food near by. When all the family are seated, and all in readiness, he will serve the guests who may be present; he will next serve the eldest lady of the household, then the ladies and gentlemen as they come in order. The hostess will sit opposite her husband, and preside over the tea, sauces, etc.

ERRORS TO BE AVOIDED.

DO NOT speak disrespectfully to the waiters, nor apologize to them for making them trouble; it is their business to bring forward the food called for.

It is courtesy, however, when asked if you desire a certain article, to reply, "If you please;" "Not any, I thank you," etc.; when calling for an article, to say, "Will you please bring me," etc.; and when the article has been furnished, to say, "Thank you."

Never eat very fast.

Never fill the mouth very full.

Never open your mouth when chewing.

Never make noise with the mouth or throat.

Never attempt to talk with the mouth full.

Never leave the table with food in the mouth.

Never soil the table-cloth if it is possible to avoid it.

Never carry away fruits and confectionery from the table.

Never encourage a dog or cat to play with you at the table.

Never use anything but fork or spoon in feeding yourself.

Never explain at the table why certain foods do not agree with you.

Never introduce disgusting or unpleasant topics for conversation.

Never pick your teeth or put your hand in your mouth while eating.

Never cut bread; always break it, spreading with butter each piece as you eat it.

Never come to the table in your shirt-sleeves, with dirty hands or disheveled hair.

Never express a choice for any particular parts of a dish, unless requested to do so.

Never hesitate to take the last piece of bread or the last cake; there are probably more.

Never call loudly for the waiter, nor attract attention to yourself by boisterous conduct.

Never hold bones in your fingers while you eat from them. Cut the meat with a knife.

Never use your own knife when cutting butter. Always use a knife assigned to that purpose.

Never pare an apple, peach or pear for another at the table without holding it with a fork.

Never wipe your fingers on the table-cloth, nor clean them in your mouth. Use the napkin.

Never allow butter, soup or other food to remain on your whiskers. Use the napkin frequently.

Never wear gloves at the table, unless the hands from some special reason are unfit to be seen.

Never, when serving others, overload the plate nor force upon them delicacies which they decline.

Never pour sauce over meat and vegetables when helping others. Place it at one side, on the plate.

Never make a display of finding fault with your food. Very quietly have it changed if you want it different.

Never pass your plate with knife and fork on the same. Remove them, and allow them to rest upon a piece of bread.

Never make a display when removing hair, insects or other disagreeable things from your food. Place them quietly under the edge of your plate.

Never make an effort to clean your plate or the bones you have been eating from too clean; it looks as if you left off hungry.

Never tip back in your chair nor lounge upon the table; neither assume any position that is awkward or ill-bred.

Never, at one's own table or at a dinner-party elsewhere, leave before the rest have finished without asking to be excused. At a hotel or boarding house this rule need not be observed.

Never feel obliged to cut off the kernels with a knife when eating green corn; eaten from the cob, the corn is much the sweetest.

Never eat so much of any one article as to attract attention, as some people do who eat large quantities of butter, sweet cake, cheese or other articles.

Never expectorate at the table; also avoid sneezing or coughing. It is better to arise quietly from the table if you have occasion to do either. A sneeze is prevented by placing the finger firmly on the upper lip.

Never spit out bones, cherry pits, grape skins, etc., upon your plate. Quietly press them from your mouth upon the fork, and lay them upon the side of your plate.

Never allow the conversation at the table to drift into anything but chit-chat; the consideration of deep and abstruse principles will impair digestion.

Never permit yourself to engage in a heated argument at the table. Neither should you use gestures, nor illustrations made with a knife or fork on the table-cloth. The accompanying engraving (Fig. 11) very forcibly illustrates several faults to which many people are addicted.

FIG. 11. BAD MANNERS AT THE TABLE.

No. 1.	Tips back his chair.
" 2.	Eats with his mouth too full.
" 3.	Feeds a dog at the table.
" 4.	Holds his knife improperly.
" 5.	Engages in violent argument at the meal-time.
" 6.	Lounges upon the table.
" 7.	Brings a cross child to the table.

No. 8.	Drinks from the saucer, and laps with his tongue the last drop from the plate.
" 9.	Comes to the table in his shirt-sleeves, and puts his feet beside his chair.
" 10.	Picks his teeth with his fingers.
" 11.	Scratches her head and is frequently unnecessarily getting up from the table.

Never pass forward to another the dish that has been handed to you, unless requested to do so; it may have been purposely designed for you, and passing it to another may give him or her what is not wanted.

Never put your feet so far under the table as to touch those of the person on the opposite side; neither should you curl them under nor at the side of your chair.

Never praise extravagantly every dish set before you; neither should you appear indifferent. Any article may have praise.

POLITENESS AT THE TABLE.

PROPERLY conducted, the dinner-party should be a pleasant affair; and if rightly managed, from the beginning to the end, it may prove a very enjoyable occasion to all in attendance, the dinner being from 5 to 8 P. M., the guests continuing at the table from one to two hours.

For a very pleasant social affair the rule is not to have the company when seated exceed twelve in number. With a party of that size the conversation can be general, and all are likely to feel more at ease than if the number be larger, provided a selection of guests is made that are congenial to each other. None of them should be conspicuously superior to the others, and all should be from the same circle of society.

Having determined upon the number of guests to be invited, the next thing in order will be the issuing of notes of invitation, by special messenger, which should be sent out ten or twelve days before the dinner is given. Their form will be—

Mr. and Mrs. L—— request the pleasure of the company of Mr. and Mrs. T—— at dinner on Wednesday, the 10th of March, at six o'clock P. M.
R. S. V. P.

The answer accepting the invitation may read—

Mr. and Mrs. T—— accept with much pleasure Mr. and Mrs. L——'s invitation for dinner on the 10th of March.

If declined, the form may be as follows:

Mr. and Mrs. T—— regret that a previous engagement (or for other reasons which may be given) *will prevent their accepting Mr. and Mrs. L——'s kind invitation for dinner on the 10th of March.*

Should the invitation be declined, the declination, which should state the reason for non-acceptance of the invitation, should be sent immediately by a messenger, that the hostess may have an opportunity for inviting other guests in the place of those who decline.

Should the invitation be accepted, nothing but serious difficulty should prevent the appointment being fulfilled. Should anything happen to prevent attendance, notification should be given the hostess immediately.

It is of the utmost importance that all of the company be punctual, arriving from ten to fifteen minutes before the appointed time. To be ten minutes late, keeping the dinner waiting, is a serious offense which no one should be guilty of.

The host, hostess and other members of the family should be early in the drawing-room to receive guests as they arrive, each of whom should be welcomed with a warm greeting.

The hostess having determined who shall accompany each other to the table, each gentleman should be informed what lady he is expected to escort. The hour having arrived, the host offers his right arm to the most honored or possibly the eldest lady guest, and the gentleman most distinguished will escort the lady of the house.

Proceeding to the dining-room when all is in readiness, the host will take his seat at the foot of the table, and the hostess at the head, the lady escorted by the host taking her seat at his right, and the escort of the hostess sitting also at *her* right. The next most honored seat is at the *left* of the hostess. The illustration (Fig. 12) upon this page shows a company thus seated.

It is fashionable to have cards laid upon the table, bearing the name, sometimes printed very beautifully upon silk, indicating where each guest shall sit, which saves confusion in being seated. The ladies having taken their places, the gentlemen will be seated, and all is in readiness for the dinner to be served, unless grace be said by a clergyman present or by the host.

Let us hope if there is any carving, it will be done before the meat is brought to the table, and the time of the company saved from this sometimes slow and tedious work. Should soup be passed, it is well for each one to take it, and also the various courses as they are served, making no special comment on the food.

The gentleman will, when a dish is brought, having seen the lady he escorted provided for, help himself and pass it on; he will pay no attention to the other lady near him, but will leave that to her escort. In all cases he will be careful and attentive to the wants of the lady in his charge, ascertaining her wishes and issuing her orders to the waiters.

No polite guest will ever fastidiously smell or examine any article of food before tasting it. Such conduct would be an insult to those who have invited him; neither will the host or hostess apologize for the cooking or find fault with each other, the cook or the waiters; all having done the best they could, there is nothing left to do but to make the best of everything that is provided.

Especial pains should be taken by the host and hostess, as well as all the company, to introduce topics of conversation that shall be agreeable and pleasing, that the dinner hour may be in the highest degree entertaining. When all the guests have finished their eating, the hostess, with a slight nod to one of the leading members of the party, will rise, as will all the company, and repair to the drawing-room, where, in social converse, the time should be spent for the next two or three hours. Etiquette demands that each member of the company remain at least an hour after the dinner is finished, it being impolite to hurry away immediately after rising from the table. Should he do so, however, he will ask to be excused.

FIG. 12. GENTILITY IN THE DINING-ROOM.

The evidences of good breeding with a party of ladies and gentlemen seated about a table, who are accustomed to the usages of polite society, are many. Among these will be the fact that the table is very beautifully and artistically spread. This need not require much wealth, but good taste is necessary to set it handsomely.

Again, the company evince gentility by each assuming a genteel position while eating. It is not necessary that an elaborate toilet be worn at the table, but careful attention should always be given to neatness of personal appearance, however plain may be the dress which is worn.

Another evidence of good manners is the self-possession with which the company deport themselves throughout the meal.

CORRECT AND INCORRECT POSITIONS.

Fig. 13. Incorrect Position for Holding Knife
and Fork.

HEREWITH is shown a fault common with many people of holding knife and fork above the hand (Fig. 13) when mashing potatoes, cutting meat, etc. The position is not only unfavorable for obtaining a good command of knife and fork, but it is likewise ungraceful. The contrasting illustration (Fig. 14) represents an easy, graceful posture for hands, when eating. The habit of holding the hands thus in correct positions can be acquired as easily as any other.

It is well to become accustomed to eating with the left hand, so as to avoid the necessity of changing the fork from the left to the right hand frequently when eating meat. When no knife is required for spreading, mashing or cutting, lay it aside entirely and eat only with the fork, holding it with the right hand.

Drinking from the Teacup.

Formerly it was the fashion to pour tea into the saucer; not so now. Tea should be gently sipped from the spoon or cup, taking cup and spoon in hand (Fig. 15) when drinking, as shown in the accompanying diagram.

The spoon should never be removed from the cup when the guest is satisfied with its contents. Should the cup be empty, and more be desired, to take the spoon out and place it beside the cup in the saucer is an intimation to the waiter to have it refilled. If not empty, and the spoon is placed thus beside the cup, it is an intimation to the waiter that you want the tea or coffee changed. Do not call for "milk;" call for and speak only of "cream." Never set your teacup upon the table-cloth. In taking sugar, use only the sugar-spoon.

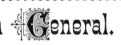

Fig. 15. Position for Holding Cup and
Spoon. *

Fig. 14. Correct Position for Holding Knife
and Fork.

As in all the affairs of life, common sense must always rise superior to fashion or forms of etiquette. In this chapter on "The Table" we have aimed to give the leading outlines which should govern conduct in the dining-room. Much judgment will be required to always understand where these rules should be applied. Certainly to meet a company of people at the table, appear to advantage, carry forward an intelligent conversation, be agreeable and finish the meal, having eaten, in kind and quantity, sufficient to preserve health and vigor, requires much wisdom and experience.

* The cup with handle, or of unusual size, may be held differently.

Etiquette of Parties in General.

Sociables, Tea-Parties, Private Theatricals, Picnics, Etc.

THERE are many other kinds of gatherings, aside from the formal dinner-party and the ball, where less formality is required, but where the rules of etiquette, nevertheless, must be continually brought into service. These comprise conversations, or sociables, private concerts, readings, tea-parties, private theatricals, card-playing, etc. At these entertainments some prefer dancing, some music, some conversation, and some the playing of games.

Whatever may be the nature of the entertainment, it is well to specify it in the invitation. Thus, for a large, full-dress party, the invitation will read:

Miss J——'s compliments to Miss H——, requesting the pleasure of her company for Friday evening, March 10, at eight o'clock.

For the small party meeting for a specific purpose, the invitation will read thus:

Miss B—— requests the pleasure of Miss K——'s company on Friday evening next at 8 o'clock, to meet the members of the Salem Literary Club, to which Miss B—— belongs.

Or,

Miss B—— would be happy to have Miss K—— take part in an entertainment consisting of readings and recitations, at her residence, on Wednesday evening, March 15th, at eight o'clock.

Like the dinner-party and ball, an answer should be promptly returned. The reply may read:

Miss K—— accepts with pleasure Miss B——'s kind invitation for next Wednesday evening.

Unable to accept the invitation, the reply may read as follows:

Miss K—— regrets that a previous engagement (or other reason) will prevent her accepting Miss B——'s kind invitation for Wednesday evening next.

Should there be any probability of mistake as to time, and identity of the person sending the invitation, the date should be explicitly given in the body of the note, and the full name and address may be placed in the lower left-hand corner.

As upon other occasions, it is the duty of the host and hostess to welcome arrivals and make all the guests feel at ease. To do this, much depends upon the hostess, who, by self-possession, geniality and continual movement among the guests, will make all feel at home. More especially if the entertainment partakes of the character of a sociable, much tact is necessary upon the part of the family to have the gathering entertained.

To keep the attention of the company occupied, as many rooms should be thrown open as possible, and many objects of interest should be scattered around the apartments to interest, amuse and instruct.

If among the company there are those particularly eminent, there should be also other notables, that attention may not be entirely concentrated upon the few.

Special pains should be taken that the party does not divide itself up into cliques, twos, threes or more, leaving a number out who seem to possess no power to get into conversation.

While it is not always advisable to break up a pleasant conversation going forward between two, three or four, care must be exercised that those inclined to drop aside and spend the time in conversing with each other are prevented by the hostess as much as possible from so doing, as the best conversationalists, thus going by themselves, would cause the remainder of the company to be wanting in spirit and animation. The introduction of others into the group, the calling for a story, the reading of a poem, the singing of a song, with instrumental music, will thus effectually break up the monotony.

Piano-Playing.

Should dancing form a principal feature of the entertainment, and the piano be used to furnish music, the hostess or one of the family should play the instrument. One of the guests should not be depended upon to furnish all of the music. If the hostess cannot play, a pianist for the occa 'on should be engaged. Either a lady or gentleman-guest may with propriety volunteer to play, if they choose ; but the hostess cannot expect that music, thus voluntarily offered, will be cheerfully furnished for more than one dance.

It is courtesy, while anyone is playing an instrument, or singing, to preserve as much stillness as possible. Should you converse, do it so quietly as not to be heard by those near the piano. Should your conversation be animated, it is well to retire to another room.

Amateur performers upon the piano should thoroughly commit to memory a few pieces to play independently of notes, as to take sheet-music to a party is a hint that they expect to be invited to play. If possible, have the voice in good condition also, so as not to be obliged to complain of a cold. To eat a small amount of horse-radish just previous to reading, singing or speaking, will quite effectually remove hoarseness.

Any lady-guest being invited to play the piano, it is courtesy for the gentleman nearest her to offer his arm and escort her to the instrument. While she is playing he will hold her bouquet, fan and gloves, and should also turn the leaves if he can readily read music, but he should not attempt it otherwise.

When a guest is invited by another guest to play the piano, it will be well to wait until the request is seconded by others; and even then the guest may not play unless it should meet the favor of the hostess, and it is believed to be the pleasure of the majority of the company. If certain that the playing will be acceptable, it is well to suggest to the hostess to invite your friend.

It is very impolite to speak disparagingly of the piano, however much it may be out of tune, or however inferior it may be. More especially is it a breach of etiquette to draw unfavorable comparisons between the instrument and another elsewhere.

How to Entertain the Party.

If it happens to be stormy on the evening of your party, an awning erected from the carriage-landing to the house, or a large umbrella carried by a servant, will be a kind provision for the comfort of the guests as they alight from their carriages.

Suppers have wisely been dispensed with of late years at the ordinary evening party. To furnish a full, late supper is a piece of folly for various reasons; among them being the fact that it is positively injurious to the health of the company to eat it. The majority of the party, in all probability, do not desire it; and consequently it is time, labor and expense, upon the part of the hostess, worse than thrown away. She should have all of her time to devote to her company ; to do which, she can provide only light refreshments, which may be passed around.

Among the methods of entertainment resorted to, aside from conversation and dancing, may be those of a literary character. Thus a debatable question may be propounded, a presiding officer selected, assisted by two, four or six others, two leading disputants appointed, debaters chosen upon each side, and the speakers given each two, three or five minutes to talk; the president and board of arbitration to decide the question according to the weight of argument. This is a pleasant and profitable way of spending the evening, if all can be enlisted and be interested in listening or have something to say.

Another intellectual and pleasant mode of spending an evening is for each member of the company to read or recite something that shall interest, amuse, instruct and entertain the audience. To do this rightly, some one should be appointed to act as master of ceremonies for the evening, being assisted by two or three others, who will make suggestions. It will be the duty of the presiding officer, at these parlor recitations, to ascertain in the beginning what each one will recite, make out a programme, and then announce the various readers and speakers of the evening, as they come in turn, having the exercises suitably interspersed with music. The pleasure of the occasion will much depend upon having every piece upon the programme short, and clearly announced by the presiding officer.

Parlor-theatricals and parlor-concerts are a pleasant means of entertaining an evening gathering — a company of six, eight, or more, thoroughly mastering a play and giving it to an audience that may assemble in the parlors. To have an entertainment of this kind pass smoothly through, some competent person must take upon himself or herself the duties of manager. Each player should be consulted before parts are assigned, and it is of the utmost importance that the players be each prompt in rendering their parts. It is the province of the hostess to act the part of stage-manager, unless she appoints some one from the audience to conduct the exercises.

Croquet parties are very fashionable, and are a healthful, pleasant means of diversion. The essentials necessary to make the game pleasant are good grounds that can be shaded, and clean, comfortable, cool seats. A table may be set in the shade, and refreshments served thereon ; or they may be passed to the guests as they sit in their seats.

On all occasions when a number of people convene together, whether indoors or out, the laws of courtesy should be obeyed. It is the duty of the gentlemen to be ever attentive to the ladies. If it be a picnic, the gentlemen will carry the luncheon, erect the swings, construct the tables, bring the water, provide the fuel for boiling the tea, etc. On the fishing excursion they will furnish the tackle, bait the hooks, row the boats, carry the fish, and furnish comfortable seats for the ladies. In gathering nuts, they will climb the trees, do the shaking, carry the nuts, and assist the ladies across the streams and over the fences. If possible, in crossing the fields, go through the bars or gateway, and avoid the necessity of compelling the ladies to clamber over the fences. Should it be necessary to climb them, it is etiquette for the gentleman to go over first, and when the lady is firmly on the top, he will gently help her down.

It should ever be the rule, with both ladies and gentlemen, upon all such occasions, to render every assistance possible to entertain the company. Self should be forgotten. More or less assistance is all the time required by the managers of the outdoor gatherings, and labor is continually necessary to make the occasion pleasant. To aid in rendering the affair agreeable by needed assistance will very likely give you more pleasure than to be entertained yourself.

Etiquette for Public Places.

It is not etiquette for a young lady to visit a place of public amusement with a gentleman, alone, with whom she is but slightly acquainted. Her escort should the first time invite another member of the family to accompany her.

The gentleman should make a point of extending his invitation to the lady long enough before the entertainment to be able to secure desirable seats. Most of the pleasure of the occasion will depend upon being so seated as to be able to witness the performance to advantage.

The lady having received a note of invitation, she should reply to the same immediately, that the gentleman may make his arrangements accordingly.

Should the weather be stormy, and for other reasons, it will be a very graceful way of complimenting the lady to provide a carriage for the occasion.

Seats having been secured, it is not necessary to arrive until about five minutes before the commencement of the performance. It is bad manners to go late to a public entertainment; the bustle and noise incident to the late arrival is often a serious interference with the exercises of the occasion.

Upon entering the hall, secure a programme for each member of your party, and follow the usher to the designated seats. The gentleman will go first, and pause at the entrance, allowing the lady to pass into the seat, when he will follow.

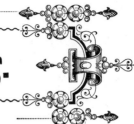

Etiquette of Visiting.

WHEN, WHERE AND HOW TO VISIT.

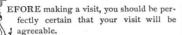

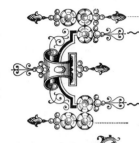

EFORE making a visit, you should be perfectly certain that your visit will be agreeable.

It is common for some people to be very cordial, and even profuse in their offers of hospitality. They unquestionably mean what they say at the time, but when they tender you an invitation to come and tarry *weeks*, it may seriously incommode them if you should pay them a visit of even a few *days*.

As a rule, a visit should never be made upon a general invitation. Should you visit a city where a friend resides, it will be best to go first to the hotel, unless you have a special invitation from the friend. From the hotel you will make a polite call, and if then you are invited, you can accept of the hospitality.

In all cases when you contemplate a visit, even with relatives, it is courtesy to write and announce your coming, giving, as nearly as possible, the day and exact time of your arrival.

An invitation to visit a friend should be answered as soon as may be; stating definitely when you will come, and how long you intend to stay.

When near your destination, it is well to send a prepaid telegram, stating upon what train you will arrive. As a reward for this forethought, you will probably find your friends waiting for you at the depot, and the welcome will be very pleasant.

What is Expected of the Guest when Visiting.

You are expected to pleasantly accept such hospitality as your friends can afford.

If no previous understanding has been had, the visit should be limited to three days, or a week at most.

You should make your visit interfere as little as possible with the routine work of the household in which you are a guest.

You should aim to conform your action, as much as may be, to the rules of the house, as to times of eating, retiring to rest, etc.

You should state upon your arrival how long you intend to stay, that your friends may arrange their plans to entertain accordingly.

Letters and papers being received in the presence of the host, hostess and others, the guest should ask to be excused while reading them.

Furnish your own materials in doing work for yourself when you are visiting, as much as possible, and never depend upon your entertainers.

A kind courtesy, while you remain, will be to execute some work representing your own skill, to be given the hostess as a memento of the occasion.

You should in shopping or transacting business, when you desire to go alone, select the hours of the day when your friends are engaged in their own duties.

The guest should beware of making unfavorable comment about the friends of the host and hostess, or of offering unfavorable criticism upon what they are known to favor or admire.

Should you happen to injure any article or other property while visiting, you should have the same immediately repaired, and, if possible, the article put in better condition than it was before.

You should not treat your friend's house as if it was a hotel, making your calls, visiting, transacting business about the town, and coming and going at all hours to suit your own convenience.

Never invite a friend who may call upon you to remain to dinner or supper. This is a right which belongs to the hostess, and it is for her to determine whether she wishes your guest to remain or not.

The guest should aim to render efficient assistance in case of sickness or sudden trouble at the house where the visit may be made. Oftentimes the best service will be rendered by considerately taking your leave.

Invitations accepted by the lady-guest should include the hostess, and those received by the hostess should include the guest. Thus, as much as possible, at all places of entertainment hostess and guest should go together.

While husbands and wives are always expected to accompany each other, where either may be invited, it is a trespass upon the generosity of the friend to take children and servants unless they are included in the invitation.

Never invite a friend who calls upon you into any other room than the parlor, unless it is suggested by the hostess that you do so. While you may have the right to enter various rooms, you have no authority for extending the privilege to others.

Immediately upon the return to your home, after paying a visit, you should write to your hostess, thanking her for hospitality and the enjoyment you received. You should also ask to be remembered to all of the family, mentioning each one by name.

Expenses which the friends may incur in removal and care of baggage, in repairs of wardrobe, or any other personal service requiring cash outlay, the guest should be careful to have paid. Washing and ironing should be sent elsewhere from the place where the guest is visiting.

The lady-guest should beware of receiving too many visits from gentlemen, and if invited to accompany them to places of amusement or on rides, she should consult with the hostess and learn what appointments she may have, and whether the going with others will be satisfactory to her.

Should a secret of the family come into your possession while on a visit, you should remember that the hospitality and privileges extended should bind you to absolute secrecy. It is contemptibly mean to become the possessor of a secret thus, and afterwards betray the confidence reposed in you.

Be careful that you treat with kindness and care servants, horses, carriages and other things at your friend's house which are placed at your disposal. To pluck choice flowers, to handle books roughly, to drive horses too fast, to speak harshly to servants—all this indicates selfishness and bad manners.

The visitor should beware of criticism or fault-finding with the family of the hostess. It is also in extremely bad taste for the guest to speak disparagingly of things about the home or the town where the visit is being made, being at the same time enthusiastic in praise of people and places elsewhere.

When a child is taken along, the mother should be very watchful that it does no injury about the house, and makes no trouble. It is excessively annoying to a neat housekeeper to have a child wandering about the rooms, handling furniture with greasy fingers, scattering crumbs over the carpets, and otherwise making disturbance.

The gentleman visitor should be certain that smoking is not offensive to the various members of the family, before he indulges too freely in the pipe and cigar about the house. For the guest, without permission, to seat himself in the parlor (Fig. 16), and scent the room with the fumes of tobacco, is a serious impoliteness.

When you can at times render assistance to those you are visiting, in any light work, you will often make your visit more agreeable. A lady will not hesitate to make her own bed if there be few or no servants, and will do anything else to assist the hostess. If your friend, however, declines allowing you to assist her, you should not insist upon the matter further.

Guests should enter with spirit and cheerfulness into the various plans that are made for their enjoyment. Possibly some rides will be had, and some visits made, that will be tiresome, but the courteous guest should find something to admire everywhere, and thus make the entertainers feel that their efforts to please are appreciated.

Of various persons in the family where the guest may be visiting, gifts may most appropriately be given to the hostess, and the baby or the youngest child. If the youngest has reached its teens, **then it may** be best to give it to the mother. The visitor will, however, use discretion in the matter. Flowers and fancy needle-work will always be appropriate for the lady. Confectionery and jewelry will be appreciated by the children. Small articles of wearing apparel or money will be suitable for servants who have been particularly attentive to the guest.

Special pains should be taken by guests to adapt themselves to the religious habits of those with whom they are visiting. If daily prayers are had, or grace is said at meals, the most reverent attention should be given; though when invited to participate in any of these exercises, if unaccustomed to the same, you can quietly ask to be excused. As a rule, it is courtesy to attend church with the host and hostess. Should you have decided preferences, and go elsewhere, do so quietly and without comment, and under no circumstances should there be allowed religious discussion afterwards. You visit the home of your friends to entertain and be entertained. Be careful that you so treat their opinions that they will wish you to come again.

Hints to the Host and Hostess.

Take the baggage-checks, and give personal attention to having the trunks conveyed to your residence, relieving the guest of all care in the matter.

Having received intelligence of the expected arrival of a guest, if possible have a carriage at the depot to meet the friend. Various members of the family being with the carriage will make the welcome more pleasant.

Have a warm, pleasant room especially prepared for the guest, the dressing-table being supplied with water, soap, towel, comb, hair-brush, brush-broom, hat-brush, pomade, cologne, matches, needles and pins. The wardrobe should be conveniently arranged for the reception of wearing apparel. The bed should be supplied with plenty of clothing, a side-table should contain writing materials, and the center-table should be furnished with a variety of entertaining reading matter.

Arrange to give as much time as possible to the comfort of the guest, visiting places of amusement and interest in the vicinity. This should all be done without apparent effort on your part. Let your friends feel that the visit is a source of real enjoyment to you; that through their presence and company you have the pleasure of amusements and recreation that would, perhaps, not have been enjoyed had they not come. Treat them with such kindness as you would like to have bestowed upon yourself under similar circumstances.

At the close of their stay, if you would be happy to have the visitors remain longer, you will frankly tell them so. If they insist upon going, you will aid them in every way possible in their departure. See that their baggage is promptly conveyed to the train. Examine the rooms to find whether they have forgotten any article that they would wish to take. Prepare a lunch for them to partake of on their journey. Go with them to the depot. Treat them with such kindness and cordiality to the close that the recollection of their visit will ever be a bright spot in their memory. Remain with them until the train arrives. They would be very lonely waiting without you. You will ever remember with pleasure the fact that you made the last hours of their visit pleasant. And thus, with the last hand-shaking, and the last waving of adieu, as the train speeds away, keep up the warmth of hospitality with your guests to the very end. It is, perhaps, the last time you will ever see them.

CONDUCT AT PLACES OF PUBLIC AMUSEMENT.

While a quiet conversation is allowable in the intervals after the opening of the performance, close attention should be given to the stage. Should it be a concert, the utmost stillness should be observed, as the slightest whisper will disturb the singers. This considerate attention should be given to the very end. It is in exceedingly bad taste, near the close of the last act, for the audience to commence moving about, putting on wraps and outer clothing, preparatory to leaving. Those who do so, lose the choicest part of the entertainment; they distract others who wish to be attentive, and they advertise the fact that they have no private carriage of their own, but on the contrary go by some public conveyance, and with characteristic selfishness they intend to rush out first and secure the best seats.

Fig. 17. The Visitor who Converts the Parlor into a Smoking-Room.

If the entertainment be a fancy fair, where goods which have been manufactured by a company of ladies are sold for church or charitable purposes, good sense will immediately suggest that as large a price should be realized as possible, and hence it is not etiquette for the purchaser to attempt to buy under price. It is also courtesy for the saleswoman, when a larger sum is presented than is charged, to deduct the price and promptly return the change, unless the surplus be donated to the charity.

Bad Manners.

Do not forget, while you make yourself comfortable, that others have rights which should be always considered.

Do not talk loudly, laugh boisterously, or make violent gestures.

Do not talk or whisper so loudly during the entertainment as to disturb those sitting near you.

Do not make a display of secrecy, mystery, or undue lover-like affection with your companion.

Do not prevent your companion from giving attention to the exercises, even though they may be without interest to yourself.

Do not, in a picture-gallery, stand conversing too long in front of pictures. Take seats, and allow others to make examination.

Do not, if a lady, allow a gentleman to join you, and thus withdraw your attention from your escort. And do not, if a gentleman, allow your attention to be taken up, to any great extent, with a lady other than the one you have in charge.

Do not, if a gentleman, be continually going from the hall between the acts of the play. To be passing up and down the aisle, eating peppers and cardamom seeds, advertises the fact that you are addicted to the too frequent use of liquors.

Do not join a party about to visit a place of amusement unless invited to do so. Should the party consist of one gentleman and two ladies, a gentleman, if well acquainted, may ask the privilege of attending one of the ladies. Should a ticket be furnished him, he should return the favor by an equal politeness bestowed upon the party, if possible, during the evening.

Courtship and Marriage.

CONDITIONS THAT PROMOTE HAPPINESS.

THE happiness of married life comes from pleasant, harmonious relations existing between husband and wife. If rightly mated in the conjugal state, life will be one continual joy. If unhappily wedded, the soul will be forever yearning, and never satisfied; happiness may be hoped for, may be dreamed of, may be the object ever labored for, but it will never be realized.

In view, therefore, of the great influence that marriage has upon the welfare and happiness of all those who enter the conjugal relation, it becomes the duty of everyone to study the laws which make happy, enduring companionships between husbands and wives. It is a duty which not only the unmarried owe themselves, but it is an obligation due to society, as the well-being of a community largely rests upon the permanent, enduring family relation.

Very properly does the highest civilization not only recognize one woman for one man, and one man for one woman, but it ordains that marriage shall be publicly solemnized; and in view of its sacred nature and its vast influence on the welfare of society, that its rights shall be jealously guarded, and that a separation of those who pledge themselves to each other for life shall be as seldom made as possible.

The young should, therefore, be thoroughly imbued with the idea that the marriage state may not be entered upon without due and careful consideration of its responsibilities, as explained in the introductory remarks found in the department devoted to "Love Letters."

The province of this chapter is to consider the etiquette of courtship and marriage, not its moral bearings; and yet we may in this connection very appropriately make a few suggestions.

Whom to Marry.

There are exceptions to all rules. Undoubtedly parties have married on brief acquaintance, and have lived happily afterwards. It is sometimes the case that the wife is much older than the husband, is much wiser, and much his superior in social position, and yet happiness in the union may follow. But, as a rule, there are a few fundamental requisites, which, carefully observed, are much more likely to bring happiness than does marriage where the conditions are naturally unfavorable.

Of these requisites, are the following:

Marry a person whom you have known long enough to be sure of his or her worth—if not personally, at least by reputation.

Marry a person who is your equal in social position. If there be a difference either way, let the husband be superior to the wife. It is difficult for a wife to love and honor a person whom she is compelled to look down upon.

Marry a person of similar religious convictions, tastes, likes and dislikes to your own. It is not congenial to have one companion deeply religious, while the other only ridicules the forms of religion. It is not pleasant for one to have mind and heart absorbed in a certain kind of work which the other abhors; and it is equally disagreeable to the gentle, mild and sweet disposition to be united with a cold, heartless, grasping, avaricious, quarrelsome person. Very truthfully does Luna S. Peck, in the "Vermont Watchman," describe one phase of inharmony, in the following poem:

MISMATED.

A HAWK once courted a white little dove,
With the softest of wings and a voice full of love;
And the hawk—O yes, as other hawks go—
Was a well-enough hawk, for aught that I know.
　　But she was a dove,
　　And her bright young life
　　Had been nurtured in love,
　　Away from all strife.

Well, she married the hawk. The groom was delighted;
A feast was prepared, and the friends all invited.
(Does anyone think that my story's not true?
He is certainly wrong—the facts are not new.)
　　Then he flew to his nest,
　　With the dove at his side,
　　And soon all the rest
　　Took a squint at the bride.

A hawk for his father, a hawk for his mother,
A hawk for his sister, and one for his brother,
And uncles and aunts there were by the dozens,
And oh, such a number of hawks for his cousins!
　　They were greedy and rough—
　　A turbulent crew,
　　Always ready enough
　　To be quarrelsome, too.

To the dove all was strange; but never a word
In resentment she gave to the wrangling she heard.
If a thought of the peaceful, far-away nest
Ever haunted her dreams, or throbbed in her breast,
　　No bird ever knew;
　　Each hour of her life,
　　Kind, gentle and true
　　Was the hawk's dove-wife.

But the delicate nature too sorely was tried;
With no visible sickness, the dove drooped and died;
Then loud was the grief, and the wish all expressed
To call the learned birds, and hold an inquest.
　　So all the birds came,
　　But each shook his head:
　　No disease could he name
　　Why the dove should be dead;

'Till a wise old owl, with a knowing look,
Stated this: "The case is as clear as a book;
No disease do I find, or accident's shock;
The cause of her death was *too much hawk!*
Hawk for her father, and hawk for her mother,
Hawk for her sister, and hawk for her brother,
Was more than the delicate bird could bear;
She hath winged her way to a realm more fair!
　　She was nurtured a dove;
　　Too hard the hawk's life—
　　Void of kindness and love,
　　Full of hardness and strife."

And when he had told them, the other birds knew
That this was the cause, and the verdict was true!

Natural Selection.

In the first place, observation proves that selections made in nature by the beasts of the field and fowls of the air, of couples which pair, the male is always the strongest, generally the largest, the most brave, and always the leader. The female follows, trusting to her companion, leaving him to fight the heavy battles, apparently confident in his bravery, strength and wisdom.

If nature teaches anything, it is what observation and experience in civilized life has also proved correct, that of husband and wife, rightly mated, the husband should represent the positive—the physical forces, the intellectual and the strongly-loving; while the wife will represent the negative—the sympathetic, the spiritual, and the affectional. The husband should be so strong as to be a natural protector to his family. He should be brave, that he may defend his companion. He should be wise, and he should be so thoroughly true and devoted to his wife that he will delight in being her guardian and support.

The wife, confident in the husband's strength and wisdom, will thus implicitly yield to his protecting care. And thus both will be happy— he in exercising the prerogatives which belong naturally to the guardian and protector; and she in her confidence, love and respect for her companion, whom she can implicitly trust.

Peculiarities Suitable for Each Other.

Those who are neither very tall nor very short, whose eyes are neither very black nor very blue, whose hair is neither very black nor very red, —the mixed types—may marry those who are quite similar in form, complexion and temperament to themselves.

Bright red hair and a florid complexion indicate an excitable temperament. Such should marry the jet-black hair and the brunette type.

The gray, blue, black or hazel eyes should not marry those of the same color. Where the color is very pronounced, the union should be with those of a decidedly different color.

The very corpulent should unite with the thin and spare, and the short, thick-set should choose a different constitution.

The thin, bony, wiry, prominent-featured, Roman-nosed, cold-blooded individual, should marry the round-featured, warm-hearted and emotional. Thus the cool should unite with warmth and susceptibility.

The extremely irritable and nervous should unite with the lymphatic, the slow and the quiet. Thus the stolid will be prompted by the nervous companion, while the excitable will be quieted by the gentleness of the less nervous.

The quick-motioned, rapid-speaking person should marry the calm and deliberate. The warmly impulsive should unite with the stoical.

The very fine-haired, soft and delicate-skinned should not marry those like themselves; and the curly should unite with the straight and smooth hair.

The thin, long-face should marry the round-favored; and the flat nose should marry the full Roman. The woman who inherits the features and peculiarities of her father should marry a man who partakes of the characteristics of his mother; but in all these cases where the type is not pronounced, but is, on the contrary, an average or medium, those forms, features and temperaments may marry either.

Etiquette of Courtship.

But however suitable may be the physical characteristics, there are many other matters to be considered before a man and woman may take upon themselves the obligation to love and serve each other through life, and these can only be learned by acquaintance and courtship, concerning which the following suggestions may be appropriate:

Any gentleman who may continuously give special, undivided attention to a certain lady, is presumed to do so because he prefers her to others. It is reasonable to suppose that others will observe his action. It is also to be expected that the lady will herself appreciate the fact, and her feelings are likely to become engaged. Should she allow an intimacy thus to ripen upon the part of the gentleman, and to continue, it is to be expected that he will be encouraged to hope for her hand; and

hence it is the duty of both lady and gentleman, if neither intends marriage, to discourage an undue intimacy which may ripen into love, as it is in the highest degree dishonorable to trifle with the affections of another. If, however, neither has objections to the other, the courtship may continue.

The Decisive Question.

At length the time arrives for the gentleman to make a proposal. If he is a good judge of human nature, he will have discovered long ere this whether his favors have been acceptably received or not, and yet he may not know positively how the lady will receive an offer of marriage. It becomes him, therefore, to propose.

What shall he say? There are many ways whereby he may introduce the subject. Among these are the following:

He may write to the lady, making an offer, and request her to reply. He may, if he dare not trust to words, even in her presence write the question on a slip of paper, and request her laughingly to give a plain "no" or "yes." He may ask her if in case a gentleman very much like himself was to make a proposal of marriage to her, what she would say. She will probably laughingly reply that it will be time enough to tell what she would say when the proposal is made. And so the ice would be broken. He may jokingly remark that he intends one of these days to ask a certain lady not a thousand miles away if she will marry him, and asks her what answer she supposes the lady will give him; she will quite likely reply that it will depend upon what lady he asks. And thus he may approach the subject, by agreeable and easy stages, in a hundred ways, depending upon circumstances.

Engaged.

An engagement of marriage has been made. The period of courtship prior to marriage has been passed by the contracting parties, doubtless pleasantly, and we trust profitably.

Let us hope that they have carefully studied each other's tastes, that they know each other's mental endowments, and that by visits, rides and walks, at picnics, social gatherings and public entertainments, they have found themselves suited to each other.

Upon an engagement being announced, it is courtesy for various members of the gentleman's family, generally the nearest relatives, to call upon the family of the lady, who in turn should return the call as soon as possible. Possibly the families have never been intimate; it is not necessary that they should be so, but civility will demand the exchange of visits. If the betrothed live in different towns, an exchange of kind and cordial letters between the families is etiquette, the parents or near relatives of the gentleman writing to the lady or her parents.

A present of a ring to the lady, appropriately signalizes the engagement of marriage. This is usually worn on the fore-finger of the left hand. If the parties are wealthy, this may be set with diamonds; but if in humble circumstances, the gift should be more plain. Other presents by the gentleman to the lady, of jewelry, on birthdays, Christmas or New Year's, will be very appropriate; while she, in turn, may reciprocate by gifts of articles of fancy-work made with her own hands.

Aside from the engagement-ring, a gentleman should not, at this period of acquaintance, make expensive presents to his intended bride. Articles of small value, indicative of respect and esteem, are all that should pass between them. Should the marriage take place, and coming years of labor crown their efforts with success, then valuable gifts will be much more appropriate than in the earlier years of their acquaintance.

Arrangements for a Permanent Home.

It remains to be seen whether the intended husband will prove a financial success or not. He may be over benevolent; he may be too ready to become security for others; he may prove a spendthrift; he may lose his property in a variety of ways. It is therefore wise for the lady and her friends to see that, previous to the marriage, if she have money in her own right, a sufficient sum be settled upon her to provide for all contingencies in the future. This is a matter that the gentleman should himself insist upon, even using his own money for the purpose, as many a man has found, when his own fortune was wrecked, the provision made for his wife to be his only means of support in declining years.

Conduct During the Engagement.

An engagement having been made, it is desirable that it be carried to a successful termination by marriage. To do this, considerable depends upon both parties.

The gentleman should be upon pleasant terms with the lady's family, making himself agreeable to her parents, her sisters and her brothers. Especially to the younger members of her family should the gentleman render his presence agreeable, by occasional rides and little favors, presents of sweetmeats, etc.

He should also take pains to comply with the general regulations of the family during his visits, being punctual at meals, and early in retiring; kind and courteous to servants, and agreeable to all.

He should still be gallant to the ladies, but never so officiously attentive to anyone as to arouse uneasiness upon the part of his affianced. Neither should he expect her to eschew the society of gentlemen entirely from the time of her engagement.

The lady he has chosen for his future companion is supposed to have good sense, and while she may be courteous to all, receiving visits and calls, she will allow no flirtations, nor do anything calculated to excite jealousy on the part of her fiancé.

The conduct of both after the engagement should be such as to inspire in each implicit trust and confidence.

Visits should not be unduly protracted. If the gentleman makes them in the evening, they should be made early, and should not be over two hours in length. The custom of remaining until a late hour has passed away in genteel society. Such conduct at the present time, among the acquaintance of the lady, is certain to endanger her reputation.

For the gentleman and lady who are engaged to isolate themselves from others when in company, or do anything that shall attract the attention of the company to themselves, is in bad taste. Such conduct will always call forth unfavorable comments. The young ladies will sneer at it from jealousy, the young men will pronounce it foolish, and the old will consider it out of place.

And yet, by virtue of engagement, the gentleman should be considered the rightful escort, and upon all occasions the lady will give him preference; and he will especially see, however thoughtful he may be of others, that her wants are carefully attended to.

Should a misunderstanding or quarrel happen, it should be removed by the lady making the first advances towards a reconciliation. She thus shows a magnanimity which can but win admiration from her lover. Let both in their conduct towards the other be confiding, noble and generous.

The Wedding.

The wedding-day having arrived, the presents for the bride, if there be any, which may be sent at any time during the previous week, will be handsomely displayed before the ceremony. The presents, which have the names of the donors attached, are for the bride — never the bridegroom, although many of them may be sent by friends of the latter.

The form and ceremony of the wedding will be as various as are the peculiarities of those who marry, and comprise every description of display, from the very quiet affair, with but a few friends present, to the elaborate occasion when the church is filled to repletion, or in the palatial residence of the father of the bride, "the great house filled with guests of every degree."

We will suppose that the parties desire a somewhat ostentations wedding, and the marriage takes place in church. In arranging the preliminaries, the bride may act her pleasure in regard to bridesmaids. She may have none; she may have one, two, three, four, six or eight; and, while in England it is customary to have but one groomsman, it is not uncommon in the United States to have one groomsman for every bridesmaid.

The bridegroom should make the first groomsman the manager of affairs, and should furnish him with money to pay necessary expenses.

Ushers are selected from the friends of the bride and groom, who, designated by a white rosette worn on the left lapel of the coat, will wait upon the invited guests at the door of the church, and assign them to their places, which will be a certain number of the front seats.

The bridegroom should send a carriage at his expense for the officiating clergyman and his family. He is not expected to pay for the carriage of the parents of the bride, nor for those occupied by the bridesmaids and groomsmen.

The latter will furnish the carriages for the ladies, unless otherwise provided. The invited guests will go in carriages at their own expense.

The clergyman is expected to be within the rails, and the congregation promptly in their seats, at the appointed hour. The bridegroom will proceed to the church, accompanied by his near relatives, and should precede the bride, that he may hand her from the carriage, if not waited upon by her father or other near relative.

The bride goes to the church in a carriage, accompanied by her parents, or those who stand to her in the relation of parents (as may other relatives, or legal guardian), or she may be accompanied by the bridesmaids.

When the bridal party is ready in the vestibule of the church, the ushers will pass up the center aisle, the first groomsman, accompanied by the first bridesmaid, coming next, the others following in their order. The groom walks next with the bride's mother upon his arm, followed by the father with the bride. At the altar, as the father and mother step back, the bride takes her place upon the left of the groom.

Another mode of entering the church is for the first bridesmaid and groomsman to lead, followed by the bride and groom. When in front of the altar, the groomsman turns to the right, the bridesmaid to the left, leaving a space in front of the minister for the bride and groom; the near relatives and parents of the bride and groom follow closely, and form a circle about the altar during the ceremony.

The former mode is, however, established etiquette. At the altar the bride stands at the left of the groom, and in some churches both bride and groom remove the right-hand glove. In others it is not deemed necessary. When a ring is used, it is the duty of the first bridesmaid to remove the bride's left-hand glove. An awkward pause is, however, avoided by opening one seam of the glove upon the ring finger, and at the proper time the glove may be turned back, and the ring thus easily placed where it belongs, which is the third finger of the left hand.

The responses of the bride and groom should not be too hastily nor too loudly given.

Following the ceremony, the parents of the bride speak to her first, succeeded by the parents of the groom before other friends.

Essentially the same ceremonies will be had, the same positions will be assumed, and the same modes of entering will be observed, in the parlors at the residence, as at the church.

The bride and groom, after the ceremony, will go in the same carriage from the church to the home or to the depot.

Should a breakfast or supper follow the ceremony, the bride will not change her dress until she assumes her traveling apparel. At the party succeeding the ceremony, the bridesmaids and groomsmen should be invited, and all may, if they prefer, wear the dresses worn at the wedding.

The Wedding Trousseau.

It is customary, at the wedding, for the young bride to wear only pure white, with a wreath of orange flowers to adorn the full veil of lace. The widow or elderly lady will wear pearl color or tinted silk, without wreath or veil. The bridesmaid of the youthful bride may wear colors, but a very beautiful effect is produced by pure white, with colored trimmings. In some cases, one-half of the bridesmaids will wear one color, and the other half another color. No black dresses should be worn by the guests. Any in mourning may, for the time, wear purple, lavender, iron-gray and other quiet colors.

The bridegroom and groomsmen will wear white gloves, vest and neckties.

The bride's traveling dress should be very quiet and modest, and not such as in any way to attract attention.

Only the bridegroom is congratulated at the wedding; it is he who is supposed to have won the prize. Acquaintances of both should speak to the bride first; but if acquainted with but one, they will address that one first, when introductions will take place.

At the wedding breakfast or supper the bride sits by the side of her husband, in the center of the table, at the side; her father and mother occupy the foot and head of the table, and do the honors of the occasion, as at the dinner-party.

The festivities of the occasion being over, and the hour of departure having arrived, the guests disperse, it being etiquette for them to make a formal call on the mother of the bride in the succeeding two weeks.

Etiquette Between Husbands and Wives.

Let the rebuke be preceded by a kiss.

Do not require a request to be repeated.

Never should both be angry at the same time.

Never neglect the other, for all the world beside.

Let each strive to always accommodate the other.

Let the angry word be answered only with a kiss.

Bestow your warmest sympathies in each other's trials.

Make your criticism in the most loving manner possible.

Make no display of the sacrifices you make for each other.

Never make a remark calculated to bring ridicule upon the other.

Never deceive; confidence, once lost, can never be wholly regained.

Always use the most gentle and loving words when addressing each other.

Let each study what pleasure can be bestowed upon the other during the day.

Always leave home with a tender good-bye and loving words. They may be the last.

Consult and advise together in all that comes within the experience and sphere of each individually.

Never reproach the other for an error which was done with a good motive and with the best judgment at the time.

The Wife's Duty.

Never should a wife display her best conduct, her accomplishments, her smiles, and her best nature, exclusively away from home.

Be careful in your purchases. Let your husband know what you buy, and that you have wisely expended your money.

Let no wife devote a large portion of her time to society-work which shall keep her away from home daytimes and evenings, without the full concurrence of her husband.

Beware of entrusting the confidence of your household to outside parties. The moment you discuss the faults of your husband with another, that moment an element of discord has been admitted which will one day rend your family circle.

If in moderate circumstances, do not be over ambitious to make an expensive display in your rooms. With your own work you can embellish at a cheap price, and yet very handsomely, if you have taste. Let the adornings of your private rooms be largely the work of your own hands.

Beware of bickering about little things. Your husband returns from his labors with his mind absorbed in business. In his dealings with his employes, he is in the habit of giving commands and of being obeyed. In his absent-mindedness, he does not realize, possibly, the change from his business to his home, and the same dictatorial spirit may possess him in the domestic circle. Should such be the case, avoid all disputes. What matters it where a picture hangs, or a flower-vase may sit. Make the home so charming and so wisely-ordered that your husband will gladly be relieved of its care, and will willingly yield up its entire management to yourself.

Be always very careful of your conduct and language. A husband is largely restrained by the chastity, purity and refinement of his wife.

A lowering of dignity, a looseness of expression and vulgarity of words, may greatly lower the standard of the husband's purity of speech and morals.

Whatever may have been the cares of the day, greet your husband with a smile when he returns. Make your personal appearance just as beautiful as possible. Your dress may be made of calico, but it should be neat. Let him enter rooms so attractive and sunny that all the recollections of his home, when away from the same, shall attract him back.

Be careful that you do not estimate your husband solely by his ability to make display. The nature of his employment, in comparison with others, may not be favorable for fine show, but that should matter not. The superior qualities of mind and heart alone will bring permanent happiness.

To have a cheerful, pleasant home awaiting the husband, is not all. He may bring a guest whom he desires to favorably impress, and upon you will devolve the duty of entertaining the visitor so agreeably that the husband shall take pride in you. A man does not alone require that his wife be a good housekeeper. She must be more; in conversational talent and general accomplishment she must be a companion.

The Husband's Duty.

A very grave responsibility has the man assumed in his marriage. Doting parents have confided to his care the welfare of a loved daughter, and a trusting woman has risked all her future happiness in his keeping. Largely will it depend upon him whether her pathway shall be strewn with thorns or roses.

Let your wife understand fully your business. In nearly every case she will be found a most valuable adviser when she understands all your circumstances.

Do not be dictatorial in the family circle. The home is the wife's province. It is her natural field of labor. It is her right to govern and direct its interior management. You would not expect her to come to your shop, your office, your store or your farm, to give orders how your work should be conducted; neither should you interfere with the duties which legitimately belong to her.

If a dispute arises, dismiss the subject with a kind word, and do not seek to carry your point by discussion. It is a glorious achievement to master one's own temper. You may discover that you are in error, and if your wife is wrong, she will gladly, in her cooler moments, acknowledge the fault.

Having confided to the wife all your business affairs, determine with her what your income will be in the coming year. Afterwards ascertain what your household expenses will necessarily be, and then set aside a weekly sum, which should regularly and invariably be paid the wife at a stated time. Let this sum be even more than enough, so that the wife can pay all bills, and have the satisfaction besides of accumulating a fund of her own, with which she can exercise a spirit of independence in the bestowal of charity, the purchase of a gift, or any article she may desire. You may be sure that the wife will very seldom use the money unwisely, if the husband gives her his entire confidence.

Your wife, possibly, is inexperienced; perhaps she is delicate in health, also, and matters that would be of little concern to you may weigh heavily upon her. She needs, therefore, your tenderest approval, your sympathy and gentle advice. When her efforts are crowned with success, be sure that you give her praise. Few husbands realize how happy the wife is made by the knowledge that her efforts and her merits are appreciated. There are times, also, when the wife's variable condition of health will be likely to make her cross and petulant; the husband must overlook all this, even if the wife is at times unreasonable.

Endeavor to so regulate your household affairs that all the faculties of the mind shall have due cultivation. There should be a time for labor, and a time for recreation. There should be cultivation of the social nature, and there should be attention given to the spiritual. The wife should not be required to lead a life of drudgery. Matters should be so regulated that she may early finish her labors of the day; and the good husband will so control his business that he may be able to accompany his wife to various places of amusement and entertainment. Thus the intellectual will be provided for, and the social qualities be kept continually exercised.

The wise husband will provide for the moral and spiritual growth of his family by regular attendance at church; the spiritual faculties of our nature are given for a beneficent purpose; their exercise and cultivation leads up into the higher and the better; one day in seven, at least, should therefore be set apart for the spiritual improvement of the family. Select a church, the religious teaching in which is nearest in accord with the views of yourself and wife, and be regular in your attendance; accompany your wife; give her the pleasure of your escort; see that she is provided with a good seat and all the advantages which the church has to give; enter fully and freely into the religious work of your church, and your family will be blessed in consequence.

Give your wife every advantage which it is possible to bestow. Shut up with her household duties, her range of freedom is necessarily circumscribed, and in her limited sphere she is likely to remain stationary in her intellectual growth. Indeed, oftentimes, if her family be large and her husband's means are limited, in her struggle to care for the family she will sacrifice beauty, accomplishments, health — life, almost — rather than that her husband shall fail. In the meantime, with wide opportunities and intellectual advantages, he will be likely to have better facilities for growth and progression. There is sometimes thus a liability of the husband and wife growing apart, an event which both should take every pains to avert. In avoiding this, much will depend upon the wife. She must resolutely determine to be in every way the equal of her companion. Much also will depend upon the husband. The wife should have every opportunity whereby she may keep even pace with him.

Possibly the wife in social position, intellectual acquirement, and very likely in moral worth, may be superior to her husband. It is equally necessary, therefore, that the husband put forth every effort to make himself worthy of his companion. It is a terrible burden to impose on a wife to compel her to go through life with a man whom she cannot love or respect.

ETIQUETTE OF TRAVELING.

HE reader will call to mind people who always appear at ease when they are traveling. Investigation will prove that these individuals have usually had a wide experience in journeying, and an extensive acquaintance with the world. The experienced traveler has learned the necessity of always being on time, of having baggage checked early, of purchasing a ticket before entering the cars, and of procuring a seat in a good location before the car is full.

The inexperienced traveler is readily known by his flurry and mistakes. He is likely to be behind time, and he is likely to be an hour too early. For want of explicit direction, his baggage often fails to reach the train in time, or does not come at all. His trunks, from lack of strength, are liable to be easily broken. In his general confusion, when he buys a ticket he neglects to place it where it will be secure, and consequently loses it. He forgets a portion of his baggage, and thus in a dozen ways he is likely to be in trouble.

If the person be a lady who is unacquainted with travel, she reveals the fact by a general impatience, restlessness, and absent-mindedness. In her want of self-possession she forgets several things she had intended to bring, and her continual fault-finding at flies, dust, heat, delay and other trials, all betray the fact that she has not heretofore been accustomed to these difficulties.

The following suggestions relating to railway traveling may be of service:

Whenever you contemplate a journey, consider carefully what route you want to take, and decide it definitely. Learn accurately what time the train leaves, and provide yourself with a table giving the running time of the road, stations on the way, etc., which will save you the trouble of asking many questions.

If you desire to ride in a sleeping-car, secure your berth a day or two previous to the time of going, in order that you may be in time to take your choice. The most desirable sections are in the center of the car, away from the annoyance of dust, drafts of air and sudden noises resulting from opening and closing doors.

At least a day before you go, consider carefully what baggage you need to take, and have it packed. Take just as little as possible. Have your trunks very secure, and pack all articles of baggage in such a manner that they cannot shake and thus be broken.

Provide among your baggage necessary toilet articles — a linen wrap to exclude the dust from your finer clothing, and a small amount of reading-matter with very coarse type. See that your baggage is perfectly in order, and an hour before you start engage an authorized expressman to take your baggage to the depot. State very distinctly where you want the baggage taken, and for what train. It is also a wise provision to have your trunk labeled with a card bearing your name and destination.

Take the number of the expressman, ascertain his charge, and withhold payment until he has assisted in finding baggage, and has aided in getting it checked at the depot. Be very sure that your watch or clock is perfectly correct with railroad time, and that you, half an hour before the starting time of the train, arrive at the depot, buy a ticket, and take your seat in the car. You are probably early enough to take your choice of location in the seats.

If in the summer time, and the train runs east or west, the north side will probably be most pleasant. Seats midway in the car are easiest to ride in, and the left side is freest from sudden gusts of wind which may come in at the open doors.

Fig. 17. The couple that make themselves appear ridiculous when traveling.

Having selected a seat, it is customary to deposit the satchel, umbrella or some article of wearing-apparel in the same, should you not be ready to occupy it; and it is etiquette for anyone finding a seat so occupied to look further.

You should carry just as little baggage into the car as possible, and all separate pieces should have your name plainly written or printed upon them, which will secure their being forwarded to you in case they are left upon the seat.

Having paid for one ticket, you are entitled to only one seat. It shows selfishness, therefore, when the coach is quite full to deposit a large amount of baggage in the surrounding seats and occupy three or four, and engage in reading, while others look in vain for a place to sit down.

It is courtesy for a gentleman when sitting alone to offer the vacant seat beside himself to a lady who may be unattended. He will also give his seat to two ladies, or a lady and gentleman who desire to sit together, and take a seat elsewhere. Such attention will often be a great kindness, while the individual bestowing it may suffer but very little inconvenience.

The true lady or gentleman will always consult the convenience of others when traveling. Thus, care should be exercised that no one be incommoded by your opening doors or windows in a railway coach. If possible, so arrange that the air of a window that you may open shall strike full upon yourself, and not upon those in the rear; certainly not if it is unpleasant to them.

What to Avoid when Traveling.

A lady and gentleman should avoid evidences of undue familiarity in the presence of strangers. Couples who may evince a silly affection by overfondling of each other in public (Fig. 17) make themselves appear extremely ridiculous to all who may see them.

People with weak eyes should avoid reading on the train, and those having weak lungs should avoid much talking, as an undue effort will be required to talk above the noise of the train.

Passengers should avoid eating at irregular times on the journey, and gentlemen should avoid smoking in the presence of those to whom it may be offensive.

Avoid leaving the pockets so open and money so exposed that thieves may steal your effects. In the sleeping-car the valuables should be put in some article of wearing-apparel and placed under the pillow.

Avoid undue haste and excitement when traveling, by forethought. Have a plan matured, and when the time comes to act you will know what to do, and with self-possession you accomplish your work very much better.

Avoid wearing laces, velvets, or any articles that naturally accumulate and hold dust. Excessive finery or a lavish display of jewelry are in bad taste on extended journeys. Before commencing a journey, consider carefully what will be most suitable to wear, and study how little baggage may be taken.

CONDUCT FOR GENTLEMEN
WHEN
TRAVELING WITH LADIES.

If the gentleman is an authorized escort he will, if an old acquaintance, accompany the lady in his charge from her residence to the depot. If the acquaintance is of short duration, it will be sufficient to meet her at the depot in ample time to purchase tickets and see that her baggage is checked, while she remains in the sitting-room at the station.

Arrangements being made, he will secure her a seat upon the train, will find a place for packages, will attend to her wants in adjusting the window, and will aim to put her entirely at ease.

In getting on and off the train, the gentleman will care for all parcels and see that nothing is left. He will assist the lady into the coach or omnibus before getting in himself, and in getting out he will precede her, and afterwards turn and help her carefully down.

If requested by the lady to defray her expenses from her purse, the gentleman may take the same and keep it the entire journey, or he may pay from his own pocket and keep an account of expenses which she will refund at the end of the journey.

He should purchase the needed confections or literature on the train. He should be fruitful in the introduction of topics that will enliven, amuse and instruct the lady, if she is inclined to be reticent; and at her journey's end he should go with her to her home, or the place where she is to stop. He may call next day, and if the acquaintance seems desirable it may be continued. The gentleman should be very careful not to continue his visits unless certain that they are acceptable.

If a hotel be the point of destination, the gentleman will accompany the lady to the parlor. He will then secure for her a room, and leave her in care of a waiter; her desire being probably to proceed to her apartments at once, where she will remove the dust and travel stains of the journey, and meet him again at a concerted hour in the parlor.

Ladies and gentlemen who are strangers, being thrown into the company of each other for a long journey, need not necessarily refuse to speak to each other. While the lady should be guarded, acquaintance may be made with certain reserve.

FIG. 18. THE RIDE ON HORSEBACK.

The gentleman takes his position at the right of the lady.

THE HORSEBACK RIDE,
AND THE
RULES THAT GOVERN IT.

A gentleman who may act as escort for a lady when riding should be very careful that the horse selected for her is entirely reliable and gentle. If he has no horse of his own, and she has none to which she is accustomed, he must understand that there is considerable danger in allowing her to use a horse that has not been tried, no matter what may be the representations of the liverymen or servant.

A trustworthy horse having been secured for the lady, it is the gentleman's duty before mounting to give a very thorough examination of the saddle and bridle, to see that all are secure. It will not do to leave this matter to the stablemen. They are accustomed to such continuous handling of harness that they become careless, and are liable to overlook defects in buckles, girths, etc., that might cause a severe accident.

When all is in readiness, it is the gentleman's province to assist the lady in mounting. To do this, it is well to have some one hold the horse, otherwise he holds the bridle with his left hand. The lady, then, with her skirt in her left hand, will take hold of the pommel of the saddle with her right, her face turned towards the horse's head. The gentleman will stand at the horse's shoulder, facing the lady, and stoop, allowing her to place her left foot in his right hand. She will then spring, while he lifts her gently and steadily into her seat, following which he will place her left foot in the stirrup and arrange her riding habit.

After the lady is in position, the gentleman will still remain with her until she has whip and reins properly in hand and is securely in her seat, when he will mount his horse and take his place (Fig. 18) upon her right, as shown in the accompanying illustration.

Should there be two ladies on horseback, the gentleman should ride to the right of both of them, unless they may need his assistance, in which case he will ride between them.

In dismounting, the gentleman should take the lady's left hand in his right, remove the stirrup and take her foot in his left hand, lowering her gently to the ground.

CONDUCT WHICH IS APPROPRIATE.

SHOULD there be no competent, near friend of the family to take charge of the funeral, then its management should devolve upon the sexton of the church, the undertaker, or other suitable person.

It is the duty of the person having the funeral in charge to have one interview with the nearest relatives as to the management, after which they should be relieved of all care in the matter.

The expense of the funeral should be in accordance with the wealth and standing of the deceased, both ostentation and parade being avoided, as should also evidences of meanness and parsimony. It is well, in the interview between the manager and the relatives, to have a definite understanding as to the expense that should be incurred.

In the large city, where many friends and even relatives may not hear of the death, it is common to send invitations to such friends as might not otherwise hear of the fact, worded somewhat as follows:

Yourself and family are respectfully invited to attend the funeral of H. H. B——, on Thursday, the 27th of June, 1878, at 2 o'clock P. M., from his late residence, No. 16, —— street, to proceed to Rosehill Cemetery.

Or, if the services are conducted at a church:

Yourself and family are respectfully invited to attend the funeral of H. H. B——, from the church of the Redeemer, on Thursday, the 27th of June, 18——, at 2 o'clock P. M., to proceed to Rosehill Cemetery.

It is customary to have these invitations printed according to the forms shown elsewhere under the head of "notes of invitation," and to send them by private messenger. The list of invited persons should be given to the manager, that he may provide a suitable number of carriages for the invited friends who may be likely to attend. It is a breach of etiquette for any who have been thus personally invited not to attend.

Persons attending a funeral are not expected to be present much before the hour appointed. Previous to this time it is well for the family of the deceased to take their last view of the remains, and thus avoid confusion.

In assembling at the house, it is customary for some near relative, but not of the immediate family, to act as usher in receiving and seating the people. The ladies of the family are not expected to notice the arrival of guests. With gentlemen it is optional whether they do so or not.

The clergyman, or person chosen to make remarks upon the funeral occasion, should be one whose religious views would be most nearly in accord with those entertained by the deceased. But even if the deceased had no religious convictions, and a clergyman of any denomination may be chosen, he should use the courtesy of saying nothing in his discourse which could in the least offend the mourners.

The remains should be so placed, either in the house or church, that when the discourse is finished, if the corpse is exposed to view, the assembled guests may see the same by passing in single file past the coffin, going from foot to head, up one aisle and down another.

While in the house of mourning, the hat should be removed from the head of the gentlemen, and not replaced again while in the house.

Loud talk or laughter in the chamber of death would be a great rudeness. All animosities among those who attend the funeral should be forgotten, and interviews with the family at the time should not be expected.

The exercises at the house or church being finished, the clergyman enters a carriage, which heads the procession. The coffin being placed in the hearse, the bearers, who are usually six in number, will go in threes, on each side of the hearse, or in a carriage immediately before, while the near relatives directly follow the hearse, succeeded by those more distantly connected. As the mourners pass from the house to the carriages, no salutations are expected to take place, the gentlemen among the guests in the meantime standing with uncovered heads, as they do also when the coffin is carried from the house to the hearse.

The master of ceremonies should precede the mourners to the carriages, see that the proper carriages are in attendance, assist the ladies to their place, and signal the drivers to pass forward as their carriages are filled. Should the attending physician be present, he will occupy the carriage immediately following the near relatives of the deceased.

The pall-bearers are selected from among the immediate friends of the deceased, and should be as near as possible of corresponding age, worth and intelligence.

It is common, upon the coffin of the infant or young person, to lay a wreath of white flowers, and upon that of a married person a cross of white blossoms. Upon the coffin of a navy or army officer, the hat, epaulets, sash, sword and the flag may be borne; while his horse, if a mounted officer, will, without a rider, be led behind the hearse. It is sometimes the case that the private carriage of the deceased, with no occupant save the driver, follows the hearse in the procession.

Arriving at the cemetery, the clergyman will precede the mourners to the grave; when gathered around, the bearers will place the coffin in its last resting place, and the final prayer will be said. This done, the guests will depart for their several homes, each informing the drivers where they desire to be left.

With the more hopeful view of death which comes with the Christian belief, there is less disposition to wear evidences of mourning. It is well, however, to drape the door-knob, especially of the residence, with crape, during the days between the death and the funeral; and the family should go out as little as possible during that time. The dress of all guests at the funeral should be of subdued and quiet colors, and, while for the young person it is customary to trim the hearse in white, it is common to drape it in dark, with black plumes, for the person of mature years.

Should the deceased have been a member of an organization that might desire to conduct the funeral, immediate notification of his death should be sent to the organization, that its members may have time to make arrangements for attending the funeral.

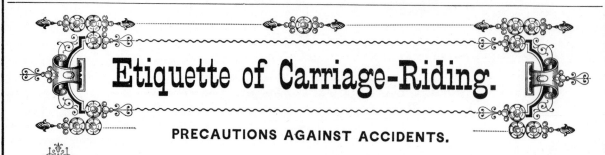

Etiquette of Carriage-Riding.

PRECAUTIONS AGAINST ACCIDENTS.

THE mode of entering a carriage will depend somewhat upon circumstances. Should the team be very restive, and the gentleman remain in the carriage the better to control his horses, the lady will enter upon the left side, the gentleman assisting her by the hand. While circumstances may sometimes prevent, it is always etiquette for the gentleman to see that the lady enters the carriage first. To aid in entering and alighting from a carriage easily and safely, every residence should be provided with an elevated platform near the walk, beside which the vehicle may be driven, as represented in the illustration.

Of two seats in the carriage facing each other, that in the rear, and facing the horses, is the most desirable, is the place of honor being the right side of this seat, which should be given to any elderly person, an honored guest or ladies, during the carriage ride.

The ladies being in place, the gentlemen will take the seat with their backs to the horses, care being observed that dresses and shawls are not shut in the door when it is closed. The

Fig. 19. Assisting the lady into the carriage.

gentleman last in will sit on the right, and upon him should devolve the giving of orders to the driver, and any other directions which the company may determine upon.

At the close of the ride, the gentlemen will dismount first, and afterwards help the ladies carefully from the carriage, taking care to keep their dresses from being soiled upon the wheels.

The single carriage should be driven as near the curbstone as possible, on the right side. The driver, having the top of the carriage down, should then turn the horses to the left, spreading the wheels on the right side, giving an opportunity for the lady to get into the carriage without soiling her dress upon the wheels. The lady should have both of her hands free to assist herself, while the gentleman (Fig. 19) should aid her, as shown in the illustration. The lady being in her place, her escort will take his seat upon the right side, will spread a lap-robe in front of the lady and himself to ward off dust and mud, and all is in readiness for the ride.

In getting from the carriage, the gentleman should alight first. He should quiet the team, and turn them, that the wheels may spread apart, retaining the reins in his hand, that he may hold the horses in case of

fright. The lady should then place her hands upon the gentleman's shoulders (Fig. 20), while her escort, taking her by the elbows, will assist her carefully to the ground. Being aided thus in safely alighting, a lady will, oftentimes, be saved from severe injury.

The gentleman on the pleasure ride should not drive so fast as to throw mud upon the occupants of the carriage. He should avoid fast driving if the lady is timid, and at the close of the ride he should take the friend to his or her residence.

Horses should not have their heads checked painfully high. They will be less shy if trained and driven without blinds. They should be driven with tight rein, and care should be observed to avoid accidents.

Ladies Unattended.

For the advantage of the unattended lady who may be stopping at a hotel, the following suggestions are made:

Fig. 20. Assisting the lady when alighting from the carriage.

The lady should enter a hotel by the ladies' entrance. When in the parlor, she should send for the proprietor or clerk, present her card, and state the length of time that she designs to remain.

By requesting the waiter to do so, he will meet the lady at the entrance to the dining-room and conduct her to a seat; thus saving her the necessity of crossing the room without an escort.

Meeting friends at the table, the lady should converse in a voice so low and quiet as not to attract attention from strangers. Particularly should she avoid loud laughter or any conspicuous evidence of commenting upon others.

To make the time spent at the hotel pass agreeably, care should be taken to obtain a pleasant room that will allow the entrance of sunshine and fresh air.

Orders at the table should be given in a low, yet clear, distinct voice. In the interval while waiting to be served, it is allowable to read a paper. Staring about the room, handling of the knife, spoons, or other articles upon the table, should be avoided.

Do not point to a dish wanted. A look in the direction of the article desired, and a request to the waiter that it be passed, will secure the dish without trouble.

The lady in the dining-room, unless accompanied by an escort, should avoid dressing ostentatiously. A very modest dress is in best taste.

The lady should not take her supper very late in the evening, in the dining-room, without an escort. It is in better taste to have the meal sent to her room. A lady should also avoid loitering in the halls or standing alone at the hotel-windows.

Unless invited, a lady should not play upon the piano in the hotel-parlor nor sing if there are others in the room, neither should she sing or hum tunes when passing through the halls.

Trunks and rooms should be carefully locked when leaving them, and valuables should be given into the hands of the proprietor for deposit in the safe, the guest ringing whenever she may require them during her stay.

The lady in her unattended condition will probably require considerable assistance from some one of the waiters, who should be suitably remunerated when she leaves.

Instead of scolding at servants who are neglectful of their duty, complain to the housekeeper or proprietor. Polite requests of the servants will, however, usually secure an immediate and pleasant response.

When intending to leave upon a special train, care should be had that trunks are packed, tickets purchased and all arrangements made sufficiently long before the time of starting to avoid hurry and mistakes.

ETIQUETTE IN CHURCH.

A CHURCH should be entered with a most reverent feeling. The object of attending divine service is to improve the spiritual nature, and hence business and everything of a secular character should be left behind when you enter the church portals.

If a stranger, you will wait in the vestibule until the arrival of the usher, who will conduct you to a seat.

Enter the church quietly, removing the hat, and never replacing it until the door is reached again at the close of the service.

If a stranger, and accompanied by a lady, you will precede her, and follow the usher up the aisle until the pew is reached, when you will pause, allow her to pass in, and you will follow, taking seats at the further end if you are first, so that you will not be disturbed by later arrivals. It is no longer a custom, as formerly, for the gentleman to step into the aisle and allow ladies that are strangers to pass to the inside.

The gentleman will place his hat, if possible, under the seat, and while in church the occupant should avoid making a noise, staring around the building, whispering, laughing or nodding to others.

All greetings, recognitions and conversation should be conducted in the vestibule after service. While in church, the passage of a fan or hymn-book to another should be recognized by merely a quiet bow.

Should you see a stranger waiting, you may invite him to enter your pew. No speaking is necessary then, nor when you open the book and point out the service.

If a stranger, it is best to conform to the rules of the service, rising and sitting down with the congregation; and, although the forms may be radically different from what you are accustomed to, you should comport yourself with the utmost attention and reverence.

Avoid making a noise when you enter a church after the services have commenced. It is disrespectful to come late, and shows bad manners to leave before the service is through. You should wait until the benediction is pronounced before you commence putting your articles in order for leaving.

It is a breach of etiquette for a number of young men to congregate in the vestibule, and there carry forward a conversation, commenting upon the services and various members of the congregation present.

If a member of a church, you should be regular in attendance. While the pastor has put forth, possibly, extra effort to prepare an effective sermon, it is poor encouragement to find members of the congregation absent because of a trivial storm, or away upon the pleasure drive.

ETIQUETTE IN THE SCHOOL.

THE following are the requisites for successful management in the schoolroom:

The teacher must be a good judge of human nature. If so, his knowledge will teach him that no two children are born with precisely the same organization. This difference in mentality will make one child a natural linguist, another will naturally excel in mathematics, another will exhibit fondness for drawing, and another for philosophy. Understanding and observing this, he will, without anger or impatience, assist the backward student, and will direct the more forward, ever addressing each child in the most respectful manner.

As few rules as possible should be made, and the object and necessity for the rule should be fully explained to the school by the teacher. When a rule has been made, obedience to it should be enforced. Firmness, united with gentleness, is one of the most important qualifications which a teacher can possess.

Everything should be in order, and the exercises of the day should be carried forward according to an arranged programme. The rooms should be swept, the fires built, and the first and second bells rung, with exact punctuality. In the same manner each recitation should come at an appointed time throughout the school hours.

The programme of exercises should be so varied as to give each pupil a variety of bodily and mental exercise. Thus, music, recreation, study, recitation, declamation, etc., should be so varied as to develop all the child's powers. Not only should boys and girls store their minds with knowledge, but they should be trained in the best methods of writing and speaking, whereby they may be able to impart the knowledge which they possess.

The teacher should require the strictest order and neatness upon the part of all the students. Clean hands, clean face and neatly combed hair should characterize every pupil, while a mat in the doorway should remind every boy and girl of the necessity of entering the schoolroom with clean boots and shoes. Habits of neatness and order thus formed will go with the pupils through life.

At least a portion of each day should be set apart by the teacher, in which to impart to the pupils a knowledge of etiquette. Students should be trained to enter the room quietly, to always close without noise the door through which they pass, to make introductions gracefully, to bow with ease and dignity, to shake hands properly, to address others courteously, to make a polite reply when spoken to, to sit and stand gracefully, to do the right thing in the right place, and thus, upon all occasions, to appear to advantage.

All the furnishings of the schoolroom should be such as to inspire the holiest, loftiest and noblest ambition in the child. A schoolroom should be handsomely decorated. The aquarium, the trailing vine, the blossom and the specimens of natural history should adorn the teacher's desk and the windows, while handsome pictures should embellish the walls. In short, the pupils should be surrounded with such an array of beauty as will constantly inspire them to higher and nobler achievements.

Boys and girls should be taught that which they will use when they become men and women. In the first place they will talk more than they will do anything else. By every means possible they should be trained to be correct, easy, fluent and pleasant speakers; and next to this they should be trained to be ready writers. To be this, they should be schooled in penmanship, punctuation, capitalization, composition and the writing of every description of form, from the note of invitation to an agreement, from the epistle to a friend to the promissory note, from the letter of introduction to the report of a meeting.

Above all, the teacher should be thoroughly imbued with the importance of inculcating in the mind of the student a knowledge of general principles. Thus, in the study of geography, the pupil should be taught that the earth is spherical in form; that its outer surface is divided into land and water; that the land is divided into certain grand divisions, peopled with different races of human beings, who exhibit special characteristics. That civilization is the result of certain causes, and progress in the human race arises from the inevitable law of nature that everything goes from the lower steadily toward the higher. A study of the causes which make difference in climate, difference in animals, difference in intellectual and moral developments among the races—a general study of causes thus will make such an impression upon the child's mind as will never be effaced; while the simple study of facts, such as load the mind with names of bays, islands, rivers, etc., is the crowding of the memory with that which is likely, in time, to be nearly all forgotten.

Thus, in the study of history, dates will be forgotten, while the outlines of the rise and fall of kingdoms, and the causes which produced the same, if rightly impressed by the teacher, will be ever stored in the mind of the pupil.

So should the teacher instruct the student in every branch of study, remembering that facts are liable to be forgotten, but fundamental principles and causes, well understood, will be forever remembered.

It is of the utmost importance, also, that the teacher continuously and persistently keep before the student the importance of temperance, justice and truth; as without these, however superior the education, the individual is entirely without balance, and is always liable to fall. The teacher should never relax his efforts in this direction.

The good teacher will be a living example in all that he teaches to others. If wise, he will seldom if ever resort to the infliction of corporal pain on the pupil, although if a law or rule be violated, it is of the utmost importance that a just punishment follow the violation, but this should never be such as will destroy the child's self-respect.

Duty of the Pupil.

It should be the aim of the student to be punctual in attendance at school, to be thorough in study, and good in the recitation. The boy or girl who would be successful in after life must lay the foundation of success in youth. They should fully understand the importance of improving their school-days for this purpose.

The student that seeks every opportunity to idle away his time in making sport and amusement for himself and fellow-students, will live to regret that he thus wasted his time. The happy, sportive, joyous, laughing boy and girl shed happiness wherever they go, if they are careful to control their gayety, and allow its flow only in the proper place; but they should never permit the love of the mirthful to infringe on the rules of the schoolroom or the laws of etiquette. On the contrary, true courtesy should teach them to use every endeavor to aid the teacher in his work, as in so doing they are themselves reaping the benefit.

The boy and the girl at school foretell the future man or woman. Those who are prompt, punctual and orderly, will be so in after life. Those who are truthful, reliable and honest in childhood, will be trusted in position and place in after years; and those who store the mind in youth with valuable knowledge, will possess that which can never be lost, but on the contrary will always be a means by which they may procure a livelihood; and, if united with energy and perseverance, will be sure to give them reputation, eminence of position, and wealth.

The boy should never take pride in disobedience to the rules of school. To be a truant, to be indolent, to be working mischief, evinces no talent; any rowdy could do this; most worthless men did this when they attended school. It requires effort to be a good scholar; it evinces brain-power to be a good student.

The youth should earnestly resolve to achieve an honorable and noble position in life. With the wide opportunities which open to the ambitious and the enterprising in this age of progression, there is no limit to the greatness which the thoroughly earnest student may attain. The idle and the dissolute will naturally, of their own weight, drop out by the wayside and sink from sight. The plodder who is content to go the dull, daily round in the same narrow rut will get the reward of his labor, though he never betters his condition. But the earnest, original, aspiring, energetic, intelligent worker, can always be sure of new fields to enter, nobler victories to gain, and grander work to be accomplished.

ETIQUETTE IN THE HOME.

PARENTS AND CHILDREN.

IN temperament, physical characteristics, mental development and moral inclinations, the child is what it has been made by its inheritance and the training it has received since infancy. If born of parents happy in disposition, harmonious in conjugal relation, and pleasant in circumstances, the child will as certainly be sweet in temper as that sweet fluid will flow from a maple tree. More especially will this be true if the child was welcome, and the days of the mother prior to its birth were full of sunshine and gladness.

If, on the contrary, a badly-developed and unhappy parentage has marked the child, then a correspondingly unfortunate organization of mind and unhappy disposition will present itself for discipline and training.

Fortunate is it for the parent who can understand the cause of the child's predilections thus in the beginning. As with the teacher, when the causes that affect the child's mind are understood, the correct system of government to be pursued is then more easily comprehended. The result of this early appreciation of the case is to teach the parent and teacher that, whatever may be the manifestation of mind with the child, it should never be blamed. This is a fundamental principle necessary to be understood by any person who would be successful in government. When thoroughly imbued with that understanding, kindness and love will take the place of anger and hatred, and discipline can be commenced aright.

One of the first things that the child should understand is that it should implicitly obey. The parent should therefore be very careful to give only such commands as should be observed, and then the order should be firmly but kindly enforced.

To always secure obedience without trouble, it is of the utmost importance that the parent be firm. For the parent to refuse a request of a child without due consideration, and soon afterward, through the child's importunities, grant the request, is to very soon lose command. The parent should carefully consider the request, and if it be denied the child should feel that the denial is the result of the best judgment, and is not dictated by momentary impatience or petulance. A child soon learns to discriminate between the various moods of the fickle parent, and very soon loses respect for government that is not discreet, careful and just.

If a command is disobeyed, parents should never threaten what they will do if the order is disobeyed again, but at once withhold, quietly, yet firmly and pleasantly, some pleasure from the child in consequence of the disobedience. The punishment should be very seldom, if ever, the infliction of bodily pain. A slight deprivation of some pleasure—it may be very slight, but sufficient to teach the child that it must obey—will be of great service to its future discipline and government by the parent. Commencing thus when the child is very young, treating it always tenderly and kindly, with mild and loving words, the child will grow to womanhood or manhood an honor to the parents.

What Parents Should Never Do.

Never speak harshly to a child.

Never use disrespectful names.

Never use profane or vulgar words in the presence of a child.

Do not be so cold and austere as to drive your child from you.

Never misrepresent. If you falsify, the child will learn to deceive also.

Never withhold praise when the child deserves it. Commendation is one of the sweetest pleasures of childhood.

Never waken your children before they have completed their natural slumbers in the morning. See that they retire early, and thus get the requisite time for sleep. Children require more sleep than older persons. The time will come soon enough when care and trouble will compel them to waken in the early morning. Let them sleep while they can.

Do not reproach a child for a mistake which was done with a good motive at the time. Freely forgive, wisely counsel, and the child will thus be taught that there is no danger in telling the truth.

Never give your children money indiscriminately to spend for their own use. However wealthy you may be, teach the child the value of money by requiring it to earn it in some manner. Commencing young, let the child perform simple duties requiring labor, which the parent may reward by pennies and very small sums. Let the child thus spend only money of its own earning. The boy who thus early learns by labor the value of a dollar, knows how to accumulate the same in after-life, and how to save it.

Never demean yourself by getting angry and whipping a child. The very fact of your punishing in anger arouses the evil nature of the child. Some day this punishment thus inflicted will react upon yourself.

What Parents Should Do.

Always speak in a pleasant voice.

Teach your children how to work; how to obtain a living by their own efforts. Teach them the nobility and the dignity of labor, that they may respect and honor the producer.

Explain the reason why. The child is a little walking interrogation point. To it all is new. Explain the reason. Your boy will some day repay this trouble by teaching some other child.

Teach your children the evil of secret vice, and the consequences of using tobacco and spirituous liquors; teach them to be temperate, orderly, punctual, prompt, truthful, neat, faithful and honest.

Encourage your child to be careful of personal appearance; to return every tool to its place; to always pay debts promptly; to never shirk a duty; to do an equal share, and to always live up to an agreement.

Teach your children to confide in you, by conference together. Tell them your plans, and sometimes ask their advice; they will thus open their hearts to you, and will ask *your* advice. The girl who tells all her heart to her mother has a shield and a protection about her which can come only with a mother's advice and counsel.

Give your children your confidence in the affairs of your business. They will thus take interest, and become co-workers with you. If you enlist their respect, then their sympathy and coöperation, they will quite likely remain to take up your work when you have done, and will go ahead perfecting what you have commenced.

If you are a farmer, do not overwork your children, and thus by a hard and dreary life drive them off to the cities. Arise at a reasonable hour in the morning, take an hour's rest after meals, and quit at five or six o'clock in the afternoon. Let the young people, in games and other amusements, have a happy time during the remainder of the day. There is no reason why a farmer's family should be deprived of recreation and amusement, any more than others.

Teach your child the value of the Sabbath as a day for the spiritual improvement of the mind; that on the Sabbath morn the ordinary work of the week should not be resumed if it is possible to avoid it; that the day should be passed in attendance upon religious service of some kind, or exercises that will ennoble and spiritualize the nature. While rest and recreation may be a part of the day's programme, true philosophy dictates that the spiritual faculties of the nature should be cultivated by setting apart a portion of the time for their improvement.

Teach your children those things which they will need when they become men and women. As women they should understand how to cook, how to make a bed, how to preserve cleanliness and order throughout the house, how to ornament their rooms, to renovate and preserve furniture and clothing, how to sing, and play various games, that they may enliven the household. They should be taught how to swim, how to ride, how to drive, how to do business, and how to preserve health. The mother should early intrust money to the girl, with which to buy articles for the household, that she may learn its value. Think what a man and woman need to know in order to be healthy, happy, prosperous and successful, and teach them that.

SAY "NO" POLITELY.

 COMMON saying is, "A man's manners make his fortune." This is a well-known fact, and we see it illustrated every day. The parents who considerately train a child amid kindness and love, rear a support for their declining years. The teacher that rules well and is yet kind, is beloved by his pupils. The hotel proprietor, by affability and an accommodating spirit, may fill his hotel with guests. The railway conductor, who has a pleasant word for the lonely traveler, is always remembered with favor. The postoffice clerk who very carefully looks through a pile of letters and says, "not any," very gently, pleasantly adding a word of hope by saying, "it may come on the afternoon train," we always gratefully recollect. When the time comes that we can return the kindness, we take great pleasure in doing so.

The man who shows himself to be a gentleman, even though he may not buy what we have to sell when we solicit him, we always know will get his reward. His affability, when he declined, demonstrated that he could say "no" with a pleasant word. The very fact of impressing us so favorably, even when he did not purchase, clearly indicated that he was thoroughly schooled in the ways of politeness, and that he lived up to the golden rule of doing to others as he desired others to do to him.

Thus every day, in the multifarious relations of life, it is in the power of persons to grant favors by at least kind words. And when pleasant manners are exhibited, how strongly these stand out in contrast with the short, curt, rough, uncouth manner which so frequently accompanies the refusal of a favor. We realize, as we see the contrast, that no one can be a gentleman who ignores the laws of etiquette.

TREATMENT OF EMPLOYES.

 T takes every grade of society to make the complete whole. One class is just as necessary as the other. In carrying forward great enterprises, how plainly do we see this manifested. Take the building of a railroad as an illustration:

A certain grade of mind is essential to prepare the road-bed and lay the track. This class of men must have strong physical natures, and the qualities that give the necessary force and energy to hew down rocks, tunnel mountains and remove all obstructions. Another class will act as foremen of the laborers, another will serve as engineers, another is fitted to act as officers, while still another grade of mind projected the enterprise and furnished the means for carrying it to a successful conclusion.

As in the materials that enter into the erection of the building, the foundation stones that support the superstructure down deep in the earth, while they are never seen, are nevertheless just as essential to the completion of the building as are the ornamental capstones above the windows; so, in associated labor, each grade of mind does its appropriate work. We could not dispense with either, and all should have due praise.

Each class being thus dependent, one upon the other, all should labor in harmony together. The workman should guard his employer's interest. He should always be promptly on time and faithful to the last hour. He should make his work a study; he should give it thought, as thereby he renders his services so much the more valuable, and his compensation in the end so much better. Probably, if faithful, he may succeed to the business of his employer, or may enter a separate field. It is certain, at any rate, if he proves himself a competent assistant he is the more likely, in time, himself to become a manager of others.

The employer, through kind and pleasant manner, may do much toward making the subordinate worthy and competent. The workman should thoroughly understand what the duty is which he is expected to perform, and he should be required pleasantly yet firmly to execute it to the letter. When once there is a definite understanding on his part as to what is explicitly required, it is not necessary that an employer use harsh means or a manner in any way discourteous in order to secure obedience to his commands.

The Toilet.

ELEMENTS OF THE BEAUTIFUL.

THE love of beautiful adornment is innate in the human mind, and in reality has a great influence in elevating and refining the race. It is true that the mind may sometimes be too much given to personal decoration, but the instincts which cause us to clothe ourselves beautifully are all refining and elevating in character.

The desire to please and to be beautiful surrounds us on every hand with grace, elegance and refinement.

The person who cares nothing for personal appearance is a sloven. Were all to be thus, the human race would rapidly degenerate toward barbarism. The person who is careless of dress is likely to be equally regardless concerning purity of character.

The little girl that studies her features in the mirror, while she evinces possibly a disposition to be vain, nevertheless in this act shows herself to be possessed of those instincts of grace which, rightly directed, will beautify and embellish all her surroundings through life.

The boy that cares nothing for personal appearance, that does not appreciate beauty in others, is likely to develop into the man who will be slovenly in habits, whose home will quite probably be a hovel, and himself very likely a loafer or a tramp. But the boy—the rolicsome, frolicsome boy, ready to roll in the dirt, possibly—who, under all this, aspires to appear handsome, who desires a clean face, clean hands and a clean shirt, who admires a well-dressed head of hair and a good suit of clothes—that boy possesses the elements which in the man, in an elegant home, will surround him with the artistic and the charming.

The love of the beautiful ever leads to the higher, the grander and the better. Guided by its impulses, we pass out of the hut into the larger and better house; into the charming and elegantly-adorned mansion. Actuated by its influence, we convert the lumbering railway carriage into a palace-car, the swamp into a garden, and the desolate place into a park, in which we wander amid the trees, the streams of limpid water, and the fragrance of beautiful flowers.

All along the world's highway are the evidences, among the most elevated and refined, of the love of the beautiful, which, perhaps more than in any other manner, finds expression in dress.

This love of personal adornment being an inherent, desirable, refining element of character, it does not, therefore, become us to ignore or to suppress it. On the contrary, it should be our duty to cultivate neatness of appearance and artistic arrangement in dress, the whole being accompanied by as much personal beauty as possible.

In the cultivation of beauty in dress, it will become necessary to discriminate between ornament as displayed by the savage, and the science of beauty as observed in a more highly civilized life. Ornament is one thing; beauty is quite another.

To develop beauty, it is necessary to understand that the combination of a few fundamental principles forms the basis in the construction of all that we admire as beautiful. Of these are—

1. CURVED LINES. 2. SYMMETRY. 3. CONTRAST. 4. HARMONY OF COLOR. 5. HARMONY OF ASSOCIATION.

The Curved Line.

A prominent feature of beauty everywhere is the curved line. The winding pathway, the graceful outline of tree, cloud and mountain in the distance, the arched rainbow, the well-trimmed shrub, the finely-featured animal, the rounded form of everything that is beautiful—all illustrate this principle. The delicately, finely rounded face, hands and general features, are essential to the highest forms of beauty in the person, and the same principles apply in the manufacture of dress. Every line and seam should run in curves.

Symmetry of Proportion.

As harmonious proportions always please the eye in every object, so we are pleased with the symmetry displayed in the human form and features. Thus symmetry will give a well-shaped head, a moderate length of neck, a clearly-defined nose, mouth not too large, shoulders of even height, and all parts of the body of proportionate length and size. The clothing should be made to set off the natural features of the body to the best advantage. Thus the coat should be so cut as to make the shoulders of the man look broad. The dress should be so fitted as to cause the shoulders of the woman to appear narrow and sloping.

Long garments will make the individual appear taller. Short garments will cause the person to seem shorter. Lines that run perpendicularly add to the apparent height; horizontal lines shorten it.

Contrast.

Another feature of beauty in personal appearance is contrast, or those qualities which give animated expression and vivacity of manner. Thus the sparkling eye, clear-cut features, a color of hair that contrasts with the skin; happy, lively expression of face; graceful, animated movement of body; interesting conversational powers—all these make the face attractive by variety and contrast.

The lady's dress is relieved by flounce, frill, and various other trimmings, with colors more or less pronounced, according to the complexion of the wearer. The gentleman's dress, as now worn, does not admit of so great variety.

Harmony.

The harmony of colors suitable for various complexions is quite fully detailed elsewhere. Harmony of association will include those principles that derive their beauty chiefly from their association with other objects. Thus the best height and form for man or woman will be the average form of men and women with whom they associate. Anything unusual will detract from this beauty.

Any article of jewelry or dress which may appear out of place for the occasion, or not appropriate with the other articles worn, is also included under this head.

CARE OF THE PERSON.

It is assumed that the reader desires health and beauty, and is willing to govern habits accordingly. Observe then the following regulations:

Retire sufficiently early to get the necessary rest and sleep, that you may arise early in the morning.

Be sure that plenty of fresh air is admitted to the room throughout the night, by the opening of windows. Avoid feathers. A perfectly clean, moderately hard bed is best for health.

The Bath.

Upon arising, take a complete bath. A simple washing out of the eyes is not sufficient. The complete bathing of the body once each day is of the utmost importance to health and beauty. Not more than a quart of water is necessary. Use the hands the same as you do upon the face. No sponge is required, and water is more agreeable to the skin when applied with the bare hand. Use rainwater; and, for a healthy person, the temperature of that which has been in the room throughout the night is about right. Use plenty of soap, and wash quickly. Follow by wiping the skin perfectly dry with a soft towel, and afterward give the body and limbs a thorough rubbing. The glow that is diffused throughout the face and body by this exercise is worth more in giving a ruddy, beautiful complexion, than all the rouge and powder in the world.

The arrangements for this bath are very simple. There is nothing required but a small amount of soft water, a piece of soap, and a towel. No elaborately-fitted-up bathroom is necessary. We have detailed all the appliances that are essential, and they are so simple that the laboring classes and the poor can have them, and be clean, as well as the rich. Occasionally, warm water, with sponge, may be necessary to remove completely all the oily exudations from the body, but for the ordinary bath this is not essential.

The sun and air bath is very excellent for health; therefore to leave the body exposed in the sun for a short time previous to dressing is very invigorating.

Before the breakfast hour the lungs should be completely inflated with fresh air. The meals should be partaken of with regularity, while more or less of fruit, oatmeal, rice, cracked wheat, graham bread, etc., will be found necessary as a diet, in order to keep the skin clear.

The Breath.

The breath should be watched, lest it become offensive. Unfortunately, it is one of the troubles which we may not be aware of, as our friends may not feel at liberty to inform us of the difficulty. Offensive breath may arise from the stomach, the teeth, the lungs, or catarrhal affection of the throat and nose.

Unquestionably, the best remedy for bad breath is a system of diet and treatment that shall remove the cause. As a temporary expedient, when offensiveness arises from a peculiar food or drink which has been partaken of, a few grains of coffee, or cassia buds, cloves, cardamom seeds or allspice, may be used; although if the breath be very strong these will not always prove effective. It is better to remove the cause.

The following remedies for offensive breath are commended by those who have had experience in testing the matter:

Powdered sugar, ½ ounce; vanilla, ½ ounce; powdered charcoal, ½ ounce; powdered coffee, 1½ ounces; gum arabic, ½ ounce. Make into pellets of 18 grains each, and take six a day. Bad breath will disappear.

Disagreeable breath arising from decay or secretions about the teeth may be removed by the following:

Rose-water, 1 ounce, and permanganate of potash, 1 grain. Rinse the mouth every three hours.

To remove catarrh, the following is highly commended:

In a pint of water put two tablespoonfuls of common fine table salt. Heat the water in a tin cup. With the aid of a nasal douche, obtained at the drugstore, or even without that, snuff about a teaspoonful of the brine up each nostril, requiring it to pass into the mouth. Use twice a day — morning and night.

For offensive breath arising from foul stomach, the following is recommended:

To a wine-glass of water add 3 grains of chloride of lime. Take a tablespoonful three times a day, before the meal, and eat of simple food which is easily digested.

Another remedy for foul breath is powdered charcoal, half a teaspoonful, spread on a piece of bread, and eaten once a day for two or three days. Another is a drink of pure water, taken twice a day, containing each time 20 grains of bisulphate of soda. The taste is made pleasant by a few drops of peppermint essence.

The following is recommended as beneficial for the teeth, and effective in removing the acidity of the stomach:

Take of gum arabic 5 drachms; vanilla sugar, 3 drachms; chlorate of lime, 7 drachms, and mix with water to a stiff paste. Roll and cut into the ordinary-sized lozenge, and eat six each day.

The Skin.

Beware of exterior application of cosmetics for the purpose of beautifying the skin. The greatest beautifiers in existence are plenty of exercise in the fresh air, the keeping of the pores of the skin completely open by bathing, the feeding of the body with a sufficiency of simple, healthy food, and the obtaining of the requisite amount of sleep.

It is true that sometimes a slight touch of art may improve the personal appearance. The very sallow complexion may be improved by a small amount of color applied; the hair, if naturally dry and stiff, may be kept in place by a simple hair preparation, and a white eyebrow may be brought into harmonious color with the hair of the head by a dye; all this being done so adroitly that the external application cannot be detected. But, as a rule, greatest beauty is obtained by a strict observance of the laws of health.

The following preparations, culled from De la Banta's "Advice to Ladies," are recommended for improving the complexion:

Take a teaspoonful of powdered charcoal (kept by druggists), mixed with sweetened water or milk, for three nights successively. This should be followed by a gentle purge afterwards, to remove it from the system. Taken once in two or three months, this remedy will prove efficacious in making the complexion clear and transparent.

ANOTHER.

Tincture of balsam of Peru, 2 drachms; tincture of tolu, 2 drachms; tincture of benzoin, 2 drachms. Mix with one gill of distilled water, and take of melted white wax, 1 ounce; spermaceti, ½ ounce; sweet almond oil, 8 drachms, and rose-water, 1 ounce. Mix all the ingredients together, and beat thoroughly, applying to the skin with a sponge.

This may be used with benefit where the skin presents a greasy appearance:

To ½ pint of rose-water, add chlorate of potash, 18 grains; glycerine, 1 ounce. Mix carefully, and use in a pure state. Apply with a sponge or linen cloth. Should it irritate the skin, dilute with more water. These lotions should be applied with care, and are best used at night.

The greasy skin, inclined to pimples, is benefited by the following preparation:

Bicarbonate of soda, 18 grains; essence of Portugal, 6 drops; distilled water, ½ pint. Mix, and bathe the face.

The shiny, polished skin, which is caused by fatty secretions beneath it, may have the difficulty removed by this preparation:

Take 1 quart of camphor water, pure glycerine 1 ounce, and ½ ounce of powdered borax. Mix, and bathe the face. Let it dry and remain a few minutes after applying it, then wash the face thoroughly with soft water.

If the skin is very pallid, it is improved by the bath in lukewarm water, followed by brisk rubbing with a coarse towel, and exercise in the air and sun. The pale skin is improved also by the sunshine. The rough skin is made smooth by the application of glycerine at night, followed by its removal with water and fine soap in the morning.

The skin may be whitened by the following prescription:

To one pint of water add 1 wineglass of fresh lemon juice, and 10 drops of ottar of roses. Mix, and keep in a well corked bottle. Use once a day.

The sallow and muddy skin is improved by this preparation

To one pint of water add 2 drachms of iodide of potassium and 1 ounce of glycerine. Mix, and apply with a sponge once a day.

To keep the skin clear, beware of pork, cheese and other substances containing much grease. Also avoid alcoholic drinks. Keep the bowels loose by fruit and a sufficiency of coarse food. Take exercise sufficient, if possible, to produce a gentle perspiration each day; bathe daily, and get into the sunshine and open air.

The Hand.

Various are the recipes for keeping the hand beautiful. If not engaged in hard manual labor, and it is very desirable to make the hands present as handsome an appearance as possible, there are a few directions necessary to keep them well preserved. Among these is perfect cleanliness, which is produced by a thorough washing, using an abundance of good toilet soap, and frequently a nail-brush.

Should the hands be inclined to chap, they will be relieved of the difficulty by washing them in glycerine before going to bed. In the winter season, to wash them in snow and soap will leave them smooth and soft.

To make the hands very white and delicate, the person is assisted by washing them several times for two or three days in milk and water, and, upon retiring to rest, bathing in palm oil, and encasing them in a pair of woolen gloves, cleaning with warm water and soap the next morning. They should be thoroughly rubbed to promote circulation, and a pair of soft leather gloves should be worn during the day.

Should the hands become sunburned, the tan may be removed by using lime-water and lemon-juice.

Should warts make their appearance, they may be removed by paring them on the top and applying a small amount of acetic acid on the summit of the wart, with a camel's hair brush, care being taken that none of the acid gets upon the surrounding skin. To prevent this, wax may be placed upon the finger or hand during the operation, or an old kid glove may be used, the wart being allowed to project through.

The nails should be cut about once a week, directly after a bath, and should never be bitten. In rough, hard labor, if it is desired to protect the hands, gloves should be worn.

But however beautiful it may be, the hand should do its full share of work. The hand that is beautiful from idleness is to be despised.

The Feet.

Much care should be taken to keep the feet in good condition. The first important consideration in their management is perfect cleanliness. Some people find it necessary to wash the feet morning and evening. Many find it indispensably necessary to wash them once a day, and no one should fail of washing them at least three times a week, and the stockings should be changed as frequently if much walking be done.

Without washing, the feet are liable to become very offensive to others in a short time. The feet of some persons will become disagreeably so sometimes within a week if they are not washed, more especially if they perspire freely.

A foot bath, using warm water, followed by wiping the feet completely dry, and afterward putting on clean stockings, is very invigorating after a long walk, or when the feet are damp and cold.

To escape chilblains, avoid getting the feet wet. Should they become damp, change shoes and stockings at once. Wear woolen stockings, and do not toast the feet before the fire. The approach of the chilblain is frequently prevented by bathing the feet in a strong solution of alum.

With the first indications of chilblains, as revealed by the itching sensation, it is well to rub them with warm spirits of rosemary, adding to the same a little turpentine. Lint, soaked in camphorated spirits, opodeldoc, or camphor liniment, may be applied and retained when the part is affected.

It is claimed also that chilblains may be cured by bathing the feet in water in which potatoes have been boiled.

Wear boots and shoes amply large for the feet, but not too large, and thus escape corns. A broad heel, half an inch in height, is all that comfort will allow to be worn.

The Hair.

The head should be washed occasionally with soap and water. Follow by wiping perfectly dry, and afterward brush the hair and scalp with a hairbrush of moderate hardness. When the hair is inclined to be harsh and dry, a moderate supply of olive oil, bear's grease or other dressing may be used. With many heads no oil is necessary, and with any an over-abundance is to be avoided. Frequent brushing with a perfectly clean brush is of great service in giving a glossy, beautiful appearance to the hair. The brush may be kept clean by washing every day or two in warm water and soda, or in diluted ammonia.

For removing dandruff, glycerine diluted with a little rosewater is recommended. Rosemary in almost any preparation is a very cleansing wash.

The yolk of an egg, beaten up in warm water, makes an excellent application for cleansing the scalp.

To clip the ends of the hair occasionally is an excellent plan for ladies, as it prevents the hair from splitting.

It is doubtful if a hair-dye is ever advisable, though an eyebrow is sometimes improved by a light application, to bring it into harmonious color with the hair, as is also hair which grows white in patches. There is no objection to the hair growing gray. Indeed the gray is often fully as beautiful as the former color.

Baldness is usually avoided by keeping the head cool. Women seldom have bald heads, but men often do, the baldness commencing upon the head at a point which is covered by the hat. In order to preserve the hair, gentlemen must avoid warm hats and caps, and whatever is worn must be thoroughly ventilated by apertures sufficient in quantity and size to allow all the heated air to escape. The silk hat should have at least twenty holes punched in the top to afford sufficient ventilation.

The beard is nature's badge to indicate manhood. It was an unwise fashion that ordained that the face should be shaved. Gradually men begin to learn that health, comfort and improved appearance come with the full beard, and in later years the beard is acquiring the prestige it held in olden times. Care should be taken to keep the beard and hair so cut and trimmed that they may present a handsome appearance.

The Teeth.

The teeth should be thoroughly cleaned with a toothbrush each morning after breakfast. Some persons clean the teeth after every meal, which is a most excellent habit. By cleaning the teeth regularly, no washes are necessary, though occasionally castile soap will be beneficial. Should tartar collect in such quantity as to be difficult to remove, the dentist should be consulted. Should the teeth begin to decay, they should be immediately cared for by the dentist. Powdered charcoal easily removes stains, and makes the teeth white.

The following also is an excellent wash for the teeth:

Tincture of myrrh, 1 ounce; compound tincture of cinchona, 1 ounce; water, 1 ounce. Put five drops on the toothbrush, dip the brush then in water, and wash the teeth.

Keep the teeth clean. They look badly if not perfectly white and clean.

Ears, Eyes and Nose.

In the daily bath, all the crevices of the ears should be thoroughly cleaned, and the earwax carefully removed whenever it shows itself.

Special pains should be taken to keep the eyes clean. It shows filthy habits to see matter gathered in the corners. If dirt accumulates between washings, the eyes should be carefully wiped with a soft handkerchief.

Keep the nasal passages perfectly clear. If there is an inclination for accumulations to stop there, snuff water up the nose, and afterward blow it, placing the thumb on one side while you blow the other. Keep the nose so clear that you can breathe through it with ease, and avoid the coarse habit of picking it.

Regularity of Habits.

It is of the utmost importance, if the individual would enjoy health and possess beauty, that all the personal habits be perfectly regular, and that attention be given to these each twenty-four hours at a regular time.

Do not let visiting, traveling or business interfere with them. You must be regular in sleep, in evacuation of the bowels, in bathing and in eating. Nature will not be cheated. She requires perfect attention to certain duties. If you attempt to violate her requirements, you will be certainly punished.

Whenever the person complains of sickness, he confesses to a violation, consciously or unconsciously, unavoidably or otherwise, of some of nature's requirements. (See remarks on "Health," in the "Letters of Advice," elsewhere in this volume.)

WHAT COLORS MAY BE WORN.

Nature has her peculiar shades and contrasts, with which she embellishes all her works.

Over the retreating dark gray cloud in the east does the rainbow show itself, strong by contrast, and beautiful in the harmony of its surroundings. Surpassingly lovely are the brilliant rays of the golden sunset, as they lie reflected upon the fleecy clouds at eventide, their charm coming from their surroundings of the gray and azure blue. Dazzlingly bright are the twinkling stars as they smile upon us in their bed of cerulean blue; and very beautiful is the rose, as it perfumes the air and charms the eye amid its accompaniments of green.

Nature thus robes all her works with shades that complement and harmonize; the result being to show the object to the best advantage.

In the higher civilization, men have donned the conventional suit of black, and have abandoned the domain of color to woman, who with her keenly æsthetic nature can never be induced to forego the pleasure that comes from brilliant and harmonious hues. Alive as woman is, therefore, to the principles that make beauty, it becomes us to investigate the subject of personal appearance as affected by color.

Colors that Suit Different Complexions.

Two distinct types of complexion exist among the white race, namely, the light-haired, fair and ruddy complexions, termed Blondes; and the dark-haired and dark-skinned, called Brunettes.

Between these are several intermediate tints and shades, all requiring much close observation to fully discriminate as to the colors most suitable to be worn, to harmonize with the different shades of complexion.

Investigation has proven that the light-haired and rosy-cheeked, with red or golden hair and ruddy complexion, require certain colors in head-dress and drapery to harmonize; and the same is true of the dark complexion, with dark hair and eyebrows.

The Shades that Blondes May Wear.

Dark violet, intermixed with lilac and blue, give additional charms to the fair-haired, ruddy blonde. Green, also, with lighter or darker tints, is favorable. With the very ruddy, the blue and green should be darker rather than lighter. An intermixture of white may likewise go with these colors.

The neutral colors are also suitable to the ruddy blondes. Of these are the russet, slate, maroon, and all the hues of brown. Light neutral tints are also pleasing, such as gray, drab, fawn and stone colors.

Transparent and delicate complexions, with light, chestnut or brown hair, should have the same set off by contrast. Thus blue, pale yellow, azure, lilac and black, trimmed with rose or pink, are suitable, as are also the various shades of gray.

Colors that become the Brunette.

Glossy black becomes the brunette; so do white, scarlet, orange and yellow. The scarlet blossom in the hair, gold-colored ribbon and poppy colors, deftly but not too conspicuously woven about the neck and breast, will display the face to fine advantage. Green also befits the dark complexion.

The sallow complexion is improved by the different shades of dark green and red. A yellow complexion is made handsomer by the reflection of yellow about it; especially if relieved by poppy colors or black.

The red and yellow face is benefited by coming in contact with blue or orange. The red face is improved by red around it, red and blue tints being developed thereby. Red and blue are relieved by purple, and the blue and yellow by green. White and black become the pale face, but red and blue become it better. Light colors harmonize with and befit the pale skin, while the dark skin is improved by the darker tints.

Colors in Bonnets.

Black Bonnets, with white, pink or red flowers and white feather, become the fair complexion. They also become the black-haired type when trimmed with white, red, orange or yellow.

White Bonnets, made of lace, muslin or crape, suit all complexions, though not so becoming to the rosy complexion as other colors. A white bonnet may be trimmed with white or pink, but with the blonde is handsomest when trimmed with blue flowers. For the brunette, preference should be given to trimmings of red, pink, orange and yellow—never blue.

Blue Bonnets are suitable only for fair or light, rosy complexions. They should never be worn by the brunette.

Yellow and Orange Bonnets suit the brunette, their appropriate trimming being poppy colors, scarlet, white and black, black and scarlet, black, scarlet and yellow.

Light Blue Bonnets are very suitable for those having light hair. They may be trimmed with white flowers, and in many cases with orange and yellow.

Green Bonnets best become the fair and rosy complexion. White flowers will harmonize in the trimmings, but pink is preferable.

Colors Suitable for the Different Seasons.

Red, in its various tints, being a warm color, when worn in dress, has a pleasing effect in winter.

Purple is appropriate in winter, spring and autumn.

Green is becoming in late summer and in autumn, by contrast with the general somber appearance of dead foliage at that season of the year.

White and light tints in clothing give an appearance of coolness and comfort in summer.

Black and dark colors are appropriate at all seasons.

Colors We See First.

Of a variety of colors to be seen, the white or light-colored will usually attract attention first and farthest, from the fact that, most objects being of dark shades of color, it is strongest in contrast. Next to white comes the scarlet red, which, close by, is one of the most brilliant and attractive colors. Yellow is one of the most noticeable, succeeded by the orange, crimson, blue and purple.

Colors in Dress Most Beautiful at Night.

A dress of a color that may be beautiful during the day, may be lacking in beauty at night, owing to the effect of gaslight; and another, most charming in the evening, may possess little beauty in the daytime. Thus, crimson, which is handsome in the evening, loses its effect upon the complexion in the daytime. So white and yellow, that add beauty at night, are unbecoming by day.

The scarlet, orange and the light brown are also most charming at night.

Colors Most Beautiful by Daylight.

Pale yellow, which is handsome by day, is muddy in appearance by gaslight. So purple and orange, that harmonize and are beautiful by daylight, lose their charm at night.

The beauty of rose color disappears under the gaslight; and all the shades of purple and lilac, the dark blues and green lose their brilliancy in artificial light. Ordinarily, the complexion will bear the strongest color at night.

Apparent Size Affected by Color.

The apparent size is affected by colors. As white upon the building will make it appear larger, so a light-colored dress will have the same effect upon the person. Thus the large figure will appear best in close-fitting black, and next best in the sober hues. The smaller figure will show to advantage in the light colors. Black, however, for a person of any size, is the most suitable color for nearly all occasions; and, handsomely made, well fitted, artistically trimmed, and suitably relieved at throat and bodice with ribbons, lace and flowers corresponding with the complexion, makes always a most beautiful costume.

Persons whose resources are limited and who cannot afford a varied wardrobe should by this fact be guided to a constant preference for black.

Colors that Contrast and Harmonize.

The object of two or more different tints in dress is to obtain relief by variety, and yet the two shades brought thus in contrast should harmonize, else the beauty of each will be lessened. Thus, a lady with a blue dress would greatly injure its effect by wearing a crimson shawl; as she would also a lilac-colored dress by trimming it with a dark brown.

That the reader may understand the colors that will contrast and yet blend, the following list of harmonizing colors is given:

Blue and gold; blue and orange; blue and salmon color; blue and drab; blue and stone color; blue and white; blue and gray; blue and straw color; blue and maize; blue and chestnut; blue and brown; blue and black; blue, brown, crimson and gold.

Black and white; black and orange; black and maize; black and scarlet; black and lilac; black and pink; black and slate color; black and buff; black, white, yellow and crimson; black, orange, blue and yellow.

Crimson and gold; crimson and orange; crimson and maize; crimson and purple; crimson and black; crimson and drab.

Green and gold; green and yellow; green and orange; green and crimson; green, crimson and yellow; green, scarlet and yellow.

Lilac and gold; lilac and maize; lilac and cherry; lilac and scarlet; lilac and crimson; lilac, scarlet, white and black; lilac, gold and chestnut; lilac, yellow, scarlet and white.

Orange and chestnut; orange and brown; orange, lilac and crimson; orange, red and green; orange, blue and crimson; orange, purple and scarlet; orange, blue, scarlet, green and white.

Purple and gold; purple and orange; purple and maize; purple, scarlet and gold color; purple, white and scarlet; purple, orange, blue and scarlet; purple, scarlet, blue, yellow and black.

Red and gold; red, white or gray; red, green and orange; red, black and yellow; red, yellow, black and white.

Scarlet and purple; scarlet and orange; scarlet and blue; scarlet and slate color; scarlet, black and white; scarlet, white and blue; scarlet, gray and blue; scarlet, yellow and blue; scarlet, blue, yellow and black.

Yellow and red; yellow and brown; yellow and chestnut; yellow and violet; yellow and blue; yellow and purple; yellow and crimson; yellow and black; yellow, purple and crimson; yellow and scarlet.

FASHION--WHY DOES IT CHANGE?

Because change is one of nature's laws. If there was no change, there would be no motion; and without motion there would be no life.

Change is ever going forward in nature. To-day it is spring, and all nature is waking to new life. A few weeks hence, and every tree and shrub will be clothed in a garb of green, sprinkled with blossoms. Later, the green of various shades will merge into the autumn tints; and later still, nature will doff her garb entirely, only to clothe herself in the coming years again with various changes, according to the seasons.

So mankind instinctively changes in style of costume, oftentimes for better, and sometimes, it must be admitted, for the worse. But the change ever goes forward, fashion repeating itself within the century, often within a generation, almost as certainly as the seasons do within the year.

There is no use, therefore, in issuing a fiat against changes of fashion. Best judgment is shown in accepting of the inevitable and adapting ourselves to the circumstances.

Hints to Gentlemen.

It is best taste to conform to fashion, avoiding extremes.

While it is well to guard against the adoption of a decidedly unwise fashion, it is well also to avoid an oddity in dress.

Well dressed gentlemen wear dark clothing cut and made to measure. Watch-chain, one ring, shirt-stud and sleeve-buttons are all the jewelry allowable for the gentleman.

Other colors than black will be appropriate in their season and for various kinds of employment.

Hints to Parents.

Give the boy a good suit of clothes, if you wish him to appear manly. An ill-fitting, bad-looking garment destroys a boy's respect for himself.

To require the boy to wear men's cast-off clothing, and go shambling around in a large pair of boots, and then expect him to have good manners, is like giving him the poorest of tools, because he is a boy, and then expecting him to do as fine work with them as a man would with good tools.

Like the man or woman, the boy respects himself, and will do much more honor to his parents, when he is well dressed in a neatly fitting suit of clothes. Even his mother should relinquish her rights, and let the barber cut his hair.

As a rule, well dressed children exhibit better conduct than children that are careless in personal appearance. While vanity should be guarded against, children should be encouraged to be neat in person and dress.

The mother should strive also to make her boy manly. Possibly, as a pet, her boy has in infancy had his hair curled. Even now, when he is six or eight years of age, the curls look very pretty. But the mother must forego her further pleasure in the curls; for the boy, to take his place along with the others, to run and jump, to grow manly and strong, must wear short hair. His mother can no longer dress it like a girl's. It will be necessary and best to cut off his curls.

Hints to Ladies.

Best taste will dictate an observance of fashion, avoiding extremes.

Dress the hair so that it will exhibit variety and relief, without making the forehead look too high.

Have one pronounced color in the dress, all other colors harmonizing with that. See "Harmony of Colors."

A dress should fit the form. Well fitted and judiciously trimmed, a calico dress is handsomer than an ill-fitting silk dress.

To present a handsome appearance, all the appurtenances of the lady's dress should be scrupulously neat and clean. Every article that is designed to be white should be a pure white, and in perfect order.

Much taste may be displayed in dress about the neck, and care should be observed not to use trimmings that will enlarge the appearance of the shoulders. The dress should be close-fitting about the waist and shoulders, though the lady should not lace too tightly.

As with the gentleman, quiet colors are usually in best taste. Heavy, rich, dark materials best suit the woman of tall figure; while light, full draperies should be worn only by those of slender proportions. Short persons should beware of wearing flounces, or horizontal trimmings that will break the perpendicular lines, as the effect is to make them appear shorter.

Care should be taken to dress according to the age, the season, the employment and the occasion. As a rule, a woman appears her loveliest when, in a dress of dark color, we see her with the rosy complexion of health, her hair dressed neatly, her throat and neck tastefully cared for, her dress in neither extreme of fashion, while the whole is relieved by a moderate amount of carefully selected jewelry.

We have aimed, in this chapter on the toilet, to present the scientific principles of dress — principles that can be applied at all times, whatever may be the fashion. It will now become the reader to study these principles, and apply them in accordance with the rules of common sense and the fashions as they may prevail.

RULES OF CONDUCT TO BE OBSERVED.

LADIES and gentlemen, when meeting on the sidewalk, should always pass to the right. Should the walk be narrow or dangerous, gentlemen will always see that ladies are protected from injury.

Ladies should avoid walking rapidly upon the street, as it is ungraceful and unbecoming.

Running across the street in front of carriages is dangerous, and shows want of dignity.

The gentleman should insist upon carrying any package which the lady may have, when walking with her.

Before recognizing a lady on the street, the gentleman should be certain that his recognition will meet with favor.

No gentleman should stand on the street-corners, steps of hotels, or other public places, and make remarks about ladies passing by.

A gentleman may take two ladies upon his arms, but under no circumstances should the lady take the arms of two gentlemen.

Upon the narrow walk, for her protection, the gentleman should generally give the lady the inside of the walk (Fig. 21), passing behind her when changing at corners.

Allowing a dress to trail on the street is in exceedingly bad taste. Such a street costume simply calls forth criticism and contempt from the more sensible people.

A gentleman walking with a lady should accommodate his step and pace to hers. For the gentleman to be some distance ahead, presents a bad appearance.

Should protection on the street be necessary, it is customary for the gentleman to give his right arm to the lady; but if more convenient, he may give the left.

Fig 21. The street-promenade. The gentleman gives the lady the inside of the walk. *

A gentleman will assist a lady over a bad crossing, or from an omnibus or carriage, without waiting for the formality of an introduction. When the service is performed, he will raise his hat, bow, and pass on.

In a street car or an omnibus, the passengers who are seated should strive to give seats to those who are standing, rendering such accommodation as they would themselves desire under similar circumstances.

When crossing the pavement, the lady should raise her dress with the right hand, a little above the ankle. To raise the dress with both hands, is vulgar, and can be excused only when the mud is very deep.

No gentleman will smoke when walking with, or standing in the presence of, a lady on the street. He should remove the cigar from her presence entirely, even though permission be granted to continue the smoking.

A gentleman should give his seat to any lady who may be standing in a public conveyance. For this favor she should thank him, which courtesy he should acknowledge by a slight bow. In an omnibus he will pass up the ladies' fares.

A true lady will go quietly and unobtrusively about her business when on the street, never seeking to attract the attention of the opposite sex, at the same time recognizing acquaintances with a courteous bow, and friends with pleasant words of greeting.

Swinging the arms when walking, eating upon the street, sucking the parasol handles, pushing violently through a crowd, very loud and boisterous talking and laughing on the streets, and whispering in public conveyances, are all evidences of ill-breeding in ladies.

A lady should have the escort of a gentleman in the evening. A gentleman at the house where she may call may return with her if she goes unattended; gossip and scandal are best avoided, however, if she have some one from her home call for her at an appointed hour.

It is courtesy to give silent, respectful attention as a funeral procession passes. It shows want of respect to pass between the carriages while the procession is moving.

Staring at people, spitting, looking back after they pass, saluting people across the street, calling out loudly or laughing at people as they go by, are all evidences of ill-breeding.

The gentleman accompanying a lady should hold the door open for the lady to enter first. Should he be near the door when a lady, unattended, is about to enter, he will do the same for her.

In the evening, or whenever safety may require, a gentleman should give a lady his arm. It is not customary in other cases to do so on the street, unless with an elderly lady, or the couple be husband and wife.

On the narrow street-crossing the gentleman will allow the lady to precede him, that he may see that no injury befalls her.

Should a lady stop in the street, when meeting a gentleman, it is courtesy for him to stop also. Should his business be urgent, he will apologize for not continuing the conversation, and ask to be excused. Should it be desirable to lengthen the interview, and the lady resumes her walk in the midst of her conversation, it is courtesy for him to turn and accompany her. Should she desire to end the conversation, a slight bow from her will indicate the fact, when he should bid her "good day" and take his leave.

* Some authorities claim that it is most sensible for the lady to walk always at the right of the gentleman, whether on the street or indoors; her right hand being thus free to hold trail, fan, or parasol.

Unclassified LAWS OF Etiquette.

IMPORTANT RULES OF CONDUCT.

NEVER exaggerate.

Never point at another.

Never betray a confidence.

Never wantonly frighten others.

Never leave home with unkind words.

Never neglect to call upon your friends.

Never laugh at the misfortunes of others.

Never give a promise that you do not fulfill.

Never send a present, hoping for one in return.

Never speak much of your own performances.

Never fail to be punctual at the time appointed.

Never make yourself the hero of your own story.

Never pick the teeth or clean the nails in company.

Never fail to give a polite answer to a civil question.

Never question a servant or a child about family matters.

Never present a gift saying that it is of no use to yourself.

Never read letters which you may find addressed to others.

Never fail, if a gentleman, of being civil and polite to ladies.

Never call attention to the features or form of anyone present.

Never refer to a gift you have made, or favor you have rendered.

Never associate with bad company. Have good company, or none.

Never look over the shoulder of another who is reading or writing.

Never appear to notice a scar, deformity, or defect of anyone present.

Never arrest the attention of an acquaintance by a touch. Speak to him.

Never punish your child for a fault to which you are addicted yourself.

Never answer questions in general company that have been put to others.

Never, when traveling abroad, be over boastful in praise of your own country.

Never call a new acquaintance by the Christian name unless requested to do so.

Never lend an article you have borrowed, unless you have permission to do so.

Never attempt to draw the attention of the company constantly upon yourself.

Never exhibit anger, impatience or excitement, when an accident happens.

Never pass between two persons who are talking together, without an apology.

Never enter a room noisily; never fail to close the door after you, and never slam it.

Never forget that, if you are faithful in a few things, you may be ruler over many.

Never exhibit too great familiarity with the new acquaintance; you may give offense.

Never will a gentleman allude to conquests which he may have made with ladies.

Never be guilty of the contemptible meanness of opening a private letter addressed to another.

Never fail to offer the easiest and best seat in the room to an invalid, an elderly person, or a lady.

Never neglect to perform the commission which the friend entrusted to you. You must not forget.

Never send your guest, who is accustomed to a warm room, off into a cold, damp, spare bed, to sleep.

Never enter a room filled with people, without a slight bow to the general company when first entering.

Never fail to answer an invitation, either personally or by letter, within a week after the invitation is received.

Never accept of favors and hospitalities without rendering an exchange of civilities when opportunity offers.

Never cross the leg and put out one foot in the street-car, or places where it will trouble others when passing by.

Never fail to tell the truth. If truthful, you get your reward. You will get your punishment if you deceive.

Never borrow money and neglect to pay. If you do, you will soon be known as a person of no business integrity.

Never write to another asking for information, or a favor of any kind, without inclosing a postage stamp for the reply.

Never fail to say kind and encouraging words to those whom you meet in distress. Your kindness may lift them out of their despair.

Never refuse to receive an apology. You may not revive friendship, but courtesy will require, when an apology is offered, that you accept it.

Never examine the cards in the card-basket. While they may be exposed in the drawing-room, you are not expected to turn them over unless invited to do so.

Never, when walking arm in arm with a lady, be continually changing and going to the other side, because of change of corners. It shows too much attention to form.

Never should the lady accept of expensive gifts at the hands of a gentleman not related or engaged to her. Gifts of flowers, books, music or confectionery may be accepted.

Never insult another by harsh words when applied to for a favor. Kind words do not cost much, and yet they may carry untold happiness to the one to whom they are spoken.

Never fail to speak kindly. If a merchant, and you address your clerk; if an overseer, and you address your workmen; if in any position where you exercise authority, you show yourself to be a gentleman by your pleasant mode of address.

Never attempt to convey the impression that you are a genius, by imitating the faults of distinguished men. Because certain great men were poor penmen, wore long hair, or had other peculiarities, it does not follow that you will be great by imitating their eccentricities.

Never give all your pleasant words and smiles to strangers. The kindest words and the sweetest smiles should be reserved for home. Home should be our heaven.

> "We have careful thought for the stranger,
> And smiles for the sometimes guest;
> But oft for our own the bitter tone,
> Though we love our own the best.
> Ah! lips with the curl impatient—
> Ah! brow with the shade of scorn,
> 'T were a cruel fate were the night too late
> To undo the work of the morn."

Etiquette Among Neighbors.

DIVISION FENCES BETWEEN HOUSES.

TO BE kind, and to treat politely the persons with whom we are immediately associated, is not all, nor should civility cease with the casual intercourse between neighbors; it should go beyond. We should regard the rights of the individual. Were all to do so, mankind would take a long stride in advance of the present selfish and thoughtless conduct which too often actuates even those who are reputed to be good and respectable.

This want of regard for the rights of others is shown in many ways. To illustrate:

The individual **who** will conduct a house or an establishment that is unpleasant, injurious to health, or detrimental to the community, evinces a disregard for the courtesy that is due to his neighbors.

The parents who allow children to annoy their neighbors, are always a most undesirable people to have in the vicinity.

The people of a community who will deliberately turn horses, cattle and hogs into the street, entirely disregarding the fact that the animals are liable to do much damage to others, demonstrate a lack of regard for neighbors which is inexcusable, and can only be explained on the ground that the habit is so common that they do not realize the injury they are doing.

The fact that we accosted Mr. Jones politely, and said pleasant things in his presence, was good so far as it went, but the further fact that we turned our cattle into the street, well knowing they were liable to trample Mr. Jones' sidewalk to pieces, and break down his trees, demonstrates that, while we are very agreeable to his face, we care but little what we may do behind his back.

This utter disregard for the wants of others causes people generally to become suspicious of their neighbors. It is true that this suspicion is gradually becoming lessened. The time was when the inhabitants built a castle as nearly as possible impregnable; around that was built a high enclosure, and still outside of that was a canal with a drawbridge. Gradually the fact has dawned that we need not be thus suspi-

cious. We need not build a house of stone, we need not construct a canal, but we still adhere to the high wall or fence, as we are oftentimes compelled to because of the disposition of the neighbor to trample upon our rights by allowing his animals to destroy our property.

The reader has doubtless seen a town in which the people allowed their domestic animals to run at large, the hogs to root the turf to pieces by the roadside, the cattle to destroy sidewalks, to break through fences and to tear down trees. This want of courtesy is not uncommon. In short, it is altogether too common in many towns of the country, and upon the part of the owners of animals it shows a complete disregard of the rights of those who would beautify their homes, and thus correspondingly beautify the town.

The code of etiquette should not alone apply among individuals when directly associated together. It should extend further. It should go out and permeate a neighborhood. It should diffuse itself throughout a town. It should bind together the people of a State— of a nation. It should be a rule of action among all nations. Already the evidences of courtesy among nations begins to manifest itself. The International Congress is based upon this principle. The idea of friendly association of the representatives of nations for mutual adjustment of differences, is the beginning of a recognition of the rights of each other.

This is evidence of a higher civilization. When we can rise superior to selfishness,

FIG. 22. PEOPLE WHO ARE TROUBLED BY THEIR NEIGHBORS.

The above illustration represents a common scene. The neighbors suspect each other, and they destroy the beauty of their grounds in the attempt to shut each other out. Suspicion and selfishness rule. Regardless of the rights of others, animals are allowed to trample to pieces the sidewalks, to destroy shade trees and to despoil the neighbor's yard. Inharmony, disorder, and ill-feeling among the people are characteristics of the neighborhood.

when we are willing to consider the rights and the requirements of others, when we are governed by the generous spirit of doing unto others as we would that they should do unto us, then we are directed by a power that will make an entire people, as a whole, what the laws of etiquette determine they shall be individually, in their intercourse with each other.

The illustration (Fig 22) upon this page represents a scene which may be observed in many villages or cities—a group of residences, modern and beautiful in architecture, surrounded and disfigured by high inclosures put up to guard against people who allow their cattle and other animals to destroy their neighbor's property.

Important Facts and Tables for Reference

Tabulated and Arranged for Writers and Speakers.

VALUE OF FOREIGN COINS IN U. S. MONEY.

Proclaimed by the Secretary of the Treasury, Jan. 1, 1884.

Country.	Monetary Unit.	Standard.	Value in U S Money.	Standard Coin.
Austria..	Florin	Silver	39.8.	
Belgium..	Franc	Gold and silver	19.3.	5, 10 and 20 francs
Bolivia	Boliviano	Silver.	80.6	Boliviano
Brazil	Milreis of 1000 reis.	Gold.	54.6.	
British Poss. in N. A.	Dollar	Gold	$1.00	
Chili	Peso	Gold	91.2.	Condor, doubloon and escudo.
Denmark	Crown	Gold	26.8.	10 and 20 crowns
Ecuador	Peso	Silver.	80.6.	Peso
Egypt	Piaster	Silver	04.9.	5, 10, 25, 50, and 100 piasters
France	Frank	Gold and silver	19.3.	5, 10 and 20 francs
Great Britain	Pound Sterling	Gold	4.86.6½	⅓ sovereign and sovereign.
Greece	Drachma	Gold and silver	19.3.	5, 10, 20, 50 and 100 drachmas.
German Empire.	Mark	Gold	23.8.	5, 10 and 20 marks.
India	Rupee of 16 annas.	Silver	38.3	
Italy	Lira	Gold and silver	19.3.	5, 10, 20, 50 and 100 lire.
Japan	Yen (gold)	Gold and silver	86.9.	5, 2, 5, 10 and 20 yen.
Liberia	Dollar	Gold	1.00	
Mexico	Dollar.	Silver	87.5.	Peso or dollar, 5, 10, 25 and 50
Netherlands.	Florin	Gold and silver	40.2.	[centavo
Norway	Crown	Gold	26.8.	10 and 20 crowns
Peru.	Sol	Silver	80.6.	Sol
Portugal	Milreis of 1000 reis.	Gold	1.08.	2, 5 and 10 milreis
Russia	Rouble of 100 copecks.	Silver.	64.5	¾, ½ and 1 rouble.
Sandwich Islands.	Dollar	Gold	1.00.	
Spain	Peseta of 100 centimes	Gold and silver.	19.3.	5, 10, 20, 50 and 100 pesetas.
Sweden	Crown	Gold	26.8.	10 and 20 crowns.
Switzerland	Franc	Gold and silver	19.3.	5, 10 and 20 francs.
Tripoli	Mahbub of 20 piasters.	Silver	72.7.	
Turkey	Piaster	Gold	04.4.	25, 50, 100, 250 and 500 piasters
U. S. of Columbia.	Peso	Silver.	80.6	Peso
Venezuela	Bolivar	Gold and silver	19.3.	5, 10, 20, 50 and 100 Bolivar

GOVERNORS, STATE SENATORS AND REPRESENTATIVES.

Salaries and Terms of Office.*

States and Territories.	Salary of Governors.	Term of office of Governors.	Pay of Members of the Legislature.	Term of office of Senators.	Term of Representatives.	When the Legislature meets.	Limit of Session.
Alabama	$ 3,000.	2 years.	$4 per day	4 years	2 years	Biennially	50 days
Arizona	2,600.	4 "	4. "	2 "	2 "	Biennially	40. "
Arkansas	3,500.	4 "	6. "	4 "	2 "	Biennially	60. "
California	6,000.	4 "	8. "	4 "	4 "	Biennially	60. "
Colorado	3,000.	2 "	4. "	4 "	2 "	Biennially	40. "
Connecticut	2,000.	2 "	300 per session	2 "	1 "	Annually	None.
Dakota	2,600.	4 "	4 per day	2 "	2 "	Biennially	40 days
Delaware	2,000.	4 "	3. "	4 "	2 "	Biennially	None
Florida	3,500.	4 "	6. "	4 "	2 "	Biennially	60 days
Georgia	4,000.	2 "	4. "	4 "	2 "	Biennially	40. "
Idaho	2,600.	4 "	4. "	2 "	2 "	Biennially	40. "
Illinois	6,000.	4 "	5. "	4 "	2 "	Biennially	None
Indiana	6,000.	4 "	6. "	4 "	2 "	Biennially	60 days
Iowa	3,000.	2 "	550 per session	4 "	2 "	Biennially	None
Kansas	3,000.	2 "	3 per day	4 "	2 "	Biennially	50 days
Kentucky	5 000.	4 "	5. "	4 "	2 "	Biennially	60 days
Louisiana	4,000.	4 "	4. "	4 "	4 "	Biennially	90. "
Maine	1,500.	2 "	150 per session	2 "	2 "	Biennially	None
Maryland	4,500.	4 "	5 per day	4 "	2 "	Biennially	90 days
Massachusetts.	5,000.	1 "	650 per session.	1 "	1 "	Annually	None
Michigan	1,000.	2 "	3 per day	2 "	2 "	Biennially	None
Minnesota	3,000.	2 "	5. "	2 "	1 "	Biennially	60 days
Mississippi	4,000.	4 "	300 per session	4 "	2 "	Biennially	None
Missouri	5,000.	4 "	5 per day	4 "	2 "	Biennially	70 days
Montana	2,600.	4 "	4. "	2 "	2 "	Biennially	40. "
Nebraska	2,500.	2 "	3. "	4 "	2 "	Biennially	40. "
Nevada	6,000.	4 "	8. "	4 "	2 "	Biennially	60. "
New Hampshire	1,000.	2 "	3. "	2 "	2 "	Biennially	None
New Mexico.	2,600.	4 "	4. "	2 "	2 "	Biennially	40 days
New Jersey	5,000.	3 "	500 per session	3 "	1 "	Annually	None
New York	10,000.	3 "	1500. "	2 "	1 "	Annually	None
North Carolina.	3,000.	4 "	4 per day	4 "	2 "	Biennially	60 days
Ohio	4,000.	2 "	5. "	2 "	2 "	Annually	None
Oregon	1,500.	4 "	3. "	4 "	2 "	Biennially	40 days
Pennsylvania	10,000.	4 "	1000 per session	4 "	2 "	Biennially	None
Rhode Island.	4,000.	1 "	1 per day	1 "	1 "	Annually	None
South Carolina.	4,500.	2 "	5. "	4 "	2 "	Annually	None
Tennessee.	4,000.	2 "	4. "	4 "	2 "	Biennially	75 days
Texas	4,000.	2 "	5. "	4 "	2 "	Biennially	60 days
Utah	2,600.	4 "	4. "	4 "	2 "	Biennially	40. "
Vermont	1,000.	2 "	3. "	2 "	2 "	Biennially	None
Virginia	5,000.	4 "	540 per session	4 "	2 "	Biennially	90 days
Washington	2,600.	4 "	4 per day	2 "	2 "	Biennially	40. "
West Virginia.	2,700.	4 "	4. "	4 "	2 "	Biennially	45. "
Wisconsin	5,000.	2 "	500 per session	2 "	2 "	Biennially	None
Wyoming	2,600.	4 "	4 per day	2 "	2 "	Biennially	40 days

*From 5 cents to 40 cents per mile is allowed representatives, in some States, in going to and from the seat of government.

Annual Salaries of Principal United States Civil, Military and Naval Officers.

Legislative.

President	$50,000
Vice President	8,000
Secretary of State	8,000
Secretary of Treasury	8,000
Secretary of Interior	8,000
Secretary of Navy	8,000
Secretary of War	8,000
Postmaster General	8,000
Attorney General	8,000
Speaker House of Representatives.	8,000
United States Senators	5,000
Representatives in Congress	5,000

U. S. Minister to

England	$17,500
Germany	17,500
France	17,500
Russia	17,500
China	12,000
Brazil	12,000
Spain	12,000
Japan	12,000
Mexico	12,000
Central America	10,000
Chili	10,000
Peru	10,000
Venezuela	7,500
Turkey	7,500
Sweden and Norway	7,500
Netherlands	7,500
Denmark.	5,000
Greece	5,000
Uruguay	5,000
Portugal	5,000
Switzerland	5,000
Liberia	4,000

Judges.

Chief Justice U. S. Supreme Court	$10,500
Associate Judges	10,000
United States Circuit Judges	6,000
U. S. District Judges, from 3,500 to	5,000
Judge of U. S. Court of Claims	4,500

Heads of Departments.

Director of Geological Surveys	$6,000
Auditor of Railroad Accounts	5,000
Superintendent of Census	5,000
Superintendent Naval Observatory	5,000
Commissioner of Patents	4,500
Director of the Mint.	4,500
Commissioner of General Land Office.	4,000
Superintendent Signal Service.	4,000
Commissioner of Pensions.	3,600
Superintendent Nautical Almanac	3,500
Commander of Marine Corps.	3,500
Commissioner of Agriculture.	3,000
Commissioner of Indian Affairs.	3,000
Commissioner of Education.	3,000

Army and Navy.

MILITARY OFFICERS.

General of the Army	$13,500
Lieutenant General	11,000
Major Generals.	7,500
Brigadier Generals.	5,500
Colonels	3,500
Lieutenant Colonels	3,000
Majors	2,500
Captains, Mounted.	2,000
Captains, not Mounted	1,800
First Lieutenants, Mounted	1,600
First Lieutenants, not Mounted	1,500
Second Lieutenants, Mounted	1,500
Second Lieutenants, not Mounted	1,400
Chaplains	1,500

NAVAL OFFICERS.

Admirals	$13,000
Vice Admirals	9,000
Rear Admirals	6,000
Commodores	5,000
Captains	4,500
Commanders	3,500
Lieutenant Commanders	2,800
Lieutenants	2,400
Masters	1,800
Ensigns	1,200
Midshipmen	1,000

TABLES OF WEIGHTS, MEASURES, AND VARIATION OF TIME.

WEIGHTS.

Troy.

24 grains (gr.) 1 pennyw'ht,—dwt.
20 dwts ....1 ounce,— oz.
3.2 grains, 1 carat, diamond wt.

By this weight gold, silver, and jewels only are weighed. The ounce and pound in this, are the same as in apothecaries' weight.

Apothecaries'.

20 grains................1 scruple.
3 scruples.............1 drachm.
8 drs.....................1 ounce.
12 ozs........ ...... 1 pound.

Avoirdupois.

16 drams (drs.) 1 ounce,— oz.
16 ozs. ....1 pound,— lb.
25 lbs. ....1 quarter,—qr.*
4 quarters.....100 weight,— cwt.
20 cwts......... 1 ton.

* Formerly 28 lbs. were allowed to the quarter, but the practice is now nearly out of use excepting in the coal mines in Pennsylvania, the Eastern fish markets, and the U.S. Custom House.

Grains are the same in each of the above weights.

5,760 grains, apothecaries' or troy weight.................1 lb.
7,000 grains, avoirdupois weight...................1 lb.
Therefore, 144 lbs. avoir. equal 175 lbs. apoth. or troy.

Of Liquids.

1 gallon oil weighs 9.32 lbs. avoir.
1 gallon distilled water, 8.35 lbs.
1 gallon sea water, 10.32 lbs.
1 gallon proof spirits, 9.08 lbs.

Miscellaneous.

IRON, LEAD, ETC.

14 lbs.....................1 stone.
21½ stones...............1 pig.
8 pigs....................1 fother.

BEEF, PORK, ETC.

200 lbs....................1 barrel.
196 lbs. (flour)..........1 barrel.
100 lbs. (fish)...........1 quintal.

MEASURES.

Dry.

2 pints .... 1 quart,— qt.
8 quarts .... 1 peck,— pk.
4 pecks .... 1 bushel,— bu.
36 bushels.. .... 1 chaldron.

1 United States standard (Winchester) bushel — 18½ inches in diameter, and 8 inches deep—contains 2150.42 cubic inches.

Liquid or Wine.

4 gills ....1 pint—pt,
2 pints ....1 quart—qt.
4 quarts........1 gallon—gal.
31½ gallons.....1 barrel—bbl.
2 barrels.......1 hogshead—hhd.
U. S. standard
gallon........231 cubic inches.
Beer gallon ...231 " "
31 " ....1 bbl.

Time.

60 seconds ...1 minute.
60 minutes........1 hour.
24 hours.........1 day.
7 days............1 week.
4 weeks.........1 lunar month.
28, 29, 30, or } 1 calendar month.
31 days, }
30 days.....1 month, (in computing interest).
52 weeks and 1 day.... } 1 year.
12 calendar months... }
365 days, 5 hours, 48 minutes, and 49 seconds.....1 solar year.

Circular.

60 seconds........... 1 minute,
60 minutes...........1 degree.
30 degrees.............1 sign.
90 degrees...........1 quadrant.
4 quadrants.......... } 1 circle.
360 degrees............. }

A convenient method of finding the difference in time between two places, is to notice their distance apart in degrees of longitude, and allow 4 minutes to each degree, based on the following

CALCULATION:

1440 minutes........... ....1 day, or revolution of the earth.
1 revolution of the earth is 360 degrees; therefore,
1 degree............4 minutes.

MEASURES.

Long.

DISTANCE.

3 barleycorns..1 inch,— in.
12 ins. ....1 foot,— ft.
3 ft.............1 yard,— yd.
5½ yds..........1 rod,— rd.
40 rds ....1 furlong,— fur.
8 fur ....1 mile.

CLOTH.

2¼ inches............1 nail.
4 nails.................1 quarter.
4 quarters........ ...1 yard.

MISCELLANEOUS.

3 inches............1 palm.
4 inches............1 hand.
6 inches............1 span.
18 inches............1 cubit.
21.8 inches.........1 Bible cubit.
2½ feet..........1 military pace.
3 feet............1 common pace.

Square.

144 sq. ins.............1 sq. foot.
9 sq. ft.............1 sq. yard.
30¼ sq. yds...........1 sq. rod.
40 sq. rods...........1 rood.
4 roods..................1 acre.

Surveyors'.

7.92 inches.........1 link.
25 links..............1 rod.
4 rods................1 chain.
10 square chains. } 1 acre.
160 square rods.... }
640 acres.............1 square mile

Cubic.

1728 cubic inches... ..1 cubic foot.
27 cubic feet.....1 cubic yard.
128 cubic feet .....1 cord (wood.)
40 cubic feet...1 ton (shipping.)
2150.42 cubic in...1 standard bu.
268.8 " ..1 " gal.
1 cubic ft., four-fifths of a bushel.

To find the number of bushels in a bin of any dimensions, find the number of cubic feet by multiplying the three dimensions of the bin in feet; deduct one-fifth, and the result is the number of bushels.

PAPER.

The Sizes in Inches.

Flat Writing-Papers.

Flat Letter....................10 x 16
Flat Cap...................14 x 17
Double Flat Letter.......16 x 20
Flat Foolscap.........13 x 16
Crown.....................15 x 19
Folio Post..................17 x 22
Demy.....................16 x 21
Medium ....18 x 23
Check Folio...............17 x 24
Bank Folio...............19 x 24
Double Cap...............17 x 28
Royal.....................19 x 24
Super Royal.............20 x 28
Imperial ....23 x 31

Of the different sizes there are also several different weights of each size, as Demy 20, 22, 24, 26, and 28 lbs. per ream.

Stationers usually rule, cut and fold the sizes required to make the various styles of letter and note papers—a flat sheet making one, two or four sheets of letter or note paper.

Ledger Papers.

Flat Cap....................14 x 17
Crown ....15 x 19
Folio......................17 v 22
Demy......................16 x 21
Medium ....18 x 23
Royal ....19 x 24
Super Royal............20 x 28
Imperial...................23 x 31
Elephant...................23 x 28

Book Papers.

The usual sizes of these, from the different American and English manufacturers, differ but little from the above, except to fill special orders.

Paper Counts.

24 sheets..................1 quire.
10½ quires..............1 token.
20 quires................1 ream.
2 reams.................1 bundle.
5 bundles...............1 bale.

Units of Anything.

12 pieces...........1 dozen.
12 dozen..... ....1 gross.
12 gross.... ....1 great gross.
20 units ....1 score,

Railway Signals.

One pull of bell-cord signifies "stop."
Two pulls mean "go ahead."
Three pulls signify "back up."
One whistle signifies "down brakes."
Two whistles mean " off brakes."
Three whistles signify "back up."
Continued whistles indicate "danger."
Rapid short whistles, "a cattle alarm."
A sweeping parting of the hands, on a level with the eyes, signifies " go ahead."
A slowly sweeping meeting of the hands, over the head, means "back slowly."
Downward motion of the hands, with extended arms, signifies "stop."
Beckoning motion of one hand, indicates "back."
A red flag waved up the track, signifies "danger."
A red flag standing by the roadside, means "danger ahead."
A red flag carried on a locomotive, signifies "an engine following."
A red flag raised at a station, is a signal to stop."
A lantern at night raised and lowered vertically, is a signal to "start."
A lantern swung at right angles across the track, means "stop."
A lantern swung in a circle, signifies "back the train."

Difference of Time between Washington and other Cities of the World.

12.00 o'clock (noon) at.........WASHINGTON.		
12.12 .. " .....P.M..............New York.		
12.24 .. " ...... " ....Boston.		
12.27 .. " ...... " ....Portland.		
1.37 .. " ...... " ....St. John (N. F.)		
3.19 .. " ...... " ....Angra (Azores).		
4.31 .. " ...... " ....Lisbon.		
4.43 .. " ...... " ....Dublin.		
4.55 .. " ...... " ....Edinburgh.		
5.07 .. " ...... " ....London.		
5.17 .. " ...... " ....Paris.		
5.58 .. " ...... " ....Rome.		
6.02 .. " ...... " ....Berlin.		
6.14 .. " ...... " ....Vienna.		
6.23 .. " ...... " ....Cape Town.		
7.04 .. " ...... " ....Constantinople.		
11.01 .. " ...... " ....Calcutta.		
12.54 .. " .....A.M..............Pekin.		
2.48 .. " ...... " ....Melbourne.		
4.51 .. " ...... " ....Auckland.		
8.58 .. " ...... " ....San Francisco.		
9.40 .. " ...... " ....Salt Lake.		
11.08 .. " ..... " ....New Orleans.		
11.18 .. " ...... " ....Chicago.		
11.52 .. " ...... " ....Buffalo.		
12.00 .. " ....(noon)............Lima (Peru).		

United States Land Measure.†

TOWNSHIP.

6	5	4	3	2	1
7	8	9	10	11	12
18	17	16	15	14	13
19	20	21	22	23	24
30	29	28	27	26	25
31	32	33	34	35	36

SECTION.

N. W.	N. E.
S. W.	S. E.

Each section has four quarter-sections, designated as above, each containing 160 acres.

† In Several States.

The township is six miles square, divided into 36 square miles or sections, numbered as above, each containing 640 acres.

SMALLER LAND DIVISIONS.

The following table will assist in making an estimate of the amount of land in fields and lots.

§ 10 rods x 16 rods...............1 acre.
† 5 yards x 968 yards...............1 "
‡ 220 feet x 198 feet.................1 "
25 feet x 125 feet.................0717 "
4356 sq. ft., .10 acre. 10890 sq. ft., .25 "
21780 " .50 " 32670 " .75 "
§ Or any two numbers whose product is 160.
† Or any two numbers whose product is 4,840.
‡ Or any two numbers whose product is 43,560.

Weights of a Cubic Foot.

Metals.

WEIGHT OF A CUBIC FOOT.

Substance.	*Lbs.*	*Oz.*
Platina	1,218	12
Pure Gold*	1,203	10
Mercury	848	12
Lead	709	8
Pure Silver†	625	13
Steel	487	12
Tin	455	11
Cast Iron	450	7
Copper	547	4
Brass	543	12
Zinc	428	13

*The value of a ton of pure gold is $602,799.21.

†The value of a ton of silver is $37,704.84.

*$1,000,000 gold coin weigh 3,685.8 lbs. avordupois.

†$1,000,000 silver coin weigh 58,929.9 lbs. avordupois.

Earth, Stone, &c.

Substance.	*Lbs.*	*Oz.*
Italian Marble	169	4
Vermont Marble	165	9
Window Glass	165	2
Common Stone	157	8
Moist Sand	128	2
Clay	120	10
Brick	118	12
Mortar	109	6
Mud	101	14
Loose Earth	93	12
Lehigh Coal, loose,	56	4
Lackawanna, loose,	48	10

Liquids.

Substance.	*Lbs.*	*Oz.*
Honey	90	10
Vinegar	67	8
Blood	65	14
Beer	64	10
Milk	64	8
Cider	63	10
Tar	63	7
Rain Water	62	8
Linseed Oil	58	12
Brandy	57	12
Ice	57	8
Alcohol	49	10

Groceries.

WEIGHT OF A CUBIC FOOT.

Substance.	*Lbs.*	*Oz.*
Sugar	100	5
Beeswax	60	5
Lard	59	3
Butter	58	14
Tallow	58	13
Castile Soap	56	15

Miscellaneous.

Substance.	*Lbs.*	*Oz.*
India Rubber	56	7
Pressed Hay	25	
Pressed Cotton	25	

Woods.

Substance.	*Lbs.*	*Oz.*
Lignum Vitæ	83	5
Ebony	83	5
Boxwood	75	2
Mahogany	66	7
White Oak	53	12
Ash	52	13
Red Hickory	52	6
Apple	49	9
Maple	46	14
Cherry	44	11
Shellbark Hickory	43	2
Pitch Pine	41	4
Chestnut	38	2
Birch	35	7
Cedar	35	1
White Poplar	33	1
Spruce	31	4
Yellow Pine	28	13
Butternut	23	8
Cork	15	...

Difference in Weight of Wood, Green and Dry.

GREEN.		
Substance.	*Lbs.*	*Oz.*
English Oak	71	10
Beech	60	
Ash	58	3
American Pine	44	12
DRY.		
English Oak	43	8
Beech	53	4
Ash	52	6
American Pine	30	11

Woods for Fuel.

Taking shellbark hickory as the highest standard of our forest trees, and calling that one hundred, other trees will compare with it in real value, for fuel, as follows·

Shellbark Hickory	100
Pignut Hickory	95
White Oak	84
White Ash	77
Dogwood	75
Scrub-Oak	73
White Hazel	72
Apple Tree	70
White Beech	69
Black Birch	65
Hard Maple	65
Black Walnut	62
Yellow Oak	60
White Elm	58
Red Oak	56
Red Cedar	56
Wild Cherry	55
Yellow Pine	54
Chestnut	52
Yellow Poplar	51
Butternut	43
White Birch	43
White Pine	30

Quantity Per Acre.

The following shows the average yield of different grasses and vegetables per acre.

Article.	*Amount.*
Barley	30 bushels
Buckwheat	25 bushels
Beans, bush	20 bushels
Beets	10 tons
Cabbages, without stalks	20 tons
Carrots	10 tons
Corn	30 bushels
Clover hay	2 tons
Millet seed	50 bushels
Meadow hay	1½ tons
Oats	40 bushels
Peas	20 bushels
Parsnips	10 tons
Potatoes	200 bushels
Rice	25 bushels
Rye	20 bushels
Rutabagas	10 tons
Turnips	10 tons
Wheat	20 bushels

Heat and Cold.

Degrees of heat above zero at which substances melt.

Substance.	*Deg.*
Wrought Iron	3,980
Cast Iron	3,479
Platinum	3,080
Gold	2,590
Copper	2,548
Steel	2,500
Glass	2,377
Brass	1,900
Silver	1,250
Antimony	951
Zinc	740
Lead	594
Tin	421
Arsenic	365
Sulphur	226
Beeswax	151
Gutta Percha	145
Tallow	97
Lard	95
Pitch	91
Ice	33

Degrees of cold above zero at which substances freeze.

Olive Oil	36
Water	32
Milk	30
Sea Water	28
Vinegar	28
Wines	20
Spirits of Turpentine	14

Degrees below zero at which the following freeze:

Brandy	7
Proof Spirit	7
Mercury	40

Cold experienced by Arctic Navigators.....70

Greatest Artific'l Cold. 220

Degrees of heat above zero at which substances boil.

Ether	98
Alcohol	173
Water	212
Petroleum	306
Linseed Oil	640

Blood Heat............ 98

Eggs Hatch............104

AGES OF ANIMALS.

Periods of Gestation and Incubation

Animals and Birds.	Age to which they live.	Period of Gestation and Incuba'n
Elephant	100	23 mo's
Camel	100	12 "
Swan	100	1½ "
Raven	100	¾ "
Crow	100	¾ "
Parrot	100	1½ "
Goose	80	1 "
Lion	70	5 "
Horse	30	11 "
Cow	20	9 "
Swine	20	4 "
Wolf	20	3 "
Peafowl	20	1 "
Pigeon	20	½ "
Cat	15	2 "
Fox	15	2 "
Dog	14	2 "
Sheep	10	5 "
Hen	10	¾ "
Canary	10	½ "
Rabbit	7	¾ "

Rates of Speed

At which Birds Fly.

PER HOUR.

Birds.	*Miles.*
Hawks	150
Sparrows	92
Ducks	90
Falcon	75
Crows	25

Fair winds make their flight much more rapid.

Interest.

Money Doubles at Compound Interest as follows:

At	3	per cent.	in	23	years.
"	4	"	"	17	"
"	5	"	"	14	"
"	6	"	"	12	"
"	7	"	"	10	"
"	8	"	"	9	"
"	9	"	"	8	"
"	10	"	"	7	"

TABLE OF WAGES;

COMPUTED ON A BASIS OF TEN HOURS LABOR PER DAY.

Hours	$1.00	$1.50	$2.00	$2.50	$3.00	$3.50	$4.00	$4.50	$5.00	$5.50	$6.00	$6.50	$7.00	$7.50	$8.00	$9.00	$10	$11	$12
½	.1	.1¼	.1⅔	.2	.2½	3	.3⅓	.3¾	.4⅙	.4½	.5	.5½	.6	.6¼	.6⅔	.7½	.8⅓	.9	.10
1	.1⅔	.2½	.3⅓	.4⅙	.5	.6	.6⅔	.7½	.8⅓	.9⅙	.10	.11	.11⅔	.12½	.13⅓	.15	.16⅔	.18⅓	.20
2	.3⅓	.5	.6⅔	.8⅓	.10	.11⅔	.13⅓	.15	.16⅔	.18⅓	.20	.21⅔	.23⅓	.25	.26⅔	.30	.33⅓	.36⅔	.40
3	.5	.7½	.10	.12½	.15	.17½	.20	.22½	.25	.27½	.30	.32½	.35	.37½	.40	.45	.50	.55	.60
4	.6⅔	.10	.13⅓	.16⅔	.20	.23⅓	.26⅔	.30	.33⅓	.36⅔	.40	.43⅓	.46⅔	.50	.53⅓	.60	.66⅔	.73⅓	.80
5	.8⅓	.12½	.16⅔	.21	.25	.29⅙	.33⅓	.37½	.41⅔	.46	.50	.54⅙	.58⅓	.62½	.66⅔	.75	. 83⅓	.91⅔	1.00
6	.10	.15	.20	25	.30	.35	.40	.45	.50	.55	.60	.65	.70	.75	.80	.90	1.00	1.10	1.20
7	.11⅔	.17½	.23⅓	.29⅙	.35	.41	.46⅔	.52½	.58⅓	.64⅙	.70	.76	.81⅔	.87½	.93⅓	1.05	1.16⅔	1.28⅓	1.40
8	.13⅓	.20	.26⅔	.33⅓	.40	.46⅔	.53⅓	.60	.66⅔	.73⅓	.80	.86⅔	.93⅓	1.00	1.06⅔	1.20	1.33⅓	1.46⅔	1.60
9	.15	.22½	.30	.37½	.45	.52½	.60	.67½	75	.82½	.90	.97½	1.05	1.12½	1.20	1.35	1.50	1.65	1.80
Days........																			
1	.16⅔	.25	.33⅓	.41⅔	.50	.58⅓	.66⅔	.75	.83⅓	.91⅔	1.00	1.08⅓	1.16⅔	1.25	1.33⅓	1.50	1.66⅔	1.83⅓	2.00
2	.33⅓	.50	.66⅔	.83⅓	1.00	1.16⅔	1.33⅓	1.50	1.66⅔	1.83⅓	2.00	2.16⅔	2.33⅓	2.50	2.66⅔	3.00	3.33⅓	3.66⅔	4.00
3	.50	.75	1.00	1.25	1.50	1.75	2.00	2.25	2.50	2.75	3.00	3.25	3.50	3.75	4.00	4.50	5.00	5.50	6.00
4	.66⅔	1.00	1.33⅓	1.66⅔	2.00	2.33⅓	2.66⅔	3.00	3.33⅓	3.66⅔	4.00	4.33⅓	4.66⅔	5.00	5.33⅓	6.00	6.66⅔	7.33⅓	8.00
5	.83⅓	1.25	1.66⅔	2.08⅓	2.50	2.91⅔	3.33⅓	3.75	4.16⅔	4.58⅓	5.00	5.41⅔	5.83⅓	6.25	6.66⅔	7.50	8.33⅓	9.16⅔	10.00
6	1.00	1.50	2.00	2.50	3.00	3.50	4.00	4.50	5.00	5.50	6.00	6.50	7.00	7.50	8.00	9.00	10.00	11.00	12.00

EXPLANATION.

The large figures at the top of the columns show the rate per week, while the smaller figures indicate the amount per hour or per day. Thus if it is desired to find the amount per hour when working for **$8.00** per week, we commence with the figure **1**, in the left hand column under the head of "hours," and trace towards the right till we reach the column headed by **$8.00**, where we find 13⅓ cents, the equivalent of one hour's labor at $8.00 per week. In like manner we find the price of several hours, one day, or several days.

To find wages at **$13**, **$14**, **$15**, **$16**, or more, per week, find the amount at **$6.50**, **$7**, **$7.50**, **$8**, etc., and multiply by **2**.

POPULATION AND GROWTH OF THE UNITED STATES.

STATES AND TERRITORIES.	AREA IN SQUARE MILES.	NO. OF INHABITANTS. 1870	1880	No. Inhab. to Sq. Mile in 1880.*	M's R. R. in each State Jan. 1, 1884
Albaama	52,250	996,992	1,262,505	24	2,059
Arkansas	53,850	484,471	802,525	44	1,732
California	158,360	560,247	864,694	5	2,881
Colorado	103,925	39,864	194,327	1	2,832
Connecticut	4,990	537,454	622,700	124	963
Delaware	2,050	125,015	146,608	71	282
Florida	58,680	187,748	269,493	4	1,157
Georgia	59,475	1,184,109	1,542,180	25	2,933
Illinois	56,650	2,539,891	3,077,871	54	9,028
Indiana	36,350	1,680,637	1,978,301	54	5,543
Iowa	56,025	1,191,792	1,624,615	28	7,216
Kansas	82,080	364,399	996,096	12	3,964
Kentucky	40,400	1,321,011	1,648,690	40	1,852
Louisiana	48,720	726,915	939,946	19	1,204
Maine	33,040	626,915	648,936	19	1,099
Maryland	12,210	780,894	934,943	76	1,098
Massachusetts	8,315	1,457,351	1,783,085	214	1,979
Michigan	58,915	1,184,059	1,636,937	27	5,151
Minnesota	83,365	439,706	780,773	9	3,906
Mississippi	46,810	827,922	1,131,597	24	1,616
Missouri	69,415	1,721,295	2,168,380	31	4,619
Nebraska	76,855	123,993	452,402	5	2,696
Nevada	110,700	42,491	62,266		948
New Hampshire	9,305	318,300	346,991	37	1,042
New Jersey	7,815	906,096	1,131,116	144	1,874
New York	49,170	4,382,759	5,082,871	103	7,349
North Carolina	52,250	1,071,361	1,399,750	26	1,812
Ohio	41,060	2,665,260	3,198,062	77	7,217
Oregon	96,030	90,923	174,768	1	950
Pennsylvania	45,215	3,521,791	4,282,891	94	7,236
Rhode Island	1250	217,353	276,531	221	211

STATES AND TERRITORIES.	AREA IN SQUARE MILES.	NO. OF INHABITANTS. 1870	1880	No. Inhab. to Sq. Mile in 1880.*	M's R. R. in each State Jan. 1, 1884
South Carolina	30,570	705,606	995,577	32	1,549
Tennessee	42,050	1,258,520	1,542,359	36	2,112
Texas	265,780	818,579	1,591,749	5	6,075
Vermont	9,565	330,551	332,286	34	937
Virginia	42,450	1,225,163	1,512,565	34	2,553
West Virginia	24,780	442,014	618,457	24	948
Wisconsin	56,040	1,054,670	1,315,497	23	4,039
TERRITORIES					
Alaska	557,390		30,178		
Arizona	113,020	9,658	40,440		866
Dakota	149,100	14,181	135,177	1	2,495
Dist. of Columb	70	131,700	177,624	2,537	21
Idaho	84,800	14,999	32,610		777
Indian Territory	64,690		75,000	1	353
Montana	146,080	20,595	39,159		1,032
New Mexico	122,580	91,874	5,119,565		1,140
Utah	84,970	86,786	143,963	1	1,124
Washington	69,180	23,955	75,116	1	498
Wyoming	97,890	9,118	20,789		625
Other lands	5,740				
	3,602,270	38,555,983	50,155,783		121,592

* In several States there is nearly one person more to the square mile than is here mentioned.

₊ Between Jan. 1, 1884, and Nov. 7, 1884, in addition to the above, there were constructed 3,192 miles of Railroad in the United States and Territories.

Principal Countries of the World; Population, Area, Religion and Government.

Country.	Population.	Date of Census.	Area of Square Miles.	Inhabitants to Sq. Mile.	Capital.	Population.	Prevailing Religion.	Form of Government.
China (Est), including Corea	388,631,975	1882	4,503,788	86.3	Peking	1,648,890	Buddhic	Empire
India	253,906,449	1881	1,383,504	184	Calcutta	871,504	Hindoo	Empire
Russia (Estimated)	102,682,124	1884	8,520,637	12	St. Petersburg	929,100	Greek Church	Empire
United States, and Territories	50,497,057	1880	38,629,012	14.5	Washington	147,307	Protestant	Republic
German Empire	45,234,061	1880	212,028	213	Berlin	1,122,360	Protestant	Monarchy
Austria-Hungary	37,786,346	1880	210,942	157	Vienna	1,103,857	Catholic	Monarchy
France	37,672,048	1881	204,092	184	Paris	2,239,928	Catholic	Republic
Japan	36,700,118	1882	148,456	247.3	Tokio	823	Buddhic	Empire
Great Britain and Ireland	35,026,108	1881	120,832	290	London	4,764,312	Protestant	Monarchy
Italy	28,459,451	1881	114,926	249	Rome	273,268	Catholic	Monarchy
Turkish Empire (Estimated)	42,209,359	1883	2,406,492	17.5	Constantinople	600,000	Mohammedan	Monarchy
Spain (Estimated)	16,061,859	1877	182,752	85	Madrid	397,690	Catholic	Monarchy
British America	4,324,810	1881	3,470,392	1.2	Ottawa	27,412	Protestant	Monarchy
Brazil	9,448,233	1872	3,275,326	3	Rio Janeiro	350,000	Catholic	Monarchy
Mexico (Estimated)	10,008,882	1882	743,948	13.5	Mexico City	300,000	Catholic	Republic
Belgium	5,655,197	1882	11,373	497	Brussels	389,782	Catholic	Monarchy
Bavaria	5,284,778	1880	29,375	180	Munich	230,023	Catholic	Monarchy
Sweden	4,603,595	1883	170,979	27	Stockholm	194,469	Protestant	Monarchy
Persia (Estimated)	7,653,600	1881	610,000	12.5	Teheran	100,000	Mohammedan	Monarchy
Portugal	4,160,315	1878	36,510	114	Lisbon	246,343	Catholic	Monarchy
Holland-Netherlands	4,225,065	1883	12,648	334.8	The Hague	131,417	Protestant	Monarchy
Columbia	4,000,000	1881	504,773	7.9	Bogota	100,000	Catholic	Republic
Switzerland	2,846,102	1880	15,992	178	Berne	44,087	Protestant	Confederation
Peru	3,049,945	1876	503,718	6	Lima	101,488	Catholic	Republic
Australasia	3,091,897	1883	3,075,135	1	*		Protestant	Monarchy
Chili (Estimated)	2,377,949	1884	256,390	9.3	Santiago	200,000	Catholic	Republic
Bolivia	2,300,000	1880	Unknown		La Paz	76,372	Catholic	Republic
Denmark (Estimated)	2,018,432	1882	13,784	146.4	Copenhagen	273,323	Protestant	Monarchy
Wurttemberg	1,971,118	1880	7,675	256.8	Stuttgart	117,303	Protestant	Monarchy
Norway	1,925,000	1881	122,869	15	Christiania	124,155	Protestant	Monarchy
Venezuela	2,121,988	1884	632,695	3.3	Caracas	55,638	Catholic	Republic
Argentine Republic	3,026,000	1882	1,125,086	2.7	Buenos Ayres	295,000	Catholic	Republic
Greece	1,979,305	1881	25,041	79	Athens	84,903	Greek Church	Monarchy
Baden	1,570,254	1880	5,851	271.8	Karlsruhe	49,998	Catholic	Grand Duchy
Guatemala	1,278,311	1884	41,830	2.9	New Guatemala	55,728	Catholic	Republic
Ecuador (Estimated)	1,066,137	1875	251 22	4.3	Quito	80,000	Catholic	Republic
Hesse	947,224	1882	2,866	330.5	Darmstadt	48,153	Protestant	Grand Duchy
Liberia	1,068,000	1880	14,300	74.7	Monrovia	13,000	Protestant	Republic
Hayti (Estimated)	800,000	1880	10,204	78.2	Port au Prince	35,000	Catholic	Republic
Uruguay	700,000	1884	73,538	9.4	Montevideo	115,500	Catholic	Republic
San Salvador	554,785	1883	7,225	77	San Salvador	18,500	Catholic	Republic
Nicaragua	275,815	1884	49,500	5.6	Managua	12,000	Catholic	Republic
Honduras	458,000	1884	39,600	10.6	Tegucigalpa	12,000	Catholic	Republic
San Domingo	350,000	1883	18,045	22	San Domingo	10,000	Catholic	Republic
Paraguay	476,048	1879	91,970	5	Asuncion	16,000	Catholic	Republic
Costa Rica	180,000	1879	26,040	7	San Jose	2,000	Catholic	Republic
Hawaii (Estimated)	73,000	1883	6,677	10.8	Honolulu	7,000	Protestant	Monarchy

* Australasia has seven organized colonies—New South Wales, Victoria, Queensland, South Australia, Western Australia, New Zealand and Tasmania, whose respective capitals, with the population of each city, are as follows: Sidney (1884). 250,000; Melbourne (1883), 282.947; Brisbane (1883), 36,109; Adelaide (1881), 38,479; Perth (1881), 5.044; Auckland (1881), 39,966; Hobart (1881), 21,118. There is no general seat of government in Australasia, the whole being controlled by the home government in England.

Area and Population of the Earth.

Divisions.	*Area in Sq. Miles.*	*Population.*	*Pop. to Sq. Mile.*
America	15,258,686	100,415,400	6.6
Europe	3,700,000	327,743,400	88.6
Asia	16,770,000	795,591,000	47.4
Africa	12,000'000	205,823,200	17.1
Australasia	3,156,841	2,862,103	
Other Countries		1,452,397	
Total	50,885,527	1,433,887,500	28.1

All these collectively are estimated to speak more than 3,000 languages.

The amount of deaths per annum is 33,333,333, or 91,954 per day, 3,730 per hour, 60 per minute, or 1 per second. It is estimated that the population of the earth, at the present time, is being increased at the rate of about 16,500,000 annually.

The average duration of life throughout the globe is 33 years. One-fourth of its population dies before the seventh year, and the half before the seventeenth. Out of 10,000 persons only one reaches his hundredth year, only one in 500 his eightieth; and only one in 100 his sixtieth.

Another estimate of the earth's population is as follows:

Races.		*Religions.*	
Whites	600,000,000	Pagans	830,600,000
Mongolians	600,000,000	Christians	380,000,000
Blacks	250,000,000	Mohammedans	122,400,000
Copper Colored	12,000,000	Jews	7,500,000
		All Infidels (Est.)	93,387,500

The Christians are divided as follows:

Church of Rome.	Protestants.	East and Greek Church.
201,000,000.	106,000,000.	81,000,000.

Oceans, Seas, Bays and Lakes.

Oceans.	*Sq. Miles.*
Pacific, about	80,000,000
Atlantic, "	40,000,000
Indian, "	20,000,000
Southern, "	10,000 000
Arctic, "	5 000 000

NOTE. The seas, bays, gulfs, etc., connected with each ocean, are included in the foregoing estimate. It may be proper to remark, however, that the exact superficial extent of the several oceans is not known with certainty, nor the exact proportion of land and water.

Seas.	*Length in Miles.*
Mediterranean, about	2,000
Caribbean "	1,800
China "	1,700
Red "	1,400
Japan "	1,000
Black "	932
Caspian "	640
Baltic "	600
Okhotsk "	600
White "	450
Aral "	250

Bays.	*Length in Miles.*
Hudson's, about	1,200
Baffin's "	600
Chesapeake "	250

Lakes.	*Length. Miles.*	*Width. Miles.*
Superior	380	120
Baikal	360	35
Michigan	330	60
Great Slave	300	45
Huron	250	90
Winnipeg	240	40
Erie	270	50
Athabasca	200	20
Ontario	180	40
Maracaybo	150	60
Great Bear	150	40
Ladoga	125	75
Champlain	123	12
Nicaragua	120	40
L. of the Woods	70	25
Geneva	50	10
Constance	45	10
Cayuga	36	4
George	36	3

Highest Mountains and Cities in the World.

NAME.	COUNTRY.	FEET	MILES.
Mt. Everest (Himalayas)	Thibet	29,002	5¾
Aconcagua	Chili	22,422	4¼
Sahama	Bolivia	22,350	4¼
Chimborazo	Ecuador	21,422	4⅔
Sorato	Bolivia	21,284	4
Illimani	Bolivia	21,145	4
Mt. Demavend	Persia	20,000	3¾
Cotopaxi	Ecuador	19,496	3¾
St. Elias	Alaska	17,850	3⅓
Popocatapetl	Mexico	17,540	3⅓
Pichinca	Ecuador	15,924	3
Mt. Blanc	Savoy	15,732	3
Mt. Rosa	Savoy	15,150	2⅞
Mt. Whitney	California	14,887	2¾
Mt. Fairweather	Alaska	14,500	2¾
Mt. Blanca	Colorado	14,464	2¾
Mt. Ranier	Washington Territory	14,444	2¾
Mt. Shasta	California	14,442	2¾
Mt. Harvard	Colorado	14,383	2¾
Gray's Peak	Colorado	14,341	2¾
Mt. Ararat	Armenia	14 320	2⅔
Long's Peak	Colorado	14,271	2⅔
Pike's Peak	Colorado	14,216	2⅔
Mt. Holycross	Colorado	14,176	2⅔
Mt. Yale	Colorado	14,101	2⅔
Cameron's Cone	Colorado	14,000	2⅔
Mt. St. Helens	Washington Territory	13,400	2½
Peak of Teneriffe	Canary Isles	12,182	2⅛
Miltzin	Morocco	11,500	2
Mt. Hood	Oregon	11,225	2
Mt. Ætna	Sicily	10,835	2
Mt. Lebanon	Syria	10,533	2
Mt. Olympus	Greece	9,754	1¾
Black Mountain	North Carolina	6,760	1¼
Mt. Sinai	Arabia	6,541	1¼
Mt. Washington	New Hampshire	6,285	1¼
Mt. Marcy	New York	5,402	1
Mt Hecla	Iceland	5,104	1
Ben Nevis	Scotland	4,406	⅞
Mt. Vesuvius	Italy	4,253	¾
Round Top, highest of Catskills	New York	3,804	¾
CITIES.			
Montezuma	Colorado	10,295	1¾
Leadville	Colorado	10,200	1¾

The Longest Rivers of the World.

Rivers.	Locality.	Rise.	Discharge.	Miles
Missouri	N. America	Rocky Mountains	Gulf of Mexico	4 194
Mississippi	N. America	Lake Itaska	Gulf of Mexico	2, 616
Amazon	Brazil	Andes	Atlantic Ocean	3, 944
Hoang-Ho	China	Koulkoun Mountains	Yellow Sea	3,000
Murray	Australasia	Australian Alps	Encounter Bay	3,000
Obi	Siberia	Altaian Mountains	Arctic Ocean	2,800
Nile	Egypt, Nubia	Blue Nile, Abyssinia	Mediterranean	2,750
Yang-tse-Kia	China	Thibet	China Sea	2,500
Lena	Siberia	Heights of Irkutsk	Arctic Ocean	2,500
Niger	Soudan	Base of Mt. Loma	Gulf of Guinea	2,300
St. Lawrence	Canada	River St. Louis	G'f St. Lawrence	1,960
Volga	Russia	Lake in Volhonsky	Caspian Sea	1,900
Maykiang	Siam	Thibet	Chinese Gulf	1,700
Indus	Hindostan	Little Thibet	Arabian Sea	1,700
Danube	Germany	Black Forest	Black Sea	1,630
Mackenzie	N. America	River Athabasca	Arctic Ocean	2,500
Brahmapootra	Thibet	Himalaya	Bay of Bengal	1,500
Columbia	N. America	Rocky Mountains	Pacific Ocean	1,090
Colorado	N. America	San Iaba	Gulf of Califor	1,000
Susquehanna	N. America	Lake Otsego	Chesapeake Bay.	400
James	N. America	Allegheny Mountains	Chesapeake Bay.	500
Potomac	N. America	Gr. Black Bone Mount'n.	Chesapeake Bay.	400
Hudson	N. America	Adirondacks, Mt. Marcy	Bay of N. Y.	325

Historical Facts Relating to the United States.

Year Settled	States.	Where Settled.	By Whom.	Admit'd to the Union	Capitals.
1565	Florida	St. Augustine	Spaniards	1845	Tallahassee.
1607	Virginia*	Jamestown	English	1788†	Richmond.
1614	New York*	Manhattan	Dutch	1788†	Albany.
1620	Massachusetts*	Plymouth	English Puritans	1788†	Boston.
1623	N. Hampshire*	Dover	English	1788†	Concord.
1624	New Jersey*	Bergen	Dutch and Danes	1787†	Trenton.
1625	Maine	Bristol	English	1820	Augusta.
1627	Delaware*	Cape Henelopen.	Swedes and Finns.	1787†	Dover.
1633	Connecticut*	Windsor	From Massachu'ts	1788†	Hartford.
1634	Maryland*	St. Mary's	English	1788†	Annapolis.
1636	Rhode Island*	Providence	English	1790†	Prov. & N'port
1663	North Carolina*	Albemarle	English	1789†	Raleigh.
1669	Wisconsin	Green Bay	French	1848	Madison.
1670	Michigan	Detroit	French	1837	Lansing.
1670	South Carolina*	Port Royal	English	1788†	Columbia.
1682	Pennsylvania.*	Philadelphia	English	1787†	Harrisburg.
1685	Arkansas	Arkansas Post	French	1836	Little Rock.
1690	Texas	San Antonia	Spaniards	1845	Austin.
1690	Indiana	Vincennes	French	1816	Indianapolis.
1699	Louisiana	Iberville	French	1812	Baton Rouge.
1711	Alabama	Mobile	French	1814	Montgomery.
1716	Mississippi	Natchez	French	1817	Jackson.
1720	Illinois	Kaskaskia	French	1818	Springfield.
1725	Vermont	Fort Dummer	From Massachu'ts	1791	Montpelier.
1733	Georgia*	Savannah	English	1788†	Atlanta.
1757	Tennessee	Fort London	From N. Carolina.	1796	Nashville.
1764	Missouri	St. Louis	French	1821	Jefferson City.
1769	California	San Diego	Spaniards	1850	Sacramento.
1775	Kentucky	Boonesboro	From Virginia	1792	Frankfort.
1788	Ohio	Marietta	From N. England.	1803	Columbus.
1811	Oregon	Astoria	From New York	1859	Salem.
1833	Iowa	Burlington	From N. England.	1846	Des Moines.
1846	Minnesota	St. Paul	From N. England.	1857	St. Paul.
1850	Kansas	Ft. Leavenworth.	Fr. N.E. & W. States.	1861	Topeka.
1861	Nevada	Washoe	From California	1864	Carson City.
1862	West Virginia	(See Virginia)	Formed fr. Va.	1862	Charleston.
1854	Nebraska		Fr. N.E. & W. States.	1867	Lincoln.
1858	Colorado	Denver	Fr. Western States	1876	Denver.

* The thirteen original States. † Date of adoption of Constitution.

Principal Exports of Various Countries.

ARABIA—Coffee, aloes, myrrh, frankincense, gum arabic.
BELGIUM—Grain, flax, hops, woolens, linens, laces, various manufactures.
BRAZIL—Cotton, sugar, coffee, tobacco, gold, diamonds, wheat, dye-woods.
CANADA, NOVA SCOTIA and NEW BRUNSWICK—Flour, furs, lumber, fish.
CAPE COLONY—Brandy, wine, ostrich feathers, hides, tallow.
CENTRAL AMERICA—Logwood, mahogany, indigo, cocoa.
CHILI—Silver, gold, copper, wheat, hemp, hides, sugar, cotton, fruits.
CHINA—Tea, silks, nankeens, porcelain, opium, articles of ivory and pearl.
DENMARK—Grain, horses, cattle, beef, pork, butter, and cheese.
EASTERN, WESTERN and SOUTHERN AFRICA—Gold, ivory, ostrich feathers.
EGYPT—Rice, grain, linseed, fruits, indigo, cotton, sugar.
ECUADOR and NEW GRENADA—Coffee, cotton, indigo, fruits, sugar, cocoa.
FRANCE—Silks, woolens, linens, cottons, wine, brandy, porcelain, toys.
GERMANY—Linen, grain, various manufactures of silver, copper, etc.
GREAT BRITAIN—Woolens, cottons, linens, hardware, porcelain, etc.
GREENLAND—Whale oil, whale bone, seal skins.
HINDOSTAN—Cotton, silks, rice, sugar, coffee, opium, indigo.
HOLLAND—Fine linens, woolens, butter, cheese, various manufactures.
ITALY—Silks, wines, grain, oil, fruits.
IRELAND—Linens, beef, butter, tallow, hides, potatoes, barley, etc.
JAPAN—Silk and cotton goods, Japanware, porcelain.
MEXICO—Gold, silver, logwood, cochineal, fruits.
PERSIA—Carpets, shawls, wine, silk, cotton, rice, rhubarb, guns, swords, etc.
PERU—Silver, gold, Peruvian bark, mercury, sugar, cotton, fruits.
RUSSIA—Hemp, iron, linen, grain, timber, furs, tallow, platina.
SPAIN and PORTUGAL—Silks, wool, wine, oil, fruits, salt, etc.
SWEDEN and NORWAY—Iron, steel, copper, timber, fish.
SWITZERLAND—Watches, jewelry, paper, laces, linen, cotton and silk goods, etc.
TURKEY—Grain, fruits, cotton, oil, wines, carpets, muslin, swords.
UNITED STATES—*Eastern States*—Lumber, beef, pork, fish, cottons, woolens, etc.
Middle States—Flour, wheat, salt, coal, cottons, woolens, etc.
Southern States—Cotton, rice, tobacco, corn, lumber, pitch, fruits.
Western States—Corn, wheat, lead, coal, iron, salt, lime, beef, pork.
VENEZUELA—Sugar, coffee, cocoa, cotton, indigo, fruits.
WEST INDIES—Sugar, rum, molasses, coffee, spice, cotton, indigo, fruits.

Presidents of the United States.

NAME.	Residence.	Born.	Instal'd into Office.	Age at that time.	Term of Office.	Died.	Age at Death.
George Washington	Va.	1732	1789	57	8 yrs.	Dec. 14, 1799	68
John Adams	Mass.	1735	1797	62	4 "	July 4, 1826	91
Thomas Jefferson	Va.	1743	1801	58	8 "	July 4, 1826	83
James Madison	Va.	1751	1809	58	8 "	June 28, 1836	85
James Monroe	Va.	1758	1817	58	8 "	July 4, 1831	72
John Quincy Adams	Mass.	1767	1825	58	4 "	Feb. 23, 1848	80
Andrew Jackson	Tenn.	1767	1829	62	8 "	June 8, 1845	78
Martin Van Buren	N. Y.	1782	1837	55	4 "	July 24, 1862	80
William H. Harrison	Ohio	1773	1841	68	1 month	April 4, 1841	68
John Tyler	Va.	1790	1841	51	3 yrs. 11 mos.	Jan. 17, 1872	72
James K. Polk	Tenn.	1795	1845	49	4 "	June 15, 1849	54
Zachary Taylor	La.	1784	1849	65	1 y. 4 m. 5 d.	July 9, 1850	66
Millard Fillmore	N. Y.	1800	1850	50	2 y. 7 m. 26 d.	March 8, 1874	74
Franklin Pierce	N. H.	1804	1853	49	4 yrs.	Oct. 8, 1869	65
James Buchanan	Penn.	1791	1857	66	4 "	June 1, 1868	77
*Abraham Lincoln	Ill.	1809	1861	52	4 y. 1 m. 10 d.	April 15, 1865	56
Andrew Johnson	Tenn.	1808	1865	57	3 y. 10 m. 20 d.	July 31, 1875	67
Ulysses S. Grant	Ill.	1822	1869	47	8 yrs.		
Rutherford B. Hayes	Ohio	1822	1877	55	4 "		
† James A. Garfield	Ohio	1831	1881	50	6 ms. 15 dys.	Sept. 19, 1881	50
Chester A. Arthur	N. Y.	1830	1881	51	3 y. 5 m. 15 d.		
Grover Cleveland	N. Y.	1837	1885	48			

* Abraham Lincoln died from the effects of a pistol shot, fired by John Wilkes Booth, at Ford's theater, Washington, on the evening of April 14, 1865. He lived ten hours, and died the next morning.
†President Garfield was shot by Charles J. Guiteau, at Washington, July 2, 1881, and died at Long Branch, N. J., Sept. 19, 1881. For this crime, Guiteau was hung at Washington, D. C., June 30, 1882.

Height of Monuments, Towers, Etc.

NAME.	PLACE.	FEET.
Washington Monument	Washington, D. C.	555
Cathedral of Cologne	Germany	525
Pyramid of Cheops	Egypt	486
Cathedral of St. Stephen	Vienna, Austria	470
Cathedral at Strasburg	Germany	468
Pyramid of Cephrenes	Egypt	456
Nicolai Church	Hamburg	450
St. Peter's Church at Rome	Italy	448
St. Michael's Church	Hamburg, Germany	428
St. Martin's Church	Landshut, Germany	411
Cathedral at Antwerp	Belgium	408
Cathedral at Cremona	Lombardy	396
Cathedral at Florence	Italy	387
Cathedral at Fribourg	Germany	386
St. Paul's Church	London, Eng.	365
Cathedral of Seville	Spain	360
Cathedral of Utrecht	Holland	356
Cathedral of Milan	Lombardy	355
Cathedral of Notre Dame	Munich, Bavaria	348
Church of St. Mark	Venice, Italy	323
Board of Trade	Chicago, Ill.	320
Trinity Church	New York, N. Y.	284
Town Hall at Berlin	Germany	274
Column at Delhi	India	262
Porcelain Tower at Nankin	China	260
Church of Notre Dame	Paris, France	224
Bunker Hill Monument	Boston, Mass.	221
Leaning Tower of Pisa	Italy	179
Washington Monument	Baltimore, Md.	175

Capacity of Large Rooms.

Estimating a person to occupy an area of 19.9 inches square.

CHURCHES.	Will Contain No. Persons.
St. Peter's, Rome	54,000
Cathedral, Milan	37,000
St. Paul's, Rome	32,000
St. Paul's, London	25,600
St. Petronio, Bologna	24,400
Cathedral, Florence	24,300
Cathedral, Antwerp	24,000
St. Sophia's, Constantinople	23,000
St. John's, Lateran	22,900
Notre Dame, Paris	21,000
Cathedral, Pisa	13,000
St. Stephen's, Vienna	12,400
St. Dominic's, Bologna	12,000
St. Peter's, Bologna	11,400
Cathedral, Vienna	11,000
St. Mark's, Venice	7,500

Opera-Houses and Theaters.

Barnum's Hippodrome, New York	8,433
Stadt Theater, New York	3,000
Academy of Music, Philadelphia	2,865
Carlo Felice, Genoa	2,560
Acad. of Music, Brooklyn	2,000
Opera-House, Munich	2,307
Alexander, St. Petersburg	2,332
San Carlos, Naples	2,240
Haverly's Theatre, Chicago	2,300
Imperial, St. Petersburg	2,160
La Scala, Milan	2,113
Academy of Paris, Paris	2,092
Covent Garden, London	2,684
Academy of Music, N. Y.	2,526
Boston Theater, Boston	2,972
Music Hall, Boston	2,585
Grand Opera-Hall, New Orleans	2,052
St. Charles Theater, New Orleans	2,178
Grand Opera-House, N. Y.	1,883
Booth's Theater, N. York	1,807
Opera-House, Detroit	1,790
McVicker's Theater, Chicago	1,786
Grand Opera-House, Chicago	1,786
Ford's Opera-House, Baltimore	2,001
National Theater, Washington	1,500
De Bar's Opera-House, St. Louis	1,696
California Theater, San Francisco	1,651
Euclid Ave. Opera-House, Cleveland	1,650
Opera-House, Berlin	1,636
Opera-House, Albany	1,404
Hooley's Theater, Chicago	1,373
Coulter Opera-House, Aurora, Ill.	1,004
Opera-House, Montreal	928

Periods of Digestion.

Substance.	Hrs.	Min.
Rice, boiled	1	
Eggs, whipped, raw	1	30
Trout, fresh, fried	1	30
Soup, Barley, boiled	1	30
Apples, sweet, mellow, raw	1	30
Venison steak, broiled	1	45
Sago, boiled	1	45
Tapioca, boiled	2	
Barley, boiled	2	
Milk, boiled	2	
Liver, beef, fresh, broiled	2	
Eggs, fresh, raw	2	
Apples, sour, mellow, raw	2	
Cabbage, with vinegar, raw	2	
Milk, raw	2	15
Eggs, fresh, roasted	2	15
Turkey, domestic, roasted	2	30
Goose, wild, roasted	2	30
Cake, sponge, baked	2	30
Hash, warmed	2	30
Beans, pod, boiled	2	30
Parsnips, boiled	2	30
Potatoes, Irish, baked	2	30
Cabbage, head, raw	2	30
Custard, baked	2	45
Apples, sour, hard, raw	2	50
Oysters, fresh, raw	2	55
Eggs, fresh, soft boiled	3	
Beefsteak, broiled	3	
Mutton, fresh, broiled	3	
Mutton, fresh, boiled	3	
Soup, bean, boiled	3	
Chicken soup, boiled	3	
Dumpling, apple, boiled	3	
Oysters, fresh, roasted	3	15
Pork, salted, broiled	3	15
Porksteak, broiled	3	15
Mutton, fresh, roasted	3	15
Bread, corn, baked	3	15
Carrot, orange, boiled	3	15
Sausage, fresh, broiled	3	20
Oysters, fresh, stewed	3	30
Butter, melted	3	30
Cheese, old, raw	3	30
Oyster soup, boiled	3	30
Bread, wheat, fresh, baked	3	30
Turnips, flat, boiled	3	30
Potatoes, Irish, boiled	3	30
Eggs, fresh, hard boiled	3	30
Eggs, fresh, fried	3	30
Green corn & beans, boiled	3	45
Beets, boiled	3	45
Salmon, salted, boiled	4	
Beef, fried	4	
Veal, fresh, broiled	4	
Fowls, domestic, boiled	4	
Beef, old, salted, boiled	4	15
Pork, salted, fried	4	15
Pork, salted, boiled	4	30
Veal, fresh, fried	4	30
Cabbage, boiled	5	15
Pork, roasted	5	30
Suet, beef, boiled	5	30

Capacity of a Freight Car.*

A load, nominally, is 20,000 pounds.
The following number can be carried.

Whisky	60	barrels.
Salt	70	"
Lime	70	"
Flour	90	"
Eggs	130 to 160	"
Flour	200	sacks.
Wood	6	cords.
Cattle	18 to 20	head.
Hogs	50 to 60	"
Sheep	80 to 100	"
Lumber	6,000	feet.
Barley	300	bushels.
Wheat	340	"
Flax Seed	360	"
Apples	370	"
Corn	400	"
Potatoes	430	"
Oats	680	"
Bran	1,000	"
Butter	20,000	pounds.

* This table is for 10-ton cars. Freight cars of larger capacity have been made of late.

Quantity of Seed to Plant.

Asparagus Roots.—1,000 plants to bed 4 x 225 feet.
Beans.—1 qt. plants 150 ft. of row.
Beets.—1 oz. plants 150 ft. of row.
Cabbage.—1 oz. gives 2,500 plants.
Celery—1 oz. gives 7,000 plants.
Cucumber.—1 oz. for 150 hills.
Lettuce.—1 oz. gives 7,000 plants.
Melon.—1 oz. for 120 hills.
Onion.—Four pounds to the acre.
Radish.—1 oz. to 100 ft. of ground.
Spinage.—1 oz. to 250 ft. of row.
Squash.—1 oz. to 75 hills.
Tomato.—1 oz. gives 2,500 plants.
Turnip.—1½ pound to the acre.

CHRONOLOGY OF IMPORTANT EVENTS.

Before Christ.

The Deluge	2348
Babylon built	2247
Birth of Abraham	1993
Death of Joseph	1635
Moses born	1571
Athens founded	1556
The Pyramids built	1250
Solomon's Temple finished	1004
Rome founded	753
Jerusalem destroyed	587
Babylon taken by Jews	538
Death of Socrates	400
Rome taken by the Gauls	385
Paper invented in China	170
Carthage destroyed	146
Cæsar landed in Britain	55
Cæsar killed	44
Birth of Christ	0

After Christ.

Death of Augustus	14
Pilate, governor of Judea	27
Jesus Christ crucified	33
Claudius visited Britain	43
St. Paul put to death	67

After Christ.

Death of Josephus	93
Jerusalem rebuilt	131
The Romans destroyed 580,000 Jews and banished the rest from Judea	135
The Bible in Gothic	373
Horseshoes made of iron	481
Latin tongue ceased to be spoken	580
Pens made of Quills	635
Organs used	660
Glass in England	663
Bank of Venice established	1157
Glass windows first used for lights	1180
Mariner's compass used	1200
Coal dug for fuel	1234
Chimneys first put to houses	1236
Spectacles invented by an Italian	1240
The first English House of Commons	1258
Tallow candles for lights	1290
Paper made from linen	1302
Gunpowder invented	1340
Woolen cloth made in England	1341
Printing invented	1436
The first almanac	1470
America discovered	1492
First book printed in England	1507

After Christ.

Luther began to preach	1517
Interest fixed at ten per cent. in England	1547
Telescopes invented	1549
First coach made in England	1564
Clocks first made in England	1568
Bank of England incorporated	1594
Shakspeare died	1616
Circulation of the blood discovered	1619
Barometer invented	1623
First newspaper	1629
Death of Galileo	1643
Steam engine invented	1649
Great fire in London	1666
Cotton planted in the United States	1759
Commencement of the American war	1775
Declaration of American Independence	1776
Recognition of American Independence	1782
Bank of England suspended cash paym't	1791
Napoleon I. crowned emperor	1804
Death of Napoleon	1821
Telegraph invented by Morse	1832
First daguerreotype in France	1839
Beginning of the American civil war	1861
End of the American civil war	1865
Great fire in Chicago	1871

POPULATION OF CITIES OF THE UNITED STATES,

Having 10,000 inhabitants and over, by the census of 1880, accompanied by a statement of the public debt of each city, to which is added a table showing the debt per person of each man, woman and child of each city.

Name of City.	Population 1880.	Debt 1880.	Debt per each Person.
Akron, Ohio	16,512	$17,619	$1.06
Albany, N. Y.	90,903	3,138,500	34.52
Alleghany, Pa.	78,681	1,596,429	20.29
Allentown, Pa.	18,063	430,443	23.83
Alexandria, Va.	13,658	1,037,088	75.92
Altoona, Pa.	19,716	368,830	18.70
Amsterdam, N. Y.	11,711		
Atchison, Kan.	15,106	449,687	29.76
Atlanta, Ga.	34,398	2,180,000	63.38
Attleborough, Mass.	11,111	16,600	1,49
Auburn, N. Y.	22,924	530,000	23.12
Augusta, Ga.	23,023	1,961,319	85,18
Aurora, Ill.	11,825	25,506	2.16
Austin, Tex.	10,960	106,744	9.74
Baltimore, Md.	332,190	27,092,690	81.55
Bangor, Maine.	16,827	2,661,000	158.13
Bay City, Mich.	20,693	433,100	20,93
Belleville, Ill.	10,682	217,712	20.38
Biddeford Maine	12,652	183,874	14.53
Binghamton, N. Y.	17,315	299,500	17,29
Bloomington, Ill.	17,184	221,463	12.88
Boston, Mass.	362,535	28,244,017	77.90
Bridgeport, Conn.	29,145	831,000	28.51
Brockton, Mass.	13,608	71,200	5.23
Brooklyn, N. Y.	566,689	38,040,000	67.13
Buffalo, N. Y.	155,137	8,211,934	52.93
Burlington, Vt.	11,364	383,427	33.74
Burlington, Iowa.	19,450	128,062	6.58
Brookhaven, N. Y.	11,544		
Cambridge, Mass.	52,740	3,403,723	64.53
Camden, N. J.	41,658	1,164,900	27.96
Canton, Ohio	12,258	180,657	14.73
Castleton, N. Y.	12,679		
Cedar Rapids, Iowa	10,104	40,876	4.04
Charleston, S. C.	49,999	4,129,102	82.58
Chattanooga, Tenn.	12,892	71,566	5.55
Chelsea, Mass.	21,785	1,554,496	71,35
Chester, Pa.	14,996	357,084	23.81
Chicago, Ill.	503,304	12,794,271	25.42
Cincinnati, Ohio	255,708	21,992,500	86.00
Cleveland, Ohio	160,142	4,076,946	25.45
Columbia, S. C.	10,040		
Columbus, Ohio	51,665	1,259,162	24.37
Covington, Ky.	29,720	1,030,000	34.66
Cohoes, N. Y.	19,417	141,214	7,27
Council Bluffs, Iowa.	18,059	138,400	7.66
Concord, N. H.	13,838	615,500	44.48
Chickopee, Mass.	11,325	100,050	8.83
Chillicothe, Ohio	10,938	None	
Detroit, Mich.	116,342	1,282,772	11.02
Dayton, Ohio	38,677	1,101,520	28.48
Denver, Col.	35,630	20,000	56
Des Moines, Iowa	22,408	578,000	25.79
Dubuque, Iowa	22,254	804,611	36.15
Dover, N. H.	11,687	458,830	39.25
Danbury, Conn.	11,669	255,415	21.88
Derby, Conn	11,649	80,243	6.88
Dallas, Tex.	10,358	304,356	29.36
Davenport, Iowa.	21,834	290,675	13.31
Evansville, Ind	29,280	None	
Elizabeth, N. J.	28,229	5,512,638	195.28
Erie, Pa.	27,730	1,201,229	43.31
Elmira, N. Y.	20,541	270,400	13.17
East Saginaw, Mich.	19,016	611,055	32.13
Easton, Pa.	11,924	219,949	18.45
Eau Claire, Wis.	10,118	101,000	9.98
Fall River, Mass	49,006	3,169,765	64,68
Fort Wayne, Ind.	26,880	856,900	31.87
Flushing, N. Y.	15,919		
Fond du Lac, Wis.	13,091	165,000	12.60
Fitchburg, Mass.	12,405	770,788	62.11
Fishkill, N. Y.	10,732		
Georgetown, D. C.	12,578		
Grand Rapids, Mich.	32,015	$471,000	$14.71
Galveston, Tex.	22,253	1,023,249	45.97
Gloucester, Mass.	19,329	193,370	10.00
Galesburg, Ill.	11,446	53,250	4.65
Hempstead, N. Y.	18,160		
Hartford, Conn.	42,553	3,689,855	86.71
Hoboken, N. J.	30,999	1,099,250	35.46
Harrisburg, Pa.	30,762	1,065,300	34.63
Holyoke, Mass.	21,851	878,454	40.20
Houston, Tex.	18,646	1,501,591	80.53
Haverhill, Mass.	18,475	393,428	21.29
Hyde Park, Ill.	15,716		
Hamilton, Ohio.	12,122	48,067	3.96
Hannibal, Mo.	11,074	144,027	13.00
Indianapolis, Ind.	75,074	1,914,500	25.50
Jersey City, N. J.	120,728	15,598,435	129.16
Johnstown, N. Y.	16,626		
Joliet, Ill.	16,145	54,000	3.34
Jackson, Mich.	16,105	183,500	11,39
Jacksonville, Ill.	10,927	273,336	25.10
Jeffersonville, Ind.	10,422	240,350	23.06
Jamaica, N. Y.	10,089		
Kansas City, Mo	55,813	1,339,224	23.99
Kingston, N. Y.	18,342	644,880	35.15
Keokuk, Iowa.	12,117	372,375	30,73
Kalamazoo, Mich.	11,937	25,000	2.09
Louisville, Ky.	123,645	4,842,935	39.16
Lowell, Mass.	59,485	1,554,275	26.12
Lawrence, Mass.	39,187	1,712,000	43.68
Lynn, Mass.	38,284	2,072,815	54.1₄
Lancaster, Pa.	25,769	464,142	18.01
Lewiston, Maine.	19,083	1,038,102	54.39
Long Island City, N. Y.	17,117	950,000	55.50
Lexington, Ky.	16,656	84,316	5.06
Leavenworth, Kan.	16,550	396,573	23.96
Lynchburg, Va.	15,959	794,837	49.80
Lafayette, Ind.	14,860	None	
Leadville, Col.	14,820		
La Crosse, Wis.	14,505	135,000	9.30
Lincoln, R. I.	13,765	50,000	3.63
Lockport, N. Y.	13,522	108,667	8.03
Little Rock, Ark.	13,185	335,243	25.42
Lincoln, Neb.	13,000	199,615	15.35
Los Angeles, Cal.	11,311	310,177	27.42
Logansport, Ind.	11,198	456,276	40,77
Lennox, N. Y.	10,249		
Milwaukee, Wis.	115,578	2.160,289	18.69
Minneapolis, Minn.	46,887	1,137,467	24.25
Memphis, Tenn.	33,593	None	
Manchester, N. H.	32,630	929,000	28.19
Mobile, Ala.	31,205	2,671,100	85.91
Meriden, Conn.	18,340	788,317	42,98
Montgomery, Ala.	16,714	567,900	33.91
Macon, Ga.	12,748	743,000	58.28
Malden, Mass.	12,017	483,523	40.23
Middletown, Conn.	11,731		
Muskegon, Mich.	11,262	180,000	15.98
Madison, Wis.	10,325	136,768	13.24
Marlborough, Mass.	10,126	151,951	15.00
Newburyport, Mass.	13,537	428,706	31.66
New York, N. Y.	1,206,590	109,425,414	90.69
New Orleans, La.	216,140		
Newark, N. J.	136,400	9,070.032	66.41
New Haven, Conn.	62,882	1,359,619	21.62
New Bedford, Mass.	26,875	1,086,000	40.37
Norfolk, Va.	21,966	2,187,371	99.57
Norwich, Conn.	21,141	1,191,256	56.34
Newport, Ky.	20,433	966,618	42.41
Newburgh, N. Y.	18,050	313,400	17.36
New Brunswick, N. J.	17,167	1,618,946	94.30
Newton, Mass.	16,995	993,591	58,46
New Albany, Ind.	16,422	358,482	21.82
Newport, R. I.	15,693	$116,408	$7.41
New Britain, Conn.	13,978	494,843	35.40
Norwalk, Conn.	13,956	522,495	37.43
New Lots, N. Y.	13,681		
Nashua, N. H.	13,397	458,661	34.23
Norristown, Pa.	13,064	81,200	6.21
Northampton, Mass.	12,172	537,500	44.15
New London, Conn.	10,529	496,611	47.16
North Adams, Mass.	10,192	267,894	26.28
Nashville, Tenn.	43,461	1,606,200	36.95
Oakland, Cal.	34,556	669,126	19.35
Omaha, Neb.	30,518	227,578	7.45
Oswego, N. Y.	21,117	1,264,224	59.86
Oshkosh, Wis.	15,749	130,500	8.28
Orange, N. J.	13,206	253,832	19,29
Oyster Bay, N. Y.	11,923		
Ogdensburg, N. Y.	10,340	135,000	13.05
Pittsburgh, Pa.	156,381	14,134,296	90.37
Providence, R. I.	104,850		
Paterson, N. J.	50,887	1,359,500	26.71
Portland, Maine.	33,810	4,332,154	128.13
Peoria, Ill.	29,315	716,500	24.44
Petersburg, Va.	21,656	1,136,100	52.46
Poughkeepsie, N. Y.	20,207	1,939,198	95.96
Pawtucket, R. I.	19,030	935,000	49.13
Pittsfield, Mass.	13,367	385,341	28.82
Pottsville, Pa.	13,253		
Portsmouth, Va.	11,388	283,014	24.85
Portsmouth, Ohio.	11,314	317,809	28.09
Philadelphia, Pa.	846,984	16,251,696	19.18
Quincy, Ill.	27,275	1,917,888	70.31
Quincy, Mass.	10,529	65,980	62.66
Rochester, N. Y.	89,363	5,701,686	63.80
Richmond, Va.	63,803	4,399,021	68.93
Reading, Pa.	43,280	999,000	23.08
Racine, Wis.	16,031	218,512	13.63
Rockford, Ill.	13,136	178,090	13.55
Richmond, Ind.	12,743	167,000	13.10
Rutland, Vt.	12,149	202,460	16.66
Rome, N. Y.	12,045	160,000	13.28
Rock Island, Ill.	11,660	289,050	24.78
St. Louis, Mo.	350,522	22,847,761	65.18
San Francisco, Cal.	232,956	3,059,285	13.12
Syracuse, N. Y.	51,791	1,351,500	26.09
Scranton, Pa.	45,850	325,202	7.09
St. Paul, Minn.	41,498	1,526,715	36.74
Springfield, Mass.	33,340	1,928,000	57.82
St. Joseph, Mo.	32,484	2,445,600	73.74
Savannah, Ga.	30,681	3,425,000	111.63
Salem, Mass.	27,598	1,162,487	42,08
Somerville, Mass.	24,985	1,596,974	63.56
Sacramento, Cal.	21,420	861,000	40.19
Salt Lake City, Utah	20,768	67,000	3.22
Springfield, Ohio.	20,729	58,627	2.82
San Antonio, Tex.	20,561	155,266	7.55
Springfield, Ill.	19,749	778,780	39.40
Sandusky, Ohio.	15,838	381,215	24.07
Schenectady, N. Y.	13,675	118,000	8.60
South Bend, Ind.	13,279	337,600	25.30
San Jose, Cal.	12,567	None	
Steubenville, Ohio.	12,093	30,190	2.91
Stamford, Conn.	11,298	165,000	14.50
Shreveport, La.	11,017		
Saratoga Springs, N. Y.	10,822	297,600	27.50
Saugerties, N. Y.	10,375		
Saginaw, Mich.	10,525	202,800	19.00
Stockton, Cal.	10,287	385,615	37.40
Shenandoah, Pa.	10,148		
Troy, N. Y.	56,747	958,296	16.80
Toledo, Ohio.	50,143	3,232,660	64.46
Trenton, N. J.	29,910	1,664,501	55.70
Terre Haute, Ind.	26,040	267,224	10.26
Taunton, Mass.	21,213	449,735	21.20
Topeka, Kan.	15,451	333,249	21.50

Name of City.	Population 1880.	Debt. 1880.	Debt per each Person.	Name of City.	Population 1880.	Debt. 1880.	Debt per each Person.	Name of City.	Population 1880.	Debt. 1880.	Debt per each Person.
Utica, N. Y.	33,913	$766,000	$22.88	Wheeling, W. V.	31,266	$531,882	$17.02	Watertown, N. Y.	10,697	$407,500	$38.00
				Wilkesbarre, Pa.	23,339	95,096	4.07	Weymouth, Mass.	10,571	64,392	6.09
Virginia City, Nev.	13,705	112,000	8.17	Watervliet, N. Y.	22,202			Winona, Minn.	10,208	183,000	17.92
Vicksburg, Miss.	11,814	373,218	31.50	Waterbury, Conn.	20,269	361,508	17.80	Waltham, Mass.	11,711	477,000	40.76
				Williamsport, Pa.	18,934	651,272	34.40				
Washington, D. C.	147,307	23,310,146	158.25	Wilmington, N. C.	17,361	539,845	31.09	Yonkers, N. Y.	18,892	1,388,000	73.47
Warwick, R. I.	12,163	57,500	4.72	Woonsocket, R. I.	16,053	230,000	14.30	Youngstown, Ohio	15,431	193,406	12.50
Worcester, Mass.	58,295	2,447,543	41.98	Wallkill, N. Y.	11,483			York, Pa.	13,940	33,000	2.38
Wilmington, Del.	42,499	1,372,450	32.05	Woburn, Mass.	10,938	626,602	57.26	Zanesville, Ohio	18,120	529,097	29.91

Great Cities of the World, Outside of the United States, Having 100,000 Inhabitants. *

Cities.	Countries.	Census.	Population.	Cities.	Countries.	Census.	Population.	Cities.	Countries.	Census.	Population.
Alexandria	Egypt	1882	212,054	Genoa	Italy	1881	179,515	Oldham	England	1881	152,511
Agra	India	1881	160.207					Osaka	Japan	1877	284,105
Ahmenabad	India	1881	127,621	Hangtscheu-fu	China	Est.	400,000				
Allahabad	India	1881	148,547	Hangjang	China	Est.	100,000	Patna	India	1881	170,654
Amsterdam	Holland	1881	328,047	Hankkow	China	Est.	600,000	Puna	India	1881	129,751
Antwerp	Belgium	1881	577,232	Hutscheu	China	Est.	200,000	Pernambuco	South America	1872	116,671
Aberdeen	Scotland	1881	105,189	Hutscheu-fu	China	Est.	100,000	Prague	Austria-Hun'y.	1880	162,323
Amritsur	India	1881	151,896	Hwangjuer	China	Est.	120,000	Paris	France	1881	2,269,023
Abeokuta	Africa	Est.	130,000	Hyderabad	India	Est.	200,000	Portsmouth	England	1881	127,953
				Hakodate	Japan	1877	112,494	Palermo	Italy	1881	244,991
Berlin	Germany	1881	1,122,360	Hamburg	Germany	1880	290,054	Porto	Portugal	1878	108,346
Bahia	Brazil	1872	129,109	Hanover	Germany	1880	122,843	Porto Novo	Africa	Est.	100,000
Buenos Ayres	South America	1881	289,925	Hague	Holland	1881	123,499	Peking	China	Est.	1,648,800
Bombay	India	1881	773,196								
Bareilly	India	1881	109,844	Jangtschau	China	Est.	360,000	Rio de Janeiro	South America	1872	274,972
Benares	India	1881	199,700	Jongpin	China	Est.	200,000	Rangoon	India	1881	134,176
Brussels	Belgium	1881	394,940	Jondpore	India	Est.	150,000	Rouen	France	1881	105,906
Bangalore	India	1871	142,513					Rome	Italy	1880	300,467
Bangkok	India	Est.	600,000	Kesho	India	Est.	150,000	Rotterdam	Holland	1881	157,270
Baroda	India	1871	112,057	Kagoshima	Japan	1877	200,000	Riga	Russia	1881	168,844
Bordeaux	France	1881	221,305	Kanagawa	Japan	1877	108,263				
Barmen	Germany	1880	95,941	Kiota	Japan	1877	229,810	Santiago	South America	1875	129,807
Bremen	Germany	1880	112.158	Konigsberg	Germany	1881	140,909	Shaohing	China	Est.	500,000
Breslau	Germany	1880	272,390	Kingston	England	1881	154,250	Shanghai	China	Est.	300,000
Belfast	Ireland	1881	207,671	Kijew	Russia	1874	127,250	Siangtan	China	Est.	1,000,000
Birmingham	England	1881	400,757	Kischenew	Russia	1881	102,427	Singan-fu	China	Est.	1,000,000
Blackburn	England	1881	104,012					Sutschau	China	Est.	500,000
Bolton	England	1881	105,422	Lima	South America	1876	101,488	Saoul	Corea	Est.	100,000
Bradford	England	1881	180,459	Leinkong	China	Est.	250,000	Sainagar	India	1873	132,681
Brighton	England	1881	128,407	Lahore	India	1881	149,349	Surat	India	1871	107,149
Bristol	England	1881	206,503	Lucknow	India	1881	261,303	Smyrna	Turkey-in-Asia	Est.	150,000
Bucharest	Roumania	1876	221,805	Lille	France	1881	178,144	Sydney	Australia	1881	220,427
Bologna	Italy	1881	123,274	Lyons	France	1881	376,613	St. Etienne	France	1881	123,813
Barcelona	Spain	1877	249,106	Leipzig	Germany	1880	148,760	Strasburg	Germany	1880	104,471
Buda-Pesth	Austria-Hun'y.	1880	360,551	Leeds	England	1881	309,126	Stuttgart	Germany	1880	117,303
				Leicester	England	1881	122,351	Salford	England	1881	176,233
Constantinople	Turkey	1879	1,075,000	Liverpool	England	1881	552,425	Sheffield	England	1881	284,410
Cairo	Egypt	1878	349,883	London	England	1881	4,764,312	Sunderland	England	1881	124,960
Canton	China	1881	1,600,000	Lisbon	Portugal	1878	246,343	St. Petersburg	Russia	1881	876,575
Calcutta	India	1881	684,658	Lemberg	Austria-Hun'y.	1880	109,726	Seville	Spain	1877	133,938
Cawnpore	India	1881	151,444	Liege	Belgium	1880	663,607	Stockholm	Sweden	1880	168,775
Columbo	Ceylon	1881	111,942								
Copenhagen	Denmark	1880	273,323	Marseilles	France	1881	360,099	Tunis	Africa	Est.	120,000
Cologne	Germany	1880	144,772	Manchester	England	1881	393,676	Taiwan-fu	China	Est.	235,000
Charkow	Russia	1879	101,175	Messina	Italy	1881	126,497	Tengtschau-fu	China	Est.	230,000
Christiania	Sweden	1880	119,407	Munich	Bavaria	1880	230,023	Tientsin	China	Est.	950,000
				Milan	Italy	1881	321,839	Tschantschau-fu	China	Est.	1,000,000
Delhi	India	1881	173,393	Madrid	Spain	1877	397,690	Tschaujang	China	Est.	200,000
Dhar	India	Est.	100,000	Malaga	Spain	1877	115,882	Tschingtu-fu	China	Est.	800,000
Damascus	Turkey-in-Asia	Est.	150,000	Moscow	Russia	1882	748,000	Tschungking-fu	China	Est.	600,000
Danzig	Germany	1880	108,551	Madras	India	1881	405,848	Tokio	Japan	1877	811,510
Dresden	Germany	1880	220,818	Mandalah	India	Est.	100,000	Tabris	Persia	Est.	165,000
Dublin	Ireland	1881	249,486	Manilla	Indian Arch'go.	Est.	160,000	Teheran	Persia	Est.	200,000
Dundee	Scotland	1881	140,239	Melbourne	Australia	1881	252,000	Tiflis	Russia-in-Asia	1876	104,024
				Montreal	Canada	1881	140,747	Trieste	Austria-Hun'y.	1880	144,844
Edinburgh	Scotland	1881	236,002	Mexico	Mexico	1879	236,500	Toulouse	France	1881	140,289
				Mukden	China	Est.	170,000	Turin	Italy	1881	252,832
Fez	Africa	Est.	100,000								
Frankfort-on-Main	Germany	1880	136,819	Nangkin	China	Est.	450,000	Valencia	Spain	1877	143,856
Florence	Italy	1881	169,001	Nantes	France	1881	124,319	Victoria	China	Est.	102,000
Fatschan	China	Est.	400,000	Newcastle	England	1881	145,228	Vienna	Austria-Hun'y.	1880	726,105
Foochow	China	Est.	630,000	Nottingham	England	1881	111,631	Venice	Italy	1881	132,826
				Naples	Italy	1881	494,314				
Glasgow	Scotland	1881	674,095	Nagoya	Japan	1877	135,715	Warsaw	Russia	1881	383,973
Gwalior	India	Est.	200,000					Weihein	China	Est.	250,000
Ghent	Belgium	1881	131,431	Odessa	Russia	1877	193,513	West Ham	England	1881	128,692

*For population of great cities not here given, see "Principal Countries of the World," mentioned elsewhere in this volume.

GOLD AND SILVER PRODUCTION AND AMOUNT OF MONEY IN CIRCULATION.

From reports by the Director of the United States mint.   Corrected to the latest date.

Precious Metals in the United States.

Statistics showing where our gold and silver come from.

Where Gold Comes From.

Deposit of domestic productions of gold at the U. S. Mints from 1793 to June 30, 1884.

State.	Amount.
California	$729,782,449.08
Montana	54,345,342.33
Colorado	44,431,821.87
Idaho	26,684,498.37
Nevada	20,497,510.25
Dakota	20,332,531.76
Oregon	17,835,054.76
North Carolina	10,931,022.38
Georgia	8,158,184.83
Arizona	3,451,186.51
New Mexico	1,950,546.38
Virginia	1,710,641.48
South Carolina	1,515,629.82
Wyoming	734,201.00
Utah	676,027.52
Washington Ter	315,315.34
Alabama	222,984.45
Alaska	138,719.50
Tennessee	87,286.00
Vermont	32,076.10
New Hampshire	11,020.55
Maryland	2,559.91
Michigan (L. Superior)	159.58
Indiana	40.13

Where Silver Comes From.

Deposits of domestic productions of silver at the U. S. Mints from 1793 to June 30, '84.

State.	Amount.
Nevada	$88,995,652.43
Colorado	22,566,463.12
Utah	17,627,286.38
Arizona	13,242,548.99
Montana	10,071,448.14
New Mexico	4,914,811.16
California	3,670,866.84
Michigan	3,559,116.89
Idaho	1,230,285.07
Dakota	237,200.97
Oregon	51,166.65
North Carolina	48,012.72
Wyoming	11,856.77
Georgia	2,134.42
Alaska	1,050.36
Massachusetts	917.56
Washington Ter	967.02
South Carolina	746.06
Virginia	177.85
Vermont	49.94
Tennessee	7.68

Amount of Specie

In the United States July 1, 1884, according to the report of the Director of the Mint, was

Gold	$595,825,492
Silver	255,568,142
Total	$851,393,634

Amount of Paper Money

In circulation in the United States July 1, 1884, was as follows:

Paper money..... $911,874,411

Amount of paper in excess of specie in U. S.....$60,480,777

The Total Production

Of precious metals from surface and mines of the earth, from the earliest period to the close of 1879, is estimated to be as follows:

Gold	$14,068,375,000
Silver	11,315,000,000
Total	$25,383,375,000

Estimate of the Total Production of Gold and Silver.

Gold From All Countries.

Estimated total yield of gold in all countries, from 1493 to 1875.

United States	$995,126,015
Austria	889,963,800
New Granada	596,501,675
Brazil	509,347,107
Russia	507,749,653
Africa	359,325,340
Austria-Hungary	226,248,247
Bolivia	144,398,100
Mexico	130,174,396
Chili	129,467,140
Various countries	74,458,340
Peru	80,327,582
Total	4,643,087,395

Silver From All Countries.

Estimated total yield of silver, in all countries, from 1493 to 1875.

Mexico	$2,600,280,659
Bolivia	1,286,999,947
Peru	1,065,357,084
Austria-Hungary	264,961,603
Other European countries	251,888,604

United States	179,874,123
Chili	89,024,298
Russia	82,880,291
Various countries	68,244,000
Germany	269,731,339
Total	6,159,241,948

Total Gold and Silver from 1493 to 1875.

Mexico	2,730,455,055
Bolivia	1,431,398,047
United States	1,175,000,138
Peru	1,145,684,666
Austria	889,963,800
New Granada	596,501,675
Russia	590,629,944
Brazil	509,347,107
Austria-Hungary	491,209,850
Africa	359,325,340
Germany	269,731,339
Other European countries	251,888,604
Chili	218,491,438
Various countries	142,702,340
Total	$10,802,329,343

AMOUNT OF MONEY IN CIRCULATION FOR EACH PERSON IN DIFFERENT COUNTRIES.

Estimated amount of gold and silver and paper money in circulation in twenty-four countries, from the report of the Director of the Mint, Oct. 1883.

Countries.	Year.	Paper.	Specie.	Money per each person.	Countries.	Year.	Paper.	Specie.	Money per each person.	Countries.	Year.	Paper.	Specie.	Money per each person.
Austria	1883	$8.34	$3.31	$11.65	France	1883	15.16	39.41	54.57	Norway-Sweden	1881	5.19	2.77	7.96
Australia	1882	9.03	25.01	34.04	Germany	1883	4.59	12.31	16.90	Peru	1879	4.29	.62	4.91
Belgium	1883	11.38	23.93	35.31	Great Britain	1883	5.77	19.31	25.08	Portugal	1879	1.10	8.79	9.89
Brazil	1883	9.18		9.18	Greece	1883	12.00	2.73	14.73	Russia	1883	5.18	1.21	6.39
Brit. India	1882	.24	4.07	4.31	Italy	1883	10.36	7.73	18.09	Spain	1883	4.14	12.03	16.17
Canada	1883	11.33	3.07	14.40	Japan	1881	3.82	3.80	7.62	Switzerland	1883	6.42	11.14	17.56
Colombia	1879	.63	1.50	2.13	Mexico	1883	.21	5.23	5.44	Turkey	1882	.21	3.00	3.21
Denmark	1881	9.62	8.74	18.36	Netherlands	1883	18.92	18.34	37.26	United States	1883	17.63	16.88	34.51

LUMBER MEASURE.

To find the number of feet in a board 1 inch thick from 3 to 30 inches wide, and from 4 to 24 feet long, see the following table. *Explanation.*—The figures at the top of the columns indicate the number of feet in length; those at the extreme left the width of the board in inches. To ascertain the number of feet multiply the number of feet in length by the number of inches in width and divide the product by 12, the result will be the number in feet and inches. Thus, multiply 9 inches wide by 13 feet long, and the result will be 117. Divide this by 12 and we have the product 9 feet and 9 inches. See the table.

LENGTH IN FEET.

	4 feet	5 feet	6 feet	7 feet	8 feet	9 feet	10 feet	11 feet	12 feet	13 feet	14 feet	15 feet	16 feet	17 feet	18 feet	19 feet	20 feet	21 feet	22 feet	23 feet	24 feet
	ft. in.	ft. in.	ft. in.	ft. in.	ft. in.	ft. in.	ft. in.	ft. in.	ft. in.	ft. in.	ft. in.	ft. in.	ft. in.	ft. in.	ft. in.	ft. in.	ft. in.	ft. in.	ft. in.	ft. in.	ft. in.
3 inches wide	1...00	1...03	1...06	1...09	2...00	2...03	2...06	2...09	3...00	3...03	3...06	3...09	4...00	4...03	4...06	4...09	5...00	5...03	5...06	5...09	6...00
4 inches wide	1...04	1...08	2...00	2...04	2...08	3...00	3...04	3...08	4...00	4...04	4...08	5...00	5...04	5...07	6...00	6...04	6...08	7...00	7...05	7...08	8...00
5 inches wide	1...08	2...01	2...06	2...11	3...04	3...09	4...02	4...07	5...00	5...05	5...10	6...03	6...08	7...01	7...11	8...04	8...09	9...02	9...07	10...00	
6 inches wide	2...00	2...06	3...00	3...06	4...00	4...06	5...00	5...06	6...00	6...06	7...00	7...06	8...00	8...06	9...00	9...06	10...00	10...06	11...00	11...06	12...00
7 inches wide	2...04	2...11	3...06	4...01	4...08	5...03	5...10	6...05	7...00	7...07	8...02	8...09	9...04	9...11	10...06	11...01	11...08	12...03	12...10	13...05	14...00
8 inches wide	2...08	3...04	4...00	4...08	5...04	6...00	6...08	7...04	8...00	8...08	9...04	10...00	10...08	11...04	12...00	12...08	13...04	14...00	14...08	15...04	16...00
9 inches wide	3...00	3...09	4...06	5...03	6...00	6...09	7...06	8...03	9...00	9...09	10...06	11...03	12...00	12...09	13...06	14...03	15...00	15...09	16...06	17...03	18...00
10 inches wide	3...04	4...02	5...00	5...10	6...08	7...06	8...04	9...02	10...00	10...10	11...08	12...06	13...04	14...02	15...00	15...10	16...08	17...06	18...04	19...02	20...00
11 inches wide	3...08	4...07	5...06	6...05	7...04	8...03	9...02	10...01	11...00	11...11	12...10	13...09	14...08	15...07	16...06	17...05	18...04	19...03	20...02	21...01	22...00
12 inches wide	4...00	5...00	6...00	7...00	8...00	9...00	10...00	11...00	12...00	13...00	14...00	15...00	16...00	17...00	18...00	19...00	20...00	21...00	22...00	23...00	24...00
13 inches wide	4...04	5...05	6...06	7...07	8...08	9...09	10...10	11...11	13...00	14...01	15...02	16...03	17...04	18...05	19...06	20...07	21...08	22...09	23...10	24...11	26...00
14 inches wide	4...08	5...10	7...00	8...02	9...04	10...06	11...08	12...10	14...00	15...02	16...04	17...06	18...08	19...10	21...00	22...02	23...04	24...06	25...08	26...10	28...00
15 inches wide	5...00	6...03	7...06	8...09	10...00	11...03	12...06	13...09	15...00	16...03	17...06	18...09	20...00	21...03	22...06	23...09	25...00	26...03	27...06	28...09	30...00
16 inches wide	5...04	6...08	8...00	9...04	10...08	12...00	13...04	14...08	16...00	17...04	18...08	20...00	21...04	22...08	24...00	25...04	26...08	28...00	29...04	30...08	32...00
17 inches wide	5...08	7...01	8...06	9...11	11...04	12...09	14...02	15...07	17...00	18...05	19...10	21...03	22...08	24...01	25...06	26...11	28...04	29...09	31...02	32...07	34...00
18 inches wide	6...00	7...06	9...00	10...06	12...00	13...06	15...00	16...06	18...00	19...06	21...00	22...06	24...00	25...06	27...00	28...06	30...00	31...06	33...00	34...06	36...00
19 inches wide	6...04	7...11	9...06	11...01	12...08	14...03	15...10	17...05	19...00	20...07	22...02	23...09	25...04	26...11	28...06	30...01	31...08	33...03	34...10	36...05	38...00
20 inches wide	6...08	8...04	10...00	11...08	13...04	15...00	16...08	18...04	20...00	21...08	23...04	25...00	26...08	28...04	30...00	31...08	33...04	35...00	36...08	38...04	40...00
21 inches wide	7...00	8...09	10...06	12...03	14...00	15...09	17...06	19...03	21...00	22...09	24...06	26...03	28...00	29...09	31...06	33...03	35...00	36...09	38...06	40...03	42...00
22 inches wide	7...04	9...02	11...00	12...10	14...08	16...06	18...04	20...02	22...00	23...10	25...08	27...06	29...04	31...02	33...00	34...10	36...08	38...06	40...04	42...03	44...00
23 inches wide	7...08	9...07	11...06	13...05	15...04	17...03	19...02	21...01	23...00	24...11	26...10	28...09	30...08	32...07	34...06	36...05	38...04	40...03	42...02	44...01	46...00
24 inches wide	8...00	10...00	12...00	14...00	16...00	18...00	20...00	22...00	24...00	26...00	28...00	30...00	32...00	34...00	36...00	38...00	40...00	42...00	44...00	46...00	48...00
25 inches wide	8...04	10...05	12...06	14...07	16...08	18...09	20...10	22...11	25...00	27...01	29...02	31...03	33...04	35...05	37...06	39...07	41...08	43...09	45...10	47...11	50...00
26 inches wide	8...08	10...10	13...00	15...02	17...04	19...06	21...08	23...10	26...00	28...02	30...04	32...06	34...08	36...10	39...00	41...02	43...04	45...06	47...08	49...10	52...00
27 inches wide	9...00	11...03	13...06	15...09	18...00	20...03	22...06	24...09	27...00	29...03	31...06	33...09	36...00	38...03	40...06	42...09	45...00	47...03	49...06	51...09	54...00
28 inches wide	9...04	11...08	14...00	16...04	18...08	21...00	23...04	25...08	28...00	30...04	32...08	35...00	37...04	39...08	42...00	44...04	46...08	49...00	51...04	53...08	56...00
29 inches wide	9...08	12...01	14...06	16...11	19...04	21...09	24...02	26...07	29...00	31...05	33...10	36...03	38...08	41...01	43...06	45...11	48...04	50...09	51...06	55...07	58...00
30 inches wide	10...00	12...06	15...00	17...06	20...00	22...06	25...00	27...06	30...00	32...06	35...00	37...06	40...00	42...06	45...00	47...06	50...00	52...06	55...00	57...06	60...00

FINANCIAL HISTORY OF THE UNITED STATES.

This financial statement represents the gross total public expenditure and total yearly public debt, gathered from the U. S. Treasurer's report, made July 1 of each year.

Yr.	President.	Vice-President.	Public Expenditures.	Public Debt.
1789	G. Washington	John Adams ...... *F		
1790	G. Washington	John Adams ...... F		
1791	G. Washington	John Adams ...... F	$3,797,436 78	$75,463,476 52
1792	G. Washington	John Adams ...... F	8,962,920 00	77,227,924 66
1793	G. Washington	John Adams ...... F	6,479,977 97	80,352,634 04
1794	G. Washington	John Adams ...... F	9,041,593 17	78,427,404 77
1795	G. Washington	John Adams ...... F	10,151,240 15	80,747,587 39
1796	G. Washington	John Adams ...... F	8,367,776 84	83,762,172 07
1797	John Adams	Thomas Jefferson...F	8,625,877 37	82,064,479 33
1798	John Adams	Thomas Jefferson...F	8,583,618 41	79,228,529 12
1799	John Adams	Thomas Jefferson...F	11,002,396 97	78,408,669 77
1800	John Adams	Thomas Jefferson...F	11,952,534 12	82,976,294 35
1801	Thos. Jefferson	Aaron Burr........R	12,273,376 94	83,638,050 80
1802	Thos. Jefferson	Aaron Burr........R	13,270,487 31	80,712,632 25
1803	Thos. Jefferson	Aaron Burr........R	11,258,983 67	77,054,686 30
1804	Thos. Jefferson	Aaron Burr........R	12,615,113 72	86,427,120 88
1805	Thos. Jefferson	George Clinton....R	13,598,309 47	82,312,150 50
1806	Thos. Jefferson	George Clinton....R	15,021,196 26	75,723,270 66
1807	Thos. Jefferson	George Clinton....R	11,292,292 99	69,218,398 64
1808	Thos. Jefferson	George Clinton....R	16,762,702 04	65,196,317 97
1809	Jas. Madison	George Clinton....R	13,867,226 30	57,023,192 09
1810	Jas. Madison	George Clinton....R	13,309,994 49	53,173,217 52
1811	Jas. Madison	George Clinton....R	13,592,604 86	48,005,587 76
1812	Jas. Madison	George Clinton....R	22,279,122 15	45,209,737 90
1813	Jas. Madison	Elbridge Gerry....R	39,190,520 36	55,962,827 57
1814	Jas. Madison	Elbridge Gerry†...R	38,028,230 32	81,487,846 24
1815	Jas. Madison	John Gaillard.....R	39,582,493 35	99,833,660 15
1816	Jas. Madison	John Gaillard.....R	48,244,495 51	127,334,933 74
1817	James Monroe	D. D. Tompkins....R	40,877,646 04	123,491,965 16
1818	James Monroe	D. D. Tompkins....R	35,104,875 40	103,466,633 83
1819	James Monroe	D. D. Tompkins....R	24,004,199 73	95,529,648 25
1820	James Monroe	D. D. Tompkins....R	21,763,024 85	91,015,566 18
1821	James Monroe	D. D. Tompkins....R	19,090,572 69	89,987,427 66
1822	James Monroe	D. D. Tompkins....R	17,676,592 63	93,546,676 98
1823	James Monroe	D. D. Tompkins....R	15,314,171 00	90,875,877 28
1824	James Monroe	D. D. Tompkins....R	31,898,538 47	90,269,777 77
1825	John Q. Adams	John C. Calhoun...R	23,585,804 72	83,788,432 71
1826	John Q. Adams	John C. Calhoun...R	24,103,398 46	81,054,059 99
1827	John Q. Adams	John C. Calhoun...R	22,656,764 04	73,987,357 20
1828	John Q. Adams	John C. Calhoun...R	25,450,479 52	67,475,043 87
1829	A. Jackson	John C. Calhoun...D	25,044,358 40	58,421,413 67
1830	A. Jackson	John C. Calhoun...D	24,585,281 55	48,565,406 50
1831	A. Jackson	John C. Calhoun...D	30,038,446 12	39,123,191 68
1832	A. Jackson	John C. Calhoun...D	34,356,698 06	24,332,235 18
1833	A. Jackson	Martin Van Buren..D	24,257,298 49	7,301,698 83
1834	A. Jackson	Martin Van Buren..D	24,601,982 44	4,760,082 08
1835	A. Jackson	Martin Van Buren..D	17,573,141 56	37,513 05
1836	A. Jackson	Martin Van Buren..D	30,868,164 04	336,957 83
1837	M. Van Buren	R. M. Johnson.....D	37,265,037 15	3,408,124 07
1838	M. Van Buren	R. M. Johnson.....D	39,455,438 35	10,434,221 14
1839	M. Van Buren	R. M. Johnson.....D	37,614,936 15	3,573,343 82
1840	M. Van Buren	R. M. Johnson.....D	28,226,533 81	5,250,875 54
1841	W. H. Harrison	John Tyler‡.......W	31,797,530 03	13,594,480 73
1842	John Tyler	Wm. P. Mangum.....W	32,936,876 53	20,601,226 28
1843	John Tyler	Wm. P. Mangum.....W	12,118,105 15	32,742,922 00
1844	John Tyler	Wm. P. Mangum.....W	33,642,010 85	23,461,652 50
1845	Jas. K. Polk	George M. Dallas...D	30,490,408 71	15,925,303 01
1846	Jas. K. Polk	George M. Dallas...D	27,632,282 90	15,550,202 97
1847	Jas. K. Polk	George M. Dallas...D	60,520,851 74	38,826,534 77
1848	Jas. K. Polk	George M. Dallas...D	60,655,143 19	47,044,862 23
1849	Zach. Taylor	Millard Fillmore§..W	56,386,422 74	63,061,858 69
1850	M. Fillmore	Wm. R. King......W	44,604,718 26	63,452,773 55
1851	M. Fillmore	D. R. Atchison.....W	48,476,104 31	68,304,796 02
1852	M. Fillmore	D. R. Atchison.....W	46,712,608 83	66,199,341 71
1853	Frank. Pierce	Wm. R. King‖.....D	54,577,061 74	59,803,117 70
1854	Frank. Pierce	D. R. Atchison.....D	75,473,170 75	42,242,222 42
1855	Frank. Pierce	Jesse D. Bright....D	66,164,775 96	35,586,558 56
1856	Frank. Pierce	Jesse D. Bright....D	72,726,341 57	31,972,537 90
1857	Jas. Buchanan	J. C. Breckenridge. D	71,274,587 37	28,699,831 85
1858	Jas. Buchanan	J· C. Breckenridge. D	82,062,186 74	44,911,881 03
1859	Jas. Buchanan	J. C. Breckenridge. D	83,678,642 92	58,496,837 88
1860	Jas. Buchanan	J. C. Breckenridge. D	77,055,125 65	64,842,287 88
1861	A. Lincoln	Hannibal Hamlin...R	85,387,313 08	90,580,873 72
1862	A. Lincoln	Hannibal Hamlin...R	565,667,563 74	524,176,412 13
1863	A. Lincoln	Hannibal Hamlin...R	899,815,911 25	1,119,772,138 63
1864	A. Lincoln	Hannibal Hamlin...R	1,295,541,114 86	1,815,784,370 57
1865	A. Lincoln	Andrew Johnson¶..R	1,906,433,331 37	2,680,647,869 74
1866	A. Johnson	Lafayette S. Foster.R	1,139,344,081 95	2,773,236,173 69
1867	A. Johnson	Benj. F. Wade.....R	1,093,079,655 27	2,678,126,103 87
1868	A. Johnson	Benj. F. Wade....R	1,069,889,970 74	2,611,687,851 19
1869	U. S. Grant	Schuyler Colfax....R	584,777,996 11	2,588,452,213 94
1870	U. S. Grant	Schuyler Colfax....R	702,907,842 88	2,480,672,427 81
1871	U. S. Grant	Schuyler Colfax....R	691,680,858 90	2,353,211,332 32
1872	U. S. Grant	Schuyler Colfax....R	682,525,270 21	2,253,251,328 78
1873	U. S. Grant	Henry Wilson.....R	524,044,597 91	2,234,482,993 20
1874	U. S. Grant	Henry Wilson.....R	724,698,933 99	2,251,690,468 43
1875	U. S. Grant	Henry Wilson**...R	682,000,885 32	2,232,284,531 95
1876	U. S. Grant	Thos. W. Ferry....R	707,805,070 13	2,180,395,067 15
1877	R. B. Hayes	Wm. A. Wheeler...R	477,320,017 86	2,205,301,392 10
1878	R. B. Hayes	Wm. A. Wheeler...R	473,928,653 59	2,256,205,892 53
1879	R. B. Hayes	Wm. A. Wheeler...R	533,895,767 06	2,245,495,072 00
1880	R. B. Hayes	Wm. A. Wheeler...R	535,285,915 56	2,120,415,370 63
1881	J. A. Garfield	C. A. Arthur*⁎*....R	312,114,688 64	2,089,962,227 33
1882	C. A. Arthur	David Davis......R	257,981,439 57	1,918,312,994 03
1883	C. A. Arthur	Geo. F. Edmunds...R	265,408,137 54	1,884,171,728 00
1884	C. A. Arthur	Geo. F. Edmunds...R	245,498,578 00	1,842,036,163 98
1885	G. Cleveland	Thos. A. Hendricks.D		
1886				
1887				
1888				
1889				
1890				
1891				
1892				
1893				
1894				
1895				
1896				
1897				
1898				
1899				
1900				

* The political complexion of the different Presidential terms is indicated by a single letter opposite each year, defined as follow: F, Federalist; R, Republican; D, Democrat; W, Whig. Owing to changes in political principles, Jefferson's administration, which is marked Republican, at a later date would have been classed under another head.

† Elbridge Gerry died November 13, 1814, and was succeeded by John Gaillard, Vice-President *pro tem.*

‡ William H. Harrison died April 4, 1841, after being one month in office. John Tyler succeeded to the Presidency, and Willie P. Mangum became Vice-President *pro tem.*

§ Zachary Taylor died July 9, 1850, being succeeded by Millard Fillmore; William R. King succeeding to the Vice-Presidency the first half of the Presidential term, and David R. Atchison the last half.

‖ William R. King died April 17, 1853; David R. Atchison becoming Vice-President *pro tem,* for the first half of the Presidential term, and Jessee D. Bright for the last half.

¶ Abraham Lincoln was assassinated by J. Wilkes Booth, April 14, 1865. Andrew Johnson succeeded to the Presidency, Lafayette S. Foster to the Vice-Presidency the remainder of the first half of the Presidential term, and Benjamin F. Wade the last half.

** Henry Wilson died November 22, 1875, and was succeeded by Thomas W. Ferry, Vice-President *pro tem.*

⁎* James A. Garfield was assassinated by Charles J. Giteau, July 2, 1881. Through his death, Sept. 19, 1881, Chester A. Arthur succeeded to the Presidency and David Davis to the Vice-Presidency. Judge David Davis was succeeded by Geo. F. Edmunds as acting Vice-President.

United States Soldiers in the Late Civil War.

Number of men furnished from April 10, 1861, to June 30, 1865.

States and Territories.	Men Furnished.	States and Territories.	Men Furnished.	States and Territories.	Men Furnished
New York	467,047	Maryland	50,316	Colorado Ter.	4,903
Pennsylvania	366,107	New Hampshire	34,629	Indian Nations	3,530
Ohio	319,659	Vermont	35,262	Nebraska Ter.	3,157
Illinois	259,147	West Virginia	32,068	North Carolina	3,156
Indiana	197,147	Tennessee	31,092	Alabama	2,576
Massachusetts	152,048	Minnesota	25,052	Texas	1,965
Missouri	109,111	Rhode Island	23,699	Oregon	1,810
Wisconsin	96,424	Kansas	20,151	Florida	1,290
Michigan	89,372	Dist. of Columbia	16,872	Nevada	1,080
Iowa	76,309	California	15,725	Washington Ter.	964
New Jersey	81,010	Delaware	13,670	Mississippi	545
Kentucky	79,025	Arkansas	8,289	Dakota Ter.	206
Maine	72,114	New Mexico Ter.	6,561	Colored Troops	186,017
Connecticut	57,379	Louisiana	5,224	Total	2,951,708

Religious Denominations in the United States.

Denominations.	No. of Members.	No. of Churches.	No. of Ministers.
Roman Catholics—adherents and church members, claimed	6,370,858	5,975	6,366
Baptist	2,133,044	24,794	15,401
Methodist Episcopal	1,680,779	16,721	9,261
Methodist Episcopal (South)	828,013		3,593
Lutheran	684,570	5,556	3,102
Presbyterian	573,377	5,338	4,920
Christian (Disciples of Christ)	567,448	4,681	3,658
Congregational	383,685	3,689	3,589
Protestant Episcopal	342,590	3,049	3,496
United Brethren in Christ	155,437	2,207	2,200
Reformed Church in the United States	154,742	1,384	752
United Evangelical	144,000	366	363
Presbyterian Church (South)	119,970	1,928	1,031
Protestant Methodist	118,170	1,501	2,120
Cumberland Presbyterians	111,855	2,474	1,386
Mormons	110,377	654	3,906
Evangelical Association	99,607	1,332	1,340
Dunkards—The Brethren	90,000	710	1,665
United Presbyterians	80,236	793	658
Reformed Church in America	78,917	489	519
Free-Will Baptists	76,706	1,485	1,286
Methodist Episcopal (colored)	74,195	1,038	648
Friends	67,643	621	876
Second Adventists	63,500	583	501
Anti-Mission Baptists	40,000	1,090	888
Universalists	26,238	719	713
Winnebrennerians (Church of God)	20,224	569	498
Unitarian Congregational	17,960	342	394
Wesleyan Methodist	17,847	260	472
Moravians	16,112	74	96
Seventh-Day Adventists	14,733	608	138
Jews	13,683	269	202
Free Methodists	12,120	287	601
Adventists	11,100	91	107
Reformed Episcopal	10,459	55	68
Seventh-Day Baptist	8,606	87	103
Reformed Presbyterian	6,020	41	31
New Jerusalem—Swedenborgian	4,734	91	81
Primitive Methodist	3,370	121	50
New Mennonite	2,990	31	44
American Communities	2,838	14	8
Shakers	2,400	17	68
Independent Methodists	2,100	13	14
Six-Principle Baptist	2,075	20	17
Total	15,345,328	92,167	77,230

Foreigners in the United States.

ACCORDING TO CENSUS OF 1880.

Where Born.	Number.	Where Born.	Number.
German Empire	1,966,742	West Indies	9,484
Ireland	1,854,571	Portugal	8,138
British America	717,084	Atlantic Islands	7,512
England	662,676	Cuba	6,917
Sweden	194,337	Spain	5,121
Norway	181,729	Australia	4,906
Scotland	170,136	South America	4,566
France	106,971	At Sea, under foreign flags	4,068
China	104,541	Europe, not specified	3,314
Switzerland	88,621	Africa, not specified	2,204
Bohemia	85,361	India	1,707
Wales	83,302	Great Britain, not specified	1,484
Mexico	68,399	Turkey	1,205
Denmark	64,196	Sandwich Islands	1,147
Holland	58,090	Asia, not specified	1,054
Poland	48,557	Pacific Islands	806
Italy	44,230	Greece	776
Austria	38,663	Central America	707
Russia	35,722	Japan	401
Belgium	15,535	Malta	305
Luxemburg	12,836	Gibraltar	167
Hungary	11,526	Greenland	129

Strength of Ice.

Thickness.	Strength.	Thickness.	Strength.
Two inches—Will support a man.		**Eight inches**—Will support a battery of artillery, with carriages and horses attached.	
Four inches—Will support a man on horseback.			
Five inches—Will support an eighty-pounder cannon.		**Ten inches**—Will support an army; an innumerable multitude.	

Education of Presidents.

Washington.. Fair English education.
Adams. Harvard.
Jefferson. William and Mary
Madison. Princeton.
Adams, J. Q.. Harvard.
Jackson. Limited education
Van Buren. Academic course.
Harrison. Hampden College.
Tyler. William and Mary.
Polk. University of N. C.
Taylor. Slight rudiments.
Fillmore. Limited education.
Pierce. Bowdoin.
Buchanan. Dickinson.
Lincoln. Education limited.
Johnson. Self-educated.
Grant. West Point.
Hayes. Kenyon College.
Garfield. Williams College.
Arthur. Union College.
Cleveland. Academic course.

Monroe and Harrison did not graduate. Monroe left college to join the revolutionary army. Financial embarrassment prevented Harrison from pursuing a full course. Polk graduated at 23, Tyler at 17. The majority graduated at 20.

Political Representation.

Number of Presidential Electors, United States Senators and Representatives in Congress that each State is entitled to by Congressional apportionment between 1883 and 1893.

States.	Electors.	Senators.	Representatives.
Alabama	10	2	8
Arkansas	7	2	5
California	8	2	6
Colorado	3	2	1
Connecticut	6	2	4
Delaware	3	2	1
Florida	4	2	2
Georgia	12	2	10
Illinois	22	2	20
Indiana	15	2	13
Iowa	13	2	11
Kansas	9	2	7
Kentucky	13	2	11
Louisiana	8	2	6
Maine	6	2	4
Maryland	8	2	6
Massachusetts	14	2	12
Michigan	13	2	11
Minnesota	7	2	5
Mississippi	9	2	7
Missouri	16	2	14
Nebraska	5	2	3
Nevada	3	2	1
N. Hampshire	4	2	2
New Jersey	9	2	7
New York	36	2	34
North Carolina	11	2	9
Ohio	23	2	21
Oregon	3	2	1
Pennsylvania	30	2	28
Rhode Island	4	2	2
South Carolina	9	2	7
Tennessee	12	2	10
Texas	13	2	11
Vermont	4	2	2
Virginia	12	2	10
West Virginia	6	2	4
Wisconsin	11	2	9
Totals	401	76	325

The Territories of Arizona, Dakota, Idaho, Montana, New Mexico, Utah, Washington and Wyoming, have each one delegate.

The Time of Fast Trotters.

Horses that have trotted a mile in 2 minutes and 19 seconds and in less time, during the following years, up to and including the season of 1884.

Horse.	Time.	Year.
Maud S.	2:09¼	1884
Jay-Eye-See	2:10	1884
St. Julien	2:11¼	1880
Rarus	2:13¼	1878
Maxy Cobb	2:13¼	1884
Phallas	2:13¾	1884
Clingstone	2:14	1882
Goldsmith Maid	2:14	1874
Trinket	2:14	1881
Lulu	2:14¼	1883
Hopeful	2:14¾	1878
Smuggler	2:15¼	1876
Hattie Woodward	2:15½	1880
Lucille Golddust	2:16¼	1877
Edwin Thorne	2:16¼	1884
Wilson	2:16¼	1883
Minnie R.	2:16½	1884
American Girl	2:16½	1874
Darby	2:16½	1879
Maud Messenger	2:16½	1884
Phil. Thompson	2:16½	1884
Jerome Eddy	2:16½	1882
Charlie Ford	2:16¾	1880
Occident	2:16¾	1873
Gloster	2:17	1874
Phyllis	2:17	1884
Harry Wilkes	2:17	1884
Fanny Witherspoon	2:17	1883
Clemmie G.	2:17	1883
Director	2:17	1883
Majolica	2:17	1883
Black Cloud	2:17¼	1882
Dexter	2:17¼	1867
Piedmont	2:17¼	1881
So-So	2:17¼	1881
Santa Claus	2:17¼	1881
Robert McGregor	2:17¼	1883
Hannis	2:17¾	1882
Duquesne	2:17¾	1883
Red Cloud	2:18	1874
Lady Thorne (2)	2:18	1883
Nettie	2:18	1874
Judge Fullerton	2:18	1875
Great Eastern	2:18	1878
Edwin Forrest	2:18	1878
Protine	2:18	1878
Dick Swiveller	2:18	1879
Josephus	2:18	1881
Kate Sprague	2:18	1881
Catchfly	2:18	1884
Lady Thorn (1)	2:18¼	1869
Lucy	2:18¼	1872
Lady Maud	2:18¼	1875
Midnight	2:18¼	1878
Monroe Chief	2:18¼	1882
Rosa Wilkes	2:18¼	1882
Slow-Go	2:18½	1877
Col. Lewis	2:18½	1878
Nutwood	2:18¾	1880
J. B. Thomas	2:18¾	1882
William H.	2:18¾	1882
Patchen	2:18¾	1880
Cleora	2:18¾	1882
Bonita	2:18¾	1883
Cozette	2:19	1876
Albemarle	2:19	1878
Edward	2:19	1878
Alley	2:19	1879
Bonesetter	2:19	1879
Alexander	2:19	1881
Daisy dale	2:19	1880
Graves	2:19	1882
Kittie Bates	2:19	1882
Wedgwood	2:19	1882
Adele Gould	2:19	1882

₊ Maud S., at Cleveland, O., August 2, 1884, trotted one mile in 2:09 3-4; and, at Lexington, Ky., November 4, 1884, she trotted one mile in 2:09 1-4—the best time ever recorded.

Jay-Eye-See trotted one mile, at Providence, R. I., August 1, 1884, in 2:10.

Seven Wonders of the World.

Pyramids of Egypt.

Tower, Walls and Terrace Hanging Gardens of Babylon.

Statue of Jupiter Olympus, on the Capitoline Hill, at Rome.

Temple of Diana, at Ephesus.

Pharos, or watch-tower, at Alexandria, Egypt.

Colossus of Rhodes, a statue 105 feet high, overthrown by an earthquake 224 B. C.

Mausoleum at Halicarnassus, a Grecian-Persian city in Asia Minor.

EXPENSE OF BOARD PER DAY.

The following table will be found convenient for the proprietors of hotels and boarding-houses in giving the price per day where the board is a certain specified price per week. Thus, if it is desired to find the price of five days' board at $5.00 per week, it will be found by reference to be $3.57. (See table). When the board exceeds $10.00 per week, double the numbers.

Days.	50c.	75c.	$1.00	$1.25	$1.50	$1.75	$2	$2.25	$2.50	$3	$3.50	$4	$4.50	$5	$6	$7	$8	$9	$10
1	.7	.11	.14	.18	.21	.25	.29	.32	.36	.43	.50	.57	.64	.71	.86	1.00	1.14	1.29	1.43
2	.14	.21	.29	.36	.43	.50	.57	.64	.71	.86	1.00	1.14	1.29	1.43	1.71	2.00	2.29	2.57	2.86
3	.21	.32	.43	.54	.64	.75	.86	.96	1.07	1.29	1.50	1.71	1.93	2.14	2.57	3.00	3.43	3.86	4.29
4	.29	.43	.57	.71	.86	1.00	1.14	1.29	1.43	1.71	2.00	2.29	2.57	2.86	3.43	4.00	4.57	5.14	5.71
5	.36	.54	.71	.89	1.07	1.25	1.43	1.61	1.79	2.14	2.50	2.86	3.21	3.57	4.29	5.00	5.71	6.43	7.14
6	.43	.64	.82	1.07	1.29	1.50	1.71	1.93	2.14	2.57	3.00	3.43	3.86	4.29	5.14	6.00	6.86	7.71	8.57
7	.50	.75	1.00	1.25	1.50	1.75	2.00	2.25	2.50	3.00	3.50	4.00	4.50	5.00	6.00	7.00	8.00	9.00	10.00

LEGAL WEIGHT OF A BUSHEL IN DIFFERENT STATES.*

States and Territories.	Wheat.	Rye.	Oats.	Barley.	Buckwheat.	Shelled Corn.	Corn on Cob.	Corn Meal.	Potatoes.	Sweet Potatoes.	Onions.	Turnips.	Beans.	Peas.	Dried apples.	Dried peaches.	Flax-seed.	Timothy seed.	Bluegrass seed.	Clover-seed.	Coal, anthracite.
	lbs.	lbs.	lbs.	lbs.	lbs.	lbs.	lbs.	lbs.	lbs.	lbs.	lbs.	lbs.	lbs.	lbs.	lbs.	lbs.	lbs.	lbs.	lbs.	lbs.	lbs.
Arkansas	60	56	32	48	52		70	50	60	50	57		60	46	24	33	56	45	14	60	80
Arizona	60	56	32	45		54							60								
California	60	54	32	50	40	52															
Colorado	60	56	32	48	52	56	70	50	60		57		60					45	14	60	
Connecticut	60	56	32	48	48	56		50	60		50	50	60	60							
Dakota	60	56	32	48	42	56	70		60	46	52	60	60	60			56	42		60	80
Delaware	60					56		48													
District Columbia	60	56	32			56		48	60												
Georgia	60	56	32	47	52	56	70	48	60		55	57	55	60	60	24	33	56	45	14	60	80
Illinois	60	56	32	48	52	56	70	48	60		55	57	55	60		24	33	56	45	14	60	80
Indiana	60	56		48	50	56	68	50	60			48		60		25	33		45	14	60	
Iowa	60	56	32	48	52	56	70		60		46	57		60		24	33	56	45	14	60	80
Kansas	60	56	32	48	50	56	70	50	60	50	57	55	60		24	33	54	45	14	60	80
Kentucky	60	56	32	47	55	55	70	50	60	55	57	60	60	60	24	39	56	45	14	60	76
Louisiana	60	32	32	32				50													
Maine	60	56	30	48	48	56		50	60		52	50	64	60							
Maryland	60	56	32	47	48	56	70	48		56	56		60				45	14	64		
Massachusetts	60	56	32	48	48	56		50	60	56	52										
Michigan	60	56	32	48	48	56	70	50	60	56	54	58	60	60	22	28	56	45	14	60	
Minnesota	60	56	32	48	42	56			60				28	28						60	
Missouri	60	56	32	48	52	56			60		57		60		24	33	56	45	14	60	
Montana	60	56	35	48	52	56		50	60		57	50	60				45	14	60		
Nebraska	60	56	32	48	52	56	70	50	60	50	57	55	60	60	24	33	56	45	14	60	80
Nevada	60	56	32	50	40	52	70		60				60								
New Hampshire	60	56	32			56		50					60	60							
New Jersey	60	56	30	48	50	56			60	54	57		60	60	25	33	55			64	
New York	60	56	32	48	48	56			60			62	60			55	44			60	
North Carolina	60	56	30	48	50	54		46					50							64	
Ohio	60	56	32	48	50	56	70		60	50	50		60	60	22	33	56	45		60	
Oregon	60	56	36	46	42	56			60				28	28					60	
Pennsylvania	60	56	32	47	48	56			60				60						62	
Rhode Island	60	56	32	48		56		50	60		50										
South Carolina	60	56	33	48	56		70	50	60	50	57		60	60	26	33	44		14	60	
Tennessee	56	32	48	50	56	72	50	60	50	56		60	60	26		56	45			
Vermont	60	56	32	48	46	56			60		52	60	60	60			45		60	
Virginia	60	56	32	48	52	56	70	50	60	56	57	55	60	60	28	32	56	45	14	60	80
Washington Ter.	60	56	36	45	42	56			50		50	50	60	60	28	28		40		60	
West Virginia	60	56	32	48	52	56			60				60		25	33	56	45		60	
Wisconsin	60	56	32	48	50	56	70		60		50	42	60		28	28	56	45		60	

* Some States, not here mentioned, only legalize and recognize the Standard United States bushel, without reference to weight.

SHORT INSURANCE RATES.

By the following table may be seen the customary short rates of insurance for periods less than a year or month.

EXPLANATION.—When the rate is one per cent., or $1 on $100 for a year, the rate for one month is 4-20 of the annual rate, or 20 cents. (See table.) For six months it would be 14-20, or 70 cents. (See following table, which, by a little study, will be readily understood.)

For Periods of Several Years.

1 YEAR.	2 YEARS.	3 YEARS.	4 YEARS.	5 YEARS.	Charge this Proportion of whole Premium.
1 mo.	2 mo.	3 mo.	4 mo.	5 mo.	$\frac{4}{20}$ or 20 per cent.
2 "	4 "	6 "	8 "	10 "	$\frac{6}{20}$ " 30 " "
3 "	6 "	9 "	12 "	15 "	$\frac{8}{20}$ " 40 " "
4 "	8 "	12 "	16 "	20 "	$\frac{10}{20}$ " 50 " "
5 "	10 "	15 "	20 "	25 "	$\frac{12}{20}$ " 60 " "
6 "	12 "	18 "	24 "	30 "	$\frac{14}{20}$ " 70 " "
7 "	14 "	21 "	28 "	35 "	$\frac{15}{20}$ " 75 " "
8 "	16 "	24 "	32 "	40 "	$\frac{16}{20}$ " 80 " "
9 "	18 "	27 "	36 "	45 "	$\frac{17}{20}$ " 85 " "
10 "	20 "	30 "	40 "	50 "	$\frac{18}{20}$ " 90 " "
11 "	22 "	33 "	44 "	55 "	$\frac{19}{20}$ " 95 " "

For Periods Less than One Year.

1 month,	$\frac{4}{20}$ of annual rate		7 mo's,	$\frac{15}{20}$ of annual rate.
2 "	$\frac{6}{20}$ " "		8 "	$\frac{16}{20}$ " "
3 "	$\frac{8}{20}$ " "		9 "	$\frac{17}{20}$ " "
4 "	$\frac{10}{20}$ " "		10 "	$\frac{18}{20}$ " "
5 "	$\frac{12}{20}$ " "		11 "	$\frac{19}{20}$ " "
6 "	$\frac{14}{20}$ " "			

For Periods Less than One Month.

5 days,	$\frac{35}{100}$ of monthly rate	15 days,	$\frac{65}{100}$ of monthly rate
10 "	$\frac{50}{100}$ " "	20 "	$\frac{80}{100}$ " "

AGRICULTURAL TABLES FOR FARMERS, GARDENERS AND OTHERS.

For many facts and figures in these various reference tables, credit is due the "American Almanac," edited by A. R. Spofford, "Moore's Universal Assistant," by R. Moore, the "American Farm and Home Cyclopædia," by H. R. Allen, "Farmers' and Mechanics' Manual," by Geo. E. Warring, "Statesman's Year Book," by Frederick Martin, "The Circle of Useful Knowledge" and other valuable works.

Vitality of Seeds.

Length of time that the seeds of various herbs and vegetables retain their powers of germination.

Vegetables.	*Years.*	*Vegetables.*	*Years.*
Cucumber	8 to 10	Leek	2 to 3
Melon	8 to 10	Onion	2 to 3
Pumpkin	8 to 10	Parsley	2 to 3
Squash	8 to 10	Parsnip	2 to 3
Broccoli	5 to 6	Pepper	2 to 3
Cauliflower	5 to 6	Salsify	2 to 3
Artichoke	5 to 6	Tomato	2 to 3
Endive	5 to 6	Egg-plant	1 to 2
Pea	5 to 6	*Herbs.*	
Radish	4 to 5		
Beets	3 to 4	Anise	3 to 4
Cress	3 to 4	Hyssop	3 to 4
Lettuce	3 to 4	Balm	2 to 3
Mustard	3 to 4	Caraway	2....
Okra	3 to 4	Coriander	1....
Rhubarb	3 to 4	Dill	2 to 3
Spinach	3 to 4	Fennel	2 to 3
Turnip	3 to 6	Lavender	2 to 3
Asparagus	2 to 3	Sweet Marjoram	2 to 3
Beans	2 to 3	Summer Savory	1 to 2
Carrots	2 to 3	Sage	2 to 3
Celery	2 to 3	Thyme	2 to 3
Corn (on cob)	2 to 3	Wormwood	2 to 3

Number to an Acre

Of plants or trees set at regular distances apart.

Distances apart.	No. of plants.	*Distances apart.*	No. of Plants.
3 inches by 3 inches	696,960	6 feet by 6 feet	1,210
6 inches by 4 inches	392,040	6½ feet by 6½ feet	1,031
6 inches by 6 inches	174,240	7 feet by 7 feet	881
9 inches by 9 inches	77,440	8 feet by 8 feet	680
1 foot by 1 foot	43,560	9 feet by 9 feet	537
1½ feet by 1½ feet	19,360	10 feet by 10 feet	435
2 feet by 1 foot	21,780	11 feet by 11 feet	360
2 feet by 2 feet	10,890	12 feet by 12 feet	302
2½ feet by 2½ feet	6,960	13 feet by 13 feet	257
3 feet by 1 foot	14,520	14 feet by 14 feet	222
3 feet by 2 feet	7,260	15 feet by 15 feet	193
3 feet by 3 feet	4,840	16 feet by 16 feet	170
3½ feet by 3½ feet	3,555	16½ feet by 16½ feet	160
4 feet by 1 foot	10,890	17 feet by 17 feet	150
4 feet by 2 feet	5,445	18 feet by 18 feet	134
4 feet by 3 feet	3,630	19 feet by 19 feet	120
4 feet by 4 feet	2,722	20 feet by 20 feet	108
4½ feet by 4½ feet	2,151	25 feet by 25 feet	69
5 feet by 1 foot	8,712	30 feet by 30 feet	48
5 feet by 2 feet	4,356	33 feet by 33 feet	40
5 feet by 3 feet	2,904	40 feet by 40 feet	27
5 feet by 4 feet	2,178	50 feet by 50 feet	17
5 feet by 5 feet	1,742	60 feet by 60 feet	12
5½ feet by 5½ feet	1,417	66 feet by 66 feet	10

Cost of Producing Pork.

The cost of producing a pound of pork depends upon the cost of corn per bushel, as follows:

Corn per Bushel in Cents.	Will make the cost of pork per hundred.
12½ cts	$1.50
15	1.78
17	2.00
20	2.38
22	2.62
25	2.96
30	3.57
33	3.92
35	4.00
38	4.52
40	4.76
42	5.00
45	5.35
50	5.95
55	6.54
60	7.14
65	7.74
70	8.57

Cost of Small Quantities of Hay.

Price per Ton.	50 lbs. worth.	100 lbs. worth.	200 lbs. worth.	300 lbs. worth	400 lbs. worth.
Four dollars	10 cts.	20 cts.	40 cts.	60	$ .80
Five dollars	12	25	50	75	1.00
Six dollars	15	30	60	90	1.20
Seven dollars	17	35	70	1.05	1.40
Eight dollars	20	40	80	1.20	1.60
Nine dollars	22	45	90	1.35	1.80
Ten dollars	25	50	1.00	1.50	2.00
Eleven dollars	27	55	1.10	1.65	2.20
Twelve dollars	30	60	1.20	1,80	2.40
Thirteen dollars	32	65	1.30	1.95	2.60
Fourteen dollars	35	70	1.40	2.10	2.80
Fifteen dollars	37	75	1.50	2.25	3.00

Facts About Sheep.

The weight of any animal at a certain age, will, of course, depend upon the manner in which it is fed and cared for. Supposing sheep to be well fed and sheltered, the following presents an average yield of flesh and wool at a certain age.

Breeds.	Bucks weigh.	Ewes weigh.	Age at maturity. Years.	Annual yield of wool lbs.
Cotswold	300	200	2	14
Lincoln	300	200	2	11
Leicester	250	150	2½	8
Merino, American	150	130	2	9
Merino, Spanish	125	110	3	10
Southdown	200	140	2	6
Shropshire	200	140	2	6
Common "Scrub"	120	90	3	4

Weight of Horses.

Breeds.	Stallions.	Geldings and Mares.	Age when Matured.
Cleveland Bay	1,400	1,300	6
Clydesdale	1,900	1,700	4½
English draft	1,800	1,650	6
Hambletonian	1,150	1,100	5
Mambrino	1,200	1,150	5
Morgan	950	900	5
Percheron—Norman	1,750	1,550	4
Pony—Canadian	950	900	4
Pony—Mustang	500	450	3
Pony—Shetland	300	250	3
"Scrub," or Native	1,000	950	4½
Thoroughbred	1,150	1,000	2
Ass	700	600	6
Mule		1,000	5

Quantity of Seed Required to Sow or Plant an Acre.

Kind of Seed.	*Quantity.*
Asparagus in 12-inch drills	16 qts
Asparagus plants, 4 by 1½ feet	8,000
Barley	2½ bu
Beans, bush, in drills 2½ feet	1½ bu
Beans, pole, Lima, 4 by 4 feet	20 qts
Beans, Carolina, prolific, etc., 4 by 3	10 qts
Beets and mangold, drills, 2½ feet	9 lbs
Broom corn in drills	12 lbs
Cabbage, outside, for transplanting	12 oz
Cabbage, sown in frames	4 oz
Carrot in drills, 2½ feet	4 lbs
Celery, seed	8 oz
Celery, plant, 4 by ½ feet	25,000
Clover, white Dutch	13 lbs
Clover, Lucerne	10 lbs
Clover, Alsike	6 lbs
Clover, large red with timothy	12 lbs
Clover, large red without timothy	16 lbs
Corn, sugar	10 qts
Corn, field	8 qts
Corn, salad, drill 10 inches	25 lbs
Cucumber, in hills	3 qts
Cucumber, in drills	4 qts

Kind of Seed.	*Quantity.*
Egg plant, plants 3 by 2 feet	4 oz
Endive, in drills 2½ feet	3 lbs
Flax, broadcast	20 qts
Grass, timothy with clover	6 qts
Grass, timothy without clover	10 qts
Grass, orchard	25 qts
Grass, red top or herds	20 qts
Grass, blue	28 qts
Grass, rye	20 qts
Grass, millet	32 qts
Hemp, broadcast	½ bu
Kale, German greens	3 lbs
Lettuce, in rows 2½ feet	3 lbs
Leek	4 lbs
Lawn grass	35 lbs
Melons, water, in hills 8 by 8 feet	3 lbs
Melons, citrons, in hills 4 by 4 feet	2 lbs
Oats	2 bu
Okra, in dril's 2½ by ¼ feet	20 lbs
Onion, in beds for sets	50 lbs
Onion, in rows for large bulbs	7 lbs
Parsnip, in drills 2½ feet	5 lbs
Pepper, plants, 2½ by 1 foot	17,500

Kind of Seed.	*Quantity.*
Pumpkin, in hills 8 by 8 feet	2 qts
Parsley, in drills 2 feet	4 lbs
Peas, in drills, short varieties	2 bu
Peas, in drills, tall varieties	1 to 1½ bu
Peas, broadcast	3 bu
Potatoes	8 bu
Radish, in drills 2 feet	10 lbs
Rye, broadcast	1½ bu
Rye, drilled	1½ bu
Salsify, in drills 2½ feet	10 lbs
Spinach, broadcast	30 lbs
Squash, bush, in hills 4 by 4 feet	3 lbs
Squash, running, 8 by 8 feet	2 lbs
Sorghum	4 qts
Turnips, in drills 2 feet	3 lbs
Turnips, broadcast	3 lbs
Tomatoes, in frames	3 oz
Tomatoes, seed in hills 3 by 3 feet	8 oz
Tomatoes, plants	3,800
Wheat, in drills	1½ bu
Wheat, broadcast	2 bu

Facts Concerning Production of Soil, Amount of Rainfall, Condition of Temperature, Weights, Foods, Etc.

Foreigners in the U. S.

By the census of 1880 there was in the States and Territories a population as follows:

Males	25,518,820
Females	24,636,963
Native born	43,475,840
Foreign born	6,679,943

Summary of the Bible.

The following table is published as containing accurate particulars of the English version of the Bible:

In the Old Testament.	
Letters	2,728,100
Words	592,493
Verses	23,214
Chapters	929
Books	39
In the New Testament.	
Letters	838,380
Words	181,253
Verses	7,959
Chapters	260
Books	27
Total.	
Letters	3,566,480
Words	773,746
Verses	31,173
Chapters	1,189
Books	66

Average Annual Rainfall

—At different parts of the United States and Territories.

Place.	*Inches.*
Neah Bay, Wash. Ter.	123
Sitka, Alaska	83
Ft. Haskins, Or.	66
Mt. Vernon, Ala	66
Baton Rouge, La	60
Meadow Valley, Cal	57
Ft. Tonson, Ind. Ter.	57
Ft. Myers, Fla.	56
Washington, Ark	54
Huntsville, Ala.	54
Natchez, Miss.	53
New Orleans, La	51
Savannah, Ga	48
Springdale, Ky.	48
Fortress Monroe, Va.	47
Memphis, Tenn.	45
Newark, N. J.	44
Boston, Mass.	44
Brunswick, Me.	44
Cincinnati, O.	44
New Haven, Conn.	44
Philadelphia, Pa.	44
Charleston, S. C.	43
New York City	43
Gaston, N. C.	43
Richmond, Ind.	43
Marietta, O.	43
St. Louis, Mo.	43
Muscatine, Ia.	42
Baltimore, Md.	41
New Bedford, Mass.	41
Providence, R. I.	41
Fort Smith, Ark.	40
Hanover, N. H.	40
Ft. Vancouver	38
Cleveland, O.	37
Pittsburgh, Pa.	37
Washington, D. C.	37
White Sulphur Springs, Va.	37
Ft. Gibson, Ind. Ter.	36
Key West, Fla.	36
Peoria, Ill.	35
Burlington, Vt.	34
Buffalo, N. Y.	33
Ft. Brown, Tex.	33
Ft. Leavenworth, Kan.	31
Detroit, Mich.	30
Milwaukee, Wis.	30
Penn Yan, N. Y.	28
Ft. Kearney	25
Ft. Snelling, Minn.	25
Salt Lake City, U. T.	23
Mackinac, Mich.	23
San Francisco, Cal.	21
Dallas, Or.	21
Sacramento, Cal.	21
Ft. Massachusetts, Col.	17
Ft. Marcy, N. M.	16
Ft. Randall, D. T.	16
Ft. Laramie, Wy. T.	15
Ft. Defiance, Ariz.	14
Ft. Craig, N. M.	11
San Diego, Cal.	9
Ft. Colville, Wash. Ter.	9
Ft. Bliss, Tex.	9
Ft. Bridger, Utah	6
Ft. Garland, Col.	6

Average Temperature

—In different States and Territories.

Place of Observation.	State or Territory.	Average Temperature.
Tucson	Ariz.	69
Jacksonville	Fla.	69
New Orleans	La	69
Austin	Tex.	67
Mobile	Ala.	66
Jackson	Miss.	64
Little Rock	Ark.	63
Columbia	S. C.	62
Ft. Gibson	Ind. Ter.	60
Raleigh	N. C.	59
Atlanta	Ga.	58
Nashville	Tenn.	58
Richmond	Va.	57
Louisville	Ky.	56
San Francisco	Cal.	55
Washington	D. C.	55
St. Louis	Mo.	55
Baltimore	Md.	54
Harrisburg	Pa.	54
Wilmington	Del.	53
Trenton	N. J.	53
Columbus	O.	53
Portland	Or.	53
Ft. Boise	Idaho	52
Salt Lake City	Utah	52
Romney	W. Va.	52
Indianapolis	Ind.	51
Leavenworth	Kan.	51
Santa Fe	N. M.	51
Sterlacoom	W. Ter.	51
Hartford	Conn.	50
Springfield	Ill.	50
Camp Scott	Nev.	50
Des Moines	Iowa	49
Omaha	Neb.	49
Denver	Col.	48
Boston	Mass.	48
Albany	N. Y.	48
Providence	R. I.	48
Detroit	Mich.	47
Ft. Randall	Dak.	47
Sitka	Alaska	46
Concord	N. H.	46
Augusta	Maine	45
Madison	Wis.	45
Helena	Mont.	43
Montpelier	Vt.	43
St. Paul	Minn.	42

Weights by Railroad.

When not able to ascertain the weight definitely, railway companies make the following standard of weights in bulk.

Articles.		*Pounds.*
Salt	Per bushel	70
Eggs	Barrel	200
Bark	Cord	2,000
Barley	Bushel	45
Apples	Bushel	50
Liquors	Per gallon	10
Charcoal	Bushel	22
Buckwheat	Bushel	48
Wood—oak	Cord	3,500
Clover seed	Bushel	62
Hides (green)	Each	85
Ice, coal, lime	Bushel	80
Stone, dressed	Cubic feet	180
Plastering lath	Per 1,000	600
Wood—hickory	Cord	4,500
Bricks, common	Each	5
Nails and spikes	Keg	106
Sand, gravel, etc.	Per cubic feet	150
Stone, undressed	Perch	4,000
Beef, pork, bacon	Per hhd.	1,000
Salt fish and meat	Per firkin.	100
Ashes, pot or pearl	Barrel	450
Butter, tallow, lard	Per bbl.	333
Coke, and cake meal	Bushel	40
Resin, tar, turpentine	Barrel	300
Onions, wheat, potatoes	Bushel	60
Bran, feed, shipstuffs, oats	Bushel	35
Liquors, malt and distilled	Barrel	350
Apples, and barrelled fruits	Barrel	200
Grain and seeds, not stated	Bushel	60
Timothy and light grass seed	Bushel	40
Hides (dry), salted or Spanish	Each	33
Shingles	Per M., short, 900 lbs., Long	1,400
Lumber—pine, poplar, hemlock	Ft. b. m.	4
Lumber—oak, walnut, cherry, ash	Ft. b. m.	5
Oysters	Per bushel, 100 lbs., per 1,000	350
Flour and meal	Per bushel, 56 lbs., Barrel	216

Landholders of Great Britain.

The English law of entailment, which provides that the eldest son shall inherit his parents' lands and tenements, has brought about the following results:

Amount of Land.	*Number Owners.*	*Acres Land.*
Less than 1 acre	816,294	179,348
From 1 to 10 acres	131,454	508,006
From 10 to 50 acres	76,109	1,827,698
From 50 to 100 acres	27,052	1,878,088
From 100 to 500 acres	34,684	7,383,718
From 500 to 1,000 acres	5,625	3,900,419
From 1,000 to 2,000 acres	3,310	4,634,549
From 2,000 to 5,000 acres	2,402	7,372,568
From 5,000 to 10,000 acres	831	5,701,593
From 10,000 to 20,000 acres	382	5,248,785
From 20,000 to 50,000 acres	169	4,988,804
From 50,000 to 100,000 acres	47	3,220,554
100,000 acres and over	25	5,113,500
No acres stated	6,945	
No rentals stated	124	2,570

Facts Concerning Poultry,

—Different breeds, their live weight, when full grown, the annual number of eggs they will lay, etc.

Breeds.	Live weight of Males.	Live weight of Hens.	No. of Eggs laid per year.	No. of Eggs to the pound.
Brahmas, light	11½	8	150	7
Brahmas, dark	10½	7	150	8
Cochins, black	10	7	170	9½
Cochins, buff	10	7½	120	8
Cochins, white	11	9	140	8
Cochins, partridge	11	8	150	8
Common	3½	3	160	11
Dorkings	6½	5	120	9
Dominiques, American	5	4	170	10
Games, black-breast'd, red	7½	5	170	10
Hamburgs	4	3	180	12
Houdans	7½	5	170	9
Leghorns, black	4½	3½	200	10
Leghorns, brown	4½	3½	200	10
Leghorns, dominique	4½	3½	200	10
Leghorns, white	4½	3½	200	10
Plymouth Rocks	8½	6½	175	8½
Polish	5½	3½	170	9
Spanish, black	7	6	170	9½
Ducks, common	3	3	90	9
Ducks, Aylesbury	7	6	80	6
Ducks, Cayuga	6	5½	100	8
Ducks, Pekin	6	5½	75	8
Ducks, Rouen	7½	6½	80	6
Geese, common	8	7	20	4
Geese, African	20	18	30	4
Geese, Egyptian	7	6	40	4
Geese, Embden	18	15	20	3¾
Geese, Toulouse	22	20	40	3½
Turkeys, common	12	10	50	7
Turkeys, black	15	12	50	6
Turkeys, bronze	24	15	50	6
Turkeys, buff	15	12	50	7
Turkeys, Narragansett	22	14	50	6

Foods for Sheep.

In the course of several experiments by De Raumer, a French scientist, it was found that 1,000 pounds of different kinds of foods produced the following results. It will be seen by examination that wheat proved the most valuable food, barley came next, while mangolds stood lowest in the scale.

Substances.	Increase of weight in living animals.	Wool produced.	Tallow. produced
Potatoes with salt	46½ lbs.	6½ lbs.	12½ lbs.
Potatoes without salt	44 lbs.	6½ lbs.	11½ lbs.
Mangold-Wurzels	38½ lbs.	5¼ lbs.	6½ lbs.
Wheat	155 lbs.	14 lbs.	59½ lbs.
Oats	146 lbs.	10 lbs.	42½ lbs.
Barley	136 lbs.	11½ lbs.	60 lbs.
Peas	134 lbs.	14½ lbs.	41 lbs.
Rye, with salt	133 lbs.	14 lbs.	35 lbs.
Rye, without salt	90 lbs.	12 lbs.	43 lbs.
Corn-meal, wet	129 lbs.	13½ lbs.	17½ lbs.
Buckwheat	120 lbs.	10 lbs.	33 lbs.

Healthiest Regions, Value of Foods, Educational Advancement, Etc.

Healthiest Regions for Consumptives.

The following table, in a scale of 100, shows the per cent. of deaths from consumption. From this it will be seen that the Atlantic States have a much higher death rate from this disease than most of the Western States and Territories.

State.	No. of Deaths in each 100.
Vermont	26
Maine	25
Massachusetts	25
New Hampshire	25
Rhode Island	25
Connecticut	20
Delaware	20
District of Columbia	20
New Jersey	20
New York	20
Maryland	16
Michigan	16
Ohio	16
Pennsylvania	16
Washington Territory	16
West Virginia	16
California	14
Indiana	14
Kentucky	14
Minnesota	14
Wisconsin	14
Dakota	12
Iowa	12
Oregon	12
Tennessee	12
Virginia	12
Illinois	11

State.	No. of Deaths in each 100.
Nebraska	9
Missouri	9
Montana	9
Colorado	8
Kansas	8
Louisiana	8
North Carolina	8
Alabama	6
Florida	6
Mississippi	6
Utah	6
Arkansas	5
Georgia	5
South Carolina	5
Texas	5
New Mexico	3

Relative Value of Foods.

One hundred pounds of good hay for stock are equal to—

Articles.	Pounds.
Beets, white silesia	669
Turnips	469
Rye-straw	429
Clover, red, green	373
Carrots	371
Mangolds	368½
Potatoes, kept in pit	350
Oat-straw	317
Potatoes	260
Carrot leaves (tops)	135
Hay, English	100
Lucerne	89
Clover, red, dry	88

Articles.	Pounds.
Buckwheat	78½
Corn	62½
Oats	59
Barley	58
Rye	53½
Wheat	44½
Oil-cake, linseed	43
Peas, dry	37½
Beans	28

Amount of Oil in Seeds.

The amount of oil in a certain seed will vary according to conditions of growth. In a scale of 100 this is considered about an average per cent.

Kind of Seeds.	Per Cent. of Oil.
Rapeseed	55
Sweet almond	47
Turnip seed	45
White mustard	37
Bitter almond	37
Hempseed	19
Linseed	17
Indian corn	7
Oats	6½
Clover hay	5
Wheat bran	4
Oat-straw	4
Meadow hay	3½
Wheat-straw	3
Wheat flour	3
Barley	2½
Potatoes, turnips, cabbages	1½

Canning Fruit.

A general rule for the canning of fruit is to add one pound of sugar to four pounds of fruit, and water sufficient to keep it from burning. If the fruit be very tart, more sugar may be added if desired. Whether glass or tin, the cans must, of course, be air-tight. The following gives the requisite time for boiling and the amount of sugar it is well to add at the time of canning.

Fruit.	Time for boiling. Min.	Quantity of sugar per qt. Oz.
Small pears, whole	30	8
Siberian apples	25	8
Bartlett pears	20	6
Tomatoes	20	None
Quinces, sliced	15	10
Pine apples, sliced	15	6
Peaches, whole	15	4
Pie-plant, sliced	10	10
Plums	10	8
Wild grapes	10	8
Sour apples	10	5
Blackberries	9	6
Strawberries	8	8
Gooseberries	8	8
Peaches, halved	8	4
Ripe currants	6	8
Raspberries	6	4
Cherries	5	6
Whortleberries	5	4

Cannot Read or Write.

The per cent. of illiteracy in the scale of 100 among the people of different countries is shown in the following table, as taken from Kiddle & Schem's Cyclopædia of Education, New York, 1877:

Country.	Year.	Per Ct. of Illiteracy.
India	1871	95
Mexico	Recent	93
Poland	Recent	91
Russia	Recent	91
Argentine Rep.	Recent	83
Greece	Recent	82
Spain	1860	80
Italy	1861	73
Hungary	Recent	51
China	Recent	50
Austria	Recent	49
Ireland	Recent	46
England	Recent	33
Belgium	Recent	30
France	1872	30
United States	1870	20
Netherlands	Recent	18
Scotland	Recent	16
Japan	Recent	10

Illiteracy in the U. S.

By the census of 1880, persons over ten years old that could not write:

Whites	2,851,911
Colored	2,798,689
Natives	4,880,271
Foreigners	777,873
Could not read, total	4,528,084

Salaries of Kings, Queens, Presidents and other Rulers.

The following table, condensed from the "Statesman's Year Book," shows the yearly salary paid to kings, queens and members of royal households and presidents of various republics, according to the most reliable authorities in 1880. Out of these salaries some rulers have much to pay, in order to maintain the character of their position, so that their actual clear savings, annually, cannot be easily shown.

Country.	Ruler.	Salary.	Country.	Ruler.	Salary.	Country.	Ruler.	Salary.
Turkey	Sultan and royal household	$10,000,000.00	Great Britain and Ireland, including queen and members of the royal household, making a total annual salary for the government to pay of $1,292,210	Queen (Privy Purse)	$290,400.00	Saxe Meiningen	Duke	$91,960.00
Russia	Emperor and royal household	9,608,000.00		Prince of Wales	400,000.00	Sweden and Norway	King	80,663.44
Italy	King	3,146,000.00		Princess of Wales	48,400.00		Royal family	418,926.20
	Prince Amadeo	58,080.00		Duke of Edinburgh	121,000.00	Saxe-Coburg-Gotha	Duke	72,600.00 to 97,342.08
	Duke of Genoa	38,720.00		Duke of Connaught	121,000.00			
Germany Prussia	Emperor and King and royal family	2,957,077.86		Prince Leopold	88,720.00	Oldenburg	Grand Duke	60,500.00
				Princess Fredrich Wilhelm of Prussia	38,720.00		Royal family	Private income
Morocco	Sultan	2,420,000.00		Princess Christian of Schleswig-Holstein	29,040.00	Schwarzburg-Rudolstadt	Prince	58,080.00
Austria-Hungary	As Emperor	2,250,600.00		Princess Louise, Marchioness of Lorne	29,040.00	United States	President	50,000.00
	As King	2,250,600.00		Duchess of Cambridge	29,040.00	Victoria	Governor	48,400.00
Spain	King	1,355,200.00		Grand Duchess of Mecklenb'g-Strelitz	14,520.00	Lippe	Prince	48,400.00 and Private income
	Queen	87,120.00		Princess Teck	24,250.00			
	Parents of King	203,280.00		Duke George of Cambridge	58,080.00	Canada	Governor-General	48,400.00
	King's Sisters	154,880.00	Denmark	King	268,886.20	Ceylon	Governor	38,720.00
Bavaria	King and royal family	1,293,940.12		Heir apparent	32,263.44	New Zealand	Governor	36,300.00
Japan	Mikado and royal family	845,548.00	Greece	King	252,541.52	New South Wales	Governor	33,880.00
Egypt	Khedive	726,000.00	Netherlands	King	242,000.00	Hong Kong	Governor	29,040.00
	His father	242,000.00		Royal family	60,500.00	Mauritius	Governor	29,040.00
	Royal family	338,800.00	Brunswick	Duke	242,000.00	Cape Colony, Africa	Governor	24,200.00
Saxony	King	711,480.00	Saxe Weimar	Grand Duke	203,280.00	Queensland	Governor	24,200.00
	Royal family	123,855.60	Roumania	Prince	174,240.00	South Australia	Governor	24,200.00
Belgium	King	543,840.00	Anhalt	Duke and royal family	140,360.00	Chili	President	21,780.00
Wurtemberg	King	447,985.56	India	Governor-General	121,000.00	Argentine Republic	President	19,360.00
	Royal family	80,319.80	Schaumberg-Lippe	Prince	121,000.00	Tasmania	Governor	16,940.00
Portugal	King	396,880.00	France	President	116,160.00	Natal, Africa	Governor	12,100.00
	Queen	64,372.00		State household	58,080.00	Western Australia	Governor	12,100.00
	Royal family	182,468.00	Schwarzburg-Sonderhausen	Prince	106,480.00	Switzerland	Federal Council— President	2,904.00
Baden	Grand Duke and royal family	362,666.04	Saxe-Altenburg	Duke and royal family	103,818.00		Members	1,323.20
Hesse	Grand Duke and royal family	318,191.28						

Astronomical Tables, Giving Facts Relative to the Heavenly Bodies,

Condensed from chapter on Astronomy in "HILL'S ALBUM OF BIOGRAPHY AND ART."

Distant From the Sun.

Distances of the different planets from the sun.

Name of Planet.	Miles distant from the sun.
Neptune	2,745,998,000
Uranus	1,822,360,000
Saturn	872,132,000
Jupiter	480,000,000
Mars	145,000,000
Earth	92,000,000
Venus	68,000,000
Mercury	37,000,000
Earth's Moon distant from Earth	240,000

The enormous distances from us of the fixed stars, which are supposed to be suns, are beyond conception. One of these, Sirius (the Dog Star), is supposed to be twenty trillion miles away.

Size of Planets.

The following gives the diameter of the sun and the known principal planets that revolve around it, together with the number of moons belonging to the several planets.

Heavenly Body.	Diameter Miles.	No. of Moons.
Sun	882,000	
Jupiter	91,000	4 moons
Saturn	71,903	8 moons
Neptune	38,000	1 moon
Uranus	34,331	6 moons
Venus	7,621	
Mars	4,222	2 moons
Mercury	2,984	
Earth	8,000	1 moon

Diameter of Earth's Moon, 2,162 miles.

Time of Revolution.

The following is the time of revolution of the various planets around the sun.

Planet.	Time in going around the sun.
Neptune	164½ years
Uranus	84 years
Saturn	29½ years
Jupiter	12 years
Mars	1 yr. 10½ months
Earth	1 year
Venus	224 2-3 days
Mercury	88 days

Our moon makes its revolution around the earth in 29 days, 12 hours, 44 minutes and 3 seconds, and is supposed to revolve once upon its own axis in that time.

Velocity of Motion.

The velocity of speed with which the various planets move through space as they go around the sun, is shown in the following:

Planet.	Miles per hour.
Mercury	110,725
Venus	80,000
Earth	68,000
Jupiter	30,000
Saturn	22,309
Uranus	15,000
Neptune	12,000

Light moves at the rate of 192,000 miles a second, and yet passing with that velocity it would take three years and nine months to reach Alpha, the nearest star, which is nineteen trillions of miles away.

Revolution on its Axis.

The length of the day on each planet is indicated by the following table, which shows the length of time required for revolution on its axis.

Planet.	Daily revolution in hours, minutes and seconds.
Mars	24 h. 39 m. 2½ s.
Mercury	24 h. 5 m. 28 s.
Venus	23 h. 21 m. 7 s.
Earth	24 h.
Saturn	10½ h.
Jupiter	9 h. 56 m.
Uranus	7 h. 5 m.

The sun revolves upon its own axis at the rate of 4,564 miles per hour, and yet requires 25¼ days to complete one entire revolution.

Solidity of Foods, Strength of Liquors, Weights, Measures, Etc.

Solidity of Different Foods.

Showing the proportion of solid matter and water in 100 parts each of the following articles of diet:

Articles.	Solid Matter.	Water	*Articles.*	Solid Matter.	Water.
Wheat	87	13	Pork	24	76
Peas	87	13	Codfish	21	79
Rice	86	14	Blood	20	80
Beans	86	14	Trout	19	81
Rye	86	14	Apples	18	82
Corn	86	14	Pears	16	84
Oatmeal	74	26	Carrots	13	87
Wheat Bread	51	49	Beets	13	87
Mutton	29	71	Milk	13	87
Chicken	27	73	Oysters	13	87
Lean Beef	26	74	Cabbage	8	92
Eggs	26	74	Turnips	7	93
Veal	25	75	Watermelons	5	95
Potatoes	25	75	Cucumbers	3	97

Bricks Required.

Number of bricks required in a wall of different thickness per square foot of surface wall. The dimensions of common bricks are from 7¾ to 8 inches long by 4¼ wide, and 2¼ inches thick.

Thickness of wall.	Bricks.
4 inches	7½
8 inches	15
12 inches	22½
16 inches	30
20 inches	37½
24 inches	46
28 inches	52½
32 inches	60
36 inches	67½
42 inches	75

Per Cent. of Alcohol in Liquors.

In a scale of 100, the following shows the per cent. of alcohol in various kinds of liquors. The reader will understand that the per cent. here given is founded upon the fact that each liquor is tested under the most favorable conditions. Various conditions would change the rate per cent.

Kind of Liquor.	*Per cent.*	*Kind of Liquor.*	*Per cent.*
Scotch Whisky	54½	Malaga	17¼
Rum	53¾	Claret	15
Brandy	53¼	Burgundy	14
Irish Whisky	53	Champagne (still)	13¾
Gin	51	Champagne (sparkling)	12½
Madeira	22¼	Rhenish	12
Port	22	Gooseberry Wine	11½
Currant Wine	20½	Elder	8¾
Teneriffe	19¾	Ale	6¾
Constantia	19¾	Cider	5 to 9
Sherry	19¾	Porter	4
Cape Muscat	18¼	Small Beer	1..

Weights and Measures for Cooks.

1 lb. of Wheat Flour is equal to	1 quart
1 lb. 2 oz. of Indian Meal make	1 quart
1 lb. of Soft Butter is equal to	1 quart
1 lb. of Broken Loaf Sugar is equal to	1 quart
1 lb. 2 oz. of Best Brown Sugar make	1 quart
1 lb. 1 oz. of Powdered White Sugar make	1 quart
10 Eggs make	1 pound
4 Large Tablespoonfuls make	½ gill
1 Common-sized Tumbler holds	½ pint
1 Common-sized Wine-glass is equal to	½ gill
1 Tea-cup holds	1 gill.
1 Large Wine-glass holds	2 ounces
1 Tablespoonful is equal to	½ ounce

Cost of Street Pavement.

The cost of paving will vary slightly in different sections, according to the supply of materials near by. The following is the average cost in Chicago, Ill.:

Kind of Pavement.	*Per Square Yard.*
Stone block, about	$2.50 to $3.25
Asphaltum block	2.25 to 2.50
Cedar block	1.25 to 1.50
Macadam	1.40 to 1.60
Curbstone, per lineal foot	.70 to .75

On a street eighty feet wide there will be two and two-thirds yards, and on a sixty-six foot street two and one-ninth yards of pavement for each foot of frontage on each side of the street, excepting on streets occupied by railway tracks.

Interest Table.

The following will be found convenient in the absence of extended interest tables.

To find the interest on a given sum, for any number of days, at any rate of interest.

At five per cent., multiply the principal by the number of days, and divide by	72
At 6 per cent., as above, and divide by	60
At 7 per cent., as above, and divide by	52
At 8 per cent., as above, and divide by	45
At 9 per cent., as above, and divide by	40
At 10 per cent., as above, and divide by	36
At 12 per cent., as above, and divide by	30
At 15 per cent., as above, and divide by	24
At 20 per cent., as above, and divide by	18

Distances Around the World.

The following includes the principal stopping places, and distances between them, in a direct line around the world.

	Miles.
New York to San Francisco	3,450
San Francisco to Yokohama	4,764
Yokohama to Hong Kong	1,620
Hong Kong to Singapore	1,150
Singapore to Calcutta	1,200
Calcutta to Bombay	1,409
Bombay to Aden	1,664
Aden to Suez	1,308
Suez to Alexandria	250
Alexandria to Marseilles	1,300
Marseilles to Paris	536
Paris to London	316
London to Liverpool	205
Liverpool to New York	3,000

Average Velocity.

Object.	*Per hour.*	*Per sec.*
Electricity moves	288,000 miles	
Light moves	192,000 miles	
A rifle ball moves	1,000 miles, or	1,466 feet
Sound moves	743 miles, or	1,142 feet
A hurricane moves	80 miles, or	117 feet
A storm moves	36 miles, or	52 feet
A horse runs	20 miles, or	29 feet
Steamboat runs	18 miles, or	26 feet
Sailing vessel runs	10 miles, or	14 feet
Slow rivers flow	3 miles, or	4 feet
Rapid rivers flow	7 miles, or	10 feet
A moderate wind blows	7 miles, or	10 feet
A horse trots	7 miles, or	10 feet
A man walks	3 miles, or	4 feet

Boxes of Different Measure.

A box 24 inches long by 16 inches wide, and 28 inches deep, will contain a barrel (3 bushels).

A box 24 inches long by 16 inches wide, and 14 inches deep, will contain half a barrel.

A box 16 inches square and 8 2-5 inches deep, will contain one bushel.

A box 16 inches by 8 2-5 inches wide, and 8 inches deep, will contain half a bushel.

A box 8 inches by 8 2-5 inches square, and 8 inches deep, will contain one peck.

A box 8 inches by 8 inches square, and 4 1-5 inches deep, will contain one gallon.

A box 7 inches by 4 inches square, and 4 4-5 inches deep, will contain half a gallon.

A box 4 inches by 4 inches square, and 4 1-5 inches deep, will contain one quart.

In purchasing anthracite coal, 20 bushels are generally allowed for a ton.

Debt of Different Countries, How Various Colors are Made, Length and Cost of American Canals, Center of Gravity of Population, Etc.

Average Height and Weight

Of Human Beings, at Different Ages.

Males.			Females.		
Age.	Feet.	Lbs.	Age.	Feet.	Lbs.
Birth	1⅔	7	Birth	1⅔	6½
2 years	2⅔	25	2 years	2½	23½
4 years	3	31⅛	3 years	3	28⅔
6 years	3½	38 4-5	6 years	4	35⅛
9 years	4	50	9 years	4	47
11 years	4⅛	59¾	11 years	4¼	56½
13 years	4¾	75 4-5	13 years	4 3-5	72 2-3
15 years	5	96½	15 years	5	89
17 years	5⅛	116½	17 years	5	104⅛
18 years	5½	127½	18 years	5⅛	112½
20 years	5½	132½	20 years	5 1-6	115⅛
30 years	5½	140⅛	30 years	5 1-6	119 4-5
40 years	5½	140½	40 years	5 1-6	121 4-5
50 years	5½	140	50 years	5	123 4-5
60 years	5⅛	136	60 years	5	119¾
70 years	5⅛	131¼	70 years	5	113½
80 years	5⅛	127½	80 years	5	108 4-5
90 years	5⅛	127½	90 years	5	108 4-5

Bait for Different Game.

Animal.	Bait Required.
Squirrel	Grain, nuts, or ear of corn.
Muskrat	Carrots, potatoes, apples, etc.
Woodchuck	Roots, fruit, corn or bread.
Mink	Fowl, flesh or roasted fish.
Skunk	Mice, meat, piece of a fowl.
Fox	Fowl, flesh, fish, toasted cheese.
Opossum	Nuts, corn, mice, piece of fowl.
Raccoon	Chicken, fish or frog.
Badger	Mice, or flesh of any kind.
Otter	Fish, piece of a bird, or otter musk.
Marten	Head of a fish, piece of meat, or fowl.
Beaver	Fresh roots.
Wolf	Waste parts of tame or wild fowl.

The Pulse in Health.

New-born infants	From 140 down to 130
During 1st year	From 130 down to 115
During 2d year	From 115 down to 100
During 3d year	From 105 down to 95
From 7th to 14th year	From 90 down to 80
From 14th to 21st year	From 85 down to 75
From 21st to 60th year	From 75 down to 70
In old age	From 75 up to 80

Center of Gravity of Population.

The change of center of population each ten years, in the United States, is shown in the following table. In ninety years the center of gravity has moved westward 467 miles, on almost a straight line from east to west. The very rapid settlement of the northwest of late would indicate that the line will move considerably northward in the next ten years.

Date.	Location.	Westward move. Miles.
1790,	23 miles east of Baltimore	
1800,	18 miles west of Baltimore	41
1810,	40 miles northwest by west of Washington	36
1820,	16 miles north of Woodstock, Va.	50
1830,	19 miles southwest of Moorefield, W. Va.	39
1840,	16 miles south of Clarksburg, W. Va.	55
1850,	23 miles southeast of Parkersburg, W. Va.	65
1860,	20 miles south of Chillicothe, O.	81
1870,	48 miles east by north of Cincinnati, O.	42
1880,	8 miles west by south of Cincinnati, O.	58
	Total	467

Capacity of Cisterns.

In calculating the capacity of cisterns, 31½ gallons are estimated to one barrel and 63 gallons to one hogshead.

Circular Cistern one foot in depth.

5 feet in diam. holds	4½ barrels.
6 feet in diam. holds	6¾ barrels.
7 feet in diam. holds	9 barrels.
8 feet in diam. holds	12 barrels.
9 feet in diam. holds	15 barrels.
10 feet in diam. holds	18½ barrels.

Square Cistern one foot in depth.

5 feet by 5 feet holds	6 barrels.
6 feet by 6 feet holds	8½ barrels.
7 feet by 7 feet holds	11½ barrels.
8 feet by 8 feet holds	15¼ barrels.
9 feet by 9 feet holds	19½ barrels.
10 feet by 10 feet holds	23¾ barrels.

Audible Sounds.

The distance at which sounds can be distinguished depends much on favoring winds.

Description of Sound.	Feet.	Miles
A powerful human voice in the open air and no wind	460	
Beating a drum	10,560	2
Music of a heavy brass band	15,840	3
A strong human voice with a breeze barely felt	15,840	3
Report of a musket	16,000	3
Cannonading, very strong	475,000	90

American Canals---Their Length and Cost.

The following table comprises the canals of the United States and Canada, of which the cost has exceeded $1,000,000.

Name.	State.	Miles.	Cost.
Chesapeake and Ohio	Maryland	191	$10,000,000
Delaware and Hudson	New York and Pa	108	9,000,000
Illinois and Michigan	Illinois	102	8,654,337
Erie	New York	363	7,143,789
Welland	Canada	36	7,000,000
Central Division	Pennsylvania	173	5,307,252
James River and Kanawha	Virginia	147	5,020,050
Ohio and Erie	Ohio	307	4,695,824
Lehigh	Pennsylvania	85	4,455,099
Miami	Ohio	178	3,750,000
North Branch Extension	Pennsylvania	90	3,528,302
Morris and Essex	New Jersey	101	3,100,000
West Division	Pennsylvania	104	3,096,522
Wabash and Erie	Indiana	469	3,057,120
Chesapeake and Delaware	Delaware and Md	13½	2,750,000
Delaware and Raritan	New Jersey	43	2,844,103
Schuylkill Division	Pennsylvania	108	2,500,176
Chenango	New York	97	2,419,950
Cornwall	Canada	12	2,000,000
Lachine	Canada	8½	2,000,000
Beauharnois	Canada	21	1,500,000
Sandy and Beaver	Ohio	76	1,500,000
Delaware Division	Pennsylvania	60	1,275,715
Champlain	New York	63	1,257,604
North Branch	Pennsylvania	73	1,096,178
Susquehannah	Pennsylvania	39	1,039,256
St. Lawrence	Canada	10	1,000,000

National Debt of Principal Countries.

The following table, from Porter's Census Book, shows the increase and decrease of the public debt of these different countries in the past twenty years:

Countries.	1860.	1870.	1880.
France	$1,854,136,500	$2,777,522,000	$3,829,982,399
Great Britain	3,893,230,000	3,883,467,000	3,766,671,000
Russia	1,124,161,500	1,070,630,000	3,318,953,000
Spain	525,582,000	1,386,952,500	2,579,245,000
Italy	436,985,900	1,900,000,000	2,540,313,000
United States	64,842,288	2,480,672,428	2,120,415,371
Austria-Hungary	1,163,093,500	1,654,610,000	1,881,115.350
Turkey	160,594,500	603,446,000	1,376,486,500
Portugal	136,262,000	291,990,000	457,451,000
Australia		180,065,500	442,851,500
Holland	442,850,500	369,854,000	389,320,000
Canada		82,730,500	175,191,000
Roumania		63,000,000	118,742,600
Sweden-Norway		29,199,000	97,330,000
Greece	28,932,000	60,000,000	94,361,438
German Empire*	494,436,400	720,242,000	49,317,595
Denmark	63,264,500	63,264,500	48,665,000

* The debt given for the German Empire in 1880 does not include the debts of any of the States composing it, but only the Empire Proper.

Combinations of Shades that Make Different Colors.

Mixing Red and Black	makes	Brown
Mixing Lake with White	makes	Rose
Mixing Umber and White	makes	Drab
Mixing White and Brown	makes	Chestnut
Mixing Yellow and Brown	makes	Chocolate
Mixing Red with Light Blue	makes	Purple
Mixing Carmine with Straw	makes	Flesh Color
Mixing Blue with Lead Color	makes	Pearl
Mixing Carmine with White	makes	Pink
Mixing Lamp-Black with Indigo	makes	Silver Gray
Mixing Lamp-Black with White	makes	Lead Color
Mixing Paris Green with White	makes	Bright Green
Mixing Yellow Ochre and White	makes	Buff
Mixing White tinted with Purple	makes	French White
Mixing Black with Chrome Green	makes	Dark Green
Mixing Chrome Green with White	makes	Pea Green
Mixing Emerald Green with White	makes	Brilliant Green
Mixing Vermilion with Chrome Yellow	makes	Orange
Mixing Chrome Yellow with White Lead	makes	Straw Color
Mixing White tinted with Red and Yellow	makes	Cream
Mixing White with tints of Black and Purple,	makes	Ashes of Roses
Mixing White, tinted with Black and Purple,	makes	French Gray
Mixing Chrome Yellow, Blue, Black and Red,	makes	Olive

SIZE OF ANIMALS, LEGAL HOLIDAYS IN THE UNITED STATES, Etc.

189

Size of Animals.

Man—4 to 5 feet in Lapland and Labrador; 5½ to 6½ feet in Europe and Asia; 5 to 5¾ in Africa and America; and 6 to 8 feet in Patagonia.

Name of Animal.	Size.
Fox	1½ to 2 feet
Mole	6 inches
Stag	4 to 5 feet
Wolf	2½ to 3 feet
Lion	6 to 8 and 9 feet
Otter	3¼ feet
Lynx	4 feet
Civet	2 feet
Sable	11 inches
Lama	6 feet
Tapir	6 feet
Hyena	3 feet
Jackal	2¼ feet
Ferret	14 inches
Ermine	10 inches
Polecat	17 inches
Weasel	7½ inches
Badger	2¼ feet
Giraffe	15 or 16 feet high
Marmot	10 inches
Roebuck	3¾ feet
Raccoon	2 feet
Vampire	6 to 12 inches

Name of Animal.	Size.
Wild Cat	2 to 5 feet
Antelope	3¼ feet
Chamois	3 feet
Opossum	15 to 18 inches
Dormouse	6 inches
Kangaroo	3 to 4 feet
Hedgehog	10 inches
Porcupine	2½ feet
Musk-Deer	3¼ feet
Ichneumon	15 inches
Maned Seal	10 to 14 feet
Pigmy Apes	2 feet
Barbary Ape	3½ feet
Common Bat	4 or 5 inches
Spectrum Bat	7 inches
Common Seal	4 to 6 feet
Hippopotamus	12 to 20 feet
Flying Squirrel	6 inches
Ourang Outang	4½ to 5½ feet
Great Ant-eater	4 feet
Pigmy Antelope	10 inches
Walrus or Morse	15 to 18 feet
Vaulting Monkey	13 inches
Bottle-nosed Seal	11 to 18 feet
Ordinary Squirrel	8 inches
Dog-faced Baboon	5 feet
Armadillo and tail	5 feet
Elephant	10 or 11 feet, 8 to 11 feet high
Lioness	5 to 6 and 7 feet, Tail 3 feet, height 3 to 5

Name of Animal.	Size.
Tiger	8 to 9 feet, Tail 3 feet, height 4 feet
Ant-eater	1 foot, Spines 4 feet
Dromedary	6 or 7 feet, 9 feet high to top of head
Rhinoceros	12 feet, 6 or 7 feet high

Legal Holidays in the U. S.

Fourth of July—in all the States and Territories.

Christmas Day—Dec. 25—in all the States and Territories.

Thanksgiving Day—usually the last Thursday in November—whenever appointed by the President of the United States or the Governors of States—in all the States and Territories.

Fast Days—whenever appointed by the Presidents of the United States or by the Governors—in all the States.

New Year's Day—Jan. 1—in all States except Arkansas, Delaware, Georgia, Kentucky, Maine, Massachusetts, New Hampshire, North Carolina, Rhode Island and South Carolina.

Washington's Birthday—Feb. 22—in all States except Alabama, Arkansas, Florida, Indiana, Iowa, Kansas, Maine, Missouri, North Carolina, Ohio, Oregon, Tennessee and Texas.

General Election Day—usually on Tuesday after the first Monday in November—in California, Maine, Missouri, New Jersey, New York, Oregon, South Carolina, and Wisconsin.

Decoration Day — May 30 — in Colorado, Connecticut, Maine, Michigan, New Hampshire, New Jersey, New York, Pennsylvania, Rhode Island and Vermont.

Good Friday — Friday before Easter Sunday—in Florida, Louisiana, Minnesota and Pennsylvania. Easter Sunday is the first Sunday after the full moon which happens on or after March 21st. If full moon happens on Sunday, Easter Sunday is the Sunday thereafter.

Shrove Tuesday — the Tuesday preceding the first day of Lent—in Louisiana, and the cities of Selma, Mobile, and Montgomery, Ala.

Memorial Day — April 26 — in Georgia.

March 2 — Anniversary of the Independence of Texas, in Texas.

April 21 — Anniversary of the Battle of San Jacinto, in Texas.

January 8—Anniversary of the Battle of New Orleans, fought 1815, in Louisiana.

February 12 — Lincoln's Birthday, in Louisiana.

March 4—Firemen's Anniversary, in Louisiana.

Different Nations, the Name of their People and the Language they Speak.

Country.	Name of People.	Language they Speak.
Austria	Austrians	German, Hungarian and Slavonic.
Arabia	Arabs, Arabians	Arabic.
Afghanistan	Afghans	Persian and Hindoostanee.
Algeria	Algerines	Chiefly Arabic.
Abyssinia	Abyssinians	Abyssinian.
Australasia	Australasians	Dutch and English. Various native languages are spoken.
Brazil	Brazilians	Portuguese.
Bolivia	Bolivians	Spanish.
Belgium	Belgians	Flemish and French.
Beloochistan	Beloochees	Beloochee and Hindoostanee.
Canada	Canadians	English and French.
Chili	Chilians	Spanish.
China	Chinese	Chinese.
Denmark	Danes	Danish.
Egypt	Egyptians	Chiefly Arabic and Italian.
England	English	English.
East Indies	East Indians	Hindoostanee, Bengalee, Siamese, Malay, etc.
France	French	French.
Greenland	Greenlanders	Danish and Esquimaux.
Germany	Germans	German.
Greece	Greeks	Greek.
Holland	Dutch	Dutch.
Hindoostan	Hindoos	Hindoostanee and others.

Country.	Name of People.	Language they Speak.
Iceland	Icelanders	Icelandic.
Ireland	Irish	English and Irish.
Italy	Italians	Italian.
Japan	Japanese	Japanese.
Mexico	Mexicans	Spanish.
Norway	Norwegians	Danish.
Poland	Poles	Polish.
Peru	Peruvians	Spanish.
Paraguay	Paraguayans	Spanish.
Prussia	Prussians	German.
Portugal	Portuguese	Portuguese.
Persia	Persians	Persian.
Russia	Russians	Russian.
Sweden	Swedes	Swedish.
Switzerland	Swiss	German, French, and Italian.
Spain	Spaniards	Spanish.
Siberia	Siberians	Russian (mostly).
Siam	Siamese	Siamese.
Scotland	Scotch	English and Gaelic.
Turkey	Turks	Turkish.
United States	Americans	English.
Venezuela	Venezuelans	Spanish.
West Indies	West Indians	Spanish.
Wales	Welsh	English and Welsh.

MULTIPLICATION TABLE.

For the convenience of those who, though once familiar with the Multiplication Table, may have forgotten portions of it, or may not at the moment be able to recall the amount which results from one number being multiplied by another, this table is given. The $\times$ signifies multiplied by, and $=$ signifies equal to.

$1 \times 0 = 0$	$2 \times 0 = 0$	$3 \times 0 = 0$	$4 \times 0 = 0$	$5 \times 0 = 0$	$6 \times 0 = 0$	$7 \times 0 = 0$	$8 \times 0 = 0$	$9 \times 0 = 0$	$10 \times 0 = 0$	$11 \times 0 = 0$	$12 \times 0 = 0$
$1 \times 1 = 1$	$2 \times 1 = 2$	$3 \times 1 = 3$	$4 \times 1 = 4$	$5 \times 1 = 5$	$6 \times 1 = 6$	$7 \times 1 = 7$	$8 \times 1 = 8$	$9 \times 1 = 9$	$10 \times 1 = 10$	$11 \times 1 = 11$	$12 \times 1 = 12$
$1 \times 2 = 2$	$2 \times 2 = 4$	$3 \times 2 = 6$	$4 \times 2 = 8$	$5 \times 2 = 10$	$6 \times 2 = 12$	$7 \times 2 = 14$	$8 \times 2 = 16$	$9 \times 2 = 18$	$10 \times 2 = 20$	$11 \times 2 = 22$	$12 \times 2 = 24$
$1 \times 3 = 3$	$2 \times 3 = 6$	$3 \times 3 = 9$	$4 \times 3 = 12$	$5 \times 3 = 15$	$6 \times 3 = 18$	$7 \times 3 = 21$	$8 \times 3 = 24$	$9 \times 3 = 27$	$10 \times 3 = 30$	$11 \times 3 = 33$	$12 \times 3 = 36$
$1 \times 4 = 4$	$2 \times 4 = 8$	$3 \times 4 = 12$	$4 \times 4 = 16$	$5 \times 4 = 20$	$6 \times 4 = 24$	$7 \times 4 = 28$	$8 \times 4 = 32$	$9 \times 4 = 36$	$10 \times 4 = 40$	$11 \times 4 = 44$	$12 \times 4 = 48$
$1 \times 5 = 5$	$2 \times 5 = 10$	$3 \times 5 = 15$	$4 \times 5 = 20$	$5 \times 5 = 25$	$6 \times = 30$	$7 \times 5 = 35$	$8 \times 5 = 40$	$9 \times 5 = 45$	$10 \times 5 = 50$	$11 \times 5 = 55$	$12 \times 5 = 60$
$1 \times 6 = 6$	$2 \times 6 = 12$	$3 \times 6 = 18$	$4 \times 6 = 24$	$5 \times 6 = 30$	$6 \times 6 = 36$	$7 \times 6 = 42$	$8 \times 6 = 48$	$9 \times 6 = 54$	$10 \times 6 = 60$	$11 \times 6 = 66$	$12 \times 6 = 72$
$1 \times 7 = 7$	$2 \times 7 = 14$	$3 \times 7 = 21$	$4 \times 7 = 28$	$5 \times 7 = 35$	$6 \times 7 = 42$	$7 \times 7 = 49$	$8 \times 7 = 56$	$9 \times 7 = 63$	$10 \times 7 = 70$	$11 \times 7 = 77$	$12 \times 7 = 84$
$1 \times 8 = 8$	$2 \times 8 = 16$	$3 \times 8 = 24$	$4 \times 8 = 32$	$5 \times 8 = 40$	$6 \times 8 = 48$	$7 \times 8 = 56$	$8 \times 8 = 64$	$9 \times 8 = 72$	$10 \times 8 = 80$	$11 \times 8 = 88$	$12 \times 8 = 96$
$1 \times 9 = 9$	$2 \times 9 = 18$	$3 \times 9 = 27$	$4 \times 9 = 36$	$5 \times 9 = 45$	$6 \times 9 = 54$	$7 \times 9 = 63$	$8 \times 9 = 72$	$9 \times 9 = 81$	$10 \times 9 = 90$	$11 \times 9 = 99$	$12 \times 9 = 108$
$1 \times 10 = 10$	$2 \times 10 = 20$	$3 \times 10 = 30$	$4 \times 10 = 40$	$5 \times 10 = 50$	$6 \times 10 = 60$	$7 \times 10 = 70$	$8 \times 10 = 80$	$9 \times 10 = 90$	$10 \times 10 = 100$	$11 \times 10 = 110$	$12 \times 10 = 120$
$1 \times 11 = 11$	$2 \times 11 = 22$	$3 \times 11 = 33$	$4 \times 11 = 44$	$5 \times 11 = 55$	$6 \times 11 = 66$	$7 \times 11 = 77$	$8 \times 11 = 88$	$9 \times 11 = 99$	$10 \times 11 = 110$	$11 \times 11 = 121$	$12 \times 11 = 132$
$1 \times 12 = 12$	$2 \times 12 = 24$	$3 \times 12 = 36$	$4 \times 12 = 48$	$5 \times 12 = 60$	$6 \times 12 = 72$	$7 \times 12 = 84$	$8 \times 12 = 96$	$9 \times 12 = 108$	$10 \times 12 = 120$	$11 \times 12 = 132$	$12 \times 12 = 144$

Expectation of Life and Present Value of Widow's Dower.

Age.	Expectation in years.	Age.	Expectation in years.	Age.	Expectation in years.	Age.	Expectation in years.	Age.	Expectation in years.
0	28.15	20	34.22	40	26.04	60	15.45	80	5.85
1	36.78	21	33.84	41	25.61	61	14.86	81	5.50
2	38.74	22	33.46	42	25.19	62	14.26	82	5.16
3	40.01	23	33.08	43	24.77	63	13.66	83	4.87
4	40.73	24	32.70	44	24.35	64	13.05	84	4.66
5	40.88	25	32.33	45	23.92	65	12.43	85	4.57
6	40.69	26	31.93	46	23.37	66	11.96	86	4.21
7	40.47	27	31.50	47	22.83	67	11.48	87	3.90
8	40.14	28	31.08	48	22.27	68	11.01	88	3.67
9	39.72	29	30.66	49	21.72	69	10.50	89	3.56
10	39.23	30	30.25	50	21.17	70	10.06	90	3.73
11	38.64	31	29.83	51	20.61	71	9.60	91	3.32
12	38.02	32	29.43	52	20.05	72	9.14	92	3.12
13	37.41	33	29.02	53	19.49	73	8.69	93	2.40
14	36.79	34	28.62	54	18.92	74	8.25	94	1.98
15	36.17	35	28.22	55	18.35	75	7.83	95	1.62
16	35.76	36	27.78	56	17.78	76	7.40	----	----
17	35.37	37	27.34	57	17.20	77	6.99	----	----
18	34.98	38	26.91	58	16.63	78	6.59	----	----
19	34.59	39	26.47	59	16.04	79	6.21	----	----

as she may live, it becomes necessary that some definite calculation be made as to how long the widow will probably live to receive this interest. This matter being determined, a calculation can readily be made as to how much she is entitled to at present, which being ascertained, the estate can be satisfactorily settled. To illustrate, by the above table, which is generally adopted in the settlement of estates, it will be seen that, if the widow be 60 years of age, she will probably live 15 and 45-100 years longer, or until her age is 75 and 45-100 years.

By the following table is given the value of an annuity of one dollar from 1 to 35 years at 5 per cent. per annum. Thus for 15 years the value of one dollar will be $10.3796. Suppose the widow's dower interest in the estate to be $100 per year. To find the present value of the widow's interest, therefore, multiply the $100 by 10.3796, and the result is $1,037.96, which is the amount that the widow is entitled to in the settlement.

Years	Dollars, Cents and 100ths	Years	Dollars, Cents and 100ths	Years	Dollars, Cents and 100ths	Years	Dollars, Cents and 100ths
1	.9523	10	7.7217	19	12.0853	28	14.8981
2	1.8594	11	8.3064	20	12.4622	29	15.1401
3	2.7232	12	8.8632	21	12.8211	30	15.3724
4	3.5459	13	9.3935	22	13.1630	31	15.5928
5	4.3294	14	9.8986	23	13.4880	32	15.8026
6	5.0756	15	10.3796	24	13.7986	33	16.0025
7	5.7863	16	10.8377	25	14.0939	34	16.1929
8	6.4632	17	11.2740	26	14.3751	35	16.3741
9	7.1078	18	11.6895	27	14.6430	--	--------

In the settlement of estates where the widow is entitled to a third interest in the real estate, or a "dower" interest, as it is termed, as long

Distances From New York City to

Place	Miles.	Place	Miles.	Place	Miles.	Place	Miles.
Adrian, Mich	775	Chattanooga, Tenn	980	Lafayette, Ind	903	Quincy, Ill	1,176
Akron, Ohio	610	Chicago, Ill	911	Lansing, Mich	785	Racine, Wis	976
Albany, N. Y	143	Chillicothe, Ohio	645	Lawrence, Mass	262	Raleigh, N. C	669
Alexandria, Va	238	Cincinnati, Ohio	744	Leavenworth, Kan	1,385	Reading, Pa	128
Algiers, La	1,551	Circleville, Ohio	640	Lexington, Ky	840	Richmond, Va	356
Allegheny, Pa	434	Cleveland, Ohio	581	Lexington, Mo	1,354	Rochester, N. Y	386
Allentown, Pa	92	Columbia, S. C	744	Little Rock, Ark	1,430	Rock Island, Ill	1,093
Alton, Ill	1,060	Columbus, Ohio	624	Lockport, N. Y	507	Rome, N. Y	264
Annapolis, Md	222	Concord, N. H	308	Louisville, Ky	900	Roxbury, Mass	238
Ann Arbor, Mich	716	Covington, Ky	745	Lowell, Mass	261	Sacramento, Cal	2,900
Atchison, Kansas	1,368	Cumberland, Md	364	Lynchburg, Va	404	St. Joseph, Mo	1,384
Atlanta, Ga	1,018	Davenport, Iowa	1,093	Macon, Ga	1,121	St. Louis, Mo	1,084
Auburn, N. Y	328	Dayton, Ohio	804	Madison, Wis	1,049	St. Paul, Minn	1,441
Augusta, Me	407	Denver City, Col	1,980	Memphis, Tenn	1,289	Salem, Mass	252
Augusta, Ga	887	Des Moines, Iowa	1,251	Milledgeville, Ga	1,100	Salt Lake City, Utah	2,410
Aurora, Ill	951	Detroit, Mich	679	Milwaukee, Wis	996	San Francisco, Cal	3,038
Baltimore, Md	188	Dover, N. H	304	Mobile, Ala	1,370	Sandusky, Ohio	642
Bangor, Me	482	Dubuque, Iowa	1,100	Montgomery, Ala	1,193	Savannah, Ga	974
Bath, Me	382	Dunkirk, N. Y	460	Montpelier, Vt	454	Scranton, Pa	142
Baton Rouge, La	1,320	Elmira, N. Y	274	Nashua, N. H	275	Springfield, Ill	1,062
Belfast, Me	424	Erie, Pa	508	Nashville, Tenn	1,085	Springfield, Mass	138
Bellefontaine, Ohio	658	Evansville, Ind	1,021	New Albany, Ind	903	Springfield, Ohio	828
Binghamton, N. Y	215	Fall River, Mass	180	New Bedford, Mass	181	Staunton, Va	486
Blackstone, Mass	272	Fitchburg, Mass	218	New Brunswick, N.J	32	Stonington, Conn	143
Bloomington, Ill	1,037	Fort Kearney, Neb	1,598	Newburg, N. Y	53	Syracuse, N. Y	302
Boston, Mass	236	Fort Wayne, Ind	763	New Haven, Conn	76	Taunton, Mass	210
Bristol, R. I	215	Fredericksburg, Va	296	New Orleans, La	1,550	Tallahassee, Fla	1,100
Bucyrus, Ohio	632	Galena, Ill	1,083	Newport, Ky	744	Terre Haute, Ind	912
Buffalo, N. Y	433	Galesburg, Ill	1,076	Newport, R.I	162	Toledo, Ohio	742
Burlington, N. J	74	Galveston, Texas	1,900	Norwalk, Conn	45	Tonawanda, N.Y	463
Burlington, Iowa	1,122	Georgetown, D. C	228	Omaha, Neb	1,455	Trenton, N.J	58
Burlington, Vt	280	Hamilton, Ohio	766	Oswego, N.Y	237	Troy, N. Y	148
Cambridge, Mass	239	Harrisburg, Pa	182	Paterson, N. J	17	Utica, N. Y	249
Camden, N. J	91	Hartford, Conn	112	Peoria, Ill	1,072	Vicksburg, Miss	1,542
Canandaigua, N. Y	377	Indianapolis, Ind	838	Petersburg, Va	378	Washington, D. C	230
Carson City, Nevada	2,800	Jackson, Miss	1,498	Philadelphia, Pa	88	Wheeling, W. Va	522
Chambersburg, Pa	246	Jefferson City, Mo	1,210	Pittsburgh, Pa	431	Wilmington, Del	116
Charleston, S. C	874	Kalamazoo, Mich	822	Portland, Me	344	Wilmington, N. C	604
Charlestown, Mass	235	Kansas City, Mo	1,361	Providence, R. I	193	Worcester, Mass	192

Distances by Water From New York City to

Place	Miles.	Place	Miles.	Place	Miles.	Place	Miles.
Amsterdam	3,510	Chagres	2,308	Lisbon	3,175	Rio Janeiro	3,840
Barbadoes	1,906	Charleston	750	Liverpool	3,210	Sandwich Islands	15,300
Batavia	13,066	Columbia River	15,965	London	3,375	San Francisco	15,858
Bermudas	660	Constantinople	5,140	Madras	11,850	St. Petersburg	4,420
Bombay	11,574	Copenhagen	3,640	Melbourne	12,844	Singapore	12,710
Bordeaux	3,310	Dublin	3,225	Monrovia	3,825	Smyrna	5,000
Boston	310	Gibraltar	3,300	Naples	4,330	Stockholm	4,050
Botany Bay	13,294	Halifax	612	New Orleans	2,045	Tahiti	12,225
Buenos Ayres	7,110	Hamburg	3,775	Panama	2,358	Trieste	5,130
Calcutta	12,425	Havana	1,420	Pekin	15,325	Valparaiso	9,750
Canton	13,900	Havre	3,210	Pernambuco	4,760	Vera Cruz	2,250
Cape Horn	8,115	Kingston	1,640	Philadelphia	240	Washington	400
Cape of Good Hope	6,830	Lima	11,310	Quebec	1,400	Round the Globe	25,000

The Influence of the Moon on the Growth of Plants.

Does the light of the moon affect the growth of plants? Does it make any difference in the growth of a plant what time in the moon it is planted? Undoubtedly it does.

Light is a great promoter of growth, and, the more brilliant the light, the stronger and more vigorous the growth, all the other conditions being favorable. It is a fact, also, with certain plants, that when young they require, like young animals, considerable time for rest and sleep. To have this sleep is to give them ultimate strength and vigor, which is essential to their subsequent complete development.

To illustrate: the seeds of certain vines and other plants sown in the new of the moon will vegetate, and the plants are likely to appear above ground, near the old of the moon, at a time when the moon's radiance is so brilliant that they are compelled to grow under its strong light. Upon the rising of the sun, the growth is still forced forward, and the tender plant, thus in its infancy, gets no rest.

The seed sown in the old of the moon will bring forth the plant in the new of the moon, or during the dark nights; at which time it obtains the needed rest and sleep, in the darkness, which is essential to its future productiveness.

That the light of the moon has thus a very perceptible and important influence upon the growth of plants when very young and tender, is a fact which thousands have verified, though few understand the philosophy of the same.

FOREIGN WORDS AND PHRASES.

LATIN WORDS AND PHRASES.

Ad captandum, For the purpose of captivating.
Ad infinitum, To an unlimited extent.
Ad libitum, At pleasure.
Alias, Otherwise.
Alibi, Elsewhere.
Alma mater, Gentle mother; often applied to the institution where one is educated.
Amor patriæ, Love of country.
Anglicè, In English.
Annus mirabilis, A year of wonders.
A priori, Beforehand; from previous knowledge.
Bona fide, In good faith; genuine.
Beatæmemoriæ, Of blessed memory.
Cocoæthes scribendi, A ridiculous fondness for writing.
Casus belli, A case for war.
Caveat, Let him beware.
Contra, On the other hand; against.
De facto, In fact.
De jure, By right.

Dramatis personæ, Characters of the play.
Ergo, Therefore.
Et id genusomne, And all of that sort.
Ex officio, By virtue of the office.
Exit, He (or she) goes out.
Exeunt omnes, They all go out.
Ex parte, On one side only.
Ex tempore, On the moment.
Facetiæ, Witty sayings.
Fac simile, An exact copy.
Fiat, Let it be done; a command.
Fiat justitia ruat cœlum, Let justice be done though the heavens crash.
Finis, The end.
Genius loci, The genius of the place.
In propria persona, In person.
In transitu, On the way.
Imprimis, In the first place.
Impromptu, Off-hand.
Interim, In the mean time.
Item, Also.
Lapsus linguæ, A slip of the tongue.
Magna charta, The great charter.

Maximum, The greatest quantity.
Mens sana in corpore sano, A sound mind in a healthy body.
Meum et tuum, Mine and thine.
Minimum, The least quantity.
Ne plus ultra, The greatest extent attainable.
Nil desperandum, Never despair.
Nolens volens, Willing or not.
Non compos mentis, Not of sound mind.
Non est inventus, Not to be found.
Non sequitur, It does not follow.
Nota bene, Mark well.
Omnia vincit amor, Love conquers all things.
Onus probandi, Burden of proving.
Orator fit, poeta nascitur, The orator is made, but the poet is born.
Otium cum dignitate, Ease with dignity.
Par nobile fratrum, A noble pair of brothers; two alike.

Passim, Everywhere.
Paterfamilias, Father of a family.
Per capita, By the head.
Per diem, By the day.
Per fas et nefas, Through right or wrong.
Per se, By itself.
Prima facie, On the first view.
Pro et con, For and against.
Pro forma, For form's sake.
Pro tempore, For the time being.
Quondam, Former.
Quid nunc? What now?
Rus in urbe, The country in town.
Semper idem, Always the same.
Sub rosa, Privately.
Sui generis, Of its own kind; unique.
Tempus fugit, Time flies.
Vale, Farewell.
Veni, vidi, vici, I came, I saw, I conquered.
Verbum sat, A word is enough.
Viva voce, By the living voice.
Vice versa, The case being reversed.

FRENCH WORDS AND PHRASES, With Pronunciation.

A bas (ah-bah), Down with.
A bon marché (ah-bong-mar-shai), Cheap.
A cheval (ah-sheh-val), On horseback.
Affaire d'amour (ah-faire-dah-moor), A love affair.
Affaire d'honneur (af-faire-don-ai-ur), An affair of honor.
A la mode (ah-lah-mod), In the fashion.
A l'improviste (ah-lam-pro-vist), Unawares.
Amateur (ah-ma-tair), An admirer of and unprofessional practitioner in any art.
Amour (ah-moor), Love.
A l'outrance (ah-loo-trangsse), To the utmost.
A propos (ah-pro-poe), By the way; to the purpose.
A tout prix (au-too-pree), At any cost.
A contraire (o-kong-trayre), On the contrary.
Au fait (o-fay), All right; instructed.
Au revoir (o-ruh-voo-ar), Till we meet again.
Avant coureur (ah-vang-koo-rayre), Forerunner.
A votre santé (au-vottr-sang-tai), To your health.
Bas bleu (bah-bluhe), Blue-stocking.
Beau monde (bo-mongde), The gay world.
Belles-lettres (bell-lay-tr), Polite literature.
Blâse (blah-zai), Time-worn, faded.
Bijou (be-joo), a jewel or gem.
Billet-doux (be-yay-doo), A love letter.
Bongré malgré (bon-grai-mai-grai), Willing or not.
Bonhomie (bun-no-mee), Good nature.
Bon jour (bong-joor), Good-day.
Bon-mot (bong-mo), A witticism.
Bon soir (bong-sooar), Good night.
Bon ton (bong-tong), High fashion.
Bon vivant (bong-vi-vang), A high liver.
Bonne bouche (bun-booshe), A tid-bit.
Bonne foi (bun-foo-ah), Good faith.
Canaille (kan-ayh), The rabble.
Carte blanche (kart-blansh), Full power.
Chacun a son goût, Every one to his taste.
Château en Espagne, Air-castles.
Chef d'œuvre (shay-duhvr), A masterpiece.

Cher ami (shair-ah-me), Dear friend (male.)
Chère amie (shayre-ah-mee), Dear friend, (female.)
Ci-devant (se-duh-vang), Formerly.
Comme il faut (kom-ill-foh), As it should be.
Compagnon de voyage (kong-pang-yong), Traveling companion.
Contretemps (kongtr-tang), Disappointment, accident.
Coup d'état (koo-daih-tah), A stroke of policy.
Coup de grâce (koo-de-grass), The finishing stroke.
Coup d'œil, A glance.
Coûte qu'il coûte (koot-key-koot), Cost what it may.
Début (dai-boo), First appearance.
Dénouement (dai-noo-mang), Solution; result.
Dieu et mon droit, God and my right.
Dot (doh), A dowry.
Double entendre (doo-bl-ang-tangdr), Double meaning.
Doux yeux (dooz-yuhe), Tender glances.
Éclat (ai-klah), Splendor; brilliancy.
Élite (ai-litt), Choice; select.
Embonpoint (ong-bong-poo-aing), Plumpness, fatness.
En ami (ang-ah-me), As a friend.
Encore (ong-kor), Again.
Enivre (ai-ne-vrai), Intoxicated.
En masse (ong-mass), In a body.
Ennui (ah-noo-e), Weariness.
En revanche (ung-ruh-vanghshe), In return.
Entente cordiale (ong-tangte-kor-dyol), Good understanding.
Entrée (ang-traie), Entrance.
Entre nous (angtr-noo), Between ourselves.
Esprit de corps (es-pree-duh-kor), Pride of association.
Faux pas (foe-paw), False step; misconduct.
Fête (fayte), A festival.
Feu de joie (fuh-dh-joo-au), Bonfire; illumination.
Gensdarmes (jang-darm), Soldier police.
Haut ton (ho-tong), Highest fashion.

Honi soit qui mal y pense, Shamed be he that evil thinks.
Jeu de mots, A play upon words.
Jeu d'esprit (juh-des-pree), A witticism.
Le bon temps viendra There is a good time coming.
L'homme propose et Dieu dispose, Man proposes and God disposes.
Matinée (mah-te-naie), A daytime entertainment.
Mise en scène (meeze-ang-seyne), Putting on the stage; getting up.
Nom de plume (nong-du-ploom), Literary nickname.
Nous verrons (noo-vai-rong), We shall see.
On dit (ong-de), It is said.
Outré (oo-tray), Extravagant; outlandish.
Papier maché (pah-pyai-ma-shai), Paper pulp prepared for use and ornament.
Par exemple, For example.
Parvenu, An upstart.
Petit (puh-te), Small, little; (feminine, *petite.*)
Protégé (pro-tai-hjai), One protected by another; (feminine, *protégée.*)
Qui vive (ke-viv), (On the), On the alert.
Recherché (ruh-sher-sha), Of rare attraction.
Résumé (rai-zoo-mai), A summary.
Rôle (role), Part in a drama or performance.
Sans façon (sang fah song), Without formality.
Sans peur et sans reproche, Without fear and without reproach.
Sans souci (sang-sou-se), Without care.
Savant (sah-vang), A man of science.
Savoir vivre, Good breeding.
Soi-disant (soo-ah-de-zang), Self-styled.
Soirée (soo-ah-raie), An evening entertainment.
Tête à tête (tayte-ah-tayte), Face to face.
Tout à vous (toot-ah-voo), Wholly yours.
Tout ensemble (too-ang-sangbl), The whole together.
Vis à vis (vee-zah-vee), Opposite.
Vive le roi (vivv-luh-roo-ah), Long live the king.
Voila tout (voo-ah-lah-too), That is all.

SPANISH WORDS AND PHRASES.

A Dios, Good-bye.
Adobe, A sun-baked brick.
Alma mia, My dear.
Cañon, A deep gulch or gorge.
Carrai! Zounds!

Chaparral, A thicket of shrub oak.
Corral, An inclosure for horses, etc.
Hacienda, A farm.
Hidalgo, An aristocrat.
Olla podrida, An incongruous mass.

Poco tempo, In a little while.
Poco dinero, Little money.
Pronunciamento, A declaration.
Quien sabe? Who knows?
Señor, Mr. or Master.

Señora, Mrs. or Mistress.
Señorita, Miss.
Sierra, Chain of mountains.
Vamos! Let us go.

ITALIAN WORDS AND PHRASES.

Cantatrice, A singer.
Conversazione, Social gathering.
Dilettante, A lover of the fine arts.

Dolce far niente, Pleasant idleness.
Impresario, A theatrical proprietor or manager.

Prima donna, First lady, or "star," in an opera.
Signor, Mr. or Master.

Signora, Mrs. or Mistress.
Signorina, Miss.
Virtù, Curious or fine.

List of Modern Abbreviations.

Abbreviations Alphabetically Arranged
For use in Writing.

a.—In commerce, *to.*

@.—In commerce, *at.*

A. A. G. — Assistant Adjutant-General.

A. A. P. S.—American Association for the Promotion of Science.

A. A. S.—*Academiæ Americanæ Socius,* Fellow of the American Academy (of Arts and Sciences).

A. A. S. S.—*Americanæ Antiquarianæ Societatis Socius,* Member of the American Antiquarian Society.

A. B.—*Artium Baccalaureus,* Bachelor of Arts.

A. B. C. F. M. — American Board of Commissioners for Foreign Missions.

Abp.—Archbishop.

Abr.—Abridgment.

Abbr.—Abbreviation.

A. B. S.—American Bible Society.

A. C.—*Ante Christum,* before Christ; Arch-Chancellor.

Acad.—Academy.

Acct.—Account; Accent.

A. C. S.—American Colonization Society.

A. D.—*Anno Domini,* in the year of our Lord.

A. D. C.—Aid-de-camp.

Ad. — Advertisement.

Adj.—Adjective.

Adjt.—Adjutant.

Adjt.-Gen.—Adjutant-General.

Ad lib.—*Ad libitum,* at pleasure.

Adm.—Admiral; Admiralty.

Adm. Ct.—Admiralty Court.

Admr.—Administrator.

Admx.—Administratrix.

Ad v.—*Ad valorem,* at (or on) the value.

Adv.—Adverb; Advent; Advertisement.

Æt.—*Ætatis,* of age, Aged.

A. F. & A. M. — Ancient Free and Accepted Masons.

A. F. B. S.—American and Foreign Bible Society.

A. G.—Adjutant-General.

Alaska—Alaska Territory.

Agr.—Agriculture.

A. G. S. S.—American Geographical and Statistical Society.

Agt.—Agent.

A. H.—*Anno Hegiræ,* in the year of the Hegira.

A. H. M. S—American Home Missionary Society.

Ala.—Alabama.

Ald.—Alderman.

A. L. of H. — American Legion of Honor.

Alex.—Alexander.

Alg.—Algebra.

Alt.—Altitude.

A. M.—*Anno Mundi,* in the year of the world. *Artium Magister,* Master of Arts. *Ante meridiem,* before noon; morning.

Amb.—Ambassador. (See Emb.)

Amer.—American.

AMM.—*Amalgama,* amalgamation.

Amt.—Amount.

An.—*Anno,* in the year.

An. A. C.—*Anno ante Christum,* in the year before Christ.

Anat.—Anatomy.

Anc.—Ancient; Anciently.

And.—Andrew.

Ang.-Sax.—Anglo-Saxon.

Anon.—Anonymous.

Ans.—Answer.

Ant.—Antiquity.

Anth.—Anthony.

Aor. or aor.—Aorist.

A. O. S. S.—*Americanæ Orientalis Societatis Socius,* Member of the American Oriental Society.

A. O. U. W.—Ancient Order of United Workmen.

Ap.—Apostle; Appius.

Ap.—*Apud,* in the writings of; as quoted by.

Apo.—Apogee.

Apoc.—Apocalypse.

App.—Appendix.

Apr.—April.

A. Q. M. G.—Assistant Quartermaster-General.

A. R.—*Anna Regina,* Queen Anne. *Anno regni,* year of the reign.

A. R. A. — Associate of the Royal Academy.

Arab.—Arabic, or Arabia.

Ariz. Ter.—Arizona Territory.

Arg.—*Argumento,* by an argument drawn from such a law.

Arith.—Arithmetic.

Ark.—Arkansas.

A. R. R.—*Anno regni regis,* in the year of the reign of the king.

Arr.—Arrived. Arrs., Arrivals.

A. R. S. S.—*Antiquariorum Regiæ Societatis Socius,* Fellow of the Royal Society of Antiquaries.

Art.—Article.

A. S. or Assist. Sec.—Assistant Secretary.

A. S. A.—American Statistical Association.

A. S. S. U.—American Sunday-School Union.

Astrol.—Astrology.

Astron.—Astronomy.

A. T.—Arch-Treasurer.

A. T. S.—American Tract Society.

Ats.—At suit of.

Atty.—Attorney.

Atty.-Gen.—Attorney-General.

A. U. A.—American Unitarian Association.

Aub. Theol. Sem. — Auburn Theological Seminary.

A. U. C.—*Anno urbis conditæ,* or *ab urbe condita,* in the year from the building of the city (Rome).

Aug.—August.

Aur.—*Aurum,* gold.

Auth. Ver.—Authorized Version (of the Bible.)

Av.—Average; Avenue.

Avoir.—Avoirdupois.

A. Y. M.—Ancient York Masons.

b.—Born.

B. A.—Bachelor of Arts.

Bal.—Balance.

Balt.—Baltimore.

Bar.—Baruch.

Bart. or Bt.—Baronet.

Bbl.—Barrel.

B. C.—Before Christ.

B. C. L.—Bachelor of Civil Law.

B. D. — *Baccalaureus Divinitatis,* Bachelor of Divinity.

Bds. or bds.—Boards (bound in).

Benj.—Benjamin.

Bk.—Book.

B. LL.—*Baccalaureus Legum,* Bachelor of Laws.

B. M.—*Baccalaureus Medicinæ,* Bachelor of Medicine.

B. R.—Bills Receivable.

B. P.—Bills Payable.

Bost.—Boston.

Bot.—Botany.

Bp.—Bishop.

B. R.—*Banco Regis* or *Reginæ,* the King's or Queen's Bench.

Brig.—Brigade; Brigadier.

Brig.-Gen.—Brigadier-General.

Brit. Mus.—British Museum.

Bro.—Brother.

Br. Univ.—Brown University.

B. S.—Bachelor in the Sciences.

B. V.—*Beata Virgo,* Blessed Virgin. *Bene vale,* farewell.

B. V. M.—Blessed Virgin Mary.

C., Ch. or Chap.—Chapter.

C. or Cent.—*Centum,* a hundred.

cæt. par.—*Cæteris paribus,* other things being equal.

Cal.—California; Calends.

Can.—Canon.

Cant.—Canticles.

Cap. or c. — *Caput, capitulum,* chapter.

Caps.—Capitals.

Capt.—Captain.

Capt.-Gen.—Captain-General.

Cash.—Cashier.

ca. resp.—*Capias ad respondendum,* a legal writ.

ca. sa.—*Capias ad satisfaciendum,* a legal writ.

Cath.—Catherine.

C. B.—Companion of the Bath. *Communis Bancus,* Common Bench.

C. C.—Caius College; Account Current; Chancellor Commander; County Commissioner.

C. C. C.—Corpus Christi College.

C. C. P.—Court of Common Pleas.

C. E.—Canada East; Civil Engineer.

Cel. or Celt.—Celtic.

Cf. or cf.—*Confer,* compare.

C. G.—Commissary-General; Consul-General.

C. H.—Court-house.

Ch.—Church; Chapter.

Chanc.—Chancellor.

Chap.—Chapter.

Chas.—Charles.

Chem.—Chemistry.
Chic.—Chicago.
Chr.—Christopher.
Chron.—Chronicles.
Cin.—Cincinnati.
C.J.—Chief-Justice.
Clk.—Clerk.
C.M.—Common Meter.
C.M.G.—Companion of the Order of St. Michael and St. George.
Co.—Company; County.
C.O.D.—Cash (or collect) on delivery.
Cochl.—A spoonful.
Col.—Colonel; Colossians.
Coll.—Collector; Colloquial; College; Collection.
Colo.—Colorado.
Com.—Commerce; Committee; Commentary; Commissioner; Commodore.
Com. Arr.—Committee of Arrangements.
Comdg.—Commanding.
Comm.—Commentary.
Comp.—Compare; Compound: Compositor.
Com. Ver.—Common version (of the Bible).
Con.—*Contra*, against; in opposition.
Con. Cr.—Contra, credit.
Conch.—Conchology.
Cong.—Congress.
Conj. or conj.—Conjunction.
Conn. or Ct.—Connecticut.
Const.—Constable; Constitution.
Cont.—Continent; Contract; Continued.
Cor.—Corinthians.
Corol.—Corollary.
Cor. Sec.—Corresponding Secretary.
C.P.—Common Pleas; Court of Probate.
C.P.S. — *Custos Privati Sigilli*, Keeper of the Privy Seal.
C.R.—King (*Rex*) Charles.
C.R.—*Custos Rotulorum*, Keeper of the Rolls.
Cr.—Creditor; Credit.
Crim. Con.—Criminal conversation; Adultery.
C.S.—Court of Sessions. *Custos Sigilli*, Keeper of the Seal.
Ct., cts.—Cent; Cents.
C. Theod.—*Codice Theodosiano*, in the Theodosian Code.
C.W.—Canada West.
Cwt.—Hundredweight.
Cyc.—Cyclopedia.

d.—*Denarius* or *Denarii*, penny or pence; Died.
D.—Five hundred.
Dak.—Dakota.
Dan.—Daniel; Danish.
D.C.—*Da Capo*, again; District of Columbia.
D.C.L.—Doctor of Civil Law.
D.D.—*Divinitatis Doctor*, Doctor of Divinity.
Dea.—Deacon.
Dec.—December; Declaration; Declination.
Deg.—Degree or degrees.
Del.—Delaware; Delegate.
Del. or del.—*Delineavit*, he (or she) drew it.
Dep.—Deputy.
Dept.—Department.
Deut.—Deuteronomy.

D.F.—Dean of the Faculty.
Dft. or Deft.—Defendant.
D.G.—*Dei gratia*, by the grace of God.
D.G.—*Deo gratias*, thanks to God.
Diam.—Diameter.
Dict.—Dictator; Dictionary.
Dim.—Diminutive.
Disc.—Discount.
Diss.—Dissertation.
Dist.—District.
Dist.Atty.—District-Attorney.
Div.—Division; Dividend.
D.M.—Doctor of Music.
Do.—*Ditto*, the same.
Dols.—Dollars.
D.O.M. — *Deo optimo maximo*, to God, the best, the greatest.
Doz.—Dozen.
D.P.—Doctor of Philosophy.
Dr.—Debtor; Doctor; Drachm.
D.S.—*Dal segno*, from the sign.
d.s.b.—*Debit sans breve*.
D.T.—*Doctor Theologiæ*, Doctor of Theology.
D.V.—*Deo volente*, God willing.
Dwt.—Pennyweight.

E.—East.
ea.—Each.
E. by S.—East by South.
Eben.—Ebenezer.
Eccl.—Ecclesiastes.
Ecclus.—Ecclesiasticus.
Ed.—Editor; Edition.
Edm.—Edmund.
Edw.—Edward.
E.E.—Errors excepted.
e.g.—*Exempli gratia*, for example. *Ex grege*, from the flock; Among the rest.
E.I.—East Indies, or East India.
E.I.C.—East India Company.
Elec.—Electric; Electricity.
Eliz.—Elizabeth.
E. lon.—East longitude.
Emb.—Embassador.
Encyc.—Encyclopedia.
E.N.E.—East-Northeast.
Eng.—England; English.
Ent.—Entomology.
Env. Ext.—Envoy Extraordinary.
Ep.—Epistle.
Eph.—Ephesians; Ephraim.
Esd.—Esdras.
E.S.E.—East-Southeast.
Esq.—Esquire.
Esth.—Esther.
et al.—*Et alii*, and others.
et seq.—*Et sequentia*, and what follows.
etc. or &c.—*Et cæteri, et cæteræ, et cætera*, and others; and so forth.
Ex.—Example; Exodus.
Exc.—Excellency; Exception.
Exch.—Exchequer.
Exec. Com.—Executive Committee.
Execx.—Executrix.
Exr. or Exec.—Executor.
Ez.—Ezra.
Ezek.—Ezekiel.
E.&O.E.—Errors and omissions excepted.
Fahr.—Fahrenheit.
F.A.M.—Free and Accepted Masons.
Far.—Farthing.
F.A.S.—Fellow of the Antiquarian Society.
fcap. or fcp.—Foolscap.
F.D.—*Fidei Defensor* or *Defensa-*

trix, Defender of the Faith.
Fe.—*Ferrum*, iron.
Feb.—February.
Fec.—*Fecit*, he did it.
Fem.—Feminine.
F.E.S.—Fellow of the Entomological Society; of the Ethnological Society.
Ff.—The Pandects.
F.G.S.—Fellow of the Geological Society.
F.H.S.—Fellow of the Horticultural Society.
fi. fa.—*Fieri facias*, cause it to be done.
Fid. Def.—Defender of the Faith.
Fig.—Figure.
Fir.—Firkin.
Fla.—Florida.
F.L.S.—Fellow of the Linnæan Society.
F.O.B.—Free on Board.
Fol.—Folio.
For.—Foreign.
Fort.—Fortification.
F.P.S.—Fellow of the Philological Society.
Fr.—Franc; francs; French. *Fragmentum*, fragment. Francis.
F.R.A.S.—Fellow of the Royal Astronomical Society.
F.R.C.S.L.—Fellow of the Royal College of Surgeons, London.
Fred.—Frederick.
F.R.G.S.—Fellow of the Royal Geographical Society.
Fri.—Friday.
F.R.S.—Fellow of the Royal Society.
Frs.—Frisian.
F.R.S.E.—Fellow of the Royal Society, Edinburgh.
F.R.S.L.—Fellow of the Royal Society, London; Fellow of the Royal Society of Literature.
F.S.A.—Fellow of the Society of Arts.
F.S.A.E.—Fellow of the Society of Antiquaries, Edinburgh.
Ft.—Foot; feet; Fort.
Fur—Furlong.
F.Z.S.—Fellow of the Zoological Society.

G. or g.—Guineas.
G.A.—General Assembly.
Ga.—Georgia.
Gal.—Galatians; Gallon.
G.B.—Great Britain.
G.C. — Grand Chancellor; Grand Chapter.
G.C.B.—Grand Cross of the Bath.
G.C.H.—Grand Cross of Hanover.
G.C.L.H. — Grand Cross of the Legion of Honor.
G.E.—Grand Encampment.
Gen.—Genesis; General.
Gent.—Gentleman.
Geo.—George; Georgia.
Geog.—Geography.
Geol.—Geology.
Geom.—Geometry.
Ger.—Germany; German.
G.L.—Grand Lodge.
Gl.—*Glossa*, a gloss.
G.M.—Grand Master.
G.O.—General Order.
Goth.—Gothic.
Gov.—Governor.
Gov.-Gen.—Governor-General.
G.R.—*Georgius Rex*, King George.
Gr.—Greek; Gross; Grains.

Gram.—Grammar.
Gro.—Gross.
Grot.—Grotius.
h.a.—*Hoc anno*, this year.
Hab.—Habakkuk.
Hab. corp. — *Habeas corpus*, you may have the body.
Hab. fa. poss.—*Habere facias possessionem*.
Hab. fa. seis.—*Habere facias seisinam*.
Hag.—Haggai.
Ham. Coll.—Hamilton College.
H.B.C.—Hudson's Bay Company.
H.B.M.—His (or Her) Britannic Majesty.
H.C.—House of Commons.
Hdkf.—Handkerchief.
h.e.—*Hoc est*, that is, or this is.
Heb.—Hebrews.
Her.—Heraldry.
Hf.-bd.—Half-bound.
Hg.—*Hydrargyrum*, mercury.
Hhd.—Hogshead.
H.H.S.—Fellow of the Historical Society.
Hist.—History.
H.J.S.—*Hic jacet sepultus*, Here lies buried.
H.L.—House of Lords.
H.M.—His (or Her) Majesty; Hill's Manual.
H.M.P.—*Hoc monumentum posuit*, Erected this monument.
H.M.S.—His (or Her) Majesty's Ship.
Hon.—Honorable.
Hon'd.—Honored.
Hort.—Horticulture.
Hos.—Hosea.
h.p.—half-pay.
H.R.—House of Representatives.
H.R.E.—Holy Roman Emperor.
H.R.H.—His Royal Highness.
H.R.I.P.—*Hic requiescat in pace*, Here rests in peace.
H.S.—*Hic situs*, Here lies.
H.S.B.Co. — Hill Standard Book Company.
H.S.H.—His Serene Highness.
h.t.—*Hic titulus*, this title; *hoc titulo*, in or under this title.
h.v.—*Hoc verbum*, this word; *his verbis*, in these words.
Hund.—Hundred.

I, II, III.—One, two, three, or first, first, second, third.
Ia.—Iowa.
Ib. or ibid.—*Ibidem*, in the same place.
Ich.—Ichthyology.
Ictus.—*Jurisconsultus*, Counselor at Law.
Id.—*Idem*, the same.
Idaho.—Idaho Territory.
i.e.—*Id est*, That is.
I.H.S.—*Jesus hominum Salvator*, Jesus the Saviour of men.
ij.—Two (*medical*).
Ill. — Illinois, Illustrious; Illustrated.
Imp.—Imperial.
In.—Inch; inches.
incog.—*Incognito*, unknown.
Incor.—Incorporated.
Ind.—Indiana, Index.
Ind. Ter.—Indian Territory.
Indef.—Indefinite.
Inf.—*Infra*, beneath or below.
in f.—*In fine*, at the end of the title, law, or paragraph quoted.

in lim.—*In limine*, at the outset.

in loc.—*In loco*, in the place; on the passage.

in pr.—*In principio*, in the beginning and before the first paragraph of a law.

I.N.R.I.—*Jesus Nazarenus, Rex Judœorum*, Jesus of Nazareth, King of the Jews.

Inst.—Instant, of this month; Institutes.

In sum.—*In summa*, in the summary.

Int.—Interest.

Interj.—Interjection.

In trans.—*In transitu*, on the passage.

Introd.—Introduction.

I.O.G.T. — Independent Order of Good Templars.

I.O.F.—Independent Order of Forresters.

I.O.O.F. — Independent Order of Odd-Fellows.

I.O.U.—I owe you.

I.q.—*Idem quod*, the same as.

Isa.—Isaiah.

Isl.—Island.

I.S.M.—*Jesus Salvator mundi*, Jesus the Saviour of the world.

Ital.—Italic; Italian.

Itin.—Itinerant, or Itinerary.

IV.—Four or fourth.

IX.—Nine or ninth.

J.—Justice or Judge.   JJ.—Justices.

j.—One (*medical*).

J.A.—Judge-Advocate.

Jac.—Jacob.

Jam.—Jamaica.

Jan.—January.

Jas.—James.

J.C.D.—*Juris Civilis Doctor*, Doctor of Civil Law.

J.D. — *Jurum Doctor*, Doctor of Laws.

Jer.—Jeremiah.

Jno.—John.

Jona.—Jonathan.

Jos.—Joseph.

Josh.—Joshua.

J.P.—Justice of the Peace.

J. Prob.—Judge of Probate.

J.R.—*Jacobus Rex*, King James.

Jr. or Jun.—Junior.

J.U.D. or J.V.D.—*Juris utriusque Doctor*, Doctor of both Laws (of the Canon and the Civil Law).

Jud.—Judith.

Judg.—Judges.

Judge-Adv.—Judge-Advocate.

Jul.—July; Julius.

Jul. Per.—Julian Period.

Jun.—June; Junius; Junior.

Jus. P.—Justice of the Peace.

Just.—Justinian.

J. W.—Junior Warden.

K.—King.

K.A.—Knight of St. Andrew, in Russia.

K.A.N. — Knight of St. Alexander Nevskoj, in Russia.

Kas.—Kansas.

K.B.—King's Bench; Knight of the Bath.

K.B.A.—Knight of St. Bento d'Avis, in Portugal.

K.B.E.—Knight of the Black Eagle, in Russia.

K.C.—King's Council; Knight of the

Crescent, in Turkey.

K.C.B.—Knight Commander of the Bath.

K.C.H. — Knight Commander of Hanover.

K.C.S.—Knight of Charles III. of Spain.

K.E.—Knight of the Elephant, in Denmark.

K.F.—Knight of Ferdinand of Spain.

K.F.M. — Knight of St. Ferdinand and Merit, in Sicily.

K.G.—Knight of the Garter.

K.G.C.—Knight of the Grand Cross.

K.G.C.B. — Knight of the Grand Cross of the Bath.

K.G.F. — Knight of the Golden Fleece, in Spain.

K.G.H.—Knight of the Guelphs of Hanover.

K.G.V.—Knight of Gustavus Vasa, in Sweden.

K.H.—Knight of Hanover; Knights of Honor.

Ki.—Kings.

Kil. or kil.—Kilderkin.

Kingd.—Kingdom.

K.J.—Knight of St. Joachim.

K.L. or K.L.A.—Knight of Leopold of Austria.

K.L.H.—Knight of the Legion of Honor; Knights and Ladies of Honor.

K.M.—Knight of Malta.

K.Mess.—King's Messenger.

K.M.H.—Knight of Merit, in Holstein.

K.M.J. — Knight of Maximilian Joseph, in Bavaria.

K.M.T.—Knight of Maria Theresa, in Austria.

K.N.—Know-Nothing.

Knick.—Knickerbocker.

K.N.S.—Knight of the Royal North Star, in Sweden.

Knt.—Knight.

K.P.—Knight of St. Patrick; Knight of Pythias.

K.R.C.—Knight of the Red Cross.

K.R.E.—Knight of the Red Eagle, in Prussia.

K.S. — Knight of the Sword, in Sweden.

K.S.A.—Knight of St. Anne, in Russia.

K.S.E.—Knight of *St. Esprit*, in France.

K.S.F.—Knight of St. Fernando, in Spain.

K.S.G.—Knight of St. George, in Russia.

K.S.H.—Knight of St. Hubert, in Bavaria.

K.S.J.—Knight of St. Janaurius of Naples.

K.S.L. — Knight of the Sun and Lion, in Persia.

K.S.M. & S.G. — Knight of St. Michael and St. George, in the Ionian Islands.

K.S.P.—Knight of St. Stanislans, in Poland.

K.S.S.—Knight of the Southern Star, in Brazil; Knight of the Sword, in Sweden.

K.S.W.—Knight of St. Wladimir, in Russia.

K.T.—Knight of the Thistle; Knight Templar.

Kt.—Knight.

K.T.S.—Knight of the Tower and Sword, in Portugal.

K.W.—Knight of William, in the Netherlands.

K.W.E.—Knight of the White Eagle, in Poland.

Ky.—Kentucky.

L.—Fifty or fiftieth. *Liber*, book. Latin.

L, £, or l.—*Libra* or *Libræ*, pound or pounds sterling.

L, or £, s. d.—*Libræ, solidi, denarii*, Pounds, shillings, pence.

La.—Louisiana.

Lam.—Lamentations.

Lat.—Latitude; Latin.

Lb. or lb.—*Libra* or *Libræ*, Pound or pounds in weight.

L.C.—Lord Chancellor; Lord Chamberlain; Lower Canada.

l.c.—Lower-case.

L.C.B.—Lord Chief Baron.

L.C.J.—Lord Chief-Justice.

L.D.—Lady-Day.

Ld.—Lord.

Ldp.—Lordship.

Leg.—Legate.

Legis.—Legislature.

Lev.—Leviticus.

Lex—Lexicon.

L.I.—Long Island.

Lib.—*Liber*, book.

Lieut.—Lieutenant.

Lieut.-Col.—Lieutenant-Colonel.

Lieut.Gen.—Lieutenant-General.

Lieut.-Gov.—Lieutenant-Governor.

Linn.—Linnæan.

Liq.—Liquidation.

Lit.—Literally; Literature.

Liv.—*Livre*, book.

LL.B.—*Legum Baccalaureus*, Bachelor of Laws.

LL.D.—*Legum Doctor*, Doctor of Laws.

loc. cit.—*Loco citato*, in the place cited.

Lon.—Longitude.

Lond.—London.

L.S.—*Locus sigilli*, place of the seal.

Lt.—Lieutenant.

LX.—Sixty or sixtieth.

LXX. — Seventy or seventieth; The Septuagint (Version of the Old Testament).

LXXX.—Eighty or eightieth.

M.—*Meridies*, noon.

M.—*Mille*, a thousand.

M. or Mons.—*Monsieur*, Sir.

M.A.—Master of Arts.

Macc.—Maccabees.

Mad.—Madam.

Mad. Univ.—Madison University.

Maj.—Major.

Maj.-Gen.—Major-General.

Mal.—Malachi.

Man.—Manasses.

Mar.—March.

March.—Marchioness.

Marg.—Margin.

Marg. Tran.—Marginal Translation.

Marq.—Marquis.

Masc.—Masculine.

Mass.—Massachusetts.

Math. — Mathematics; Mathematician.

Matt.—Matthew.

Max.—Maxim.

M.B. — *Medicinœ Baccalaureus*, Bachelor of Medicine.

M.B.—*Musicœ Baccalaureus*, Bachelor of Music.

M.B.G. et H.—*Magna Britannia, Gallia et Hibernia*, Great Britain, France, and Ireland.

M.C.—Member of Congress.

Mch.—March.

M.D.—*Medicinœ Doctor*, Doctor of Medicine.

Md.—Maryland.

Mdlle.—*Mademoiselle*.

Mdse.—Merchandise.

M.E.—Methodist Episcopal; Military or Mechanical Engineer.

Me.—Maine.

Mech.—Mechanics, or Mechanical.

Med.—Medicine.

Mem.—Memorandum. *Memento*, remember.

Merc.—Mercury.

Messrs. or MM.—*Messieurs*, Gentlemen.

Met.—Metaphysics.

Metal.—Metallurgy.

Meteor.—Meteorology.

Meth.—Methodist.

Mex.—Mexico, or Mexican.

M.-Goth. —Mœso-Gothic.

M.H.S. — Massachusetts Historical Society; Member of the Historical Society.

Mic.—Micah.

Mich.—Michigan.

Mil.—Military.

Mil. Acad.—Military Academy.

Min.—Mineralogy; Minute.

Minn.—Minnesota.

Min. Plen. — Minister Plenipotentiary.

Miss.—Mississippi.

M.L.A. — Mercantile-Library Association.

MM. — Their Majesties. *Messieurs*, Gentlemen, Two thousand.

M.M.S.—Moravian Missionary Society.

M.M.S.S. — *Massachusettensis Medicinœ Societatis Socius*, Fellow of the Massachusetts Medical Society.

Mo.—Missouri; Month.

Mod.—Modern.

Mon.—Monday.

Mons.—*Monsieur*, Sir.

Mos.—Months.

Mont. Ter.—Montana Territory.

M.P.—Member of Parliament; Member of Police.

M.P.P.—Member of Provincial Parliament.

M.R.—Master of the Rolls.

Mr.—Mister.

M.R.A.S. — Member of the Royal Asiatic Society; Member of the Royal Academy of Science.

M.R.C.C. — Member of the Royal College of Chemistry.

M.R.C.S.—Member of the Royal College of Surgeons.

M.R.G.S. — Member of the Royal Geographical Society.

M.R.I.—Member of the Royal Institute.

M.R.I.A. — Member of the Royal Irish Academy.

Mrs.—Mistress.

M.R.S.L. — Member of the Royal Society of Literature.

M.S.—*Memoriæ sacrum*, Sacred to the Memory; Master of the Sciences.

MS.—*Manuscriptum*, manuscript.

MSS.—Manuscripts.

Mt.—Mount, or Mountain.

Mus. B.—Bachelor of Music.

Mus. D.—Doctor of Music.

M.W.—Most Worthy; Most Worshipful.

Myth.—Mythology.

N.—North; Number; Noun; Neuter.

n.—Note.

N.A.—North America.

Nah.—Nahum.

Nat.—Natural.

Nat. Hist.—Natural History.

Nath.—Nathanael, or Nathaniel.

N.B.—New Brunswick; North British. *Nota Bena*, mark well; take notice.

N.C.—North Carolina; New Church.

N.E.—New England; Northeast.

Neb.—Nebraska.

Neh.—Nehemiah.

n.e.i.—*Non est inventus*, He is not found.

nem. con. or nem. diss.—*Nemine contradicente*, No one opposing; unanimously.

Neut.—Neuter (gender).

Nev.—Nevada.

New Test. or N.T.—New Testament.

N.F.—Newfoundland.

N.G.—New Granada; Noble Grand.

N.H.—New Hampshire; New Haven.

N.H.H.S.—New Hampshire Historical Society.

Ni. pri.—*Nisi prius* (law).

N.J.—New Jersey.

n.l.—*Non liquet*, It does not appear.

N. lat.—North latitude.

N.Mex.—New Mexico.

N.N.E.—North-Northeast.

N.N.W.—North-Northwest.

N.O.—New Orleans.

No.—*Numero*, number.

Nol. pros.—*Nolens prosequi*, Unwilling to prosecute.

Nom. or nom.—Nominative.

Non con.—Not content; dissenting (House of Lords).

Non cul.—*Non culpabilis*, Not guilty.

Non obst.—*Non obstante*, notwithstanding.

Non pros.—*Non prosequitur*, He does not prosecute.

Non seq.—*Non sequitur*, It does not follow

Nos.—Numbers.

Nov.—November.

N.P.—Notary Public; New Providence.

N.S.—New Style (after 1752); Nova Scotia.

N.T.—New Testament.

N.u.—Name, or names, unknown.

Num.—Numbers; Numeral.

N.V.M.—Nativity of the Virgin Mary.

N.W.—Northwest.

N.W.T.—Northwestern Territory.

N.Y.—New York.

N.Y.H.S.—New York Historical Society.

O.—Ohio.

Ob.—*Obiit*, He (or she) died.

Obad.—Obadiah.

Obj.—Objection; Objective.

O.K.—A slang phrase for "All correct."

Obt. or obdt.—Obedient.

Oct.—October.

O.F.—Odd-Fellow, or Odd-Fellows.

O.F.P.—Order of Friar Preachers.

Old Test. or O.T.—Old Testament.

Olym.—Olympiad.

Ont.—Ontario.

Opt.—Optics; Optical; Optional.

Or.—Oregon.

Ord.—Ordinance; Order; Ordnance; Ordinary.

Orig.—Originally.

Ornith.—Ornithology.

O.S.—Old Style (before 1752).

O.S.F.—Order of St. Francis.

O.T.—Old Testament.

O.U.A.—Order of United Americans.

Oxf.—Oxford.

Oxon.—*Oxoniensis Oxonii*, of Oxford, at Oxford.

Oz.—Ounce.

P.—*Pondere*, by weight.

P. or p.—Page; Part; Participle.

Pa.—Pennsylvania.

Pal.—Palæontology.

Par.—Paragraph.

Par. Pas.—Parallel passage.

Parl.—Parliament.

Pathol.—Pathology.

Payt.—Payment.

Pb.—*Plumbum*, lead.

P.B.—*Philosophiæ Baccalaureus*, Bachelor of Philosophy.

P.C.—*Patres Conscripti*, Conscript Fathers; Senators.

P.C.—Privy Council; Privy Councilor.

P.D.—*Philosophiæ Doctor*, Doctor of Philosophy.

Pd.—Paid.

P.E.—Protestant Episcopal.

P.E.I.—Prince Edward Island.

Penn.—Pennsylvania.

Pent.—Pentecost.

Per or pr.—By the.

Per an.—*Per annum*, by the year.

Per cent.—*Per centum*, by the hundred.

Peri.—Perigee.

Pet.—Peter.

P.G.—Past Grand.

Phar.—Pharmacy.

Ph. B.—*Philosophiæ Baccalaureus*, Bachelor of Philosophy.

Ph.D.—*Philosophiæ Doctor*, Doctor of Philosophy.

Phil.—Philip; Philippians; Philosophy; Philemon.

Phila. or Phil.—Philadelphia.

Philom.—*Philomathes*, Lover of Learning.

Philomath.—*Philomathematicus*, A lover of the mathematics.

Phil. Trans.—Philosophical Transactions.

Phren.—Phrenology.

P.H.S.—Pennsylvania Historical Society.

Pinx.—*Pinxit*, He (or she) painted it.

Pk.—Peck.

Pl. or plur.—Plural.

Plff.—Plaintiff.

P.M.—*Post Meridiem*, Afternoon; Evening; Postmaster; Passed Midshipman.

P.M.G.—Postmaster-General; Professor of Music in Gresham College.

P.O.—Post-Office.

Poet.—Poetical.

Pop.—Population.

Port.—Portugal; Portuguese.

Pos.—Position; Positive; Possession.

P.P.—*Pater Patriæ*, Father of his Country; Parish Priest.

P.P.C.—*Pour prendre conge*, to take leave.

Pp. or pp.—Pages.

Pph.—Pamphlet.

Pr.—By.

P.R.—*Populus Romanus*, the Roman People; Porto Rico; Proof-reader; Prize Ring.

P.R.A.—President of the Royal Academy.

P.R.C.—*Post Romam conditam*, After the building of Rome.

Pref.—Preface.

Prep.—Preposition.

Pres.—President.

Prin.—Principally.

Pro.—For; in favor of.

Prob.—Problem.

Prof.—Professor.

Pron.—Pronoun; Pronunciation.

Prop.—Proposition.

Prot.—Protestant.

Pro tem.—*Pro tempore*, for the time being.

Prov.—Proverbs; Provost.

Prox.—*Proximo*, next (month).

P.R.S.—President of the Royal Society.

P.S.—*Post scriptum*, Postscript.

P.S.—Privy Seal.

Ps.—Psalm or Psalms.

Pt.—Part; Pint; Payment; Point; Port; Post-town.

P.Th.G.—Professor of Theology in Gresham College.

Pub.—Publisher; Publication; Published; Public.

Pub. Doc.—Public Documents.

P.v.—Post-village.

Pwt.—Pennyweight; pennyweights.

Pxt.—*Pinxit*, He (or she) painted it.

Q.—Queen; Question.

q.—*Quasi*, as it were; almost.

Q.B.—Queen's Bench.

Q.C.—Queen's College; Queen's Counsel.

q.d.—*Quasi dicat*, as if he should say; *quasi dictum*, as if said; *quasi dixisset*, as if he had said.

q.e.—*Quod est*, which is.

q.e.d.—*Quod erat demonstrandum*, which was to be proved.

q.e.f.—*Quod erat faciendum*, which was to be done.

q.e.i.—*Quod erat inveniendum*, which was to be found out.

q.l.—*Quantum libet*, as much as you please.

Q.M.—Quartermaster.

qm.—*Quomodo*, how; by what means.

Q.M.G.—Quartermaster-General.

q.p. or q.pl.—*Quantum placet*, as much as you please.

Qr.—Quarter.

Q.S.—Quarter-sessions; Quartersection.

q.s.—*Quantum sufficit*, a sufficient quantity.

Qt.—Quart.

qu. or qy.—*Quære*, inquire; query.

Quar.—Quarterly.

Ques.—Question.

q.v.—*Quod vide*, which see; *quantum vis*, as much as you will.

R.—*Recipe*, take. *Regina*, Queen; *Rex*, King. River; Rod; Rood; Rises.

R.A.—Royal Academy; Royal Academician; Royal Arch; Royal Arcanum; Royal Artillery.

RC.—*Rescriptum*, a Rescript, rewritten.

R.E.—Royal Engineers.

Rec.—Recipe, or Recorder.

Recd.—Received.

Rec. Sec.—Recording Secretary.

Rect.—Rector; Receipt.

Ref.—Reference; Reform.

Ref. Ch.—Reformed Church.

Reg.—Register; Regular.

Reg. Prof.—*Regius Professor*.

Regr.—Registrar.

Regt.—Regiment.

Rel.—Religion.

Rep.—Representative; Reporter; Republic.

Rev.—Reverend; Revelation (Book of); Review; Revenue; Revise.

Rhet.—Rhetoric.

R.I.—Rhode Island.

Richd.—Richard.

R.I.H.S.—Rhode Island Historical Society.

R.M.—Royal Marines; Royal Mail.

R.M.S.—Royal Mail Steamer.

R.N.—Royal Navy.

R.N.O.—*Riddare af Nordstjerne Orden*, Knight of the Order of the Polar Star.

Ro.—*Recto*, Right-hand page.

Robt.—Robert.

Rom.—Romans (Book of).

Rom. Cath.—Roman Catholic.

R.P.—*Regius Professor*, the King's Professor.

R.R.—Railroad.

R.S.—Recording Secretary.

Rs.—*Responsum*, answer; *respondere*, to answer.

R.S.A.—Royal Society of Antiquaries; Royal Scottish Academy.

R.S.D.—Royal Society of Dublin.

R.S.E.—Royal Society of Edinburgh.

R.S.L.—Royal Society of London.

R.S.V.P.—*Repondez s'il vous plait*, Answer, if you please.

Rt. Hon.—Right Honorable.

Rt. Rev.—Right Reverend.

Rt. Wpful.—Right Worshipful.

R.W.—Right Worthy.

R.W.O.—*Riddare af Wasa Orden*, Knight of the Order of Wasa.

S.—South; Saint; Scribe; Sulphur; Sunday; Sun; Series.

S—*Solidus*, a shilling.

S.A.—South America; South Africa; South Australia.

s.a.—*Secundum artem*, according to art.

Sam.—Samuel.

Sancs.—Sanscrit.

S.A.S.—*Societatis Antiquariorum Socius*, Fellow of the Society of Antiquaries.

Sat.—Saturday.

Sax.—Saxon.

Sax. Chron.—Saxon Chronicle.

S.C.—*Senatus Consultum*, A decree of the Senate; South Carolina.

Sc.—*Sculpsit*, he (or she) engraved it.

sc. or scil.—*Scilicet*, namely.

Scan. Mag.—*Scandalum magnatum*, scandal; or *scandalum magnum*, great scandal.

S. caps.—Small capitals.

Schol.—*Scholium*, a note.

Schr.—Schooner.

Sci. fa.—*Scire facias*, make known (legal).

Sclav.—Sclavonic.

Sculp. or sculp.—*Sculpsit*, he (or she) engraved it.

Scot.—Scotland; Scottish; Scotch.

Scr.—Scruple.

S.D.—*Salutem dicit*, sends health.

S.E.—Southeast.

Sec.—Secretary; Second; Section.

Sec. Leg.—Secretary of Legation.

Sec. leg.—*Secundum legem*, according to law.

Sec. reg.—*Secundum regulam*, according to rule.

Sect.—Section.

Sem.—*Semble*, it seems.

Sen.—Senate; Senator; Senior.

Sept.—September; Septuagint.

Seq.—*Sequentia*, following; *sequitur*, it follows.

Ser.—Series.

Serg.—Sergeant.

Serg.-Maj.—Sergeant-Major.

Serv.—Servant.

S.G.—Solicitor-General.

Shak.—Shakspeare.

S.H.S.—*Societatis Historiæ Socius*, Fellow of the Historical Society.

Sing.—Singular.

S. Isl.—Sandwich Islands.

S. J.—Society of Jesus; Society of Jesus, or Jesuits.

S.J.C.—Supreme Judicial Court.

Skr.—Sanscrit.

S.L.—Solicitor at Law (Scot).

S. lat.—South latitude.

S.M.—State Militia; Short Meter; Sergeant-Major; Sons of Malta.

S. M. Lond. Soc. Cor.—*Societatis Medicæ Londinensis Socius Correspondens*, Corresponding Member of the London Medical Society.

s. n.—*Secundum naturam*, according to nature.

Soc. Isl.—Society Islands.

Sol.—Solomon; Solution.

Sol.-Gen.—Solicitor-General.

Sp. or Span.—Spanish.

Sp.—Special.

S. of Sol.—Song of Solomon,

S.P.—*Sine prole*, without issue.

S.P.A.S.—*Societatis Philosophicæ Americanæ Socius*, Member of the American Philosophical Society.

S.P.G.—Society for the Propagation of the Gospel.

Sp. gr.—Specific gravity.

S.P.Q.R.—*Senatus Propulusque Romani*, the Roman Senate and people.

Sq. ft.—Square foot or square feet.

Sq. in.—Square inch or inches.

Sq. m.—Square mile or miles.

Sq. r.—Square rood or roods.

Sq. yd.—Square yard.

Sr.—Sir or Senior.

S. R. I.—*Sacrum Romanum Imperium*, Holy Roman Empire.

S.R.S.—*Societatis Regiæ Socius*, Fellow of the Royal Society.

S.S.—Sunday-school.

SS.—Saints.

SS. or ss.—*Scilicet*, to wit.

ss.—*Semis*, half.

S.S.C.—Solicitor before the Supreme Court (Scotland).

S.S.E.—South-Southeast.

S.S.W.—South-Southwest.

St.—Saint; Street; Strait; Stone.

Stat.—Statute.

S. T. D.—*Sacræ Theologiæ Doctor*, Doctor of Sacred Theology.

Ster. or Stg.—Sterling.

S.T.P.—*Sacræ Theologiæ Professor*, Professor of Sacred Theology.

Su.—Sunday.

Subj.—Subjunctive.

Subst.—Substantive.

Su.-Goth.—Suio-Gothic.

Sun. or Sund.—Sunday.

Sup.—Supplement; Superfine; Superior.

Supt.—Superintendent.

Surg.—Surgeon; Surgery.

Surg.-Gen.—Surgeon-General.

Surv.—Surveyor.

Surv.-Gen.—Surveyor-General.

Sus.—Susannah.

s. v.—*Sub verbo*, under the word or title.

S.W.—Southwest.

Switz.—Switzerland.

Syn.—Synonym; Synonymous.

T.—Territory; Town; Township; *Tutti*, all together.

T. or tom.—*Tome*, volume.

Ta.—*Tantalum* (Columbium).

T.E.—Topographical Engineers.

Tenn.—Tennessee.

Ter.—Territory.

Tex.—Texas.

Text. Rec.—*Textus Receptus*, the Received Text.

Th. or Thurs.—Thursday.

Theo.—Theodore.

Theol.—Theology; Theological.

Theoph.—Theophilus.

Thess.—Thessalonians.

Tho'.—Though.

Thos.—Thomas.

Thro'.—Through.

Tim.—Timothy.

Tit.—Titus.

T.O.—Turn over.

Tob.—Tobit.

Topog.—Topography; Topographical.

Tr.—Transpose; Translator; Translation; Trustee. Trs.—Trustees.

tr.—*Trillo*, a shake.

Trans.—Translator; Translation; Transactions.

Treas.—Treasurer.

Trin.—Trinity.

Tues. or Tu.—Tuesday.

Typ.—Typographer.

U.C.—*Urbis conditæ*, year of Rome.

U.E.I.C.—United East India Company.

U.J.D.—*Utriusque Juris Doctor*, Doctor of both Laws (Civil and Canon).

U.K.—United Kingdom.

ult.—*Ultimo*, last; of the last month.

Unit.—Unitarian.

Univ.—University.

U.S.—United States.

u.s.—*Ut supra* or *uti supra*, as above.

U.S.A.—United States Army; United States of America.

U.S.M.—United States Mail; United States Marine.

U.S.M.A.—United States Military Academy.

U.S.N.—United States Navy

U.S.N.A.—United States Naval Academy.

U.S.S.—United States Senate.

Utah—Utah Territory.

V.—Five or fifth; Violin.

VV.—Violins.

v. or vid.—*Vide*, see.

v. or vs.—*Versus*, against; *Versiculo*, in such a verse.

Va.—Virginia.

Vat.—Vatican.

V.C.—Vice-Chancellor.

V.D.M.—*Verbi Dei Minister*, Minister of God's Word.

Ven.—Venerable.

Ver.—Verse.

V.G.—Vicar-General.

v. g.—*Verbi gratia*, as for example.

VI.—Six or sixth.

VII.—Seven or seventh.

VIII.—Eight or eighth.

Vice-Pres. or V.P.—Vice-President.

Visc.—Viscount.

viz. or vi.—*Videlicet*, to wit; namely; that is to say.

Vo.—*Verso*, left-hand page.

Vol.—Volume.

V.R.—Victoria Regina, Queen Victoria.

V.S.—Veterinary Surgeon.

Vt.—Vermont.

Vul.—Vulgate (Latin version of the Bible).

W.—West.

Wash. Ter.—Washington Territory.

Wed.—Wednesday.

West. Res. Coll.—Western Reserve College.

w. f.—Wrong font.

Whf.—Wharf.

W.I.—West Indies.

Wis.—Wisconsin.

Wisd.—Wisdom (Book of).

Wk.—Week.

W. lon.—West longitude.

W.M.—Worshipful Master.

Wm.—William.

W.M.S.—Wesleyan Missionary Society.

W.N.W.—West-Northwest.

W.P.—Worthy Patriarch.

Wp.—Worship.

Wpful.—Worshipful.

W.S.—Writer to the Signet.

W.S.W.—West-Southwest

Wt.—Weight.

W. Va.—West Virginia.

Wyo. Ter.—Wyoming Territory.

X.—Ten or tenth.

XI.—Eleven.

XII.—Twelve.

XIII.—Thirteen.

XIV.—Fourteen.

XV.—Fifteen.

XVI.—Sixteen.

XVII.—Seventeen.

XVIII.—Eighteen.

XIX.—Nineteen.

XX.—Twenty.

XXX.—Thirty.

XL.—Forty.

XC.—Ninety.

X. or Xt.—Christ.

Xmas or Xm.—Christmas.

Xn. or Xtian.—Christian.

Xnty or Xty.—Christianity.

Xper or Xr.—Christopher.

Yd.—Yard.

y. or yᵉ.—The.

yᵐ.—Them.

yⁿ.—Then.

yʳ.—Their; Your.

yˢ.—This.

yᵗ.—That.

Y.M.C.A.—Young Men's Christian Association.

Yrs.—Years; Yours.

Zach.—Zachary.

Zech.—Zechariah.

Zeph.—Zephaniah.

Zool.—Zoology.

Zn.—Zinc.

&.—And.

&c.—*Et cætera*, and the rest; and so forth.

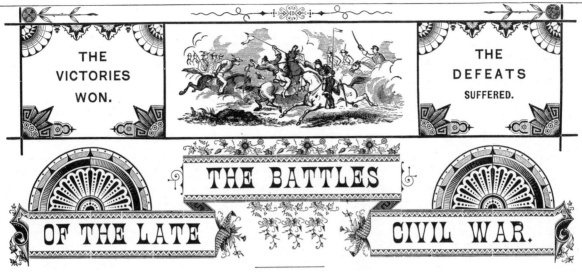

THE VICTORIES WON.

THE DEFEATS SUFFERED.

THE BATTLES OF THE LATE CIVIL WAR.

The Causes of the Rebellion.

LEAVING DESOLATION in its track, throughout many parts of the South, was a four-years' war, waged between the people of the Northern and Southern portions of the United States, extending over a period of time from April 12, 1861, to the surrender of Lee, April 9, 1865.

Among the causes that produced the war, briefly stated, were these: The staple productions in the South, prior to the war, were cotton and sugar. To sell these productions in the markets of the world at the highest figures, and purchase the necessaries of life at the lowest price, was regarded by the Southern people as legitimate. To have unrestricted commercial intercourse, therefore, with the people of all nations, being free to export their productions without hindrance, and import goods from abroad free of duty, was considered for the best interests of the South.

There existed a decided difference of opinion between the people of the Northern and Southern States on this subject. A large body of people at the North believed that home industries could best be built up through the shutting out of foreign production by a high protective tariff. This party favored the placing of a high tax on all goods from abroad.

Protective tariff against free trade, which became a sectional issue, was one of the causes. Another was the black man. For generations the colored people had been regarded by most persons at the South as property that could be rightfully bought and sold.

In many parts of the North, in the early history of the country, slavery was common. Washington was a prominent owner of slaves, as were many other great and good men; and the institution of slavery having for generations been protected by legislation, a vast body of people at the South regarded it as perfectly right to buy, sell, and own slaves.

Gradually a public sentiment grew up in the North antagonistic to the idea of one class owning another class. This feeling extended into the halls of national legislation, and in time developed very bitter sectional feeling.

The final result was that the Southerners, thinking of the triumph of the United States when they cut loose from England, and that the people of the South should have the right to make such laws as they deemed best for their own interests, inaugurated the work of separating the South from the North by the act of secession, passed by the legislature of South Carolina, in which that State seceded from the Union, December 20, 1860. This example was followed by others of the Southern States in the following order, eleven States passing ordinances of secession between the fifteenth day of December, 1860, and June 10, 1861: Mississippi, January 9, 1861; Florida, January 10, 1861; Alabama, January 11, 1861; Georgia, January 19, 1861; Louisiana, January 26, 1861; Texas, February 1, 1861; Virginia, April 17, 1861; Arkansas, May 6, 1861; North Carolina, May 21, 1861; Tennessee, by a vote of the people, June 8, 1861. The Western portion of Virginia refused to secede, and in 1863 was admitted into the Union as the loyal State of West Virginia.

The people of the South were then desirous of having the authorities of the United States withdrawn from the seceded States, and in order to hasten and compel this, an attack was made on Fort Sumter, April 12, 1861. This precipitated the war of the Rebellion—a four-years' struggle—that caused a loss of near 500,000 lives, and fastened upon the United States a debt, at the close of the war, of near $3,000,000,000.

An outline of each prominent battle, the numbers killed, wounded and taken prisoners, are given in the succeeding pages:

THE BATTLES OF THE FIRST YEAR OF THE WAR.

Battle of Fort Sumter — Fort Sumter, in Charleston harbor, S. C., occupied by Major Robert Anderson and a force of 47 effective United States soldiers and 62 other persons, and mounting 52 cannon, was bombarded by General Beauregard, commanding 7,000 Confederates, in Charleston, April 12 and 13, 1861. The fort was set on fire by the Confederates, and evacuated, after a fair defense, by Major Anderson. His loss was only one man, who was killed by the bursting of a gun inside the fort; the Confederate losses are not generally known.

Skirmish at Fairfax Court House, Va. — Fought May 31, 1861, between 47 Unionist cavalry, under Lieutenant Tompkins, and a force of 1,500 Confederates.

Battle at Phillippi—Fought June 3, 1861, at Phillippi, W. Va., between 2,000 Confederates and several regiments of Unionists, under Colonel Kelly and Colonel Lander, resulting in the retreat of the Confederates, with a loss of 15 killed, a number wounded and taken prisoners, and $25,000 worth of arms surrendered. Colonel Kelly was severely wounded.

Battle of Big Bethel — Fought June 10, 1861, at Big Bethel, Va., between 2,500 Unionists, under General Pierce, and 1,800 Confederates.

The Unionists were defeated, with a loss of 16 killed, 34 wounded, and 5 missing. The Confederate loss is unknown.

Skirmish at Cole Camp — A body of Confederates attacked a company of Home Guards at Cole Camp, Mo., June 10, 1861. The latter were defeated, with a loss of 10 killed, 20 wounded, and 30 prisoners.

Skirmish at Falling Waters — Fought near Hainesville, W. Va., July 2, 1861, between five Confederate regiments and a battery, under General Johnston and a portion of the Unionists in General Patterson's division. After a sharp fight the Confederates retired to Martinsburg. Their loss was about 80 killed and wounded. The Unionists had 3 killed and 10 wounded.

Battle of Carthage—Fought at Carthage, Mo., July 5, 1861, between 1,500 Unionists, under General Sigel and 6,000 Confederates, under Generals Parsons and Rains. The Unionists were defeated, and lost 14 killed and 31 wounded. The Confederate loss was estimated at about 500.

Battle of Rich Mountain — Fought at Rich Mountain, Va., July 11, 1861, between a detachment of Unionists, under General Rosecrans, and about 1,000 Confederates, under Colonel Pegram. The Confederates lost 150 killed and wounded, and 800 others surrendered as prisoners. The Unionists, during that and the succeeding three days' campaign, lost only 13 killed and 40 wounded; the Confederates 200 killed, and 7 guns.

Battle of Carrick's Ford — Fought July 13, 1861, at Carrick's ford, Va., between 10,000 Confederates, under General Garnett, and a column of Unionists, under General Morris. After a sharp action the former retreated, General Garnett having been killed. The Union loss was 2 killed and 10 wounded.

Skirmish at Screytown—Fought at Screytown, Va., July 13, 1861, between a body of Confederates, and a party of Unionists under Colonel Lowe; the latter were defeated with a loss of 9 killed, and 40 wounded and missing.

Battle of Blackburn Ford—Fought July 18, 1861, near Blackburn ford, Va., between Colonel Richardson's brigade of Unionists and a body of Confederates. The latter received the Unionists with a raking fire from a battery. The Unionists maintained their position, however, for three hours, until ordered to retire to Centerville. Their loss was 19 killed and 64 wounded and missing; that of the Confederates about 60.

First Battle of Bull Run—Fought July 21, 1861, at Manasses, on Bull Run river, in Northeastern Virginia, between General McDowell and about 28,000 Unionists and about 30,000 Confederates, commanded by Generals Beauregard and Joseph E. Johnston. The Unionists fought well at first, but, the Confederates being reinforced, a panic ensued in the Union army, and it fled in great disorder toward Washington. The Union loss was 481 killed, 1,011 wounded, and 1,460 missing; the Confederates lost 378 killed, 1,489 wounded, and 30 missing. The Unionists also lost 4,000 muskets and 4,500 sets of accoutrements, 20 cannon, and a considerable quantity of ammunition.

Battle of Dug Spring, Mo. — A body of Confederates, under General Rains, was defeated by General Lyon's command, August 2, 1861. The latter lost 8 killed and 30 wounded.

Battle of Wilson's Creek—Fought August 10, 1861, at Wilson's Creek, Mo., between 5,000 Unionists, under General Lyon, and about twice as many Confederates, under Generals McCulloch and Price. After six hours' hard fighting, during which General Lyon was killed, the Unionists retired to Springfield, Mo. The Union loss in killed, wounded and missing was 1,256 men; that of the Confederates was 1,768 men.

Skirmish at Charleston, Mo. — August 21, 1861, Colonel Doherty, with 300 Illinois soldiers, dispersed a rebel force, losing 1 killed and 6 wounded.

Battle at Summerville, Va.—The seventh Ohio regiment, 900 strong, was surprised while at breakfast, August 26, 1861, by a Confederate force, under General Floyd, but fought their way out, with the loss of six officers.

Capture of Forts Hatteras and Clark —These two Confederate defenses of Hatteras inlet, N. C., were captured August 29, 1861, by a Union naval squadron, under Commodore Stringham, U. S. N., and a land force of 300 men, under General Butler. The Confederate loss was 691 officers and men taken prisoners, 49 killed and 51 wounded; 29 cannon, 1,000 stand of arms, 6 regimental colors, and a large amount of military trappings and stores. The Unionists had none killed and but few wounded. The forts were commanded by Commodore Barron, Colonel Martin and Major Andrews.

Battle of Boonville—Fought at Boonville, Mo., September 1, 1861, between Unionists and Confederates. The former were the victors, with a loss of 6 wounded, and they destroyed the town.

Battle of Carnifex—Fought near Carnifex ferry, Va., September 10, 1861, between 4,500 Unionists, under General Rosecrans, and six regiments of Confederates, with 16 cannon, under General Floyd. After several hours' fighting, darkness came, and the contest ended. The Confederates retreated, leaving a large quantity of stores and war material in the hands of their foes. The loss in men by the Unionists was 15 killed and 70 wounded; the Confederates lost but a few men.

Skirmish at Blue Mills, Mo.—September 17, 1861, the Third Iowa regiment encountered a band of Confederates, and was compelled to retreat. Receiving reinforcements, they again rallied, when the Confederates retired. The Union loss was 12 killed and 85 wounded.

Battle of Cheat Mountain—Fought September 12-17, 1861, at Cheat Mountain Pass, Va., between 9,000 Confederates, under General Lee, and the Unionists under General Reynolds, who held the Pass. After several days' skirmishing at a number of points, the Confederates retired, without dislodging the Unionists. Their loss was 100 killed, including Colonel John A. Washington; the Unionists lost 9 killed and 12 wounded.

Siege of Lexington — Lexington, Mo., on the Missouri river, about 300 miles above St. Louis, was held by 2,460 Unionists, under Colonel Mulligan, in fortifications of earthworks. On the 21st of September, 1861, they were attacked by four times their number of Confederates, under General Price. For several days Mulligan defended his position, but not receiving expected reinforcements, and being without water, he surrendered. His men were paroled, but some 3,000 muskets and rifles, 5 cannon, wagons, 750 horses, army stores, ammunition and gold belonging to Missouri banks, fell into the hands of the enemy. The Unionists had also 39 men killed and about 120 wounded. Price abandoned Lexington a few days afterwards.

Skirmish at Papinsville — September 21, 1861, General Lane, with a body of Unionists, encountered a Confederate force at Papinsville, Mo., losing 17 men, killed.

Fight at Chapmanville, W. Va.—Fought, October 2, 1861, between a party of Confederates and Colonel Envartz's Kentucky volunteers, in which the former were defeated, with a loss of 47 prisoners. The Union loss was 4 killed and 8 wounded.

Fight at Greenbrier, W. Va.—October 3, 1861, General Reynolds, with 5,000 Unionists, reconnoitred the position at Buffalo hill, Va., occupied by from 12,000 to 15,000 Confederates. A brisk action ensued, chiefly carried on with artillery. The Confederates were driven from some of their intrenchments, and lost a number of prisoners, horses and baggage. The Union loss was 8 killed and 32 wounded. General Reynolds then returned to Cheat Mountain, his headquarters.

Battle of Chicamacomico — Fought at Chicamacomico, October 4, 1861, between a large force of rebels, under Colonel Barlow, and the Twentieth Indiana regiment. The latter retreated, leaving their wounded in the hands of the enemy. Next day the Union steamer Monticello shelled the Confederates and drove them to their boats.

Skirmish at Flemington, W. Va.—Fought October 6, 1861, between the Unionist Home Guards and a band of Confederates, the latter being defeated.

Fight at Santa Rosa Island — Fought at Santa Rosa island, Fla., October 9, 1861, where a Confederate force attacked the Unionist occupants, but was defeated. The Union loss was 13 killed and 21 wounded.

Skirmish at Big River Bridge, Mo.—Fought between a force of 600 Confederates, under Jeff. Thompson, and a Union Guard of 50, near Potosi, Mo., October 15, 1861; the Confederates captured the guard and destroyed the bridge.

Battle of Ball's Bluff — Fought at Ball's bluff, Va., October 21, 1861, between 1,900 Unionists, under Colonel Baker, and 4,000 Confederates. After a severe fight, in which Colonel Baker was killed, the Unionists, not being reinforced by General Stone, as they expected, retreated, having lost 223 killed, 266 wounded, and 455 prisoners. The Confederates lost about 350 killed and wounded.

Fight at Camp Wild Cat—Fought October 21, 1861, in Laurel county, Ky., between 6,000 Confederates, under General Zollicoffer, and four regiments (with artillery) of Unionists, under General Schoepf and Colonels Steadman and Garrard. The approach of the Confederates was repulsed at several points, and they retreated, pursued by the loyal inhabitants of the country and the Union troops. The Confederate loss was about 1,000 men, with their camp equipage, arms, etc. The Union loss was 4 killed and 21 wounded.

Skirmishes in Missouri — At Fredericktown, Mo., October 21, 1861, a body of Unionists defeated a party of Confederates. The Unionists lost 6 killed and about 60 wounded.

October 22, 1861, a skirmish occurred at Buffalo mills, Mo., in which the Confederates lost 17 killed and 90 prisoners. The Union loss is not stated.

Fight at Romney—Fought at Romney, W. Va., October 25, 1861, between a party of Unionists, under General Kelley, and a force of Confederates. After a two hours' fight the latter were vanquished, losing 450 prisoners, 200 horses, 3 cannon, and their camp equipage.

Zagonyi's Charge—October 26, 1861, Major Zagonyi, of General Fremont's command, with 150 of the latter's body-guard, charged upon a Confederate force of some 3,000 men, near Springfield, Mo. The Confederates were routed, with the loss of 106 killed and 27 prisoners. Zagonyi brought only 80 of his men out of the charge unhurt.

Capture of Beaufort — An expedition of naval and military forces, under the Unionist Commodore Dupont and Generals Sherman, Viele, Stevens and Wright, with about 15,000 men, on November 7, 1861, attacked and captured the two Confederate forts, Walker and Beauregard, at Port Royal, S. C., both mounting more than 40 cannon. Before the superior force of the assailants, the Confederates retreated. The same attacking force also took possession of the town of Beaufort, S. C., and Hilton island. The Unionists lost 8 men killed and 25 wounded. The Confederate loss is believed to have been heavy. They left most of the military equipments in the hands of the enemy.

Battle of Belmont — Fought at Belmont, Mo., November 7, 1861, between 2,850 Unionists, under General Grant, and about 6,000 Confederates under General Polk. The latter receiving reinforcements, after a severe engagement the Unionists retired, with a loss of 84 killed, 288 wounded, and 235 missing. The Confederates probably lost about 1,000 men.

Skirmishes in Virginia—Guyandotte was attacked by Confederates, November 10, 1861, but they were repulsed by the Unionists, the latter having several men killed. The next day the Unionists burned the town.

At Hunter's hill, November 26, a sharp skirmish occurred between Unionists and Confederates, in which the former had 28 killed and wounded.

Fight at Pensacola—Fort Pickens and the United States war vessels, Niagara and Colorado, November 23, 1861, bombarded the Confederate fortifications at Pensacola, Fla. The port of Warrenton was burned.

Skirmish in Missouri—At Warsaw, November 29, 1861, a fight occurred between Confederates and Unionists, and a portion of the town was destroyed.

Fight at Salem, Mo. — Fought between Unionists and Confederates, November 30, 1861, in which the latter were defeated, with a loss of 39 killed and wounded.

Bombardment of Freestone Point, Va. — December 9, 1861, Freestone Point was shelled by Unionist gunboats. The Confederate batteries were silenced, and the buildings containing Confederate stores were destroyed.

Fight at Camp Alleghany, Va.—Fought December 13, 1861, between a Union force, under General Milroy, who defeated a party of rebels, under Colonel Johnston. The former lost 21 killed and 107 wounded.

Fight at Munfordsville, Ky. — A drawn battle was fought at Munfordsville, December 17, 1861, between a portion of the Thirty-second Indiana (German) regiment, under Colonel Willich, and three regiments and a battery of Confederates, under General Hindman, in which the former lost 10 killed and 17 wounded. The Confederates lost 62 killed, and a large number wounded. The rout of the Confederates was complete.

General Pope in Missouri—Two brigades of General Pope's command, under Colonels Steele and Jeff. C. Davis, December 17 and 18, 1861, surprised rebel camps at Osceola and Milford, Mo., securing 360 Confederate prisoners at Osceola, and 1,300 Confederates, with 1,000 stand of arms, 400 horses, 65 wagons, and a large amount of camp equipage and stores at Milford. The Union loss was 2 killed and 17 wounded.

Battle of Drainsville, Va. — Fought 17 miles southwest of Washington, D. C., between a portion of General Ord's brigade of Unionists and a force of Confederates, under General Stuart, December 20, 1861. The Confederate loss was 43 killed and 143 wounded; that of the Unionists was 7 killed and 61 wounded. It was a victory for the Unionists.

Fight of Mount Zion — Fought in Boone county, Mo., December 28, 1861, between Unionists and Confederates; the latter were dispersed with considerable loss in killed, wounded and prisoners, while the Union loss was only 3 killed and 11 wounded.

BATTLES OF THE SECOND YEAR OF THE WAR.

Fight in South Carolina—In a cannon-fight at Fort Pickens, January 1, 1862, General Stevens, commanding a Union land force, advanced from Beaufort, and, with the assistance of the gunboats, captured the (Confederate) Coosaw batteries, held by General Bragg, losing 2 killed and 8 wounded.

Fight at Huntersville, W. Va.—January 4, 1862, the Union troops, under General Milroy, defeated a Confederate force at Huntersville, and captured $80,000 worth of stores.

Battle of Prestonburg, Ky.—Fought January 10, 1862, between about 3,000 Unionists, under General Garfield, and about 2,500 Confederates, with three guns, under General Humphrey Marshall. Garfield, after fighting for several hours, and then being reinforced, finally routed the Confederates, whose loss was about 60 killed, besides prisoners, horses and stores.

A River Combat—Fought January 11, 1862, between two Union steamers and four Confederate boats, about 20 miles south of Cairo, Ill. The latter were compelled to seek refuge under the Confederate batteries at Columbus, Ky.

Battle of Mill Springs, Ky.—Fought January 19, 1862, between about 8,000 Confederates, under Generals Crittenden and Zollicoffer, and 3,000 Union troops, under Generals Thomas and Schoepf. The Confederates were defeated, with the loss of Generals Zollicoffer and Peyton, and 192 killed and 62 wounded, 8 cannon, 1,000 stand of arms, 1,700 horses and mules, a drove of cattle, 100 wagons, quartermaster's stores, etc. The Union loss was 39 killed and 203 wounded.

Capture of Fort Henry, Tenn.—General Grant, with a force of Unionists, and Commodore Foote, with 7 Union gunboats, formed an expedition which left Cairo, Ill., to reduce Fort Henry, on the Tennessee river, then in possession of the Confederates, under General Tighlman. On the 6th of February, 1862, without waiting for General Grant, who was detained by bad roads, Commodore Foote attacked the fort with his squadron. Within two hours General Tighlman unconditionally surrendered the fort, mounting 20 cannon, with barracks and tents, and about 130 prisoners. The Union loss was 2 killed and 37 wounded; the Confederates had 6 killed and 10 wounded.

Battle of Roanoke Island, N. C.—Fought February 8, 1862, between a Union expedition by land and sea, and the Confederate fortifications on the islands held by 2,000 men. The Union force consisted of more than 100 vessels and 11,500 troops, commanded by Commodore Goldsborough and General Burnside. The result was the capture of 6 Confederate forts, 40 guns, 2,000 Confederate prisoners, 3,000 small arms, ammunition, etc. The Union loss was 50 killed and 212 wounded, the Confederates had 5 killed and 18 wounded.

Battle of Fort Donelson, Tenn.—Fought February 15 and 16, 1862, between 20,000 Confederates, under Generals Pillow, Floyd and Buckner, within the fort and its outworks, and about 20,000 Unionists under General Grant, assisted by Commodore Foote, with his fleet of gunboats. On the second day General Buckner unconditionally surrendered the fort, with between 12,000 and 15,000 prisoners, 40 cannon, and a large amount of stores. The Union losses included 321 in killed, 1,046 wounded, and 150 missing. Floyd escaped with part of the Confederate force.

Battle of Fort Craig, N. M.—Fought February 21, 1862, between Union troops under General Canby and a Texan force. The Unionists were defeated with a loss of 62 killed and 162 wounded.

Captures on the Sea-coast—Commodore Dupont, commanding the Union fleet on the Southern coast, on the 4th of March, 1862, captured Brunswick, Ga., and Forts Clinch, Fernandina, and St. Mary's, Fla.

Battle of Pea Ridge, Ark.—Fought March 6, 7 and 8, 1862, between about 12,000 Unionists, under General Curtis, and 20,000 Confederates, under Van Dorn, Price and McCulloch, resulting in the defeat of the latter. The Unionists lost 203 killed, 972 wounded, and 176 missing. The loss of the Confederates was much greater.

The Fight at Hampton Roads—On the 8th of March, 1862, the Confederate steam war-vessels Merrimack, Jamestown and Yorktown, attacked the Union fleet at Hampton roads, Va., destroying the Cumberland and Congress, and damaging several other Government vessels. Next day occurred the battle between the iron-clad Monitor (Union), commanded by Lieutenant Worden, and the Merrimack (Confederate), in which the latter was disabled. The Federal loss of men, killed and drowned, besides the vessels, was 224, and 62 wounded and prisoners. The Confederate loss was 6 killed and a number wounded.

Surrender of New Madrid, Mo.—The Confederates had fortified Island No. Ten, in the Mississippi river, a few miles above New Madrid, which was also fortified and defended by a Confederate force. Commodore Foote, with his river fleet of armed boats, and General Pope, with a land force, having threatened their works, the Confederates, March 13, 1862, evacuated New Madrid, leaving 25 cannon, and military stores valued at $1,000,000 in the hands of the Unionists.

Capture of Newbern, N. C.—Newbern was occupied by a Confederate force. On the 14th of March, 1862, General Burnside attacked the city with a fleet of gunboats and three brigades of Unionists. A four-hours' fight ensued, when the Confederates retreated, and the Unionists took possession of the city, with 69 heavy cannon and field-pieces, large quantities of ammunition, naval and military stores, steamers, vessels, etc., valued at $2,000,000. The Union loss was 91 killed and 466 wounded, many mortally. The Confederate loss was not so heavy, they being under cover.

Battle of Winchester, Va.—Fought March 23, 1862, between Union troops, numbering 8,000 men and 24 cannon, under Generals Banks and Shields, and 13,200 Confederate infantry and cavalry, with 28 cannon, under Jackson and Garnett. After five hours' fighting, the Confederates were defeated, and retreated to Strasburg, followed by their victors. The Union loss was 103 killed, 441 wounded, and 46 missing. The loss of the Confederates was very large, 270 being buried on the field.

Battle of Pigeon Ranch, N. M.—Fought March 28, 1862, between 3,000 Unionists, under Colonel Hough, and 1,100 Texan Confederates; a drawn battle.

Battles of Pittsburg Landing and Shiloh—General Grant was encamped at Pittsburg Landing, on the Tennessee river, with 45,000 Unionists, awaiting reinforcements under General Buell. April 6, 1862, they were attacked by 40,000 Confederates, under Generals Johnston and Beauregard, and driven back to the river, with the loss of a number of prisoners. Next day, General Buell, with more Unionists, having arrived, the battle was resumed, lasting throughout the day. The Confederates, however, were finally defeated and driven to their fortifications at Corinth, Miss. The Confederates lost General A. S. Johnston. The Union loss is set down at 1,700 killed, 7,495 wounded, and 3,022 prisoners. The Confederate losses, as reported by Beauregard, were 1,728 killed, 8,012 wounded, and 959 missing.

Capture of Island No. Ten.—The Confederates having fortified Island No. Ten, in the Mississippi river, 10 miles above New Madrid, and so commanding a strong position, General Pope, with a force of Unionists, also secured another commanding position, just below the island. After several ineffectual attempts to dislodge him by the Confederate gunboats, on the 16th of March, 1862, Commodore Foote and his flotilla arrived to assist General Pope. The island was well fortified with earthworks and heavy cannon, and manned by 20,000 Confederates. The bombardment was so hot and heavy, however, as to seriously incommode the Confederates, and on April 8, 1862, the Unionists attacked them with such vigor that the works were carried. The result was the capture of 5,000 prisoners, 124 cannon, 5,000 stand of small arms, 2,000 hogsheads of sugar and a large quantity of clothing, tents, ammunition, etc.

Bombardment of Fort Pulaski, Ga.—Fort Pulaski, twelve miles from Savannah, occupied by the Confederates and defended by 128 cannon and mortars, was invested by 11 Union batteries, under command of General Gilmore. On the 10th of April, 1862, the bombardment of the fort began, and on the 11th the fort was unconditionally surrendered to the Unionists, who had lost 1 killed and 3 wounded. The Confederates had 5 wounded, and 380 prisoners were taken with the fort.

Capture of Huntsville, Ala.—On the 11th of April, 1862, General Mitchel, Unionist, occupied Huntsville, capturing 200 Confederate prisoners, 15 locomotives and a number of cars.

Skirmish at Monterey, Va., and Capture at Chattanooga.—April 12, 1862, Confederates attacked General Milroy's Union force at Monterey, but were repulsed. On the same day, the Union general, Mitchel, captured 2,000 Confederates at Chattanooga.

Second Siege of Yorktown, Va.—Yorktown was strongly fortified by the Confederates, under General J. E. Johnston, who occupied it on April 17, 1862, with 53,000 men, exclusive of cavalry. The siege of this stronghold, which began April 5, 1862, was conducted by General McClellan, who had a force of 118,000 Unionists. It continued for a month. On the 4th of May, Johnston and his men evacuated the place, with whatever he could take, and started toward Richmond. Union cavalry, under Hancock and Hooker's division, engaged 30,000 of them near Williamsburg, and a severe fight ensued. The Confederates at length retired, but most of their trains had by that time escaped beyond the lines. The Unionists lost 1,856 killed and wounded and 372 missing. The Confederate loss is believed to have been at least 2,600 killed and wounded.

Bombardment of Forts Jackson and Saint Philip, La.—Commodore Farragut and the Union fleet designed to capture New Orleans from the Confederates, and sailed early in February, 1862. On the 18th of April, 1862, he began the bombardment of the two Confederate forts, Saint Philip and Jackson, in the Mississippi, below New Orleans, with such success that the obstructions were removed, and the fleet passed the forts on its way to New Orleans, April 24.

Fights in North Carolina—April 19, 1862, the Unionists, under General Burnside, defeated a body of Confederates near Elizabeth City, N. C. The Union loss was 11 killed. On the same day, General Reno, with 2,000 Unionists, defeated some Confederate troops at Camden, N. C., in which the former lost 99 wounded and 14 killed.

Capture of New Orleans—Part of Commodore Farragut's fleet of Union vessels, nine in number, and a land force of Unionists, under General Butler, appeared before New Orleans, then held by the Confederates, April 25, 1862. Forts Saint Philip and Jackson, the Confederate strongholds, capitulated April 28; General Lovell, with his Confederate troops, retreated into the interior of the State, and General Butler took possession of the city, May 1, 1862. The Confederate loss, besides the forts, included 11 gunboats, the ram Manassas, and the iron-clad Louisiana. The Confederates destroyed immense quantities of cotton, steamboats, ships, sugar, and other property in the city, to prevent its falling into the hands of the Unionists. The loss of the Unionists in passing the Confederate forts was 30 killed and 110 wounded.

Fight at Lebanon, Tenn.—Fought May 5, 1862, between the Union troops under General Dumont and Morgan's Confederate cavalry. The latter had 66 killed and 183 taken prisoners; the Unionists lost 10 killed and 26 wounded and missing.

Battle of West Point, Va.—Fought May 7, 1862, between a formidable force of Confederates—a part of Lee's army—and Generals Franklin and Sedgwick's divisions of about 30,000 Unionists. The battle lasted six hours, when the Confederates were repulsed. The Union loss was 194 killed and wounded.

Battle at McDowell's, Va.—On the 8th of May, General Milroy's force of Unionists attacked a body of Confederates, but after a fight of five hours he was obliged to withdraw, having sustained a loss of 29 killed and about 200 wounded.

Evacuation of Pensacola, Fla.—The 3,000 Confederates, under General Bragg, who had occupied Pensacola since January 12, 1861, fearing a visit from Commodore Porter's Union mortar-fleet, evacuated the city May 9, 1862. When leaving, they fired the navy-yard, destroying the extensive workshops, warehouses, forts McRae and Barrancas, the lighthouse and the magnificent naval hospital. The Unionists at Fort Pickens, by a heavy cannonade, succeeded in driving the Confederates from the forts and buildings, thus arresting the work of destruction.

Capture of Norfolk, Va.—May 10, 1862, the Confederate authorities of Norfolk surrendered the city to General Wool and his 5,000 Unionists, without a fight. The navy-yard was in ruins, the iron-clad Merrimack had been blown up, and many guns spiked. The Confederates left behind them some 200 cannon and considerable ammunition.

A Naval Fight—May 10, 1862, a fight occurred between 8 Confederate and 6 Union gunboats on the Mississippi river, near Fort Wright, in which the former were defeated, losing 2 of their vessels.

Surrender of Natchez, Miss.—May 12, 1862, Commodore Farragut's fleet captured Natchez, which was then occupied by a small Confederate force, and was soon after abandoned by the Unionists.

Naval Fight in Virginia—A squadron of 4 Union war vessels, under Commodore Rodgers, encountered a Confederate force at Fort Darling, on the James river, eight miles from Richmond, May 16, 1862, and after a sharp fight the fleet withdrew, having lost 13 killed and 16 wounded.

On the Chickahominy—May 17, 1862, McClellan's left wing, drove a body of Confederates across the Chickahominy, at Bottom bridge, 13 miles from Richmond.

Battle at Lewisburgh, Va.—May 23, 1862, a force of Confederates, under Colonel Heath, attacked a body of Unionists, and, after an hour's contest, were defeated. The Unionists lost 14 killed and wounded.

Battle of Front Royal, Va.—Fought May 23, 1862, between Colonel Kenley, commanding a Union regiment, three companies and part of a battery, and a large force of Confederates, near Manassas gap, Va. After a desperate defense, Kenley retired across the Shenandoah, and rallied again; but was finally compelled to retreat, with a very heavy loss.

A Union Defeat — May 25, 1862, General Banks, with about 4,000 Unionists, encountered more than 25,000 Confederates, under Jackson and Ewell, at Strasburg, Va. Against such odds, after the first attack, and having held Winchester for two hours, Banks retreated to Williamsburgh to await reinforcements.

Battle of Hanover Court House, Va. —Fought May 27, 1862, between Fitz John Porter's division of Unionists and 13,000 Confederates. The latter were dislodged with the loss of about 200 killed, 730 prisoners, 2 railroad trains, arms, and ammunition. The Union loss was 53 killed and 344 wounded and missing.

Movements at Corinth, Miss.—May 28, 29 and 30, 1862, Corinth was invested by the Unionists under Generals Halleck, Pope and W. T. Sherman. On the 29th the Confederates, under Beauregard, evacuated their position, and on the 31st the Unionists, under General Halleck, occupied the town. General Pope, with 40,000 Unionists, pursued the fugitives (whose retreat had been obstructed by another Union force), and took many prisoners. Beauregard, however, again rallied his forces at Okolono, Miss.

Battle of Seven Pines, Va.—Fought May 31, 1862, between a large force of Confederates, under Longstreet, D. H. Hill, and Smith, and the Union troops in Casey's division of McClellan's army. Casey sustained his position for three hours against superior numbers, but finally fell back to the Seven Pines. They were dislodged from that position by the Confederates, and driven to a belt of woods, where the 1,800 Unionists, under Heintzelman, made so strong a resistance as to check the assault. Both armies then separated and encamped for the night.

Battle of Fair Oaks, Va. — While the battle of the Seven Pines was in progress, May 31, 1862, another battle was fought at Fair Oaks, hardly a mile away, between the Unionists in Sumner's division of McClellan's army and about 38,000 Confederates, under Johnston and Smith. The contest continued from four o'clock in the afternoon until twilight, when the Unionists charged upon the foe, driving them back in confusion at about the time that the struggle at the Seven Pines closed. Johnston was severely wounded in the last attack. Both armies bivouacked on the field, but a short distance from each other. Next morning hostilities were resumed at Fair Oaks, but not at the Seven Pines. Sumner being reinforced by Hooker, after an hour's hard fighting the Confederates were driven from the shelter of the woods, and retreated in confusion to Richmond.

Losses at the Seven Pines and Fair Oaks—The losses of the Unionists in both battles were 890 killed, 3,627 wounded, 1,222 missing. The total loss of the Confederates is estimated at 6,733.

Fort Pillow Besieged—Fort Pillow, about 40 miles north of Memphis, Tenn., was erected by the Confederates. After a siege of 54 days by Union gunboats, under Commodore Foote, the fort, occupied by 6,000 Confederates, under General Villipigue, was abandoned, it having been dismantled and destroyed, June 5, 1862.

Battle Near Memphis, Tenn. — Fought June 6, 1862, between 8 Confederate war-vessels, under Commodore Montgomery, and a Union fleet of 5 gunboats and 9 rams, commanded by Colonel Ellet. Four of the Confederate vessels were sunk and 3 were run ashore. After the battle, the city of Memphis was surrendered to the Unionists, and was always afterwards retained by them.

Skirmish Near Harrisonburg, Va. — Fought June 6, 1862, between Unionists and Confederates, under General Ashby, who was killed.

Battle of Cross-Keys, Va.—Fought June 8, 1862, between a Union force under General Fremont, and 5,000 Confederates under General Ewell, a contest that retarded Fremont's advance. The Union loss was 664; that of the Confederates is unknown.

Battle of James Island, S. C. — Fought near Charleston, June 16, 1862, between Unionists, under General Stevens, and Confederates, the former being defeated with a loss of 85 killed, 172 wounded, and 128 missing.

Battle at Saint Charles, Ark.—Fought June 17, 1862, between Unionists, under Colonel Fitch, and a Confederate battery, which was destroyed. An explosion in a Union gunboat killed 125.

Battles Before Richmond—June 26, 1862, McClellan's Union army of 103,000 was gathered on the Chickahominy, confronted by about 100,000 Confederates, under Robert E. Lee. Richmond, the Confederate capital, was in no condition to withstand a siege. Lee, therefore, decided to attack McClellan and raise the siege. He, therefore, divided his army and posted it at several points. The contest opened at Mechanicsville, where the Confederates attacked McClellan's right wing. In this action 6,000 Unionists contended with 12,000 Confederates. The latter were repelled, and fell back, having lost 1,500 men, while the Union loss was barely 300, owing to their sheltered position. On the 27th the battle of Cold Harbor was fought with great severity, between about 56,000 Confederates and 33,000 Unionists. During this day's fight the Confederates lost 9,500 in killed and wounded, and the Unionists 4,000 killed and wounded, 2,000 prisoners, and 22 cannon. During one skirmish the Confederates lost 200 out of 650 men. The victory at the close of the day was apparently with Lee, although he had suffered double the losses that he had inflicted, and his position was perilous. June 29, a series of engagements occurred at Savage's Station, McClellan having fallen back from his advantageous position. At Peach Orchard the Confederates attacked the Unionists, but were repulsed. Later in the day they renewed the attack at Savage's Station, which lasted until nine o'clock in the evening. The Union loss was about 600; that of the Confederates about 400. The Union wounded and sick (2,500) fell into the hands of the Confederates. June 30, McClellan continued his retreat to the James river. On this day was fought the battle of Frazier's Farm, between the Union divisions of McCall, Hooker, and Kearney, and the Confederates under A. P. Hill and Longstreet. The attempt to break the Union line failed. The Unionists lost about 300 killed, and 1,500 wounded; the Confederates, 325 killed and 1,700 wounded. The battle of Malvern Hill was fought July 1, 1862. McClellan had about 90,000 men; Lee only about 60,000 with which to attack McClellan's position. McClellan's artillery and musketry, well-placed, served to repel the Confederates' repeated charges upon his lines. The attacking party was not more than 28,000 strong. At dark the contest ceased, the Confederates having been repulsed at every point. The Union loss, that day, was about 375 killed and 1,800 wounded; the Confederate loss, 900 killed and 3,500 wounded. During the engagements from June 26 to July 1, it is estimated that the Unionists lost 1,582 killed, 7,709 wounded, and 5,958 missing; while the Confederates lost 3,150 killed, 15,255 wounded, and about 1,000 prisoners.

Skirmish at Bayou Cache, Ark. — Fought July 7, 1862, between a portion of General Curtis' Union army and the Confederates under General Rust, the latter being defeated, with 110 killed. Curtis lost but 8 killed and 45 wounded.

Skirmish at Jasper, Ala. — Fought July 7, 1862, between Unionists and Confederates, the former being worsted.

Capture of Hamilton, N. C. — July 9, 1862, Hamilton was captured by the Unionists.

Battle of Murfreesboro, Tenn.—Fought July 13, 1862, between a small force of Unionists, by whom it had been previously occupied, and a body of Confederates, under Forrest, a Michigan regiment being taken prisoners, and $30,000 worth of commissary stores were captured.

Capture of Kentucky Towns — July 11, 1862, the Confederate, General Morgan, raided Lebanon, Ky., burned part of the town and despoiled the bank. July 17, he captured Cynthiana, Ky., and burned several railroad bridges.

A Raid in Indiana — July 18, 1862, a band of Confederates raided Newburgh, Ind., destroyed some hospital stores, captured 250 stand of arms, and retreated across the Ohio.

Skirmish at Memphis, Tenn. — Fought July 19, 1862, between Unionists and Confederates, the former losing 6 killed and 32 wounded.

Bombardment of Vicksburg, Miss. — In June, 1862, the Union fleets of gunboats, respectively commanded by Commodore Farragut, from below, and Commanders Davis and Ellet, from above, met at Vicksburg, which was then strongly fortified and occupied by a Confederate force estimated at 10,000, and from time to time bombarded the city without any definite results. July 14, 1862, the commanders made a general attack upon the fortifications and heavily bombarded them for two hours. The upper batteries were silenced, and the city was set on fire in several places. Farragut's fleet passed the batteries and steamed down the river. The Confederates were not dislodged. On the 22d of July, the siege was abandoned.

Battle at Moore's Hill, Mo. — Fought between Confederates and Unionists, July 28, 1862, the former being defeated. The Unionists lost 10 killed and 30 wounded.

Capture of Orange Court House, Va. —August 1, 1862, Union cavalry, under General Crawford, after a short skirmish, drove out 2 regiments of Confederates, killing 11, and taking over 50 prisoners.

Skirmish Near Memphis, Tenn. — Fought August 3, 1862, between a Confederate force, under General Jeff. Thompson, and Union troops, in which Thompson was defeated.

A Naval Fight — Fought August 4, 1862, between 3 Union gunboats, under Commodore Porter, and the monster ram Arkansas, belonging to the Confederates. They met above Baton Rouge, on the Mississippi river, and on being attacked with incendiary shells the Arkansas was set on fire and destroyed.

Battle at Baton Rouge, La. — Fought August 5, 1862, between Confederates, under General Breckinridge, and a small force of Unionists, under General Williams. Confederate and Union gunboats were also engaged. Under a sharp shelling by the Union boats the Confederates were repulsed. The Unionists lost 56 killed, including General Williams, and 175 wounded and missing.

Battle of Cedar Mountain, Va.—Fought August 9, 1862, between the Confederate army, numbering about 21,000, under Generals Jackson, Ewell and Longstreet, and about 7,000 Unionists, under General Banks. The latter was forced to retire about 1½ miles from his first position. Banks being reinforced, the Confederates next day fell back two miles, and on the 11th retired across Robertson river. The Union loss was 450 killed, 660 wounded, and 290 prisoners, besides cannon and a large quantity of ammunition. The Confederate loss was nearly as heavy in killed, wounded and missing, including Generals Winder and Trimble.

Fight at Fort Donelson, Tenn.—August 25, 1862, the Confederates made an unsuccessful attack on the Unionists at Fort Donelson.

Fights at Manassas and Haymarket, Va.—August 26, 1862, the Confederates, under General Ewell, attacked a portion of the Union army, under Pope, at Manassas, and drove them out. Next day Pope fell back toward Warrenton, and was reinforced by Hooker's command. Overtaking the Confederates at Haymarket, a severe fight ensued between Hooker and Ewell, in which the Confederates were vanquished, Ewell losing his camp with 300 killed and wounded.

Reduction of City Point, Va. — On the 27th of August, 1862, the Union gunboats destroyed the Confederate fortifications at City Point.

Skirmish Near Centerville, Va. — Fought August 28, 1862, between Gibbon's brigade of McDowell's Union corps, and a force of Confederates under Stonewall Jackson. The fight was severe, but ended with the coming on of darkness.

Battle of Gainsville, Va.—Fought August 29, 1862, between Sigel and Reynolds' divisions of McDowell's Union corps, reinforced by Reno and Heintzelman's divisions, and the Confederate army under Stonewall Jackson, with reinforcements arriving. The battle raged furiously for several hours, in which the enemy was driven back, leaving his dead and wounded on the field. Darkness put an end to the contest, and General Pope claimed a victory. His losses were estimated at between 6,000 and 8,000 men, and those of the Confederates much greater.

The Second Battle of Bull Run — Fought August 30, 1862, between Stonewall Jackson's entire army of Confederates, reinforced by Longstreet and the advance of Lee's army (about 46,000 in all), and 35,000 Unionists under Pope. The contest was severe, lasting all day; at dark, exhausted, the Unionists retired to Centerville, in good order, leaving the Confederates in possession of the field. The Unionists lost at least 11,000 in killed and wounded, and, perhaps, 9,000 prisoners; the Confederates about 8,500 killed and wounded.

Battle at Richmond, Ky. — Fought August 30, 1862, between the Confederates, under Kirby Smith, and the Unionists, under Generals Manson and Nelson. The latter were defeated with a loss of about 200 killed, 700 wounded, and 2,000 prisoners.

Skirmish at Bolivar, Tenn. — Fought August 30, 1862, between Unionists and Confederates, the latter being defeated.

Destruction of Bayou Sara, La. — August 31, 1862, Bayou Sara, a prosperous shipping port of Louisiana, on the Mississippi river, 165 miles from New Orleans, was almost entirely destroyed by the Union fleet of Admiral Porter, in consequence of his being fired upon by Confederate guerrillas.

Battle at Britton's Lane, Tenn. — Fought September 1, 1862, between Unionists and Confederates, the latter retiring and leaving their dead on the field. The Unionists lost 5 killed, 78 wounded and 92 missing.

Battle at Chantilly, Va.—Fought September 1, 1862, between the Unionists under Generals Hooker, Reno, and Kearney, and the Confederate army under Ewell and Hill. General Pope endeavored to transfer his forces from Centerville to Germantown, and while doing so was attacked. The fight lasted for several hours, ending with the darkness. The Union generals,

Kearney and Stevens, were killed. Under an impetuous bayonet charge the Confederates were driven from the field; but the losses of the Unionists were heavy.

Battle at Washington, N. C.—September 6, 1862, the Confederates attacked the Union garrison, but were repulsed. The Unionists lost 8 killed and 36 wounded.

Battle at Middletown, Md. — Fought September 12, 1862, between Unionists and Confederates, the former losing 80 killed and wounded.

Battle of South Mountain, Md. — Fought September 14, 1862, between the Union army under Generals Hooker, Reno, Franklin, Cox and others, and the Confederate forces under Longstreet and Hill. The engagement was general and severe, and resulted in the retreat of the Confederates. The Union general, Reno, was killed. The Union losses were 312 killed, 1,234 wounded, and 22 missing. The Confederate loss was quite as large, including 1,500 prisoners.

Surrender of Harper's Ferry—A force of 12,000 Unionists, under General Miles, who held Harper's Ferry, W. Va., was attacked September 12, 1862, by a strong Confederate army, under Stonewall Jackson, and after a two-days' contest, the place was surrendered on the 15th to the Confederates. General Miles was killed, and the Unionists sustained a loss of about 11,000 prisoners, 73 cannon, 13,000 small arms, and a considerable amount of stores. Union cavalry, 2,000 strong, cut their way through the rebel lines, and escaped.

Battle of Munfordsville, Ky.—Fought between about 5,000 Unionists, under Colonel Dunham, who held the place, and a strong force of Confederates under Price. After three days' fighting, September 14, 15 and 16, 1862, Dunham surrendered about 4,500 men and their artillery, and turned the town over to the Confederates. September 21, General McCook and a force of Unionists recaptured the place.

Battle of Antietam, Md.—Fought September 17, 1862, near Sharpsburg, Md., between 65,000 Confederates, under Lee and Jackson, and 85,000 Unionists, under McClellan, Hooker, Burnside, Sumner, and Mansfield. The contest was severe, and lasted from early morning until evening. During the succeeding night the Confederates retreated, leaving in the hands of their foes 3,500 prisoners, 39 stand of colors, and 13 cannon. Their total loss was about 9,000 men. The Unionists lost 2,010 killed, 9,416 wounded, and 1,043 missing. The Union General Mansfield lost his life while endeavoring to regain the ground lost by Hooker. It is classed as a drawn battle.

The Evacuation of Maryland and Harper's Ferry—On the 18th of September, 1862, the Confederate army of Lee and Jackson withdrew from Maryland to Virginia, after having invaded the first-named State for a fortnight. Harper's Ferry, W. Va., was also evacuated by the Confederates on the same day.

Battle of Iuka, Miss. — General Price, with about 15,000 Confederates, occupied Iuka early in September, 1862. On the 19th of September, Generals Rosecrans and Ord advanced with a force of Unionists to capture this point, and for two hours the contest was severe and bloody. During the following night the Confederates evacuated the town. Their losses included more than 300 buried on the field, and 500 severely wounded, 200 of whom died within a few days. The Union losses were 300 killed and 500 wounded.

Battle of Augusta, Ky.—Fought September 27, 1862, between an attacking force of Confederates and the Union garrison of 120. The latter surrendered with a loss of 9 killed, 15 wounded, and the rest taken prisoners.

Battle of Corinth, Miss.—Fought October 3 and 4, 1862, between 25,000 Unionists, under General Rosecrans, who held the town and its outposts, and more than 35,000 Confederates, under Generals Van Dorn, Price, and Lovell. On the first day, the Unionists outside were driven into the town. The battle was renewed with terrible severity next morning, the Unionists having been reinforced by McPherson, and the Confederates were obliged to retreat, leaving in the hands of their foes 2,248 prisoners, 14 stand of colors, 2 cannon, 3,300 stand of small arms, a large amount of ammunition, etc. The Confederates had 1,423 men and officers killed, and more than 5,000 wounded. The Unionists lost 315 killed, 1,812 wounded, and 232 prisoners and missing.

Battle at Lavergne, Tenn. — Fought October 6, 1862, between a Confederate force and a brigade of Unionists, under General Palmer; the former were repulsed, with a loss to the latter of 5 killed and 13 wounded and missing. The Confederate loss was about 80 killed and wounded, 175 prisoners, 2 cannon, provisions, camp equipage, etc.

Battle of Perryville, Ky. — Fought October 8, 1862, between 15,000 Unionists, under Colonel Daniel McCook, of Buell's army, and four divisions of the Confederate army, under Generals Bragg, Polk, and Hardee. The battle lasted from three o'clock in the morning until after dark that evening, and resulted in a victory for the Unionists. The loss of the latter, besides the killing of Generals Jackson and Terrell, was 466 killed, 1,463 wounded and 160 missing. The Confederate loss is estimated at about the same figures.

Raid on Chambersburg, Pa. — On the 10th of October, 1862, the Confederate general, Stuart, with 2,000 cavalry, made a dash on Chambersburg, seized a considerable amount of clothing designed for McClellan's Union army, destroyed property belonging to the government, burned the railroad depot, captured fresh horses, passed clear around McClellan's army, and escaped without loss.

Battle Near Gallatin, Tenn. — October 19, 1862, the Confederates, under General Forrest, were defeated by a force of Unionists.

Operations in Florida—During the latter part of October, 1862, an expedition of Unionists, under Colonel Beard, of New York, destroyed 9 large salt works on Florida rivers, and brought back 150 good colored recruits for the Northern army.

Battle of Pocotaligo, S. C. — Fought October 22, 1862, between about 5,000 Union soldiers, with three batteries and an engineer corps, under General Brannon, and a force of Confederates. In the struggle of nearly six hours to gain possession of the Charleston and Savannah railroad, the Unionists were repulsed, with the loss of 30 killed and 180 wounded.

Battle of Maysville, Ark. — Fought October 22, 1862, between 10,000 Unionists, under General Blunt, and 7,000 Confederates. After a severe action of an hour's duration, the latter were totally routed, with the loss of all their artillery, a large number of horses, and a part of their garrison equipments.

Battle of Labadie, La.—Fought October 27, 1862, between a party of Confederates and a Union force. The latter won the field, with a loss of 17 killed and 74 wounded.

Fight at Garrettsburg, Ky. — Fought November 11, 1862, between Unionists under General Ransom, and Confederates under General Woodward. The latter were defeated.

Battle of Kinston, N. C.—Fought November 17, 1862, between 6,000 Confederates, under General Evans, and a Union force under General Foster. After a fight of five hours the Confederates were defeated, with the loss of 11 cannon and about 400 prisoners. The Union loss was about 200 killed and wounded. This fight and several other encounters of more or less importance occurred during a ten-days' expedition of General Foster from Newbern to Goldsboro, for the purpose of cutting off railroad communication between Richmond, Va., and Charleston, S. C. He appears to have been successful.

Battle of Cane Hill, Ark. — Fought November 28, 1862, between 2,000 Unionists (cavalry and artillery), under Generals Blunt and Heron, and 2 regiments of Confederate cavalry. After a sharp skirmish the latter retreated to Van Buren, leaving their killed and some of their wounded on the field. The Unionists followed them to Van Buren, and completely routed them there, capturing 100 prisoners, 4 steamers, a large quantity of corn, camp equipage, mules and horses. The Confederates retreated, leaving behind 600 wounded and sick soldiers.

Skirmish near Charleston, Va.—Fought December 2, 1862, between Unionists and Confederates. The latter were defeated, with a loss of 70 killed and wounded and 145 prisoners.

Battle of Prairie Grove, Ark.—Fought December 7, 1862, between about 7,000 Unionists (infantry and artillery), under General Heron, reinforced by about 5,000 more and 24 cannon, under General Blunt, and 28,000 men of Hindman's Confederate army, with 18 cannon, under Marmaduke, Parsons, Frost, and Rains. The Confederates were defeated with a loss of more than 2,000 killed and wounded, and during the succeeding night retreated from the field. The Union army lost 495 killed and 500 wounded, including upward of 40 field and line officers.

Fight at Hartsville, Tenn. — Fought December 7, 1862, between Morgan's Confederate cavalry and a brigade of Unionists of Dumont's command, under Colonel Moore. After an hour's fight, the brigade, consisting of the 104th Illinois, the 106th and 108th Ohio, part of the 2d Indiana cavalry and a battery, surrendered to the Confederates and were paroled. The Unionists also lost 55 killed.

Battle of Fredericksburg, Va. — December 11, 1862, the Union army, under Burnside, began the bombardment of Fredericksburg, then occupied by the Confederates under Lee. During this bombardment Burnside transferred 100,000 of his men across the Rappahannock, in front of Fredericksburg. December 13, the battle was fought, Burnside bringing about 32,000 men into action, under Sumner, Hooker and Franklin. Lee had of his 80,000 troops only about 25,000 in the fight, under Jackson and Longstreet. The Unionists, after a severe contest, were repulsed. Their losses were 1,152 killed, 9,101 wounded, 3,234 missing. The Confederates lost only 595 killed, 4,061 wounded, and 653 missing.

Skirmish at Zurich, Va.—Fought on the 13th December, 1862, between Unionists and Confederates, the latter being defeated, with the capture of a portion of their force.

Capture of Baton Rouge, La. — On December 14, 1862, a part of General Banks' command, under General Grover, took peaceable possession of Baton Rouge, the capital of the State, the Confederates having evacuated the town.

Capture of Holly Springs, Miss. — December 19, 1862, the Confederate general, Van Dorn, with several thousand cavalry, invested Holly Springs, which was then occupied by the Unionists. Once in, after a feeble resistance by the Unionists, they destroyed and carried off public and private property valued at nearly $5,000,000. They then evacuated the town.

A Raid into East Tennessee—A notable cavalry raid was made into East Tennessee, beginning December 21, 1862, by the Unionist General Carter, with about 1,000 men. They were gone from Winchester, Ky., 20 days, during which, without tents, they marched 470 miles (170 in the enemy's country); burned 2 important railroad bridges across the Holston and Wautaga rivers; damaged 10 miles of track; had 2 skirmishes with the Confederates; captured 400 prisoners, 700 stand of arms, and a train of cars with a locomotive, besides a considerable quantity of stores, and returned with the loss of 2 men killed and 8 others wounded, captured or missing.

Skirmish at Dumfries, Va. — Fought December 23, between the Unionists, under General Sigel, and a party of Confederates. The latter were repulsed.

Battle of Davis' Mills, Miss. — Fought between the Confederates, under Van Dorn, and a small force of Unionists, under Colonel Morgan, of the 25th Indiana regiment, December 21, 1862. After a severe conflict the Confederates retreated, leaving their dead and wounded on the field.

Second Siege of Vicksburg, Miss. — December 27, 1862, General Sherman attacked the advanced works of the Confederate defenses, about six miles from Vicksburg, on the Yazoo river. At the same time the gunboats attacked the Confederate batteries on Haines' Bluff. December 28, the Unionists drove the Confederates from the first and second lines of defense, and advanced to within 2½ miles of Vicksburg. December 29, the Confederates attacked General Sherman with their whole force, and drove him back to the first line of defense. December 30, after burying their dead and transferring their wounded to transports, the Unionists abandoned the siege, General Sherman returning to camp at Milliken's Bend. The Union loss was about 600 killed, 1,500 wounded, and 1,000 missing.

Battles of Stone River, Tenn.—Fought December 31, 1862, and January 1, 2, 3, 1863, between 43,400 Unionists under General Rosecrans, and 62,490 Confederates under Hardee, Polk, and Kirby Smith. The main attack of the Confederates was made December 31, on General Rosecrans' right, commanded by General McCook. This Union division was driven back four miles, and lost 26 cannon, but being reinforced from the left and center, the Confederates were in turn repulsed and the lost ground regained. Confederate attacks were made on the Federal lines January 1 and 2, but were repulsed. On the night of January 3 the Confederates retreated. The Union losses were 1,553 killed, 7,000 wounded, and 3,000 prisoners. The Confederate loss is estimated at 10,000 in all.

Battle of Parker's Cross Roads, Tenn.—Fought December 31, 1862, between 7,000 Confederate cavalry, under Forrest, with 10 cannon, and a body of Unionists under Generals Dunham and Sullivan. After a sharp fight, the Confederates retreated, losing their cannon, 500 horses, caissons, ammunition, small arms, wagons, camp equipage, and more than 1,000 men killed, wounded, or taken prisoners.

BATTLES OF THE THIRD YEAR OF THE WAR.

Battle of Galveston, Tex. — Fought January 1, 1863, between a Confederate force of 3,000 men, under General Magruder, and the 300 Unionists who occupied the town. At the same time the Confederate batteries and 2 steamers attacked the Union blockading fleet in the harbor. After a contest of several hours, the small Union force on shore and the Union steamer Harriet Lane were captured by the Confederates. The Union vessel Westfield was blown up to prevent her falling into the hands of the enemy, and Commodore Renshaw perished with her. The Confederates captured, also, a large quantity of arms, ammunition, etc. The Unionists lost 25 killed.

Fight at Springfield, Mo. — Fought January 7, 1863, between a force of Confederates, and a force of Unionists under General Brown, who held the place and defeated the Confederates. The place contained a large quantity of stores owned by the Unionists, whose loss in the defense was 17 killed.

Battle of Arkansas Post, Ark. — Fought January 10 and 11, 1863, by the Union river fleet under Admiral Porter, and the Union land forces under General McClernand, against the Confederate force who held the post. On the second day the fortifications were carried by the Unionists. The Confederate loss was about 200 killed, 4,500 prisoners, about 4,500 stand of arms, and 20 cannon. The Unionists lost about 100 killed and 500 wounded.

A Naval Battle—January 10, 1863, two Confederate iron-clads undertook to break up the Union blockade at Charleston, S. C. Two Union vessels were seriously injured, and the inner line of the fleet disturbed. Otherwise the attack was a failure.

Capture of Transports—January 12, 1863, three Union transports and a gunboat surrendered to the Confederates on the Cumberland river, Tenn.

Battle at Bayou Teche, La. — Fought January 15, 1863, between a party of Unionists and the Confederate force which held the place. The latter were captured, and the Confederate gunboat Cotton was destroyed.

Battle at Sabine City, Tex. — Fought January 20, 1863, between Confederates and 2 vessels of the blockading squadron. The latter were captured, and 1 was destroyed.

Third Siege of Vicksburg—January 22, 1863, General McClernand resumed the Union siege of Vicksburg, Miss., and work was renewed on the Union cut-off canal at that point. The Union ram, Queen of the West, ran the blockade at Vicksburg, February 2, but was afterwards captured by the Confederates. February 13, the iron-clad Indianola also ran the blockade, and was captured by the Confederates. February 18, 1863, the Union gunboats began to shell Vicksburg, but without accomplishing anything.

Fight at Fort McAllister, Ga.—Fought between the Union iron-clad Montauk, sailed by Commander Worden, and 3 wooden gunboats and a force of Confederates in the fort. Two unsuccessful efforts were made, January 27 and February 1, 1863, to capture the fort. February 27, the Confederate steamer Nashville, while attempting to run the Union blockade, got aground and was destroyed by the fleet.

Battle of Blackwater, Va. — Fought January 30, 1863, between a force of Confederates, under General Pryor, and the Union army, under Generals Peck and Corcoran. After 2 severe engagements, the Confederates were repulsed, with a Union loss of 24 killed and 80 wounded.

Skirmish at Rover, Tenn. — Fought January 31, 1863, between a party of Unionists and another of Confederates, the latter being defeated with a loss of 12 killed and 300 wounded.

Battle Near Middletown, Tenn. — Fought February 2, 1863, between Stokes' Union Tennessee cavalry and a Kentucky Union regiment and a Confederate camp. The camp was captured, the occupants dispersing.

Fight at Bradyville, Tenn. — Fought March 1, 1863, between 2,300 infantry and cavalry, under General Stanley, and a force of about 800 Confederate cavalry. After a sharp skirmish the latter were routed and driven more than three miles, some of them being cut down as they ran.

Skirmish at Eagleville, Tenn.—Fought March 2, 1863, between a brigade from the regular Union army and a force of Confederates, in which the latter were routed.

Skirmish Near Thompson's Station, Tenn. — Fought March 5, 1863, between 7 regiments of Union soldiers, with a battery, under Colonel Coburn, and a force of Confederates, numbering 30,000 men, under Van Dorn. Overcome by superior numbers, after an unequal struggle, Coburn surrendered, part of his command escaping safely. The Unionists lost 100 killed, 300 wounded, and about 1,200 prisoners. The Confederates admitted a loss of 150 killed and 450 wounded.

Battle at Unionville, Tenn. — Fought March 7, 1863, by a force of Unionists under General Minty and a body of Confederate cavalry, the latter being defeated, with the loss of their wagons, horses and tents and about 60 prisoners.

Battle of Fairfax, Va.—Fought March 9, 1863, between General Stoughton, with a Union force, and a band of rebel cavalry. The latter passed through the Union lines, and captured the General and some of his men.

Fight at Newbern, N. C. — Fought March 13, 1863, between an attacking force of Confederates and the Unionists who held the place. The attempt resulted in a failure to recapture the place.

Battle at Port Hudson, La.—March 13, 1863, Commodore Farragut's Union fleet attempted to pass the Confederate batteries, but only a part of the vessels succeeded. One—the Mississippi—ran aground and was destroyed.

Battle Near Kelly's Ford, Va.—March 17, 1863, a force of 200 Union cavalry, under General Averill crossed the Rappahannock river, where only one horseman could pass the ford at once, and, notwithstanding a galling fire from the Confederate rifle-pits and sharpshooters, charged upon the Confederate intrenchments, killing or capturing nearly the entire force of their enemies. They then encountered a body of Confederate cavalry, under Stuart, with whom they had a hand-to-hand encounter for five hours. The Confederates were routed with great slaughter, and the Unionists took 80 of them prisoners.

Battle at Milton, Tenn. — Fought March 20, 1863, between 4,000 Confederates under Wheeler and Morgan, and 1,323 mounted Unionists, under Colonel Hall. The Confederates were totally defeated, with a loss of 400.

Capture of Jacksonville, Fla.— March 20, 1863, the Confederates were driven from the city by a Union brigade of colored soldiers.

Battle of Steele's Bayou, Miss. — Fought March 22, 1863, between about 4,000 Confederates and General Sherman's division of the Union army, assisted by Union gunboats. The brief contest resulted in the retreat of the Confederates, with heavy loss, while the Unionists lost but one man, who was killed.

Capture of Mount Sterling, Ky. — March 22, 1863, a force of Confederates, under Clark, captured Mount Sterling.

The Brentwood, Tenn., Affair — March 25, 1863, Brentwood was occupied by about 500 Unionists. That day the place was captured and sacked by about 3,000 Confederates under Wheeler, Forrest, Armstrong and Stearns. Green Clay Smith, with a body of Union cavalry pursued them as they departed with their spoils and prisoners, in the direction of Columbia. About nine miles from Brentwood he overtook them, charged upon them, killing many and driving them six miles further. The Confederates having been reinforced by Wheeler's cavalry, 2,500 strong, Clay slowly withdrew from the advancing foe, retreating two miles, when the Confederates gave up the pursuit. The Confederate loss was estimated at fully 400 men, many horses, ambulances, etc. Smith did not lose a man as prisoner, but brought away 47 of the enemy.

Battle of Somerset, Ky. — Fought March 29, 1863, between a force of Unionists, under Carter and Gilmore, and a body of Confederate cavalry, under Pegram. The battle resulted in the total defeat of the Confederates, and their evacuation of Kentucky.

Battle near Woodbury, Tenn.—Fought April 1, 1863, between a Union force under General Hazen, and 600 Confederates, under Colonel Smith. The latter were defeated, with a loss of 20 killed and wounded, 30 prisoners, 50 horses, besides mules and wagons.

Battle near Nashville, Tenn. — Fought between General Mitchell, with 300 Union cavalry, and an encampment of Confederates, April 6, 1863. Mitchell made a sabre charge, killing 15 Confederates, taking 5 prisoners and capturing all their arms, tents, horses and equipments.

Attack on Charleston, S. C.—April 7, 1863, Commodore Dupont, with nine Union iron-clad war-vessels, attacked Charleston. The fight continued for two hours, under a sharp fire from Forts Sumter and Moultrie, when the Union fleet retired, five of the vessels being disabled, and one —the Keokuk—subsequently sank at her anchorage. The Union loss was 16 wounded—1 fatally.

Fight at Franklin, Tenn.—Fought April 10, 1863, between a large Confederate force under Van Dorn, and the Union troops occupying the town, under General Granger. After a protracted fight the Confederates were driven off and pursued until nightfall.

Three Battles in Louisiana — April 11, 1863, General Banks, with the Union troops under Emory and Weitzel, started from Berwick, at the mouth of the Atchafalaya river. In three sharp engagements with the Confederate forces in the Bayou Teche region, on April 15, 16 and 17, he took nearly 2,000 prisoners, caused the destruction of their 3 gunboats and several transport vessels, with a large amount of other Confederate property, dispersing their army in that section. The Union loss was 700.

Porter's Fleet Runs Past Vicksburg —April 17, 1863, Commodore Porter succeeded in running six vessels of his Union fleet safely past the Confederate batteries at Vicksburg.

Battle of Fayetteville, Ark. — Fought April 18, 1863, between 2,000 Union troops occupying the town and an attacking party of Confederates, numbering 3,000, with four cannon. The Confederates were repulsed, the Unionists losing 5 killed and 17 wounded.

Capture of a Union Steam-Ram — April 22, 1863, the Union ram, Queen of the West, was captured by the Confederates, in Grand Lake, La., with her commander, Captain Fuller, and all her officers and crew, numbering 90. The same day General Banks occupied Washington and Opelousas, Miss.

Battle at Fairmont, W. Va. — Fought April 30, 1863, between the Union forces, under Colonel Mulligan, and Confederate troops. The former were repulsed, and the Baltimore & Ohio railroad bridges, at Fairmont and Cheat river were blown up.

Battle at Monticello, Ky.—Fought May 1, 1863, between 5,000 Union troops, under General Carter, and the Confederate forces under Pegram. The latter were driven from the field, with a loss of 66 men. On the same day the Confederate troops, under Marmaduke, were driven out of Missouri by the Union General Vandever.

Battle of Port Gibson, Miss.—Fought May 1, 1863, between the united Union armies of Generals Grant and McClernand and the Confederate force under General Bowen. The latter, after a severe fight, were defeated with the loss of 1,550 men and 5 cannon.

Grierson's Raid in Mississippi—Colonel Grierson, of the 6th Illinois regiment, with his own and the 7th Illinois cavalry, 900 strong, and 6 cannon, started from La Grange, Tenn., April 17, 1863, to march southerly through the center of Mississippi. May 2, 1863, they reached Baton Rouge, La., having traveled nearly 800 miles in 16 days, and having passed through 17 counties. As they went they destroyed Confederate railroads, bridges, cars, locomotives and stores of all kinds, fought successfully against several attempts to capture them, and brought into Baton Rouge more than 1,000 horses and a large number of cattle, besides 500 colored people who followed them.

Battle of Chancellorsville, Va. — The Army of the Potomac, under General Hooker, made its second attempt to capture the Confederate fortifications at Fredericksburg, Va., between April 27 and May 3, 1863. The main body of the Union army crossed the Rappahannock river April 27, at Kelly's ford, about 20 miles northwest of Fredericksburg, taking a position 10 miles west of that stronghold, at Chancellorsville. The main battle, after two days' severe skirmishing, took place May 3, between the Confederate army, under Lee and Jackson, and Hooker's army. The Unionists, in this battle, were defeated. In the meantime the Union General Sedgwick had crossed the Rappahannock river and occupied Fredericksburg, but he, too, was defeated and compelled to retire. Hooker's army recrossed the river on the night of May 5. Hooker's whole effective force was about 95,000; Lee's, in all, 60,000. The Union losses were about 17,000—12,000 killed and wounded—5,000 missing; the Confederates, 13,000—10,300 killed and wounded.

Stoneman in Virginia.—During the battles of Chancellorsville, May 1-4, 1863, the Union General Stoneman, with a large body of cavalry, raided Virginia destroying large quantities of Confederate provisions at different points and a portion of the railroad between Gordonsville and Charlottesville, and considerably damaging one or two other railroads.

Capture of Alexandria, La.—May 5, 1863, Admiral Porter and his Union gunboats captured this town.

Streight's Surrender—After effective service and hard fighting in the enemy's country, May 8, 1863, Union Colonel Streight, with 1,700 men, was captured by the Confederate cavalry under Forrest, near Cedar Bluff, Ala.

Fight on the Cumberland River—Fought May 9, 1863, between Union Kentucky cavalry, under Colonel Jacobs, and a Confederate guerrilla force, near Horseshoe Bend, Tenn. The latter were defeated, with the loss of a number killed, 8 prisoners and the destruction of their camp.

Battle at Raymond, Miss.—Fought May 12, 1863, between a Union force, under General McPherson, of Grant's army, and two divisions of Confederates, under Gregg and Walker. After a fierce fight of two hours, the place was captured, the Confederates losing 103 killed, 720 wounded and prisoners. Union loss, 69 killed, 341 wounded, and 32 missing.

Battle Near Jackson, Miss. — Fought May 13, 1863, between Grant's Union army and Confederate troops under Joseph S. Johnson. The latter was defeated, losing the town, 7 cannon, 400 prisoners, and large quantities of military stores. The State House was burned.

Fight at Linden, Tenn. — Fought May 13, 1863, between 55 men of the 1st Tennessee cavalry, under Colonel Breckenridge, and twice that number of Confederates. The latter were defeated, with the loss of 43 officers and privates, 50 horses and a quantity of other property.

Battle at Suffolk, Va.—Fought May 15, 1863, between a Confederate detachment and a party of Unionists, in which the former were defeated.

Battle Near Holly Springs, Miss. — Fought May 15, 1863, between Faulkner's Confederate cavalry and a Union force, the former being defeated.

Battle of Baker's Creek, Miss. — Fought May 16, 1863, between the Confederates, under General Pemberton, and the Union army, under General Grant, about 25,000 men being engaged on each side. The fight ended in the defeat of the Confederates, who lost 2,600 killed and wounded, 2,000 prisoners and 29 cannon.

Battle of Big Black River, Miss.—Fought May 17, 1863, between the Confederates under Pemberton and Grant's Union army, the former being again defeated, with a loss of 2,600 men and 17 cannon.

Destruction at Austin, Miss.—May 24, 1863, Colonel Ellet's Union marine brigade burned the town, which had been occupied by the Confederates.

A Navy-Yard Destroyed—May 25, 1863, the Unionists destroyed the Confederate navy-yard at Yazoo city, Miss.

Loss of a Union Gunboat—May 28, 1863, in an encounter between the Union gunboat Cincinnati, on the Mississippi river, and the Confederate batteries at Vicksburg, Miss., the former was sunk, going down with flying colors. The Union loss was 25 killed and wounded and 15 drowned.

A Raid in South Carolina—June 3, 1863, the second South Carolina Union regiment (colored), under Colonel Montgomery, numbering 200 men, passed up the Coosa river, landing in full view of two Confederate regiments, who retreated. Penetrating 25 miles into the country, Montgomery brought away 725 negroes, a lot of blooded horses, and other property belonging to the Confederates, valued at $600,000.

Battle at Triune, Tenn. — Fought June 11, 1863, between 5,000 Confederate cavalry and two batteries, under Forrest, and a force of Union cavalry, under Colonel R. B. Mitchell. The Confederates were defeated, with a loss of 21 killed and 70 others wounded and taken prisoners. Mitchell's loss was 6 killed.

Sinking of a Blockade-Runner — Off Charleston, June 11, 1863, the Confederate and notorious blockade-runner, the Herald, was sunk by a broadside from the Union blockading fleet.

Battle of Winchester, Va. — Fought June 14, 1863, between about 7,000 Unionists, under Milroy, and the advance of Lee's army on its way to Pennsylvania. Besides a small number killed and wounded, Milroy lost 4,000 prisoners, about 30 guns, many small arms, and 300 wagons.

A Naval Fight — Fought June 17, 1863, in Wilmington waters, off the coast of North Carolina, between the Confederate ram Atlanta and the Union war vessel Weehawken, commanded by Captain John Rodgers. The Atlanta was decoyed and captured.

Battle Near Aldie, Va.—Fought June 17, 1863, between Union troops, under Colonel Kilpatrick, and 5 regiments of Confederate cavalry, under Fitzhugh Lee, with artillery. After a desperate hand-to-hand encounter, the Confederates retreated, leaving 100 prisoners in the hands of the Unionists.

Second Battle of Big Black River, Miss. — Fought June 23, 1863, between a Confederate force, under Johnston, and a division of the Union army, under Osterhaus. The latter was defeated.

Fights in Tennessee — June 24, 1863, the Union general, Rosecrans, began his advance from Murfreesboro, Tenn. On the same day, Willich's brigade, of McCook's division of the Union army, wrested Liberty Gap from the Confederates, sustaining a loss of 75 killed and wounded. Next day, Willich, Wilder and Carter's brigades of Rosecrans' army defeated a division of Confederates, under Claiborne. The Unionists lost 40 killed and 100 wounded; the Confederates, who retreated in disorder, suffered a much greater loss. June 24, 1863, Wilder's mounted Union brigade captured Hoover's Gap from the Confederates. His loss was 53 killed and wounded. June 26, 1863, Wilder's Union brigade destroyed the Decherd bridge in the rear of the Confederate general, Bragg, between Tullahoma and Chattanooga. Other fights and skirmishes were features in this nine days' campaign by the Unionists under Rosecrans, whose total loss was 85 killed, 462 wounded and 13 missing. The Confederates lost 1,364 prisoners and 11 cannon, and were expelled from Middle Tennessee.

Morgan's Raids — June 27, 1863, John Morgan, with 2,500 Confederate guerrillas and 4 cannon, began a raid in Kentucky. On the 3d of July, a sharp fight occurred between them and a reconnoitering party of Unionists under Captain Carter. The captain was killed, his men retreated, and Morgan occupied Columbia. On the 4th of July, Morgan fought 200 Unionists, under Colonel Moore, at Tebb's Bend, on Green river, Ky. For four hours the battle raged, when Morgan was repulsed and retreated, leaving his dead on the field. At Lebanon, Morgan captured 300 Union militia, robbed and paroled them. Morgan then raided Southern Ohio and Indiana. At Corydon, Ind., in a fight, Morgan had 2 men killed and 7 wounded, while the opposing Unionists lost 15 killed and wounded. There and at other places large amounts of merchandise and horses were seized by the raiders, money was extorted as a ransom for property, and their operations created general excitement. In the meantime, a pursuit by armed men to capture Morgan was vigorously prosecuted. At Buffington's island, in the Ohio river, July 19, Morgan encountered a force of Unionists under General Judah, Lieutenant O'Neil (of the 5th Indiana cavalry), and two gunboats, and a bloody battle ensued, which resulted in the utter rout and dispersion of Morgan's band. They left behind them about 1,000 prisoners, all their artillery, and large quantities of stolen plunder. John Morgan and 500 of his men escaped, but were hotly pursued by General Shackleford, of the Union army, and on July 26, at West Point, Ohio, Morgan, finding himself surrounded by a superior force, unconditionally surrendered, his band having been slain, dispersed or captured.

Battle of Grey's Gap, Tenn.—Fought June 30, 1863, between Union cavalry and infantry under Stanley and Granger and a force of Confederate cavalry and infantry. The latter were driven from point to point, hotly pursued, and many of them were killed, drowned and wounded in their flight. The capture of Shelbyville, Tenn., by the Unionists, with a large number of prisoners and a quantity of arms and commissary stores, were the results of this day's work.

Capture of Tullahoma, Tenn.—July 1, 1863, the Unionists under Brannon, Negley and Sheridan occupied Tullahoma, which the Confederates had evacuated on the previous night. This was one step in the campaign which drove the Confederates from Middle Tennessee.

Battle of Gettysburg, Pa.—Fought July 1–3, 1863, between the invading Confederate army under General R. E. Lee, and the Union army of the Potomac under General Meade. The forces engaged or near at hand, July 2, were about equal, each numbering between 70,000 to 80,000 infantry and artillery. The battle, one of the most terrible of the war, resulted in the defeat of the Confederates, their compulsory evacuation of Pennsylvania and Maryland, their withdrawal from the valley of the Shenandoah, and heavy losses, as follows: 5,000 killed, 23,000 wounded left on the field, 8,000 prisoners, 3 cannon and 41 battle flags; 24,978 small arms were collected on the battle field. The Union loss was 2,834 killed, 13,713 wounded, and 6,643 missing.

Battle at Helena, Ark.—Fought July 4, 1863, between about 4,000 Unionists, under General Prentiss, and 7,600 Confederates under General Holmes, the latter being defeated with the loss of of 173 killed, 687 wounded, and 776 missing. The Union loss did not exceed 250 in killed and wounded.

Surrender of Vicksburg, Miss.—General Grant began his siege of Vicksburg, May 18, prosecuting it with great vigor until July 4, 1863, when Pemberton, the Confederate General occupying the place, surrendered to the Union army 27,000 prisoners, 132 cannon and 50,000 stand of arms. Thus the Mississippi river was opened to the Gulf of Mexico.

Battle of Port Hudson, La.—General Banks' Union army invested Port Hudson in May, 1863, the place being strongly fortified and defended by a force of Confederates under General Gardner. Three important assaults were made upon this stronghold by land and water, May 27, June 11 and 14, in which some of the Confederate works were captured, but the Unionists were on both days repulsed, with the loss of about 3,000 men. The siege was continued until July 7, when Gardner capitulated (owing to the surrender of Vicksburg), and on the 9th of July, 1863, General Banks entered the town, taking 6,408 prisoners, 2 steamers, 51 cannon, and a quantity of small arms.

Draft Riots at the North.—From July 13 to 16, 1863, New York, Boston and other Northern cities, were the scene of riots in opposition to the drafting of soldiers for the Union army. In New York mobs held possession of the city for three days; the drafting offices were demolished and the buildings burned. A colored orphan asylum was pillaged and burned down. Collisions were frequent between the authorities and the mob, and many persons were killed. These riots cost the city more than $1,500,000 for losses by them.

Battle at Jackson, Miss.—Fought July 17, 1863, between the Union army under Sherman and the Confederates under Johnston. The result was the occupation of the city by Sherman, the capture of a large quantity of stores, 40 locomotives and the rolling stock of three railroads.

Capture of Natchez, Miss.—July 17, 1863, General Ransom and a party of Unionists captured this city from the Confederates, taking a large quantity of ammunition, 13 cannon, 2,000 cattle and 4,000 hogsheads of sugar.

Battle of Elk Creek, Ark.—Fought July 17, 1863, between 2,400 Unionists under General Blunt, and 5,000 Confederates under General Cooper. The latter were defeated, with the loss of 184 men. The Unionists lost 40 men.

Union Cavalry in North Carolina—July 20, 1863, the cavalry expedition sent out by the Union General Foster, attacked the Wilmington & Weldon railroad at Rocky Mount, burned the long bridge over Tar river, tore up two miles of track, destroyed the depot, a large cotton factory, a supply train and 5,000 bales of cotton belonging to the Confederates.

Battle at Wytheville, Va.—Fought July 20, 1863, between Union cavalry under Colonel Tolland, of the 34th Ohio mounted infantry, and a Confederate force; it resulted, after a severe conflict, in the defeat of the Confederates, the burning of the town, the seizure of 3 cannon, 700 stand of arms and 120 prisoners. The Confederates also lost 75 men killed and many wounded. The Unionists lost 65 killed and wounded, including among the former Colonel Tolland.

Bombardment of Chattanooga, Tenn.—July 22, 1863, Colonel Wilder, of Rosecrans' army, shelled Chattanooga, creating considerable agitation among its Confederate occupants, but without definite results.

Recapture in Louisiana—July 22, 1863, the Union gunboat Sachem recaptured Brashear city from the Confederates.

Battle Near Manassas Gap, Va. — Fought July 23, 1863, between 800 Unionists, under General Spinola, and about twice as many Confederate troops from Georgia and North Carolina. The latter were utterly routed.

Battle in the Southwest—Fought July 23, 1863, between Kit Carson's Union 1st New Mexico regiment and a party of Navajos, near Fort Canby. The Indians were defeated.

Kentucky Invaded—The Confederates re-invaded Kentucky, July 23, 1863. July 31, 1863, the Unionists in that State, commanded by Colonel Sanders, completely routed the Confederate forces under Scott and Pegram, and martial law was declared.

Battle at Culpeper, Va. — Fought August 2, 1863, between Union cavalry under Buford, and Confederate cavalry under Stuart. The battle was indecisive, but 100 prisoners were taken by the Unionists.

Battle of Grenada, Miss.—Fought 17th of August, 1863, between a Union expedition sent out by General Hurlbut, under Lieutenant-Colonel Phillips, of the 9th Illinois mounted infantry, and a Confederate force of 2,000 men under General Slimmer, who occupied Grenada. The Confederates were so hardly pressed by the attacking party that they fled in confusion, leaving behind an immense quantity of ordnance and stores. These, with the depot, the machine-shop, the railroad track, 57 locomotives, and more than 400 cars, were destroyed by the Unionists.

The War in Arkansas—August 22, 1863, the Union force under General Blunt, numbering 4,500, attacked 11,000 Confederates under General Cooper, in the Indian Territory, and compelled the latter to retreat to Red river. On the same day, Union cavalry under Colonel Woodson, successfully attacked numerous Confederate guerrilla bands in Arkansas, capturing the Confederate general, Jeff. Thompson, with his entire staff. On the 29th of July, 1863, the Confederate army under General Price, then in Arkansas, was severely pressed by the Union forces under General Steele. The same day, Steele's advance, under General Davidson, drove 3,000 Confederates, under Marmaduke, out of Brownsville and across the Arkansas river. September 1, 1863, General Blunt defeated the Confederates under Cooper and Cabell, and captured Fort Smith, Ark. The same day the Confederates evacuated Little Rock, and General Steele occupied it September 10, 1863.

Quantrell's Raid—A force of Confederate guerrillas, numbering 350, collected in Cass county, Mo., under the leadership of Quantrell. In the dead of night, August 25, 1863, they unexpectedly attacked the town of Lawrence, in Kansas, set it on fire, burned 182 buildings to the ground, destroying $2,000,000 of property; killed 145 persons, including helpless women and children, and wounded 591 citizens, many of them mortally. Soon afterwards, the guerrillas having departed, the citizens organized a force, commanded by General James H. Lane, and pursued the marauders to Grand River, Mo. There, when attacked, the murderers dispersed in various directions, but about 80 of them were slain.

Occupation of Knoxville, Tenn.—The Confederate General Buckner, evacuated Knoxville, leaving behind a considerable quantity of quartermaster's stores, with other valuable property, and General Burnside, with his Union force, occupied the place September 3, 1863, to the delight of the inhabitants.

Battle at Sabine City, Texas—Fought September 8, 1863, between the Confederate force occupying the fortifications of the town and the 19th Union army corps under General Franklin, with 4 Union gunboats. The fight was quite severe, but resulted in the repulse of the Unionists and the loss of 2 of their gunboats.

Affairs at Chattanooga, Tenn.—After the battle of Stone river, at the beginning of 1863, the Confederate army under Bragg occupied Chattanooga. September 8, 1863, when Rosecrans and his Union army approached, the Confederates abandoned the place, and, on the 9th, Crittenden's division of the Union army occupied it. Bragg's army having been reinforced by Longstreet, managed to drive the Unionists out of Chattanooga, while Rosecrans attempted to force the Confederates from their threatening position in that vicinity. The result was the battle of Chickamauga.

Affairs at Cumberland Gap, Tenn.—This narrow pass, which separates Kentucky from Tennessee, and became an important point during the civil war, was occupied early in the contest by the Confederates, then by the Unionists, and again by the Confederates. September 9, 1863, General Burnside's Union army recaptured it, with 2,000 prisoners and 14 cannon, from General Frazer.

Battle of Chickamauga, Tenn.—Fought September 19 and 20, 1863, between about 50,000 Confederates, under Bragg, who began the contest, and about 55,000 Union soldiers, besides cavalry, under Rosecrans. The cavalry and about 10,000 of Bragg's infantry were not, however, long in the action. At the close of the first day both armies occupied nearly the same position that they did in the morning. The battle occupied the whole of both days, and resulted in defeat and the retreat of the Unionists to Chattanooga. The Union loss was 1,644 killed, 9,262 wounded, and 4,945 prisoners. The Confederate loss is estimated at not far from 18,000 men.

A Cavalry Defeat—Confederate cavalry, under Wheeler, which had come north of the Tennessee river for the purpose of operating against Rosecrans' Union army, encountered Union forces October 9, 1863, at Farmington, Tenn., and near Shelbyville, Ky., and was defeated, with considerable loss, at both points.

Battle of Missionary Ridge, Tenn.—General Thomas, who succeeded Rosecrans in command of the Union army, was practically besieged by the Confederates at Chattanooga. A battle was fought November 24, 25 and 26, 1863, at this point, between about 80,000 Unionists, under Grant, who had partially raised the siege and reinforced the garrison, and about 50,000 Confederates under Bragg. The latter's army occupied strong positions above Chattanooga, on Lookout mountain at the south and Missionary ridge on the east. Hooker, with 10,000 Unionists, went to Lookout mountain to assail the Confederate left. Sherman, Sheridan, and other Union commanders, with their several divisions, stormed and carried the Confederate redoubts, as did Hooker those on Lookout mountain. The Confederates fled from a galling fire from their own cannon, and were vigorously pursued. The Union losses were 757 killed, 4,529 wounded, and 330 missing. The Confederate loss in killed and wounded did not, probably, exceed 4,000; but they lost 6,142 prisoners, 40 cannon, and 7,000 stand of small arms. This battle ended the war in Tennessee for a year.

The Storming of Knoxville, Tenn.—Under instructions from superior officers, General Burnside prepared for a vigorous defense of Knoxville. The second division of the 23rd army corps under General Julius White, and other troops, was to co-operate with Burnside. November 14, 1863, a fight occurred in the vicinity between General White's command and Confederates on Huff's hill, in which the Confederates were dislodged with considerable loss on both sides. November 16, another severe fight occurred near Knoxville, between the 23rd and 9th Army corps, with artillery, and a Confederate force at Campbell's station, but the Unionists were obliged to retreat, which they did in good order, although hotly pursued. On the 17th a close siege of Knoxville began, which terminated, November 28, in an attempt of the Confederates to carry the fortifications by storm, commanded by General Longstreet. The assault, however, was repulsed with so much vigor, that, in connection with the defeat of Bragg at Missionary Ridge, the Confederates deemed it advisable to raise the siege. Longstreet, therefore, retreated, followed by Burnside's forces, while another army, under Foster, started from Cumberland Gap to cut off their retreat. The number of Unionists engaged in this siege was about 12,000; their loss was less than 50; the loss of the attacking party was about 500.

BATTLES OF THE FOURTH YEAR OF THE WAR.

Battles Near Newbern, N. C.—February 1, 1864, a Confederate force, estimated at 15,000, attacked a small number of Union troops, under General Palmer, at Bachelor's creek, an outpost of the Unionists at Newbern. The latter, finding themselves outnumbered, fell back in good order, with only a slight loss, although the fight was severe, and they were pursued by the Confederates. Next morning a Confederate force in boats boarded the Union gunboat Underwriter, which had run aground and, after a sharp struggle, captured her with about one-third of her crew. Engineer Allen and part of the crew of the gunboat, rose up against the crew of the Confederate barge that was carrying them off, overcame them and rescued the commander and crew, bringing them safely into port.

Battle at Stevensburg, Va.—Fought all day, February 6, 1864, between the second and third corps of the Union army, under General Sedgwick, and a Confederate force. The Unionists withdrew, having lost 200 men in killed and wounded.

Sherman's Raid in Mississippi—February 3, 1864, General Sherman, with a Union force of 25,000 men, marched from Big Black river on a grand raid through the Confederate State of Mississippi, returning to Vicksburg, March 4, 1864. At Messenger's station there was a sharp skirmish with a Confederate force, resulting in a Union loss of 12 killed and 35 wounded, and a much larger one on the part of the Confederates. At Canton Sherman's troops captured artillery, ammunition and prisoners. Jackson, Brandon, Morton, and Meridian were visited, with some opposition, but with loss to the Confederates. At Meridian the Unionists remained seven days, destroying Confederate stores, ammunition and public buildings, the arsenal, hotels, etc. Other places visited by the Unionists were Enterprise, Marion, Quitman, Hillsboro, Lake station, Decatur, Bolton and Lauderdale springs. At these places railroad property, machine shops, lumber and flour mills were destroyed. Near Decatur a skirmish occurred, in which the Confederates were repulsed with the loss of 5 killed and three prisoners. The expedition marched more than 400 miles in 24 days, liberated 10,000 slaves, and brought away an immense amount of booty. The estimated losses of the Unionists during this raid were 50 men killed and wounded and about 100 prisoners. The Confederate losses in killed and wounded were considered much larger, and in deserters and prisoners were estimated at more than 600.

Escape of Union Prisoners—February 9, 1864, a large number of Union prisoners escaped from the Confederate Libby prison, at Richmond, Virginia.

Battle of Plymouth, N. C.—Fought February 17, 1864, between about 10,000 Confederates, under General R. F. Hoke, and about 1,500 Unionists, under General Wessel, who occupied Fort Williams, one of the defenses of Plymouth. Six times the Confederates assaulted this stronghold without capturing it, but on the fourth day, after fighting six times his own force, Wessel gave up the unequal contest and surrendered.

Battle of Olustee, Fla.—Fought February 20, 1864, between a Union force of about 4,500 infantry and 400 cavalry, with 20 cannon, under General Seymour, and an estimated Confederate force, under General Finnegin, of 3,000. The fight lasted three and a half hours, and resulted in the retreat of the Unionists before a superior force to Barber's station. Union loss 2,000 men, besides artillery, ammunition and wagon trains. Confederate loss about 1,000 men.

A Raid on Richmond, Va.—February 28, 1864, a Union cavalry expedition, under General Kilpatrick, started from the army of the Potomac to liberate Union prisoners at Richmond. After several skirmishes, March 4, 1864, Kilpatrick withdrew from the raid, having destroyed a large amount of Confederate property in the vicinity. Colonel Ulric Dahlgren had command of a branch expedition of Union cavalry in another direction, which also destroyed a large amount of property; but on the third of March his command fell into a Confederate ambush, and he lost his life, and a large number of his men were taken prisoners.

Capture of Fort de Russey, La.—March 15, 1864, a large Union force under General Mower, of Smith's Red river expedition, stormed this formidable fortress of the Confederates. The veterans, however, after a short but sturdy fight, carried the fort, capturing 12 cannon, 2,000 barrels of powder, a large supply of army stores and ammunition, with 325 prisoners.

Surrender of Union City, Tenn.—March 24, 1864, between the Confederate force under Forrest and 500 Unionists under Hawkins, who occupied the place. The latter repulsed the attacking party several times, but at length surrendered.

Battle at Paducah, Ky.—Fought March 25, 1864, between 6,000 Confederates under Forrest, Buford, Harris and Thompson, and the 40th Illinois regiment under Colonel S. G. Hicks, numbering 655 Unionists, assisted by some Union gunboats. Hicks made a stand at Fort Anderson, and repelled several attacks and refused to surrender. Three more attacks were then made on the fort, but were repulsed with heavy losses each time, Thompson being killed. The Confederates retired next day, having suffered an estimated loss of 300 killed and from 1,000 to 1,200 wounded. The Union loss was 14 killed and 46 wounded.

Battles in Arkansas—March 26, 1864, a small Union force, from Rosecrans' army, marched from Pine Bluff, Ark., to Mount Elba and Longview, on the Washita river, destroying at the latter place several pontoon bridges, 35 wagons loaded with camp and garrison equipage, ammunition, stores, etc., and capturing 320 prisoners. March 30, 1864, this Union force encountered 1,200 Confederates at Monticello, routing them, capturing a large quantity of arms, wagons, and 300 horses and mules, and losing but 15 men during the expedition.

Battle of Natchitoches, La.—Fought March 31, 1864, between a cavalry division, under Lee, of General Banks' Union army, and a Confederate force under Taylor, estimated at 1,000. After a brisk but brief skirmish the Confederates were completely routed, with a loss of 6 or 8 killed and wounded and 25 prisoners. The Unionists lost none.

Battle of Crump's Hill, La.—Fought April 2, 1864, between 3 brigades of Union troops under Lee, and a body of Confederates. The former made a charge which caused the Confederates to retreat, and the Unionists pursued them seven miles, killing and wounding a number. The Confederates made a stand, however, and a severe fight of an hour's duration ensued. Then the Confederates again retreated. A number of prisoners fell into the hands of the Unionists.

Fight Near Pleasant Hill, La.—Fought April 7, 1864, between the cavalry of Banks' and Smith's Union armies and about 3,000 Confederate cavalry under Green. At first it was a running fight, but the Confederates being reinforced, Colonel Haral Robinson, of Lee's Union cavalry brigade, dashed upon them with so much vigor that Green's force was whipped and driven from the field. This engagement lasted two and a half hours, and the losses on each side were estimated at 40 killed and wounded. Robinson pursued the retreating enemy until the latter reached a superior reinforcement. He then retired.

Battle Near Sabine Cross Roads, La.—Fought April 8, 1864, between the advance of General Banks' Union army, under General Stone, and from 18,000 to 22,000 Confederates under Kirby Smith, Dick Taylor, Green, Price and Mouton. The Unionists were repulsed on that day, but on the next, after a severe conflict, the Confederates were defeated, 2,000 of them throwing away their arms during their flight. The losses in killed and wounded were very heavy, being estimated at 2,000 on each side. The Confederate General Mouton was slain, and 700 Confederate prisoners were captured.

Battle of Fort Pillow, Tenn. — The Unionists occupied the garrison with 19 officers, 276 white infantry and 262 colored infantry, a section of light artillery (colored), and 1 battalion of white cavalry, the whole being commanded by Major Booth. On April 12, 1864, the Confederates under Forrest attacked the fort, but by the aid of a gunboat they were kept at bay by the garrison. Major Booth was killed, and Major Bradford took command of the beleaguered fort. A demand to surrender from Forrest was refused by Bradford. New and commanding positions having been gained by the Confederates, their attack was resumed, and they soon carried the fort. No quarter was shown to its inmates, either black or white, male or female, and even children were slain by the invaders. Thus the Unionists were destroyed.

Gunboat Battles in North Carolina — April 17 and 18, 1864, at Plymouth, N. C., the Confederate iron-clad ram Albemarle, with the aid of a battery, destroyed 2 Union gunboats. On May 5, 1864, an effort was made by Union gunboats to destroy the Albemarle, but the attempt failed. October 27, 1864, Lieutenant Cushing, of the Union navy, succeeded with a torpedo in blowing this formidable craft to pieces, narrowly escaping his own destruction.

Battles of the Wilderness, Va. — May 4, 1864, General Grant, commanding the Union army of the Potomac, about 130,000 strong, crossed the Rapidan river into the "wilderness" of Virginia, to dislodge the Confederate General Lee and his 60,000 troops from their position between the Unionists and the Confederate capital. As Grant advanced, Lee prepared for a stubborn contest. From May 5 to May 31 there was fought a terrible series of battles, unprecedented in American annals for their sanguinary results. During those 27 bloody days various fortunes of war were experienced by both armies, and closed, leaving Lee on the south side of the North Anna river, and the Union force on the shores of the Pamunky river. The Union losses during these battles were 5,584 killed, 28,364 wounded, and 7,450 missing—a total of 41,398—which does not include the losses in Burnside's corps. No trustworthy statement of the Confederate losses was made, but they are estimated at about 20,000.

Butler's Operations on the James River, Va. — On May 5, 1864, General Butler and a Union force started from fortress Monroe, for a cruise up the James river in transports toward Richmond, destroying railroads, bridges, etc. Occasional skirmishes were had with Confederates, and on the 16th of May occurred

The Battle of Fort Darling, Va. — Fought between Butler's Union army and a force of Confederates under Beauregard. Butler's troops were forced to retire, with the loss of about 5,000 men, mostly prisoners, and several cannon. The fight was resumed on the 19th, and after a short conflict the Confederates were repulsed. Next day the Confederates drove the Unionists out of their intrenchments. Another fight ensued, and the Unionists recovered their rifle-pits.

Second Battle of Fort Darling—Fought May 21, 1864, between the Unionists under Gilmore, of Butler's army, occupying the intrenchments, and a large force of Confederates of Beauregard's army, who advanced upon the fort. Gilmore's batteries opened upon them at short range, and the several fierce charges of the Confederates were repulsed, with heavy loss. The Union gunboats also assisted in shelling the Confederates during this battle.

Battle of the Kulp House, Va.—Fought May 22, 1864, between a force of Confederates, under Hood and Hooker, and Schofield's divisions of Sherman's Union army. Hood made the attack, but was repulsed and driven off, leaving his dead and wounded on the field, and losing many prisoners.

Battle of Wilson's Wharf, Va. — Fought May 24, 1864, between a brigade of Confederate cavalry, under Fitzhugh Lee, and two regiments of negro Union troops, under General Wild, who occupied a strong position on the north bank of the James river. Lee demanded the surrender of the post, which was refused. A severe conflict followed for several hours, but the Confederate attempts to capture the position proved fruitless, and they finally abandoned the assault.

Battle of New Hope Church, Ga.—Sherman's Union army, in pursuit of Johnston's

Confederate forces in Georgia, after several unimportant skirmishes, found themselves confronted with the Confederates about three miles from Dallas, Ga., May 25, 1864. After a general action the Confederates were driven three miles and into their inner intrenchments.

Battle of Powder Springs, Ga. — Fought in May, 1864, between McPherson's division of Sherman's Union army and a considerable force of Confederates of Johnston's army. After a sharp engagement the latter were driven toward Marietta, with a loss of 2,500 killed and wounded (left on the field), and about 300 prisoners. The Union losses did not, it is officially stated, exceed 300.

Sherman's Expedition from Chattanooga, Tenn., to Atlanta, Ga. — In the spring of 1864, General Sherman, with a force of 100,000 Unionists and 254 cannon, aided by Generals Thomas, McPherson and Schofield, commanding divisions, started to march from Chattanooga, through the Confederates' country, to Atlanta. Opposing this expedition was the Confederate General J. E. Johnston, aided by Hardee, Hood, and Polk, with Wheeler's cavalry, their entire force numbering about 60,000 men, including 10,000 cavalry and artillery. The Union expedition began its operations May 7, 1864, and closed them successfully at Atlanta, Ga., September 2, of the same year, occupying Dalton, May 8.

Sheridan's Raid in Virginia — May 13, 1864, General Sheridan, with his Union cavalry force, reached the rear of Lee's army, near Hanover junction, breaking 2 railroads, capturing several locomotives, and destroying Lee's depot for supplies at Beaver Dam, containing more than 1,000,000 rations.

Battle of Resaca, Ga. — Fought May 15, 1864, between General Sherman's Union troops and Johnston's Confederate army. The battle lasted two days, and resulted in the evacuation of Resaca by the Confederates and their pursuit by the Unionists. The losses were estimated at 3,600 killed and wounded, including among the latter Generals Hooker, Willich, Kilpatrick, and Manson. The Confederates lost, it is estimated, 2,000 killed and wounded, including 3 general officers reported among the former, several hundred prisoners, and 7 cannon.

Second Battle of Cold Harbor, Va.—Fought June 3, 1864, between the Union army, under Grant and Meade, and the Confederate forces, under Lee and Longstreet. Grant had about 150,000, and Lee about 50,000 men. The fight was brief but desperate, lasting less than half an hour, and resulted in the repulse of the Union army at every point. Grant's loss in killed, wounded and missing, including 3 brigadier-generals killed, was about 7,000 men; Lee's loss, including one general officer, was less than half that number.

Battle of Pine Mountain, Ga.—Fought June 14, 1864, between a body of Confederates, who held the place, and a force of Union artillery under Sherman. During this fight the Confederate General Leonidas Polk was killed, and on the next day the stronghold was found to have been abandoned, the Confederates having intrenched themselves along the lines of hills connecting Kenesaw and Lost mountains; this line was abandoned, however, on the 17th. Being pressed by the Unionists under McPherson, the Confederates took to Kenesaw mountain and there were strongly intrenched.

Sheridan's Raid in Virginia—June 7, 1864, General Sheridan and a Union cavalry force set out to destroy the Confederate railroads leading from Gordonsville. On the 11th, at Buck Childs', he encountered a force of Confederate cavalry, which was driven back and outflanked. The result was a complete rout of the Confederates, who left their dead and nearly all their wounded on the field, besides the capture of 20 officers, 500 men and 300 horses by the Unionists. About five miles from Gordonsville the Confederates had constructed rifle-pits, and on the 12th there was a cavalry engagement of considerable importance. The Confederates lost heavily, including several general officers. Sheridan lost about 85 killed and 490 wounded. The raid was successful.

Morgan's Second Guerrilla Raid—The Confederate guerrilla General Morgan again invaded Kentucky, June 7, 1864. After plundering Lexington and taking Cynthiana, he was attacked and had nearly all his force captured or dispersed by the Union General Burbridge. By the 17th of June, Morgan was discomfited and his raid ended. Morgan's operations were finally ended September 5, 1864, at Greenville, Tenn., where he was killed.

Averill's Raid in the Shenandoah Valley, Va.—June 16, 1864, General Averill, with a body of Unionists proceeded to destroy the Virginia and East Tennessee railroad, in order to cut off Lee's communications with Richmond. He

succeeded in destroying 15 miles of the track, and burned five bridges, depots, cars, large quantities of Confederate stores, and captured 200 prisoners and 150 horses. His loss was 6 men drowned, 5 wounded, and 14 missing, during his rugged expedition of 355 miles.

First Battle at Petersburg, Va.—Fought June 15 and 16, 1864, between the Confederate army under Lee (about 70,000 strong), which occupied the town, and Grant's army, about 100,000. A series of engagements resulted first in the repulse of the Unionists under W. F. Smith, and subsequently other repulses, which cost the Union army a loss of 1,198 killed, 6,853 wounded, and 2,217 missing. June 21, 1864, an attempt was made by the Unionists to seize the Weldon railroad, which cost them 3,000 men. Afterwards this and other roads were seized by them, which prevented supplies reaching Lee's army at Petersburg. July 30, 1864, a mine containing 8,000 pounds of powder was exploded under a Confederate fort at Petersburg by the Unionists. The effect was not so beneficial as was expected by the Unionists, the earth being blown into an inaccessible position, so that entrance to the city was extremely difficult by that route. The Confederates poured in shell upon the attacking party, and after four hours' ineffectual assault the Union forces withdrew, having lost 4,003 men killed, wounded and missing, while the Confederate loss is set down at less than 1,000. August 5, the Confederates exploded a mine in front of a Union corps, without inflicting serious injury, and considerable fighting ensued, without important results or serious losses on either side.

Battle of Rood's Hill, Va. — Fought in June, 1864, between 6 regiments of Unionists under General Sigel and about 7,000 Confederate infantry, with cavalry and artillery, of Breckenridge's army. Sigel was defeated with the loss of about 600 killed, wounded and missing, and 5 cannon.

A Naval Victory—June 19, 1864, in the French port of Cherbourg, the famous Confederate ocean-cruiser Alabama, commanded by Raphael Semmes, was defeated and sunk by the United States war-ship Kearsarge, commanded by Commodore Winslow. Semmes escaped.

Battles of Kenesaw Mountain, Ga.—Finding the Confederates strongly intrenched upon Kenesaw mountain, June 27, 1864, General Sherman ordered his Union troops to attempt to dislodge them. This assault was participated in by McPherson, Thomas, Blair, Dodge, Logan and other division commanders of the Union army. The assault was well made, but the Confederate intrenchments could not be carried. A flank movement was at once made, with such effect that early on the morning of July 3, 1864, the Union skirmishers appeared on the mountain above the Confederate intrenchments, which had been abandoned on the previous night. In the attack of June 27, the Unionists lost from 2,000 to 3,000 men.

Battle of Monocacy River, Md.—On the 9th July, 1864, an action occurred between 15,000 Confederates, under Early, and Rickett's division of the sixth Union army corps, under General Wallace. The latter were outflanked and forced to fall back, with the loss of about 1,200, including about 600 prisoners.

Battle Near Washington, D. C.—Fought July 11, 1864, about 5 miles from the city between Union troops, under General Augur—a brigade of veteran infantry—and Confederate skirmishers. The former were the attacking party. The Confederates were completely routed, leaving about 100 of their dead and wounded on the field. The Union loss was about 200.

Battle of Peach-Tree Creek, Ga.—Fought July 20, 1864, between Sherman's Union army and the Confederate forces under Johnston. Hooker's Union corps suffered in the severe conflict, but the Confederates were driven to their intrenchments, leaving more than 500 of their number killed and over 1,000 wounded on the field, 7 stand of colors and many prisoners. Their entire loss was estimated at 5,000. Sherman lost 1,500 killed, wounded and missing.

Battle of the Howard House, Ga. — Fought July 22, 1864, between the Confederate army under Hood (who had superseded Johnston) and Sherman's Union army, the former attacking the latter. The conflict was general and stubborn until the Confederates gave way, repulsed. Sherman's loss, including the death of General McPherson, was 3,722 killed, wounded and prisoners. The Confederates, it is estimated, lost 3,240 killed, or 8,000 in all.

Another Fight in Front of Atlanta, Ga. — Fought July 24, 1864, between the Confederate army, under Hood, and a portion of Sherman's Union army, under Howard and Logan, the former coming out of their Atlanta intrenchments to attack the latter. This bloody conflict resulted in the complete repulse of the attacking party, with a loss of about 650 killed, and probably not less than 4,300 wounded. Sherman lost less than 600 in killed, wounded and missing.

Battle Near Winchester, Va.—General Crook, with a small Union force, was defeated on the 24th of July, 1864, by the Confederates under General Early.

Union Raids in Georgia—In the latter part of July, 1864, General Sherman organized two cavalry expeditions to destroy the Macon railroad, which was a source of Confederate supplies. They consisted of General Stoneman, with 5,000 Union cavalry, and General McCook with 4,000 cavalry. Another object was to release the Union prisoners at Andersonville. In making a premature descent upon Andersonville, Stoneman encountered a superior force of Confederates, who defeated him and took him and 700 of his men prisoners. McCook proceeded to the Macon railroad, but Stoneman failing to meet him there, he withdrew to Newman, Ga., where he fell in with a considerable force of Confederate infantry. Surrounding McCook's command they forced him into a battle, compelling him to fight his way out, which he did with the loss of 500 of his men. He then returned to the main army at Marietta. Substantially the raid was a serious failure.

Chambersburg, Pa., Plundered and Burned—July 30, 1864, a cavalry force under the Confederate General McCausland, entered Chambersburg, plundered the citizens, and burned about 250 buildings, at an estimated loss of $1,000,000.

Battle of Moorefield, W. Va.—Fought August 7, 1864, between Union cavalry under Averill and a body of Confederate cavalry, the latter being defeated with the loss of all their artillery, 50 prisoners, many wagons and small arms. The remainder were driven to the mountains.

Farragut's Fleet at Mobile, Ala.—August 5, 1864, the Union fleet commanded by Rear-Admiral Farragut, commenced the attack in Mobile bay by blowing up and causing the evacuation of the Confederate Fort Powell, permitting the passage of 17 Union vessels into the bay. One had been sunk by the fort batteries; the Confederate war-vessel Tennessee surrendered after a sharp engagement, and her commander, Buchanan, was killed; another Confederate vessel was captured and another was beached. On August 7, Farragut opened fire on the Confederate Fort Gaines, which contained 600 men. On the 8th this fort was surrendered by its officer. A co-operating federal force, under General Granger, assisted in the reduction of another Confederate fort on August 23, leaving Farragut in control of the entrance of the bay.

Sheridan in the Shenandoah Valley, Va.—From August 9 to the 15th, 1864, General Sheridan's Union cavalry had several encounters of more or less severity with the Confederates under Early. Skirmishes occurred within ten miles of Winchester; Sulphur Springs bridge, where Custer's Union cavalry were repulsed; near White Post, the Confederates retiring after a 3 hours' contest; at Newtown, which Early succeeded in holding; near Strasburg, Early retiring, and the Unionists occupying the town; at Berryville, where Mosby's force captured Sheridan's supply train, destroying a large number of wagons and driving off several hundred horses, mules and beef cattle. Sheridan's force, August 15, 1864, retired to Charlestown.

Battle at Deep Bottom, Va.—Fought August 16, 1864, between the Federal forces and a superior number of Confederates, the former being obliged to retire, though without heavy losses.

Fights on the Weldon Railroad, Va.,—August 18, 1864, the Unionists made an advance upon this road, in order to cut off the enemy's supplies, but were driven back by the Confederates. A sharp fight followed, and the lost ground retaken and fortified. Next day the fight was renewed and the Union lines were broken. This battle cost the Unionists about 3,000 men, a great proportion being taken prisoners. On the 21st the Confederates made another vigorous attempt to dislodge the Unionists from the road, but were repulsed with a severe loss; the Unionists suffered but slightly in comparison.

Battle of Ream's Station, Va.—Fought August 25, 1864, between the Union corps under Hancock and a heavy force of Early's Confederate army, the latter being the attacking party. Both sides fought desperately, and Hancock withdrew from Ream's station, having lost 9 cannon and 3,000 men killed, wounded and taken prisoners. The Confederates lost 1,500 killed and wounded. This battle gave the Confederates repossession of the Weldon railroad southward, although the track had previously been destroyed by the Unionists.

Kilpatrick's Raid in Georgia—General Kilpatrick, of Sherman's Union army, with 5,000 cavalry, August 18, 1864, broke the track of the

West Point railroad, near Fairburn, and then struck the Macon road, near Jonesboro. Here he encountered a heavy force of Confederates, under Ross, but maintained possession of the road for several hours. Finding himself likely to be overwhelmed by numbers, he retreated, made a circuit and again struck the road at Lovejoy's station. Here he was once more menaced by the Confederates. Making a charge upon them, capturing 4 cannon and a number of prisoners, he retired to Decatur, without having very seriously broken up the Macon railroad.

Battle of Jonesboro, Ga.—Fought August 31, 1864, between a force under Howard, of Sherman's Union army, and a heavy force of Confederates from Hood's army, under Hardee, and Lee's command. The conflict in front of Jonesboro lasted two hours, when the Confederates withdrew to their fortifications. Their loss, as officially reported by Hood, was 1,400 killed and wounded. Union losses were comparatively light. On the first of September General Davis, with a body of Union cavalry, attacked the Confederate lines at Jonesboro, carrying their fortifications, and the Confederates effected their escape southward. In the meantime the Unionists were busily engaged in destroying the Macon railroad.

Raiders in Georgia, Tennessee and Kentucky—The Confederate cavalry under Wheeler, after breaking the Union railroad and destroying property at Adairsville and Calhoun, Ga., August 14, 1864, demanded the surrender of Dalton, then occupied by less than 500 Unionists under Colonel Laibold. This was refused, and Wheeler sharply attacked Laibold's position, but the latter having been reinforced next morning, Wheeler was driven off. Wheeler then passed into Tennessee, and formed a Union with Forrest and other raiders; but the whole were driven from the State by the Union forces under Generals Rousseau, Steadman and Granger. September 4, 1864, the famous Confederate guerrilla, John Morgan, was surprised and killed near Greenville, Tenn., by a Union force under General Gillem, his band being dispersed or captured. September 8, 1864, the Confederate raider, Jessie, and 100 of his men were captured at Ghent, in Kentucky.

Surrender of Atlanta, Ga.—The grand object of Sherman's Union expedition to Atlanta was achieved on the night of September 1, 1864, by the Confederate General Hood and his forces evacuating the city and its fortifications. Before leaving, he blew up seven trains of cars and destroyed other property. General Slocum, of the 20th Union Army corps, occupied the city September 2, and it then became the headquarters of the Federal army in Georgia. Hood withdrew to Macon.

Battle of Winchester, Va.—Fought September 19, 1864, between a heavy force of Confederates under Early, in position near Winchester, and Union troops under Averill and Sheridan. The fight lasted from noon until five o'clock in the evening, when the Confederates retreated, pursued by Sheridan's troops. Union loss 653 killed, 3,719 wounded, and 618 captured. Confederate loss, about 6,000—2,000 wounded were found in the hospitals at Winchester, and about 3,000 were taken prisoners.

Battle of Fisher's Hill, Va.—Fought September 22, 1864, between Sheridan's Union army and Early's Confederate troops, who were intrenched at that point. A flanking movement and a general charge along the Confederate lines compelled the latter to evacuate their fortifications, the Unionists pursuing them through the night. Early's loss was about 300 killed and wounded, and also 1,100 prisoners, 16 cannon, with his camp equipage, wagons, horses, small arms, and ammunition. Sheridan's loss was about 300 men. By the 29th of September, the Confederates had been driven from the Shenandoah valley.

Battle of Pilot Knob, Mo.—The Confederate General Price, with a force estimated at 10,000 men invaded Missouri, from Arkansas, September 23, 1864, raiding the country with apparently but little opposition. On the 26th Price attacked the little town of Pilot Knob, then occupied by a Union brigade under General Ewing, but was repulsed in all his attempts with severe losses. Price then occupying Shepherd's mountain, in that vicinity, Ewing blew up his magazine and retired to Harrison's station, where he intrenched. Price closely pursued him, breaking up the railroad, but Ewing finally escaped to Rolla, with little loss, from the dangers that surrounded him.

Price Defeated—During the month of October, 1864, the Confederate General Price committed various depredations in Missouri, although harassed and watched by Union forces under several commanders. October 25, when on the Fort Scott (Kas.) railroad, Price was beaten with serious loss. On the 26th, at Mine Creek, his Generals Marmaduke and Cabell, with a large number of their men, were captured; and he was

defeated also at Des Cygnes, Kas., on the 27th, and on the 28th at Newtonia. This ended the invasion of Missouri. Price lost 10 cannon, a large number of small arms, 1,958 prisoners (besides his killed, wounded and deserters), and nearly all his trains and plunder. His defeat was caused by the exertions of 7,000 Union cavalry, whose total losses in killed, wounded and missing, were less than 350.

Battle of Allatoona, Ga.—On the 5th October, 1864, a strong force of Confederates under General French, unsuccessfully attacked the small Union garrison under General Corse, with a loss of 2,000 men, killed and captured. Union loss 700 men, over one-third of the entire command. General Corse was wounded in the face.

Battle of Thoms' Brook, Va.—Fought October 8, 1864, between Union cavalry, under Generals Merritt and Custer, and the Confederate cavalry divisions of Generals Rosser and Lomax. The latter were defeated and driven twenty miles, with the loss of about 330 prisoners and several cannon. The Union loss was less than 100.

Battle of Cedar Creek, Va.—Fought October 19, 1864, between Sheridan's Union army (he being temporarily absent, but returning before the fight was over), and Early's Confederate forces in the valley of the Shenandoah. The latter were the attacking party, but their assault was steadily met, after the first panic, by the Unionists, who subsequently repulsed and routed their foes. During the first part of the battle it is estimated that the Unionists lost 1,300 prisoners, 20 cannon, considerable camp equipage, ambulances, wagons and medical supplies. Before the close of the contest the Unionists, it is estimated, captured and recaptured the following: 1,264 prisoners, 48 cannon, 398 horses and mules, 65 ambulances, 50 wagons, 15,000 rounds of artillery ammunition, 1,580 small arms, 10 battle-flags, harness, medical stores, etc. The Confederates lost about 3,000 men in killed, wounded and prisoners. The Unionists lost 5,990, including 2,000 temporarily missing, and a large number of officers. But the victory, though gained at heavy loss, was considered decisive for the Unionists.

Bombardment and Capture of Plymouth, N. C.—Commodore Macomb, with 7 Union gunboats, began bombarding the Confederate stronghold of Plymouth, N. C., October 29, 1864. The attack lasted until the 31st, when a Union shell exploded the Confederate magazine, and soon afterwards the Union commander took possession of the place without further resistance.

Sherman's March from Atlanta to Savannah, Ga.—On the 1st of November, 1864, the Confederate force under Hood in Georgia was estimated at 35,000 infantry and 10,000 cavalry. About this time Sherman arranged the details for his expedition from Atlanta to the sea-coast through the Confederate State of Georgia. The Union army for this enterprise comprised 60,000 infantry, 5,500 cavalry, and between 60 and 70 pieces of artillery. On the 14th of November the storehouses, depot buildings and machine shops, covering 200 acres in the city of Atlanta, were burned by the Unionists, and but little more than the dwellings and churches of the place survived the flames. On the 15th of November the advance guard of the expedition left Atlanta, followed on the next day by the main army.

Battle Near Morristown, Tenn.—Fought November 13-14, 1864, between General Breckenridge, with a Confederate force estimated at 3,000 strong, and General Gillem, with 1,500 Unionists and 6 cannon. The latter were routed losing several hundred prisoners and artillery. Gillem then escaped, with the remainder of his force, to Knoxville.

Battle of Hollow-Tree Gap, Tenn.—Four miles from Franklin, Thomas' Union cavalry overtook Hood's retreating Confederate army, November 17, 1864, and attacked it in front and rear, capturing 413 prisoners and three battle-flags.

Another Battle at Franklin, Tenn.—Hood's Confederate army then fell back to Franklin, but Johnson's division of Thomas' Union army repulsed them on the Harpeth river bank, and Union cavalry took possession of the town, capturing the Confederate hospitals, containing more than 2,000 wounded men, 200 of whom were Unionists. Hood was still pursued after leaving Franklin, but escaped into the interior of Georgia, with but little additional loss.

Battle of Griswoldville, Ga.—Fought November 22, 1864, between a detachment of Kilpatrick's Union cavalry (from Sherman's army) with a brigade of Union infantry, and about 5,000 Confederates, mostly militia, with some of Hardee's corps. The latter were the attacking party. The fight was brief but sanguinary, and resulted in the retreat of the Confederates, who left more than 300 of their dead on the field, and lost more than 2,000 in wounded and prisoners. The Union loss was about 40 killed and wounded.

Occupation of Milledgeville, the Capital of Georgia — Sherman's Union army occupied Milledgeville, November 23, 1864. The Confederate legislature, in session there, hastily adjourned, and the citizens were panic-stricken. The Unionists burned the magazines, arsenals, depot-buildings, various factories, store-houses, containing large amounts of Confederate public property, and about 1,700 bales of cotton. Private property was everywhere respected. Railroads were generally torn up and destroyed.

Capture of Fort McAllister, near Savannah, Ga. — The fort was manned by about 200 men, Confederate infantry and artillery, and lay in Sherman's way to the objective point of his expedition, the city of Savannah. December 13, 1864, the fort was carried, in a single assault, by nine regiments of Unionists. On the same day Sherman was enabled to communicate with the Union naval squadron at the mouth of the Ogeechee river, under Admiral Dahlgren and General Foster.

Capture of Savannah, Ga.—A demand from the Union General Sherman upon the Confederate General Hardee, who then occupied Savannah, for the surrender of the city, November 17, 1864, was refused. Sherman, therefore, prepared to carry the place by a military and naval assault. Hardee, recognizing the exigencies of the times, evacuated the city on the night of November 20, first destroying the Confederate war vessels in the harbor; and thus Sherman's expedition successfully terminated. Hardee's command moved toward Charleston, S. C.

Results of Sherman's Expedition from Atlanta to Savannah—Sherman's Union army brought with them to Savannah 15,000 slaves, more than 1,000 prisoners, 150 cannon, 13 locomotives in good order, 190 railroad cars, a very large supply of ammunition and other war material, three steamers and 32,000 bales of cotton, besides achieving national benefits growing out of the success of his expedition.

Hood in Tennessee and Alabama—The Confederate General Hood, who had retired before Sherman's Union army to Gaylesville, in Northeastern Alabama, visited Jacksonville, and thence proceeded northwesterly toward the Tennessee river, watched by the Union forces under General Thomas. The Confederate troops began their northward march about November 20, 1864, approaching Pulaski, Tenn. At this point, General Schofield and General A. J. Smith concentrated their Union forces, on learning of Hood's approach. The latter moved directly upon Gaynesboro, thus flanking Schofield, who fell back to Columbia, and being pursued by Hood, retreated to Franklin.

Battle of Spring Hill, Tenn. — Hood, with his Confederate army, attacked Schofield's Union cavalry November 29, 1864. A fight ensued, in which Schofield lost less than 300 men, and then he retreated to Franklin, 18 miles from Nashville. Here he formed his lines in a strong position and prepared for a battle with Hood.

Battle of Franklin, Tenn. — Fought November 30, 1864, between Schofield's Union force, consisting of two army divisions, commanded by Generals Stanley and Cox, and two corps of Hood's Confederate army, under Generals Lee and Cheatham. The fight was extremely hot, the Confederates making repeated charges upon the Union batteries; but the Confederates were finally repulsed, and Schofield was reinforced by General Smith's corps. The Union loss was 189 killed, 1,033 wounded, and 1,104 missing. Hood's loss was 1,750 killed, 3,800 wounded, and 702 taken prisoners.

Skirmish at Overall's Creek, Tenn.—Fought December 4, 1864, at the blockhouse, occupied by a Union force and Bates division of Cheatham's Confederate corps, the latter attacking the former, and using artillery. The Union General Milroy coming up with infantry, cavalry and artillery, attacked the Confederates and drove them off.

Battle Near Murfreesboro, Tenn. — Fought December 5, 6, and 7, 1864. General Rousseau and about 8,000 Unionists were occupying Fortress Rosecrans, and were approached by two divisions of Lee and Cheatham's Confederate corps, with 2,500 of Forrest's Confederate cavalry. The Confederates hesitating to attack the fort General Milroy, with seven regiments of Union infantry, was sent out to engage them. He found them a short distance off, posted behind rail breastworks. A fight ensued, in which the Confederates were routed, with the loss of 30 killed, 175 wounded, 207 prisoners, and two cannon. On the same day Buford's Confederate cavalry entered Murfreesboro and shelled it, but were speedily driven out by a regiment of Union infantry and a section of artillery.

A Union Raid in Virginia — By orders from General Grant, December 6, 1864, a Union force of 20,000 men, with 22 cannon, proceeded down the line of the Weldon railroad, with instructions to destroy the road and penetrate the enemy's country, capturing such points and supplies as should come in their way. The weather was bad, but the expedition, which was absent a week, was mainly successful. Some opposition was encountered, but the entire loss of the Unionists did not exceed 100 men. They destroyed 3 railroad bridges, 15 miles of track, burned Sussex Court-house, and brought in a few prisoners.

Battle of Nashville, Tenn.—Fought December 15 and 16, 1864, between General Thomas, with four corps of Union infantry and Wilson's cavalry, dismounted, aided by a division of Rear Admiral Lee's Mississippi naval squadron, and Hood's concentrated army of Confederates. The first day's fight resulted in driving the Confederates from their intrenchments with a loss of about 600 killed and wounded, 1,000 prisoners and 16 great guns. The Union loss that day was about 500 killed and wounded. The attack was renewed by the Unionists next morning on Hood's new position, and resulted, soon after noon in the complete rout of the Confederates, suffering severe losses. All their dead and wounded were left on the field of battle. The Confederate losses in the two days' contests footed up about 2,000 killed and wounded, 4,462 prisoners captured, including 287 officers, 53 cannon and thousands of small arms. The Confederates were pursued.

Stoneman's Raid in Virginia—December 15, 1864, Generals Stoneman and Burbridge of the Union army in Tennessee, sallied out to Glade's Spring, W. Va., destroying a railroad track east of Abingdon, and mining the principal salt works in that region. This movement severed the Confederate communication between Richmond and East Tennessee, and deprived the Confederates of important public property.

The Flash at Fort Fisher, N. C.—In December, 1864, an expedition was fitted out under the Union Generals Butler and Weitzel and the North Atlantic naval squadron, under Admiral Porter, to break up the Confederate blockade-runner's depot at Wilmington, N. C. A preliminary explosion, December 23, 1864, having failed to reduce the fort to splinters, the fleet attacked it next day. Five hours' cannonading, resisted by the Confederate garrison, resulted in blowing up two magazines within the inclosure and setting it on fire in several places. December 25 the assault was renewed on sea and shore by the Union forces, but General Weitzel reporting, after a reconnoissance, that it would be inexpedient to carry the fort by assault, the attempt was abandoned, leaving the fort substantially uninjured, and the expedition retired.

BATTLES OF THE FIFTH YEAR OF THE WAR.

Battle at Beverly, W. Va.—Fought January 11, 1865, between a Union force occupying the town and Confederate troops under General Rosser. The former were defeated, the latter capturing the town and a large portion of the force defending it.

Capture of Fort Fisher, N. C.—The Union assault upon Fort Fisher, the formidable Confederate stronghold at Wilmington, N. C., mounting 72 great guns, was resumed January 13, 1865, by about 8,000 Union troops under General Terry, with Admiral Porter's fleet and 1,000 or more marines—a Confederate force of 2,300 men occupying the fort. The fleet began the bombardment of the fort on that day, and in the afternoon of the 15th the Union soldiers, with the sailors and marines, attacked the fort by land and sea. At 4 o'clock one-half of the fort had been captured. That evening reinforcements of Union soldiers arrived, and the Confederate defense surrendered. The fighting had been very severe. Of the garrison, 217 were killed or wounded, besides the force surrendered. The Union loss was about 1,000, besides which were 200 men killed or wounded on the next day by the accidental blowing up of a magazine.

Fight at Fort Anderson, N. C. — Fort Anderson, one of the defenses of the mouth of Cape Fear river, near Wilmington, defended by about 6,000 Confederates, under General Hoke, strongly intrenched, was attacked, January 18, 1865, by 8,000 Union soldiers of Cox's division, under General Schofield, and Admiral Porter, with 14 gunboats and a monitor. A heavy fire from the fleet and the operations of the land force continued during the day, and before daylight on the 19th the Confederates evacuated the fort. The Confederate loss was 12 cannon, a quantity of ammunition, and about 50 prisoners. The Unionists lost 3 killed and 5 wounded in the fleet, and less than 50 killed and wounded in the skirmishes of the land forces.

Skirmishes on Town Creek, N. C.—Fought January 20, 1865, between a Confederate force in rifle-pits and Union troops under Terry. The latter lost 10 killed and 47 wounded, but drove the Confederates inside their works. A similar Union force soon afterwards charged upon some Confederates in the same vicinity. They were met with grape and canister. Another charge was then made by the Union soldiers, and the Confederates were routed, with the loss of 2 cannon and 373 prisoners, the rest escaping. The Union loss was about 30.

Evacuation of Wilmington, N. C. — January 21, 1865, finding themselves beleaguered with a heavy Union force, the Confederates prepared to evacuate Wilmington. That night they burned their war material and stores, about 1,000 bales of cotton, 15,000 barrels of resin, extensive cotton-sheds and presses, an unfinished iron-clad, three steam-mills, three large turpentine factories, with wharves, railroad bridges and other property, and moved out. At daylight on the 22d, the Union troops under Generals Terry and Cox occupied the city, taking about 700 prisoners, and capturing a large amount of Confederate property.

Sherman's March to Wilmington, N. C., from Savannah, Ga. — January 13, 1865, Sherman's Union advance corps left Beaufort, N. C. On the 15th a skirmish occurred with a Confederate force on the Charleston railroad for the possession of a Confederate pontoon and trestle bridge. The Unionists succeeded in saving the bridge from being burned and drove off the Confederates. The Union loss was about 50 killed and wounded. January 19, the march of the main Union army from Savannah, under Sherman, began. By a system of feints the Unionists misled the Confederates as to their intentions. At the Salkehatchie river, Mower and Smith's divisions captured a bridge from the Confederate force which held it, losing 18 killed and 70 wounded in the struggle. February 16, the Confederates surrendered the city of Columbia, S. C., to Colonel Stone, of the 25th Iowa infantry. The Confederate soldiers set fires in the city, and that night the city was burned, and within two or three days afterwards the arsenal, railroad depots, and tracks, machine shops, foundries, etc., were destroyed by the Unionists. March 9, Wade Hampton's Confederate troops surprised Kilpatrick's and Spencer's Union forces, rescuing their jeopardized camp equipage, artillery and horses, and driving off the Unionists. March 12-14 the Unionists spent in destroying all the buildings and much valuable military and public property. March 8, the Confederates under Hoke captured two Union regiments, commanded by Colonel Upham, securing over 1,000 prisoners. March 10, Hoke's Confederate force fought Cox's Union brigade, but the latter were the victors, driving off Hoke, who left his killed and wounded on the field, besides losing about 200 prisoners.

Battles at Fort Steadman and Hatcher's Run, Va. — Fought February 6 and 7, 1865, between the 2d, 6th and 9th corps and Griffin's division of the 5th corps of Grant's army in Virginia and Lee's Confederate army. Steadman's fort, occupied by the 14th New York Union heavy artillery, was carried by the Confederates at the outset, and its guns were turned against the Unionists. The Confederates also captured two Union batteries between Fort Steadman and Fort Haskell, and with them fought the Union troops. They failed, however, to carry the Union Fort Haskell. A tremendous cannonade followed, the Union batteries being massed against Fort Steadman with so much vigor that some of the Confederates retreated, first into the fortress and then out of it, leaving all the guns that they had captured. A large portion of the escaping Confederates, 1,758 in all, were captured. The Confederate loss at this point was estimated at 2,500. The Union forces on the left then moved out against the Confederate intrenched lines of pickets, which were swept right and left, resulting in the capture of about 300 prisoners. Another attack by the Unionists, reconnoitering across Hatcher's Run, resulted in driving in another Confederate picket line, with the capture of 70 more prisoners. Subsequently the Confederates rallied their forces and attacked the 6th and 2d corps of Grant's army. The fight was severe and continued until dark and even into the night, but the Unionists were the victors. The Confederate total losses in both battles were set down at 5,000 men—1,883 prisoners. The Unionists lost 171 killed, 1,236 wounded, and 983 missing.

Evacuation of Charleston, S. C.—February 18, 1865, the city of Charleston was evacuated by the Confederates, and occupied by the Union General Gilmore. A large amount of valuable property was destroyed, including 6,000 bales of cotton. Ammunition stored in the railroad depot exploded, and many lives were lost. General Gilmore displayed the American flag over the ruins of Fort Sumter.

Sheridan's March Through the Shenandoah Valley, Va.—General Sheridan, with a strong Union force, left Winchester, Va., February 24, 1865. This expedition was principally distinguished by

Sheridan's Capture of Early's Army. —March 2, 1865, near Waynesboro, Va., Sheridan's Union force encountered the Confederates under Early. The latter fired one volley, when General Custer's division advanced upon them. The Confederate line suddenly broke, and Custer's force surrounded them, capturing 87 Confederate officers, 1,165 enlisted men, 13 flags, 5 cannon, more than 100 horses and mules and about 100 wagons and ambulances. Custer's brigades immediately pursued the fleeing Confederates, destroying the depot at Greenwood station, with their artillery and other captured war material. Next day the prisoners were sent to Winchester. An attempt to rescue them by the Confederate General Rosser only succeeded in his being beaten off, with the loss of 27 more prisoners. March 26, 1864, Sheridan arrived at City Point, Va., having made a most successful raid. His total losses were 2 officers and about 50 men in killed, wounded and prisoners.

Battle of Averysboro, N. C.—Fought March 16, 1865, between four divisions of Sherman's Union army, under General Slocum, and about 20,000 Confederates under Hardee. After a severe action the latter retreated, leaving 108 of his dead on the field. The Union loss was 77 killed, 477 wounded and no prisoners.

Battles near Bentonville, N. C.—Fought March 18-21, 1865, between General Sherman's Union army and Johnston's Confederate army.

The latter were defeated, with heavy losses, including 267 killed and 1,625 prisoners. The Union loss in killed, wounded and missing, was 1,643. Sherman now had possession of Goldsboro, N. C., and concentrated his army there.

Skirmish on the Quaker Road, Va.—Fought March 29, 1865, between one division of Meade's Union 5th corps, with 3 batteries, and a detachment of Lee's Confederate army. After a short and sharp conflict, the Confederates withdrew to their original position, they having made the attack. The Union loss was 458 killed, wounded and missing. That night, under a heavy Confederate cannonade, the Union 9th corps lost 51 men.

Skirmish on the Boydton Road, Va.—Fought March 30, 1865, between Merritt's corps of Meade's Union army and Confederate infantry and cavalry. Another smart skirmish occurred between detachments of the same armies on the same day, and the total Union losses were something less than 200 men.

A Federal Repulse—Proceeding along the Boydton (Va.) road toward Five Forks, March 31, 1865, Meade's Union advance and Sheridan's Union cavalry encountered a strong force of Confederates, who stubbornly resisted the Federal advance and brought on a conflict, which resulted in the repulse of the Unionists, with a loss of from 2,500 to 3,000 men. Between 300 and 400 Confederate prisoners were captured. Subsequently, under the fire of the Union batteries, the Confederates withdrew.

Battle of Five Forks, Va.—Fought April 1, 1865, between a part of Lee's Confederate army and three divisions of Union infantry and four of Union cavalry, commanded by Sheridan, while Meade's army threatened the Confederate line from Dinwiddie to Petersburg. After a preliminary contest, Sheridan broke through the Confederate lines, inclosing the Five Forks fortification and its Confederate garrison and capturing it. The battle for two hours was one of the most terrific of the war, and resulted in the utter defeat of the Confederates. They lost nearly 3,000 killed and wounded and 5,000

prisoners. The Union loss was about 1,000 men, including General Winthrop, who was killed.

Evacuation of Petersburg, Va.—Saturday night and Sunday morning, April 1 and 2, 1865, Grant's Union army, under Meade and Sheridan, invested Petersburg with such vigor that on the afternoon of the second day Lee evacuated the place, his communications with Richmond being severed. The losses were very heavy on both sides.

Evacuation of Richmond, Va.—Petersburg having been lost, President Davis, of the Southern Confederacy, retired from its capital, on Sunday, April 2, 1865, and on the following morning General Weitzel with his force entered Richmond, capturing about 500 cannon, 5,000 stand of arms, and 6,000 prisoners. Thirty locomotives and 300 cars were abandoned by the Confederates. The Confederate fleet was destroyed, and as the rear-guard of Lee's army moved out of the city they fired it, burning considerable property and stores.

Surrender of General Lee—Lee's army was followed by Grant's Union forces after the evacuation of Richmond, and on the 9th of April, 1865, Lee surrendered to General Grant, at Appomattox Court House, Virginia, and his officers and men were paroled as prisoners of war. They numbered over 27,000. Lee's losses in killed and wounded, from March 25 to April 3, 1865, were something more than 10,000. There were released 350 wagons, 10,000 small arms, and 30 great guns.

Capture of Southern Cities — April 12, 1865, Mobile was captured by the Union army under General Canby, who captured 1,000 Confederate prisoners, 150 cannon, and 3,000 bales of cotton. On the same day the Unionists captured Salisbury, N. C., and Columbus, Ga. On the following day they captured Raleigh, N. C., taking Governor Vance prisoner.

The End of the War—General Johnston, of the Confederate army, surrendered to the Unionists, April 26, 1865, at Durham's station, near Greensboro, N. C. This closed the war of the Rebellion.

Distinguished Officers in the Union Service During the Civil War.†

Robert Anderson. Maj.-Gen.; b. near Louisville, Ky.; died in France in 1871.

Edward D. Baker. Colonel; U. S. Sen. from Or.; b. in London, Eng., in 1811; killed at Ball's Bluff, Va., in 1861.

Don Carlos Buell. Maj.-Gen.; b. at Marietta, O., in 1818.

Ambrose E. Burnside. Maj.-Gen.; b. at Liberty, Ind., 1824; Gov. R. I., and M. C.; d. in 1880.

Benjamin F. Butler. Maj.-Gen.; b. at Deerfield, N. H., in 1818; has been M. C. from Mass.

Edward R. S. Canby. Brig.-Gen.; b. in Ky. in 1819; shot by Modoc Indian chief, in Cal. in 1873.

John C. Fremont. Maj.-Gen.; b. at Savannah, Ga., in 1813; Repub. can. for Pres. in 1856; has been U. S. Sen. from Cal., and later Gov. of Ariz.

Ulysses S. Grant.* Gen.-in-Chief of the U. S. A. during the latter part of the war; was b. at Pt. Pleasant, O., in 1822. Eight years Pres. of the U. S.

Henry W. Halleck. Gen.-in-Chief of the U. S. Army for a time; b. at Waterville, N. Y., in 1815; d. at Louisville, Ky., in 1872.

Winfield S. Hancock. Maj.-Gen.; b. in Montg. Co., Pa., in 1824; Dem. can. for Pres., 1880.

Joseph Hooker. Brevet Maj.-Gen.; b. at Hadley, Mass., in 1815; d. in 1879.

Oliver O. Howard. Brevet Maj.-Gen; b. at Leeds, Me.

Philip Kearney. Maj.-Gen.; b. in N. Y. City, in 1815; wounded at Second Bull Run, where he d., in 1862.

John A. Logan. Maj.-Gen.; b. in Jefferson Co., Ill., in 1826; U. S. Sen. from Ill.

Nathaniel Lyon. Brig.-Gen.; b. at Ashford, Conn., in 1819; slain at Wilson's Creek, Mo., in 1861.

Geo. B. McClellan. Gen.-in-Chief of the U. S. Army, for a time; b. at Phila., Pa., in 1826; was Dem. can. for Pres. in 1364; elected Gov. of N. J. in 1878.

Ervin McDowell. Maj.-Gen.; b. at Franklinton, O., in 1818.

James B. McPherson. Maj.-Gen. of vols. B. at Clyde, O., in 1828; k. at Atlanta, in 1864.

Geo. G. Meade. Maj.-Gen.; b. at Cadiz, Spain, in 1815; d. at Phila. in 1872.

T. F. Meagher. Brig.-Gen.; b. at Waterford, Ireland, in 1823; accidentally drowned by falling from a steamer near Ft. Benton, Montana, in 1867.

John A. McClernand. Maj.-Gen.: b. in Breckenridge Co., Ky.; has been M. C.

Ormsby M. Mitchel. Maj.-Gen.; b. in Union Co., Ky., in 1810; d. of yellow fever at Beaufort, S. C., in 1862.

Richard J. Oglesby. Maj.-Gen.; b. in Oldham Co., Ky., in 1824; has been Gov. of Ill., and U. S. Sen. from that State.

Alfred Pleasanton. Maj.-Gen.; b. at Washington, D. C., in 1824; author of treatise on healing effect of sunlight passing through blue glass.

John Pope. Maj.-Gen.; b. at Kaskaskia, Ill., in 1823.

Fitz John Porter. Maj.-Gen.; b. at Portsmouth, N. H., in 1823.

Thomas E. G. Ransom. Brig.-Gen.; b. in 1834; d. in Chicago in 1864.

Wm. S. Rosecrans. Maj.-Gen.; b. at Kingston, O., in 1809.

Franz Sigel. Maj.-Gen.; b. at Zinsheim, Baden, Germany.

John M. Schofield. Maj.-Gen.; b. in Chautauqua Co., N. Y., in 1831; U. S. Secretary of War in 1868.

John Sedgwick. Maj.-Gen.; b. at Cornwall, Conn., in 1813; k. at Spottsylvania, Va., in 1864.

Philip H. Sheridan. Maj.-Gen.; b. at Somerset, O., in 1831; present Lieut.-Gen. U. S. A.

Wm. T. Sherman. Maj.-Gen. in the war; present Gen. U. S. A.; b. at Lancaster, O., in 1820.

Alfred H. Terry. Brig.-Gen.; b. at Hartford, Conn., in 1827.

Geo. H. Thomas. Maj.-Gen.; b. in Southham Co., Va., in 1816; d. at San Fran., Cal., in 1870.

Leading Officers in the Confederate Service.†

Peter G. T. Beauregard.* Gen.; b. at New Orleans, La., in 1818.

Braxton Bragg.* Maj.-Gen.; born in N. C. about 1815; d. at Galveston, Tex., in 1875.

Jefferson Davis. Col.; b. in Christian Co., Ky., in 1808; was President of the Southern Confederacy; formerly U. S. Senator from Miss., and was Sec. of War under Pres. Pierce.

J. A. Early.* Maj.-Gen.; b. in Va. about 1815.

Richard S. Ewell. Lieut.-Gen.; born in D. C., in 1820; d. at Springhill, Tenn., in 1872.

Wade Hampton, Jr. Lieut.-Gen.; b. at Columbia, S. C., in 1818; has been Gov. of S. C. and member of the U. S. Senate.

Wm. J. Hardee.* Brig.-Gen.; b. at Savannah, Ga., in 1818; d. at Wytheville, Va., in 1873.

Ambrose P. Hill.* Maj.-Gen.; b. in Culpeper Co., Va., about 1825; k. at Petersburg, Va., in 1865.

Dan'l H. Hill.* Gen.; b. in S. C. about 1822.

John B. Hood.* Lieut.-Gen.; b. in Bath Co., Ky., about 1830.

Benj. Huger.* Maj.-Gen.; b. at Charleston, S. C., in 1806.

Thos. J. Jackson (Stonewall).*** Lieut.-Gen.; b. at Clarksburg, Va., in 1824, ·d. from wounds received at battle of Chancellorsville.

Albert S. Johnston.* Gen.; b. in Mason Co., Ky., in 1803; k. at Shiloh, in 1862.

Joseph E. Johnston.* Maj.-Gen.; b. in Pr. Edward Co., Va., in 1807.

George W. C. Lee.* Gen.; b. in Va. about 1833.

Robert E. Lee.* Gen.-in-Chief of the Confederate army: b. at Stafford, Va., in 1807; d. at Lexington, Va., in 1870.

Fitz Hugh Lee.* Gen.; b. in Va. about 1835.

James Longstreet.* Lieut.-Gen.; b. in S. C. about 1820.

Benj. McCulloch. Maj.-Gen.; b. in Rutherford Co., Tenn., in 1814; k. at Pea Ridge, Ark., Mar. 7, 1862.

Leonidas Polk.* Maj.-Gen.; b. at Raleigh, N. C., in 1806; k. at Pine Mountain, near Marietta, Ga., in 1864.

Sterling Price. Maj.-Gen.; b. in Pr. Edward Co., Va., 1809; M. C. from Mo., and was Gov. of that State; d. at St. Louis in 1867.

Kirby E. Smith.* Maj.-Gen.; b. at St. Augustine, Fla., about 1825.

Jas. E. B. Stuart. Maj.-Gen.; b. in Patrick Co., Va., in 1832; k. in battle near Richmond in 1864.

Earl Van Dorn. Maj.-Gen.; b. in Miss. in 1821; d. in 1863.

EXPLANATORY.—* Graduated at West Point; b., born; d., died; k., killed.   † Many other distinguished names should be here mentioned, but lack of space prevents.

1. Alabama.
2. Arkansas.
3. California.
4. Colorado.
5. Connecticut.
6. Delaware.
7. Florida.
8. Georgia.
9. Illinois.
10. Indiana.
11. Iowa.
12. Kansas.
13. Kentucky.
14. Louisiana.
15. Maine.
16. Maryland.
17. Massachusetts.
18. Michigan.
19. Minnesota.

20. Mississippi.
21. Missouri.
22. Nebraska.
23. Nevada.
24. N. Hampshire.
25. New Jersey.
26. New York.
27. N. Carolina.
28. Ohio.
29. Oregon.
30. Pennsylvania.
31. Rhode Island.
32. S. Carolina.
33. Tennessee.
34. Texas.
35. Vermont.
36. Virginia.
37. West Virginia.
38. Wisconsin.

OW THE UNITED STATES ARE GOVERNED.

Duties and Privileges of

PERSONS IN OFFICIAL POSITIONS.

Early Discovery, Settlement and Government of the Country.

THE RECORD of North American discovery and settlement may be thus briefly told: Greenland, by Icelanders, in A. D. 980; Bahama islands, by Christopher Columbus, in 1492; Isthmus of Darien, by Columbus, in 1494; Florida, by Sebastian Cabot, in 1497; Newfoundland and Canada, by John and Sebastian Cabot, in 1497; North and South Carolina, by Sebastian Cabot, in 1498; Hudson bay, by Sebastian Cabot, in 1512; the Mississippi river, by De Soto, about 1541; Davis' strait, by John Davis, in 1585; the Hudson river, by Henry Hudson, in 1608; and Baffin bay, by William Baffin, in 1616. In 1500, Amerigo Vespucci explored Brazil, S. A., and gave his name to both of the American continents.

The Spaniards early settled the West India Islands and New Mexico. The French occupied Canada in 1534, with the valley of the Mississippi, and other regions south and west. The English made their first permanent settlement at Jamestown, Va., in 1607, and a few years later several districts (including the present city of New York) were populated by Hollanders and Swedes. In 1620, the Puritan Pilgrims landed on the bleak coast of Massachusetts. By 1770, England, after a series of conflicts, had captured the country, occupied by the French, Dutch, and Swedish settlers, and was in possession of nearly the whole of North America, except Mexico, which was held by Spain. Soon afterwards, Russia acquired territory on the northwestern coast. Such was the ownership of the continent when the war of the Revolution began, in 1775.

At that time there were thirteen American colonies. These afterwards became the thirteen original States.

The colonists, who were subjects of Great Britain, became restive under various restrictions placed upon them by the mother country. Among these were a species of search warrant, which permitted government officials to enter stores and private houses to search for goods upon which prescribed taxes had not been paid.

Another was a stamp tax, which required every document used in the trade or legal business of the colonies to bear a stamp costing not less than an English shilling each, and a larger sum in proportion to the value of the document used.

This tax was afterwards repealed, but in 1767 another act of parliament provided for taxing paper, glass, tea and other goods imported into the colonies.

This enactment being resisted upon the part of the people, the English government sent troops to Boston to enforce the law, when a collision ensued between the troops and the citizens, in which several of the latter were killed and wounded.

Owing to the bitter opposition these taxes were soon repealed, excepting that of threepence on each pound of tea imported. But even this tax the colonists refused to pay, and when the first shipload of tea arrived in Boston harbor, the citizens went upon the vessel and threw the tea overboard.

In order to subdue and punish her American subjects, the English government thereupon devised other oppressive measures and annoyances, which, in the spring of 1775, resulted in the conflicts between the British soldiers and citizens at Concord and Lexington, and commenced the seven years war, known as the War of the Revolution for American Independence. The war had been in progress for about a year, when the Continental Congress in session at Independence Hall, in Philadelphia, July 2, 1776, adopted a resolution, introduced by Richard Henry Lee, declaring:

That these united colonies are, and of right ought to be, free and independent States; that they are absolved from all allegiance to the British crown, and that all political connection between them and the State of Great Britain is, and ought to be, totally dissolved.

Two days later the Declaration of Independence, prepared by Thomas Jefferson, was brought into Congress, and, amid intense excitement on the part of the citizens, was adopted. The announcement that it had been signed was made by the ringing of a bell in the cupola of the building. Such was the birth of American freedom.

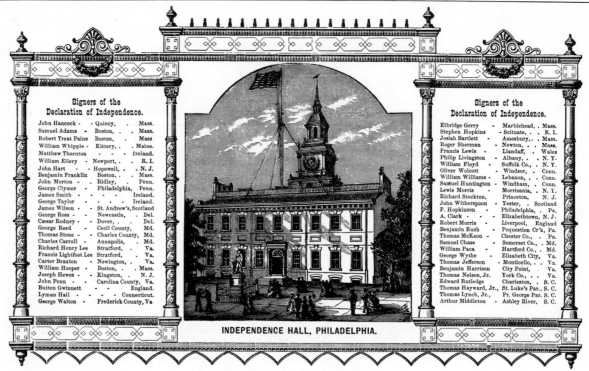

Signers of the Declaration of Independence.

John Hancock - - - Quincy, . . Mass.
Samuel Adams - - Boston, . . Mass.
Robert Treat Paine Boston, . . Mass
William Whipple - Kittery, . . Maine.
Matthew Thornton - - - Ireland.
William Ellery - Newport, . . R. I.
John Hart - - Hopewell, . . N. J.
Benjamin Franklin Boston, . . Mass.
John Morton - . Ridley, . . Penn.
George Clymer - Philadelphia, Penn.
James Smith - - - - Ireland.
George Taylor - - - - Ireland.
James Wilson - - St. Andrew's, Scotland
George Ross - - Newcastle, . Del.
Cæsar Rodney - - Dover, . . Del.
George Reed - - Cecil County, Md.
Thomas Stone - - Charles County, Md.
Charles Carroll - Annapolis, . Md.
Richard Henry Lee Stratford, . Va.
Francis Lightfoot Lee Stratford, . Va.
Carter Braxton - Newington, . Va.
William Hooper - Boston, . . Mass.
Joseph Hewes - Kingston, . N. J.
John Penn - - Carolina County, Va.
Button Gwinnett - - - England.
Lyman Hall - - - Connecticut.
George Walton - Frederick County, Va

INDEPENDENCE HALL, PHILADELPHIA.

Signers of the Declaration of Independence.

Elbridge Gerry - Marblehead, . Mass.
Stephen Hopkins - Scituate, . . R. I.
Josiah Bartlett - Amesbury, . . Mass.
Roger Sherman - Newton, . . Mass.
Francis Lewis - Llandaff, . Wales
Philip Livingston - Albany, . . N. Y.
William Floyd - Suffolk Co., . N. Y.
Oliver Wolcott - Windsor, . Conn.
William Williams - Lebanon, . . Conn.
Samuel Huntington - Windham, . Conn.
Lewis Morris - Morrisania, . N. Y.
Richard Stockton - Princeton, . N. J.
John Witherspoon - Yester, . Scotland
F. Hopkinson - Philadelphia, . Pa.
A. Clark - - Elizabethtown, N. J.
Robert Morris - Liverpool, England
Benjamin Rush - Poquestion Cr'k, Pa.
Thomas McKeon - Chester Co., . Pa.
Samuel Chase - Somerset Co., . Md.
William Paca - Hartford Co., . Md.
George Wythe - Elizabeth City, Va.
Thomas Jefferson - Monticello, . . Va.
Benjamin Harrison City Point, . . Va.
Thomas Nelson, Jr. York Co., . . . Va.
Edward Rutledge Charleston, . S. C.
Thomas Hayward, Jr., St. Luke's Par.,. S. C.
Thomas Lynch, Jr., Pr. George Par. S. C.
Arthur Middleton - Ashley River, S. C.

The Declaration of Independence.

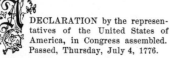

DECLARATION by the representatives of the United States of America, in Congress assembled. Passed, Thursday, July 4, 1776.

When, in the course of human events, it becomes necessary for one people to dissolve the political bands which have connected them with another, and to assume among the powers of the earth the separate and equal station to which the laws of nature, and of nature's God, *entitle them*, a decent respect to the opinions of mankind requires that they should declare the causes which impel them to the separation.

We hold these truths to be self-evident: that all men are created equal; that they are endowed, by their Creator, with certain inalienable rights; that among these are life, liberty, and the pursuit of happiness. That, to secure these rights, governments are instituted among men, deriving their just powers from the consent of the governed; that, whenever any form of government becomes *destructive of* these ends, it is the right of the people to alter or to abolish it, and to institute a new government, laying its foundation on such principles, and organizing its powers in such form, as to them shall seem most likely to effect their safety and happiness. Prudence, indeed, will dictate that governments, long established, should not be changed for light and transient causes; and accordingly, all experience hath shown, that mankind are more disposed to suffer, while evils are sufferable, than to right themselves, by abolishing the forms to which they are accustomed. But when a long train of abuses and usurpations, pursuing invariably the same object, evinces a design to reduce them under absolute despotism, it is their right, it is their duty, to throw off such government, and to provide new

guards for their future security. Such has been the patient sufferance of these colonies; and such is now the necessity which constrains them to alter their former systems of government. The history of the present king of Great Britain is a history of repeated injuries and usurpations, all having, in direct object, the establishment of *an absolute* tyranny over these states. To prove this, let facts be submitted to a candid world.

He has refused his assent to laws the most wholesome and necessary for the public good.

He has forbidden his governors to pass laws of immediate and pressing importance, unless suspended in their operation till his assent should be obtained; and, when so suspended, he has utterly neglected to attend to them.

He has refused to pass other laws for the accommodation of large districts of people, unless those people would relinquish the right of representation in the legislature; a right inestimable to them, and formidable to tyrants only.

He has called together legislative bodies at places unusual, uncomfortable, and distant from the depository of their public records, for the sole purpose of fatiguing them into compliance with his measures.

He has dissolved representative houses, repeatedly, for opposing, with manly firmness, his invasions on the rights of the people.

He has refused, for a long time, after such dissolutions, to cause others to be elected; whereby the legislative powers, incapable of annihilation, have returned to the people at large for their exercise; the state remaining, in the meantime, exposed to all the dangers of invasion from without, and convulsions within.

He has endeavored to prevent the population of these states; for that purpose, obstructing the laws for naturalization of foreigners; refusing to

pass others to encourage their migration hither, and raising the conditions of new appropriations of lands.

He has obstructed the administration of justice, by refusing his assent to laws for establishing judiciary powers.

He has made judges *dependent on* his will alone, for the tenure of their offices, and the amount and payment of their salaries.

He has erected a multitude of new offices, and sent hither swarms of officers to harrass our people, and eat out their substance.

He has kept among us, in time of peace, standing armies, without the consent of our legislatures.

He has affected to render the military independent of, and superior to, the civil power.

He has combined with others, to subject us to a jurisdiction foreign to our constitution, and unacknowledged by our laws; giving his assent to their acts of pretended legislation:

For quartering large bodies of armed troops among us:

For protecting them, by a mock-trial, from punishment for any murders which they should commit on the inhabitants of these states:

For *cutting off* our trade with all parts of the world:

For imposing taxes on us, without our consent:

For depriving us, in many cases, of the benefits of trial by jury:

For transporting us beyond seas, to be tried for pretended offences:

For abolishing the free system of English laws in a neighboring province, establishing therein *an arbitrary* government, and enlarging its boundaries, so as to render it, at once, an example and a fit instrument for introducing the same absolute rule into these colonies:

For taking away our charters, abolishing our most valuable laws, and altering fundamentally, the forms of our government; for suspending our own legislatures, and declaring themselves invested with power to legislate for us, in all cases whatsoever.

He has abdicated government here, by declaring us *out of his protection*, and waging war against us.

He has plundered our seas, ravaged our coasts, burnt our towns, and destroyed the lives of our people.

He is at this time, transporting large armies of foreign mercenaries, to complete the works of death, desolation, and tyranny, already begun with circumstances of cruelty and perfidy, scarcely paralleled in the most barbarous ages, and totally unworthy the head of a civilized nation.

He has constrained our fellow-citizens, taken captive on the high seas, to bear arms against their country, to become the *executioners of* their friends and brethren, or to fall themselves by their hands.

He has excited domestic insurrections amongst us, and has endeavored to bring on the inhabitants of our frontiers, the merciless Indian savages, whose known rule of warfare is an undistinguished destruction of all ages, sexes, and conditions. In every stage of these oppressions, we have petitioned for redress, in the most humble terms; our repeated petitions have been answered only by repeated injury. A prince, whose character is thus marked by every act which may define a tyrant, is unfit to be the ruler of a free people. Nor have we been wanting in attentions to our British brethren. We have warned them, from time to time, of attempts, by their legislature, to extend an unwarrantable jurisdiction over us. We have reminded them of the circumstances of our emigration and settlement here. We have appealed to their native justice and magnanimity, and we have conjured them, by the ties of our common kindred, to disavow these usurpations, which would inevitably interrupt our connections and correspondence. They too, have been deaf to the voice of justice and of consanguinity. We must, therefore, *acquiesce in* the necessity which

denounces our separation, and hold them, as we hold the rest of mankind, enemies in war, in peace friends.

We, therefore, the representatives of the UNITED STATES OF AMERICA IN GENERAL CONGRESS assembled, appealing to the Supreme Judge of the world, for the rectitude of our intentions, do, in the name, and by the authority, of the good people of these colonies, solemnly publish and declare, That these united colonies are, and of right ought to be, FREE AND INDEPENDENT STATES; and that they are absolved from all allegiance to the British crown, and that all political connection between them and the State of Great Britain is, and ought to be, totally dissolved; and that, as FREE AND INDEPENDENT STATES, they have full power to levy war, conclude peace, contract alliances, establish commerce, and to do all other acts and things, which independent states may of right do. And, for the support of this declaration, with a firm reliance on the protection of *Divine Providence*, we mutually pledge to each other, our lives, our fortunes, and our sacred honor.

The End of The Revolution. — Adoption of The Constitution.

The Ratification of the Constitution by the Thirteen Original States.

AFTER the signing of the Declaration of Independence, the thirteen British colonies were known as the "Thirteen United States of America." Beyond the efforts of Congress to sustain the conflict between the States and the "mother country," and to encourage Washington in his design to free the soil from British domination, the political changes were unimportant, until England dispatched a messenger to New York with offers of peace, about the beginning of the year 1782. November 30, 1782, the preliminaries of peace were signed at Paris, France, and, on September 3, 1783, the treaty was concluded, the independence of each of the

several States was acknowledged, and boundary lines established.

The government of the States was then principally vested in Congress and their own legislation; but, May 14, 1787, a national convention met at Philadelphia. After four months' deliberation, the present Constitution of the United States was adopted, and submitted to the people of each State for ratification or rejection. Their action was tardy in the extreme, for although Delaware, the first State to accept it, voted for it December 7, 1787, Rhode Island, the last, did not ratify it until May 27, 1790; but every State voted in its favor. Congress ratified it March 4, 1789, at which time it became the law of the land.

THE CONSTITUTION OF THE UNITED STATES.

WE, THE PEOPLE of the United States, in order to form a more perfect union, establish justice, insure domestic tranquility, provide for the common defense, promote the general welfare, and secure the blessings of liberty to ourselves and our posterity, do ordain and establish this Constitution for the United States of America.

ARTICLE I.—Section 1. All legislative powers herein granted shall be vested in a

Congress of the United States, which shall consist of a Senate and House of Representatives.

House of Representatives.

Sect. II—1. The House of Representatives shall be composed of members chosen every second year by the people of the several States, and the electors in each State shall have the qualifications requisite for electors of the most numerous branch of the State Legislature.

2. No person shall be a Representative who shall not have attained to the age of twenty-five years, and been seven years a citizen of the United States, and who shall not, when elected, be an

inhabitant of that State in which he shall be chosen.

3. Representatives and direct taxes shall be apportioned among the several States which may be included within this Union, according to their respective numbers, which shall be determined by adding to the whole number of free persons, including those bound to service for a term of years, and excluding Indians not taxed, three-fifths of all other persons. The actual enumeration shall be made within three years after the first meeting of the Congress of the United States, and within every subsequent term of ten years, in such manner as they shall by law direct.

The number of Representatives shall not exceed one for every thirty thousand, but each State shall have at least one Representative; and until such enumeration shall be made, the State of New Hampshire shall be entitled to choose three, Massachusetts eight, Rhode Island and Providence Plantations one, Connecticut five, New York six, New Jersey four, Pennsylvania eight, Delaware one, Maryland six, Virginia ten, North Carolina five, South Carolina five and Georgia three.

4. When vacancies happen in the representation from any State, the executive authority thereof shall issue writs of election to fill such vacancies.

5. The House of Representatives shall choose their Speaker and other officers, and shall have the sole power of impeachment.

The Senate.

Sect. III. The Senate of the United States shall be composed of two senators from each State, chosen by the Legislature thereof for six years, and each senator shall have one vote.

1. Immediately after they shall be assembled in consequence of the first election, they shall be divided as equally as may be into three classes. The seats of the senators of the first class shall be vacated at the expiration of the second year, of the second class at the expiration of the fourth year, and of the third class at the expiration of the sixth year, so that one-third may be chosen every second year: and if vacancies happen by resignation or otherwise during the recess of the Legislature of any State, the Executive thereof may make temporary appointments until the next meeting of the Legislature, which shall then fill such vacancies. No person shall be a Senator who shall not have attained to the age of thirty years, and been nine years a citizen of the United States, and who shall not, when elected, be an inhabitant of that State for which he shall be chosen.

2. The Vice-President of the United States shall be President of the Senate, but shall have no vote, unless they be equally divided.

3. The Senate shall choose their other officers, and also a President *pro tempore*, in the absence of the Vice-President, or when he shall exercise the office of President of the United States.

4. The Senate shall have the sole power to try all impeachments. When sitting for that purpose, they shall be on oath or affirmation. When the President of the United States is tried, the Chief Justice shall preside; and no person shall be convicted without the concurrence of two-thirds of the members present.

5. Judgment in cases of impeachment shall not extend further than to removal from office and disqualification to hold and enjoy any office of honor, trust or profit under the United States; but the party convicted shall nevertheless be liable and subject to indictment, trial, judgment and punishment according to law.

Election of Congressmen.

Sect. IV. Times, places and manner of holding elections for Senators and Representatives shall be prescribed in each State by the Legislature thereof; but the Congress may at any time by law make or alter such regulations, except as to the places of choosing Senators. The Congress shall assemble at least once in every year, and such meeting shall be on the first Monday in December, unless they shall by law appoint a different day.

Sect. V.—1. Each House shall be the judge of the elections, returns, and qualifications of its own members, and a majority of each shall constitute a quorum to do business; but a smaller number may adjourn from day to day, and may be authorized to compel the attendance of absent members, in such manner and under such penalties as each House may provide.

General Rules.

2. Each House may determine the rules of its proceedings, punish its members for disorderly behavior, and, with the concurrence of two-thirds, expel a member.

3. Each House shall keep a journal of its proceedings, and from time to time publish the same, excepting such parts as may in their judgment require secrecy; and the yeas and nays of the members of either House on any question shall, at the desire of one-fifth of those present, be entered on the journal.

4. Neither House, during the session of Congress, shall, without the consent of the other, adjourn for more than three days, nor to any other place than that in which the two Houses shall be sitting.

Sect. VI—1. The Senators and Representatives shall receive a compensation for their services, to be ascertained by law, and paid out of the Treasury of the United States. They shall in all cases, except treason, felony, and breach of the peace, be privileged from arrest during their attendance at the session of their respective Houses, and in going to or returning from the same; and for any speech or debate in either House, they shall not be questioned in any other place.

2. No Senator or Representative shall, during the time for which he was elected, be appointed to any civil office under the authority of the United States, which shall have been created, or the emoluments whereof shall have been increased during such time; and no person holding any office under the United States shall be a member of either House during his continuance in office.

Sect. VII—1. All bills for raising revenue shall originate in the House of Representatives; but the Senate may propose or concur with amendments as on other bills.

How Law is Made.

2. Every bill which shall have passed the House of Representatives and the Senate, shall, before it becomes a law, be presented to the President of the United States. If he approve, he shall sign it; but if not, he shall return it, with his objections, to that House in which it shall have originated, who shall enter the objections at large on their journal, and proceed to reconsider it. If, after such reconsideration, two-thirds of that House shall agree to pass the bill, it shall be sent, together with the objections, to the other House, by which it shall likewise be reconsidered, and if approved by two-thirds of that House, it shall become a law. But in all such cases the votes of both Houses shall be determined by yeas and nays, and the names of the persons voting for and against the bill shall be entered on the journal of each House respectively. If any bill shall not be returned by the President within ten days (Sundays excepted) after it shall have been presented to him, the same shall be a law, in like manner as if he had signed it, unless the Congress, by their adjournment, prevent its return, in which case it shall not be a law.

3. Every order, resolution, or vote to which the concurrence of the Senate and House of Representatives may be necessary (except on a question of adjournment) shall be presented to the President of the United States; and before the same shall take effect, shall be approved by him, or, being disapproved by him, shall be repassed by two-thirds of the Senate and House of Representatives, according to the rules and limitations prescribed in the case of a bill.

The Powers of Congress.

Sect. VIII. The Congress shall have power—

1. To lay and collect taxes, duties, imposts and excises, to pay the debts and provide for the common defense and general welfare of the United States; but all duties, imposts, and excises, shall be uniform throughout the United States;

2. To borrow money on the credit of the United States;

3. To regulate commerce with foreign nations and among the several States, and with the Indian tribes;

4. To establish a uniform rule of naturalization, and uniform laws on the subject of bankruptcy throughout the United States.

5. To coin money, regulate the value thereof, and of foreign coin, and fix the standard of weights and measures;

6. To provide for the punishment of counterfeiting the securities and current coin of the United States;

7. To establish post offices and post roads;

8. To promote the progress of science and useful arts, by securing for limited times to authors and inventors the exclusive right to their respective writings and discoveries;

9. To constitute tribunals inferior to the Supreme Court;

10. To define and punish piracies and felonies committed on the high seas, and offenses against the law of nations;

11. To declare war, grant letters of marque and reprisal, and make rules concerning captures on land and water;

12. To raise and support armies, but no appropriations of money to that use shall be for a longer term than two years;

13. To provide and maintain a navy;

14. To make rules for the government and regulation of the land and naval forces;

15. To provide for calling forth the militia to execute the laws of the Union, suppress insurrections, and repel invasions;

16. To provide for organizing, arming, and disciplining the militia, and for governing such parts of them as may be employed in the service of the United States, reserving to the States respectively, the appointment of the officers, and the authority of training the militia according to the discipline prescribed by Congress;

17. To exercise exclusive legislation in all cases whatsoever, over such district (not exceeding ten miles square) as may, by cession of particular States and the acceptance of Congress, become the seat of government of the United States, and to exercise like authority over all places purchased by the consent of the Legislature of the State in which the same shall be, for the erection of forts, magazines, arsenals, dock-yards, and other needful buildings; and,

18. To make all laws which shall be necessary and proper for carrying into execution the foregoing powers and all other powers vested by this Constitution in the Government of the United States, or in any department or officers thereof.

Emigration and Taxes.

Sect. IX.—1. The migration or importation of such persons as any of the States now existing shall think proper to admit, shall not be prohibited by the Congress prior to the year one thousand eight hundred and eight, but a tax or duty may be imposed on such importation, not exceeding ten dollars for each person.

2. The privilege of the writ of habeas corpus shall not be suspended, unless when in cases of rebellion or invasion the public safety may require it.

3. No bill of attainder or ex post facto law shall be passed.

4. No capitation, or other direct tax shall be laid, unless in proportion to the census or enumeration hereinbefore directed to be taken.

5. No tax or duty shall be laid on articles exported from any State. No preference shall be given by any regulation of commerce or revenue to the ports of one State over those of another; nor shall vessels bound to or from one State, be obliged to enter, clear, or pay duties in another.

6. No money shall be drawn from the Treasury, but in consequence of appropriations made by laws; and a regular statement and account of the receipts and expenditures of all public money shall be published from time to time.

Titles Forbidden.

7. No title of nobility shall be granted by the United States, and no person holding any office of profit or trust under them shall, without the consent of the Congress, accept of any present, emolument, office, or title, of any kind whatever, from any king, prince, or foreign state.

Sect. X.—1. No State shall enter into any treaty, alliance, or confederation; grant letters of marque and reprisal; coin money; emit bills of credit; make anything but gold and silver coin a tender in payment of debts; pass any bill of attainder, ex post facto law, or law impairing the obligation of contracts, or grant any title of nobility.

2. No State shall, without the consent of the Congress, lay any impost or duties on imports or exports, except what may be absolutely necessary for executing its inspection laws; and the net produce of all duties and imposts, laid by any State on imports or exports, shall be for the use of the Treasury of the United States; and all such laws shall be subject to the revision and control of the Congress.

3. No State shall, without the consent of Congress, lay any duty of tonnage, keep troops, or ships of war, in time of peace, enter into any agreement or compact with another State, or with a foreign power, or engage in war, unless actually invaded, or in such imminent danger as will not admit of delay.

Election of President.

ARTICLE II.—Sect. I.—1. The executive power shall be vested in a President of the United States of America. He shall hold his office during the term of four years, and, together with the Vice-President, chosen for the same term, be elected, as follows:

2. Each State shall appoint, in such manner as the Legislature thereof may direct, a number of electors, equal to the whole number of Senators and Representatives to which the State may be entitled in the Congress; but no Senator or Representative, or person holding an office of trust or profit under the United States, shall be appointed an elector.

3. (Annulled, see amendments, Article XII.)

4. The Congress may determine the time of choosing the electors, and the day on which they shall give their votes; which day shall be the same throughout the United States.

5. No person except a natural-born citizen, or a citizen of the United States at the time of the adoption of this Constitution, shall be eligible to the office of President; neither shall any person be eligible to that office who shall not have attained to the age of thirty-five years, and been fourteen years a resident within the United States.

6. In case of the removal of the President from office, or of his death, resignation, or inability to discharge the powers and duties of the said office, the same shall devolve on the Vice-President, and the Congress may by law provide for the case of removal, death, resignation, or inability, both of the President and Vice-President, declaring what officer shall then act as President, and such officer shall act accordingly, until the disability be removed, or a President shall be elected.

7. The President shall, at stated times, receive for his services, a compensation, which shall neither be increased or diminished during the period for which he shall have been elected, and he shall not receive within that period, any other emolument from the United States, or any of them.

8. Before he enters on the execution of his office, he shall take the following oath or affirmation:

"I DO SOLEMNLY SWEAR (OR AFFIRM) THAT I WILL FAITHFULLY EXECUTE THE OFFICE OF THE PRESIDENT OF THE UNITED STATES; AND WILL, TO THE BEST OF MY ABILITY, PRESERVE, PROTECT, AND DEFEND THE CONSTITUTION OF THE UNITED STATES."

Powers of the President.

Sect. II.—1. The President shall be commander-in-chief of the army and navy of the United States, and of the militia of the several States when called into the actual service of the United States; he may require the opinion, in writing, of the principal officer in each of the executive departments, upon any subject relating to the duties of their respective offices, and he shall have power to grant reprieves and pardons for offenses against the United States, except in cases of impeachment.

2. He shall have power, by and with the advice and consent of the Senate, to make treaties, provided two-thirds of the Senators present concur; and he shall nominate, and by and with the advice and consent of the Senate, shall appoint embassadors and other public ministers and consuls, judges of the Supreme Court, and all other officers of the United States, whose appointments are not herein otherwise provided for, and which shall be established by law; but the Congress may, by law, vest the appointment of such inferior officers as they think proper, in the President alone, in the courts of law, or in the heads of departments.

3. The President shall have power to fill up all vacancies that may happen during the recess of the Senate, by granting commissions which shall expire at the end of their next session.

Sect. III. He shall from time to time give to the Congress information of the state of the Union, and recommend to their consideration, such measures as he shall judge necessary and expedient; he may, on extraordinary occasions, convene both Houses, or either of them, and in case of disagreement between them, with respect to the time of adjournment, he may adjourn them to such time as he shall think proper; he shall receive embassadors and other public ministers; he shall take care that the laws be faithfully executed and shall commission all officers of the United States.

Sect. IV. The President, Vice-President, and all civil officers of the United States, shall be removed from office on impeachment for, and conviction of, treason, bribery, or other high crimes and misdemeanors.

Administration of Justice.

ARTICLE III.—Sect. I. The Judicial power of the United States, shall be vested in one Supreme Court, and in such inferior courts as the Congress may from time to time ordain and establish. The Judges, both of the Supreme and Inferior Courts, shall hold their offices during good behavior, and shall, at stated times, receive for their services a compensation, which shall not be diminished during their continuance in office.

Sect. II.—1. The Judicial power shall extend to all cases in law and equity, arising under this Constitution, the laws of the United States, and treaties made, or which shall be made, under their authority; to all cases affecting embassadors, other public ministers and consuls; to all cases of admiralty and maritime jurisdiction; to controversies to which the United States shall be a party; to controversies between two or more States; between a State and citizens of another State; between citizens of different States; between citizens of the same State claiming lands under grants of different States, and between a State or the citizens thereof and foreign States, citizens, or subjects.

2. In all cases affecting embassadors, other public ministers and consuls, and those in which a State shall be a party, the Supreme Court shall have original jurisdiction. In all the other cases before mentioned, the Supreme Court shall have appellate jurisdiction, both as to law and fact, with such exceptions, and under such regulations as the Congress shall make.

3. The trial of all crimes, except in cases of impeachment, shall be by jury; and such trial shall be held in the State where the said crimes shall have been committed; but when not committed within any State, the trial shall be at such place or places as the Congress may by law have directed.

Sect. III.—1. Treason against the United States shall consist only in levying war against them, or in adhering to their enemies, giving them aid and comfort. No person shall be convicted of treason unless on the testimony of two witnesses to the same overt act, or on confession in open court.

2. The Congress shall have power to declare the punishment of treason, but no attainder of treason shall work corruption of blood or forfeiture, except during the life of the person attainted.

Rights of the Several States.

ARTICLE IV.—Sect. I. Full faith and credit shall be given in each State to the public acts, records and judicial proceedings of every other State. And the Congress may by general laws, prescribe the manner in which such acts, records and proceedings shall be proved, and the effect thereof.

Sect. II.—1. The citizens of each State shall be entitled to all privileges and immunities of citizens in the several States.

2. A person charged in any State with treason, felony, or other crime, who shall flee from justice and be found in another State, shall, on demand of the executive authority of the State from which he fled, be delivered up, to be removed to the State having jurisdiction of the crime.

3. No person held to service or labor in one State under the laws thereof, escaping into another, shall, in consequence of any law or regulation therein, be discharged from such service or labor, but shall be delivered up on claim of the party to whom such service or labor may be due.

Sect. III.—1. New States may be admitted by the Congress of this Union; but no new States shall be formed or erected within the jurisdiction of any other State; nor any State be formed by the junction of two or more States, or parts of States, without the consent of the Legislatures of the States concerned as well as of the Congress.

2. The Congress shall have power to dispose of and make all needful rules and regulations respecting the territory or other property belonging to the United States; and nothing in this Constitution shall be so construed as to prejudice any claims of the United States, or of any particular State.

Sect. IV. The United States shall guarantee to every State in this Union a Republican form of government, and shall protect each of them against invasion; and on application of the Legislature or of the executive (when the Legislature cannot be convened), against domestic violence.

How Amendments May be Made

ARTICLE V. The Congress, whenever two-thirds of both Houses shall deem it necessary, shall propose amendments to this Constitution, or, on the application of the Legislatures of two-thirds of the several States, shall call a convention for proposing amendments, which, in either case, shall be valid to all intents and purposes, as part of this Constitution, when ratified by the Legislatures of three-fourths of the several States, or by conventions in three-fourths thereof, as the one or the other mode of ratification may be proposed by the Congress; provided that no amendment which may be made prior to the year one thousand eight hundred and eight, shall in any manner affect the first and fourth clauses in the ninth section of the first article; and that no State, without its consent shall be deprived of its equal suffrage in the Senate.

ARTICLE VI.—1. All debts contracted, and engagements entered into, before the adoption of this Constitution, shall be as valid against the United States under this Constitution, as under the confederation.

2. This Constitution, and the laws of the United States which shall be made in pursuance thereof; and all treaties made or which shall be made, under authority of the United States, shall be the supreme law of the land; and the judges in every State shall be bound thereby, anything in the constitution or laws of any State to the contrary notwithstanding.

3. The Senators and Representatives before mentioned, and the members of the several State Legislatures, and all executive and judicial officers both of the United States and of the several States, shall be bound by oath or affirmation to support this Constitution; but no religious test shall ever be required as a qualification to any office or public trust under the United States.

ARTICLE VII. The ratification of the conventions of nine States, shall be sufficient for the establishment of this Constitution between the States so ratifying the same.

AMENDMENTS TO THE CONSTITUTION.

ARTICLE I. Congress shall make no law respecting an establishment of religion, or prohibiting the free exercise thereof; or abridging the freedom of speech or of the press; or the right of the people peaceably to assemble and to petition the government for a redress of grievances.

ARTICLE II. A well regulated militia being necessary to the security of a free State, the right of the people to keep and bear arms shall not be infringed.

ARTICLE III. No soldier shall, in time of peace, be quartered in any house without the consent of the owner; nor in time of war, but in a manner to be prescribed by law.

ARTICLE IV. The right of the people to be secure in their persons, houses, papers, and effects, against unreasonable searches and seizures, shall not be violated; and no warrants shall issue, but upon probable cause, supported by oath or affirmation, and particularly describing the place to be searched, and the persons or things to be seized.

ARTICLE V. No person shall be held to answer for a capital or otherwise infamous crime, unless on a presentment or indictment of a Grand Jury, except in cases arising in the land or naval forces, or in the militia, when in actual service in time of war or public danger; nor shall any person be subject for the same offense to be twice put in jeopardy of life or limb; nor shall be compelled in any criminal case to be a witness against himself, nor be deprived of life, liberty, or property, without due process of law; nor shall private property be taken for public use, without just compensation.

Trial by Jury.

ARTICLE VI. In all criminal prosecutions, the accused shall enjoy the right to a speedy and public trial, by an impartial jury of the State and district wherein the crime shall have been committed, which district shall have been previously ascertained by law, and to be informed of the nature and cause of the accusation; to be confronted with the witnesses against him; to have compulsory process for obtaining witnesses in his favor; and to have the assistance of counsel for his defense.

ARTICLE VII. In suits at common law, where the value in controversy shall exceed twenty dollars, the right of trial by jury shall be preserved, and no fact tried by a jury shall be otherwise re-examined in any court of the United States, than according to the rules of the common law.

ARTICLE VIII. Excessive bail shall not be required, nor excessive fines imposed, nor cruel and unusual punishments inflicted.

ARTICLE IX. The enumeration, in the Constitution, of certain rights, shall not be construed to deny or disparage others retained by the people.

ARTICLE X. The powers not delegated to the United States by the Constitution, nor prohibited by it to the States, are reserved to the States respectively, or to the people.

ARTICLE XI. The judicial power of the United States shall not be construed to extend to any suit in law or equity, commenced or prosecuted against one of the United States by citizens of another State, or by citizens or subjects of any foreign State.

The Electoral Vote.

ARTICLE XII.—1. The electors shall meet in their respective States, and vote by ballot for President and Vice-President, one of whom at least shall not be an inhabitant of the same State with themselves. They shall name in their ballots the person voted for as President, and in distinct ballots the person voted for as Vice-President; and they shall make distinct lists of all persons voted for as President, and of all persons voted for as Vice-President, and of the number of votes for each, which lists they shall sign and certify, and transmit sealed to the seat of the Government of the United States, directed to the President of the Senate. The President of the Senate shall, in the presence of the Senate and House of Representatives, open all the certificates, and the votes shall then be counted. The person having the greatest number of votes for President shall be the President, if such number be a majority of the whole number of electors appointed; and if no persons have such majority, then from the persons having the highest numbers, not exceeding three on the list of those voted for as President, the House of Representatives shall choose immediately, by ballot, the President. But in choosing the President, the votes shall be taken by States, the representation from each State having one vote. A quorum for this purpose shall consist of a member or members from two-thirds of the States, and a majority of all the States shall be necessary to a choice. And if the House of Representatives shall not choose a President whenever the right of choice shall devolve upon them, before the fourth day of March next following, then the Vice-President shall act as President, as in the case of the death or other constitutional disability of the President.

2. The person having the greatest number of votes as Vice-President shall be the Vice-President, if such number be a majority of the whole number of electors appointed; and if no person have a majority, then from the two highest numbers on the list, the Senate shall choose a Vice-President. A quorum for the purpose shall consist of two-thirds of the whole number of Senators, and a majority of the whole number shall be necessary to a choice.

3. But no person constitutionally ineligible to the office of President, shall be eligible to that of Vice-President of the United States.

ARTICLE XIII.—1. Neither slavery nor involuntary servitude, except as a punishment for crime, whereof the party shall have been duly convicted, shall exist within the United States or any place subject to their jurisdiction.

2. Congress shall have power to enforce this article by appropriate legislation.

Who are Citizens.

ARTICLE XIV. — Sect. 1. All persons born or naturalized in the United States, and subject to the jurisdiction thereof, are citizens of the United States and of the State in which they reside. No State shall make or enforce any law which shall abridge the privileges or immunities of citizens of the United States. Nor shall any State deprive any person of life, liberty, or property, without due process of law, nor deny to any person within its jurisdiction the equal protection of the laws.

Sect. II. Representatives shall be apportioned among the several States according to their respective numbers, counting the whole number of persons in each State, excluding Indians not taxed. But when the right to vote at any election for the choice of electors for President and Vice-

President of the United States, Representatives in Congress, the executive and judicial officers of a State, or the members of the Legislatures thereof, is denied to any of the male inhabitants of such a State, being twenty-one years of age and citizens of the United States, or in any way abridged, except for participation in rebellion or other crime, the basis of representation therein shall be reduced in the proportion which the number of such male citizens shall bear to the whole number of male citizens twenty-one years of age in such State.

Sect. III. No person shall be a Senator or Representative in Congress, or elector of President and Vice-President, or hold any office, civil or military, under the United States or under any State, who, having previously taken an oath as a member of Congress, or as an officer of the United States, or as a member of any State Legislature, or as an executive or judicial officer of any State, to support the Constitution of the United States, shall have engaged in insurrection or rebellion against the same, or given aid or comfort to the enemies thereof, but Congress may, by

a vote of two-thirds of each House, remove such disability.

What Debts Shall be Paid.

Sect. IV. The validity of the public debt of the United States, authorized by law, including debts incurred for payment of pensions and bounties for services in supressing insurrection or rebellion, shall not be questioned; but neither the United States nor any State shall assume or pay any debt or obligation incurred in aid of insurrection or rebellion against the United States, or any claim for the loss or emancipation of any slave; but all such debts, obligations, and claims, shall be held illegal and void.

Sect. V. The Congress shall have power to enforce, by appropriate legislation, the provisions of this article.

ARTICLE XV.—Sect. I. The right of citizens of the United States to vote shall not be denied or abridged by the United States or any State on account of race, color, or previous condition of servitude.

Sect. II. The Congress shall have power to enforce this article by appropriate legislation.

The First Congresses.

HE first Continental Congress, formed while the thirteen colonies were yet under British dominion, exerted no political influence, and had no part in the government of the United States, for it dissolved before the signing of the Declaration of Independence. It met in Carpenters' Hall, Philadelphia, Pa., September 5, 1774, and adjourned October 26, the same year.

The second Congress assembled at the Pennsylvania State House, Philadelphia, May 10, 1775, and on July 4, 1776, adopted the Declaration of Independence.

The third Congress was held at Baltimore, Md., beginning December 20, 1776.

The fourth Congress opened at Philadelphia, March 4, 1777.

The fifth Congress began its session at Lancaster, Pa., September 27, 1777.

The sixth Congress met at York, Pa., September 30, 1777.

The seventh Congress gathered at Philadelphia, July 2, 1778.

The eighth Congress was held at Princeton, N. J., June 30, 1783.

The ninth Congress opened at Annapolis, Md., November 26, 1783, and here, December 23, 1783, Washington resigned his office of commander-in-chief of the army.

The tenth Congress began at Trenton, N. J., November 1, 1784.

The eleventh Congress assembled at the City Hall, in New York, January 11, 1785, where the new government was organized, and Washington, the first president, was inaugurated in 1789. The Federal capital remained at New York until 1790.

Congress met again at Philadelphia, December 6, 1790, and the seat of government remained here until 1800, at which time the Federal capital was permanently established at Washington, D. C., Congress first assembling in that city November 17, 1800.

The First Presidential Election.

ACH of the thirteen original States having duly accepted the Federal Constitution, it was ratified by Congress, and went into operation in 1789. At this time public opinion pointed unmistakably to General Washington as the first President of the new republic. The first Wednesday of January, 1789, was set apart for the choice of presidential electors in each of the States by the voters thereof; the first Wednesday of February, 1789, was fixed upon for the selection of a President by the chosen electors, and the first Wednesday of March, 1789, as the date when the new administration of governmental affairs should commence operations.

The first Congress of the Federal Union met without a quorum in the House of Representatives, and did not organize until March 30, 1789, nor did the Senate convene until April 6, following, at which time presidential ballots were counted. All the States, except New York (which neglected, through indifference, to hold an election), had chosen presidential electors, and Washington was their unanimous choice for President, receiving sixty-nine votes, while John Adams, having received thirty-four votes, was declared Vice-President.

April 30, 1789, the new executive officers were publicly inaugurated at the City Hall, in New York; and thus the Republic began its long career of prosperity, with a government as complete as that of either Great Britain or France.

Duties of Principal Federal Officers.

N ORDER to become acquainted with the general government of the country, the reader should first carefully study the Constitution of the United States, which is herewith given, with headings, displayed in a manner such as to make it easily understood.

To become familiar with the State, county, town and municipal government, and the duties of persons in the several State, county, town and city offices, the student should acquaint himself or herself with the Constitution of the State in which he or she may be a resident, and follow with a reading of the statutes of that particular State.

The object of this chapter is to give the reader an understanding of the duties of some of the leading federal officers, together with a view of the manner in which Congressional law is made and the country governed.

The article on the duties of Congressmen very fully reveals the method of procedure in the passage of bills that make up the laws of the land, some of which may be only for personal benefit, while others are necessary and are framed for the general good.

Through laws thus passed by Congress, have the general federal offices been created. The succeeding pages quite fully outline the frame-work of the general government.

President's Mansion, Washington, D. C.

The President of the United States.

THE PRESIDENT must be thirty-five years old, a native of the United States, and a resident of the United States fourteen years.

He holds office for four years, and swears to preserve, protect and defend the Constitution of the United States, to the best of his ability.

He is commander-in-chief of the army and navy of the United States, and of the militia of the several States, when it is called into actual service of the nation; and may require the opinion, in writing, of the principal officer in each of the executive departments upon any subject relating to the duties of their respective offices.

He has power to grant pardons for offenses against the United States, except in cases of impeachment; has power, by and with the advice and consent of the United States Senate, to make treaties (provided that two-thirds of the Senators present concur); and shall nominate and, by and with the advice and consent of the Senate, appoint embassadors, ministers, and consuls to foreign countries, judges of the Supreme Court of the United States, and all other officers of the United States, whose appointments are not otherwise provided for in other ways or established by law. If vacancies occur during the recess of the Senate, the President may grant commissions to new appointees which shall expire at the end of the next session of the Senate.

From time to time he is to give Congress information of the state of the Union, and recommend such legislation as shall to him seem necessary and expedient; on extraordinary occasions, or in a national emergency, he may call either house of Congress, or both, as he pleases, to convene, and if they disagree as to the time when they shall adjourn, he may adjourn them, as he may deem best.

He shall sign all bills passed by Congress before they can become law; but he may return to the house where it originated, any bill, order, or resolution, with his objections, which he cannot approve. If he fails to sign it, or return it to Congress within ten days after its passage, it becomes a law without his approval.

His term of office begins on the 4th day of March next succeeding his election; his salary shall be $50,000 a year, to be paid monthly, and he has the use of the furniture and other effects, belonging to the United States, that are usually kept in the President's mansion known as the "White House," where he resides.

WASHINGTON
1st President.

J. ADAMS
2d President.

JEFFERSON
3d President.

MADISON
4th President.

MONROE
5th President.

J. Q. ADAMS
6th President.

JACKSON
7th President.

VAN BUREN
8th President.

HARRISON
9th President.

TYLER
10th President.

ARTHUR.
21st President.

CLEVELAND
22nd President.

POLK
11th President.

TAYLOR
12th President.

FILMORE
13th President.

PIERCE
14th President.

BUCHANAN
15th President.

LINCOLN
16th President.

JOHNSON
17th President.

GRANT
18th President.

HAYES.
19th President.

GARFIELD.
20th President.

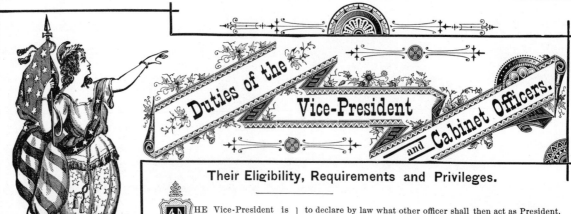

Their Eligibility, Requirements and Privileges.

THE Vice-President is elected at the same time and by the same process as the President of the United States. No man who is ineligible for the office of President can be elected Vice-President. He goes into office with the President, and their terms of office expire on the same day.

In case the President resigns or dies, or becomes unable to exercise the functions of his office, or is removed from it, the duties of his position shall be performed by the Vice-President during the remainder of the term for which both were elected. In case both die or resign or become unable to perform the duties required of them, or are removed from office, Congress has the power to declare by law what other officer shall then act as President.

The Vice-President is, by virtue of his office, the President of the United States Senate, and in case of his death, removal, resignation, or inability, the Senate may elect a presiding officer of the Senate, who shall also be President of the United States should any cause create a vacancy in that office. The Vice-President may be removed from his office on impeachment for, and conviction of, treason, bribery, or other high crimes or misdemeanors.

As presiding officer of the Senate, he cannot vote except when there is an equal division of the Senate on any question, and his vote is decisive.

It is his duty, also, as presiding officer of the Senate, to open, in the presence of the assembled Senate and House of Representatives, all the certificates of the election of the President and Vice-President of the United States, and superintend the counting of the votes accompanying the certificates.

Duties of the Several Members of the President's Cabinet.

THE EXECUTIVE departments of the United States government are seven in number: the Department of State, the Department of War, the Department of the Treasury, the Department of Justice, the Department of the Navy, the Department of the Interior, the Post-office Department. The Department of Justice is governed by the Attorney-General, the Post-office Department by the Postmaster-General, and the others by secretaries, respectively. Each head of a department is entitled to a salary of $8,000 a year, payable monthly.

The head of each department is authorized to prescribe regulations, not inconsistent with law, for its government, the conduct of its officers and clerks, the distribution and performance of its business, and the custody, use and preservation of the records, papers and property pertaining to it.

From the first day of October until the first day of April, in each year, all the bureaus and offices in the State, War, Treasury, Navy and Post-office Departments, and in the General Land Office (at Washington) are required to be open for the transaction of the public business at least eight hours in each day; and from the first day of April until the first day of October, in each year, at least ten hours in each day, except Sundays and days designated by law as public holidays.

The clerks in the departments are arranged in four classes, distinguished as the first, second, third and fourth classes. No clerk can be appointed in either of these classes, in any department, until he has been examined and found qualified by a board of three examiners, consisting of the chief of the bureau or office into which such clerk is to be appointed, and two other clerks to be selected by the head of the department. Women may, at the discretion of the head of any department, be appointed to any of the clerkships therein authorized by law, upon the same qualifications, requisites and conditions, and with the same compensations as are prescribed for men. Each head of a department may, from time to time, alter the distribution among the various bureaus and offices of his department of the clerks prescribed by law, as he may find it proper and necessary so to do.

Clerks and employes in the departments, whose compensation is not otherwise prescribed, receive the following salaries per year:

First Class Clerks.	$1,200	Fourth Class Clks..	$1,800	Asst. Messengers...	$720
Second do ..	1,400	Women Clerks.....	900	Laborers	720
Third do ..	1,600	Messengers	840	Watchmen	720

Temporary clerks, performing duties similar to those in either class, are entitled to a salary of the same rate as permanent clerks.

Each head of a department is authorized to employ as many clerks of all classes, and such other employes, at such rates of compensation, respectively, as Congress may, from year to year, appropriate money for paying them. No money can be paid to any clerk employed in either department at an annual salary, as compensation for extra services, unless expressly authorized by law. Further restrictions are also placed upon the employment of extra and temporary clerks and subordinate assistants in the departments, and the law prescribes the rates of their compensation, in case their employment becomes necessary.

The chief clerks in the several departments and bureaus and other offices connected therewith have supervision, under their immediate superior, over the duties of the other clerks therein, and see that they are faithfully performed. And it is also the business of the chief clerks to take care, from time to time, that the duties of the other clerks are distributed among them with equality and uniformity, according to the nature of the case. The chief clerks also report monthly to their superior officers any existing defects that they may know of in the arrangement or dispatch of the public business; and each head of a department, chief of a bureau, or other superior officer must examine the facts as stated, and take proper measures to amend such existing defects.

The disbursing clerks authorized by law in any department are appointed by the heads of the departments from clerks of the fourth class. Each of these clerks is required to give a bond to the United States for the faithful discharge of the duties of his office, according to law, in such amount as may be directed by the Secretary of the Treasury, and with sureties approved by the Solicitor of the Treasury, and renew, strengthen and increase the amount of such bond, from time to time, as the Secretary of the Treasury may direct.

Each disbursing clerk, except the one employed in the Treasury Department, may, when so directed by the head of his department, superintend the building which it occupies.

Each disbursing clerk, in addition to his salary as a clerk of the fourth class, is entitled to receive $200 more a year, or $2,000 in all.

In case of the death, resignation, absence or sickness of the head of any department, the first or sole assistant thereof, unless the President directs otherwise, performs the duties of such head until a successor is appointed or the sickness or absence ceases.

In case of the death, resignation, absence or sickness of the chief of any bureau, or any officer thereof whose appointment is not vested in the head of the department, the assistant or deputy of such chief or officer, or his chief clerk, may perform the duties of his superior, unless the President orders otherwise.

The President, in case of the vacancies created as above mentioned, may authorize and direct the head of any other department, or any other officer in either department (whose appointment is vested in the President) to perform the duties of the vacant office until a successor is appointed, or the sickness or absence of the incumbent ceases. But no vacancy of this kind, occasioned by death or resignation, may be temporarily filled for a longer time than ten days. And any officer performing the duties of another office, during such vacancy, is not entitled to any compensation beyond his own proper salary.

Officers or clerks of any department, when lawfully detailed to investigate frauds or attempts to defraud the government, or any official misconduct or irregularity, are authorized to administer oaths to witnesses; and any head of a department or bureau may, when any investigation in his department requires it, subpœna witnesses before the proper officer, to testify in the case, and resort to compulsion by the court to enforce the attendance of such witnesses. Heads of departments or bureaus are furnished the necessary legal assistance by the Attorney-General; and evidence is to be furnished by the departments in suits pending in the court of claims.

Each department is allowed to expend $100 a year for newspapers, to be filed in that department. The head of each department makes an annual report to Congress, giving a detailed statement of the manner in which the contingent fund for his department has been expended, the names of every person to whom any of it has been

President Lincoln and His Cabinet.

THE above pictorial illustration is from F. B. Carpenter's painting, made at the White House, in Washington, in 1864, representing the memorable meeting of Lincoln and his cabinet assembled to listen to the first reading of the Emancipation Proclamation.

Some of the sketches will be readily recognized. In the picture William H. Seward, Secretary of State, who sits in front of the table, is evidently considering certain features of the document. Edwin M. Stanton, head of the War Department, sitting at the extreme left, listens intently; so, also does Salmon P. Chase, Secretary of the Treasury, who stands with arms folded. Lincoln, as he sits with paper in hand, is all attention; so is Gideon Welles, head of the Navy, who, in long, white beard, sits opposite Seward. Caleb Smith, Secretary of the Interior, stands next to Welles; Montgomery Blair, Postmaster-General, stands beside Smith, and Edward Bates, Attorney-General sits at the extreme right.

Altogether the faces and the scene represented will go down into the future as one of the memorable events connected with the efforts made for the preservation of the American Union in the dark and troublous days of the rebellion.

paid, the nature of the service rendered, the kind of property furnished, and its price, etc. ; he also reports to Congress, annually, the names of the clerks and other persons who have been employed in his department and its offices, the time and manner of their employment, the sums paid to each, whether they have been useful, need to be removed, etc.

The Secretaries of State, the Treasury, the Interior, War and Navy, the Postmaster-General, the Attorney-General and the Commissioner of Agriculture, are required to keep a complete inventory of all the property belonging to the United States in the buildings, rooms, offices and grounds occupied by them, respectively, and under their charge, as well as an account of the sale or other disposition of

any of such property, except supplies of stationery and fuel in the public offices, and books, pamphlets and papers in the library of Congress.

The head of each department is required, as soon as practicable after the last day of September, in the year whenever a new Congress assembles, to cause to be filed in the office of the Secretary of the Interior, a full and complete list of all officers, agents, clerks and employes in his department, or in any of the offices or bureaus connected with it. Such list must include, also, all the statistics peculiar to his department required to enable the Secretary of the Interior to prepare the Biennial Register.

THE SECRETARY OF STATE.

A Summary of His Duties.

HE duties of the Secretary of State are from time to time prescribed by the President of the United States, and relate principally to carrying on correspondence, issuing commissions or instructions to or with public ministers or consuls from the United States, or to negotiations with public ministers from foreign states or princes, or to memorials or other applications from foreign public ministers or other foreigners, or to such other matters respecting foreign affairs as the President of the United States assigns to the department; and he conducts the business of the department in such manner as the President shall direct. He has custody of the seal of the United States, and of the seal of the Department of State, and of all the books, records, papers, furniture, fixtures and other property in or belonging to the department.

When the President has approved and signed any bill, order, resolution or vote passed by Congress, or which becomes a law in any other prescribed manner, the Secretary of State shall receive it from the President or the Speaker of the House of Representatives, and give it due publication in print in the manner ordered by law. Also, when any new amendment to the national Constitution has been legally adopted, the Secretary of State shall give it due publication as prescribed in the statutes.

Annual Reports.

He shall report annually to Congress the following particulars:

An abstract of all the returns made to him pursuant to law by customs collectors at the various ports of the country, of seamen registered by them, and impressments of seamen and detention of vessels by foreign authorities.

A statement of all such changes and modifications in the commercial systems of other nations, in any manner made, as shall have been communicated to his department.

Important information communicated by diplomatic and consular officers if he deems it valuable for publication to the people.

A full list of all consular officers.

A report of any rates or tariff of fees to be received by diplomatic or consular officers, prescribed by the President during the preceding year.

A statement of such fees as have been collected and accounted for by such officers during the preceding year.

A statement of lists of passengers arriving in the United States from foreign places, returned to him every three months by collectors of customs.

Names of any consular officers of foreign citizenship who may have been employed under salaries, and the circumstances of their appointment.

A statement of expenditures from the contingent fund required to be made by him, which must include all the contingent expenses of foreign intercourse and of all foreign ministers and their offices, except such expenditures as are settled upon the certificate of the President.

Every act of Congress that becomes a law of the land by regular process, together with every foreign treaty, postal convention, or congressional joint resolution adopted, must be sent to the public printer for legal publication by the Secretary of State, who is also to publish in one or more newspapers (not exceeding three) such commercial information that he may receive from diplomatic and consular officers as he may consider important to the public interests.

Passports.

It is from this department, also, that passports are furnished, free of charge, to all persons who desire to travel in foreign countries where passports are necessary. Copies of records in this department are copied by clerks for all persons at a cost to the applicant of ten cents for each 100 words in the desired statement.

Annual Salaries of Assistant Officers.

The subordinate officers of this department, with their salaries, are as follows:

3 Asst. Secretaries $3,500	11 Clerks $1,800	2 Clerks $1,000
1 Chief Clerk..... 2,500	4 do 1,600	10 do 900
1 Translator...... 2,100	2 do 1,400	1 Engineer 1,200
4 Bureau Chiefs.. 2,100	10 do 1,200	1 Assistant 1,000

Messengers, Watchmen, Firemen, Laborers, etc., ranging from $660 to $840.

Each chief clerk has the supervision of the clerks in his bureau or division of the department, and regulates the amount and character of the duties of each, reporting particulars concerning such clerks, their short-comings, etc., to his superior officer monthly. In case of the death, removal, resignation, sickness, or incapacity of the head of any bureau, the next officer below him performs his duties until a successor is appointed.

SECRETARY ... OF WAR.

An Outline Sketch of His Official Work, the Number of His Assistants and their Salaries.

THE EXECUTIVE of War is appointed by the President to assist in carrying on the government of the country, and performs such duties as shall from time to time be enjoined on or intrusted to him by the President relative to military commissions, the military forces, the warlike stores of the United States, or to other matters respecting military affairs.

He must prepare and communicate to Congress estimates of necessary expenditures and needed appropriations for his department, including estimates for such sums as will be required to print and bind documents relating to his department, and for the compensation of his subordinate officers and clerks, and estimates for the construction of public works. All estimates for the public service in this and all other Cabinet departments are transmitted to Congress by the Secretary of the Treasury.

The Secretary of War has the custody and charge of all the books, records, papers, furniture, fixtures, and other property belonging to his department; controls the collection at the seat of government of all flags, standards, and military colors captured by the army from the enemies of the country; defines and prescribes the kinds and amounts of supplies to be purchased by the subsistence and quartermasters' departments of the army; regulates the transportation of supplies from the places of purchase to the several military posts or stations at which they are required, and the safe-keeping and storage of such supplies, provisions, etc., and the transportation of troops, munitions of war, equipments and stores; provides for the taking of weather observations at military stations in the interior of the continent, and other points in the States and Territories; for giving notice on the Northern lakes and sea-coast, by magnetic telegraph, of the approach and force of storms, and for the establishment and reports of signal offices in various parts of the country concerning the weather, for the benefit of agricultural and commercial interests, with telegraph lines to connect weather-reporting stations, etc. ; furnishes non-commissioned officers and soldiers who have in any manner lost their certificates of discharge from the army with duplicate certificates; details employes of the department to administer proper oaths in the settlement of officers' accounts for clothing, camp and garrison equipage, quartermasters' stores, cannon, etc.

The Secretary of War must report to Congress annually a statement of the appropriations of the preceding fiscal year (beginning always July 1) for his department, showing how much was appropriated under each specific bureau or branch of the department, and the balance that remained on hand unexpended, together with his estimates of the amounts of appropriations, specifically stated, that will probably be needed for the ensuing year, aside from what may remain of the balances in his hand; also a statement of all his official contracts for supplies or services during the preceding year, military expenses, etc.

Another important duty of the Secretary is to submit to Congress reports of river and harbor examinations and surveys made by order of Congress, with statements showing the extent to which the commerce of the country will be promoted by the contemplated improvement of these rivers and harbors, with a view to the wisest appropriation and expenditure of the public money in this direction.

Once a year, he reports to Congress an abstract of the returns of the Adjutants-General relative to the militia of the several States.

The annual reports of the Secretary to Congress are made at the beginning of each regular session, and embrace the transactions of his department during the preceding year.

The War Department is divided into branches, governed by the following army officers: The Adjutant-General, Quartermaster-General, Paymaster-General, Commissary-General, Surgeon-General, Chief of Engineers, Chief of Ordnance, and the Court of Military Justice.

Annual Salaries of Assistant Officers.

1 Chief Clerk.... $2,750	1 Printer......... $1,600	6 Compositors ... $1,000
1 Disbursing Clk. 2,000	95 Clerks.......... 1,400	32 Clerks.......... 900
7 Bureau Chiefs. 2,000	1 Engineer....... 1,400	1 Messenger 840
52 Clerks.......... 1,800	390 Clerks......... 1,200	64 Messengers, etc. 720
1 Draughtsman.. 1,800	2 Engineers..... 1,200	50 Laborers....... 660
52 Clerks.......... 1,600	1 Pressman...... 1,200	8 Charwomen.... 180
1 Anatomist..... 1,600	191 Clerks......... 1,000	

There are also 125 private physicians, at Washington and various military posts, who receive $100 a month, with quarters and fuel; 185 hospital stewards, at $20 to $35 a month, with rations, quarters, fuel, and clothing; about fifty paymaster's clerks, at $1,200 a year; ninety national cemetery keepers, at from $720 to $900 a year, with residences; 450 weather observers in the Signal service, at from $25 to $100 a month, with allowances; about 500 employes at armories and arsenals, and 450 clerks, superintendents, janitors of the several buildings of the department, at rates ranging from $40 to $200 a month.

Equipment, Salaries and Duties of Army Officers.

THE PRESIDENT of the United States is the commander-in-chief of the army.

The army of the United States, on a peace footing, consists of five regiments of artillery, ten regiments of cavalry, twenty-five regiments of infantry, an Adjutant-General's department, an Inspector-General's department, a Quartermaster's department, a Subsistence department, a corps of engineers, a battalion of engineer soldiers, an Ordnance department, the enlisted men of the Ordnance department, a Medical department, with its corps of hospital stewards, a Pay department, a Bureau of Military Justice, a force of Indian scouts, not exceeding 1,000; officers on the army retired list, and the Professors and corps of Cadets, and a military band at the West Point Military academy.

What Constitutes a Regiment.

A regiment of artillery consists of twelve batteries of artillery (or cannoniers), and each battery has not exceeding 122 private soldiers attached to it. One battery in each regiment is equipped as light or flying artillery, so called from the rapidity with which it can be moved; seats being contrived for the men who work it, with sufficient horses to enable them to proceed at a gallop.

A regiment of cavalry consists of twelve troops of mounted soldiers, each troop containing not more than seventy-eight enlisted privates. Two regiments of the cavalry are made up of enlisted colored privates. Any of the cavalry force may be dismounted and armed and drilled as infantry, at the discretion of the President.

A regiment of infantry consists of ten companies, each company containing from fifty to 100 privates, as the exigencies of the service may require. The enlisted men of two regiments of infantry are colored men.

There can not be in the army, at one time, more than 30,000 enlisted men.

Duty of Quartermasters.

The Quartermaster's department has charge of purchasing and distributing to the army (and marines in land service) all military stores and supplies requisite for their use, which other corps are not directed by law to provide; to furnish means of transportation for the army, its military stores and supplies, and to pay for, and to provide for and pay all incidental expenses of the military service, which other corps are not directed to provide for and pay.

The Subsistence department is in charge of picked subordinate officers, whose duty it is to receive, at each military post or place of deposit and preserve, the subsistence supplies of the army, under regulations prescribed by the Secretary of War, and to purchase and issue to the army such supplies as enter into the composition of the army ration.

Duty of Military Engineers.

The Corps of Engineers regulates and determines, with the approval of the Secretary of War, the number, quality, form, and dimensions of the necessary vehicles, pontoons, tools, implements, arms and other supplies for the use of the battalion of engineer soldiers. This battalion consists of five companies of enlisted privates of the first and second class, each company containing not more than sixty-four privates of each class. This battalion is recruited and organized, with the same limitations, provisions, allowances, and benefits, in every respect like other troops on a peace footing.

The enlisted men are instructed in, and perform the duties of, sappers, miners, and pontooniers; aid in giving practical instruction in those branches at the West Point military academy, and may be detailed to oversee and aid laborers upon fortifications and other works in charge of the engineer corps of the government, and, as fort-keepers, to protect and repair finished fortifications; but engineers cannot assume nor be ordered on any duty beyond the line of their immediate profession, except by a special order of the President, who may also transfer engineers from one corps to another, regard being paid to rank.

Ordnance Department.

The Ordnance department has in charge the enlistment, under the direction of the Secretary of War, of master-armorers, master-carriage makers, and master-blacksmiths, who are mustered in as sergeants; subordinate armorers, carriage-makers and blacksmiths are mustered as corporals; artificers, as privates of the first-class, and laborers, as privates of the second-class. The Chief of Ordnance, subject to the approval of the Secretary of War, organizes and details to other military organizations or garrisons such numbers of ordnance enlisted men, furnished with proper tools, carriages and apparatus as may be necessary, and makes regulations for their government; he also furnishes estimates, and, under the direction of the Secretary of War, makes contracts and purchases, for procuring the necessary supplies of ordnance and ordnance stores for the use of the United States army; directs the inspection and proving of the same, and the construction of all cannon and carriages, and ammunition wagons, traveling forges, arti-ficers' wagons, and of every implement and apparatus for ordnance, and the preparation of all kinds of prescribed ammunition and ordnance stores; establishes depots of ordnance and ordnance stores, in such parts of the United States, and in such numbers as may be deemed necessary; executes, or causes to be executed, all orders of the Secretary of War, and (in time of war) the orders of any general or field officer commanding an army or detachment, for the required supply of all ordnance and ordnance stores for active service; and, half-yearly, or oftener, he makes a report to the Secretary of War of all the officers and enlisted men in his department, and of all ordnance and ordnance stores under his control.

The Army Medical Department.

The Medical department furnishes surgical or medical aid to members of the army; has supervision of the purchase and distribution of the hospital and medical supplies; unites with the line officers of the army, under the rules and regulations of the Secretary of War, in superintending the cooking done by the enlisted men; attends, under the direction of the Surgeon-General, to the proper preparation of the rations for the enlisted men; provides such quantities of fresh or preserved fruits, milk, butter and eggs, as may be necessary for the proper diet of the sick in hospitals, and trusses for ruptured soldiers or pensioners.

The Pay department is charged with the punctual payment of the troops, and is presided over by the Paymaster-General, and as many assistant paymasters as are required to perform that duty.

The Bureau of Military Justice has control of the proceedings of courts-martial, courts of military inquiry, military commissions, etc.

Salaries of Leading Army Officers.

The General of the army ranks next in command to the President in the control of the national troops. He has a salary of $13,500 a year, and selects from the army such a number of aids, not exceeding six, as he may deem necessary, who, while serving on his staff, bear the rank of colonels of cavalry.

The Lieutenant-General of the army ranks next below the General; has a salary of $11,000 a year, and is allowed to select from the army two aids and a military secretary, who rank as lieutenant-colonels of cavalry while serving on his staff.

Three Major-Generals have command under the Lieutenant-General. Each is entitled to $7,500 a year, forage for five horses, and three aids, whom he may select from captains or lieutenants in the army, whose pay over and above the pay of their rank is $200 a year.

Six Brigadier-Generals, each drawing $5,500 a year, and each having two aids, who may be selected by him from lieutenants in the army. Each draws forage for four horses.

Officers of a Regiment of Artillery.

Each regiment of artillery is commanded by one Colonel, one Lieutenant-Colonel, one Major for every four batteries, one Adjutant, one Quartermaster and Commissary, one Sergeant-Major, one Quartermaster-Sergeant, one chief musician (who is an instructor of music), and two principal musicians; the Adjutant and Quartermaster and Commissary are extra Lieutenants, selected from the first or second lieutenants of the regiment. Each battery of artillery is officered by one Captain, one First Lieutenant, one Second Lieutenant, one First Sergeant, one Quartermaster-Sergeant, four Sergeants, four Corporals, two musicians, two artificers and one wagoner; but one First Lieutenant, one Second Lieutenant, two Sergeants and four Corporals may be added to each battery, at the discretion of the President.

Officers of a Regiment of Cavalry.

Each regiment of cavalry has for its officers one Colonel, one Lieutenant-Colonel, three Majors, one Surgeon, one Assistant-Surgeon, one Adjutant, one Quartermaster, one Veterinary Surgeon (with the rank of regimental Sergeant-Major), one Sergeant-Major, one Quartermaster-Sergeant, one Saddler-Sergeant, one chief musician (who is an instructor of music), and one chief trumpeter. Two Assistant-Surgeons may be allowed to each regiment, and four regiments have an additional Veterinary Surgeon. The Adjutant and the Quartermaster of each regiment are extra Lieutenants, selected from the first or second lieutenants of the regiment. Each troop of cavalry is officered by one Captain, one First Lieutenant, one Second Lieutenant, one First Sergeant, one Quartermaster-Sergeant, five Sergeants, four Corporals, two trumpeters, two farriers, one saddler and one wagoner.

Officers of a Regiment of Infantry.

The officers of each infantry regiment consist of one Colonel, one Lieutenant-Colonel, one Major, one Adjutant, one Quartermaster, one Sergeant-Major, one Quartermaster-Sergeant, one chief musician, two principal musicians. The Adjutant and the Quartermaster are extra lieutenants, selected from the first or second lieutenants of the regiment. Each company of infantry is officered by one Captain, one First Lieutenant, one Second Lieutenant, one First Sergeant, one Quartermaster-Sergeant, four Sergeants, four Corporals, two artificers, two musicians, and one wagoner.

Salaries of Regimental Officers.

Colonels receive as compensation $3,500 a year, and forage for two horses; Lieutenant-Colonels, $3,000 a year, and forage for two horses; Majors, $2,500 a year, and forage for two horses; Captains, mounted, $2,000 a year, and forage for two horses; Captains, not mounted, $1,800 a year; Adjutants, $1,800 a year, and forage for two horses; Regimental Quartermasters, $1,800 a year, and forage for two horses: First Lieutenants, mounted, $1,600 a year, and forage for two horses; First Lieutenants, not mounted, $1,500 a year; Second Lieutenants, mounted, $1,500 a year, and forage for two horses; Second Lieutenants, not mounted, $1,400 a year; Chaplains, $1,500 a year, and forage for two horses; Acting Assistant Commissaries, $100 a year in addition to the pay of their rank; Ordnance Store-keeper and Paymaster at the Springfield (Mass.) Armory, $2,500, and forage for

two horses; all other Store-keepers, $2,000 a year, and forage for two horses. Each commissioned officer below the rank of a Brigadier-General, including Chaplains and others whose rank or pay assimilates, are allowed 10 per cent. of their current yearly pay for each term of five years of service.

The Pay of Enlisted Men.

The following enlisted men are paid these sums monthly during their first terms of enlistment, with some modifications prescribed by law: Sergeant-Majors of cavalry, artillery and infantry, $23 each; Quartermaster-Sergeants of cavalry, artillery and infantry, $23 each; chief trumpeters of cavalry, $22; principal musicians of artillery and infantry, $22; chief musicians of regiments, $60, and the allowances of a Quartermaster-Sergeant; Saddler Sergeants of cavalry, $22; First Sergeants of cavalry, artillery and infantry, $22; Sergeants of cavalry, artillery and infantry, $17; Corporals of cavalry and light artillery, $15; Corporals of artillery and infantry, $15; saddlers of cavalry, $15; blacksmiths and farriers of cavalry, $15; trumpeters of cavalry, $13; musicians of artillery and infantry, $13; privates of cavalry, artillery and infantry, $13; Sergeant-Majors of engineers, $36; Quartermaster-Sergeants of engineers, $36; Sergeants of engineers and ordnance, $34; Corporals of engineers and ordnance, $20; musicians of engineers, $13; privates (first class) of engineers and ordnance, $17; privates (second class) of engineers and ordnance, $13. To these rates of pay $1 a month is added for the third year of enlistment, $1 for the fourth year, and one more for the fifth year, making $3 a month increase for the last year of enlistment; but this increase is "retained pay," and is not given to the soldier until his term is ended, and it is forfeited if he misbehaves himself before he receives his discharge. Occasional extra services by soldiers and non-commissioned officers also entitle them to additional pay.

Hospital Stewards.

Hospital stewards are either enlisted for that position, or appointed from the enlisted men in the army, and are permanently attached to the medical corps, under the regulations of the Secretary of War. There is one hospital steward for each military post; and they are graded as of the first, second and third classes. The first class receive $30 a month, the second $22, and the third $20. Hospital matrons in post or regimental hospitals receive $10 a month, and female nurses in general hospitals, 40 cents a day; but one military ration, or its equivalent, is allowed to each. Women are employed as matrons and nurses in post or regimental hospitals in such numbers as may be necessary, and as nurses in general or permanent hospitals at such times and in such numbers as the Surgeon-General or the medical officer in charge of any such hospital deems proper.

Pay Department in the Army.

The pay department of the army consists of one Paymaster-General, with the rank of colonel, two Assistant Paymasters-General, with the rank of colonel of cavalry, two Deputy Paymasters-General, with the rank of lieutenant of cavalry, and sixty Paymasters, with the rank of major of cavalry. Officers of the pay department are not entitled, by virtue of their rank, to command in the line or in other staff corps. When volunteers or militia are called into the service of the United States, and the officers in the pay department are not deemed by the President sufficient for the punctual payment of the troops, he may appoint and add to such corps as many paymasters, called

additional paymasters, ranking as majors (not exceeding one for every two regiments of volunteers or militia) as he may deem necessary; but these additional paymasters may only be retained in service so long as they are required to perform the special duty for which they are appointed. Paymasters and additional paymasters are allowed a capable non-commissioned officer or private as a clerk. If suitable persons for this office cannot be found in the army, they are authorized, with the approval of the Secretary of War, to employ citizens as clerks, at a salary of $1,200 a year.

The Paymaster-General performs his duties under the direction of the President. The army is paid in such a manner that the arrears shall at no time exceed two months, unless circumstances render further arrears unavoidable. The Deputy Paymasters-General, in addition to paying troops, superintend the payment of armies in the field. The paymasters and additional paymasters pay the regular troops and all other troops in the service of the United States, when required to do so by order of the President.

The Signal Service.

The chief signal officer is of high rank in the army, with a corps of seven or more first lieutenants as acting signal officers, one scientific professor, and assistants, besides six inspectors ranking as first and second lieutenants. The work is divided into several divisions, each in charge of a proper officer, as follows: General correspondence—in charge of letters and records; property and disbursing—in charge of supplies and accounts; station—for instructing observers; telegraph—in charge of army telegraph lines; indications—issues weather warning, etc.; weather review and international bulletin; scientific and study; instruction; printing; instrument and observatory.

Judge Advocates.

The Bureau of Military Justice consists of one Judge Advocate-General, with the rank of Brigadier-General, and one Assistant Judge Advocate-General, with the rank of colonel of cavalry. It is the duty of the Judge Advocate-General to receive, revise and cause to be recorded the proceedings of all courts-martial, courts of inquiry and military commissions, and perform such other duties as have been prescribed for that office, from time to time, by the laws of the country.

There are eight Judge Advocates of the army, holding the rank of major of cavalry. They perform their duties under the direction of the Judge Advocate-General, and preside over courts-martial, courts of inquiry, etc.; have power to issue a like process to compel witnesses to appear and testify which courts of criminal jurisdiction within the State, Territory or district where such military courts are held may lawfully issue, and have power to appoint a reporter, who records the proceedings of such court and the testimony taken before it, and sets down the same, in the first instance, in short-hand writing. The reporter, before entering upon this duty is sworn, or makes affirmation, faithfully to perform the same.

Brevet Officers.

In the army, promotions of officers to higher grades in the service are regulated by law. In time of war, the President may confer commissions by brevet (giving a higher rank and title, without increase of pay) upon commissioned officers of the army for distinguished conduct and public service in presence of the enemy. Such commissions bear date from the particular action or service for which the brevet rank was conferred. Such officers may be assigned to duty or command according to their brevet rank by a special assignment of the President; but brevet rank does not entitle an officer to precedence or command, except when so assigned, nor is he entitled to wear, while on duty, any uniform other than that of his actual rank, nor to be addressed in orders or official communications by any title other than that of his actual rank.

Military Cadets.

When any cadet (student) of the United States Military Academy at West Point has gone through its classes and received a regular degree from the academical staff, he is considered a candidate for a commission in any portion of the army for whose duties he may be deemed competent. But should there be no vacancy then existing in such corps, he may be brevetted as a supernumerary officer, with the rank of second lieutenant, until a vacancy occurs.

Non-commissioned Officers.

Under regulations established by the Secretary of War, non-commissioned officers may be examined by a board of four officers as to their qualifications for the duties of commissioned officers in the line of the army, and are eligible for appointment as second lieutenants in any corps for which they are qualified.

Meritorious Privates.

Whenever a private soldier distinguishes himself in the army, the President may, on the recommendation of the commanding officers of the regiment to which such private soldier belongs, grant him a certificate of merit.

Educational.

Schools are established at all posts, garrisons, and permanent camps, at which troops are stationed, in which the enlisted men are instructed in the common English branches of education, and especially in the history of the United States. It is the duty of the post or garrison commander to set apart a suitable room or building for school and religious purposes, and the Secretary of War details such officers and enlisted men as may be necessary to carry out this measure.

Retiring Boards---Veteran Officers.

From time to time the Secretary of War, under the direction of the President, assembles an Army Retiring Board, consisting of not more than nine, nor less than five, officers, two-fifths of whom are selected from the Medical corps, and besides these the board is composed, as far as may be, of seniors in rank to the officer whose disability is the subject of inquiry. The members of the board are sworn to discharge their duties honestly and impartially. The board inquires into and determines the facts touching the nature and occasion of the disability of any officer who appears to be incapable of performing the duties of his office, and shall have such powers of a court-martial and of a court of inquiry as may be necessary for that purpose. The proceedings and decision of the board are transmitted to the Secretary of War, and are by him laid before the President for his approval or disapproval and orders in the case.

When an officer has served forty consecutive years as a commissioned officer, he may, upon making application to the President, be retired from active service and placed upon the retired list, at the discretion of the President. When any officer has served forty-five years as a commissioned officer, or is sixty-two years old, he may, at the discretion of the President, be retired from active service.

When any officer has become incapable of performing the duties of his office, he shall either be retired from active service, or wholly retired from the service by the President, in the manner provided by law. Officers are retired from active service upon the actual rank held by them at the date of their retirement; are withdrawn from command and the line of promotion; are entitled to wear the uniform of their rank; continue to be borne on the army register; are subject to the rules and articles of war, and to trial by court-martial for any breach thereof. The whole number of officers on the retired list cannot at any time exceed 300.

Retired officers may be assigned to duty at the Soldiers' Home (Dayton, Ohio) when selected by the commissioners of the home, approved by the Secretary of War; and a retired officer cannot be assigned to any other duty, but may, on his own application, be detailed to serve as professor in any college. No retired officer, in these positions, however, will be allowed any additional compensation—only his regular pay as a retired officer.

Rights of Enlisted Men.

No enlisted man can, during his term of service, be arrested on mesne process, or taken or charged in execution for any debt unless it was contracted before his enlistment and amounted to $20 when first contracted.

Cooks.

Cooks for the army are detailed, in turn, from the privates of each company of troops in the service of the United States, at the rate of one cook for each company numbering less than thirty men, and two cooks for each company numbering more than thirty men, and they serve on each detail ten days.

Officers as Teachers.

The President may, upon the application of any established college or university within the United States, having capacity to educate at the same time not less than 150 male students, detail an officer of the army to act as president, superintendent or professor thereof, but the number of such officers may not exceed thirty at any time; are to be apportioned throughout the United States, as nearly as practicable, according to population, and are governed by general rules prescribed, from time to time, by the President.

Officers' Reports.

Every officer commanding a regiment, corps, garrison or detachment, is required, once in two months, or oftener, to make a report to the chief of ordnance, stating all damages to arms, implements or equipments belonging to his command, noting those occasioned by negligence or abuse, and naming the officer or soldier by whose negligence or abuse such damages were occasioned.

Every officer who receives clothing or camp equipage for the use of his command, or for issue to troops, must render to the Quartermaster-General, quarter-yearly, returns of such supplies, according to prescribed forms, with the requisite vouchers.

Army Officers as Civil Officers.

No army officer in active service can hold any civil office, either by election or appointment, and if he accepts or exercises the functions of a civil office he ceases to be an officer of the army and his commission is vacated. Should he accept a diplomatic or consular appointment under the government, he is considered as having resigned his place in the army, and it is filled as a vacancy.

Musicians and Their Pay.

The leader of the band at the military academy receives $75 a month, and the chief musicians of regiments $60 and the allowances of a quartermaster sergeant.

Army Clothing.

The uniform of the army, and the quantity and kind of clothing issued annually to the troops, are prescribed by the President.

West Point Military Academy.

The officers of the West Point Academy consist of a superintendent, a commandant of cadets, a senior instructor of artillery tactics, a senior instructor of cavalry tactics, a senior instructor of infantry tactics, a professor and an assistant professor of civil and military engineering, a professor and an assistant professor of natural and experimental philosophy, a professor and an assistant professor of mathematics; one chaplain, who is also professor of history, geography and ethics, aided by an assistant professor; a professor and an assistant professor of chemistry, mineralogy and geology, a professor and an assistant professor of drawing, a professor and an assistant professor of the French language, a professor and an assistant professor of the Spanish language, one adjutant, one master of the sword, and one teacher of music.

The superintendent, the commandant of cadets and the professors are appointed by the President, and the assistant professors, acting assistant professors and the adjutant are officers of the army, detailed to such duties by the Secretary of War, or cadets (students) assigned by the superintendent, under the direction of the Secretary of War.

The superintendent and commandant of cadets may be selected, and all other officers on duty at the Military academy may be detailed from cavalry, infantry or artillery; but the academic staff (as such) is not entitled to any command in the army, outside of the academy. The superintendent and the commandant of cadets, while serving as such, have, respectively, the local rank of colonel and lieutenant-colonel of engineers.

The superintendent, and, in his absence, the next in rank, has the immediate government and military command of the academy, and is commandant of the military post at West Point.

The commandant of cadets has the immediate command of the battalion of cadets, and is the instructor in the tactics of artillery, cavalry and infantry.

Supervision of the Military Academy.

The supervision and charge of the academy is vested in the War Department, under such officers, or officer, as the Secretary of War may assign to that duty.

Leaves of absence are granted by the superintendent, under regulations prescribed by the Secretary of War, to the professors, assistant professors and other officers of the academy for the entire period of the suspension of the ordinary academic studies, without deductions from their respective pay or allowances.

The professors are placed on the same footing, as to retirement from active service, as officers of the army.

Salaries of Military Teachers.

Pay of the Academic staff: Superintendent, same as a colonel; Commandant of cadets, same as a lieutenant-colonel; Adjutant, same as an adjutant of the cavalry service; Professors, who have served more than ten years at the academy, the pay and allowances of a colonel, and all other professors those of a lieutenant-colonel; the instructors of ordnance and science of gunnery and of practical engineering have the pay of a major, besides ten per centum of their current yearly pay for each and every term of five years' service in the army and at the academy, and such professors are placed upon the same footing, as regards restrictions upon pay and retirement from active service, as officers of the army; each assistant professor and each senior instructor of cavalry, artillery and infantry tactics, and the instructor of practical military engineering, receives the pay of a captain; the master of the sword receives at the rate of $1,500 a year, with fuel and quarters; the librarian and assistant librarian of the academy each receive $120 additional pay; the non-commissioned officer in charge of mechanics and other labor at the academy, the soldier who acts as clerk in the adjutant's office, and the four enlisted men in the philosophical and chemical departments and the lithographic office, receive each $50 additional pay.

Requirements of Military Cadets.

The corps of cadets consists of one from each congressional district in the United States, one from each Territory, one from the District of Columbia and ten from the United States at large, and are appointed by the President.

Appointees to cadetships are required to be between seventeen and twenty-two years old; but if they had served faithfully in the Southern rebellion as Union volunteers, the law allowed tnem to be two years older, and no person who served in the rebellion against the Union could receive a cadet's appointment. Cadets are appointed one year in advance of the time of their admission to the academy; they draw no pay or allowances until they are admitted; they are examined under regulations prescribed by the Secretary of War before their admission, and they are required to be well-versed in reading, writing and arithmetic, and to have a knowledge of the elements of English grammar, descriptive geography (particularly of our country), and of the history of the United States. Previous to admission, also, each cadet is required to take an oath of fidelity to his country and his duties, and to sign articles binding himself to serve the Government eight years, unless sooner discharged.

How Cadets are Drilled.

The cadets are arranged into companies, under the direction of the superintendent, each of which is commanded by an officer of the army for the purpose of military instruction. Each company is allowed four musicians. The corps is taught and trained in all the duties of a private soldier, non-commissioned officer and officer, goes into encampment at least once a year for three months, and is instructed and drilled in all the duties incident to a regular camp. Cadets are also subject to do duty in such places and on such service as the President may direct.

No cadet who is reported as deficient in either conduct or studies, and recommended to be discharged from the academy, can, except upon the recommendation of the academic board, be returned or re-appointed, or appointed to any position in the army before his class have left the academy and received their commissions.

The superintendent of the academy has power to convene general courts-martial for the trial of cadets, and to execute the sentences of such courts (except sentences of suspension or dismission), subject to the limitations and conditions existing as to other general courts-martial.

The Board of Visitors.

A Board of Visitors is appointed once a year to attend the annual examination of cadets at the Military academy. Seven persons are appointed by the President of the United States, and two United States Senators and three Representatives in Congress are designated by the presiding officers in the Senate and House of Representatives, respectively, at the session of Congress next preceding the examination.

It is the duty of this Board of Visitors to inquire into the actual state of the discipline, instruction, police administration, financial affairs, and other concerns of the academy. The visitors appointed by the President report the results of their

examination to the Secretary of War, for the information of Congress at the beginning of the next session; the Congressional visitors report directly to Congress, within twenty days after its meeting, their action as visitors, with their views and recommendations concerning the academy.

These visitors receive no compensation for their services, except the payment of their expenses for board and lodging while visiting West Point, and an allowance of not more than eight cents per mile for traveling expenses, going and returning by the shortest mail routes.

Articles of War.

The statutes of the United States contain a code of laws for the government of the army, known as the "Articles of War," and to these every officer and soldier is required to yield implicit obedience or suffer the penalties therein provided. These articles number 128. They include all ranks and conditions of the army, the formation, jurisdiction and conduct of general courts-martial, field-officers' courts, regimental courts, and garrison courts. Officers can only be tried by general courts-martial. (See "Judge Advocates-General.") The other courts are composed of officers chosen by commandants in the field, in the regiment, and in the garrison for the trial of minor offenses committed by soldiers and non-commissioned officers.

Military Prison.

A military prison has been established at Rock Island, Ill., by the government, for the confinement and reformation of offenders against the rules, regulations and laws for the government of the army of the United States, in which are confined and employed at labor, and governed according to law, all such offenders as have been convicted before any court-martial or military commission of the United States and sentenced to imprisonment therein.

The Secretary of War appoints a board of five members, consisting of three officers of the army and two civilians, who each hold their office for three years (unless sooner removed), and are each paid $5 a day while on duty, besides their necessary traveling expenses. With the Secretary of War, twice a year, and oftener if deemed expedient, they visit the prison for the purposes of examination, inspection and correction, and to inquire into all abuses and neglect of duty on the part of the officers or other persons in charge of the prison, and make such changes in the general discipline of the institution as they deem essential.

The officers of the prison consist of a commandant and such subordinate officers as may be necessary, a chaplain, a surgeon and a clerk, all of whom are detailed by the Secretary of War from the commissioned officers of the army, and he also details a sufficient number of enlisted men to act as turnkeys, guards and assistants in the prison.

The commandant controls the prison, has charge of the prisoners and their employments, and custody of all the property of the government connected with the prison, receives and pays out all money used for the prison, causes accounts to be kept of all the property, expenses, income, business and concerns of the prison, and transmits full and regular reports thereof to the Secretary of War. Under the direction of the Secretary of War, he employs (for the benefit of the United States) the convicts at such labor and in such trades as may be deemed best for their health and reformation, has power to sell and dispose of the articles manufactured by the convicts, regularly accounting for the proceeds thereof; takes note and makes record of the good conduct of the con-

victs, and shortens the daily time of hard labor for those who earn such consideration by their obedience, honesty, industry or general good conduct.

One of the inspectors of the army, at least once in three months, visits the prison for the purpose of examining into the books and all the affairs thereof, and to ascertain whether the laws, rules and regulations relating to it are complied with, whether the officers are competent and faithful, and whether the convicts are properly governed and employed and humanely and kindly treated. Of the results of his inspection he makes full and regular reports to the Secretary of War.

National Service.

Should the United States be invaded or be in imminent danger of invasion from any foreign nation or Indian tribe, or of rebellion against the government of the United States, the President may call forth such number of the militia of the State or States most convenient to the place of danger or scene of action as he may deem necessary to repel such invasion, or to suppress such rebellion, and issue his orders for that purpose to such officers of the militia as he may think proper. If the militia of more than one State is called into the active service of the United States by the President, he apportions them among such States according to representative population. In a time of rebellion the militia is subject to the same rules and articles of war as the regular troops of the United States.

When called into actual service, however, the militia is reorganized in a manner similar to regular troops. Each regiment of infantry then has one colonel, one lieutenant-colonel, one major, one adjutant (a lieutenant), one quartermaster (a lieutenant), one surgeon, two assistant surgeons, one sergeant-major, one regimental quartermaster-sergeant, one regimental commissary-sergeant, one hospital steward and two principal musicians; the regiment composed of ten companies, each company consisting of one captain, one first lieutenant, one second lieutenant, one first sergeant, four sergeants, eight corporals, two musicians, one wagoner, and from sixty-four to eighty-two privates. The militia is then also further organized into divisions of three or more brigades each, and each division has a major-general, three aids-de-camp, and one assistant adjutant-general (with the rank of major). Each brigade is made up of four or more regiments, and has one brigadier-general, two aids-de-camp, one assistant adjutant-general (with the rank of captain), one surgeon, one assistant quartermaster, one commissary of subsistence, and sixteen musicians as a band.

When thus called into actual service, the President may specify the period for which such service will be required of the militia, not exceeding nine months. During the time of service they will be entitled to the same pay, rations, clothing, and camp equipage provided by law for the regular army of the United States. They are also allowed mileage for the distance between their places of residence and the place of rendezvous from which they start for the field of military operations, with forage for the animals of mounted regiments, loss of horses, etc.

Courts-martial for the trial of militia are composed of militia officers only.

National Armories.

At each United States arsenal (or place where military arms and munitions of war are stored) is established a national armory, where muskets and carbines for the military service are manufactured. These armories are each in charge of one superintendent, who must be an officer of the ordnance corps of the army.

His Duties as Manager of the United States Moneys.

MONG THE requirements it is stipulated that the Secretary of the Treasury shall not be interested, directly or indirectly, in carrying on any business of trade or commerce, or own any interest in a sea-vessel; that he shall not purchase or own any public lands or public property, or be concerned in buying or selling government securities, whether of the United States or any State thereof, or profit by any negotiation or transaction relating to the business of his department, other than his legal allowances, under penalty of fine and removal from his office, and he shall further be incapable of holding any other office under the United States Government. Every clerk in the department is also under similar restrictions and subject to similar penalties in a lighter degree.

The general duties of the Secretary require him, from time to time, to consider and prepare plans for the improvement and management of the national revenue and the support of the public credit; to superintend collection of the revenue; to prescribe the forms of keeping and rendering all public accounts and making proper returns; granting, under certain restrictions, all warrants for moneys to be issued from the Treasury in accordance with the laws of Congress; report to, or inform, either house of Congress, in person or in writing, respecting all matters referred to him by the Senate or House of Representatives, or which pertain to his office, and to perform such general duties relative to the national finances as he shall be directed, with considerable discretionary power: such as the collection of duties on imports and tonnage, under his superintendence. Whenever it is possible, he shall cause all accounts of the expenditure of public money to be settled within the fiscal year.

It is the duty of the Secretary of the Treasury to make and issue, from time to time, such instructions and regulations to the several collectors, receivers, depositaries, officers and others who may receive Treasury notes, United States notes, or other securities of the United States, and to those employed to prepare and issue such notes and securities, as he shall deem best to promote the convenience and security of the public, and protect the government or individuals against loss or fraud.

He prescribes forms of entries, oaths, bonds and other papers, with rules and regulations, in accordance with law, to be used in carrying out the various provisions of the internal revenue law, or the law relating to raising revenue from imported goods by duties or warehouse charges.

He prescribes such directions, rules, and forms to revenue collectors as are necessary for the proper observation of the law.

He prescribes the forms of the annual statements to Congress, which show the actual condition of commerce and navigation between the United States and foreign countries, or along the coasts between the collection districts of the government, in each year.

He, under the direction of the President, from time to time, establishes regulations to secure a just, faithful, and impartial appraisal of all goods, wares and merchandise imported into the United States, with proper entries of their true values and amounts.

When the revenue received at any port of the United States by collections does not amount to $10,000 a year, the Secretary may discontinue it as a port of delivery.

The Secretary of the Treasury is authorized to receive deposits of gold coin or bullion, by the Treasurer or Assistant-Treasurers of the United States, in sums of not less than $20, and issue certificates of deposit therefor of not less than $20 each; and these certificates shall be received in payment of public dues, as duties on imported goods, etc., the same as gold or bullion.

The Secretary may designate any recognized officer of the government as a disbursing agent, for the payment of all moneys appropriated for the construction of government buildings in the district to which such officer belongs.

When any person or corporation unjustly withholds from the government any moneys belonging to it, the Secretary may employ individuals (not exceeding three) to recover such moneys upon terms and conditions prescribed by himself; and the persons so employed receive no compensation except out of the moneys so recovered, and if they accept money or emolument for themselves from the persons from whom they attempt to recover said moneys, they become liable to fine and imprisonment by the government.

Plans for Raising Money.

In his annual report to Congress the Secretary shall present: Estimates of the public revenue and public expenditures for the current fiscal year, with plans for improving and increasing the revenues from time to time; a statement of all contracts for supplies or services which have been made by him, or under his direction, during the preceding year; a statement of the expenditure of moneys appropriated for the payment of miscellaneous claims against the government not otherwise provided for; a statement of the rules and regulations made by him, with his reasons for making them, to secure a just and faithful appraisal of all goods, wares, and merchandise imported into the United States, and their amounts and values; a full and complete statement of the sums collected from seamen, and expended for sick and disabled seamen, as a hospital tax for that purpose.

The secretary shall make other reports to Congress, at prescribed times: A statement of the amount of money expended at each custom-house during the preceding fiscal year, with the detailed number, occupation and salaries of all persons employed at each custom-house during the same period.

A statement showing the results of the information collected during the preceding year by the Bureau of

Treasury Building, Washington, D. C.

Statistics concerning the condition of the agriculture, manufactures, domestic trade, currency, and banks in the States and Territories.

The reports made to him by the auditors relating to the accounts of the war and navy departments respectively, showing the application of the money appropriated by Congress for those departments for the preceding year.

An abstract, in tabular form, of the separate accounts of moneys received from internal duties or taxes in each of the States, Territories and collection districts, required to be kept at the Treasury.

A copy of each of the accounts kept by the superintendent of the Treasury buildings of all contingent expenses of the several bureaus of the department, and of all amounts paid for furniture, repairs of furniture, or of the sale of old furniture.

Also the number, names, and salaries of persons employed in surveying the lake and sea-coasts, their respective duties, and the amounts expended by the superintendent of this branch of the government service.

Statistics of Commerce.

The secretary is also charged with the duty, under prescribed regulations, of printing and presenting to Congress the annual report of the statistics of commerce and navigation, prepared by the Bureau of Statistics; of printing annually a condensed statement of the whole amount of the exports and imports to and from foreign countries during the preceding fiscal year; of publishing in some newspaper at Washington, every three months, a statement of the whole receipts, during the previous quarter-year, showing the amounts received from customs, public lands, and miscellaneous sources, and also the payments made during said quarter to civil officers and employes, the army or the navy, for Indian affairs, fortifications or pensions; of publishing in some newspaper at Washington, on the first day of each month, the last preceding weekly statement of the Treasurer of the United States, showing the amount to his credit in the different banks, in the mints or other depositories, the amounts for which drafts have been given and those unpaid, the amount remaining subject to his draft, and any recent changes in the depositories of the Treasury.

Bureau of Statistics.

The Bureau of Statistics is superintended by a division clerk, who is appointed for that purpose by the Secretary of the Treasury.

The purpose of the bureau is the collection, arrangement and classification of such statistical information as may be procured, tending to show, each year, the condition of the agriculture, manufactures, domestic trade, currency and banks of the several States and Territories. Under the direction of the Secretary of the Treasury, the chief of the Bureau of Statistics prepares annually a report, containing in detail statements substantially showing: Statistics concerning the commerce and navigation of the United States with foreign countries, to the close of the fiscal year; comprehending all goods, wares and merchandise exported from the United States to foreign countries, and all goods, wares and merchandise imported into the United States from foreign countries, and all navigation employed in the foreign trade of the United States. These statistics exhibit the kinds, qualities and values of the articles exported or imported, minutely stated; also what articles are of foreign or native production. The statistics of navigation show the amount of tonnage of all vessels arriving from foreign countries in the United States, and all vessels departing from the United States to foreign ports; the amount of tonnage of vessels belonging to the United States, and the amount of tonnage of vessels owned in foreign countries, arriving in and departing from the United States, with other particulars.

Bureau of the Mint.

The Bureau of the Mint is under the general direction of the Secretary of the Treasury. Its chief officer is the Director of the Mint, who is appointed by the President; serves five years, unless he dies, resigns or is removed for cause, and has a salary of $4,500, besides his necessary traveling expenses. The Bureau of the Mint has under its control all the government mints for the manufacture of gold, silver and other coins, and all the assay offices for the stamping of bullion in order to establish its fineness and coin value. In his annual report to the Secretary of the Treasury, the Director of the Mint sets forth what and how valuable have been the operations of the mints during the preceding fiscal year, and the estimates for their operation during the next succeeding year.

The Secretary of the Treasury appoints the number of classified clerks necessary to carry on the duties of this bureau.

First Home in the Wilderness.

How to Secure a Home on Government Land. *

THE Government of the United States owns and controls the public lands, not previously disposed of, where the Indian title has been extinguished by purchase or otherwise.

The public lands are open to pre-emption by citizens of the United States, except in the following cases: Lands reserved by any treaty, law or Presidential proclamation, for any purpose; lands lying within the limits of any incorporated city or town; lands actually settled or used for business purposes, and not for farming, and lands on which salt-springs or mines are situated.

Who May Pre-empt Land.

Every head of a family, or widow, or single person, more than twenty-one years old, being a citizen of the United States, or having filed his written intention to become such, or who may, himself or herself, actually settle on land subject to pre-emption, inhabiting, building a residence thereon, and improving the land, may enter at the proper land-office any quantity of such land, not exceeding 160 acres, upon which he or she may reside, by paying to the government the sum of $1.25 per acre.

Who May Not Pre-empt Land.

No person who owns 320 acres of land in any State or Territory, or who abandons his or her own land to settle on public lands in the same State or Territory, has a right to pre-emption.

No person is entitled to more than one pre-emption, and cannot secure a second tract of public land by this means.

Where the Land-Offices are Located.

Most of the public lands subject to pre-emption lie west of the Mississippi river. Land-offices, where all necessary information relative to the settlement and entry of these lands may be obtained, are located in the several States and Territories, as follows:

Alabama—Huntsville and Montgomery.

Arkansas—Little Rock, Camden, Harrison and Dardanelle.

Arizona Ter.—Prescott and Tucson.

California—San Francisco, Marysville, Humboldt, Stockton, Visalia, Sacramento, Los Angeles, Shasta, Susanville and Bodie.

Colorado—Denver City, Leadville, Central City, Pueblo, Del Norte, Lake City, Gunnison, Durango and Glenwood Springs.

Dakota Ter.—Mitchell, Watertown, Fargo, Yankton, Bismarck, Deadwood, Aberdeen, Grand Forks, Huron and Devil's Lake.

Florida—Gainesville.

Idaho Ter.—Boise City, Lewiston, Oxford, Hailey and Coeur d' Alene.

Iowa—Des Moines.

Kansas—Topeka, Salina, Independence, Larned, Wichita, Kirwin, Concordia, Wa-Keeny, Oberlin and Garden City.

Louisiana—New Orleans and Natchitoches.

Michigan—Detroit, East Saginaw, Reed City and Marquette.

Minnesota—Taylor's Falls, Saint Cloud, Duluth, Fergus Falls, Worthington, Tracy, Benson, Crookston and Redwood Falls.

Mississippi—Jackson.

Missouri—Boonville, Ironton and Springfield.

Montana Ter.—Miles City, Bozeman and Helena.

Nebraska—Neligh, Beatrice, Lincoln, Niobrara, Grand Island, North Platte, Bloomington, Mc Cook and Valentine.

Nevada—Eureka.

New Mexico Ter.—Santa Fe and Las Cruces.

Oregon—Oregon City, Roseburg, Le Grand, Lakeview and The Dalles.

Utah Ter.—Salt Lake City.

Washington Ter.—Olympia, Vancouver, Walla Walla, Spokane Falls and Yakima.

Wisconsin—Menasha, Falls of St. Croix, Eau Claire, Wausau, La Crosse and Bayfield.

Wyoming Ter.—Cheyenne and Evanston.

The Pre-emptor's Oath.

Previous to making a pre-emption, every citizen must make oath before the land register or receiver in the district where the desired tract is located, that he has never availed himself, on a former occasion, of his privilege to pre-empt public land; that he does not own 320 acres of land in any State or Territory; that he has not settled upon and improved such land to sell it on speculation, but for his own exclusive use; that he has not, in any way, contracted or agreed with any other person that the title of the said land, in whole or part, shall be for the benefit of any one except himself.

The certifiate of this oath is filed in the land office of each district, and a copy of it is also sent to the General-Land Office for preservation.

Penalty for False Swearing.

Any person taking this oath and swearing falsely forfeits the money he has paid for the specified land and all his right and title to the land itself, and if he has previously bargained to transfer his pre-emptive title to any other person, that conveyance is null and void.

Preliminary Steps.

Before any person can enter land as above described, he must give satisfactory proof to the register and receiver of the land-office that he has properly settled upon and improved the land that he desires to pre-empt.

Within thirty days after first settling upon said land, the pre-emptor must file with the register of the proper land-office a written declaration of his intention to enter such tract of land under the pre-emption laws. Failing to make this statement within the prescribed time, or in furnishing the necessary proof of settlement and improvement of such land, or make the required payment, within one year after settling upon it, any other person may enter the same tract.

When two or more persons settle on the same tract of land, the right of pre-emption is in the one who made the first settlement.

The head of any family, or single person, twenty-one years old, being a citizen of the United States, is entitled to enter one quarter-section (160 acres), or less, but no more, of public lands not otherwise disposed of, after having filed a pre-emption claim, (if such land is subject to pre-emption), at $1.25 per acre, or eighty acres or less, in one tract, at $2.25 per acre.

Those possessing land may enter adjoining public land, if the tracts do not exceed 160 acres.

Upon applying to the register of the proper land office, he must swear that he is the head of a family, or twenty-one years old, or has served in the army or navy of the United States, as the case may be, and that he is securing the desired tract for his own use, for actual settlement and cultivation; taking this oath, and paying to the register of the land-office the sum of five dollars, where the land does not exceed eighty acres, and ten dollars for a larger amount.

When Ownership is Actually Acquired.

The certifiate of the register of the land-office, however, does not issue to the applicant for five years, at the end of which time, or two years later, he, or his widow, or his heirs, must prove by competent witnesses that he, she, or they

❋ Though belonging to the Department of the Interior this subject is treated here, as the revenues from land sales belong to the Treasury Department.

resided upon or cultivated the tract for five successive years after the the above affidavit was made, and that they still retain the land, and then take an oath of allegiance to the United States Government. He, she, or they will then be entitled to receive a patent for the land. Any false swearing concerning these particulars is punished, as in other cases of perjury.

The register of the land-office keeps a record of all the proceedings touching each tract of land claimed as a homestead.

No such homestead can be levied upon and sold for any debt contracted before the government patent is issued.

When the Payment Must be Made.

The payment for the homestead, besides the five or ten dollars prepaid when the land is entered, must be all paid before the expiration of the five years previous to the issue of the patent. Further information on this and other points can be obtained by applying to the land-office.

Tree Culture on Homesteads.

Any settler who has cultivated for two years as much as five acres in trees to an eighty-acre homestead, or ten acres on a homestead of 160 acres, is entitled to a free patent for his land at the end of three years. Each settler may claim as many quarter sections of homestead lands, not adjoining each other, as have been improved by the culture, for ten years, of forty acres of timber thereon.

Land Officers.

The President appoints a Register of the Land-Office and a Receiver of public moneys for each of the land districts of the United States, and each is required to reside at the place where the land-office to which he is appointed is directed to be kept. Each receives a salary of $500 a year, with liberal fees and commissions for locating land-warrants, issuing land-certificates, etc; but the salary, fees and commissions cannot in any case exceed an aggregate of $3,000. All balances received and remaining in the hands of registers and receivers above this amount, must be paid into the United States Treasury, as other public moneys.

The receivers make to the Secretary of the Treasury monthly returns of the moneys received in their several offices. and pay them over pursuant to his instructions.

Applicants for Land.

Should any person apply to any register to enter any land whatever, and the Register knowingly and falsely informs the person so applying that the same has been already entered, and refuses to permit the person so applying to enter such land, the Register is liable therefor to the applicant for five dollars for each acre of land which the latter offered to enter, to be recovered in an action for debt in any proper court.

Custom-House Officers.

The laws of the United States provide for the collection of duties on imported goods and merchandise in 110 collection districts of the Union, with one Collector of Customs, appointed by the President, for each district.

Collectors of Customs.

Collectors of customs at the various ports of entry of the United States are appointed by the President, for the term of four years.

The oath of office, taken and subscribed by each collector before some magistrate authorized to administer oaths within the collector's own district, affirms his past and present fidelity to the Government of the United States, and that he will use his best endeavors to detect and prevent frauds against the laws of the United States imposing duties upon imports.

Duty of the Collector.

At each of the ports to which there are appointed (by the President) a collector, naval officer and customs surveyor, it is the duty of the collector to receive all reports, manifests and documents to be made or exhibited on the entry of any ship or vessel, according to the customs laws of the United States; to record all manifests; to receive the entries of all ships or vessels, and of the goods, wares, and merchandise imported in them; to estimate, with the naval officer, when there is one, or alone, when there is none, the amount of the dues payable thereon, indorsing such amount upon the respective entries; to receive all moneys paid for duties, and take all bonds for securing the payment thereof; to grant all permits for the unlading and delivery of goods; to employ, with the approval of the Secretary of the Treasury, proper persons as weighers, gaugers, measurers, and inspectors at the several ports within his district; to provide, with the like approval, at the public expense, storehouses for the safe keeping of goods, and such scales, weights and measures as may be necessary.

It is his business to furnish statistics of commerce and navigation for the use of the Bureau of Statistics, at Washington, relating to the kinds and quantities of all imported articles free from duty, subject to specific and ad valorem duties; the value of articles exported from his district to foreign countries; an accurate account of the characters and tonnage of all vessels sailing from his district to foreign countries; a similar record of all vessels arriving within his district from foreign countries, and an account of the kinds, quantities and value of merchandise entered and cleared coastwise at ports within his collection district.

It is his duty to cause the seizure of any vessel fitted out for piratical or aggressive purposes in violation of the law of nations.

Duties of Naval Officers.

The Naval Officer of any port is appointed by the President, and holds his office four years, unless sooner removed. His duties are as follows: To examine quarter-yearly, or oftener, if directed so to do by the Secretary of the Treasury, the books, accounts, returns and money on hand of the collector, and make a full, accurate and faithful report of their condition to the Secretary of the Treasury; to receive copies of all manifests and entries; to estimate, together with the collector, the duties on all merchandise subject to duty, and no duties can be received without such estimates; to keep a separate record of such estimates, to countersign all permits, clearances, certificates, debentures and other documents to be granted by the collector; to examine the collector's abstract of duties (taxation) and other accounts of receipts, bonds and expenditures, and certify to their correctness if found right.

Every naval officer is entitled to a maximum compensation of $5,000 a year out of any and all fees and emoluments received by him. Deputy naval officers may be appointed by the respective naval officers, when necessary, and in several of the largest commercial cities of the United States they each receive a salary of $2,500 a year. The naval officers are responsible for the acts of their respective deputies.

Duty of Surveyors of Customs.

The Surveyor of Customs at any port is appointed by the President, and holds his office four years, unless sooner removed.

At ports where a collector, naval officer and surveyor are appointed, it is the duty of the latter, subject to the direction of the collector, to superintend and direct all inspectors, weighers, measurers, gaugers at his port, to report weekly to the collector the name or names of all the above-named subordinates who are absent from or neglect their business; to visit or inspect the vessels which arrive in his port from foreign ports each day, and to report the same, with all necessary particulars concerning them, to the collector every morning; to put on board of each of such vessels, immediately after their arrival in port, one or more inspectors of cargoes; to ascertain the proof, quantities and kinds of distilled spirits imported, rating such spirits according to their respective degrees of proof as defined by the laws imposing duties on this class of merchandise; to examine whether the goods imported in any vessel, and the deliveries thereof, agreeably to the inspector's returns, correspond with the permits for landing the same, and to report any disagreement or error in the same to the collector, and to the naval officer, if there is one; to superintend the lading for exportation of all goods entered for the benefit of any drawback, bounty or allowance, and examine and report whether the kind, quantity and quality of the goods so laden on any vessel for shipment to a foreign port correspond with the entries and permits granted therefor; to examine, and from time to time, especially twice a year, try the weights, measures, and other instruments used in ascertaining the duties on imports, with standards provided by each collector for that purpose, to report errors and disagreements in the same to the collector, and to obey and execute such directions as he may receive for correcting the same agreeably to the standards.

Authority to Employ Assistance.

Every collector of customs has authority, with the approval of the Secretary of the Treasury, to employ within his district as many proper persons as deputy-collectors as he deems necessary, and they are declared to be officers of the customs. During the absence or sickness of collectors, such deputy may exercise the powers of a collector, the collector being responsible for the acts of his deputies.

The Secretary of the Treasury has power, except in cases otherwise provided, to limit and fix the number and compensation of the clerks employed by collector, surveyor or naval officer, and may fix and limit the salaries of their respective deputies.

Rules Must be Posted Up.

Every collector, naval officer and surveyor is required to keep posted up in his office a fair table of the rates of fees and duties demandable by law, and to give receipts for fees received by him whenever they may be requested, under a penalty of $100 for non-compliance, recoverable to the use of the informer. And every officer of the customs who demands or receives any other or greater fee or compensation than the law allows for any duty of his office, is liable to the aggrieved party in the sum of $200 for each offense.

Restrictions upon Collectors.

No person employed in the collection of duties on imports or tonnage may own, either in whole or in part, any vessel, or act as agent, attorney or consignee for the owner of any vessel, or of any cargo or lading on any vessel, or import, or be concerned in the importation of any merchandise for sale, under a penalty of $500.

Collectors, naval officers and surveyors must attend in person at the ports to which they are respectively appointed, keeping fair and true accounts and records of all their transactions as officers of the customs, subject to the inspection of the Secretary of the Treasury, who prescribes the form and manner of keeping such accounts and records, or to the inspection of such persons as he may appoint for that purpose; the neglect of this duty involves a penalty of $1,000.

Appraisers of Merchandise.

Four appraisers of merchandise are appointed by the President, who are employed in visiting such ports of entry, under the direction of the Secretary of the Treasury as may be deemed useful by him for the security of the revenue, and who at such ports afford such aid and assistance in the appraisement of merchandise as may be deemed necessary by the secretary to protect and insure uniformity in the collection of customs duties.

Whenever an appraisement of imported merchandise is to be made at any port for which no appraiser is provided by law, the collector of that district may appoint two respectable resident merchants, who shall be the appraisers of such merchandise. Any such merchant who refuses to assist at such appraisement, is liable to a fine not exceeding $50 and the costs of prosecution.

Assistant Treasurers.

Assistant Treasurers are appointed by the President, to serve for four years, at Boston, New York, Philadelphia, Baltimore, New Orleans, St. Louis, San Francisco, Chicago and Cincinnati.

The Assistant Treasurers have the charge and care of the rooms, vaults and safes assigned to them respectively, and there perform the duties required of them relating to the receipt, safekeeping, transfer and disbursement of the public moneys.

All collectors and receivers of public money of every description in the cities where there are sub-treasuries are required to deposit with the sub-treasurers all the public moneys collected by them or in their hands, there to be safely kept until otherwise disposed of according to law.

If any assistant treasurer fails safely to keep all public moneys deposited by any person, he is deemed guilty of embezzlement and punished by fine and imprisonment.

Officers of Internal Revenue.

The United States are divided into 131 internal revenue collection districts.

The President appoints for each of these districts one Collector of Internal Revenue, who must be a resident of the district for which he is appointed.

Appointment of Deputy Collectors.

Each collector is authorized to appoint, in writing, as many deputy-collectors as he may think proper, to be by him compensated for their services; to revoke any such appointment, giving notice thereof to the Commissioner of Internal Revenue, and to require and accept bonds or other security from such deputies.

Duty of Internal Revenue Collectors.

It is the duty of the collector and his deputies (each of whom has equal authority with the collector) to collect all internal revenue taxes levied or assessed against individuals or corporations within the portion of the district assigned to him; but each collector is in every respect responsible both to the United States and to individuals, as the case may be, for all moneys collected, and for every act done or neglected to be done by any one of his deputies while acting in that position.

Superintendent of Exports.

In any port of the United States where there is more than one Collector of Internal Revenue, the Secretary of the Treasury may designate one of them to have charge of all matters relating to the exportation of articles subject to tax under the internal revenue laws, and there may be appointed under such collector an officer to superintend all matters of exportation and drawback. This officer is known as Superintendent of Exports.

Inspectors of Tobacco and Cigars.

In every collection district where it is necessary the Secretary of the Treasury appoints one or more inspectors of tobacco and cigars. This officer is entitled by authority of the Secretary of the Treasury to receive such fees as the latter may prescribe to be paid by the owner or manufacturer of the inspected articles.

Internal Revenue Gaugers.

In every collection district where it may be necessary, the Secretary of the Treasury appoints one or more internal revenue gaugers, whose duty it is to determine the amount of articles which he is called to examine.

Requirements and Penalties.

Collectors of internal revenue are required to report violations of the revenue laws to the district attorney of his district for prosecution.

Every collector, deputy collector and inspector is authorized to administer oaths and take evidence in reference to matters in his department of the public service.

Any officer of internal revenue may be specially authorized by the commissioner to make seizures of property which may become forfeited or jeopardized by a violation of the revenue laws.

Any revenue officer who discloses to any other person the operations, style of work or apparatus of any manufacturer whose establishment comes under his inspection, is liable to be fined heavily and imprisoned. Neither can any internal revenue officer be or become interested in the manufacture of tobacco, snuff, cigars or spirits, under penalty of being dismissed from office, besides a heavy fine; and the law also provides severe penalties for extortion, receiving unlawful fees, etc., by revenue officers.

Superintendents of the Manufacture of Money.

The United States Government has mints at Philadelphia, San Francisco, New Orleans, Carson, (Nev.), and Denver, and assay offices at New York, Boise City (Idaho), and Charlotte, N. C. The officers of a mint are a superintendent, an assayer, a melter and refiner, a coiner, and, at Philadelphia, an engraver. Besides these are various assistants and clerks, and numerous workmen.

Restrictions upon Employes.

Every officer, assistant and clerk of a mint must take the oath of fidelity, which oath is deposited with the Secretary of the Treasury, and the superintendent may require any employe of the mint to take such an oath.

The assayer, the melter and refiner, and the coiner of every mint, before entering upon the duties of his office, is required to execute a bond to the United States, with one or more securities.

In the temporary absence of the superintendent, the chief clerk acts in his place; and in that of the Director of the Mint, the Secretary of the Treasury designates some one to act for him.

Duties of the Superintendent of the Mint.

The Superintendent of each mint has the control of it, the superintendence of the officers and other persons employed in it, and the supervision of its business, subject to the direction of the Director of the Mint, to whom he makes reports at such times and in such form as the director prescribes. These reports exhibit in detail, and classified, the deposits of bullion, the amount of gold, silver and minor coinage, and the amount of unparted, standard and refined bars issued, and such other statistics and information as may be required.

He receives and safely keeps, until legally withdrawn, all moneys or bullion designed for the use or expenses of the mint. He receives all bullion brought to the mint for assay or coinage; is the keeper of all bullion or coin in the mint, except when it is in the hands of other officers, and delivers all coins struck at the mint to the persons to whom they are lawfully payable.

From the report of the assayer and the weight of the bullion, he computes the value of each deposit and the amount of the charges or deductions, if any, of all which he gives a detailed memorandum to the depositor; and he also gives, at the same time, a certificate of the net amount of the deposit, to be paid in coins or bars of the same species of bullion as that deposited, the assayer verifying the correctness of such certificate by countersigning it.

Duties of the Assayer.

The Assayer assays all metals and bullion whenever assays are required in the operations of the mint. From every parcel of bullion deposited for coinage or bars, the superintendent delivers to the assayer a sufficient portion for the purpose of being assayed, and the assayer reports to the superintendent the quality or fineness of the bullion assayed by him, with such information as will enable the superintendent to compute the amount of charges to be made against the depositor.

Duty of the Melter and Refiner.

The Melter and Refiner executes all the operations necessary to form ingots of standard silver or gold and alloys for minor coinage, suitable for the coiner, from the metals legally delivered to him for that purpose, or to form bars conformably with the law from gold and bullion delivered to him for that purpose. He keeps a careful record of all transactions with the superintendent, noting the weight and character of the bullion, and is responsible for all bullion placed in his care until he returns it to the superintendent, receiving proper vouchers therefor.

Duty of the Coiner.

The Coiner executes all the operations necessary in order to form coins, conformable in all respects to the law, from the standard gold and silver ingots and alloys for minor coinage legally delivered to him for that purpose, and is responsible for it until it is returned to the superintendent. As coins are prepared from time to time, the coiner delivers them to the superintendent, who receipts for them and keeps a careful record of their kind, number and actual weight. The coiner, also, from time to time, delivers to the superintendent the clippings and other portions of bullion remaining, after the process of coining, the superintendent receipting for the same and keeping a careful record of their weight and character.

At the end of every calendar year the coiner, in the presence of the superintendent and assayer, defaces and destroys the obverse (or date) working-dies, so that no more coins of that date can be issued.

Duty of the Engraver.

The Engraver prepares all the working-dies (or moulds) required for use in the coinage of the mint, and when new coins or devices are required, under the supervision of the Director of the Mint, he engraves the models, moulds and matrices, or original dies for the same; but the director has power to engage, temporarily, the services of other artists for such work.

The Light-House Board.

The President appoints two officers of the navy, of high rank; two officers of the corps of engineers of the army, and two citizens in civil life, of high scientific attainments, whose services are at the disposal of the President, together with an officer of the navy and an officer of engineers of the army as secretaries; and these gentlemen constitute the lighthouse board.

This board is attached to the office of the Secretary of the Treasury, and under his superintendence discharges all administrative duties relating to the construction, illumination, inspection and government of light-houses, light-vessels, beacons, sea-marks, and whatever belongs to them, embracing the foundations of works already in existence, procuring illuminating and other apparatus, supplies, and materials of all kinds for building and for rebuilding, when necessary, and keeping in good repair the light-houses, light-vessels, beacons and buoys of the United States; has charge and custody of all the archives, books, documents, drawings, models, returns, apparatus and other things pertaining to the light-house service. Upon the requisition of the Secretary of the Treasury, the board furnishes all the estimates of expense which the several branches of the light-house system may require, and such other information as it may be necessary to lay before Congress at each session.

The board is authorized, whenever an appropriation may be made by Congress for a new light-house on land not belonging to the United States, to purchase the necessary site for such light-house with money appropriated for that purpose.

Who Build Light-Houses.

The President causes, from time to time, such officers to be detailed from the engineer corps of the army as are necessary to superintend the construction and renovation of light-houses. The plans, drawings, specifications and estimates of cost of all illuminating and other apparatus, and of construction and repair of towers, buildings, etc., connected with the light-house service, are prepared by the engineer-secretary of the board.

Who May be Light-House Inspectors.

The Atlantic, Gulf of Mexico, Pacific and lake coasts of the United States are divided into fifteen light-house districts, each of which is under the supervision of either a commodore, captain or commander of the navy, who is called the inspector. The engineer in charge of each district is either a colonel, lieutenant-colonel, major or captain of the Engineer Corps of the United States.

The laws provide that there be detailed from the engineer corps of the army such officers as may be necessary to superintend the construction and renovation of light-houses; also, that an officer of the army or the navy be assigned to each district as a light-house inspector, subject to the orders of the light-house board, who receives no pay or emolument beyond his own lawful compensation in the regular line of his profession, with mileage while traveling under orders connected with his duties.

Working Force in Light-House Offices.

Each inspector and engineer has an office in every district to which they are assigned, and are allowed (according to their various locations and duties) the assistance of certain employes, paid by the Government, as follows: In the inspector's offices—one or two clerks, one messenger, one keeper of the buoy depot, one superintendent of construction, one or more assistant superin-

tendents of construction, a store-keeper, a foreman of depot, a copyist, and a watchman of the buoy depot.

Engineers in Light-House Department.

In the engineer's department are employed, but not in every office: One assistant engineer, a superintendent of construction, and one or more assistant superintendents of construction, a foreman of the lamp-shop, one lampist, a foreman of laborers, a draughtsman, and a messenger.

In both the inspectors' and engineers' departments are employed steam-tugs, or vessels, for the conveyance of supplies, implements, etc., generally officered as follows: One master, one mate, one engineer, assistant engineer, and a pilot occasionally.

The Light-House Keeper.

At light-houses are employed: One keeper, at from $375 to $1,000 a year, according to location, with assistant keepers, with salaries ranging from $160 to $450 a year; keepers of light-ships receive $800 or $1,000 a year.

The Life-Saving Service.

By law the Secretary of the Treasury is authorized to establish stations at certain points on the Atlantic coast and the shores of the Northern lakes, for affording aid to the shipwrecked vessels and rescuing their crews and passengers.

Articles Used for Saving Life.

This life-saving service is divided into seven ocean districts and three lake districts. The various stations are supplied with the requisite apparatus as may, in the judgment of the Secretary of the Treasury, be best adapted to the purposes of each station, such as life-boats, ropes, mortars for sending ropes on board wrecked vessels, contrivances for getting passengers safely on shore, etc. Each district is in charge of a superintendent, who possesses the powers and performs the duties of an inspector of the customs for each of the coasts on which stations are established. These districts number seven on the Atlantic coast, and three on the great lakes; and each superintendent receives from the Secretary of the Treasury the proper instructions relative to the duties required of them.

Each station is in charge of a keeper, who is instructed in his duties by the Secretary of the Treasury. At some stations experienced surfmen are engaged to assist in aiding wrecked vessels.

Quarantines.

The law provides for the restraint, stoppage and government of all vessels arriving at sea-ports and inland ports from places where infectious diseases prevail, or vessels on which cases of such infectious diseases exist.

This law, the health-laws of the several States, and the regulations of the Secretary of the Treasury, are required to be duly observed by the officers of the customs-revenue of the United States, by the masters and crews of the several revenue-cutters belonging to the Government, and by the military officers commanding in any fort or station upon the coast, and all such officers of the United States must faithfully aid in the execution of such quarantines and health-laws, according to their respective powers and within their respective precincts, as directed, from time to time, by the Secretary of the Treasury.

The Revenue Marine Service.

The President, for the better security of the collection of import or tonnage duties on commercial vessels and cargoes, causes the maintenance of as many revenue-cutters as may be necessary for the protection of the Government revenues,

the expense of which is paid out of the sum annually appropriated by Congress for this service.

Duties of Officers in this Service.

The officers of the revenue-cutters are respectively deemed officers of the customs, and are subject to the direction of such collectors of the revenue, or other customs officers, as, from time to time, may be designated for that purpose. They are required to board all vessels arriving within the United States or within twelve miles of the United States coasts, if bound for United States ports, and search and examine every part of such vessels, and demand and receive and certify the manifests required to be on board of certain vessels; to affix and put proper fastenings on the hatches and other communications with the hold of such vessels, and remain on board such vessels until they arrive at the port or place of their destination.

How Revenue-Cutters are Known.

The revenue-cutters on the Northern and Northwestern lakes are specially charged with the duty of aiding vessels in distress on the lakes.

Revenue-cutters are distinguished by a peculiar flag or ensign; and the officers are empowered to stop any vessel liable to seizure or examination by firing upon her after hoisting the revenue flag, if the merchant-vessel's officers refuse to let the revenue officers board her.

The Coast Survey.

Surveys of the sea-coasts and lake-coasts of the United States may be authorized by the President for the purpose of aiding navigation by the production of correct charts of courses, distances, depth of water, etc., along such coasts. The public vessels in actual service and officers of the navy and army are employed, as far as practicable, in this survey.

What is Done With the Surveys.

The Secretary of the Treasury is authorized to dispose of the maps and charts of the survey of the coast, from time to time, and under such regulations as he may prescribe, besides those distributed gratuitously among foreign governments, the departments of our own Government, and literary and scientific associations.

Steamboat Inspectors.

The laws of the United States provide for the inspection of the hulls and steamboilers of merchant, passenger, and excursion vessels propelled by steam in United States waters, owned in the United States, except on canals.

From time to time the President appoints a Supervising Inspector-General, who is selected with reference to his fitness and ability to reduce to a system and carry into effect all the provisions of the law relating to steamboat inspection.

Under the direction of the Secretary of the Treasury, it is his business to superintend the administration of the steamboat inspection laws and regulations; preside at the meetings of the board of supervising inspectors; receive all reports of inspectors; receive and examine all accounts of inspectors, and report fully, at stated periods, to the Secretary of the Treasury, upon all matters pertaining to his official duties.

Inspection Districts.

The United States are divided into ten inspection districts, each of which is in charge of a supervising inspector, appointed by the President, each of whom is chosen for his knowledge, skill and practical experience in the uses of steam for navigation, and who must be a competent judge of the character and qualities of steam vessels and all parts of the machinery used in steaming.

Annual Meetings.

The supervising inspectors and Supervising Inspector-General assemble as a board at Washington once a year (in January), and at such other times as the Secretary of the Treasury may require, for joint consultation, and assign to each supervising inspector the limits of territory in which he is to perform his duties. The board also establishes all essential regulations necessary to carry out in the most effective manner the provisions of the laws. These regulations, when approved by the Secretary of the Treasury, have the force of law.

Each supervising inspector watches over all parts of the territory assigned to him; visits and confers with, and examines into the doings of the local boards of inspectors within his district, and instructs them in the proper performance of their duties; and, whenever he deems it expedient, he visits any licensed vessels at his discretion, and examines their condition with reference to the inspection laws and regulations having been observed and complied with, both by the owners or masters, or the board of inspectors.

Restrictions Upon Inspectors.

No person who is directly or indirectly interested in any patent required to be used on any steamer by the steamboat inspection laws, or who is a member of any association of owners, masters, engineers or pilots of steamboats, or who is directly or indirectly interested in any steam-vessel, or who is intemperate in his habits, or who does not possess the required skill or experience, may not hold the office of either supervising or local inspector, and if any such person attempts to perform the functions of an inspector, he is punishable by a fine of $500 and dismissal from office.

Must Not Employ Unlicensed Officers.

The boards of local inspectors license and classify the masters, chief mates, engineers and pilots of all steam-vessels, and it is a punishable offense for any steamboat owner to employ an unlicensed officer of these grades.

Whenever a supervising inspector ascertains that any of the above-named steamboat officers fails to perform his duty according to law, he is required to report him to the board of local inspectors in the district where the vessel was inspected or belongs, and if necessary or expedi-

ent, to have the offending party prosecuted; and if the local board is in fault for licensing him the facts must be investigated, and the delinquent inspectors are liable to removal from office.

It is the duty of the inspecting supervisors to see that the local boards faithfully perform their duties of inspection; to inspect boats and grant licenses in districts where there are no local boards, or where it is difficult to apply to them; to furnish to local inspectors all needful information concerning licensed persons, individuals from whom licenses have been withheld, or whose licenses have been revoked or suspended; boats whose owners have refused or neglected to have them properly repaired, and persons who have been refused certificates.

United States Fish Commissioner.

The laws provide that the President shall appoint from among the civil officers or employes of the government a Commissioner of Fish and Fisheries, who must be a person of proved scientific and practical acquaintance with the fishes of the sea-coast, and who receives no salary additional to that which he drew before his appointment. It is his business to prosecute investigations and inquiries on the subject, with the view of ascertaining whether any, and what, diminution in the number of the food fishes of the coast and lakes of the United States has taken place, and, if so, to what causes this diminution is due, and, also, whether any, and what, protective, prohibitory, or precautionary measures should be adopted in the premises, and report the same to Congress. He may take, or cause to be taken, at all times, in the waters of the sea-coast of the United States, where the tide ebbs and flows, and also in the waters of the lakes, such fish or specimens thereof as may, in his judgment, from time to time, be needful or proper for the conduct of his duties, any law, custom, or usage of any State to the contrary notwithstanding.

Pension Agents.

The President is authorized to appoint all pension-agents, who hold their respective offices for four years, unless sooner removed or suspended. Each pension-agent, whether man or woman, is required to execute an official bond, with sufficient security, for such an amount and in such form as the Secretary of the Interior may approve. The President may establish pension-agencies, not exceeding three in any State or

Territory, whenever in his judgment the public interest and the convenience of pensioners require.

Agents for paying pensions receive a commission of two per centum on all disbursements made by them to pensioners. They are also allowed, where an agent disburses $50,000 annually to pensioners, not exceeding $500 for clerk-hire, office-rent, and office expenses; where an agent disburses $100,000 annually, not exceeding $750 a year for such office expenses; and for every $50,000 additional disbursed by an agent, he or she is allowed not more than $250 a year additional income; but no agent can receive from fees and commissions more than $4,000 a year. Each agent is, however, entitled to thirty cents in full for each voucher prepared and paid by him or her, including necessary postage, which sum is paid to the United States. Pension-agents and their clerks are authorized to take and certify the affidavits of all pensioners and their witnesses who come before them for that purpose, but they receive no fee for this service. In paying a pension the pension-agent is authorized to deduct from the amount of it the attorney's fee for aiding the pensioner, as agreed upon or as prescribed by the Commissioner of Pensions, where no sum was agreed upon. For this service the pension-agent may retain thirty cents.

Pension Surgeons.

The Commissioner of Pensions is authorized to organize, at his discretion, boards of examining surgeons, not to exceed three members, to examine the physical condition of pensioners or applicants for pensions in the interest of the government. In ordinary examinations each surgeon receives a fee of one dollar, and for special cases three dollars each. The Secretary of the Interior also appoints a surgeon as medical referee, who, under the control and direction of the Commissioner of Pensions, has charge of the examination and revision of the reports of examining surgeons, and performs other duties touching medical and surgical questions in the Pension-Office as the interests of the service may demand. His salary is $2,500 a year.

The Secretary of the Interior may also appoint qualified surgeons, not exceeding four in number, to perform the duties of examining surgeons when so required, and they are borne on the rolls of his office as clerks of the fourth class, with salaries of $1,800 a year each.

A Sketch of the Work in the Department of the Interior.

THE DEPARTMENT of the Interior, at Washington, is governed by the Secretary of the Interior. There is also an Assistant Secretary of the Interior, appointed by the President, whose duties are prescribed by the Secretary, or by law.

There are in the Department of the Interior the following bureaus, controlled by their respective commissioners: The General Land Office, Bureau of Indian Affairs, Pension Office, Patent Office, and Office of Education.

Duties of the Secretary of the Interior.

The Secretary of the Interior has supervision of the census, when directed by law; the public lands, including mines; the Indians; pensions and bounty lands; patents for inventions; the custody and distribution of government publications; the educa-tional interests; the Government Hospital for the Insane, and the Columbia Asylum for the Deaf and Dumb.

He exercises all the powers and performs all the duties in relation to the Territories of the United States that were by law or custom performed, previous to March 1, 1873, by the Secretary of State. He has, also, supervisory and appellate powers in relation to all acts of United States marshals, and others, in taking and returning the census of the country. He has also supervision of all the expenditures of his department. He also reports annually to Congress the nature, character, and amounts of all claims presented to him during the preceding year, under laws or treaty stipulations for compensation for depredations committed by Indians, whether allowed by him or not, and the evidence on which he based his action; also, the quantity and kind of the copies of public journals, books and documents received from the government for distribution, and the manner of their distribution in detail.

DUTIES OF OFFICERS IN THE INTERIOR DEPARTMENT.

General Land Office.

The Commissioner of the General Land-Office performs, under the directions of the Secretary of the Interior, all executive duties pertaining to the survey and sale of the public lands of the United States, or in anywise respecting such public lands, such as relate, also, to private claims of land, and the issue of patents for all grants of land under the authority of the government. He makes plats of lands surveyed under the authority of the United States, and gives such information respecting the public lands and concerning the business of his office as may be directed.

All patents issued from the Land-office bear the authority of the United States, are signed by the President, countersigned by the Commissioner of the General Land-Office, and are recorded in that office.

Duty of the Recorder.

It is the duty of the Recorder of the General Land-Office, under instructions from the commissioner, to certify and affix the seal of the office to all patents for public lands, and to attend to their correct engrossing, recording and transmission; to prepare alphabetical indexes of the names of persons entitled to patents and those who receive them, and to prepare copies and exemplifications of matters on file or records in the General Land-Office as the commissioner may direct.

Duties of the Commissioner of Indian Affairs.

The Commissioner of Indian Affairs has the management of all Indian affairs and all matters arising out of Indian relations. To him are transmitted, for examination, all accounts and vouchers for claims and disbursements connected with Indian affairs, and by him they are passed to the proper accounting officer of the department of the Treasury for settlement.

The President may prescribe such regulations as he deems proper for carrying into effect the various legal provisions relating to the control of Indian affairs; and the Secretary of the Interior also prepares and publishes regulations, at his discretion, establishing the method of presenting claims, arising under treaty stipulations or Congressional laws, for compensation for depredations committed by Indians, and the character of the evidence brought to support such claims.

It is the duty of the Secretary of the Interior, also, to make and maintain such rules as are necessary to prohibit the sale of arms or ammunition within any district or country occupied by uncivilized or hostile Indians.

It is the duty of the Commissioner of Indian Affairs to report annually to Congress a tabular statement showing distinctly the separate objects of expenditure under his supervision, during the fiscal year next preceding each report. In his annual report he embodies the statements of all agents or commissioners issuing food, clothing or supplies of any kind to Indians, with the number of Indians present and actually receiving such supplies.

Commissioner of Pensions.

The Commissioner of Pensions performs such duties in the execution of the various pension and bounty-land laws of the United States as the President directs.

The commissioner is authorized, with the approval of the Secretary of the Interior, to appoint a person to sign the name of the commissioner to certificates or warrants for bounty lands to soldiers, sailors, etc.

The commissioner is authorized to detail, from time to time, any of the clerks in his office to investigate any suspected attempts to defraud the United States in or affecting the adminstration of any law relative to pensions, and to aid in the prosecution of any person implicated, with such additional compensation as is customary in cases of special service; and such person is empowered to administer oaths in the course of such investigation.

Officers of Indian Affairs.

The Board of Indian Commissioners consists of not more than ten persons, appointed by the President; men eminent for intelligence and philanthropy, who receive no compensation for performing their duties under such appointment. The board has power to appoint one of its members as its secretary, who is entitled to such reasonable salary as may be agreed upon by the board, to be paid from any moneys appropriated by the government for the expenses of the commission. The board supervises all expenditures of money appropriated for the benefit of Indians within the limits of the United States, and inspects all goods purchased for Indians, in connection with the Indian service, and has access to all books and papers relating thereto in any government office; but the examination of vouchers and accounts by the executive committee of the board is not necessary to secure their payment.

Duty of Indian Inspectors.

The President is authorized to appoint several Indian inspectors, not exceeding five in number, each of whom holds his office for four years, unless sooner removed.

As often as twice a year one or more of the inspectors is required to visit each Indian superintendency and agency and fully investigate all matters pertaining to the business of each, including an examination of its accounts, the manner of expending money, the number of Indians provided for, contracts of all kinds connected with the business, the condition of the Indians, their advancement in civilization, the extent of the reservations, and what use is made of the lands set apart for that purpose, and, generally, all matters belonging to the Indian service.

Each inspector has power to examine on oath all officers and other persons in and about the superintendencies and agencies, and to suspend from office any superintendent, agent, or employe, and appoint another person temporarily to fill the vacancy created by the suspension, reporting his action to the President. The inspectors are, also, each empowered to enforce the laws and prevent the violation of the laws in the several agencies and superintendencies. It is so arranged that the same inspector may not investigate the affairs of any superintendency or agency twice in succession.

Indian Superintendents.

The President is authorized, from time to time, to appoint four or more superintendents of Indian affairs, and each holds his office four years.

Each superintendent, within his district, exercises a general supervision and control over the official conduct and accounts of all officers and persons employed by the government in Indian affairs, under such regulations as are established by the President, and may suspend such officers and persons from their offices or employments for reasons forthwith to be communicated to the Secretary of the Interior; and, also, to perform within his district such duties as may be properly assigned to him. The Secretary of the Interior may, at his discretion, authorize the temporary employment of clerks by superintendents of Indian affairs whenever the public interests seem to require it.

Whenever a superintendency is discontinued by the President, or abolished by law, the agents in that district report directly to the Commissioner of Indian Affairs.

Indian Agents.

From time to time the President is authorized to appoint numerous Indian agents, locating them among the Indian tribes west of the Mississippi river, and from Texas to Oregon. The President has power to discontinue any agent at his discretion, or to require one agent to perform duty at two agencies for one salary. Each agent holds his office four years, and before entering upon his duties is required to give a bond with such security as the President or Secretary of the Interior may require. Within his agency he manages and superintends the intercourse with the Indians according to law, and executes and performs such regulations and duties as may be prescribed by the President, the Secretary of the Interior, the Commissioner of Indian Affairs, or the Superintendent of Indian Affairs.

Where Indian Agents Must Live.

Every agent is required to reside and keep his agency within or near the tribe of Indians to which he is assigned, and at such place as the President may designate, and may not leave the limits of his agency without permission.

The President may require any military officer of the United States to execute the duties of an Indian agent, and such officer receives no other compensation than his army pay and actual traveling expenses.

Legal Powers of Agents.

Indian agents are authorized to take acknowledgments of deeds and other instruments of writing, and to administer oaths in investigations committed to them in the Indian country, under rules and regulations prescribed by the Secretary of the Interior.

The President also appoints a competent number of sub-Indian agents, to be employed and to reside wherever the President may direct.

Location of Each Agency.

The limits of each superintendency, agency and sub-agency are established by the Secretary of the Interior, either by tribes or geographical boundaries. All special agents and commissioners not appointed by the President are appointed by the Secretary of the Interior.

Indian Interpreters.

An interpreter is allowed to each agency. Where there are several tribes in the same agency speaking different languages, one interpreter may be allowed by the Secretary of the Interior for each of such tribes. Interpreters may be nominated by the proper agents to the Department of the Interior for approval, and may be suspended by the agent, for cause, from pay and duty, and the circumstances reported to the Department of the Interior for final action.

Indian Interpreters Preferred.

Whenever persons of Indian descent can be found who are properly qualified for the performance of the necessary duties, preference is given to them in all cases of appointments of interpreters and other persons employed for the benefit of the Indians.

The Secretary of the Interior must, under the direction of the President, cause the discontinuance of the services of such agents, sub-agents, interpreters, etc., as may from time to time become unnecessary in consequence of the emigration of the Indians, or other causes.

No person employed in Indian affairs may have

any interest or concern in any trade with the Indians, except for and on account of the United States, under a penalty of $5,000 and removal from office.

Teachers Among the Indians.

In every case where the President may judge improvement in the habits and condition of Indians practicable, and ascertains that the means of instruction can be introduced among them with their own consent, he may employ capable persons of good moral character to instruct them in the mode of agriculture suited to their situation, and to teach their children in reading, writing and arithmetic, under such regulations as the President may prescribe. And when any of the Indian tribes are, in the opinion of the Secretary of the Interior, competent to direct the employment of their blacksmiths, mechanics, teachers, farmers or other persons engaged for them, the direction of such persons may be given to the proper authority of the tribe.

Indian Traders.

Any loyal citizen of the United States, of good moral character, may be permitted to trade with any Indian tribe upon giving a bond to the United States of not less than $5,000, with good security, approved by the proper authorities, conditioned that he will faithfully observe all laws and regulations made for the government of trade and intercourse with the Indian tribes, and in no respect violate the same.

United States Surveyors.

The President appoints one Surveyor-General in the States and Territories named below, each embracing one surveying district: Louisiana, Florida, Minnesota, Kansas, Nebraska, Iowa, Dakota Territory, Oregon, Washington, Colorado, New Mexico, California, Idaho, Nevada, Montana, Utah, Wyoming and Arizona. Each Surveyor-General has but one office in his district, located, from time to time, as the President shall direct, and must reside in the district to which he is appointed. The term of office of Surveyors-General is four years.

The Records of Surveys.

The Secretary of the Interior takes the necessary measures for the completion of the surveys in the general surveying districts for which Surveyors-General have been appointed, at the earliest practicable period; and when the surveys are finished, the field-notes, maps, records and other papers pertaining to land-titles within the same are turned over to the Secretary of State of the respective States, and the office of Surveyor-General in every such district ceases and is discontinued.

Every Surveyor-General is authorized to employ a sufficient number of skillful surveyors as his deputies, who are sworn to a faithful performance of their duties. He frames regulations for their direction, and has power to remove them for negligence or misconduct in office.

What Shall be Surveyed.

Each Surveyor-General is required to cause to be surveyed, measured, and marked all base and meridian lines through such points, and perpetuated by such monuments and such other correction parallels and meridians as are prescribed by law and instructions from the General Land-Office, in respect to the public lands within his surveying district to which the Indian title has been or may be extinguished. He causes to be surveyed all private land-claims within his district after they have been confirmed by authority of Congress, so far as may be necessary to complete the survey of the public lands. He transmits to the register of the respective land-offices within his district general and particular plats of all lands surveyed by him for each land district, forwarding copies of such plats to the Commissioner of the General Land-Office.

As far as is compatible with his other duties, he is required occasionally to inspect the surveying operations in his district, sufficiently to satisfy himself that the field-work is being faithfully executed according to contract. In case he cannot give his personal attention to such inspection, he is authorized to appoint a confidential deputy to make the required examination.

There is allowed for the several offices of the Surveyors-General, for clerk-hire, office-rent, fuel, books, stationery, and other incidental expenses, such sums as Congress may appropriate from year to year.

Whenever he thinks that the public interest requires it, the President is authorized to transfer the duties of Land Register and Receiver in any district to the Surveyor-General of the district in which such land district is located.

The Patent-Office.

The Patent-Office is a bureau of the Interior Department, wherein are kept and preserved all the records, books, models, drawings, specifications and other papers and things pertaining to patents for inventions.

In the Patent-Office are the following officers, appointed by the President: A Commissioner of Patents, an Assistant Commissioner of patents, and three Examiners-in-chief.

All the other officers, clerks and employes, named below, are appointed by the Secretary of the Interior, on the nomination of the Commissioner of Patents, their salaries varying from $900 to $2,500 per year: A chief clerk, an examiner in charge of interferences, one examiner in charge of trade-marks, twenty-four principal examiners, twenty-four first assistant examiners, twenty-four second assistant examiners (two of whom may be females), twenty-four third assistant examiners, a librarian, one machinist, three skilled draughtsmen, thirty-five copyists of drawings, one messenger and purchasing clerk, one skilled laborer, eight attendants in the model room, and eight others in the same room.

The Patent-Office has a seal, with which letters-patent and papers issued from it are authenticated.

The Commissioner of Patents and the chief clerk are severally required to give a bond for the faithful discharge of their duties, and a true accounting of public moneys coming into their hands.

Must Not be Pecuniarily Interested.

No officer or employe of the Patent-Office is allowed to acquire or take, during his or her term of service, any right or interest, directly or indirectly, except by inheritance or bequest, in any patent issued by the office.

Under the direction of the Secretary of the Interior, the Commissioner of Patents superintends or performs all duties respecting the granting and issuing of patents directed by the laws, and has charge of all books, records, papers, models, machines and other things belonging to the Patent-Office.

He, subject to the approval of the Secretary of the Interior, from time to time, establishes regulations, consistent with law, for the conduct of proceedings in his office. He also causes to be classified and arranged in suitable cases, in rooms and galleries of the Patent-Office, set apart for that purpose, the models, specimens of composition, fabrics, manufactures, works of art and designs which are deposited in the Patent-Office;

and these rooms and galleries are kept open during suitable hours for inspection by visitors.

He may restore to the respective applicants such models accompanying rejected applications for patents as he deems it unnecessary to preserve, or he may sell or otherwise dispose of them after the application has been finally rejected for a year, paying the purchase-money into the Treasury, as other patent-moneys are directed to be paid.

Description of Patents.

He may cause to be printed copies of the patent-claims of current issue, and copies of such laws, decisions, regulations and circulars as may be necessary for the information of the public.

He is authorized to have printed, from time to time, for free distribution a limited number of the complete specifications and drawings of each patent, together with suitable indexes, one copy being placed for free public inspection in each State-house of every State and Territory, copies for the like purpose in the clerks' offices of the Federal district courts, and one in the library of Congress—all being certified under the hand of the Commissioner and seal of the Patent-Office, and not to be taken from their places of deposit for any other purpose than as evidence in suits at law.

He is also authorized to have printed such additional copies of these specifications and drawings, duly certified, for sale at a price as low as may be warranted by the actual cost and demand for them, and to furnish a complete set of them to any public library that will pay for binding and transporting them and will provide suitable places of deposit, open to the public.

The lithographing and engraving are done by contract after competitive bidding, and the printing is done at the Government Printing-office.

Report of Commissioner of Patents.

Annually, the Commissioner of Patents lays before Congress a report, setting forth the amount of moneys received for patents, for copies of records or drawings, and all other sources; details of all the moneys paid out for contingent and miscellaneous expenses; a list of all the patents granted during the preceding year, generally classified; an alphabetical list of all the patentees and their places of residence; a list of all the patents that have been extended during the year, with such other information of the condition of the Patent-Office as may be useful to Congress or the public.

Superintendent of Public Documents.

The Superintendent of Public Documents, appointed by the Secretary of the Interior, collects, arranges, preserves, packs and distributes the publications received at the Department of the Interior for distribution, and performs other duties belonging to his office, including the compiling and supervising of the "Biennial Register," for the use of Congress and the several States.

The Returns Office.

The Secretary of the Interior is directed to provide, from time to time, a proper apartment in his department, to be called the Returns office, in which he causes to be filed the returns of contracts made by the Secretary of War, the Secretary of the Navy and the Secretary of the Interior, and appoints a clerk to attend to its business. His duty is to file all returns made to the office, so that they may be easy of access, keeping all returns made by the same officer in the same place, and numbering them in the order in which they are made. He also keeps an index-book, with the names of the contracting parties and the number of each contract opposite to the names, and this book is to be open for public

inspection. He also furnishes copies of these returns to any person who is willing to pay five cents for copying every 100 words; he has also to certify to the correctness of each copy made.

The Office of Education.

The Office of Education is a bureau of the Department of the Interior, the duties of which include the collection of facts and figures showing the condition and progress of education in the several States and Territories, and to diffuse such information respecting the organization and management of schools and methods of teaching as shall aid the people of the United States in the establishment and maintenance of efficient school systems, and otherwise promote the cause of education throughout the country.

The office of education is managed by a commissioner of education, who is appointed by the President.

The persons employed in the office of education include a chief clerk, one statistician, and one translator.

Hospitals.

Besides the foregoing bureaus and offices of the Department of the Interior, the Secretary of the Interior is charged with the supervision of the Government Hospital for the Insane, in the District of Columbia, which has for its objects the most humane care and enlightened curative treatment of the insane of the army and navy of the United States and the District of Columbia; and the Columbia Institution for the Deaf and Dumb, in the District of Columbia, which was established for the education of deaf mutes from the several States and Territories.

Department of Agriculture.

Congress, some years since, made provision for a Department of Agriculture at Washington.

The general design and duties of the Government Department of Agriculture are to acquire and distribute among the people of the United States useful information on subjects connected with agriculture in the most general and comprehensive sense of that word, and to procure, propagate, and distribute among the people new and valuable plants and seeds. The chief officer of this department is the Commissioner of Agriculture, who is appointed by the President. Besides a chief clerk, the commissioner appoints the following assistants: One chemist, one assistant chemist, one entomologist, one microscopist, one botanist, one statistician, one superintendent of experimental gardens and grounds, one assistant superintendent of the same, one disbursing clerk, one superintendent of the seed-room, one assistant superintendent of the seed-room, one librarian, one engineer, one superintendent of the folding-room, two attendants in the museum, and one carpenter.

Duties of the Commissioner of Agriculture.

The Commissioner of Agriculture has charge of the building and premises appropriated to the use of that department at Washington, and of the library, furniture, fixtures, records, and other property belonging to it.

It is his duty to procure and preserve all information concerning agriculture which he can obtain by means of books and correspondence, and by practical and scientific experiments (official records, accurately kept, are made in his office), by the collection of statistics, and by any appropriate means within his power.

He is also required to collect new and valuable seeds and plants. and to test, by cultivation, the value of such of them as ought to be thus tested; propagate such as may be worthy of propagation, and distribute them among agriculturists.

The Bureaus of the Naval Department.

ROMINENT in the President's cabinet is the Secretary of the Navy. The business of the naval department is distributed among the following eight bureaus: The Bureau of Yards and Docks, presided over by an officer selected from the navy, not below the grade of commander; the Bureau of Equipment and Recruiting, presided over by a similar naval officer; a Bureau of Navigation, presided over by a similar officer; a Bureau of Ordnance, and Bureau of Construction and Repair, presided over by similar officers, the latter being also a skillful navy constructor; the Bureau of Steam-engineering, presided over by one of the chief engineers of the navy, who is also a skillful engineer; the Bureau of Provisions and Clothing, presided over by a paymaster of the navy, of not less than ten years' standing; the Bureau of Medicine and Surgery, presided over by one of the surgeons of the navy. The chiefs of these bureaus are appointed by the President, hold their offices for four years, and receive only the salary pertaining to each of their official grades in the navy.

Duties of the Secretary of the Navy.

The duties of the Secretary of the Navy are as follows: To execute such orders as he shall receive from the President relative to procuring naval stores and materials, and the construction, armament, equipment and employment of vessels of war, and other matters connected with the naval establishment; to have custody and charge of all the books, records and property in and belonging to the Navy Department; to cause the collection of all flags, standards and colors taken by the navy from the enemies of the United States.

The annual reports of the secretary to Congress shall present: A statement of the appropriations of the preceding fiscal year, how much money was expended, and in what manner, and the probable demand of the balances of appropriations remaining unused in each department of the navy; a statement of all offers for contracts for supplies and services made during the year, and accepted, by classes; a statement showing how much money was expended during the preceding fiscal year for wages of mechanics and laborers employed in building, repairing or equipping vessels, or in handling stores, and how much money was spent in purchasing stores and materials, with the cost and value of articles received, used, and remaining on hand, at the navy-yards; a statement of all sales of vessels and materials of the navy, by whom bought, the amounts realized from such sales, etc. The respective bureaus of the department furnish to the secretary all estimates for the specific, general and contingent expenses of the department and bureaus.

The Hydrographic Office.

Attached to the Bureau of Navigation in the Navy Department is a hydrographic office, for improving the means for navigating safely the vessels of the navy and merchant marine by providing, under the authority of the Secretary of the Navy, accurate and cheap nautical charts, sailing directions, navigators and manuals of instruction for the use of all such vessels. The Secretary of the Navy is authorized to provide such charts, maps, etc., to be prepared and printed and distributed to navigators at the cost of printing and paper. The moneys thus received from the sale of maps, charts, etc., is to be applied to the purchase and preparation of more of the same articles.

Nautical Observations.

The Naval Observatory at Washington is in charge of a naval officer, who receives only the pay of an officer of his grade for shore duty. The "Nautical Almanac," containing the result of naval and astronomical observations, is supervised annually by a naval officer or professor of mathematics in the navy, appointed by the secretary for that purpose.

The meridian of the Naval Observatory, at Washington, is established as the American meridian for all astronomical purposes, and the meridian of Greenwich, England, for all nautical purposes.

Facts Concerning the Various Branches of the United States Navy.

THE ACTIVE officers of the United States Navy are graded as follows:

Admiral, Vice-Admiral, rear-admirals, commodores, captains, commanders, lieutenant-commanders, lieutenants, masters, ensigns, and midshipmen.

When the present Admiral and Vice-Admiral die, resign, or are removed, the grade will cease to exist, as no vacancy in it can be filled by promotion from the next lower rank.

The relative rank between officers of the navy and officers of the army is as follows:

The Vice-Admiral ranks with the lieutenant-general, Rear-admirals with major-generals, Commodores with brigadier-generals, Captains with colonels, Commanders with lieutenant-colonels, Lieutenant-Commanders with majors, Lieutenants with captains, Masters with first lieutenants, and Ensigns with second lieutenants.

How Many Naval Officers are Allowed.

There are allowed on the active list of naval officers of the line, one Admiral, one Vice-Admiral, ten rear-admirals, twenty-five commodores, fifty captains, ninety commanders, eighty lieutenant-commanders, 280 lieutenants, 100 masters and 100 ensigns. During war, rear-admirals are selected from those officers on the active list, not below the grade of commanders, who eminently distinguish themselves by their courage, skill and genius in their profession, and not then unless they have, upon the recommendation of the President, received the thanks of Congress for distinguished service. During peace, vacancies in the grade of rear-admiral are filled by regular promotion from the list of commodores.

Requisites in the Medical Service.

The active list of the Medical corps of the navy consists of fifteen medical directors, fifteen medical inspectors, fifty surgeons, and 100 assistant surgeons. All appointments in the Medical corps are made by the President. No person can be appointed assistant surgeon until he has been examined and approved by a board of naval surgeons, nor be less than twenty-one years old, nor more than twenty-six. No person can be appointed surgeon until he has served as an assistant surgeon at least two years in the navy, at sea, nor until he has been approved for such appointment by a board of naval surgeons.

The President selects the surgeons, and appoints to every fleet or squadron one who is denominated "surgeon of the fleet," and is surgeon of the flag-ship.

The Pay Department of the Navy.

The active list of the Pay corps of the Navy consists of thirteen pay directors, thirteen pay inspectors, fifty paymasters, thirty passed assistant paymasters and twenty assistant paymasters. All appointments in the pay corps are made by the President.

No person can be appointed assistant paymaster who is less than twenty-one years old or more than twenty-six years, nor until his physical, mental and moral qualifications have been approved by a board of paymasters appointed by the Secretary of the Navy.

The President may designate among the paymasters in the service, and appoint one to every fleet or squadron, who is denominated "paymaster of the fleet."

The Engineer Corps of the Navy.

The active list of the Engineer corps of the Navy consists of seventy chief engineers, divided into three grades, ten having the relative rank of captain, fifteen of commander, and forty-five of lieutenant-commander, or lieutenant. One engineer-in-chief is selected by the President to serve in each fleet or squadron of the navy, and is denominated "engineer of the fleet." There are also in the navy 100 first assistant engineers, who have the relative rank of lieutenant or master in the navy, and 100 second assistant engineers, with the relative rank of master, or ensign.

Religious Service in the Navy.

The laws provide for the appointment by the President, for service in the public armed vessels of the United States, a number of chaplains (or ministers of the gospel), not exceeding twenty-four. A chaplain must not be less than twenty-one, nor more than thirty-five years old at the time of his appointment. Every chaplain is permitted to conduct public worship according to the manner and forms of the church of which he may be a member, and each chaplain must report annually to the Secretary of the Navy the official services performed by him during the previous year.

Mathematicians in the Naval Service.

The number of professors of mathematics

employed in the navy cannot exceed twelve, and they are appointed and commissioned by the President. They perform such duties as may be assigned to them by order of the Secretary of the Navy, at the Naval Academy, at the Naval Observatory, and in ships of war, instructing midshipmen of the navy, or otherwise. Three have the relative ranks of captains, four of commanders, and five of lieutenant-commanders, or lieutenants.

Naval Constructors.

The President may appoint naval constructors, who have rank and pay as naval officers, and are required to perform duty at any navy-yard or other station. Cadet engineers, who graduate with credit in the scientific and mechanical class of the Naval Academy, may, upon the recommendation of the academic board, be immediately appointed as assistant naval constructors.

Store-Keepers.

The President may appoint a civil engineer and a naval store-keeper at each of the navy-yards where such officers are necessary. The Secretary of the Navy may appoint citizens who are not officers of the navy to be store-keepers at foreign stations, when suitable officers of the navy cannot be ordered on such service, or when, in his opinion, the public interest will be thereby promoted.

Number Who May Enlist, and their Age.

The number of persons who may at one time be enlisted in the navy, including seamen, ordinary seamen, landsmen, mechanics, firemen, coal-heavers, apprentices, and boys, may not exceed 7,500.

Boys between the ages of sixteen and eighteen years may be enlisted to serve in the navy until they arrive at the age of twenty-one years, and other persons may be enlisted to serve for a period not exceeding five years unless sooner discharged by the direction of the President. No minor between sixteen and eighteen years old can be enlisted without the consent of his parents or guardian. No boy less than sixteen years old, no insane or intoxicated person, and no deserter from the navy or army can be enlisted in the naval service. Any person enlisted in the military service may, on application to the Navy Department, approved by the President, be transferred to the navy or marine corps, to serve therein the remainder of his term of enlistment, subject to the laws and regulations of the naval service. But such tranfer does not release the soldier from any indebtedness to the government. Provision is also made in the laws for sending men from distant stations to the places of their enlistment at the expiration of their terms of service. Honorable discharges may be granted to seamen, ordinary seamen, landsmen, firemen, coal-heavers and boys who have enlisted for three years; and it is the duty of every commanding officer, on returning from a cruise, to report to the Secretary of the Navy a list of his crew who enlisted for three years as being entitled to an honorable discharge as a testimonial of obedience and fidelity. And every commanding officer of a vessel is required to discourage his crew from selling any part of their prize-money, bounty-money, or wages.

Flag-Officers.

The President may select any officer not below the grade of a commander on the active list, and assign him to the command of a squadron, with the rank and title of "flag-officer;" and any officer so assigned has the same authority and receives the same obedience from the commanders of ships in his squadron, even though they hold commissions of an older date than his, that he would be entitled to receive if his commission were the oldest.

The laws prescribe with great minuteness the naval system of promotion from a lower rank to a higher one.

The Naval Academy.

The Naval Academy of the United States is established at Annapolis, Md. The students are styled " cadet midshipmen," and of these one is allowed to be appointed for every member or delegate of the House of Representatives in Congress, one for the District of Columbia, and ten are appointed annually from the United States at large.

How Cadets are Appointed.

In March, every year, the Secretary of the Navy notifies (in writing) every member and delegate in Congress of any cadet vacancy that may exist in his district. The nomination of a candidate to fill such vacancy is made upon the recommendation of the member or delegate, if made before the first day of July of that year; but if it is not made by that time, the Secretary of the Navy must fill the vacancy. The candidates for the District of Columbia and the United States at large are selected by the President. All candidates from Congressional or Territorial districts and the District of Columbia must be actual residents, respectively, of the localities from which they are nominated.

Age of Candidates.

All candidates must be between the ages of fourteen and eighteen years, and physically sound, well formed and robust, and each is examined, how and where the Secretary of the Navy may prescribe. Any candidate rejected at such examination does not have the privilege of another examination for admission to the same class, unless recommended by the board of examiners. Should any candidate be found to be mentally or morally disqualified for admission, the member of Congress or Territorial delegate is notified to appoint another, who will be also duly examined and admitted or rejected.

Length of Time in School.

The academic course of cadet midshipmen continues for six years. Cadet midshipmen who are found to be deficient at any examination shall not be continued at the academy or in the service, unless the academic board of examiners so recommend.

When cadet midshipmen have successfully passed the graduating examination at the academy, they receive appointments as midshipmen in the navy, and take rank according to their proficiency in academic studies.

Who Determines the Course of Study.

The Secretary of the Navy has authority to issue regulations for the education, at the naval academy, as naval constructors and steam engineers, of midshipmen and other persons who exhibit a peculiar aptitude for such professions. For this purpose such persons are formed into a separate class at the academy, to be styled cadet engineers, or are otherwise supplied with all proper facilities for such a scientific mechanical education as will fit them for their proposed professions. These students may not at any time exceed fifty in number, and are selected by the Secretary of the Navy. No person other than a midshipman can be eligible for appointment to this class unless he first produces satisfactory evidence of mechanical skill and proficiency, and passes an examination as to his mental and physical qualifications.

The course of study for cadet engineers is four years, including two years' service on naval steamers. They are examined from time to time, and if found deficient, or if dismissed for misconduct, they cannot remain at the academy or in the service, except upon the recommendation of the academic board.

How Vessels are Ranked and Classified.

The classification of vessels in the navy includes four grades, commanded as follows: First rate vessels by commodores, second rate by captains, third rate by commanders, and fourth rate by lieutenant-commanders. Steamships, carrying forty or more guns, are classed as first rates, those of twenty guns and under forty as second rates, and all those of less than twenty guns as third rates.

How Vessels are Named.

The vessels of the navy are named by the Secretary of the Navy, under the direction of the President, according to the following rule: Sailing vessels of the first class, after the States of the Union, those of the second class after the rivers and principal cities and towns of the United States, and those of the third class as the President may direct. Steamships of the several classes are named in the same manner precisely, care being taken that not more than one vessel in the navy shall have the same name.

The Secretary of the Navy may change the names of any vessels purchased for the naval service.

Punishment for Offenses.

Congress has prepared sixty articles for the government of the officers and men in the navy. They have special reference to offenses committed against discipline, good order and morality, and the penalties attached to these and infractions of duty; the composition and powers of courts-martial and courts of inquiry, the sale or misuse of government property, the treatment of prize vessels and prisoners of war, the general conduct of all persons in the navy, etc.

Punishment with Death.

The following offenses are punishable with death, and the code applies to all persons in the navy: Mutiny, disobedience of orders, striking a superior officer, murder, acting as a spy, intercourse with an enemy without leave, receiving secret messages from an enemy, desertion in time of war, deserting a trust, sleeping on watch, leaving a station without orders, willful stranding or injuring of a vessel, unlawful destruction of public property, striking his flag or treacherously yielding to an enemy, cowardice in battle, deserting duty in battle, neglecting orders to prepare for battle, neglecting to clear ship for action, or to join in attack when signal is made to give battle, failing to encourage the men to fight, failing to seek an encounter with an enemy when duty requires it, or failing to relieve and assist other vessels of the fleet or squadron when in battle.

Other Punishment.

Courts-martial may adjudge the penalties of imprisonment for life, or for a stated term, at hard labor, and have jurisdiction in this respect over the offenses of profanity, falsehood, drunkenness, gambling, fraud, theft or other conduct tending to the destruction of good morals; cruelty; oppression; quarreling and fomenting quarrels; challenging or fighting duels, or acting as a second in a duel; contempt of superior officers; seeking to form combinations against a commanding officer to weaken his authority; using mutinous words; neglect of orders; not endeavoring to prevent the destruction of public property; negligent stranding of any vessel of the navy; misconduct in convoying merchant or other vessels; receiving goods or merchandise for freight on board of a naval vessel without high authority; aiding or abetting in making false muster-roll; wasting public property; plundering or abusing citizens on shore; refusing to apprehend offenders or to receive prisoners; absence from duty without leave; violating general orders or regulations; desertion in time of peace; harboring deserters, etc.

Duties of commanders in active service are designated respecting accurate accounts of men transferred to and from their respective ships, showing their exact positions in the navy at the date of transfer; complete lists of the officers, men and passengers, sent quarterly to headquarters; noting deaths and desertions on board ship; care of the property of deceased persons; inspection of provisions; the health of their crews; presence at the final payment of crews; promulgation of the articles for the government of the navy, etc., and liability to be court-martialed for neglect of these rules and restrictions.

What Constitutes a Court-Martial.

Rules prescribe that no officer shall be dismissed from the service except by an order of the President, or by the sentence of a general court-martial. A general court-martial may be convened by the President, the Secretary of the Navy, or the commander-in-chief of a fleet or squadron. It consists of not more than thirteen nor less than five commissioned officers, not more than one-half of lower rank than the officer to be tried.

The Duty of a Court-Martial.

It is the duty of a court-martial, in all cases of conviction, to adjudge a punishment adequate to the nature of the offense. In a sentence to suffer death, two-thirds of the members must vote in favor of such sentence, or it cannot be inflicted; in all other cases, sentences are decided by a majority of the votes of the members. No sentence of a court-martial extending to the taking of life or to the dismissal of a commissioned or warrant-officer can be carried into execution until confirmed by the President. All other sentences may be carried into execution on confirmation of the commander of the fleet or officer ordering the court.

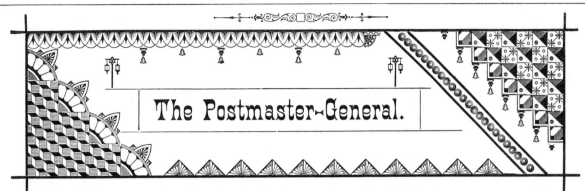

The Postmaster-General.

An Insight into the Workings of the Postal Service.

HIS EXECUTIVE department of the Government is superintended by the Postmaster-General. His term continues through that of the President, by whom he is appointed, and one month more, unless he sooner dies or resigns, or is removed for cause.

In this department are also three Assistant Postmasters-General, appointed by the President. There is also in this department an Assistant Attorney-General, appointed by the Postmaster-General.

Oath of Persons in the Postal Service.

Before entering upon his or her duties, or drawing any salary, every person employed in the postal service, from the Postmaster-General down, has to go before some civil or military officer and take the following oath of office:

I, A. B., do solemnly swear, (or affirm) that I will faithfully perform all the duties required of me, and abstain from everything forbidden by the laws in relation to the establishment of post-offices and post-roads within the United States; and that I will honestly and truly account for, and pay over, any money belonging to the said United States which may come into my possession or control: So help me God.

Duties of the Postmaster-General.

The duties of the Postmaster-General are as follows: To establish and discontinue post-offices; to instruct all persons in the postal service with reference to their duties; to decide on the forms of all official papers; prescribe the manner of keeping and stating postal accounts; to inforce the prompt rendering of postal returns relative to said accounts; to control, subject to the settlement of the Sixth Auditor of the Treasury Department, all expenses incident to the service of his department; to superintend disposal of the moneys of his department; to direct the manner in which balances shall be paid over; issue warrants to deposit money into the treasury, and to pay it out; to superintend generally the business of the department, and execute all laws relative to the postal service; to keep an account of all property in charge of the department, and report the same to Congress annually; to negotiate and conclude postal arrangements with foreign countries, and may reduce or increase the rates of postage between this and foreign countries; to publish the results of postal conventions with foreign countries; to deliver to the Sixth Auditor of the Treasury a copy of mail-carrying contracts; to issue warrants (on the quarterly statements of the Sixth Auditor) of payments of postmasters on account of the postal service, for carrying such amounts to the credit of the postal revenues on the books of the Auditor; to discharge from custody any person confined in jail on a judgment in a civil case in favor of the department if the defendant can show that he has no property of any kind; to prepare estimates and transmit them to Congress annually through the Secretary of the Treasury, for the necessary appropriations of money for his department, specifying in detail the purposes for which it is needed, such as printing, binding, salaries of employes, and other items.

Postmaster-General's Reports.

The Postmaster-General shall report to Congress annually: All contracts for carrying the mails made within the preceding year, with all particulars concerning them, and no person employed in the Post-Office Department shall become interested in any such contract, or act as agent, with or without compensation, for any mail-contractor, under pain of instant dismissal from office and other penalties; a statement of all land and water mail routes established or ordered within the preceding year, besides those contracted for at the annual mail-lettings, with the particulars attending them, and of all allowances made to mail contractors within the preceding year above the original contract prices, and the reasons therefor, etc.; a statement in detail of all expenses curtailed within the preceding year; a detailed statement of the finances of the department for the preceding year, showing its resources, engagements, and liabilities; a report of the fines assessed against mail contractors and deductions from their pay, with the particulars; a copy of each contract for carrying mails between the United States and foreign countries, and a statement showing its benefits to the department; a report of all contracts, except for carrying mails, with the details thereof. a report on the postal business and agencies in foreign countries; a statement of the money expended in the department for the preceding fiscal year, with details. All of these reports and statements are to be printed at the public printing office, together or separately.

THE UNITED STATES POSTAL SERVICE.

Division of Labor in Large Post-Offices.

The postmaster, with a private secretary, has an office, where he maintains a general supervision over the entire post-office and its business, answering correspondence relating to postal business, and giving the public such information concerning the postal service as may be necessary for the general good. In his office, also, is an "inquiry clerk," whose business it is to receive all complaints concerning missing letters and other mail-matter, to institute searches therefor in his own or other interested post-offices, etc.

In the larger post-offices, like that at Chicago, the work is divided into sections. The general laws provide for clerks, at various salaries, and the postmasters, with the consent of the Postmaster-General, assign to each a distinctive branch of labor. In the Chicago Post-Office, for instance, there are five divisions, embracing all the operations of the office, as follows:

THE EXECUTIVE DEPARTMENT—Composed of the assistant postmaster, the auditor of post-office accounts, the book-keeper, the cashier, the watchmen, etc.

THE MAILING DEPARTMENT—Devoted to the reception and sending-off of mail-matter passing into and through the office, and out of it, in the regular course of business.

THE LETTER DELIVERY—Including the superintendent of free delivery and the letter-carriers, with the general delivery, the box-delivery, etc.

THE REGISTERED-LETTER DEPARTMENT—For the registry and mailing of valuable letters and the delivery of registered letters to the proper parties.

THE MONEY-ORDER DEPARTMENT—In which money-orders upon other post-offices in the United States and several foreign countries are issued, and similar orders from other post-offices are paid to the proper persons.

Special Postal Agents.

Connected with the principal post-offices are also two or more special agents of the Post-Office Department, whose business it is to superintend the railway postal service, and special agents employed in the free delivery and money-order service, in the interest of the Department.

Assistant Postmaster.

This officer is appointed by the postmaster, who is responsible for his acts. He is, as his title indicates, the active assistant of the postmaster in supervising the work of the post-office. He cannot be a contractor for carrying any mail, nor be interested in any mail-carrying contract, and his salary varies according to the location and circumstances of his appointment.

Post-Office Auditor.

The auditor is charged with the examination and correction of the accounts of the postmaster with the Government, his subordinate officers, clerks and employes of the post-office.

The Post-Office Book-keeper.

The book-keeper is charged with the duty of correctly opening, keeping and closing, from time to time, the accounts of the postmaster with the Government and with every individual doing business with or for his post-office, subject to the orders of the postmaster and assistant postmaster, by whom his salary is fixed.

The Post-Office Cashier.

This officer has supervision of all the money paid into or out of the post-office, subject to the orders of the postmaster and assistant postmaster, and provides for its safe keeping and proper deposit with the United States Sub-Treasurer, or in some other designated place.

The Post-Office Watchmen.

The duties of the watchmen are principally confined to the custody of the post-office building and its contents at night and other designated periods during the absence of officers and employes.

Interior Work of Large Post-Offices.

The duties of mailing clerks are varied according to the departments in which they are employed, as for instance: To open all packages of letters addressed to that office, to count and compare them with the post-bill accompanying the package and to check any error in the bill; to file the bill, and send the letters to the letter-carriers' department, the general delivery, the box-delivery, the registry office or the money-order office, as may be necessary for their proper care and safe delivery.

If the office is a "distributing post-office," letters for various other places within the distributing limits of the office are sorted, billed, repacked and forwarded to their proper destination by mail.

Some of the clerks sort out newspapers and periodicals, and send them to the proper delivery, or mail them for other points. Newspapers and periodicals for other newspapers and periodicals within the delivery of that office are sent to the "exchange clerks," to be sorted and properly distributed; so, also, transient newspapers and periodicals are sorted and sent to the proper deliveries in the post-office.

Other clerks receive, sort, stamp, bill and mail letters designed for other places. Others receive, examine and mail transient packages of newspapers and periodicals directed to other post-offices. Others receive regular daily, weekly and other newspapers and periodicals sent from publishing houses direct to subscribers, exchanges, etc., weigh them, to ascertain the amount of postage to be prepaid by the publishers, and send the accounts to the proper officer, after which such papers and periodicals can be forwarded by mail to any part of the country without further charge to the publishers or subscribers.

Delivery clerks receive domestic and foreign letters, newspapers, periodicals not directed to any special box, street or number. These go into the general delivery, to be there called for by their owners. Other letters and papers, directed to a specified box, are placed in that box to remain until called for.

Post-Office Stamp Department.

In large offices there is a wholesale stamp department and a retail stamp department. In the first, stamps are sold to merchants and others by the sheet, or in greater quantities; stamped envelopes by the package or larger quantity, and postal cards by packages or hundreds.

In the retail department sales extend from a single one-cent stamp to a dozen or more of any required sorts. In this department, also, the clerk weighs transient packages to be sent by mail, to ascertain the required amount of postage to be prepaid, if requested so to do.

Letter Delivery.

The superintendent of free delivery is placed in charge of the letter-carriers and their work. He sees that letters are promptly and properly sorted by the clerks for the branch offices or the various letter-carriers.

One or more clerks are stationed in the general delivery to promptly and carefully assort and deliver the letters and papers, domestic and foreign, sent to their department. In some offices there is a foreign-letter delivery, conducted like the ordinary general delivery. When letters remain a designated time in the general delivery uncalled for, they are advertised in some public newspaper, kept a certain time longer, and are then forwarded to the dead-letter office of the Post-Office Department at Washington.

All letters not properly directed for mailing, or on which the postage is not prepaid, are also sent to the dead-letter office at stated periods. In the box-delivery, clerks are stationed to wait upon those who call for the contents of their boxes, and properly distribute whatever mail-matter is sent to their department. Those persons who rent lock-boxes and drawers wait upon themselves, having the proper keys to their respective compartments of this delivery.

Registered-Letter Division.

For the greater security of valuable mail-matter, the Postmaster-General established a uniform system for the registration of letters. Mail-matter can only be registered on the application of the party who posts the same, and the fee for registration, in addition to the regular postage, is ten cents, to be in all cases prepaid. The registry clerk in the post-office gives the person registering the letter a receipt for it, properly describing it. The letter is classified on the books of the office sending it as a registered letter; it is then carefully mailed to the postmaster at the post-office to which it is directed; is classified there as a registered letter, and delivered to the person to whom it is addressed only upon his giving a receipt therefor as a registered letter. The proper number of clerks is detailed to the registered-letter department of a large office by the postmaster thereof. In smaller offices the postmaster and his ordinary clerks attend to the registration of letters, as they are presented, and the delivery thereof whenever they arrive.

The Money-Order Division.

In order to promote public convenience, and to insure greater security in the transfer of money through the mails, the Postmaster-General has established and maintains, under rules and regulations which he deems expedient, a uniform money-order system at all suitable post-offices, known as "money-order offices." The postmaster of every city where branch post-offices are in operation subject to his supervision, is authorized, under the direction of the Postmaster-General, to issue, or cause to be issued, by his clerks and assistants in charge of such branch offices or stations, postal money-orders, payable at his own or at any other money-order office, or at any branch post-office or station of his own or any other money-order office, as the remitters thereof may direct; and the postmaster and his sureties are, in every case, held accountable upon his official bond for all moneys received by him or his designated assistants or clerks in charge of stations, from the issue of money-orders, and for all moneys which may come into his or their hands, or be placed in his or their custody by reason of the transaction by them of money-order business.

Any postmaster who issues a money-order without having previously received the money therefor, is deemed guilty of a misdemeanor, and may be fined not less than $50 nor more than $500.

Prices of Postal Money-Orders.

Money-orders not exceeding $15, ten cents.
    "   "   30, fifteen cents.
    "   "   40, twenty cents.
    "   "   50, twenty-five cents.

None are sold exceeding $50, nor can one individual or firm send more than three orders amounting to $50 to one and the same party on the same day.

Money-orders are payable only to the persons in whose names they are drawn, but the right to collect the amount may be transferred in writing on the money-order to one other (and no other) individual by the person in whose favor the order is originally drawn.

Blank applications for money-orders are kept at money-order offices, which each applicant can fill up with his name, the name and address of the party to whom the order is to be paid, the amount and date of the application, and all such applications are preserved in the money-order office for a stated time after the money-order is issued.

The postmaster who issues a money-order sends a notice thereof by mail, without delay, to the postmaster on whom it is drawn.

After a money-order has been issued, if the purchaser desires to have it modified or changed, the postmaster who issued it can take it back and give a new one instead, for which a new fee has to be paid.

The postmaster who issues a money-order shall repay the amount of it upon the application of the person who obtained it and the return of the order, but the fee paid for it is not returned.

The Postmaster-General transfers money-order funds from one postmaster to another, and from the postal revenue to the money-order fund; and also to the postmaster at any money-order office, by a warrant on the United States Treasury, and payable out of the postal revenues, such sums as may be required over and above the current revenues at his office to pay the money-orders drawn upon him. He also requires each postmaster at a money-order office to render to the Post-Office Department weekly, semi-weekly, or daily accounts of all money-orders issued and paid, of all fees received for issuing them, of all transfers and payments made from money-order funds, and of all money received to be used for the payment of money-orders or on account of money-order business.

Commissions to Postmasters.

Postmasters at money-order offices are allowed, as compensation for issuing and paying money-orders, not exceeding one-third of the whole amount of fees collected on orders issued, and one-fourth of one per cent. on the gross amount of orders paid at their respective offices, provided that such compensation, together with the postmaster's salary, does not exceed $4,000 a year, except in the case of the postmaster at New York city.

There is at Washington an officer of the Government known as the superintendent of the money-order system, whose salary is $3,000 a year.

Officers in the Money-Order Department.

The officers in charge of the postal money-order division of the Chicago Post-Office, aside from the postmaster and assistant postmaster, are a superintendent, an examiner and a cashier. The superintendent supervises and controls the direct operations of his office under the instructions of the Postmaster-General and the postmaster. The examiner examines the correctness of each money-order presented from another post-office before passing it to the cashier for payment, reserving a minute of it, which must compare with the order in name, place of issue, number and amount. The cashier, upon receiving the order from the examiner, pays it to the proper person waiting to receive the money.

The cost of the stationery and incidental expenses of the money-order division of each post-office are, if possible, paid out of the fees received from the sale of money-orders.

The Dead-Letter Office.

The dead-letter office is a branch of the Post-Office Department at Washington, for the purposes herein named.

The Postmaster-General regulates the period during which undelivered letters may remain in any post-office, and when they shall be returned to the dead-letter office, and he makes regulations for their return from the dead-letter office to the writers when they cannot be delivered to the persons to whom they are addressed.

When Letters are Advertised.

As often as the Postmaster-General may prescribe, but not oftener than once a week, postmasters are required to advertise the list of letters remaining uncalled-for and unclaimed in their respective offices. This is done by inserting the list in a newspaper of the vicinity having the largest circulation within that post-office delivery, or by a written list posted in some public place. After the list has been published, the postmaster is required to post up in a conspicuous place in his office a copy of such list.

Sent to the Dead-Letter Office.

At the end of the time prescribed by the Postmaster-General for keeping undelivered letters in his office after advertising them, the postmaster sends them to the dead-letter office, together with the following other letters: Letters deposited in that office to be mailed to other offices, on which the name of the post-office was accidentally omitted, or on which the address was too imperfect to be properly understood; letters on which prepayment of postage was neglected, and letters addressed to a known fraudulent institution or firm.

What is Done With Dead Letters.

At the dead-letter office, all letters sent to it are opened and examined. If they contain valuable inclosures they are registered, and when they cannot be delivered to the party addressed nor to the writer, the contents are disposed of, and a careful account is kept of the amount realized in each case, and may be reclaimed within four years by the sender or the party addressed. All other letters of value or importance to the party addressed or the writer, and which cannot be returned to either, are disposed of as the Postmaster-General directs.

Letters with Writer's Address on Envelope.

Prepaid letters, bearing upon the outside the name and address of the writer, are not advertised, but if not called for within a time set by the writers, are returned to the persons sending them, without charge.

Mail Contractors.

Before making any contract for carrying the United States mails, except on railways, and, under certain circumstances, upon steamboats or other vessels, the Postmaster-General must give public notice by advertising once a week for six weeks, in one or more newspapers published in the State or Territory where the mail service is to be performed (one of which papers must be published at the State or Territorial capital), and such notice must describe the route, the time at which the mail is to be made up, the time at which it is to be delivered, and the frequency of the service.

Proposals for Carrying the Mail.

Every proposal for carrying the mail over any specified route must be accompanied by the oath of the bidder, that he has the pecuniary ability to fulfill his obligations and that his bid is made in good faith and with the intention to enter into contract and perform the service in case his bid is accepted; that the signatures of his guarantors are genuine, and that he believes them pecuniarily responsible for and able to pay all damages to the United States arising from his failure to fulfill his contract. The guarantors must be one or more responsible persons. Proposals for carrying mails are delivered sealed, and are kept sealed until the bidding is closed, and are then opened and marked in the presence of the Postmaster-General and one or two of the Assistant Postmasters-General, or any other two officers of the Post-Office Department, to be designated by the Postmaster-General. Any bidder may withdraw his bid, in writing, twenty-four hours before the time for opening it.

Bids are Recorded.

All bids are recorded and preserved by the Postmaster-General. Postmasters are forbidden to give any bidder a certificate of the sufficiency of his guarantor or surety before the guarantee or contract is signed by such guarantor or surety, and if he "knowingly makes any false or illusory certificate," may be forthwith dismissed from office and fined or imprisoned, or both.

Contracts Run for Only Four Years.

No contract for carrying mails on land can be made for a longer term than four years, nor on the sea for more than two years. No mail contractor can receive any pay until he has executed his contract according to law and the regulations of the department. The laws prescribe the manner of carrying mails in detail, prohibit sending letters by private expresses, provide for carrying letters on vessels, steamboats, etc., and punishment for obstructing or delaying the mail.

The Railway Postal Service.

Railway routes on which mails are carried, including those in which the service is partly by railway and partly by steamboat, are divided into three classes, according to the size of the mails, the speed at which they are carried and the frequency and importance of the service, so that each railway company receives, as far as practicable, a proportionate and just rate of compensation, according to the service performed. The pay for carrying mails on any railway of the first class does not exceed $300 per mile a year, on railways of the second class not more than $100 per mile a year, and on those of ,the third class not more than $50 per mile a year, unless one-half the service on any railway is required to be performed in the night, when twenty-five per cent. additional may be paid by the Postmaster-General.

Postal Clerks Carried Free.

On all railways carrying mails, the person in charge of them is transported free, and mail-matter and the route agent are to be carried on any train. The pay for carrying mails on railways which receive government aid is fixed by Congress.

Postal Car Accommodations.

Among the conditions of the railway postal service are the following: That the railway shall furnish mail trains with postal cars sufficiently large, properly fitted up, furnished, warmed and lighted for the accommodation of route-agents and the necessary clerks to accompany and distribute the mails.

The clerks sort the mails for each station on the route and the post-roads connecting therewith, while traveling, and deliver the mail-bag thus made up at mail-stations, by kicking or throwing it from the car at places where the train does not stop, or by handing it to the authorized mail-messengers at depots where the train halts.

Different Classes of Postmasters.

The Postmaster-General establishes post-offices at all such places on post-roads defined by law as he may deem expedient.

Postmasters are divided into five classes. Those of the fourth and fifth classes, who do the least business, are appointed and may be removed by the Postmaster-General, and the others are appointed by the President, holding their offices for four years, unless sooner removed.

Where Postmasters Must Live.

Every postmaster must reside within the delivery of the office to which he is appointed, and before entering upon its privileges, emoluments and responsibilities, must execute a bond to the Government with good and approved security; and if it is designated as a money-order office, his bond contains an additional condition for the performance of his duties and obligations in connection with the money-order business.

The bond of any married woman who may be appointed postmaster is as binding upon her and her sureties, and she is as liable for misconduct in office, as if she were a man.

What the Post-Office Department Requires.

Every person employed in the postal service must take and subscribe to an oath that he (or she) will faithfully perform all the duties required of him (or her), and abstain from everything forbidden by the laws in relation to the establishment of post-offices and post-roads within the United States; and that he (or she) will honestly and truly account for and pay over any money belonging to the United States which may come into his (or her) possession or control. Every person employed in the postal service is subject, however, to all penalties and forfeitures for violations of the laws relating to such service, whether he has taken the oath of office or not.

Requirements of Postmasters.

Every postmaster keeps an office in which one or more persons must be on duty during such hours of the day as the Postmaster-General directs, for the purpose of receiving, delivering, making up and forwarding all mail-matter received thereat. He must also keep a record, in prescribed form, of all postage-stamps, envelopes, postal books, blanks, and property received from his predecessor, or from the Post-Office Department or its agents; of all receipts of money for postage and box-rents, and of all other receipts on account of the postal service, and of any other transactions which are required by the Postmaster-General. These records are preserved and delivered to his successor, and shall at all times be subject to examination by any special agent of the department.

He renders to the Postmaster-General, under oath, once in three months, in such form as the latter prescribes, an account of all moneys received or charged by him, or at his office, for postage, rent of boxes or other receptacles for mail-matter, or by reason of keeping a branch post-office, or for the delivery of mail-matter in any manner whatever.

The Postmaster-General may also require him to send with his quarterly accounts a sworn statement of the truth of such accounts, showing, besides, that he has not knowingly delivered, or permitted to be delivered, any mail-matter on which the postage was not at the time paid.

Penalty for Neglect.

If he neglects for a month to make his quarterly returns to the department, he and his sureties forfeit and pay double the amount of the gross receipts at such office during any previous or subsequent equal period of time; and if at the time of trial no account has been rendered, they are liable to a penalty in such sum as the court and jury estimate to be equivalent thereto.

Where Postmasters Must Keep Money.

He is required to safely keep, without loaning, using, depositing in an unauthorized bank, or exchanging for other funds, all public money collected by him, or which comes into his possession, until it is ordered by the Postmaster-General to be transferred or paid out. Postmasters in cities where there is an Assistant Treasurer of the United States, must deposit the postal revenues and all money accruing at their offices with such assistant treasurer as often as once a week, and oftener if the Postmaster-General requires it. Every postmaster must promptly report to the Postmaster-General every delinquency, neglect or malpractice of mail-contractors, their agents or mail-carriers, that comes to his knowledge.

When More Post-Office Clerks are Allowed.

Whenever unusual business accrues at any post-office, the Postmaster-General may make a special order allowing reasonable compensation for clerks, and a proportionate increase of salary to the postmaster during the time of such extraordinary business.

The Postmaster-General may designate offices at the intersection of mail-routes as distributing or separating offices, and if any such office is of the third, fourth, or fifth class, he may make a reasonable allowance to the postmaster for the necessary cost of clerk-hire arising from such duties. The Postmaster-General may discontinue any post-office where the safety and security of the postal service and revenues are endangered from any cause, or where the efficiency of the service requires it.

What Persons in the Postal Service May Not Do.

No postmaster, assistant postmaster or clerk employed in any post-office, may be a mail-contractor or concerned in any contract for carrying the mail. No postmaster can act as an agent for any lottery office, or, under any pretense of purchase, or otherwise, sell lottery-tickets; nor can he receive or send any lottery-scheme, circular or ticket free of postage, under penalty of $50 for each violation of this regulation.

Salaries of Postmasters.

The salaries of postmasters must be readjusted by the Postmaster-General once in two years, and in special cases as much oftener as he may deem expedient. The salary of a postmaster, and such other expenses of the postal service authorized by law as may be incurred by him, and for which appropriations have been made by Congress, may be deducted out of the receipts of his office, under the direction of the Postmaster-General.

Whenever, by reason of the extension of the free delivery of letters, the box-rents of any post-office are decreased, the Postmaster-General may allow, out of the receipts of that office, a sum sufficient to maintain the salary at the amount fixed upon before the decrease in box-rents. No postmaster can, under any pretense whatever, have, receive, or retain for himself, in the aggregate, more than the amount of his salary and his commission on the money-order business of his office.

When a Town May Have Letter-Carriers.

As frequently as the public convenience may require, at every city or town containing a population of 20,000 within the delivery of its post-office, letter-carriers may be employed for the free delivery of mail-matter.

Letter-Boxes.

The Postmaster-General may establish, in places where letter-carriers are employed, and in other places where, in his judgment, the public convenience requires it, receiving-boxes for the deposit of mail-matter, and cause the matter deposited therein to be collected as often as may be for general accommodation.

The compensation of letter-carriers is established by a law of Congress, and graded according to service or location.

The uniform dress worn by letter-carriers is prescribed by the Postmaster-General, and it is a penal offense for any person not connected with the letter-carriers' department of the postal service to wear such uniform.

Every letter-carrier must execute a bond, with sureties, to be approved by the Postmaster-General, for the safe custody and delivery of all mail-matter and the faithful account and payment of all money received by him.

If any person willfully or maliciously injures, tears down or destroys any public letter-box, or assaults a letter-carrier while performing his duty, he is liable to prosecution, a fine of not less than $100 nor more than $1,000, or to imprisonment from one to three years.

The Postmaster-General may establish branch offices for the receipt and delivery of mail-matter and the sale of postage-stamps and envelopes, within any post-office delivery, and prescribe the rules and regulations for their government.

No Gifts to Letter-Carriers.

No extra postage or carriers' fees may be charged or collected upon any mail-matter collected or delivered by carriers, nor can any person employed in the postal service receive any fees or perquisites on account of duties performed by him in his official position.

All expenses of letter-carriers, branch offices and receiving boxes, or incident thereto, are kept and reported in a separate account by the postmaster, and the Postmaster-General is guided in the expenditures for this branch of the service by the income derived from it.

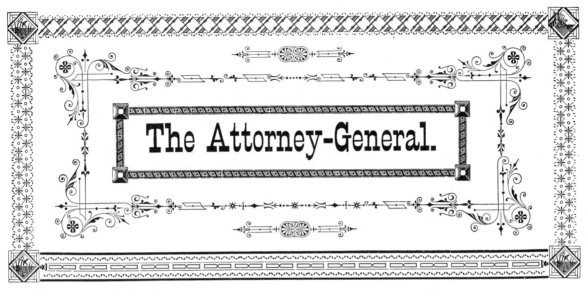

The Judiciary Department of the United States.

HIS EXECUTIVE department of the Government is in charge of the Attorney-General of the United States. He is assisted by another officer, learned in the law, called the Solicitor-General; also three officers, learned in the law, called Assistant Attorneys-General; a Solicitor of the Treasury, an Assistant Solicitor of the Treasury, a Solicitor of Internal Revenue, a Naval Solicitor, and an Examiner of Claims for the Department of State. All of the officers above designated are appointed by the President, each and all of whom hold their positions for four years, unless for sufficient cause they are sooner removed.

Duties of the Attorney-General.

It is the duty of the Attorney-General to give his advice and opinion upon questions of law whenever required by the President. No public money can be expended upon any building, site or land purchased by the Government on which to erect any armory, arsenal, fort, fortification, navy-yard, custom-house, lighthouse or other public building until the Attorney-General, in writing, decides upon the validity of the land-title and the Legislature of the State in which the land is located has given its consent to such purchase; and other government officers are named as assistants in procuring sound title to such lands.

The head of any executive department may require the Attorney-General to give his opinion concerning any question of law arising in his department, including the Secretary of War and the Secretary of the Navy, who may call upon him for legal advice.

Most of the questions of law referred to the Attorney-General, he may submit to his subordinate officers for examination and opinion, but not any questions involving a construction of the Constitution of the United States, and his approval of their opinions is required to make them valid.

He has a general superintendence over district attorneys and marshals of the United States in any State or district, and when the public interest requires it, he may employ other counsel to aid district attorneys in their duties. Should the head of any department require the attendance of counsel in examining witnesses in any claim case, the Attorney-General must furnish a subordinate lawyer for that purpose, and regulations exist for the appointment and preparation of such counsel. He may also send the Solicitor-General, or any officer of the Department of Justice, to any State or district of the United States to attend to the interests of the Government in any Federal or State court. He has also a general supervision of the accounts of district attorneys, marshals, clerks or other officers of United States courts. He shall also sign all requisitions for the advance or payment of all moneys in the Treasury, appropriated for the use of the Department of Justice. He is also authorized to publish in book form, from time to time, such opinions of the officers of the Department of Justice as he shall deem valuable for preservation, with indexes and foot-notes, the work to be done at the Government Printing-office.

At the beginning of each regular session of Congress, he has to make a report of the business of the Department of Justice for the last preceding fiscal year, including the expense accounts of the Federal courts, statistics of crime in the United States, the number of pending suits, etc.; also a report of the additional counsel and attorneys employed to assist in United States law cases.

The officers of the Department of Justice, under the direction of the Attorney-General, shall assist in performing all legal services required for other departments, in prosecuting or defending government claims, suits, etc., and the Attorney-General may require any solicitor or officer of his department to perform any duty required of the department or any of its officers.

Unless the Attorney-General otherwise directs, he and the Solicitor-General shall conduct and argue suits and writs of error and appeals in the Supreme Court, and suits in the courts of claims, in which the Government is interested.

The traveling expenses of the officers of this department, while visiting courts, etc., in remote States and districts, are paid in addition to their salaries.

Administration of Justice.

The United States Supreme Court.

HE CONSTITUTION declares that the judicial power of the United States is vested in one Supreme Court and in such inferior courts as Congress may, from time to time, ordain and establish. The judges, both of the Supreme and inferior courts, hold their offices during good behavior, and receive for their services compensation that may not be diminished during their continuance in office.

This judicial power extends to all cases in law and equity arising under the Constitution, the laws of the United States, and all treaties with foreign countries made under their authority.

The Supreme Court of the United States consists of a Chief Justice and eight associate justices, appointed by the President, any six of whom constitute a quorum. The associate justices have precedence according to the dates of their commissions, or, when the commissions of two or more of them bear the same date, according to their ages. Should a vacancy occur in the office of Chief Justice, or he become unable to perform the labors and exercise the powers of his office, his duties devolve upon the associate justice who is first in precedence, until such disability is removed or another associate justice is appointed and qualified. This provision applies to every associate justice who succeeds to the office of Chief Justice.

The Supreme Court has power to appoint a clerk, a marshal, and a reporter of its decisions.

The clerk is under the same obligations, the same restrictions, the same oath or affirmation of office, and the same bond, as is the clerk of a United States district court.

One or more deputy clerks may be appointed by the court on the application of the clerk, and may be removed at the pleasure of the court; and their duties and responsibilities are similar to those of deputy clerks in a United States district court.

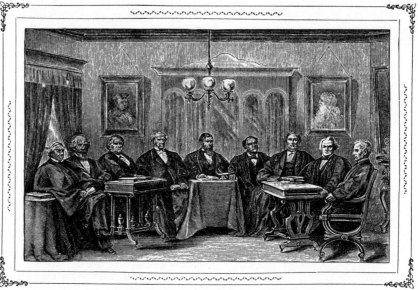

The Judges of the United States Supreme Court.

Jos. P. Bradley,   Stephen J. Field,   Sam. F. Miller,   Nathan Clifford,   M. R. Waite,   N. A. Swayne,   David Davis,   W. Strong,   Ward Hunt.

THE above illustration, from a photograph by S. M. Fassett, of Washington, represents the Judges of the Supreme bench, as they appeared in 1876. The picture is valuable as showing the dress worn and the position assumed by the judges when together in session, the Chief Justice being in the center, and the eight Associate Justices sitting four upon each side.

The marshal of the Supreme Court is required to attend the court at its sessions; to serve and execute all processes and orders issuing from it, or made by the Chief or associate justices, in pursuance of law, and to take charge of all property of the United States used by the court or its members; and with the approval of the Chief Justice he may appoint assistants and messengers to attend the court, with the same compensation allowed to similar officers in the lower house of Congress.

The reporter of the Supreme Court is required to see that its decisions, made during his term of office, are printed and published within eight months after they are made, and in any subsequent year he must print and publish another volume of the same sort. He also delivers a specified number of copies of such printed decisions to the Secretary of the Interior. At the completion of his first volume of reports he is entitled to receive $2,500, and for every subsequent volume prepared and published by him, $1,500; but all his work must be done within the legally-prescribed time and manner. The law also provides for the proper distribution of these decisions to officers of the United States Government, and the price at which other persons may buy them. Thus are preserved, from year to year, most valuable additions to our national legal lore, which, substantially bound in volumes, are gradually enlarging the law libraries of the land.

The Supreme Court holds one session annually, beginning on the second Monday in October, and such adjourned or special terms as it may deem necessary for the dispatch of its business.

The Supreme Court has exclusive jurisdiction of all controversies of a civil nature where a State is a party, except between a State and its citizens, or between a State and citizens of other States, or aliens, in which last-named cases it has original, but not exclusive, jurisdiction. And it has, exclusively, all such jurisdiction of suits or proceedings against embassadors, or other public ministers, or their domestics, or domestic servants, as a court of law can have consistently with the law of nations; and original, but not exclusive, jurisdiction of all suits brought by public ministers or embassadors, or in which a consul or vice-consul is a party.

It has power, also, to issue writs of prohibition in the district courts when proceeding as courts of admiralty and maritime jurisdiction; and writs of mandamus in cases warranted by the principles and usages of law to any courts appointed under the authority of the United States, or to persons holding office under the authority of the Government, where a State, or an embassador, or other public minister, or a consul or vice-consul is a party. The trial of issues of fact in the Supreme Court, in all actions at law against citizens of the the United States, are by jury. The laws provide largely for the character of the practice in this Supreme tribunal, which is final in its action and decrees.

What is Required of Judges.

The Justices of the Supreme Court and the United States district and circuit courts, before entering upon their public duties, are solemnly sworn, or made to affirm, that they will administer justice without respect to persons, and do equal right to the poor and to the rich, and that they will faithfully and impartially discharge and perform all the duties incumbent on them, according to the best of their abilities and understanding, agreeably to the Constitution and laws of the United States.

Continuance of Salary in Old Age.

None of these judges may exercise the profession or employment of counsel or attorney, or be engaged in the practice of the law, and disobedience in this direction is deemed a high misdemeanor and treated accordingly.

When any one of these judges resigns his office after having held it at least ten years, and has attained the the age of seventy years, he receives, during the remainder of his life, the same salary that was by law payable to him at the time of his resignation.

Division into Districts.

The United States are divided into fifty-five federal judicial districts. A district judge is appointed for each district by the President of the United States, unless otherwise provided for by the statutes. Each judge must reside in the district for which he is appointed. The records of the district court are kept at the place where it is held.

The jurisdiction of the district courts in suits, and the places and times of holding such courts, are regulated by law. The law also provides for the government of the judges in holding, changing or postponing courts, according to circumstances.

Restrictions upon Clerks.

No clerk, assistant, or deputy clerk of any United States court is allowed to act as solicitor, proctor, attorney or counsel in any cause pending in either of said courts, or in any district for which he is acting as said officer, and, if he does, he may be stricken from the roll of attorneys upon complaint.

Within thirty days after the adjournment of each term of court, the clerk is required to forward to the Solicitor of the Treasury a list of all judgments and decrees, to which the United States are parties, that have been entered in said court during such term, showing the amount

adjudged or decreed in each case, for or against the United States, and the term to which execution thereon will be returnable.

Duties of Clerks.

At each regular session of any court of the United States, the clerk presents to the court an account of all moneys remaining therein or subject to its order, stating in detail in what causes they are deposited, and in what causes payments have been made.

In the absence or disability of the judges the clerks administer oaths to all persons who identify papers in admiralty causes.

The Attorney-General exercises general supervisory powers over the accounts of clerks and other officers of United States courts.

Judges of district courts, in cases of absence or sickness, hold terms of court for each other, with the same powers and effects as if held in their own district.

United States Circuit Courts.

The judicial districts of the United States are divided into nine circuits. The Chief Justice and associate justices of the Supreme Court of the United States are allotted among these circuits by an order of that court. For each circuit there is also appointed a circuit judge, who has the same power and jurisdiction as the justice of the Supreme Court allotted to the circuit.

Circuit courts are usually held in each judicial district of the United States, (see District Courts), and are presided over by the circuit justice of the United States Supreme Court, or by the circuit judge, or by the district judge of the district sitting alone, or by any two of said judges sitting together.

It is the duty of the Chief Justice of the Supreme Court, and of each justice of that court, to attend at least one term of the circuit court in each district of the circuit to which he is allotted during every period of two years. Cases may be heard and tried by each of the judges holding a circuit court sitting apart, by direction of the presiding justice or judge, who designates the business to be done by each.

Circuit courts may be held at the same time in the different districts of the same circuit. Special terms are arranged in certain circuits of the United States. The law also regulates the circumstances under which district judges may sit in circuits, in cases of error or appeal from their own decisions; when suits may be transferred from one circuit to another; when causes may be certified back to the courts from which they came, and under what circumstances circuit justices may hold courts of other circuits at the request of another circuit justice, or when no justice has been allotted to a circuit, after a vacancy occurs.

The circuit judge of each circuit, except in cases otherwise provided for by law, appoints a clerk for each circuit court. The court also, at the request of the circuit clerks, appoints deputy clerks, and both clerks and deputies are governed by the regulations concerning district clerks and their deputies.

District Attorneys.

In nearly every district where United States circuit and district courts are established throughout the nation, the President appoints a person learned in the law to act as attorney for the United States in such district, who holds his position for four years, and is sworn to the faithful execution of his office.

It is the duty of each district attorney to prosecute, in his district, all delinquents for crimes and offenses cognizable under the authority of the United States, and all civil actions in which the United States are concerned,

and, unless otherwise instructed by the Secretary of the Treasury, to appear in behalf of the defendants, in all suits or proceedings pending in his district against collectors or other officers of the revenue, for any act done by them or for the recovery of money exacted by or paid to such officers, and by them paid into the Treasury. On instituting any suit for the recovery of any fine, penalty or forfeiture, he is required to immediately transmit a statement of the case to the Solicitor of the Treasury. Also, immediately after the close of every term of the circuit and district courts for his district, he forwards to the Solicitor of the Treasury (except in certain cases, as provided by law) a full and particular statement, accompanied by the certificates of the clerks of the respective courts, of all causes pending in said courts, and of all causes decided therein during the term in which the United States are party.

Marshals and their Duties.

A marshal is appointed in nearly every district, by the President, and holds his office for four years.

It is the duty of the marshal of each district to attend the district and circuit courts when in session, and to execute throughout the district all lawful precepts directed to him and issued under the authority of the United States; and he has power to command all necessary assistance in the execution of his duty.

The marshals and their deputies have, in each State, the same powers as sheriffs and their deputies, in executing the laws of the United States.

If a marshal dies, his deputies continue to perform their official duties, and are held responsible for their acts under the bond of the deceased marshal, the same as if he were still alive.

Marshals and their deputies whose term of office expires, or who are removed, have legal power to execute all processes remaining in their hands.

Within a month before the commencement of each term of the circuit and district courts in his district, every marshal is required to make returns to the Solicitor of the Treasury of the proceedings had upon all writs of execution or other processes in his hands for the collection of moneys adjudged and decreed to the United States, respectively, by such courts. And every marshal to whom any execution upon a judgment in any suit for moneys due on account of the Post-Office Department has been directed, is required to make returns to the sixth auditor, whenever he directs, of the proceedings which have taken place upon such process of execution.

When Vacancies Occur.

Should a vacancy occur in the office of the district attorney or marshal within any circuit, the circuit justice of such circuit may fill it, and the person so appointed serves until an appointment is made by the President; and the marshal thus appointed must give a bond, as if he had been appointed by the President, and the bond shall be approved by the circuit justice, and filed in the office of the clerk of the court.

Juries.

Jurors chosen to serve in the courts of the United States, in each State respectively, must possess the same qualifications (subject to modifications), and be entitled to the same exemptions, as the jurors in the highest court of law in such State may have and be entitled to at the time when such jurors for service in the United States courts are summoned; and they are selected by ballot, lot, or otherwise, in accordance with the custom in such State court, so far as that mode may be found practicable in a United States court or by its officers. And for this purpose the United States courts may, by rule or order, conform the selection and impaneling of juries, in substance, to the laws and usages relating to jurors in the State courts in such State.

Number of the Grand Jury.

Every grand jury impaneled before any district or circuit court must consist of not less than sixteen, nor more than twenty-three persons. If less than sixteen attend they are placed on the grand jury, and the marshal is ordered, at a date fixed by the court, to summon from the body of the district, and not from bystanders, a sufficient number of persons to complete the grand jury. Vacancies in the jury arising from the challenging of jurors are also filled in a similar manner. From the persons summoned and accepted as grand jurors, the court appoints a foreman, who has power to administer oaths and affirmations to witnesses appearing before such jury.

Grand juries are not summoned to attend the United States courts, except at the discretion and upon the orders of the presiding judge. The circuit and district courts of the States and Territories and the supreme court of the District of Columbia, discharge their juries whenever they consider their attendance unnecessary.

No person can be summoned as a juror in any circuit or district court oftener than once in two years, and any juror summoned to serve oftener than once in two years is ineligible, if challenged.

The grand jury impaneled and sworn in any district court may take cognizance of all crimes and offenses within the jurisdiction of the circuit court for such district as well as of the district court. Laws in relation to grand jurors, however, differ in certain localities.

Who May Not Serve on Juries.

Every person summoned to serve as a grand or petit juror in United States courts, are disqualified and subject to challenge who have willfully or voluntarily taken up arms or joined in any rebellion or insurrection against the United States, giving it aid and comfort, or any assistance, directly or indirectly, in money, arms, horses, clothes, or anything whatever for the benefit of any person engaged in such insurrection, or about to join it; or who has resisted, or is about to resist, with force and arms, the execution of the laws of the United States.

At every term of any United States court, the district attorney, or other person acting in behalf of the United States in such court, may move, and

the court may require the clerk to administer to every person summoned to serve as a grand or petit jury in that court, an oath embodying the substance of the above-named cause for disqualification as a juror, and liable to be challenged; and unless such persons can truly take such oath, they cannot be allowed to serve on juries in that court.

Nor can any person serve as a juror in a United States court in any proceeding or prosecution based upon or arising under the provisions of laws enforcing the fourteenth amendment of the Federal Constitution (relative to the equality of civil rights of all citizens, regardless of their color), unless such person can take and subscribe an oath, in open court, that he has never counseled, advised or voluntarily aided in any combination or conspiracy against said amendment and the laws enforcing it.

The Court Room.

THE illustration shown above represents the usual attendants upon a lawsuit during its trial in court.

Behind the desk is seated the judge; in front is the clerk of the court and beside him sits the court crier. Seated in a chair by the judge's desk is the witness being questioned by the lawyer who sits with his client at the end of the table. At the adjoining table several reporters are writing; at the extreme right are the twelve jurymen; on the opposite side of the room are four lawyers, one of whom is standing and is objecting to the course pursued by the lawyer who is examining the witness. Inside the railing and near the entrance sits the deputy sheriff, who has general charge of the court-room; at the extreme left and outside the railing sit spectators and individuals who may be called as witnesses.

The United States court of claims, is located at Washington, in apartments provided at the expense of the Government. It consists of one chief justice and four judges, who are appointed by the President, and hold their offices during good behavior. Each of them is required to take an oath to support the Constitution and faithfully discharge his duties.

When Court is in Session.

The court of claims holds one annual session. beginning early in December and continuing as long as the prompt transaction of its business may require. Any two of the judges constitute a quorum and can hold a court.

The court appoints a chief clerk, an assistant clerk (if necessary), a bailiff and a messenger. The clerks are required to take the constitutional oath of fidelity, and perform their duties under the direction of the court. For misconduct or incapacity they may be removed by the court, but

the court must report to Congress the causes of such removal.

The chief clerk has authority to disburse, under the direction of the court, the contingent fund which may from time to time be appropriated to its use by Congress; and his accounts are settled by the proper accounting officers of the Treasury in the same way as the accounts of other disbursing agents of the Government are adjusted.

Statement of Judgments Rendered.

At the beginning of the annual session of Congress, the clerk transmits to it a full and complete statement of all the judgments rendered by the court during the previous year, stating the amounts thereof and the parties in whose favor they were rendered, together with a brief synopsis of the nature of the claims; and at the end of every term of the court he transmits copies of its decisions to the heads of the various departments of the Government, to specified government officials, and to other officers charged with the adjustment of claims against the United States.

No member of either branch of Congress can practice as an attorney or counselor in the court of claims.

The court of claims has jurisdiction over all claims founded on statutes or contracts, or which are referred to it by either house of Congress; all set-off and counterclaims of the Government against persons presenting claims upon it; the claims of disbursing officers for relief from responsibility on account of the capture, while in the line of his duty, of Government funds, vouchers, records or papers in his charge, and claims for captured or abandoned property, arising from the exigencies of insurrection or other cause. The methods of procedure and practice in such court of claims are particularly described in the United States statutes. It has also power to appoint commissioners to take testimony to be used in the investigation of claims that come before it, to prescribe the fees which they receive for their services, etc.

Any final judgment against a claimant on any claim prosecuted in the court of claims according to the provisions of the law forever bars any further claim or demand against the United States arising out of the matters involved in the controversy.

These brief sketches of the various United States tribunals will serve to give the reader a faint idea of the power and dignity that distinguish in our national judicial system.

A Sketch of the Capitol at Washington.

ABOUT one and one-half miles easterly from the President's Mansion is the United States Capitol, a structure distinguished as much by its size and elegance of finish as by being the place in which the two houses of Congress assemble to enact the national laws.

The corner-stone was laid by Washington in September, 1793, and it was first occupied by Congress in November, 1800. In 1814 it was partially burned by the British soldiery; the reconstruction of the burned wings was begun in 1815; the corner-stone of the main building was laid in March, 1818, and it was finished in 1827. In 1850 it was decided to extend the structure, and the corner-stone of the new work was laid July 4, 1851, with an address by Daniel Webster. The structure was completed in 1867.

The whole edifice has an eastern front, and its entire length is 751 feet four inches, and its greatest depth, including steps and porticoes, is 348 feet. The building covers about three and a half acres of ground. The main or old portion is built of sandstone, painted white, and the extensions are of white marble, slightly variegated with blue. The outside of the building is adorned with architectural ornaments and several groups of sculpture. An iron dome rises from the center to a height of 287½ feet above the basement floor, having a diameter of 135½ feet. The top of this dome is surmounted by Crawford's bronze statue of Liberty, nineteen and a half feet high. The inside of the Capitol is liberally decorated with frescoes, sculptures and paintings. The rotunda, inside of the dome, is a circular apartment, ninety-six feet in diameter and 180 feet high.

The chamber occupied by the United States Senate is situated in the center of the northern extension of the Capitol; is of rectangular form, being over 113 feet in length, more than eighty feet in width, and thirty-six feet in height. The galleries surrounding it will seat 1,200 persons.

The House of Representatives occupies the center of the southern extension of the Capitol, and is 139 feet long, ninety-three feet wide and thirty-six feet high. The galleries will seat 1,000 people.

The Supreme Court of the United States holds its sessions in the old Senate chamber, on the east side of the north wing of the central building. It is a semicircular apartment, seventy-five feet long and forty-five feet high. The former Hall of Representatives, also of a semi-circular form, ninety-six feet long, and fifty-seven feet high, is in the south wing of the central building, and is used as a depository for the historical statues contributed by the several States, in accordance with the invitation of Congress, in 1864, with other statuary and paintings. It is considered the most stately and beautiful apartment in the Capitol.

The Library of Congress is another attractive room, ninety-one and a half feet long, thirty-four feet wide and thirty-eight feet high, on the west side of the rotunda, together with two wings, each ninety and a half feet long, twenty-nine and a half feet wide.

The Capitol grounds cover an area of fifty-one and a half acres, handsomely laid out, and containing a great variety of trees.

THE PRESIDENT'S MANSION.*

T THE western end of the city of Washington stands the staid and venerable home of the Presidents of the United States, during their terms of office. Close by it, and surrounding it, are the Government buildings occupied by the State Department, the Treasury Department, the War Department and the Navy Department, representing, in one group, the executive, diplomatic, pecuniary, and defensive sinews of the nation. Having an attractive location, with handsomely ornamented grounds in front, and a fine park in its rear reaching to the Potomac river, the President's house occupies a prominent position in the national capital.

The corner-stone of the mansion was laid October 13, 1792, and the structure was first occupied in 1800 by President John Adams. It is properly called the "White House," owing to its freestone walls having been painted white. Its designer was Mr. James Hoban, who embodied in it a resemblance to the palace of the Duke of Leinster, in Great Britain. It contains two stories and a basement, is 170 feet long and eighty-six feet wide. The portico on the north front is supported by eight columns of the Ionic order of architecture; on the south front is a semicircular colonnade of six other Ionic columns, and the roof is surrounded with a handsome balustrade.

During the war of 1812, when the British army invaded Washington, President Madison was forced to flee, and the English troops destroyed the mansion. This was in 1814. In the following year Congress authorized its reconstruction, and in 1818 the new edifice was first occupied by President Monroe.

The main entrance to the mansion is in the north front, where a massive door-way opens into the main hall, divided midway by a row

* For view of President's mansion see page devoted to President's Duties.

of pillars resembling marble, and along its walls are ranged the portraits of the chief magistrates who formerly occupied it. On the left of the hall the visitor is ushered into the celebrated "East room," which occupies the entire lower eastern portion of the mansion. It is in this apartment, which is handsomely furnished, that the Presidents hold their levees and state assemblages. It is eighty-six feet long, forty feet wide and twenty-eight feet high, and is warmed with four fire-places.

Three other apartments of some celebrity, — the "Green," the "Blue," and the "Red," — adjoin the East room, each deriving its name from the color which distinguishes it from the adjacent ones,

and all are handsomely furnished. The Red room is sometimes used as a general reception parlor. The north front of the mansion has six rooms, which are chambers used by the President and his family, and on the south front are seven rooms, described as the ante-chamber, audience room, cabinet-room, ladies' parlor, the President's private office, and two others used for various purposes. The main or state dining-room is west of the Red room, and joining it is the ordinary dining-room used by the President's family. The ladies' parlor is for the private use of the President's family, and is considered the handsomest apartment in the building. The basement contains eleven rooms, including kitchens, pantries, etc.

The Duties of a Congressman.

How Bills are Passed and Laws Made.

ALTHOUGH the Constitution of the United States quite fully details the work to be done by Congress, the following outline of the form of procedure will doubtless be interesting, it being much the same as that observed in the State legislatures in the passage of State laws:

The day having arrived for the regular meeting of a new Congress, the members of the House of Representatives gather in their hall in the Capitol at Washington, at three o'clock in the afternoon, and come to order.

The Clerk of the last previous Congress rises and says: "The hour fixed by law for the meeting and organization of the House of Representatives of the Forty-—— Congress having arrived, the Clerk of the House of Representatives of the Forty-—— Congress will proceed to read the list of members-elect to the House of Representatives for the Forty-—— Congress, prepared by him in accordance with law."

He then reads the list by States, comprising about 200 names. During the reading, some member, whenever a certain name is called (each member answering to his name), says: "I reserve a point of order on that name," intimating that he has objections to the called member's right to a seat in Congress.

The list being called through, the Clerk says: "One hundred and ninety-three persons have answered to the call. Being a quorum of the body, the Clerk is now ready to receive motions."

Sometimes, at this point, members rise and state their objections to seating certain new members, making motions to refer the credentials of such members to the Committee on Elections, etc. This business consumes considerable time in discussion, with more or less bitterness of feeling and speech.

At length the Clerk says: "The Clerk appeals to members of the House to preserve order."

Sometimes the confusion continues after this. At length the Clerk is heard to say: "The gentleman from Tennessee is out of order. The tellers will please take their places"—to aid in the organization of the House.

Selection of a Speaker.

Nominations for Speaker are then made by several members. A vote is taken by voice, counted by the tellers, and announced: "Whole number of votes cast, ——; necessary to a choice, ——; Mr. A. has ——; Mr. B., ——."

The Clerk announces: "Mr. A., of New York, having received a majority of all the votes given, is duly elected Speaker of the House of Representatives for the Forty-—— Congress. The gentleman from Wisconsin (Mr. Brown) and the gentleman from Connecticut (Mr. Jones) will please conduct the Speaker-elect to the chair, and the gentleman from Pennsylvania (Mr. Robinson), the senior member of the body, will please administer to him the oath required by the Constitution and laws of the United States."

Mr. Brown and Mr. Jones then conduct Mr. A. to the chair, where he stands and expresses, in a brief speech, his thanks for the honor conferred upon him, and pays a handsome compliment to the intelligence and political strength of the new Congress. The oath of fidelity to the Constitution, the laws and his duties, is then administered to him by Mr. Robinson.

Admitting the Members.

The Speaker then says: "The first business in order is the swearing-in of members. The various delegations (by States) will present themselves in a convenient number as they are called."

As the various members present themselves, the other members listen in silence, or occasionally interpose an objection to a certain member being qualified. These objections properly take a written form, and are referred to the Committee on Elections for examination; with the necessary affidavits to show why the members objected to should not have a seat in Congress. Long discussions sometimes intervene, and if the objec-

tions are not withdrawn, the oath is not administered to the member in dispute until the Committee on Elections report favorably in his case.

The Delegates elect from the several Territories are also sworn in.

Ready for Business.

A member offers a resolution, which meets with no opposition, but is immediately read, considered and agreed to, as follows: "That the Senate be informed that a quorum of the House of Representatives has assembled, and that Mr. A., one of the Representatives from New York, has been chosen Speaker, and that the House is now ready to proceed to business."

Mr. C., of Illinois, rises and presents a resolution, which is read, considered and adopted, appointing the Speaker and four members a committee to revise the rules of the House for its better government, to report at an early day.

Mr. G., the Secretary of the Senate, now appears on the floor of the House to announce: "Mr. Speaker—I am directed to inform the House that a quorum of the Senate has assembled, and that the Senate is ready to proceed to business."

Sometimes discussions as to the rights of certain members to seats in the House are then resumed.

Presently, a member rises and asks unanimous consent to take up and concur in a resolution just received from the Senate. No objection being made, the resolution is read, announcing the appointment of two members of the Senate to join certain members of the House (to be selected by the House) to wait upon the President of the United States, and inform him that a quorum of each House has assembled, and that Congress is ready to receive any communication that he may be pleased to make.

Waiting Upon the President.

Mr. E. moves that the House appoint three members to join the committee on the part of the Senate. The motion being agreed to, the Speaker appoints Mr. L., of Georgia; Mr. M., of Tennessee, and Mr. N., of New Jersey, as the committee on the part of the House.

During the absence of this committee but little business is done, beyond discussions upon the eligibility of certain members, or the election of the following officers of the House of Representatives: A Clerk, a Sergeant-at-Arms, a Door-keeper, Postmaster and Chaplain, in the order named. Members nominate candidates for each office as their own names are called, if they choose; the Speaker appoints tellers, and the voting is done by voice.

The vote having been announced, the successful candidate is declared elected by the Speaker. He then comes forward and qualifies for his new position by taking the Constitutional oath of fidelity. Sometimes the election of Chaplain is postponed, in order to find a candidate who is entirely satisfactory to the majority.

Somebody then proposes a regular hour for the daily meeting of the House, and the hour of twelve, noon, is usually adopted.

The drawing of seats for the members of the House is usually next in order, either by themselves or their colleagues.

This is also considered a good time to lay before the House the papers in the various contested election cases of members of the House, to be referred to the Committee on Elections when that committee has been appointed by the Speaker, within a few days after the organization.

The Joint Committee of the two Houses of Congress, appointed to announce to the President the readiness of Congress to receive any communication from him, having fulfilled their duty, return to their respective houses and report what they have done, and are then discharged from further duty in the case.

The President's annual or inaugural message is, about this time, delivered to both houses, in joint session in the House of Representatives, being usually read by the Clerk of the House and his assistants. After it has been read, the Senate retires to its own chamber and both houses proceed to refer certain portions of the message to appropriate committees for consideration and future action.

A resolution is usually adopted in the House of Representatives, authorizing the printing of several thousand copies of the message for the use of members and others.

By this time the first day's session has drawn to a close. A motion to adjourn is therefore made, seconded and adopted, and the House dissolves until the next hour of meeting.

In the Senate Chamber.

In the Senate, on the first day of the new session, the proceedings are usually marked by less feeling and confusion, but the organization is similarly effected. The Vice-President of the United States is inducted into the chair of the Senate; the new Senators are sworn in, or have their credentials referred to the Committee on Elections, and but little other business is, generally, transacted.

The New Member.

Among the members of the House of Representatives whose credentials were found to be all right, and whose eligibility and claim to a seat in Congress are therefore undisputed, is Mr. Sempronius Smith, from the Tenth District of Wisconsin. Mr. Smith has been a prosperous merchant, and mill-owner, a wide-awake and useful citizen, and his popularity resulted in his being sent to Congress to represent the interests of a large and thrifty constituency. For a few days after the organization, he wisely refrains from making himself conspicuous in the councils

Interior of House of Representatives, Washington, D. C.

THIS ILLUSTRATION represents the members of the House of Representatives in session during the meeting of Congress. The full number entitled to vote, from 1888 to 1893 is 325. The speaker of the house occupies the upper seat; at one end of his desk sits the door-keeper, at the other end the sergeant-at-arms; at the desk in front are the clerks, and at the lower desk, are the official reporters. In the gallery above the speaker, newspaper correspondents have their seats; the remainder of the gallery, which will hold about 1,000 persons, being allotted to spectators.

The members occupy the seats in the body of the house, the individuals standing on the floor being pages, who serve the members when they desire to communicate with the clerks or with each other.

of the nation. He is "learning the ropes." He confers with his colleagues and a few new acquaintances in the House upon national topics. Naturally he is shrewd and honest, and he comes to Congress fully decided to do his duty.

A Local Bill for Personal Gain.

That more or less of personal selfishness should sometimes reveal itself in Congressional legislation is a natural consequence. In order to show the routine work of introducing a bill, the nature of the lobby, the means which may influence the passage of a law in Congress, where personal benefits are conferred, the following illustration is given. This class of bill is presented as illustrative of the work of the lobby and the means sometimes used to influence legislation in securing appropriations for personal profit.

Mr. Smith does not believe that any man ever goes to Congress without at least one selfish motive—one "axe to grind." Pott, his predecessor, had half a dozen axes to grind, and came very near ruining a good portion of his constituency by advocating his selfish measures. Smith confesses (to himself only, however,) that he has one motive of a personal nature in coming to Congress. The city in which he lives—Smithtown (named after his uncle, its first settler)—is located on the west bank of the Nippewisset river, near its headwaters. Fifteen miles below, on the east bank, is Poppleton, another thriving city, in which Smith and his relatives own large real estate and commercial interests. The Grand Trunk Through-route Railroad runs around Smithtown to the north, and completely ignores it, while passing trains from Iowa to Milwaukee. On the other hand, the Great Occidental Railroad, running from Chicago to a junction with the Northern Pacific, has a station at Poppleton, and receives and delivers freight and passengers, regularly. Smith's idea is to connect Smithtown and Poppleton by steamers running on the Nippewisset river as a means of benefiting both towns. But the Nippewisset can hardly be called a navigable stream, for although it is forty rods wide and seventy miles long, and empties into the Mississippi, it is full of shallow water between Smithtown and Poppleton, and in the summer time an empty pontoon could hardly be floated between the two points. Smith has formed an idea to remedy this evil, and it is taking shape in his brain. In his seat in Congress and in his private lodgings he is engaged in putting it upon paper.

INTRODUCTION OF THE BILL.

One day, when the introduction of bills is in order, he rises in his seat in the House, and, catching the Speaker's eye, he says:

"Mr. Speaker—I hold in my hand a bill entitled: 'An Act to build a dam across the Nippewisset river at a point three miles below the town of Poppleton, Lomax county, Wisconsin, and appropriating $15,000 for that purpose.' This bill, sir, is in the interest of a large and populous section of my district, and is offered for the purpose of facilitating trade and commerce between the great Northwest and the metropolitan city of Chicago and the Atlantic sea-board. I desire, sir, to have it read and referred to the Committee on Appropriations." Smith "fairly ached" to make a speech on his bill, but he wisely refrained until it should regularly come before the House. He sent it to the Speaker by a page. Smith's colleague (Benson) requested that it be read before being referred, as it was short. He thought that an internal improvement bill of this sort had sufficient public interest to demand this consideration.

The fact is that Benson only preferred his request to satisfy his own curiosity. He had no special interests in Smith's district, and if the bill did no injury to the State, it might pass and welcome.

The Speaker said: "If there are no objections, the bill will be read by the Clerk."

TEXT OF THE BILL.

The Clerk read as follows:

"Be it enacted by the Senate and House of Representatives of the United States of America in Congress assembled, That permission is hereby granted to Robert Sweet, Thomas P. Glade and John Q. A. Sweet to construct and maintain a substantial dam across the Nippewisset river, three miles below the city of Poppleton, in the county of Lomax and State of Wisconsin.

"SECTION 2. The said dam shall be constructed of natural stone and timber, and earth, put together as crib-work, and extend from the present east shore of the Nippewisset river, at a point known as Winkle's ford, to the west shore of said river to a point known as the northeast corner of Tripp's farm.

"SECTION 3. The lands likely to be overflowed by reason of the construction of the said dam are swamp-lands, owned by the State of Wisconsin; and the said Robert Sweet, Thomas P. Glade and John Q. A. Sweet, their heirs and successors, are hereby authorized and required to build and maintain strong and substantial dykes, or levees along the line of the banks of said river, between the river and said swamp-lands, to prevent the overflow of the river into said swamps.

"SECTION 4. There is also appropriated to the said Robert Sweet, Thomas P. Glade and John Q. A. Sweet, to aid in the construction of said dam and dykes, or levees, the sum of $15,000, to be paid from moneys in the Treasury of the United States not otherwise appropriated."

One word of explanation which was not granted to the House by Smith. The parties named in this bill were brothers-in-law to Smith.

REFERRED TO A COMMITTEE.

The Speaker: "If there is no objection, the bill will be sent to Committee on Appropriations."

A Member: "I move that it be ordered printed and sent to the Committee on Commerce."

Another Member: "I second that motion."

The yeas and nays being called for, the motion prevailed, Smith himself voting in the affirmative.

That afternoon Smith's bill was sent to the room of the Committee on Commerce by a messenger, with other bills that had been referred to them during the day.

THE WORK OF THE LOBBY.

Smith had a lobby force at the capital, a number of personal friends from Smithtown and Poppleton, who knew the value of Smith's project to the interests of their respective towns and their own pockets. Ostensibly the surrounding country was to be greatly benefited by the passage of the bill. Now the lobby went to work in good earnest. They advocated the measure to every member of the House who would listen to them. They were liberal in dinners, wines and cigars. They had an argument to meet every objection. It was not a trumpery affair. A whole district would be benefited; towns would flourish, farmers be encouraged, commerce be increased, and labor enlisted. They all understood the merits of the bill. Smith was modest; he only pleaded the best interests of his constituents. Glade, one of the parties named in the bill, was there. He got in some good arguments also. Smith knew two or three of the Committee on Commerce, and by his manly bearing and quiet demeanor gave them a favorable impression of himself.

THE BILL BEFORE THE COMMITTEE.

When the full bill came up in the committee for consideration, Smith was requested to be present with one or two of his friends to explain anything that might be deemed questionable. Smith and his friends did their best to convince the committee of the fairness and utility of the measure. They described the geographical position with neat diagrams, and the commercial interests with nicely-arranged statistics. They represented the value of the Nippewisset river below the proposed dam as already worthless for commercial purposes—a thing of swamps and shoals and bars. They pointed with much enthusiasm to the increased value of lots and lands made available by making the river navigable above the dam. The committee courteously dismissed Smith and his friends, and then discussed the question of reporting the bill favorably to the House. One or two opposition members argued against the measure on political grounds, and one or two more objected otherwise, but the value of the levees or dykes to the commerce of that section of country was a strong argument. The chairman thought the improvement was richly worth the sum it would cost for its promotion of commerce in the Northwest. He had known railroads that promised less to receive large grants of land and great subsidies of money without a murmur of opposition. Now 15,000 people and 500 farms were to be benefited by

the appropriation of an insignificant sum of money. He believed in encouraging steamboats, canal-boats, sail vessels or railroads impartially, in proportion to their relative business. A railroad company needed more help than a steamboat company, and always got it. He should vote for the measure as one of the committee, or as its chairman with his casting vote. Then the vote was taken. It stood five to three before the chairman voted; then it stood six to three.

REPORT OF THE COMMITTEE.

Next day the chairman of the Committee on Commerce stood up in the House and favorably reported Smith's bill without amendment.

The House went into Committee of the Whole that afternoon to consider some appropriations for special objects. Smith's bill was among them. Smith was a little nervous. It is true he had won an important victory. The Committee on Commerce was made up of men of good common sense and ability, and their recommendation was on the side of the dominant political party in the House. But now the bill had to run the gauntlet of the entire House—friends and foes. Smith made an able plea in behalf of it, and his colleague (Benson) made another. One or two Eastern members, with pardonable sectional indifference, briefly objected to the West swallowing up so much of the public money; but an old stalwart veteran from Massachusetts said that the East had no reason to be ashamed of the West and its energetic commercial prosperity. The two sections were no longer divided in their interests. Massachusetts was the older and the better cultivated State in the matter of intellect and commercial affairs, but Wisconsin was fast overtaking any of the New England States in both of these advantages. Then he wound up with an oratorical slap at New York's overgrown steamship and railroad monopolies, and said he should vote for Smith's bill. Two or three other gentleman spoke of Wisconsin in the most favorable terms. Her war record was briefly reviewed and compared favorably with her agricultural, manufacturing and political position in the Union. Many members listened to the discussion with perfect indifference. One man suggested an amendment by striking out the appropriation. This bit of waggery caused a general smile and hastened the vote on the bill. The yeas and nays were called for and taken; the bill received a handsome majority on the question of reporting it favorably to the House, and then the committee rose.

One secret of the success of Smith's bill, thus far, is found in the real benefit that it proposed to bring to everybody living above the dam; the population below the dam had not yet found out enough about it to oppose it intelligently.

On the following day, the action of the Committee of the Whole was duly reported to the assembled House, and the bills favorably passed upon by the committee were called up in rotation for action by the House. That is, the members moved the second reading of each one as it came up, and it was so ordered.

Debate followed the second reading. Some of the bills were discussed at length; some were laid on the table; some were postponed; others were ordered to be engrossed for a third reading and put upon their passage. One or two were passed by good majorities. One or two more were recommitted to their respective committees for further consideration and amendment.

A SPEECH IN FAVOR OF THE BILL.

Smith's bill was read a second time. Benson good-naturedly spoke in favor of its passage. He had been in Congress one or two terms, and always spoke to the point and pleasantly. In consideration of its having favorably passed the Committee on Commerce and the Committee of the Whole, he felt it due to his colleague (Smith) and the State which they both represented, to move its third reading and passage by the House.

An opposition member, from a district in another portion of the Union, wished to know if the lobby had come well-primed to urge this bill through the House.

Benson indignantly repelled the insinuation of corrupting influences. The parties named in the bill were business men in good standing—not millionaires, and men who had no money to throw away in buying votes for a paltry sum of $15,000. Suppose they had a prospective money interest in the bill. So had every business man in the county. The lobby were a unit in advocating the measure, and not a word of genuine opposition had been heard except from the opponents of the dominant party in this House. "I," said Benson, in conclusion, "I move, sir, that the bill go to a third reading and be put upon its passage."

Smith seconded the motion. The crisis had come in the House, but he felt rather sure of success. The men from below the dam had not been heard from. The other eight members from Wisconsin knew of no good reason why the bill should not pass, and they said little or nothing in

regard to it. Besides, they might need the votes of Smith and Benson in some little measures of their own during the session; so they were a unit on this question.

The yeas and nays on the passage of the bill were called. The vote showed political bias and considerable indifference as to the result. It stood: Yeas, 94; nays, 65; not voting, 37. So the bill was passed.

THE BILL GOES TO THE SENATE.

A day later, Smith's bill, with others, is taken to the Senate Chamber by the Clerk of the House of Representatives and handed to the Secretary of the Senate. The latter officer, at the proper time, announces to the Senate the receipt of these bills, which have been sent to that branch of Congress for its concurrence. As the title of each is read, some Senator moves its reference to a committee, or to be laid on the table, or to be read in full a first or a first and second time.

A Senator, hearing the title of Smith's bill read, requested that it be read in full. Having heard it read, the Senator moved that the bill be sent to the Committee on Commerce.

Another Senator moved that it go to the Committee on Appropriations. This last motion being seconded, the first Senator withdrew his motion.

The President: "Unless objection is made, the bill will be sent to the Committee on Appropriations."

No one objected; and the bill was referred to the Committee on Appropriations.

PERSONAL INTERVIEWS WITH A CONGRESSMAN.

One of the Senators from Wisconsin was on this committee. When Smith learned the reference of his bill in the Senate, he sought the Senator from Wisconsin, with whom he had considerable acquaintance; had a conference with him in regard to its merits, and reported the action of the House Committees and the House in detail. Some of Smith's lobby friends also interviewed the Senator from Wisconsin, and favorably impressed him with the merits of the enterprise.

In the afternoon of the following day, Smith's bill was brought up in the committee. Smith was not present, nor was it necessary. He had fully explained matters to the Senator from his State. When the bill had been read by the clerk of the committee, the members of the committee naturally turned to the Senator from Wisconsin, with gentlemanly deference, and he briefly and comprehensively expressed a favorable opinion of it. Smith could not have done better. The State would really derive benefit from the passage of the bill. He would not deprecate the value of any other public work authorized by Congress, but this comparatively insignificant appropriation would have an effect upon the interests of inter-State commerce far outside of Wisconsin. The whole Union was more or less benefited, frequently, by these little aids to commerce.

One of the committee objected to the largeness of the amount of the appropriation. In his opinion the dam and dykes ought not to cost more than the amount named in the bill, but the parties to be benefited directly by this appropriation and improvement ought to pay at least one-third of the expense out of their own pockets. He proposed to amend the bill by striking out "$15,000," and substituting therefor "$10,000." The Senator from Wisconsin was on his feet in a moment. Only the week before he had assisted the objecting Senator to increase the appropriation in a bill of a similar character, but of no more merit than this. He made a little speech, in which he denounced the niggardly spirit in public enterprises, under a senseless cry of "retrenchment and reform." He begged permission to introduce a witness to show that $15,000 was the smallest possible sum that could be beneficially expended in making the Nippewisset river navigable for boats. The parties who requested the passage of the bill had asked nothing for the erection of the necessary wharves and piers at Poppleton or Smithtown. They were willing to bear the burden of this expense themselves. He sent a messenger for one of Smith's lobby, a gentleman familiar with the entire county mentioned in the bill. The committee questioned him in reference to the amount of work that $15,000 would accomplish. He said it might possibly build the dam, and, perhaps, most of the dykes, yet he thought that $20,000 would be none too much to finish the work proposed; but the county would willingly make up any deficiency remaining after the expenditure of the appropriation.

FAVORABLE CONSIDERATION BY THE COMMITTEE.

The committee was favorably impressed by this testimony, and the Senator cheerfully withdrew his proposed amendment. No other objection was made to the bill as it came from the House. One member of the committee thought the matter should have been put into the general appropriation for rivers and harbors; but that was all. A vote was taken on the concurrence of the committee on the merits of the measure. There are always members of committees who talk and vote against the dominant party in Congress. There was one in this committee, and he voted against Smith's bill. Otherwise the committee agreed unanimously to report the bill favorably to the Senate.

Next day the chairman of the committee so reported it to the Senate, without amendment.

The Tenure-of-Office law being then under consideration, a Senator moved that Smith's bill be read a second time, ordered printed, and laid on the table for future consideration. To this the Senate agreed.

Several days passed, for the discussion of the Tenure-of-Office law was vigorously and extensively pressed.

As soon as he saw his way clearly to gain the attention of the Senate, the Senator from Wisconsin, who had considered Smith's bill in the Committee on Appropriations, having in the meantime conferred with Smith, called up the Nippewisset river-dam bill for a third reading.

This motion brought the bill squarely before the Senate. The Senator from Wisconsin recited the action of the committee in favorably recommending it for passage without amendment, and also the favor with which it had passed the House. He briefly dwelt upon the benefit which the bill endeavored to confer upon a large class of intelligent and industrious citizens in Lomax county and upon the interests of inter-State commerce.

It was in the days when the civil service and tenure-of-office questions deeply agitated both branches of Congress. The debates had been exciting and tedious, and the minds of the Senators were filled with conflicting views upon these subjects. They gave little attention to minor matters; hence the explanations of the Senator from Wisconsin easily served to settle any doubts of the constitutionality or practical benefits of Smith's bill.

So the bill was read a third time and put upon its final passage without a dissenting voice. The vote on its passage stood: Yeas, 37, nays, 15, absent or not voting, 13.

Then the Secretary of the Senate announced that the bill had passed

An hour afterwards, in the House of Representatives, the Secretary of the Senate announced that the Senate had passed, and the Vice-President had signed, the House bill to construct a dam across the Nippewisset river, in Lomax county, Wisconsin.

SIGNED THE BILL.

The Speaker of the House thereupon signed Smith's bill also, and it was dispatched to the President of the United States for his approval or veto. (See "Duties of the President.")

A day or two subsequent to this, the President's Private Secretary appeared in the House of Representatives and announced that the President had approved and signed the bill to build a dam across the Nippewisset river, in Lomax county, Wisconsin.

Smith was happy, and received the congratulations of his friends for so successfully getting his first bill safely through Congress, within ten days.

Smith now owns two steamboat lines on the Nippewisset river.

A Bill of General Interest.

IN THE HOUSE.

On the last day of the last session of the Fortieth Congress, the President of the United States signed, and thus approved, a bill, which had been regularly passed by both Houses of Congress, entitled "An Act making appropriations for sundry civil expenses of the Government for the year ending June 30, 1870, and for other purposes."

On the 9th of April, 1869, at the first session of the Forty-first Congress, in the House of Representatives, Mr. Dawes, from Massachusetts, addressed the speaker as follows: "I ask unanimous consent to report from the Committee on Appropriations a bill making available an appropriation heretofore made for furniture for the Presidential Mansion. The appropriation made at the last session of Congress cannot be made available until next July, unless this bill is passed."

The bill introduced by Mr. Dawes, who was at that time chairman of the Standing Committee of the House on Appropriations, was a perfectly legitimate piece of legislation. He also presented to the House, at the same time a letter from the Secretary of the Treasury, Mr. Boutwell, who stated that the appropriation bill of the previous session, mentioned above, had been referred to the Comptroller of the Currency for his views, and that the comptroller had expressed the opinion that the money appropriated to purchase furniture for the President's House could not be drawn before July 1, 1869. The Secretary also requested that a bill similar to that now introduced by Mr. Dawes might be passed by Congress.

The House received the bill presented by Mr. Dawes, which was read a first and second time, without opposition. It was in substance as follows:

"Be it enacted by the Senate and House of Representatives of the United States of America, in Congress assembled, That the sum of $25,000 appropriated by the act approved March 3, 1869, entitled 'An act making appropriations for sundry civil expenses of the government for the year ending June 30, 1870,' for the purpose of refurnishing the President's House, may be made available for that purpose without increasing the amount."

Mr. Brooks, of New York, asked: "Can the gentleman name what is the amount appropriated for the White House this year?"

Mr. Dawes replied: "There has been none made by this Congress. The last Congress appropriated $25,000—the usual amount at the coming in of a new administration. It has never been less than that. On one occasion it was more."

No further remarks being made, the bill was ordered to be engrossed and read a third time, and being engrossed, it was accordingly read a third time, and passed by the House as it was introduced by Mr. Dawes.

For some unexplained cause, Mr. Dawes then moved to reconsider the vote by which the House had passed the bill, and also moved that the motion to reconsider such vote be laid on the table.

The bill was now ready to go to the Senate for concurrence, amendment or defeat.

IN THE SENATE.

On the following day, in the Senate, a message was received from the House of Representatives, by its Clerk, Mr. McPherson, announcing that the House had passed the bill making available an appropriation heretofore made for furniture for the Presidential Mansion, and requesting the concurrence therein of the Senate.

Mr. Fessenden, of Maine, said: "That is a very short bill, and I move that it be taken up at once and acted upon. It is absolutely necessary to pass it, because the money which has been appropriated for that purpose cannot be used in the present fiscal year as the law stands. This bill is merely to allow the money to be used at once."

He then called attention to the letter from the Secretary of the Treasury, expressing the opinion of the Comptroller of the Currency as to the unavailability of the appropriation in its present condition.

Mr. Stewart, referring to the bill, said: "It had better be read."

By unanimous consent, the bill was read twice by its title, and was then considered as in Committee of the Whole.

Mr. Conkling said: "Let us hear the letter read of which the chairman told us."

The Chief Clerk then read Secretary Boutwell's letter in reference to the appropriation.

Mr. Fessenden said: "I notice that the bill reads that 'the sum of $25,000, etc., is hereby made available for such purpose.' It is available now, but not until the close of the fiscal year. I think, therefore, that it will be necessary to amend it. I move to amend it by inserting after the word 'available' the words, 'during the present fiscal year.'"

The amendment was agreed to as in Committee of the Whole.

The bill was next reported to the Senate as amended, and the Senate concurred in the amendment.

It was ordered that the amendment be engrossed, and the bill read a third time.

So the bill was read a third time and passed.

IN THE HOUSE.

A message from the Senate, by its Secretary, Mr. Gorham, announced to the House that the Senate had passed the bill, with an amendment, in which he was directed to ask the concurrence of the House.

Mr. Dawes said: "I ask unanimous consent that the bill just returned from the Senate may be taken up, and the amendment of the Senate concurred in.

Messrs. Kerr, Brooks, and others objected.

IN THE SENATE.

Mr. Fessenden, in the Senate, on the same day, said: "In regard to the bill authorizing the $25,000 appropriated for furnishing the President's House to be used during the current year, which we sent back to the other House with an amendment, I understand that it cannot be got up in the House,"—owing to the objections of Messrs. Kerr, Brooks and others,—"and it is sent back to me informally, with the request that it be passed as it is. I move, therefore, regarding the bill as here by unanimous consent, that we reconsider the vote by which it was passed, and then vote down the amendment, and pass it"—the bill as it came from the House at first—"without amendment."

Mr. Edmunds, of Vermont, said: "It has not been returned formally."

Mr. Edmunds said: "No, but informally."

The President of the Senate said: "The vote will be regarded as reconsidered if there be no objection."

Mr. Edmunds and others said: "Let it be done by unanimous consent."

The President of the Senate said: "There being no objection, the vote on the passage of the bill making available an appropriation heretofore made for furniture for the Presidential Mansion will be regarded as reconsidered. The amendment will be regarded as rejected, and the bill passed without amendment—if there be no objection."

IN THE HOUSE.

In the House a message from the Senate, by its Clerk, Mr. Gorham, announced that the Senate had passed, without amendment, an act making available the appropriation heretofore made for furniture for the Presidential Mansion.

IN THE SENATE.

A message from the House, by its Clerk, Mr. McPherson, announced that the Speaker of the House had signed the bill making available the appropriation for furniture for the White House; and the President of the Senate then signed it. It was then ready to be sent to the President of the United States for approval and signature, in the same form as that in which Mr. Dawes introduced it in the House of Representatives on the previous day

REMARKS.

The history of this bill is something unusual, and the action upon it irregular, but the legality of the measure is unquestioned. After the Senate had passed the bill with the amendment, it was the duty of the House to either accept or reject the amendment by ballot. This it failed to do. It was irregular, also, for the Senate to reject its own amendment without having the bill before it, as it should have had, but it could not have it. The bill having, therefore, finally passed both houses without amendment, and the presiding officers having both signed it, it became a law, for it is not likely that the President would veto a bill of so much importance to the house in which he lived. It was something unusual, too, for the Senate to first consider the bill "as in Committee of the Whole," there agree to it, report it to the Senate as a body, and then put it on its passage.

Congressional Committees.

Committees are appointed in the different houses of Congress to consider bills relating to the following.

- Elections.
- Ways and Means.
- Appropriations.
- Judiciary.
- Banking and Currency.
- Weights and Measures.
- Commerce.
- Agriculture.
- Foreign Affairs.
- Military Affairs.
- Post-Office and Post-Roads.
- Public Lands.
- Indian Affairs.
- Territories.
- Railways and Canals.
- Manufactures.
- Miners and Mining.
- Public Buildings and Grounds.
- Pacific Railroad.
- Improvement of the Mississippi River.
- Education and Labor.
- Militia.
- Patents.
- Invalid Pensions.
- Pensions.
- Claims.
- War Claims.
- Public Expenditures.
- Private Land Claims.
- District of Columbia.
- Revision of the Laws.
- Expenditures in the Department of State.
- Expenditures in the Treasury Department.
- Expenditures in the War Department.
- Expenditures in the Navy Department.
- Expenditures in the Post-Office Department.
- Expenditures in the Interior Department.
- Expenditures in the Department of Justice.
- Expenditures in Public Buildings.
- Rules.
- Accounts.
- Mileage.
- Public Library.
- Printing.
- Enrolled Bills.
- Census.
- Civil Service.
- Ventilation of Hall.

The Duties of United States Officers in the Territories.

THE executive power of the Territories of the United States is vested in a governor, who is appointed by the President, and who holds his office for four years, unless sooner removed. He resides in the Territory to which he is assigned, although appointed from some other portion of the United States.

Powers of the Governor.

In his office he is commander-in-chief of the militia of his Territory, grants pardons and reprieves, remits fines and forfeitures for offenses against the laws of the Territory; issues respites for offenses against the laws of the United States, till the decision of the President can be made known thereon; commissions all officers appointed under the laws of such Territory, and takes care that the statutes are faithfully executed. The governor has also the same powers to either approve or veto any bill passed by the Territorial legislature, and the process in either case is similar to that indicated in the description of the government of the several States of the Union.

Duties of the Territorial Secretary.

The President also appoints a secretary for each Territory, who resides in the Territory to which he is appointed, and who holds his office for four years, unless sooner removed. In case of the death, removal, resignation or absence of the governor from the Territory, the secretary executes all the powers and performs all the duties of the governor during such vacancy or absence. It is the duty of the secretary, also, to record and preserve all the laws and proceedings of the legislative assembly, and all the acts and proceedings of the governor in the executive department; transmit copies of the laws and journals of the legislature, after each session thereof, to the President and Congress, and copies of the executive proceedings and official correspondence of the Territory to the President twice a year; prepare the laws passed by the legislature for publication, and furnish the copy to the public printer of the Territory.

Territorial Legislature.

The legislature consists of two branches—the council and house of representatives, members of both branches being duly qualified voters, are elected by the people in the various districts in the Territory. They remain in office two years, and hold their regular sessions once in two years, each legislature appointing its own day of meeting. Members must reside in the county or district from which they are respectively elected. The apportionment of districts and the election of legislators are established by the laws of the United States.

Territorial Laws Submitted to Congress.

Laws passed in certain Territories have to be submitted to Congress, and if they are not there approved, they become null and void. The Territorial legislatures are not allowed to pass laws interfering with the primary disposal of the soil, imposing taxes upon property of the United States, or taxing the land or property of non-resident owners higher than that of persons residing in the Territory.

Length of Time Legislature is in Session.

The sessions of each Territorial legislature are limited to forty days. The president of the council and the speaker of the house are both elected by their respective branches of the legislature. The qualifications of members and their rights to hold other offices while they are members, etc., are regulated by United States law. The legislature cannot pass any law altering the salary of the governor, the secretary, or the officers or members of the legislature as fixed by the laws of the United States.

The subordinate officers of each branch of every Territorial legislature consist of one chief clerk, one assistant clerk, one enrolling clerk, one engrossing clerk, one sergeant-at-arms, one door-keeper, one messenger and one watchman.

Territorial Representation in Congress.

Every Territory has a right to send a Delegate to the House of Representatives of the Congress of the United States, to serve during each term of Congress, and this Delegate is elected by a majority of the qualified voters of the Territory. Such Delegate has a seat in Congress with the right of debating, but not of voting.

How Minor Offices are Filled.

Justices of the peace, and all general officers of the militia of the Territory, are appointed or elected by the people in such manner as may be prescribed by the governor and legislature; all other officers not otherwise provided for by the laws of the Territory are appointed by the governor, with the advice of the Territorial council, vacancies being filled temporarily by the governor's appointment during a recess of the legislature until it meets again.

When a Resident May Vote.

Voters must be twenty-one years old, and citizens of the United States, or persons who have legally declared their intentions of becoming such, and without regard to "race, color or previous condition of servitude." No officer, soldier, seamen, mariner or other person in the service of the United States can vote in any Territory until he has been permanently domiciled there for six months, and no person belonging to the army or navy can be elected to, or hold, any civil office or appointment in any Territory.

All township, district and county officers, except justices and general officers of the militia, are appointed or elected in such manner as the governor and legislature provide.

Territorial Supreme Courts.

The supreme court of every Territory consists of a chief justice and two associate justices, any two of whom constitute a quorum for business. They are appointed by the President, hold their offices for four years, unless sooner removed, and open a term of their court annually at the seat of Territorial government.

Each Territory is divided into three judicial districts, in each of which a Territorial district court is held by one of the justices of the supreme court, at such time and place as the law prescribes; and each judge, after his assignment, resides in the district to which he is assigned.

The supreme court and the district courts, respectively. of the Territories, possess chancery as well as common law jurisdiction.

Territorial Prisoners.

A penitentiary established in some of the Territories when ready for the reception of convicts, is placed in charge of the attorney-general of the Territory, who makes all needful rules and regulations for its government, and the marshal having charge over such penitentiary must cause them to be duly executed and obeyed; and the reasonable compensation of the marshal and his deputies for their services under such regulations are fixed by the attorney-general.

Diplomatic Officers of the United States.

THE diplomatic officers of the United States include the following:

EMBASSADORS. — Persons sent by one sovereign power to another sovereign power to transact public business of importance and interest to one or both of them.

ENVOYS—Extraordinary—Public ministers, or officers, sent from one sovereignty to another on special business of importance.

MINISTERS — Plenipotentiary—Embassadors, or negotiators, or envoys, sent to a foreign seat of government with full diplomatic powers.

MINISTERS—Resident—Embassadors with diplomatic powers who reside continually at a foreign seat of government.

COMMISSIONERS—Persons appointed by a sovereign power to confer with similar persons from another sovereign power, and decide any special and disputed question of international interest or importance.

CHARGES D'AFFAIRES—Ministers of the third or lowest class, sent to a foreign seat of government.

AGENTS—Officers sent to a foreign country, with limited powers, to treat upon specified international matters.

SECRETARIES OF LEGATION — Officers appointed by the President to accompany ministers to foreign governments to assist them in their official duties.

Appointed by the President.

The foregoing diplomatic officers are appointed by the President, and confirmed by the United States Senate.

But one minister resident is accredited to Guatemala, Costa Rica, Honduras, Salvador, and Nicaragua, living in either of these States that he may select.

Ministers resident and consuls-general, combined in the same person, are accredited to the Republics of Hayti and Liberia.

The consul-general at Constantinople is the secretary of legation to Turkey, but receives compensation only as a consul-general.

Any regularly-appointed diplomatic officer upon whom devolves another similar office while holding the first, is allowed 50 per cent. additional pay as long as he holds the second office.

All fees collected at the legations are accounted for to the Secretary of the Treasury.

Consular Officers.

"Consul general," "consul," and "commercial agent," denote full, principal and permanent consular officers, as distinguished from subordinates and substitutes.

Either of these terms designate an officer of greater or less degree, appointed to reside at a certain place in a foreign country, to protect the commerce and commercial interests of the United States.

"Deputy-consul" and "consular agent" denote consular officers who are subordinate to such principals, exercising the powers and performing the duties within the limits of their consulates or commercial agencies, respectively, the former at the same ports or places, and the latter at ports or places different from those at which such principals are respectively located.

"Vice-consuls" and "vice-commercial agents" denote consular officers who are temporarily substituted to fill the places of consuls-general, consuls or commercial agents when they are temporarily absent, or relieved from duty.

The term "consular officer" includes the foregoing persons and none others.

No consul-general or consul may hold those offices at any other place than that to which each is appointed.

Restrictions Upon Consuls.

All consular officers whose salaries exceed $1,000 a year, cannot, while holding office, be interested in or transact any business as merchants, factors, brokers or other traders, or as clerks or agents for any such persons.

Consular Clerks.

The President has authority to appoint consular clerks, not exceeding thirteen in number, who must be citizens of the United States and over eighteen years old when appointed, and assign them from time to time to such consulates and with such duties as he shall direct. Such clerks must be duly examined as to their qualifications by an examining board, who report to the Secretary of State, before their appointment.

Duties of Consular Officers.

Consuls and vice-consuls have the right, in the ports or places to which they are severally appointed, of receiving the protests or declarations which captains, masters, crews, passengers

or merchants, who are citizens of the United States, may choose to make there, and also such as any foreigner may make before them relative to the personal interest of any citizen of the United States. Every consular officer is also required to keep a list of all seamen and mariners shipped and discharged by him, giving the particulars of each transaction, the payments made on account of each man, if any; also, of the number of vessels arrived and departed, the amounts of their tonnage, the number of their seamen and mariners, and of those who are protected, and whether citizens of the United States or not, and as nearly as possible the nature and value of their cargoes and where produced, making returns of the same to the Secretary of the Treasury; also to take possession of the personal estate left by any citizen of the United States (other than seamen belonging to any vessel), who dies within the jurisdiction of that consulate, leaving no representative or relative by him to take care of his effects.

The consul inventories the effects, collects debts due to the deceased, pays those due from him, sells such of the property of the deceased as is perishable in its nature, and after one year the remainder, unless, in the meantime, some relative or representative of the deceased comes to claim his effects, paying the accrued fees. In case no relative or representative appears, the consul forwards the remainder of the effects, the accounts, etc., to the Secretary of the Treasury in trust for the legal claimants.

Persons dying abroad may appoint consular officers their agents for the disposal of their effects, etc., or any other person instead, and the consular officer may be called upon to assist in caring for the property and interests of the deceased.

Consular officers are required to procure and transmit to the Department of State authentic information concerning the commerce of such countries, of such character, in such manner and form, and at such times as the Department of State may prescribe; also, the prices-current of all articles of merchandise usually exported to the United States from the port or place at which the consular officer is stationed. Other duties of a commercial character are fully prescribed by the laws, with restrictions and penalties for violations of the rules and regulations governing consulates.

Public Speaking

HOW TO SPEAK WELL IN PUBLIC
AND INFLUENCE AN AUDIENCE TO YOUR POINT OF VIEW

HE speakers and essayists whom we know as wielding the greatest influence in the world's history, added to the graces of oratory a depth of investigation, independence of thought, and freedom of expression. They scorned to traverse the beaten paths, simply because of custom and popularity. They chose to be independent. Rather than follow, they preferred to lead the opinion of others.

The following suggestions give an outline of what is necessary for the production of a ready, easy speaker.

First. The foundation of the discourse should be thoroughly fixed in the mind, and the order of succession in which the arguments are to follow.

Second. These should be so arranged that one thought should be the natural outgrowth of the other, and each idea should be so distinctly marked out as to be in readiness the moment it is wanted.

Third. The speaker should vividly feel all that he may design to speak, in order that clear ideas may be expressed. The mind should not, however, be so absorbed with the subject in hand as to prevent its acting readily in the development of the topic under consideration. It is possible for the feelings to become so vehement in their expression as to paralyze utterance from their very fullness.

Fourth. The feelings, in speaking, must be resolved into ideas, thought into images, to express which there must be suitable language. While the main idea should be firmly grasped, in its elucidation it should be separated into its principal members, and these again divided into subordinate parts, each under perfect command of the speaker, to be called upon and used at will, until the subject is exhausted.

Fifth. The full, complete and ready use of the imagination is of the greatest importance to the extemporaneous speaker, which power may be greatly cultivated by reading the works of Walter Scott, Dickens, and other standard writers who excel in imaginative description. To hold up before the audience a clear, distinct outline of the subject in hand, and paint the picture in fitting language so vividly that the auditors will delightedly follow its progress, step by step, is the distinguishing excellence of the off-hand speaker. With many persons of real talent, the powers of imagination work too slowly to hold the attention of the audience. This hindrance, however, can be largely overcome by practice.

Sixth. The difficulty of embarrassment, which afflicts some people upon public appearance, is overcome by practice, and by having a perfectly distinct understanding of what is to be said, which consciousness tends to give confidence and self-possession. To obtain the ability to present this clear conception of the subject, the speaker should study logic, geometry, and kindred subjects, that arrive at conclusions through a process of analytical reasoning. The speaker should be able to think methodically, being able to decompose his thoughts into parts, to analyze these into their elements, to recompose, regather, and concentrate these again in a manner such as will clearly illustrate the idea sought to be conveyed.

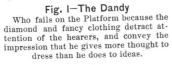

Fig. I—The Dandy
Who fails on the Platform because the diamond and fancy clothing detract attention of the hearers, and convey the impression that he gives more thought to dress than he does to ideas.

Fig. 2—Solid Man
Whose unostentatious yet substantial appearance is so much in his favor, when before an audience, as to make him a person of very considerable power, however little he may say.

Seventh. One of the most efficient aids to public speaking is the ability to write. The public speaker will do well to commence by writing in full what he is desirous of saying. He should, at the same time, make a study of the various masters of oratory. Writing gives great clearness to the expression of thought, and, having plenty of time in its composition, the mind is able to look at the subject in every phase. With the main idea clearly defined and kept constantly in view, let the speaker examine the subject in every light, the different faculties of the mind concentrating upon a single point. Thus, step by step, the subject is considered in all its bearings, the various details of the idea being completely studied, and the whole matter thoroughly developed, until the subject has reached its perfect form.

Eighth. The daily study of synonymous words and their meanings will give greater facility of expression. The mind should also be stored with a variety of information on subjects pertaining to the arts and sciences, from which one can constantly draw in cases of emergency. It is impossible for the speaker to extemporize what is not in the mind. And, further, all reading and study should be done with such care that every idea thus acquired will be so thoroughly impressed on the mind as to be available when we wish to communicate our ideas to others.

Ninth. In public speaking, one of the great secrets of success is a knowledge of human nature. To acquire this, the speaker should carefully study men—the passions and impulses that influence mankind—their phrenological characteristics, and know them as they are. To do this, he should freely mingle in society, interchanging ideas, and seeking every opportunity for the practice of extempore speaking.

Tenth. An important element necessary to success in the off-hand speaker is courage. While it is essential that he use choice and fitting language in the expression of ideas, let him not hesitate, when he has commenced a sentence, because he cannot readily call to mind the exact language necessary to beautifully clothe the thought. Push vigorously through to the end, even though at a sacrifice, for a time, of the most perfect forms of speech. This courage that dare stand up and speak a sentence ungrammatically, even, is necessary to make the good speaker of the future.

Finally, while all cannot become equally proficient in oratory, the industrious student of average talent, who earnestly resolves to win success as an extempore speaker, will find himself, in the majority of cases, in time, self-possessed in the presence of others. With ideas clear and distinct, vivified and quickened by imagination, clothed in fitting words and beautiful language, he will be enabled to instruct and entertain an audience in a manner vastly better than most people would suppose who may have listened to his maiden efforts in the commencement of his public speaking.

Instruction and Practice in Elocution.

Facts relative to Oratory, Eloquence, Expression, Gesture and Personal Appearance.

AS MEN began to multiply upon the earth, the uses of language increased and assumed new expressions in accordance with the desires and needs of individuals. Thus, affection required one tone of voice and one collection of words and phrases especially adapted to its communications. The voice of petition gave utterance to another class of

Fig. 1.—Careless,
Ungainly and slovenly in appearance, consequently lacks the power to favorably impress his hearers as a public speaker, although he may possess real talent of a high order.

Fig. 2. —Orderly,
Self-poised, genteelly dressed, and has large influence with his auditors, because of fine personal presence, though he may lack the genius that makes the finished orator.

to sweetness and the earnestness of true confidence. In the school, in the various trades and occupations of men, in the halls of legislation, in the courts, on the platform, in the pulpit, and in the drama, nature and art have established utterances greatly diversified. Language has thus become a power in our human existence, and on the lips of the orator can sway the nations, as the winds

tones and sentences expressive of its wishes. Anger, and fear, and hope, and every sentiment common to humanity, each found a rhetoric of its own, of such a distinctive character that it could not be easily mistaken for another. The cry of grief, the exultation of joy, differed then, as now, as widely as the East from the West, and the ear conveyed to the brain the peculiar sound of each. By-and-bye, when savage-life gave way to civilization, new sentiments were born, and nature and custom have given language to all.

In the calm home-life the voice is modulated awaken and arouse the sleeping ocean.

The human voice has been created an instrument in which are united the melody of the flute, the violin and the organ. The lungs supply the air, and the throat and nostrils serve as pipes for the construction of sweet sounds, producing tunes and all the changes of expression required by every consonant and vowel, and by every varying sentiment. So perfect is this arrangement for the formation of language, that rapid speakers are enabled to pronounce from 7,000 to 7,500 words an hour, or about two words in a second.

The art of correct and impressive speaking embraces elocution, oratory, eloquence, rhetoric, emotion, feeling, agitation, and logic, or the power of demonstration.

Elocution is the correct method of giving utterance to a connected discourse, either long or brief, before an audience, accompanied with appropriate gestures.

Oratory is the highest degree of elocution, and is the art of presenting a subject in its most effective and eloquent manner.

Eloquence is the expression of a great degree of emotion, whether pleasurable or sad, with such earnestness and skill as to excite a similar emotion in the breasts of the audience. With fervency and fluency it utters the most elevating thoughts in the choicest language, and with the most appropriate and graceful movements of the entire physical organization.

Rhetoric is the art of framing correct, forceful and elegant sentences, either in writing or speaking, and these may, on the lips of an acknowledged orator, supply the place of genuine emotion. Rhetoric may thus become an artificial eloquence, conveying powerful sentiments which the speaker may not feel in his heart. A true actor on the stage, or platform, may become so perfect in the rhetoric of his performance as to represent the

Disadvantages in Public Speaking.

THE above illustration shows the following unfavorable conditions for the speaker.

1. If in the day-time, the light in the hall, coming wholly from windows in the rear of the speaker, throws a shadow whereby his face cannot be seen.

2. If in the night, the unshaded lights, in the vicinity of the speaker, upon which the audience are compelled to look, will pain the eyes and divert attention of the hearers.

3. The disordered condition of maps, pictures, etc., upon the wall will annoy and hold the attention of some auditors who have large order and are keenly sensitive to disorder.

4. The holding of the manuscript by the speaker, in front of his face, will break the magnetic connection between

himself and hearers, and then the audience will become listless and inattentive.

5. The balustrade and table in front of the speaker prevent the effect that may be exerted upon an audience by gesture and posture of the lower limbs.

6. The seating of a small audience in the rear of a hall gives an empty appearance to the room, alike depressing to speaker and hearers.

7. The scattering of an audience apart breaks magnetic conditions that are favorable to a speaker when the audience is seated closely together and near the platform.

8. Members of the audience communicating one with another, reading newspapers, moving about the room, or going out, make conditions unfavorable to the speaker and those who would listen to the discourse.

most varied and strongest emotions of human nature without experiencing them.

Emotion, Feeling, and **Agitation** are varying results of true oratory, and are produced by the eloquence of the speaker. Emotion is a mental excitement, inducing pity, grief, fear, joy, enthusiasm, or other natural passions. Feeling applies to a sympathetic condition of either mind or body, and is manifested with less excitement than emotion. Agitation is the violence of intense excitement, arising from physical or mental disorder.

Logic is the art of reasoning systematically upon any subject, and embraces its cause, progress and effect. "Pure logic" is the formal expression, governed by general rules, of any idea that may present itself. "Applied logic" is the application of this method and these rules to any specific topic on which an argument is proposed.

Logic was first used as a form of reasoning by Aristotle, the great Greek philosopher, who, indeed, gave form and character to the principles and practice of public speaking.

Aristotle divided oratory into three classes, as follows:

The Demonstrative, which embraces praise in a high degree, as eulogies of great men; censure, reproach, or severe accusation against individuals, the acts of public bodies, or of governments; philosophic addresses, etc.

The Deliberative, which includes debates on subjects of national or district importance, in the halls of legislation or other public places, educational or moral lectures, etc.

The Judicial, which relates to the oratory of the courts of justice, where cases are pleaded or defended under the rules of current law practice.

All of these classes admit of the purest and most brilliant elocutionary efforts. Aristotle also classified rhetoric into three distinct parts—persuasion, expression, and arrangement. In *persuasion*, the orator presents himself, his motives, and the object of his discourse, in a persuasive attitude, with the design of obtaining the confidence of his hearers. In *expression* he treats of the arguments to be advanced in support of his object, and in this division he exemplifies the use of logic as a means of making his arguments clear and strengthening them. In *arrangement*, he teaches the proper method of presenting the argument, arranging propositions in the most effective manner, delivering them in appropriate language, and enforcing them with suitable and impressive gestures.

In Oratory, the features and the hands perform an important part, introducing illustrations of the topic under discussion, emphasizing the language as it varies

"From grave to gay, from lively to severe,"

and vividly depicting each emotion or passion as it is indicated by the tongue.

Conditions Favorable for the Public Speaker.

THE following arrangements in a hall favor the speaker, who would have the best conditions by which he may have influence with an audience.

1. The stand used for manuscript should occupy as little room upon the platform as possible.

2. All lights in the vicinity of the speaker, or upon the platform, should be so shaded that the audience cannot see them.

3. If convenient, the auditors upon the platform should be so seated that the speaker can occasionally turn and address them also.

4. The less the speaker is confined to manuscript, if thoroughly conversant with the subject, the better will be the effect of his speech with the audience.

5. The speaker should be carefully and well dressed, but not in the extreme of fashion. A Prince-Albert or dress-coat becomes the platform speaker who would appear to the best advantage before a fashionable audience.

6. The front part of the platform should have nothing upon it that can obstruct the view of the entire figure of the speaker. The position of the feet and lower part of the body frequently have much to do in enforcing an idea when accompanied by suitable words.

7. A large audience, a congregation well dressed, a handsomely furnished hall, an audience composed of the most respectable and influential in the community, and who give close attention—all these are favoring conditions, calculated to assist the public speaker in making a good impression.

True oratory springs from the impulses of the inner life as affected by outward circumstances, and the true orator is "a man terribly in earnest." Such a speaker needs no manuscript to aid him in his discourse. Observe the impassioned eloquence of Patrick Henry, on the eve of the American Revolutionary war:

"There is no retreat but in submission and slavery. Our chains are forged! Their clanking may be heard on the plains of Boston...The next gale that sweeps from the North will bring to our ears the clash of resounding arms! ...I know not what course others may take; but as for me,—give me liberty, or give me death!"

That was *natural oratory*, and no studied composition could carry with it the eloquence and power of these few simple sentences.

The man who is confined to his manuscript composition on the platform is not an orator—he is only a *reader*. In this respect he lacks freedom of gesture, and is unable to face his audience and allow them to see the varying emotions caused by his subject reflected in his features.

How differently does the true orator appear! Untrammeled on the platform by papers, he stands before his audience in the dignity of human nature, every feature enlivened by the thoughts that fill his brain, a clear, ringing voice to give them expression, and body and limbs all alive with harmonious and touching gestures. Such a man is a power in the land, for good or evil, swaying the masses, pleading the cause he advocates with earnestness, fidelity and eloquence, and leaving the impress of his intellect upon the minds and hearts of his hearers.

The distinguishing mechanical features of a finished address are distinct articulation, inflections, accent, emphasis, modulation and gesture.

Articulation is the art of using the vocal organs, including the teeth, with such ease and perfection that every portion of a word or sentence is distinctly uttered, every vowel and consonant fully pronounced, and no words or letters clipped off, as it were, or omitted from any sentence. Beginners, especially children, in their haste to get through a sentence, when "speaking a piece," often do this in a very ridiculous manner, but no finished orator is guilty of the practice. In the sentence, "He could pay nobody," the words, by careless speaking become, "He could pain nobody." This example will serve to show the necessity of a clear enunciation of every word and syllable, lest the entire passage be changed and its sense destroyed.

Inflection is a slide, or a change of the voice. The monotone is devoid of any rising or falling changes; hence the term "monotonous" is ap-

plied to a continuous flow of words in a single tone of voice. Still, the monotone, as the expression of great sublimity of thought, is sometimes used by the best orators and readers. While it may serve to express earnestness, it does not convey the idea of deep emotion.

The rising inflection may start a sentence with a monotone, but becomes louder and more significant as it proceeds. It is strongly marked in the asking of a question, as: "Where were you yesterday?"—throwing the emphasis on "yesterday," with a gradual raising of the voice.

The falling inflection begins with a high tone of voice and ends the sentence in a moderate one; for example: "Yesterday I stayed at home," answering the question and emphasizing "yesterday," also, because that word covered the principal object in asking the question.

The circumflex tone begins with the falling inflection and ends with the rising one, as: "I went out *yesterday*, but I stay here *to-day*,"—"to-day" elevated.

Fig. 1—Bashfulness.   **Fig. 2—Self-possession.**

The above illustrations represent the effect of practice and culture. While speaker No. 1, by his unpolished manner and diffidence, is an object of pity or ridicule, as a public speaker, No. 2, representing a well-known orator, as he apostrophizes a glass of water, entrances his audience by his self-possession, his earnestness, and his naturalness.

The word *or* in the sentence: "Will you stay —or go?"—throws the rising inflection on "stay," and the falling on "go."

In the negative sentence: "Study not for recreation, but for instruction," the rising inflection is on the affirmative, "instruction," while "recreation" has the falling tone.

Affection or tender emotion requires the rising inflection, coupled with softness: "Then spake the father, Come hither, my child."

These inflections enter into all the expressions of the human voice, ever varying, according to the sentiment to be promulgated. Nature teaches them and frames their utterances, while art acquires and simulates them on the stage, on the platform, in the pulpit, in the halls of legislation, or in the legal tribunal.

Accent is a peculiar force of the voice displayed in the pronunciation of a particular syllable in a word, or a particular word in a sentence, to make it more effective. A variety of English words have two or more accentuations. Thus the word "ac-cent," in the sense here used, has the accent on the first syllable —"ac"; but if we say that such a word should be accented, the "cent" is most strongly pronounced.

Emphasis is a stronger expression given to the utterance of a word or sentence, for the purpose of impressing it upon the mind, than can be given by inflection or accent alone; requiring elevation of tone, indicating either earnestness or emotion, or calling attention to some peculiarity of thought or argument advanced by the speaker. In writing, the emphasized word is usually underscored; in type, it is put in *italic* letters.

Modulation is the natural or acquired melodious form of utterance to suit the sentiment with musical precision. Indeed, modulation is a feature of music as well as of elocution, giving sweetness of tone and variation to the voice. It combines articulation, inflection, accent and emphasis, and enriches the entire discourse with harmony of expression.

Gesture is any natural movement of the limbs or body that indicates the character of the prevailing feeling or emotion of the heart. It appeals at once to our sympathies with far greater eloquence than words, and when combined with oratory makes the latter more effective. Without proper gestures, an orator loses much of his power to control the thoughts and opinions of his auditors; they add to the earnestness of his expressions, increasing his eloquence, and carrying conviction with every proposition advanced. In real oratory the eye speaks as well as the lips; the motions of the arms, and hands, and head, and body, are all brought into subjection to the dominant argument, and the grace and dignity of the human form are exhibited in all their

brilliancy. "Hamlet's" advice to the players —"Suit the word to the action, and the action to the word," is worth heeding. A downward movement of the arm or hand at a rising inflection would be but a burlesque.

Volume is the character of the voice as determined by the utterance of various emotions, in which the throat expands or contracts, producing whispers, wailings, etc., and is expressive of the inward emotion, whatever it may be.

Time is a slight pause made by the speaker, with the design of giving an opportunity to consider the importance of the word or phrase to which he would call specific attention.

Pitch represents the proper elevation of the voice, and its use in elocution is to regulate the tone of the discourse to its character. If not regarded as it should be, the delivery becomes faulty and disagreeable.

Force applies to the energy which is given to certain words and phrases, as expressive of the earnestness with which they should be received. It is *mental emphasis*, laying stress, in degrees, upon whatever is uttered.

Avoid talking through the nose and getting into a sing-song strain of delivery. Do not take the other extreme and become too grand in language for the subject. Speak of common things naturally, distinctly and intelligently. Do not use great, swelling words, chosen from the dictionary, for the sake of "showing off." The Anglo-Saxon tongue is filled with short, expressive words—words of one or two syllables, that point a sentence with wit and eloquence better than a flow of dissyllables.

Pitch the tone of voice no higher than is necessary to reach the ears of the person farthest from you in the audience, but be sure that it reaches its limit without losing its distinctness. In this lay one of the strongest features of the eloquence of the lamented Wendell Phillips.

Oratory should express in the features, the position of the body, and the movements of the head and limbs, the emotions which govern the utterances of the speaker, as indicated in the figures, explanations and examples which follow:

FACIAL EXPRESSION AND GESTURE.

As Illustrated by Drawings Prepared Expressly for this Work.

FOR THE purpose of setting clearly before the student in elocution and oratory the gesture, posture, and expression of face appropriate to the delineation of an emotion or thought of the mind the accompanying illustrations are given.

They are prepared by us from attitudes representing Prof. Walter C. Lyman, a teacher of elocution and voice culture in Chicago, who has graduated from his classes many superior readers, several of whom have been successful in attracting to themselves upon the stage much attention, because of their faithful rendition of character.

Following these fourteen illustrations, representing the Professor in various attitudes, are twelve representations by Miss Mamie T. Short, of Chicago, a pupil of Professor Lyman's.

Much care has been taken in the production of these illustrations to truthfully represent natural posture, and a correct, clearly defined expression of the face, when actuated by passion, sentiment, or emotion. To the multitude of students in the field of elocutionary study, these examples from life will be invaluable as giving needed instruction in this important art.

An interesting study is found in the contrasts of the appearance of the individual when representing these various sentiments and emotions.

While Dignity expresses manhood in its self-possessed and energetic mood, Fear cringes and shrinks, and trembles, and the two serve to show the effect of inward emotions upon the outer man. Expectation displays eagerness, hope and forwardness of purpose, while Horror reverses the *pose* and the expression, with shrinking, repulsive movements.

Supplication exhibits desire and humility, while Despair indicates the absence of all emotions but one —the sense of loss in its most extreme form. Other contrasts are shown in the following:

Unexcited.

ALL the muscles of the features, limbs and body are relaxed; the eyes assume a mild and quiet expression; the brow is expanded and unwrinkled; the arms and hands hang idly by the side; one foot is slightly advanced, but the body rests lightly upon both; the voice is natural and cheerful, as illustrated in the following example:

LADIES AND GENTLEMEN—In compliance with the request of the publishers of this work, I herewith submit to you the following illustrations as representations of the gesture, posture and facial expression, indicative of the emotion, thought, or sentiment, which may stir the heart under varying circumstances.

The highest degree of power by the orator is attained when burning words, born of the time and appropriate to the occasion, are accompanied by natural and graceful gesture.

Weeping—Violent Grief.

THE head droops, inclining to one side; the eyes overflow with tears; the lips and countenance are drawn downward; the body inclines forward; the hands are wrung; the lower limbs are relaxed and retiring; the movements are slow, and the voice low, unless the grief is excessive, and the breath comes and goes with agitation, broken by moans and sobs.

EXAMPLE—"Oh, my sorrow is more than I can bear!

My wife, my child, all gone—wrecked—swallowed in the great deep, and that too, when I was so anxiously watching—waiting their coming; and they so near the land!

A few hours more I would have clasped them to my heart. Alas, that the storm should rise when they, in glad anticipation, were so near their haven, and so near the husband's and father's arms!"

IN this illustration, representing the emotion of **Love,** the whole being is subdued, the head and body inclining forward; the forehead is tranquil; the eyebrows droop; the eye sparkles with affection; the palm of the right hand is pressed over the heart, and the left hand, with open fingers, is folded over the right wrist; the lower limbs stand together in easy position, with the right foot in advance; the voice is low and musical, and often there is an air of melancholy thought.

Love.

EXAMPLE—"I love you, Margery dear, because you are young and
    fair,
For your eyes' bewild'ring blueness, and the gold of your curling hair.
No queen has hands that are whiter, no lark has a voice so sweet,
And your ripe young lips are redder than the clover at our feet.
My heart will break with its fullness, like a cloud o'ercharged with rain,
Oh!—tell me, Margery darling, how long must I love in vain?"

THE head is either erect or thrown slightly back, in **Laughter** and **Mirth;** the forehead is smooth; the eyes are partly closed and full of cheerful expression, sometimes filled with tears of joy; the mouth is open and extended; the shoulders are elevated; the elbows are spread, the hands resting on the sides of the body below the waist; and the voice is loud and joyous in tone. Should the mirth, however, be inward and silent, the form is convulsed with emotion, as in the expression of grief.

Laughter—Mirth.

EXAMPLE—"So he took me for a Priest, did he?
    Ha! Ha!! Ha!!! Ha!!!!
Couldn't he tell the difference between a saint and a sinner?
    Ha! Ha!! Ha!!! Ha!!!!
Why, that man don't know the difference between his heels and
  his head,
    Ha! Ha!! Ha!!! Ha!!!!"

THE height of enthusiasm, the wildness of **Madness** or insanity, the struggle going on within, are manifested in this character. The head is dishevelled and uneasy; the arms and hands are moved about—now pressing the head, now thrown convulsively from it. Every movement of the body is irregular, rapid and reckless; the eyes, with fearful effect, turn uneasily from object to object, dwelling on none; the countenance is distorted, and the world is a blank.

Madness—Insanity.

EXAMPLE—"Mark how yon demon's eyeballs glare.
    He sees me; now, with dreadful shriek,
    He whirls a serpent high in air.
    Horror! the reptile strikes its tooth
    Deep in my heart, so crushed and sad.
    Aye, laugh, ye fiends, I feel the truth,
    Your work is done—I'm mad!—I'm mad!!"

FIRST, in **Horror,** the head is thrown forward, then upward, and then drawn back; the eyes, with fierce expression, stare wildly at the object; the countenance is distorted and affrighted; the form is contracted and half-turned away from the object; the lower limbs droop and are slightly thrown apart; the elbows are thrust out from the body; the hands are raised and open, with the palms outward, while the fingers seem contracted; and the voice is an excited half-whisper.

Horror.

EXAMPLE—"Which of you have done this?
    Avaunt and quit my sight! Let the earth hide thee!
    Thy bones are marrowless, thy blood is cold;
    Thou hast no speculation in those eyes,
    Which thou dost glare with.
    Hence, horrible shadow!
    Unreal mockery, hence!"

UNDER a feeling of **Disgust,** the head and body are turned away from the object; the lower limbs are parted, with the feet at right angles, the left being advanced; the forehead and the eyebrows are contracted; the mouth is slightly open; the eyes indicate the feeling within; the left hand is held partly in front of the face, with the fingers extended and the palm outward, as if pushing away the hated object, while the tongue utters a short and sharp guttural exclamation.

Disgust.

EXAMPLE—" She did not all too early die....
　　　Unchecked the course of true love ran;
　　　I married my Louisa Ann.
　　　There the romance, however, ends;
　　　Dear reader, you and I are friends!
　　　You don't *like* my Louisa Ann—
　　　No more do I—I never *can !*"

WHEN the individual is moved with **Anger,** the head is erect; the eye burns and flashes; the lips are compressed; the brows contracted, the nostrils are distended; the body is convulsed with passion, the fists are clinched; and the lower limbs are spread, with one foot strongly planted in advance of the other; the voice is either low or suppressed, or harsh, loud and quick; the whole appearance indicates agitation, fierceness and conflict, and every movement indicates energy.

Anger.

EXAMPLE—" Now imitate the action of the tiger,
　　　Stiffen the sinews, summon up the blood;
　　　Lend fierce and dreadful aspect to the eye,
　　　Set the teeth close, and stretch the nostrils wide;
　　　Hold hard the breath,
　　　And bend up every spirit to its full height. "
" In the contempt and anger of his lip. "

IMBUED with **Earnestness,** the entire form stands erect; the brow is expanded; the eyes express sincerity and a desire to convince the hearers of the truth and importance of the subject under discussion; the chest is thrown well forward; the lower limbs are slightly parted, with the feet at right angles; the left arm is extended, with open hand; the right hand is closed, and the voice is full and distinct, and moderate or elevated, as the theme or the feelings may suggest.

Earnestness.

EXAMPLE—" Ye call me chief; and ye do well to call him chief, who for twelve long years has met upon the arena every shape of man or beast the broad empire of Rome could furnish, and who never yet lowered his arm.   If there be one among you who can say that ever, in public fight or private brawl, my actions did belie my tongue, let him stand forth, and say it.   If there be three in all your company dare face me on the bloody sands, let them come on. "

WITH the sense of **Dignity,** or self-valuation, the head is held erect, or thrown slightly back; the form is straightened and raised to its fullest height; the forehead is expanded; the eyebrows are raised; the eyes indicate a subdued fierceness; the lips are compressed, and the countenance firm; the arms are folded across the chest, or the left hand is thrust into the bosom; the lower limbs are straight and together, with the feet at right angles; the movements are slow and methodical.

Dignity.

EXAMPLE—" I am a Roman citizen....Here, in your capital, do I defy you. Have I not conquered your armies, fired your towns, and dragged your generals at my chariot wheels, since first my youthful arms could wield a spear? And do you think to see me crouch and cower before a tamed and shattered senate? The tearing of flesh and rending of sinews is but pastime compared with the mental agony that heaves my frame. "

EXCITED with joyous **Expectation,** the chin is thrown forward; the eyes open, and beaming with anticipation, are directed towards the desired object; the countenance and lips express earnestness; the body inclines towards the object; the hands are clasped; one foot is advanced; the movements are slow and graceful; the voice is cheerful and moderate; the forehead is unwrinkled, and the expression, not only of the countenance, but of the whole being, is pleasing.

Expectation.

EXAMPLE—"There has fallen a splendid tear
From the passion-flower at the gate.
She is coming, my dove, my dear:
She is coming, my life, my fate;
The red rose cries, 'She is near, she is near;'
The larkspur listens, 'I hear, I hear,'
And the lily whispers, 'I wait.' "

DISTRACTED by **Fear,** the head is thrown forward, especially the chin; the eyes stare wildly at the object; then turn away; the shoulders are elevated; the body shrinks and contracts; the lower limbs are relaxed and droop, with one foot thrown back; the hands are contracted, with the palms outward, in front of the breast; there is a convulsive motion of the chest, the breathing is explosive, and the voice is rapid, high and broken. Fear causes the form and limbs to contract.

Fear.

EXAMPLE—" In thoughts from the visions of the night, when deep sleep falleth on men, fear came upon me, and trembling, which made all my bones to shake. Then a spirit passed before my face; the hair of my flesh stood up ; it stood still, but I could not discern the form thereof; an image was before my eyes; there was silence, and I heard a voice saying, Shall mortal man be more just than God ?—shall a man be more pure than his Maker?"

BORNE down with a feeling of **Despair,** the head is bowed, the chin resting upon the breast; the eyebrows are depressed; the eyes are rolled downward and express agony; the muscles of the face are convulsed and tremulous; the mouth is opened; the nostrils are expanded; the hands are tightly clasped, or wrung as if in pain; the teeth gnash; the body sways violently to and fro; the voice, if heard at all, is little better than a groan, and the breath is a succession of sighs.

Despair.

EXAMPLE—" O my offence is rank, it smells to heaven;
It hath the primal eldest curse upon 't,
A brother's murder!—Pray I cannot,
Though inclination be as sharp as will;
My stronger guilt defeats my strong intent;
And, like a man to double business bound,
I halt in pause where I shall first begin. "

IN the act of **Supplication,** the head is held back; the eyes, lips and countenance express earnestness; the body is bent forward; the hands are either spread heavenward, are clasped, or wrung, in intense emotion; one or both knees are bent to the ground; the movements are still or restless, according to the condition of the mind, and the voice is regulated by the same influence—sometimes slow, moderately fast, low and pleading, or high and exultant with praise and thanksgiving.

Supplication.

EXAMPLE—" 'Gitchie Manito, the mighty,'
Cried he, with his face uplifted,
In that bitter hour of anguish;'give your children food,
O Father!—
Give us food, or we must perish;
Give me food for Minnehaha!
For my dying Minnehaha!' "

RESULTS OF HIGHER CIVILIZATION.

THE civilization of the age is signalized by the advancement of woman to a higher plane of thought and action than she formerly occupied. Among the savage nations, woman's condition is that of the very lowest; in the semi-civilized countries she is largely regarded as fit only for menial labor, and even in civilized Europe, to-day, among the lower classes, the woman, harnessed with a dog, transports a large share of the produce to market, and in the same manner she serves as a creature of burden in scavenger and other work.

Only back to the first of this century, among the most intelligent of our best society in America and Europe, woman was thought unworthy and incompetent to perform work requiring any great degree of intellectuality. She was permitted to teach primary schools at a very low salary; beyond that, very few intellectual pursuits were open to her outside of literature.

Gradually, however, woman has beaten her way to the front, in spite of ridicule, jealousy and opposition. College trustees have resisted the opening of their doors to her; the managers of higher institutions of learning have opposed the idea of employing her as the superintendent of their schools. Physicians have fought against her invading their domain. Church-goers have insisted that they would never listen to a woman-preacher. Lawyers have laughed at the suggestion that she might enter their profession, and judges in authority have refused her admission to practice in certain courts.

But the march of progress has been forward, and the intelligent sentiment of the age has demanded that woman be allowed to enter any pursuit, the work of which she could perform just as well as men. The result has been the filling of hundreds of clerkships in the Treasury Department at Washington with women, very satisfactorily to the government and all parties concerned. Large numbers have entered the postal service, holding various important positions. Thousands have gone into the educational field, and as teachers, managers, and heads of academies, seminaries, and advanced public schools, have demonstrated both business capacity and intellectual talent of a high order.

A large percentage of women are successfully engaged in mercantile pursuits. She is well represented in the medical profession, she is fast entering the pulpit, and the time is not far distant when on the platform, whether engaged in general lecture, moral teaching, political discussion, or legal argument, she will be found the exponent of truth and co-worker with man in reform. And while all this transpires she will be no less the kind mother, and the devoted, faithful wife.

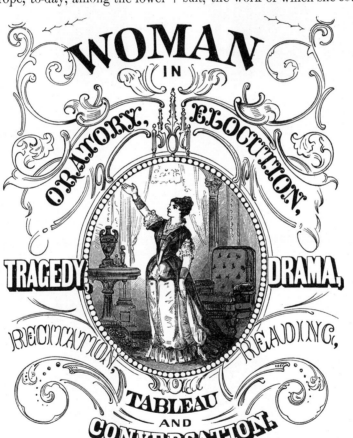

IN the illustration of **Dignified Repose**, the position is erect, quiet and graceful; the right foot is a little in advance of the left; the right arm and hand listlessly pend at the side, with the left forearm resting easily upon a book or table; all the muscles are relaxed; the eyes express tranquillity; the forehead is free from lines of care; the voice is subdued, but natural and cheerful, and the whole appearance of the individual evinces inward and outward contentment.

Dignified Repose.

EXAMPLE—"DEAR LADIES: With the multitude of ignorant people about us who need education, shall we not lend our assistance towards making the world wiser and better? To do this we should make the most of the privileges presented through the power of language; but to give words their greatest effect, these arts, including tone of voice, facial expression and gesture, must be studied and mastered, if we would use language to the best advantage."

BOTH feet, in **Anger,** are firmly planted apart upon the floor; the upper part of the form and head energetically incline forward; the forehead contracts; the eyebrows lift; the eyes fiercely flash; the arms rigidly stretch down the sides, with the hands clinched; the breath comes quick and heavily; the voice is shrill and harsh. The emotion of anger, under a sense of personal injury, may develop into resentment or revenge, and become furious or sullen, according to temperament.

Anger.

EXAMPLE—" Smile on, my lords!
I scorn to count what feelings, withered hopes,
Strong provocations, bitter, burning wrongs,
I have within my heart's hot cells shut up,
To leave you in your lazy dignities;
But here I stand and scoff you! here I fling
Hatred and full defiance in your face!"

EVERY indication of **Laughter** is represented here. The face, beaming with wreathed smiles, is slightly elevated; the form is sprightly and elastic, and convulsed with joyousness; the right arm and hand are extended, with the open palm turned towards the object of ridicule; the mouth opens widely to give vent to laughter, and the voice is loud and musical with gayety. Laughter is also a peculiar feature in representations of scorn. This is easily distinguished.

Laughter.

EXAMPLE—"What *I* in love! ha! ha!—the idea! and with *that* fellow! The thought is so supremely ridiculous! My name to be changed to Mrs. Philander Jacob Stubbs! And on the strength of the report—ha! ha!—Philander Jacob came around to see mother last night! I think I feel a pain in my heart already—ha! ha! Mrs. Philander Jacob Stubbs, indeed! Laughable, isn't it—ha! ha! ha! Mrs. Stubbs!—Mrs. *Stubbs!*—ha! ha! ha!"

ABSENCE of all hope creates **Despair,** and according to the sharpness of suffering the expression varies—sometimes indicating bewilderment and distraction; a look of wildness, and then a laxation of vitality bordering on insensibility; again, a terrific gloom of countenance; the eyes are fixed; the features shrunken and livid, and the muscles of the face are tremulous and convulsive; occasionally tears and laughter alternate, but frequently stupidity and sullenness appear.

Despair.

EXAMPLE—" Me miserable!—which way shall I fly
Infinite wrath and infinite despair?
Which way I fly is hell; myself am hell;
And in the lowest deep a lower deep,
Still threatening to devour me, opens wide,
To which the hell I suffer seems a heaven!
....Farewell, remorse! All good to me is lost!"

TO represent the expression of **Love** with fidelity to nature, the gaze should be intently fixed upon the object of affection, with mingled tenderness and admiration; the hands are clasped in the fervency of emotion; the head and body incline forward; the features indicate earnestness, the lips being slightly parted; the lower limbs are firmly balanced upon the feet, and the voice is mild and melodious, in harmony with the thoughts of the heart. Love is a beautifier.

Love.

EXAMPLE—"Come in the evening, come in the morning,
Come when you're looked for, or come without warning;
Kisses and welcome you'll find here before you,
And the oftener you come the more I'll adore you!
Light is my heart since the day we were plighted,
Red is my cheek that they told me was blighted;
How sweet is the thought, to be ever united!"

REPRESENTING **Dignity,** the step is firm; the body is stretched to its full height; the head is elevated and poised a little to one side; the eyes are wide-open, "with a downward tendency;" the brow is expanded; the right arm is thrown energetically across the chest, asserting the right to speak and the will to enforce that right; every muscle is firmly set, and the voice is slightly raised, with a tone of command that signifies possession of a perfect womanhood.

Dignity.

EXAMPLE—"I perjure myself,—I sink my soul in falsehood to gratify your greed for gold?—never! Out, wretch! leave my sight forever! Think you that I have no knowledge of the difference between right and wrong? Think you I would blast the happiness of another and carry in my heart forever the knowledge of a lie for a few paltry dollars? And you thought to tempt me to this by an offer of money. Base creature,–I despise you! Begone!–never let me see you more!"

AGITATION and disorder mark the whole appearance in **Madness.** Every movement is sudden and irregular, quick and uncontrolled; the eyes, extended to their utmost limit, protrude wildly and turn rapidly from object to object; the hair is tossed loosely about the head and face; the open hands are thrown upward to the head, and press and clasp and tousle it as if to drive away the agony of the brain; the breath comes and goes excitedly; the countenance is distorted.

Madness.

EXAMPLE—"Here have I watched, in this dungeon cell,
Longer than memory's tongue can tell;
Here have I shrieked in my wild despair,
When the damned fiends from their prison came,
Sported and gamboled, and mocked me here,
With their eyes of fire, and their tongues of flame,
Shouting forever and aye my name."

IN **Earnestness,** the form assumes its full height; the head is erect, with the features slightly elevated; the breath has a firm, quickened movement; the eyes are clear and the brows knit; the voice is deep; the lips are slightly compressed; the countenance is fearless; the right arm is extended, with the open palm of the hand turned upward, and there is a dignified air.

Earnestness.

EXAMPLE—"You think I love it! If this nerveless hand
Could gain immortal strength, this very hour,
I'd sweep this hellish traffic from the land,
And crush its blighting, maddening, nightmare power
Yea, now, with all my latest dying breath,
I'll curse the thing that drags me down to death!—
Aye, curse it ever, ever!"

THE head and bust, in **Fear,** are first thrown forward and then recede: the chin is drawn toward the chest; the mouth opens; the eyes are expanded and gaze upon the fearful object; the face is distorted, and contracted; the lower limbs tremble; the hands, outspread, are held, with the palms outward, before the face and chest in great disorder; the voice is very high and abrupt, and the breathing convulsive. Fear, protracted, becomes dread, terror and fright.

Fear.

EXAMPLE—" Oh, take it away!—take it away—the evil thing! Ah, how its cruel eyes, and blasting breath, and flashing tongue, image of Eden's destroyer, blight my very soul! Take it away! Oh, how it chills my blood and clogs my breath! Away with it—away! Its ghostly hiss, its slimy folds, whisper of death! O! Save me from its fangs! Oh, this is terrible!—Help! help! help!—I faint!—Help! help! Oh, take it from me!"

AN exaggerated species of dignity, **Scorn,** is expressed in the straightened and rigid form; the elevated eyebrows; the scowl upon the forehead, as the lady turns slightly away from the object; the closed lips; the right hand thrown well forward, with the palm bent downward; and the voice, as manifested in bitter laughter, sarcasm, or disgust, varies in its tone and expression. The emotion of scorn frequently involves the display of either derision, mockery, contempt, or all combined.

Scorn.

EXAMPLE—" Is the obligation to our fathers discharged? Is the debt we owe posterity paid? Answer me, thou coward, who hidest thyself in the hour of trial! If there is no reward in this life, no prize of glory in the next, capable of animating thy dastardly soul? Think and tremble, thou miscreant! at the whips and stripes thy master shall lash thee with on earth,—and the flames and scorpions thy second master shall torment thee with hereafter!"

VIOLENT agitation pervades the form in the expression of **Horror;** the chest and head are thrown backward and to one side; one hand flies to the head, while the other, with open palm and outspread fingers, appears to be warding off the terrible vision; the eyes stare wildly at the object, with elevated brows; the lips and other features have a contorted appearance, and there is an inward shrinking of the entire form, one foot being thrown far back.

Horror.

EXAMPLE—"Oh, Horror! horror!—The vessel is on fire! See the red flames bursting through the deck, twining and climbing up mast and rope! The sails are a sheet of flame, and higher, higher still, the fire ascends! See the poor men and women huddling at the stern as the fierce winds blow the vessel onward! Oh, who will save them now? Is there no hand to help—no power to quench the flame?— Oh, horror, horror, horror! They are lost!"

THE attitude and the expression of **Supplication** are represented as follows: Either one or both knees rest upon the ground; the features assume an earnest appearance; the hands are tightly clasped beneath the chin, and the emotions of the heart are reflected in the movements of the entire form. These and the voice are regulated by the fervency of the petitions offered, being sometimes very subdued in tone; at times rising to an ardent key, and tremulous with feeling.

Supplication.

EXAMPLE—" With flashing eye and burning brow,
The mother followed heedless how,
And kneeling in his presence now—
'O, spare my child, my joy, my pride!
O, give me back my child!' she cried:
'My child! my child!' with sobs and tears
She shrieked upon his callous ears.'"

Forms of Speeches for Public Meetings.

While These May not be Followed Literally, They will Give Suggestions.

THE forms for organizing a meeting are explained upon another page. The president of the assemblage, when called to the chair, will sometimes briefly thank the audience for the honor bestowed upon him, and will then suggest that the meeting select a secretary, after which the meeting will proceed with the usual business.

The following are among the forms frequently used at the opening, and in the early portion of meetings.

Appropriate Remarks for Presiding Officer upon taking the Chair.
Form No. 1.

I thank you, Ladies and Gentlemen, for the honor you bestow in electing me to this position.

Form No. 2.

With a deep sense of the responsibility resting upon me in assuming the duties of this position, I nevertheless fully appreciate the honor you bestow upon me in electing me as the presiding officer of your society. I hope the confidence you have given me may be fully repaid upon my part by an able and impartial discharge of my duty.

Form No. 3.

GENTLEMEN: I suppose it would become me, in accepting the presidency of this organization, as is customary, to assert that in choosing me you have made a very poor selection as a chairman of your meeting. But as that would be a reflection upon your judgment, and as you will doubtless soon discover all this, there is no need of parading that fact before you at this time.

I have one consolation in taking the chair. The presiding officer is not expected to make speeches. It is his business to listen. It is not his mission to inaugurate new measures. His duty is to serve the will of the meeting. My work, therefore, being light while in the chair, I accept of the position. But I am not disposed at this time to make a speech. I thank you for the trust you repose in me, and I will endeavor to perform my duty here as I understand it. The meeting being now organized, I await your further pleasure.

Form No. 4.

My thanks are due you, Ladies and Gentlemen, for the honor you confer in selecting me to preside over the deliberations of your society in the coming year. I value the compliment especially as coming from a company—a society, the members of which are, in the highest sense, intelligent and well-informed. I esteem the honor, also, because you have bestowed upon me this favor of your own free will, entirely unsolicited upon my part, and I prize it because I hope in my humble way, through this position, to very materially aid you in the accomplishment of that for which we labor in common.

I cannot promise what the future will be. The hereafter is always uncertain; but I can hope, with you, that our work together will be effective, pleasant, and productive of good results.

I enter upon my duties with a full realization of the fact, also, that my success will depend upon your support and co-operation. Hoping for that, I assume the position, trusting that I may discharge its duties, partially at least, to your satisfaction.

Speech of President Stating Object of Meeting
Organized for the general suppression of vice.

MY FRIENDS: If I do my duty here I will not regret your selecting me as the president of this convention. I especially appreciate the compliment when I consider the fact that the gathering includes several who have, in the various meetings of this society, honored the same position to which I am now chosen.

We meet again on this occasion to proclaim our vows of fidelity to the cause, to detail the work that has been accomplished, the good that has resulted, and the victory we hope yet to achieve. We do not hesitate to gird on our armor and continue in the service fearlessly. Very many of those I see before me have done battle in the work for long years. They have performed much hard labor, and they have given freely of time and money to carry the cause forward, and the result has been that we have seen the crime, once so common upon our streets, very largely suppressed. Our young men have been educated to spend their evenings amid the refining influences of home, while hundreds of debauchees have been rescued, and have returned as faithful husbands and tender fathers to their families.

Our labor has been long and arduous, but the grand results have justified the effort.

Fruitful, however, as has been our work, we are not done. Its full completion is yet in the future. But however distant away, as long as there is a soul to save from the terrible thraldom of passion and vice, so long will we press forward in this cause. As we have met, and taken counsel in the past, so do we meet in consultation again.

Rejoicing in the good, grand work this society has wrought in the past, I can only hope, with yourselves, that this convention of earnest men and women will be fruitful in the suggestion and adoption of measures that will give peace to unhappy homes, and blessing to the righteous cause.

Another Speech Explaining Object of Meeting,
Upon being chosen as the president of a society established for philosophical inquiry and investigation of religious subjects.

LADIES AND GENTLEMEN: I appreciate the compliment you bestow in choosing me to be the presiding officer at this meeting, from the fact that whatever the attendance may be, I deem the purpose of this gathering to be one of very considerable importance. Important, because in a certain sense it is the only organization of the kind in this city, and important because in a free interchange of opinion, such as is proposed here, there is opportunity for enlargement of mental vision and intellectual growth, such as will make this society of great service to its members because of its educational privileges.

There exists great need of such an organization as will give full and free opportunity for the expression of opinions upon political, moral, social, and religious events of the hour, because in the utterance of our peculiar ideas we are liable to give a new thought, and in listening to a wide variety of opinions we learn many things.

In saying this, I am not disposed to hold the church or our clergy in light esteem. It is a fact that every well-balanced human mind possesses the organs of spirituality and veneration,—faculties that tend to worship. It is natural for every people to have a religion of some kind. It is best that they should, because, through the exercise of the religious in man's nature, the lower and base in man's nature is held in subjection. It is well, therefore, for people to assemble at least one day in seven at some stated place, at some regular time, and there, under the administration of some competent person, receive spiritual and moral instruction, such as is calculated to make mankind better and happier. This involves the necessity for a Sabbath, a church and a clergyman. I grant that religious teaching frequently inculcates nothing but superstition and bigotry. But this does not argue against the fact that one day in seven should be set apart as a day for religious instruction and spiritual improvement. From the fact, also, that the free-thought participants in a meeting of this character so often give expression to feelings of bitterness toward the church, I am inclined to ask you to give credit to the religious organization of the church for the following:

The furnishing of a place where we can meet for moral teaching. An earnest effort to give moral instruction. The opening of Sunday-schools, whereby the young, under the guidance of good teaching, may be taught the ways of morality. The doing of an immense amount of charitable work, the founding of hospitals and many institutions of benevolent character, by which the sufferings of people are relieved and their condition made better. In addition to this, the church, through its efficient organization, affords opportunity for social privileges among the young; in socials, pic-nics, and entertainments, while it gives social privileges to all its members of the greatest importance to any one who would pass through life successfully and happily.

I am turning out of my course, ladies and gentlemen, to give this eulogy of the church, though slightly foreign to the purpose of our meeting, from the fact that many so-called liberals are so very *illiberal* as to spend much of their time, when speaking, in denunciation of those who may not meet with us on these occasions. As all organized reform-effort, in whatever direction, whether religious or secular, is a step in the scale of progress, it does not become us to come here to spend time in denunciation. The purpose of the organization which we form to-day should be the presentation and discussion of those principles, methods of action, and reforms, which tend to the improvement and elevation of manhood. Whoever will give us another truth, whoever will tell us a new plan, whoever will present us something better than we have known heretofore—that person will be welcomed as a speaker, and a colaborer in this organization. With an earnest hope that this society we are organizing to-day may serve a beneficent purpose, I am pleased thus to aid in its beginning. Ladies and gentlemen, what is the further pleasure of the meeting?

Suitable Forms for Presiding Officer when Introducing Speaker.

Form No. 1.

LADIES AND GENTLEMEN: Mr. Henry K. Williams.

Form No. 2.

LADIES AND GENTLEMEN: I have the pleasure of introducing to you Mr. Henry K. Williams.

Form No. 3.

LADIES AND GENTLEMEN: I have the honor to introduce to you Mr. Henry K. Williams, of Boston, who will now address you.

Form No. 4.

LADIES AND GENTLEMEN: In order that you may be well-informed concerning the prohibition movement throughout the West, I introduce to you Hon. Henry K. Williams, of Boston, who will address you on the subject at issue.

Form No. 5.

LADIES AND GENTLEMEN: Thanking you for the honor bestowed by selecting me as the chairman of this meeting, I now have the pleasure of introducing the speaker of the evening, the Hon. Martin W. Wilson, of Cleveland, who will address you on the subject of Tariff-Reform.

Form No. 6.

FELLOW CITIZENS: I am not unmindful of the honor you bestow in choosing me as your presiding officer for this occasion. Tendering you my thanks for the compliment, I proceed to the business of the meeting by introducing to you General Thos. M. Snow, of Wisconsin, who will detail to you some of the scenes through which he has passed during the last six months.

Form No. 7.

As the chairman of this meeting, I will explain the object of this gathering. As is well-known, the property of no person in this section is secure from robbery. Thieves are abroad night and day, and persons in this region, especially farmers, have been heavy losers, particularly of horses. Feeling that definite and positive action should be taken to more effectually guard ourselves, this meeting is called for the purpose of organizing a protective association. In order that we may better understand how such an organization may be formed and be made beneficial to our community, Mr. Walter D. Hammond, the secretary of the Home Protective Association of Mount Hope, has been invited to visit us and detail how the Mount Hope Association was organized and what good it has accomplished. In accord with that invitation Mr. Hammond is now here, and to you I now introduce him.

Speech Announcing Change of Programme.

It becomes necessary to announce to you a change of programme for the exercises of to-day. By a letter just received from the Hon. William Marsh, we learn that he cannot be with us until Thursday afternoon; and through a telegram, received a short time since, we are informed that the band must delay their coming until to-morrow. Under these circumstances we vary the arrangement of exercises considerably, but fortunately, in no sense, to the disadvantage of our audience. The fact is we have now present with us two superior vocalists, who have promised us songs; a well-known pianist, who has volunteered to furnish us instrumental music, and the time assigned this afternoon to Mr. Marsh will be occupied by Professor Holland, with a paper on " Universal Suffrage." Earnestly desiring that our audience may be all in their seats promptly at the opening of each session, we now begin the exercises of the day.

Forms of Oral Announcements,

The most important features of the announcement being repeated, in order that time and place be thoroughly understood.

The meetings of this society during the week will be as follows: The Literary Society on Wednesday evening, at the residence of Charles N. Brown, at 88 Lincoln street—Wednesday evening, at 88 Lincoln street. The Ladies Aid Society at Mrs. Ira Minard's, 971 Maple Avenue, at two o'clock Thursday afternoon—Thursday afternoon at two o'clock. Mrs. Minard's residence is 971 Maple Avenue. The Young Folks' Prayer-meeting in the vestry of this church, Friday afternoon at three o'clock—Friday afternoon, in the church vestry.

The Patrick Henry Debating Club will hold their meeting at Everett Hall, 101 Seminary Avenue, Thursday evening, October 14. An essay by Miss Helen Williams, and a recitation by Arthur D. Cummings, followed by a variety of instrumental and vocal music, will be among the attractions of the occasion—Everett Hall, 101 Seminary Avenue, next Thursday evening.

Brief Inaugural Address of a Mayor.

GENTLEMEN OF THE COUNCIL; In meeting with you this evening for the first time as the municipal directors of the affairs of this city, I am glad to find among you so many with whom in the past I have been permitted to sustain most pleasant business relations and social intercourse. Such relations and such intercourse it is my wish to perpetuate in our deliberations in this chamber.

We are here to-night, however, as the servants of a numerous and prosperous people, who have laid upon us the responsibility of maintaining good government. While we gather here from every section of this municipality, representing different wards, I trust that every one of us has a lively interest in the welfare of all our citizens.

There is work for us all to do. We have many things to regulate, to establish, to perform, in our official capacity. In my hands I hold the latest reports from the chiefs of the fire department, the city treasury, the health office, and the magistrates. From these I have learned facts that show the necessity of a better organization and equipment of our firemen; the judicious expenditure of our limited city funds; the cleansing of various unhealthy districts in certain wards, and a more efficient enforcement of several of our city ordinances.

It should be our duty, gentlemen, at the earliest moment, to see that these several interests are cared for, while the general good of the entire city should receive our attention throughout our term of office.

I trust that in our deliberations we may be so united in sentiment that our labors will be less arduous than if hampered by the delays and vexations of inharmonious discussions. Let us now proceed to business.

Form of a President's Inaugural.

MEMBERS OF THE INDUSTRIAL LEAGUE: We meet to-day in the third annual convention of this association. As in the past, we come together to consider the interests of the laboring classes, and in our discussions I wish to direct your attention to the following subjects pertaining to the cause of Labor.

1. The interests of the country as affected by a protective tariff.
2. The benefits resulting from Labor unions.
3. Strikes, whether beneficial or not, and their results upon the laboring classes.
4. Arbitration, as a means of settling misunderstandings between employers and employes.
5. New lands. Where they are, and how to reach them, and the inducements offered the unemployed in going there.
6. Convict labor. What course should be pursued by the State and general government, to prevent it from coming too strongly in competition with our workingmen.
7. Less hours for general labor. The attention of the convention is especially called to the need of working less hours in all manufacturing institutions, and in all the industries, in order that the unemployed may have an opportunity to work.

While much important matter will doubtless come before the meeting, I direct the attention of the members to these topics, as subjects exciting general comment, worthy of your careful thought.

Trusting that the harmony which has prevailed in our meetings heretofore may be shown in this, I will now read the programme of exercises for to-day.

Remarks by a Teacher at the Opening of School.

YOUNG LADIES AND GENTLEMEN: It has fallen to my lot to become your instructor during the coming term of school, and the hope is that in our intercourse together our time spent in each others' society may be pleasant and profitable. It should be understood, in the beginning, that I have not come here to govern you. I trust you have such kindly dispositions as to make it useless for any one to come here to rule. The real mission of the teacher should be to assist, to aid pupils in acquiring an education.

While we hope it will not be necessary to have many laws established here, there is one rule that it will be very important to have observed, and that is, "the golden rule"—the doing unto others as we would have others do unto us. I expect you to do to me as you would be done by were you a teacher and I the pupil, and I will try and do the same by you.

I doubt not you all hope to grow to be men and women, having such an education as will fit you to take any place that may be assigned you in life. I expect you to have an ambition to get this learning, and having that, I expect to assist you a good deal in getting it.

Now, to accomplish what we have undertaken to perform, it will be necessary for you to do some things. And of these will be coming to the school regularly; punctuality at the opening of each session; carefully abstaining from whispering during school-hours, and a thorough resolve that you will be perfect in your lessons.

But I will lay down no rules now. I hope and expect you will be such good pupils that few rules will be needed. We will now begin the exercises of the school.

Speech of Welcome to a Distinguished Guest.

GOVERNOR RAYMOND: These gentlemen and myself represent the citizens of Chicago and by them we have been instructed to give you, and the ladies who accompany you, a hearty welcome to the hospitality of the "Garden City."

Although this may possibly be your first visit to our city, we do not consider you at all in the light of a stranger in a strange land; for your fame has preceded you, and in our homes your name is known in connection with your enviable war-record and the important measures which have distinguished you in our national councils. Nor are you in any sense a stranger to the great metropolis of the Central States of our Union, for you have often spoken brave words in our behalf as a commercial and manufacturing city—words for which we heartily thank you and gladly welcome you here to-day.

As we have been informed that your visit has no political or commercial significance, we do not propose, in welcoming you, to beset you with an imposing array of facts and figures relating to our municipal position in the Union, but, instead, to make your sojourn with us a source of pleasure and recreation. For this purpose all our arrangements have been perfected for escorting you to such places as we deem will give you most delight, and to provide such other entertainments as hospitality may suggest for your comfort and convenience.

We have provided suitable apartments for you at the ———— Hotel, and shall be pleased to regard you as our guest while you remain in the city.

We ask, however, that should it be consistent with your wishes and arrangements, you will allow us to announce a public reception to-morrow evening, at your hotel, in order that your numerous friends, embracing the wealth and culture of our population, may be enabled to express their welcome to you in person.

The Reply.

GENTLEMEN: The warm greeting which meets me at the threshold of your thrifty and renowned city, I believe, is an earnest of the esteem which the people of Chicago desire to express for me, and I fully appreciate their kindness and very generous reception.

My first visit to Chicago, gentlemen, was in 1832, when General Scott (under whom I was then only a subaltern officer) came to Fort Dearborn, in pursuance of military orders from headquarters. The city was not then in existence, and the place was a wilderness. General Scott, for want of better accommodations, slept in a wooden trough, and I, a mere lad, was glad to "bunk" upon the ground in a blanket. The fort was a hospital, for the cholera was making fearful ravages in the little garrison.

To-day I come to a city, they tell me, of 600,000 inhabitants, where not a vestige of the old Indian village or the fort remains. A city so great that the most terrific conflagration of modern times has not been able to destroy its vigor or wealth. A city that controls the trade of nations. A city that has no equal for rapid growth and augmentation in the world. A city that contains the elements of high civilization in great profusion.

Gentlemen, I am telling you nothing new, and I desist; but I am come prepared to be still farther astounded than I now am at your prosperity and the magnitude of your business and social institutions. With the Queen of Sheba, I feel that " the half has not been told." I therefore submit myself to your care and direction, believing that as your guest I shall find new causes for enlarging my views of Chicago and her hospitable citizens.

Speeches Nominating a Candidate for Office.

No. 1.

MR. PRESIDENT: I suggest the name of Henry L. Smith as that of our Assessor for the coming year.

No. 2.

MR. PRESIDENT: As a gentleman every way competent to fill the office, I will nominate John H. Williams as our candidate for the office of County Treasurer.

No. 3.

MR. PRESIDENT: I desire to place in nomination for the Presidency of this convention a gentleman whose long acquaintance with educational work, prominent position in his profession, and thorough fitness for the place make him eminently fitted to hold this office. I therefore nominate, as the President of this organization in the coming year, Colonel Abner D. Kellogg.

No. 4.

The needs of this convention, in the coming year, make it imperative that we select as the first officer of this organization a person of extended experience and large executive ability, coupled with the ability to preside over the deliberations of this body in a manner such as to do our meetings credit. As such, I suggest, as the President of our convention, William H. Daniels.

No. 5.

MR. PRESIDENT: I present the name of Cyrus D. Fillmore as that of our candidate for Mayor. I, in common with others, believe him to be, in the present contest, the strongest man that can be selected. Whatever may be the personal choice of individuals, it becomes us, upon this occasion, to choose as a candidate an individual whose personal popularity, with all classes, will carry the largest vote.

We have many important issues before the people at the present time. There are principles involved in which we are deeply interested. We cannot afford to lose the coming election. We must not. Hence the need of selecting a man who will unite all factions, and, while he can be sure of election, will, when in the place, fill the office with honor to himself and credit to the city. I nominate, as our candidate for Mayor, Cyrus D. Fillmore.

Speech Declining a Nomination for Office.

GENTLEMEN: I thank you for your expression of approval and for your selection of myself as a candidate for office. But circumstances will prevent my acceptance of any office you might tender me at present. Under other conditions I might be pleased to serve you, but at the present time I must content myself with being simply a humble constituent of the person who may be elected.

Ingersoll's Speech Nominating James G. Blaine,

At Republican Convention held at Cincinnati in 1876.

MR. PRESIDENT: The Republicans of the United States demand, as their leader in the great contest of 1876, a man of intelligence, a man of integrity, a man of well-known and approved political opinion. They demand a statesman. They demand a reformer after, as well as before, the election. They demand a politician in the highest, broadest, and best sense,—a man of superb moral courage. They demand a man acquainted with public affairs, with the wants of the people, with not only the requirements of the hour, but with the demands of the future. They demand a man broad enough to comprehend the relation of this government to the other nations of the earth. They demand a man well versed in the powers, duties, and prerogatives of each and every department of this government. They demand a man who will sacredly preserve the financial honor of the United States ; one who knows enough to know that the national debt must be paid through the prosperity of this people; one who knows enough to know that all the financial theories in the world cannot redeem a single dollar; one who knows enough to know that all the money must be made, not by law, but by labor; one who knows enough to know that the people of the United States have the industry to make the money and the honor to pay it over just as fast as they make it.

The Republicans of the United States demand a man who knows that prosperity and resumption, when they come, must come together; that when they come they will come hand in hand through the golden harvest-fields; hand in hand by the whirling spindlers and the turning wheels; hand in hand past the open furnace doors; hand in hand by the flaming forges; hand in hand by the chimneys filled with eager fire, greeted and grasped by the countless sons of toil.

This money has to be dug out of the earth. You cannot make it by passing resolutions in a political convention.

The Republicans of the United States want a man who knows that this government should protect every citizen at home and abroad; who knows that any government that will not defend its defenders, and protect its protectors, is a disgrace to the map of the world. They demand a man who believes in the eternal separation and divorcement of church and school. They demand a man whose political reputation is spotless as a star, but they do not demand that their candidate shall have a certificate of moral character signed by a Confederate Congress. The man who has, in full, heaped and rounded measure, all these splendid qualifications, is the present grand and gallant leader of the Republican party,—James G. Blaine.

Our country, crowned with the vast and marvelous achievements of its first century, asks for a man worthy of the past and prophetic of her future; asks for a man who has the audacity of genius; asks for a man who has the grandest combination of heart, conscience, and brain beneath her flag. Such a man is James G. Blaine.

For the Republican host, led by this intrepid man, there can be no defeat.

This is a grand year,—a year filled with the recollection of the Revolution; filled with proud and tender memories of the past, with the sacred legends of liberty,—a year in which the sons of freedom will drink from the fountains of enthusiasm,—a year in which the people call for a man who has preserved in Congress what our soldiers won upon the field,—a year in which they call for the man who has torn from the throat of treason the tongue of slander; for the man who has snatched the mask of Democracy from the hideous face of rebellion; for the man who, like an intellectual athlete, has stood in the arena of debate and challenged all comers, and who is still a total stranger to defeat.

Like an armed warrior, like a plumed knight, James G. Blaine marched down the halls of the American Congress and threw his shining lance full and fair against the brazen forehead of the defamers of his country and the maligners of his honor. For the Republican party to desert this gallant leader now is as though an army should desert their general upon the field of battle.

James G. Blaine is now and has been for years the bearer of the sacred standard of the Republican party. I call it sacred, because no human being can stand beneath its folds without becoming and without remaining free.

Gentlemen of the Convention: In the name of the great Republic, the only Republic that ever existed upon this earth; in the name of all her defenders and of all her supporters; in the name of all her soldiers living; in the name of all her soldiers dead upon the field of battle, and in the name of those who perished in the skeleton clutch of famine at Andersonville and Libby, whose sufferings he so vividly remembers, Illinois—Illinois nominates for the next President of this country that prince of parliamentarians, that leader of leaders, James G. Blaine.

PRESENTATION AND OTHER SPEECHES.

THE presentation speech should be short. It may allude to the work that the individual has accomplished, by which he or she is entitled to the gift. It may appropriately speak of the high regard in which the recipient is held by the donors of the gift, and it may bespeak a delightful, prosperous future for the person addressed, besides being brimful of good wishes; but the speech should come early to the point and close.

In the meantime it may be well for the managers of the affair to have some one besides the recipient of the gift appointed to make an appropriate response, unless he or she is thoroughly capable of making a suitable reply. In most cases it is a relief to the recipient to be informed of the intended presentation, as he or she, in that case, can make a response that will be more satisfactory than if taken by surprise and without time for preparation. As a rule, the article should be concealed from view until it is spoken of in the presentation, when it will create renewed interest.

Lady Presenting a Flag.

Presentation of a Flag by a Lady

To a volunteer company of the state militia, the flag being held by a gentleman while the lady makes the address.

CAPTAIN ARTHUR BENSON AND MEMBERS OF COMPANY H OF THE FIRST REGIMENT OF THE NEW YORK VOLUNTEER MILITIA—GENTLEMEN: In recognition of the public spirit, the patriotism and the bravery that move you to form an organization for the protection of your homes and your country, should you be called upon to fight in their defense, it becomes my duty, in behalf of the ladies of this town, to present you a silken flag.

This emblem of our nationality has been fashioned into these stars and stripes, has been trimmed and embellished as you see it here, by hands that will never tire of working for you. As you look upon its silken folds you may understand that it is the grand emblem of our country's greatness, and it is more. It is the bearer of the hope and love of the donors who present it—whose hearts will go with you to the end, should fate determine that it shall be carried into the battlefield.

Our hope is that it may never do other duty than rustle peacefully above your heads, a silent token of our respect and regard, but should necessity require, we are confident that in brave hands it will lead to success, and in the hours of trial will be wherever it shall wave the signal of victory. Into your hands we now place it. God grant that the need of trailing it in blood may never arise, but should duty or your country call, we know it will wave over the heads of brave men —we know you will do it honor.

Response of the Captain.

MISS CHANDLER: Responding, in behalf of my company, to the sentiments you express, I but speak the words which my comrades would utter, when I say that we deeply feel and most highly appreciate this appropriate and beautiful gift which we receive at your hands.

If it shall be our mission to unfurl it only when peace and harmony shall prevail, it will be well. Should it be our fate to go forth in defense of home and loved friends, we shall carry it as a token of the love, the respect and the solicitude we bear for those who remember us thus kindly.

The sight of this will ever nerve our men to greater bravery—it will be an inspiration. We thank you for this offering, and for the sentiment that comes with its presentation.

We shall carry it fearlessly in peace and in war; and throughout the length and breadth of this country we propose it shall wave over States ever loyal and true to the government—we resolve that it shall ever be the emblem of a nation that shall never be dismembered or disunited. Again tendering you our high regard for this testimonial, our color-bearer will now receive it, while the band will express our heartfelt appreciation of your gift as they render the "Star-Spangled Banner."

Presentation Speech at a Silver Wedding.

MR. AND MRS. ———: It becomes my pleasant duty, in behalf of your friends assembled here to-night, to remind you that we are not forgetful of the fact that you have turned a quarter of a century in wedded life. This of itself, in an age when marital separations are so common, is worthy of recognition; but it is not alone that fact that causes your friends to convene at this time.

For years it has been our privilege to know your household in genial friendship. In the varied walks of neighborly and social intercourse, you have contributed abundantly toward the making of life pleasant in the circle in which we have moved. We do not forget that when the laugh was merriest your happy presence added pleasure to the scene; and when sorrow visited our homes your words of consolation and sympathy made the sorrow lighter.

There comes a time, at various periods in life, when we can honor and reward those whom we esteem. Such is the present occasion.

Recollecting our many obligations for kindness you have rendered, and the pleasant years made agreeable through your acquaintance, your friends herewith present you this tea-service and desire your acceptance of the same.

The gift, while appropriate as a memorial of twenty-five years of wedlock, is presented as a token of the high favor in which you are held by your many friends.

May it adorn your table in the future, and may the refreshing beverage you shall sip from these silver goblets be such as will aid in prolonging your lives to that time when, at your golden wedding, we shall, by the sight of these present gifts, be reminded of the pleasant scene that took place twenty five years before—the delightful occasion which we celebrate to-night.

Reply to the Presentation Speech.

DEAR FRIENDS: It is at such a time as this that words fail to express the feelings of the heart. There comes occasionally a period in life when our unworthiness is made all the more manifest by the bestowal of kindness upon us. It is true that we have mingled in your society for years. But while, in our humble way, we may have contributed some pleasure to those about us, we have ever been the recipients of continued enjoyment at your hands; and it is *we* who are under obligation—not yourselves.

We accept these gifts to-night, dear friends, with a full appreciation of the kind motives which presented them, and not that we deserve them as free gifts at your hands.

There may be some things in our lives commendatory. We have journeyed together in married life for twenty-five years. Some shadows have crossed our path in that time, and many joys have illumined our way. Upon the whole, we have had more happiness than sorrow; more roses than thorns have strewn our pathway. Thus in this twenty-five years of consort together we have our recompense.

We have striven to do our duty as neighbors and friends, and for the little we have done we have, in all our intercourse with you, been repaid a thousand-fold.

We accept these gifts, therefore, with a sense of deep obligation to those kind friends by whom they are presented, and we shall use and cherish them, in all the years to come, with the earnest hope that, at like anniversary festal gatherings we may have frequent opportunity to repay the kindness which you have thus bestowed.

Speech, Presenting a Book,

By the pupil of a school to a teacher at the close of her last term.

MISS WILLIAMS: I am appointed by the pupils of this school to present you, in their name, this volume—a cyclopedia of poetry, containing the poetic gems of ancient and modern times.

In presenting this testimonial, I assure you in behalf of your pupils that, as a patient teacher, a wise counselor and a most excellent instructor, you will ever be remembered by the students of this school with feelings of the highest regard and esteem.

We look back over the period during which we have received instruction from you with sincere pleasure. We recollect your efforts in our behalf with grateful remembrance, and we learned of your intended resignation as a teacher, and the leaving of this school, with sincere regret.

In the turning of the pages of this volume you will, we hope, be reminded of those who presented it. In that remembrance of us please do not recollect the dullness we have often shown, and the disobedience, we fear, we have sometimes manifested. But please remember that we shall strive, in the hereafter, to profit by the instruction you have given, and when we are far separated from each other, it may please you to know that we consider that we are better and wiser from the instruction we have received from you.

Response of the Teacher.

MY DEAR PUPILS: I receive and accept of your elegant gift with much pleasure; first, because the volume, of itself, is one of rare value, which I shall highly prize, and, second, because it comes to me as a token of your appreciation of my efforts since I have had the pleasure of being with you.

I assure you I will turn its pages in happy recollection of the pleasant faces I have met in this room during my school duties. I will always remember your willing hearts, your kind intentions, your many evidences of love and regard for me, and your unceasing efforts to make my work as light and agreeable as possible.

I thank you for this beautiful testimonial, and also for the assurance you give me, that, as I read its pages, I may be reminded that the donors not only hold me in kindly remembrance, but they are resolved to profit by the teaching that has been given here.

My earnest hope is that your future life may realize all that your studious habits and school-days now seem to promise. Knowing you as I do, I expect you, in noble manhood and womanhood, to honor this school by your future lives of usefulness, prosperity and happiness.

Speech Upon being Nominated as a Candidate for Office.

MR. PRESIDENT AND FELLOW CITIZENS: My thanks are due for the compliment paid in selecting me to represent this district in the State senate. As I desire to go into the legislature unpledged and untrammeled, I shall make few promises as to what I shall do if elected.

It may not be amiss, however, to state that there is certain work which our representative, whoever he may be, should feel himself bound to perform, should he occupy a seat in the legislative councils. And of this may be mentioned the establishment of a reform school in this portion of the State in which can be received and trained a large number of boys who now bid fair to become ultimately permanent inmates of our prisons. The law should be stronger relating to the preservation of game. The rate of taxation on certain manufacturing industries should be lessened. The law relating to less hours for laboring men in the State service should be enforced, and much other needed legislation is evident.

So far as *I* am concerned, I can only say, if elected, I propose to do my duty as I understand it. That duty

Speech of the Candidate for Congress.

I conceive to be consists in working for the best interests of the constituency, and in serving the State and the entire people faithfully. Should it be my fate not to be chosen to fill the place for which you have placed me in nomination, the sun will probably rise and set as it has done heretofore, and I will console myself with the thought that there is a blessing in defeat. But should I be elected, I shall hope that my efforts may avail in accomplishing some work that will be beneficial to yourselves and the State.

Again thanking you, gentlemen, for your generous support, I can only hope that the expression you give here will be the voice of the people, and that our party in the coming election may carry the banner of victory.

Speech of Congressional Candidate from Hotel Balcony,

In reply to a serenade at the Clarendon House.

FELLOW CITIZENS: In response to your call for a talk from me, I beg to assure you that I appreciate the honor you do me in this gathering. But while I tender you my thanks for this ovation, I am not unmindful of the fact that the cause on this occasion is greater than any man. We are in the midst of an exciting political contest, in which principles are involved of the utmost importance, and whether those principles shall triumph or not, in the coming election, is the question of vital significance.

It must be clearly evident to the unprejudiced mind that the machinery of government is seriously destroyed, when so many of our people, in the midst of an abundance, should be compelled to beg for common necessaries of life. The fact is as plain as the unclouded noonday sun, that a government is wofully weak that will compel tens of thousands of strong, able-bodied men, anxious to work, to stand idle, while their families suffer for the means of maintaining existence. We are in the midst of plenty. The factories, shops and warehouses are full to repletion with goods that people require. The fields are teeming with grain, the banks are plethoric with money, and yet, in the midst of all this abundance, there is not wisdom enough in our national legislators to secure a proper division of this wealth among those who have produced it. But, fellow-citizens, I shall not now take your time in a discussion of the cause of hard times and the remedy.

I can only say that as your candidate for Congress, I deeply feel the need of prompt and efficient action by our general government; and if I am elected, I hope to faithfully perform my part in the work that so greatly needs to be done. I thank you, gentlemen, for this personal compliment to me, and with you I pray for the success of that cause which is righteous and just.

Speech when Presenting a Prize

To the successful competitors in a boat-race.

GENTLEMEN: Much discussion has been developed from time to time (in country school-houses and village debating clubs) as to the relative superiority of mind over muscle. Indeed, the question has been many times definitely settled (by these authorities), and yet it is ever bobbing up in actual life and begging for a final decision. Gentlemen, I am not here to solve the problem—I only rise to do honor to the union of mind and muscle that has brought victory to your banner and made you the proud recipients of this beautiful prize, the gift of fair hands, which you have so gallantly won.

I see in your frank and youthful features the glow of health and energy; I see in your bared arms the cord-like sinews that denote strength and endurance; and I see in the successful management of your boat the expression of an iron will to accomplish, whatever the opposition, and of a skill indicative of the intellect that controls your muscles and makes your manhood great.

Yours was not an easy triumph. Seven clubs competed with you for this rare and beautiful prize. I see in their crews, as they stand around you, skill and energy which you may be proud to have defeated. But in you they acknowledge the possession of superior skill, a superior force, and I doubt not that next to winning this prize for their respective clubs they rejoice most in your talents and success.

Gentlemen, you are young. Soon you will be entering for a greater race than this. The contest of life is before you. The prizes are honor, prosperity, wealth and influence. These are within your reach, for the same energy, the same skill, the same spirit of emulation, that you have manifested to-day, will be requisite if you desire to "go in and win" fame and fortune in the future.

There are lessons to be learned in this regatta from which you will be the gainers if you heed them. In the systematic training, the physical preparation for this contest, you have been taught the value of healthful diet and judicious exercise. To everything that tended to insure success you gave the closest attention. You avoided anything that was likely to weaken your bodily energies. You practiced temperance and sobriety. You gave up late hours and dissipation; you studied your own organization, and day by day you saw the benefit you received from systematic and self-denying regimen. All pointed to this crowning victory.

So, in the mastery of life, in business vocations, in hours of recreation, the same careful watchfulness over yourself—the same sobriety and temperance, the same healthful treatment of your vital powers, will well repay you.

There is one thing, however, in this regatta that you will have to avoid in the race of life. As your oars harmoniously swept your boat along towards the home-stake, I noticed that you looked one way and sped another. In the life-contest you will do otherwise—or fail. You will be your own look-out, your own steersman, and you will need to keep a keen watch before you if you would win. To-day the course has been clear. In the course of life you will encounter snags and fogs, and other boats will cross your bows, and all your skill and energy will be required to keep your way clear, to avoid damaging collisions, and to hold your own.

But you tire of these allusions, and wonder where I will take you to in these airy flights. So I return to this present place and time.

Gentlemen, this richly ornamented silver vase that I hold before you is yours. You have worn it fairly, and these fair donors gladly give it to you. Altogether it is a fair operation. And as I hand it over to you, Mr. Captain, and retire to private life, I but echo the sentiment that so generally lights up every face about me when I say, "Long life and success to the Arrow Club."

Speech Accompanying Presentation of a Watch to a Clergyman.

REVEREND AND DEAR SIR: For more than twelve months past, we, as members of your church and congregation, have profited by your ministrations, and within that period you have greatly endeared yourself to us by your suavity, your amiable character, your earnest devotion to duty, and the hearty interest you have ever manifested in our welfare as a people.

In the sacred desk you have faithfully advocated your religion and ours, have wisely warned us against the evils that beset us in our everyday life, and have earnestly pleaded with us to seek our truest happiness in the paths of rectitude and sobriety.

In our homes you have been our sincere and sympathizing counselor and friend. In our hours of pain and sorrow you have spoken gentle and soothing words to our troubled hearts; our children have profited by your instruction; you have united our sons and daughters in holy wedlock; your benediction has rested upon us in our domestic and business affairs, and in all things you have proven yourself our competent and loving pastor.

With a deep sense of your many benefactions, those assembled here have requested me, in their name, to present to you this WATCH, as a token of our mutual and increasing admiration and esteem for yourself, and of our gratitude for your labors in our behalf. We ask you, dear sir, to accept it as freely as we offer it; for it is fitting that you who are daily and hourly preparing us for the joys of Eternity, should bear about you this monitor of passing Time, ever marking, as we sincerely hope, hours, days and many years of happiness for you and yours.

The Clergyman's Reply.

FRIENDS AND BRETHREN: Rapidly as time has passed with me since I first came among you, a perfect stranger, you have in one short year become very near and dear to me, and we are no more strangers. On the contrary, you have so freely bestowed upon me your confidence and generosity that it seems as if I had always known and loved you in the bonds of gospel truth. Busy as I have been in forwarding the interests of this church and society, I have received from you so many tokens of esteem and affection that my duties have been greatly lightened, and I have found time to institute new labors in your behalf. At all times your sympathy and encouragement has been freely given, and gratefully appreciated. As I receive this beautiful WATCH, which all must greatly admire, my heart warms with renewed joy in your service, for it assures me that your friendship is not for an hour, or a day, or a year, but for all time; and it shall be my heart's endeavor to merit in future, with renewed energy, the esteem which you have thus so bountifully expressed. I pray you to accept my thanks for your beautiful gift and the kind words accompanying it. As pastor and people, may our ties unite us closer and closer in the bonds of Christian love throughout time and eternity.

Address to a Retiring Public Officer,

Accompanying a testimonial from the employes.

MR. HAZLITT: We have learned with unfeigned regret of your intention to resign your office as Superintendent of this railway at the close of the present month, and avail ourselves of this occasion to express, in some degree, the esteem with which we regard you in your official capacity, and our admiration for your private character.

During the many years in which you have so ably controlled the machinery of this great corporation, each one of us, from conductor to engine-wiper, has had reason to remember your many acts of forbearance and words of kindness; for many times, when we have unintentionally neglected duty, or done that which we ought not to have done, we have experienced undeserved consideration at your hands. Instead of discharging us, and thus making our lives miserable, you have given us gentle counsel and encouragement to perform our duties better; and in this way you have made us your sincere friends, and taught us faithfulness in our respective departments. For all these acts and lessons we now gratefully thank you.

But we would not confine our gratitude to mere empty words. With the means which your generosity has enabled us to save from our wages we have purchased this gold-cased chronometer watch, which we ask you to accept as our parting gift. It is not much; but as a railway officer you know the value of correct time, and the necessity of always being " on time," and we deemed it not only an appropriate present, but one which you might be induced daily to wear near your kind and generous heart. Whenever you look upon its face, will you not think of us who gave it as a memento of our now-ending long and pleasant relations? And our blessing goes with you wherever you may go.

Speech at a Wooden Wedding.

LADIES AND GENTLEMEN: An occasion like this is eminently calculated for the reception of congratulations. Here are two hearts that have beat as one full five years without desiring to be two again. Five years! Ask *them* how long it *seems*, and they will tell you—*five months!* Fortunately the calendar attests the truth of the record, and if any further proof is necessary, we offer in evidence their three curly-headed children, the largest four years old.

Why this should be called a *wooden* wedding I don't know. None of us is willing to confess being a blockhead, and it would be dangerous to insinuate that our excellent host and hostess are either sappy or wooden-headed, gnarly or knotty in disposition, or inclined to *leave.* Why, then, this array of washtubs, washboards, pails, clothespins, rolling-pins, potato-mashers and pudding-sticks? All are useful in their way, especially the rolling-pins and potato-mashers (in case of domestic war), and I have read of one woman, whose husband neglected to provide sufficient firewood for the kitchen, who bought and burned about a hundred and fifty dozen clothes-pins for cooking purposes. But she was a rare exception. *Our* hostess is better treated than that.

Well, I suppose wood has its uses as well as everything else, and if on this occasion it tends to unite in warmer friendship our host and hostess and their guests, it serves a good purpose, and leads us to look forward with hope and satisfaction to the next important anniversary of their married life—the *tin* wedding of five years hence. May we all be there!

Speech Accompanying a Testimonial of Esteem.

SIR: A few more days and the term of your office will expire. We had hoped, until after the recent election, that you might have held it still longer; but the people have determined otherwise, and it only remains for us to bow submissively to the will of the majority.

You step down from public to private life without the loss of one worthy qualification that you possessed when you entered upon your official duties. Nor has the tongue of slander, in all the lapse of time since then, been able to stain a single attribute of your private character. Malice has been unable to overcome you by its persistent opposition, and your course has been every way satisfactory to your constituents.

We have, indeed, been proud of you in your high position, and we are none the less proud of you now. On the contrary, we are so proud of you that at the first opportunity we propose to elect you to a higher office than that which you now relinquish.

Looking about for some suitable testimonial to present to you, as a token of our admiration and good wishes, we remembered your public spirit, benevolence and love of country, and decided, Sir, to ask your acceptance of this elegantly engrossed and richly framed copy of Washington's Farewell Address when he was about to retire, like you, to private life. Its money-value is small; but with it we offer you, also, our unfeigned appreciation of your labors in our behalf and that of our common country.

The Reply.

GENTLEMEN: I thank you not less for your hearty words of encouragement and esteem than for this beautiful memento of the honest patriotism and counsels of the Father of his Country.

In all my experiences of public life, it has been my endeavor to avoid sectional prejudices and to labor entirely for the best interests of our entire nation. Yet, in all those hours of solicitude concerning public affairs, my heart has warmly turned to my constituents for encouragement and approbation, and I have not failed to receive at your hands the most gratifying assurance that I was pursuing a satisfactory course in whatever I undertook in behalf of the whole people.

You say you are proud of me. I believe you; but you are not prouder of me than I am of my constituents, and it has been a pleasure to serve you to the best of my ability. I know not to what fields of public duty I may be called in the future, but I now "step down and out" with a feeling of relief, and the assurance that my labors have not been in vain.

Again thanking you for your kind appreciation and this elegant testimonial of your esteem, I bid you good-night and pleasant dreams.

Speech of a Candidate When Serenaded.

GENTLEMEN: I love music, but especially that kind that wakes me in the night to assure me of the esteem, kind remembrance and hearty support of my friends in the exciting contest upon which we have entered. The poet may praise "the music of the spheres," but the stalwart warrior best delights his senses by the "music of the spears," on the eve of a great battle. These are *not* "piping times of peace," gentlemen, in *our* camp. We have our armor on, our swords by our sides, and our hands on the hilts, ready for service, keeping step with "the music of the Union," and marching on, I trust, to certain victory. Still the strains of martial music on the midnight air are very inspiriting. They serve to arouse our energies, to drive away our cares, and bid us hope for the best.

The principles involved in this campaign should be our strongest reliance. Good men may be nominated on a bad platform, and be defeated, while ordinary candidates, backed by sound political principles, to which they stand solemnly pledged, are honored by their election. It is of course best to advocate good measures and nominate good men to enforce them; but, whatever the man, let the principles of the party be such that every good citizen-voter can support them, and then our confidence in the cause will spur us on to victory. Gentlemen, I congratulate you upon the very broad and wise platform on which we base our prospects at the coming election. Your candidates may be defeated, but such defeat cannot injure or destroy your principles. Stand by them, therefore, till you have vindicated them and the justice of our cause.

Thanking you again for this delightful " concord of sweet sounds," and rejoicing in your confidence, I bid you good-night and pleasant dreams.

Speech of Welcome

By Gen. W. T. Sherman, at reunion of the Army of the Tennessee.

FELLOW-SOLDIERS: I am glad to meet those here present on this day, and in this place. It is said that we could not meet on any day which is not the anniversary of some battle, but it was not accident that we hold this reunion of the Army of the Tennessee in St. Louis.

The day was chosen to do honor to those who took part in the capture of Camp Jackson in the suburbs of St. Louis. We have malice toward none, and charity to all. Forgiving the past, but not forgetting it, we will cherish the memories of the war forever. Each year diminishes the members of our society, but not the glorious memories of the civil war of 1861-'65; beneath this we have the kindliest feelings toward all. I am glad to see this hall filled with faces that come back to me as plainly as when we parted at Raleigh.

Mayor's Address of Welcome to Secretary of War.

SIR: In extending to you the hospitalities of this city, its municipal authorities and citizens unite in offering you a hearty welcome, worthy not only of the high position which you hold in the government of this nation, but of the respect and admiration that we cherish for your private character.

We welcome you as the chief of one of the most important departments at the National Capital—a department upon which the integrity and defense of our country greatly depend.

We welcome you as one who in other distinguished political offices has left a proud and unsullied record of duties performed in the spirit of patriotism and fidelity to our institutions.

We claim for our city a population of 500,000 people, with a large mercantile and manufacturing business, which it will be our pleasure to exhibit to you as fully as your inclination and opportunity may demand.

We have those among us who are deeply interested in the higher branches of literature, art and science, whom we would like to present to you as worthy representatives of the culture of our city.

In brief, Sir, whatever our city affords in all its social and industrial departments that may attract your special attention, we shall be pleased to submit it to your inspection and enjoyment. Our desire is to make your visit here so agreeable that you will take away with you none but the most gratifying assurances of our prosperity and hospitality, and that you may be induced to revisit us with delight.

The Reply.

MR. MAYOR AND GENTLEMEN OF ———— The warmth of your reception merits a grateful response in my bosom; for in becoming your guest, even for a day or two, I feel that while I minister to your pleasure, I reap the purest gratification on my part.

The past of your city is replete with historical, commercial, political and social associations, which possess great interest for me; and I see in her near future a wealth of augmented prosperity no less certain than deserved.

Since you accord to me the privilege of seeing for myself the works which make your city great, and of meeting those ladies and gentlemen who have wrought these triumphs of art, science and literature, I most confidently place myself in your hospitable hands.

I thank you, gentlemen, for your cordial greeting, and none the less heartily because I have reason to believe that your esteem attaches to my person no less than to the position which I hold as a public servant.

Defeated Candidate's Reply to a Serenade,

By Daniel Webster at the time of defeat for the candidacy of the presidency, at the Baltimore convention, 1862.

FELLOW-CITIZENS: I thank you for your friendly and respectful call. I am very glad to see you. Some of you have been engaged in an arduous public duty at Baltimore, the object of your meeting being the selection of a fit person to be supported for the office of President of the United States. Others of you take an interest in the result of the deliberations of that assembly of Whigs. It so happened that my name among others was presented on the occasion; another candidate, however, was preferred. I have only to say, gentlemen, that the convention did, I doubt not, what it thought best, and exercised its discretion in the important matter committed to it. The result has caused me no personal feeling whatever, nor any change of conduct or purpose. What I have been, I am in principles and character; and what I am, I hope to continue to be. Circumstances or opponents may triumph over my fortunes, but they will not triumph over my temper or self-respect.

Gentlemen, this is a serene and beautiful night. Ten thousand thousand of the lights of heaven illuminate the firmament. They rule the night. A few hours hence their glory will be extinguished—

> "Ye stars that glitter in the skies,
> And gaily dance before mine eyes,
> What are ye when the sun shall rise?"

Gentlemen, there is not one among you who will sleep better tonight than I shall. If I wake, I shall learn the hour from the constellations, and I shall rise in the morning, God willing, with the lark; and though the lark is a better songster than I am, yet he will not leave the dew and the daisies and spring up and greet the purpling east with a more blithe and jocund spirit than I possess. Gentlemen, I again repeat my thanks for this mark of respect, and commend you to the enjoyment of a quiet and satisfactory repose. May God bless you all.

Speech of Congratulation to a Candidate

For office, immediately after his nomination.

SIR: At the very outset of this political contest we hail you as our standard-bearer, congratulating you upon your harmonious, almost unanimous nomination for Congressman, and ourselves upon the prospect of being so ably represented in our national councils.

Since you first came among us you have, by your affability, industry in your profession, and public spirit, won deserved consideration at the hands of our citizens. Especially have your political principles, and the eloquent earnestness with which on several important occasions you have advocated them, produced the happiest effect in convincing the opposition of their errors and leading them to embrace the views of our own party. Your arguments in behalf of your principles have been unanswered, and where you have not succeeded in converting our opponents, you have very thoroughly silenced them.

We feel that with you for our leader in this contest we are going straight on to victory, and that, when elected, you will ably advance our national and local interests. We feel that you will be no mere ornamental figure-head in the halls of Congress, but believe that on every question of importance your voice will be lifted and your vote cast in the advocacy of good government.

We are well-acquainted with your views of protection, financial retrenchment and reform, the Mormon question, and internal improvements, and we are satisfied that upon these and other issues you will capably represent your party and constituents. Trusting that our efforts to elect you may be successful, and we believe they will be, we pledge you our untiring and hearty support.

The Candidate's Reply.

GENTLEMEN: The genuine heartiness of your congratulations, and the unanimity with which you have labored for my nomination, together with your pledges to support me throughout this campaign, serve to strengthen the determination which I had already formed, should I be elected, to be the consistent representative of my constituents.

The political contest upon which we are now entering will require us to exert all the energies we possess to overcome the political chicanery and vindictive animosity of our opponents; but I assure you that, as your leader, I will not flinch a moment, whatever the opposition to our success may be. If "eternal vigilance is the price of liberty," like ————'s detectives, our motto should be, "we never sleep!" Money and trickery will confront us on every hand; but when

I look into your faces, gentlemen, and see written there the determination to fight this battle to the bitter end, I feel that it will be manfully fought. It is too soon to figure the result. Ours will be no easy victory, and energy and watchfulness alone can decide whether we triumph or succumb to a superior force. We all *hope* for the best—we will work for it—we will fight for it.

> "Who does the best his circumstance allows,
> Does well—acts nobly—angels could no more."

Gentlemen, you well know my principles, and I am glad to know that they are yours. Together let us give "a long pull, a strong pull, and a pull altogether," and after the votes are counted I trust to return your congratulations of to-day with compound interest.

Speech of Mayor at a Volunteer Firemen's Review,

The different fire companies being grouped in the vicinity of city hall, the mayor occupying a position where he can overlook the firemen as he addresses them.

FRIENDS OF AURORA: An examination and review of the different fire companies of Aurora by the city council recalls the fact that one hundred and twenty firemen report here for duty at the present time, who, in case of fire, are assisted in extinguishing it by fifteen hundred feet of hose, two miles of Holly water-pipe, ten hydrants, three Holly pumps, hose-carts, and three excellently equipped fire-steamers. All in all, in her fire-extinguishing appliances, Aurora can safely challenge comparison with any of her sister cities; not only is this so in number of men, number of steamers, hose-carts and accessories thereto, but particularly are we fortunate in having always at hand, in the central and business portion of the city, a great abundance of never-failing water.

Two parties are to be thanked for this very superior fire-extinguishing equipment we see here to-day—namely, the men who have so generously volunteered, in many cases at personal loss and discomfort, to do the firemen's duty, and the taxpayers who have at various times, in all, appropriated some $50,000 in furnishing the necessary machinery to aid our firemen in subduing a conflagration.

That the department has attained an excellent degree of efficiency is shown in the fact that, at all ordinary times, within a reasonable distance from the engine-houses, water is thrown upon a fire, in the day-time, within ten minutes after the first tap of the bell, and at night the time for getting to a fire need not exceed fifteen minutes.

How efficiently our fire department does its work, and the large amount of property it saves, has been repeatedly demonstrated to our people.

We have seen several wooden buildings completely wrapped in flames and nearly burned down when the alarm was given, following which our firemen came to the rescue and the conflagration was subdued, while an adjoining wooden building, directly alongside, not two feet away, was scarcely scorched.

It is not many months since we saw, through the efficiency of our fire department, a fine church edifice saved from destruction. We saw the Hoyt Brothers' manufactory rescued from the flames, while the sparks danced like hail-stones upon its roof, and but a few months ago the valuable central school-building was preserved to us through the gallantry of our firemen—a saving vastly greater than the entire amount ever appropriated for the support of the fire department.

For this, and much other noble work done by our firemen in the past year, I desire, in behalf of the city council and the people of Aurora, to tender you our warmest thanks.

The people have voted liberally to furnish you the needed appliances for extinguishing fires. They now, as exhibited in this review, have the consciousness of knowing that the money they expended has been wisely appropriated—that we have a most excellent body of firemen, and that this department of our municipal protection is in a very high degree efficient.

Thankful for our general freedom from large fires in the past twelve months, grateful to you for the thorough manner in which you have guarded us from conflagration, the hope is, that through your continued efficiency we may be alike fortunate in the year to come.

Speech at a Christmas Festival.

To Sunday-school pupils; the room being decorated with evergreens, while one or two Christmas-trees laden with gifts stand near by.

FRIENDS OF THE SABBATH-SCHOOL AND SUNDAY-SCHOOL PUPILS: In the midst of our festival rejoicings we assemble here to-night to make our holiday still more pleasant by the exercises of this occasion, and as I look into the expectant faces of these boys and girls, these young ladies and gentlemen that I see before me, we ask what does this evergreen, hung with a profusion of articles to be distributed among the pupils of this school, mean?

It means that good parents and kind friends have made it possible for you to attend this Sabbath-school in the past year. It means that you have been blessed with a most able and efficient pastor, who presides over the ministrations of this church. It means that your school has been managed by a superintendent who is solicitous for your welfare. It means that faithful teachers have labored throughout the year for your welfare; and together, with pastor, superintendent, teachers and friends, all hold you in kindly remembrance to-night.

And now, my young friends, what do you propose to give back in exchange for all this kindness bestowed upon you in the last twelve months? These gifts cannot all be upon one side, and you do not wish them to be. You do not desire to be under obligation. You hope to pay for all this kindness; and I will tell you how you may, to the entire satisfaction of your parents, your pastor, your superintendent and your teachers. And that will be by emulating, in the coming year, the teaching of that one whose birth we celebrate in this Christmas festivity.

As Christ taught forgiveness to all, so you must carry no hatreds, no animosities into the coming year. As Christ taught love to all, so you must exercise the kindliest of feelings to every one. You should emulate the Divine Master in seeking to do good to every one with whom you come in contact; and particularly by bringing into this Sabbath-school, in the next year, every boy and girl whom you know may be benefited by its influence. As Christ taught charity to all, so you must lend a helping hand to those who need assistance; and as Jesus said, Honor thy father and mother, so may you be that obedient to parents, that kind, that watchful of their needs, as to make them a thousand-fold glad that you are their children.

As your teachers and superintendent have labored in your behalf in the past year, so must you be very careful to remember their admonitions and practice their teaching. Doing that, your parents and your teachers will feel abundantly repaid for all they have done for you, even down to the distribution of these gifts to you to-night.

President Garfield used to say that he never stood in the presence of a boy without a feeling of veneration at the thought of what that boy might achieve in after-life.

As I stand in your presence to-night and look into the faces of these happy boys and girls—all all before you, with its privileges and opportunities—I can well understand the sentiment that moved the martyred President as he studied the life of a child and thought of its future possibilities.

How soon this little girl—the very youngest—will develop through girlhood to maidenhood. How very soon she will pass out from home —out into the great world, with confiding step and heart, leaning on the arm of a trusted companion, to assume the duties of wifehood, motherhood and womanhood.

And these boys—how soon they will take the helm to do our work. How the great world of travel, adventure, agriculture, invention, manufacture, teaching, legislation, and finance will absorb them.

And who of this audience will be the good, the true, the noble, and the successful in the coming time? May *you* so heed the teaching of this Sabbath-school that you will *all* be of that number.

May the year just opening before you in your Sabbath-school be one of real profit. May you each bring one new pupil to this school in the coming year, to enjoy these blessings with you. May we all meet here again next Christmas-time.

And now, hoping that you will enjoy the Christmas-tree to the full, I wish you, in behalf of parents, friends and teachers, a most delightful, happy New-Year.

Speech at Old Settlers' Reunion.

FELLOW CITIZENS—OLD NEIGHBORS AND PIONEERS IN HALLOCK COUNTY: Forty years ago, in company with Old Benjamin Crawford, who died last year, I hunted for ducks on this very block of ground, worth to-day a large fortune of itself. At that time there were only seventeen white persons in the town, three or four blacks, and a tribe of Winnebago Indians, encamped, at that time, about three miles west of our village.

There were two frame-houses in the place. The rest were made of logs, containing usually about three rooms, with sometimes a chamber. In a careful review of my own life and recollection of those who were here in those early days, I doubt if there has ever been a period in all our experience when we had a greater amount of happiness than fell to our lot in those pioneer days.

Everybody had work—plenty of it. Nobody feared being discharged on Saturday night because of over production. Good health generally prevailed, the result of exercise, fresh air, hard work and sound sleep. There were no cliques in society, no aristocracy, no snobbery, no bankruptcies, no envy, and no distress because certain men were getting very rich while others were very poor.

There were no heart-burnings because one neighbor had a better furnished house than the others, and the women—they were women in those days—had no worry because they had nothing to wear.

Old Deacon Towne told me, on one occasion, when we were talking of the old times, that himself and family came from a handsomely furnished house in Troy, New York, to his log cabin, up near the big woods, and in all his experience he never saw such genuine hospitality, nor such a genial and happy time as his neighbors all had on their plain fare and the few opportunities around them. Yes, we lived right down to the barest necessaries in those days, and in doing that we learned that our real wants, in order to make us happy, are very few.

Forty winters, since some of us came here, have spread their white covering, and as many beautiful springs have brought the birds and flowers to us, returning every season to a vastly larger population than we had the year before. But I cannot tell you how, step by step, we have grown. I will leave that for others, who will give you the history of these forty years more in detail. Suffice it to say, the early settlers in this locality have been most fortunate in the peace and happiness which surrounded them in their pioneer days, in the wealth which has been showered upon them, and in the privileges which they enjoy to-day.

Speech at an Improvement Meeting.

MR. PRESIDENT: While it is unquestionably true that the manufacturing of articles that may be sold abroad is a most prolific source of revenue and ultimate wealth to a town, it is equally important that a healthy atmosphere be about us, and that our homes, by their charming surroundings, be such as will cultivate those graces of nature which enable a people to make the right use of wealth when it is acquired. I have therefore this to suggest as a means of beautifying this city: That the inhabitants upon any street, for the space of one block, form an improvement society for that block, to do the following:

First—To take away all front fences from before dwellings.

Second—To set elms by the roadside and a sufficiency of ornamental trees to suitably shade the streets.

Third—To secure a smooth stone sidewalk, at least eight feet in width.

Fourth—To grade the front lot from the house to the roadway, and cover the same with sod.

Fifth—To have the street swept as often as may be necessary to keep it clean, and the lawns all mown and kept in excellent order.

Sixth—To have all alleys and foul places carefully cleaned, and put into a condition such as will make the atmosphere in the immediate vicinity perfectly healthy.

The taking down of fences, setting trees, and putting grounds in order, will not be very expensive in the first place, and the keeping of them in fine condition afterwards can be done with comparatively small expense, the labor being performed by men who need this employment.

When these improvements which I have indicated are carried into effect generally, throughout the town, ours will be one of the healthiest and one of the most beautiful cities in the world.

Selling Goods at Auction.

The business of disposing of goods at auction is one of large magnitude. Frequently, when all other means prove futile in getting rid of property, the auctioneer's persuasive language, added to the inherent impression that auction prices are invariably *low*, entails spirited competition, and thus the figures realized often exceed the most sanguine expectations. As in other classes of trade, there are men engaged in this pursuit who are utterly unprincipled, and who are very properly dubbed "Peter Funks;" while on the other hand individuals, whose character and honor are as high as the highest and as good as the best, also discourse on the auction-block. In Trinity building, the great real-estate mart of New York city, millions of dollars of property change ownership "under the hammer" each year—and in all the leading cities of the Union vast quantities of dry-goods, boots and shoes, and other staple articles, reach the jobber through the same channel.

At the beginning of an auction, the terms of sale are stated. If it be a vendue of merchandise, the crier or auctioneer commences about as follows:

The Words of the Auctioneer.

LADIES AND GENTLEMEN: These goods are to be sold to the highest bidder, without reserve. If I accept the first bid and get the second, then the article must be sold. Strangers will be required, in every case, to pay a deposit. Bid promptly, and I will dispose of the goods quickly. I begin the sale by offering this splendid photograph album, known as the Superdonbonsical brand; it is manufactured in the city of Berlin by Henri Von Hytenschnitzenheimer and cost twelve dollars, besides import-duties. How much am I bid to start it? Start it along,—it is for sale at your own price; how much do I hear for it? One dollar! One dollar is no money for it,—but no matter—I'm bid a dollar for it—One dollar. One dollar—one dollar—one dollar—one dollar—one dollar; at one dollar—one dollar—and a quarter I *have*—one dollar and a quarter—and a quarter—and a quarter—will you go the half?—*half*, I'm bid; one dollar and fifty, one dollar and fifty—will you give the seventy-five? Why what are you people thinking about?—one dollar and fifty cents would not pay the import-duties on this magnificent, hand-made, morocco-bound album, with separation pages, a hinge to every leaf and a patent back and spring clasp—seventy five—one dollar and seventy-five I am bid—and now will you make it two dollars? *at* one dollar and seventy-five—two dollars will you make it? Will you *go* the two—do I *hear* the two—shall I have the *two?* One dollar and seventy-five—going at one dollar and seventy-five—going going at the low price of one dollar and three-quarters—once! twice! one dollar and seventy-five,—fair warning and a fair sale—going, going, going, gone! Next lot.

Fourth of July Oration.

FELLOW CITIZENS: The Declaration of American Independence, adopted by the Continental Congress at the State House, Philadelphia, July 4, 1776, to the reading of which we have just been listening, stands to day the charter of our national liberty. It was the first grand step of American freedom and progress in their march across this continent, whose influence now binds together a nation extending from Lake Itasca, on the north, to Mexico, on the South, and bounded respectively, on the east and on the west, by the Atlantic and Pacific oceans. It was the death-knell of England's power over her American colonies, and severed the ties that bound them to contribute to her support without a voice in their own government.

At this distance from the occurrences of that day, when the enthusiastic and just indignation that prompted this immortal State paper has passed away, the allegations against King George and his ministers have, to a certain degree, lost much of their interest; and yet those wrongs still stand, and will continue to stand while the world lasts, a momentous page in our national history. At this period, when all nations have learned to respect us, and we count England among our best friends and commercial allies, the bitterness of these charges against her has, in *our* minds, faded away. In the bosoms of the Revolutionary fathers, however, they created a fervor of patriotism stronger than the love of life and property, and in defense of their principles these men took up arms, defied tyranny, fought, bled and died. With them, as the great orator, Patrick Henry, defined it, the issue was simply "liberty, or death!" To gain the one, they braved the other, regarding their sufferings as a sacrifice to secure the prosperity and political freedom of their posterity. Nowhere is this sentiment more forcefully, more brilliantly expressed than in the closing sentences of the Declaration itself: "With a firm reliance on the protection of Divine Providence, we mutually pledge to each other our lives, our fortunes, and our sacred honor."

It was no empty boast. Living or dying, whatever might be the result, they went forth to battle for their rights with such earnestness, such fidelity to each other and their country, that they won the prize for which they fought, and the American Republic, born of patriotism and of strife, won victory and peace for succeeding generations. Such a spectacle entranced the nations, and the colonies did then, in deed and in truth, "assume among the powers of the earth the separate and equal station to which the laws of nature and of nature's God entitled them."

The one great principle established by the triumph of the American colonies was this: The equality of all men under the law, possessing the inalienable rights of life, liberty, and the pursuit of happiness, as one common heritage.

That principle prevailed, with one exception, through all the vicissitudes of the young republic, fortified by the wisdom of a Washingson, a Jefferson, an Adams, and a Hamilton, and the result of their deliberations was that grand guarantee of our liberties, the Constitution of 1788–'79. At that time negro slavery was viewed with different eyes from those that witnessed its horror in after-years, and its enormity was not appreciated by the founders of the government; a fact that has led to many sneers, that while the continental patriots fought for their own liberty, they forged the chains of their slaves, and thus cast discredit upon their motives for freedom. This criticism, though severe, had a particle of reason in it; but in that day, and among that people, slavery was considered no offense against Divine or human law.

The benefits secured to every individual (excepting slaves) were representation in the national councils, the right of equal suffrage, trial by jury, freedom from unjust and onerous taxation, protection to life, and peaceful possession of individual property. And these rights and privileges are our heritage to-day.

It is in honor of these rights and privileges under the Constitution, secured to us by the valor of our forefathers, that we celebrate this day. In the long strides of the civilization of the nineteenth century, our nation has kept step with the progress of the world, and, under our Constitution and beneficent laws, every encouragement has been afforded us for the development of the arts and sciences; labor has been appreciated as a source of wealth and improvement, and has attained to a high position in the work of perfecting the great enterprises of the age; inventors and inventions have been encouraged and patronized; literature has achieved honor by its freshness and brilliancy, and everything that comfort or luxury could suggest has been multifariously furnished at prices within the reach of moderate incomes. To enumerate the blessings we have in this way enjoyed under the provisions of our national charter would be a herculean labor; and in any other country such progress as we have made in one hundred years would have required two or three centuries.

Above me wave the stars and stripes of our country among the peaceful branches of the grove, and the shadows of the flag we love and venerate as the ensign of our liberties flit over the happy faces of our sturdy yeomanry and their comely wives and daughters. The birds are singing in our leafy bowers; flowers and fruits, and waving fields of grain, enrich our soil; peaceful homes dot the landscape all around us, and the voices of merry children fall sweetly upon our ears. These are the blessings of peace wrought out for us by the hardy Continentals and their brave and wise leaders of the American Revolution. To-day we venerate their memory; and if from their spirit-homes they are permitted to witness our happiness and the blessings they purchased for us in those rugged times and dark days, I am sure they must rejoice with us in the triumph of the principles they established, and in behalf of which they laid down their lives by the wayside and on the battlefield. Let us never forget these men, nor those noble mothers, wives and daughters of the Revolution, whose patriotism was no less sincere and enthusiastic than that of the men they encouraged to take up arms against tyranny, and was only less demonstrative because of the gentleness of their sex.

The lessons which the lives and deaths of these brave and noble men and women bequeathed to us are worthy of our consideration, and I would dwell upon some of the peculiarities which made them great and sustained them in the hour of trial and danger. I have already referred to the deep, inborn patriotism which the rule of oppression to which they were subjected so thoroughly developed. It was a sentiment born of the period and the circumstances of their existence—a sentiment that subdued all selfish propensities and found expression in actions of just defiance and heroism.

They were men of simple habits, living lives of industry in their several vocations, and overcoming difficulties by their energy and perseverance.

They were men of integrity and honor, knowing and doing their duty as citizens in all the relations of life.

They possessed no false ambition to become rich by speculation and fraud, nor to aspire to stations of honor and profit for selfish purposes; nor did they encourage hurtful extravagance.

They respected the laws of the government under which they lived, until those laws became unjustly oppressive and destructive to the best interests of the entire colonies.

They encouraged morality and truth in their dealings with each other and also toward strangers with whom they came in contact, and were severe in punishing infractions of law and evil practices.

Such were the men and women in "the times that tried their souls," and such were the examples which they left for us to follow.

Young ladies and gentlemen, whose beaming eyes gaze into mine as I look around over this assemblage, in your blooming manhood and womanhood remember these dead heroes and their families, their sufferings and their endurance, their unselfish patriotism, and, above all, the examples of their private virtues. The world needs such men and women as they were every day, and it is in your power to emulate them in all that reflects honor upon their memories. There are battles to be fought against wrong and oppression in numerous forms, social obstacles to overcome, love of country to cherish and maintain, truth and honor to be upheld, and it will soon devolve upon you to govern this broad nation, with all its interests confided to your care. In the near future this responsibility will fall like a mantle upon your shoulders, and it will behoove you to see that the trust is not misplaced. To-day there is not one of the old Revolutionary patriots alive. They did their work, and did it well, and then passed on. Other generations came upon the stage of action, but through all the years that intervened between then and now, their staunch principles and sturdy teachings were owned and heeded. Will you own and heed them also? If you will, I may safely prophesy from this stand that the glory of the Union will not depart from it in your day and generation, and I foresee, in that case, greater wonders awaiting our second centennial birthday than we in the last century have witnessed. Revere the stars and stripes forever. They are the symbols of our prosperity as well as our integrity—the mementoes of a past age—the hope of our country's future.

CELEBRATING THE FOURTH OF JULY.

History of the Day and Forms for its Observance.

FROM 1761 to 1773 the thirteen American colonies owned and controlled by Great Britain were in a continuous state of excitement caused by the excessive taxation imposed upon them, the arbitrary rule of the home government in their affairs, and their insufficient representation in the national councils of legislation. The colonists felt justly aggrieved, and the spirit of revolution was strongly manifested on several occasions; so much so that in one or two instances their public demonstrations of indignation resulted in the repeal of certain obnoxious measures.

After several serious collisions between the colonists and the national authorities, owing to the increased taxation and oppression of the government, this spirit of rebellion culminated, in 1773, in the destruction of three cargoes of tea sent to Boston, on which the colonists were required to pay an onerous tax. This bold act brought a new crisis into colonial affairs. The colonists were in open rebellion, and the military forces of the government were increased, with new powers, to subjugate the rebels. In the contest which ensued the colonists were frequently victorious, and their enthusiasm in the work of freeing themselves from the dominion of Great Britain was unbounded.

The legislative body which they formed, known as the Continental Congress, was organized and composed of the most brilliant intellects and patriotic spirits in the country. It began its first session at Carpenter's Hall, Philadelphia (afterward known as Independence Hall), September 5, 1774, continuing until near the end of October. Little was accomplished at this session, beyond giving earnest expression to their determination to secure civil and political liberty.

The year 1775 was marked by the battles of Lexington and Concord, the capture of Fort Ticonderoga, the battle of Bunker Hill, the evacuation of Boston by the British, and other stirring events. The second session of the Continental Congress began at the Pennsylvania State House, May 10, and continued throughout the year, encouraging the efforts of the patriots in the field, and stimulating the project for an early separation of the colonies from the home government.

June 7, 1776, Richard Henry Lee introduced in Congress his famous resolution, "That these united colonies are, and of right ought to be, free and independent states; that they are absolved from all allegiance to the British crown, and that all political connection between them and the state of Great Britain is, and ought to be, totally dissolved." This resolution was adopted by twelve of the colonies, July 2, 1776. On the fourth, the Declaration of Independence, prepared by Thomas Jefferson, was adopted amid great rejoicings and the wildest enthusiasm. Wherever the news spread, it was greeted with shouts, bonfires, processions, and other unusual demonstrations of delight.

This is "the day we celebrate," and the reason why its joyful observance is so general throughout the land and in other countries wherever Americans can assemble in its honor. That it should be so widely recognized and celebrated is only a just tribute to the patriots who secured to us the liberties we enjoy.

Years ago John Adams said: "It will be celebrated by succeeding generations as the great anniversary festival. It ought to be commemorated as the day of deliverance

How to Organize a Fourth of July Procession.

THIS illustration represents a lengthy procession, composed of many distinct parts, among them the various trades organized to celebrate the Fourth of July. In this the orator of the day occupies a central position. Before his carriage come the fire companies, the military display, chief marshal and the police, who may be detailed for the day; next behind is the orator's carriage, with the distinguished guests and others to appear on the platform; next follow the mayor and aldermen, in carriages, succeeded by the civic societies; next come the different trades-wagons, the rear being made up of citizens in carriages; several bands scattered throughout the procession, each placed at the head of a distinct division, add much to the attractiveness of the occasion. The interest is increased when the cavalcade exhibits a large amount of variety.

by solemn acts of devotion to Almighty God. It ought to be solemnized with pomp and parade, with shows, games, sports, guns, bells, bonfires, and illuminations, from one end of the continent to the other, from this time forth, forevermore."

In the celebration of the day the managers should seek to present a large and varied programme, both in the procession and upon the speaker's stand. No exercise should be unduly long. The procession, formed at ten o'clock, and commencing to move at eleven, should exhibit a variety of that which will instruct and amuse; bands of music being judiciously distributed through the same so that the music of one will not interfere with the other. On the platform, there should be prayer, singing by glee-club, poem, reading Declaration of Independence, music by the band, oration, singing by quartette, announcement of afternoon exercises, music, and benediction.

EXERCISES AT BURIAL SERVICE.

Forms in Use on certain Occasions.

DECORATION-DAY, one of the American national holidays, occurs May 30 of each year, and is devoted, with appropriate ceremonies, to decorating with flowers the graves of the soldiers who fell in the civil war between the Northern and Southern States, from 1861 to 1865, both inclusive. The custom originated among the women of the Southern States in the early years of the contest, and was annually observed by them. This touching memorial of the honored dead soon became general throughout the country, and in 1868 and 1869 the 30th day of May was set apart for its observance by order of General John A. Logan, who was then commander-in-chief of the military association known as the "Grand Army of the Republic." Since then it has been regularly observed by the society, the following being some of the established forms.

The Post Commander of each post having previously issued an order for the meeting of all its members at the Post Hall, or elsewhere, on Decoration-Day, the comrades, in uniform, gather at the appointed time and place, and quietly take their usual stations.

Order; make it an instrument of great good; keep our names on the roll of Thy servants, and at last receive us into that Grand Army above, where Thou, O God, art the Supreme Commander."

Decoration of Unknown Graves.

If a monument in memory of unknown or unreturned soldiers is to be decorated, a firing party of comrades, with three rounds of blank cartridges, is detailed to do escort duty. These march to the cemetery with arms unloaded and reversed. At the cemetery the Post may be divided into detachments, or may keep in phalanx, until all the graves are decorated, and then assembles in some proper portion of the grounds for services, conducted as follows:

First, there is usually performed music by the band or a hymn. Prayer by the Chaplain. After which, the Commander delivers the following:

Address at Cemetery.

"To-day is the festival of our dead. We unite to honor the memory of our brave and our beloved, to enrich and ennoble our lives by recalling a public heroism and a private worth that are immortal, to encourage by our solemn service a more zealous and stalwart patriotism.

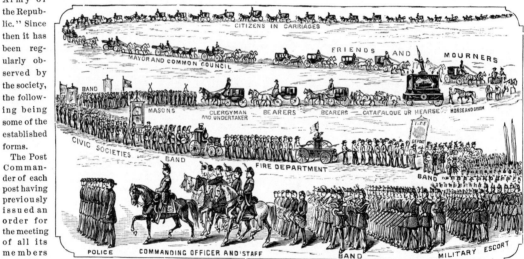

The Arrangement of a Funeral Procession.

THE procession here shown represents a funeral conducted by the masonic fraternity, the deceased having been not only a mason, but prominent in military circles, and in municipal affairs, as well as a patron of the various civic societies, The attendance at the burial service by various orders and different classes being large, the above diagram will be of assistance, as showing the proper position for each in the procession. In this the catafalque, or hearse, is immediately preceded by the bearers, the next before being the clergyman and undertaker, the masons, civic societies, fire-department and military companies. Following is the riderless horse of deceased, mourners, friends, city councilmen and citizens. Numerous bands distributed through the cavalcade enhance the impressiveness of the affair.

The Chaplain's Prayer.

While the comrades stand at ease, the Chaplain offers this prayer:

ALMIGHTY FATHER! humbly we bow before Thee, our Creator, Preserver, Guide and Protector. We thank Thee for our lives; for the mercy which has kept us until this hour; for Thy guidance in our marches by day and by night; for Thy constant care in the hour of danger; and for the preservation of our national integrity and unity. Be graciously near to our comrades who suffer from disease or wounds, and to the widows and orphans of those who fell in our holy cause; in all distress comfort them, and give us willing hearts and ready hands to supply their needs. Grant that the memory of our noble dead, who freely gave their lives for the land they loved, may dwell ever in our hearts. Bless our country; bless our

Festival of the dead! Yes, though many eyes are clouded with tears, though many hearts are heavy with regret, though many lives are still desolate because of the father or brother, the husband or lover, who did not come back; though every grave, which a tender reverence or love adorns with flowers, is the shrine of a sorrow whose influence is still potent though its first keen poignancy has been dulled—despite of all, to-day is a festival, a festival of our dead; no less a festival because it is full of solemnity.

"And now, as in this silent camping-ground of our dead, with soldierly tenderness and love, we garland these passionless mounds, let us recall those who made their breasts a barricade between our country and its foes. Let us recall their toils, their sufferings, their heroism, their supreme fidelity in camp, in prison-pen, or on the battle-field, and in hospital, that the flag under which they fought, and from the shadow of whose folds they were promoted, may never be dishonored; that the country for whose union and supremacy they surrendered life may have the fervent and enthusiastic devotion of every citizen; that, as we stand by every grave as before an altar, we may pledge our manhood that, so help us God, the memory of our dead shall encourage and strengthen in us all a more loyal patriotism."

Words of the Officer and Chaplain.

At the close of this address, the Officer of the Day says:

"In your name, my comrades, I scatter (or deposit) these memorial flowers upon this grave (or monument), which represents the graves of all who died in the sacred cause of our country. Our floral tribute shall wither. Let the tender fraternal love for which it stands endure until the touch of death shall chill the warm pulse-beats of our hearts."

The Chaplain then adds:

"Comrades, by this service, without distinction of race or creed, we renew our pledge to exercise a spirit of fraternity among ourselves, of charity to the destitute wards of the Grand Army, and of loyalty to the authority and union of the United States of America, and to our glorious flag, under whose folds every Union soldier's or sailor's grave is the altar of patriotism."

G. A. R. Public Exercises in a Hall.

Should inclement weather interfere with the foregoing exercises at the cemetery, the public is invited to join the comrades in celebrating the day in some hall.

The audience having been seated, the Post enter in uniform, with their heads covered, and stand in the portion of the hall assigned to them. On the platform sit invited guests, the orator of the day, and the Chaplain.

The Commander, standing before the comrades, or on the platform, calls the Post to order, to hear the Adjutant read such portions of instructions from departmental headquarters as may have been previously selected by the Commander.

The Commander's Speech on Decoration.

When the Adjutant has finished reading, the Commander says:

"Obedience is a soldier's duty. It is not, however, merely in obedience to the orders read that we assemble here. The most generous instincts of our hearts prompt us to do what the orders from headquarters command. This day commemorates a valor on sea and on land that is illustrious. This day is eloquent with a patriotism which did not speak only from the lips. This day is sacred with the almost visible presence of those who, out of prison-pens and hospitals, from camps and battlefields, have joined the innumerable company of those who muster to-day upon the parade-ground of heaven. Comrades, salute the dead!"

At this order the Commander, with each comrade, places his left hand upon his heart, and with his right hand raises his hat from his head. After remaining in this position, in silence, for a moment, the Commander drops his left hand by his side, replaces his hat on his head, and commands the Post to uncover and be seated.

Words of Welcome.

Removing his hat, after quiet is restored, the Commander says to the audience:

"Friends: As Commander of this Post, I welcome you, in the name of my comrades, to this public service. To us Decoration-Day is the memorial day of stalwart bravery, of patriotic heroism, of national faith. It is the freedom day of a race emancipated from bondage, and of a nation redeemed from iniquity. It is dear to every soldier. It deepens in our hearts a memory of our brave and our beloved,—the grand army of the immortals; and that memory makes precious to us the badge of the G. A. R., which we wear upon our breasts. May we join so reverently in these exercises that what we call a decoration-day may be to our dead their day of coronation."

Dedication Services.

The following are the forms of dedicating memorial shafts, statues, tablets, etc., as established by the Grand Army of the Republic.

The city or town officials and other guests of the society, by invitation, assemble at the hall, monument, or other designated place, and are seated on the platform. At the front of the platform stands a table or desk, covered with an American flag, upon which rest two crossed swords, with their points toward the audience, and upon these an open Bible. The comrades of the dedicating Post are drawn up in front of the platform, and, if in the outer air, as near the object of dedication as possible.

After music by the band, or choir, the civil authority, usually the mayor of a city, president of the village, chairman of the town board, or some other selected officer, addresses the Commander of the Post, in substance, as follows:

"Commander—I have been authorized to invite you at this time to accept from the citizens of ——, at the hands of its accredited representatives, this memorial, and to request that it may be dedicated by you to the noble purpose for which it has been set up (or erected.)"

The Commander's Speech of Thanks.

The Commander responds, addressing the civil officer by his title:

"In the name of my comrades of the Grand Army of the Republic, representing as they do all soldiers and sailors who defended the integrity and authority of the nation, I thank you and those whom you represent, for this memorial, (naming it.) Its very silence is impressive. Without articulate speech it is eloquent. It needs no words. It is itself an oration. It assures us that our dead are held in remembrance—those dead who gave their lives for the security of the citizen and the union of the States. It is significant of brave and loyal obedience to the command of the nation always and everywhere, since the obligations of citizenship are not restricted to time or place, or to the conflict of arms. It gives encouragement for the future, since the recognition and approval it gives of patriotic fidelity and heroism will be an incentive for the display of public valor and virtue in all coming time. There can be no doubt that the honor you pay to the patriot dead, and to their memorable deeds, will serve not only to make American citizenship in these days more reputable, but also to maintain and perpetuate, through all future generations, the union and authority of the United States of America."

Commander's Dedication Speech.

The Commander, giving the order, "Attention, Post!" here says:

"In the name of the Grand Army of the Republic, I now dedicate this memorial (naming it.) I dedicate it to the memory of those who in the navy (*the sailor on guard salutes*) guarded our inland seas and ocean coasts, and fell in defense of the flag. I dedicate it to the memory of those who in the army (*the soldier on guard salutes*) fought for our hillsides and valleys and plains, and fell in defense of the flag. I dedicate it to the memory of those who on land and sea fought for the Union, and fell in defense of the flag; (*the guard of honor salutes and stands at salute*) who on land and sea fought for the authority of the Constitution, and fell in defense of the flag; who on land and on sea fought for their country, and fell in the defense of the flag. Comrades, salute the dead!"

G. A. R. Burial Service

Of soldiers or sailors belonging to the society of the Grand Army of the Republic.

At the request of the family or friends of a deceased soldier or sailor who has been honorably discharged from the national service, a Post may participate in the funeral ceremonies, if so disposed.

Assembling at the recent residence of the deceased, or wherever the religious services have been appointed, the Commander details the usual number of comrades to act as pall-bearers, if no others have already been selected.

The corpse is then escorted to the grave by comrades, as set forth in army regulations, the left in front, a guard of honor surrounding the remains, and the hearse preceded by the Post, in charge of the Officer of the Day.

At the grave the Post halts, forming two lines, between which the remains pass to the front, where they are placed upon a bier.

Ceremonies at the Grave.

If the nature of the ground permits, the Post forms about the grave in the manner best suited to participation in the obsequies, and the ceremony proceeds as follows:

The Commander stands at the head of the coffin; the Chaplain at its foot; the officers and Past-Commander in the rear of the Commander; the Post behind the Chaplain, and the Post colors stationed in the front.

This arrangement having been completed, the Commander says:

"Assembled to pay our last tribute of respect to this dead soldier (or sailor) of our Republic, let us unite in prayer. The Chaplain will invoke the Divine blessing."

The Chaplain offers a brief and appropriate prayer, to which the comrades add a simultaneous "Amen!" If a choir is present, a hymn is sung; after which the Commander delivers a short address in unison with the occasion.

At its close, a comrade, laying a wreath of evergreens or flowers upon the coffin, says: "In behalf of the Post, I give this tribute, a symbol of undying love, for comrades of the war."

A second comrade, laying upon the coffin a rose or other flower, says: "Symbol of purity, we offer at this lowly grave a rose. May future generations emulate the unselfish devotion of even the lowliest of our heroes."

A third comrade, laying a laurel-leaf upon the coffin, says: "Last token of affection from comrades in arms, we crown these remains with a symbol of victory."

Chaplain's Address at the Grave.

The Chaplain's address, which immediately follows, is of the following import:

"The march of another comrade is over, and he lies down after it in the house appointed for all the living. Thus summoned, this open grave reminds us of the frailty of human life and the tenure by which we hold our own. 'In such an hour as ye think not, the Son of man cometh.'

"It seems well that we should leave our comrade to rest where over him will bend the arching sky, as it did in great love when he pitched his tent, or lay down, weary and footsore, by the way or on the battlefield for an hour's sleep."

[Should it be a sailor's funeral, the Chaplain substitutes for the foregoing paragraph the following: "As we leave our comrade to rest, no longer to hear the sound of the waves, or float upon the bosom of the deep, no longer to sail beneath peaceful skies, or to be driven before the angry storm, may he find welcome in that land where there is no more sea."]

"As he was then, so he is still—in the hands of the Heavenly Father. 'God giveth his beloved sleep.'

"As we lay him down here to rest, let us in great charity forget each foible of our deceased comrade as human, and cherish only his virtues. Reminded also, forcibly, by the vacant place so lately filled by our deceased brother that our ranks are thinning, let each one be so loyal to every virtue, so true to every friendship, so faithful in our remaining march, that we shall be ready to fall out here to take our places at the great review, not with doubt, but in faith; the merciful Captain of our salvation will call us to that fraternity which, on earth and in heaven, may remain unbroken." (A moment's pause.) "Jesus saith, 'Thy brother shall rise again. I am the Resurrection and the Life.'" (The remains are here deposited in the grave.) "Behold, the silver cord having been loosed, the golden bowl broken, we commit this body to the grave, where dust shall return to the earth as it was, and the spirit to God who gave it. Earth to earth, ashes to ashes, dust to dust, looking for the resurrection and the life to come through our Lord Jesus Christ."

After a prayer, the Post forms again in marching order and returns to its hall.

Address at the Funeral

Of an active, useful man who dies in middle-life.

FRIENDS: A broken column most fittingly represents the untimely death of a man thus in middle-life. And when to live was so desirable—when the work to be done had been but just commenced, it is doubly painful to bid adieu to the friend thus passing into the unknown. And yet, in the mysterious way by which great blessings are wrought, we are compelled to admit that possibly in this dispensation some good will come to these mourning friends that cannot now be seen.

He has laid his burdens suddenly down. We can hardly reconcile ourselves to the thought that others should take them up, and yet the future may reveal the good, the discipline that there may be in this— He goes out into the unknown, and all is blank. He leaves his labor here unfinished, and unskilled hands must carry to completion the work which he has begun. All seems wrong, and we refuse to be comforted, and yet who shall say it is not best?

Other hands and minds may assume his task and do it so well that

his labor and influence shall not be lost. And he—well, we do not know what grand fields of thought and action he may enter upon, but we feel that he is not dead. To say that death ends all is to admit creation a failure. Why be born? Why be brought into existence, merely to toil, to suffer and die, with no compensation on earth?

To millions, if this earth was all, life would not be worth the living. To create man simply to live out his brief time here without purpose and then die, would be like the construction of a machine for the simple purpose of making it. But as we do not construct for simple experiment, as we do not build to simply tear down again, so we do not believe the God of nature makes anything in vain; but, on the contrary, that in the creation of man he had a great, grand plan, the fulfillment of which we see but dimly shadowed on earth.

Change is constantly going forward, but annihilation and death never take place in nature.

> "There is no such thing as death—
> In nature nothing dies;
> From each sad remnant of decay
> Some forms of life arise.
> The little leaf that falls
> All brown and sere to earth,
> Ere long will mingle with the buds
> That give the flower its birth."

And as in nature nothing dies, so man does not. Life here is but the budding to a life beyond, the first steps, the primer school. And what we call death is but another birth—the passing through of the real self into a broader sphere beyond, to be great and good and blessed there, in proportion to the life well-lived and the good done on earth.

The house in which our brother dwelt is left behind. It was but the simple habitation fitted for his use while he remained here. Always frail, it took but a breath to shatter it, and when at length there came a shock strong enough to weaken it, and our friend could no longer remain, he passed into the unseen, and we behold left only the tenement in which he lived.

Between himself and where we stand there hangs a curtain, beyond which, wisely, we cannot in this life see. But we can hope and believe. And as in nature there is no death, so faith tells us our brother is not dead, but living—wiser, greater, grander than ever before, because he was great and good here, with opportunities multiplied for happiness and advancement, a thousand fold. For do we not, if we live rightly here, advance from a lower to a higher sphere on earth, and shall not our advancement be always?

Glorious thought! As we cannot live a twelvemonth on earth without increased knowledge, so, as the cycles of time go their unceasing rounds, man must, in obedience to the eternal law of progress, be forever growing wiser and richer in the knowledge of truth and justice and right.

We gather to-day to mourn as for the departure of a friend whom we shall not soon see again, but we have faith that we shall meet him a little way on in the future. And the eye that shone so brilliantly, and the voice that addressed us so kindly, and the hand that grasped our own so cordially, will again greet us on the other side.

Remarks on the Death of a Child.

DEAR FRIENDS: I know how impossible it is to silence your grief with words. The heart pleads for utterance in tears, and let it speak thus. We bow in sorrow at the taking of our little one, feeling that while the ripened fruit may be gathered, it is unkind that the bud should be taken before it has even opportunity to unfold into blossom. But in nature fruits fall, and so do blossoms and buds. In the ways of kind nature this is perhaps best, and in the taking from our arms this little one we accept the cross and bear it, believing that the bud will yet blossom and bear fruit in the angel-land whither the spirit of this little one has so early flown.

Perhaps it is best that this child's life on earth went out so soon. With the trials that meet struggling human kind on every side, with the sorrows that line the pathway from childhood to old age, who can contemplate the passing of an innocent soul thus into the beautiful beyond without feeling that possibly our loss is to this young soul a great gain.

We do not fully know the future life. It is well that we should not. It is best that we rest content on earth until we are called to go. A cloud is therefore wisely placed between this life and eternity, through which we may not see; but we may hope, and we do hope with a belief that becomes an absolute faith, that the sun is radiantly shining beyond this portal called death, and into a beautiful sunshine, with glad arms to welcome our little one, our child has been taken and is now amid the pleasures and the beauties that await the pure and the innocent in the hereafter.

Parents, kindred, friends—very beautifully has Longfellow pictured the sunny future of this child, so early taken from us, as he asks that we accept our loss in

Resignation.

THERE is no flock, however watched and tended,
  But one dead lamb is there!
There is no fireside, howsoe'er defended,
  But has one vacant chair!

The air is full of farewells to the dying,
  And mournings for the dead;
The heart of Rachel, for her children crying,
  Will not be comforted!

Let us be patient! These severe afflictions
  Not from the ground arise,
But oftentimes celestial benedictions
  Assume this dark disguise.

We see but dimly through the mists and vapors;
  Amid these earthly damps,
What seem to us but sad, funereal tapers
  May be heaven's distant lamps.

There is no Death! What seems so is transition;
  This life of mortal breath
Is but a suburb of the life elysian,
  Whose portal we call Death.

She is not dead,—the child of our affection,—
  But gone unto the school
Where she no longer needs our poor protection,
  And Christ himself doth rule.

In that great cloister's stillness and seclusion,
  By guardian angels led,
Safe from temptation, safe from sin's pollution,
  She lives, whom we call dead.

Day after day we think what she is doing
  In those bright realms of air;
Year after year, her tender steps pursuing,
  Behold her grown more fair.

Thus do we walk with her, and keep unbroken
  The bond which nature gives,
Thinking that our remembrance, though unspoken,
  May reach her where she lives.

Not as a child shall we again behold her;
  For, when with raptures wild
In our embraces we again enfold her,
  She will not be a child,—

But a fair maiden, in her Father's mansion,
  Clothed with celestial grace;
And beautiful with all the soul's expansion
  Shall we behold her face.

And though at times, impetuous with emotion
  And anguish long suppressed,
The swelling heart heaves, moaning like the ocean
  That cannot be at rest,—

We will be patient, and assuage the feeling
  We may not wholly stay;
By silence sanctifying, not concealing,
  The grief that must have way.

Address on the Death of a Young Lady.

FRIENDS: How feeble are words to carry consolation to hearts bereaved of a loved daughter in the household. A tender, clinging vine, interwoven in sweet memories from the hour the angel first gave her to our home; a gentle spirit of light that flitted in and out like a gleam of sunshine. No one can fill her place in the vacant chair; no one will take her place in our hearts. And we would not have the void filled, even if we could. It will be a sacred thought in all the years to come, to parents and friends, that she shed radiance in the home as long as she did. It will be a blessed recollection that she grew up to love and be loved by those who will ever cherish her memory so tenderly.

It is in such an hour as this that hope spreads her pinion, and we rest our faith on the belief that our darling is not dead. She is only gone from us for a little while. Out among the angels she is a star, and her loving ways and bright eyes are just as beautiful as they were here. We lower the corse into the tomb, but not our darling Minnie. We strew with flowers and wet with our tears only the frail casement in which she lived. Over the river she has gone only a little in advance of us. Some one must go first. Perhaps in the ways of a kind Providence it is best that it should be she who is to welcome us on the other shore.

WHEN falls the night upon the earth,
  And all in shadow lies,
The sun's not dead; his radiance still
  Beams bright on other skies.

And when the dawn-star groweth dim
  Upon the brow of morn,
It still shines on, though earthly eyes,
  That miss it, grow forlorn.

Some other world is glad to see
  Our star that's gone away;
The light whose going makes our night
  Makes somewhere else a day.

And she is just our loved one still,
  And loves us now no less;
She goes away to come again,—
  To watch us, and to bless.

Grace for a Morning Repast.

OUR HEAVENLY FATHER, we returns thanks for Thy bountiful goodness that has brought us to the beginning of this day in life and health. We thank Thee for this evidence of Thy continued favor, and, bowing in gratitude to Thee, our generous Benefactor, desire Thy blessing upon this food. Amen.

Grace for Noon Repast.

SUPREME POWER: Creator of all things, wilt Thou be pleased to bless this food to our use? May we be so guided by Thy guardian care, that all we undertake and do shall be prospered? Go with us, and watch over us for the remainder of this day, and for the good we may accomplish, and the happiness we shall enjoy, Thine shall be the glory. Amen.

Grace at an Evening Repast.

OUR FATHER, who art in heaven, and art ever mindful of our needs, at the close of this day's labor we gather around this board, which Thy bounty has so graciously supplied with nourishing refreshment, and return our grateful thanks. And we beseech Thee that what Thou hast so freely provided may be blessed to our use and Thy glory. Amen.

Various Forms of Ministerial Benedictions and Ascriptions.

The grace of our Lord Jesus Christ be with you.   Amen.

The grace of our Lord Jesus Christ, the love of God, and the fellowship of the Holy Ghost be with you all.   Amen.

Glory be to the Father, and to the Son, and to the Holy Ghost, as it was in the beginning, is now, and ever shall be, world without end.

And now unto the Father, the Son, and the Holy Ghost, one God ever blessed, be ascribed all glory and honor, praise, power, majesty and dominion forever.   Amen.

The peace of God, which passeth all understanding, keep your hearts and minds in the knowledge and love of God and of His Son Jesus Christ; and the blessing of God Almighty, the Father, the Son, and the Holy Ghost, be with you, and remain with you, always.   Amen.

Now the God of peace, who brought again from the dead the great Shepherd of the sheep with the blood of the eternal covenant, even our Lord Jesus Christ, make you perfect in every good thing to do His will, working in us that which is well-pleasing in His sight, through Jesus Christ, to whom be glory for ever and ever.   Amen.

Speech Soliciting Funds for Church Edifice.

WORDS OF THE PASTOR.

BELOVED: Before pronouncing the benediction I wish to call your kind attention to the Rev. Charles Peabody, of Brooklyn, who has a few remarks to offer. Mr. Peabody, as most of you know, is the authorized agent of the Church Extension Committee of our Eastern Synod, and whatever he has to present to your consideration you will doubtless receive with interest.

WORDS OF MR. PEABODY.

I do not propose to detain you long, lest the good effect of the excellent sermon to which we have just listened should be marred, but will merely present the object of my visit in a few brief sentences and lay the claim of the Synod before you. At the beginning of the year 1883, we had a church extension fund of about $45,000, and pledges, to be paid during the year, of some $25,000 more, leaving us a working fund of about $60,000. On the first of January, 1883, we owed upon unfinished church edifices nearly $20,000, which we had to pay, and did pay, within the first six months of 1883. Between the first of January, 1883, and Christmas of that year, we contracted for the erection of thirty new churches, in various parts of the Synod, at an average cost of $3,000 each—an aggregate of $90,000, most of which will become due June 1, 1884. At the beginning of July, 1883, we had on hand about $40,000 of the old fund, and had received, in fresh subscriptions, bequests, etc., $15,000 more—so that our available working fund was some $55,000. On the first of January, 1884, we had paid out of this amount $15,000, which was required for sundry expenditures, in addition to the sum already contracted for the thirty new churches. In the meantime, by business failures and slow contributions, our working fund had become reduced (including the $15,000 for extra expenditures) to about $35,000, leaving a surplus to be raised before the first of June of $55,000. The time is near at hand, and although money has been contributed, we are still behind about $40,000, which, for the honor of our religion and our own character as a benevolent people, we are very anxious to raise. If by the first of June we can wipe out these contract debts, we shall only be about even, for any surplus funds received since the first of January last will have been absorbed in the incidental expenses of the work. I am, therefore, here to-day to ask you to contribute as liberally to our church extension fund as your benevolence may dictate. Remember that this debt of $40,000 represents the freedom of thirty new churches and as many increasing congregations in new and thinly settled districts of the Great West—people who, in their Eastern homes, enjoyed the same blessed gospel privileges as you do now, but who, after emigrating West, find themselves in straitened circumstances, dependent upon their farm-labor for their support, yet anxious to worship in their own old way, and once more enjoy the benefits of stated preaching, with Sunday-school and other religious privileges.

We have been careful, this year, to refrain from making any important contracts for more new churches, preferring to release the Synod from debt and begin again anew when our funds shall commence flowing in for future operations. With the wealth and prosperity enjoyed by churches like this, we hope to clear our books. I have stated our necessities plainly, and earnestly call upon you to contribute your quota this morning to the extinction of our mutual obligations. Remember, " it is more blessed to give than to receive;" " freely ye have received, freely give;" " God loveth a cheerful giver."

Let me not appeal to you in vain for aid. The cause is worthy, and with the help of your faith and good works, under the Divine blessing, will prosper and redound to the glory of the Master.

Speech Soliciting Funds for a Park.

LADIES AND GENTLEMEN: You have responded so generally to the call for this meeting, that I am encouraged to hope its object is popularly appreciated and will be generously sustained by your influence and money.

The circumstances which led to this movement in favor of establishing a village park, in the enjoyment of which all may participate, are these. The village, now five years old, was laid out with an eye only to the conveniences of daily life, having facilities for such domestic business in groceries, stores and shops of various kinds, as the present wants of the citizens demanded. At that time no thought of future improvement was practically cherished, and as a consequence the omission of a park from the village plat was not especially considered important. Now, however, we begin to feel the necessity of having a place suitable for village gatherings, holiday celebrations and general enjoyment, under the blue skies and in the open air, apart from the business centre of the village. At an opportune moment Mr. Blank offers to sell us fifteen acres of excellent land on the borders of the village, convenient of access, and every way suitable for the purposes of a park. His price is forty dollars an acre, or $600 for the lot, with its beautiful shade-trees and a living spring of water. To improve this park, and make it an agreeable resort for young and old, will require $1,000. As the years go by, more and better improvements will be needed, but for the present this sum will be sufficient to put it in excellent order, clearing up the underbrush, destroying unsightly weeds and stumps, plowing, grass-seeding and flower-planting. For myself, I would recommend that it never be fenced; but others will say, how shall we keep the cattle out of it? Gentlemen, common law does not require a man to fence his land to keep off intruders; it simply makes the intruder responsible for all damages done to property on another's land. If any one has a cow, or a horse, or sheep, he must provide proper pasture for his animal within an inclosure, or be held responsible for the ravages it commits. It is cheaper to hire cows pastured than to suffer them to run at large, if bills of damages are taken into the account. Let the village authorities regulate this matter, promptly and stringently, and every man of the village may remove his front and his line fences, and feel perfectly safe from the incursions of intruding bovines.

We have figured up the cost of the proposed park at $1,600, which, divided among our 1,000 inhabitants, is only $1.60 per head, and I am grandly mistaken if we have not among us ten substantial men who will subscribe for immediate use at least $50.00 each, so that the cost to each of the others will only be $1.10.

A subscription paper has been prepared, and every property-holder within the corporation is expected to subscribe not less than $1.00, and from that up to $5.00 or $10.00, according to his means.

As soon as $1,000 has been subscribed, the meeting will select a committee from gentlemen and ladies present to purchase the park and arrange for its immediate improvement and ornamentation. Subscriptions are now in order.

Speech Soliciting Funds for a Public Fountain.

LADIES AND GENTLEMEN: The winter is past, the time of the singing of birds has come, and hot weather will soon be upon us. Everything betokens a heated term of considerable duration, and it is well, for the sake of our own comfort as citizens of this growing town, and that of our dumb animals, that we should provide a public fountain at the junction of two of our principal thoroughfares, where young and old, man and beast, may come and slake their thirst, freely and fully, until winter resumes its icy sway.

How has it been in the past with us in this respect? True, for years we had Collins' old well, at the corner of Main and Clay streets, but midsummer always made water scarce in it; the curb was high; the windlass was ungainly and even dangerous; the worn-out bucket leaked like a sieve, and the old thing creaked and dragged until it became a terror to all who undertook to draw water from it.

Then Phillips, at his own expense, tore away the old curb and windlass, and put in a log-pump, with a handle that tired out everybody who used it before the pail was full. Finally some one choked up the pump with potatoes, and nobody could use it any longer.

Carter was then hired by the council to take out the old pump and put in a chain-pump, with an iron casing, which worked much better and easier, but one day the bottom fell out of the well, and no more water could be had.

At this stage of affairs some one proposed to dig a new well and refit the iron pump; but the council, in a fit of economy, voted down the measure, because it would cost too much.

Last summer the farmers from the surrounding country, with their families, and horses, and dogs, together with our own citizens and teamsters, were put to great inconvenience, and some distress, for want of a public drinking resort, where pure, cold water—nature's own beverage!—could be obtained. In consequence, private wells and houses were visited, and much unnecessary trouble ensued.

In view of these difficulties, a few of our public-spirited citizens, whose generosity has more than once been successfully appealed to in behalf of suffering humanity, met together and discussed the feasibility of procuring a public fountain for the village, and the cost of so useful an ornament to our Main street. Correspondence with proper parties at the metropolis adduced the fact that a good substantial street fountain, properly placed, with all the machinery necessary to supply it freely with water for six months, would cost $800. This information led a number of us to call this meeting for the purpose of debating the subject of the contemplated fountain, to decide by our votes whether we shall have it, or not, and to ask each and every one present to subscribe to a fund for its purchase.

I have gone over the ground of our past failures of wells and pumps, and have endeavored to explain the necessity that exists for speedy action. Several of our prominent business men have pledged themselves to pay one-half of the expense out of their own pockets, in order to encourage this laudable enterprise, and we have prepared subscription papers for the balance of the fund, which we cordially ask you to sign this evening. We are sure that the sum is so small—$400.00—that a limited subscription from each will ensure the entire sum and give us a lasting and beautiful monument to your liberality. I see many here who, we are satisfied, will keenly appreciate this public improvement as a benefit to themselves and their households, and these undoubtedly will feel greatly disposed to help others to participate in its purchase. The papers will now be circulated.

A Visitor Speaks to the Pupils of a Public School.

MY DEAR YOUNG FRIENDS: I have been listening with much pleasure to your recitations to-day, and with no less delight to the encouraging words of your teachers whenever you faltered in your answers. For I remember when I was a boy, like some of you little ones, I was always very sorry to have the teacher speak harshly to me, if I could not, at first thought, answer correctly to his question. But when he spoke kindly to me, he always encouraged me, and I could more quickly remember what I should say.

Boys and girls, you are very much like men and women in your likes and dislikes, and you feel, quite as keenly as I should, any harsh or unjust word or action on the part of your instructor. In old times, years before you were born, we had no such noble schools as you have. We had but few books, and I think, now, they could not have been as attractive and interesting to study as those I see lying upon your desks. We used to deem them very dull; and then, too, our teachers were not so wise and skillful in imparting instruction as yours are in the public schools to-day. They were usually young men attending college, and teaching to earn money to pay for their education; sometimes they were cross to us, and at others they were very unjust in punishing us for not learning faster than we did. Our school-houses were also very inconvenient places, and often really uncomfortable for teachers and pupils.

But now all this has been changed by the improvements of the age, and the school-houses and books and teachers are all of a better class, so that learning may be made pleasant and much more easily gained. If a boy could read, write and cipher through the "rule of three," it was quite as much as he had reason to expect from the district school. Perhaps he could not spell half the words in the spelling-book aright, nor write a ten-line letter without making fifty mistakes, nor cipher a sum in compound addition correctly. But now you may easily master all these things and many more and better ones, and if you pay proper attention to the lessons you receive, you can go into the high-school, and there gain a sensible, practical education that will either fit you for the business of life, or prepare you to take a higher course in college.

I spoke about cross and harsh teachers. I do not know of any in this school, and I do not think there are any here. But if they never speak harshly to you, they may yet feel very sad that some one of you is not doing what you ought to do,—that is when you play on the sly in school-hours, when you whisper, and when you neglect your studies. Now, if you are obedient and studious children, you will make the teacher happy and have the satisfaction of knowing you are doing right.

You young people should recollect, and I trust that you do, that in a few years you will be on the stage of action, doing the work of men and women. Will you be successful? That will depend upon what you know. And what you know then will largely depend upon what you learn in this school. The years are going by very quickly, and you will be obliged to put your knowledge to the test very soon.

I say this because some young people do not know the value of school. They look upon the school-yard and the school-room as one vast play-ground—not you—but *some* boys and girls I have known—and they never wake up to a sense of what they need, and what they have lost, until it is too late.

Have a mark, young people; aim for it, and you will rise vastly higher than you will if you have no purpose in life. Your teachers are here to assist you. They are not here to punish. They do not want to spend their time in governing you. They desire to aid in the securing of that education which shall fit you to do your work nobly in life.

It is pleasant to witness the opportunities you possess. It is very satisfactory to see the drill, the system, and methods pursued in your studies and recitations; and I doubt not it will be equally satisfactory to witness your success in after-years, the result of your attending this school.

Response to Speech of Welcome,

By James G. Blaine when visiting Chicago Board of Trade.

GENTLEMEN: I consider it a compliment that this welcome should be extended to me by a commercial body whose business is conducted amid a torrent of confusion which it would seem as hopeless to attempt to check as it is to stem the flow of the Atlantic tide. Remembering that well, I thank you very sincerely for the cordiality of your reception. I had the honor, nine years ago this very month—or possibly the month of October — to have a similar reception in this room. It had just then been completed, as I remember, and it was considered and believed, at that time, to be far beyond any anticipated needs of the commerce of Chicago. To-day it is so far behind that you are building a new and grander and larger structure, and well you may. Within the past week I have visited five cities to the west of you, and I find them all directly tributary to Chicago as the Queen City of coming years. They look to this as the Mecca of their commercial pilgrimage, and every frontiersman tells the story of its greatness, and every arrangement that adds to his herds is increasing and prospering the growth and business and building up the commerce of your city.

Ten years ago you were waiting for telegrams from London as to prices of produce before you could trade. To-day London is waiting for telegrams from New York and Chicago. We have ceased to wait for Europe to fix a market. You have such absolute control of it that you make Europe wait till you fix the prices. But, gentlemen, it is a dangerous thing to get on the strain of what Chicago is to become. This much is certain: That it is to be the second city of this continent—that it is to outstrip every other commercial centre except New York. I hope no Chicago man of this generation will take offense at this exception. But that it is to be second only to New York is to see clearly the prophecy of present facts, and that should be open to no objection.

I see a majority of you are young men. You will grow older by-and-by. I see very few gray hairs among you, but occasionally a bald head. You know a preacher once said that a man in his church who was bald got it through the truth glancing off the top of his head. I venture you have had some such experience to increase the want of hair on the Chicago Board of Trade.

I thank you sincerely; I thank you more than I can express for the cordiality of your reception.

Speech at a Base-Ball Dinner.

FELLOW-PLAYERS: As I look around this table I see honest, manly faces, strong limbs, and genial companions, which do my heart good, especially as I fail to see a single " muff " among you.

Everything, it is said, has its uses; and we who know the arduous, active life of a professional base-ball player are willing to accord to him the righteous award of skill, energy and endurance. He may not move senates by his eloquence, nor determine intricate points of international law, but he understands the physical requirements of a first-class base-ball player and how to gain them by careful training and temperate habits. He sets a good example for professional men by striving to excel in his calling, lest he should be defeated in the very first contest and render future games extremely doubtful in point of victory. As a pitcher, he graduates his muscular power to the proper momentum, so as not to under or over-pitch, economizes his strength, and becomes as vigilant as a detective on a doubtful

scent. If he is a batter, he must exercise the same sort of endurance, energy and vigilance, always being sure to knock the ball so far that he can run all the bases and reach home before the fielders can recover it. With all this training, this professional and physical development, come robust health and the acquirement of faculties that he can exercise to the best advantage in other kinds of business. Nor would I withhold all due honor to fielders, whose usefulness in our favorite game should not be underrated. Like the rank and file of a fighting army, they may not make much individual display, but in the result their activity and vigilance greatly adds to the renown of the pitcher and batter. Gentlemen, as one of yourselves, proud of our organization, and desiring nothing so much as our success, trusting in you all as abundantly able to crown yourselves with glory, I unite with you in the earnest effort to succeed.

Reception of a Visiting Fire Company.

MR. FOREMAN, AND FIREMEN ALL: During the weeks that we have been anticipating your coming, we have also been studying plans by which we might make your visit a pleasant one; for we designed, as we now do, to offer you our heartiest welcome. We welcome you to our municipality, our homes, our engine-houses, and as many agreeable sights and sounds as the city affords.

We are glad to welcome you as brothers in the cause of protection against the ravages of fire. Such a brotherhood as ours ought to be united, for it is a dangerous service, often requiring the utmost skill to prevent serious catastrophes, with unity of purpose and prompt obedience to the commands of our officers.

It is understood that you have brought with you your machine, and we judge from your appearance that you have also brought sterling material to man it. A little healthful emulation as to the merits of our respective engines and companies, on whichever banner victory may perch, we trust will result in cementing us still closer as members of our worthy profession.

We have heard something of your superiority in your own city, and we shall be proud to furnish you every facility for displaying your gallantry here. Indeed, our citizens purpose to give you a public reception to-morrow afternoon, in connection with a friendly contest between our local companies and yourselves.

In the meantime we have assigned you comfortable apartments and a free table at the Park House, where we shall be pleased to have you make yourselves entirely at home as friends and guests whom we greatly esteem.

Reply by the Foreman of the Visiting Company.

MR. FOREMAN AND GENTLEMEN: We anticipated a generous reception at your hands, for the fame of your hospitality has become general among the firemen of our city.

Although this is our first professional visit, we have heard that your fire department keeps abreast with the improvements and the demands of the age, and that in you we should find " foemen worthy of our steel." A glance at your numbers and make-up convinces us that the report was true, and the test of skill which you propose for to-morrow afternoon meets with our warm approval.

We fully appreciate the genuine heartiness of your welcome, and the excellent quarters which you have provided for us during our visit. We hope, before the snow falls, to be able to reciprocate these favors with interest.

We believe that under your guidance we shall greatly enjoy this visit. Enterprise and activity are visible on every hand, and as these are qualities entirely in harmony with the fireman's profession, we anticipate, in your society, a " high old time."

Again thanking you for your kindness, we await your further pleasure.

THE BAPTISMAL SERVICE.

According to the General Church Forms.

GENERALLY the baptism of children forms a part of the morning services of the church, after the opening prayer, the first hymn, and the responsive reading of selections from the Psalms. The minister coming from the pulpit into the chancel, the parents, guardians, godfathers and godmothers (if there are any) range themselves before him, with the child, or children, uncovered, in front of the baptismal font. Then the minister addresses the congregation:

Address to the Congregation.

DEARLY BELOVED: You have heard in the Gospel the words of our Saviour, commanding children to be brought to him; how he blamed all those who would have kept them from him; how he exhorts all men to follow innocency as little children. You perceive how by his outward conduct and gentle words, he declared his good-will toward them; for he took them into his arms, laid his hands upon them and blessed them. You are not to doubt, therefore, but earnestly believe, that he will likewise favorably receive these infants now presented here for baptism; that he will embrace them with the arms of his love and mercy; that he will make them partakers of his everlasting kingdom.

Being thus persuaded, let us devoutly return thanks:

Almighty God, our Heavenly Father, we thank Thee that Thou hast brought us to a certain knowledge of the truth, and that Thou wilt make these children inheritors of eternal life. We pray Thee to increase in us knowledge. Bestow upon these infants Thy heavenly blessing, and enable them by Thy grace to overcome evil and to accept Thee for their best friend, Saviour, counselor and guide, following Thee in all wisdom, humility and obedience. Bless these parents and guardians, and help them by Thy grace and Spirit to bring up these children in the nurture and admonition of the Lord, so that both parents and children may be united to Thee on earth and together enjoy the pleasures of the world to come. Amen.

Naming each one separately and distinctly, as he comes to it, the minister, who usually baptizes by sprinkling water upon the child's head, says:

(Naming it), I baptize thee in the name of the Father, and of the Son, and of the Holy Ghost. Amen.

When all have been baptized, the minister addresses the parents and guardians as follows:

The Baptism of Children.

ON certain days throughout the year, it is customary, in most churches, to baptize those children that may be presented by their parents. At that time, in commemoration of the occasion, it is usual to decorate the church beautifully with flowers. The view here displayed shows the position taken before the altar by the fathers and mothers, as they present their little ones for the reception of this very beautiful ordinance. As will be seen, when standing before the clergyman, the husband or godfather stands at the right of the lady.

BELOVED: The children of our love should come to us as blessings, gathering like "olive-plants about our table," living "wellsprings of pleasure" in our homes. Yet while we enjoy their presence, their winning ways, their loving smiles and innocent amusements, we should never forget our responsibility in bringing them into this world, nor the duty which their coming imposes upon us. From the moment that they enter into our households, until they go hence in the strength of manhood and womanhood, upon us rests the burden of preparing them for good and useful lives.

Not only have we to provide, day by day, for their bodily needs, their comfort and their education, but a heavier responsibility rests upon us of instilling into their innocent minds the principles of virtue and truth. The wisest man that ever lived has left it on record for our instruction that if we "train up a child in the way he should go, when he is old he will not depart from it." Thus much for our encouragement to teach the right thing in the right way; to guide the young to do the right and avoid the wrong; to lead them in the paths of moral integrity, to respect the rights of others, and to become sober, industrious, honest, polite and trustworthy men and women.

In accordance with our religion, we may—nay, we should—devote ourselves to this service, believing that the Divine blessing attends the proper instruction of an infant soul. Therefore, by this act of baptism, we to-day consecrate them to the cause of truth and purity, believing that with the blessing of heaven upon our endeavors they may become happy and prosperous, and be helpful to others who are not so.

In the water which we place upon their foreheads we behold the representative of that purity and innocency which we would preserve in their existence.

And to you who have brought these children into being, and have presented them at this altar, we look for the solemn promise that as your circumstances permit, will you follow the injunction to lead them carefully in wisdom's ways, always having their best interests, spiritual and moral, as well as physical and mental, at heart, encouraging them in seeking after truth and embracing it; by your example, also, teaching them to live aright?

Answer—We will.

We, therefore, welcome these little ones into the visible and corporate church of Christ on earth. Then follows a brief prayer.

Parents and children then retire, and the regular service proceeds.

THE BANQUET HALL.

Order and Arrangement of the Banquet.

BANQUETS are given in honor either of some noted occasion, or some distinguished foreigner or prominent citizen, generally by an organization or association of men. A committee of arrangements is appointed, which has the entire control and management of the affair, and which is subdivided into committees on invitation, finance, supper, etc., etc. Invitations, handsomely gotten up, are issued several days before the banquet is to come off, and read generally in this wise:

"The Chamber of Commerce of the city of —— request the pleasure of your presence at a banquet to be given at the —— House, on Thursday evening, the 21st of December next, at 8 o'clock, in honor of the Centennial of American Independence. You are invited to respond to the toast, 'Our Pilgrim Fathers.'"

On the evening named the guest is expected to present his card of invitation (which he generally retains as a memento or souvenir), at the time and place named, when he is shown into a parlor or reception room, where he is received by the committee and introduced to such of the guests as he may be unacquainted with. Some little time having been spent in conversation, the guests are gradually marshalled, and at the signal from the headwaiter that the banquet is served, the guests are escorted by the committee to the hall, and, while the more prominent are conducted to the center-table, the others are ushered to seats at the tables on either hand, the reporters being favorably placed at a table of their own, or interpersed among the other guests. All are expected to stand opposite their respective places until a signal be given by the presiding officer, who, if a clergyman be present, generally requests him to ask a blessing.

Being seated, each guest finds before him a plate, with a napkin, on which rests a button-hole bouquet, a finger-bowl with its doiley, a goblet for water, and a variety of glasses for wines of different kinds, should wine be admitted, together with an elaborately gotten up menu, or bill of fare. The bouquet he is expected to attach to his coat, and he is privileged to retain the menu as a souvenir of the occasion, if he desires so to do.

The guests being seated, the waiter immediately serves them through the various courses, from oysters to nuts and apples and cream or roman punch. Etiquette forbids that the guest shall eat heartily of any of the viands, or drink deeply of the wines which in some instances are served with each course. On no account should he ask that his plate or his glass be replenished, as this would mark him as vulgar. An exception to this rule may be made in the case of champagne, as this wine is not considered intoxicating, and it is generally served with the dessert. It is the wine in which the toasts are drank.

After the various courses are served, which usually requires from an hour to an hour and a half, the presiding officer raps to order, and in a short and pithy speech announces the object of the meeting, the purpose of the banquet, and, if it is in honor of an individual, proposes the health of such individual, whereupon the guests all rise, except the party toasted, drink the toast standing, and generally give cheers to the distinguished guest. Should the banquet be given in honor of an occasion, the chairman proposes as a toast, "The day we celebrate," which likewise is

The Banquet.

ON the occasion of a banquet, the hall is usually trimmed with decorations suitable for the event, and various methods are pursued in arranging the tables, the one here shown being a common one. Two long tables extend lengthwise of the room. At the end of these is a table across the end of the hall and situated upon a platform. The guests at this table occupy one side, the president being in the center, with the most honored guest at the right, and other guests and speakers upon each side. Thus the speaking is distinctly heard.

frequently drank standing. A series of toasts are then read, and responded to by parties who have been invited to do so, and who are expected to prepare and deliver a short, witty and mirth-provoking speech. Music follows each toast—if it has been provided —or a quartette of male voices is introduced; a good singer among the guests is frequently called upon to entertain his fellow-guests, and it is esteemed unkind for him to decline. After the regular toasts have been responded to, the chairman may call upon any individual in the company for remarks, until the hour for adjournment has arrived, when the musicians are called upon for "Auld Lang Syne," or "Home, Sweet Home," and the party is dispersed.

Brief, appropriate banquet speeches follow on succeeding pages.

Speech of a Sentimentalist,

In response to the toast of " The Ladies."

GENTLEMEN: With all my heart I respond to this toast! I assure you it inspires me like one of Miss Braddon's delightful love-stories. The ladies! Yes, I admire them greatly in the aggregate; I honor them in the abstract, and some of them I absolutely love!

> " Why should I fear to own to all
> That beauty does my heart enthrall?"

Gentlemen, in proposing this toast you honor your manhood and every daughter of Eve; in responding to it I can only echo the sentiment of Sir Walter Scott:

> " O woman, in our hours of ease,
> Uncertain, coy, and hard to please,
> And variable as the shade
> By the light quivering aspen made;
> When pain and anguish wring the brow,
> A ministering angel thou!"

And speaking of angels, what a delightful combination some fine genius has made in writing of "mother, home and heaven!"

Yes, my mother! Sacredly to her honored gray hairs I answer to this toast.

To my sister, my earliest playmate, beloved guide and helper in my infantile pilgrimage, I sacredly respond to this toast.

My sweetheart! What words can paint her beauty and her goodness? I wish her happiness, sleeping or waking !

My friend! Truest of the true, faithful among the many that are untrue; always bright, tractable, hopeful and wise—I respond for her!

My cousin! poor child, she was older than I, but we loved each other in our childhood, and when she married unfortunately, and died of a broken heart, last year, she left me only the memory of her beautiful character to cherish forever.

My wife—that is to be!

> " She's all my fancy painted her;
> She's lovely—she's divine!"

But the rest of that verse does not apply in my case, for she has surely promised to be mine! I hope for her good health and happiness!

Did I hear somebody whispering near me, " How about mother-in-law?" Gentlemen, excuse me if I stand up squarely before you, and defend that much-maligned relative. Fortunately I know whom she will be, and I tell you that should my wife and I, in the far future, marry our daughter (that is to be) to some heartless, dissipated fellow, I hope that he may find his mother-in-law a terror to his soul, and I'll back her up in it, you may believe. I tell you sons-in-law determine the mother-in-law question every time! Show me a man who respects himself and his wife as he ought, and proves himself an honorable gentleman on all occasions, and his mother-in-law will love him better, if possible, than his wife ever did. *That's my mother-in-law.* Gentlemen, I take pleasure in responding to the toast—The Ladies—all the ladies of our land!

Speech at a Dry-Goods-Merchants' Reunion.

FELLOW TRADESMEN: When the formation of this society was conceived it had no higher purpose than to unite us for mutual protection and companionship, and on that basis it has proved itself a useful and social union. From a small membership it has risen to the dignity of a thoroughly organized, popular and powerful association, perfectly able to carry out its proposed beneficent measures, and enjoying a fund of prosperity commensurate with its usefulness. We have now been in existence for five years, and within that period no less than twenty-five similar organizations have been formed in this county alone; so that the dry-goods trade of this section has been greatly benefited and improved by our co-operation. To-night we celebrate the fifth anniversary of our society, and I am happy to an-

nounce that its records have never yet been sullied by the business failure of any of its members, nor saddened by the hand of death. We meet, therefore, under peculiarly gratifying circumstances, for the exchange of our congratulations upon the success of the movement, with high hopes for the future, and to commemorate the fame of those distinguished manufacturers and merchants of America who have made dry-goods the great element of mercantile prosperity that it has now become. Gentlemen, I therefore heartily propose as a toast—" All honor to the Dry-goods Merchants of America—Living or Dead !"

A Landsman's Response to the Toast of " The Navy."

MR. CHAIRMAN, AND GENTLEMEN: It was rather remarkable that the committee should have designated me, above all others, to respond to this important toast. For my marine experiences have been limited in number and extent, and while they have sometimes proved exceedingly unpleasant to myself, I must acknowledge that they have been a source of considerable amusement to my fellow-voyagers. For my navigation has been strictly confined to steam-vessels, in which I rated as a first-class cabin-passenger, with my fare paid and state-room secured in advance; and in all my voyages I have never encountered worse marine disasters than wretched attacks of sea-sickness.

Fortunately, however, my knowledge of naval affairs has not been restricted to my own experiences. As the years have rolled by, I have frequently been thrown into the society of many distinguished gentlemen who belonged to the United States Navy, and am ready to bear testimony to all the good qualities claimed for this sterling branch of our government defenses.

Around the names of Decatur, McDonough, Biddle, Bainbridge, Lawrence, Perry, Chauncey, Elliott, Farragut, Dahlgren, and a host of other true " hearts of oak," circle brilliant halos of fame for their gallant services by sea and land, and all patriotic Americans point to them with proud appreciation. Gentlemen, these men are dead, but their victories illumine our history as a nation with a lustre that charms the mind of youth as it reads the story of their triumphs.

We may praise our army for its deeds of valor on the tented field, and well does it deserve the highest encomiums for its gallantry; but I have noticed that in numerous sieges on the sea-coast without the aid of the Navy the success of the Army would have been exceedingly doubtful. And in the list of noble vessels whose names we love to cherish, stand the veteran " Constitution" (our " Old Ironsides"), the " United States," the " Chesapeake," the " Wasp," the " Hornet" and the " Monitor."

Gentlemen, I must not dwell too long in recalling the past. We hear the press occasionally sneering at the apparent insignificance of our Navy in " these piping times of peace." Let them sneer; for there never was a time, as yet, in our history when the United States *needed* a Navy that she did not have it, with a force of fighting men to make it glorious. In the future, as in the past, I look for the renewal of this phenomenon at the proper time, and I believe there will never come a period in our national existence when our Navy will yield its prestige to a foreign or domestic foe, or fail to add new laurels to its victorious record.

Response to the Toast of " The Army."

MR. PRESIDENT AND GENTLEMEN: It devolves upon me as a duty to reply to the sentiment just offered. To a soldier, duty should ever be a pleasure; and as one of the great Army thus brought to the front, I willingly and proudly respond to the good wishes embodied in this toast.

I could have wished, gentlemen, that some one else had been chosen to perform what I am called upon to do, for it would probably have been done far better. I see before me many who could more eloquently speak of the value and exploits of our military organization, because they have been longer in it and have seen more service.

I am happy, on this occasion, to meet so many old comrades—stalwart young fellows whom I knew before they aspired to shoulder-straps; with whom, side by side, I carried a musket into many bloody fights, which *their* valor turned to victories. I am glad to see them here to-night, safe and sound, and by their high-rank uniforms attesting that republics are not always ungrateful.

Gentlemen, the record of the United States Army is brilliant with deeds of bravery and distinguished conquests. Tracing it from the first fight of the Revolution, in 1775, to this day, when peace is in all our borders, Americans have reason to glory in its achievements, and we know that it stands well in the estimation of the world.

What the Army has been in the past, and it owes much to the courage and energy of our citizen-soldiery, we may safely rely upon it in the future, when the alarum of invasion or intestinal conflict shall be sounded. As in the past, the nation will rise as one man, and the cry of " to-arms !" will again meet with a hearty response.

There is another reason why all honor should be accorded to this important bulwark of our nation, and it is this: While in most foreign countries military service has to be enforced by conscription, or draft, or by royal edict, here the latent patriotism of the people, and the liberal provisions of the government, lead them to volunteer freely for the maintenance of the Army.

The Army also owes much to the moral and substantial support of the people at large. Who so honored as General Washington, General Grant, General Sherman and General Sheridan? Who so esteemed as the men who have fallen in defense of our flag, whose graves we decorate with spring-time flowers from year to year? My comrades, we have reason to rejoice that the American soldier, living or dead, may count his admirers by the thousands.

At a Party--Prefacing the Toast, " Our Host and Hostess."

GENTLEMEN: I think you will all agree with me when I refer to this occasion as one of those bright oases in ordinary life which release us from business cares and afford us opportunity to unbend and mingle in cheerful recreation with our esteemed friends. I am sure that we all need a stimulus of this sort after a season of drudgery at the desk or counter, in order to clear away the dust and cobwebs from our brains, to revive our social natures, and to develop the finer sentiments and feelings of humanity. When I look around this generous board and see so many friendly faces, my heart warms, and there comes bubbling up the desire that these happy reunions might be more frequent in our existence. But while I rejoice with you that the hour has been a triumph of social enjoyment, we should not be forgetful of those to whose thoughtful care and hospitality we are indebted for it. Certainly we can, each one of us, appreciate the bounty and good taste that have provided this delightful banquet, and I, therefore, have no hesitation in asking you to pledge to them our warmest regards while I propose the healths of our excellent host and hostess.

The Host's Reply.

GENTLEMEN—FRIENDS: It would ill become me to sit still with that hearty sentiment ringing in our ears and nestling in our hearts, and, in my own name and that of my wife, I rise to thank you, sincerely and earnestly, for your very kind expressions of esteem and friendship for us. True gratitude does not require to be clothed in many words. Language is frequently inadequate, in such cases, to convey more than a mere and remote idea of the feelings that are prompted by such very gratifying and generous sentiments as you have so unanimously uttered. In all sincerity and earnestness, as your friends, we hope for your individual prosperity in all the relations of life and business, trusting that in the early future we may have the pleasure of again meeting you, under as agreeable circumstances, to renew our mutual and harmonious enjoyment.

A Toast---" The Ladies."

Response by a tender-hearted bachelor.

GENTLEMEN: I think you must have known me and my sentiments pretty well when you assigned to me the duty of responding to the toast of " the ladies;" for I confess it is a subject to which I have given much thought, and of which I have expressed much admiration. Really, it touches a tender chord in my bosom, and I suppose I am peculiarly sensitive about it because my mother was a lady. Oh, these mothers! how much we owe to them! Our being, our earliest nourishment, our consolation, our training in the ways of life. They are our guardian-spirits, our lovers, our helpers, our teachers, our best friends. I pity the man who has never felt a mother's love, or her—slipper, when he has wandered into forbidden paths and been caught at it! I tell you these are things to remember. In imagination I can feel them *tingling* still; but far better comes the remembrance to my heart, that while she caused *my* tears to flow, she had all she could do to keep her own from mingling with mine.

And my sister! I heartily respond for her, because, being older than I, she guided my infant footsteps over many rough places, carried me when I was tired—and boxed my ears when I was naughty.

My sweetheart! I cannot tell you how many there were of her! I never knew—but no school-room could seat all of her. I don't know which of her I loved the best. I know some of her loved me well, but my stolen cherries, nuts and candy better! She was of all ages, all styles of beauty—white and brown—pale and quiet—rosy and a romp; but I loved her dearly, and for her I respond to-night.

My cousin! Yes, I respond in memory of her, hateful and aggravating though she was; stealing my gum, begging half my apple, cuffing me when I kissed her, wheedling me into writing her compositions for her after school—and making me like her whether I wanted to or not!

My friend! I remember her in all sweetness! She never sauced me; she never tormented me by word or deed; she never " went back " on me; I could trust her with all I had; she always kept my secrets; always gave me good advice; always sewed on my buttons, and never grumbled; taught me how to be good, and how to be polite, and how to be manly; I tell you she was a friend, indeed, to be proud of. But she is dead!

My wife!—Don't laugh. It is true that I have none now; but in the future, when I join hands with her at the altar, and proudly call her mine—though I do not now even know her name or the number of her shoe—I shall marry her because I love her. I wish for her good health wherever she is to-night!

And now, gentlemen, when the roosters are waking up and dawn is appearing, it is time to close our festivities and retire to our couches. May pleasant dreams await us there!

Response to the Toast of " The Press."

GENTLEMEN: To speak ably to a toast relating to a subject so important and of so much magnitude might well stagger the confidence of any individual, unless he be an editor; and the smaller the circulation of his paper, so much greater, ordinarily, would we expect to find his confidence on an occasion like this.

That I have been announced as the speaker to respond to this toast seems to me a pleasant parody, when I consider the genuine eloquence and intelligent comprehension of the topic that some older and more experienced journalist would have brought to bear upon it. But the fiat has gone forth, and I rise, in accordance with your behest, to utter a few words about my chosen profession.

Gentlemen, what the power of the press has been in the past, in shaping public opinion, correcting public morals, rebuking social and political abuses, and instructing the people, is too well-known to be repeated here in detail. Whatever progress the arts and sciences, domestic culture, legislation, education, and commerce, have achieved, is largely due to the influence of the press. Our national integrity, advancement and prosperity owe much to types and printers' ink. In truth " the press, the lever that moves the world," has done good service and with Archimedean energy *has* moved the world as no other earthly power could move it. Show me an enterprise of man that the newspaper has not developed and strengthened, and I will show you an enterprise that the dark ages would be ashamed to encourage.

We find much fault with the press for revealing crime and wickedness, and clothing it with attractiveness and " sensation " that it does not deserve. We accuse it of shaping public opinion to the detriment of society. Gentlemen, remember that the *people* rule in this country, and that the press, like Abraham Lincoln in the war, can only echo and fulfill the wishes of the people. Educate the people to think for themselves, to study and maintain their own opinions, regardless of the press, and the press will find its true level and be the exponent of the real sentiments of the public. As it is, the average citizen prefers to let the press think for him; and when he is called to serve upon a jury, his mind is so imbued with the opinions of the reporter and editor that he is incompetent to form an honest judgment on the evidence of sworn witnesses.

This is all wrong. Gentlemen, believe me the brains of the community are not all in the editor's skull. I accord to my profession all the influence, all the wisdom, that it has any reason to claim; but it is not infallible. Men and women should be more independent of it. Like the lawyer, the editor, trammeled by political ambition and personal motives, does very much special pleading as the advocate of many things which he should be ashamed to approve.

But still the press is a mighty engine for reform. It can gather and disseminate really important information with greater rapidity than the slower process of book-making and distributing can possibly do, and reach a larger class of readers. If all the motives and energies of the press are on the side of morality and truth, it will fulfill the functions of a missionary in a good cause; but if the paper is " satanic " in its principles, and its readers lack the moral stamina to resist its influences, the effect must be more or less evil.

No, the man or woman who is willing to sit calmly down, and say, " Well, my paper says so and so is right, and I suppose it is, because the editor is a sharp fellow and knows, probably, better than I do," does not comprehend the privileges he or she possesses to think and act independently.

All honor to the press as a power for good, but none for it as the conservator of immorality.

Speech at a Printers' Banquet.

FELLOW-PRINTERS: It having devolved upon me to respond to the sentiment just offered—" The Art Preservative of All Arts, and the Artists of the Composing-Room "—I may as well say right here that I know all about those fellows—of whom I am proud to be one on this occasion.

The dinner we have just eaten was one to make each of us perfectly satisfied with ourselves and our vocation. In our office phrase, it was a " fat-take," and counted immensely in the " make-up " of this evening's enjoyment. With the exception of a feeling of unwonted tightness under the lower button of my vest, I am unusually self-satisfied and happy, and I see by your pleasant faces that our feelings are reciprocal.

But I was to speak about " the art preservative of all arts." Trusting to my present condition of mind and body, I should say it must be a good dinner, like this we have just eaten; for I think that if there is anything more preservative or congenial in the arts than such cookery, it can only be found in the " black art " which we practice.

But seriously, gentlemen, the subject is too broad, too magnificent, and comes up at too late an hour this evening, to receive more than a passing mention. All honor to our profession—I would say " trade," but *art* is a profession, and I am talking about art. I say, all honor to all our art—to the men who invented and perpetuated it until *we* came upon the stage—sad bunglers as they were in the business. All honor to the typos and the pressmen who are covering themselves and their profession with honor by the skill and beauty with which they have invested it. All honor to the press of the country—even to those editors whose sharpest, most pungent articles are written with shears and paste, instead of pen and ink. All honor to the men who advertise their business, and grow corpulent and wealthy by their free use of printers' ink. All honor to the men

who write and publish books. All honor to each and every reading man, woman and child in the universe, for their appreciation of our art. All honor to the men who design and draft the beautiful alphabets and ornaments with which we adorn our finest work. All honor to the pressman who " over-lays " his fellows and makes our art more brilliant by his clear " impressions." All honor to the paper-men who understand our needs and strive to make our art finer and better by the variety and excellence of their products.

Finally, all honor to our art itself—the art that is working wonders in the education and the reformation of the world—and to you, my fellow-typos, whose nimble fingers and good taste furnish lasting monuments of the progress of the age.

Speech at an Iron Manufacturers' Festival.

MR. PRESIDENT AND GENTLEMEN: In an epoch so filled with surprising inventions, improved methods of living, and important benefits to all classes of society, it is difficult to determine the specific name that should be given to this age. After some considerable deliberation I have decided in my own mind that this is, really and truly, the IRON AGE—not the one of which we have read so much in the history of the past, when life was a burden and held under a tenure of doubtful stability—when men's hearts were wrung by cruelty and oppression—but an age into whose composition iron and steel have so largely entered that it has reformed society and business, and greatly changed all our commercial relations. Look at the perfect network of railroads now traversing this continent and that of Europe, and pushing through the deserts and cities of the great East. Look at the majestic iron steamers that plow all navigable seas and oceans. Look at the immense forges, rolling-mills and factories that illumine the skies in all civilized countries with their lurid furnace-flames. Look at all these, and then ask, what power so potent as that of iron in this century? Without it all branches of industry would cease, and the clock of time would be set back five hundred years. No, gentlemen, in this era of progress, *Iron* is King! Accord whatever credit we may to science, art and literature, as motors in the great work of civilization, *Iron* holds its own in the scale, and is one of the world's greatest industrial agents in providing labor for workingmen. Indeed, the value of the iron-trade to all classes of society is incalculable, for it is universal—not for any one age or country, but for all time and in every land. Mr. President and Gentlemen, when I consider this subject and endeavor to estimate its true worth, I am bewildered at its greatness and the inadequateness of figures to represent it intelligibly. To-night I shall go no further with it, but leave it in its vastness for future political economists to investigate and assess. For one I am glad to be here to testify to its gigantic powers and increasing influence upon the world at large. Gentlemen, I give you: " The Iron Trade and its Artisans."

Artists' Reunion.

Response by the president to the toast, " Our Art and Artists."

FELLOW-ARTISTS: I suppose that most of us are aware of the very important part which fidelity to nature and the higher principles of art bear in the success of our profession; and I fancy, sometimes, that the lessons which we have received in this direction, while pursuing our studies, may have a meaning that extends beyond our canvas and our easels.

I doubt not that in the experiences of most of us here present we have more than once had occasion to note the similarity between the work of perfecting a superior painting and of shaping our lives to our ideal of honor and usefulness. In the studio, when the picture has gathered form and awaits the finer touches of the pencil, we carefully scan it from different points of vision, noting each defect in coloring and expression, and toning down, heightening, obliterating and retouching, as our skill and tastes may dictate, until we confess that in our eyes it is perfect. Thus it behooves us, as artists—

as men who revere art—who strive for excellence and fame—who respect ourselves and our talents—to stand aside occasionally and critically examine ourselves—our outer and inner lives—and note wherein we have come short of being the ideal men that we were designed to be. In the painting we have created with our pencils, a few movements of the hand will effect a wonderful transformation. If defects exist in character may we be equally adroit in the removal of blemishes and in the attainment of that which is wanting.

We are told that "an undevout astronomer is mad." Gentlemen, if our art is at all inferior to the sublime science of astronomy, it is because it is doing business more with our earth than with the immense universe beyond. We may with the utmost fidelity transfer to our canvas the finest landscapes and wildest charms of nature, and so win the highest applause from hosts of admirers. But alas! our choicest paintings are but types and shadows of the real grandeur of the works of nature which inspire our genius and should fill us with the spirit of devotion to the bounteous Providence which has spoken these beautiful things of earth into existence. An undevout artist is no less mad than the unbelieving astronomer.

Gentlemen, I am aware that this is an unusual train of thought to be introduced upon a festive occasion like this, but I am here to accord to my calling, and yours, all the dignity and emphasis to which it is entitled. I revere the memory of the dead and gone masters of our art; I rejoice in the perpetuation of their works and genius, and I believe that we who are endeavoring to leave to a grateful posterity paintings worthy of our profession should feel the importance of our mission, be faithful in our representations of nature, true artists in spirit as well as in works, and carry with us the character of high-minded, broad, generous, faithful men.

And now, turning to lighter matters connected with our profession, allow me to suggest that you who are expert portrait-painters should be "sharper than a serpent's tooth." I have observed that you paint portraits of gentlemen very conscientiously, for where the original possesses a pug-nose, you invariably give him one in your picture, and oftentimes, no doubt, it causes the poor man a world of uneasiness. As a remedy, I would suggest a schedule for such emergencies, fixing the price of an aquiline nose at so much, and a pug for something less, and let the gentleman decide for himself which he will have portrayed. This, brother artists, is the true mission of art—to make every one satisfied with himself and with your work. Should a cross-eyed man desire to be taken with straight visual organs, always be ready to accommodate him. What else should you do? He pays for the work, and takes his choice, preferring straight eyes to crooked ones. Who can blame him?

These are little things, gentlemen, but very suggestive, and you will do well to heed them.

I have thus responded to the toast in accordance with the assignment of the committee, and from the fullness of my heart, every sentiment of which is fraught with veneration for Art, and esteem for my fellow-artists

Response to a Speech of Congratulation,

Made by John A. Logan to Illinois Republican Association.

Mr. President, and Fellow-Citizens of Illinois: I welcome you heartily, and tender you my sincere thanks for the expression of good will manifested to-night in this voluntary visit. It is pleasant at all times to meet with one's co-workers, and it is especially so to meet with those with whom our labors have been most immediately cast. Born and reared in the State of Illinois, a flood of personal and agreeable recollections rushes upon me as I behold your familiar faces. Some of you stood with me as boys upon the shore of life's great ocean, panting with eagerness to explore the inviting but untried expanse before you. Some of you were side by side with me when our young manhood, full of vigor and latent possibilities, began the struggle with forbidding fortune, and in the face of obstacles which magnified and ennobled your subsequent success. With some of you I have rejoiced in the accomplishment of objects for which we

have striven, and with some of you I have grieved over the nonfruition of your best-grounded hopes. With all of you I have been closely associated during some portion of our respective careers, and can dwell with gratification over the retrospect of our personal acquaintances—a retrospect which, while full of pleasures, should not fail to remind us that, though we have passed the heyday of youth, and are standing under the more subdued light of middle-age, we are still in the prime of usefulness, and with life's mission still unfilled. Some of you that are here have come upon the field of labor at a more recent period, but are no less my friends and fellow-laborers. To one and all of you, gentlemen, I desire to manifest my deep appreciation of the spirit which prompts your visit at this time, and to extend the hand of fellowship and of hearty greeting to my friends of Illinois here assembled.

Speech at a Manufacturers' Convention,
Giving the Causes of Depression in Business.

The periods of financial depression come frequently in late years. Why? Does anybody know why? Apparently very few people have any distinct idea as to the causes that produce general financial distress throughout the community. Ask a dozen of the best business men of your town to-day the reason for the present hard times, and you will get a dozen different answers. One will tell you that it is "presidential year." Another will tell you that it is "wildcat speculation." Another, that it is "over-trading." Another, that it is "lack of sufficient protection." Another, that it is "wasteful extravagance," etc. etc. Evidently there is no clearly defined idea in the minds of business men relative to the causes that produce commercial stagnation. For this reason I have chosen this subject.

To explain, I will go back in history. Primitive man had no labor-saving implements to aid him in securing warmth and food. To obtain these necessaries, he had to labor with every possible physical effort all throughout his working hours. Time passed, and inventive genius produced labor-saving devices, such as the sickle, the hoe, the plough, the fanning-mill, the spinning-wheel, etc.

With these came opportunity for rest from long hours; and, with greater leisure for study and intellectual advancement, labor-saving machinery began to rapidly multiply. The result was, with the productive power of the country increased, the time of labor has been shortened from sixteen hours to fourteen, from fourteen to twelve, and from twelve to ten.

The history of these shortenings of the hours would fill a volume. Working the long hours with labor-saving machinery would make an over-production, succeeded by stagnation in business, bankruptcies, strikes, riots, and general disturbance. This was followed by a shortening of the hours, when, the productive power being lessened for a time, the demand for goods equaled or exceeded the supply, and then came an era of better times. The hours of factory labor have never been shortened without great effort, and whenever they have been reduced, the periods soon following have been those of great financial prosperity to the country.

During a period of several years preceding the civil war, our mechanics, with the aid of improved machinery, working twelve hours a day, had produced a vast overabundance, and the business of the country was at a standstill. The time of a day's labor was lessened two hours near the opening of the war, and nearly a million of men went to the battlefields. This made an immense reduction of the productive power of the country; and then came that era of great financial prosperity which the people enjoyed for several years, known as "war-times."

Good times stimulated invention to its utmost, and the planing-machine, the mower, the reaper, threshing-machines, telegraphs, telephones, and a vast array of other machines came to our aid, and along with them the laborers from other countries. Added to all this, the war closed, and the soldiers returned, also to enter the field of production. The result was—what? In the fall of 1873 an immense overstock of every description of goods that could not be immediately consumed.

Then followed the general failures among business men who had not foreseen the crisis that was approaching.

What made the panic of 1873? An immense overproduction, brought about by laboring men working in the manufactories ten hours each day, aided by steam and labor-saving machinery. Or, in other words, the power of production was in excess of the ability to consume. The balance was destroyed, and financial disturbance was the result.

Fortunately, soon after this panic, the Territories offered mining inducements, and thousands of our discharged laborers went there. Millions of acres of new lands were opened to settlers, and hundreds of thousands of surplus laborers have found themselves homes and employment there. These avenues of employment, besides furnishing homes for large numbers of immigrants from foreign lands, have made a fairly active and prosperous trade for business men for several years.

The immense productive power of the country, however, assisted by a general introduction of steam and labor-saving machinery, has been, of late, greatly overbalancing the power to consume, and the certain results are following. The hundreds of thousands of men who have gone to the new lands are producing wheat in such abundance as to bring the price below the cost of production. The result is disappointment to the farmer. He does not realize the price he had expected. He does not carry forward the improvement he had anticipated; he does not patronize the merchant—and the merchant does not order goods. Dull times at the factories are realized because merchants do not order; more mechanics are discharged; few goods are shipped; railroads do not pay dividends, their stocks shrink in value, and financial distress prevails among those who hold this class of securities.

It is clearly evident that the power to consume must balance the capacity to produce, or a general stoppage of production must cease. Such is the fact. When production has been stimulated by great demand, and the power to produce is in excess of consumption, then comes an overproduction. Then follows a lowering of the working-man's wages, and, finally, the discharge of large numbers of mechanics from the factory. With the power to buy destroyed among the great mass of the common people, manufacturers cannot sell, and then the discharge of laborers goes forward all the more rapidly, and general idleness prevails.

The business man who, a few years since, saw and realized the immense productive power of the country, consisting of great armies of foreign laborers who have come to our shores, aided by steam and labor-saving-machinery, could have readily understood that in the near future there must be a great overproduction, and, consequently, a lowering of prices, and cessation of trade.

Such are the facts to-day. We produce more than we consume, and we have the result. While other causes may have their remote effects, this is the real cause of hard times. When there is a scarcity of carpets in the market, the carpet business is good. When there is an overabundance of carpets in stock, the business is dull. And so throughout the entire range of production.

An excess of production being the cause of dull times, what is the remedy? Clearly, a less production. How shall this be brought about? There are various ways. One is, to do as we are doing now, and as we always do in a panic; shut down the mills and factories for a few months, until we have eaten up and worn out the goods on hand, and wait until scarcity shall cause trade to revive. Another, is to lessen the productive power of the country. How shall the latter be accomplished? Clearly, the most sensible way is by short-

ening the hours of labor. Beyond question, the interests of all classes would be subserved to-day by shortening time to eight hours for a day's work. Estimating that we have twenty millions of laboring men in the country, each working ten hours daily, two hours less each day would be one-fifth of their time to be taken from production, or the equivalent of four millions of laborers taken from the producing classes. That immense reduction of the working force would soon create such scarcity of production as would set every idler at work, in order to produce what we now have. Every person earning money, and consequently enabled to buy and consume, would greatly increase the consumptive power; so that, with the production decreased, and the ability to consume increased, there would not be an overstock of goods, and there would be, constantly, an active demand—which makes good times.

How shall we effect a reduction of time to eight hours a day? It is a matter very difficult to accomplish, from the fact that the laborer does not want to work eight hours for eight hours' pay, and the manufacturer, in the close competition with which he has to contend, is not willing to give ten hours' pay for eight hours' labor.

At this point laborers and employers divide. Each admits the necessity for a reduction of the hours, but neither is willing to bear the expense of the reduction. Under the circumstances, the most feasible plan seems to be that of a gradual reduction, which may be effected by all business men, first giving their employes a half-holiday on Saturday, without a reduction of pay. This would be a reduction of one-twelfth of the working-time; and this reduction of time, with twenty millions of men, would, in order to produce what we now make, give employment to 1,600,000 more men than we now employ.

From the half-day the time might be gradually extended until it should include all of Saturday; and this reduction of working-time should be favored by our business educators, being, as it is, for the best interests of all classes.

Our laborers need recreation. If they cannot get it on the secular days, they will take it on Sunday. Give them the opportunity to have it on Saturday, that they may spend the Sabbath in moral and spiritual improvement, and all will be the gainers.

Then may follow the going to labor at a later hour in the morning; and so on, by gradual reduction, the hours of toil may be lessened, and the intellectual opportunities of our laborers may be improved, while the productive and consumptive power of the country may be so balanced as to give continual prosperity to all its interests.

That the lessening of the hours of daily labor brings better pay to the workman, and greater prosperity to the employer and the business man, is proven by a single illustration:

Suppose stove manufacturers, finding an overstock on hand, decide to reduce their working-time to eight hours per day, and pay accordingly. The first probability of a scarcity of stoves will increase the demand, and very soon, working their foundries only eight hours a day, the orders will come in faster than they can fill them. The stove-maker goes to the boot and shoe manufacturer, whom he knows has been discharging men, for some of his idle workmen, and is told that, as the proprietors are working only eight hours a day in making boots and shoes, they are not discharging any men. On the contrary, they are employing more. The same reply is made at the reaper-factory, at the woolen-mills, and the various manufactories in town.

The stove-maker returns to his office, marks up the price of his stoves to correspond with their scarcity in the market, and then bids for workmen, and pays them even a higher price than he paid when they worked ten hours, because men are scarce. But he must have them even at an advanced price, in order to fill his orders—orders that are profitable because the price of stoves has been advanced; and yet, with this advance, workmen can buy more freely than before, because they have regular, steady employment at better wages than formerly.

We may anticipate many objections that will arise, one being that raising the price of home-made goods, similar articles will flow in from foreign countries, so that our manufacturers could not compete with low-priced goods produced by cheap labor and long hours abroad. The reply to this may be, that a tariff should protect us from this invasion; but, better yet, what applies to our industries here applies equally throughout all the civilized world. An International Congress, composed of representatives from all nations, should consider this matter and have a gradual reduction of working-time throughout the entire world, so that with the incoming of the labor-saving machine mankind may get the advantage of it as a labor-saver.

It is designed to benefit the world, and it should do so. As it comes forward to do our work, the hours of physical toil should be lessened accordingly, and they must be, as the permanent prosperity of any people can only be preserved when the ability to produce is balanced by an equal power to consume.

Speech at a County Agricultural Fair.

LADIES AND GENTLEMEN: Another year of seed-time and harvest has passed away since we last assembled on these grounds to witness the excellence of this county in producing the necessaries and luxuries of life. Rain and sunshine, spring and autumn, and summer and winter, have wrought their mysteries of nature, and here we see the noble work that they have perfected. On every hand we behold these generous products of the soil, the fruits of the orchard, the flowers of the garden, the handiwork of the dairy, the loom, and the kitchen. Delicate fingers have wrought this beautiful embroidery, these artificial flowers, these dainty quilts and rugs, which excite our admiration by the skill which they display, and appeal to our senses by the air of comfort and luxury which surrounds them.

It is gratifying to me to observe these triumphs of the outer and inner life of the farm, for it indicates a good degree of prosperity, praiseworthy industry, and the exercise of a taste that only needs specific culture to excel in the fine-arts that make home beautiful and elevate the sentiment of the household.

Not far off I hear the lowing of sightly cattle, the bleating of sheep, the sonorous utterances of swine, the cackling of hens, and the defiant crow of the Shanghai. It is only another indication that other branches of farm-life as well as the raising of grain, vegetables and fruit, have prospered during the past twelve months. For my part, I am glad it does not devolve on me to award the prizes upon this exhibition. If it did, I think the blue ribbon would grace everything here offered for competition. But that should not be, and the managers, with a greater wisdom and a better sense of justice, have entrusted that labor to men and women more competent to judge between good and evil than I am. No doubt you will all be satisfied, and some of you very happy, when their awards are made.

Near by I observe that the manufacturers of farm-machinery have not forgotten to be present with their labor-saving instrumentalities, glittering with bright paint and gold, to decorate the space allotted to them. The interest that *you* have in these things, however, goes below the gilding and the paint, and you have long since learned to appreciate the usefulness and value of them as important agents in your agricultural success.

I have been at many county fairs in my time. I was at twenty last year. Some of you may remember seeing me here. I thought then that in all points you rather excelled your neighbors by the variety and true excellence of your exhibition, and now I am convinced that ——— county yields the palm to none in these particulars.

Last year Senate county raised an average of thirty-five bushels of winter wheat to the acre, and No. 1 at that. But since I came here to-day I am assured that you overlap Senate county by three bushels per acre, and you ought to be very proud of the record, for Senate county claims to be the best in the State.

I hear that your county is also furnishing many very fine road and draught horses of the Norman and some other lighter breeds. I have seen several specimens of travelers while on my way hither, and I am satisfied that in this direction you are making gradual and important improvements.

Of course, in making this branch of industry successful, you import blooded stock to mix with your best domestic animals, and so, from year to year, the improvement will increase. At your trials on the course, however, you will, I hope, be careful not to let the love of money or fast horses outweigh other superior qualities in your estimation.

Farmers' boys and girls, I have a word for you! Don't leave the farm. Stay there and work, and earn an honest, healthful living in the pure air of the country, rather than rush headlong into the crowded streets and contaminated atmosphere of city life. There may be more excitement, more to see and hear and learn, than on the farm, but it is dangerous to health and morals and comfort. Make your homes, with the assistance of your parents, pleasant places by exercising your own good taste and skill in devising new attractions and decorations; and, above all, read, learn and master the arts and sciences that are most easily reached in the retirement of the country fireside. Good books cost little now, comparatively, and are easily obtained. From them gather wisdom and entertainment as you can—but however much you may visit the city, stick to the farm.

And, farmers, a word to you. Cease making farm-life a drudgery. Dress up and put your homes in attractive condition. Commence your labors at a reasonable hour in the morning, and close at a reasonable hour at night. Beginning work at four o'clock in the morning and ending at nine at night, the year round, will drive the best boy living off to the city. Make your homes charming. Why not? Must your children go to the city to find beauty! Must they go there to see beautiful pleasure-grounds, attractive architecture and handsomely decorated homes? Must they go away from home in order to find that pleasure, beauty, and attraction, which young people love? In landscape-gardening, and floriculture, you have the finest of opportunities. In the growing of fruit and ornamental trees, in opportunity for sports and games, you have a thousand advantages where the city has one.

"Can't afford it?" You can't afford to do otherwise. The noblest mission of man is to live long, be happy, and make others happy about him. No man that overworks can live to a great age. No man's family living in the midst of constant toil, drudgery, and lack of recreation, can have perfect health and real enjoyment.

Nature will not be cheated. The body will endure so much toil and no more. The innate love of the beautiful will not be deprived of its gratification. Make your farm a treadmill of hard, grinding toil; let your house go unpainted, and the door-yard grow up to weeds; let your horses go uncleaned, and your wagon be covered with mud; let your pig-pen be close upon one side, and the cow-yard near by the other; let this spirit of neglect and hard work characterize your farm-life, and the children will quit, and you will be deprived of their assistance long before they are grown to an age whereby they can aid you.

"Can't afford to spend time and money to fix up about the house?" Do you wish to have your children interested with you in all your labors? Would you like to have one of them carry forward the farm, after you have done with it, while the rest settle in the immediate vicinity? Then give plenty of time for growth and recreation to the children.

Reduce your work to a system. Take down your fence in the near vicinity of the house, and give yourself several acres of beautiful green lawn about your home. Leave an abundance of open space for air, light and view in the front of your house; but on this broad lawn, on either side of the residence, set groups of evergreens, fruit and ornamental trees. Not too many, but enough to give variety.

Cultivate a love of the beautiful, and show it in your works about your homes. It does not cost much money to do this. It is mostly a matter of taste and love of order and neatness. The rustic summer-house, with trailing vines that hang upon it, need not be expensive. The preparation of the flower-beds will cost you but little time. The floral beauties that will make your home brilliant will cost you nothing. The ladies and the children of the household will care for them with the greatest pleasure. Place a broad piazza on the front of your house, upon which the family can sit when they rest from the active labors of the day in the warm season. Trim your house and outbuildings handsomely and paint them; keep the grass cleanly cut upon your lawns, and with the accessories I have mentioned your homes will be beautiful; they will be attractive to the children—they will be charming to all that come within their influence; and in them you will be vastly happier than when living in homes and on farms that present, as many do, only dreariness and evidences of bare, hard life.

Washington's Birthday.

Speech at a gathering in honor of the occasion.

LADIES AND GENTLEMEN: That a little child should have been born of respectable people in moderate circumstances, in the British colony of Virginia, February 22, 1732, is not of itself a remarkable fact, especially as the child differed little from other children at birth. It is a very common occurrence in these days, in Virginia, and in all parts of the globe. But once in a while it has happened that the nativity of one of these little ones who are continually coming into the world derives great interest from the wit, wisdom, genius, or prowess of the individual, gradually displayed after he has entered " the world's broad field of battle,'' and has won victories, in either war or peace, which Fame proudly blazons on her scroll. A baby seems a very little thing—a toy, a doll—to be loved and petted and played with. An apple-seed is another little thing, seemingly of no special value in itself; but the seed and the child, if properly treated, grow up together and may become a valuable, fruit-bearing tree and an energetic, wise and useful man. So when the boy-baby came into the household of Augustine Washington, one hundred and fifty years ago to-day, in Westmoreland county, Virginia, there was really nothing to distinguish him from any other child born into that county about that time, except the family to which he belonged, and that was not particularly noted. But the tremendous consequences that this event wrought in the history of Great Britain, America and the world at large have filled the trump of Fame for a hundred years, and founded one of the grandest nations of the globe. I am not here, to-day, to recount in detail the early trials, the noble acts of the youth, the arduous labors of the man, the steps by which he climbed to his honored niche in the history of mankind. With these things we are familiar; but we are here to rejoice, with millions of our countrymen, that ever George Washington was born; to rejoice that he was the great and good man appointed by Providence to cheer and guide an oppressed people to a better and nobler condition of life, where they could enjoy personal and political freedom, pursue happiness and found a nation of such breadth, such grandeur, such liberty, that it might become the asylum of the poor and downtrodden of all nations. Washington was only human; subject to the errors and infirmities of our common nature; yet by will and circumstances fitted far above his fellows for the mission which he had to fulfill. As a man he was noble; as a soldier he was firm and brave and shrewd; as a hero he won the confidence of the people; as a patriot he triumphed over tyranny; as a statesman he left the impress of his character upon the institutions of his country. He was emphatically '' the man of the time,'' and there seldom comes a time in human affairs when a good and great man—great in manhood, wisdom and energy—is not useful. There is one other in our national history, who, like Washington, came from the ranks of ordinary life to leave the stamp of his sturdy integrity, wisdom, and usefulness upon his age and country. It was Abraham Lincoln; and it is very difficult to refer to either Washington or Lincoln, in thought or word, without remembering the other and the services each rendered in behalf of humanity and good government. If Washington possessed a peculiar talent, a shrewdness, an executive power fitted

to the destiny he accomplished, so did Lincoln, more than any other living man, possess attributes which admirably fitted him for his great work. And as with one, so with the other; when his mission on earth was fully accomplished he lay down, blessed and honored, to a hero's rest. Well may we, year by year, assemble in honor of the birth of Washington, and on the same day unite in one grand sentiment—'' The memory of Washington and Lincoln.''

Speech of a Speaker who had Nothing to Say.

LADIES AND GENTLEMEN: If there is one comfort greater than another, to a person who has nothing to say at such a time as this, it is the realization of the fact that having nothing to say, he can announce that fact, take his seat and enjoy the remainder of the programme unmolested.

I can truly say that I have not burdened my mind with the smallest idea to present you on this occasion. I have not taxed my memory with anything, and hence I have no taxes to pay. I comply simply because you call, and, whatever one's calling may be, it is his duty to respond, especially if—he cannot escape. Of course, if I had had about a week of preparation, I might now arise and make you a dashing extemporaneous speech. The subjects are upon every side that would inspire me. It would be easy to dwell upon the wealth of beauty that we see around us. I should like to speak of the flashing wit, the brilliant oratory and the burning eloquence to which we have listened. This elegant repast, this genial gathering, the importance of this reunion, the glorious benefit resulting from this meeting—all these—any one of them—afford themes for a speech. Of course there are a thousand subjects incidental to this gathering that suggest a speech, but should I enter upon a consideration of any one of them I would regret it, and so would you.

It is an old, trite saying that the time to sit down is when the audience wants you to speak longer. In my case, if I wanted to speak longer you would want me to sit down. I will therefore retire, humbly hoping that this speech will not be misreported and that when you want a brilliant speech you will always call upon me.

Valedictory Address,

Delivered before a class graduating at college.

MR. PRESIDENT AND FELLOW-STUDENTS: It has devolved upon me, as the senior member of the class of 1884, to give expression to a few thoughts appropriate to this occasion. I do so with a keen appreciation of the relations we have so long sustained with each other, the faculty of this college, and the world of affairs into which we are about to emerge, and with which we are henceforth to mingle, not knowing what is before us, but hoping in the ardor of young manhood for the best.

Fellow Students, we have been companions for four years—four years, to some of us, of diligent application to our studies; four years of light and shade to all of us; four years of social fellowship and pleasant recreation; four years of mental and physical improvement. We have sympathized with each other in troubles and sorrows; have lightened each other's hearts in times of sadness, and have enjoyed college-life in each other's society, I will venture to say, as well as any other class that ever graduated from these classic halls. We go hence with our diplomas, which the world looks upon as the keys that are to unlock the doors of science, art, literature, theology, physic and merchandise for us, and open the avenues of wealth and honor to us. We go hence, as we are, to the battle of life. What success we shall have, what victories we may win, the future alone can tell.

But we go forth with strong hope and abiding faith that all will be well with us if we perform our duty faithfully in whatever calling or sphere fate may assign us.

Where will fate or fortune place us in the great sea of the future? I see in imagination this class all scattered, many the heads of families, engaged in the peaceful pursuits of agriculture and trade; others on the rough sea of political life, some of whom will doubtless reap honor in State and Congressional legislation, bestowing benefit upon their fellow-men, while they hold high and responsible positions in official life.

But as we go forth, each to fulfill his destiny, let us forget all our boyish prejudices, if any we have, against each other, and through our lives be helpful friends to each other as opportunities may offer. For myself, and I think I speak for all, these college friendships are too sacred to be lightly broken or forgotten, and in our farewells and final pressure of our hands together, let us renew the bonds which our fellowship in our *Alma Mater* has woven.

Mr. President and Professors—one and all—we go hence with the profoundest esteem for the wisdom, forbearance and uniform justice and kindness that you have ever manifested toward us within these walls. We have been often hasty, heedless of your feelings and our own best interests, and have at times caused you great annoyance by our boyish follies; but in all these things you have proven yourselves our true friends and mentors, and in our hearts we have cherished no malevolence, no hatred toward you. In whatever we have given you offense we would ask your forgiveness, and carry away with us a heartfelt gratitude for all the many favors we have received at your hands.

Fellow Students of the Freshmen and Sophomore classes, I take a restrospective view, as I look into your youthful faces, and I see this graduating class as it was four years ago, a handful of inexperienced, puzzled freshmen, the sport of the sophomores, and unheeded or plagued by the seniors. What we felt and endured then, half-discouraged by our outward circumstances and our inward fears, you now feel and endure; but look up, boys, look up! The freshmen will soon be sophomores, and the sophomores seniors; and the troubles of the present will fade away in the future like a morning dream. On your part you have youth, good intellects and capable teachers, and if you fail—and I do not believe you will—you will have only your want of assiduity to study to blame for it. The four years' course is not the bugbear that you fear it is, and its difficulties will dissolve before the energy and application that you (I am sure) are now determined to exercise. We leave you here to so maintain the honor of this institution that you may depart from it with its blessing.

The hour of parting draws nigh. In spite of hope and faith in the future, there is a tinge of sadness in the present, which I, for one, do not fear to cherish and confess, for it testifies to the genuineness of our human sympathy and heartfelt friendship. Farewell, and peace go with you all '

Opening a New Railroad.

Speech at the driving of the last spike by the president.

MESSRS. DIRECTORS AND OFFICERS: No one knows better than yourselves the difficulties which we encountered at the outset in the establishment and construction of this railroad. You recall to memory, if you have ever forgotten it, the distrust and doubt with which we placed its stock upon the market, at a time when we had nothing to show but our unfledged charter and the right of way over about one-third of the distance which we proposed to build our line. I recollect, if you do not, the timidity with which I approached the first capitalist whose aid we sought, and laid our plans before him. He listened patiently to the story of our prospects and condition, and generously subscribed for five hundred shares, paying for one hundred, and wishing us success. The magic of his name was worth a thousand shares more. Our confidence was restored, and that of the people along the line was strengthened by the announcement of his interest in the road. The shares were rapidly sold, money flowed in briskly, and the work went on with proportionate energy, and with every confidence in the final result. To-day the track of 567 miles is laid, and well-laid; the rolling-stock has been purchased and will begin to run to-morrow morning; the shares are all sold; the assessed installments have been promptly paid, and in five minutes more

the spike will be driven that unites the distant cities of C—— and S—— by many ties of wood and iron of such strength and durability that the most important interests of both cities will be entrusted to it. I am not (*turning to the spectators*), Ladies and Gentlemen, advertising the stock of this road on this occasion—for none of it is for sale, and it stands at *par*—the best evidence that the confidence of capitalists and the public is secured in our favor. But we thank you for the encouragement you give us by your attendance upon this ceremony, and we trust that you will not withhold from us your patronage. We are not, properly speaking, a "grand-trunk line," but wherever our cars shall run you are welcome to ride—at regular rates. (*Taking the sledge-hammer and the spike, and placing the latter where it belongs:*) C—— and S——, with this sledge I unite you in the bonds of commercial sisterhood. (*Drives the spike.*) The work is done,—the road is finished. Let on the steam! (*Chorus of steam-whistles, and cheering by the audience.*

Fourth of July Celebration Abroad.

Speech by the United States consul at a reunion of Americans.

LADIES AND GENTLEMEN: Assembled as we are to-day beneath the blue skies and amid the luxuriant products of a foreign nation, our hearts beat warmly at the recurrence of this cherished anniversary of American freedom. Some of us have come from the sterile hills of New England, some from the sunny South, some from the prairies of the West, and we all sit down together at one table to celebrate the day made glorious by our forefathers in the declaration of our national independence. At that time in our history they were in the midst of the great struggle for social and political freedom; the end was uncertain; blood had yet to be spilt before peace could be conquered; yet, trusting in a just and overruling Providence, jeopardizing their lives and fortunes, they feared not to proclaim the equal freedom of all men under the law. The victory was not yet won, but they went forth, in the spirit of that declaration, to seal it with liberty or death, hopeful of the triumph which awaited them. To-day we remember their bravery, their energy, and their patriotism; to-day we rejoice in the principles which they maintained; to-day we are proud to be citizens of the great and prosperous nation which they founded. More keenly do we feel this pride when we look around us where we are to-day, when we see the errors and inconsistencies of other governments, and miss the educational, social and political advantages which we enjoy in our own country. Let us be thankful for our native land; for the stars and stripes which wave over us; for our prerogatives of national and individual freedom. I propose "The Memory of the Revolutionary Fathers."

Celebration of Queen Victoria's Birthday in America.

Speech by an American at a reunion of English and American ladies and gentlemen.

LADIES AND GENTLEMEN: I don't know what kind of weather prevailed in England on the twenty-fourth of May in the year of grace 1819; but it was a blessed day for Great Britain, for it gave the kingdom one of its most esteemed and favored sovereigns—the Lady in whose honor we have gathered here. Fulfilling the destiny of every true woman, she united herself in marriage to the man of her choice —a Prince every way worthy of her confidence and affection, and so public-spirited and progressive and intelligent as to endear himself to the better classes of the Queen's subjects. To the regret of all civilized nations he was taken away in the prime of his manhood; and I believe that if man was ever sincerely mourned and his memory revered, that man was Prince Albert of Coburg. True to his memory, faithful to the trusts imposed upon her in rearing her fatherless children aright, Victoria proved herself equal to the emergency, and with unswerving fidelity has ruled judiciously over the greatest nation of the globe. It is no disgrace for any civilized people to honor her by celebrating this her natal day, whatever their political government, and it is with pride and pleasure that I propose: "Queen Victoria—Sovereign, Wife and Mother—Long may she reign!"

AMONG the delightful titbits that afford variety and merriment on certain festal occasions, may be toasts and sentiments, thus:

For a Christmas Dinner.

" Christmas hospitality: And the ladies who make it delightful by their *mincing* ways."

" The sports of the holidays: Sleighing the *Dears*, and taking comfort among the *Buffaloes*."

For the Thanksgiving Festival.

" Our opinion on the Eastern Question: We agree with Russia, that *Turkey* ought to be *gobbled*."

" The health of our venerable host: Although an American citizen, he is one of the best *Grand Seniors* that ever presided over *Turkey*."

" Thanksgiving: The magnetic festival that brings back erratic wanderers to the Old Folks at Home."

" The thanksgiving board: While it *groans* with plenty within, who cares for the whistling of the wind without."

" Thanksgiving: The religious and social festival that converts every family mansion into a Family Meeting House."

For the Fourth of July.

" The American Eagle: The older he grows the louder he screams, and the higher he flies."

" The Union of the States, and the Union of the Sexes: The one was the beginning of man's independence, the other is the end of it."

" Our Standard Sheet: It has often been badly mangled, and terribly scorched, but is, nevertheless, the noblest sheet that ever covered a hero on the bed of glory."

For a Wooden Wedding.

" Our Host and Hostess: The fire of affection they mutually kindled five years ago has not gone out; on the contrary, we are glad to see them *wooding up*."

" The Wooden Wedding of our Friends: And may all the children be *chips of the old block*."

" The Hero and Heroine of this Wooden Festival: May they flourish like green bay trees in their youth, and retain all their *pith* when they become elders."

For the Tin Wedding.

" The Golden Rule of Matrimony: Marry the first time for love — the second time for *Tin*."

" The Fair Bride: She blushed at her first marriage, but she shows more *metal* to-day."

" Tin Weddings: And the bright reflections to which they give rise."

For the Crystal Wedding.

" Crystal Weddings: The medium through which the bliss of enduring affection is *magnified*, *reflected*, and made *transparent* to everybody."

" The fifteenth year of Wedlock: A matrimonial *Stage*, chiefly remarkable for its *Tumblers*."

" Our Hospitable Hostess: And may it never be her fate to look on life 'as through a glass darkly.'"

" The New Married Couple: They will not find the friendship of their friends as brittle as their gifts."

For a Silver Wedding.

" A quarter of a century of Married Happiness: The best five-twenty bond in the world."

" The Bridal Pair: Their admirable performances in double harness well entitle them to the plate."

" Our Kind Entertainers: Know all men, by these presents, how sincerely we love them."

For the Golden Wedding.

" Matrimony's Pleasant Autumn: May it always bear golden fruit."

" The Bridegroom's Prize: Not toys of gold, but the more attractive metal by his side."

* Selected from Barber's Ready-made Speeches, published by Dick & Fitzgerald, New York.

Writing for the Press.

IN writing for the Press, while being explicit, the writer should make the statement as brief as possible.

Though in ordinary conversation talk may be cheap, in the newspaper, words cost money. If sent by telegraph, they cost for transmission ; time is consumed in their examination by the editor and proofreader ; money is expended in putting them in type ; ink and paper must be furnished on which they make their impress ; and time is to be occupied by the reader in their perusal ; therefore, each word should convey as much significance as possible.

General Directions.

1. If, unavoidably, a long article is written relating to a variety of subjects, it is well to break the sameness of the appearance by *sub-heads*, scattered through the article, relating to different subjects considered in the composition.

2. Write very plainly, on white paper with black ink, taking care to write names of persons, dates and places, with the utmost distinctness.

3. Use sheets of paper about six by nine inches in size, numbered in their order if more than one sheet be used. Very large sheets, on the compositor's case, make it inconvenient for the type setter.

4. Write on but one side of the sheet. Thus the paper containing your communication may be, if necessary, cut into parts, and distributed among several compositors who will place your composition in type.

5. As a rule, in short news articles, never use the pronouns *I* or *you*. A plain, succinct record of the news is all that is required. If necessary for the writer to refer to himself, it is better to say " Our reporter " or " The writer."

6. Never waste time in complimenting the editor or his paper, when writing a letter for publication. Commence at once with the subject in hand, and close when you have done.

Local Reporting.

That kind of journalistic writing most easily taken up, and yet quite difficult to do well, is that of presenting in attractive form a judicious report of home news.

Much demand exists for more reportorial talent, especially on the country newspaper. Thousands of exciting incidents and events transpire, the details of which, written up for the press, would greatly edify the readers of the country journal, the editor of which, knowing nothing of the affair, is compelled to fill his paper with foreign news of less interest to his subscribers.

As a general rule, there is not sufficient local matter to be obtained, nor space to be filled, in the weekly country journal, to make it an object for the publisher to employ, at a weekly salary, a person whose exclusive business shall be collecting local news ; and yet the editor is desirous of obtaining all the important home intelligence there is, and will willingly pay for such as he may publish, at the rate of from $1 to $5 per column, when an arrangement may be made for the correspondent to write regularly.

Of course no writer should expect compensation until it is clearly shown that his or her writings are of decided service to the paper in which they are published. When they become so, editors and publishers readily concede the fact, and are willing to pay what the articles are worth.

Important Reportorial Qualifications.

The reporter should be truthful. In writing of any event, great care should be taken to state the actual facts. To do this, the reporter should possess the energy to go to the scene of action, if possible, himself, and learn the exact condition of affairs. It is often unsafe to depend upon hearsay.

The reporter should carefully guard against allowing his own opinions to warp or bias his report of the sayings or doings of others, thus giving, almost without his being conscious of the fact, an untruthful representation. A plain, unvarnished report should be made, and nothing else.

Much discretion should be exercised in the personal mention of individuals. A dozen words, thoughtlessly written, may do irreparable injury to the reputation of an innocent person: a paragraph in praise may add to the life-long happiness and prosperity of the individual upon whom it is bestowed. As a general rule, while praise may be personally given, if wrongs exist, it is better to speak of them in general terms, rather than couple them with names of the individuals at fault; though, if the person be notoriously persistent in a course of wrong doing, justice demands newspaper exposure.

Subjects of Local and General Interest.

ITEMS FOR THE NEWSPAPER.

For the advantage of the inexperienced writer, making record of home news, the following partial list is given, containing subjects of general interest to the public.

Accidents.—When, where, to whom.

Amusements, Excursions, Etc.—When, where; character of amusement, etc.

Births.—When, where, name of parents and sex of child.

Burglary.—When, where, by whom, amount stolen, etc.

Change of Business Firms.—When, and names of the parties.

Crops.—Present condition and future prospects.

Crime of any kind.—Names of offenders; nature of the crime.

Churches.—Change of pastors, revivals, election of church officers, etc.

Dissolutions of Partnership.—Names of parties, where going, what to do.

Deaths.—Who, when, where, cause.

Discoveries.—Of curiosities, or anything new or valuable.

Distinguished Arrivals.—At the hotels or elsewhere.

Divorces.—Who, when, where, cause. When and where married.

Elopements.—Names of parties and circumstances.

Election Intelligence.—Election takes place when, candidates to be, or are elected, etc.

Fires.—Whose property, when, where, cause, amount of insurance, names of companies insured in.

Facts and Figures.—Concerning any products raised in the vicinity, amount sold, profits, etc.

Festivals.—Held by whom, for what object, amount realized, etc.

Improvements.—By whom, where, and costs.

Inventions.—Patents granted to whom, what for, nature of the improvement.

Lectures.—Past, or to come; when, where, by whom, substance of what was said.

Marriages.—Who, when, where, by whom married, where gone on bridal tour.

Murders.—When, where, who, by whom, object of the murder, circumstances.

New Comers.—Their business, where located, where from, etc.

New Manufactures.—In prospect, when, where, by whom established, kind, etc.

New Buildings.—To be or built, erected by whom, for what purpose, cost, etc.

Price of Staple Commodities.—In the market, prospect for the future, etc.

Parties Leaving Town.—Who, when, where going, business going into.

Presentations.—By whom, to whom, where given, what presented, why.

Railroads.—New roads in prospect, profits of present roads, etc.

Sales of Real Estate.—By whom, to whom, who will occupy, amount paid, etc.

Shows, Exhibitions, Fairs.—Where, when, who gives them, character of entertainment.

Schools.—Facts and figures concerning them, change of teachers, improvements needed, etc.

Secret Societies.—Election of officers, prosperity and condition of the society.

Strange Phenomena.—In the heavens, in the elements, on or in the earth, where, when.

Suggestions of Improvements Needed.—Where, when, by whom, cost, etc.

Surgical Operations.—By whom performed, of what character, condition of patient.

Sickness. — Who sick, cause, by what physician attended, health of the community.

Telegraphs. — What new lines are to be established, present cost of telegraphing, etc.

Violation of Law. — Whereby parties are arrested and fined, what offense, when, where, etc.

Writing for the Metropolitan Press.

In every locality something will occasionally transpire the details of which will be of general interest to the public at large, in which case the publishers of papers in the large cities will esteem it a favor for some person to give them the facts.

Should the town in which the correspondent is stationed be sufficiently large, and the news frequently occurring important, the publisher will pay an accepted regular correspondent for news that he prints, from $1 to $10 per article, as may be agreed between publisher and correspondent.

Only such matter is desired for the metropolitan journal as will interest the people throughout the entire country. Of such news are facts concerning : — *Enactments of Law. Severe accidents. Fires. Crops. Murders. Elopements. Burglary. Schools. Churches. New manufactures. Railroads. Elections. Weather. Discoveries. Inventions. Strange phenomena. Important Statistics. Personal mention of distinguished persons, etc.*

RESULTS OF BAD PENMANSHIP.

Especial pains should be taken, when writing for the press, to write legibly. The error is very common with some authors and prominent men, of writing in a manner such as to seriously trespass upon the time and patience of printers and correspondents upon whom they inflict their penmanship.

This fault is a very serious one, and causes much waste of time and pecuniary loss to printers. Lawyers frequently prepare their briefs, clergymen their sermons, and others their copy, in a penmanship so entirely illegible as to compel several re-settings of much of the same, in type, before it is correct. Of course this loss of time must be borne by the compositor, and frequently, with those printers employed in setting type by the thousand, bad manuscript entails a loss in their earnings of several dollars per week.

While to filch from the pocket of the printer, in this manner may not be deemed so dishonorable as to steal his purse, the result is, however, all the same.

Again, business men who would regard it a great intrusion for another to trespass on their time for even a half hour, will show the discourtesy to write a letter to a correspondent which may consume hours and even days of his time in deciphering the same.

This evil would be less if it stopped here. Unfortunately, however, it goes beyond and afflicts the coming penmanship of our youth. The boy that will pick up the half consumed cigar and smoke out the balance of the stump, thinking that thereby he makes a man of himself, will look upon bad penmanship, when executed by distinguished men, as an evidence of genius, and is not unlikely to imagine himself a great man, because he imitates their pot-hooks and scrawls.

Eminent men are liable to have faults. If the error is an illegible penmanship, this defect is none the less a fault, because the man may have distinguished reputation and redeeming qualities in other directions.

Young writers should not therefore ape bad penmanship as an evidence of genius. Of two articles written for the newspaper, all things else being equal, that one stands much the best chance for publication which is most plain in penmanship. Let the young author see that the composition is not only correctly written, when prepared for the press, but that it is so perfectly legible that its merit may be readily seen upon examination.

BOOKS.

THE accompanying illustrations, upon this page, represent the principal sizes of books, namely: *Folio*, a long book; *Quarto* (*4to*), nearly square, (shape of HILL'S MANUAL); *Octavo* (*8vo*), the general size; and *Duodecimo* (*12mo*), a small book, as seen below.

FOLIO.

The standard size of book paper is 25 x 38 inches; one half of the sheet being 19 x 25 inches, which folded in two leaves, having four pages, makes a book of the size called a *folio*.

QUARTO.

When the half sheet is folded in four leaves, making eight pages, it forms a *quarto* in size.

OCTAVO.

The half sheet folded again, eight leaves, sixteen pages, forms an *octavo*, or folded into sixteen leaves forms a *sixteenmo*.

DUODECIMO.

By folding the same into twelve leaves, making twenty-four pages, we have a *duodecimo*. Folded into eighteen leaves, or thirty-six pages, we form an *18mo*; into 24 leaves, and we have a *24mo*, &c.

The words Post, Crown, Demy, Royal, etc., used in connection, as Royal Octavo, designate the sizes of paper of which books are made.

Modern facilities for the manufacture of paper enable publishers to have any desired size made to order, as has been done in the case of this book.

The marks a, b, c; 1, 2, 3; 1*, 2*, 3*, 1A, &c., occasionally found at the bottom of a page, are what printers term *signature* marks, being printed for the direction of the binders in folding the sheets.

The art of covering books in a superior manner, was in use long before the art of printing was discovered, some of the most beautiful and elaborate binding being executed as early as the 11th century. Books, which were in manuscript, in those days, were few, and so very valuable that great care was taken in their preservation, jewelers and other artisans engaging in the manufacture and ornamentation of their covers.

With the advanced civilization of the 19th century, however, the superior machinery for book binding has not only cheapened the cost, but the facilities in some large establishments, are such as to enable manufacturers to elegantly bind, in muslin, one hundred and fifty copies per hour.

FOLIO.

QUARTO, "4to."

OCTAVO, "8vo."

Duodecimo, "12mo."

NAMES OF THE DIFFERENT SIZES OF BOOK AND NEWSPAPER TYPE.

The poetry and other matter occupying the lower portion of the following oblong spaces, it will be seen, are printed in a style much more open than the matter occupying the upper part of the space. This results from placing a thin piece of metal, called a *lead*, between the lines. Reading matter having these leads between the lines is called *leaded:* thus, the reading matter in the following spaces is what is termed *solid* and *leaded;* the upper portion being *solid*, and the lower part *leaded*.

This page contains a specimen of fourteen kinds of n

This page contains a specimen of fourteen kinds of newsp

This page contains a specimen of fourteen kinds of newspaper and book type, fr

This page contains a specimen of fourteen kinds of newspaper and book type, from Bri

This page contains a specimen of fourteen kinds of newspaper and book type, from Brilliant to Tw

This page contains a specimen of fourteen kinds of newspaper and book type, from Brilliant to Two-line

This page contains a specimen of fourteen kinds of newspaper and book type, from Brilliant to Two-line Small Pica.

This page contains a specimen of fourteen kinds of newspaper and book type, from Brilliant to Two-line Small Pica. A

This page contains a specimen of fourteen kinds of newspaper and book type, from Brilliant to Two-line Small Pica. A B C D E

This page contains a specimen of fourteen kinds of newspaper and book type, from Brilliant to Two-line Small Pica. A B C D E 1 2 3 4

This page contains a specimen of fourteen kinds of newspaper and book type, from Brilliant to Two-line Small Pica. A B C D E F G 1 2 3 4 5 6 7 8 9 10

This page contains a specimen of fourteen kinds of newspaper and book type, from Brilliant to Two-line Small Pica. A B C D E F G H I J K L M N O P 1 2 3 4 5 6 7 8 9 10 11 12

This page contains a specimen of fourteen kinds of newspaper and book type, from Brilliant to Two-line Small Pica. A B C D E F G H I J K L M N O P Q R S T U V W X Y Z & 1 2 3 4 5 6 7 8 9 10

This page contains a specimen of fourteen kinds of newspaper and book type, from Brilliant to Two-line Small Pica. A B C D E F G H I J K L M N O P Q R S T U V W X Y Z & 1 2 3 4 5 6 7 8 9 10 11 12 13 14 15 16 17 18

BRILLIANT.

Experience proves that the apprentice foreshadows the workman, just as surely as the bend of a twig foretells the in-lination of the tree. The upright, obedient, industrious lad will graduate a steady, skillful, and capable man, as unmistakably as the perverse, idling, careless boy will ripen into the lazy, dissolute fellow. The fact is, a boy is measurably the maker of his own destiny; and if he fail to acquire a master-knowledge of the trade to which he is put, it will mainly be because he did not, at the outset, determine to be a master-workman. Good morals and steady industry are indispensable. Among the business habits, that are highly valued in the apprentice, are punctuality, order, neatness and dispatch. The boy who is promptly at his work in the morning soon wins the esteem of his employer. The lad who keeps the shop and store in a neat and orderly manner ere long becomes a valuable assistant, and the youth who, in addition to these qualifications, is activ) in the dispatch of business, is certain to make himself useful to those with whom he may engage. The boy should also recollect that ere long he may be called upon to fill the place of employer, if he is true to the trusts imposed upon him, while an apprentice and employee. To attain the highest success as a tradesman and worthy citizen, he should not only form these correct habits of business, but he should carefully cultivate and maintain a pure, untarnished morality ; upon which rests all permanent happiness and success. To do this he should avoid bad associates, and thoroughly resolve, in the commencement, to be economical, prudent, temperate, truthful, and scrupulously honest.

THE FUTURE LIFE.
By Wm. C. Bryant.

How shall I know thee in the sphere which keeps
The disembodied spirits of the dead,
When all of thee that time could wither, sleeps
And perishes among the dust we tread ?

DIAMOND.

Experience proves that the apprentice foreshadows the workman, just as surely as the bend of a twig foretells the inclination of the tree. The upright, obedient, industrious lad will graduate a steady, skillful, and capable man, as unmistakably as the perverse, idling, careless boy will ripen into the lazy, dissolute fellow. The fact is, a boy is measurably the maker of his own destiny ; and if he fail to acquire a master-knowledge of the trade to which he is put, it will mainly be because he did not at the outset determine to be a master-workman. Good morals and steady industry are indispensable. Among the business habits that are highly valued in the apprentice are punctuality, order, neatness and dispatch. The boy who is promptly at his work in the morning soon wins the esteem of his employer. The lad who keeps the shop and store in a neat and orderly manner ere long becomes a valuable assistant, and the youth who, in addition to these qualifications, is active in the dispatch of business, is certain to make himself useful to those with whom he may engage. The boy should also recollect that ere long he may be called upon to fill the place of employer, if he is true to the trusts imposed upon him while an apprentice and employee. To attain the highest success as a tradesman and worthy citizen, he should not only form these correct habits of business, but he should carefully cultivate and maintain a pure, untarnished morality ; upon which rests all permanent happiness and success.

For I shall feel the sting of ceaseless pain,
If there I meet thy gentle spirit not;
Nor hear the voice I love, nor read again,
In thy serenest eyes, the tender thought.

PEARL.

Experience proves that the apprentice foreshadows the workman, just as surely as the bend of a twig foretells the inclination of the tree. The upright, obedient, industrious lad will graduate a steady, skillful, and capable man, as unmistakably as the perverse, idling, careless boy will ripen into the lazy, dissolute fellow. The fact is, a boy is measurably the maker of his own destiny ; and if he fail to acquire a master-knowledge of the trade to which he is put, it will mainly be because he did not at the outset determine to be a master-workman. Good morals and steady industry are indispensable. Among the business habits that are highly valued in the apprentice are punctuality, order, neatness and dispatch. The boy who is promptly at his work in the morning soon wins the esteem of his employer. The lad who keeps the shop and store in a neat and orderly manner ere long becomes a valuable assistant, and the youth who, in addition to these qualifications, is active in the dispatch of business, is certain to make himself useful to those with whom he may engage. The boy

Will not thy own meek heart demand me there ?
That heart whose fondest throb to me was given ?
My name on earth was ever in thy prayer,
And wilt thou never utter it in heaven ?

AGATE.

Experience proves that the apprentice foreshadows the workman, just as surely as the bend of a twig foretells the inclination of the tree. The u p-right, obedient, industrious lad will graduate a steady, skillful and capable man, as unmistakably as the perverse, idling, careless boy will ripen into the lazy, dissolute fellow. The fact is, a boy is measurably the maker of his own destiny, and if he fail to acquire a master-knowledge of the trade to which he .s put, it will mainly be because he did not at the outset determine to be a master-workman. Good morals and steady industry are indispensable. Among the business habits that are highly valued in the apprentice are punctuality, order, neatness and dispatch. The boy who is promptly at his work in the morning soon wins the esteem of his employer. The lad who keeps the shop and store in a neat and orderly manner ere long becomes a

In meadows fanned by heaven's life-breathing wind,
In the resplendence of that glorious sphere,
And larger movements of the unfettered mind,
Wilt thou forget the love that joined us here?

NONPAREIL.

EXPERIENCE proves that the apprentice foreshadows the workman, just as surely as the bend of a twig foretells the inclination of the tree. The upright, obedient, industrious lad will graduate a steady, skillful, and capable man, as unmistakably as the perverse, idling, careless boy will ripen into the lazy, dissolute fellow. The fact is, a boy is measurably the maker of his own destiny; and if he fail to acquire a master-knowledge of the trade to which he is put, it will mainly be because he did not at the outset determine to be a master-workman. Good morals and steady industry are indispensable. Among the business habits that are highly valued in the apprentice are punctuality, order, neatness and dispatch. The boy who is

The love that lived through all the stormy past,
And meekly with my harsher nature bore,
And deeper grew, and tenderer to the last,
Shall it expire with life, and be no more?

MINION.

EXPERIENCE proves that the apprentice foreshadows the workman, just as surely as the bend of a twig foretells the inclination of the tree. The upright, obedient, industrious lad will graduate a steady, skillful, and capable man, as unmistakably as the perverse, idling, careless boy will ripen into the lazy dissolute fellow. The fact is, a boy is measurably the maker of his own destiny; and if he fail to acquire a master-knowledge of the trade to which he is put, it will mainly be because he did not at the outset determine to be a master-workman.

A happier lot than mine, and larger light,
Await thee there; for thou hast bowed thy will
In cheerful homage to the rule of right,
And lovest all, and renderest good for ill.

BREVIER.

EXPERIENCE proves that the apprentice foreshadows the workman, just as surely as the bend of a twig foretells the inclination of the tree. The upright, obedient, industrious lad will graduate a steady, skillful, and capable man, as unmistakably as the perverse, idling, careless boy will ripen into the lazy, dissolute fellow. The fact is, a boy is measurably the maker of his own destiny; and if he fail to acquire a master-knowledge of the trade to which he is

For me, the sordid cares in which I dwell,
  Shrink and consume my heart as heat the scroll,
And wrath has left its scar—that fire of hell
  Has left its frightful scar upon my soul.

LONG PRIMER.

EXPERIENCE proves that the apprentice foreshadows the workman, just as surely as the bend of a twig foretells the inclination of the tree. The upright, obedient, industrious lad will graduate a steady, skillful, and capable man, as unmistakably as the perverse, idling, careless boy will ripen into the lazy, dissolute fellow. The fact is, a boy is

Shalt thou not teach me in that calmer home
  The wisdom that I learned so ill in this—
The wisdom which is love—till I become
  Thy fit companion in that land of bliss?

PICA.

EXPERIENCE proves that the apprentice foreshadows the workman, just as surely as the bend of a twig foretells the inclination of the tree. The upright, obedient, industrious lad will graduate a steady,

skillful, and capable man, as unmistakably as the perverse, idling, careless boy will ripen into the lazy, dissolute fellow. The fact is, a boy is measurably the maker of

GREAT PRIMER.

Experience proves that the apprentice foreshadows the workman, just as surely

as the bend of a twig foretells the inclination of the tree. The upright, obedient,

BOURGEOIS.

EXPERIENCE proves that the apprentice foreshadows the workman, just as surely as the bend of a twig foretells the inclination of the tree. The upright, obedient, industrious lad will graduate a steady, skillful, and capable man, as unmistakably as the perverse, idling, careless boy will ripen into the lazy, dissolute fellow. The fact is, a boy is measurably the maker of his own destiny; and if he fail to acquire a master-knowledge of the trade

Yet, though thou wearest the glory of the sky,
  Wilt thou not keep the same beloved name,
The same fair, thoughtful brow, and gentle eye,
  Lovelier in heaven's sweet climate, yet the same?

SMALL PICA.

EXPERIENCE proves that the apprentice foreshadows the workman, just as surely as the bend of a twig foretells the inclination of the tree. The upright, obedient, industrious lad will graduate a steady, skillful, and capable man, as unmistakably as the perverse, idling, careless boy

will ripen into the lazy, dissolute fellow. The fact is, a boy is measurably the maker of his own destiny; and if he fail to acquire a master-knowledge of the trade to which he is put, it

ENGLISH.

Experience proves that the apprentice foreshadows the workman, just as surely as the bend of a twig foretells the inclination of the tree. The up-

right, obedient, industrious lad will graduate a steady, skillful, and capable man, as unmistakably as the perverse, idling, careless boy will ripen into the

TWO LINE SMALL PICA.

Experience proves that the apprentice foreshadows the workman, just as

surely as the bend of a twig foretells the inclina-

DIRECTIONS FOR READING PROOF.

TYPOGRAPHICAL MARKS

[1] *a*/ Though several differing opinions exist as to
the individual by whom the art of printing was [2] ℔
first discovered, yet all authorities concur in
admitting Peter Schoeffer to be the person [3] *Caps*
who invented *cast metal types*, having learned
[4] ℔ the art of of *cutting* the letters from the Gut-
[5] :/ enbergs/ he is also supposed to have been
[6] ✳ the first whoengraved on copper plates. The [7] /-/
following testimony is preseved in the family, [8] *z*/
[9] ‿ by Jo. Fred. Faustus, of Ascheffenburg:
[10] ☐ > 'Peter Schoeffer, of Gernsheim, perceiving [5] < ✳
[11] ⩘ his master Fausts design, and being himself *S. Caps.*
[12] *tr.* (desirous ardently) to improve the art, found
out (by the good providence of God) the
method of cutting (*incidendi*) the characters [13] *stet.*
in a *matrix*, that the letters might easily be
[5] / singly *cast*/ instead of bieng *cut*. He pri- [12] *ei*/
[14] ⊥ vately *cut matrices*| for the whole alphabet: ∧ [15]
Faust was so pleased with the contrivance,
/that he promised Peter to give him his only [17] *w.f.*
[16] /daughter Christina in marriage, a promise [3] *Ital.*
/which he soon after performed.
[19] *as*/ (But there were many difficulties at first [18] *no* ¶
with these *letters*, as there had been before [3] *Rom.*
[20] + with wooden ones, the metal being too soft [3] *Ital.*
to support the force of the impression: but [9] ⌒/
this defect was soon remedied, by mixing
a substance with the metal which sufficiently *tr.* [12]
[5] ⊙ hardened it/'

and when he showed his master the
letters cast from these matrices.

EXEMPLIFIED.

Though several differing opinions exist as to
the individual by whom the art of printing was
first discovered, yet all authorities concur in
admitting PETER SCHOEFFER to be the
person who invented *cast metal types*, having
learned the art of *cutting* the letters from the
Gutenbergs: he is also supposed to have been
the first who engraved on copper-plates. The
following testimony is preserved in the family,
by Jo. Fred. Faustus, of Ascheffenburg:

'Peter Schoeffer, of Gernsheim, perceiving his master Faust's design, and being himself ardently desirous to improve the art, found
out (by the good providence of God) the
method of cutting (*incidendi*) the characters in
a *matrix*, that the letters might easily be singly
cast, instead of being *cut*. He privately *cut*
matrices for the whole alphabet: and when he
showed his master the letters cast from these
matrices, Faust was so pleased with the contrivance, that he promised Peter to give him
his only daughter *Christina* in marriage, a
promise which he soon after performed. But
there were as many difficulties at first with
these letters, as there had been before with
wooden ones, the metal being too soft to support the force of the impression: but this defect
was soon remedied, by mixing the metal with
a substance which sufficiently hardened it.'

EXPLANATION OF THE CORRECTIONS.

Mackellar's American Printer gives the following rules for correcting proof which will be found
of convenience to all who write for the press:

A wrong letter in a word is noted by drawing a short perpendicular line through it, and making another short line in
the margin, behind which the right letter is placed. (See No. 1.)
In this manner whole words are corrected, by drawing a line
across the wrong word and making the right one in the margin
opposite.

A turned letter is noted by drawing a line through it, and
writing the mark No. 2 in the margin.

If letters or words require to be altered from one character
to another, a parallel line or lines must be made underneath
the word or letter,—viz. for capitals, three lines; small capitals, two lines; and Italics, one line; and, in the margin opposite the line where the alteration occurs, *Caps*, *Small Caps*, or
Ital. must be written. (See No. 3.)

When letters or words are set double, or are required to be
taken out, a line is drawn through the superfluous word or
letter, and the mark No. 4 placed opposite in the margin.

Where the punctuation requires to be altered, the correct
point, marked in the margin, should be encircled.

When a space is omitted between two words or letters which should be separated, a caret must be made where the separation ought to be, and the sign No. 6 placed opposite in the margin.

No. 7 describes the manner in which the hyphen and ellipsis line are marked.

When a letter has been omitted, a caret is put at the place of omission, and the letter marked as No. 8.

Where letters that should be joined are separated, or where a line is too widely spaced, the mark No. 9 must be placed under them, and the correction denoted by the marks in the margin.

Where a new paragraph is required, a quadrangle is drawn in the margin, and a caret placed at the beginning of the sentence. (See No. 10.)

No. 11 shows the way in which the apostrophe, inverted commas, the star and other references, and superior letters and figures, are marked.

Where two words are transposed, a line is drawn over one word and below the other, and the mark No. 12 placed in the margin; but where several words require to be transposed, their right order is signified by a figure placed over each word, and the mark No. 12 in the margin.

Where words have been struck out, that have afterward been approved of, dots should be marked under them, and *Stet.* written in the margin. (See No. 13.)

Where a space sticks up between two words, a horizontal line is drawn under it, and the mark No. 14 placed opposite, in the margin.

Where several words have been left out, they are transcribed at the bottom of the page, and a line drawn from the place of omission to the written words (see No 15); but if the omitted matter is too extensive to be copied at the foot of the page, *Out, see copy*, is written in the margin, and the missing lines are enclosed between brackets, and the word *Out*, is inserted in the margin of the copy.

Where letters stand crooked, they are noted by a line (see No. 16); but, where a page hangs, lines are drawn across the entire part affected.

When a smaller or larger letter, of a different font, is improperly introduced into the page, it is noted by the mark No. 17, which signifies wrong font.

If a paragraph is improperly made, a line is drawn from the broken-off matter to the next paragraph, and *No* ¶ written in the margin. (See No. 18.)

Where a word has been left out or is to be added, a caret must be made in the place where it should come in, and the word written in the margin. (See No. 19.)

Where a faulty letter appears, it is marked by making a cross under it, and placing a similar one in the margin (see No. 20); though some prefer to draw a perpendicular line through it, as in the case of a wrong letter.

MARKS USED IN CORRECTING PROOF.

⊘	Turn letter.
☐	Indent line one em quadrat.
ℒ	Take out ; expunge.
∧	The caret shows where the letter or word is omitted.
#	Insert space.
⌢	Less space.
⌣	Close up entirely.
ℒ #	Remove type, and insert a space, in place of what is removed.
ℒ ⌣	Take out type, and close up.
✕	Bad type.
⟂	Push down space.
⊥	Plane down a letter.
⌇	No paragraph.
------	Placed under erased words, restores them.
Stet.	Written in the margin, restores a cancelled word or words that have dots under them.
¶	Begin a paragraph.
/	Letters stand crooked.
/-/	Should be a compound word.
⊏ or ∟	Remove to the left.
⊐ or ⌐	Remove to the right.
⌐	Carry higher up on page.
∟	Carry down.
≡	Three lines, beneath writing, denote capitals.
=	Two lines, beneath writing, denote small capitals.
—	One line, beneath writing, denotes italics.
w. f.	Wrong font type.
tr.	Transpose letters, words or sentences.
l. c.	Lower case, or small letters.
s. c.	Small capitals.
⊙	Period.
⊙	Colon.
⁊	Calls attention to some doubtful word or sentence.

Pen and Pencil Flourishing.

Carrie Belden.

Down where the lilies grow wild and white,
I'll bathe in the waters, sparkling and bright.

FLORENCE GERTRUDE.

'The path of sorrow and that path alone
Leads to the land where sorrow is unknown.'

"For Time will teach thee soon the truth,
There are no birds in last year's nests."

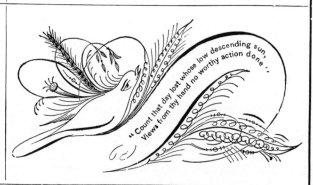

"Count that day lost whose low descending sun,
Views from thy hand no worthy action done."

Adelaide.

A. McCOLLINS.

JACKSON, N.Y.

BRUSH LETTERS FOR MARKING PURPOSES—MODERN STYLE.

ABCDEFGHIJKLMNOPQRSTUVWX
YZ&...abcdefghijklmnopqrstuvwxyz.
1234567890.

Enquire,Huntington,Chicago,Rochester,
Buffalo,Cleveland,Milwaukee,Ohio.

Hill Standard Book Co.,
No. 103 State St.,
Chicago, Ill's.

PLAIN ROMAN LETTERS.

A B C D E F G H I J K L
M N O P Q R S T U V W
X Y Z . & Æ Œ
a b c d e f g h i j k l m n o p q
r s t u v w x y z . æ œ 1 2 3 4 5
6 7 8 9 0 . $ £

ANTIQUE POINTED EXTENDED.

A B C D E F G H I J K
L M N O P Q R S T U V
W X Y Z & .
1 2 3 4 5 6 7 8 9 0 .

ONE-HAND DEAF AND DUMB ALPHABET.

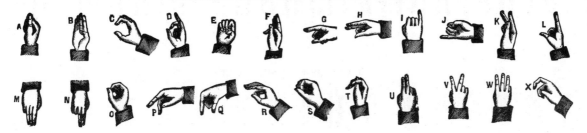

DORIC.

A B C D E F G H I J K L M N O P
Q R S T U V W X Y Z ?
a b c d e f g h i j k l m n o p q r s
t u v w x y z & $ 1 2 3 4 5 6 7 8 9 0 .

POINTED CONDENSED.

A B C D E F G H I J K L M N O P Q R S T
U V W X Y Z & $ 1 2 3 4 5 6 7 8 9 0 ? .

OLD ENGLISH TITLE TEXT.

A B C D E F G H I J K L M

N O P Q R S T U V W X Y Z

a b c d e f g h i j k l m n o p q r s t u v w x y z

OLD ENGLISH FANCY TEXT.

A B C D E F G H I J K L M N O P

R S V W X Y Z &

a b c d e f g h i j k l m n o p q r s t u v w x y z.

MEDIEVAL.

A B C D E F G H I J K L M N

O P Q R S T U V W F Y Z C

a b c d e f g h i j k l m n o p q r s t u

v w x y z. 1 2 3 4 5 6 7 8 9 0.

FIREMAN'S HERALD.

PRIZE.

WHEREAS,

THE · PUBLISHERS · OF · THE

Fireman's Herald,

OF

New York City,

UPON THE 19TH DAY OF   JANUARY, 1882,

a prize of an engrossed OFFERED Pen and ink premium for the best set of

COMPANY BY LAWS, BLANKS AND ROLL,

THIS IS TO CERTIFY THAT

THE Passaic Steam Fire

Engine Co. No. 1,

OF

PATERSON, N.J.

HAS BEEN AWARDED THE

SAID PRIZE.

In Testimony Whereof we the undersigned Judges have hereunto affixed our signatures on this the twelfth day of October A.D. 1882.

(The signatures of the committee of award are here omitted for want of room.)

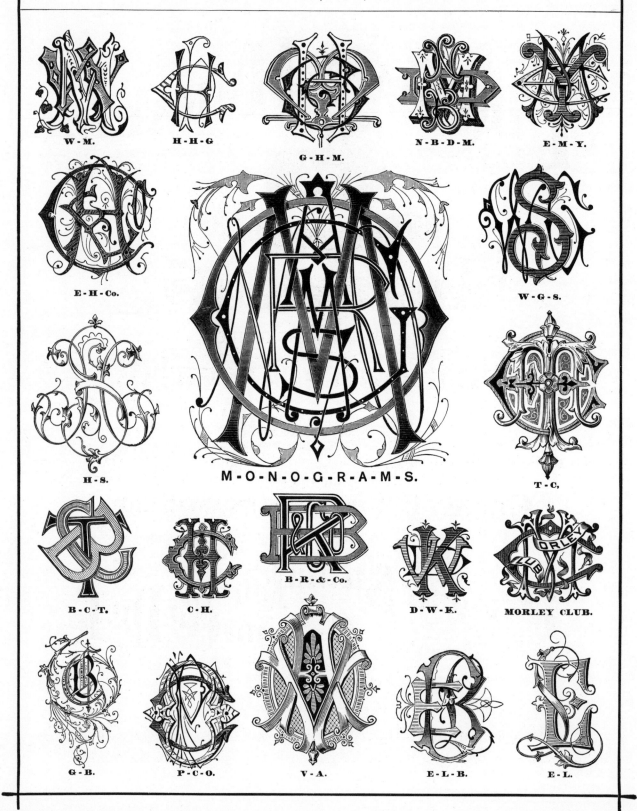

W · M.

H · H · G

G · H · M.

N · B · D · M.

E · M · Y.

E · H · Co.

W · G · S.

H · S.

M · O · N · O · G · R · A · M · S.

T · C,

B · C · T.

C · H.

B · R · & · Co.

D · W · K.

MORLEY CLUB.

G · B.

P · C · O.

V · A.

E · L · B.

E · L.

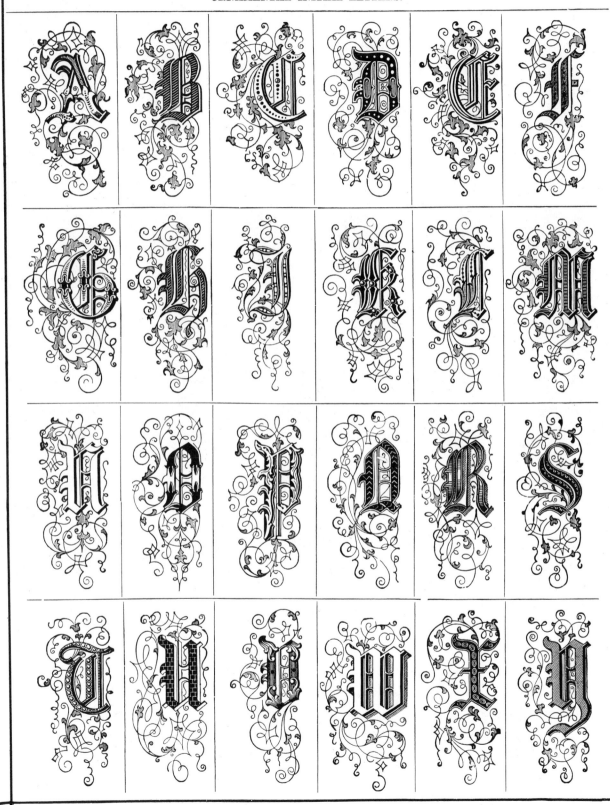

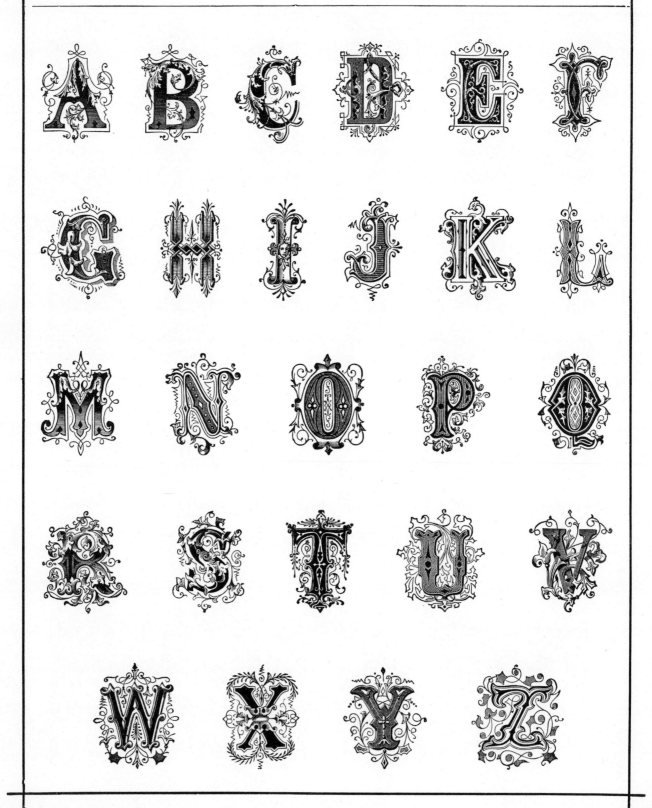

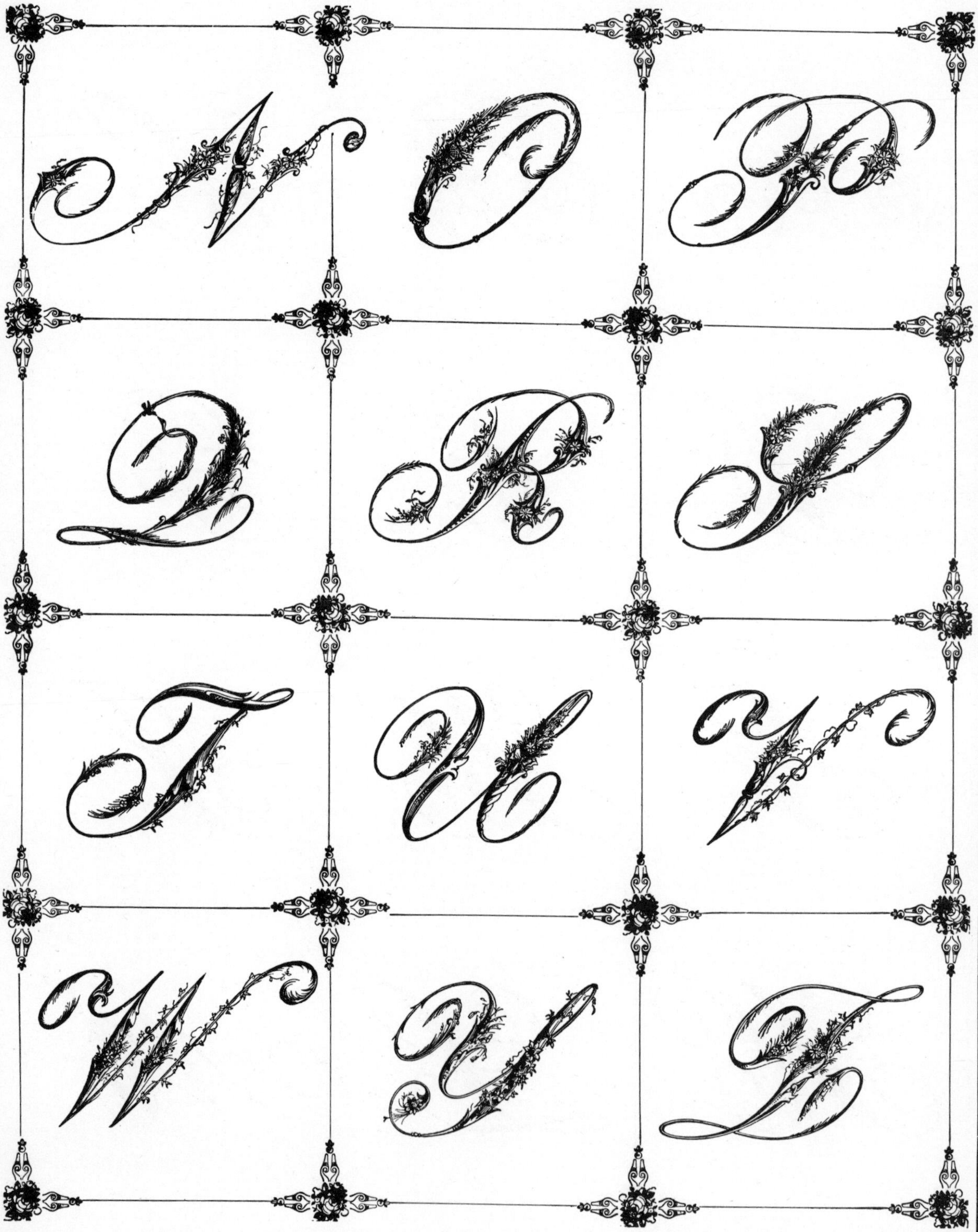
N O P
Q R S
T U V
W X Z

Illustrations of the Proper Wording and Punctuation of Sign Writing.

Unusually Large Marks are used to Distinctly Illustrate Punctuation.

The following samples of Signs will be found convenient by Sign Writers as showing correct punctuation.

BANK.

POST-OFFICE.

JOHN SMITH.

JOHN HENRY SMITH.

J. H. SMITH.

JOHN H. SMITH.

CHARLES SMITH. HENRY JONES.

C. SMITH & H. JONES.

SMITH & JONES.

The period (.) is used at the end of every sentence, even if it be but one word; as, *Bank. Merchant Tailor. John Smith. William Jones, Dealer in Hats, Caps and Furs.* The period is also used to show the omission of letters, at the last of a name or word, called abbreviation; as *Co.* for *Company; H. J. Smith* for *Henry James Smith.* In the abbreviation of *Chas., Wm., Thos., Jas., Robt., Bros.,* and *Saml.,* while the rule is to use the apostrophe, it is customary to use the period.

The comma (,) is used, in sign painting, to show the omission of words. This is shown in the following sentences:

Brown and West and Co. are Dealers in Paints and Oils and Glass, and so forth.

To avoid repeating the *and* we use the comma, thus:

Brown, West & Co., Dealers in Paints, Oils, Glass, &c.

The apostrophe (') is used to show the omission of letters, in the beginning or middle of a word, thus: *'t is* for *it is;* *'t were* for *it were;*

'73 for 1873; *comp'y* for *company*; *pack'g* for *packing*; *d's* for *days*; *m's* for *months*; *y's* for *years*; *gen'l ag't* for *general agent*, etc.

The apostrophe is also used to show the possessive, thus: *Brown's Bank.* If the owner's name terminates with an *s*, the apostrophe follows the *s*; as, *Wells' Bank, Briggs' Store.* If two or more persons are spoken of, in the possessive, the apostrophe follows the *s*; as, *Ladies' Entrance; Gents' Parlor; Tomlinson Brothers' Bank.* If, however, the person's name takes the character of an adjective, describing the article, no apostrophe is required; as, *Briggs House; Merchants Bank.*

This character (*&*) stands for *and*, and came originally from *Et.*, Etc. in script, the Latin abbreviation for *et cetera*—"and the rest." The first is used in connecting firm names, and the other at the end to avoid details. Thus, *Smith & Brown;* or *Smith, Brown & Co., Dealers in Groceries, Provisions, &c.*

Where the placing of a period or other mark, after a letter or figure, would decidedly injure the appearance of the same, good taste may suggest that such mark be omitted. See Nos. 44 and 42, next page.

For other marks in punctuation, see page 52.

A light faced letter is used in the following advertisements, to illustrate the punctuation conspicuously.

NORTH AMERICA

FIRE & MARINE INSURANCE COMPANY,

ST. LOUIS, MISSOURI.

CAPITAL, - - - - $200,000.

OFFICERS:

J. HARTLEY WELLS, *Pres't.*   DAVID BRIGGS, *Sec'y.*

S. & J.

EDITOR.

EDITOR'S ROOM.

SUPT'S OFFICE.

LADIES' PARLOR.

TREASURER'S OFFICE.

DRY GOODS.

MERCHANT TAILOR.

JONES SCHOOL.

BRIGGS HOUSE.

METROPOLITAN HOTEL.

JONES' STORE.

FRESH AND SALT MEATS.

FIRST NATIONAL BANK.

PROF. A. B. COOK.

DR. HENRY WING.

SAML. H. SMITH, M.D.

FIRE INS. COMP'Y.

A. M. EXPRESS CO.

AMERICAN PACK'G CO.

JONES BROS., WEST & HOYT.

PAGE BROS.' BLOCK.

WELLS, WADE BROS. & COOK.

Mc MICKEN & St. CLAIR.

St. CLAIR BROS.' EXCHANGE.

MEN'S AND BOYS' CLOTHING.

CHILDREN'S UNDERGARMENTS.

BENNETT & PETERS.

STOVES AND HARDWARE.

SMITH, JONES & BLACK.

HARDWARE, CUTLERY, ETC.

MRS. WM. HENRY WEST.

MILLINERY AND FANCY GOODS.

C. CLINTON BROWN,

ATTORNEY AND COUNSELOR.

DE LAND & Mc GANN.

44   BROWN BROTHERS.   44

42   BRAINARD'S SONS.   42

C. S. BELDON, CLARK & CO.

DRUGGISTS' SUNDRIES.

F. BURT, SHAW & SONS,

REAL ESTATE AND LOAN AG'TS.

St. CLAIR BROS. & SONS,

GEN'L AGENTS.

D. O. WELLS, BRIGGS & SONS,

AG'TS N. W. MANUF'G CO.

HIRAM BROWN,

DEALER IN

BOOTS AND SHOES.

H. O. SMITH,

DEALER IN

LUMBER.

HOYT & WEBSTER,

DEALERS IN

PAINTS, OILS, GLASS, ETC.

WILLIAMS & CO.,

DEALERS IN

HATS, CAPS, FURS, ETC.

BRIGGS, WELLS & CO.,

WHOLESALE AND RETAIL DEALERS IN

BOOKS, WALL-PAPER & STATIONERY.

JONES, COX & CO.,

MANUFACTURERS AND DEALERS IN

HARDWARE, CUTLERY AND STOVES ;

ALSO, GEN'L AG'TS FOR

AURORA SILVER-PLATE MANUF'G CO.

WEBB & GREEN,

GEN'L AG'TS FOR THE

N. W. MANUFACTURING COMPANY ;

AND DEALERS IN

R. R. SUPPLIES, PIG IRON AND LEAD.

FIRE AND MARINE INSURANCE.

WESTERN INSURANCE COMPANY ;

CLEVELAND, O.

PAID-UP CAPITAL, $2,000,000 IN U. S. BONDS.

CHARLES D. SMITH, AGENT.

A. E. SMALL.   P. D. COOK.

SMALL & COOK,

ATTORNEYS AND COUNSELORS AT LAW ;

ROOM 15, STEVENS BLOCK,

OFFICE HOURS: { 9 TO 12 A. M.
               { 2 TO 6 P. M.   MILWAUKEE.

NORTHERN LIGHT, NO 8 ;

MANUFACTURED BY

FRIDLEY, ST. ANNE & BROTHER,

ELKHART, IND.

PATENTED, AUG. 1, 1870. RE-ISSUED, SEPT. 10, 1872.

SHNIEDEWEND, LEE & CO.,

ELECTROTYPERS ;

MANUFACTURERS OF

LABOR-SAVING SLUGS, METAL FURNITURE, AND SUPERIOR
FINISHED LEADS.

NO. 111 E. MADISON ST., CHICAGO, ILL.

ST. CLAIRE & McCLURE,

SUCCESSORS TO HATCH BROS. ;

HEADQUARTERS FOR THE

" COSMOPOLITAN," " STEWART," AND
" WESTERN HOME," COOKING STOVES.

NO. 44 MAPLE ST., ST. LOUIS, MO.

PUSH ALONG !   KEEP MOVING !

CHAS. McGILL,

THE HOUSE-MOVER.

ADDRESS P. O. BOX 1,108, OR CALL AT 91 PECK AVE.,

SALEM, MASS.

BLACK BROS. & CO.,

WHOLESALE CLOTHING HOUSE ;

HEADQUARTERS FOR

GENTS' FURNISHING GOODS AND FURS.

70 BROADWAY, UP STAIRS, ST. CROIX, ILL.

THE LARGEST GENTS' FURNISHING HOUSE IN THE WORLD.

OAK HALL CLOTHING EMPORIUM,

NOS. 148, 150, 152 AND 154 PRINDLE ST.

HOWARD'S LARGE OVEN,

AIR-TIGHT, SUMMER AND WINTER COOKING STOVE.

PAT'D MAY 4, 1871.

OSCAR D. HOWARD.

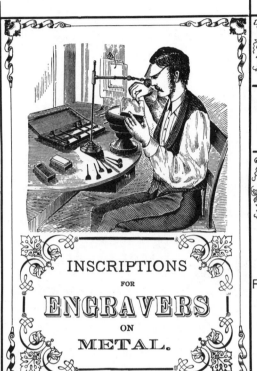

INSCRIPTIONS
FOR
ENGRAVERS
ON
METAL.

Engravers' Inscriptions.

Wording and Punctuation of Inscriptions for Engraving.

Forms of Wording, appropriate in marking Rings, Spoons, Pins, Coffin-Plates, Cane-Heads, Watches, Silverware, etc., for use in Presentation on the occasion of Weddings, Marriage Anniversaries, Birthdays, etc., etc.

STYLES OF LETTERING.

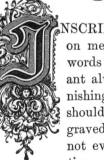

INSCRIPTIONS to be engraved on metal, should be in as few words as possible. It is important always that the person furnishing the copy to the engraver should write the words to be engraved in the plainest manner, not even omitting the punctuation. Care should be taken to plainly distinguish the I from the J, and other letters, that in script are likely to be taken for others. Special care should also be observed in spelling.

The following forms of wording, styles of lettering, punctuation, and arrangement of sentences will be found serviceable, both for the engraver and those persons who wish to have engraving executed.

Carrie Jane.	I. O. O. F.	Charles Horton.
MINE EVER.	To My Husband.	REMEMBER.
Mrs. D. Williams.	To My Sister.	FORGET ME NOT.

From a Friend.

Gift of Friendship.

A. F. A. M.

Mary.

Christmas, 1870.

Chas. O. Wilson;

From a Friend.

Susan.

XMAS. 1872.

C. D. Briggs & Minnie Buck.

July 7, 1871.

Martin Wells to May King.

December 26, 1869.

William H. Brown.

JANUARY 1, 1869.

Jas. H. Kendall.

Aged 25 y'rs, 3 m's.

OUR

Little Willie.

George R. Hoyt.

Born, May 12, 1835.

PRESENTED
—TO—
Hoyt L. Wilson;
BY
EMPLOYEES, CAR DEP'T,
N. W. R. R.
April 4th, 1873.
Chicago, Ill.

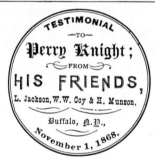

TESTIMONIAL
—TO—
Perry Knight;
FROM
HIS FRIENDS,
L. Jackson, W. W. Coy & H. Munson.
Buffalo, N. Y.,
November 1, 1868.

TO
Capt. A. Benson;
FROM
His Comrades of Co. E,
44th Regt., Ill. Vol's.
CHICAGO, ILL.
Jan. 1, 1863.

Mother;

From MARY.

CHRISTMAS, 1873.

Kittie;

FROM HER FATHER.

Lizzie D. Smith;

From Her Father. May 12, 1873.

Fannie W. Brown;

From Her Mother.

18th Birthday, June 10th, 1873.

Harvey D. Kent;

FROM

Father and Mother.

21st Birthday.

Mother;

From HER CHILDREN.

Christmas, 1872.

Mr. & Mrs. Jas. C. Black.

25th Anniversary Wedding;

August 17th, 1873:

FROM

THEIR MANY FRIENDS.

PRESENTED TO

Mr. & Mrs. R. Coy;

BY

Mr. & Mrs. Browning.

Apr. 1, 1868.

Mr. & Mrs. King;

FROM

Their Many Friends,

AS A TOKEN OF

Esteem and Respect.

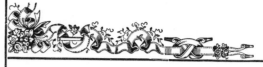

Tomb-Stone Inscriptions.

Wording and Punctuation.

USUAL recent wording of Tomb-Stone Inscriptions is shown in the following. In comparison, it will be seen that the modern inscription is generally much more brief than that of the olden time. Formerly it was customary to chisel in rude letters epitomized biographical histories of the deceased on the tomb-stones that marked their last resting place. Among such are many quaint, curious and foolish inscriptions that, so far as perpetuating the memories of the deceased was concerned, had better never have been engraved on the headstones.

The lesson taught in these examples is, that the more concise the inscription, the more favorably coming generations will judge of the handful of dust that lies beneath the leaning tombstone. The most approved modern forms, accompanied by epitaphs, are shown herewith, together with the correct grammatical wording and punctuation of the same. The following appropriately accompany the inscription.

Brief Epitaphs.

Father.	Our Mother.	Charlie.
All is Well.	Gone Home.	Christ is my Hope.
Darling Sister.	Gone, but not Forgotten.	The Morning Cometh.
We will Meet again.	Rest, Darling Sister, Rest.	Dying is but Going Home.
Over in the Summer Land.	In after Time we'll meet Her.	There shall be no Night there.
Absent, not Dead.	Gentle, Sweet little Freddie.	They are not Dead.

Lillie.

She faltered by the wayside, and
the Angels took her home.

MINNIE,

INFANT DAUGHTER OF

L. & M. Binninger,

DIED

Sept. 15th, 1873. AGED 1 Mo. & 15 D's.

Beneath this stone, in soft repose,
Is laid a mother's dearest pride;
A flower that scarce had waked to life
And light and beauty, ere it died.

TRUMAN MARTIN,

Aged 60 Years. August 2, 1870.

Harriet Theresa,

WIFE OF

F. D. Stevenson,

AGED 41 Years. Oct. 4, 1872.

"I Fear not Death."

Little Johnny,

DIED

November 1st, 1871. AGED 5 Y's & 8 M's.

" 'Tis a little grave, but O, have care,
For world-wide hopes are buried there,
How much of light, how much of joy,
Is buried with a darling boy."

Harvey J. Belden,

CAPT. OF

51st Regiment, Illinois Vols.,

Killed at the Battle of Perryville,

October 8th, 1863.

Aged 51 Y's, 6 M's, 10 D's.

Darling Freddie.

The Angels called Him.

MARY ELLEN,

WIFE OF

Chas. Williamson,

Born at Keene, N. H., Jan. 8, 1805.

Born into Spirit Life Sept. 6th, 1865.

NOT DEAD, BUT GONE BEFORE.

H. W. Billings.

December 1, 1872. Aged 36 Years.

CHARLES H.,

SON OF

Thos. & A. Smith,

DIED

December 25th, 1870. AGED 4 Y'S, 3 M'S & 4 D'S.

SACRED

to the Memory of

WHO DEPARTED THIS LIFE

August 10, 1871. Aged 50 Years.

"I go to prepare a place for thee."

Rev. G. Wells,

BORN, DIED,

Sept. 21st, 1841. Nov. 21st, 1872.

He Died as He Lived—a Christian.

Hon. M. Randall,

DIED

August 15, 1869. AGED 61 Years.

A Member of the U.S. Congress for 20 Years, he
died as he lived, a pure and upright man.

Wm. D. Hubbard,

Dec. 28th, 1873. Aged 92 Y's, 8 M's.

"Farewell to thee, my house of clay!
Long have we two been bound together,
But I forsake thy porch to-day,
And yield thee up to wind and weather.
Sleep, sleep at last ! thy sleep shall be
My rest, my strength, my victory !"

Our Mother,

Died October 5, 1869. AGED 61 Years.

MINNIE B. PHELPS,

BORN INTO SUMMER LAND

Sept. 1st, 1872. Aged 19 Y's, 3 M's.

DARLING SISTER ;

" Yet, though thou wear'st the glory of the sky,
We know thou'lt keep the same beloved name ;
The same fair, thoughtful brow and gentle eye,
Lovelier in heaven a sweet climate, yet the same."

Mary L. Palmer,

ENTERED SPIRIT LIFE

September 9, 1872. Aged 38 Y's, 6 M's.

"O land beyond the setting sun !
O realm more fair than poet's dream !
How clear thy silvery streamlets run,
How bright thy golden glories gleam !
For well we know that fair and bright,
Far beyond human ken or dream,
Too glorious for our feeble sight,
Thy skies of cloudless azure beam."

Herbie :

The angels called him on a sunny day,
August 15th, 1872.

AGED 5 Y'S, 6 M'S, 4 D'S.

" We shall all go home to our Father's house,
To our Father's house in the skies,
Where the hope of our souls shall have no blight,
And our love no broken ties :
We shall roam on the banks of the River of Peace,
And bathe in its blissful tide :
And one of the joys of our heaven shall be,
The little boy that died."

Selections for Epitaphs.

GLEANINGS FROM THE POETS.

Brief Extracts from the Best Poems, suitable to accompany Tomb-Stone Inscriptions.

EVERY inscription on tomb-stones may appropriately be accompanied by an epitaph, which should be expressive yet very brief. Formerly it was customary oftentimes to inscribe several stanzas of poetry upon the headstone. With the improved taste of later years, however, it is considered best to condense the epitaph into a few words, usually not exceeding four lines in length.

The following appropriate stanzas for epitaphs are culled from the best poems:

'We saw not the angels who met him there,
The gates of the city we could not see.
Over the river, over the river,
My darling stands waiting to welcome me."

"Amiable, she won all; intelligent, she charmed all; fervent, she loved all; and dead, she saddened all."

"He carries the lambs in his bosom."

"Rest in peace, thou gentle spirit,
Throned above —
Souls like thine with God inherit
Life and love."

"I love them that love me, and those that seek me early shall find me."

"Judge not the Lord by feeble sense,
But trust Him for His grace;
Behind a frowning providence,
He hides a smiling face."

"Not thus his nobler part shall dwell
A prisoner in this narrow cell;
But he, whom we now hide from men,
With youth renewed, shall live again."

"Death, thou art but another birth,
Freeing the spirit from the clogs of earth."

"Ay, hold it true, whate'er befall,
And feel it, when we sorrow most,
'T is better to have loved and lost,
Than to have never loved at all."

"Shed not for her the bitter tear,
     Nor give the heart to vain regret;
'T is but the casket that lies here,
     The gem that filled it sparkles yet."

———

"Sheltered and safe from sorrow."

———

"Ere sin could harm, or sorrow fade,
     Death came with friendly care;
The opening bud to heaven conveyed,
     And bade it blossom there."

———

"Happy infant, early blest!
     Rest, in peaceful slumbers, rest."

———

"This lovely bud, so young, so fair,
     Called hence by early doom,
Just came to show how sweet a flower
     In Paradise would bloom."

———

"Suffer little children to come unto me."

———

"There, in the Shepherd's bosom,
     White as the drifted snow,
Is the little lamb we missed one morn,
     From the household flock below."

———

"Sweet flower, transplanted to a clime
     Where never comes the blight of time."

———

"So the bird of my bosom fluttered up to the dawn,
A window was opened — my darling was gone!
A truant from time, from tears, and from sin,
For the angel on watch took the wanderer in."

———

"O Death! where is thy sting? O Grave! where
     is thy victory?"

———

"From meadows fanned by heaven's life-breathing
     wind,
In the resplendence of that glorious sphere,
And larger movements of the unfettered mind,
Come darling, oft, and meet me here."

———

"A happier lot than ours, and larger light, sur-
     rounds thee there."

———

"Gone to a land of pure delight,
     Where saints immortal reign;
Infinite day excludes the night,
     And pleasures banish pain."

———

"Though I walk through the valley of the shadow
     of death, I will fear no evil, for Thou
               art with me."

———

"Triumphant smiles the victor's brow,
     Fanned by some angel's purple wing.
Where is, O grave, thy victory now?
     And where, insidious death, thy sting?"

———

"Thy rod and Thy staff, they comfort me."

———

"Sweet is the scene when virtue dies!
     When sinks a righteous soul to rest,
How mildly beam the closing eyes,
     How gently heaves the expanding breast!"

———

"Here I lay my burden down,
     Change the cross into the crown."

———

"I shall know the loved who have gone before,
     And joyfully sweet will the meeting be,
When over the river, the peaceful river,
     The angel of death shall carry me."

———

"Because I lived, ye shall live also."

———

"Life is real, life is earnest,
     And the grave is not its goal;
'Dust thou art, to dust returnest,'
     Was not spoken of the soul."

———

"Of such is the kingdom of Heaven "

" Dear is the spot where Christians sleep,
 And sweet the strains that angels pour.
O ! why should we in anguish weep ?
 They are not lost, but gone before."

————

" I am the resurrection and the life."

————

" From darkness and from woe,
 A power like lightning darts ;
A glory cometh down to throw
 Its shadow o'er our hearts."

————

" Heaven's eternal year is thine."

————

" Known and unknown, human, divine,
 Sweet darling hand and lips and eye ;
Dear heavenly one, thou canst not die,
 Mine, mine forever, ever mine."

————

" Death loves a shining mark."

————

" Life's duty done, as sinks the day,
 Light from its load the spirit flies ;
While heaven and earth combine to say,
 How blest the righteous when he dies."

————

" He giveth his beloved sleep."

————

" Gone before us, O our brother,
 To the spirit land !
Vainly look we for another,
 In thy place to stand."

————

" Her children rise up and call her blessed."

" She was but as a smile,
 Which glistens in a tear,
Seen but a little while,
 But, oh ! how loved, how dear !"

————

" We loved her."

————

" We only know that thou hast gone,
 And that the same returnless tide,
Which bore thee from us, still glides on,
 And we, who mourn thee, with it glide."

————

" There shall be no night there."

————

" Green be the turf above thee,
 Friend of my better days ;
None knew thee but to love thee,
 Nor named thee but to praise."

————

" I know his face is hid
 Under the coffin lid ;
Closed are his eyes ; cold is his forehead fair.
 My hand that marble felt,
 O'er it in prayer I knelt ;
Yet my heart whispers that — he is not here."

————

" Far off thou art, but ever nigh ;
 I have thee still, and I rejoice."

————

" To us for sixteen anxious months,
 His infant smile was given,
And then he bade farewell to earth
 And went to live in heaven."

————

" Where immortal spirits reign,
 There we shall meet again."

"Poetry is the blossom and fragrance of all human knowledge, human thoughts, human passions, emotions, language."—COLERIDGE.

GENTLE stillness of a spring-time evening, when, with heart attuned to the glories of the twilight scene, we listen enraptured to the closing song of busy nature, hushing to repose — *this is poetry!*

The coming storm, preceded by the rushing wind; the dark, angry, approaching clouds, capped with the flashing, darting lightning, with the low muttering, and anon the deep-toned thunder, coming nearer and nearer in its awful grandeur! To the lover of the grand and sublime — *this is poetry!*

The silvery quiet of the moonlight night, when we wander amid the jessamines and roses, with our darling, whispering words of love, and dreaming of the future — *this is poetry!*

The midnight hour in the attic, when, through the crevices of the roof and windows, we catch glimpses of the flashing lightning, and listen, slumber, and dream to the music of the pattering rain-drops on the roof — *this is poetry!*

The roaring cataract, the silvery rivulet, the towering mountain, the dark ravine, the open-ing rosebud, the cherub child, the waving grain, the modest violet, — *all breathe the music of poetry!*

The beautiful face, the gentle, thrilling pressure of the hand, the kettle singing for tea, the joyous meeting of the husband and wife on the return from labor at the twilight hour, the smile, the kiss — *all this is poetry!*

It flashes in the sky, it blossoms on the earth, it breathes music in the air, delighting the eye, charming the ear, and filling the soul with ineffable happiness — *all this is poetry!*

To appreciate, to comprehend, and to interpret this golden, sunny halo of beauty, is the gift of the poet.

Poetry is not necessarily told in rhyme. It is oftentimes revealed as beautifully in prose. B. F. Taylor illustrates this very strikingly in the following description of

The Old Church.

"Last evening we were walking leisurely along. The music of choirs in three churches came floating out into the darkness around us, and they were all new and strange tunes but one; and that one, it was not sung as we had heard it, but it awakened a train of long buried memories, that rose to us even as they were before the cemetery of the soul had a tomb in it. It was sweet old 'Corinth' they were singing—strains that we have seldom heard since the rose-color of life was blanched—and we were in a moment back again to the old church ; and it was a summer afternoon, and yellow sunbeams were streaming through the west windows, and the silver hair of the old deacon who sat in the pulpit was turned to gold in its light, and the minister, who, we used to think, could never die, so good was he, had concluded 'application' and 'exhortation,' and the village choir were singing the last hymn, and the tune was 'Corinth.'

"It is years—we dare not think how many—since then, and the prayers of 'David the son of Jesse' are ended, and the choir scattered and gone—the girl with blue eyes that sang alto, and the girl with black eyes that sang air ; the eyes of one were like a June heaven at noon, and the other like the same heaven at night. They both became wives, and both mothers, and both died. Who shall say they are not singing 'Corinth' still, where Sabbaths never wane, and congregations never break up ? There they sat, Sabbath after Sabbath, by the square column at the right of the 'leader,' and to our young ears their tunes were 'the very soul of music.' That column bears still their penciled names, as they wrote them in those days in life's June, 183—, before dreams of change had overcome their spirits like a summer's cloud.

"Alas ! that with the old singers most of the sweeter tunes have died upon the air ! But they linger in memory, and they shall yet be sung in the sweet reunion of song that shall take place by and by, in a hall whose columns are beams of morning light, whose ceiling is pearl, whose doors are gold, and where hearts never grow old. Then she that sang alto, and she that sang air, will be in their places once more."

More frequently, however, the poet gives expression to his emotions in rhyme, such form of expression having the advantage of musical sound, accompanied by sentiment. Unfortunately, however, much of that which passes for poetry is but rhyme, being devoid of sense or moral.

For the assistance and guidance of those who would correctly write poetry, we give herewith the rules of versification, accompanied by a vocabulary of rhymes, followed by a number of standard poems from the best authors, that are models in their respective kinds of verse.

Versification.

ERSIFICATION is the art of making verse. Verse is rhythmical language, keeping time like music ; having syllables arranged according to accent, quantity, and generally rhyme ; being so divided into lines as to promote harmony.

Two kinds of verse are in use by poets, namely, *blank verse* and *rhyme*. Rhyme is characterized by a similarity of sound at the end of one line with another ; as

" Perhaps in this neglected spot is . . . . laid
   Some heart once pregnant with celestial . . . fire ;
Hands, that the rod of empire might have . . swayed,
   Or waked to ecstasy the living . . . . lyre."

" The Assyrian came down like a wolf on the . . fold,
   And his cohorts were gleaming with purple and gold."

Blank Verse.

Blank verse is the name given to a kind of poetry without rhyme, which was the form that the earlier poets almost entirely made use of. The poetry of the Greeks and Romans was generally without rhyme, and not until the Middle Ages, when introduced by the Goths from the North, did rhyme come into the Latin and the vernacular tongues of modern Europe.

Blank verse is particularly suited to the drama, and was very popular in the sixteenth century, during which time, and the beginning of the seventeenth century, Shakespeare wrote his plays. The following from Milton's " Paradise Lost " representing Eve's lament and farewell to Eden, written in 1667, illustrates the power of expression in blank verse :

"O unexpected stroke, worse than of death !
Must I thus leave thee, Paradise ? thus leave
Thee, native soil ! these happy walks and shades,
Fit haunt of gods ? where I had hoped to spend,
Quiet though sad, the respite of that day
That must be mortal to us both. O, flowers
That never will in other climate grow,
My early visitation and my last
At even, which I bred up with tender hand
From the first spring bud, and gave ye names !
Who now shall rear thee to the sun, or rank
Your tribes, and water from the ambrosial fount ?
Thee lastly, nuptial bower ? by me adorn'd
By what to sight or smell was sweet ! from thee
How shall I part, and whither wander down
Into a lower world, to this obscure
And wild ? How shall we breathe in other air
Less pure, accustom'd to immortal fruits ?"

Accent and Feet.

Upon careful observation, it will be seen that we involuntarily divide a line of rhythmical verse into meter, by a sort of keeping time with hands and *feet:* accenting at regular intervals certain syllables, thus giving the peculiar musical accompaniment which makes poetry attractive.

There are four kinds of feet in English verse called *Iambus, Trochee, Anapest* and *Dactyl.* The distinguishing characteristic of *Iambic* verse is, that we always accent the second syllable in reading the same; as " Behóld, how gréat."

The *Trochee,* like the Iambus, consists of two syllables, with the accent on the first syllable; as " Sée the dístant fórest dárk and wáving."

The *Anapest* has the first two syllables unaccented, and the last accented; as " O'er the lánd of the frée and the hóme of the bráve."

The *Dactyl* contains three syllables, with the accent on the first; as *dúrable, brávery.*

Meters.

Verse is also named according to the *number* of feet in each line; a foot in Iambic being two syllables. *Monometer* is a line of one foot; *dimeter,* of two feet; *trimeter,* of three feet; *tetrameter,* of four feet; *pentameter,* of five feet; *hexameter,* of six feet; *heptameter,* of seven feet; *octometer,* of eight feet.

Examples.

The following examples represent the *Iambic, Trochaic, Anapestic,* and *Dactylic,* in the different kinds of *meter.* A straight line (ˉ) over a syllable, shows that such syllable is accented. A curved line (˘) indicates the unaccented.

IAMBIC.—*One foot.*

" Thĕy gō
To sow."

IAMBIC.—*Two feet.*

" Tŏ mĕ | thĕ rōse
No longer glows,"

" Thĕir lōve | ănd āwe
Supply | the law."

IAMBIC.—*Three feet.*

" Blŭe lĭght | nĭngs sĭnge | thĕ wāves,
And thunder rends the rock."

IAMBIC.—*Four feet.*

" Ănd cōld | ĕr stĭll | thĕ wīnds | dĭd blōw,
And darker hours of night came on."

IAMBIC.—*Five feet.*

" Fŏr prāise | tŏo dēar | lў lōv'd | ŏr wārm | lў sōught,
Enfeebles all internal strength of thought."

IAMBIC.—*Six feet.*

" Hĭs heārt | ĭs sād, | hĭs hōpe | ĭs gōne, | hĭs lĭght | ĭs pāssed;
He sits and mourns in silent grief the lingering day."

IAMBIC.—*Seven feet.*

" Thĕ lōf | ty hĭll, | thĕ hŭm | blĕ lāwn, | wĭth cŏunt | lĕss beaŭ | tĭes shīne ;
The silent grove, the solemn shade, proclaim thy power divine."

NOTE.—It has become common in writing modern poetry to divide this kind of verse into four lines; alternate lines having four and three feet; thus,—

" The lofty hill, the humble lawn,
With countless beauties shine;
The silent grove, the solemn shade,
Proclaim thy power divine."

IAMBIC.—*Eight feet.*

O āll | yĕ pēo | plĕ, clāp | yŏur hānds, | ănd wĭth | trıum | phănt vōic | ĕs sīng ;
No force the mighty pow'r withstands of God the universal King.

NOTE.—It is common at present to reduce this verse into lines of eight syllables, as follows,—

" O all ye people, clap your hands,
And with triumphant voices sing,
No force the mighty pow'r withstands
Of God the universal King."

Stanza—Long, Short, and Common Meter.

A *stanza* is a combination of several lines in poetry, forming a distinct division of the poem; thus,—

" The curfew tolls the knell of parting day,
The lowing herd winds slowly o'er the lea,
The ploughman homeward plods his weary way,
And leaves the world to darkness and to me."

A Verse.

Verse is but a single line of a stanza, thus,—

" The curfew tolls the knell of parting day."

Long Meter.

The long, short, and common meters are known by the number of feet or syllables found in them. Long meter stanzas contain in each line four Iambic feet, thus —

> "Through every age, eternal God
> Thou art our rest, our safe abode ;
> High was thy throne ere heaven was made,
> Or earth, thy humble footstool, laid."

Short Meter.

Short meter stanzas contain three lines of six syllables, and one of eight syllables — the third line being the longest, and containing four Iambic feet, thus —

> "Sweet is the time of Spring,
> When nature's charms appear ;
> The birds with ceaseless pleasure sing,
> And hail the opening year."

Common Meter.

Iambic verse of seven feet, divided into two lines, the first containing four, and the latter three feet, makes what is known as common meter ; thus —

> "When all thy mercies, O, my God !
> My rising soul surveys,
> Transported with the view, I 'm lost
> In wonder, love, and praise."

Each species of Iambic verse will admit of an additional short syllable ; as

> Ŭpŏn ă mōunt | ăin,
> Bĕsīde ă fōunt | ăin.

Trochaic Verse.

The accent in *Trochaic* verse occurs on the first syllable. The foot consists of two syllables.

TROCHAIC.— *One foot.*

> Chāngĭng.
> Ranging.

TROCHAIC.— *Two feet.*

> Fancў | viĕwĭng,
> Joys ensuing.

TROCHAIC.— *Three feet.*

> "Whĕn thў | heărt ĭs | mōurnĭng."
> "Go where comfort waits thee."

TROCHAIC.— *Four feet.*

> "Rōund ă | hōlў | cālm dĭf | fūsĭng,
> Love of peace and lonely musing."

TROCHAIC.— *Five feet.*

> Āll thăt | wālk ŏn | fōot ŏr | rĭde ĭn | chāriŏts,
> All that dwell in palaces or garrets.

TROCHAIC.— *Six feet.*

> Ōn ă | mōuntăin | strĕtch'd bĕ | nĕath ă | hōarў | wĭllŏw,
> Lay a shepherd swain and viewed the roaring billow.

TROCHAIC.— *Seven feet.*

> Hāstĕn | Lŏrd tŏ | rĕscŭe | mĕ, ănd | sĕt mĕ | sāfe frŏm | trōublĕ,
> Shame thou those who seek my soul, reward their mischief double.

TROCHAIC.— *Eight feet.*

NOTE.— Trochaic and Iambic are frequently found combined in one stanza.

> Ōnce ŭp | ŏn a | mĭdnight | drĕary | whĭle I | pōndered | wĕak and | wĕary
> Over many a quaint and curious volume of forgotten lore.

Anapestic Verse.

Anapestic verse contains three syllables to the foot, with the accent on the last syllable.

ANAPESTIC.— *One foot.*

> "Ŏn thĕ lānd,
> Lĕt mĕ stănd."

ANAPESTIC.— *Two feet.*

> "Bŭt hĭs coŭr | ăge 'găn fāil,
> Fŏr nŏ ârts cŏuld ăvāil."

This form admits of an additional short syllable ; as

> "Bŭt hĭs coŭr | ăge găn fāil | hĭm,
> For no arts could avail him."

ANAPESTIC.— *Three feet.*

> Ŏ yĕ wōods | sprĕad yŏur brănch | ĕs ăpāce,
> Tŏ yŏur deĕpĕst rĕcĕssĕs I hīe ;
> I wŏuld hĭde wĭth thĕ bĕasts ŏf thĕ chāse,
> I wŏuld vănĭsh frŏm ĕvĕrў ēye.

ANAPESTIC.—*Four feet.*

Măy Ĭ gŏv | ĕrn mў pāss | iŏns wĭth āb | sŏlūte swāy,
Ănd grŏw wīsĕr ănd bĕttĕr ăs lĭfe weărs ăwāy.

This measure admits of a short syllable at the end; as

Ŏn thĕ wārm | cheĕk ŏf youth | smīles ănd rŏ | sĕs ăre blēnd | ĭng.

Dactylic Verse.

In *Dactylic* verse the accent occurs on the first syllable of each successive three, being on the first, fourth, seventh, and tenth syllables.

DACTYLIC.—*One foot.*

Cheĕrfullў,
Fearfully.

DACTYLIC.—*Two feet.*

Fāthĕr ăll | glŏrĭoŭs
O'er all victorious.

DACTYLIC.—*Three feet.*

Weărĭng ă | wăy ĭn hĭs | yoŭthfŭlnĕss,
Loveliness, beauty, and truthfulness.

DACTYLIC.—*Four feet.*

" Bŏys wĭll ăn | tĭcĭpăte, | lăvĭsh ănd | dĭssĭpăte,
Āll thăt yoŭr bŭsў păte hŏardĕd wĭth cāre ;
And, in their foolishness, passion, and mulishness,
Charge you with churlishness, spurning your pray'r."

DACTYLIC.—*Five feet.*

" Nŏw thŏu dŏst | wĕlcŏme mĕ, | wĕlcŏme mĕ, | frŏm thĕ dărk | sēa,
Land of the beautiful, beautiful land of the free."

DACTYLIC.—*Six feet.*

" Tīme, thŏu ărt | ĕvĕr ĭn | mōtiŏn, ŏn | wheĕls ŏf thĕ | dāys, yĕars, ănd | āges,
Restless as waves of the ocean, when Eurus or Boreas rages."

DACTYLIC.—*Seven feet.*

" Oŭt ŏf thĕ | kĭngdŏm ŏf | Chrīst shăll bĕ | gătherĕd, by | ăngĕls ŏ'er Sātăn vĭctŏrĭoŭs,
All that offendeth, that lieth, that faileth to honor his name ever glorious."

DACTYLIC.— *Eight feet.*

Nĭmrŏd thĕ | hŭntĕr wăs | mĭghty ĭn | hŭntĭng, ănd | fāmed ăs thĕ | rŭlĕr ŏf | cĭtĭes ŏf | yŏre ;
Babel, and Erech, and Accad, and Calneh, from Shinar's fair region his name afar bore.

Other Kinds of Poetical Feet.

Besides the foregoing there are other kinds of feet that sometimes occur. These are named the *pyrrhic*, the *spondee*, the *amphibrach*, and the *tribrach*. The *pyrrhic* consists of two short and the *spondee* of two long syllables. The *amphibrach* contains three syllables, of which the first and third are short and the second long. The *tribrach* consists of three short syllables.

Examples.

PYRRHIC.— " Ŏn thĕ tall tree."
SPONDEE.— " The pāle mŏōn."
AMPHIBRACH. — " Dĕlīghtfŭl, Dŏmĕstĭc."
TRIBRACH.-" Nŭmĕrăblĕ, cŏnqŭĕrăblĕ."

Poetical Pauses.

The full effect in reading poetry is most completely given when a slight pause is made at the close of every line, even though the sense may not require a pause. Frequently a pause for sense is found in or near the middle of the line, particularly of long lines, in which it improves the rhythm, and brings out the meaning of the poem with much better effect. This pause is called the *cæsural* pause, and is shown in the following examples.

Cæsural Pause.

On her white breast | a sparkling cross she wore—
Which Jews might kiss | and infidels adore.
Her lively looks | a sprightly mind disclose,
Quick as her eyes | and as unfixed as those ;
Favors to none, | to all she smiles extends,
Oft she rejects, | but never once offends.

" Then her cheek | was pale, and thinner | | than should be | for one so young ;
And her eyes, | on all my motions, | | with a mute observance hung."

The *final pause* occurs at the end of each line whether the sense requires it or not, though it should not be too distinctly marked, as it consists merely in a brief suspension of the voice without any change in tone or accent. The following example shows its effect.

Final Pause.

Ye who have anxiously and fondly *watched*
Beside a fading friend, unconscious *that*
The cheek's bright crimson, lovely to the view,
Like nightshade, with unwholesome beauty bloomed.

Varieties of Poetry.

EVERAL leading kinds of poetry are named as follows: *Epic, Dramatic, Lyric, Elegiac, Pastoral, and Didactic.*

Epic Poetry.

Epic poetry pertains to the narrative, descriptive, and heroic in character, and is the highest and most difficult of poetry to write well. Among the best of the Epic poems may be mentioned, Homer's "*Iliad*" in Greek, Virgil's "*Æneid*" in Latin, and Milton's "Paradise Lost" in English.

Dramatic Poetry.

Dramatic poetry is also an elevated species of poetry, and takes nearly equal rank with the Epic. This kind of poetry includes the dramas, tragedies, comedies, melodramas, and operas.

Lyric Poetry.

Lyric poetry, as its name indicates, was the kind of verse originally written to be sung as an accompaniment to the lyre. This class of poetry is the oldest in the language of all nations, comprising, as it does, the songs of the people. In the Lyric are included the Songs, Hymns, Odes, and Sonnets.

Elegiac Poetry.

Elegiac poetry includes the elegies, such as Milton's "Lycidias," Tennyson's "In Memoriam," and poems of grave, solemn, and mourn-ful character. Gray's "Elegy, Written in a Country Churchyard" is undoubtedly the most complete specimen of this class of poetry to be found in any language.

Pastoral Poetry.

In the early history of the world, throughout certain portions of Europe, a distinct occupation was that of the shepherd, whose duty was to care for the flocks, as they roamed in the valleys and among the hills. Leading thus a life of dreamy ease among the charms of nature, the shepherds of better culture took readily to the writing of verse, which poetry, usually descriptive of rustic life, became known as Pastoral poetry.*

This class of poetry includes the poems that relate to country scenes, and the quiet, the simplicity, and the happiness found in rural life.

Of these may be included, in modern poems, "The Old Oaken Bucket," "The Sower," "Twenty Years Ago," "Maud Muller," and others of like character.

Didactic Poetry.

Didactic poetry pertains chiefly to the meditative and instructive, and includes such poems as Bryant's "Thanatopsis," Campbell's "Pleasures of Hope," Thomson's "Seasons," Pope's "Essay on Man," and kindred poems.

Kinds of Poems.

ARIOUS kinds of poems are known by certain names, which are defined as follows:

Odes.— Sacred hymns, such as are sung in church.

Pæans.— Songs of praise and triumph.

Ballads.— An easy form of descriptive verse, written in such style as to be easily sung by the people, who may have little acquaintance with music.

* From the Latin word *pastor*, a shepherd.

Epigrams.— A short poem, witty and concise, treating of a single subject, usually ending with an unexpected, ingeniously expressed natural thought.

Sonnets.— The Sonnet is a poetical composition, consisting of fourteen lines, so constructed that the first eight lines shall contain but two rhymes, and the last six but two more; and so arranged that, in the first part, the first line is made to rhyme with the fourth, fifth, and eighth —the second rhyming with the third, sixth, and seventh, while in the second part, the first, third, and fifth; and the second, fourth, and sixth also rhyme with each other, as shown in the following:

Autumn.

" The blithe birds of the summer tide are flown;
     Cold, motionless, and mute, stands all the wood,
     Save as the restless wind, in mournful mood,
Strays through the tossing limbs with saddest moan.
The leaves it wooed with kisses, overblown
     By gusts capricious, pitiless and rude,
     Lie dank and dead amid the solitude;
Where-through it waileth, desolate and lone.
But with a clearer splendor sunlight streams
     Athwart the bare, slim branches; and on high
Each star, in Night's rich coronal that beams,
     Pours down intenser brilliance on the eye;
Till dazzled Fancy finds her gorgeous dreams
     Outshone in beauty by the autumn sky."

Cantatas.—The Cantata is a musical composition, partaking of the nature of an anthem, being intermixed with airs and recitatives; and may be adapted to a single voice, or many.

Charades. The Charade may be in either prose or poetry, and contains as a subject a word of two syllables, each forming a distinct word; these to be concealed in an enigmatical description, first separately and then together.

Canzonets.—A short song consisting of one, two, or three parts is termed a Canzonet. The following, of two parts, is an illustration.

BLACK EYES AND BLUE.

Black eyes most dazzle in the hall;
Blue eyes most please at evening fall.
The black a conquest soonest gain;
The blue a conquest most retain;
The black bespeak a lively heart
Whose soft emotions soon depart;

The blue a steadier flame betray,
That burns and lives beyond a day;
The black may features best disclose;
In blue may feelings all repose;
Then let each reign without control,
The black all MIND — the blue all SOUL.

Epitaphs.—An Epitaph is usually a stanza in poetry, which follows the inscription on a tombstone.*

Satires. — The Satire is a poem used in exposing folly and wickedness, in keen, cutting words; holding the same up to ridicule and contempt.

Parodies.—A ludicrous imitation of a serious subject, usually in rhyme, is termed a Parody, as follows —

" Hands that the rod of empire might have swayed —
     Close at my elbow stir their lemonade."

Prologues.—The Prologue is a short poem, introductory to a play or discourse, usually recited before the performance begins.

Epilogues.—The Epilogue is a short poem, which frequently reviews the principal incidents of the play, delivered by one of the actors at the close of a dramatic performance.

Impromptus.—An Impromptu is a poetical composition, made at the moment, without previous study.

Acrostics.—An Acrostic is a stanza of several lines, the first letters of which, taken in their order from top to bottom, make a word or sentence.

Friendship, thou 'rt false! I hate thy flattering smile!
Return to me those years I spent in vain,
In early youth, the victim of thy guile,
Each joy took wing, ne'er to return again —
Ne'er to return; for, chilled by hopes deceived,
Dully the slow-paced hours now move along;
So changed the time, when, thoughtless, I believed
Her honeyed words, and heard her syren song.
If e'er, as me, she lure some youth to stray,
Perhaps, before too late, he 'll listen to my lay.

---

*See chapter on Epitaphs.

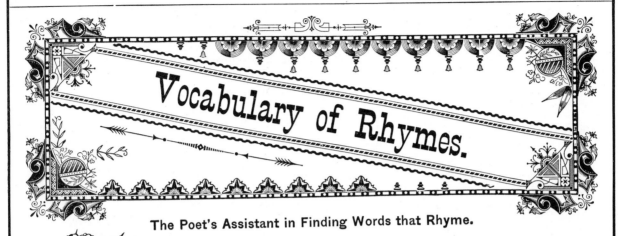

The Poet's Assistant in Finding Words that Rhyme.

AMONG the gems of literature that will live longest in the history of the world, will be various beautiful poems. Poetry is not always in rhyme, but generally it is.

As a rule, a prominent feature of beauty in the poem is the pleasant sensation produced by words coming near each other of similar sound.

In the stanza,

"Maud Muller, on a summer's day,
Raked the meadow, sweet with hay,"

it is seen that the pleasant jingling of "DAY" and "HAY" has much to do in making the verse attractive.

To express the same idea without rhyme thus:

Maud Muller raked one day in summer,
In a meadow where the hay was sweet,

is to deprive the sentiment of much of its charm.

Rhyme is, in fact, one of the prominent essentials of sweet verse, though to make the complete poem, common sense and truth must be expressed with rhyme.

It is sometimes the case that rhyme can be so ingeniously arranged, however, as to make a poem a success from the simple arrangement of rhyming words. Thus:

"Hi diddle diddle, the cat and the fiddle,
The cow jumped over the moon;
The little dog laughed to see such a craft,
And the dish ran away with the spoon."

Though nonsensical and ridiculous, this, with many others of the Mother Goose Melodies, is more attractive to the child than any of the choicest stanzas in Gray's Elegy.

A pleasant and intellectual pastime may be had by a company of young people, in the construction of impromptu rhymes. To conduct the exercise, one of the number is seated at the table, provided with paper and pencil. When all are in readiness, the hostess of the occasion announces a subject upon which they are to write a poem. Suppose the subject to be "SPRING." The person sitting next to the secretary will give the first line, the poetic feet decided upon, perhaps, being eight syllables to the line. The first line presented to the secretary may read,

In spring-time when the grass is green.

It is now in order for the second person in the group to give the next line ending with a word that rhymes with "green." Half a minute only will be allowed for the line to be produced. The individual, whose turn it is, gathers thought and says:

A thousand blossoms dot the scene.

This may not be very good poetry, but the

rhyme is complete and the poetry is as good as may be expected with so short a time in which to produce it. The next continues by presenting the third line as follows:

A perfume sweet loads down the air.

The fourth says,

The birds now sing, and mate, and pair.

The fifth continues,

O! charming season of the year.

The sixth may be at a loss for the suitable word to rhyme with "year," but must produce something in the half-minute, and here it is:

I wish that you was always here.

Whether the word "you" is a suitable word in this place, the rhymsters have not time to de-termine, as the composition must progress rapidly so that a twenty-line metrical composition may be produced in ten minutes.

As poetry this extemporaneous effusion, when finally read by the secretary, will not be very good—it may be only doggerel rhyme—but it will be amusing to see it produced, and its production will be a decidedly intellectual exercise.

For the advantage of the student who may aim to write the best of verse, as well as the impromptu poet in the social circle, who may wish to test the ability to rapidly make rhyme, the following vocabulary, from Walker's Rhyming Dictionary, is given:

Classification of Words that Rhyme.

AB.—Bab, cab, dab, mab, nab, blab, crab, drab, scab, stab. *Allowable rhymes*, babe, astrolabe, etc.

ACE.—Ace, dace, pace, face, lace, mace, race, brace, chace, grace, place, space, trace, apace, deface, efface, disgrace, displace, misplace, embrace, grimace, interlace, retrace, populace, etc. *Perfect rhymes*, base, case, abase, debase, etc. *Allowable rhymes*, grass, glass, etc., peace, cease, etc., dress, less, etc.

ACH.—Attach, detach, etc. *Perfect rhymes*, batch, match, etc. *Allowable rhymes*, fetch, wretch, etc.

ACK.—Back, cack, hack, jack, lack, pack, quack, tack, sack, rack, black, clack, crack, knack, slack, snack, stack, track, wrack, attack, zodiac, demoniac, symposiac, almanac. *Allowable rhymes*, bake, take, etc., neck, speck, etc.

ACT.—Act, fact, pact, tract, attract, abstract, extract, compact, contract, detract, distract, exact, protract, enact, infract, subtract, transact, cataract, *with the preterits and participles of verbs in* ack *as* backed, hacked, etc. *Allowable rhymes, the preterits and participles of verbs in* ake, *as* baked, caked, etc.

AD.—Add, bad, dad, gad, had, lad, mad, pad, sad, brad, clad, glad, plad, shad, etc. *Allowable rhymes*, cade, fade, etc., glede, bead, read, etc.

ADE.—Cade, fade, made, jade, lade, wade, blade, glade, shade, spade, trade, degrade, evade, dissuade, invade, persuade, blockade, brigade, esplanade, cavalcade, masquerade, renegade, retrograde, serenade, ambuscade, cannonade, palisade, etc. *Perfect rhymes*, aid, maid, braid, afraid, upbraid, etc., *and the preterits and participles of verbs in* ay, ey, *and* eigh, *as* played, obeyed, weighed, etc. *Allowable rhymes*, ad, bad, etc., bed, dead, etc., bead, mead, etc., heed, need, etc.

AFE.—Safe, chafe, vouchsafe, etc. *Allowable rhymes*, leaf, sheaf, etc., deaf, etc., laugh, staff, etc.

AFF.—Gaff, chaff, draff, quaff, staff, engraff, epitaph, cenotaph, paragraph, etc. *Perfect rhyme*, laugh. *Allowable rhymes*, safe, chafe, etc.

AFT.—Aft, haft, raft, waft, craft, shaft, abaft, graft, draft, ingraft, handicraft. *Perfect rhymes*, draught, *the preterits and participles of verbs in* aff *and* augh *as* quaffed, laughed, etc. *Allowable rhymes, the preterits and participles of verbs in* afe, *as* chafed, vouchsafed, etc.

AG.—Bag, cag, fag, gag, nag, rag, tag, wag, brag, crag, drag, flag, knag, shag, snag, stag, wrag, scrag, Brobdignag.

AGE.—Age, cage, gage, page, rage, sage, wage, stage, swage, assuage, engage, disengage, enrage, presage, appendage, concubinage, heritage, hermitage, parentage, parsonage, personage, pasturage, patronage, pilgrimage, villanage, equipage. *Allowable rhymes*, edge, wedge, etc., liege, siege, oblige, etc.

AID, *see* ADE. **AIGHT**, *see* ATE. **AIGN**, *see* ANE.

AIL.—Ail, bail, fail, hail, jail, mail, nail, pail, quail, rail, sail, tail, wail, flail, frail, snail, trail, assail, avail, detail, bewail, entail, prevail, retail, countervail, etc. *Perfect rhymes*, ale, bale, dale, gale, hale, male, pale, sale, tale, vale, wale, scale, stale, swale, whale, impale, exhale, regale, veil, nightingale, etc. *Allowable rhymes*, peal, steal, etc., bell, cell, etc.

AIM, *see* AME.

AIN.—Cain, blain, brain, chain, fain, gain, grain, lain, main, pain, rain, vain, wain, drain, plain, slain, Spain, stain, swain, train, twain, sprain, strain, abstain, amain, attain, complain, contain, constrain, detain, disdain, distrain, enchain, entertain, explain, maintain, ordain, pertain, obtain, refrain, regain, remain, restrain, retain, sustain, appertain. *Perfect rhymes*, bane, cane, dane, crane, fane, Jane, lane, mane, plane, vane, wane, profane, hurricane, etc., deign, arraign, campaign, etc., feign, reign, etc., vein, rein, etc. *Allowable rhymes*, lean, mean, etc., queen, seen, etc., ban, can, etc., den, pen, etc.

AINT.—Faint, paint, plaint, quaint, saint, taint, acquaint, attaint, complaint, constraint, restraint, etc. *Perfect rhyme*, feint. *Allowable rhymes*, cant, pant, etc., lent, rent, etc.

AIR, *see* ARE. **AISE**, *see* AZE. **AIT**, *see* ATE. **AITH**, *see* ATH. **AIZE**, *see* AZE.

AKE.—Ake, bake, cake, lake, make, quake, rake, sake, take, wake, brake, drake, flake, shake, snake, stake, strake, spake, awake, betake, forsake, mistake, partake, overtake, undertake, bespake. *Perfect rhymes*, break, steak, etc. *Allowable rhymes*, back, rack, etc., beck, deck, etc., speak, weak, etc.

AL.—Cabal, canal, animal, admiral, cannibal, capital, cardinal, comical, conjugal, corporal, criminal, critical, festival, funeral, general, hospital, interval, liberal, madrigal, literal, magical, mineral, mystical, musical, natural, original, pastoral, pedestal, personal, physical, poetical, political, principal, prodigal, prophetical, rational, satirical, reciprocal, rhetorical, several, temporal, tragical, tyrannical, carnival, schismatical, whimsical, arsenal. *Allowable rhymes*, all, ball, etc., ail, mail, etc., ale, pale, etc.

ALD.—Bald, scald, emerald, etc. *Perfect rhymes, the preterits and participles of verbs in* all, aul *and* awl, *as* called, mauled, crawled, etc.

ALE, *see* AIL.

ALF.—Calf, half, behalf, etc. *Allowable rhymes*, staff, laugh, etc.

ALK.—Balk, chalk, stalk, talk, walk, calk, etc. *Perfect rhyme*, hawk. *Allowable rhymes*, sock, clock, etc.

ALL.—All, ball, call, etc. *Perfect rhymes*, awl, bawl, brawl, crawl, scrawl, sprawl, squall. *Allowable rhymes*, cabal, equivocal. etc. *See* AL.

ALM.—Calm, balm, becalm, psalm, palm, embalm, etc., *and verbs whose plurals and third persons singular rhyme with* alms, *as* calms, becalms, etc.

ALT.—Halt, malt, exalt, salt, vault, assault, default *and* fault, *the last of which is, by Pope, rhymed with* thought, bought, etc.

ALVE.—Calve, halve, salve, valve.

AM.—Am, dam, ham, pam, ram, cram, dram, flam, sham, swam, epigram, anagram, etc. *Perfect rhyme*, lamb. *Allowable rhymes*, dame, lame, etc.

AME.—Blame, came, dame, same, flame, fame, frame, game, lame, name, tame, shame, inflame, became, defame, misname, misbecame, overcame, etc. *Perfect rhymes*, aim, claim, maim, acclaim, declaim, exclaim, proclaim, reclaim. *Allowable rhymes*, dam, ham, etc., hem, them, etc., theme, scheme, etc., dream, gleam, etc.

AMP.—Camp, champ, cramp, damp, stamp, vamp, lamp, clamp, decamp, encamp, etc.

AN.—Ban, can, Dan, man, Nan, pan, ran, tan, van, bran, plan, scan, span, than, unman, fore-ran, began, trepan, courtesan, partisan, artisan, pelican, caravan, etc. *Allowable rhymes*, bane, cane, plain, mane, etc., bean, lean, wan, swan, etc., gone, upon, etc.

ANCE—Chance, dance, glance, lance, trance, prance, entrance, romance, advance, mischance, complaisance, circumstance, countenance, deliverance, consonance, dissonance, extravagance, ignorance, inheritance, maintenance, temperance, intemperance, exorbitance, ordinance, concordance, sufferance, sustenance, utterance, arrogance, vigilance, expanse, enhance.

ANCH.—Branch, stanch, blanch, ranch, hanch. *Perfect rhymes*, launch, paunch.

AND.—And, band, hand, land, rand, sand, brand, bland, grand, gland, stand, strand, command, demand, countermand, disband, expand, withstand, understand, reprimand, contraband, etc. *Allowable rhymes*, wand, fond, bond, etc., *and the preterits and participles of verbs in* ain *and* ean, *as* remained, leaned, etc.

ANE, *see* AIN.

ANG.—Bang, fang, gang, hang, pang, tang, twang, sang, rang, harangue, clang. *Allowable rhymes*, song, long, etc.

ANGE.—Change, grange, range, strange, estrange, arrange, exchange, interchange. *Allowable rhymes*, revenge, avenge, etc.

ANK.—Bank, blank, shank, clank, dank, drank, slank, frank, spank, stank, lank, plank, prank, rank, thank, disrank, mountebank, etc.

ANSE, *see* ANCE.

ANT.—Ant, cant, chant, grant, pant, plant, rant, slant, aslant, complaisant, displant, enchant, gallant, implant, recant, supplant, transplant, absonant, adamant, arrogant, combatant, consonant, cormorant, protestant, significant, visitant, covenant, dissonant, disputant, elegant, elephant, exorbitant, conversant, extravagant, ignorant, insignificant, inhabitant, militant, predominant, sycophant, vigilant, petulant, etc. *Allowable rhymes*, faint, paint, etc. *See* **AINT** *and* **ENT**.

AP.—Cap, gap, hap, lap, map, nap, pap, rap, sap, tap, chap, clap, trap, flap, knap, slap, snap, wrap, scrap, strap, enwrap, entrap, mishap, etc. *Allowable rhymes*, cape, tape, etc., cheap, heap *and* swap.

APE.—Ape, cape, chape, grape, rape, scrape, shape, escape, mape, crape, tape, etc. *Allowable rhymes*, heap, keep, etc.

APH, *see* **AFF.**

APSE.—Lapse, elapse, relapse, perhaps, *and the plurals of nouns and third persons singular of the present tense in* ap, *as* caps, maps, etc., he raps, he laps, etc. *Allowable rhymes, the plurals of nouns and third persons singular of verbs in* ape *and* eap, *as* apes, heaps, he heaps, etc.

APT.—Apt, adapt, etc. *Rhymes, the preterits and participles of the verbs in* ap, *as* tapped, slapped, etc. *Allowable rhymes, the preterits and participles of the verbs in* ape, *as* aped, escaped, etc.

AR.—Bar, car, far, jar, mar, par, tar, spar, scar, star, chair, afar, debar, unbar, catarrh, particular, perpendicular, secular, angular, regular, popular, singular, titular, vinegar, scimitar, calendar, collender. *Perfect rhyme, the plural verb* are. *Allowable rhymes*, bare, prepare, etc., pair, repair, wear, tear, war, etc, *and words ending in* er *or* or, *having the accent on the last syllable, or last but two.*

ARB.—Barb, garb, etc.

ARCE.—Farce, parse, Mars, etc. *Allowable rhyme*, scarce.

ARCH.—Arch, march, parch, starch, countermarch, etc.

ARD.—Bard, card, guard, hard, lard, nard, shard, yard, bombard, discard, regard, interlard, retard, disregard, etc., *and the preterits and participles of verbs in* ar, *as* barred, scarred, etc. *Allowable rhymes*, cord, reward, etc.

ARD.—Ward, award, reward, etc. *Allowable rhymes*, hard, card, *see the last article*, hoard, lord, bird, curd, *and the preterits and participles of the verbs in* ar, or, *and* ur, *as* barred, abhorred, incurred, etc.

ARE.—Bare, care, dare, fare, hare, mare, pare, tare, rare, ware, flare, glare, scare, share, snare, spare, square, stare, sware, prepare, aware, beware, compare, declare, ensnare. *Perfect rhymes*, air, hair, fair, lair, pair, chair, stair, affair, debonnair, despair, impair, repair, etc., bear, pear, swear, tear, wear, forbear, forswear, etc., there, were, where, ere, e'er, ne'er, elsewhere, whate'er, howe'er, howsoe'er, whene'er, where'er, etc., heir, co-heir, their. *Allowable rhymes*, bar, car, etc., err, prefer, *and* hear, here, etc., regular, singular, war, etc.

ARES.—Unawares. *Rhymes*, their's, *and the plurals of nouns and third persons singular of verbs in* are, air, eir, ear, *as* care, he cares, pair, he pairs, heirs, bear, he bears, etc. *The allowable rhymes are the plurals of nouns and the third persons singular of verbs which are allowed to rhyme with the termination* ars, *as* bars, cars, errs, prefers, etc.

ARF.—Scarf. *Allowable rhymes*, dwarf, wharf.

ARGE.—Barge, charge, large, targe, discharge, o'ercharge, surcharge, enlarge. *Allowable rhymes*, verge, emerge, gorge, forge, urge, etc.

ARK.—Bark, cark, Clark, dark, lark, mark, park, shark, spark, stark, embark, remark, etc. *Allowable rhymes*, cork, fork, etc.

ARL.—Snarl, marl, parl. *Allowable rhymes*, curl, furl, etc.

ARM.—Arm, barm, charm, farm, harm, alarm, disarm. *Allowable rhymes*, warm, swarm, storm, etc.

ARN.—Barn, yarn, etc. *Allowable rhymes*, warn, forewarn, etc., horn, morn, etc.

ARN.—Warn, forewarn. *Perfect rhymes*, horn, morn, etc. *Allowable rhymes*, barn, yarn, etc.

ARP.—Carp, harp, sharp, counterscarp. *Allowable rhyme*, warp.

ARSH.—Harsh, marsh, etc.

ART.—Art, cart, dart, hart, mart, part, smart, tart, start, apart, depart, impart, dispart, counterpart. *Perfect rhymes*, heart, etc. *Allowable rhymes*, wart, thwart, etc., hurt, etc., dirt, flirt, etc., pert, etc.

ART (*sounded* **ORT**).—Wart, thwart, etc. *Perfect rhymes*, short, retort, etc. *Allowable rhymes*, art, sport, court, etc.

ARTH, *see* **EARTH.**

ARVE.—Carve, starve, etc. *Allowable rhymes*, nerve, deserve, etc.

AS.—Was. *Allowable rhymes*, has, as.

ASS.—Ass, brass, class, grass, lass, mass, pass, alas, amass, cuirass, repass, surpass, morass, etc. *Allowable rhymes*, base, face, deface, etc., loss, toss, etc.

ASE, *see* **ACE.**

ASH.—Ash, cash, dash, clash, crash, flash, gash, gnash, hash, lash, plash, rash, thrash, slash, trash, abash, etc. *Allowable rhymes*, wash, quash, etc., leash, etc.

ASH.—Wash, quash, etc. *Allowable rhymes*, cash, dash, etc.

ASK.—Ask, task, bask, cask, flask, mask.

ASP.—Asp, clasp, gasp, grasp, hasp. *Allowable rhymes*, wasp, etc.

AST.—Cast, last, blast, mast, past, vast, fast, aghast, avast, forecast, overcast, outcast, repast. *Perfect rhymes, the preterits and participles of verbs in* ass, *as* classed, amassed, etc. *Allowable rhymes, the preterits and participles of verbs in* ace, *as* placed, etc. *Nouns and verbs in* aste, *as* taste, waste, etc.

ASTE.—Baste, chaste, haste, paste, taste, waste, distaste. *Perfect rhymes*, waist, *and the preterits and participles of verbs in* ace, *as* faced, placed, etc. *Allowable rhymes*, cast, fast, etc., best, nest, etc., *and the preterits and participles of verbs in* ess, *as* messed, dressed, etc.

AT.—At, bat, cat, hat, fat, mat, pat, sat, rat, tat, vat, brat, chat, flat, plat, sprat, that, gnat. *Allowable rhymes*, bate, hate, etc.

ATCH.—Catch, match, hatch, latch, patch, scratch, smatch, snatch, despatch.

ATE.—Bate, date, fate, gate, grate, hate, tate, mate, pate, plate, prate, rate, sate, state, skate, slate, abate, belate, collate, create, debate, elate, dilate, estate, ingrate, innate, rebate, relate, sedate, translate, abdicate, abominate, abrogate, accelerate, accommodate, accumulate, accurate, adequate, affectionate, advocate, adulterate, aggravate, agitate, alienate, animate, annihilate, antedate, anticipate, antiquate, arbitrate, arrogate, articulate, assassinate, calculate, capitulate, captivate, celebrate, circulate, coagulate, commemorate, commiserate, communicate, compassionate, confederate, congratulate, congregate, consecrate, contaminate, corroborate, cultivate, candidate, co-operate, considerate, consulate, capacitate, debilitate, dedicate, degenerate, delegate, deliberate, denominate, depopulate, dislocate, deprecate, discriminate, derogate, dissipate, delicate, disconsolate, desperate, educate, effeminate, elevate, emulate, estimate, elaborate, equivocate, eradicate, evaporate, exaggerate, exasperate, expostulate, exterminate, extricate, facilitate, fortunate, generate, gratulate, hesitate, illiterate, illuminate, irritate, imitate, immoderate, impenetrate, importunate, imprecate, inanimate, innovate, instigate, intemperate, intimate, intimidate, intoxicate, intricate, invalidate, inveterate, inviolate, legitimate, magistrate, meditate, mitigate, moderate, necessitate, nominate, obstinate, participate, passionate, penetrate, perpetrate, personate, potentate, precipitate, predestinate, predominate, premeditate, prevaricate, procrastinate, profligate, prognosticate, propagate, recriminate, regenerate, regulate, reiterate, reprobate, reverberate, ruminate, separate, sophisticate, stipulate, subjugate, subordinate, suffocate, terminate, tolerate, temperate, vindicate, violate, unfortunate. *Perfect rhymes*, bait, plait, strait, wait, await, great. *Nearly perfect rhymes*, eight, weight, height, straight. *Allowable rhymes*, beat, heat, etc., bat, cat, etc., bet, wet, etc.

ATH.—Bath, path, etc. *Allowable rhymes*, hath, faith, etc.

ATHE.—Bathe, swathe, lathe, rathe.

AUB, *see* **OB.** **AUCE,** *see* **AUSE.** **AUCH,** *see* **OACH.**

AUD.—Fraud, laud, applaud, defraud. *Perfect rhymes*, broad, abroad, bawd, *and the preterits and participles of verbs in* aw, *as* gnawed, sawed, etc. *Allowable rhymes*, odd, nod, etc., ode, bode, etc., *also the word* load.

AVE.—Cave, brave, gave, grave, crave, lave, nave, knave, pave, rave, save, shave, slave, stave, wave, behave, deprave, engrave, outbrave, forgave, misgave, architrave. *Allowable rhyme, the auxiliary verb* have.

AUGH, *see* **AFF.** **AUGHT,** *see* **OUGHT.** **AULT,** *see* **ALT.**

AUNCH.—Launch, paunch, haunch, staunch, etc.

AUNCE, *see* **ONSE.**

AUNT.—Aunt, daunt, gaunt, haunt, jaunt, taunt, vaunt, avaunt. *Perfect rhymes*, slant, aslant. *Allowable rhymes*, want, etc., pant, cant, etc.

AUSE.—Cause, pause, clause, applause, because. *Perfect rhymes, the plurals of nouns, and third persons singular of verbs in* aw, *as* laws, he draws, etc. *Allowable rhyme*, was.

AUST, *see* **OST.**

AW.—Craw, daw, law, chaw, claw, draw, flaw, gnaw, jaw, law, maw, paw, raw, straw, thaw, withdraw, foresaw.

AWD, *see* **AUD.** **AWK,** *see* **ALK.**

AWL.—Bawl, brawl, drawl, crawl, scrawl, sprawl, squall. *Perfect rhymes*, ball, call, fall, gall, small, hall, pall, tall, wall, stall, install, forestall, thrall, inthrall.

AWN.—Dawn, brawn, fawn, pawn, spawn, drawn, yawn, lawn, withdrawn.

AX.—Ax, tax, wax, relax, flax. *Perfect rhymes, the plurals of nouns and third persons singular of verbs in* ack, *as* backs, sacks, etc., he lacks, he packs, etc. *Allowable rhymes, the plurals of nouns and third persons singular of verbs in* ake, *as* cakes, lakes, etc., he makes, he takes, etc.

AY.—Bray, clay, day, dray, tray, flay, fray, gay, hay, jay, lay, may, nay, pay, play, ray, say, way, pray, spray, slay, spay, stay, stray, sway, affray, allay, array, astray, away, belay, bewray, betray, decay, defray, delay, disarray, display, dismay, essay, forelay, gainsay, inlay, relay, repay, roundelay, virelay. *Perfect rhymes*, neigh, weigh, inveigh, etc., prey, they, convey, obey, purvey, survey, disobey, grey. *Allowable rhymes*, tea, sea, fee, see, glee, etc.

AZE.—Craze, daze, blaze, gaze, glaze, maze, raze, amaze, graze. *Perfect rhymes*, raise, praise, dispraise, etc., paraphrase, etc., *and the nouns plural, and third persons singular of the present tense of verbs in* ay, eigh, *and* ey, *as* days, he inveighs, he obeys, etc. *Allowable rhymes*, ease, tease, seize, etc., *and* keys, *the plural of* key, *also the auxiliaries* has *and* was.

E

E and EA, *see* **EE.** **EACE,** *see* **EASE.**

EACH.—Beach, breach, bleach, each, peach, preach, teach, impeach. *Nearly perfect rhymes*, beech, leech, speech, beseech. *Allowable rhymes*, fetch, wretch, etc.

EAD, *see* **EDE and EED.** **EAF,** *see* **IEF.**

EAGUE.—League, Teague, etc. *Perfect rhymes*, intrigue, fatigue, etc. *Allowable rhymes*, Hague, vague, etc., leg, beg, etc,, bag, rag, etc.

EAK, *see* **AKE.**—Beak, speak, bleak, creak, freak, leak, peak, sneak, squeak, streak, weak, tweak, wreak, bespeak. *Nearly perfect rhymes*, cheek, leek, creek, meek, reek, seek, sleek, pique, week, shriek. *Allowable rhymes*, beck, speck, etc., lake, take, thick, lick, etc.

EAL.—Deal, heal, reveal, meal, peal, seal, steal, teal, veal, weal, zeal, squeal, repeal, conceal, congeal, anneal, appeal. *Nearly perfect rhymes*, eel, heel, feel, keel, kneel, peel, reel, steel, wheel. *Allowable rhymes*, bell, tell, etc., bale, tale, etc., bill, fill, etc., ail, fail, etc.

EALM, *see* **ALM.**

EALTH.—Health, wealth, stealth, commonwealth, etc.

EAM.—Bream, cream, gleam, seam, scream, steam, stream, team, beam, dream. *Perfect rhymes*, fleame, scheme, theme, blaspheme, extreme, supreme. *Nearly perfect rhymes*, deem, teem, beseem, misdeem, esteem, disesteem, redeem, seem, etc. *Allowable rhymes*, dame, lame, etc., limb, him, etc., them, hem, etc., lamb, dam, etc. *See* **AME.**

EAN.—Bean, clean, dean, glean, lean, mean, wean, yean, demean, unclean. *Perfect rhymes*, convene, demesne, intervene, mien. *Nearly perfect rhymes*, machine, keen, screen, seen, green, spleen, between, careen, foreseen, serene, obscene, terrene, etc., queen, etc. *Allowable rhymes*, bane, mane, etc., ban, man, etc., bin, thin, begin etc.

EANS, *see* **ENSE.** **EANT,** *see* **ENT.** **EAP,** *see* **EEP and EP.** **EAR,** *see* **EER.**

EARD—Heard, herd, sherd, etc. *Perfect rhymes, the preterits and participles of verbs in* er, *as* erred, preferred, etc. *Allowable rhymes,* beard, *the preterits and participles of verbs in* ere, ear, *and* ar, *as* revered, feared, barred.

EARCH.—Search, perch, research. *Allowable rhymes,* church, smirch, lurch, parch, march, etc.

EARN, *see* **ERN. EARSE,** *see* **ERSE. EART,** *see* **ART.**

EARTH.—Earth, dearth. *Perfect rhymes,* birth, mirth, etc. *Allowable rhymes,* hearth, etc.

EASE, *sounded* **EACE.**—Cease, lease, release, grease, decease, decrease, increase, surcease. *Perfect rhyme,* peace. *Nearly perfect rhymes,* piece, niece, fleece, geese, frontispiece, apiece, etc. *Allowable rhymes,* less, mess, etc., lace, mace, etc., miss, hiss, etc., nice, vice, etc.

EASH, *see* **ESH.**

EAST.—East, feast, least, beast. *Perfect rhymes, the preterits and participles of verbs in* ease, *as* cease, increased, etc. *Nearly perfect rhyme,* priest. *Allowable rhymes,* haste, taste, etc., best, chest, etc., fist, list, etc., *and the preterits and participles of verbs in* ess *and* iss, *as* dressed, hissed.

EAT.—Bleat, eat, feat, heat, meat, neat, seat, treat, wheat, beat, cheat, defeat, estreat, escheat, entreat, retreat. *Perfect rhymes,* obsolete, replete, concrete, complete. *Nearly perfect rhymes,* feet, fleet, gleet, greet, meet, sheet, sleet, street, sweet, discreet. *Allowable rhymes,* bate, grate, hate, etc., get, met, etc., bit, hit, etc. *See* **ATE.**

EATH.—Breath, death, etc. *Allowable rhymes,* heath, sheath, teeth.

EATHE.—Breathe, sheathe, etc. *Perfect rhymes,* wreath, inwreath, bequeath, beneath, underneath, etc. *Nearly perfect rhymes,* seethe, etc.

EAVE.—Cleave, heave, interweave, leave, weave, bereave, inweave. *Perfect rhymes,* receive, conceive, deceive, perceive. *Nearly perfect rhymes,* eve, grieve, thieve, aggrieve, achieve, believe, disbelieve, relieve, reprieve, retrieve. *Allowable rhymes,* live, give, etc., lave, cave, etc., *and* have.

EBB.—Ebb, web, etc. *Allowable rhymes,* babe, astrolabe, etc., glebe, etc.

ECK.—Beck, check, deck, neck, speck, wreck. *Allowable rhymes,* break, take, etc., beak, sneak, etc.

ECT.—Sect, abject, affect, correct, incorrect, collect, deject, detect, direct, disrespect, disaffect, dissect, effect, elect, eject, erect, expect, indirect, infect, inspect, neglect, object, project, protect, recollect, reflect, reject, respect, select, subject, suspect, architect, circumspect, dialect, intellect. *Perfect rhymes, the preterits and participles of verbs in* eck, *as* decked, checked, etc. *Allowable rhymes, the preterits and participles of verbs in* ake *and* eak, *as* baked, leaked.

ED.—Bed, bled, fed, fled, bred, led, shred, shed, sped, wed, abed, inbred, misled. *Perfect rhymes,* said, bread, dread, dead, head, lead, read, spread, thread, tread, behead, o'erspread. *Allowable rhymes,* bead, mead, etc., blade, fade, etc., maid, paid, etc., *and the preterits and participles of verbs in* ay, ey, *and* eigh, *as* bayed, obeyed, weighed, etc.

EDE, *see* **EED.**

EDGE.—Edge, wedge, fledge, hedge, ledge, pledge, sedge, allege. *Allowable rhymes,* age, page, etc., siege, oblige, etc., privilege, sacrilege, sortilege.

EE.—Bee, free, glee, knee, see, three, thee, tree, agree, decree, degree, disagree, foresee, o'ersee, pedigree, he, me, we, she, be, jubilee, Lee. *Nearly perfect rhymes,* sea, plea, flea, tea, key. *Allowable rhymes, all words of one syllable ending in* y, ye, *or* ie, *or polysyllables of these terminations having the accent on the ultimate or antepenultimate syllable.*

EECE, *see* **EASE. EECH,** *see* **EACH.**

EED.—Creed, deed, indeed, bleed, breed, feed, need, meed, heed, reed, speed, seed, steed, weed, proceed, succeed, exceed. *Perfect rhymes,* knead, read, intercede, precede, recede, concede, impede, supersede, etc., bead, lead, mead, plead, etc. *Allowable rhymes,* bed, dead, etc., bid, hid, etc., made, blade, etc.

EEF, *see* **IEF. EEK,** *see* **EAK. EEL,** *see* **EAL. EEM,** *see* **EAM. EEN,** *see* **EAN.**

EEP.—Creep, deep, sleep, keep, peep, sheep, steep, sweep, weep, asleep. *Nearly perfect rhymes,* cheap, heap, reap, etc. *Allowable rhymes,* ape, rape, etc., step, nep, etc., hip, lip, etc.

EER.—Beer, deer, fleer, geer, jeer, peer, meer, leer, sheer, steer, sneer, cheer, veer, pickeer, domineer, cannoneer, compeer, engineer, mutineer, pioneer, privateer, charioteer, chanticleer, career, mountaineer. *Perfect rhymes,* here, sphere, adhere, cohere, interfere, persevere, revere, austere, severe, sincere, hemisphere, etc., ear, clear, dear, fear, hear, near, sear, smear, spear, tear, year, appear, besmear, disappear, endear, auctioneer. *Allowable rhymes,* hare, dare, etc., preter, deter, character, etc.

EESE, *see* **EEZE. EET,** *see* **EAT. EETH,** *see* **EATH. EEVE,** *see* **EAVE.**

EEZE.—Breeze, freeze, wheeze, sneeze, squeeze, *and the plurals of nouns and third persons singular, present tense, of verbs in* ee, *as* bees, he sees. *Perfect rhymes,* cheese, these, etc. *Nearly perfect rhymes,* ease, appease, disease, displease, tease, seize, etc., *and the plurals of nouns in* ea, *as* teas, pleas, etc., *and the polysyllables ending in* es, *having the accent on the antepenultimate, as* images, monarchies, etc.

EFT.—Cleft, left, theft, weft, bereft, etc. *Allowable rhymes,* lift, sift, etc., *and the third person singular, present tense, of verbs in* afe, aff, augh, *and* iff, *as* chafed, quaffed, laughed, whiffed, etc.

EG.—Egg, leg, beg, peg. *Allowable rhymes,* vague, plague, etc., league, Teague, etc.

EIGH, *see* **AY. EIGHT,** *see* **ATE. EIGN,** *see* **AIN. EIL,** *see* **AIL. EIN,** *see* **AIN. EINT,** *see* **AINT. EIR** *see* **ARE. EIT,** *see* **EAT. EIVE,** *see* **EAVE. EIZE,** *see* **EEZE.**

ELL.—Ell, dwell, fell, hell, knell, quell, sell, bell, cell, dispel, foretell, excel, compel, befell, yell, well, tell, swell, spell, smell, shell, parallel, sentinel, infidel, citadel, refel, repel, rebel, impel, expel. *Allowable rhymes,* bale, sail, etc., heal, peal, etc., eel, steel, etc.

ELD.—Held, geld, withheld, upheld, beheld, etc. *Perfect rhymes, the preterits and participles of verbs in* ell, *as* swelled, felled, etc. *Allowable rhymes, the preterits and participles of verbs in* ale, ail, etc., heal, seal, etc., *as* impaled, waled, etc., healed, sealed, etc.

ELF.—Elf, pelf, self, shelf, himself, etc.

ELK.—Elk, whelk, etc.

ELM.—Elm, helm, realm, whelm, overwhelm, etc. *Allowable rhymes,* palm, film, etc.

ELP.—Help, whelp, yelp, etc.

ELT.—Belt, gelt, melt, felt, welt, smelt, pelt, dwelt. *Perfect rhyme,* dealt.

ELVE.—Delve, helve, twelve, etc.

ELVES.—Elves, themselves, etc. *Perfect rhymes, the plurals of nouns and third persons singular of verbs in* elf *and* elve, *as* twelves, delves, shelves, etc.

EM.—Gem, hem, stem, them, diadem, stratagem, etc. *Perfect rhymes,* condemn, contemn, etc. *Allowable rhymes,* lame, tame, etc., team, seam, theme, etc.

EME, *see* **EAM.**

EMN.—Condemn, contemn, etc. *Perfect rhymes,* gem, hem, etc. *Allowable rhymes,* lame, tame, etc., team, seam, etc.

EMPT.—Tempt, exempt, attempt, contempt.

EN.—Den, hen, fen, ken, men, pen, ten, then, when, wren, denizen. *Allowable rhymes,* bane, fane, etc., mean, bean, etc.

ENCE.—Fence, hence, dense, pence, thence, whence, defense, expense, offense, pretense, commence, abstinence, circumference, conference, confidence, consequence, continence, benevolence, concupiscence, difference, diffidence, diligence, eloquence, eminence, evidence, excellence, impenitence, impertinence, impotence, impudence, improvidence, incontinence, indifference, indigence, indolence, inference, intelligence, innocence, magnificence, munificence, negligence, omnipotence, penitence, preference, providence, recompense, reference, residence, reverence, vehemence, violence. *Perfect rhymes,* sense, dense, cense, condense, immense, intense, propense, dispense, suspense, prepense, incense, frankincense.

ENCH.—Bench, drench, retrench, quench, clench, stench, fench, trench, wench, wrench, intrench.

END.—Bend, mend, blend, end, fend, lend, rend, send, spend, tend, vend, amend, attend, ascend, commend, contend, defend, depend, descend, distend, expend, extend, forefend, impend, misspend, obtend, offend, portend, pretend, protend, suspend. transcend, unbend, apprehend, comprehend, condescend, discommend, recommend, reprehend, dividend, reverend. *Perfect rhymes,* friend, befriend, *and the preterits and participles of verbs in* en, *as* penned, kenned, etc. *Allowable rhymes, the preterits and participles of verbs in* ean, *as* gleaned, yeaned, etc.

ENDS.—Amends. *Perfect rhymes, the plurals of nouns and third persons singular, present tense, of verbs in* end, *as* friends, he mends, etc.

ENE, *see* **EAN.**

ENGE.—Avenge, revenge, etc.

ENGTH.—Length, strength, etc.

ENSE (*sounded* **ENZE**).—Cleanse. *Perfect rhymes, the plurals of nouns and third persons singular, present tense, of verbs in* en, *as* hens, fens, he pens, he kens, etc.

ENT.—Bent, lent, rent, pent, scent, sent, shent, spent, tent, vent, went, absent, meant, ascent, assent, attent, augment, cement, content, consent, descent, dissent, event, extent, foment, frequent, indent, intent, invent, lament, misspent, o'erspent. present, prevent, relent, repent, resent, ostent, ferment, outwent, underwent, discontent, unbent, circumvent, represent, abstinent, accident, accomplishment, admonishment, acknowledgment, aliment, arbitrament, argument, banishment, battlement, blandishment, astonishment, armipotent, bellipotent, benevolent, chastisement, competent, compliment, complement, confident, continent, corpulent, detriment, different, diffident, diligent, disparagement, document, element, eloquent, eminent, equivalent, establishment, evident, excellent, excrement, exigent, experiment, firmament, fraudulent, government, embellishment, imminent, impenitent, impertinent, implement, impotent, imprisonment, improvident, impudent, incident, incompetent, incontinent, indifferent, indigent, innocent, insolent, instrument, irreverent, languishment, ligament, lineament, magnificent, management, medicament, malcontent, monument, negligent, nourishment, nutriment, occident, omnipotent, opulent, ornament, parliament, penitent, permanent, pertinent, president, precedent, prevalent, provident, punishment, ravishment, regiment, resident, redolent, rudiment, sacrament, sediment, sentiment, settlement, subsequent, supplement, intelligent, tenement, temperament, testament, tournament, turbulent, vehement, violent, virulent, reverent. *Allowable rhymes,* paint, saint, etc.

ENTS.—Accoutrements. *Perfect rhymes, the plurals of nouns and third persons singular, present tense, of verbs in* ent, *as* scents, he assents, etc.

EP.—Step, nep, etc. *Allowable rhymes,* leap, reap, etc., rape, tape, etc.

EPT.—Accept, adept, except, intercept, etc. *Perfect rhymes,* crept, slept, wept, kept. *Allowable rhymes, the preterits and participles of verbs in* ape, eep *and* eap, *as* peeped, reaped, shaped, etc.

ERR.—Err, aver, defer, infer, deter, inter, refer, transfer, confer, prefer, parterre, administer, wagoner, islander, arbiter, character, villager, cottager, dowager, forager, pillager, voyager, massacre, gardener, slanderer, flatterer, idolater, provender, theater, amphitheater, foreigner, lavender, messenger, passenger, sorcerer, interpreter, officer, mariner, harbinger, minister, register, canister, chorister, sophister, presbyter, lawgiver, philosopher, astrologer, loiterer, prisoner, grasshopper, astronomer, sepulcher, thunderer, traveler, murderer, usurer. *Allowable rhymes,* bare, care, etc., ear, fear, etc., bar, car, etc., sir, fir, her, etc.

ERCH, *see* **EARCH. ERCE,** *see* **ERSE. ERD,** *see* **EARD. ERE,** *see* **EER.**

ERGE.—Verge, emerge, absterge, immerge. *Perfect rhyme,* dirge. *Nearly perfect rhymes,* urge, purge, surge. *Allowable rhymes,* barge, large, etc.

ERN.—Fern, stern, discern, concern. *Perfect rhymes,* learn, earn, yearn, etc. *Allowable rhymes,* barn, yarn, etc., burn, turn, etc.

ERSE.—Verse, hearse, absterse, adverse, averse, converse, disperse, immerse, perverse, reverse, traverse, asperse, intersperse, universe. *Perfect rhymes,* amerce, coerce, etc., fierce. tierce, pierce, etc. *Allowable rhymes,* farce, parse, Mars, etc., purse, curse, etc.

ERT.—Wert, advert, assert, avert, concert, convert, controvert, desert, divert, exert, expert, insert, invert, pervert, subvert. *Allowable rhymes,* heart, part, etc., shirt, dirt, etc., hurt, spurt, etc.

ERVE.—Serve, nerve, swerve, preserve, deserve, conserve, observe, reserve, disserve, subserve. *Allowable rhymes*, starve, carve, etc., curve, etc.

ESS.—Bless, dress, cess, chess, guess, less, mess, press, stress, acquiesce, access, address, assess, compress, confess, caress, depress, digress, dispossess, distress, excess, express, impress, oppress, possess, profess, recess, repress, redress, success, transgress, adulteress, bashfulness, bitterness, cheerfulness, comfortless, comeliness, dizziness, diocese, drowsiness, eagerness, easiness, embassadress, emptiness, evenness, fatherless, filthiness, foolishness, forgetfulness, forwardness, frowardness, fruitfulness, fulsomeness, giddiness, greediness, gentleness, governess, happiness, haughtiness, heaviness, idleness, heinousness, hoaryness, hollowness, holiness, lasciviousness, lawfulness, laziness, littleness, liveliness, loftiness, lioness, lowliness, manliness, masterless, mightiness, motherless, motionless, nakedness, neediness, noisomeness, numberless, patroness, peevishness, perfidiousness, pitiless, poetess, prophetess, ransomness, readiness, righteousness, shepherdess, sorceress, sordidness, spiritless, sprightliness, stubbornness, sturdiness, surliness, steadiness, tenderness, thoughtfulness, ugliness, uneasiness, unhappiness, votaress, usefulness, wakefulness, wantonness, weaponless, wariness, willingness, willfulness, weariness, wickedness, wilderness, wretchedness, drunkenness, childishness. *Allowable rhymes*, mass, pass, etc., mace, place, etc.

ESE, *see* **EEZE.**

ESH.—Flesh, fresh, refresh, thresh, afresh, mesh. *Allowable rhymes*, mash, flash, etc.

ESK.—Desk. *Perfect rhymes*, grotesque, burlesque, etc. *Allowable rhymes*, mask, ask, etc.

EST.—Best, chest, crest, guest, jest, nest, pest, quest, rest, test, vest, west, arrest, attest, bequest, contest, detest, digest, divest, invest, infest, molest, obtest, protest, retest, suggest, unrest, interest, manifest, etc. *Perfect rhymes*, breast, abreast, etc., *and the preterits and participles of verbs in* ess, *as* dressed, expressed, etc. *Allowable rhymes*, cast, fast, etc., haste, waste, etc., beast, least, etc. *See* **EAST.**

ET.—Bet, jet, fret, get, let, met, net, set, wet, whet, yet, debt, abet, beget, beset, forget, regret, alphabet, amulet, anchoret, cabinet, epithet, parapet, rivulet, violet, counterfeit, coronet, etc. *Perfect rhymes*, sweat, threat, etc. *Allowable rhymes*, bate, hate, etc., beat, heat, etc.

ETCH.—Fetch, stretch, wretch, sketch, etc. *Allowable rhymes*, match, latch, etc., peach, bleach, etc.

ETE, *see* **EAT.** **EVE**, *see* **EAVE.** **EUM**, *see* **UME.**

EW.—Blew, chew, dew, brew, drew, flew, few, grew, new, knew, hew, Jew, mew, view, threw, yew, crew, slew, anew, askew, bedew, eschew, renew, review, withdrew, screw, interview, etc. *Perfect rhymes*, blue, clue, cue, glue, hue, rue, sue, strue, accrue, ensue, endue, imbue, imbrue, pursue, subdue, adieu, purlieu, perdue, residue, avenue, revenue, retinue.

EWD, *see* **EUD.** **EWN**, *see* **UNE.**

EX.—Sex, vex, annex, convex, complex, perplex, circumflex, *and the plurals of nouns and third persons singular of verbs in* eck, *as* checks, he checks, etc. *Allowable rhymes*, ax, wax, etc., *and the plurals of nouns and third persons singular of verbs in* ake, ack, eak, eke, ique, ike, etc., breaks, rakes, etc., he takes, he breaks, racks, he ekes, pikes, he likes, he pipes, etc.

EXT.—Next, pretext, *and the preterits and participles of verbs in* ex, *as* vexed, perplexed, etc. *Allowable rhymes, the preterits and participles of verbs in* ax, *as* waxed, etc.

EY, *see* **AY.**

I

IB.—Bib, crib, squib, drib, glib, nib, rib. *Allowable rhymes*, bribe, tribe, etc.

IBE.—Bribe, tribe, scribe, ascribe, describe, superscribe, prescribe, proscribe, subscribe, transcribe, inscribe. *Allowable rhymes*, bib, crib, etc.

ICE.—Ice, dice, mice, nice, price, rice, spice, slice, thrice, trice, advice, entice, vice, device. *Perfect rhymes*, rise, concise, precise, paradise, etc. *Allowable rhymes*, miss, kiss, hiss, artifice, avarice, cockatrice, benefice, cicatrice, edifice, orifice, prejudice, precipice, sacrifice, etc., piece, fleece, etc.

ICH, *see* **ITCH.**

ICK.—Brick, sick, chick, kick, lick, nick, pick, quick, stick, thick, trick, arithmetic, asthmatic, choleric, catholic, phlegmatic, heretic, rhetoric, schismatic, splenetic, lunatic, politic, empiric. *Allowable rhymes*, like, pike, etc., weak, speak, etc.

ICT.—Strict, addict, afflict, convict, inflict, contradict, etc. *Perfect rhymes, the preterits and participles of verbs in* ick, *as* licked, kicked, etc. *Allowable rhymes, the preterits and participles of verbs in* ike, eak, *as* liked, leaked, etc.

ID.—Bid, chid, hid, kid, lid, slid, rid, bestrid, pyramid, forbid. *Allowable rhymes*, bide, chide, parricide, etc., *and the preterits and participles of verbs in* y *or* ie, *as* died, replied, etc., lead, bead, mead, deed, need, etc., *and the preterits and participles of verbs in* ee, *as* freed, agreed, etc.

IDE.—Bide, chide, hide, glide, pride, ride, slide, side, stride, tide, wide, bride, abide, guide, aside, astride, beside, bestride, betide, confide, decide, deride, divide, preside, provide, subside, misguide, subdivide, etc. *Perfect rhymes, the preterits and participles of verbs in* ie *and* y, *as* dyed, replied, etc., *and the participle* sighed. *Allowable rhymes*, bead, mead, etc., bid, hid, etc.

IDES.—Ides, besides. *Perfect rhymes, the plurals of nouns and third persons singular of verbs in* ide, *as* tide, he rides, etc. *Allowable rhymes, the plurals of nouns and third persons singular of verbs in* ead, id, *as* beads, he leads, etc., kids, he bids, etc.

IDGE.—Bridge, ridge, abridge, etc.

IDST.—Midst, amidst, etc. *Perfect rhymes, the second person singular, of the present tense of verbs in* id, *as* thou biddest, thou hiddest, etc. *Allowable rhymes, the second persons singular of the present tense of verbs in* ide, *as* thou hidest, thou readest, etc.

IE, or Y.—By, buy, cry, die, dry, eye, fly, fry, fie, hie, lie, pie, ply, pry, rye, shy, sly, spry, sky, sty, tie, try, vie, why, ally, apply, awry, belie, comply, decry, defy, descry, deny, imply, espy, outvie, outfly, rely, reply, supply, untie, amplify, beautify, certify, crucify, deify, dignify, edify, falsify, fortify, gratify, glorify, indemnify, justify, magnify, modify, mollify, mortify, pacify, petrify, purify, putrefy, qualify, ratify, rectify, sanctify, satisfy, scarify, signify, specify, stupefy, terrify, testify, verify, vilify, vitrify, vivify, prophesy. *Perfect rhymes*, high, nigh, sigh, thigh. *Allowable rhymes*, bee, she, tea, sea, etc., pleurisy, chemistry, academy, apostasy, conspiracy, confederacy, ecstasy, democracy, embassy, fallacy, legacy, supremacy, lunacy, privacy, piracy, malady, remedy, tragedy, comedy, cosmography, geography, geometry, etc., elegy, certainty, sovereignty, loyalty, disloyalty, penalty, casualty, ribaldry, chivalry, infamy, constancy, fealty, cavalry, bigamy, polygamy, vacancy, inconstancy, infancy, company, accompany, dittany, tyranny, villainy, anarchy, monarchy, lethargy, incendiary, infirmary, library, salary, sanctuary, votary, auxiliary, contrary, diary, granary, rosemary, urgency, infantry, knavery, livery, recovery, robbery, novelty, antipathy, apathy, sympathy, idolatry, galaxy, husbandry, cruelty, enemy, blasphemy, prophecy, clemency, decency, inclemency, emergency, regency, progeny, energy, poverty, liberty, property, adultery, artery, artillery, battery, beggary, bribery, bravery, delivery, drudgery, flattery, gallery, imagery, lottery, misery, mystery, nursery, raillery, slavery, sorcery, treachery, discovery, tapestry, majesty, modesty, immodesty, honesty, dishonesty, courtesy, heresy, poesy, poetry, secrecy, leprosy, perfidy, subsidy, drapery, symmetry, drollery, prodigy, policy, mutiny, destiny, scrutiny, hypocrisy, family, ability, activity, avidity, assiduity, civility, community, concavity, consanguinity, conformity, congruity, diuturnity, facility, falsity, familiarity, formality, generosity, gratuity, humidity, absurdity, adversity, affability, affinity, agility, alacrity, ambiguity, animosity, antiquity, austerity, authority, brevity, calamity, capacity, captivity, charity, chastity, civility, credulity, curiosity, finery, declivity, deformity, duty, dexterity, dignity, disparity, diversity, divinity, enmity, enormity, equality, equanimity, equity, eternity, extremity, fatality, felicity, fertility, fidelity, frugality, futurity, gravity, hostility, humanity, humility, immanity, immaturity, immensity, immorality, immortality, immunity, immutability, impartiality, impossibility, impetuosity, improbity, inanity, incapacity, incivility, incongruity, inequality, indemnity, infinity, inflexibility, instability, invalidity, jollity, lenity, lubricity, magnanimity, majority, mediocrity, minority, mutability, nicety, perversity, perplexity, perspicuity, prosperity, privity, probability, probity, propensity, rarity, rapidity, sagacity, sanctity, sensibility, sensuality, solidity, temerity, timidity, tranquillity, virginity, visibility, university, trumpery, apology, genealogy, etymology, simony, symphony, soliloquy, allegory, armory, factory, pillory, faculty, treasury, usury, augury, importunity, impunity, impurity, inaccuracy, inability, incredulity, indignity, infidelity, infirmity, iniquity, integrity, laity, liberality, malignity, maturity, morality, mortality, nativity, necessity, neutrality, nobility, obscurity, opportunity, partiality, perpetuity, prosperity, priority, prodigality, purity, quality, quantity, scarcity, security, severity, simplicity, sincerity, solemnity, sterility, stupidity, trinity, vacuity, validity, vanity, vivacity, unanimity, uniformity, unity, anxiety, gaiety, impiety, piety, satiety, sobriety, society, variety, customary, melody, philosophy, astronomy, anatomy, colony, gluttony, harmony, agony, gallantry, canopy, history, memory, victory, calumny, injury, luxury, penury, perjury, usury, industry.

IECE, *see* **EASE.**

IEF.—Grief, chief, fief, thief, brief, belief, relief, etc. *Perfect rhymes*, reef, beef, etc. *Nearly perfect rhymes*, leaf, sheaf, etc.

IEGE.—Liege, siege, oblige, disoblige, assiege, besiege.

IELD.—Field, yield, shield, wield, afield. *Nearly perfect rhymes, the preterits and participles of verbs in* eal, *as* healed, repealed, etc.

IEN, *see* **EEN.** **IEND**, *see* **END.** **IERCE**, *see* **ERSE.** **IEST**, *see* **EAST.** **IEVE**, *see* **EAVE.**

IFE.—Rife, fife, knife, wife, strife, life. *Allowable rhymes*, cliff, skiff, stiff, whiff, etc.

IFF, *see* **IFE.**

IFT.—Gift, drift, shift, lift, rift, sift, thrift, adrift, etc., *and the preterits and participles of verbs in* iff, *as* whiffed, etc.

IG.—Big, dig, gig, fig, pig, rig, sprig, twig, swig. *Allowable rhymes*, léague, Teague, fatigue, etc.

IGE, *see* **IEGE.** **IGH**, *see* **IE.** **IGHT**, *see* **ITE.** **IGN**, *see* **INE**, **IGUE**, *see* **EAGUE.**

IKE.—Dike, like, pike, spike, strike, alike, dislike, oblique. *Allowable rhymes*, leak, speak, antique, etc., lick, pick, etc.

ILL.—Bill, chill, fill, drill, gill, hill, ill, kill, mill, quill, rill, shrill, skill, spill, still, swill, thrill, till, trill, will, distill, fulfill, instill, codicil, daffodil, utensil. *Perfect rhymes, all words ending in* ile, *with the accent on the antepenultimate syllable, as* volatile, etc. *Allowable rhymes*, byle, chyle, file, feel, reel, etc., meal, peal, seal, etc., *and words in* ble, *having the accent on the antepenultimate; as* suitable, etc.

ILD.—Child, mild, wild, etc. *Perfect rhymes, the preterits and participles of verbs of one syllable in* ile, *or of more syllables, provided the accent be on the last, as* piled, reviled, etc. *Allowable rhymes, the preterits and participles of verbs in* ill, *as* filled, willed, etc., *in* oil, *as* oiled, boiled, foiled, etc.

ILD. Gild, build, rebuild, etc. *Perfect rhymes, the preterits and participles of verbs in* illed, *as* filled, willed, etc. *Allowable rhymes*, child, mild, *and their allowable rhymes, which see.*

ILE.—Bile, chyle, file, guile, isle, mile, pile, smile, stile, style, tile, vile, while, awhile, compile, revile, defile, exile, erewhile, reconcile, beguile. *Allowable rhymes*, oil, boil, etc., bill, fill, etc.

ILK.—Milk, silk, bilk, etc.

ILT.—Gilt, jilt, built, quilt, guilt, hilt, spilt, stilt, tilt.

ILTH.—Filth, tilth, etc.

IM.—Brim, dim, grim, him, rim, skim, slim, trim, whim, prim. *Perfect rhymes*, limb, hymn, limn. *Allowable rhymes*, lime, time, climb, etc., team, gleam, etc.

IMB, *see* **IM.**

IME.—Chime, time, grime, climb, clime, crime, prime, mime, rhyme, slime, thyme, lime, sublime. *Allowable rhymes*, brim, dim, maritime, etc.

IMES.—Betimes, sometimes, etc. *Perfect rhymes, the plurals of nouns and third persons singular, present tense, of verbs in* ime, *as* chimes, he rhymes, etc. *Allowable rhymes, the plurals of nouns and third persons singular, present tense, of verbs in* eam *and* im, *as* dreams, brims, he swims, etc.

IMN, *see* **IM.**

IMP.—Imp, pimp, limp, gimp.

IMPSE.—Glimpse. *Rhymes, the plurals of nouns, third person present, of verbs in imp, as imps, he limps, etc.*

IN.—Chin, din, fin, gin, grin, in, inn, kin, pin, shin, sin, spin, skin, thin, tin, win, within, assassin, javelin, begin. *Allowable rhymes, chine, dine, etc., lean, bean, etc., machine, magazine, etc.*

INCE.—Mince, prince, since, quince, rinse, wince, convince, evince.

INCH.—Clinch, flinch, winch, pinch, inch.

INCT.—Instinct, distinct, extinct, precinct, succinct, etc., *and the preterits and participles of verbs in ink, as linked, pinked, etc.*

IND.—Bind, find, mind, blind, hind, kind, grind, rind, wind, behind, unkind, remind, etc., *and the preterits and participles of verbs in ine, as* refined. *Allowable rhymes, rescind, prescind, and the noun wind, as it is frequently pronounced, also the participles of verbs in oin, as joined.*

INE.—Dine, brine, mine, chine, fine, line, nine, pine, shine, shrine, kine, thine, trine, twine, vine, wine, whine, combine, confine, decline, define, incline, inshrine, intwine, opine, calcine, recline, refine, repine, superfine, interline, countermine, undermine, supine, concubine, porcupine, divine. *Perfect rhymes,* sign, assign, consign, design, etc. *Allowable rhymes,* bin, thin, tin, origin, join, loin, etc., *polysyllables ending in ine, pronounced in, as* masculine, feminine, discipline, libertine, heroine, etc.

ING.—Bring, sing, fling, cling, ring, sling, spring, sting, swing, wing, wring, thing, etc., *and the participles of the present tense in ing, with the accent on the antepenultimate, as* recovering, altering, etc.

INGE.—Cringe, fringe, hinge, singe, springe, swinge, tinge, twinge, infringe.

INK.—Ink, think, wink, drink, blink, brink, chink, clink, link, pink, shrink, sink, slink, stink, bethink, forethink.

INT.—Dint, mint, hint, flint, lint, print, squint, asquint, imprint.

IP.—Chip, lip, hip, clip, dip, drip, nip, sip, rip, scrip, ship, skip, slip, snip, strip, tip, trip, whip, equip, eldership, fellowship, workmanship, rivalship, *and all words in ship, with the accent on the antepenultimate. Allowable rhymes,* wipe, gripe, etc., leap, heap, etc.

IPE.—Gripe, pipe, ripe, snipe, type, stripe, wipe, archetype, prototype. *Allowable rhymes,* chip, lip, workmanship, etc.

IPSE.—Eclipse. *Rhymes, the plurals of nouns and third persons singular, present tense, of verbs in ip, as* grips, strips, etc. *Allowable rhymes, the plurals of nouns and third persons singular, present tense, of verbs in ipe, as* gripes, wipes, etc.

IR, see UR. IRCH, see URCH. IRD, see URD.

IRE.—Fire, dire, hire, ire, lyre, mire, quire, sire, spire, squire, wire, tire, attire, acquire, admire, aspire, conspire, desire, inquire, entire, expire, inspire, require, retire, transpire, Tyre. *Perfect rhymes,* friar, liar, brier, *and nouns formed from verbs ending in ie or y, as* crier, dyer, *as also the comparative of adjectives of the same sounding terminations, as* nigher, shyer, etc.

IRGE, see ERGE.

IRL.—Girl, whirl, twirl. *Nearly perfect rhymes,* curl, furl, churl, etc.

IRM.—Firm, affirm, confirm, infirm. *Nearly perfect rhymes,* worm, term, etc.

IRST, see URST. IRT, see URT.

IRTH.—Birth, mirth. *Perfect rhymes,* earth, dearth, *which see.*

ISS.—Bliss, miss, hiss, kiss, this, abyss, amiss, submiss, dismiss, remiss. *Allowable rhymes,* mice, spice, etc., peace, lease, etc.

IS, *pronounced like* **IZ.**—Is, his, whiz.

ISE, see ICE and IZE.

ISH.—Dish, wish, fish, cuish, pish.

ISK.—Brisk, frisk, disk, risk, whisk, basilisk, tamarisk.

ISP.—Crisp, wisp, lisp.

IST.—Fist, list, mist, twist, wrist, assist, consist, desist, exist, insist, persist, resist, subsist, alchemist, amethyst, anatomist, antagonist, annalist, evangelist, eucharist, exorcist, herbalist, humorist, oculist, organist, satirist, etc., *and the preterits and participles of verbs in iss, as* missed, hissed, etc. *Allowable rhymes, the preterits and participles of verbs in ice, as* spiced, sliced, etc.

IT.—Bit, cit, hit, fit, grit, flit, knit, nit, pit, quit, sit, split, twit, wit, whit, writ, admit, acquit, commit, emit, omit, outwit, permit, remit, submit, transmit, refit, benefit, perquisite. *Allowable rhymes,* beat, heat, etc., bite, mite, light, etc.

ITCH and HITCH.—Ditch, pitch, rich, which, Fitch, bitch, flitch, hitch, itch, stitch, switch, twitch, witch, bewitch, niche, enrich.

ITE and IGHT.—Bite, cite, kite, mite, quite, rite, smite, spite, trite, white, write, contrite, disunite, despite, indite, invite, excite, incite, polite, requite, unite, reunite, aconite, appetite, parasite, proselyte, expedite. *Perfect rhymes,* blight, benight, bright, fight, flight, fright, height, light, knight, night, might, plight, right, tight, slight, sight, spright, wight, affright, alight, aright, foresight, delight, despite, unsight, upright, bedight, oversight. *Allowable rhymes,* eight, weight, etc., bit, hit, etc., favorite, hypocrite, infinite, requisite, opposite, apposite, exquisite, etc.

ITH.—Pith, smith, frith.

ITHE.—Hithe, blithe, tithe, scythe, writhe, lithe. *Allowable rhyme,* with.

IVE.—Five, dive, alive, gyve, hive, drive, rive, shrive, strive, thrive, arrive, connive, contrive, deprive, derive, revive, survive. *Allowable rhymes,* give, live, sieve, forgive, outlive, fugitive, laxative, narrative, prerogative, primitive, sensitive, vegetive, affirmative, alternative, contemplative, demonstrative, diminutive, distributive, donative, inquisitive, lenitive, massive, negative, perspective, positive, preparative, provocative, purgative, restorative.

IX.—Fix, six, flix, mix, affix, infix, prefix, transmix, intermix, crucifix, etc., *and the plurals of nouns and third persons of verbs in ick, as* wicks, licks, etc. *Allowable rhymes, the plurals of nouns and third persons singular of verbs in ike, as* pikes, likes, etc.

IXT—Betwixt. *Rhymes, the preterits and participles of verbs in ix, as* fixed, mixed, etc.

ISE and IZE.—Prize, wise, rise, size, guise, disguise, advise, authorize, canonize, chastise, civilize, comprise, criticise, despise, devise, enterprise, excise, exercise, idolize, immortalize, premise, revise, signalize, solemnize, surprise, surmise, suffice, sacrifice, sympathize, tyrannize, *and the plurals of nouns and third persons singular, present tense, of verbs ending in ie or y, as* pies, lies, he replies, etc. *Allowable rhymes,* miss, hiss, precipice, etc.

O

O, *see* **OO** *and* **OW.**

OACH.—Broach, croach, proach, abroach, approach, encroach, reproach. *Perfect rhyme,* loach. *Allowable rhymes,* botch, notch, etc., mutch, hutch, etc.

OAD, *see* **AUD** *and* **ODE.** **OAF,** *see* **OFF.** **OAK,** *see* **OKE.** **OAL,** *see* **OLE.** **OAM,** *see* **OME.** **OAN,** *see* **ONE.** **OAP,** *see* **OPE.** **OAR,** *see* **ORE.** **OARD,** *see* **ORD.** **OAST,** *see* **OST.** **OAT,** *see* **OTE.** **OATH,** *see* **OTH.**

OB,—Fob, bob, mob, knob, sob, rob, throb. *Perfect rhymes,* swab, squab. *Allowable rhymes,* daub, globe, robe, dub, etc.

OBE.—Globe, lobe, probe, robe, conglobe. *Allowable rhymes,* fob, mob, etc., rub, dub, etc., daub, etc.

OCE, *see* **OSE.**

OCK.—Block, lock, cock, clock, crock, dock, frock, flock, knock, mock, rock, shock, stock, sock. *Allowable rhymes,* oak, poke, cloak, etc., look, took, etc., buck, suck, etc.

OCT.—Concoct. *Rhymes, the preterits and participles of verbs in ock, as* blocked, locked, etc. *Allowable rhymes, the preterits and participles of verbs in oak and oke, as* croaked, soaked, yoked, etc.

OD.—Clod, God, rod, sod, trod, nod, plod, odd, shod. *Allowable rhymes,* ode, code, mode, etc., *and the preterits and participles of verbs in ow, as* sowed, did sow, etc.

ODE and OAD.—Bode, ode, code, mode, rode, abode, corrode, explode, forbode, commode, incommode, episode, etc. *Perfect rhymes,* road, toad, goad, load, etc., *and the preterits and participles of verbs in ow, as* owed, showed, etc. *Allowable rhymes,* blood, flood, clod, hod, nod, broad, fraud, etc. *See* **OOD.**

OE, *see* **OW.**

OFF and OUGH.—Off, scoff, etc. *Perfect rhymes,* cough, trough, etc. *Allowable rhymes,* oaf, loaf, etc., proof, roof, etc. *See* **OOF.**

OFT.—Oft, croft, soft, aloft, etc., *and the preterits and participles of verbs in* off *and* uff, *as* ruffed, scoffed, etc.

OG.—Hog, bog, cog, dog, clog, fog, frog, log, jog, etc. *Perfect rhymes,* dialogue, epilogue, agog, synagogue, catalogue, pedagogue. *Allowable rhymes,* rogue, vogue, etc.

OGUE.—Rogue, vogue, prorogue, collogue, disembogue. *Allowable rhymes,* bog, log, dialogue, etc.

OICE.—Choice, voice, rejoice. *Allowable rhymes,* nice, vice, rice, etc.

OID.—Void, avoid, devoid, etc., *and the preterits and participles of verbs in oy, as* buoyed, cloyed, etc. *Allowable rhymes,* hide, bide, ride, etc.

OIL.—Oil, boil, coil, moil, soil, spoil, toil, despoil, embroil, recoil, turmoil, disembroil. *Allowable rhymes,* isle, while, tile, etc.

OIN.—Coin, join, subjoin, groin, loin, adjoin, conjoin, disjoin, enjoin, purloin, rejoin. *Allowable rhymes,* whine, wine, fine, etc. *See* **INE.**

OINT.—Oint, joint, point, disjoint, anoint, appoint, disappoint, counterpoint. *Allowable rhymes,* pint.

OISE.—Poise, noise, counterpoise, equipoise, etc., *and the plurals of nouns and third persons singular, present tense, of verbs in oy, as* boys, cloys, etc. *Allowable rhymes,* wise, size, prize, *and the plurals of nouns and third persons singular, present tense, of verbs in* ie *or* y, *as* pies, tries, etc.

OIST.—Hoist, moist, foist. *Perfect rhymes, the preterits and participles of verbs in oice, as* rejoiced. *Allowable rhymes, the preterits and participles of verbs in ice, as* spiced.

OIT.—Coit, exploit, adroit, etc. *Allowable rhymes,* white, light, might, sight, mite, etc.

OKE.—Broke, coke, smoke, spoke, stroke, yoke, bespoke, invoke, provoke, revoke, etc. *Perfect rhymes,* choke, cloak, oak, soak. *Allowable rhymes,* stock, mock. etc., buck, luck, etc., talk, walk, etc., look, book, etc. *See* **OCK** *and* **OOK.**

OL.—Loll, doll, droll, extol, capitol, etc. *Allowable rhymes,* all, ball, etc., bawl, etc., hole, mole, etc., dull, mull, etc.

OLD.—Old, bold, cold, gold, hold, mold, scold, sold, told, behold, enfold, unfold, uphold, withhold, foretold, manifold, marigold. *Perfect rhymes, preterits and participles of verbs in* oll, owl, ole *and* oal, *as* rolled, cajoled, foaled, bowled, etc.

OLE.—Bole, dole, jole, hole, mole, pole, sole, stole, whole, shole, cajole, condole, parole, patrol, pistole, etc. *Perfect rhymes,* coal, foal, goal, sole, bowl, droll, prowl, roll, scroll, toll, troll, control, enroll, etc., soul, etc., to roll, etc. *Allowable rhymes,* gull, dull, etc., bull, full, etc., loll, doll, etc., tool, cool, etc.

OLEN.—Stolen, swollen.

OLT.—Bolt, colt, jolt, holt, dolt, molt, revolt, thunderbolt. *Allowable rhymes,* vault, fault, salt, etc.

OLVE.—Solve, absolve, resolve, convolve, involve, devolve, dissolve, revolve.

OM, *see* **UM.**

OME.—Loam, dome, home, tome. *Perfect rhymes,* foam, roam, comb. *Allowable rhymes,* dum, hum, come, bomb, etc., troublesome, etc. *See* **OOM.**

OMB, *see* **OOM.** **OMPT,** *see* **OUNT.** **ON.** *see* **UN.**

ON.—Don, on, con, upon, anon, etc. *Perfect rhymes,* gone, undergone, etc. *Allowable rhymes,* dun, run, won, etc., own, moan, etc., lone, bone, etc., Amazon, cinnamon, comparison, caparison, garrison, skeleton, union, jupon.

OND.—Pond, bond, fond, beyond, abscond, correspond, despond, diamond, vagabond, etc., *and the preterits and participles of verbs in* on, *as* donned, conned, etc. *Allowable rhymes, the preterits and participles of verbs in* one, oan *and* un, *as* stoned, moaned, stunned, etc.

ONCE, *see* **UNCE.**

ONE.—Prone, bone, drone, throne, alone, stone, tone, lone, zone, atone, enthrone, dethrone, postpone, etc. *Perfect rhymes*, grown, flown, disown, thrown, sown, own, loan, shown, overthrown, groan, blown, moan, known. *Allowable rhymes*, dawn, lawn, etc., on, con, etc., none, bun, dun, etc., moon, boon, etc.

ONG.—Long, prong, song, thong, strong, throng, wrong, along, belong, prolong. *Allowable rhymes*, bung, among, hung, etc.

ONGUE, *see* **UNG. ONK,** *see* **UNK.**

ONSE.—Sconse, ensconce, etc. *Allowable rhymes*, once, nonce, askance, etc.

ONT.—Font. *Perfect rhyme*, want. *Allowable rhymes*, front, affront, etc., confront, punt, runt, etc., *the abbreviated negatives*, won't, don't, etc.

OO.—Coo, woo. *Nearly perfect rhymes*, shoe, two, too, who, etc., do, ado, undo, through, you, true, blue, flew, strew, etc. *Allowable rhymes*, know, blow, go, toe, etc.

OOD.—Brood, mood, food, rood, etc. *Nearly perfect rhymes, the preterits and participles of verbs in* oo, *as* cooed, wooed, etc. *Allowable rhymes*, wood, good, hood, stood, withstood, understood, brotherhood, livelihood, likelihood, neighborhood, widowhood, etc., blood, flood, etc., feud, allude, habitude, etc., *the preterits and participles of verbs in* ue *and* ew, *as* brewed, strewed, etc., imbued, subdued, etc., bud, mud, etc., *and the three apostrophized auxiliaries*, would, could, should, *pronounced* wou'd, cou'd, shou'd, etc., ode, code, *and the preterits and participles of verbs in* ow, *as* crowed, rowed, etc., *also* nod, hod, etc.

OOF.—Hoof, proof, roof, woof, aloof, disproof, reproof, behoof. *Allowable rhymes*, huff, ruff, rough, enough, etc., off, scoff, etc.

OOK.—Book, brook, cook, crook, hook, look, rook, shook, took, mistook, undertook, forsook, betook. *Allowable rhymes*, puke, fluke, etc., duck, luck, etc., broke, spoke, etc.

OOL.—Cool, fool, pool, school, stool, tool, befool. *Allowable rhymes*, pule, rule, etc., dull, gull, etc., bull, pull, etc., pole, hole, etc.

OOM.—Gloom, groom, loom, room, spoom, bloom, doom, etc. *Perfect rhymes*, tomb, entomb, *and the city* Rome. *Nearly perfect rhymes*, whom, womb, etc. *Allowable rhymes*, come, drum, etc., bomb, thumb, clomb, etc., plume, spume, etc., *and* from, home, comb, etc.

OON.—Boon, soon, moon, noon, spoon, swoon, buffoon, lampoon, poltroon. *Allowable rhymes*, tune, prune, etc., bun, dun, etc., gone, done, etc., bone, alone, etc., moan, roan, etc. *See* **ONE.**

OOP.—Loop, poop, scoop, stoop, troop, droop, whoop, coop, hoop, etc. *Perfect rhymes*, soup, group, etc. *Allowable rhymes*, dupe, up, sup, tup, etc., cop, top, etc., cope, hope, etc.

OOR.—Boor, poor, moor, etc. *Perfect rhymes*, tour, amour, paramour, contour. *Allowable rhymes*, bore, pore, etc., pure, sure, etc., your, pour, etc., door, floor, etc., bur, cur, etc., sir, stir, etc.

OOSE.—Goose, loose, etc. *Nearly perfect rhymes, the nouns* deuce, use, etc., profuse, seduce. *Allowable rhymes*, dose, jocose, globose, etc., moss, toss, etc., us, pus, thus, etc.

OOT.—Root, boot, coot, hoot, shoot. *Nearly perfect rhymes*, suit, fruit, etc., lute, impute, etc. *Allowable rhymes*, rote, vote, etc., goat, coat, etc., but, hut, soot, etc., foot, put, etc., hot, got, etc.

OOTH.—Booth, sooth, smooth. *Allowable rhymes*, tooth, youth, uncouth, forsooth, etc. *Though these are frequent, they are very improper rhymes, the* th *in one class being flat, and in the other sharp.*

OOZE.—Ooze, noose. *Perfect rhymes*, whose, choose, lose. *Nearly perfect rhymes, the verbs* to use, abuse, etc. *Allowable rhymes*, doze, hose, etc., buzz *and* does, *the third persons singular of* do, *with the plurals of nouns and third persons singular, present tense, of verbs in* ow, o, oe, ew, ue, *as* foes, goes, throws, views, imbues, flues, etc.

OP.—Chop, hop, drop, crop, fop, top, prop, flop, shop, slop, sop, stop, swap, underprop. *Allowable rhymes*, cope, trope, hope, etc., tup, sup, etc., coop, etc.

OPE.—Sope, hope, cope, mope, grope, pope, rope, scope, slope, tope, trope, aslope, elope, interlope, telescope, heliotrope, horoscope, antelope, etc., *and* ope, *contracted in poetry for* open. *Allowable rhymes*, hoop, coop, etc., lop, top, etc., tup, sup, etc.

OPT.—Adopt *rhymes perfectly with the preterits and participles of verbs in* op, *as* hopped, lopped, etc. *Allowable rhymes, the preterits and participles of verbs in* ope, upe, oop, *and* up, *as* coped, duped, hooped, cupped, etc.

OR.—Or, for, creditor, counselor, confessor, competitor, emperor, ancestor, ambassador, progenitor, conspirator, successor, conqueror, governor, abhor, metaphor, bachelor, senator, etc., *and every word in* or, *having the accent on the last, or last syllable but two, as* abhor, orator, etc. *Allowable rhymes*, bore, tore, etc., boar, hoar, etc., pure, endure, etc., pur, demur, etc., stir, sir, etc.

ORCH.—Scorch, torch, etc. *Allowable rhymes*, birch, smirch, church, etc., porch, etc.

ORCE.—Force, divorce, enforce, perforce, etc. *Perfect rhymes*, corse, coarse, hoarse, course, discourse, recourse, intercourse, source, resource, etc. *Allowable rhymes*, worse, purse, etc., horse, endorse, etc.

ORD.—Cord, lord, record, accord, abhorred. *Allowable rhymes*, hoard, board, aboard, ford, afford, sword, etc., word, curd, bird, etc., *and the preterits and participles of verbs in* ore, ur *and* ir, *as* bored, incurred, stirred, etc

ORE.—Bore, core, gore, lore, more, ore, pore, score, shore, snore, sore, store, swore, tore, wore, adore, afore, ashore, deplore, explore, implore, restore, forbore, forswore, heretofore, hellebore, sycamore. *Perfect rhymes*, boar, oar, roar, soar, four, door, floor, *and* o'er *for* over. *Allowable rhymes*, hour, sour, etc., pow'r *for* power, show'r *for* shower, etc., bur, cur, etc., poor, your, etc., abhor, orator, senator, etc. *See* **OOR** *and* **OR.**

ORGE.—Gorge, disgorge, regorge, etc. *Allowable rhymes*, forge, urge, dirge, etc.

ORK.—Ork, cork, fork, stork, etc. *Allowable rhymes*, pork, work.

ORLD.—World *rhymes perfectly with the preterits and participles of verbs in* url, *as* hurled, curled, etc.

ORM and ARM.—Form, storm, conform, deform, inform, perform, reform, misinform, uniform, multiform, transform. *Allowable rhymes*, form (*a seat*) *and* worm.

ORN, *rhyming with* **HORN.**—Born, corn, morn, horn, scorn, thorn, adorn, suborn, unicorn, Capricorn. *Allowable rhymes, the participles* borne, (*suffered*) shorn, etc., *the verb* mourn, *the nouns* urn, turn, etc.

ORN, *rhyming with* **MORN.**—Born, shorn, torn, worn, lorn, love-lorn, sworn, forsworn, overborn, forlorn. *Perfect rhyme*, mourn. *Allowable rhymes*, born, corn, etc., urn, burn, etc.

ORSE, *see* **ORCE.**—Horse, endorse, unhorse. *Allowable rhymes*, worse, curse, etc., remorse, coarse, course, corse, etc.

ORST, *see* **URST. ORT,** *see* **ART.**

ORT, *rhyming with* **WART.**—Short, sort, exhort, consort, distort, extort, resort, retort, snort. *Allowable rhymes*, fort, court, port, report, etc., dirt, shirt, etc., wort, hurt, etc.

ORT, *rhyming with* **COURT.**—Fort, port, sport, comport, disport, export, import, support, transport, report. *Allowable rhymes*, short, sort, etc., dirt, hurt, etc.

ORTH.—Forth, fourth. *Allowable rhymes*, north, worth, birth, earth, etc.

OSE, (*sounded*) **OCE.**—Close, dose, jocose. *Perfect rhymes*, morose, gross, engross, verbose. *Allowable rhymes*, moss, cross, etc., us, thus, etc.

OSE (*sounded*) **OZE.**—Close, dose, hose, pose, chose, gloze, froze, nose, prose, those, rose, compose, depose, disclose, dispose, discompose, expose, impose, inclose, interpose, oppose, propose, recompose, repose, suppose, transpose, arose, presuppose, foreclose, etc., *and the plurals of nouns and apostrophized preterits and participles of verbs in* ow, oe, o, etc., *as* rows, glows, foes, goes, etc. *Allowable rhymes, the verbs* choose, lose, etc., *and the plurals of nouns and third persons singular of verbs in* ow, *rhyming with* now, *as* cows, *and the word* buzz.

OSS.—Boss, loss, cross, dross, moss, toss, across, emboss. *Allowable rhymes, the nouns* close, dose, jocose, etc., *and* us, thus, etc.

OST.—Cost, frost, lost, accost, etc., *and the preterits and participles of words in* oss, *as* mossed, embossed, etc., *the verb* exhaust, *and the noun* holocaust. *Allowable rhymes*, ghost, host, post, compost, most, etc., coast, boast, toast, etc., bust, must, etc., roost, *and the preterits and participles of verbs in* oose, *as* loosed, etc.

OT, *see* **AT.**—Clot, cot, blot, got, hot, jot, lot, knot, not, plot, pot, scot, shot, sot, spot, apricot, trot, rot, grot, begot, forgot, allot, besot, complot, counterplot. *Allowable rhymes*, note, vote, etc., boat, coat etc., but, cut, etc.

OTCH.—Botch, notch, etc. *Perfect rhyme*, watch. *Allowable rhymes*, much, such, etc.

OTE.—Note, vote, mote, quote, rote, wrote, smote, denote, promote, remote, devote, anecdote, antidote, etc. *Perfect rhymes*, boat, coat, bloat, doat, gloat, float, goat, oat, overfloat, afloat, throat, moat. *Allowable rhymes*, bout, flout, etc., hot, cot, etc., but, cut, etc., boot, hoot, etc.

OTH.—Broth, cloth, froth, moth, troth, betroth. *Perfect rhyme*, wrath. *Allowable rhymes*, both, loth, sloth, oath, growth, etc., forsooth, *the noun* mouth, *and the solemn auxiliary* doth, *to which some poets add* loathe, clothe, *but I think improperly. See* **OOTH.**

OU, *see* **OO** *and* **OW. OUBT,** *see* **OUT.**

OUCH.—Couch, pouch, vouch, slouch, avouch, crouch. *Allowable rhymes*, much, such, etc., coach, roach, etc.

OUD.—Shroud, cloud, proud, loud, aloud, crowd, overshroud, etc., *and the preterits and participles of verbs in* ow, *as* he bowed, vowed, etc. *Allowable rhymes, the preterits and participles of verbs in* ow, *as* owed, flowed, etc., blood, flood, etc., bud, mud, etc.

OVE.—Wove, inwove, interwove, alcove, clove, grove, rove, stove, strove, throve, drove. *Allowable rhymes*, dove, love, shove, glove, above, etc., move, behoove, approve, disprove, disapprove, improve, groove, prove, reprove, etc.

OUGH, *see* **OFF, OW** *and* **UFF.**

OUGHT.—Bought, thought, ought, brought, forethought, fought, nought, sought, wrought, besought, bethought, methought, etc. *Perfect rhymes*, aught, naught, caught, taught, etc., *sometimes* draught. *Allowable rhymes*, not, yacht, etc., note, vote, etc., butt, hut, etc., hoot, root, etc.

OUL, *see* **OLE** *and* **OWL.**

OULD.—Mould. *Perfect rhymes*, fold, old, cold, etc., *and the preterits and participles of verbs in* owl, ol *and* ole, *as* bowled, tolled, cajoled, etc. *Allowable rhymes, the preterits and participles of verbs in* ull, *as* gulled, pulled, etc.

OUNCE.—Bounce, flounce, renounce, pounce, ounce, denounce, pronounce.

OUND.—Bound, found, mound, ground, hound, pound, round, sound, wound, abound, aground, around, confound, compound, expound, profound, rebound, redound, resound, propound, surround, etc., *and the preterits and participles of verbs in* own, *as* frowned, renowned, etc. *Allowable rhymes, the preterits and participles of verbs in* one, oan *and* un, *as* toned, moaned, sunned, etc., *consequently* fund, refund, etc., *and* wound (*a hurt*), *pronounced* woond.

OUNG, *see* **UNG.**

OUNT.—Count, mount, fount, amount, dismount, remount, surmount, account, discount, miscount. *Allowable rhymes*, want, font, don't, won't, etc.

OUP, *see* **OOP.**

OUR.—Hour, lour, sour, our, scour, deflour, devour, etc., *rhymes perfectly with* bower, cower, flower, power, shower, tower, etc., *pronounced* bow'r, tow'r, etc. *Allowable rhymes*, bore, more, roar, pour, tour, moor, poor, etc., pure, sure, etc., sir, stir, bur, cur, etc.

OURGE, *see* **URGE, OURNE,** *see* **ORN** *and* **URN.**

OURS.—Ours *rhymes perfectly with the plurals of nouns and third persons present of verbs in* our *and* ower, *as* hours, scours, deflours, bowers, showers, etc. *Allowable rhymes, the plurals of nouns and third persons present of verbs in* oor *and* ure, *as* boors, moors, etc., cures, endures, etc.

OURS.—Yours *rhymes perfectly with the plurals of nouns and third persons present of verbs in* ure, *as* cures, endures, etc. *Allowable rhymes,* ours, *and its perfect rhymes and the plurals of nouns and third persons present of verbs in* oor, ore *and* ur, *as* boors, moors, etc., shores, pores, etc., burs, slurs, stirs, etc.

OURSE, *see* **ORCE. OURT,** *see* **ORT. OURTH,** *see* **ORTH. OUS,** *see* **US.**

OUS, *pronounced* **OUCE.**—House, mouse, chouse, etc. *Allowable rhymes, the nouns* close, dose, jocose, etc., deuce, use, produce, etc., us, thus, etc., moose, *and the noun* noose.

OUSE, *pronounced* **OUZE,** *see* **OWZE.**

OUT.—Bout, stout, out, clout, pout, gout, grout, route, scout, shout, snout, spout, stout, sprout, trout, about, devout, without, throughout, etc., *rhymes perfectly with* doubt, redoubt, misdoubt, drought, etc. *Allowable rhymes,* note, vote, etc., boat, coat, etc., lute, suit, etc., got, not, etc., nut, shut, hoot, boot, etc.

OUTH.—Mouth, south, *when nouns have the* th *sharp. The verbs* to mouth, to south, *may allowably rhyme with* booth, smooth, etc., *which see.*

OW, *sounded* **OU.**—Now, bow, how, mow, cow, brow, plow, sow, vow, prow, avow, allow, disallow, endow, etc. *Perfect rhymes,* bough, plough, slough, (*mire*), etc., thou. *Allowable rhymes,* go, no, blow, so, etc.

OW, *sounded* **OWE.**—Blow, stow, crow, bow, flow, glow, grow, know, low, mow, row, show, sow, strow, stow, slow, snow, throw, trow, below, bestow, foreknow, outgrow, overgrow, overflow, overthrow, reflow, foreshow, etc. *Perfect rhymes,* go, no, toe, foe, owe, wo, oh, so, lo, though, hoe, ho, ago, forego, undergo, dough, roe, sloe, *and the verb* to sew (*with the needle*). *Allowable rhymes,* now, cow, vow, do, etc. *See the last article.*

OWL, *see* **OLE.**—Cowl, growl, owl, fowl, howl, prowl, etc. *Perfect rhymes,* scowl, foul, etc. *Allowable rhymes,* bowl, soul, shoal, goal, etc., dull, gull, etc.

OWN, *see* **ONE.**—Brown, town, clown, crown, down, drown, frown, grown, adown, renown, embrown, etc. *Perfect rhyme,* noun. *Allowable rhymes,* tone, bone, moan, own, *and the participles* thrown, shown, blown.

OWSE, *see* **OUSE.**—Blouse. *Perfect rhymes,* brouse, trouse, rouse, spouse, carouse, souse, espouse, *the verbs* to house, mouse, etc., *and the plurals of nouns and third persons, present tense, of verbs in* ow, *as* brows, allows, etc. *Allowable rhymes,* hose, those, to dose, etc.

OX.—Ox, box, fox, equinox, orthodox, heterodox, etc. *Perfect rhymes, the plurals of nouns and third persons present of verbs in* ock, *as* locks, stocks, etc. *Allowable rhymes, the plurals of nouns and third persons present of verbs in* oke, oak, *and* uck, *as* strokes, oaks, cloaks, sucks, etc.

OY.—Boy, buoy, coy, employ, cloy, joy, toy, alloy, annoy, convoy, decoy, destroy, enjoy, employ.

OZE, *see* **OSE.**

U

UB.—Cub, club, dub, drub, grub, rub, snub, shrub, tub. *Allowable rhymes,* cube, tube, etc., cob, rob, etc.

UBE.—Cube, tube. *Allowable rhymes,* club, cub, etc.

UCE.—Truce, sluice, spruce, deuce, conduce, deduce, induce, introduce, produce, seduce, traduce, juice, reduce, etc., *rhyme perfectly with the nouns* use, abuse, profuse, abstruse, disuse, excuse, misuse, obtuse, recluse.

UCH, *see* **UTCH.**

UCK.—Buck, luck, pluck, suck, struck, tuck, truck, duck. *Allowable rhymes,* puke, duke, etc., look, took, etc.

UCT.—Conduct, deduct, instruct, obstruct, aqueduct. *Perfect rhymes, the preterits and participles of verbs in* uck, *as* ducked, sucked, etc. *Allowable rhymes, the preterits and participles of verbs in* uke *and* ook, *as* puked, hooked, etc.

UD.—Bud, scud, stud, mud, cud, *rhyme perfectly with* blood *and* flood. *Allowable rhymes,* good, hood, etc., rood, food, etc., beatitude, latitude.

UDE.—Rude, crude, prude, allude, conclude, delude, elude, exclude, exude, include, intrude, obtrude, seclude, altitude, fortitude, gratitude, interlude, latitude, longitude, magnitude, multitude, solicitude, solitude, vicissitude, aptitude, habitude, ingratitude, inaptitude, lassitude, plenitude, promptitude, servitude, similitude, etc. *Perfect rhymes,* leud, feud, etc., *and the preterits and participles of verbs in* ew, *as* stewed, viewed, etc. *Allowable rhymes,* bud, cud, etc., good, hood, etc., blood, flood, etc.

UDGE.—Judge, drudge, grudge, trudge, adjudge, prejudge.

UE, *see* **EW.**

UFF.—Buff, cuff, bluff, huff, gruff, luff, puff, snuff, stuff, ruff, rebuff, counterbuff, etc. *Perfect rhymes,* rough, tough, enough, slough (*cast skin*), chough, etc. *Allowable rhymes,* loaf, oaf, etc.

UFT.—Tuft. *Perfect rhymes, the preterits and participles of verbs in* uff, *as* cuffed, stuffed.

UG.—Lug, bug, dug, drug, hug, rug, slug, snug, mug, shrug, pug. *Allowable rhymes,* vogue, rogue, etc.

UICE, *see* **USE. UISE,** *see* **ISE** *and* **USE. UIE,** *see* **IE.**

UKE.—Duke, puke, rebuke, etc. *Nearly perfect rhymes,* cook, look, book, etc. *Allowable rhymes,* duck, buck, etc.

UL and ULL.—Cull, dull, gull, hull, lull, mull, null, trull, skull, annul, disannul. *Allowable rhymes,* fool, tool, etc., wool, bull, pull, full, bountiful, fanciful, sorrowful, dutiful, merciful, wonderful, worshipful, *and every word ending in* ful, *having the accent on the antepenultimate syllable.*

ULE.—Mule, pule, yule, rule, overrule, ridicule, misrule. *Allowable rhymes,* cull, dull, wool, full, bountiful. *See the last article.*

ULGE.—Bulge, indulge, divulge, etc.

ULK.—Bulk, hulk, skulk.

ULSE.—Pulse, repulse, impulse, expulse, convulse.

ULT.—Result, adult, exult, consult, indult, occult, insult, difficult. *Allowable rhymes,* colt, bolt, etc.

UM.—Crum, drum, grum, gum, hum, mum, scum, plum, stum, sum, swum, thrum. *Perfect rhymes,* thumb, dumb, succumb, come, become, overcome burthensome, cumbersome, frolicsome, humorsome, quarrelsome, troublesome, martyrdom, christendom. *Allowable rhymes,* fume, plume, rheum, *and* room, doom, tomb, hecatomb.

UME.—Fume, plume, assume, consume, perfume, resume, presume, deplume.

UMP.—Bump, pump, jump, lump, plump, trump, stump, rump, thump.

UN.—Dun, gun, nun, pun, run, sun, shun, tun, stun, spun, begun. *Perfect rhymes,* son, won, ton, done, one, none, undone. *Allowable rhymes,* on, gone, etc., tune, prune, etc. *See* **ON.**

UNCE.—Dunce, once, etc. *Allowable rhyme,* sconce.

UNCH.—Bunch, punch, hunch, lunch, munch.

UND.—Fund, refund. *Perfect rhymes, the preterits and participles of verbs in* un, *as* shunned, etc.

UNE.—June, rune, untune, jejune, prune, importune, etc. *Nearly perfect rhymes,* moon, soon, etc. *Allowable rhymes,* bun, dun, etc.

UNG.—Clung, dung, flung, hung, rung, strung, sung, sprung, slung, stung, swung, unsung. *Perfect rhymes,* young, tongue, among. *Allowable rhymes,* song, long, etc.

UNGE.—Plunge, spunge, expunge, etc.

UNK.—Drunk, sunk, shrunk, stunk, spunk, punk, trunk, slunk. *Perfect rhyme,* monk.

UNT.—Brunt, blunt, hunt, runt, grunt. *Perfect rhyme,* wont (*to be accustomed*).

UP.—Cup, sup, up. *Allowable rhymes,* cope, scope, *and* dupe, group.

UPT.—Abrupt, corrupt, interrupt. *Perfect rhymes, the participles of verbs in* up, *as* supped, etc.

UR. Blur, cur, bur, fur, slur, spur, concur, demur, incur. *Perfect rhymes,* sir, stir. *Nearly perfect rhymes,* fir, etc. *Allowable rhymes,* pore, oar, etc.

URB.—Curb, disturb. *Nearly perfect rhymes,* verb, herb, etc. *Allowable rhyme,* orb.

URCH.—Church, lurch, birch. *Nearly perfect rhymes,* perch, search. *Allowable rhyme,* porch.

URD.—Curd, absurd. *Perfect rhymes,* bird, word, *and the preterits and participles of verbs in* ur, *as* spurred. *Allowable rhymes,* board, ford, cord, lord, etc., *and the preterits and participles of verbs in* ore, oar *and* or, *as* goared, oared, abhorred, etc., *also the preterits and participles of verbs in* ure, *as* cured, immured, etc. *See* **ORD.**

URE.—Cure, pure, dure, lure, sure, adjure, allure, assure, demure, conjure, endure, manure, enure, insure, immature, immure, mature, obscure, procure, secure, calenture, coverture, epicure, investiture, forfeiture, furniture, miniature, overture, portraiture, primogeniture, temperature. *Allowable rhymes,* poor, moor, power, sour, etc., cur, bur, etc.

URF.—Turf, scurf, etc.

URGE.—Purge, urge, surge, scourge. *Perfect rhymes,* verge, diverge, etc. *Allowable rhymes,* gorge, George, etc., forge, etc.

URK.—Lurk, Turk. *Perfect rhyme,* work. *Nearly perfect rhymes,* irk, jerk, perk.

URL, *see* **IRL.**—Churl, curl, furl, hurl, purl, uncurl, unfurl. *Nearly perfect rhymes,* girl, twirl, etc., pearl, etc.

URN.—Burn, churn, spurn, turn, urn, return, overturn. *Perfect rhymes,* sojourn, adjourn, rejourn.

URSE.—Nurse, curse, purse, accurse, disburse, imburse, reimburse. *Perfect rhyme,* worse. *Allowable rhymes,* coarse, corse, force, verse, disperse, horse, etc.

URST.—Burst, curst, accurst, etc. *Perfect rhymes,* thirst, worst, first.

URT.—Blurt, hurt, spurt. *Perfect rhymes,* dirt, shirt, flirt, squirt, etc. *Allowable rhymes,* port, court, short, snort, etc.

US.—Us, thus, buss, truss, discuss, incubus, overplus, amorous, boisterous, clamorous, credulous, dangerous, degenerous, generous, emulous, fabulous, frivolous, hazardous, idolatrous, infamous, miraculous, mischievous, mountainous, mutinous, necessitous, numerous, ominous, perilous, poisonous, populous, prosperous, ridiculous, riotous, ruinous, scandalous, scrupulous, sedulous, traitorous, treachorous, tyrannous, venomous, villainous, vigorous, adventurous, adulterous, ambiguous, blasphemous, dolorous, fortuitous, sonorous, gluttonous, gratuitous, incredulous, lecherous, libidinous, magnanimous, obstreporous, odoriferous, ponderous, ravenous, rigorous, slanderous, solicitous, timorous, valorous, unanimous, calamitous. *Allowable rhymes, the nouns* use, abuse, diffuse, excuse, *the verb* to loose, *and the nouns,* goose, deuce, juice, truce, etc., close, dose, house, mouse, etc.

USE, *with the* **S** *pure.*—*The nouns* use, disuse, abuse, deuce, truce. *Perfect rhymes, the verb* to loose, *the nouns* goose, noose, moose. *Allowable rhymes,* us, thus, buss, etc.

USE (*sounded*) **UZE.**—Muse, *the verbs* to use, abuse, amuse, diffuse, excuse, infuse, misuse, peruse, refuse, suffuse, transfuse, accuse. *Perfect rhymes,* bruise, *the plurals of nouns and third persons singular of verbs in* ew *and* ue, *as* dews, imbues, etc. *Allowable rhymes,* buzz, does, etc.

USH.—Blush, brush, crush, gush, flush, rush, hush. *Allowable rhymes,* bush, push.

USK.—Busk, tusk, dusk, husk, musk.

UST.—Bust, crust, dust, just, must, lust, rust, thrust, trust, adjust, adust, disgust, distrust, intrust, mistrust, unjust, robust. *Perfect rhymes, the preterits and participles of verbs in* uss, *as* trussed, discussed, etc.

UT.—But, butt, cut, hut, gut, glut, jut, nut, shut, strut, englut, rut, scut, slut, smut, abut. *Perfect rhyme,* soot. *Allowable rhymes,* boot, etc., dispute, etc., boat, etc.

UTCH.—Hutch, crutch, Dutch. *Perfect rhymes,* much, such, touch,

UTE.—Brute, lute, flute, mute, acute, compute, confute, dispute, dilute, depute, impute, minute, pollute, refute, repute, salute, absolute, attribute, constitute, destitute, dissolute, execute, institute, irresolute, persecute, prosecute, prostitute, resolute, substitute. *Perfect rhymes,* fruit, recruit, etc. *Allowable rhymes,* boot, etc., boat, etc., note, etc., hut, etc.

UX.—Flux, reflux, etc. *Perfect rhymes, the plurals of nouns and third persons of verbs in* uck, *as* ducks, trucks, etc. *Allowable rhymes, the plurals of nouns and third persons of verbs in* ook, uke, oak, etc., *as* cooks, pukes, oaks, etc.

Y, *see* **IE.**

CHOICE
SELECTIONS
FROM
THE POETS.

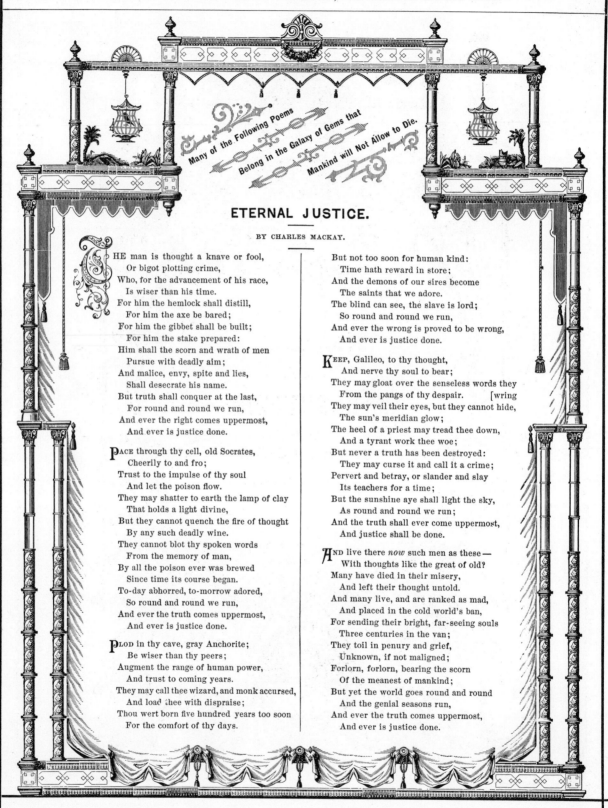

Many of the Following Poems Belong in the Galaxy of Gems that Mankind will Not Allow to Die.

ETERNAL JUSTICE.

BY CHARLES MACKAY.

THE man is thought a knave or fool,
 Or bigot plotting crime,
Who, for the advancement of his race,
 Is wiser than his time.
For him the hemlock shall distill,
 For him the axe be bared;
For him the gibbet shall be built;
 For him the stake prepared:
Him shall the scorn and wrath of men
 Pursue with deadly aim;
And malice, envy, spite and lies,
 Shall desecrate his name.
But truth shall conquer at the last,
 For round and round we run,
And ever the right comes uppermost,
 And ever is justice done.

PACE through thy cell, old Socrates,
 Cheerily to and fro;
Trust to the impulse of thy soul
 And let the poison flow.
They may shatter to earth the lamp of clay
 That holds a light divine,
But they cannot quench the fire of thought
 By any such deadly wine.
They cannot blot thy spoken words
 From the memory of man,
By all the poison ever was brewed
 Since time its course began.
To-day abhorred, to-morrow adored,
 So round and round we run,
And ever the truth comes uppermost,
 And ever is justice done.

PLOD in thy cave, gray Anchorite;
 Be wiser than thy peers;
Augment the range of human power,
 And trust to coming years.
They may call thee wizard, and monk accursed,
 And load thee with dispraise;
Thou wert born five hundred years too soon
 For the comfort of thy days.

But not too soon for human kind:
 Time hath reward in store;
And the demons of our sires become
 The saints that we adore.
The blind can see, the slave is lord;
 So round and round we run,
And ever the wrong is proved to be wrong,
 And ever is justice done.

KEEP, Galileo, to thy thought,
 And nerve thy soul to bear;
They may gloat over the senseless words they
 From the pangs of thy despair. [wring
They may veil their eyes, but they cannot hide,
 The sun's meridian glow;
The heel of a priest may tread thee down,
 And a tyrant work thee woe;
But never a truth has been destroyed:
 They may curse it and call it a crime;
Pervert and betray, or slander and slay
 Its teachers for a time;
But the sunshine aye shall light the sky,
 As round and round we run;
And the truth shall ever come uppermost,
 And justice shall be done.

AND live there *now* such men as these—
 With thoughts like the great of old?
Many have died in their misery,
 And left their thought untold.
And many live, and are ranked as mad,
 And placed in the cold world's ban,
For sending their bright, far-seeing souls
 Three centuries in the van;
They toil in penury and grief,
 Unknown, if not maligned;
Forlorn, forlorn, bearing the scorn
 Of the meanest of mankind;
But yet the world goes round and round
 And the genial seasons run,
And ever the truth comes uppermost,
 And ever is justice done.

HEREAFTER.

O LAND beyond the setting sun!
　O realm more fair than poet's
　　dream!
How clear thy silvery streamlets run,
　How bright thy golden glories
　　gleam!

Earth holds no counterpart of thine;
　The dark-browed Orient, jewel-
　　crowned,
Pales, as she bows before thy shrine,
　Shrouded in mystery so profound.

The dazzling North, the stately West,
　Whose rivers flow from mount to sea;
The South, flower-wreathed in languid rest,
　What are they all compared with thee?

All lands, all realms beneath yon dome,
　Where God's own hand hath hung the stars,
To thee with humblest homage come,
　O world beyond the crystal bars!

Thou blest hereafter! Mortal tongue
　Hath striven in vain thy speech to learn,
And fancy wanders, lost among
　The flowery paths for which we yearn.

But well we know, that fair and bright,
　Far beyond human ken or dream,
Too glorious for our feeble sight,
　Thy skies of cloudless azure beam.

We know thy happy valleys lie
　In green repose, supremely blest;
We know against thy sapphire sky
　Thy mountain peaks sublimely rest.

And sometimes even now we catch
　Faint gleamings from the far-off shore,
And still with eager eyes we watch
　For one sweet sign or token more.

For oh, the deeply loved are there!
　The brave, the fair, the good, the wise,
Who pined for thy serener air,
　Nor shunned thy solemn mysteries.

There are the hopes that, one by one,
　Died even as we gave them birth;
The dreams that passed ere well begun,
　Too dear, too beautiful for earth.

The aspirations, strong of wing,
　Aiming at heights we could not reach;
The songs we tried in vain to sing;
　Thoughts too vast for human speech;

Thou hast them all, Hereafter! Thou
　Shalt keep them safely till that hour
When, with God's seal on heart and brow,
　We claim them in immortal power!

NEVER AGAIN.

NEVER again will the roses blow
　For us as the roses we used to know.

Oh! never again will the wide sky hold
Such wealth of glory and sunset gold;

And never again will I whisper, dear,
The pleasant fancies you smiled to hear;

And never again, at the day's decline,
Shall I sit with your little hand in mine,

And look at the beauty of sunset skies,
And the sweeter beauty of your sweet eyes.

Never again! for the dream is done
That a word, and a look, and a touch begun.

Love, if we *always* could dream, ah, then!
The words are as sad as "it might have been!"

For us, there is nothing but memory,
In the coming days, *of what could not be!*

Love, you are near me, and yet as far
As the round earth is from the fartherest star.

Kiss me and smile in my eyes once more,
Tho' your lips should quiver, and tears run o'er.

Put your hand in mine for one moment, one,
And then, good-bye, for the dream is done!

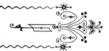

HANNAH JANE.

BY PETROLEUM V. NASBY.

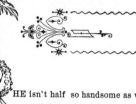

SHE isn't half so handsome as when, twenty
    years agone,
At her old home in Piketon, Parson Avery
    made us one;
The great house crowded full of guests of
    every degree,
The girls all envying Hannah Jane, the
    boys all envying me.

Her fingers then were taper, and her skin as white as milk,
Her brown hair—what a mess it was! and soft and fine as silk;
No wind-moved willow by a brook had ever such a grace,
The form of Aphrodite, with a pure Madonna face.

She had but meagre schooling; her little notes, to me,
Were full of crooked pot-hooks, and the worst orthography;
Her "dear" she spelled with double e, and "kiss" with but one s;
But when one's crazed with passion, what's a letter more or less?

She blundered in her writing, and she blundered when she spoke,
And every rule of syntax, that old Murray made, she broke;
But she was beautiful and fresh, and I—well, I was young;
Her form and face o'erbalanced all the blunders of her tongue.

I was but little better. True, I'd longer been at school;
My tongue and pen were run, perhaps, a little more by rule;
But that was all. The neighbors round, who both of us well knew,
Said—which I believed—she was the better of the two.

All's changed: the light of seventeen 's no longer in her eyes;
Her wavy hair is gone—that loss the coiffeur's art supplies;
Her form is thin and angular; she slightly forward bends;
Her fingers, once so shapely, now are stumpy at the ends.

She knows but very little, and in little are we one;
The beauty rare, that more than hid that great defect, is gone.
My parvenu relations now deride my homely wife,
And pity me that I am tied, to such a clod, for life.

I know there is a difference; at reception and levee,
The brightest, wittiest, and most famed of women smile on me;
And everywhere I hold my place among the greatest men;
And sometimes sigh, with Whittier's judge, "Alas! it might have
    been."

When they all crowd around me, stately dames and brilliant belles,
And yield to me the homage that all great success compels,
Discussing art and state-craft, and literature as well,
From Homer down to Thackeray, and Swedenborg on "Hell,"

I can't forget that from these streams my wife has never quaffed,
Has never with Ophelia wept, nor with Jack Falstaff laughed;
Of authors, actors, artists—why, she hardly knows the names;
She slept while I was speaking on the Alabama claims.

I can't forget—just at this point another form appears—
The wife I wedded as she was before my prosperous years;
I travel o'er the dreary road we traveled side by side,
And wonder what my share would be, if Justice should divide.

She had four hundred dollars left her from the old estate;
On that we married, and, thus poorly armored, faced our fate.
I wrestled with my books; her task was harder far than mine—
'Twas how to make two hundred dollars do the work of nine.

At last I was admitted; then I had my legal lore,
An office with a stove and desk, of books perhaps a score;
She had her beauty and her youth, and some housewifely skill,
And love for me and faith in me, and back of that a will.

I had no friends behind me—no influence to aid;
I worked and fought for every little inch of ground I made.
And how she fought beside me! never woman lived on less;
In two long years she never spent a single cent for dress.

Ah! how she cried for joy when my first legal fight was won,
When our eclipse passed partly by, and we stood in the sun!
The fee was fifty dollars—'t was the work of half a year—
First captive, lean and scraggy, of my legal bow and spear.

I well remember when my coat (the only one I had)
Was seedy grown and threadbare, and, in fact, most shocking bad,
The tailor's stern remark when I a modest order made:
"Cash is the basis, sir, on which we tailors do our trade."

Her winter cloak was in his shop by noon that very day;
She wrought on hickory shirts at night that tailor's skill to pay;
I got a coat, and wore it; but alas! poor Hannah Jane
Ne'er went to church or lecture till warm weather came again.

Our second season she refused a cloak of any sort,
That I might have a decent suit in which t' appear in court;
She made her last year's bonnet do, that I might have a hat:
Talk of the old-time, flame-enveloped martyrs after that!

No negro ever worked so hard; a servant's pay to save,
She made herself most willingly a household drudge and slave.
What wonder that she never read a magazine or book,
Combining as she did in one, nurse, house-maid, seamstress, cook.

What wonder that the beauty fled, that I once so adored!
Her beautiful complexion my fierce kitchen fire devoured;
Her plump, soft, rounded arm was once too fair to be concealed;
Hard work for me that softness into sinewy strength congealed.

I was her altar, and her love the sacrificial flame:
Ah! with what pure devotion she to that altar came,
And, tearful, flung thereon—alas! I did not know it then—
All that she was, and more than that, all that she might have been!

At last I won success. Ah! then our lives were wider parted:
I was far up the rising road; she, poor girl! where we started.
I had tried my speed and mettle, and gained strength in every race;
I was far up the heights of life—she drudging at the base.

She made me take each fall the stump; she said 't was my career;
The wild applause of list'ning crowds was music to my ear.
What stimulus had she to cheer her dreary solitude?
For me she lived on gladly, in unnatural widowhood.

She couldn't read my speech, but when the papers all agreed
'T was the best one of the session, those comments she could read;
And with a gush of pride thereat, which I had never felt,
She sent them to me in a note, with half the words misspelt.

I to the legislature went, and said that she should go
To see the world with me, and, what the world was doing, know.
With tearful smile she answered, "No! four dollars is the pay;
The Bates House rates for board *for one* is just that sum per day."

At twenty-eight the State-house; on the bench at thirty-three;
At forty every gate in life was opened wide to me.

I nursed my powers, and grew, and made my point in life; but she—
Bearing such pack-horse weary loads, what could a woman be?

What could she be? Oh, shame! I blush to think what she has been,
The most unselfish of all wives to the selfishest of men.
Yes, plain and homely now she is; she's ignorant, 't is true;
For me she rubbed herself quite out; I represent the two.

Well, I suppose that I might do as other men have done—
First break her heart with cold neglect, then shove her out alone.
The world would say 't was well, and more, would give great praise to me,
For having borne with "such a wife" so uncomplainingly.

And shall I? No! The contract 'twixt Hannah, God and me,
Was not for one or twenty years, but for eternity.
No matter what the world may think; I know, down in my heart,
That, if either, I'm delinquent; she has bravely done her part.

There's another world beyond this; and, on the final day,
Will intellect and learning 'gainst such devotion weigh?
When the great one, made of us two, is torn apart again,
I'll fare the worst, for God is just, and He knows Hannah Jane.

THE MOTHERLESS TURKEYS.

BY MARIAN DOUGLASS.

THE white turkey was dead! The white turkey was dead!
    How the news through the barn-yard went flying!
Of a mother bereft, four small turkeys were left,
    And their case for assistance was crying.
    E'en the peacock respectfully folded his tail,
As a suitable symbol of sorrow,
And his plainer wife said, "now the old bird is dead,
    Who will tend her poor chicks on the morrow?
And when evening around them comes dreary and chill,
    Who above them will watchfully hover?"
"Two each night I will tuck 'neath my wings," said the Duck,
    "Though I have eight of my own I must cover!"
"I have so much to do! For the bugs and the worms,
    In the garden, 't is tiresome pickin';
I've nothing to spare—for my own I must care,"
    Said then the Hen with one chicken.

"How I wish," said the Goose, "I could be of some use,
    For my heart is with love over-brimming;

The next morning that's fine, they shall go with my nine
    Little yellow-backed goslings, out swimming!"
"I will do what I can," the old Dorking put in,
    "And for help they may call upon me too,
Though I've ten of my own that are only half grown,
    And a great deal of trouble to see to;
But these poor little things, they are all head and wings,
    And their bones through their feathers are stickin'!"
"Very hard it may be, but, Oh, don't come to me!"
    Said the Hen with one chicken.

Half my care, I suppose, there is nobody knows,
    I'm the most over-burdened of mothers!
They must learn, little elves! how to scratch for themselves,
    And not seek to depend upon others."
She went by with a cluck, and the Goose to the Duck
    Exclaimed with surprise, "Well, I never!"
Said the Duck, "I declare, those who have the least care,
    You will find are complaining forever!
And when all things appear to look threatening and drear,
    And when troubles your pathway are thick in,
For some aid in your woe, Oh, beware how you go
    To a Hen with one chicken."

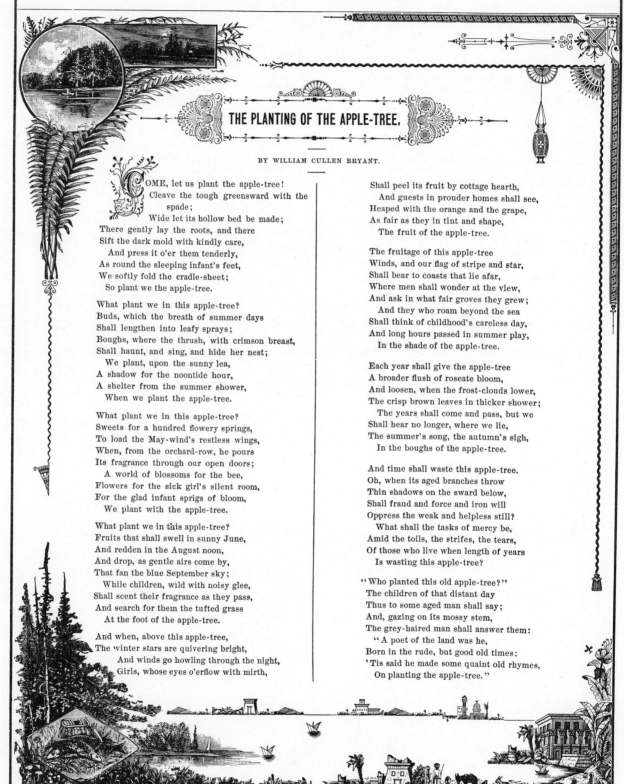

THE PLANTING OF THE APPLE-TREE.

BY WILLIAM CULLEN BRYANT.

COME, let us plant the apple-tree!
  Cleave the tough greensward with the
      spade;
    Wide let its hollow bed be made;
There gently lay the roots, and there
Sift the dark mold with kindly care,
    And press it o'er them tenderly,
As round the sleeping infant's feet,
We softly fold the cradle-sheet;
  So plant we the apple-tree.

What plant we in this apple-tree?
Buds, which the breath of summer days
Shall lengthen into leafy sprays;
Boughs, where the thrush, with crimson breast,
Shall haunt, and sing, and hide her nest;
  We plant, upon the sunny lea,
A shadow for the noontide hour,
A shelter from the summer shower,
  When we plant the apple-tree.

What plant we in this apple-tree?
Sweets for a hundred flowery springs,
To load the May-wind's restless wings,
When, from the orchard-row, he pours
Its fragrance through our open doors;
  A world of blossoms for the bee,
Flowers for the sick girl's silent room,
For the glad infant sprigs of bloom,
  We plant with the apple-tree.

What plant we in this apple-tree?
Fruits that shall swell in sunny June,
And redden in the August noon,
And drop, as gentle airs come by,
That fan the blue September sky;
  While children, wild with noisy glee,
Shall scent their fragrance as they pass,
And search for them the tufted grass
  At the foot of the apple-tree.

And when, above this apple-tree,
The winter stars are quivering bright,
  And winds go howling through the night,
  Girls, whose eyes o'erflow with mirth,

Shall peel its fruit by cottage hearth,
  And guests in prouder homes shall see,
Heaped with the orange and the grape,
As fair as they in tint and shape,
  The fruit of the apple-tree.

The fruitage of this apple-tree
Winds, and our flag of stripe and star,
Shall bear to coasts that lie afar,
Where men shall wonder at the view,
And ask in what fair groves they grew;
  And they who roam beyond the sea
Shall think of childhood's careless day,
And long hours passed in summer play,
  In the shade of the apple-tree.

Each year shall give the apple-tree
A broader flush of roseate bloom,
And loosen, when the frost-clouds lower,
The crisp brown leaves in thicker shower;
  The years shall come and pass, but we
Shall hear no longer, where we lie,
The summer's song, the autumn's sigh,
  In the boughs of the apple-tree.

And time shall waste this apple-tree.
Oh, when its aged branches throw
Thin shadows on the sward below,
Shall fraud and force and iron will
Oppress the weak and helpless still?
  What shall the tasks of mercy be,
Amid the toils, the strifes, the tears,
Of those who live when length of years
  Is wasting this apple-tree?

"Who planted this old apple-tree?"
The children of that distant day
Thus to some aged man shall say;
And, gazing on its mossy stem,
The grey-haired man shall answer them:
  "A poet of the land was he,
Born in the rude, but good old times;
'Tis said he made some quaint old rhymes,
  On planting the apple-tree."

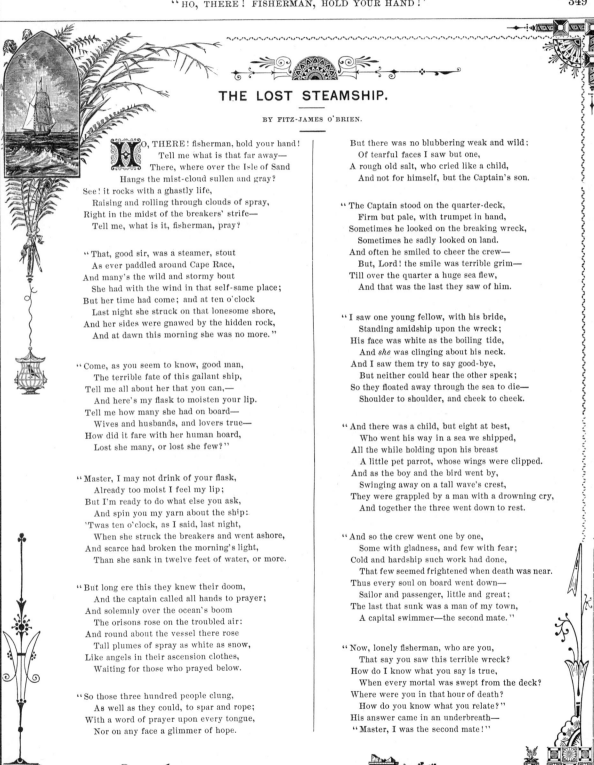

THE LOST STEAMSHIP.

BY FITZ-JAMES O'BRIEN.

HO, THERE! fisherman, hold your hand!
　　Tell me what is that far away—
There, where over the Isle of Sand
　　Hangs the mist-cloud sullen and gray?
See! it rocks with a ghastly life,
　　Raising and rolling through clouds of spray,
Right in the midst of the breakers' strife—
　　Tell me, what is it, fisherman, pray?

"That, good sir, was a steamer, stout
　　As ever paddled around Cape Race,
And many's the wild and stormy bout
　　She had with the wind in that self-same place;
But her time had come; and at ten o'clock
　　Last night she struck on that lonesome shore,
And her sides were gnawed by the hidden rock,
　　And at dawn this morning she was no more."

"Come, as you seem to know, good man,
　　The terrible fate of this gallant ship,
Tell me all about her that you can,—
　　And here's my flask to moisten your lip.
Tell me how many she had on board—
　　Wives and husbands, and lovers true—
How did it fare with her human hoard,
　　Lost she many, or lost she few?"

"Master, I may not drink of your flask,
　　Already too moist I feel my lip;
But I'm ready to do what else you ask,
　　And spin you my yarn about the ship:
'Twas ten o'clock, as I said, last night,
　　When she struck the breakers and went ashore,
And scarce had broken the morning's light,
　　Than she sank in twelve feet of water, or more.

"But long ere this they knew their doom,
　　And the captain called all hands to prayer;
And solemnly over the ocean's boom
　　The orisons rose on the troubled air:
And round about the vessel there rose
　　Tall plumes of spray as white as snow,
Like angels in their ascension clothes,
　　Waiting for those who prayed below.

"So those three hundred people clung,
　　As well as they could, to spar and rope;
With a word of prayer upon every tongue,
　　Nor on any face a glimmer of hope.

But there was no blubbering weak and wild;
　　Of tearful faces I saw but one,
A rough old salt, who cried like a child,
　　And not for himself, but the Captain's son.

"The Captain stood on the quarter-deck,
　　Firm but pale, with trumpet in hand,
Sometimes he looked on the breaking wreck,
　　Sometimes he sadly looked on land.
And often he smiled to cheer the crew—
　　But, Lord! the smile was terrible grim—
Till over the quarter a huge sea flew,
　　And that was the last they saw of him.

"I saw one young fellow, with his bride,
　　Standing amidship upon the wreck;
His face was white as the boiling tide,
　　And *she* was clinging about his neck.
And I saw them try to say good-bye,
　　But neither could hear the other speak;
So they floated away through the sea to die—
　　Shoulder to shoulder, and cheek to cheek.

"And there was a child, but eight at best,
　　Who went his way in a sea we shipped,
All the while holding upon his breast
　　A little pet parrot, whose wings were clipped.
And as the boy and the bird went by,
　　Swinging away on a tall wave's crest,
They were grappled by a man with a drowning cry,
　　And together the three went down to rest.

"And so the crew went one by one,
　　Some with gladness, and few with fear;
Cold and hardship such work had done,
　　That few seemed frightened when death was near.
Thus every soul on board went down—
　　Sailor and passenger, little and great;
The last that sunk was a man of my town,
　　A capital swimmer—the second mate."

"Now, lonely fisherman, who are you,
　　That say you saw this terrible wreck?
How do I know what you say is true,
　　When every mortal was swept from the deck?
Where were you in that hour of death?
　　How do you know what you relate?"
His answer came in an underbreath—
　　"Master, I was the second mate!"

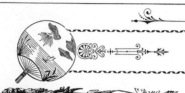

A WISH FOR THEE

BY JOHN G. C. BRAINARD.

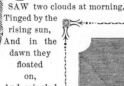

I SAW two clouds at morning,
  Tinged by the rising sun,
And in the dawn they floated on,
  And mingled into one:
I thought that morning cloud was blest,
It moved so sweetly to the west.

I saw two summer currents
  Flow smoothly to their meeting,
And join their course with silent force,

In peace each other greeting;
  Calm was their course through banks of green,
While dimpling eddies played between.

Such be your gentle motion,
  Till life's last pulse shall beat;
Like summer's beam, and summer's stream,
Float on in joy, to meet
A calmer sea, where storms shall cease,
A purer sky, where all is peace.

"I saw two clouds at morning, tinged by the rising sun."

THE SCULPTOR BOY.

CHISEL in hand stood a sculptor boy,
  With his marble block before him: —
And his face lit up with a smile of joy
  As an angel dream passed o'er him.
He carved that dream on the yielding stone
  With many a sharp incision;
In heaven's own light the sculptor shone,
  He had caught that angel vision.

Sculptors of life are *we*, as we stand,
  With our lives uncarved before us;
Waiting the hour when, at God's command,
  Our life dream passes o'er us.
Let us carve it then on the yielding stone,
  With many a sharp incision:—
Its heavenly beauty shall be our own—
  Our lives, that angel vision.

LITTLE AND GREAT.

BY CHARLES MACKAY.

A TRAVELER, through a dusty road,
  Strewed acorns on the lea;
    And one took root and sprouted up,
And grew into a tree.
Love sought its shade at evening time,
To breathe his early vows;
And Age was pleased, in heats of noon,
To bask beneath its boughs.
The dormouse loved its dangling twigs,
The birds sweet music bore;
It stood a glory in its place,
  A blessing evermore.

A little spring had lost its way
  Amid the grass and fern;
A passing stranger scooped a well,
Where weary men might turn.
He walled it in, and hung with care
A ladle at the brink:
He thought not of the deed he did,
But judged that Toil might drink.
He passed again—and lo! the well,
  By summers never dried,
Had cooled ten thousand parching tongues,
And saved a life beside.

"And Age was pleased, in heats of noon, to bask beneath its boughs."

A dreamer dropped a random thought;
  'Twas old—and yet 'twas new;
A simple fancy of the brain,
But strong in being true.
It shone upon a genial mind,
  And lo! its light became
A lamp of life, a beacon ray,
  A monitory flame.
The thought was small—its issue great;
  A watch-fire on the hill,
It sheds its radiance far adown,
And cheers the valley still.

A nameless man, amid a crowd
  That thronged the daily mart,
Let fall a word of hope and love,
Unstudied, from the heart.
A whisper on the tumult thrown,
  A transitory breath,
It raised a brother from the dust,
It saved a soul from death.
O germ! O fount! O word of love!
O thought at random cast!
Ye were but little at the first,
  But mighty at the last!

THERE IS NO SUCH THING AS DEATH.

THERE is no such thing as death—
  In nature nothing dies;
From each sad remnant of decay
  Some forms of life arise.

The little leaf that falls
  All brown and sere to earth,
Ere long will mingle with the buds
  That give the flower its birth.

THE VAGABONDS.

BY J. T. TROWBRIDGE.

WE ARE two travelers, Roger and I.
　Roger's my dog—Come here, you scamp!
Jump for the gentleman —mind your eye!
　Over the table,—look out for the lamp!—
The rogue is growing a little old;
　Five years we've tramped through wind and weather,
And slept out-doors when nights were cold,
　And ate and drank—and starved—together.

We've learned what comfort is, I tell you!
　A bed on the floor, a bit of rosin,
A bit of fire to thaw our thumbs (poor fellow!
　The paw he holds up there's been frozen,)
Plenty of catgut for my fiddle,
　(This out-door business is bad for strings,)
Then a few nice buckwheats, hot from the griddle,
　And Roger and I set up for kings!

No, thank ye, sir,—I never drink;
　Roger and I are exceedingly moral—
Aren't we Roger?—See him wink!
　Well, something hot, then, we won't quarrel,
He's thirsty, too, see him nod his head!
　What a pity, sir, that dogs can't talk!
He understands every word that's said,—
　And he knows good milk from water-and-chalk.

The truth is, sir, now I reflect,
　I've been so sadly given to grog,
I wonder I've not lost the respect
　(Here's to you, sir!) even of my dog;
But he sticks by, through thick and thin;
　And this old coat, with its empty pockets
And rags that smell of tobacco and gin,
　He'll follow while he has eyes in his sockets.

There isn't another creature living
　Would do it, and prove through every disaster,
So fond, so faithful, and so forgiving,
　To such a miserable, thankless master!
No, sir!—see him wag his tail and grin!
　By George! it makes my old eyes water—
That is, there's something in this gin
　That chokes a fellow.　But no matter!

We'll have some music, if you're willing,
　And Roger (hem! what a plague a cough is, sir!)
Shall march a little. — Start, you villain!
　Stand straight!　'Bout face!　Salute your officer!
Put up that paw!　Dress!　Take your rifle!
　(Some dogs have arms, you see!)　Now hold your
Cap while the gentleman gives a trifle,
　To aid a poor, old, patriot soldier!

March!　Halt!　Now show how the rebel shakes
　When he stands up to hear his sentence.
Now tell us how many drams it takes
　To honor a jolly new acquaintance.
Five yelps,—that's five; he's mighty knowing!
　The night's before us, fill the glasses!—
Quick, sir!　I'm ill,—my brain is going!—
　Some brandy,—thank you,—there, it passes.

Why not reform?　That's easily said;
　But I've gone through such wretched treatment,
Sometimes forgetting the taste of bread,
　And scarce remembering what meat meant,
That my poor stomach's past reform;
　And there are times when, mad with thinking,
I'd sell out heaven for something warm,
　To prop a horrible inward sinking.

Is there a way to forget to think?
　At your age, sir, home, fortune, friends,
A dear girl's love,—but I took to drink;—
　The same old story; you know how it ends.
If you could have seen these classic features,
　You needn't laugh, sir; they were not then
Such a burning libel on God's creatures;
　I was one of your handsome men:

If you had seen HER, so fair and young,
　Whose head was happy on this breast!
If you could have heard the song I sung
　When the wine went round, you wouldn't have guessed
That ever I, sir, should be straying,
　From door to door, with fiddle and dog,
Ragged and penniless, and playing
　To you to-night for a glass of grog!

She's married since;—a parson's wife:
　'Twas better for her that we should part,
Better the soberest, prosiest life
　Than a blasted home and a broken heart.
Have I seen her?　Once: I was weak and spent
　On a dusty road: a carriage stopped:
But little she dreamed as on she went,
　Who kissed the coin that her fingers dropped!

You've set me talking, sir, I'm sorry;
　It makes me wild to think of the change!
What do you care for a beggar's story?
　Is it amusing?　You find it strange?
I had a mother so proud of me!
　'Twas well she died before—Do you know
If the happy spirits in heaven can see
　The ruin and wretchedness here below?

Another glass, and strong, to deaden
　This pain; then Roger and I will start.
I wonder, has he such a lumpish, leaden,
　Aching thing, in place of a heart?
He is sad sometimes, and would weep if he could,
　No doubt remembering things that were,—
A virtuous kennel, with plenty of food,
　And himself a respectable cur.

I'm better now; that glass was warming.
　You rascal! limber your lazy feet!
We must be fiddling and performing
　For supper and bed, or starve in the street.
Not a very gay life to lead, you think?
　But soon we shall go where lodgings are free,
And the sleepers need neither victuals nor drink;
　The sooner the better for Roger and me!

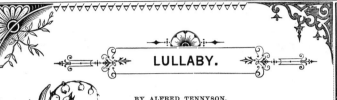

LULLABY.

BY ALFRED TENNYSON.

WEET and low, sweet and low,
　　Wind of the western sea!
Low, low, breathe and blow,
　　Wind of the western sea!
Over the rolling waters go;
Come from the dying moon, and blow,
　　Blow him again to me;
While my little one, while my pretty one sleeps.

Sleep and rest, sleep and rest!
　　Father will come to thee soon.
Rest, rest on mother's breast;
　　Father will come to thee soon!
Father will come to his babe in the nest;
Silver sails all out of the west,
　　Under the silver moon.
Sleep, my little one! sleep, my pretty one, sleep!

ROCK ME TO SLEEP, MOTHER.

BY FLORENCE PERCY.

BACKWARD, turn backward, O Time, in your flight,
Make me a child again, just for to-night!
Mother, come back from the echoless shore,
Take me again to your heart as of yore;
Kiss from my forehead the furrows of care,
Smooth the few silver threads out of my hair;
Over my slumbers your loving watch keep—
Rock me to sleep, mother—rock me to sleep!

Backward, flow backward, O tide of the years!
I am so weary of toil and of tears—
Toil without recompense—tears all in vain—
Take them, and give me my childhood again!
I have grown weary of dust and decay—
Weary of flinging my soul-wealth away;
Weary of sowing for others to reap—
Rock me to sleep, mother—rock me to sleep!

Tired of the hollow, the base, the untrue,
Mother, O Mother, my heart calls for you!
Many a summer the grass has grown green,
Blossomed and faded, our faces between;
Yet with strong yearning, and passionate pain,
Long I to-night for your presence again.
Come from the silence so long and so deep—
Rock me to sleep, mother—rock me to sleep!

Over my heart, in the days that are flown,
No love like a mother's love ever has shone
No other worship abides and endures—
Faithful, unselfish, and patient like yours;
None like a mother can charm away pain
From the sick soul and the world-weary brain.
Slumber's soft calm o'er my heavy lids creep—
Rock me to sleep, mother—rock me to sleep!

Come, let your brown hair just lighted with gold,
Fall on your shoulders again as of old;
Let it drop over my forehead to-night,
Shading my faint eyes away from the light;
For with its sunny-edged shadows once more
Happy will throng the sweet visions of yore—
Lovingly, softly, its bright billows sweep—
Rock me to sleep, mother—rock me to sleep!

Mother, dear mother, the years have been long
Since I last listened to your lullaby song;
Sing, then, and unto my heart it shall seem
Womanhood's years have been only a dream;
Clasped to your heart in a loving embrace,
With your light lashes just sweeping my face,
Never hereafter to wake or to weep—
Rock me to sleep, mother—rock me to sleep!

THE EVENING BELLS.

BY THOMAS MOORE.

THOSE evening bells, those evening
bells!
   How many a tale their music tells
Of youth, and home, and native clime,
When I last heard their soothing chime!

Those pleasant hours have passed away,
And many a heart that then was gay,

Within the tomb now darkly dwells,
And hears no more those evening bells.

And so it will be when I am gone;
That tuneful peal will still ring on,
When other bards shall walk these dells
And sing your praise, sweet evening bells.

A MESSAGE.

BY EBEN E. REXFORD.

YOU ARE dying, my friend!
   Your bark will go drifting, ere breaking of day,
Toward the shores lying over the shadowy bay;
And at morn you will see, rising fair through the
      mist,
   The hills which the sunshine eternal has kissed.

   You are going away!
You will meet on the shores, which your vessel will find,
Dear friends who sailed outward, and left us behind;
You will know them, and clasp them, and kiss them once
      more,
Grown young again there, on the beautiful shore.

   Dear friend, when you meet
The woman I loved, on the shore far away,
Will you give her the message I give you to-day?
You will know her, I know, by her face, that was fair
As the face of an angel, and beautiful hair.

   And her eyes, like a star,
In a clear summer night, shining out through the
   dew,

Falling down, like a kiss, from the furthermost blue.
And her voice, when she greets you, you'll know as of old,
Her voice, and her face in its tresses of gold.

   O, tell her, my friend,
That I miss her so much since she left me that night,
When the mists of the sea drifted over my sight,
And hid her in shadows, so dense and so deep,
That, remembering the time, even now I must weep.

   And tell her for me,
That I wait for the morn, which for her has begun,
When our ways, which were severed on earth, shall be one;
I shall come to her, over the wide solemn sea,
And clasp her, and claim her—that tell her for me.

   Friend, you will not forget?
Already your bark is afloat on the tide,
That shall bear you out over the waters so wide;
At morn you will see her, and tell her for me,
That I love her, I miss her, this side of the sea.

THERE'S BUT ONE PAIR OF STOCKINGS
TO MEND TO-NIGHT.

AN OLD wife sat by her bright fireside,
Swaying thoughtfully to and fro,
In an ancient chair whose creaky frame
Told a tale of long ago;
While down by her side, on the kitchen floor,
Stood a basket of worsted balls—a score.

The good man dozed o'er the latest news,
Till the light of his pipe went out,
And, unheeded, the kitten, with cunning paws,
Rolled and tangled the balls about;
Yet still sat the wife in the ancient chair,
Swaying to and fro in the fire-light glare.

But anon a misty tear-drop came
In her eye of faded blue,
Then trickled down in a furrow deep,
Like a single drop of dew;
So deep was the channel—so silent the stream,
The good man saw naught but the dimmed eye-beam.

Yet he marvelled much that the cheerful light
Of her eye had weary grown,
And marvelled he more at the tangled balls;
So he said in a gentle tone:
"I have shared thy joys since our marriage vow,
Conceal not from me thy sorrows now."

Then she spoke of the time when the basket there
Was filled to the very brim,
And how there remained of the goodly pile
But a single pair—for him.
"Then wonder not at the dimmed eye-light,
There's but one pair of stockings to mend to-night.

"I cannot but think of the busy feet,
Whose wrappings were wont to lie
In the basket, awaiting the needle's time,

Now wandered so far away;
How the sprightly steps, to a mother dear,
Unheeded fell on the careless ear.

"For each empty nook in the basket old,
By the hearth there's a vacant seat;
And I miss the shadows from off the wall,
And the patter of many feet;
'Tis for this that a tear gathered over my sight
At the one pair of stockings to mend to-night.

"'Twas said that far through the forest wild,
And over the mountains bold,
Was a land whose rivers and dark'ning caves
Were gemmed with the rarest gold;
Then my first-born turned from the oaken door,
And I knew the shadows were only four.

"Another went forth on the foaming waves
And diminished the basket's store—
But his feet grew cold—so weary and cold—
They'll never be warm any more—
And this nook, in its emptiness, seemeth to me
To give forth no voice but the moan of the sea.

"Two others have gone toward the setting sun,
And made them a home in its light,
And fairy fingers have taken their share
To mend by the fireside bright;
Some other baskets their garments fill—
But mine! Oh, mine is emptier still.

"Another—the dearest—the fairest—the best—
Was ta'en by the angels away,
And clad in a garment that waxeth not old,
In a land of continual day.
Oh! wonder no more at the dimmed eye-light,
While I mend the one pair of stockings to-night."

YOU AND I.

IF we could leave this world behind—
Its gains and loss, its praise and blame,
Nor seeking place, nor fearing shame,
Some fair land quite forgotten find,
We might be happy, you and I,
And let this foolish world go by.

No paradise of love and bliss,
No dreams of youth in Eden bowers,
But some dear home of quiet hours,

Where all of life we would not miss,
But find some day sweet ere we die,
And let this cruel world go by.

It will not be—we are too weak
To snatch from Time and Life one day;
But, when they both have passed away,
O Love! we will each other seek
Where none can part us, none deny
This world and all its woes gone by.

A SNOW-STORM.

BY CHARLES G. EASTMAN.

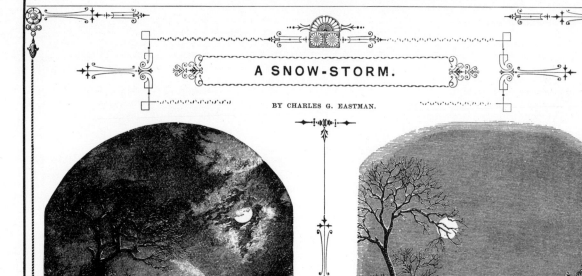

IS A fearful night in the winter time,
　As cold as it ever can be;
The roar of the blast is heard, like the chime
　Of the waves on an angry sea;
The moon is full, but her silver light
The storm dashes out with its wings to-night;
And over the sky from south to north
Not a star is seen, as the wind comes forth
　In the strength of a mighty glee.

All day had the snow come down—all day,
　As it never came down before;
And over the hills, at sunset, lay
　Some two or three feet or more;
The fence was lost, and the wall of stone,
The windows blocked, and the well-curbs gone;
The haystack had grown to a mountain lift.
And the woodpile looked like a monster drift,
　As it lay by the farmer's door.

The night sets in on a world of snow,
　While the air grows sharp and chill,
And the warning roar of a fearful blow
　Is heard on the distant hill;
And the Norther!　See—on the mountain peak,

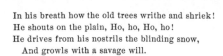

In his breath how the old trees writhe and shriek!
He shouts on the plain, Ho, ho, Ho, ho!
He drives from his nostrils the blinding snow,
　And growls with a savage will.

Such a night as this to be found abroad,
　In the drifts and the freezing air,
Sits a shivering dog in the field by the road;
　With the snow in his shaggy hair!
He shuts his eyes to the wind, and growls;
He lifts his head and moans and howls;
Then crouching low from the cutting sleet,
His nose is pressed on his quivering feet:
　Pray, what does the dog do there?

A farmer came from the village plain,
　But he lost the traveled way;
And for hours he trod, with might and main,
　A path for his horse and sleigh;
But colder still the cold wind blew,
And deeper still the deep drifts grew,
And his mare, a beautiful Morgan brown,
At last in her struggles floundered down,
　Where a log in a hollow lay.

In vain, with a neigh and a frenzied snort,
  She plunged in the drifting snow,
While her master urged, till his breath grew short,
  With a word and a gentle blow;
But the snow was deep, and the tugs were tight,
His hands were numb, and had lost their might;
So he wallowed back to his half-filled sleigh,
And strove to shelter himself till day,
  With his coat and the buffalo.

He has given the last faint jerk of the rein
  To rouse up his dying steed,
And the poor dog howls to the blast in vain,
  For help in his master's need;
For a while he strives, with a wistful cry,
To catch a glance from his drowsy eye,
And wags his tail if the rude winds flap
The skirt of the buffalo over his lap,
  And whines when he takes no heed.

The wind goes down, and the storm is o'er:
  'Tis the hour of midnight past;
The old trees writhe and bend no more
  In the whirl of the rushing blast;
The silent moon, with her peaceful light,
Looks down on the hills, with snow all white;
And the giant shadow of Camel's Hump,
The blasted pine and the ghostly stump,
  Afar on the plain are cast.

But cold and dead, by the hidden log,
  Are they who came from the town:
The man in his sleigh, and his faithful dog,
  And his beautiful Morgan brown—
In the wide snow-desert, far and grand,
With his cap on his head, and the reins in his hand,
The dog with his nose on his master's feet,
And the mare half seen through the crusted sleet,
  Where she lay when she floundered down.

LITTLE FEET.

BY FLORENCE PERCY.

TWO little feet so small that both may nestle
  In one caressing hand—
Two tender feet upon the untried border
  Of life's mysterious land;

Dimpled and soft, and pink as peach-tree blossoms
  In April's fragrant days—
How can they walk among the briery tangles
  Edging the world's rough ways?

These white-rose feet, along the doubtful future,
  Must bear a woman's load;
Alas! since woman has the heaviest burden,
  And walks the hardest road.

Love, for a while, will make the path before them
  All dainty, smooth and fair—
Will cull away the brambles, letting only
  The roses blossom there.

But when the mother's watchful eyes are shrouded
  Away from sight of men,
And these dear feet are left without her guiding,
  Who shall direct them then?

How will they be allured, betrayed, deluded,
  Poor little untaught feet—
Into what dreary mazes will they wander,
  What dangers will they meet?

Will they go stumbling blindly in the darkness
  Of Sorrow's tearful shades?
Or find the upland slopes of Peace and Beauty
  Whose sunlight never fades?

Will they go toiling up Ambition's summit,
  The common world above?
Or in some nameless vale, securely sheltered,
  Walk side by side in Love?

Some feet there be, which walk Life's track unwounded,
  Which find but pleasant ways;
Some hearts there be, to which this life is only
  A round of happy days.

But they are few. Far more there are who wander
  Without a hope or friend,
Who find the journey full of pains and losses,
  And long to reach the end!

How shall it be with her, the tender stranger,
  Fair-faced and gentle-eyed,
Before whose unstained feet the world's rude highway
  Stretches so strange and wide?

Ah! who may read the future? For our darling
  We crave all blessings sweet—
And pray that He who feeds the crying ravens
  Will guide the baby's feet.

BINGEN ON THE RHINE.

BY CAROLINE E. NORTON.

SOLDIER of the Legion lay dying in Algiers:
There was lack of woman's nursing, there was dearth
  of woman's tears;
But a comrade stood beside him, while his life-blood
  ebbed away,
And bent with pitying glances, to hear what he might say.
The dying soldier faltered, as he took that comrade's hand,
And he said, "I never more shall see my own, my native land.
Take a message and a token to some distant friends of mine;
For I was born at Bingen—at Bingen on the Rhine!

"Tell my brothers and companions, when they meet and
    crowd around,
To hear my mournful story, in the pleasant vineyard ground,
That we fought the battle bravely; and when the day was done,
Full many a corse lay ghastly pale beneath the setting sun.
And midst the dead and dying were some grown old in war,
The death wounds on their gallant breasts the last of many scars;
But some were young, and suddenly beheld life's morn decline;
And one had come from Bingen—fair Bingen on the Rhine!

"Tell my mother that her other sons shall comfort her old age,
For I was still a truant bird that thought his home a cage;
For my father was a soldier, and even as a child
My heart leaped forth to hear him tell of struggles fierce and wild;
And when he died, and left us to divide his scanty hoard,
I let them take whate'er they would—but kept my father's sword;
And with boyish love I hung it, where the bright light used to shine
On the cottage wall at Bingen—calm Bingen on the Rhine!

"Tell my sister not to weep for me, and sob with drooping head,
When the troops come marching home again, with glad and gallant
    tread;
But to look upon them proudly, with a calm and steadfast eye,
For her brother was a soldier too, and not afraid to die;
And if a comrade seek her love, I ask her in my name
To listen to him kindly, without regret or shame;
And to hang the old sword in its place, my father's sword and
    mine,
For the honor of old Bingen—dear Bingen on the Rhine!

"There's another, not a sister: in the happy days gone by
You'd have known her by the merriment that sparkled in her eye;
Too innocent for coquetry, too fond for idle scorning;
O friend! I fear the lightest heart makes sometimes heaviest mourning.
Tell her the last night of my life (for ere this moon be risen,
My body will be out of pain, my soul be out of prison),
I dreamed I stood with her, and saw the yellow sunlight shine

"A soldier of the Legion lay dying in Algiers."

On the vine-clad hills of Bingen—fair Bingen on the Rhine!

"I saw the blue Rhine sweep along; I heard, or seemed to hear,
The German songs we used to sing, in chorus sweet and clear;
And down the pleasant river, and up the slanting hill,
The echoing chorus sounded, through the evening calm and still;
And her glad blue eyes were on me, as we passed, with friendly talk
Down many a path beloved of yore, and well-remembered walk;
And her little hand lay lightly, confidingly in mine:
But we'll meet no more at Bingen—loved Bingen on the Rhine!"

His voice grew faint and hoarse—his grasp was childish weak;
His eyes put on a dying look—he sighed, and ceased to speak;
His comrade bent to lift him, but the spark of life had fled:
The soldier of the Legion in a foreign land was dead!

And the soft moon rose up slowly, and calmly she looked down
On the red sand of the battle-field, with bloody corpses strown.
Yes, calmly on that dreadful scene her pale light seemed to shine,
As it shone on distant Bingen—fair Bingen on the Rhine!

THE CLOSING SCENE.

BY T. BUCHANAN READ.

WITHIN the sober realm of leafless trees,
  The russet year inhaled the dreamy air;
Like some tanned reaper, in his hour of ease,
  When all the fields are lying brown and bare.

The gray barns looking from their hazy hills,
  O'er the dun waters widening in the vales,
Sent down the air a greeting to the mills,
  On the dull thunder of alternate flails.

All sights were mellowed, and all sounds subdued,
  The hills seemed further, and the stream sang low,
As in a dream the distant woodman hewed
  His winter log with many a muffled blow.

The embattled forest, erewhile armed with gold,
  Their banners bright with every martial hue,
Now stood like some sad, beaten host of old,
  Withdrawn afar in time's remotest blue.

On sombre wings the vulture tried his flight;
  The dove scarce heard his sighing mate's complaint;
And, like a star slow drowning in the light,
  The village church vane seemed to pale and faint.

The sentinel cock upon the hill-side crew—
  Crew thrice—and all was stiller than before;
Silent till some replying warden blew
  His alien horn, and then was heard no more.

Where erst the jay, within the elm's tall crest,
  Made garrulous trouble round her unfledged young;
And where the oriole hung her swaying nest,
  By every light wind, like a censer, swung.

Where sang the noisy martins of the eaves
  The busy swallows circling ever near—
Foreboding, as the rustic mind believes,
  An early harvest and a plenteous year;

Where every bird, that waked the vernal feast,
  Shook the sweet slumber from its wings at morn,
To warn the reaper of the rosy east;
  All now was sunless, empty, and forlorn.

Alone, from out the stubble, piped the quail;
  And croaked the crow through all the dreary gloom;
Alone the pheasant, drumming in the vale,
  Made echo in the distance to the cottage loom.

There was no bud, no bloom upon the bowers;
  The spiders wove their thin shrouds night by night,
The thistle-down, the only ghost of flowers,
  Sailed slowly by—passed noiseless out of sight.

Amid all this—in this most dreary air,
  And where the woodbine shed upon the porch
Its crimson leaves, as if the year stood there,
  Firing the floor with its inverted torch;

Amid all this, the center of the scene,
  The white-haired matron, with monotonous tread,
Plied the swift wheel, and, with her joyless mien,
  Sate like a fate, and watched the flying thread.

She had known sorrow. He had walked with her,
  Oft supped, and broke with her the ashen crust,
And in the dead leaves still, she heard the stir
  Of his thick mantle trailing in the dust.

While yet her cheek was bright with summer bloom,
  Her country summoned and she gave her all;
And twice war bowed to her his sable plume—
  Re-gave the sword to rust upon the wall.

Re-gave the sword but not the hand that drew,
  And struck for liberty the dying blow;
Nor him who, to his sire and country true,
  Fell 'mid the ranks of the invading foe.

Long, but not loud, the droning wheel went on,
  Like the low murmur of a hive at noon;
Long, but not loud, the memory of the gone
  Breathed through her lips a sad and tremulous tune.

At last the thread was snapped—her head was bowed;
  Life dropped the distaff through her hands serene.
And loving neighbors smoothed her careful shroud,
  While death and winter closed the autumn scene.

BY MARY BRADLEY.

PASSED before her garden gate:
   She stood among her roses,
And stooped a little from the state
   In which her pride reposes,
To make her flowers a graceful plea
For luring and delaying me.

"When summer blossoms fade so
      soon,"
   She said with winning sweetness,
"Who does not wear the badge of June
   Lacks something of completeness.
My garden welcomes you to-day,
Come in and gather, while you may."

I entered in: she led me through
   A maze of leafy arches,
Where velvet-purple pansies grew
   Beneath the sighing larches,—
A shadowy, still, and cool retreat
That gave excuse for lingering feet.

She paused; pulled down a trailing vine;
   And twisted round her finger
Its starry sprays of jessamine,
   As one who seeks to linger.
But I smiled lightly in her face,
And passed on to the open space.

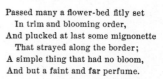

MIGNONETTE.

Passed many a flower-bed fitly set
   In trim and blooming order,
And plucked at last some mignonette
   That strayed along the border;
A simple thing that had no bloom,
And but a faint and far perfume.

She wondered why I would not choose
   That dreamy amaryllis,—
"And could I really, then, refuse
   Those heavenly white lilies!
And leave ungathered on the slope
This passion-breathing heliotrope?"

She did not know—what need to tell
   So fair and fine a creature?—
That there was one who loved me well
   Of widely different nature;
A little maid whose tender youth,
And innocence, and simple truth,

Had won my heart with qualities
   That far surpassed her beauty,
And held me with unconscious ease
   Enthralled of love and duty;
Whose modest graces all were met
And symboled in my mignonette.

I passed outside her garden gate,
   And left her proudly smiling:
Her roses bloomed too late, too late
   She saw, for my beguiling.
I wore instead—and wear it yet—
The single spray of mignonette.

Its fragrance greets me unaware,
   A vision clear recalling
Of shy, sweet eyes, and drooping hair
   In girlish tresses falling,
And little hands so white and fine
That timidly creep into mine;

As she—all ignorant of the arts
   That wiser maids are plying—
Has crept into my heart of hearts
   Past doubting or denying;
Therein, while suns shall rise and set,
To bloom unchanged, my Mignonette!

A MUSICAL BOX.

BY W. W. STORY.

THOU knowest her, the thing of
 laces, and silk,
 And ribbons, and gauzes, and
  crinoline,
With her neck and shoulders as
 white as milk,
 And her doll-like face and
  conscious mien.

A lay-figure fashioned to fit a
 dress,
 All stuffed within with straw
  and bran;
 Is that a woman to love, to
  caress?
 Is that a creature to charm a man?

Only listen! how charmingly she talks
 Of your dress and hers—of the Paris mode—
Of the coming ball—of the opera box—
 Of jupons, and flounces, and fashions abroad.

Not a bonnet in church but she knows it well,
 And Fashion she worships with downcast eyes;
A *marchande de modes* is her oracle,
 And Paris her earthly paradise.

She's perfect to whirl with in a waltz;
 And her shoulders show well on a soft divan,
As she lounges at night and spreads her silks,
 And plays with her bracelets and flirts her fan,—

With a little laugh at whatever you say,
 And rounding her "No" with a look of surprise,

And lisping her "Yes" with an air distrait,
 And a pair of aimless, wandering eyes.

Her duty this Christian never omits!
 She makes her calls, and she leaves her cards,
And enchants a circle of half-fledged wits,
 And slim *attaches* and six-foot Guards.

Her talk is of people who're nasty or nice,
 And she likes little *bon-bon* compliments;
While she seasons their sweetness by way of spice,
 By some witless scandal she often invents.

Is this the thing for a mother or wife?
 Could love ever grow on such barren rocks?
Is this the companion to take for a wife?
 One might as well marry a musical box.

You exhaust in a day her full extent;
 'Tis the same little tinkle of tunes always;
You must wind her up with a compliment,
 To be bored with the only airs she plays.

ELEGY WRITTEN IN A COUNTRY CHURCHYARD.

BY THOMAS GRAY.

HE curfew tolls the knell of parting day;
  The lowing herd winds slowly o'er the lea,
The plowman homeward plods his weary way,
  And leaves the world to darkness and to me.

Now fades the glimmering landscape on the sight,
  And all the air a solemn stillness holds,
Save where the beetle wheels his droning flight,
  And drowsy tinklings lull the distant folds;

Save that, from yonder ivy-mantled tower,
  The moping owl does to the moon complain
Of such as, wandering near her secret bower,
  Molest her ancient, solitary reign.

Beneath those rugged elms, that yew-tree's shade,
  Where heaves the turf in many a mouldering heap,
Each in his narrow cell forever laid,
  The rude forefathers of the hamlet sleep.

The breezy call of incense-breathing morn,
  The swallow twittering from the straw-built shed,
The cock's shrill clarion, or the echoing horn,
  No more shall rouse them from their lowly bed.

For them no more the blazing hearth shall burn,
  Or busy housewife ply her evening care;
No children run to lisp their sire's return,
  Or climb his knees the envied kiss to share.

Oft did the harvest to their sickle yield,
  Their furrow oft the stubborn glebe has broke:
How jocund did they drive their team afield!
  How bowed the woods beneath their sturdy stroke!

Let not Ambition mock their useful toil,
  Their homely joys, and destiny obscure;
Nor Grandeur hear, with a disdainful smile,
  The short and simple annals of the poor.

The boast of heraldry, the pomp of power,
  And all that beauty, all that wealth e'er gave,
Await, alike, the inevitable hour—
  The paths of glory lead but to the grave.

Nor you, ye proud, impute to these the fault,
  If memory o'er their tomb no trophies raise,
Where, through the long-drawn aisle and fretted vault
  The pealing anthem swells the note of praise.

Can storied urn, or animated bust,
  Back to its mansion call the fleeting breath?
Can Honor's voice provoke the silent dust,
  Or Flattery soothe the dull, cold ear of death?

Perhaps, in this neglected spot, is laid
  Some heart once pregnant with celestial fire—
Hand, that the rod of empire might have swayed,
  Or waked to ecstacy the living lyre:

But Knowledge to their eyes her ample page,
  Rich with the spoils of time, did ne'er unroll;
Chill Penury repressed their noble rage,
  And froze the genial current of the soul.

Full many a gem, of purest ray serene,
  The dark unfathomed caves of ocean bear;
Full many a flower is born to blush unseen,
  And waste its sweetness on the desert air.

Some village Hampden, that, with dauntless breast,
  The little tyrant of his fields withstood—
Some mute, inglorious Milton here may rest,
  Some Cromwell, guiltless of his country's blood.

The applause of listening senates to command,
  The threats of pain and ruin to despise,
To scatter plenty o'er a smiling land,
  And read their history in a nation's eyes,

Their lot forbade; nor circumscribed alone
  Their growing virtues, but their crimes confined;—
Forbade to wade through slaughter to a throne,
  And shut the gates of mercy on mankind;

The struggling pangs of conscious Truth to hide,
  To quench the blushes of ingenuous Shame,
Or heap the shrine of Luxury and Pride
  With incense kindled at the Muse's flame.

Far from the maddening crowd's ignoble strife,
  Their sober wishes never learnt to stray;
Along the cool, sequestered vale of life
  They kept the noiseless tenor of their way.

Yet even these bones from insult to protect,
  Some frail memorial still erected nigh,
With uncouth rhymes and shapeless sculpture decked,
  Implores the passing tribute of a sigh.

Their names, their years, spelled by th' unlettered Muse,
  The place of fame and elegy supply;
And many a holy text around she strews,
  That teach the rustic moralist to die.

For who, to dumb forgetfulness a prey,
  This pleasing, anxious being e'er resigned,—
Left the warm precincts of the cheerful day,
  Nor cast one longing, lingering look behind?

On some fond breast the parting soul relies,
  Some pious drops the closing eye requires;
Even from the tomb the voice of Nature cries,
  Even in our ashes live their wonted fires.

For thee, who, mindful of th' unhonored dead,
  Dost in these lines their artless tale relate;
If chance, by lonely contemplation led,
  Some kindred spirit shall enquire thy fate—

Haply, some hoary headed swain may say,
  "Oft have we seen him, at the peep of dawn,
Brushing, with hasty steps, the dews away,
  To meet the sun upon the upland lawn.

"There, at the foot of yonder nodding beech,
  That wreathes its old, fantastic roots so high,
His listless length at noontide would he stretch,
  And pore upon the brook that babbles by.

"Hard by yon wood, now smiling, as in scorn,
  Muttering his wayward fancies, he would rove,
Now drooping, woful-wan, like one forlorn,
  Or crazed with care, or crossed with hopeless love.

"One morn I missed him on th' accustomed hill,
  Along the heath and near his favorite tree;
Another came,—nor yet beside the rill,
  Nor up the lawn, nor at the wood was he.

"The next, with dirges due, in sad array,
  Slow through the church-way path we saw him borne;
Approach and read (for thou canst read) the lay,
  Graved on the stone beneath yon aged thorn."

EPITAPH.

Here rests his head upon the lap of earth,
  A youth to fortune and to fame unknown;
Fair Science frowned not on his humble birth,
  And Melancholy marked him for her own.

Large was his bounty, and his soul sincere;
  Heaven did a recompense as largely send:
He gave to misery all he had,—a tear;
  He gained from heaven—'twas all he wished—a friend.

No farther seek his merits to disclose,
  Nor draw his frailties from their dread abode,—
(There they, alike, in trembling hope repose,)
  The bosom of his Father and his God.

TWO LITTLE PAIRS.

BY MRS. SUSAN TEALL PERRY.

TWO little pairs of boots, to-night,
  Before the fire are drying;
Two little pairs of tired feet
  In a trundle bed are lying;
The tracks they left upon the floor
  Make me feel like sighing.

Those little boots with copper toes!
  They run the livelong day;
And oftentimes I almost wish
  They were miles away;
So tired am I to hear so oft
  Their heavy tramp at play.

They walk about the new-ploughed ground
  Where mud in plenty lies;
They roll it up in marbles round,
  They bake it into pies,
And then, at night upon the floor,
  In every shape it dries!

To-day I was disposed to scold,
  But when I look to-night
At those little boots before the fire,

With copper toes so bright,
I think how sad my heart would be
  To put them out of sight.

For in a trunk up stairs I've laid
  Two socks of white and blue;
If called to put those boots away,
  Oh God, what should I do?
I mourn that there are not to-night
  Three pairs instead of two.

I mourn because I thought how nice
  My neighbor 'cross the way,
Could keep her carpets all the year
  From getting worn or gray;
Yet well I know she'd smile to own
  Some little boots to-day.

We mothers weary get, and worn,
  Over our load of care;
But how we speak to these little ones
  Let each of us beware;
For what would our fireside be to-night,
  If no little boots were there?

THE FIRST SNOW-FALL.

BY JAMES RUSSELL LOWELL.

THE snow had begun in
  the gloaming,
  And busily, all the
    night,
Had been heaping field and
  highway
With a silence deep and
  white.

Every pine and fir and
  hemlock
Wore ermine too dear for
  an earl,
And the poorest twig on
  the elm-tree
Was ridged inch-deep with
  pearl.

From sheds new-roofed
  with carrara
Came chanticleer's muffled
  crow;
The stiff rails were softened
  to swan's-down;
And still wavered down
  the snow.

I stood and watched from
  my window
The noiseless work of the
  sky,
And the sudden flurries of
  snow-birds,
Like brown leaves whirl-
  ing by.

I thought of a mound in
  sweet Auburn
Where a little headstone
  stood:
How the flakes were fold-
  ing it gently,
As did robins the Babes in the Wood.

"*Every pine and fir and hemlock wore ermine too dear for an earl.*"

Up spoke our own little
  Mabel,
Saying, "Father, who
  makes it snow?"
And I told of the good All-
  father
Who cares for us here
  below.

Again I looked at the snow-
  fall,
And thought of the leaden
  sky
That arched o'er our first
  great sorrow
When that mound was
  heaped so high.

I remember the gradual
  patience
That fell from that cloud
  like snow,
Flake by flake, healing and
  hiding
The scar of our buried
  woe.

And again to the child I
  whispered
"The snow that husheth
  all,
Darling, the merciful
  Father
Alone can bid it fall!"

Then with eyes that saw
  not I kissed her,
And she, kissing back,
  could not know
That my kiss was given to
  her sister
Folded close under deepening snow.

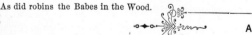

A DEATH-BED.

BY JAMES ALDRICH.

HER suffering ended with the day;
  Yet lived she at its close,
And breathed the long, long night away,
  In statue-like repose.

But when the sun, in all his state,
  Illumed the eastern skies,
She passed through glory's morning-gate,
  And walked in Paradise.

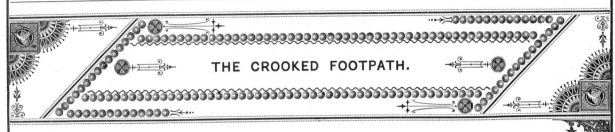

THE CROOKED FOOTPATH.

BY OLIVER WENDELL HOLMES.

AH, here it is! the sliding rail
That marks the old remembered spot,
The gap that struck our schoolboy trail,
The crooked path across the lot.

It left the road by school and church:
A pencilled shadow, nothing more,
That parted from the silver birch
And ended at the farmhouse door.

No line or compass traced its plan;
With frequent bends to left or right,
In aimless, wayward curves it ran,
But always kept the door in sight.

The gabled porch, with woodbine green,
The broken millstone at the sill,
Though many a rood might stretch between,
The truant child could see them still.

No rocks across the pathway lie,
No fallen trunk is o'er it thrown;

"*And yet it winds, we know not why, and turns as if for tree or stone.*"

And yet it winds, we know not why,
And turns as if for tree or stone.

Perhaps some lover trod the way,
With shaking knees and leaping heart;
And so it often runs astray,
With sinuous sweep or sudden start.

Or one, perchance, with clouded brain,
From some unholy banquet reeled;
And since, our devious steps maintain
His track across the trodden field.

Nay, deem not thus:—no earth-born will
Could ever trace a faultless line;
Our truest steps are human still,—
To walk unswerving were divine.

Truants from love, we dream of wrath;
O, rather let us trust the more!
Through all the wanderings of the path
We still can see our Father's door!

THE OLD LOVE.

I MET her, she was thin and old,
She stooped and trod with tottering feet;
Her locks were gray that once were gold,
Her voice was harsh that once was sweet;
Her cheeks were sunken, and her eyes,
Robbed of their girlish light of joy,
Were dim: I felt a strange surprise
That I had loved her when a boy.

And yet a something in her air
Restored to me my youthful prime;
My heart grew young and seemed to wear
The impress of that long-lost time;
I took her wilted hand in mine,
Its touch awoke a world of joy;
I kissed her with a reverent sigh,
For I had loved her when a boy!

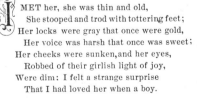

OVER THE HILL TO THE POOR-HOUSE.*

BY WILL M. CARLETON.

OVER the hill to the poor-house I'm trudgin' my weary way—
I, a woman of seventy, and only a trifle gray—
I, who am smart an' chipper, for all the years I've told,
As many another woman, that's only half as old.

Over the hill to the poor-house—I can't make it quite clear!
Over the hill to the poor-house—it seems so horrid queer!
Many a step I've taken a-toilin' to and fro,
But this is a sort of journey I never thought to go.

What is the use of heapin' on me a pauper's shame?
Am I lazy or crazy? am I blind or lame?
True, I am not so supple, nor yet so awful stout,
But charity ain't no favor, if one can live without.

I am willin' and anxious an' ready any day,
To work for a decent livin', an' pay my honest way;
For I can earn my victuals, an' more too, I'll be bound,
If anybody only is willin' to have me round.

Once I was young and han'some—I was, upon my soul—
Once my cheeks was roses, my eyes as black as coal;
And I can't remember, in them days, of hearin' people say,
For any kind of reason, that I was in their way.

'Taint no use of boastin', or talkin' over free,
But many a house an' home was open then to me;
Many a han'some offer I had from likely men,
And nobody ever hinted that I was a burden then.

And when to John I was married, sure he was good and smart,
But he and all the neighbors would own I done my part;
For life was all before me, an' I was young an' strong,
And I worked the best that I could in tryin' to get along.

And so we worked together; and life was hard but gay,
With now and then a baby, for to cheer us on our way;
Till we had half a dozen, an' all growed clean an' neat,
An' went to school like others, an' had enough to eat.

So we worked for the childr'n, and raised 'em every one;
Worked for 'em summer and winter, just as we ought to 've done;
Only perhaps we humored 'em, which some good folks condemn,
But every couple's childr'n's a heap the best to them.

Strange how much we think of our blessed little ones!—
I'd have died for my daughters, I'd have died for my sons;
And God he made that rule of love; but when we're old and gray,
I've noticed it sometimes somehow fails to work the other way.

Strange, another thing: when our boys an' girls was grown,
And when, exceptin' Charley, they'd left us there alone;
When John he nearer an' nearer come, an' dearer seemed to be,
The Lord of Hosts he come one day an' took him away from me.

Still I was bound to struggle, an' never to cringe or fall—
Still I worked for Charley, for Charley was now my all;
And Charley was pretty good to me, with scarce a word or frown,
Till at last he went a-courtin', and brought a wife from town.

She was somewhat dressy, an' hadn't a pleasant smile—
She was quite conceity, and carried a heap o' style;
But if ever I tried to be friends, I did with her, I know;
But she was hard and proud, an' I couldn't make it go.

She had an edication, an' that was good for her;
But when she twitted me on mine 'twas carryin' things too fur;
An' I told her once 'fore company (an' it almost made her sick),
That I never swallowed a grammar, or et a 'rithmetic.

So 'twas only a few days before the thing was done—
They was a family of themselves, and I another one;
And a very little cottage for one family will do,
But I have never seen a house that was big enough for two.

An' I never could speak to suit her, never could please her eye,
An' it made me independent, an' then I didn't try;
But I was terribly staggered, an' felt it like a blow,
When Charley turned ag'in me, an' told me I could go.

I went to live with Susan, but Susan's house was small,
And she was always a-hintin' how snug it was for us all;
And what with her husband's sisters, and what with childr'n three,
'Twas easy to discover that there wasn't room for me.

An' then I went to Thomas, the oldest son I've got,
For Thomas' buildings 'd cover the half of an acre lot:
But all the childr'n was on me—I couldn't stand their sauce—
And Thomas said I needn't think I was comin' there to boss.

An then I wrote to Rebecca,—my girl who lives out West,
And to Isaac, not far from her—some twenty miles at best;
And one of 'em said 'twas too warm there, for any one so old,
And t'other had an opinion the climate was too cold.

So they have shirked and slighted me, an' shifted me about—
So they have well-nigh soured me, an' wore my old heart out;
But still I've borne up pretty well, an' wasn't much put down,
Till Charley went to the poor-master, an' put me on the town.

Over the hill to the poor-house—my childr'n dear, good-bye!
Many a night I've watched you when only God was nigh;
And God 'll judge between us; but I will al'ays pray
That you shall never suffer the half I do to-day.

* From "Farm Ballads,"   Published by Harper & Brothers.

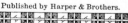

OVER THE HILL FROM THE POOR-HOUSE.

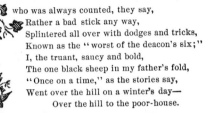

BY WILL M. CARLETON.

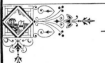

I who was always counted, they say,
Rather a bad stick any way,
Splintered all over with dodges and tricks,
Known as the "worst of the deacon's six;"
I, the truant, saucy and bold,
The one black sheep in my father's fold,
"Once on a time," as the stories say,
Went over the hill on a winter's day—
    Over the hill to the poor-house.

Tom could save what twenty could earn;
But givin' was somethin' he ne'er could learn;
Isaac could half o' the Scriptures speak,
Committed a hundred verses a week;
Never forgot, an' never slipped;
But "Honor thy father and mother" he skipped.
    So over the hill to the poor-house.

As for Susan, her heart was kind
An' good—what there was of it, mind;
Nothin' too big an' nothin' too nice,
Nothin' she wouldn't sacrifice
For one she loved; an' that 'ere one
Was herself, when all was said an' done.
An' Charley an' 'Becca meant well, no doubt,
But anyone could pull 'em about.

An' all our folks ranked well, you see,
Save one poor fellow, and that was me;
An' when, one dark an' rainy night,
A neighbor's horse went out of sight,
They hitched on me as the guilty chap
That carried one end of the halter-strap.
An' I think, myself, that view of the case
Wasn't altogether out o' place;
My mother denied it, as mothers do,
But I'm inclined to believe 'twas true.

Though for me one thing might be said—
That I, as well as the horse, was led;
And the worst of whisky spurred me on,
Or else the deed would have never been done.
But the keenest grief I ever felt,
Was when my mother beside me knelt,
An' cried an' prayed till I melted down,
As I wouldn't for half the horses in town.
I kissed her fondly, then and there,
An' swore henceforth to be honest and square.

I served my sentence—a bitter pill
Some fellows should take, who never will;
And then I decided to "go out West,"
Concludin' 'twould suit my health the best;
Where, how I prospered, I never could tell,
But Fortune seemed to like me well.
An' somehow, every vein I struck
Was always bubblin' over with luck;
An' better than that, I was steady an' true,
An' put my good resolutions through.
But I wrote to a trusty old neighbor, an' said,
"You tell 'em, old fellow, that I am dead,
An' died a Christian; 'twill please 'em more
Than if I had lived the same as before."

But when this neighbor he wrote to me,
"Your mother is in the poor-house," says he;
I had a resurrection straightway,
An' started for her that very day;
And when I arrived where I was grown,
I took good care that I shouldn't be known;
But I bought the old cottage, through and through,
Of some one Charley had sold it to;
And held back neither work nor gold,
To fix it up as it was of old;
The same big fire-place, wide and high,
Flung up its cinders toward the sky;
The old clock ticked on the corner-shelf—
I wound it an' set it a-goin' myself;
An', if everything wasn't quite the same,
Neither I nor Manly was to blame;
    Then—over the hill to the poor-house!

One bloomin', blusterin' winter's day,
With a team an' cutter I started away;
My fiery nags was as black as coal;
(They some'at resembled the horse I stole;)
I hitched an' entered the poor-house door—
A poor old woman was scrubbin' the floor;
She rose to her feet in great surprise
And looked, quite startled, into my eyes;
I saw the whole of her trouble's trace
In the lines that marred her dear old face;
"Mother!" I shouted, "your sorrows are done!
You're adopted along o' your horse-thief son.
    Come over the hill from the poor-house!"

She didn't faint; she knelt by my side,
An' thanked the Lord till I fairly cried.
An' maybe our ride wasn't pleasant and gay,
An' maybe she wasn't wrapped up that day;
An' maybe our cottage wasn't warm and bright;
An' maybe it wasn't a pleasant sight,
To see her a-gettin' the evenin's tea,
An' frequently stoppin' and kissin' me;
An' maybe we didn't live happy for years,
In spite of my brothers' and sisters' sneers,
Who often said, as I have heard,
That they wouldn't own a prison bird
(Though they're gettin' over that, I guess,
For all of them owe me more or less.)

But I've learned one thing, and it cheers a man
In always a-doin' the best he can;
That whether, on the big book, a blot
Gets over a fellow's name or not,
Whenever he does a deed that's white
It's credited to him fair and right.
An' when you hear the great bugle's notes,
An' the Lord divides his sheep and goats;
However they may settle my case,
Wherever they may fix my place,
My good old Christian mother, you'll see,
Will be sure to stand right up for me.
    So over the hill from the poor-house!

WEIGHING THE BABY.

BY ETHEL LYNN.

HOW MANY pounds does the baby weigh,—
    Baby, who came but a month ago;
How many pounds from the crowning curl
    To the rosy point of the restless toe?

Grandfather ties the handkerchief's knot,
    Tenderly guides the swinging weight,
And carefully over his glasses peers
    To read the record, "Only eight!"

Softly the echo goes around,
    The father laughs at the tiny girl;
The fair young mother sings the words,
    While grandmother smooths the golden curl.

And stooping above the precious thing,
    Nestles a kiss within a prayer;
Murmuring softly, "Little one,
    Grandfather did not weigh you fair."

Nobody weighed the baby's smile,
    Or the love that came with the helpless one;

Nobody weighed the threads of care
    From which a woman's life is spun.

No index tells the mighty worth
    Of a little baby's quiet breath!
A soft, unceasing metronome,
    Patient and faithful unto death.

Nobody weighed the baby's soul,
    For here, on earth, no weights there be
That could avail.   God only knows
    Its value in eternity.

Only eight pounds to hold a soul
    That seeks no angel's silver wing,
But shrines it in this human guise—
    Within so fair and small a thing.

Oh, mother, laugh your merry note,
    Be gay and glad, but don't forget
From baby's eyes looks out a soul
    That claims a home in Eden yet.

JUDGE NOT.

JUDGE not! The workings of his brain
    And of his heart thou canst not see;
What looks to thy dim eyes a stain,
    In God's pure light may only be
A scar, brought from some well-won field,
Where thou wouldst only faint and yield.

The look, the air, that frets thy sight,
    May be a token, that below
The soul has closed in deadly fight

With some infernal, fiery foe,
Whose glance would scorch thy smiling grace,
And cast thee shuddering on thy face.

The fall thou darest to despise—
    Perchance the slackened angel's hand
Has suffered it, that he may rise
    And take a firmer, surer stand;
Or, trusting less to earthly things,
May henceforth learn to use his wings.

THE LITTLE BOY THAT DIED.

BY JOSHUA D. ROBINSON.

AM all alone in my chamber now,
  And the midnight hour is near,
And the faggot's crack, and the clock's dull tick,
  Are all the sounds I hear;
And over my soul in its solitude
  Sweet feelings of sadness glide;
And my heart and my eyes are full when I think
  Of the little boy that died.

I went home one night to my father's house—
  Went home to the dear ones all,
And softly I opened the garden gate,
  And softly the door of the hall;
My mother came out to meet her son,
  She kissed me, and then she sighed,
And her head fell on my neck, and she wept
  For the little boy that died.

And when I gazed on his innocent face,
  As still and cold he lay,
And thought what a lovely child he had been,
  And how soon he must decay;
"O Death, thou lovest the beautiful!"
  In the woe of my spirit I cried,
For sparkled the eyes, and the forehead was fair,
  Of the little boy that died.

Again I will go to my father's house—
  Go home to the dear ones all,
And sadly I'll open the garden gate,
  And sadly the door of the hall;
I shall meet my mother, but, nevermore,
  With her darling by her side;
And she'll kiss me and sigh, and weep again
  For the little boy that died.

I shall miss him, when the flowers come,
  In the garden where he played;
I shall miss him more by the fireside,
  When the flowers have all decayed;
I shall see his toys and his empty chair,
  And the horse he used to ride;
And they will speak, with silent speech,
  Of the little boy that died.

I shall see his little sister again,
  With her playmates about the door,
And I'll watch the children at their sports,
  As I never did before;
And if, in the group, I see a child
  That's dimpled and laughing-eyed,
I'll look to see if it may not be
  The little boy that died.

We shall go home to our Father's house—
  To our Father's house in the skies,
Where the hope of our souls shall have no blight,
  And our love no broken ties;
We shall roam on the banks of the River of Peace,
  And bathe in its blissful tide;
And one of the joys of our Heaven will be
  The little boy that died.

And therefore, when I'm sitting alone,
  And the midnight hour is near,
And the faggot's crack and the clock's dull tick
  Are the only sounds I hear,
O! sweet o'er my soul in its solitude
  Are the feelings of sadness that glide,
Though my heart and my eyes are full when I think
  Of the little boy that died.

CLEON AND I.

BY CHARLES MACKAY

CLEON hath a million acres,
  Ne'er a one have I;
Cleon dwelleth in a palace,
  In a cottage, I;
Cleon hath a dozen fortunes,
  Not a penny, I;
Yet the poorer of the twain is
  Cleon, and not I.

Cleon, true, possesseth acres,
  But the landscape, I;
Half the charms to me it yieldeth,
  Money cannot buy;
Cleon harbors sloth and dullness,
  Freshening vigor, I;
He in velvet, I in fustian,
  Richer man am I.

Cleon is a slave to grandeur,
  Free as thought am I;
Cleon fees a score of doctors,
  Need of none have I;
Wealth-surrounded, care-environed,
  Cleon fears to die;
Death may come, he'll find me ready,
  Happier man am I.

Cleon sees no charm in nature,
  In a daisy, I;
Cleon hears no anthems ringing
  In the sea and sky;
Nature sings to me forever,
  Earnest listener, I;
State for state, with all attendants,
  Who would change?—Not I.

IF I SHOULD DIE TO-NIGHT.

BY BELLE E. SMITH.

If I should die to-night,
My friends would look upon my quiet face
  Before they laid it in its resting-place,
  And deem that death had left it almost fair;
  And, laying snow-white flowers against my hair,
Would smooth it down with tearful tenderness,
And fold my hands with lingering caress;
  Poor hands, so empty and so cold to-night!

  If I should die to-night,
My friends would call to mind, with loving thought,
  Some kindly deed the icy hand had wrought;
  Some gentle word the frozen lips had said;
Errands on which the willing feet had sped;
The memory of my selfishness and pride,
My hasty words, would all be put aside,
  And so I should be loved and mourned to-night.

  If I should die to night,
Even hearts estranged would turn once more to me,
  Recalling other days remorsefully.
  The eyes that chill me with averted glance
Would look upon me as of yore, perchance,
And soften, in the old, familiar way,
For who could war with dumb, unconscious clay?
So I might rest, forgiven of all, to-night.

  Oh, friends, I pray to night,
Keep not your kisses for my dead, cold brow.
  The way is lonely, let me feel them now.
  Think gently of me; I am travel-worn;
My faltering feet are pierced with many a thorn.
Forgive, oh, hearts estranged, forgive, I plead!
When dreamless rest is mine I shall not need
The tenderness for which I long to-night.

WORDS FOR PARTING.

BY MARY CLEMMER.

O WHAT shall I do, my dear,
   In the coming years, I wonder,
When our paths, which lie so sweetly near,
   Shall lie so far asunder?
O, what shall I do, my dear,
   Through all the sad to-morrows,
When the sunny smile has ceased to cheer,
   That smiles away all sorrows?

What shall I do, my friend,
   When you are gone forever?
My heart its eager need will send,
   Through the years to find you, never.
And how will it be with you,
   In the weary world, I wonder?
Will you love me with a love as true,
   When our paths lie far asunder?

A sweeter, sadder thing,
My life for having known you;
   Forever, with my sacred kin,
My soul's soul, I must own you;
Forever mine, my friend,
   From June till life's December;
Not mine to have and hold,
   Mine to pray for, and remember.

The way is short, my friend,
   That reaches out before us;
God's tender heavens above us bend,
   His love is smiling o'er us.
A little while is ours,
   For sorrow or for laughter;
I'll lay the hand you love in yours,
   On the shore of the hereafter.

LOVE LIGHTENS LABOR.

A GOOD wife rose from her bed one morn,
   And thought, with a nervous dread,
Of the pile of clothes to be washed, and more
   Than a dozen mouths to be fed.
There's the meals to get for the men in the field,
   And the children to fix away
To school, and the milk to be skimmed and churned;
   And all to be done this day.

It had rained in the night, and all the wood
   Was wet as it could be;
There were puddings and pies to bake, besides
   A loaf of cake for tea;
And the day was hot, and her aching head
   Throbbed wearily as she said:
"If maidens but knew what good wives know,
   They would be in no haste to wed."

"Jennie, what do you think I told Ben Brown?"
   Called the farmer from the well;
And a flush crept up to his bronzed brow,
   And his eyes half bashfully fell,

"It was this," he said—and coming near,
   He kiss'd from her brow the frown;—
"'Twas this," he said, "that you were the best,
   And the dearest wife in town."

The farmer went back to the field, and the wife,
   In a smiling and absent way,
Sang snatches of tender little songs
   She'd not sung for many a day.
And the pain in her head was gone, and the clothes
   Were white as the foam of the sea;
Her bread was light and her butter was sweet,
   And as golden as it could be.

"Just think," the children all called in a breath,
   "Tom Wood has run off to sea!
He wouldn't, I know, if he only had
   As happy a home as we."
The night came down, and the good wife smiled
   To herself as she softly said:
"'Tis so sweet to labor for those we love,
   It's not strange that maids will wed!"

JENNY KISSED ME.

BY LEIGH HUNT.

JENNY kissed me when we met,
    Jumping from the chair she sat in;
Time, you thief, who love to get
    Sweets into your list, put that in!
Say I'm weary, say I'm sad;
    Say that health and wealth have missed me;
Say I'm growing dull, but add,
        Jenny kissed me!

ROLL CALL.

CORPORAL Green!" the orderly cried;
    "Here!" was the answer, loud and clear,
    From the lips of a soldier who stood near,
And "Here!" was the word the next replied.

"Cyrus Drew!"—then a silence fell—
    This time no answer followed the call;
    Only his rear man had seen him fall,
Killed or wounded he could not tell.

There they stood in the failing light,
    These men of battle, with grave, dark looks,
    As plain to be read as open books,
While slowly gathered the shades of night.

The fern on the hill-side was splashed with blood,
    And down in the corn, where the poppies grew,
    Were redder stains than the poppies knew;
And crimson-dyed was the river's flood.

For the foe had crossed from the other side,
    That day in the face of a murderous fire,
    That swept them down in its terrible ire;
And their life-blood went to color the tide.

"Herbert Kline!" At the call, there came
    Two stalwart soldiers into the line,
    Bearing between them this Herbert Kline,
Wounded and bleeding, to answer his name.

"Ezra Kerr!"—and a voice answered, "Here!"
    "Hiram Kerr!"—but no man replied.
    They were brothers, these two, the sad winds sighed,
And a shudder crept through the cornfield near.

"Ephraim Deane!"—then a soldier spoke:
    "Deane carried our Regiment's colors," he said;
    "Where our Ensign was shot, I left him dead,
Just after the enemy wavered and broke.

"Close to the roadside his body lies.
    I paused a moment and gave him to drink.
    He murmured his mother's name, I think,
And death came with it and closed his eyes."

'Twas a victory; yes, but it cost us dear,—
    For that company's roll, when called at night,
    Of *a hundred* men who went into the fight,
Numbered but *twenty* that answered "Here!"

UP-HILL.

BY CHRISTINA G. ROSSETTI.

DOES the road wind up-hill all the way?
　　Yes, to the very end.
Will the day's journey take the whole long day?
　　From morn to night, my friend.

But is there for the night a resting place?
　　A roof for when the slow, dark hours begin?
May not the darkness hide it from my face?
　　You cannot miss that inn.

Shall I meet other wayfarers at night?
　　Those who have gone before.
Then must I knock, or call when just in sight?
　　They will not keep you standing at the door.

Shall I find comfort, travel-sore and weak?
　　Of labor you shall find the sum.
Will there be beds for me and all who seek?
　　Yea, beds for all who come.

"Yea, beds for all who come."

OH, WHY SHOULD THE SPIRIT OF MORTAL BE PROUD?

BY WILLIAM KNOX.

OH, why should the spirit of mortal be proud?
　Like a swift-fleeting meteor, a fast-flying cloud,
　A flash of the lightning, a break of the wave,
　Man passes from life to his rest in the grave.

The leaves of the oak and the willow shall fade,
　Be scattered around and together be laid;
　And the young and the old, and the low and the high,
　Shall moulder to dust and together shall lie.

The infant a mother attended and loved,
　The mother that infant's affection who proved;
　The husband that mother and infant who blessed,
　Each, all, are away to their dwellings of rest.

The maid on whose cheek, on whose brow, in whose eye,
　Shone beauty and pleasure—her triumphs are by;
　And the memory of those who loved her and praised,
　Are alike from the minds of the living erased.

The hand of the king that the sceptre hath borne,
　The brow of the priest that the mitre hath worn,
　The eye of the sage and the heart of the brave,
　Are hidden and lost in the depth of the grave.

The peasant, whose lot was to sow and to reap;
　The herdsman, who climbed with his goats up the steep;
　The beggar, who wandered in search of his bread,
　Have faded away like the grass that we tread.

The saint who enjoyed the communion of heaven,
　The sinner who dared to remain unforgiven,
　The wise and the foolish, the guilty and just,
　Have quietly mingled their bones in the dust.

So the multitude goes, like the flowers or the weed
　That withers away to let others succeed;
　So the multitude comes, even those we behold,
　To repeat every tale that has often been told.

For we are the same our fathers have been;
　We see the same sights our fathers have seen,—
　We drink the same stream and view the same sun,
　And run the same course our fathers have run.

The thoughts we are thinking our fathers would think,
　From the death we are shrinking our fathers would shrink,
　To the life we are clinging they also would cling;
　But it speeds for us all, like a bird on the wing.

They loved, but the story we cannot unfold;
　They scorned, but the heart of the haughty is cold;
　They grieved, but no wail from their slumbers will come;
　They joyed, but the tongue of their gladness is dumb.

They died, aye! they died; and we things that are now,
　Who walk on the turf that lies over their brow,
　Who make in their dwellings a transient abode,
　Meet the things that they met on their pilgrimage road.

Yea! hope and despondency, pleasure and pain,
　We mingle together in sunshine and rain;
　And the smiles and the tears, the song and the dirge,
　Still follow each other, like surge upon surge.

'Tis the wink of an eye, 'tis the draught of a breath;
　From the blossom of health to the paleness of death,
　From the gilded saloon to the bier and the shroud,—
　Oh, why should the spirit of mortal be proud?

UNTIL DEATH.

AKE me no vows of constancy, dear friend,
　　To love me, though I die, thy whole life long,
And love no other till thy days shall end,—
　　Nay, it were rash and wrong.

If thou canst love another, be it so;
　　I would not reach out of my quiet grave
To bind thy heart, if it should choose to go;—
　　Love should not be a slave.

My placid ghost, I trust, will walk serene
　　In clearer light than gilds these earthly morns,
Above the jealousies and envies keen,
　　Which sow this life with thorns.

Thou wouldst not feel my shadowy caress,
　　If, after death, my soul should linger here;
Men's hearts crave tangible, close tenderness,
　　Love's presence, warm and near.

It would not make me sleep more peacefully
　　That thou wert wasting all thy life in woe

For my poor sake; what love thou hast for me,
　　Bestow it ere I go!

Carve not upon a stone when I am dead
　　The praises which remorseful mourners give
To women's graves—a tardy recompense—
　　But speak them while I live.

Heap not the heavy marble on my head
　　To shut away the sunshine and the dew;
Let small blooms grow there, and let grasses wave,
　　And rain-drops filter through.

Thou wilt meet many fairer and more gay
　　Than I; but, trust me, thou canst never find
One who will love and serve thee night and day
　　With a more single mind.

Forget me when I die! The violets
　　Above my rest will blossom just as blue,
Nor miss thy tears; e'en nature's self forgets;
　　But while I live, be true!

SOMETIME.

OMETIME, when all life's lessons
　　　　have been learned,
　　And sun and stars for ever-
　　　　more have set,
　　The things which our weak
　　　　judgments here have spurned,
　　The things o'er which we
　　　　grieved with lashes wet,
Will flash before us out of
　　　　life's dark night,
As stars shine most in deeper tints of blue;
And we shall see how all God's plans were right,
　　And how what seemed reproof was love most true.

And we shall see how, while we frown and sigh,
　　God's plans go on as best for you and me;
How, when we called, He heeded not our cry,
　　Because His wisdom to the end could see.
And e'en as prudent parents disallow
　　Too much of sweet to craving babyhood,
So God, perhaps, is keeping from us now
　　Life's sweetest things because it seemeth good.

And if, sometimes, commingled with life's wine,
　　We find the wormwood, and rebel and shrink,

Be sure a wiser hand than yours or mine
　　Pours out this portion for our lips to drink.
And if some friend we love is lying low,
　　Where human kisses cannot reach his face,
Oh, do not blame the loving Father so,
　　But wear your sorrow with obedient grace!

And you shall shortly know that lengthened breath
　　Is not the sweetest gift God sends His friend,
And that, sometimes, the sable pall of death
　　Conceals the fairest boon His love can send.
If we could push ajar the gates of life,
　　And stand within, and all God's workings see,
We could interpret all this doubt and strife,
　　And for each mystery could find a key!

But not to-day. Then be content, poor heart!
　　God's plans like lilies pure and white unfold;
We must not tear the close-shut leaves apart,
　　Time will reveal the calyxes of gold.
And if, through patient toil, we reach the land
　　Where tired feet, with sandals loose, may rest,
When we shall clearly know and understand,
　　I think that we will say, "God knew the best!"

RAIN ON THE ROOF.

BY COATES KINNEY.

WHEN the humid shadows hover over
    all the starry spheres,
And the melancholy darkness gently
    weeps in rainy tears,
'Tis a joy to press the pillow of a cot
    tage chamber bed,
And listen to the patter of the soft
    rain overhead.

Every tinkle on the shingles has an
    echo in the heart,
And a thousand dreary fancies into
    busy being start;
And a thousand recollections weave their bright hues into woof,
As I listen to the patter of the soft rain on the roof.

There, in fancy, comes my mother, as she used to years agone,
To survey the infant sleepers ere she left them till the dawn;

I can see her bending o'er me, as I listen to the strain
Which is played upon the shingles by the patter of the rain.

Then my little seraph sister, with her wings and waving hair,
And her bright-eyed cherub brother—a serene, angelic pair,—
Glide around my wakeful pillow, with their praise or mild reproof,
As I listen to the murmur of the soft rain on the roof.

And another comes to thrill me with her eyes' delicious blue.
I forget, as gazing on her, that her heart was all untrue;
I remember that I loved her as I ne'er may love again,
And my heart's quick pulses vibrate to the patter of the rain.

There is naught in art's bravuras that can work with such a spell,
In the spirit's pure, deep fountains, where the holy passions swell,
As that melody of nature,—that subdued, subduing strain,
Which is played upon the shingles by the patter of the rain.

ON THE OTHER SIDE.

WE GO our ways in life too much alone;
    We hold ourselves too far from all our kind;
Too often we are dead to sigh and moan;
    Too often to the weak and helpless blind;
Too often, where distress and want abide,
    We turn and pass upon the other side.

The other side is trodden smooth, and worn
    By footsteps passing idly all the day.
Where lie the bruised ones that faint and mourn,
    Is seldom more than an untrodden way;
Our selfish hearts are for our feet the guide,
    They lead us by upon the other side.

It should be ours the oil and wine to pour
    Into the bleeding wounds of stricken ones;
To take the smitten, and the sick and sore,
    And bear them where a stream of blessing runs;
Instead, we look about—the way is wide,
    And so we pass upon the other side.

Oh, friends and brothers, gliding down the years,
    Humanity is calling each and all
In tender accents, born of grief and tears!
    I pray you, listen to the thrilling call;
You cannot, in your cold and selfish pride,
    Pass guiltlessly by on the other side.

AMBITION.

BY LORD BYRON.

He who ascends to mountain tops shall find
    The loftiest peaks most wrapt in clouds and snow;
He, who surpasses or subdues mankind,
    Must look down on the hate of those below.
Though high above the sun of glory glow,
    And far beneath the earth and ocean spread,
Round him are icy rocks, and loudly blow
    Contending tempests on his naked head;
And thus reward the toils which to those summits led.

BLESSED ARE THEY THAT MOURN.

BY WM. C. BRYANT.

There is a day of sunny rest
    For every dark and troubled night;
And grief may bide an evening guest,
    But joy shall come with early light.

For God hath marked each sorrowing day
    And numbered every secret tear,
And heaven's long age of bliss shall pay
    For all His children suffer here.

BY ALFRED TENNYSON.

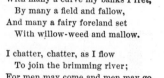

SONG OF THE BROOK.

I COME from haunts of coot and hern;
  I make a sudden sally,
And sparkle out among the fern,
  To bicker down a valley.

By thirty hills I hurry down,
  Or slip between the ridges;
By twenty thorps, a little town,
  And half a hundred bridges.

Till last by Philip's farm I flow,
  To join the brimming river;
For men may come and men may go,
  But I go on forever.

I chatter over stony ways,
  In little sharps and trebles;
I bubble into eddying bays,
  I babble on the pebbles.

With many a curve my banks I fret,
  By many a field and fallow,
And many a fairy foreland set
  With willow-weed and mallow.

I chatter, chatter, as I flow
  To join the brimming river;
For men may come and men may go,
  But I go on forever.

I wind about, and in and out,
  With here a blossom sailing,
And here and there a lusty trout,
  And here and there a grayling,

And here and there a foamy flake
  Upon me, as I travel,
With many a silvery waterbreak
  Above the golden gravel;

And draw them all along, and flow
  To join the brimming river;
For men may come and men may go,
  But I go on forever.

I steal by lawns and grassy plots;
  I slide by hazel covers;
I move the sweet forget-me-nots
  That grow for happy lovers.

I slip, I slide, I gloom, I glance
  Among my skimming swallows;
I make the netted sunbeam dance
  Against my sandy shallows.

I murmur under moon and stars,
  In brambly wildernesses;
I linger by my shingly bars;
  I loiter round my cresses.

And out again I curve and flow
  To join the brimming river;
For men may come and men may go,
  But I go on forever.

THE DOORSTEP.

BY EDMUND CLARENCE STEDMAN.

THE conference meeting through at last,
    We boys around the vestry waited,
To see the girls come tripping past
    Like snow-birds willing to be mated.

Not braver he that leaps the wall
    By level musket-flashes litten,
Than I, who stepped before them all
    Who longed to see me get the mitten.

But no, she blushed and took my arm!
    We let the old folks have the highway,
And started toward the Maple Farm
    Along a kind of lovers' by-way.

I can't remember what we said,
    'Twas nothing worth a song or story,
Yet that rude path by which we sped
    Seemed all transformed and in a glory.

The snow was crisp beneath our feet,
    The moon was full, the fields were gleaming;
By hood and tippet sheltered sweet,
    Her face with youth and health was beaming.

The little hand outside her muff—
    O sculptor, if you could but mold it!
So lightly touched my jacket-cuff,
    To keep it warm I had to hold it.

To have her with me there alone—
    'Twas love and fear and triumph blended:
At last we reached the foot-worn stone
    Where that delicious journey ended.

She shook her ringlets from her hood,
    And with a " Thank you, Ned," dissembled,
But yet I knew she understood
    With what a daring wish I trembled.

A cloud passed kindly overhead,
    The moon was slyly peeping through it,
Yet hid its face, as if it said,
    " Come, now or never, do it, *do it!* "

My lips till then had only known
    The kiss of mother and of sister,
But somehow, full upon her own
    Sweet, rosy, darling mouth—I kissed her!

Perhaps 'twas boyish love, yet still,
    O listless woman! weary lover!
To feel once more that fresh wild thrill,
    I'd give—But who can live youth over.

LITTLE BOY BLUE.

BY ABBY SAGE RICHARDSON.

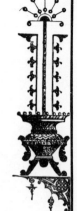

UNDER the haystack, little Boy Blue
  Sleeps with his head on his arm,
While voices of men and voices of maids
  Are calling him over the farm.

Sheep in the meadows are running wild,
  Where a poisonous herbage grows,
Leaving white tufts of downy fleece
  On the thorns of the sweet, wild rose.

Out in the fields where the silken corn
  Its plumed head nods and bows,
Where the golden pumpkins, ripen below,
  Trample the white-faced cows.

But no loud blast on the shining horn
  Calls back the straying sheep,

And the cows may wander in hay or corn,
  While their keeper lies asleep.

His roguish eyes are tightly shut,
  His dimples are all at rest;
The chubby hand tucked under his head,
  By one rosy cheek is pressed.

Waken him! No! Let down the bars
  And gather the truant sheep,
Open the barn-yard and drive in the cows,
  But let the little boy sleep.

For year after year we can shear the fleece,
  And corn can always be sown;
But the sleep that visits little Boy Blue
  Will not come when the years have flown.

EXTRACT FROM "THE BATTLE-FIELD."

BY W. C. BRYANT.

TRUTH crushed to earth shall rise again:
  The eternal years of God are hers;
But Error, wounded, writhes with pain,
  And dies among his worshipers.

KEEP PUSHING.

KEEP pushing! 'tis wiser than sitting aside,
And sighing and watching and waiting the tide;
In life's earnest battle they only prevail,
Who daily march onward and never say fail.

EXTRACT FROM "A PSALM OF LIFE."

BY H. W. LONGFELLOW.

LIVES of great men all remind us
  We can make our lives sublime,
And, departing, leave behind us
  Footprints on the sands of time.

SCATTER THE GERMS OF THE BEAUTIFUL.

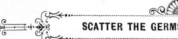
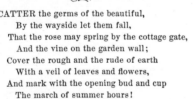

SCATTER the germs of the beautiful,
  By the wayside let them fall,
That the rose may spring by the cottage gate,
  And the vine on the garden wall;
Cover the rough and the rude of earth
  With a veil of leaves and flowers,
And mark with the opening bud and cup
  The march of summer hours!

Scatter the germs of the beautiful
  In the holy shrine of home;
Let the pure, and the fair, and graceful there
  In the loveliest lustre come;
Leave not a trace of deformity
  In the temple of the heart,
But gather about its hearth the gems
  Of nature and of art.

Scatter the germs of the beautiful
  In the temples of our God—
The God who starred the uplifted sky,
  And flowered the trampled sod!
When he built a temple for himself,
  And a home for his priestly race,
He reared each arm in symmetry,
  And covered each line in grace.

Scatter the germs of the beautiful
  In the depths of the human soul!
They shall bud, and blossom, and bear the fruit,
  While the endless ages roll;
Plant with the flowers of charity
  The portals of the tomb,
And the fair and the pure about thy path
  In paradise shall bloom.

HEAVEN BY LITTLES.

BY J. G. HOLLAND.

Heaven is not reached by a single bound;
  But we build the ladder, by which we rise
  From the lowly earth to the vaulted skies,
And we mount to its summit round by round.

I count these things to be grandly true!
  That a noble deed is a step toward God—
  Lifting the soul, from the common sod,
To a purer air and a broader view.

We rise by the things that are under our feet;
  By what we have mastered of greed and gain,
  By the pride deposed, and the passion slain,
And the vanquished ill that we hourly meet.

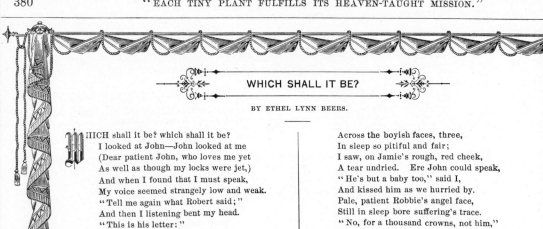

WHICH SHALL IT BE?

BY ETHEL LYNN BEERS.

WHICH shall it be? which shall it be?
I looked at John—John looked at me
(Dear patient John, who loves me yet
As well as though my locks were jet,)
And when I found that I must speak,
My voice seemed strangely low and weak.
"Tell me again what Robert said;"
And then I listening bent my head.
"This is his letter:"

       "I will give
A house and land while you shall live,
If, in return, from out your seven,
One child to me for aye is given."

I looked at John's old garments worn,
I thought of all that John had borne
Of poverty and work and care,
Which I, though willing, could not share;
I thought of seven mouths to feed,
Of seven little children's need,
And then of this.

       "Come, John," said I,
"We'll choose among them, as they lie
Asleep; so walking hand in hand,
Dear John and I surveyed our band.
First to the cradle lightly stepped
Where the new, nameless baby slept.
"Shall it be baby?" whispered John.
I took his hand, and hurried on
To Lily's crib. Her sleeping grasp
Held her old doll within its clasp;
Her dark curls lay like gold alight,
A glory 'gainst the pillow white.
Softly her father stooped to lay
His rough hand down in a loving way,
When dream or whisper made her stir,
And, huskily, John said, " Not her—not her."

We stooped beside the trundle-bed,
And one long ray of lamp-light shed

Across the boyish faces, three,
In sleep so pitiful and fair;
I saw, on Jamie's rough, red cheek,
A tear undried. Ere John could speak,
"He's but a baby too," said I,
And kissed him as we hurried by.
Pale, patient Robbie's angel face,
Still in sleep bore suffering's trace.
"No, for a thousand crowns, not him,"
We whispered while our eyes were dim.
Poor Dick! bad Dick! our wayward son,
Turbulent, reckless, idle one—
Could he be spared? "Nay, He, who gave,
Bids us befriend him to his grave;
Only a mother's heart can be
Patient enough for such as he;
And so," said John, "I would not dare
To send him from her bedside prayer."
Then stole we softly up above,
And knelt by Mary, child of love.
"Perhaps for her 'twould better be,"
I said to John. Quite silently
He lifted up a curl that lay
Across her cheek, in willful way,
And he shook his head, " Nay, love, not thee,"
The while my heart beat audibly.
Only one more, our oldest lad,
Trusty and thoughtful, good and glad—
So like his father. "No, John, no—
I cannot, will not, let him go."

And so we wrote, in courteous way,
We could not give one child away;
And after that, toil lighter seemed,
Thinking of that of which we dreamed,
Happy, in truth, that not one face
Was missed from its accustomed place;
Thankful to work for all the seven,
Trusting the rest to One in Heaven.

WEEDS.

WE call them weeds, the while with slender fingers,
   Earth's wounds and scars they seek to cover o'er;
On sterile sands, where scarce the raindrop lingers,
   They grow and blossom by the briny shore.

We call them weeds; did we their form but study,
   We many a secret might unfolded find;
Each tiny plant fulfills its heaven-taught mission,
   And bears the impress of Immortal Mind.

We call them weeds; the while their uses hidden
   Might work a nation's weal, a nation's woe;

Send thro' each wasted frame the balm of healing,
   And cause the blood with youth's quick pulse to flow.

Weeds—yet they hold in bonds the mighty ocean!
   Their slender threads bind firm the sandy shore;
Navies may sink amid its wild commotion,
   These humble toilers ne'er their work give o'er.

And who shall say the feeblest thought avails not
   To bind the shifting sands upon life's beach?
Some heart may treasure what we've long forgot,
   The faintest word some soul with power may reach.

OVER THE RIVER

BY NANCY AMELIA PRIEST.

OVER the river they beckon to me,
  Loved ones who've crossed to the farther side;
The gleam of their snowy robes I see,
  But their voices are lost in the dashing tide.
There's one with ringlets of sunny gold,
  And eyes, the reflection of heaven's own blue;
He crossed in the twilight gray and cold,
  And the pale mist hid him from mortal view.
We saw not the angels who met him there,
  The gates of the city we could not see;
Over the river, over the river,
  My brother stands waiting to welcome me.

"Over the river the boatman pale carried another, the household pet; darling Minnie! I see her yet."

Over the river the boatman pale
  Carried another, the household pet;
Her brown curls waved in the gentle gale,
  Darling Minnie! I see her yet.
She crossed on her bosom her dimpled hands,
  And fearlessly entered the phantom bark;
We felt it glide from the silver sands,
  And all our sunshine grew strangely dark.
We know she is safe on the farther side,
  Where all the ransomed and angels be:
Over the river, the mystic river,
  My childhood's idol is waiting for me.

And I sit and think, when the sunset's gold
  Is flushing river, and hill, and shore,
I shall one day stand by the water cold,
  And list for the sound of the boatman's oar;
I shall watch for a gleam of the flapping sail,
  I shall hear the boat as it gains the strand,
I shall pass from sight, with the boatman pale,
  To the better shore of the spirit land.
I shall know the loved, who have gone before,
  And joyfully sweet will the meeting be,
When over the river, the peaceful river,
  The angel of death shall carry me.

COMMENDATIONS

FROM

DISTINGUISHED EDUCATORS AND EMINENT MEN.

NO work of an educational character, of late years, has met with such universal approval from teachers and learned men as this. While the book is most warmly welcomed by the illiterate, it is equally sought for by the educated. Hundreds of testimonials from distinguished individuals might be given similar to the following:

From Samuel Fallows, ex-State Supt. Pub. Schools, Wisconsin.

"I am highly delighted with the plan and execution of Hill's Manual."

From Prof. J. G. Cross, Principal of the Northwestern Business College, Naperville, Ill.

"It is a most valuable book, which ought to be multiplied as many times as there are families in the United States. I have adopted it as a book of daily reference for our business students."

From Theodore B. Boyd, Principal of the Louisville Commercial College.

"I have examined 'Hill's Manual of Social and Business Forms,' and am surprised at the amount of useful information contained in one volume. Prof. Hill seems to have studied the wants of every one. It is one of the most useful books that was ever laid upon the counting-room desk or the drawing-room table."

From D. S. Burns, Supt. Pub. Schools, Harrisburg, Pa.

"I know of no work that contains so great a variety of valuable information on social and business topics as 'Hill's Manual of Social and Business Forms.' I think it a work of special value to those who have not had opportunities of an extended school course, or becoming familiar by contact with the conventionalities of society."

From Wm. Cornell, Supt. Pub. Schools in Fall River, Mass.

"I most cheerfully recommend "Hill's Manual of Social and Business Forms' as a very full work on the various 'Forms' which every person is likely to have occasion to use in his relations with persons in society. A thorough study of the 'book' by our young men and women would repay them by their acquiring a large fund of very valuable and practical knowledge from its pages. It should meet with a large circulation."

From M. M. Ballou, Distinguished Author, formerly Publisher of "Boston Globe," "Ballou's Monthly," etc.

"'Hill's Manual' is one of those indispensable books of reference which both business men and families should always have at hand. It is such a natural outgrowth of the spirit of the age to condense and put in available form important information upon every subject, that, while we are much gratified to possess this volume, we are also surprised that such a book has not before been produced. It is exactly what its title indicates, a book of 'Social and Business Forms'; but it would require too much space to give even a synopsis of this valuable compendium of instruction and important knowledge."

From D. P. Lindsley, Author of Lindsley's System of Tachygraphy, Andover, Mass.

"'Hill's Manual' is really the most comprehensive, thorough and elegant volume, treating on 'Social and Business Forms,' that has ever been issued in this country."

From Gov. Gaston, of Massachusetts.

"'Hill's Manual of Social and Business Forms' *contains much valuable and useful information.* I think *it well meets a public want,* and can therefore be safely and properly commended to public favor."

From President McCollister, of Buchtel College, Akron, Ohio.

"'HILL'S MANUAL' is a timely book, meeting a public want which has not been filled before. Every family should own this book. It contains information important and useful to all classes. I feel all who examine it will want it."

From Wm. M. Cubery, of Cubery & Co., Publishers of the "Pacific Churchman," San Francisco, Cal.

"'Hill's Manual of Social and Business Forms' is not only a luxury, but a necessity— eminently serviceable in the social circle, and indispensable to the man of business who would save time and money. I keep a copy in my counting-room for ready reference."

From Stephen Walkley, Treasurer of the Peck, Stow & Wilcox Co., Southington, Conn.

"Hill's Manual is remarkable as containing a great variety of forms for numberless little things which all people have to do at sometime in their lives, but which most people do so seldom that they entirely forget the methods in ordinary use, and do them awkwardly or not at all. I have known even well-educated persons travel one or two miles to have a subscription paper drawn, just for the lack of such a book as this. I am surprised at the great scope of the work, and have yet to discover any social or business form needed by people in the ordinary walks of life which is not there given."

From Newton Bateman, ex-State Supt. of Public Schools, Illinois.

"KNOX COLLEGE, GALESBURG, ILL. "'Hill's Manual of Social and Business Forms' is the best and most complete work of the kind that has yet fallen under my notice. Indeed I do not see how it could well be more comprehensive and exhaustive in respect to the matters of which it treats. It contains, in comparatively small compass, an immense amount of useful information upon a great variety of practical matters, general and special, with which every person in every community ought to be acquainted."

From Geo. Soule, President of Soule's Commercial and Literary Institute, New Orleans.

"I am pleased to say that I regard 'Hill's Manual' as one of the most valuable works for all classes of society which the nineteenth century has produced."

From Prof. Worthy Putnam, Author of Putnam's Elocution and Oratory, Berrien Springs, Mich.

"I have bought Hill's Manual—I like it—I admire it; and so says my household. It is a little encyclopædia of use, ornament, and knowledge for both men and women. It is a gem of authorship, artistic execution and usefulness."

From the venerable Jared P. Kirtland, M. D., LL.D.

"After a THOROUGH AND CRITICAL EXAMINATION of 'Hill's Manual,' I have subscribed for three copies: one to accompany Webster's Unabridged Dictionary on my writing desk for my own use, the others for my two eldest great-grandsons. * * * It should be in the possession of every class of persons, from the young student to the most active business man or woman." JARED P. KIRTLAND.

President Grant Subscribes.

The agent of Hill's Manual at Long Branch writes: "By ten A. M. I was at the president's cottage, tipped and doffed my hat, announced my business, when the president promptly said he did not want to subscribe. I obtained permission to show it to him, and did so very hurriedly. At the conclusion, he took my specimen copy, paid me the cash, and added his name to my autograph book."

From Major Merwin, Editor "American Journal of Education," St. Louis.

"After having given 'Hill's Manual' a very careful and thorough examination, I do not hesitate to say that it will be found one of the most *useful* and *practical* works to put into the schools of the country that has ever been published. IT IS A FIT AND ALMOST INDISPENSABLE COMPANION TO WEBSTER'S UNABRIDGED DICTIONARY; containing in a compact form just those things every person who transacts *any* business needs to know. There is scarcely a subject which comes within the purview of any individual, either in public or private life, but what is explained in this elegant volume. If it could be consulted in the drawing up of contracts, nearly all the mistakes which occur might be avoided, and the ill feeling and litigation growing out of misunderstandings would be a thing of the past. I wish every person in the State could be supplied with a copy."

SOLD ONLY BY SUBSCRIPTION, and not at Bookstores. AGENTS WANTED. Address, for terms,

HILL STANDARD BOOK CO., Publishers,

No. 103 State Street, CHICAGO, ILL.

[OVER]

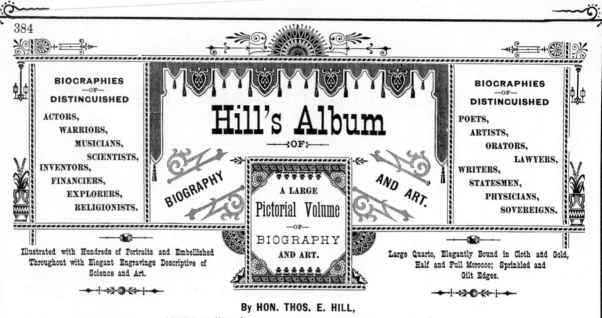

BIOGRAPHIES
—OF—
DISTINGUISHED

ACTORS,
WARRIORS,
MUSICIANS,
SCIENTISTS,
INVENTORS,
FINANCIERS,
EXPLORERS,
RELIGIONISTS.

Hill's Album
—:OF:—

BIOGRAPHY AND ART.

A LARGE Pictorial Volume
—OF—
BIOGRAPHY AND ART.

BIOGRAPHIES
—OF—
DISTINGUISHED

POETS,
ARTISTS,
ORATORS,
LAWYERS,
WRITERS,
STATESMEN,
PHYSICIANS,
SOVEREIGNS.

Illustrated with Hundreds of Portraits and Embellished Throughout with Elegant Engravings Descriptive of Science and Art.

Large Quarto, Elegantly Bound in Cloth and Gold, Half and Full Morocco; Sprinkled and Gilt Edges.

By HON. THOS. E. HILL,
AUTHOR OF "HILL'S MANUAL OF SOCIAL AND BUSINESS FORMS."

THE PURPOSE of HILL'S ALBUM has been to present in a condensed form the leading and essential facts concerning the lives of the most noted persons who have ever lived.

The Plan has been followed of arranging distinct classes together. Thus the great Religious Founders, including Moses, Buddha, Confucius, Zoroaster, Christ, Mohammed and others, accompanied by fine illustrations, biographies, History and Beliefs of Denominations, Dictionary of Religious Terms, etc., are included in one chapter. The Great Military Heroes at all times, including Wellington, Bonaparte, Washington, Grant and many others, together with a list of memorable battles fought, a Dictionary of Military Terms, etc., form another chapter, and so through the volume.

The Lessons drawn from these biographies as they are presented, are of themselves a peculiar feature of this work. In the histories of the Rothschilds, the Astors, Vanderbilt, Girard, Peabody, A. T. Stewart, Jay Gould, Longworth, Mackey, Flood and others, the secret of their success in money-getting is very clearly stated, so that the reader desirous of making money may greatly profit by the reading. And thus throughout the volume the causes that led to success, in whatever direction, is very clearly pointed out. Much light under this head is given in the chapter devoted to phrenology.

The Examples presented through the struggles of inventors, including Howe, Goodyear, Stephenson, Watt, and multitudes of others celebrated for triumphs in war, finance, exploration, science, literature and art, are worthy of careful study and imitation by the young who aspire to supremacy.

General Matter. The chapters relating to the History and Beliefs of the Great Denominations; the Illustrated Darwinian Philosophy, showing the world's progress at different epochs of time; the department devoted to Astronomy, presenting the subject in simple language, clearly illustrated; the chapter relating to Phrenology, accompanied by views and diagrams of heads; the portion concerning Household Decoration and that treating of Landscape Gardening, all profusely illustrated, are each intensely interesting and instructive.

The Scope of the work it is impossible to enumerate here; suffice it to say eleven pages are devoted to giving the table of contents. The range of the work includes the men who have formed the religious beliefs, that have been brilliant lights in the commercial world, that have wrought great improvements, that have discovered new continents, that have opened the book of science, that have made the people happy through laughter, that have written our sweetest songs, that have produced the most thrilling tales, that have presented the world the most truthful portraitures with the brush and chisel, and that have stirred the hearts of the people through powerful oratory.

The Typographic Display of the ALBUM is a distinguishing feature of the book. In elegant, artistic finish it is without a rival, the secret of its superior embellishment lying in the fact that the power to produce the book mechanically rests with the author, who, by his knowledge of the artistic, is able to produce the matter in such attractive form.

SOLD BY SUBSCRIPTION ONLY. AGENTS WANTED.

THE book is published by the Hill Standard Book Co., in Chicago, Ill., on heavy tinted super-calendered paper, in various styles of elegant binding. Full information concerning terms to agents, territory in which they may sell the book, etc., can be learned by addressing

[OVER]

HILL STANDARD BOOK CO., Publishers,
103 State Street, CHICAGO, ILL.

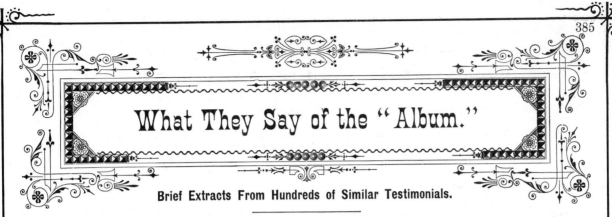

What They Say of the "Album."

Brief Extracts From Hundreds of Similar Testimonials.

The following are from papers published at Aurora, Ill., where the author of the ALBUM resided twelve years, during the last of which he was Mayor of the city.

From the Aurora Beacon.

THE business career of Mr. Thos. E. Hill, who was at one time a resident of Aurora, and mayor of the city, has been very successful, and some have been inclined to think it the result of good luck. Every enterprise of which he took hold seemed to turn him money, and schemes which would have been abortive in the hands of ordinary men blossomed into rare success under his management. The same good fortune follows him and his enterprises to this day. There is no "luck" in it at all. It grows first from his intense industry, energy and application; second from his enthusiasm; and third from his keen appreciation of *what the public desires*, drawn from long contact with it and close study. In his youth he was eminently successful as a canvasser, as a teacher of writing and lecturer on penmanship. In Aurora, for a number of years he published and edited the *Herald* with great success. When he sold his newspaper, and established the system of city messenger, which has since become so popular between minor cities and Chicago, he exploited new ground which was for a time very profitable; and it was during the hours when he was passing between Aurora and Chicago, that he conceived and did the first work upon the "Manual," that splendid product of the brain, of the compiler, the printer and the book-binder, which has made Thos. E. Hill's name familiar from the Atlantic to the Pacific oceans, and from Minnesota to Florida.

"For two years or more past, Mr. Hill has been of opinion that there existed room for another work besides the "Manual," which should be equally popular and useful—and meet a demand as universal as that enjoyed by his first great work. He has devoted a large amount of labor and inventive genius to the accomplishment of his ideal, and we now have it before us in "HILL'S ALBUM OF BIOGRAPHY AND ART." It is a large quarto volume of 451 pages, printed upon heavy tinted paper, with hundreds of fine portraits, miscellaneous illustrations, unique, artistic and elegant designs. In its preparation he has called to his aid the most modern and refined skill of the type-maker, engraver and typographer, and he has thus, in the "ALBUM," surpassed, in artistic and typographical display, all his former efforts.

"The new work is divided into eighteen departments, as follows: 1st, Religion and its Founders; 2d, Military Chieftains and Famous Battles; 3d, Discoverers and Explorers; 4th, Sketches of Leading Inventors; 5th, History of Financiers; 6th, Sketches of the Scientists; 7th, the Theory of Progression; 8th, Astronomical Science; 9th, Phrenology and Science of Mind; 10th, Humorists and Caricaturists; 11th, Physicians, Lawyers and Sovereigns; 12th, Orators and Statesmen; 13, Actors and Play Writers; 14th, Historians, Novelists, Essayists, etc.; 15th, Poets and Song Writers; 16th, Painters and Sculptors; 17th, Household Ornamentation; 18th, Beautiful Homes. Under these heads are given very many beautiful engravings of men, incidents and places, with sketches, biographical and pertinent, interspersed with very many things valuable to every person who would be reasonably well informed. We doubt if there is any one volume where so much useful information of the kind is gathered, and certainly there is none where it is put in more methodical form, or presented in a manner so pleasing to the eye and taste."

From the Aurora Blade.

"Every page of HILL'S ALBUM is *a model of typography* and originality, each differing from the other in mechanical construction, and each succeeding leaf a surprise from an artistic standpoint. The question one asks, instinctively, is, how can a man conceive so many elegant designs? The contents of the book, however, are what prove its most forcible recommendation. The name of the author of this valuable work, Hon. Thomas E. Hill, is in itself enough to recommend it to all. Our readers are advised to examine the book carefully when they have the opportunity.

From the Aurora Herald.

"'HILL'S ALBUM OF BIOGRAPHY AND ART,' is the name of a new book by Hon. Thos. E. Hill, author of "Hill's Manual of Social and Business Forms." It is gotten up very much after the style of the Manual, but more elaborate and expensive, as nearly every page has some engraving especially for it. The title of the book does not give any adequate idea of the immense amount of information it contains. We suppose it is called an ALBUM because of the many pictures it contains, but in addition thereto it contains short biographical sketches of distinguished men, from the time of Moses and Aaron down to the present. It gives a sketch of Moses, with his portrait, and an outline of his teachings; of Buddha, portrait and doctrines, also the same of Confucius, Jesus Christ, Mohammed, Swedenborg. Andrew Jackson Davis, and Joseph Smith, and an outline of the belief of the different Christian denominations. It also gives sketches and portraits of numerous warriors, inventors, financiers, scientists, actors, humorists, explorers, poets, lawyers, doctors, statesmen, orators, artists, etc., and gives as much about each as most people would care to remember. It is, in short, *a complete library in one volume*, and must have been the work of years to gather the information and put it in this condensed form. Of the typographical excellence it is unnecessary to speak, as all know that whatever Mr. Hill undertakes in that line, is done in the best style known to the art. We know of no other book which has so many new and original designs."

[OVER]

From the People and the Press in General.

The Universal Testimony is that Hill's Album is one of the Most Unique, Elegant and Useful Books in the World. Read the Verdict.

"One of the Most Instructive and Entertaining Books."
[From Rev. H. W. Thomas, Chicago.]

I THINK 'Hill's Album' is *one of the most instructive and entertaining books* I ever saw."

"Most Fascinatingly Interesting."
[From the *Passaic* (N. J.) *Item.*]

" We know of no volume so comprehensive in its information as this, and arranged in such a manner as to be *most fascinatingly interesting.*"

"The Most Beautiful and Complete."
[From the *Chicago Inter-Ocean.*]

" One of the *most beautiful and complete* books of the year. Not only is it wholly creditable as a fine specimen of the printer's art, but the elegant, unique and artistic designs are worthy of special commendation. But the value of the book is in its reading contents, and the admirable system and method of its arrangement. The author is the Hon. Thomas E. Hill, author of 'Hill's Manual of Social and Business Forms,' another of the practical books. The book, under many headings, gleans the most interesting and valuable acts of history bearing upon the subject."

"We Have Examined it and Were Captured."
[From the *Sandwich* (Ill.) *Argus.*]

"'Hill's Album' is a wonder of art and industry. *We have examined it and were captured.* Mr. Hill made a great success of his 'Manual,' and this work gives evidence of his old-time industry and thoroughness. It is full of information upon matters of science, art, architecture, mechanics, biography, religion, etc., and is embellished and illustrated in the highest perfection. The amount of persistent labor needed for Mr. Hill to accomplish this perfect 'Album,' is as wonderful as the skill shown in gathering in so small a compass the pith of the world's history."

Must be Largely Sought and Highly Prized."
[From the *Penman's Art Journal*, New York.]

"The subject-matter of the work, in its extent and skillful manner of presentation, bears unmistakable evidence of great labor and profound research, as well as a liberal expenditure of money on the part of the author. The embellishments are upon a scale most liberal and excellent in taste. The work, as a whole, is one that *must be largely sought and highly prized* by all classes, not alone as a handbook of valuable and interesting information, but as a beautiful and appropriate ornament for the parlor or drawing-room. It is a fitting companion of 'Hill's Manual,' which has proved the most popular and ready-selling work of its day, having already reached its thirtieth edition, and into the hundreds of thousands of copies sold. Like the 'Manual,' the new work is to be sold only on subscription, through agents."

"It is a Marvel."
[From the *Chicago Tribune.*]

"In the preparation of a work like this a vast amount of labor was required, and *it is a marvel* that the author was able to condense so much valuable information into so little space."

"Extreme Beauty, Wise Brevity and Charming Variety."
[From Rev. J. B. Lockwood, Mt. Joy, Pa.]

" *Extreme beauty, wise brevity, charming variety* and practical utility are some of the evident characteristics of this second venture in book-making by Mr. Hill. We predict an immense demand for the 'Album.' In the drawing-room it will be an elegant ornament; in the sitting-room an entertaining companion; in the study a handy volume of biographical reference. Like its predecessor — the 'Manual'—it will be a special educator in the family, and will largely aid in promoting intelligent citizenship in the community."

"One of the Most Valuable Works to Place in a Family."
[From the Chicago *Youths' Examiner.*]

"We supposed when we saw 'Hill's Manual of Social and Business Forms,' we saw as fine a work as was ever issued in this country, and were not satisfied until the work was numbered among our books. As we examine the new book, now before us, by Hon. Thos. E. Hill, we feel how unequal is the task of giving the work anything like the description it deserves, in a notice of this character. Nothing but a personal examination will give even a fair idea of its merits. We can honestly say that it is *one of the most valuable works to place in a family* that it has ever been our pleasure to examine."

"Far Ahead of Anything Ever Issued of Like Nature."
[From the *Joliet* (Ill.) *Signal.*]

"It is dedicated 'to those striving for excellence in the various departments of human action, and who would know how others have won success.' It comprises eighteen different departments, and it is a model, not only for the vast number of interesting subjects treated upon, and the conciseness and brevity of the articles and amount of useful and desirable information contained, but for the beauty of its typography and the charming manner in which the subjects are grouped and illustrated. It is *far ahead of anything ever issued of like nature,* and is an elegant and attractive volume for any parlor or library."

"I Consider This a Fair Test."

J. J. MOORE, *from St. Charles, Mo.*, *writes:*
"I have taken **twenty-seven** orders in this place for the 'Album,' in four days. *I consider this a fair test* of what I can do."

CHARLES N. THOMAS, *Gen. Agt. in New England*, *writes:*
"The agent I put at work in Maine took **seventeen** orders for 'Albums,' his first week, working half his time."

B. W. KRAYBILL, *reporting from Lancaster, Pa.*, *says:*
"My first day netted me **ten** sales for the 'Album.'"

[OVER]

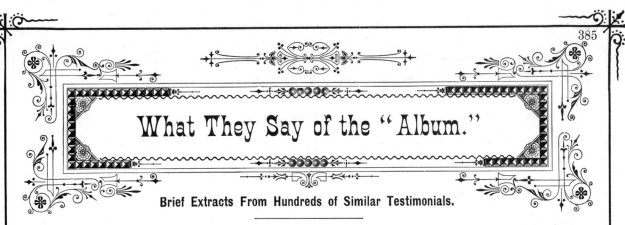

What They Say of the "Album."

Brief Extracts From Hundreds of Similar Testimonials.

The following are from papers published at Aurora, Ill., where the author of the ALBUM resided twelve years, during the last of which he was Mayor of the city.

From the Aurora Beacon.

"THE business career of Mr. Thos. E. Hill, who was at one time a resident of Aurora, and mayor of the city, has been very successful, and some have been inclined to think it the result of good luck. Every enterprise of which he took hold seemed to turn him money, and schemes which would have been abortive in the hands of ordinary men blossomed into rare success under his management. The same good fortune follows him and his enterprises to this day. There is no "luck" in it at all. It grows first from his intense industry, energy and application; second from his enthusiasm; and third from his keen appreciation of *what the public desires*, drawn from long contact with it and close study. In his youth he was eminently successful as a canvasser, as a teacher of writing and lecturer on penmanship. In Aurora, for a number of years he published and edited the *Herald* with great success. When he sold his newspaper, and established the system of city messenger, which has since become so popular between minor cities and Chicago, he exploited new ground which was for a time very profitable; and it was during the hours when he was passing between Aurora and Chicago, that he conceived and did the first work upon the "Manual," that splendid product of the brain, of the compiler, the printer and the book-binder, which has made Thos. E. Hill's name familiar from the Atlantic to the Pacific oceans, and from Minnesota to Florida.

"For two years or more past, Mr. Hill has been of opinion that there existed room for another work besides the "Manual," which should be equally popular and useful—and meet a demand as universal as that enjoyed by his first great work. He has devoted a large amount of labor and inventive genius to the accomplishment of his ideal, and we now have it before us in "HILL'S ALBUM OF BIOGRAPHY AND ART." It is a large quarto volume of 451 pages, printed upon heavy tinted paper, with hundreds of fine portraits, miscellaneous illustrations, unique, artistic and elegant designs. In its preparation he has called to his aid the most modern and refined skill of the type-maker, engraver and typographer, and he has thus, in the "ALBUM," surpassed, in artistic and typographical display, all his former efforts.

"The new work is divided into eighteen departments, as follows: 1st, Religion and its Founders; 2d, Military Chieftains and Famous Battles; 3d, Discoverers and Explorers; 4th, Sketches of Leading Inventors; 5th, History of Financiers; 6th, Sketches of the Scientists; 7th, the Theory of Progression; 8th, Astronomical Science; 9th, Phrenology and Science of Mind; 10th, Humorists and Caricaturists; 11th, Physicians, Lawyers and Sovereigns; 12th, Orators and Statesmen; 13, Actors and Play Writers; 14th, Historians, Novelists, Essayists, etc.; 15th, Poets and Song Writers; 16th, Painters and Sculptors; 17th, Household Ornamentation; 18th, Beautiful Homes. Under these heads are given very many beautiful engravings of men, incidents and places, with sketches, biographical and pertinent, interspersed with very many things valuable to every person who would be reasonably well informed. We doubt if there is any one volume where so much useful information of the kind is gathered, and certainly there is none where it is put in more methodical form, or presented in a manner so pleasing to the eye and taste."

From the Aurora Blade.

"Every page of HILL'S ALBUM is *a model of typography* and originality, each differing from the other in mechanical construction, and each succeeding leaf a surprise from an artistic standpoint. The question one asks, instinctively, is, how can a man conceive so many elegant designs? The contents of the book, however, are what prove its most forcible recommendation. The name of the author of this valuable work, Hon. Thomas E. Hill, is in itself enough to recommend it to all. Our readers are advised to examine the book carefully when they have the opportunity.

From the Aurora Herald.

"'HILL'S ALBUM OF BIOGRAPHY AND ART,' is the name of a new book by Hon. Thos. E. Hill, author of "Hill's Manual of Social and Business Forms." It is gotten up very much after the style of the Manual, but more elaborate and expensive, as nearly every page has some engraving especially for it. The title of the book does not give any adequate idea of the immense amount of information it contains. We suppose it is called an ALBUM because of the many pictures it contains, but in addition thereto it contains short biographical sketches of distinguished men, from the time of Moses and Aaron down to the present. It gives a sketch of Moses, with his portrait, and an outline of his teachings; of Buddha, portrait and doctrines, also the same of Confucius, Jesus Christ, Mohammed, Swedenborg. Andrew Jackson Davis, and Joseph Smith, and an outline of the belief of the different Christian denominations. It also gives sketches and portraits of numerous warriors, inventors, financiers, scientists, actors, humorists, explorers, poets, lawyers, doctors, statesmen, orators, artists, etc., and gives as much about each as most people would care to remember. It is, in short, *a complete library in one volume*, and must have been the work of years to gather the information and put it in this condensed form. Of the typographical excellence it is unnecessary to speak, as all know that whatever Mr. Hill undertakes in that line, is done in the best style known to the art. We know of no other book which has so many new and original designs."

[OVER]

From the People and the Press in General.

The Universal Testimony is that Hill's Album is one of the Most Unique, Elegant and Useful Books in the World. Read the Verdict.

"One of the Most Instructive and Entertaining Books."
[From Rev. H. W. Thomas, Chicago.]

I THINK 'Hill's Album' is *one of the most instructive and entertaining books* I ever saw."

"Most Fascinatingly Interesting."
[From the *Passaic* (N. J.) *Item.*]

"We know of no volume so comprehensive in its information as this, and arranged in such a manner as to be *most fascinatingly interesting.*"

"The Most Beautiful and Complete."
[From the *Chicago Inter-Ocean.*]

"One of the *most beautiful and complete* books of the year. Not only is it wholly creditable as a fine specimen of the printer's art, but the elegant, unique and artistic designs are worthy of special commendation. But the value of the book is in its reading contents, and the admirable system and method of its arrangement. The author is the Hon. Thomas E. Hill, author of 'Hill's Manual of Social and Business Forms,' another of the practical books. The book, under many headings, gleans the most interesting and valuable acts of history bearing upon the subject."

"We Have Examined it and Were Captured."
[From the *Sandwich* (Ill.) *Argus.*]

"'Hill's Album' is a wonder of art and industry. *We have examined it and were captured.* Mr. Hill made a great success of his 'Manual,' and this work gives evidence of his old-time industry and thoroughness. It is full of information upon matters of science, art, architecture, mechanics, biography, religion, etc., and is embellished and illustrated in the highest perfection. The amount of persistent labor needed for Mr. Hill to accomplish this perfect 'Album,' is as wonderful as the skill shown in gathering in so small a compass the pith of the world's history."

Must be Largely Sought and Highly Prized."
[From the *Penman's Art Journal*, New York.]

"The subject-matter of the work, in its extent and skillful manner of presentation, bears unmistakable evidence of great labor and profound research, as well as a liberal expenditure of money on the part of the author. The embellishments are upon a scale most liberal and excellent in taste. The work, as a whole, is one that *must be largely sought and highly prized* by all classes, not alone as a handbook of valuable and interesting information, but as a beautiful and appropriate ornament for the parlor or drawing-room. It is a fitting companion of 'Hill's Manual,' which has proved the most popular and ready-selling work of its day, having already reached its thirtieth edition, and into the hundreds of thousands of copies sold. Like the 'Manual,' the new work is to be sold only on subscription, through agents."

"It is a Marvel."
[From the *Chicago Tribune.*]

"In the preparation of a work like this a vast amount of labor was required, and *it is a marvel* that the author was able to condense so much valuable information into so little space."

"Extreme Beauty, Wise Brevity and Charming Variety."
[From Rev. J. B. Lockwood, Mt. Joy, Pa.]

"*Extreme beauty, wise brevity, charming variety* and practical utility are some of the evident characteristics of this second venture in book-making by Mr. Hill. We predict an immense demand for the 'Album.' In the drawing-room it will be an elegant ornament; in the sitting-room an entertaining companion; in the study a handy volume of biographical reference. Like its predecessor — the 'Manual'—it will be a special educator in the family, and will largely aid in promoting intelligent citizenship in the community."

"One of the Most Valuable Works to Place in a Family."
[From the *Chicago Youths' Examiner.*]

"We supposed when we saw 'Hill's Manual of Social and Business Forms,' we saw as fine a work as was ever issued in this country, and were not satisfied until the work was numbered among our books. As we examine the new book, now before us, by Hon. Thos. E. Hill, we feel how unequal we are to the task of giving the work anything like the description it deserves, in a notice of this character. Nothing but a personal examination will give even a fair idea of its merits. We can honestly say that it is *one of the most valuable works to place in a family* that it has ever been our pleasure to examine."

"Far Ahead of Anything Ever Issued of Like Nature."
[From the *Joliet* (Ill.) *Signal.*]

"It is dedicated 'to those striving for excellence in the various departments of human action, and who would know how others have won success.' It comprises eighteen different departments, and it is a model, not only for the vast number of interesting subjects treated upon, and the conciseness and brevity of the articles and amount of useful and desirable information contained, but for the beauty of its typography and the charming manner in which the subjects are grouped and illustrated. It is *far ahead of anything ever issued of like nature,* and is an elegant and attractive volume for any parlor or library."

"I Consider This a Fair Test."

J. J. MOORE, *from St. Charles, Mo., writes:*
"I have taken **twenty-seven** orders in this place for the 'Album,' in four days *I consider this a fair test* of what I can do."

CHARLES N. THOMAS, *Gen. Agt. in New England, writes:*
"The agent I put at work in Maine took **seventeen** orders for 'Albums,' his first week, working half his time."

B. W. KRAYBILL, *reporting from Lancaster, Pa., says:*
"My first day netted me **ten** sales for the 'Album.'"

[OVER]

In All Parts of the United States **AGENTS ARE WANTED** To Represent the Interests of

HILL'S MANUAL OF SOCIAL AND BUSINESS FORMS

THIS Book is attaining an immense circulation, the printing of the **twenty-seventh edition** having been called for within a short period from the time of its first publication; and its sale is constantly increasing with unparalleled rapidity, the prospect being that in time it will reach nearly every household in the land.

SPECIAL feature of this book favorable to agents, is, that it has a more rapid sale in any locality the more fully people become acquainted with its merits. A second and third canvass of a town is more profitable to the agent than the first. *For terms to agents, address Hill Standard Book Co., Publishers, 103 State St., Chicago, Ill.*

COMMENDATIONS.

The following are brief extracts from hundreds of similar notices received from the press and the people.

WHAT NEWSPAPERS SAY.

From the "Statesman," Austin, Texas.
"It is a book that no professional or business man ought to be without."

From the "Churchman," San Francisco, Cal.
"The work is having the rapid sale which its intrinsic value should inspire."

From the "Women's Exponent," Salt Lake City.
"We view it as one of the best books of its kind ever brought to our notice."

From the "Detroit Free Press."
"This book disarms criticism by carefully refraining from promising too much, and as carefully performing all that it promises."

From the "Daily Times," Denver, Col.
"The book is an original, elegant, and wonderfully comprehensive volume, alike indispensable in every home, counting-room and office."

From the "Republican," Red Wing, Minn.
"No one can imagine the amount of information there is in this book from its title. It is clearly the fundamental principles of a Commercial College, collated and bound, so you can carry it home with you to be studied at your leisure."

From the "Chicago Tribune."
"Prof. Hill has done an excellent service in preparing so splendid a work. With it at hand, one need never be at a loss for the form to do almost any ordinary business correctly, or to prepare a note or an answer to the many and varied calls of social life. We predict for it great popularity and an extensive sale."

OPINIONS OF PROMINENT MEN.

From Hon. Schuyler Colfax, late Vice-President of the United States.
SOUTH BEND, IND.
MY DEAR SIR: I have examined with interest, and also with surprise, your "Manual of Social and Business Forms," and find it really an encyclopedia of information of all kinds, needed in social or business life, admirably arranged and handsomely illustrated, forming the most comprehensive and satisfactory work of the kind I have ever seen. It ought to be in every library and counting-room, and the longer it is examined and used, the more highly it will be appreciated. Yours truly,
SCHUYLER COLFAX.
PROF. THOS. E. HILL, Chicago, Ill.

From Prof. A. Freese, formerly Sup't of Schools, Cleveland, Ohio.
"Hill's Manual is no ordinary affair. This you will see after examining it five minutes. For a young man who wants to know how business is done, how to put things in good shape, and the *right shape,* this book is invaluable. He could afford to pay $50 for it, in case he could not get it for less. If I could have found such a work in my boyhood, my blunders would have been less, and my *greenness* less apparent when I struck out into this sharp and critical world."

From W. W. Chandler, General Agent Star Union Line, Chicago.
CHICAGO, ILL.
It is indeed a *wonderful production,* and I am more and more astonished at the great *variety* and vast *amount* of *practical* information it contains. No young man can afford to be without a copy, and the information it contains is equally valuable and ESSENTIAL TO EVERY LADY IN THE LAND. *An offer of a hundred dollars for the book, or even five times that sum, would not buy it from me, were it an impossibility to procure another copy.*
HILL'S MANUAL IS EMPHATICALLY THE MOST COMPLETE, COMPREHENSIVE, AND RELIABLE WORK OF THE KIND EVER PUBLISHED, BEYOND THE SHADOW OF A DOUBT.

WHAT AGENTS SAY.

From J. S. Martin, Gold Hill, Nevada.
"I have canvassed for Hill's Manual seven days, and taken 127 orders."

From J. W. England, Plain City, Utah.
"The book takes well, and the more it is known the better it is liked."

From T. F. Graber, Kenosha, Wis.
"I never saw a book that I could canvass for with a will, before I saw yours."

Wm. H. Shepard, San Francisco, Cal.,
Writes: "Our canvass in Denver, Colorado, bids fair to reach 350 subscribers." This was the second canvass, six months after the first.

H. B. Mathews, Aurora, Ill.,
Says: "This is the best book in existence for an agent to sell in hard times, as it enables people to save money and make money; hence, they cannot afford to be without it.

From Mrs. L. Hoag, High Forest, Minn.
"We find by recanvassing after the book has been introduced, we can double on our subscribers, and we intend going over the ground time and again."

From Wm. Rolph, Laporte City, Iowa,
"I like the business of canvassing for Hill's Manual first-rate, because it PAYS, and it is such a work as I consider *honorable* to sell, for it is equal to all the agent can say for it."

Chas. S. Attix, Camp Brown, Wyoming,
Inquires concerning the agency of Hill's Manual, saying that many who have seen a copy of the book in his possession desire it, and adds: "I have been offered ten dollars for the copy I have, but would not part for it for double that amount."

(OVER.)

OPINIONS OF THE PRESS.

The newspapers of the country have been of one voice in the praise of HILL'S MANUAL. The following testimonials are a few of the hundreds of similar character.

IN NEW ENGLAND.

From the Boston Herald.

"A very valuable volume is 'Hill's Manual of Social and Business Forms.' It is a large quarto, handsomely produced as far as externals are concerned, but not less attractive and desirable on account of its contents, for, from its pages the self-instructing student can become familiar with all the forms in general use, and almost everything that a person should know in this practical age."

From the Nashua (N. H.) Telegraph.

"'Hill's Manual' is one of the most beautiful and useful books ever published. It is a book for everybody, man, woman and child. No one can fail to find much in it that is both entertaining and instructive, and that can be applied to practical use. It is an eminently useful book for public or private libraries, and a most valuable book for study and reference by every man in every possible business. No book on this continent was ever gotten up with such exquisite taste in its mechanical execution, and certainly none that will be of greater value to the masses of men and women—old and young. Whoever purchases the book will have in it alone a valuable library at very small cost."

From the Suffolk Co. (Mass.) Journal.

"Of its inestimable value one cannot judge fully without examining the work. Many of the most eminent men in our country have given it their unqualified praise, having bought and used it, and the general sentiment among them is, that having once possessed it and become acquainted with its worth, they could hardly be induced to part with it at any price. Among those in this section of country are Gov. Gaston, Gov. Rice, C. G. Atwood of the Boston Board of Trade, G. A. Somerby, Esq., and many others. The leading educational men of our country speak of it in the same terms of praise."

From the Fall River (Mass.) Border City Herald.

"'HILL'S MANUAL OF SOCIAL AND BUSINESS FORMS.'—This is a valuable new work of real excellence, and forms a manual comprehending instructions and examples to guide the scholar, the man of business, the teacher, and the general public in every branch of enterprise over the wide domain of human effort. The work is of the most varied character, and supplies alike the wants of the old and the demands of the young in every phase of human life. We assure all who purchase this work that a more elegant, useful, and comprehensive volume of instructions and examples, suiting all ages and conditions in life in both sexes, has never been laid upon our tables."

From the Cambridge (Mass.) Chronicle.

"'HILL'S MANUAL OF SOCIAL AND BUSINESS FORMS' is one of the most useful volumes ever placed upon the desk of a business or professional man, or upon the table of a drawing-room. It is a perfect treasure of valuable and practical information on social and business topics, which are of immense importance to every one. The items confined within the limits of the book embrace instructions and guides for the city officer, student, politician, clergyman, physician, clerk. In fact, every person who is in business or engaged in any calling whatever, will find information as to the proper manner in which to write any document entering into the various social and business relations of life."

IN THE MIDDLE STATES.

From the Phrenological (N. Y.) Journal.

"This work is exceedingly comprehensive. The author has evidently aimed to cover all the departments of practical life in which the pen is an essential instrumentality, and his endeavor has not failed of eminent success in producing a most useful book. We have been informed that upward of 50,000 copies have been sold in a short time; and no wonder, as it is such a work as an agent can talk about, if talk be at all necessary besides its examination."

From the Akron (Ohio) Beacon.

"Let it be placed where young people may have access to it; and in the hands of every family, where children can, as it were, GROW UP with it, so that its principles may become a kind of second nature to them, and many a stream will be bridged which would otherwise separate them from positions in both social and business life, which by nature they are fitted to fill. The work certainly belongs to the list of articles which should be considered a NECESSITY in every household, and a timely, helping hand to those of mature years."

From the Easton (Penn.) Free Press.

"'Hill's Manual' is a work of which no written description can give a properly adequate idea. It must be examined, that its merits may be appreciated. The author seems to have studied the wants of almost every person and family, and more perfectly met these wants than it would seem possible to do in volumes; and yet we find it in one compact book, which comes within the reach of all."

From the Syracuse (N. Y.) Daily Journal.

"It has often been remarked of individuals that 'they have forgotten more in a minute' than others have learned in a lifetime. Whether the remark is to be taken as a compliment to the former or a reflection upon the latter, matters not particularly, since it is a well-known fact, and one most frequently and sincerely regretted by everybody, that thousands of little things that contribute to daily pleasure, convenience or knowledge are absolutely forgotten and beyond recall at the very moment when most they are needed. What heart burning, what vexation of spirit would be averted, what incalculable material benefits, even, would often accrue were there at our elbow some monitor, visible or invisible, embodying in its inexhaustible resources the *multum in parvo* which forgetful mortals crave.

"Such a mentor, nearly if not altogether infallible, has been provided in 'Hill's Manual of Social and Business Forms and Guide to Correct Writing,' a copy of which lies before us, and the examination of which suggests the fitness of the above title. Its external appearance and internal composition fit it, in all respects, to be the guide of young and old, male and female, business man of whatever trade, calling or profession, and man of leisure, dunce and scholar. 'Hill's Manual' best speaks for itself, for its compactness, brevity and comprehensiveness brings within its covers thousands upon thousands of items of information in daily practical use, the topical enumeration of which, in the general index, occupies seven pages.

"The book is a marvel of patience and painstaking care. It is the work of years, and a triumph at last. No more useful book can be found in existence."

IN THE WEST AND SOUTH

From the Chicago Evening Journal, March 8, 1876.

"The people of Aurora, Ill., yesterday elected Thomas E. Hill mayor of their city, without opposition. The press and the people unanimously declared him to be so eminently fitted for the place, by wealth, public spirit and enterprise, that all classes united in choosing him for the place, irrespective of party or political feeling. Though formerly, for several years, engaged in teaching, Mr. Hill has latterly made journalism his profession. He is best known to the world, however, as the author of 'Hill's Manual of Social and Business Forms,' a book which, though a very large volume, has had the remarkable sale of over 50,000 copies in a very brief time."

From the Chicago Evening Post.

"One of the most useful volumes that was ever laid upon the counting-room desk or the drawing-room table, is 'Hill's Manual of Business Forms.' It is a perfect treasury of knowledge; a complete encyclopædia of practical information. Scanning the table of contents, it is puzzling to conceive how so much can have been crowded into the confines of a single book—impossible to believe that the half which is there promised can be fulfilled. But turning over the pages, one by one, observing the freight they bear, the method of its arrangement, its variety and completeness, incredulity is succeeded by astonishment and admiration. The work is a marvel of ingenuity and industry, a prodigy of patient and skillful labor."

The Preston (Minn.) Republican says:

"Hill's Manual, as a whole, is the outgrowth of many years of preparation, the object of the author being to give in a concise form, and in one compendium, much that has been heretofore inaccessible, and also much that could be obtained elsewhere only at great cost, thus placing this important information in convenient form for ready reference, within the reach of all. In the varied departments of practical, every-day life, it will be found at once the faithful tutor, the reliable guide, and the safe adviser.

"For the business man or mechanic, the professional man or farmer, for every lady, the student, the young or old, and pre-eminently for the family, the work has never had its equal, as regards real practical utility.

"Meeting an existing want among all classes of people, the sale of the work at the present time, in proportion to the population, has rarely, if ever, been equaled by any other work, even in the most prosperous years of the last decade."

From the Louisville Commercial.

"HILL'S MANUAL.—We learn that this useful book is meeting with the favor it so well deserves. It is a peculiar work, in the respect that no description will give a person a true idea of it, owing to the diversity of subjects treated; hence, only those who examine the work can really appreciate it. We are all, to some extent, specialists, having given more attention to some one line of business or study, leaving other matters of equal importance but partially covered; and just here this work will be found to meet a want which almost every one has felt. It certainly belongs to the list of articles which should be considered a necessity in every office and library, and is a helping hand to those of mature years."